DICTIONNAIRE

FRANÇAIS–ANGLAIS · ANGLAIS–FRANÇAIS
FRENCH–ENGLISH · ENGLISH–FRENCH

DICTIONARY

Hodder Murray
www.hoddereducation.co.uk

LAROUSSE

Concept
Valérie Katzaros, Frances Illingworth

Direction éditoriale / *Managing Editor*
Valérie Katzaros

Responsables de la rédaction / *Senior Editors*
Frances Illingworth, Laurence Larroche

Rédaction / *Editors*
Michael Janes, Lola Busuttil,
Peter Weisman,
Gearóid Cronin, Marie Ollivier, Christian Salzedo

Secrétariat d'édition / *Copy preparation*
Paloma Cabot, Marianne Ebersberg, Mercedes Escudero

Correction / *Proofreading*
Anne Landelle

Informatique éditoriale / *Data Management*
Dalila Abdelkader

Direction artistique / *Design*
Sophie Compagne

Illustrations / *Illustrations*
Jean-Pierre Lamerand, Laurent Blondel, Agathe Bouton

Remerciements / *Special thanks to*
Geneviève Wittmann, Marc Chabrier

Fabrication / *Production Manager*
Nicolas Perrier

Composition / *Typesetter*
IGS

Orders: please contact Bookpoint Ltd, 130 Milton Park, Abingdon, Oxon OX14 4SB.
Telephone: (44) 01235 827720. Fax: (44) 01235 400454. Lines are open 9.00–5.00, Monday to Saturday, with a 24-hour message
answering service. Visit our website at www.hoddereducation.co.uk

© Larousse 2006
First published in 2005 by Larousse

Hodder Murray, an imprint of Hodder Education, a member of the Hodder Headline Group
338 Euston Road - London NW1 3BH

Larousse, 21, rue du Montparnasse - 75283 Paris, Cedex 06, France

Impression number	10 9	8 7 6	5 4	3 2 1	
Year	2010	2009	2008	2007	2006

A catalogue record for this title is available from the British Library

ISBN-10: 0340 915 17X
ISBN-13: 978 0340 915 172

Préface

Ce dictionnaire est un ouvrage entièrement nouveau destiné aux collégiens qui débutent dans l'apprentissage de l'anglais. Il est fondé sur un concept pédagogique simple : à chaque mot, ou à chacun des sens d'un mot, sont associés une traduction et un exemple. Ce concept est reflété par une présentation claire en deux couleurs dans laquelle les mots, les sens et les traductions sont nettement mis en évidence.

Par ailleurs, ces mots et ces sens ont été sélectionnés avec soin pour répondre aux besoins des jeunes apprenants. Complétant le lexique, un grand nombre d'informations concernant les faux amis, l'usage des mots et des points de grammaire difficiles sont données sous formes de notes pédagogiques. En outre, parce que l'apprentissage d'une langue ne se limite pas aux mots, mais passe également par la connaissance d'une culture, des encadrés sont consacrés aux particularités culturelles des pays anglo-saxons. Enfin, la spécificité de ce nouveau dictionnaire est la pédagogie par l'image : des illustrations en couleur regroupées par thèmes permettent d'associer une image à un mot ou à une expression.

Preface

This dictionary is a completely new reference book for students in their first years of learning French. The concept is simple: each word and each different sense of a word has a translation and an example. The two-color layout ensures that each entry stands out clearly, as well as the different senses and translations. Words and senses have been carefully selected to meet the needs of young learners. The wordlist is complemented by instructive notes containing lots of useful information on false friends, usage and essential grammar points. As learning a language involves not only learning words but also learning about a different way of life, the dictionary also includes boxed notes on French culture. Last but not least this dictionary also aims to teach through pictures: themed color illustrations allow the learner to associate an image with a word or phrase.

phonetic transcription

English vowels

[ɪ] pit, big, rid
[e] pet, tend
[æ] pat, bag, mad
[ʌ] putt, cut
[ɒ] pot, log
[ʊ] put, full
[ə] mother, suppose

[iː] bean, weed
[ɑː] barn, car, laugh
[ɔː] born, lawn
[uː] loop, loose
[ɜː] burn, learn, bird

English Diphtongs

[eɪ] bay, late, great
[aɪ] buy, light, aisle
[ɔɪ] boy , foil
[əʊ] no, road, blow
[aʊ] now, shout, town
[ɪə] peer, fierce, idea
[eə] pair, bear, share
[ʊə] poor, sure, tour

Semi-vowels

you, spaniel	[j]	
wet, why, twin	[w]	
	[ɥ]	

Consonants

pop, people	[p]	
bottle, bib	[b]	
train, tip	[t]	
dog, did	[d]	
come, kitchen	[k]	
loch	[x]	
gag, great	[g]	
chain, wretched	[tʃ]	
jig, fridge	[dʒ]	
fib, physical	[f]	
vine, livid	[v]	
think, fifth	[θ]	

transcription phonétique

Voyelles françaises

[i] fille, île
[e] pays, année
[ɛ] bec, aime
[a] lac, papillon
[o] drôle, aube
[ɔ] botte, automne
[u] outil, goût
[y] usage, lune
[ø] aveu, jeu
[œ] peuple, bœuf
[ə] le, je

Nasales françaises

[ɛ̃] timbre, main
[ɑ̃] champ, ennui
[ɔ̃] ongle, mon
[œ̃] parfum, brun

Semi-voyelles

yeux, lieu
ouest, oui
lui, nuit

Consonnes

prendre, grippe
bateau, rosbif
théâtre, temps
dalle, ronde
coq, quatre

garder, épilogue

physique, fort
voir, rive

phonetic transcription

transcription phonétique

this, with	[ð]	
seal, peace	[s]	cela, savant
zip, his	[z]	fraise, zéro
sheep, machine	[ʃ]	charrue, schéma
usual, measure	[ʒ]	rouge, jabot
how, perhaps	[h]	
metal, comb	[m]	mât, drame
night, dinner	[n]	nager, trône
sung, parking	[ŋ]	dancing, smoking
	[ɲ]	agneau, peigner
little, help	[l]	halle, lit
right, carry	[r]	arracher, sabre

The symbol ['] has been used to represent the French "aspirate h", e.g. hachis ['aʃi].

The symbol ['] indicates that the following syllable carries primary stress and the symbol [ˌ] that the following syllable carries secondary stress.

The symbol [ʳ] in English phonetics indicates that the final "r" is pronounced only when followed by a word beginning with a vowel. Note that it is nearly always pronounced in American English.

Le symbole ['] représente le « h aspiré » français, p. ex. hachis ['aʃi].

Les symboles ['] et [ˌ] indiquent respectivement un accent primaire et un accent secondaire sur la syllabe suivante.

Le symbole [ʳ] indique que le « r » final d'un mot anglais ne se prononce que lorsqu'il forme une liaison avec la voyelle du mot suivant ; le « r » final est presque toujours prononcé en anglais américain.

Comment utiliser le dictionnaire

Entrée

Les entrées du dictionnaire sont classées par ordre alphabétique et sont surlignées.

Catégorie grammaticale

La catégorie grammaticale de l'entrée est donnée en toutes lettres. Certains mots ont plusieurs catégories grammaticales signalées par un carré jaune.

---

imperméable [ɛ̃pɛrmeabl] *adjectif & nom*

■ *adjectif*
waterproof : **une veste imperméable** a waterproof jacket
■ *nom masculin*
raincoat.

Prononciation

La phonétique indique la prononciation du mot.

Sens

Si mot a plus d'un sens et peut se traduire de différentes façons, les sens sont numérotés.

---

bibliothèque [biblijɔtɛk] *nom féminin*

1. **library** *(pluriel* **libraries***)* : **la bibliothèque municipale** the public library
2. **bookcase** : **une bibliothèque en bois** a wooden bookcase.

Traduction

La traduction de l'entrée se trouve à la ligne. Les pluriels irréguliers des noms anglais sont indiqués après la traduction.

Expressions

Les expressions importantes se trouvent à la fin des entrées et sont soulignées.

---

clin d'œil [klɛ̃dœj] *(pluriel* clins d'œil*) nom masculin*

➤ **faire un clin d'œil à quelqu'un** to wink at somebody ; **il m'a fait un clin d'œil !** he winked at me!

Exemples

Les exemples illustrent le sens du mot et vous aident à choisir la bonne traduction.

Sous-entrées

Les mots encadrés en jaune montrent une forme différente de l'entrée : ce sont des sous-entrées. Les verbes anglais à particule, ou **phrasal verbs**, sont des sous-entrées classées par ordre alphabétique.

---

carry ['kærɪ] *verb*

porter : **she's carrying a large bag** elle porte un grand sac

carry on *phrasal verb*

continuer : **he carried on working** il a continué à travailler.

Formes irrégulières

Les formes irrégulières anglaises sont données en entrée.

---

said [sed] *past tense & past participle of* say

I said you were right j'ai dit que tu avais raison ; **she hasn't said anything** elle n'a rien dit.

UK et US

UK (United Kingdom) indique qu'un mot ne s'utilise qu'en anglais britannique et *US* (United States) indique qu'un mot ne s'utilise qu'en anglais américain.

---

trottoir [trɔtwar] *nom masculin*

pavement *UK*, **sidewalk** *US*
➤ **un trottoir roulant** a travolator.

How to use the dictionary

bear [beəʳ] *noun & verb*

- *noun*
  ours *(masculine)* : **a polar bear** un ours polaire
- *verb (past tense* bore, *past participle* borne)
  supporter : **I can't bear him** je ne le supporte pas.

Grammatical category

The grammatical category of the word is shown in full. Some words have more than one grammatical category. Each new category is preceded by a yellow square.

Pronunciation

The phonetics show the pronunciation of the word.

cap [kæp] *noun*

1. **casquette** *(feminine)* : **he wears his baseball cap back to front** il porte sa casquette à l'envers
2. **capsule** *(feminine)* : **take the cap off the bottle** enlevez la capsule de la bouteille.

Sense

If a word has more than one sense and more than one translation, each new sense is numbered.

Translation

The translation of the entry is given on a new line. The gender of French nouns is given after the translation.

frog [frɒg] *noun*

grenouille *(feminine)*
➤ **frog's legs** cuisses *(feminine plural)* de grenouilles
➤ **to have a frog in one's throat** avoir un chat dans la gorge.

Phrases

Important phrases are shown at the end of the entry and are underlined.

Examples

The examples illustrate the meaning of a word and help you choose the right translation.

add [æd] *verb*

ajouter : **add some sugar to the mixture** ajoutez du sucre au mélange.

add up *phrasal verb*

additionner : **add the numbers up** additionnez les chiffres.

Subentries

Words that are bordered in yellow are subentries and show a different form of the main word.
Phrasal verbs are given in alphabetical order as subentries after the main entry.

lu, e [ly] *participe passé de* lire.

Irregular forms

Irregular forms appear as entries with a cross-reference to the main form.

belle ➤ beau.

a [a] ➤ avoir.

à [a] *préposition* (à + le = au [o], à + les = aux [o])

1. *Indique le lieu* **at, in** : **Denis n'est pas à la maison** Denis isn't at home ; **ils sont à l'école** they are at school ; **nous nous sommes retrouvés au restaurant** we met at the restaurant ; **ils habitent à Paris** they live in Paris ; **nous avons une maison à la campagne** we have a house in the country
2. *Indique la direction* **to** : **mes amis vont à Londres cet été** my friends are going to London this summer ; **on va à la plage ce week-end** we're going to the beach this weekend
3. *Introduit un complément d'objet indirect* **to** : **tu as parlé à Céline ?** have you spoken to Céline? ; **c'est difficile à dire** it's hard to say

> « À » peut se traduire différemment selon le verbe qu'il suit : **je pense souvent à Thomas** I often think about Thomas ; **elle croit encore au Père Noël** she still believes in Father Christmas.
> Parfois, « à » ne se traduit pas : **tu devrais téléphoner à Natacha** you should phone Natacha ; **tu as montré tes photos à Yves ?** have you shown Yves your photographs ?

4. *Indique l'heure, la date* **je t'appelle à onze heures** I'll call you at eleven ; **à Noël** at Christmas ; **au vingt et unième siècle** in the twenty-first century
5. *Dans une description* **with** : **une fille aux cheveux longs** a girl with long hair ; **le garçon à la casquette rouge** the boy with the red cap
6. *Devant un chiffre* **un livre à dix euros** a ten-euro book ; **nous allions à 50 km à l'heure** we were doing fifty kilometres per hour
7. *En relation avec « de »* **and** : **tu es libre de deux à trois ?** are you free between two and three?
8. *Indique l'appartenance* **c'est à moi** it's mine ; **ce cahier est à toi ?** is this exercise book yours? ; **ce VTT est à Raoul** this mountain bike is Raoul's ; **une amie à moi** a friend of mine
9. *Pour saluer* **à demain !** see you tomorrow! ; **à plus tard !** see you later! ; **à lundi !** see you on Monday!

abandonner [abɑ̃dɔne] *verbe*

1. **to abandon** : **ils ont abandonné le village** they abandoned the village
2. **to give up** : **c'est trop dur, j'abandonne !** it's too hard, I give up!

abat-jour [abaʒur] *nom masculin invariable*

lampshade.

abattre [abatr] *verbe*

1. **to knock down** : **les ouvriers ont abattu le mur** the workmen knocked the wall down
2. **to cut** : **le bûcheron va abattre les arbres** the woodcutter is going to cut the trees down
3. **to kill** : **les terroristes ont abattu le ministre** the terrorists killed the minister.

abbaye [abei] *nom féminin*

abbey.

abdominaux [abdɔmino] *nom masculin pluriel*

> **faire des abdominaux** to do exercises for the stomach muscles.

abeille [abɛj] *nom féminin*

bee.

abîmer [abime] *verbe*

to damage : **n'abîme pas mon livre** don't damage my book

s'abîmer *verbe pronominal*

to get damaged : **le classeur s'est abîmé dans mon cartable** the ring binder got damaged in my schoolbag.

abonné, e [abɔne] *adjectif*

> **être abonné à un magazine** to suscribe to a magazine.

abonnement [abɔnmɑ̃] *nom masculin*

subscription : **l'abonnement au journal coûte cent euros** the newspaper subscription costs a hundred euros.

s'abonner [sabɔne] *verbe pronominal*

➤ **s'abonner à quelque chose** to take out a subscription to something : **je vais m'abonner à ce nouveau magazine** I'm going to take out a subscription to this new magazine.

abord [abɔr] *nom masculin*

➤ **aux abords de** around : **aux abords du château** around the castle
➤ **d'abord** first : **je dois d'abord faire mes devoirs** I must do my homework first.

aborder [abɔrde] *verbe*

to deal with : **le prof n'a pas abordé ce problème** the teacher didn't deal with this problem.

aboutir [abutir] *verbe*

➤ **aboutir à quelque chose** to result in something : **la discussion a abouti à un compromis** the discussion resulted in a compromise.

aboyer [abwaje] *verbe*

to bark : **le chien a aboyé toute la nuit** the dog barked all night.

abréger [abreʒe] *verbe*

to abbreviate : **tu peux abréger « Madame » en « Mme »** you can abbreviate 'Madame' to 'Mme'.

abréviation [abrevjasjɔ̃] *nom féminin*

abbreviation.

abri [abri] *nom masculin*

shelter : **les enfants ont construit un abri avec des branches** the children built a shelter with branches
➤ **se mettre à l'abri** to take shelter : **mettez-vous à l'abri sous l'arbre** take shelter under the tree ; **on s'est mis à l'abri du vent** we took shelter from the wind.

abricot [abriko] *nom masculin & adjectif invariable*

apricot.

s'abriter [sabrite] *verbe pronominal*

to take shelter : **ils se sont vite abrités** they quickly took shelter ; **nous nous sommes abrités de la pluie** we took shelter from the rain OU we sheltered from the rain.

absence [apsɑ̃s] *nom féminin*

absence : **pendant son absence, nous avons beaucoup avancé** while he was absent, we made a lot of progress.

absent, e [apsɑ̃, ɑ̃t] *adjectif & nom*

■ *adjectif*
absent : **Thomas est absent, il a la grippe** Thomas is absent, he has flu
■ *nom masculin, nom féminin*
absentee : **il y a trois absents aujourd'hui** there are three absentees today OU there are three people absent today.

s'absenter [sapsɑ̃te] *verbe pronominal*

to leave : **je me suis absenté deux minutes** I left for two minutes.

absolument [apsɔlymɑ̃] *adverbe*

absolutely : **absolument pas !** absolutely not!

accéder [aksede] *verbe*

➤ **accéder à** to reach : **on accède à la maison par un petit chemin** you reach the house by a narrow path.

accélérer [akselere] *verbe*

to accelerate : **la voiture a accéléré** the car accelerated.

accent [aksɑ̃] *nom masculin*

accent : **il a l'accent américain** he has an American accent
➤ **un accent aigu** an acute accent
➤ **un accent grave** a grave accent
➤ **un accent circonflexe** a circumflex accent
➤ **l'accent tonique** the stress.

accentuer [aksɑ̃tɥe] *verbe*

1. to emphasize : **cette couleur accentue sa pâleur** this colour emphasizes her pallor ; **sa coupe de cheveux accentue son grand nez** his haircut emphasizes his big nose
2. to stress : **accentue la première syllabe** stress the first syllable.

accepter [aksɛpte] *verbe*

to accept : **ils ont accepté ma proposition** they accepted my offer
➤ **accepter de faire quelque chose** to agree to do something : **la prof a accepté de retarder l'interro** the teacher agreed to put the test back.

accès [aksɛ] *nom masculin*

access : **cette carte donne accès à toutes les expositions** this card gives you access to all the exhibitions.

accessoire [akseswar] *nom masculin*

accessory : **un appareil photo avec plusieurs accessoires** a camera with several accessories.

accident [aksidɑ̃] *nom masculin*

accident : **les parents d'Audrey ont eu un accident** Audrey's parents had an accident
➤ **un accident de la route** a road accident
➤ **un accident de voiture** a car accident.

accompagnateur, trice [akɔ̃panatœr, tris] *nom masculin, nom féminin*

il y a trois accompagnateurs pour vingt élèves there are three adults to accompany twenty pupils.

accompagner [akɔ̃paɲe] *verbe*

to go with : **je t'accompagne jusqu'au bout de la rue** I'll go to the end of the street with you.

accomplir [akɔ̃plir] *verbe*

to carry out : **il a accompli sa tâche** he carried out his task.

accord [akɔr] *nom masculin*

agreement : **mes parents ont donné leur accord** my parents gave their agreement
➤ **d'accord** OK, all right : **tu viens ? – d'accord !** are you coming? – OK!
➤ **se mettre d'accord** to agree : **ils ont fini par se mettre d'accord** they finally agreed
➤ **être d'accord avec quelqu'un** to agree with somebody : **je suis d'accord avec toi** I agree with you.

accordéon [akɔrdeɔ̃] *nom masculin*

accordion : **Louis joue de l'accordéon** Louis plays the accordion.

accorder [akɔrde] *verbe*

➤ **accorder quelque chose à quelqu'un** to give somebody something : **ils lui ont accordé une bourse** they gave him a grant.

accrochage [akrɔʃaʒ] *nom masculin*

collision : **elle a eu un accrochage avec la voiture de sa mère** she had a collision in her mother's car.

accrocher [akrɔʃe] *verbe*

to hang up : **il a accroché le tableau** he hung the painting up
➤ **accrocher quelque chose à**
1. to hang something on : **accroche ta veste au portemanteau** hang your jacket on the coat rack
2. to hitch something to : **la caravane est accrochée à la voiture** the caravan is hitched to the car

s'accrocher *verbe pronominal*

to hang on : **accroche-toi ou tu vas tomber !** hang on or you'll fall! ; **accroche-toi à la rampe** hang on to the banister.

s'accroupir [sakrupir] *verbe pronominal*

to squat down : **il s'est accroupi pour prendre la photo** he squatted down to take the photo.

accueil [akœj] *nom masculin*

1. reception : **demande à l'accueil** ask at reception
2. welcome : **un accueil chaleureux** a warm welcome.

accueillir [akœjir] *verbe*

to welcome : **ils m'ont accueilli à bras ouverts** they welcomed me with open arms.

s'accumuler [sakymyle] *verbe pronominal*

to pile up : **les papiers s'accumulent sur le bureau** papers are piling up on the desk.

accuser [akyze] *verbe*

to accuse : **ils m'ont accusé de tricher** they accused me of cheating ; **il est accusé de meurtre** he has been accused of murder.

s'acharner [saʃarne] *verbe pronominal*

➤ **s'acharner contre quelqu'un** ou **s'acharner sur quelqu'un** to hound somebody : **la presse s'acharne contre lui** the press is hounding him
➤ **s'acharner à faire quelque chose** il **s'acharne à vouloir acheter cette maison** he's determined to buy that house.

achat [aʃa] *nom masculin*

buying : **l'achat de vêtements de sport revient cher** buying sportswear is expensive
➤ **faire des achats** to go shopping.

acheter [aʃte] *verbe*

to buy : **j'ai envie d'acheter cette écharpe** I want to buy this scarf
➤ **acheter quelque chose à quelqu'un**
1. to buy somebody something : **je lui ai acheté un CD pour son anniversaire** I bought her a CD for her birthday

2. to buy something from somebody : **ma mère a acheté des fleurs chez le fleuriste** my mother bought flowers from the florist.

acide [asid] *adjectif & nom*

■ *adjectif*

1. **sour** : **ces cerises sont acides** these cherries are sour

2. **acid** : **des pluies acides** acid rain

■ *nom masculin*

acid.

acier [asje] *nom masculin*

steel

➤ **l'acier inoxydable** stainless steel.

acné [akne] *nom féminin*

acne : **elle a de l'acné** she has acne.

acquérir [akerir] *verbe*

to acquire : **acquérir des connaissances en astrologie** to acquire a knowledge of astrology.

acquis, e [aki, iz] *participe passé de* **acquérir**.

acrobate [akrɔbat] *nom masculin ou féminin*

acrobat.

acte [akt] *nom masculin*

1. **act, action** : **un acte de courage** an act of bravery ; **assez de paroles, des actes !** that's enough talk, it's time for action!

2. **act** : **une pièce en cinq actes** a play in five acts.

acteur [aktœr] *nom masculin*

actor.

actif, ive [aktif, iv] *adjectif*

active : **c'est une petite fille très active** she's a very active little girl.

action [aksjɔ̃] *nom féminin*

action : **il y a beaucoup d'action dans ce film** there's a lot of action in the film.

s'activer [saktive] *verbe pronominal familier*

to hurry up : **active-toi, on est en retard !** hurry up, we're late!

activité [aktivite] *nom féminin*

activity : **il y a des activités pour les ados au club** there are activities for teenagers at the club.

actrice [aktris] *nom féminin*

actress (*pluriel* **actresses**).

actualité [aktɥalite] *nom féminin*

current affairs : **il ne s'intéresse pas à l'actualité** he's not interested in current affairs.

actuel, elle [aktɥɛl] *adjectif*

present : **à l'heure actuelle** at the present time

> ⚠ Actuel is a false friend, it does not mean 'actual'.

actuellement [aktɥɛlmɑ̃] *adverbe*

1. **at present** : **actuellement il y a cinq cents élèves dans l'école** at present there are five hundred pupils in the school

2. **nowadays** : **actuellement les jeunes sont plus libres qu'avant** nowadays young people have more freedom than before

> ⚠ Actuellement is a false friend, it does not mean 'actually'.

s'adapter [sadapte] *verbe pronominal*

to adapt : **David s'est facilement adapté à sa nouvelle école** David has adapted easily to his new school.

addition [adisjɔ̃] *nom féminin*

1. **sum** : **faire une addition** to do a sum

2. **bill, check** *US* : **l'addition, s'il vous plaît** can I have the bill, please?

additionner [adisjɔne] *verbe*

to add up : **additionne ces nombres** add these numbers up.

adhérer [adere] *verbe*

> **adhérer à** to join : **je vais adhérer à son club de tennis** I'm going to join his tennis club.

adhésif, ive [adezif, iv] *adjectif*

adhesive, sticky.

adieu [adjø] *nom masculin*

goodbye : **dire adieu à quelqu'un** to say goodbye to somebody.

adjectif [adʒɛktif] *nom masculin*

adjective.

admettre [admɛtr] *verbe*

to admit : **admets que tu as tort !** admit that you're wrong! **Anne est admise dans la classe supérieure** Anne is admitted into the next year

administratif, ive [administratif, iv] *adjectif*

administrative.

Administration [administrasjɔ̃] *nom féminin*

➤ **l'Administration** the Civil Service : **sa mère travaille dans l'Administration** her mother works in the Civil Service.

admirer [admire] *verbe*

to admire : **je l'admire beaucoup** I really admire her.

admis, e [admi, iz] *participe passé de* admettre.

ado [ado] *(abréviation de* adolescent) *nom masculin ou féminin familier*

teenager.

adolescence [adɔlesɑ̃s] *nom féminin*

adolescence.

adolescent, e [adɔlesɑ̃, ɑ̃t] *nom masculin, nom féminin*

teenager : **un mensuel pour les adolescents** a monthly magazine for teenagers.

adopter [adɔpte] *verbe*

to adopt : **ils ont adopté un petit Chinois** they adopted a Chinese boy.

adoptif, ive [adɔptif, iv] *adjectif*

1. adopted : **leur fils adoptif** their adopted son
2. adoptive : **sa famille adoptive** his adoptive family.

adorable [adɔrabl] *adjectif*

lovely ; **quel village adorable !** what a lovely village!

adorer [adɔre] *verbe*

to love : **j'adore le chocolat** I love chocolate.

adresse [adrɛs] *nom féminin*

1. address : **je vais noter ton adresse** I'll write your address down
2. skill : **il faut beaucoup d'adresse pour faire ce métier** you need a lot of skill to do this job

➤ **une adresse électronique** an e-mail address.

s'adresser [sadrese] *verbe pronominal*

➤ **s'adresser à quelqu'un**
1. to speak to somebody : **c'est à moi que tu t'adresses ?** are you speaking to me?
2. to be aimed at somebody : **à qui s'adresse cette remarque ?** who is that remark aimed at?

adroit, e [adrwa, at] *adjectif*

skilful *UK*, skillful *US*.

adulte [adylt] *nom masculin ou féminin & adjectif*

adult : **c'est plus cher pour les adultes** it's more expensive for adults ; **une baleine adulte** an adult whale.

adverbe [advɛrb] *nom masculin*

adverb.

adversaire [advɛrsɛr] *nom masculin ou féminin*

opponent : **il a battu son adversaire en trois sets** he beat his opponent in three sets.

aérer [aere] *verbe*

to air : **tu devrais aérer ta chambre** you should air your bedroom.

aérien, enne [aerjɛ̃, ɛn] *adjectif*

une compagnie aérienne an airline.

aérogare [aerogar] *nom féminin*

terminal : **le vol part de l'aérogare 2** the flight leaves from terminal 2.

aéroglisseur [aeroglisœr] *nom masculin*

hovercraft.

aéroport [aeropɔr] *nom masculin*

airport : **je vais à l'aéroport** I'm going to the airport ; **nous sommes arrivés à l'aéroport** we've arrived at the airport.

affaire [afɛr] *nom féminin*

1. matter : **c'est une affaire très compliquée** it's a very complicated matter
2. bargain : **dix euros ? tu as fait une affaire !** ten euros? you got a bargain!
3. case : **l'affaire Duroc** the Duroc case

affaires *nom féminin pluriel*

1. things : **pose tes affaires là** put your things there
2. business *(ne s'utilise jamais au pluriel)* : **son père est dans les affaires** his father is in business ; **les affaires vont bien** business is good

➤ **un homme d'affaires** a businessman
➤ **mêle-toi de tes affaires !** mind your own business!

affection [afɛksjɔ̃] *nom féminin*

affection : **elle a besoin d'affection** she needs affection
➤ **avoir de l'affection pour quelqu'un** to be fond of somebody : **j'ai beaucoup d'affection pour ma grand-mère** I'm very fond of my grandmother.

affectueux, euse [afɛktɥø, øz] *adjectif*

affectionate.

affiche [afiʃ] *nom féminin*

poster : **il aime les vieilles affiches** he likes old posters.

afficher [afiʃe] *verbe*

1. to put up : **Marc a affiché sa photo de classe dans sa chambre** Marc put his class photograph up on his bedroom wall
2. to display : **les prix sont affichés dans la vitrine** the prices are displayed in the window.

d'affilée [dafile] *adverbe*

in a row : **trois jours d'affilée** three days in a row.

affirmer [afirme] *verbe*

to claim, to maintain : **Sandrine affirme que ce n'est pas de sa faute** Sandrine maintains that it isn't her fault.

s'affoler [safɔle] *verbe pronominal*

to panic : **ne t'affole pas, ce n'est pas grave** don't panic, it's not serious.

affranchir [afrɑ̃ʃir] *verbe*

to stamp : **n'oubliez pas d'affranchir la lettre** don't forget to stamp the letter.

affreux, euse [afrø, øz] *adjectif*

awful : **ce bâtiment est vraiment affreux** this building is really awful ; **il fait un temps affreux** the weather's awful.

affronter [afrɔ̃te] *verbe*

1. to play against, to play : **Manchester United affrontera le Real Madrid en demi-finale** Manchester United will play Real Madrid in the semifinal
2. to face : **ils ont affronté le danger avec courage** they faced the danger with courage

s'affronter [safrɔ̃te] *verbe pronominal*

to play : **les deux équipes s'affronteront samedi** the two teams will play on Saturday.

afin [afɛ̃]

➤ **afin de** in order to : **ils sont partis tôt afin d'éviter les embouteillages** they left early in order to avoid the traffic jams
➤ **afin que** so that : **donnez-moi votre numéro de téléphone afin que je puisse vous joindre** give me your phone number so that I can contact you.

africain, e [afrikɛ̃, ɛn] *adj*

African

En anglais, les adjectifs se rapportant à un continent s'écrivent avec une majuscule :

l'éléphant africain est plus grand que l'éléphant indien the African elephant is bigger than the Indian elephant

Africain, e *nom masculin, nom féminin*

African.

Afrique [afrik] *nom féminin*

➤ **l'Afrique** Africa

En anglais, il n'y a pas d'article devant les noms de continents :

l'Égypte se trouve en Afrique Egypt is in Africa ; **es-tu déjà allé en Afrique ?** have you ever been to Africa?

➤ **Afrique du Nord** North Africa
➤ **Afrique du Sud** South Africa

agaçant, e [agasɑ̃, ɑ̃t] *adjectif*

annoying : **qu'est-ce que c'est agaçant d'attendre !** it's so annoying having to wait!

agacer [agase] *verbe*

to annoy : **arrête, tu m'agaces !** stop it, you're annoying me!

âge [aʒ] *nom masculin*

age : **à son âge, je savais déjà lire** at her age, I could already read ; **une personne d'un certain âge** a middle-aged person
➤ **quel âge as-tu ?** how old are you?

âgé, e [aʒe] *adjectif*

old : **mes grands-parents sont très âgés** my grandparents are very old ; **elle est âgée de douze ans** she's twelve years old ; **un enfant âgé de trois ans** a three-year-old child.

agence [aʒɑ̃s] *nom féminin*

agency *(pluriel* agencies*)* : une agence de publicité an advertising agency
➤ une agence de voyages a travel agency.

agenda [aʒɛ̃da] *nom masculin*

diary *(pluriel* diaries*)*
➤ un agenda électronique a personal organizer.

s'agenouiller [saʒnuje] *verbe pronominal*

to kneel down : il s'est agenouillé pour prier he knelt down to pray.

agent [aʒɑ̃] *nom masculin*

agent : il est agent secret he's a secret agent
➤ un agent de police a police officer.

aggraver [agrave] *verbe*

to make worse : tu vas aggraver la situation si tu fais ça you're going to make the situation worse if you do that

s'aggraver *verbe pronominal*

to get worse : sa maladie s'est aggravée his illness has got worse.

agir [aʒir] *verbe*

1. to act : nous devons agir vite we must act quickly
2. to work : le médicament a agi tout de suite the medicine worked immediately
3. to behave : il a mal agi he behaved badly

s'agir *verbe pronominal*

➤ de quoi s'agit-il ? what is it about? ; je voudrais vous parler – de quoi s'agit-il ? I'd like to talk to you – what is it about? ; de quoi s'agit-il dans ce livre ? what's this book about? ; il s'agit d'un petit sorcier it's about a young wizard.

agité, e [aʒite] *adjectif*

1. restless : les élèves sont agités the pupils are restless
2. rough : la mer est très agitée aujourd'hui the sea is very rough today.

agiter [aʒite] *verbe*

1. to shake : agite la bouteille avant de verser le jus shake the bottle before pouring the juice
2. to wave : ils agitaient les bras pour attirer son attention they were waving their arms to catch her attention

s'agiter *verbe pronominal*

to fidget : arrête de t'agiter comme ça ! stop fidgeting!

agneau [aɲo] *(pluriel* agneaux*) nom masculin*

lamb.

agrafe [agraf] *nom féminin*

staple.

agrafer [agrafe] *verbe*

to staple : je vais agrafer les feuilles ensemble I'm going to staple the sheets together.

agrafeuse [agraføz] *nom féminin*

stapler.

agrandir [agrɑ̃dir] *verbe*

to enlarge : il a fait agrandir la photo he enlarged the photograph.

agréable [agreabl] *adjectif*

nice, pleasant : j'ai passé un moment agréable avec elle I had a nice time with her ou I had a pleasant time with her.

agresser [agrɛse] *verbe*

to attack : des jeunes l'ont agressé dans le parc some youths attacked him in the park
➤ se faire agresser to be attacked : elle s'est fait agresser she was attacked.

agressif, ive [agrɛsif, iv] *adjectif*

aggressive.

agricole [agrikɔl] *adjectif*

agricultural.

agriculteur, trice [agrikyltœr, tris] *nom masculin, nom féminin*

farmer.

agriculture [agrikyltyr] *nom féminin*

farming, agriculture : l'agriculture est l'activité principale de la région farming is the main activity in the region.

ai [e] ➤ avoir.

aide [ɛd] *nom féminin*

help : tu as besoin d'aide ? do you need any help?
➤ à l'aide ! help! : appeler à l'aide to call for help
➤ à l'aide de with the help of : il a traduit le

texte à l'aide d'un dictionnaire he translated the text with the help of a dictionary.

aider [ede] *verbe*

to help : aide-moi, la valise est trop lourde help me, the suitcase is too heavy

➤ **aider quelqu'un à faire quelque chose** to help somebody do something : **son père l'a aidée à faire ses devoirs** her father helped her do her homework.

aie, aies *etc* ➤ avoir.

aïe [aj] *interjection*

ouch! : aïe ! ça fait mal ! ouch! that hurts!

aigle [ɛgl] *nom masculin*

eagle : l'aigle est l'emblème des États-Unis the eagle is the national emblem of the United States.

aigre [ɛgr] *adjectif*

sour : cette sauce est un peu aigre this sauce is a bit sour.

aigu, aiguë [egy] *adjectif*

high-pitched : elle a une voix aiguë she has a high-pitched voice.

aiguille [egɥij] *nom féminin*

1. **needle : une aiguille à tricoter** a knitting needle
2. **hand : la petite aiguille de la pendule** the hour hand of the clock ; **la grande aiguille de la pendule** the minute hand of the clock

➤ **des aiguilles de pin** pine needles.

ail [aj] (*pluriel* ails ou aulx [o]) *nom masculin*

garlic : du pain à l'ail garlic bread.

aile [ɛl] *nom féminin*

wing : l'oiseau a une aile cassée the bird has a broken wing ; **les réacteurs sont sous les ailes de l'avion** the engines are under the wings of the plane.

aille, ailles *etc* ➤ aller.

ailleurs [ajœr] *adverbe*

somewhere else : cherche ailleurs look somewhere else

➤ **nulle part ailleurs** nowhere else

➤ **partout ailleurs** everywhere else

➤ **d'ailleurs** besides : **je n'ai pas envie d'y aller, et d'ailleurs j'ai des devoirs à faire** I don't want to go, and besides I've got homework to do.

aimable [ɛmabl] *adjectif*

kind, nice : l'infirmière a été très aimable the nurse was very kind ou the nurse was very nice.

aimant [ɛmɑ̃] *nom masculin*

magnet.

aimer [eme] *verbe*

1. **to like : tu aimes le football ?** do you like football?
2. **to love : Amélie dit qu'elle aime Cédric** Amélie says that she loves Cédric

➤ **aimer bien** to like : **j'aime bien ton manteau** I like your coat ; **Pierre aime bien aller à la pêche** Pierre likes going fishing

➤ **j'aimerais bien** I would like ; **j'aimerais bien un chocolat** I would like a chocolate ; **j'aimerais bien que tu m'aides** I would like you to help me

➤ **aimer mieux** to prefer : **le bleu n'est pas mal, mais j'aime mieux le vert** the blue one isn't bad, but I prefer the green one

➤ **j'aime mieux rester ici** I'd rather stay here

s'aimer *verbe pronominal*

to love each other : ils s'aiment vraiment they really love each other.

aîné, e [ene] *adjectif & nom*

■ *adjectif*
older, elder : ma sœur aînée my older sister ou my elder sister
■ *nom masculin, nom féminin*
oldest, eldest : l'aîné est étudiant, les deux autres sont encore à l'école the eldest is a student, the other two are still at school.

ainsi [ɛ̃si] *adverbe*

➤ **et ainsi de suite** and so on, and so forth

➤ **ainsi que** as well as : **le directeur ainsi que les professeurs** the headmaster as well as the teachers.

air [ɛr] *nom masculin*

1. **air : l'air est pur ici** the air is pure here
2. **tune : c'est un air connu** it's a well-known tune

➤ **air conditionné** air-conditioning

➤ **avoir l'air** to look : **il a l'air triste** he looks sad ; **il a l'air de bouder** he looks as if he's sulking

➤ **en plein air** open-air : **un concert en plein air** an open-air concert

➤ **prendre l'air** to get some fresh air : **viens**

prendre un peu l'air come and get some fresh air.

aise [ɛz] *nom féminin*

➤ **à l'aise** comfortable : **je ne me sens pas à l'aise avec eux** I don't feel comfortable with them

■ **mal à l'aise** uneasy : **ça me met mal à l'aise** it makes me uneasy.

ajouter [aʒute] *verbe*

to add : **n'oublie pas d'ajouter le prix des billets** don't forget to add the price of the tickets.

alarme [alarm] *nom féminin*

alarm : **l'alarme de la voiture** the car alarm.

album [albɔm] *nom masculin*

album : **tu as écouté leur dernier album ?** you listened to their latest album?

➤ **un album photos** a photo album.

alcool [alkɔl] *nom masculin*

1. **alcohol** : **elle ne boit jamais d'alcool** she never drinks alcohol
2. **brandy** : **de l'alcool de prune** plum brandy
➤ **alcool à 90 degrés** surgical spirit *UK* ou rubbing alcohol *US*.

alcoolisé, e [alkɔlize] *adjectif*

alcoholic : **des boissons alcoolisées** alcoholic drinks.

alentours [alɑ̃tur] *nom masculin pluriel*

outskirts : **les alentours de la ville** the outskirts of the city

➤ **aux alentours de**
1. **near** : **il y a des magasins aux alentours du parc** there are shops near the park
2. **around** : **ils arriveront aux alentours de dix heures** they'll arrive around ten o'clock.

alerte [alɛrt] *nom féminin*

alert : **qui a donné l'alerte ?** who gave the alert?

➤ **une alerte à la bombe** a bomb scare.

algues [alg] *nom féminin pluriel*

seaweed *(ne s'utilise pas au pluriel)* : **ces algues sont toxiques** this seaweed is toxic.

aliment [alimɑ̃] *nom masculin*

food : **il ne mange que des aliments biologiques** he only eats organic food

Food s'utilise le plus souvent au singulier.

alimentation [alimɑ̃tasjɔ̃] *nom féminin*

diet : **une alimentation équilibrée** a balanced diet

➤ **magasin d'alimentation** food store.

allé, e [ale] *participe passé de* aller.

allée [ale] *nom féminin*

1. **path** : **une allée mène au lac** there's a path that leads to the lake
2. **drive** : **l'allée qui mène au château** the drive that leads to the castle.

Allemagne [almaɲ] *nom féminin*

➤ **l'Allemagne** Germany

En anglais, à de rares exceptions près, il n'y a pas d'article devant les noms de pays :

l'Allemagne est un pays voisin de la France Germany shares a border with France ; **Elsa vit en Allemagne** Elsa lives in Germany ; **Éric va en Allemagne tous les ans** Éric goes to Germany every year.

allemand, e [almɑ̃, ɑ̃d] *adjectif*

German

En anglais, les adjectifs se rapportant à un pays ou une région s'écrivent avec une majuscule :

j'aime les saucisses allemandes I like German sausages

allemand *nom masculin*

l'allemand German : **j'apprends l'allemand** I'm learning German

Allemand, e *nom masculin, nom féminin*

German.

aller [ale] *nom & verbe*

▪ *nom masculin*
1. **outward journey** : **l'aller m'a paru plus long que le retour** the outward journey seemed longer than the return journey
2. **single ticket** *UK*, **one-way ticket** *US* : **un aller pour Londres, s'il vous plaît** a single ticket to London, please
➤ **à l'aller** on the way there : **on s'est arrêtés deux fois à l'aller** we stopped twice on the way there

▪ *verbe*
1. **to go** : **où est-ce que vous allez pour les vacances ?** where are you going for the holidays? ; **je vais à la piscine** I'm going to the swimming pool ; **ce bus va au centre-ville** this bus goes to the town centre ; **allons-y !**

let's go! ; **comment ça va à l'école ?** how is it going at school? ; **ces chaussures ne vont pas avec cette robe** these shoes don't go with this dress ; **je suis allé voir le médecin** I went to see the doctor

> Dans la langue parlée ou dans les tournures impératives, on intercale **and** entre **go** et l'infinitif pour montrer une intention. En anglais américain, le **and** est souvent omis :

je vais répondre au téléphone I'll go and answer the phone ; **va chercher du pain** go and get some bread *UK* ou go get some bread *US*

2. *Pour parler de l'état de santé* **to be** : **comment ça va ? – ça va, merci** how are you? – fine, thanks ; **Sylvian va mieux** Sylvian is better

3. *Pour indiquer le futur proche* **to be going to** : **je vais acheter un nouveau vélo** I'm going to buy a new bike ; **tu vas être en retard** you're going to be late

> En anglais, on utilise **will** + infinitif pour annoncer une action immédiate :

le téléphone sonne – j'y vais the phone's ringing – I'll go

➤ **allez !** come on! : **allez, dépêche-toi !** come on, hurry up!

➤ **vas-y !** go on! : **vas-y, Paul, n'aie pas peur !** go on, Paul, don't be scared!

➤ **aller à quelqu'un** to suit somebody : **le vert ne me va pas** green doesn't suit me

s'en aller *verbe pronominal*

1. to leave : **tu t'en vas déjà ?** are you leaving already?

2. to go away : **la tache ne veut pas s'en aller** the stain won't go away ; **va-t'en !** ou **allez-vous-en !** go away!

allergie [alɛrʒi] *nom féminin*

allergy

➤ **faire une allergie à quelque chose** to be allergic to something : **il fait une allergie aux fraises** he's allergic to strawberries.

allergique [alɛrʒik] *adjectif*

allergic : **Sandrine est allergique aux cacahuètes** Sandrine is allergic to peanuts.

aller-retour [aleratur] *nom masculin*

return ticket *UK*, return *UK*, round-trip ticket *US* : **un aller-retour pour Chartres** a return ticket to Chartres.

alligator [aligatɔr] *nom masculin*

alligator.

allô [alo] *interjection*

hello!

allongé, e [alɔ̃ʒe] *adjectif*

lying down : **il était allongé** he was lying down ; **elle est allongée sur le lit** she's lying on the bed.

allonger [alɔ̃ʒe] *verbe*

1. to make longer : **tu devrais allonger un peu la conclusion** you should make the conclusion a bit longer

2. to stretch out : **allongez vos jambes** stretch your legs out

s'allonger *verbe pronominal*

to lie down : **allonge-toi si tu es fatigué** lie down if you're tired.

allumer [alyme] *verbe*

1. to turn on, to switch on : **allume la radio** turn the radio on ou switch the radio on

2. to light : **ils ont allumé un feu pour se réchauffer** they lit a fire to keep warm.

allumette [alymɛt] *nom féminin*

match *(pluriel* **matches***)* : **une boîte d'allumettes** a box of matches.

allure [alyr] *nom féminin*

➤ **avoir une drôle d'allure** to look funny ; **ce gâteau a une drôle d'allure** this cake looks funny

➤ **à toute allure** at top speed.

allusion [alyzjɔ̃] *nom féminin*

➤ **faire allusion à** to refer to : **l'auteur fait allusion à son enfance** the author is referring to his childhood.

alors [alɔr] *adverbe*

1. so : **j'étais fatigué, alors j'ai décidé de rester à la maison** I was tired, so I decided to stay at home ; **alors, qu'est-ce qu'on fait ?** so, what shall we do?

2. then : **Paris était alors moins peuplé** Paris was less populated then

➤ **et alors ?** so what? : **il va se mettre en colère – et alors ?** he'll be angry – so what?

➤ **alors que**

1. even though : **elle est sortie alors que c'était interdit** she went out even though it was forbidden

2. whereas : **il aime le café alors que moi je bois du thé** he likes coffee whereas I drink tea.

Alpes [alp] *nom féminin pluriel*

➤ **les Alpes** the Alps : **il a un chalet dans les Alpes** he has a chalet in the Alps ; **je vais dans les Alpes** I'm going to the Alps.

alphabet [alfabɛ] *nom masculin*

alphabet.

alphabétique [alfabetik] *adjectif*

alphabetical : **par ordre alphabétique** in alphabetical order.

alpinisme [alpinism] *nom masculin*

mountaineering : **faire de l'alpinisme** to go mountaineering.

altitude [altityd] *nom féminin*

altitude : **voler à basse altitude** to fly at low altitude.

aluminium [alyminjɔm] *nom masculin*

aluminium *UK*, aluminum *US*.

amande [amɑ̃d] *nom féminin*

almond : **un gâteau aux amandes** an almond cake.

Amazonie [amazoni] *nom féminin*

➤ **l'Amazonie** the Amazon.

ambassade [ɑ̃basad] *nom féminin*

embassy (*pluriel* **embassies**) : **l'ambassade de France en Irlande** the French embassy in Ireland.

ambiance [ɑ̃bjɑ̃s] *nom féminin*

atmosphere : **il y avait une super ambiance à la soirée** there was a great atmosphere at the party.

ambitieux, euse [ɑ̃bisjø, øz] *adjectif*

ambitious.

ambition [ɑ̃bisjɔ̃] *nom féminin*

ambition : **son ambition est de devenir astronaute** his ambition is to become an astronaut

➤ **avoir de l'ambition** to be ambitious.

ambulance [ɑ̃bylɑ̃s] *nom féminin*

ambulance.

améliorer [ameljɔre] *verbe*

to improve : **il s'entraîne pour améliorer ses performances** he's training to improve his performance

s'améliorer *verbe pronominal*

to improve, to get better : **la situation s'est beaucoup améliorée** the situation has improved a lot ; **il s'améliore en anglais** he's getting better at English.

amende [amɑ̃d] *nom féminin*

fine : **avoir une amende** to get a fine.

amener [amne] *verbe*

to bring : **amène des copains si tu veux** bring some friends if you want.

amer, ère [amɛr] *adjectif*

bitter : **ce café est amer** this coffee is bitter

américain, e [amerikɛ̃, ɛn] *adjectif*

American

> En anglais, les adjectifs se rapportant à un continent s'écrivent avec une majuscule :

le continent américain the American continent.

Américain, e [amerikɛ̃, ɛn] *nom masculin, nom féminin*

American : **les Américains** the Americans.

Amérique [amerik] *nom féminin*

➤ **l'Amérique** America :

> En anglais, il n'y a pas d'article devant les noms de continents :

ils vivent en Amérique they live in America ; **elle aimerait aller en Amérique** she'd like to go to America

➤ **l'Amérique centrale** Central America
➤ **l'Amérique du Nord** North America
➤ **l'Amérique du Sud** South America
➤ **l'Amérique latine** Latin America.

ami, e [ami] *nom masculin, nom féminin*

friend : **ma meilleure amie s'appelle Élodie** my best friend's called Élodie
➤ **un petit ami** a boyfriend
➤ **une petite amie** a girlfriend.

amicalement [amikalmɑ̃] *adverbe*

best wishes : **amicalement, Sabine** best wishes, Sabine.

amitié [amitje] *nom féminin*

friendship : **une longue amitié** a long-standing friendship.

amour [amur] *nom masculin*

love : **c'est plus que de l'amitié, c'est de l'amour** it's more than friendship, it's love.

amoureux, euse [amurø, øz] *adjectif*

in love : **Lucas est amoureux de Virginie** Lucas is in love with Virginie ; **elle est tombée amoureuse de son voisin** she fell in love with her neighbour

amoureux *nom masculin pluriel*

lovers : **un couple d'amoureux sur un banc** a couple of lovers on a bench.

amphithéâtre [ɑ̃fiteatr] *nom masculin*

amphitheatre *UK*, amphitheater *US* : **un amphithéâtre romain** a Roman amphitheatre.

ample [ɑ̃pl] *adjectif*

baggy : **des vêtements amples** baggy clothes.

ampli [ɑ̃pli] *nom masculin*

amp.

ampoule [ɑ̃pul] *nom féminin*

1. bulb : **l'ampoule de la cuisine a grillé** the kitchen bulb has blown
2. blister : **j'ai des ampoules aux pieds** I have blisters on my feet.

amusant, e [amyzɑ̃, ɑ̃t] *adjectif*

funny : **il raconte toujours des histoires amusantes** he always tells funny stories.

s'amuser [samyze] *verbe pronominal*

1. to have a good time : **on s'est bien amusés à la soirée d'Arthur** we had a really good time at Arthur's party
2. to play : **les enfants s'amusent dehors** the children are playing outside
➤ **s'amuser à faire quelque chose** to be busy doing something : **elle s'amusait à lancer des cailloux dans l'eau** she was busy throwing stones into the water.

an [ɑ̃] *nom masculin*

year : **ça fait trois ans que j'apprends l'an-**glais I have been learning English for three years ; **il a 14 ans** he's 14 years old
➤ **le Nouvel An** the New Year.

analyse [analiz] *nom féminin*

1. test : **on m'a fait des analyses** I had some tests ; **une analyse de sang** a blood test
2. analysis : **l'analyse d'un texte** the analysis of a text.

ananas [anana(s)] *nom masculin*

pineapple : **une tarte aux ananas** a pineapple tart.

ancêtre [ɑ̃sɛtr] *nom masculin ou féminin*

ancestor.

anchois [ɑ̃ʃwa] *nom masculin*

anchovy *(pluriel* **anchovies***)*.

ancien, enne [ɑ̃sjɛ̃, ɛn] *adjectif*

1. old ; **un bâtiment ancien** an old building ; **c'est mon ancienne école** that's my old school
2. ex- : **tu connais son ancienne petite amie ?** do you know his ex-girlfriend?

ancre [ɑ̃kr] *nom féminin*

anchor
➤ **jeter l'ancre** to drop anchor.

âne [an] *nom masculin*

donkey : **les ânes ont de longues oreilles** donkeys have long ears.

anesthésie [anɛstezi] *nom féminin*

anaesthesia *UK*, anesthesia *US*
➤ **être sous anesthésie** to be under anaesthetic : **être sous anesthésie générale** to be under general anaesthetic ; **être sous anesthésie locale** to be under local anaesthetic.

ange [ɑ̃ʒ] *nom masculin*

angel.

angine [ɑ̃ʒin] *nom féminin*

throat infection : **Amélie est absente, elle a une angine** Amélie is absent, she has a throat infection.

anglais, e [ɑ̃glɛ, ɛz] *adjectif*

English

> En anglais, les adjectifs se rapportant à un pays ou une région, ainsi que le nom désignant la langue parlée dans ce pays, s'écrivent avec une majuscule :

la campagne anglaise the English countryside

anglais *nom masculin*

English : tu parles bien anglais you speak good English.

Anglais, e [ɑ̃glɛ, ɛz] *nom masculin, nom féminin*

Englishman *(féminin* **Englishwoman** *) :* **les Anglais** the English.

angle [ɑ̃gl] *nom masculin*

1. **angle : un angle droit** a right angle
2. **corner : il y a une boulangerie à l'angle de la rue** there's a baker's on the corner of the street.

Angleterre [ɑ̃glətɛr] *nom féminin*

➤ **l'Angleterre** England

> En anglais, à de rares exceptions près, il n'y a pas d'article devant les noms de pays :

ils sont allés en Angleterre they went to England ; **l'Angleterre fait partie du Royaume-Uni** England is part of the United Kingdom ; **Laurence vit en Angleterre** Laurence lives in England.

anglophone [ɑ̃glɔfɔn] *adjectif*

English-speaking : les pays anglophones English-speaking countries.

angoisser [ɑ̃gwase] *verbe*

to make somebody anxious : ça l'angoisse de parler en public speaking in public makes him anxious.

animal [animal] *(pluriel* **animaux** [animo])

nom masculin

animal : les animaux vivent en liberté dans le parc the animals roam free in the park
➤ **un animal domestique** a pet
➤ **un animal sauvage** a wild animal.

animateur, trice [animatœr, tris] *nom masculin, nom féminin*

1. **presenter** *UK* **: il est animateur de jeux à la télé** he's a TV quiz show presenter
2. **organiser** *UK,* **organizer** *US* **: les animateurs du club sont très sympas** the club organisers are very nice.

animation [animasjɔ̃] *nom féminin*

1. **life : il n'y a pas beaucoup d'animation dans ce quartier** there isn't much life in this area
2. **activities : il y a des animations pour les jeunes dans le camp** there are activities for young people in the camp.

animé, e [anime] *adjectif*

lively : c'est un quartier très animé la nuit it's a very lively area at night.

anneau [ano] *(pluriel* **anneaux**) *nom masculin*

ring : un anneau d'or a gold ring.

année [ane] *nom féminin*

year : la première année de collège est parfois difficile the first year at secondary school is sometimes difficult
➤ **une année bissextile** a leap year
➤ **l'année scolaire** the school year
➤ **bonne année !** Happy New Year!

anniversaire [anivɛrsɛr] *nom masculin*

1. **birthday : joyeux anniversaire !** Happy Birthday!
2. **anniversary : ils fêtent leur anniversaire de mariage** they're celebrating their wedding anniversary.

annonce [anɔ̃s] *nom féminin*

advertisement : tu pourrais passer une annonce dans le journal you could put an advertisement in the newspaper
➤ **une petite annonce** a small ad *UK* ou a classified ad *US*.

annoncer [anɔ̃se] *verbe*

to announce : le gouvernement a annoncé une baisse des impôts the government announced a cut in taxes
➤ **annoncer à quelqu'un que** to inform somebody that : **le proviseur nous a annoncé que notre professeur était absent** the headmaster informed us that our teacher was away.

annuaire [anɥɛr] *nom masculin*

phone book : j'ai trouvé ton numéro dans l'annuaire I found your number in the phone book.

annuel, elle [anɥɛl] *adjectif*

yearly : la moyenne annuelle the yearly average.

annuler [anyle] *verbe*

to cancel : nous avons dû annuler la fête we had to cancel the party.

a

anorak [anɔrak] *nom masculin*
anorak.

anse [ãs] *nom féminin*
handle : **l'anse du panier** the basket handle.

antarctique [ãtarktik] *adjectif*
Antarctic.

Antarctique [ãtarktik] *nom masculin*
➤ **l'Antarctique** Antarctica.

antenne [ãtɛn] *nom féminin*
1. aerial, antenna : **l'antenne de la télé ne marche pas bien** the TV aerial doesn't work properly
2. antenna : **les antennes du papillon** the butterfly's antennae
➤ **une antenne parabolique** a satellite dish.

antibiotique [ãtibjɔtik] *nom masculin*
antibiotics : **elle est sous antibiotiques** she's on antibiotics.

antipathique [ãtipatik] *adjectif*
unpleasant : **qu'est-ce qu'il est antipathique !** he's so unpleasant!

antiquaire [ãtikɛr] *nom masculin ou féminin*
antique dealer : **le père de Virginie est antiquaire** Virginie's father is an antique dealer.

antique [ãtik] *adjectif*
antique : **un vase antique** an antique vase ; **les civilisations antiques** ancient civilizations.

antiquité [ãtikite] *nom féminin*
antique : **un magasin d'antiquités** an antique shop.

antivol [ãtivɔl] *nom masculin invariable*
lock.

anxieux, euse [ãksjø, øz] *adjectif*
anxious.

août [u(t)] *nom masculin*
August : **je vais à Londres en août** I'm going to London in August
➤ **nous sommes le trois août** it's the third of August *UK* ou it's August third *US*

En anglais, les mois de l'année s'écrivent avec une majuscule.

apercevoir [apɛrsəvwar] *verbe*
to see : **je l'ai aperçue dans la rue** I saw her in the street

s'apercevoir *verbe pronominal*
s'apercevoir de quelque chose to notice something ; **je ne me suis pas aperçu de mon erreur** I didn't notice my mistake ; **s'apercevoir que** to notice that ; **je ne me suis pas aperçu qu'il était parti** I didn't notice that he'd left.

aperçu, e [apɛrsy] *participe passé de* apercevoir.

ap. J.-C. *(abréviation de* après Jésus-Christ)
AD : **en 55 ap. J.-C.** in 55 AD.

aplatir [aplatir] *verbe*
to flatten : **la grêle a aplati l'herbe** the hail flattened the grass.

apparaître [aparɛtr] *verbe*
to appear : **cette espèce est apparue à la fin du jurassique** this species appeared at the end of the Jurassic period.

appareil [aparɛj] *nom masculin*
1. device : **un appareil de mesure** a measuring device
2. brace *UK*, braces *US* : **Jérôme porte un appareil** Jérôme wears a brace
3. aircraft : **l'appareil a décollé tout de suite** the aircraft took off straightaway
➤ **un appareil photo** a camera : **un appareil photo numérique** a digital camera
➤ **qui est à l'appareil ?** who's speaking? : **Céline Faucheur à l'appareil** Céline Faucheur speaking.

appart [apart] *(abréviation de* appartement)
nom masculin familier
apartment, flat *UK*.

appartement [apartəmã] *nom masculin*
apartment, flat *UK*.

appartenir [apartənir] *verbe*
➤ **appartenir à** to belong to : **à qui appartient ce sac à dos ?** who does this backpack belong to? ; **cette broche a appartenu à ma grand-mère** this brooch belonged to my grandmother.

appartenu [apartəny] *participe passé invariable de* appartenir.

apparu [apary] *participe passé de* apparaître.

appel [apɛl] *nom masculin*

call : **il y a eu trois appels pour toi ce matin** there were three calls for you this morning

➤ **faire l'appel** to call the register : **la prof a oublié de faire l'appel** the teacher forgot to call the register.

appeler [aple] *verbe*

to call : **je l'ai appelé mais il ne m'a pas entendue** I called him but he didn't hear me ; **je t'appellerai ce soir** I'll call you this evening

s'appeler *verbe pronominal*

to be called : **comment s'appelle ce truc ?** what's this thing called? ; **comment tu t'appelles ?** what's your name? ; **elle s'appelle Érica** her name is Érica OU she's called Érica.

appendicite [apɛ̃disit] *nom féminin*

appendicitis : **elle a l'appendicite** she has appendicitis ; **je dois me faire opérer de l'appendicite** I have to have my appendix removed.

applaudir [aplodir] *verbe*

to clap, to applaud : **ils ont applaudi à la fin du discours** they clapped at the end of the speech OU they applauded at the end of the speech.

applaudissements [aplodismɑ̃] *nom masculin pluriel*

applause (*ne s'utilise jamais au pluriel*) : **il reçut de nombreux applaudissements** he got a big round of applause.

appliquer [aplike] *verbe*

1. to apply : **appliquer une pommade sur une plaie** to apply ointment to a wound
2. to enforce : **appliquer la loi** to enforce the law

s'appliquer *verbe pronominal*

to apply oneself : **tu pourrais t'appliquer un peu plus !** you could apply yourself a bit more!

apporter [aporte] *verbe*

to bring : **apporte-moi le journal** bring me the newspaper ; **il m'a apporté des fleurs** he brought me some flowers.

appréciation [apresjasjɔ̃] *nom féminin*

comment : **le prof a mis une appréciation**

sur ma copie the teacher put a comment on my homework.

apprécier [apresje] *verbe*

to like : **je sais qu'il ne m'apprécie pas** I know he doesn't like me ; **je n'ai pas apprécié sa remarque** I didn't like the remark he made.

apprendre [aprɑ̃dr] *verbe*

1. to learn : **elle apprend le grec** she's learning Greek ; **j'apprends à jouer au tennis** I'm learning to play tennis OU I'm learning how to play tennis
2. to teach : **ma mère m'a appris cette chanson** my mother taught me this song ; **il apprend à lire à ses enfants** he's teaching his children to read OU he's teaching his children how to read

➤ **apprendre que** to hear that : **j'ai appris qu'ils sortaient ensemble** I heard that they were going out together.

apprentissage [aprɑ̃tisaʒ] *nom masculin*

apprenticeship : **Aurélien est en apprentissage dans une boulangerie** Aurélien is serving his apprenticeship at a baker's.

appris, e [apri, iz] *participe passé de* apprendre.

approcher [aprɔʃe] *verbe*

to move closer to : **approche ta chaise de la télé** move your chair closer to the TV

s'approcher *verbe pronominal*

to move closer : **ne t'approche pas !** don't come any closer!

➤ **s'approcher de** to come up to OU to approach : **il s'est approché de moi** he came up to me OU he approached me.

approuver [apruve] *verbe*

to approve of : **ses parents n'approuvent pas son choix** his parents don't approve of his choice.

approximatif, ive [aprɔksimatif, iv] *adjectif*

approximate : **une estimation approximative** an approximate estimate.

appuyer [apɥije] *verbe*

to push : **appuie plus fort** push harder

appuyer sur quelque chose   to   press something : **appuie sur le bouton vert** press the green button

s'appuyer *verbe pronominal*

to lean : **ne t'appuie pas contre le mur, je viens de le peindre** don't lean against the wall, I've just painted it.

après [aprɛ] *préposition & adverbe*

■ *préposition*
after : **on a géographie après le déjeuner** we have a geography lesson after lunch ; **après avoir mangé, ils ont joué aux cartes** after they had eaten, they played cards OU after eating, they played cards
■ *adverbe*
1. afterwards : **qu'est-ce que tu veux faire après ?** what do you want to do afterwards?
2. later : **deux jours après, il est revenu** he came back two days later
➤ **après tout** after all : **après tout c'est de sa faute** it's his fault after all
➤ **d'après** according to : **d'après lui, demain la France va gagner** according to him, France is going to win tomorrow
➤ **d'après moi** in my opinion : **d'après moi, Julie va refuser** in my opinion, Julie is going to refuse
➤ **la semaine d'après** the week after : **pas la semaine prochaine, la semaine d'après** not next week, the week after.

après-demain [apredmɛ̃] *adverbe*

the day after tomorrow : **je t'appelle après-demain** I'll call you the day after tomorrow.

après-midi [apremidi] *nom masculin & nom féminin invariable*

afternoon : **on a passé l'après-midi à lire** we spent the afternoon reading ; **je vais chez le dentiste lundi après-midi** I'm going to the dentist on Monday afternoon ; **à trois heures de l'après-midi** at three in the afternoon.

après-ski [apreski] *nom masculin*

snow-boot.

aquagym [akwaʒim] *nom féminin*

aquarobics : **je fais de l'aquagym** I do aquarobics.

aquarelle [akwarɛl] *nom féminin*

watercolour *UK*, watercolor *US*.

aquarium [akwarjɔm] *nom masculin*

aquarium.

arabe [arab] *adjectif & nom*

■ *adjectif*
Arab : **les pays arabes** Arab countries
■ *nom masculin*
Arabic : **Leila parle arabe** Leila speaks Arabic

> En anglais, les adjectifs se rapportant à un pays ou une région, ainsi que le nom désignant la langue parlée dans ce pays, s'écrivent avec une majuscule.

Arabe *nom masculin ou féminin*

Arab.

araignée [areɲe] *nom féminin*

spider.

arbitre [arbitr] *nom masculin*

1. referee : **l'arbitre lui a donné un carton jaune** the referee gave him a yellow card
2. umpire : **elle est arbitre de tennis** she's a tennis umpire.

arbre [arbr] *nom masculin*

tree : **à l'ombre d'un arbre** in the shade of a tree
➤ **un arbre fruitier** a fruit tree
➤ **l'arbre généalogique** the family tree
➤ **un arbre de Noël** a Christmas tree.

arc [ark] *nom masculin*

bow : **ils jouent avec des arcs et des flèches** they're playing with bows and arrows.

arc-en-ciel [arkɑ̃sjɛl] (*pluriel* arcs-en-ciel) *nom masculin*

rainbow.

arche [arʃ] *nom féminin*

arch (*pluriel* **arches**).

archéologie [arkeɔlɔʒi] *nom féminin*

archaeology, archeology *US*.

archéologue [arkeɔlɔg] *nom masculin ou féminin*

archaeologist, archeologist *US* : **elle veut devenir archéologue** she wants to become an archaeologist.

architecte [arʃitɛkt] *nom masculin ou féminin*

architect : **mon père est architecte** my father is an architect.

architecture [arʃitɛktyr] *nom féminin*
architecture.

arctique [arktik] *adjectif*
Arctic.

Arctique [arktik] *nom masculin*
> l'**Arctique** the Arctic.

ardoise [ardwaz] *nom féminin*
slate : **un toit en ardoise** a slate roof.

arête [arɛt] *nom féminin*
bone : **ce poisson est plein d'arêtes** there are a lot of bones in this fish.

argent [arʒɑ̃] *nom masculin*
1. silver : **un bracelet en argent** a silver bracelet
2. money : **il te reste de l'argent ?** have you got any money left?
> l'**argent de poche** pocket money.

argot [argo] *nom masculin*
slang.

argument [argymɑ̃] *nom masculin*
argument : **des arguments contre la réforme** arguments against the reform.

arme [arm] *nom féminin*
weapon
> **une arme à feu** a firearm
> **une arme blanche** knife (*pluriel* **knives**).

armée [arme] *nom féminin*
army (*pluriel* **armies**) : **mon frère est dans l'armée** my brother's in the army
> l'**armée de l'air** the air force
> l'**armée de terre** the army.

armoire [armwar] *nom féminin*
wardrobe : **toutes tes chemises sont dans l'armoire** all your shirts are in the wardrobe.

armure [armyr] *nom féminin*
armour *UK*, armor *US*.

arôme [arom] *nom masculin*
flavour *UK*, flavor *US* : **yaourt arôme vanille** vanilla-flavoured yoghurt *UK* ou vanilla-flavored yogurt *US*.

arracher [araʃe] *verbe*
1. to pull up : **j'ai arraché des mauvaises herbes** I pulled up some weeds
2. to tear out : **il a arraché plusieurs pages de**

son cahier he tore several pages out of his exercise book
> **arracher quelque chose à quelqu'un** to snatch something from somebody ; **le voleur lui a arraché son sac** the thief snatched her bag from her
> **se faire arracher une dent** to have a tooth taken out.

arranger [arɑ̃ʒe] *verbe*
1. to arrange : **elle a arrangé les fleurs dans le vase** she arranged the flowers in the vase
2. to sort out : **ne t'inquiète pas, j'ai tout arrangé** don't worry, I've sorted everything out
3. to suit : **lundi ça ne m'arrange pas du tout** Monday doesn't suit me at all
4. to fix : **Bruno a arrangé ma montre** Bruno fixed my watch

s'arranger *verbe pronominal*
1. to manage : **je vais m'arranger, ce n'est pas un problème** I'll manage, it's not a problem
2. to work out : **ça va s'arranger** it'll work out
> **arrangez-vous pour être là à l'heure** make sure you're there on time.

arrêt [arɛ] *nom masculin*
stop : **je descends au prochain arrêt** I'm getting off at the next stop
> **un arrêt d'autobus** a bus stop
> **sans arrêt**
1. non-stop : **il a plu sans arrêt pendant deux jours** it rained non-stop for two days
2. always, constantly : **elle pose sans arrêt des questions** she's always asking questions ou she's constantly asking questions.

arrêter [arete] *verbe*
1. to stop : **arrête le moteur** stop the engine ; **arrêter de faire quelque chose** to stop doing something ; **arrête de rigoler !** stop laughing!
2. to arrest : **la police a arrêté les voleurs** the police arrested the thieves
> **ne pas arrêter de faire quelque chose** to keep doing something : **il n'arrête pas de m'embêter** he keeps pestering me

s'arrêter *verbe pronominal*
to stop : **arrête-toi au supermarché** stop at the supermarket.

arrière [arjɛr] *adjectif & nom*
▪ *adjectif invariable*
back : **le siège arrière** the back seat

■ *nom masculin*

back : **je vais m'asseoir à l'arrière** I'll sit in the back

➤ **en arrière**

1. back : **nous avons dû revenir en arrière** we had to go back

2. behind : **il est resté en arrière** he stayed behind.

arrière-grand-mère [arjɛrgrɑ̃mɛr] (*pluriel* arrière-grands-mères) *nom féminin*
great-grandmother.

arrière-grand-père [arjɛrgrɑ̃pɛr] (*pluriel* arrière-grands-pères) *nom masculin*
great-grandfather.

arrivée [arive] *nom féminin*

arrival : **le hall des arrivées** the arrivals hall ; **à mon arrivée, je l'ai appelé** I called him when I arrived.

arriver [arive] *verbe*

to arrive, to come : **ils sont arrivés à neuf heures** they arrived at nine o'clock ; **le bus arrive** the bus is coming

➤ **arriver à faire quelque chose** to manage to do something : **tu es arrivé à la convaincre ?** did you manage to convince her? ; **il n'arrive pas à faire ses devoirs** he can't do his homework

➤ **arriver à** to come up to : **l'eau m'arrivait aux genoux** the water came up to my knees

➤ **il m'arrive de ...** I sometimes ... : **il m'arrive d'oublier quel jour on est** I sometimes forget what day it is.

arrobas, arobas [arɔbas] *nom féminin*

In email address at.

arrogant, e [arɔgɑ̃, ɑ̃t] *adjectif*

arrogant : **un ton arrogant** an arrogant tone.

arrondir [arɔ̃dir] *verbe*

1. to round up : **elle me devait cinquante-neuf euros mais elle a arrondi à soixante** she owed me fifty-nine euros but she rounded it up to sixty

2. to round down : **arrondissez à la dizaine inférieure** round it down to the nearest multiple of ten.

arrondissement [arɔ̃dismɑ̃] *nom masculin*

arrondissement

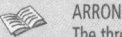
arroser [aroze] *verbe*

to water : **n'oublie pas d'arroser les plantes** don't forget to water the plants.

arrosoir [arozwar] *nom masculin*

watering can.

art [ar] *nom masculin*

art : **l'art moderne** modern art

➤ **les arts martiaux** martial arts.

artichaut [artiʃo] *nom masculin*

artichoke.

article [artikl] *nom masculin*

article : **tu as lu l'article sur la Chine ?** have you read the article on China?

articuler [artikyle] *verbe*

to speak clearly : **articule, je ne comprends pas ce que tu dis !** speak clearly, I can't understand what you're saying!

artificiel, elle [artifisjɛl] *adjectif*

artificial : **un lac artificiel** an artificial lake.

artisan, e [artizɑ̃, an] *nom masculin, nom féminin*
craftsman (*féminin* craftswoman).

artiste [artist] *nom masculin ou féminin*

artist : **il veut être artiste** he wants to be an artist

➤ **un artiste peintre** a painter.

as [a] ➤ avoir.

as [as] *nom masculin*

ace : **l'as de trèfle** the ace of clubs.

ascenseur [asɑ̃sœr] *nom masculin*

lift *UK*, elevator *US* : **prenons l'ascenseur**

let's take the lift *UK* OU let's take the elevator *US*.

Ascension [asɑ̃sjɔ̃] *nom féminin*
➤ **l'Ascension** Ascension Day.

asiatique [azjatik] *adjectif*
   Asian

   En anglais, les adjectifs se rapportant à un continent s'écrivent avec une majuscule :

   la cuisine asiatique Asian cooking

Asiatique *nom masculin ou féminin*
   Asian.

Asie [azi] *nom féminin*
➤ **l'Asie** Asia

   En anglais, il n'y a pas d'article devant les noms de continent :

   ils ont longtemps vécu en Asie they lived in Asia for a long time ; **j'aimerais beaucoup aller en Asie** I'd love to go to Asia.

aspect [aspɛ] *nom masculin*
   appearance : changer d'aspect to change in appearance
➤ **avoir un drôle d'aspect** to look strange
➤ **d'un aspect agréable** nice-looking : **une personne d'aspect agréable** a nice-looking person.

asperge [aspɛrʒ] *nom féminin*
   asparagus (*ne s'utilise jamais au pluriel*) **: je n'aime pas les asperges** I don't like asparagus.

asperger [aspɛrʒe] *verbe*
   asperger quelqu'un de quelque chose to splash somebody with something ; **la voiture m'a aspergé de boue** the car splashed me with mud.

aspirateur [aspiratœr] *nom masculin*
   vacuum cleaner, Hoover® *UK*
➤ **passer l'aspirateur** to do the vacuuming OU to hoover *UK*.

aspirer [aspire] *verbe*
   to inhale : plusieurs personnes ont aspiré du gaz several people inhaled gas.

aspirine [aspirin] *nom féminin*
   aspirine : un cachet d'aspirine an aspirin.

assassin [asasɛ̃] *nom masculin*
   murderer.

assassinat [asasina] *nom masculin*
   murder.

assassiner [asasine] *verbe*
   to murder : se faire assassiner to be murdered.

assemblée [asɑ̃ble] *nom féminin*
   assembly (*pluriel* **assemblies**)
➤ **l'Assemblée nationale** the National Assembly.

s'asseoir [saswar] *verbe pronominal*
   to sit, to sit down : assieds-toi sit down ; **il s'est assis sur le canapé** he sat on the sofa.

assez [ase] *adverbe*
1. **enough : la tarte est assez grande pour huit** the tart is big enough for eight ; **assez de** enough ; **il y a assez de lait** there's enough milk
2. **quite : Benjamin est assez sympa** Benjamin is quite nice
➤ **en avoir assez de** to have had enough of : **j'en ai assez de tes plaisanteries !** I've had enough of your jokes!

assiette [asjɛt] *nom féminin*
   plate : passe-moi ton assiette pass me your plate
➤ **une assiette creuse** OU **une assiette à soupe** a soup plate
➤ **une assiette à dessert** a dessert plate
➤ **une assiette plate** a dinner plate.

assis, e [asi, iz] *verbe & adjectif*
■ *participe passé de* asseoir.
■ *adjectif*
   sitting, sitting down : il est assis sur l'herbe he's sitting on the grass ; **elle était assise** she was sitting down.

assistant, e [asistɑ̃, ɑ̃t] *nom masculin, nom féminin*
   assistant : c'est l'assistante du directeur she's the director's assistant ; **l'assistant d'anglais** the English assistant
➤ **une assistante sociale** a social worker.

assister [asiste] *verbe*
➤ **assister à**
1. **to go, to attend : tous les parents ont as-**

sisté à la réunion all the parents went to the meeting
2. **to witness** : je n'ai pas assisté à l'accident I didn't witness the accident.

association [asɔsjasjɔ̃] *nom féminin*

association : une association de consommateurs a consumer association.

assommer [asɔme] *verbe*

to knock out : les cambrioleurs l'ont assommé the burglars knocked him out.

assorti, e [asɔrti] *adjectif*

matching : une chemise avec une cravate assortie a shirt with a matching tie.

assurance [asyrɑ̃s] *nom féminin*

1. **insurance** : une assurance auto a car insurance ; tu as pris une assurance ? have you taken out any insurance?
2. **confidence** : elle manque d'assurance she isn't very confident.

assurer [asyre] *verbe*

1. **assurer à quelqu'un que** to assure somebody that ; je t'assure que c'est vrai I assure you that it's true OU I swear it's true
2. **to insure** : leur maison n'est pas assurée their house isn't insured

s'assurer *verbe pronominal*

1. **to insure oneself** : mes parents se sont assurés contre l'incendie my parents have insured themselves against fire
2. **s'assurer que** to make sure that ; assure-toi que la porte est fermée à clé make sure that the door is locked OU make sure the door is locked.

astérisque [asterisk] *nom masculin*

asterisk.

asthme [asm] *nom masculin*

asthma : elle a de l'asthme she has asthma ; une crise d'asthme an asthma attack.

astrologie [astrɔlɔʒi] *nom féminin*

astrology.

astronaute [astrɔnot] *nom masculin ou féminin*

astronaut : elle est astronaute she's an astronaut.

astronomie [astrɔnɔmi] *nom féminin*

astronomy.

astuce [astys] *nom féminin*

trick : j'ai trouvé l'astuce pour ouvrir la boîte I've got the trick of opening the box.

atelier [atəlje] *nom masculin*

1. **workshop** : l'atelier de travaux manuels de l'école the school's arts and crafts workshop
2. **studio** : un atelier de peintre rénové a renovated artist's studio.

athlète [atlɛt] *nom masculin ou féminin*

athlete.

athlétisme [atletism] *nom masculin*

athletics *UK (singulier)*, track and field *US*.

atlantique [atlɑ̃tik] *adjectif*

Atlantic

> En anglais, les adjectifs se rapportant à un océan s'écrivent avec une majuscule :

la côte atlantique the Atlantic coast

Atlantique *nom masculin*

➤ **l'Atlantique** the Atlantic Ocean OU the Atlantic.

atlas [atlas] *nom masculin*

atlas (*pluriel* atlases).

atmosphère [atmɔsfɛr] *nom féminin*

atmosphere : l'atmosphère terrestre the earth's atmosphere.

atomique [atɔmik] *adjectif*

1. **atomic** : la bombe atomique the atomic bomb
2. **nuclear** : l'énergie atomique nuclear energy.

atroce [atrɔs] *adjectif*

terrible : j'ai un mal de tête atroce I have a terrible headache.

attacher [ataʃe] *verbe*

1. **to tie, to tie up** : ils ont attaché leur chien à un poteau they tied their dog to a post ; attache tes lacets tie your laces up
2. **to fasten** : veuillez attacher vos ceintures de sécurité please fasten your seat belts

s'attacher à *verbe pronominal*

to grow to like, to become attached to : peu à peu je me suis attachée à lui I grew to like him OU I became attached to him.

attaque [atak] *nom féminin*

1. attack : **l'armée a lancé une attaque sur la ville** the army launched an attack on the town
2. stroke : **le père de Quentin a eu une attaque** Quentin's father had a stroke.

attaquer [atake] *verbe*

to attack : **attaquer quelqu'un dans la rue** to attack somebody in the street

s'attaquer à *verbe pronominal*

to attack : **elle s'attaque toujours aux plus faibles** she always attacks people who are weaker than her.

atteindre [atɛ̃dr] *verbe*

to reach : **elle est montée sur une chaise pour atteindre le placard** she climbed onto a chair to reach the cupboard.

attendre [atɑ̃dr] *verbe*

1. to wait for : **attendez-moi !** wait for me! ; **on a attendu que la pluie s'arrête** we waited for the rain to stop
2. to wait : **attends, j'ai presque fini** wait, I've nearly finished

s'attendre à *verbe pronominal*

to expect : **personne ne s'attendait à ça** nobody expected that

> ⚠️ Attendre is a false friend, it does not mean 'attend'.

attendu, e [atɑ̃dy] *participe passé de* attendre.

attentat [atɑ̃ta] *nom masculin*

attack : **un attentat à la bombe** a bomb attack.

attention [atɑ̃sjɔ̃] *nom & interjection*

■ *nom féminin*
attention : **il essaie d'attirer leur attention** he's trying to attract their attention
■ *interjection*
watch out! : **attention, ça glisse !** watch out, it's slippery! ; **attention à la marche** mind the step

> **faire attention à**
1. to be careful of : **faites attention aux voitures** be careful of the cars
2. to pay attention to : **il ne fait pas attention à ce que dit le professeur** he's not paying attention to the teacher.

atterrir [aterir] *verbe*

1. to land : **l'avion a atterri à l'heure** the plane landed on time
2. *familier* to end up : **Jean a atterri chez le proviseur** Jean ended up in the headmaster's office.

atterrissage [aterisaʒ] *nom masculin*

landing.

attirer [atire] *verbe*

to attract : **l'aimant attire le fer** magnets attract iron

> **s'attirer des ennuis** to get into trouble : **tu vas t'attirer des ennuis** you'll get into trouble.

attitude [atityd] *nom féminin*

attitude : **je ne comprends pas leur attitude** I don't understand their attitude.

attraper [atrape] *verbe*

to catch : **essaie de m'attraper !** try and catch me! ; **j'ai attrapé un rhume** I've caught a cold.

au [o] > à.

aube [ob] *nom féminin*

dawn : **à l'aube** at dawn.

auberge [obɛrʒ] *nom féminin*

inn

> **une auberge de jeunesse** a youth hostel.

aubergine [obɛrʒin] *nom féminin*

aubergine *UK*, eggplant *US*.

aucun, e [okœ̃ , yn] *adjectif & pronom*

■ *adjectif*
ne ... aucun no ; **il n'y a aucune voiture dans la rue** there are no cars in the street ou there aren't any cars in the street
■ *pronom*
none : **aucun des enfants** none of the children

> **aucun des deux** neither of them.

au-dessous [odəsu] *loc adv*

underneath, below : **les assiettes sont là et les bols au-dessous** the plates are there and the bowls are underneath

> **au-dessous de** below : **trois degrés au-dessous de zéro** three degrees below zero ; **ils habitent au-dessous de chez nous** they live on the floor below us.

au-dessus [odəsy] *adverbe*

above : **le piano est contre le mur et il y a une glace au-dessus** the piano is against the wall and there's a mirror above ; **au-dessus du prix habituel** above the usual price ; **ils habitent au-dessus de chez nous** they live on the floor above.

augmentation [ogmɑ̃tasjɔ̃] *nom féminin*

1. increase : **une augmentation du nombre d'étudiants** an increase in the number of students
2. rise *UK*, raise *US* : **une augmentation de salaire** a pay rise *UK* ou a pay raise *US*.

augmenter [ogmɑ̃te] *verbe*

1. to go up, to increase : **le nombre d'élèves a augmenté** the number of pupils has increased
2. to increase, to put up *UK* : **ils ont encore augmenté les prix** they've increased prices again ou they've put the prices up again.

aujourd'hui [oʒurdɥi] *adverbe*

today : **nous sommes le dix-huit aujourd'hui** it's the eighteenth today.

auparavant [oparavɑ̃] *adverbe*

1. first : **répondez aux questions, mais auparavant lisez-les attentivement** answer the questions, but first read them carefully
2. before : **trois jours auparavant** three days before.

auquel [okɛl] ➤ lequel

le livre auquel je pensais the book I was thinking of.

aurai, auras *etc* ➤ avoir.

aussi [osi] *adverbe*

1. too, as well, also : **est-ce que tu veux aussi de la salade ?** do you want some salad too? ou do you want some salad as well? ; **j'y vais aussi** I'm going too ou I'm going as well ; **elle a un chat et elle a un chien aussi** she has a cat and she also has a dog ; **j'ai faim – moi aussi** I'm hungry – so am I ou I'm hungry – me too ; **j'étais en retard – Fabien aussi** I was late – so was Fabien

Too et as well s'emploient plus souvent que also. Notez que too et as well se placent toujours en fin de phrase, tandis que also se place en milieu de phrase.

2. so : **je n'ai jamais rien vu d'aussi beau** I've never seen anything so beautiful
➤ **aussi ... que** as ... as : **il n'est pas aussi grand que moi** he's not as big as me.

aussitôt [osito] *adverbe*

immediately : **il est arrivé aussitôt** he arrived immediately
➤ **aussitôt que** as soon as : **aussitôt que possible** as soon as possible.

Australie [ostrali] *nom féminin*

➤ **l'Australie** Australia

En anglais, à de rares exceptions près, il n'y a pas d'article devant les noms de pays :

l'Australie est un pays immense Australia is a huge country ; **les kangourous vivent en Australie** kangaroos live in Australia ; **ils sont allés en Australie** they went to Australia.

australien, enne [ostraljɛ̃, ɛn] *adjectif*

Australian

En anglais, les adjectifs se rapportant à un pays ou une région s'écrivent avec une majuscule :

le climat australien the Australian climate

Australien, enne *nom masculin, nom féminin*

Australian.

autant [otɑ̃] *adverbe*

so much : **je n'ai jamais autant ri** I've never laughed so much
➤ **autant de**
1. so much : **normalement, ça ne fait pas autant de bruit** it doesn't usually make so much noise
2. so many : **je n'ai jamais vu autant de gens dans la rue** I've never seen so many people in the street
➤ **autant que ...** as much as : **j'ai mangé autant que Léa** I ate as much as Léa
➤ **autant de ... que ...**
1. as much ... as ... : **je n'ai pas autant d'argent que toi** I don't have as much money as you
2. as many ... as : **il n'a pas autant d'amis que toi** he doesn't have as many friends as you
➤ **autant que possible** as much as possible
➤ **autant y aller tout de suite** we may as well go right now.

a

auteur [otœr] *nom masculin*

author : **c'est un auteur très connu** he's a very famous author.

autobus [otobys] *nom masculin*

bus *(pluriel* **buses)** : **nous sommes rentrés en autobus** we came back by bus.

autocar [otokar] *nom masculin*

coach *UK (pluriel* **coaches**), bus *US (pluriel* **buses**) : **une excursion en autocar** a coach trip.

autocollant, e [otokolã, ãt] *adjectif*

self-adhesive : **une étiquette autocollante** a self-adhesive label

autocollant *nom masculin*

sticker : **son classeur est couvert d'autocollants** her ring binder is covered in stickers.

auto-école [otoekol] *(pluriel* auto-écoles*)*
nom féminin
driving school.

autographe [otograf] *nom masculin*

autograph : **je lui ai demandé un autographe** I asked for his autograph.

automatique [otomatik] *adjectif*

automatic.

automatiquement [otomatikmã] *adverbe*

automatically : **la lumière s'éteint automatiquement** the light goes out automatically.

automne [oton] *nom masculin*

autumn, fall *US* : **en automne** in the autumn ou in autumn ou in the fall *US*.

automobiliste [otomobilist] *nom masculin*
ou féminin
driver.

autorisation [otorizasjõ] *nom féminin*

permission : **il a demandé l'autorisation à ses parents** he asked for his parents' permission.

autoriser [otorize] *verbe*

autoriser quelqu'un à faire quelque chose to give somebody permission to do something ; **la prof nous a autorisés à sortir plus tôt** the teacher gave us permission to leave earlier.

autorité [otorite] *nom féminin*

authority : **il manque d'autorité** he has no authority.

autoroute [otorut] *nom féminin*

motorway *UK*, freeway *US*.

auto-stop [otostop] *nom masculin*

hitchhiking : **l'auto-stop est interdit sur l'autoroute** hitchhiking is forbidden on the motorway ; **faire de l'auto-stop** to hitchhike ; **nous sommes allés à la plage en auto-stop** we hitchhiked to the beach.

autour [otur] *adverbe*

around : **il y a des arbres autour de la place** there are trees around the square : **on arrivera autour de cinq heures** we'll arrive around five o'clock.

autre [otr] *adjectif & pronom*

◼ *adjectif*
other : **l'autre jour** the other day ; **les autres classes** the other classes ; **j'ai d'autres amis** I have other friends
➤ **un autre, une autre** another : **je voudrais un autre morceau de gâteau** I'd like another piece of cake : **tu iras une autre fois** you'll go another time
➤ **autre chose** something else : **je parlais d'autre chose** I was talking about something else
➤ **autre part** somewhere else
◼ *pronom*
➤ **l'autre** the other one : **je préfère l'autre** I prefer the other one
➤ **les autres**
1. the other ones : **je veux les autres** I want the other ones
2. the others : **les autres ne sont pas encore arrivés** the others haven't arrived yet
➤ **un autre, une autre** another one : **est-ce que je peux en avoir un autre ?** can I have another one?
➤ **d'autres** others : **il n'y en a pas d'autres** they aren't any others
➤ **personne d'autre** nobody else ou no one else : **personne d'autre n'est venu** nobody else came.

autrefois [otrəfwa] *adverbe*

in the past : **autrefois, il n'y avait pas d'électricité** in the past, there was no electricity.

autrement [otrəmã] *adverbe*

1. **differently** : **je l'ai fait autrement** I did it differently
2. **otherwise** : **appelle-le, autrement il va se vexer** call him, otherwise he'll be offended
➤ **autrement dit** in other words.

autruche [otryʃ] *nom féminin*

ostrich (*pluriel* **ostriches**).

aux [o] ➤ **à**.

auxquels, auxquelles [okɛl] ➤ **lequel**

les mots auxquels je pense the words that I'm thinking of.

avalanche [avalɑ̃ʃ] *nom féminin*

avalanche.

avaler [avale] *verbe*

to swallow : **il a avalé le cachet** he swallowed the pill.

avance [avɑ̃s] *nom féminin*

lead : **ils ont deux points d'avance sur l'autre équipe** they have a two-point lead over the other team
➤ **avoir une heure d'avance** to be an hour early
➤ **à l'avance** in advance : **réserver à l'avance** to reserve in advance ou to book in advance
➤ **d'avance** in advance : **vous devez payer d'avance** you have to pay in advance
➤ **en avance** early : **elle arrive toujours en avance** she always arrives early ; **en avance de dix minutes** ten minutes early.

avancer [avɑ̃se] *verbe*

1. **to move forward** : **les voitures avançaient lentement** the cars moved slowly forward
2. **to progress** : **le travail avance** the work is progressing
3. **to be fast** : **ta montre avance** your watch is fast ; **avancer de deux minutes** to be two minutes fast
4. **to bring forward** : **ils ont avancé la date de la réunion** they have brought the date of the meeting forward
5. **to lend** : **tu peux m'avancer dix euros ?** can you lend me ten euros?

avant [avɑ̃] *préposition, adverbe, adjectif & nom*

■ *préposition & adverbe*
before : **Chris a répondu avant moi** Chris

answered before me ; **quelques jours avant** a few days before ; **ferme tout à clé avant de partir** lock everything before you leave ; **je dois te parler avant que tu partes** I must speak to you before you leave
■ *adjectif invariable*
front : **les roues avant** the front wheels
■ *nom masculin*
front : **l'avant de la voiture est abîmé** the front of the car is damaged.

avantage [avɑ̃taʒ] *nom masculin*

advantage : **il y a des avantages et des inconvénients** there are advantages and disadvantages.

avant-hier [avɑ̃tjɛr] *adverbe*

the day before yesterday : **j'ai vu Charlotte avant-hier** I saw Charlotte the day before yesterday.

avec [avɛk] *préposition & adverbe*

■ *préposition*
with : **tu viens avec nous ?** are you coming with us?
■ *adverbe*
tiens mon sac, je ne peux pas courir avec ! hold my bag, I can't run with it!

avenir [avnir] *nom masculin*

future : **elle dit qu'elle sait prédire l'avenir** she says she can predict the future ; **à l'avenir, soyez plus prudents** be more careful in the future.

aventure [avɑ̃tyr] *nom féminin*

adventure : **il aime l'aventure** he likes adventure ; **un film d'aventure** an adventure film.

avenue [avny] *nom féminin*

avenue.

averse [avɛrs] *nom féminin*

shower : **c'est juste une averse** it's only a shower.

avertir [avɛrtir] *verbe*

to warn : **je t'avertis, si tu continues tu vas avoir des problèmes !** I'm warning you, if you carry on you'll have problems!
➤ **avertir quelqu'un de quelque chose**
1. **to warn somebody about something** : **il l'a averti du danger** he warned him about the danger
2. **to let somebody know about some-**

thing : **avertis-moi dès que possible** let me know as soon as possible.

avertissement [avɛrtismɑ̃] *nom masculin*

warning : Elsa a déjà eu deux avertissements Elsa has already had two warnings.

aveugle [avœgl] *nom & adjectif*

■ *nom masculin ou féminin*
blind person : j'ai aidé un aveugle à traverser la rue I helped a blind person to cross the street ; **les aveugles** the blind
■ *adjectif*
blind : elle est aveugle she's blind.

avion [avjɔ̃] *nom masculin*

plane : j'ai pris l'avion pour y aller I went there by plane OU I flew there ; **c'est plus rapide en avion** it's quicker by plane
➤ **un avion à réaction** a jet plane OU a jet.

avis [avi] *nom masculin*

opinion : j'aimerais connaître ton avis I'd like to know your opinion
➤ **à mon avis** in my opinion : **à ton avis, est-ce que c'est possible ?** in your opinion, is it possible?
➤ **changer d'avis** to change one's mind : **elle a encore changé d'avis** she changed her mind again.

av. J.-C. (*abréviation de* avant Jésus-Christ)

BC : en 360 av. J.-C. in 360 BC.

avocat, e [avɔka, at] *nom masculin, nom féminin*

lawyer : Stéphanie voudrait être avocate Stéphanie would like to be a lawyer.

avocat [avɔka] *nom masculin*

avocado : une salade d'avocat an avocado salad.

avoine [avwan] *nom féminin*

oats (*s'utilise toujours au pluriel*) : **des flocons d'avoine** porridge oats.

avoir [avwar] *verbe*

1. **to have : ils ont deux chiens** they have two dogs OU they have got two dogs ; **Bertrand a trois frères** Bertrand has three brothers OU Bertrand has got three brothers ; **je n'ai pas beaucoup d'amis** I don't have many friends OU I haven't got many friends ; **ils avaient une**

villa mais ils l'ont vendue they had a villa but they sold it ; **Nath a la grippe** Nath has flu ; **elle a les cheveux bruns** she has brown hair OU she has got brown hair
2. *Suivi d'un nom indiquant une sensation*

> Dans ce cas « avoir » se traduit par **to be** + adjectif :

j'ai sommeil I'm sleepy ; **il a froid** he's cold ; **j'ai très faim** I'm really hungry
3. *En parlant de l'âge* **to be : quel âge as-tu ? – j'ai treize ans** how old are you? – I'm thirteen years old OU I'm thirteen
4. **to get : on a eu des places gratuites** we got some free tickets ; **j'ai appelé mais je n'ai pas réussi à l'avoir** I called but I didn't manage to get him
5. **to pass : il a eu son examen** he passed his exam

> « Avoir » sert à former le passé composé.
> Il se traduit par **to have** si l'on parle d'une action qui n'est pas encore terminée ou qui est située de façon peu précise dans le passé : je n'ai pas encore fini **I haven't finished yet** ; tu as déjà visité Cambridge ? **have you ever visited Cambridge ?**
> « Avoir » + participe passé se traduit par un prétérit en anglais si l'action est complètement terminée : on a joué au basket hier **we played basketball yesterday** ; pourquoi tu as dit ça ? **why did you say that ?**

➤ **j'en ai pour cinq minutes** it'll take me five minutes
➤ **se faire avoir** *familier* to be had : **dix euros, tu t'es fait avoir !** ten euros, you've been had!
➤ **il y a** ➤ **il**.

avouer [avwe] *verbe*

1. **to confess : le criminel a avoué** the criminal confessed
2. **to admit : avoue qu'il te plaît !** admit that you like him!

avril [avril] *nom masculin*

April : en avril in April
➤ **nous sommes le trois avril** it's the third of April *UK* OU it's April third *US*
➤ **le premier avril** April Fool's Day
    ➤ Poisson d'avril

> En anglais, les mois de l'année s'écrivent avec une majuscule.

baby-sitter [bebisitœr] (*pluriel* baby-sitters) *nom masculin ou féminin*
baby-sitter.

baby-sitting [bebisitiŋ] *nom masculin*
baby-sitting : **faire du baby-sitting** to baby-sit.

bac [bak] *nom masculin*
1. ➤ baccalauréat
2. ferry (*pluriel* ferries) **: nous avons pris le bac pour traverser la rivière** we took the ferry across the river
➤ **un bac à glace** an ice tray.

baccalauréat [bakalɔrea] *nom masculin*
school-leaving certificate

> BACCALAURÉAT
> In France, if you want to go on to higher education, you have to take the baccalauréat exams at the end of your final year at lycée. The baccalauréat covers many different subjects but students can focus on one main subject area, for example the Arts, Science or Engineering. This exam is the French equivalent of A levels in England or the high-school diploma in the US.

➤ Lycée.

bachelier, ère [baʃəlje, ɛr] *nom masculin, nom féminin*
student that has passed the baccalauréat.

badge [badʒ] *nom masculin*
badge.

badminton [badmintɔn] *nom masculin*
badminton : **jouer au badminton** to play badminton.

baffle [bafl] *nom masculin*
speaker : **il a acheté de nouveaux baffles pour sa chaîne** he bought new speakers for his system.

bagages [bagaʒ] *nom masculin pluriel*
luggage (*ne s'utilise pas au pluriel*) **: tes bagages sont très lourds** your luggage is very heavy
➤ **faire ses bagages** to pack ou to pack one's bags.

bagarre [bagar] *nom féminin*
fight : **tu cherches la bagarre ?** are you looking for a fight?

se bagarrer [sə bagare] *verbe pronominal*
to fight : **arrêtez de vous bagarrer !** stop fighting!

bague [bag] *nom féminin*
ring : **une bague en or** a gold ring.

baguette [bagɛt] *nom féminin*
1. baguette : **une baguette et deux croissants, s'il vous plaît** a baguette and two croissants, please
2. chopstick : **je ne sais pas manger avec des baguettes** I can't eat with chopsticks
3. baton : **la baguette du chef d'orchestre** the conductor's baton
➤ **une baguette magique** a magic wand
➤ **des baguettes de tambour** drumsticks.

baie [bɛ] *nom féminin*
1. bay : **on s'est baignés dans une petite baie** we swam in a small bay
2. berry (*pluriel* berries) **: ils se nourrissent de baies** they live on berries
➤ **une baie vitrée** a bay window.

baignade [bɛɲad] *nom féminin*
swimming : **'baignade interdite'** 'no swimming'.

se baigner [sə beɲe] *verbe pronominal*
to go swimming, to go for a swim : **Nicolas s'est baigné dans la rivière** Nicolas went swimming in the river ou Nicolas went for a swim in the river.

baignoire [bɛɲwar] *nom féminin*
bath *UK*, bathtub *US*.

bâiller [baje] *verbe*
to yawn : **tu bâilles sans arrêt, tu es fatiguée ?** you keep yawning, are you tired?

bain [bɛ̃] *nom masculin*

bath : je vais prendre un bain I'm going to have a bath *UK* ou I'm going to take a bath *US*

➤ **un bain moussant** a bubble bath

➤ **prendre un bain de soleil** to sunbathe.

baiser [beze] *nom masculin*

kiss : donner un baiser à quelqu'un to give somebody a kiss.

baisse [bɛs] *nom féminin*

fall : une baisse du chômage a fall in unemployment

➤ **être en baisse** to be falling ou to be going down : les prix sont en baisse prices are falling ou prices are going down.

baisser [bese] *verbe*

1. **to put down, to lower** : baisse la vitre, j'ai chaud put the window down, I'm hot
2. **to turn down** : vous pourriez baisser la radio ? could you turn the radio down?
3. **to fall, to go down** : le niveau de l'eau baisse the water level is falling ou the water level is going down

se baisser *verbe pronominal*

to bend down : il s'est baissé pour ramasser sa pièce he bent down to pick up the coin.

bal [bal] *nom masculin*

ball

➤ **un bal masqué** a fancy-dress ball.

balade [balad] *nom féminin familier*

walk : faire une balade to go for a walk.

se balader [səbalade] *verbe pronominal familier*

to go for a walk : on s'est baladés dans la forêt we went for a walk in the forest.

baladeur [baladœr] *nom masculin*

personal stereo, Walkman®.

balai [balɛ] *nom masculin*

broom, brush (*pluriel* **brushes**) : un placard à balais a broom cupboard ; passer le balai dans to sweep ; j'ai passé le balai dans l'entrée I swept the hall.

balance [balɑ̃s] *nom féminin*

scales (*s'utilise toujours au pluriel*) : cette balance est fausse these scales are wrong

Balance *nom féminin*

Libra : je suis Balance I'm a Libra.

se balancer [səbalɑ̃se] *verbe pronominal*

1. **to rock backwards and forwards** : arrête de te balancer sur ta chaise stop rocking backwards and forwards on your chair
2. **to swing** : elle aime se balancer très haut she likes swinging very high.

balançoire [balɑ̃swar] *nom féminin*

swing : les balançoires du parc the swings in the park.

balayer [baleje] *verbe*

to sweep : qui va balayer la cuisine ? who's going to sweep the kitchen?

balcon [balkɔ̃] *nom masculin*

balcony (*pluriel* **balconies**) : il y a des fleurs sur le balcon there are flowers on the balcony.

baleine [balɛn] *nom féminin*

whale : les Japonais chassent encore la baleine the Japanese still hunt whales.

balle [bal] *nom féminin*

1. **ball** : balle de ping-pong table-tennis ball
2. **bullet** : il a mis une balle dans le revolver he put a bullet in the gun.

ballerine [balrin] *nom féminin*

pump : Lucille porte des ballerines Lucille is wearing pumps.

ballet [balɛ] *nom masculin*

ballet.

ballon [balɔ̃] *nom masculin*

1. **ball** : attrape le ballon ! catch the ball!
2. **balloon** : la salle est décorée avec des ballons the room is decorated with balloons

➤ **un ballon de basket** a basketball

➤ **un ballon de foot** a football

➤ **un ballon de rugby** a rugby ball.

banane [banan] *nom féminin*

1. **banana** : un kilo de bananes a kilo of bananas
2. **bum bag** *UK*, **fanny pack** *US* : je porte mon argent dans une banane I carry my money in a bum bag.

b

banc [bɑ̃] *nom masculin*

bench *(pluriel* benches) : il s'est assis sur un banc he sat down on a bench.

bandage [bɑ̃daʒ] *nom masculin*

bandage : il portait un bandage au bras he had a bandage on his arm.

bande [bɑ̃d] *nom féminin*

1. strip : des bandes de papier strips of paper
2. bandage : l'infirmière lui a mis une bande au genou the nurse put a bandage on his knee
3. tape : le magnétophone abîme les bandes the tape recorder damages the tapes
4. group : une bande de jeunes a group of young people
➤ la bande dessinée comic strip

  BANDE DESSINÉE

There's a very strong comic book (bande dessinée or BD) tradition in France. It is considered a serious and important art form, for both young people and adults. Best-selling comic books in France are Astérix and Tintin. These days, comic books are also being made into video games.

bande-annonce [bɑ̃danɔ̃s] *(pluriel* bandes-annonce) *nom féminin*

trailer : as-tu vu la bande-annonce de son nouveau film ? have you seen the trailer for his new film?

bandeau [bɑ̃do] *nom masculin*

1. blindfold : ils lui ont mis un bandeau sur les yeux they put a blindfold on him ou they blindfolded him
2. headband : Lise porte un bandeau dans les cheveux Lise is wearing a headband.

bande-son [bɑ̃dsɔ̃] *(pluriel* bandes-son) *nom féminin*

soundtrack : j'aime bien la bande-son de ce film I like the soundtrack to this film.

banlieue [bɑ̃ljø] *nom féminin*

suburb : une banlieue résidentielle a residential suburb
➤ la banlieue the suburbs : ils habitent en banlieue they live in the suburbs.

banque [bɑ̃k] *nom féminin*

bank : je dois aller à la banque I have to go to the bank.

banquette [bɑ̃kɛt] *nom féminin*

seat : la banquette arrière de la voiture the back seat of the car.

banquier, ère [bɑ̃kje, ɛr] *nom masculin, nom féminin*

banker : l'oncle de Bertrand est banquier Bertrand's uncle is a banker.

baptême [batɛm] *nom masculin*

christening : on est invités au baptême we are invited to the christening
➤ un baptême de l'air a maiden flight.

baptiser [batize] *verbe*

1. to baptize, to christen : je ne suis pas baptisé I wasn't baptized
2. to call : elle a baptisé sa poupée Dorothée she called her doll Dorothée.

bar [bar] *nom masculin*

bar : les bars sont pleins le samedi soir the bars are full on Saturday nights.

barbe [barb] *nom féminin*

beard : il se laisse pousser la barbe he's growing a beard
➤ une barbe à papa candy floss *UK* ou cotton candy *US*.

barque [bark] *nom féminin*

rowing boat *UK*, rowboat *US* : on peut louer des barques you can hire rowing boats.

barrage [baraʒ] *nom masculin*

1. dam : un barrage sur le Mississippi a dam on the Mississippi
2. roadblock : il y a un barrage de police plus loin there's a police roadblock ahead.

barre [bar] *nom féminin*

bar : ils ont enfoncé la porte avec une barre de métal they broke the door down with a metal bar.

barrer [bare] *verbe*

1. to block : la route est barrée the road is blocked
2. to cross out : pourquoi tu as barré ce mot ? why did you cross that word out?

barrette [barɛt] *nom féminin*

slide *UK*, barrette *US* : elle a des barrettes dans les cheveux she has slides in her hair.

barrière [barjɛr] *nom féminin*

fence : il y a une barrière autour du champ there's a fence around the field.

bas, basse [ba, bas] *adjectif*

low : une chaise basse a low chair ; les prix sont bas prices are low

bas *nom & adverbe*

■ *nom masculin*

1. bottom : le chat a abîmé le bas du rideau the cat has damaged the bottom of the curtain
2. stocking : elle porte des bas she's wearing stockings

■ *adverbe*

1. low : l'avion volait très bas the plane was flying low ; mets le tableau plus bas put the painting lower down
2. quietly : on a parlé bas pour ne pas les déranger we talked quietly so as not to disturb them

➤ **en bas**
1. downstairs : ils habitent en bas they live downstairs
2. down : ne regarde pas en bas don't look down
➤ **en bas de** at the bottom of : signe en bas de la page sign at the bottom of the page.

base [baz] *nom féminin*

base : une base militaire a military base
➤ **une base de données** a database
➤ **à base de** made from : une boisson à base d'oranges a drink made from oranges.

basket [baskɛt] *nom*

■ *nom masculin*
basketball : jouer au basket to play basketball

■ *nom féminin*
trainer *UK*, sneaker *US* : tes baskets sont toutes sales your trainers are all dirty

> ⚠ In French the word basket does not mean 'basket'.

basket-ball [baskɛtbol] *nom masculin*

basketball : jouer au basket-ball to play basketball.

basque [bask] *adjectif*

Basque : le Pays basque the Basque country

basse [bas] *adjectif* ➤ bas.

bassin [basɛ̃] *nom masculin*

1. pond : il y a un bassin dans le parc there's a pond in the park
2. pool : tu es trop petit pour aller dans le grand bassin you're too small to go in the main pool ; le petit bassin the children's pool
3. pelvis : il s'est fracturé le bassin he fractured his pelvis.

bateau [bato] *nom masculin*

boat : nous irons en Irlande en bateau we'll go to Ireland by boat
➤ **un bateau à moteur** a motor boat
➤ **un bateau de pêche** a fishing boat
➤ **un bateau à voile** a sailing boat *UK* ou a sailboat *US*.

bateau-mouche [batomuʃ] (*pluriel* bateaux-mouches) *nom masculin* sightseeing boat in Paris.

bâtiment [batimã] *nom masculin*

building : un grand bâtiment a tall building.

bâton [batɔ̃] *nom masculin*

stick : il m'a donné un coup de bâton he hit me with a stick ; un bâton de colle a stick of glue
➤ **des bâtons de ski** ski poles.

batterie [batri] *nom féminin*

1. battery (*pluriel* batteries) : la batterie est à plat the battery is flat
2. drums : Romain joue de la batterie Romain plays the drums.

battre [batr] *verbe*

to beat : il bat son chien he beats his dog ; l'équipe de Toulouse nous a battus the team from Toulouse beat us ; battre les œufs en neige beat the egg whites until stiff
➤ **battre des mains** to clap

se battre *verbe pronominal*

to fight : arrêtez de vous battre ! stop fighting!

battu, e [baty] *participe passé de* battre.

bavard, e [bavar, ard] *adjectif*

talkative : Cyril est très bavard Cyril is very talkative ou Cyril talks too much.

bavarder [bavarde] *verbe*

to chat : elle bavardait avec ses copines she was chatting with her friends.

bazar [bazar] *nom masculin familier*

mess : **quel bazar dans cette chambre !** what a mess in this bedroom!

BD, bédé [bede] *(abréviation de* bande dessi-née*) nom féminin*

comic strip : **une bédé super rigolote** a really funny comic strip.

➤ bande dessinée.

beau, belle, beaux [bo, bɛl, bo] *adjectif*

(**bel** [bɛl] *devant une voyelle ou un « h » muet*)

1. beautiful : **une belle fille** a beautiful girl ; **quel beau temps !** what beautiful weather!
2. handsome : **un beau garçon** a handsome boy

➤ **il fait beau** the weather is nice OU it's a nice day.

Beaubourg [bobur] *nom*

Beaubourg

> BEAUBOURG
> This is another name for the Pompidou Centre, which was built in the 1970s in the Beaubourg district in central Paris. The design of this high-tech cultural centre is rather unusual, with the insides of the building, such as the pipes, on the outside. As well as art galleries and a cinema, there is a multi-media library which is free to members of the public. The centre attracts eight million visitors every year.

beaucoup [boku] *adverbe*

1. a lot : **il travaille beaucoup** he works a lot ; **elle a beaucoup d'énergie** she's got a lot of energy
2. much : **je n'ai pas beaucoup d'argent** I haven't got much money ; **c'est beaucoup mieux** it's much better.

beau-fils [bofis] *(pluriel* beaux-fils*) nom masculin*

1. son-in-law : **sa fille et son beau-fils habitent à Troyes** his daughter and son-in-law live in Troyes
2. stepson : **elle vit avec son nouveau mari et son beau-fils** she lives with her new husband and stepson.

beau-frère [bofrɛr] *(pluriel* beaux-frères*) nom masculin*

brother-in-law.

beau-père [bopɛr] *(pluriel* beaux-pères*) nom masculin*

1. father-in-law : **il s'entend bien avec son beau-père et sa belle-mère** he gets on well with his father-in-law and mother-in-law
2. step-father : **Marina vit avec sa mère et son beau-père** Marina lives with her mother and step-father.

beaux-parents [boparã] *nom masculin pluriel*

in-laws.

bébé [bebe] *nom masculin*

baby *(pluriel* babies*)* : **un gros bébé** a big baby ; **un bébé phoque** a baby seal.

bec [bɛk] *nom masculin*

beak : **l'oiseau a un brin de paille dans le bec** the bird has a piece of straw in its beak.

bédé ➤ BD.

bel ➤ beau.

belge [bɛlʒ] *adjectif*

Belgian

En anglais, les adjectifs se rapportant à un pays ou une région s'écrivent avec une majuscule :

des chocolats belges Belgian chocolates

Belge *nom masculin ou féminin*

Belgian.

Belgique [bɛlʒik] *nom féminin*

➤ **la Belgique** Belgium

En anglais, à de rares exceptions près, il n'y a pas d'article devant les noms de pays :

la Belgique a trois langues officielles Belgium has three official languages ; **elle veut faire ses études en Belgique** she wants to study in Belgium ; **tu es déjà allé en Belgique ?** have you ever been to Belgium?

bélier [belje] *nom masculin*

ram

Bélier *nom masculin*

Aries : **je suis Bélier** I'm an Aries.

belle ➤ beau.

belle-fille [bɛlfij] (pluriel belles-filles) nom
féminin

1. **daughter-in-law : son fils et sa belle-fille habitent à Reims** his son and daughter-in-law live in Reims
2. **step-daughter : elle vit avec son nouveau mari et sa belle-fille** she lives with her new husband and step-daughter.

belle-mère [bɛlmɛr] (pluriel belles-mères) nom féminin

1. **mother-in-law : il s'entend bien avec son beau-père et sa belle-mère** he gets on well with his father-in-law and mother-in-law
2. **step-mother : Marina vit avec son père et sa belle-mère** Marina lives with her father and step-mother.

belle-sœur [bɛlsœr] (pluriel belles-sœurs) nom féminin
sister-in-law.

bénéfice [benefis] nom masculin
profit : **ils ont fait un gros bénéfice cette année** they made a big profit this year.

bénévole [benevɔl] adjectif & nom
▪ adjectif
voluntary : **un travailleur bénévole** a voluntary worker
▪ nom masculin ou féminin
volunteer : **tout le travail est fait par des bénévoles** all the work is done by volunteers.

béquille [bekij] nom féminin

1. crutch (pluriel crutches) : **il marche avec des béquilles** he walks on crutches
2. stand : **il a mis sa moto sur la béquille** he put his motorbike on its stand.

berceau [bɛrso] (pluriel berceaux) nom masculin
cradle.

bercer [bɛrse] verbe
to rock : **elle berçait le bébé** she was rocking the baby.

berger, ère [bɛrʒe, ɛr] nom masculin, nom féminin
shepherd (féminin shepherdess)
➤ **un berger allemand** a German shepherd.

bermuda [bɛrmyda] nom masculin
bermudas, bermuda shorts (s'utilisent toujours au pluriel) : **il est en bermuda** he's wearing bermudas ou he's wearing bermuda shorts.

besoin [bəzwɛ̃] nom masculin
need : **un besoin urgent** an urgent need
➤ **avoir besoin de quelque chose** to need something : **je n'ai pas besoin d'aide** I don't need any help.

bestiole [bɛstjɔl] nom féminin
bug : **il y a une bestiole sur la vitre** there's a bug on the window.

bête [bɛt] nom & adjectif
▪ nom féminin
1. animal : **une bête sauvage** a wild animal
2. insect : **tu as une bête sur ta chemise** there's an insect on your shirt
▪ adjectif
stupid : **qu'est-ce qu'il est bête !** he's so stupid!

bêtise [betiz] nom féminin
j'ai fait une bêtise I've done something stupid ; **arrête de faire des bêtises** stop being stupid ; **est-ce que j'ai dit une bêtise ?** did I say something stupid? ; **il dit des bêtises** he's talking nonsense.

béton [betɔ̃] nom masculin
concrete : **un mur en béton** a concrete wall.

betterave [betrav] nom féminin
beetroot UK, beet US.

beurre [bœr] nom masculin
butter : **du beurre salé** salted butter
➤ **du beurre de cacahuètes** peanut butter.

beurrer [bœre] verbe
to butter : **il beurre son pain grillé** he's buttering his toast.

bibliothécaire [biblijɔtekɛr] nom masculin ou féminin
librarian : **Pascale est bibliothécaire** Pascale is a librarian.

bibliothèque [biblijɔtɛk] nom féminin
1. library (pluriel libraries) : **la bibliothèque municipale** the public library
2. bookcase : **une bibliothèque en bois** a wooden bookcase.

bicyclette [bisiklɛt] *nom féminin*

bicycle, bike : **je vais à l'école à bicyclette** I go to school on my bike OU I cycle to school
➤ **faire de la bicyclette** to cycle.

bien [bjɛ̃] *nom, adjectif, adverbe & interjection*

■ *nom masculin*

good : **le bien et le mal** good and evil ; **je te dis ça pour ton bien** I'm telling you this for your own good ; **ça me fait du bien** it does me good

■ *adjectif invariable* (*comparatif & superlatif* meilleur)

1. good : **il est bien comme prof** he's a good teacher ; **il est bien, ce film** it's a good film
2. good-looking : **je trouve Vincent plutôt bien** I think Vincent is rather good-looking
3. nice : **il est bien ton manteau** your coat's nice ; **tu es bien avec ce jean** you look nice in those jeans ; **c'est bien de l'avoir aidé** it was nice of you to help him ; **ce n'est pas bien de dire des gros mots !** it's not nice to swear!
4. well : **Anna n'est pas très bien en ce moment** Anna isn't very well at the moment ; **je ne me sens pas bien** I'm not feeling well
5. comfortable : **tu es bien dans ce fauteuil ?** are you comfortable in that armchair?

■ *adverbe* (*comparatif & superlatif* mieux)

1. well : **tu as bien dormi ?** did you sleep well? ; **elle dessine bien** she draws well

> « Bien » précédé d'un verbe se traduit souvent par good suivi d'un nom :

Élodie chante bien Élodie is a good singer ; **il ne conduit pas bien** he isn't a good driver ; **on s'est bien amusés** we had a good time

2. properly : **la porte n'est pas bien fermée** the door isn't shut properly
3. very, really : **vous êtes bien aimable** you're very kind OU you're really kind ; **des poires bien mûres** very ripe pears OU really ripe pears
4. much : **bien plus tard** much later ; **Bertrand est bien plus sympa que sa sœur** Bertrand is much nicer than his sister
➤ **il y a bien longtemps** a very long time ago
➤ **tu as bien fait** you did the right thing
➤ **tu ferais bien d'y aller** you should go
➤ **c'est bien fait pour lui !** serves him right!
➤ **bien de** OU **bien des** quite a lot of : **bien des gens** quite a lot of people ; **j'ai eu bien du mal à les convaincre** I had quite a lot of trouble persuading them
➤ **tu as bien de la chance !** you're very lucky!

➤ **bien que** although OU though : **je vais accepter bien que je ne sois pas convaincue** I'll accept although I'm not convinced OU I'll accept though I'm not convinced
➤ **bien sûr** of course

■ *interjection*

1. right : **bien, où en étions-nous ?** right, where were we? ; **bien, alors on se retrouve demain à cinq heures** right, so we'll meet up tomorrow at five
2. fine : **j'ai décidé de ne pas y aller – bien, fais comme tu veux** I've decided not to go – fine, do as you like.

bientôt [bjɛ̃to] *adverbe*

soon : **le magasin va bientôt fermer** the shop is going to close soon
➤ **à bientôt !** see you soon!

bienvenu, e [bjɛ̃vny] *nom masculin, nom féminin*

être le bienvenu to be welcome ; **tu seras toujours la bienvenue ici** you will always be welcome here

bienvenue *nom féminin*

welcome : **bienvenue !** welcome! ; **souhaiter la bienvenue à quelqu'un** to welcome somebody.

bière [bjɛr] *nom féminin*

beer : **je prendrai une bière** I'll have a beer
➤ **une bière blonde** a lager
➤ **une bière brune** an ale.

bifteck [biftɛk] *nom masculin*

steak : **j'ai mangé un bifteck à midi** I had a steak for lunch
➤ **du bifteck haché** minced beef *UK* OU ground beef *US*.

bijou [biʒu] (*pluriel* bijoux) *nom masculin*

jewel : **un bijou précieux** a precious jewel
➤ **des bijoux** jewellery *UK* OU jewelry *US* ; **Dorothée aime les bijoux en or** Dorothée likes gold jewellery.

bijouterie [biʒutri] *nom féminin*

jeweller's *UK*, jewelry store *US* : **il y a une bijouterie dans cette rue** there's a jeweller's in this street.

bilan [bilɑ̃] *nom masculin*

results (*pluriel*) : **le bilan du trimestre est décevant** the end-of-term results are disappointing

> **faire le bilan de quelque chose** to assess something.

bilingue [bilɛ̃g] *adjectif*

bilingual : **il est bilingue** he's bilingual.

billard [bijar] *nom masculin*

billiards (*singulier*) : **jouer au billard** to play billiards
> **le billard américain** pool.

bille [bij] *nom féminin*

marble : **jouer aux billes** to play marbles.

billet [bijɛ] *nom masculin*

1. note, bill *US* : **un billet de cinquante euros** a fifty-euro note
2. ticket : **Coralie a trois billets pour le concert** Coralie has three tickets for the concert ; **un billet de train** a train ticket.

bio [bjo] *adjectif invariable*

organic : **des légumes bio** organic vegetables.

biologie [bjɔlɔʒi] *nom féminin*

biology.

biologique [bjɔlɔʒik] *adjectif*

1. organic : **l'agriculture biologique** organic agriculture
2. biological : **une réaction biologique** a biological reaction.

bip [bip] *nom masculin*

beep, tone : **parlez après le bip** speak after the beep ou speak after the tone.

biscotte [biskɔt] *nom féminin*

toasted bread sold in packets and often eaten for breakfast.

biscuit [biskɥi] *nom masculin*

biscuit *UK*, cookie *US* : **un paquet de biscuits** a packet of biscuits
> **des biscuits salés** crackers.

bise [biz] *nom féminin familier*

kiss (*pluriel* **kisses**) : **faire la bise à quelqu'un** to kiss somebody ; **je leur ai fait la bise** I kissed them ; **grosses bises** love and kisses.

bison [bizɔ̃] *nom masculin*

bison.

bisou [bizu] *nom masculin familier*

kiss (*pluriel* **kisses**) : **faire un bisou à quelqu'un** to give somebody a kiss.

bizarre [bizar] *adjectif*

strange : **c'est bizarre, il n'y a personne ici** that's strange, there's no one here.

blague [blag] *nom féminin*

joke : **tes blagues ne sont pas drôles** your jokes aren't funny ; **il a fait une blague à son professeur** he played a practical joke on his teacher.

blanc, blanche [blɑ̃, blɑ̃ʃ] *adjectif*

1. white : **un tee-shirt blanc** a white T-shirt
2. blank : **donne-moi une feuille blanche** give me a blank sheet of paper
3. pale : **tu es tout blanc, tu es malade ?** you're very pale, are you ill?

blanc *nom masculin*

1. white : **je ne porte jamais de blanc** I never wear white
2. blank : **laisse un blanc pour la signature** leave a blank for the signature
> **un blanc d'œuf** an egg white
> **du blanc de poulet** chicken breast

Blancs *nom masculin pluriel*

whites : **les Blancs et les Noirs** whites and blacks.

blé [ble] *nom masculin*

wheat : **un champ de blé** a wheatfield.

blessé [blese] *nom masculin*

1. injured person : **il y a un blessé** one person has been injured ; **il y a eu trois blessés** three people were injured
2. wounded person : **il n'y a eu qu'un blessé dans la bataille** there was only one person wounded in the battle ; **des centaines de blessés** hundreds of wounded.

blesser [blese] *verbe*

1. to injure, to hurt : **personne n'a été blessé dans l'accident** nobody was injured in the accident ou nobody was hurt in the accident
2. to wound : **il a été blessé à la guerre** he was wounded in the war.

blessure [blesyr] *nom féminin*

1. **injury** *(pluriel* **injuries***)* : **une blessure légère** a slight injury
2. **wound** : **l'infirmière a nettoyé la blessure** the nurse cleaned the wound.

bleu, e [blø] *adjectif*

1. **blue** : **une jupe bleue** a blue skirt
2. **very rare** : **un steak bleu** a very rare steak

bleu | *nom masculin*

1. **blue** : **le bleu lui va bien** blue suits him
2. **bruise** : **elle était couverte de bleus** she was covered in bruises
➣ **bleu ciel** sky blue
➣ **bleu marine** navy blue.

bloc [blɔk] *nom masculin*

1. **block** : **un bloc de pierre** a block of stone
2. **pad** : **un bloc de papier à lettres** a writing pad.

bloc-notes [blɔknɔt] *(pluriel* blocs-notes*)*

nom masculin
notepad.

blond, e [blɔ̃, blɔ̃d] *adjectif*

blond : **elle est blonde aux yeux bleus** she's blond with blue eyes ; **Kevin a les cheveux blonds** Kevin has blond hair ou Kevin has fair hair.

bloquer [blɔke] *verbe*

1. **to jam** : **j'ai bloqué la porte** I jammed the door
2. **to block** : **les manifestants ont bloqué la rue** the demonstrators have blocked the street
➣ **être bloqué** to be stuck : **nous sommes bloqués dans un embouteillage** we're stuck in a traffic jam.

blouse [bluz] *nom féminin*

coat : **ils portent des blouses blanches pour le cours de chimie** they wear white coats for their chemistry lessons.

blouson [bluzɔ̃] *nom masculin*

jacket : **un blouson en cuir** a leather jacket.

bocal [bɔkal] *(pluriel* bocaux [bɔko]*) nom*

masculin
jar : **un bocal de cornichons** a jar of gherkins.

bœuf [bœf, *pluriel* bø] *nom masculin*

1. **ox** *(pluriel* **oxen***)* : **une charrette tirée par des bœufs** a cart pulled by oxen

2. **beef** : **du bœuf rôti** roast beef.

bof [bɔf] *interjection familier*

ça t'a plu, le concert ? – bof did you like the concert? – not really.

bogue [bɔg], **bug** [bʌg] *nom masculin*

bug : **le bogue de l'an 2000** the millennium bug.

boire [bwar] *verbe*

to drink : **tu veux boire quelque chose ?** would you like something to drink? ; **on a bu toute la bouteille** we drank the whole bottle.

bois [bwa] *nom masculin*

wood : **on pourrait traverser le bois** we could go through the wood ; **je vais couper du bois** I'm going to cut some wood.

boisson [bwasɔ̃] *nom féminin*

drink : **tu veux une boisson chaude ou froide ?** do you want a hot drink or a cold drink?
➣ **des boissons alcoolisées** alcoholic drinks
➣ **une boisson gazeuse** a fizzy drink *UK* ou a soda *US*.

boîte [bwat] *nom féminin*

1. **box** *(pluriel* **boxes***)* : **une boîte de chocolats** a box of chocolates
2. **can** : **une boîte de petits pois** a can of peas ; **des légumes en boîte** canned vegetables
3. **club** : **une boîte de nuit** a nightclub ; **sortir en boîte** to go clubbing
➣ **une boîte de conserve** a can
➣ **la boîte aux lettres** the postbox *UK* ou the mailbox *US*
➣ **une boîte vocale** a voice mail.

boiter [bwate] *verbe*

to limp : **le cheval boitait** the horse was limping.

bol [bɔl] *nom masculin*

bowl : **un bol de céréales** a bowl of cereal
➣ **avoir du bol** *familier* to be lucky.

bombarder [bɔ̃barde] *verbe*

to bomb : **l'armée a bombardé la ville** the army bombed the town.

bombe [bɔ̃b] *nom féminin*

1. **bomb** : **la bombe atomique** the atomic bomb
2. **spray** : **du déodorant en bombe** deodorant spray.

bon, bonne [bɔ̃, bɔn] (*comparatif & superlatif* meilleur) *adjectif*

1. **good** : est-ce que la viande est bonne ? is the meat good? ; **c'est un bon livre** it's a good book ; **Jérémie est bon en anglais** Jérémie is good at English ; **faire de l'exercice, c'est bon pour la santé** exercise is good for you
2. **right** : c'est la bonne réponse it's the right answer ; **est-ce que c'est le bon numéro ?** is this the right number?
3. **valid** : ton passeport n'est plus bon your passport is no longer valid
➤ **bonne année !** Happy New Year!
➤ **bon anniversaire !** happy birthday!
➤ **bon courage !** good luck!
➤ **bonne journée !** have a nice day!
➤ **bonne nuit** good night

bon *interjection, adverbe & nom*

◼ *interjection*
right! : bon, je m'en vais right, I'm going
➤ **bon, d'accord** ok then
➤ **ah bon ?** really? : **la prof de géo est absente – ah bon ?** the geography teacher is away – really?
◼ *adverbe*
➤ **il fait bon aujourd'hui** the weather's nice today ou it's a nice day today
➤ **ça sent bon** that smells nice
◼ *nom masculin*
voucher : un bon de réduction a discount voucher.

bonbon [bɔ̃bɔ̃] *nom masculin*

sweet *UK*, **candy** *US* : **un bonbon à la fraise** a strawberry-flavoured sweet ; **un paquet de bonbons** a packet of sweets *UK* ou a packet of candy *US*
➤ **un bonbon à la menthe** a mint.

bond [bɔ̃] *nom masculin*

leap : **faire un bond** to leap up ; **elle a fait un bond quand je suis entré** she leapt up when I came in.

bondé, e [bɔ̃de] *adjectif*

packed : **le bus était bondé** the bus was packed.

bondir [bɔ̃dir] *verbe*

1. **to leap on** : **le chat bondit sur le lézard** the cat leapt on the lizard
2. **to pounce on** : **le policier a bondi sur** l'agresseur the policeman pounced on the attacker.

bonheur [bɔnœr] *nom masculin*

1. **happiness** : **l'argent ne fait pas le bonheur** money doesn't buy happiness
2. **luck** : **prends cette médaille, elle te portera bonheur** take this medallion, it will bring you luck
➤ **quel bonheur de te revoir !** it's great to see you again!

bonhomme [bɔnɔm] (*pluriel* bonshommes [bɔ̃zɔm]) *nom masculin*

1. *familier* **guy** : **un bonhomme assez bizarre** an odd guy
2. **little man** (*pluriel* **little men**), **stick figure** : **elle a dessiné un bonhomme dans la marge** she drew a little man in the margin
➤ **un bonhomme de neige** a snowman.

bonjour [bɔ̃ʒur] *nom masculin*

hello : **bonjour tout le monde !** hello everybody!

> En anglais, pour dire bonjour le matin on dit **hello** ou **good morning**, l'après-midi on dit **hello** ou **good afternoon**.

bonne [bɔn] ➤ bon.

bonnet [bɔnɛ] *nom masculin*

woolly hat *UK*, **wooly hat** *US* : **mets ton bonnet, il fait froid** put your woolly hat on, it's cold
➤ **un bonnet de bain** a swimming cap.

bonsoir [bɔ̃swar] *nom masculin*

1. **hello, good evening** : **bonsoir, ça va ?** hello, how are you?
2. **good night** : **bonsoir, dormez bien** good night, sleep well
3. **goodbye** : **allez, bonsoir, je rentre** goodbye then, I'm going home.

bord [bɔr] *nom masculin*

1. **edge** : **ce verre est trop près du bord de la table** the glass is too close to the edge of the table
2. **rim** : **il y a du rouge à lèvres sur le bord du verre** there's lipstick on the rim of the glass
3. **bank** : **on s'est promenés au bord de la rivière** we went for a walk on the river bank
➤ **à bord de** on board : **à bord du ferry** on

board the ferry ; **nous sommes montés à bord** we got on board

➤ **au bord de la mer** by the sea OU at the seaside : **nous avons passé la journée au bord de la mer** we spent the day at the seaside ; **nous sommes allés au bord de la mer** we went to the seaside

➤ **être au bord des larmes** to be on the verge of tears

➤ **au bord de la route** by the roadside.

bordure [bɔrdyr] *nom féminin*

edge : **en bordure de la forêt** on the edge of the forest.

bosse [bɔs] *nom féminin*

1. bump : **Matthieu a une grosse bosse sur le front** Matthieu has a big bump on his forehead

2. hump : **les chameaux ont deux bosses** camels have two humps.

bosser [bɔse] *verbe familier*

to work : **j'ai bossé toute l'après-midi pour l'interro** I worked all afternoon for the test.

bossu, e [bɔsy] *adjectif & nom*

▪ *adjectif*
hunchbacked

▪ *nom masculin, nom féminin*
➤ **le bossu de Notre-Dame** the hunchback of Notre-Dame.

botte [bɔt] *nom féminin*

boot : **des bottes en cuir** leather boots
➤ **des bottes en caoutchouc** wellingtons *UK* OU rubber boots *US*.

bouche [buʃ] *nom féminin*

mouth : **il a une très grande bouche** he has a very big mouth
➤ **une bouche de métro** a metro entrance.

boucher[1] [buʃe] *verbe*

1. to fill : **avec quoi on va boucher ce trou ?** what are we going to fill this hole with?

2. to block : **écarte-toi, tu me bouches la vue !** move out of the way, you're blocking my view!

boucher[2], **ère** [buʃe, ɛr] *nom masculin, nom féminin*

butcher : **le père de Luc est boucher** Luc's father is a butcher.

boucherie [buʃri] *nom féminin*

butcher's, butcher's shop : **ma mère m'a envoyé à la boucherie** my mother sent me to the butcher's.

bouchon [buʃɔ̃] *nom masculin*

1. top : **où est le bouchon du dentifrice ?** where's the top to the toothpaste?

2. cork : **il y a des morceaux de bouchon dans le vin** there are bits of cork in the wine

3. traffic jam : **on était bloqués dans un bouchon** we were stuck in a traffic jam.

boucle [bukl] *nom féminin*

1. buckle : **la boucle de sa ceinture est argentée** his belt buckle is silver

2. curl : **Valérie a de longues boucles brunes** Valérie has long brown curls

➤ **des boucles d'oreille** earrings : **elle porte des boucles d'oreille en or** she's wearing gold earrings.

bouclé, e [bukle] *adjectif*

1. curly : **elle a les cheveux bouclés** she has curly hair

2. curly-haired : **un bébé tout bouclé** a curly-haired baby.

bouclier [buklije] *nom masculin*

shield : **les guerriers portaient des boucliers** the warriors were carrying shields.

bouder [bude] *verbe*

to sulk : **je me suis excusé, maintenant arrête de bouder** I said I was sorry, now stop sulking.

boue [bu] *nom féminin*

mud : **ton pantalon est plein de boue** your trousers are covered in mud.

bouée [bwe] *nom féminin*

1. rubber ring : **elle nage encore avec une bouée** she still swims with a rubber ring

2. buoy : **on a nagé jusqu'à la bouée** we swam to the buoy

➤ **une bouée de sauvetage** a lifebelt.

bouffe [buf] *nom féminin familier*

1. food : **la bouffe est vraiment mauvaise ici** the food's really bad here

2. meal : **on s'est fait une bouffe entre copains** we had a meal with some friends.

bouffer [bufe] *verbe familier*

to eat : **qu'est-ce qu'on bouffe ce soir ?**

what are we eating tonight? ; **il bouffe comme un cochon** he eats like a pig.

bouger [buʒe] *verbe*

to move : **surtout ne bouge pas, tu as une guêpe sur le bras** don't move, there's a wasp on your arm ; **ne bouge pas, j'arrive** stay where you are, I'm coming
➤ **j'ai une dent qui bouge** I've got a loose tooth.

bougie [buʒi] *nom féminin*

candle : **la pièce était éclairée par des bougies** the room was lit by candles.

bouillant, e [bujã, ãt] *adjectif*

1. boiling : **remplis la tasse d'eau bouillante** fill the cup with boiling water
2. boiling hot : **je ne peux pas boire ce café, il est bouillant** I can't drink this coffee, it's boiling hot.

bouillir [bujir] *verbe*

to boil : **est-ce que l'eau bout ?** is the water boiling?
➤ **fais bouillir de l'eau pour le thé** put the kettle on to make some tea.

boulanger, ère [bulãʒe, ɛr] *nom masculin, nom féminin*

baker : **Pierre veut devenir boulanger** Pierre wants to become a baker.

boulangerie [bulãʒri] *nom féminin*

baker's, baker's shop : **je vais à la boulangerie acheter du pain** I'm going to the baker's to buy bread.

boule [bul] *nom féminin*

1. ball ; **une boule de billard** a billiard ball ; **une boule de cristal** a crystal ball
2. scoop : **je veux une glace à deux boules** I want two scoops of ice cream
➤ **une boule de neige** a snowball

boules *nom féminin pluriel*

➤ **jouer aux boules** to play pétanque
   ➤ pétanque.

boulette [bulɛt] *nom féminin*

pellet : **une boulette de papier** a paper pellet
➤ **des boulettes de viande** meatballs.

boulevard [bulvar] *nom masculin*

boulevard : **le café est sur le boulevard** the café is on the boulevard.

boulot [bulo] *nom masculin familier*

1. work : **on a beaucoup de boulot cette semaine** we have a lot of work this week
2. job : **un boulot bien payé** a well-paid job.

boum [bum] *nom féminin familier*

party *(pluriel* **parties**) : **on s'est bien amusés à la boum de Sarah** we had a really good time at Sarah's party.

bouquet [bukɛ] *nom masculin*

bunch *(pluriel* **bunches**) : **un bouquet de roses** a bunch of roses.

bouquin [bukɛ̃] *nom masculin familier*

book : **un bouquin super intéressant** a really interesting book.

bouquiner [bukine] *verbe familier*

to read : **il passe son temps à bouquiner** he spends his time reading.

Bourgogne [burgɔɲ] *nom féminin*

➤ **la Bourgogne** Burgundy ; **Dijon est en Bourgogne** Dijon is in Burgundy ; **ils sont allés en Bourgogne en auto-stop** they hitch-hicked to Burgundy.

bourse [burs] *nom féminin*

grant *UK*, scholarship *US* : **Mahmoud a obtenu une bourse d'études** Mahmoud got a study grant *UK*
➤ **la Bourse** the stock exchange
➤ **la Bourse de Paris** the Paris Stock Exchange.

bousculer [buskyle] *verbe*

1. to push : **il m'a bousculée et il ne s'est même pas excusé !** he pushed me and he didn't even apologize!
2. to rush : **ne me bouscule pas, sinon je vais oublier quelque chose** don't rush me or I'll forget something.

boussole [busɔl] *nom féminin*

compass *(pluriel* **compasses**) : **les marins se dirigent avec une boussole** sailors use a compass to navigate.

bout [bu] *nom masculin*

1. **end : on voit le bout du tunnel** you can see the end of the tunnel ; **au bout de la rue** at the end of the street
2. **piece : un bout de pain** a piece of bread ; **un bout de papier** a piece of paper
➤ **au bout de dix minutes** after ten minutes
➤ **être à bout de souffle** to be out of breath.

bouteille [butɛj] *nom féminin*

bottle : une bouteille de lait a bottle of milk.

boutique [butik] *nom féminin*

shop *UK*, **store** *US* : **il y a beaucoup de boutiques dans ma rue** there are a lot of shops in my street.

bouton [butɔ̃] *nom masculin*

1. **button : il manque un bouton à cette chemise** there's a button missing off this shirt ; **appuie sur le bouton vert** press the green button
2. **knob : tournez le bouton vers la droite** turn the knob to the right
3. **switch** (*pluriel* **switches**) : **le bouton de la lumière** the light switch
4. **spot** *UK*, **pimple : je suis plein de boutons !** I'm covered in spots!
➤ **le bouton de la sonnette** the doorbell.

boutonner [butɔne] *verbe*

to button up : boutonne ta chemise button your shirt up.

bowling [buliŋ] *nom masculin*

1. **bowling : j'aime bien le bowling** I like bowling ; **on va faire un bowling ?** shall we go bowling?
2. **bowling alley : il y a un nouveau bowling rue Cézanne** there's a new bowling alley on rue Cézanne.

boxe [bɔks] *nom féminin*

boxing : Aurélien fait de la boxe Aurélien boxes.

bracelet [braslɛ] *nom masculin*

1. **bracelet : un bracelet en argent** a silver bracelet
2. **strap : le bracelet de ma montre est cassé** my watch strap is broken.

braguette [bragɛt] *nom féminin*

flies *UK* (*s'utilise toujours au pluriel*), **fly** *US* : **ta braguette est ouverte** your flies are undone *UK* ou your fly is undone *US*.

branche [brɑ̃ʃ] *nom féminin*

branch (*pluriel* **branches**) : **les chauves-souris s'accrochent aux branches des arbres** bats hang from tree branches.

branché, e [brɑ̃ʃe] *adjectif*

1. **plugged in : est-ce que l'ordinateur est branché ?** is the computer plugged in?
2. *familier* **trendy : un quartier branché** a trendy area.

brancher [brɑ̃ʃe] *verbe*

to plug in : tu as branché la télé ? have you plugged the TV in?
➤ **ça te branche d'aller au cinéma ?** *familier* do you feel like going to the cinema?
➤ **son idée ne me branche pas vraiment** *familier* I don't really like his idea.

bras [bra] *nom masculin*

arm : je me suis fait mal au bras I hurt my arm
➤ **prendre quelqu'un dans ses bras** to take somebody in one's arms.

brasse [bras] *nom féminin*

breaststroke : nager la brasse to swim breaststroke.

bravo [bravo] *interjection*

1. **bravo! : les spectateurs criaient « bravo ! »** the audience was shouting 'bravo!'
2. **well done! : bravo, c'est du bon travail !** well done, that's good work!

bref, brève [brɛf, brɛv] *adjectif*

brief : une lettre brève a brief letter

bref *adverbe*

in short : bref, il n'était pas content in short, he wasn't happy.

Bretagne [brətaɲ] *nom féminin*

➤ **la Bretagne** Brittany : **les Duchamp ont une maison en Bretagne** the Duchamps have a house in Brittany ; **nous allons souvent en Bretagne** we often go to Brittany.

bretelle [brətɛl] *nom féminin*

strap : on voit la bretelle de son soutien-gorge you can see her bra strap

bretelles *nom féminin pluriel*

braces *UK*, **suspenders** *US* : **il portait un pantalon avec des bretelles** he was wearing trousers with braces *UK* ou he was wearing pants with suspenders *US*.

brève ➤ bref.

brevet [brəvɛ] *nom masculin*

1. certificate : **brevet de secouriste** first-aid certificate
2. diploma : **brevet professionnel** vocational diploma
➤ **le brevet des collèges** *school exam taken at the age of 15 after four years of secondary education.*

bricoler [brikɔle] *verbe*

1. to do odd jobs : **mon père aime bricoler le dimanche** my father likes doing odd jobs on Sundays
2. to tinker with : **Simon a bricolé la radio, maintenant elle ne marche plus !** Simon has tinkered with the radio, now it's not working anymore!

brillant, e [brijɑ̃, ɑ̃t] *adjectif*

1. shiny : **de beaux cheveux brillants** lovely shiny hair
2. brilliant : **Laïla est une élève brillante** Laïla is a brilliant pupil ; **les résultats de Pierre ne sont pas brillants** Pierre's results aren't brilliant.

briller [brije] *verbe*

to shine : **les étoiles brillent dans le ciel** the stars are shining in the sky.

brin [brɛ̃] *nom masculin*

sprig : **un brin de romarin** a sprig of rosemary
➤ **un brin d'herbe** a blade of grass.

brindille [brɛ̃dij] *nom féminin*

twig : **l'oiseau a fait son nid avec des brindilles** the bird made his nest out of twigs.

brioche [brijɔʃ] *nom féminin*

brioche *(soft roll or loaf made from light dough).*

brique [brik] *nom féminin*

1. brick : **une maison en briques** a brick house
2. carton : **une brique de jus d'orange** a carton of orange juice.

briquet [brikɛ] *nom masculin*

lighter.

britannique [britanik] *adjectif*

British

En anglais, les adjectifs se rapportant à un pays ou une région s'écrivent avec une majuscule :

il a l'accent britannique he has a British accent

Britannique *nom masculin ou féminin*

British person : **il y avait plusieurs Britanniques** there were several British people
➤ **les Britanniques** the British.

brocante [brɔkɑ̃t] *nom féminin*

market selling secondhand goods.

broche [brɔʃ] *nom féminin*

brooch *(pluriel* brooches*)* : **une broche en diamants** a diamond brooch.

brochette [brɔʃɛt] *nom féminin*

kebab : **des brochettes d'agneau** lamb kebab.

brochure [brɔʃyr] *nom féminin*

brochure : **une brochure publicitaire** an advertising brochure.

broderie [brɔdri] *nom féminin*

embroidery *(ne s'utilise jamais au pluriel)* : **faire de la broderie** to do embroidery ; **des broderies rouges** red embroidery.

bronzé, e [brɔ̃ze] *adjectif*

tanned : **elle est toute bronzée** she's very tanned.

bronzer [brɔ̃ze] *verbe*

to tan : **je bronze facilement** I tan easily
➤ **se faire bronzer** to sunbathe.

brosse [brɔs] *nom féminin*

brush *(pluriel* **brushes***)*
➤ **une brosse à cheveux** a hairbrush
➤ **une brosse à dents** a toothbrush
➤ **les cheveux en brosse** a crew cut : **Marc a les cheveux en brosse** Marc has a crew cut.

brosser [brɔse] *verbe*

to brush : **brosse ton manteau, il est plein de poils de chat** brush your coat, it's covered in cat's hairs
➤ **se brosser les cheveux** to brush one's hair : **brosse-toi les cheveux** brush your hair
➤ **se brosser les dents** to brush one's teeth:

tu t'es brossé les dents ? have you brushed your teeth?

brouette [bruɛt] *nom féminin*

wheelbarrow.

brouillard [brujar] *nom masculin*

fog : **un brouillard épais** thick fog ; **il y a du brouillard** it's foggy.

brouillon [brujɔ̃, ɔn] *nom masculin*

rough copy *(pluriel* **rough copies***)* : **je vais d'abord faire un brouillon** I'll make a rough copy first.

bruit [brɥi] *nom masculin*

1. sound, noise : **j'ai entendu un bruit** I heard a noise ; **il n'y a pas un bruit** there isn't a sound ; **un bruit de pas** the sound of foodsteps

2. noise : **je n'arrive pas à travailler avec tout ce bruit** I can't work with all this noise ; **faire du bruit** to make a noise ; **ils font un bruit infernal** they're making a terrible noise

3. rumour *UK*, rumor *US* : **le bruit court que tu t'en vas** there's a rumour that you're going.

brûlant, e [brylɑ̃, ɑ̃t] *adjectif*

burning hot : **cette soupe est brûlante** this soup is burning hot.

brûler [bryle] *verbe*

1. to burn : **David a brûlé ses vieux cahiers** David burned his old exercise books

2. to be on fire : **l'immeuble brûle !** the building is on fire!

3. to be burning hot : **attention, ça brûle** be careful, it's burning hot

➤ **brûler un feu rouge** to go through a red light

se brûler *verbe pronominal*

to burn oneself : **je me suis brûlé** I burned myself ; **je me suis brûlé la main** I burned my hand.

brûlure [brylyr] *nom féminin*

burn : **il a une brûlure sur la jambe** he has a burn on his leg.

brume [brym] *nom féminin*

mist : **il y a de la brume** there's a mist *OU* it's misty.

brun, e [brœ̃, bryn] *adjectif*

1. dark : **elle a les cheveux bruns** *OU* **elle est brune** she's got dark hair *OU* she's got brown hair

2. brown : **un chien au pelage brun** a brown dog.

brusquement [bryskəmɑ̃] *adverbe*

suddenly, abruptly : **le bus s'est arrêté brusquement** the bus stopped suddenly.

brut, e [bryt] *adjectif*

1. crude : **le pétrole brut** crude oil

2. dry : **du champagne brut** dry champagne

3. gross : **le poids brut** gross weight.

brutal, e, aux [brytal, o] *adjectif*

1. rough : **il est très brutal avec les autres enfants** he's very rough with the other children

2. sudden : **un changement brutal** a sudden change.

Bruxelles [bry(k)sɛl] *nom*

Brussels : **ma cousine vit à Bruxelles** my cousin lives in Brussels ; **Clément va à Bruxelles demain** Clément is going to Brussels tomorrow.

bruyant, e [brɥijɑ̃, ɑ̃t] *adjectif*

noisy : **ce que vous êtes bruyants !** you're so noisy!

bu, e [by] *participe passé de* boire.

bûche [byʃ] *nom féminin*

log : **on va couper des bûches pour le feu** we're going to cut some logs for the fire

➤ **une bûche de Noël** a Yule log.

buée [bɥe] *nom féminin*

condensation : **il y a de la buée sur la vitre** there's condensation on the window *OU* the window is steamed.

buffet [byfɛ] *nom masculin*

1. buffet : **ils ont fait un buffet pour leur mariage** they had a buffet for their wedding ; **le buffet de la gare** the station buffet

2. sideboard : **les assiettes sont dans le buffet** the plates are in the sideboard.

bug ➤ bogue.

buisson [bɥisɔ̃] *nom masculin*

bush *(pluriel* bushes*)* : **Luc s'est caché derrière le buisson** Luc hid behind the bush.

bulle [byl] *nom féminin*

1. bubble : **des bulles de savon** soap bubbles ; **faire des bulles** to blow bubbles
2. speech balloon : **les bulles d'une BD** the speech balloons in a comic strip.

bulletin [byltɛ̃] *nom masculin*

report *UK*, report card *US* : **mon bulletin trimestriel n'est pas terrible** my end-of-term report isn't very good
> **un bulletin d'informations** a news bulletin
> **le bulletin météo** the weather forecast.

bureau [byro] *(pluriel* bureaux*) nom masculin*

1. office : **ma mère travaille dans un bureau** my mother works in an office
2. desk : **j'ai un bureau dans ma chambre** I have a desk in my bedroom
> **le bureau de poste** the post office
> **un bureau de tabac** a tobacconist's *UK*.

bus [bys] *nom masculin*

bus *(pluriel* buses*)* : **tu prends le bus pour aller à l'école ?** do you take the bus to school?

buste [byst] *nom masculin*

1. chest : **un buste musclé** a muscular chest
2. bust : **un buste de Rodin** a bust by Rodin.

but [byt] *nom masculin*

1. aim : **leur but est de gagner le championnat** their aim is to win the championship
2. goal : **Petit a marqué deux buts** Petit scored two goals
> **dans le but de faire quelque chose** in order to do something ; **ils sont venus dans le but de discuter** they came in order to talk ou they came to talk
> **quel est le but de votre visite ?** what's the purpose of your visit?

buvette [byvɛt] *nom féminin*

refreshment stall *UK* : **j'ai travaillé à la buvette de la kermesse** I worked on the refreshment stall at the fête.

ça [sa] *pronom*

1. it : **qu'est-ce que ça veut dire ?** what does it mean? ; **ça m'énerve** it gets on my nerves ; **je trouve ça marrant** I find it funny ; **est-ce que ça te plaît ?** do you like it?
2. that : **donne-moi ça** give me that
3. this : **tiens, prends ça** here, take this
> **qui ça ?** who?
> **où ça ?** where?
> **ça y est** that's it : **ça y est, j'ai fini mes devoirs** that's it, I've finished my homework.

cabane [kaban] *nom féminin*

hut : **ils ont construit une cabane dans la forêt** they built a hut in the forest.

cabine [kabin] *nom féminin*

cabin : **une cabine de première classe sur le bateau** a first-class cabin on the boat
> **les cabines d'essayage** fitting rooms
> **une cabine téléphonique** a phone box *UK* ou a phone booth *US*.

cabinet [kabinɛ] *nom masculin*

> **un cabinet médical** a doctor's surgery *UK* ou a doctor's office *US*

cabinets *nom masculin pluriel*

toilet : **il est aux cabinets** he's in the toilet

> ⚠ The French word **cabinet** is a false friend, it does not mean 'cabinet'.

câble [kabl] *nom masculin*

1. cable : **câble électrique** electric cable
2. cable TV : **ils ont le câble chez eux** they have cable TV.

cacahouète, cacahuète [kakawɛt] *nom féminin*

peanut.

cacao [kakao] *nom masculin*

cocoa : **du beurre de cacao** cocoa butter.

cache-cache [kaʃkaʃ] *nom masculin invariable*

jouer à cache-cache to play hide-and-seek.

cacher [kaʃe] *verbe*

to hide : j'ai caché son cadeau I've hidden his present

➤ **cacher la vue à quelqu'un** to block somebody's view : **pousse-toi, tu me caches la vue** move, you're blocking my view

se cacher *verbe pronominal*

to hide : il se cache derrière le garage he is hiding behind the garage.

cachette [kaʃɛt] *nom féminin*

hiding place : j'ai trouvé une bonne cachette I found a good hiding place

➤ **en cachette** secretly : ils se voient en cachette they see each other secretly

➤ **en cachette de quelqu'un** behind somebody's back : **Élodie fume en cachette de ses parents** Élodie smokes behind her parents' backs.

cadavre [kadavr] *nom masculin*

corpse : ils ont trouvé deux cadavres dans la maison they found two corpses in the house.

Caddie® [kadi] *nom masculin*

trolley *UK*, shopping cart *US* : son Caddie est plein de boîtes de conserve his trolley is full of cans.

cadeau [kado] (*pluriel* cadeaux) *nom masculin*

present : est-ce qu'on ouvre les cadeaux maintenant? shall we open the presents now?

➤ **un cadeau d'anniversaire** a birthday present

➤ **faire un cadeau à quelqu'un** to give somebody a present : **ils m'ont fait un cadeau magnifique** they gave me a beautiful present ; **mon correspondant m'a fait cadeau d'un livre** my penfriend gave me a book.

cadenas [kadna] *nom masculin*

padlock : il a mis un cadenas sur son vélo he put a padlock on his bike.

cadre [kadr] *nom masculin*

1. frame : un tableau avec un cadre doré a painting with a golden frame

2. surroundings (*s'utilise toujours au pluriel*) : le cadre est agréable, mais la nourriture n'est

pas très bonne the surroundings are pleasant, but the food isn't great

3. executive : le père de Julien est cadre supérieur dans une grande entreprise Julien's father is a senior executive in a big company.

café [kafe] *nom masculin*

1. coffee : je bois du café le matin I drink coffee in the morning ; deux cafés, s'il vous plaît two coffees, please

2. café : on a déjeuné dans un café we had lunch in a café

➤ **un café crème** OU **un café au lait** a coffee with hot milk OU a white coffee *UK*

➤ **un café liégeois** a coffee ice cream with whipped cream

➤ **un café noir** a black coffee.

cafétéria [kafeterja] *nom féminin*

cafeteria : nous avons mangé dans une cafétéria we ate in a cafeteria.

cage [kaʒ] *nom féminin*

cage : je n'aime pas voir les animaux en cage I don't like to see animals in cages.

cagoule [kagul] *nom féminin*

balaclava : les gangsters portaient des cagoules the gangsters were wearing balaclavas

⚠ The French word **cagoule** is a false friend, it does not mean 'cagoule'.

cahier [kaje] *nom masculin*

exercise book *UK*, notebook *US*

➤ **un cahier de brouillon** a rough book *UK* OU a notebook *US*

➤ **un cahier de textes** a homework book.

caillou [kaju] (*pluriel* cailloux) *nom masculin*

stone : ils lui ont lancé des cailloux they threw stones at him.

caisse [kɛs] *nom féminin*

1. crate : toutes nos affaires sont dans des caisses all our things are in crates

2. checkout : elle travaille à la caisse au supermarché she works at the checkout in the supermarket

➤ **la caisse enregistreuse** the till OU the cash register

➤ **une caisse d'épargne** a savings bank.

caissier, ère [kesje, ɛr] *nom masculin, nom féminin*

cashier : **Charlotte est caissière au Mono-prix** Charlotte is a cashier at Monoprix.

calcul [kalkyl] *nom masculin*

calculation : **tes calculs sont faux** your calculations are wrong
> **le calcul** arithmetic : **je suis nul en calcul** I'm hopeless at arithmetic
> **le calcul mental** mental arithmetic.

calculatrice [kalkylatris] *nom féminin*

calculator : **calculatrice de poche** pocket calculator.

calculer [kalkyle] *verbe*

to work out, to calculate : **elle a tout calculé de tête** she worked everything out in her head ; **j'ai calculé qu'il me faudrait deux heures** I worked out that it would take me two hours.

calculette [kalkylɛt] *nom féminin*

pocket calculator.

caleçon [kalsɔ̃] *nom masculin*

1. boxer shorts *(s'utilise toujours au pluriel)* : **ton caleçon dépasse de ton jean** your boxer shorts are showing under your jeans
2. leggings *(s'utilise toujours au pluriel)* : **Aurélie porte un caleçon** Aurélie is wearing leggings.

calendrier [kalɑ̃drije] *nom masculin*

calendar.

Californie [kaliforni] *nom féminin*

> **la Californie** California : **mon père va souvent en Californie** my father often goes to California.

câlin [kalɛ̃] *nom masculin*

cuddle : **fais-moi un câlin** give me a cuddle.

calme [kalm] *adjectif & nom*

■ *adjectif*
1. quiet : **c'est un quartier très calme** it's a very quiet area
2. calm : **restez calmes, il n'y a pas de danger** keep calm, there's no danger
■ *nom masculin*
peace and quiet : **j'ai besoin de calme pour travailler** I need peace and quiet to work
> **du calme !** calm down!

calmer [kalme] *verbe*

to ease : **cette pommade va calmer la douleur** this ointment will ease the pain

se calmer *verbe pronominal*

1. to calm down : **calme-toi, ce n'est pas grave** calm down, it's not serious
2. to ease : **la douleur s'est calmée** the pain eased
3. to die down : **le vent s'est calmé** the wind died down.

camarade [kamarad] *nom masculin ou féminin*

friend : **tous ses camarades sont là** all his friends are here
> **un camarade de classe, une camarade de classe** a classmate
> **un camarade d'école, une camarade d'école** a schoolfriend.

cambriolage [kɑ̃brijɔlaʒ] *nom masculin*

burglary *(pluriel* **burglaries***)* : **il y a eu trois cambriolages dans l'immeuble** there have been three burglaries in the building.

cambrioler [kɑ̃brijɔle] *verbe*

to burgle *UK*, to burglarize *US* : **l'école a été cambriolée** the school was burgled.

cambrioleur, euse [kɑ̃brijɔlœr, øz] *nom masculin, nom féminin*

burglar : **les cambrioleurs ont tout emporté** the burglars took everything.

caméra [kamera] *nom féminin*

camera : **une caméra vidéo** a video camera

 The French word **caméra** is only used to mean a video camera or a film camera.

Caméscope® [kameskɔp] *nom masculin*

camcorder.

camion [kamjɔ̃] *nom masculin*

lorry *UK (pluriel* **lorries***)*, truck *US* : **il y avait plein de camions sur la route** there were a lot of lorries on the road.

camionnette [kamjɔnɛt] *nom féminin*

van : **nous avons loué une camionnette pour déménager** we hired a van to move house.

campagne [kɑ̃paɲ] *nom féminin*

1. country : **ils vivent à la campagne** they live in the country
2. countryside : **la campagne est belle par ici** the countryside is beautiful round here
3. campaign : **une campagne électorale** an

election campaign : **une campagne publicitaire** an advertising campaign.

camper [kɑ̃pe] *verbe*

to camp : **on a campé sur la plage** we
camped on the beach.

camping [kɑ̃piŋ] *nom masculin*

1. camping : **j'aime bien le camping** I like
camping : **faire du camping** to go camping
2. campsite : **le camping est au bord de la rivière** the campsite is on the river bank.

Canada [kanada] *nom masculin*

➤ **le Canada** Canada

En anglais, à de rares exceptions près, il n'y a pas
d'article devant les noms de pays :

mon père vit au Canada my father lives in
Canada ; **tu es déjà allée au Canada ?** have
you ever been to Canada?

canadien, enne [kanadjɛ̃, ɛn] *adjectif*

Canadian

En anglais, les adjectifs se rapportant à un pays
ou une région s'écrivent avec une majuscule :

il a un accent canadien he has a Canadian
accent

Canadien, enne *nom masculin, nom féminin*

Canadian.

canal [kanal] (*pluriel* canaux [kano]) *nom
masculin*

canal : **on s'est promenés au bord du canal**
we went for a walk by the canal.

canapé [kanape] *nom masculin*

1. sofa : **assieds-toi sur le canapé** sit on the
sofa
2. canapé : **un buffet avec des canapés et des
olives** a buffet with canapés and olives.

canapé-lit [kanapeli] *nom masculin*

sofa bed.

canard [kanar] *nom masculin*

duck : **du canard rôti** roast duck.

cancer [kɑ̃sɛr] *nom masculin*

cancer : **M. Lubat a un cancer** Mr Lubat has
cancer ; **elle a un cancer du foie** she has liver
cancer

Cancer *nom masculin*

Cancer : **je suis Cancer** I'm a Cancer.

candidat, e [kɑ̃dida, at] *nom masculin, nom féminin*

candidate : **il est candidat aux élections**
he's a candidate in the elections.

canne [kan] *nom féminin*

walking stick : **mon grand-père marche
avec une canne** my grandfather uses a walking stick

➤ **une canne blanche** a white stick *UK* ou a
white cane *US*

➤ **une canne à pêche** a fishing rod.

canon [kanɔ̃] *nom masculin*

1. gun : **l'armée utilise des canons** the army
uses guns ; **les canons de l'armée pointaient
vers la ville** the army's guns were aimed at
the town
2. barrel : **le canon du revolver** the barrel of
the revolver
➤ **chanter en canon** to sing in a round.

cantine [kɑ̃tin] *nom féminin*

canteen *UK*, cafeteria *US* : **la cantine de
l'école est immense** the school canteen is
huge
➤ **manger à la cantine** to have school meals.

caoutchouc [kautʃu] *nom masculin*

rubber : **des gants en caoutchouc** rubber
gloves.

capable [kapabl] *adjectif*

capable : **tu crois qu'il est capable de lui
dire la vérité ?** do you think he's capable of
telling her the truth?

cape [kap] *nom féminin*

cape : **la cape de Batman** Batman's cape.

capitale [kapital] *nom féminin*

capital : **quelle est la capitale de l'Australie ?** what's the capital of Australia?

➤ **en capitales** in capitals ou in capital letters :
écrivez votre nom en capitales write your
name in capitals ou write your name in capital
letters.

capot [kapo] *nom masculin*

bonnet *UK*, hood *US* : **le capot de la voiture** the car bonnet.

capricieux, euse [kaprisjø, øz] *adjectif*

temperamental : **qu'est-ce que tu es capricieuse !** you're so temperamental!

Capricorne [kaprikɔrn] *nom masculin*

Capricorn : **je suis Capricorne** I'm a Capricorn.

capsule [kapsyl] *nom féminin*

cap : **je n'arrive pas à enlever la capsule de la bouteille** I can't get the cap off the bottle.

capuche [kapyʃ] *nom féminin*

hood : **mets ta capuche, il pleut** put your hood up, it's raining.

capuchon [kapyʃɔ̃] *nom masculin*

cap, top : **j'ai perdu le capuchon de mon stylo** I've lost the cap of my pen.

car [kar] *conjonction*

because : **il n'y aura pas cours d'informatique car le professeur est malade** there won't be a computing class because the teacher is ill.

car [kar] *nom masculin*

coach *UK (pluriel* coaches*)*, bus *US (pluriel* buses*)* : **nous sommes allés à Bruxelles en car** we went to Brussels by coach

> **le car scolaire** the school bus.

caractère [karaktɛr] *nom masculin*

personality, character : **Sophie a un caractère agréable** Sophie has a nice personality
> **avoir bon caractère** to be good-natured
> **avoir mauvais caractère** to be bad-tempered
> **en gros caractères** in large type
> **en petits caractères** in small type
> **en caractères d'imprimerie** in block capitals.

carafe [karaf] *nom féminin*

jug *UK*, carafe *US* : **mets la carafe d'eau sur la table** put the water jug on the table.

caramel [karamɛl] *nom masculin*

caramel : **une tarte avec du caramel au fond** a tart with caramel at the bottom
> **du caramel dur** toffee *UK* ou taffy *US*
> **du caramel mou** fudge.

carapace [karapas] *nom féminin*

shell : **la carapace de la tortue** the tortoise's shell.

caravane [karavan] *nom féminin*

caravan *UK*, trailer *US* : **nous partons en vacances en caravane** we're going on holiday in a caravan.

caresser [karese] *verbe*

to stroke : **j'aime bien caresser le chat** I like stroking the cat.

carie [kari] *nom féminin*

> **j'ai une carie** I've got a cavity
> **la carie dentaire** tooth decay.

carnaval [karnaval] *nom masculin*

carnival : **le carnaval de Venise** the Venice carnival.

carnet [karnɛ] *nom masculin*

1. notebook : **je vais noter le numéro dans mon carnet** I'll write the number in my notebook
2. book : **un carnet de timbres** a book of stamps ; **un carnet de tickets de métro** a book of metro tickets
> **un carnet d'adresses** an address book
> **un carnet de chèques** a chequebook *UK* ou a checkbook *US*
> **un carnet de notes** a report card.

carotte [karɔt] *nom féminin*

carrot : **des carottes râpées** grated carrots.

carré, e [kare] *adjectif*

square : **une pièce carrée** a square room ; **20 mètres carrés** 20 square metres

carré *nom masculin*

square : **dessine un carré** draw a square.

carreau [karo] *(pluriel* carreaux*) nom masculin*

1. tile : **il y a des carreaux blancs dans la salle de bains** there are white tiles in the bathroom
2. window pane : **ils ont cassé un carreau** they broke a window pane playing football
3. diamonds : **le trois de carreau** the three of diamonds
> **à carreaux** checked ; **une jupe à carreaux** a checked skirt.

carrefour [karfur] *nom masculin*

crossroads *UK (s'utilise comme un nom au singulier)*, intersection *US* : **nous sommes arrivés** à un **carrefour** we came to a crossroads *UK* ou we came to an intersection *US*.

carrelage [karlaʒ] *nom masculin*

tiles (*s'utilise toujours au pluriel*) **: le carrelage est abîmé** the tiles are damaged.

carrément [karemɑ̃] *adverbe*

1. **straight out : Marine lui a carrément dit qu'elle le détestait !** Marine told him straight out that she hated him!
2. **downright : il est carrément bête** he's downright stupid
3. **really : j'étais carrément en retard** I was really late.

carrière [karjɛr] *nom féminin*

1. **career : elle a fait carrière dans la finance** she made a career in finance
2. **quarry** (*pluriel* **quarries**) **: une carrière d'ardoise** a slate quarry.

cartable [kartabl] *nom masculin*

schoolbag : ton cartable est super lourd your schoolbag is really heavy.

carte [kart] *nom féminin*

1. **card : je vais payer par carte** I'm going to pay by card ; **jouer aux cartes** to play cards
2. **map : une carte de France** a map of France ; **une carte routière** a road map
3. **menu : ce restaurant a une carte très variée** this restaurant has a very varied menu
➤ **une carte d'anniversaire** a birthday card
➤ **une carte bancaire** a bank card
➤ **une Carte Bleue®** a Visa Card®
➤ **une carte de crédit** a credit card
➤ **une carte d'identité** an identity card
➤ **des cartes à jouer** playing cards
➤ **une carte postale** a postcard
➤ **une carte de visite** a visiting card ou a calling card *US*

> 📖 CARTE D'IDENTITÉ
> All French citizens have to carry identity cards. They show a photograph of the holder plus their name, address, age, height, etc. The police can ask to see someone's identity card at any time. A French citizen can travel within the European Union using their identity card instead of a passport.

carton [kartɔ̃] *nom masculin*

1. **cardboard : une maquette en carton** a cardboard model

2. **cardboard box** (*pluriel* **cardboard boxes**) **: on a mis toutes nos affaires dans des cartons** we put all our things in cardboard boxes.

cartouche [kartuʃ] *nom féminin*

cartridge : une cartouche de fusil a gun cartridge ; **un stylo à cartouches** a cartridge pen.

cas [ka] *nom masculin*

case : c'est un cas spécial it's a special case
➤ **au cas où ...** in case ... **: au cas où il pleuvrait** in case it rains
➤ **en tout cas** in any case ou anyway
➤ **en cas d'urgence** in an emergency.

case [kaz] *nom féminin*

box (*pluriel* **boxes**) **: tu as oublié de remplir une case** you've forgotten to fill in one of the boxes.

casque [kask] *nom masculin*

1. **helmet : il met un casque pour faire du vélo** he wears a helmet when he rides his bike
2. **headphones** (*s'utilise toujours au pluriel*) **: tu pourrais écouter ta musique au casque** you could use headphones to listen to your music.

casquette [kaskɛt] *nom féminin*

cap : Thomas porte sa casquette à l'envers Thomas is wearing his cap back to front.

casser [kase] *verbe*

to break : attention, tu vas casser le verre ! be careful, you'll break the glass! ; **la corde a cassé** the rope broke

se casser *verbe pronominal*

to break : l'assiette s'est cassée the plate broke ; **Cédric s'est cassé le bras** Cédric broke his arm.

casserole [kasrɔl] *nom féminin*

pan, saucepan : une casserole d'eau bouillante a pan of boiling water

> ⚠️ The French word **casserole** is a false friend, it does not mean 'casserole'.

cassette [kasɛt] *nom féminin*

tape, cassette : une cassette de Boyzone a Boyzone tape
➤ **une cassette vidéo** a video ou a video cassette.

catalogue [katalɔg] *nom masculin*

catalogue *UK*, catalog *US*.

catastrophe [katastrɔf] *nom féminin*

disaster : **on a raté le train, quelle catastrophe!** we missed the train, what a disaster!

catégorie [kategɔri] *nom féminin*

category *(pluriel* **categories***)* : **il y a plusieurs catégories d'hôtels** there are several different categories of hotels.

cathédrale [katedral] *nom féminin*

cathedral : **la cathédrale de Chartres** Chartres cathedral.

catholique [katɔlik] *adjectif & nom masculin ou féminin*

Catholic : **Natacha est catholique** Natacha's a Catholic

> En anglais, les adjectifs et les noms se rapportant à une religion s'écrivent avec une majuscule.

cauchemar [koʃmar] *nom masculin*

nightmare : **j'ai fait un cauchemar horrible** I had a horrible nightmare.

cause [koz] *nom féminin*

cause : **personne ne connaît la vraie cause de l'accident** nobody knows the real cause of the accident

> **quelle est la cause de son départ ?** why did he leave?

> **à cause de** because of : **je me suis fait punir à cause de toi!** I got punished because of you!

cavalier, ère [kavalje, ɛr] *nom masculin, nom féminin*

rider : **Anne est une excellente cavalière** Anne is an excellent rider.

cave [kav] *nom féminin*

cellar : **la table de ping-pong est à la cave** the ping-pong table is in the cellar

> ⚠ The French word **cave** is a false friend, it does not mean 'cave'.

CD [sede] *nom masculin*

CD : **on a offert un CD à Marianne pour son anniversaire** we gave Marianne a CD for her birthday.

CD-ROM, CD-Rom [sederɔm] *nom masculin invariable*

CD-ROM.

ce [sə] *adjectif & pronom*

◼ *adjectif* (**cet** [sɛt] *devant une voyelle ou un « h » muet, féminin* **cette** [sɛt]*, pluriel* **ces** [se]*)*

> Pour désigner une personne ou une chose qui est proche, « ce » se traduit par this :

1. this : **il habite dans ce quartier** he lives in this area ; **cette année, je vais à un cours de judo** I'm going to judo classes this year ; **cet arbre a plus de cent ans** this tree is more than a hundred years old ; **ici c'est ma chambre** this is my room ; **ce monsieur ici, c'est mon oncle** this man here is my uncle

> Pour désigner une personne ou une chose éloignée, « ce » se traduit par that :

2. that : **à cette époque, j'habitais à Toulouse** at that time, I lived in Toulouse ; **d'ici, je n'arrive pas à lire ce panneau** I can't read that sign from here ; **la dame là-bas, c'est ma tante** that woman over there is my aunt

> **ce champ-ci** this field
> **cette fois-ci** this time
> **cette chambre-là** that room
> **cette année-là** that year

◼ *pronom* (**c'** *devant une voyelle*)

it : **qu'est-ce que c'est ?** – **c'est une montre** what is it? – it's a watch ; **c'est Estelle qui me l'a dit** it was Estelle who told me ou Estelle told me ; **c'était mieux avant** it was better before

> Quand « ce » s'applique à une personne, il faut utiliser le pronom personnel correspondant en anglais :

c'est une prof très sévère she's a very strict teacher ; **c'est un Américain** he's an American ; **ce sont des gens sympa** they're nice people

> **ce qui** what ; **raconte-moi ce qui s'est passé** tell me what happened
> **ce que** what ; **ce que je trouve le plus difficile** what I find the most difficult.

ceci [səsi] *pronom*

this : **ceci est à moi** this is mine.

céder [sede] *verbe*

to give in : **on a tellement insisté qu'il a cédé** we insisted so much that he gave in.

ceinture [sɛtyr] *nom féminin*

belt : **attachez vos ceintures** fasten your seat belts

➤ **ceinture de sécurité** seatbelt.

cela [səla] *pronom*

1. that : **je n'ai pas dit cela** I didn't say that ; **cela l'a beaucoup impressionnée** that impressed her a lot
2. it : **cela vaut la peine d'y aller** it is worth going.

célèbre [selɛbr] *adjectif*

famous : **Victor Hugo est un écrivain célèbre** Victor Hugo is a famous writer.

célibataire [selibatɛr] *adjectif & nom*

■ *adjectif*
single : **il est célibataire** he's single ; **une mère célibataire** a single mother ; **un père célibataire** a single father
■ *nom masculin ou féminin*
un célibataire a single man ; **une célibataire** a single woman ; **les célibataires** single people.

celle ➤ celui.

celle-ci [sɛlsi] ➤ celui.

celle-là [sɛlla] ➤ celui.

celles ➤ ceux.

celles-ci [sɛlsi] ➤ ceux.

celles-là [sɛlla] ➤ ceux.

cellule [selyl] *nom féminin*

cell : **les cellules de la prison** the prison cells ; **les cellules du cerveau** brain cells.

celui, celle [səlɥi, sɛl] *pronom*

1. the one : **celui de devant** the one in front ; **celui dont tu parlais** the one you were talking about ; **celui qui a gagné la course** the one who won the race ; **celle qui te va le mieux** the one that suits you best
2. *Pour indiquer la possession* **je préfère celle de Théo** I prefer Théo's
➤ **celui-ci** ou **celle-ci** this one ; **je préfère celui-ci** I prefer this one ; **celle-ci n'a rien à**

voir avec l'autre this one isn't anything like the other one

➤ **celui-là** ou **celle-là** that one : **celui-là est numérique** that one is digital ; **c'est celle-là qu'elle voulait** she wanted that one.

celui-ci [səlɥisi] ➤ celui.

celui-là [səlɥila] ➤ celui.

cendre [sɑ̃dr] *nom féminin*

ash *(pluriel* **ashes***)* : **de la cendre de cigarette** cigarette ash.

cendrier [sɑ̃drije] *nom masculin*

ashtray.

censé, e [sɑ̃se] *adjectif*

➤ **être censé faire quelque chose** to be supposed to do something : **il était censé être à l'école** he was supposed to be at school.

censeur [sɑ̃sœr] *nom masculin*

deputy head *UK*, vice-principal *US* : **le censeur du lycée** the school's deputy head.

cent [sɑ̃] *adjectif numéral*

one hundred, a hundred : **il y avait au moins cent personnes** there were at least a hundred people ; **deux cent cinquante** two hundred and fifty
➤ **pour cent** percent : **trente-deux pour cent** thirty-two percent ; **cent pour cent** a hundred percent.

centaine [sɑ̃tɛn] *nom féminin*

il reste une centaine de places there are about a hundred seats left ; **des centaines de gens** hundreds of people.

centenaire [sɑ̃tnɛr] *adjectif*

hundred-year-old : **un arbre centenaire** a hundred-year-old tree ; **ma grand-mère est centenaire** my grandmother is a hundred years old.

centième [sɑ̃tjɛm] *adjectif numéral, nom masculin & nom masculin ou féminin*

hundredth : **c'est le centième nom sur la liste** it's the hundredth name on the list ; **Paul est arrivé centième** Paul came hundredth.

centimètre [sɑ̃timɛtr] *nom masculin*

centimetre *UK*, centimeter *US* : **ça fait trois centimètres de long** it's three centimetres long.

central, e, aux [sɑ̃tral, o] *adjectif*

central : **j'habite dans un quartier très**

central the area I live in is very central ; **le chauffage central** central heating.

centrale [sɑ̃tral] *nom féminin*

power plant : **une centrale nucléaire** a nuclear power plant.

centre [sɑ̃tr] *nom masculin*

centre *UK*, center *US* : **la table est au centre de la pièce** the table is in the centre of the room

➤ **un centre aéré** an activity centre for school children

➤ **un centre commercial** a shopping centre *UK* ou a shopping mall *US*.

centre-ville [sɑ̃trəvil] *nom masculin*

city centre *UK*, city center *US*, town centre *UK*, town center *US* : **Lise habite à deux minutes du centre-ville** Lise lives two minutes from the city centre.

cependant [səpɑ̃dɑ̃] *conjonction*

however, yet : **je suis d'accord avec vous, j'ai une remarque à faire cependant** I agree with you. However, I have one comment.

cercle [sɛrkl] *nom masculin*

circle : **dessine un cercle au milieu de la page** draw a circle in the middle of the page.

cercueil [sɛrkœj] *nom masculin*

coffin.

céréale [sereal] *nom féminin*

cereal : **le riz est une céréale** rice is a cereal ; **je mange des céréales au petit déjeuner** I eat cereal for breakfast.

cérémonie [seremɔni] *nom féminin*

ceremony *(pluriel* ceremonies*)* : **une cérémonie officielle** an official ceremony.

cerf-volant [sɛrvɔlɑ̃] *nom masculin*

kite : **le dimanche on joue au cerf-volant sur la plage** on Sundays we fly a kite on the beach.

cerise [səriz] *nom féminin*

cherry *(pluriel* cherries*)* : **de la confiture de cerises** cherry jam.

cerne [sɛrn] *nom masculin*

avoir des cernes to have rings under one's eyes.

certain, e [sɛrtɛ̃, ɛn] *adjectif*

1. certain : **tu es certain que c'est lui ?** are you

certain it's him? ; **je suis certain d'avoir mis mes clés là** I'm certain I left my keys here

2. some : **à certains endroits** in some places

➤ **un certain temps** a while ; **Suzanne a mis un certain temps à réagir** Suzanne took a while to react

➤ **une personne d'un certain âge** a middle-aged person

➤ **un certain M. Lebrun** a certain Mr Lebrun.

certains, certaines *pronom*

1. some : **certains d'entre eux** some of them

2. some people : **certains pensent que c'est normal** some people think it's normal.

certainement [sɛrtɛnmɑ̃] *adverbe*

1. probably : **Yacine viendra certainement** Yacine will probably come

2. of course, certainly : **vous pouvez m'aider ? – oui, certainement !** can you help me? – yes, of course!

certificat [sɛrtifika] *nom masculin*

certificate : **un certificat médical** a medical certificate.

cerveau [sɛrvo] *(pluriel* cerveaux*) nom masculin*

brain : **le cerveau humain** the human brain.

cervelle [sɛrvɛl] *nom féminin*

1. brain : **fais marcher ta cervelle !** use your brain!

2. brains *(s'utilise toujours au pluriel)* : **de la cervelle d'agneau** lamb's brains.

ces [se] *adjectif pluriel*

1. *Pour parler de quelque chose de proche* these : **je n'aime pas ces dessins** I don't like these drawings ; **à qui sont ces clés ?** whose keys are these?

2. *Pour parler de quelque chose de plus éloigné* those : **est-ce que tu connais ces gens ?** do you know those people?

➤ **ces jours-ci** these days

➤ **ces émissions-là** those programmes.

César [sezar] *nom masculin*

les Césars French cinema awards

CÉSARS
The **Césars** are the French equivalent of the Oscars. Every year since 1976, prizes are awarded for the best French film, the best director, actor, etc. The awards are named after the artist who designed the trophies.

cesse [sɛs] nom féminin

➤ **sans cesse** constantly ; **elle pose sans cesse des questions** she's constantly asking questions ou she's always asking questions.

c'est-à-dire [setadir] conjonction

that is : **à l'heure du déjeuner, c'est-à-dire à treize heures** at lunchtime, that is one o'clock.

cet ➤ ce.

ceux, celles [sø, sɛl] pronom pluriel

the ones, those : **celles d'en face** the ones opposite ou those opposite ; **pour ceux d'entre vous qui veulent venir** for those of you who want to come ; **garde ceux que tu veux** keep the ones you want ; **celles dont je te parlais** the ones I was telling you about ; **celles que tu portais hier** the ones you wore yesterday

➤ **ceux-ci** ou **celles-ci** these ones ; **ceux-ci sont meilleurs** these ones are better ; **j'ai choisi celles-ci** I chose these ones

➤ **ceux-là** ou **celles-là** those ones ; **ceux-là sont moins chers** those ones are cheaper ; **je voudrais essayer celles-là** I'd like to try those ones on.

ceux-ci [søsi] ➤ ceux.

ceux-là [søla] ➤ ceux.

chacun, e [ʃakœ̃, yn] pronom indéfini

1. each : **chacun d'entre eux** each of them ; **trente euros chacun** thirty euros each.
2. everyone, everybody : **chacun est libre de faire ce qu'il veut** everybody's free to do what they want.

chagrin [ʃagrɛ̃] nom masculin

grief

➤ **avoir du chagrin** to be upset : **il a un gros chagrin** he's very upset.

chaîne [ʃɛn] nom féminin

1. chain : **une chaîne en or** a gold chain
2. channel : **sur quelle chaîne est le film ?** what channel is the film on? ; **une chaîne à péage** a pay channel
3. stereo, hi-fi : **Nicolas a une super chaîne avec un lecteur de CD** Nicolas has a great stereo with a CD player

➤ **une chaîne hi-fi** a hi-fi system

➤ **travailler à la chaîne** to work on an assembly line.

chair [ʃɛr] nom féminin

➤ **en chair et en os** in the flesh

➤ **de la chair à saucisse** sausage meat

➤ **avoir la chair de poule** to have goose pimples.

chaise [ʃɛz] nom féminin

chair : **une chaise en bois** a wooden chair

➤ **une chaise longue** a deckchair

➤ **la chaise électrique** the electric chair.

châle [ʃal] nom masculin

shawl : **elle portait un châle** she was wearing a shawl.

chalet [ʃalɛ] nom masculin

1. chalet : **un chalet de montagne** a mountain chalet
2. Au Canada holiday cottage : **ils ont un chalet au bord de la mer** they have a cottage by the sea.

chaleur [ʃalœr] nom féminin

heat : **la chaleur est insupportable** the heat is unbearable ; **quelle chaleur !** it's so hot!

chambre [ʃɑ̃br] nom féminin

1. bedroom : **on a joué dans la chambre de Léa** we played in Léa's bedroom
2. room : **une chambre d'hôtel** a hotel room ; **une chambre pour une personne** a single room ; **une chambre pour deux personnes** a double room

➤ **une chambre d'amis** a spare room ou a guest room.

chameau [ʃamo] (pluriel chameaux) nom masculin

camel.

champ [ʃɑ̃] nom masculin

field : **un champ de blé** a field of wheat

➤ **le champ de bataille** the battlefield

➤ **un champ de courses** a racecourse.

champagne [ʃɑ̃paɲ] nom masculin

champagne : **ils ont bu du champagne** they drank champagne.

champignon [ʃɑ̃piɲɔ̃] nom masculin

mushroom : **une omelette aux champignons** a mushroom omelette

➤ **des champignons de Paris** button mushrooms.

champion, onne [ʃɑ̃pjɔ̃, ɔn] *nom masculin, nom féminin*

champion : **il est champion du monde de natation** he's the world swimming champion.

championnat [ʃɑ̃pjɔna] *nom masculin*

championship : **le championnat du monde de football** the world football championship.

chance [ʃɑ̃s] *nom féminin*

1. **luck** : **bonne chance !** good luck! ; **avoir de la chance** to be lucky ; **tu as de la chance d'aller en Australie** you're lucky to be going to Australia ; **ne pas avoir de chance** to be unlucky ; **porter chance à quelqu'un** to bring somebody good luck

2. **chance** : **il n'a aucune chance de gagner** he has no chance of winning.

changement [ʃɑ̃ʒmɑ̃] *nom masculin*

change : **il y a eu des changements pendant que je n'étais pas là** there were some changes while I was away

➤ **le changement de vitesse** the gear stick *UK* ou the gearshift *US*.

changer [ʃɑ̃ʒe] *verbe*

to change : **ne change rien, c'est bien comme ça** don't change anything, it's all right like that ; **on doit changer à Châtelet** we have to change at Châtelet ; **changer des euros en livres** to change euro into pounds ; **viens, ça te changera** come with us, it'll be a change for you

➤ **changer de** to change : **on change de place ?** shall we change places? ; **elle a encore changé d'avis** she's changed her mind again.

chanson [ʃɑ̃sɔ̃] *nom féminin*

song : **une chanson d'amour** a love song.

chant [ʃɑ̃] *nom masculin*

1. **song** : **un chant religieux** a religious song

2. **singing** : **Serge prend des cours de chant** Serge is taking singing lessons

➤ **des chants de Noël** Christmas carols.

chanter [ʃɑ̃te] *verbe*

to sing : **elle chante vraiment bien** she sings really well ou she's a really good singer

➤ **si ça te chante** *familier* if you want to : **dis-le-lui si ça te chante** tell him if you want to.

chanteur, euse [ʃɑ̃tœr, øz] *nom masculin, nom féminin*

singer : **une chanteuse de rock** a rock singer.

chantier [ʃɑ̃tje] *nom masculin*

building site : **les ouvriers sont encore sur le chantier** the workmen are still on the building site.

Chantilly [ʃɑ̃tiji] *nom féminin*

➤ **de la crème Chantilly** whipped cream.

chapeau [ʃapo] *(pluriel* **chapeaux***) nom masculin*

1. **hat** : **un chapeau de paille** a straw hat

2. *familier* **well done!** : **tu as tout fini ? chapeau !** you've finished? well done!

➤ **un chapeau melon** a bowler hat.

chapelle [ʃapɛl] *nom féminin*

chapel.

chapitre [ʃapitr] *nom masculin*

chapter : **ils se rencontrent au chapitre deux** they meet in chapter two.

chaque [ʃak] *adjectif*

1. **each** : **chaque invité a eu un petit cadeau** each guest got a small present

2. **every** : **chaque être humain a le droit d'être libre** every human being has the right to be free ; **je prends le bus chaque jour** I take the bus every day

Le plus souvent **each** et **every** ont le même sens. On emploie **each** si on veut mettre l'accent sur tous les éléments du groupe dont on parle, avec le sens de « chacun des », et on emploie **every** si on veut insister sur le groupe dans son ensemble, avec le sens de « tous les ».

char [ʃar] *nom masculin*

1. **tank** : **les chars sont entrés dans la ville** the tanks entered the city

2. **float** : **les chars du carnaval sont magnifiques** the carnival floats are beautiful

3. *Au Canada* **car** : **il a garé son char près de l'école** he parked his car near the school.

charbon [ʃarbɔ̃] *nom masculin*

coal

➤ **du charbon de bois** charcoal.

charcuterie [ʃarkytri] *nom féminin*

1. **pork butcher's** : **je dois aller à la charcuterie** I have to go to the pork butcher's

C

2. cooked pork meats *(pluriel)* : **une assiette de charcuterie** a plate of cooked pork meats.

charge [ʃarʒ] *nom féminin*

load : **charge maximum** maximum load

➤ **prendre quelque chose en charge** to pay for something ; **l'école prend les frais du voyage en charge** the school is paying for the cost of the trip

 The French word **charge** is a false friend, it does not mean 'charge'.

chargé, e [ʃarʒe] *adjectif*

1. loaded : **la voiture est chargée de provisions** the car is loaded with shopping ; **trop chargé** overloaded

2. busy : **un emploi du temps chargé** a busy schedule.

charger [ʃarʒe] *verbe*

to load : **je vais charger la voiture pendant que vous vous préparez** I'll load the car while you're getting ready

➤ **être chargé de quelque chose** to be in charge of something ou to be responsible for something : **Marc, tu es chargé des boissons** Marc, you're in charge of the drinks

se charger *verbe pronominal*

➤ **se charger de quelque chose** to take care of something : **je me charge des boissons** I'll take care of the drinks ; **je me charge d'envoyer les invitations** I'll take care of sending the invitations.

chariot [ʃarjo] *nom masculin*

trolley *UK*, **cart** *US* : **son chariot est plein de bouteilles** his trolley is full of bottles.

charmant, e [ʃarmɑ̃, ɑ̃t] *adjectif*

charming.

charme [ʃarm] *nom masculin*

charm : **elle a beaucoup de charme** she has a lot of charm.

charrette [ʃarɛt] *nom féminin*

cart.

chasse [ʃas] *nom féminin*

hunting : **la chasse au renard** fox hunting ; **aller à la chasse** to go hunting

➤ **tirer la chasse** to pull the chain ou to flush the toilet.

chasser [ʃase] *verbe*

1. to hunt : **chasser le renard** to hunt foxes

2. to throw out : **le videur les a chassés de la boîte de nuit** the bouncer threw them out from the club.

chasseur, euse [ʃasœr, øz] *nom masculin, nom féminin*

hunter : **les chasseurs se cachent derrière les buissons** the hunters are hiding behind the bushes.

chat, chatte [ʃa, ʃat] *nom masculin, nom féminin*

cat : **le chat m'a griffé** the cat scratched me ; **un chat persan** a Persian cat ; **un chat siamois** a Siamese cat

➤ **j'ai un chat dans la gorge** I have a frog in my throat

➤ **il n'y a pas un chat** *familier* there's not a soul around.

châtaigne [ʃatɛɲ] *nom féminin*

chestnut : **des châtaignes grillées** roasted chestnuts.

château [ʃato] *(pluriel* châteaux*) nom masculin*

castle : **le château du duc de Lorraine** the Duke of Lorraine's castle

➤ **un château d'eau** a water tower

➤ **un château fort** a castle

➤ **un château de sable** a sandcastle.

chaton [ʃatɔ̃] *nom masculin*

kitten : **la chatte et ses chatons** the cat and her kittens.

chatouiller [ʃatuje] *verbe*

to tickle : **ne me chatouille pas, je déteste ça !** don't tickle me, I hate it!

chatouilles [ʃatuj] *nom féminin pluriel*

➤ **faire des chatouilles à quelqu'un** to tickle somebody

➤ **craindre les chatouilles** to be ticklish.

chatte ➤ chat.

chaud, e [ʃo, ʃod] *adjectif*

1. warm : **ton café est à peine chaud** your coffee isn't very warm

2. hot : **mon bain est trop chaud** my bath is too hot

chaud *adverbe*

warm, hot : **enfin, il fait plus chaud** at last

it's getting warmer ; **il fait chaud ici, on peut ouvrir ?** it's hot in here, can we open the window ? ; **avoir chaud** to be hot ; **enlève ton manteau si tu as chaud** take your coat off if you're hot.

chauffage [ʃofaʒ] *nom masculin*

heating : **on a le chauffage central** we have central heating.

chauffer [ʃofe] *verbe*

1. to heat up : **l'eau est en train de chauffer** the water is heating up ; **faire chauffer quelque chose** to heat something up
2. to overheat : **le moteur chauffe, arrêtons-nous** the engine is overheating, let's stop
> **ça va chauffer !** *familier* there's going to be trouble!

chauffeur [ʃofœr] *nom masculin*

1. driver : **mon oncle est chauffeur de taxi** my uncle is a taxi driver
2. chauffeur : **le chauffeur du ministre** the minister's chauffeur.

chaussée [ʃose] *nom féminin*

road : **l'arbre était en travers de la chaussée** the tree was lying across the road.

chaussette [ʃosɛt] *nom féminin*

sock : **des chaussettes en laine** woollen socks ; **il était en chaussettes** he was wearing socks.

chausson [ʃosɔ̃] *nom masculin*

1. slipper : **il est en chaussons** he's wearing slippers
2. ballet shoe : **Sonia a acheté des chaussons pour son cours de danse** Sonia bought some ballet shoes for her dancing lesson.

chaussure [ʃosyr] *nom féminin*

shoe : **des chaussures en cuir** leather shoes
> **des chaussures de marche** walking boots
> **des chaussures de ski** ski boots
> **des chaussures de sport** sports shoes.

chauve [ʃov] *adjectif*

bald : **mon père devient chauve** my father is going bald.

chauve-souris [ʃovsuri] (*pluriel* chauves-souris) *nom féminin*

bat : **les chauves-souris ont de grandes ailes** bats have big wings.

chef [ʃɛf] *nom masculin*

1. leader : **le chef du parti** the leader of the party
2. boss (*pluriel* bosses) : **c'est moi le chef ici !** I'm the boss around here!
3. chef : **ce steak est cru, allez me chercher le chef !** this steak is raw, go and get the chef!
> **un chef d'entreprise** a company manager
> **un chef d'État** a head of state
> **un chef d'orchestre** a conductor.

chef-d'œuvre [ʃɛdœvr] (*pluriel* chefs-d'œuvre) *nom masculin*

masterpiece : **ces tableaux sont des chefs-d'œuvre** these paintings are masterpieces.

chemin [ʃəmɛ̃] *nom masculin*

1. path : **où mène ce chemin ?** where does this path go?
2. way : **c'est le chemin le plus court** it's the quickest way ; **nous nous sommes arrêtés en chemin** we stopped on the way
> **chemin de fer** railway *UK* ou railroad *US*.

cheminée [ʃəmine] *nom féminin*

1. fireplace : **il y a une grande cheminée dans le salon** there is a big fireplace in the living room
2. mantelpiece : **mets le vase sur la cheminée** put the vase on the mantelpiece
3. chimney : **les cheminées de l'usine** the factory chimneys.

chemise [ʃəmiz] *nom féminin*

1. shirt : **une chemise à manches longues** a long-sleeved shirt
2. folder : **la chemise où je mets mes photocopies** the folder I put my photocopies in
> **chemise de nuit** nightie *UK* ou nightgown *US*.

chemisier [ʃəmizje] *nom masculin*

blouse : **un chemisier en soie** a silk blouse.

chêne [ʃɛn] *nom masculin*

oak : **une table en chêne** an oak table.

chenille [ʃənij] *nom féminin*

caterpillar : **les chenilles mangent des feuilles** caterpillars eat leaves.

chèque [ʃɛk] *nom masculin*

cheque *UK*, check *US* : **faire un chèque** to write a cheque
> **chèque sans provision** bad cheque *UK* ou bad check *US*
> **chèque de voyage** traveller's cheque *UK* ou traveler's check *US*.

c

chéquier [ʃekje] *nom masculin*

chequebook *UK*, checkbook *US*.

cher, chère [ʃɛr] *adjectif*

1. **dear** : **Chère Caro, ...** Dear Caro, ...
2. **expensive** : **ce restaurant est trop cher** this restaurant is too expensive.
> **coûter cher** to be expensive ; **ce manteau coûte très cher** this coat is very expensive.

chercher [ʃɛrʃe] *verbe*

to look for : **je cherche mes lunettes, tu les as vues ?** I'm looking for my glasses, have you seen them?
> **aller chercher quelqu'un** to pick somebody up ; **je viendrai te chercher à la gare** I'll pick you up at the station
> **aller chercher quelque chose** to go and get something ; **va chercher les verres, s'il te plaît** go and get the glasses, please.

chéri, e [ʃeri] *nom masculin, nom féminin*

darling : **oui, chéri** yes, darling.

cheval [ʃəval] (*pluriel* **chevaux** [ʃəvo]) *nom masculin*

horse : **cheval de course** racehorse
> **faire du cheval** to ride OU to go riding : **elle fait du cheval le mercredi** she goes riding every Wednesday ; **tu sais faire du cheval ?** can you ride?

chevalier [ʃəvalje] *nom masculin*

knight : **les chevaliers du Moyen-Âge** the knights of the Middle Ages.

cheveu [ʃəvø] (*pluriel* **cheveux**) *nom masculin*

hair : **un cheveu blanc** a white hair ; **les cheveux** hair ; **Anna a les cheveux roux** Anna's got red hair ; **ses cheveux sont trop longs** her hair is too long.

cheville [ʃəvij] *nom féminin*

ankle : **je me suis foulé la cheville** I twisted my ankle.

chèvre [ʃɛvr] *nom*

■ *nom féminin*
goat
■ *nom masculin*
goat's cheese : **une salade au chèvre chaud** a salad with warm goat's cheese.

chez [ʃe] *préposition*

> **chez moi**
1. **at home** : **je suis chez moi** I'm at home

2. **home** : **je vais rentrer chez moi** I'm going home
> **chez quelqu'un**
1. **at somebody's house** OU **at somebody's place** : **je suis chez Marie** I'm at Marie's house OU I'm at Marie's place
2. **to somebody's house** OU **to somebody's place** : **je vais chez Paul** I'm going to Paul's house OU I'm going to Paul's place

> Pour indiquer que l'on est ou que l'on va chez un commerçant, chez le dentiste, chez le médecin, etc., on emploie le possessif en anglais :

> **Bruno est chez le coiffeur** Bruno is at the hairdresser's ; **je dois aller chez le médecin** I have to go to the doctor's.

chic [ʃik] *adjectif* (*invariable en genre*)

smart *UK*, **chic** *US* : **tu es très chic aujourd'hui** you look very smart today.

chien [ʃjɛ̃] *nom masculin, nom féminin*

dog : **leur chien s'appelle Arthur** their dog is called Arthur.

chienne [ʃjɛn] *nom féminin*

female dog, bitch.

chiffon [ʃifɔ̃] *nom masculin*

rag : **prends un vieux chiffon pour nettoyer les vitres** take an old rag to clean the windows
> **chiffon à poussière** duster *UK* OU dust cloth *US*.

chiffre [ʃifr] *nom masculin*

figure : **écris la somme en chiffres** write the sum in figures
> **chiffres arabes** Arabic numerals
> **chiffres romains** Roman numerals.

chignon [ʃiɲɔ̃] *nom masculin*

bun : **Mme Joly porte un chignon** Mrs Joly wears her hair in a bun.

chimie [ʃimi] *nom féminin*

chemistry : **un cours de chimie** a chemistry class.

chimpanzé [ʃɛ̃pɑ̃ze] *nom masculin*

chimpanzee.

Chine [ʃin] *nom féminin*

> **la Chine** China

En anglais, à de rares exceptions près, il n'y a pas d'article devant les noms de pays :

il a vécu en Chine he lived in China ; **j'aimerais aller en Chine** I'd like to go to China.

chinois, e [ʃinwa, az] *adjectif*

Chinese : **la cuisine chinoise** Chinese cooking

chinois *nom masculin*

Chinese : **Patrick parle chinois** Patrick speaks Chinese ; **j'ai appris le chinois** I learned Chinese

En anglais, les adjectifs se rapportant à un pays ou une région, ainsi que le nom désignant la langue de ce pays ou de cette région, s'écrivent avec une majuscule.

Chinois, e *nom masculin, nom féminin*

Chinese : **un Chinois** a Chinese man ; **une Chinoise** a Chinese woman ; **les Chinois** the Chinese.

chiot [ʃjo] *nom masculin*

puppy (*pluriel* **puppies**).

chips [ʃips] *nom féminin pluriel*

crisps *UK*, potato chips *US* : **un paquet de chips** a packet of crisps *UK* ou a packet of chips *US*

⚠ In French the word **chips** is a false friend to British English speakers, it does not mean 'chips'.

chirurgie [ʃiryrʒi] *nom féminin*

surgery : **la chirurgie esthétique** plastic surgery.

chirurgien, enne [ʃiryrʒjɛ̃, ɛn] *nom masculin, nom féminin*

surgeon : **la cousine d'Alice est chirurgienne** Alice's cousin is a surgeon.

choc [ʃɔk] *nom masculin*

1. impact : **le choc a été si violent que la vitre a explosé** the impact was so violent that the window exploded
2. shock : **ça m'a fait un choc !** it gave me a shock!

chocolat [ʃɔkɔla] *nom masculin*

chocolate : **un gâteau au chocolat** a choc-olate cake ; **une boîte de chocolats** a box of chocolates

➤ **du chocolat au lait** milk chocolate
➤ **du chocolat noir** dark chocolate
➤ **un chocolat liégeois** a chocolate ice cream with whipped cream.

choisir [ʃwazir] *verbe*

to choose : **Simon a choisi une casquette noire** Simon chose a black cap ; **choisir de faire quelque chose** to choose to do something ; **Annie a choisi de passer ses vacances à Paris** Annie chose to spend her holidays in Paris.

choix [ʃwa] *nom masculin*

choice : **tu as le choix entre le jaune et le bleu** you have a choice between the yellow one and the blue one ; **on a dû faire un choix** we had to make a choice.

chômage [ʃomaʒ] *nom masculin*

unemployment : **le chômage est en baisse** unemployment is falling
➤ **être au chômage** to be unemployed.

chose [ʃoz] *nom féminin*

thing : **j'ai plusieurs choses à faire** I've got a few things to do.

chouchou, chouchoute [ʃuʃu, ʃuʃut] *nom masculin, nom féminin familier*

teacher's pet : **c'est le chouchou de la prof de biologie** he's the biology teacher's pet

chouchou *nom masculin*

scrunchy, scrunchie.

chouette [ʃwɛt] *nom & adjectif*

◼ *nom féminin*
owl : **la chouette est un oiseau rapace** the owl is a bird of prey ; **on entend le cri de la chouette** you can hear the owl's screech
◼ *adjectif familier*
great : **elles sont chouettes, tes baskets** your trainers are great.

chou-fleur [ʃuflœr] (*pluriel* choux-fleurs) *nom masculin*

cauliflower.

chrétien, enne [kretjɛ̃, ɛn] *adjectif & nom masculin, nom féminin*

Christian

C

55

En anglais, les adjectifs et les noms se rapportant à une religion s'écrivent avec une majuscule :

il est chrétien he's a Christian.

Christ [krist] *nom masculin*

le Christ Christ.

chuchoter [ʃyʃɔte] *verbe*

to whisper : **Amélie m'a chuchoté la réponse** Amélie whispered the answer to me ; **pourquoi tu chuchotes comme ça ?** why are you whispering like that?

chut [ʃyt] *interjection*

sh!, hush!

chute [ʃyt] *nom féminin*

fall : **elle a fait une mauvaise chute** she had a bad fall
➤ **une chute d'eau** a waterfall
➤ **les chutes du Niagara** Niagara Falls.

cible [sibl] *nom féminin*

target : **elle atteint la cible chaque fois** she hits the target every time.

cicatrice [sikatris] *nom féminin*

scar : **j'ai une grosse cicatrice au bras** I've got a big scar on my arm.

cidre [sidr] *nom masculin*

cider *UK*, hard cider *US* : **du cidre doux** sweet cider ; **du cidre brut** dry cider.

ciel [sjɛl] *nom masculin*

sky : **le ciel est tout bleu** the sky is all blue.

cigarette [sigarɛt] *nom féminin*

cigarette : **fumer une cigarette** to smoke a cigarette.

cil [sil] *nom masculin*

eyelash *(pluriel* eyelashes*)*.

cimetière [simtjɛr] *nom masculin*

cemetery *(pluriel* cemeteries*)*, graveyard.

ciné [sine] *nom masculin familier*

cinema *UK*, movies *US* : **tu viens au ciné avec nous ?** are you coming to the cinema with us?

cinéma [sinema] *nom masculin*

cinema *UK*, movie theater *US* : **on pourrait aller au cinéma** we could go to the cinema *UK* ou we could go to the movies *US*.

cinq [sɛ̃k] *adjectif numéral & nom masculin*

five : **il y a cinq garçons dans ma classe** there are five boys in my class ; **elle a cinq ans** she's five
➤ **le cinq novembre** the fifth of November *UK* ou November fifth *US*.

cinquante [sɛ̃kɑ̃t] *adjectif numéral & nom masculin*

fifty : **cinquante euros** fifty euros.

cinquantième [sɛ̃kɑ̃tjɛm] *adjectif numéral & nom*

fiftieth : **c'est le cinquantième nom sur la liste** it's the fiftieth name on the list ; **Anne est arrivée cinquantième** Anne came fiftieth.

cinquième [sɛ̃kjɛm] *adjectif numéral & nom*

▪ *adjectif numéral & nom*
fifth : **c'est la cinquième fois que j'essaie** this is the fifth time I've tried ; **Anne est arrivée cinquième** Anne came fifth ; **un cinquième de la somme totale** a fifth of the total sum
▪ *nom féminin*
year eight *UK*, seventh grade *US* : **Bertrand est en cinquième** Bertrand is in year eight.

cintre [sɛ̃tr] *nom masculin*

coat hanger : **mets ta veste sur un cintre** put your jacket on a coat hanger.

cirage [siraʒ] *nom masculin*

shoe polish : **du cirage noir** black shoe polish.

circonstances [sirkɔ̃stɑ̃s] *nom féminin pluriel*

circumstances : **étant donné les circonstances** given the circumstances.

circuit [sirkɥi] *nom masculin*

tour : **on a fait un circuit dans le Tarn** we went on a tour of the Tarn
➤ **un circuit automobile** a racing circuit.

circulation [sirkylasjɔ̃] *nom féminin*

1. traffic : **il y a beaucoup de circulation sur cette route** there's a lot of traffic on this road
2. circulation : **elle a une mauvaise circulation** she's got bad circulation.

circuler [sirkyle] *verbe*

1. to move : **on peut circuler librement dans l'école** we can move freely round the school
2. to run : **est-ce que le bus numéro 12 circule ?** is bus number 12 running?

3. **to circulate** : **le sang circule dans le corps** blood circulates round the body
> **une rumeur circule** there's a rumour going round.

cire [sir] *nom féminin*

1. **wax** : **les bougies sont faites de cire** candles are made of wax ; **de la cire d'abeille** bees-wax
2. **polish** : **cette table sent la cire** the table smells of polish.

cirque [sirk] *nom masculin*

1. **circus** *(pluriel* **circuses**) : **on va au cirque ce soir** we're going to the circus tonight
2. *familier* **chaos** : **c'est le cirque dans cette classe !** it's chaos in this classroom!

ciseaux [sizo] *nom masculin pluriel*

scissors : **une paire de ciseaux** a pair of scissors.

citoyen, enne [sitwajɛ̃, ɛn] *nom masculin, nom féminin*

citizen : **un citoyen français** a French citizen

citron [sitrɔ̃] *nom masculin*

lemon : **une tarte au citron** a lemon tart
> **un citron pressé** a fresh lemon juice
> **le citron vert** lime.

citrouille [sitruj] *nom féminin*

pumpkin.

civilisation [sivilizasjɔ̃] *nom féminin*

civilization : **la civilisation grecque** Greek civilization.

clair, e [klɛr] *adjectif*

1. **clear** : **l'eau est très claire** the water is very clear
2. **light** : **vert clair** light green ; **une maison très claire** a very light house

clair *adverbe*

il fait déjà clair dehors it's already light outside ; **mon grand-père ne voit pas très clair** my grandfather can't see very clearly.

clarinette [klarinɛt] *nom féminin*

clarinet : **Charles joue de la clarinette** Charles plays the clarinet.

classe [klas] *nom féminin*

1. **class** *(pluriel* **classes**) : **Laetitia est dans ma classe** Laetitia is in my class ; **voyager en** **première classe** to travel first class ; **un billet de deuxième classe** a second-class ticket
2. **school** : **il n'y a pas classe demain** there's no school tomorrow ; **aller en classe** to go to school
> **classe de neige** school skiing trip
> **classe de mer** school trip to the seaside
> **classe verte** school trip to the countryside.

classer [klase] *verbe*

1. **to classify** : **les pays sont classés par nombre d'habitants** the countries are classified according to the number of inhabitants
2. **to file** : **je vais classer ces vieux articles** I'm going to file these old articles
> **classer quelque chose par ordre alphabétique** to put something in alphabetical order.

classeur [klasœr] *nom masculin*

folder : **mon classeur d'anglais** my English folder
> **un classeur à anneaux** a ring binder.

classique [klasik] *adjectif*

1. **classical** : **la musique classique** classical music
2. **classic** : **Julie a un style très classique** Julie has a very classic style.

clavier [klavje] *nom masculin*

keyboard : **un clavier d'ordinateur** a computer keyboard.

clé, clef [kle] *nom féminin*

key : **j'ai perdu mes clés** I've lost my keys
> **fermer quelque chose à clé** to lock something ; **il a fermé la porte à clé** he locked the door.

clémentine [klemãtin] *nom féminin*

clementine.

client, e [klijã, ãt] *nom masculin, nom féminin*

1. **customer** : **le client a toujours raison** the customer is always right
2. **client** : **les clients de l'hôtel** the hotel clients.

climat [klima] *nom masculin*

climate.

climatisation [klimatizasjɔ̃] *nom féminin*

air-conditioning : **mets la climatisation** turn the air-conditioning on.

clin d'œil [klɛ̃dœj] (*pluriel* clins d'œil) *nom masculin*

> **faire un clin d'œil à quelqu'un** to wink at somebody ; **il m'a fait un clin d'œil !** he winked at me!

clip [klip] *nom masculin*

video : **tu as vu le clip de Britney Spears ?** have you seen the Britney Spears video?

cliquer [klike] *verbe*

to click : **clique d'abord sur « OK »** first click on "OK" ; **cliquer deux fois** to double-click.

clochard, e [klɔʃar, ard] *nom masculin, nom féminin*
tramp.

cloche [klɔʃ] *nom féminin*

bell : **on entend les cloches de l'église** you can hear the church bells.

à cloche-pied [klɔʃpje] *adverbe*

sauter à cloche-pied to hop.

clocher [klɔʃe] *nom masculin*
church tower.

clou [klu] *nom masculin*

nail : **il y a un clou qui dépasse** there's a nail sticking out
> **des clous de girofle** cloves.

clown [klun] *nom masculin*

clown : **le clown était très drôle** the clown was very funny
> **faire le clown** to clown around : **arrête de faire le clown !** stop clowning around!

club [klœb] *nom masculin*

club : **je suis membre du club de voile** I'm a member of the sailing club.

cm (*abréviation de* centimètre)
cm.

coccinelle [kɔksinɛl] *nom féminin*

ladybird *UK*, ladybug *US* : **la coccinelle s'est envolée** the ladybird flew away.

cochon [kɔʃɔ̃] *nom masculin*

pig : **ils élèvent des cochons** they raise pigs
> **un cochon d'Inde** a guinea pig.

code [kɔd] *nom masculin*

code : un code secret a secret code ; **le code de la route** the highway code *UK*
> **le code barres** the bar code
> **le code postal** the postcode *UK* ou the zip code *US*
> **un code confidentiel** a PIN number.

cœur [kœr] *nom masculin*

heart : **on l'a opéré du cœur** he had a heart operation
> **avoir bon cœur** to be kind-hearted
> **apprendre quelque chose par cœur** to learn something by heart
> **avoir mal au cœur** to feel sick *UK* ou to feel nauseous *US*.

coffre [kɔfr] *nom masculin*

1. boot *UK*, trunk *US* : **les valises sont dans le coffre** the suitcases are in the boot
2. safe : **les cambrioleurs ont fait sauter le coffre** the burglars blew the safe up
3. chest : **un coffre en bois sculpté** a carved wooden chest.

se cogner [səkɔɲe] *verbe pronominal*

se cogner contre quelque chose to bump into something ; **elle s'est cognée contre la table** she bumped into the table ; **attention, ne te cogne pas la tête** be careful not to bump your head ou be careful not to bang your head.

se coiffer [səkwafe] *verbe pronominal*

to do one's hair : **je n'ai pas eu le temps de me coiffer** I didn't have time to do my hair.

coiffeur, euse [kwafœr, øz] *nom masculin, nom féminin*

hairdresser : **un coiffeur pour dames** a ladies' hairdresser ; **un coiffeur pour hommes** a men's hairdresser ou a barber ; **Rose veut être coiffeuse** Rose wants to be a hairdresser.

coiffure [kwafyr] *nom féminin*

hairstyle : **j'aime bien ta nouvelle coiffure** I like your new hairstyle.

coin [kwɛ̃] *nom masculin*

1. corner : **on va mettre le bureau dans le coin** we're going to put the desk in the corner
2. spot : **je connais un super coin pour un pique-nique** I know a great spot for a picnic
> **au coin du feu** by the fireside
> **dans le coin** in the area : **est-ce qu'il y a**

une boulangerie dans le coin ? is there a baker's in the area?

➤ le café du coin the local café

 The French word coin is a false friend, it does not mean 'coin'.

coincer [kwɛ̃se] *verbe*

to wedge : coince la porte avec un livre wedge the door open with a book

➤ être coincé to be jammed ou to be stuck ; le tiroir est encore coincé the drawer is jammed again

se coincer *verbe pronominal*

to jam : la portière s'est coincée the car door jammed

➤ se coincer le doigt to get one's finger caught ; il s'est coincé le doigt dans le tiroir he got his finger caught in the drawer.

col [kɔl] *nom masculin*

1. collar : il l'a saisi par le col he grabbed him by the collar
2. pass (*pluriel* passes) : le col est fermé à cause de la neige the pass is closed because of the snow

➤ un col roulé a polo neck *UK* ou a turtleneck *US*.

colère [kɔlɛr] *nom féminin*

anger : il est rouge de colère he's red with anger ; être en colère to be angry ; se mettre en colère to get angry.

colis [kɔli] *nom masculin*

parcel *UK*, package *US* : je vais chercher un colis à la poste I'm going to pick up a parcel from the post office.

collant [kɔlɑ̃] *nom masculin*

tights *UK* (*s'utilise toujours au pluriel*), pantyhose *US* (*s'utilise toujours au singulier*) : elle porte un collant rouge she's wearing red tights *UK* ou she's wearing red pantyhose *US*.

colle [kɔl] *nom féminin*

1. glue : de la colle forte strong glue
2. *familier* detention : il a eu deux heures de colle he got two hours' detention.

collection [kɔlɛksjɔ̃] *nom féminin*

collection : voilà un timbre pour ta collection here is a stamp for your collection ; Aurélie fait la collection de cartes postales Aurélie collects postcards.

collectionner [kɔlɛksjɔne] *verbe*

to collect : je collectionne les petites autos I collect toy cars.

collège [kɔlɛʒ] *nom masculin*

school, secondary school *UK*, high school *US* : Irène va au collège en septembre Irène starts secondary school in September ; je vais au collège en bus I go to school by bus

 The French word collège is a false friend, it does not mean 'college'.

COLLÈGE
When they are 11, schoolchildren in France leave primary school and go on to the first stage of secondary school, **collège**. They leave **collège** when they are 15, after they have taken an exam called the **brevet des collèges**. They can then go on to a **lycée** where they study for the **baccalauréat** exam.

collégien, enne [kɔleʒjɛ̃, ɛn] *nom masculin, nom féminin*

schoolboy (*féminin* schoolgirl).

collègue [kɔlɛg] *nom masculin ou féminin*

colleague : elle ne s'entend pas avec ses collègues she doesn't get on with her colleagues.

coller [kɔle] *verbe*

1. to stick : n'oublie pas de coller ta photo sur le formulaire don't forget to stick your photograph on the form ; cette enveloppe ne colle pas this envelope doesn't stick
2. *familier* to give detention to : la prof de français a collé Sacha the French teacher gave Sacha detention.

collier [kɔlje] *nom masculin*

necklace : elle porte un collier en or she's wearing a gold necklace.

colline [kɔlin] *nom féminin*

hill : elle est montée sur la colline she went up the hill.

colo [kɔlo] (*abréviation de* colonie) *nom féminin familier*

holiday camp *UK*, summer camp *US*.

colonie [kɔlɔni] *nom féminin*

colony (*pluriel* **colonies**) : **une ancienne colonie française** an ex-French colony
> **une colonie de vacances** a holiday camp *UK* ou a summer camp *US* ; **aller en colonie de vacances** to go to holiday camp *UK* ou to go to summer camp *US*

> COLONIE DE VACANCES
> For many in France, **les colonies de vacances** - summer camps for children - are an integral part of growing up. At 'les colos', as they are called, children spend all or part of the summer break under the supervision of **moniteurs**, group leaders who organize games, sports and other group activities.

colonne [kɔlɔn] *nom féminin*

column : **les chiffres sont présentés en deux colonnes** the figures are shown in two columns
> **la colonne vertébrale** the spine.

colorier [kɔlɔrje] *verbe*

to colour in *UK*, to color *US*.

combat [kɔ̃ba] *nom masculin*

fighting (*ne s'utilise jamais au pluriel*) : **les combats continuent au sud** fighting continues in the south
> **un combat de boxe** a boxing match.

combien [kɔ̃bjɛ̃] *adverbe*

1. how much : **combien valent ces bottes ?** how much are these boots? ; **combien de sucres veux-tu ?** how much sugar do you want?
2. how many : **combien étiez-vous ?** how many of you were there? ; **combien de jours ça vous a pris ?** how many days did it take you?
> **combien de temps** how long : **combien de temps est-ce que ça va durer ?** how long is it going to last ?
> **nous sommes le combien aujourd'hui ?** what's the date today?

comédie [kɔmedi] *nom féminin*

1. comedy (*pluriel* **comedies**) : **c'est quel genre de film ?** - **une comédie** what kind of film is it? - it's a comedy
2. act : **elle ne pleure pas vraiment, c'est de la comédie** she isn't really crying, it's an act
> **une comédie musicale** a musical

> LA COMÉDIE–FRANÇAISE
>
> This is a famous French theatre company, founded in the seventeenth century. Most plays performed by the 'Comédie-Française' are classical works, although modern plays are sometimes performed. The plays of Molière, the seventeenth-century playwright, are performed more than those of any other playwright. He is a symbol of the company.

comédien, enne [kɔmedjɛ̃, ɛn] *nom masculin, nom féminin*

> **un comédien** an actor
> **une comédienne** an actress

> ⚠ **Comédien** is a false friend, it does not mean 'comedian'.

comique [kɔmik] *adjectif & nom*

■ *adjectif*
1. comic : **un acteur comique** a comic actor ; **un film comique** a comedy
2. funny, comical : **c'était trop comique !** it was so funny!
■ *nom masculin ou féminin*
comedian : **un comique très connu** a very famous comedian.

commande [kɔmɑ̃d] *nom féminin*

order : **passer une commande** to place an order

commandes *nom féminin pluriel*

controls : **les commandes de l'avion** the controls of the plane.

commander [kɔmɑ̃de] *verbe*

1. to order : **on a commandé un lecteur DVD sur catalogue** we ordered a DVD player from a catalogue ; **j'ai commandé un steak** I ordered steak
2. to be in charge : **c'est moi qui commande ici !** I'm the one in charge here!

comme [kɔm] *conjonction & adverbe*

■ *conjonction*
1. like : **il veut être médecin, comme son père** he wants to be a doctor, like his father ; **ne parle pas comme ça** don't talk like that ; **les fêtes comme Halloween** celebrations like Hallowe'en
2. as : **fais comme tu veux** do as you like ; **comme prévu** as planned ; **son frère travaille comme guide** his brother works as a guide

3. as, since : **comme il pleut, la sortie est an-nulée** as it's raining, the outing has been cancelled OU since it's raining, the outing has been cancelled

> **comme ci comme ça** so-so
> **comme si** as if : **comme s'il allait sauter** as if he was about to jump
> **qu'est-ce que tu aimes comme musique ?** what music do you like?

■ *adverbe*

so : **comme c'est beau !** it's so beautiful! ; **comme tu as changé !** you've changed so much!

> **comme il faut** properly ; **mange comme il faut !** eat properly!

commencer [kɔmɑ̃se] *verbe*

to start, to begin : **tu as commencé le livre que je t'ai prêté ?** have you started the book I lent you? ; **le film a déjà commencé** the film has already started OU the film has already begun ; **tu commences à m'énerver !** you're starting to get on my nerves! OU you're beginning to get on my nerves!

> **ça commence bien !** that's a great start!

comment [kɔmɑ̃] *adverbe*

how : **comment dit-on « ordinateur » en anglais ?** how do you say "ordinateur" in English? ; **comment ça va ?** how are you?

> **comment ?** pardon? OU sorry : **comment, qu'est-ce que tu as dit ?** pardon, what did you say? OU sorry, what did you say?
> **comment t'appelles-tu ?** what's your name? OU what are you called?

> ⚠ The French word **comment** is a false friend, it does not mean 'comment'.

commentaire [kɔmɑ̃tɛr] *nom masculin*

comment : **Bertrand n'a fait aucun commentaire** Bertrand made no comment ; **sans commentaire !** no comment!

commérages [kɔmeraʒ] *nom masculin pluriel*

gossip (*ne s'utilise jamais au pluriel*) : **ce ne sont que des commérages** it's only gossip.

commerçant, e [kɔmɛrsɑ̃, ɑ̃t] *nom masculin, nom féminin*

shopkeeper, storekeeper *US* : **le père d'Élodie est commerçant** Élodie's father is a shopkeeper.

commerce [kɔmɛrs] *nom masculin*

1. trade : **le commerce extérieur** foreign trade
2. shop *UK*, store *US* : **les petits commerces** small shops OU small stores.

commercial, e, aux [kɔmɛrsjal, o] *adjectif*

commercial : **Harry Potter a été un succès commercial** Harry Potter was a commercial success.

> **un centre commercial** a shopping centre *UK* OU a shopping mall *US*.

commettre [kɔmɛtr] *verbe*

to commit : **la personne qui a commis ce meurtre** the person who committed this murder.

commis, e [kɔmi, iz] *participe passé de* **commettre**.

commissaire [kɔmisɛr] *nom masculin*

un commissaire de police a police superintendent *UK*, a police captain *US*.

commissariat [kɔmisarja] *nom masculin*

un commissariat de police a police station.

commode [kɔmɔd] *nom & adjectif*

■ *nom féminin*

chest of drawers : **tes chaussettes sont dans la commode** your socks are in the chest of drawers

■ *adjectif*

handy : **c'est commode d'être près du collège** it's handy being near the school

> **il n'est pas commode** he's not an easy person.

commun, e [kɔmœ̃, yn] *adjectif*

1. shared : **il y a quatre chambres et un salon commun** there are four bedrooms and a shared living room
2. joint : **une décision commune** a joint decision

> **avoir quelque chose en commun** to have something in common : **nous n'avons rien en commun** we don't have anything in common
> **faire quelque chose en commun** to do something together : **on lui a fait un cadeau en commun** we bought her a present together.

communauté [kɔmynote] *nom féminin*

community (*pluriel* **communities**) : **la Communauté européenne** the European Community.

communication [kɔmynikasjɔ̃] *nom féminin*

communication
> **communication téléphonique** telephone call.

compact, e [kɔ̃pakt] *adjectif*

compact : **un appareil photo compact** a compact camera

compact *nom masculin*

j'ai demandé des compacts pour Noël I asked for some CDs for Christmas.

compagne ➤ compagnon.

compagnie [kɔ̃paɲi] *nom féminin*

company *(pluriel* **companies***)* : **une compagnie d'assurances** an insurance company
une compagnie aérienne an airline
> **tenir compagnie à quelqu'un** to keep somebody company.

compagnon , [kɔ̃paɲɔ̃] **compagne** ,

[kɔ̃paɲ] *nom masculin, nom féminin*
partner : **Cédric a présenté sa nouvelle compagne à ses parents** Cédric introduced his new partner to his parents.

comparaison [kɔ̃parɛzɔ̃] *nom féminin*

comparison : **en comparaison avec son frère, elle est sympa** in comparison with her brother, she's nice
> **faire une comparaison entre deux choses** to compare two things.

comparer [kɔ̃pare] *verbe*

to compare : **ce n'est pas juste de le comparer avec sa sœur** it's not fair to compare him with his sister.

compas [kɔ̃pa] *nom masculin*

compass : **utilise ton compas pour tracer le cercle** use your compass to draw the circle.

compétition [kɔ̃petisjɔ̃] *nom féminin*

event, competition : **une compétition d'athlétisme** an athletics event
> **faire de la compétition** to take part in competitive events.

compil [kɔ̃pil] *(abréviation de* compilation*)*

nom féminin familier
compilation album.

compilation [kɔ̃pilasjɔ̃] *nom féminin*

compilation album : une compilation de Madonna a Madonna compilation album.

complément [kɔ̃plemɑ̃] *nom masculin*

complement
> **le complément d'objet direct** the direct object
> **le complément d'objet indirect** the indirect object.

complètement [kɔ̃plɛtmɑ̃] *adverbe*

completely : **il est complètement fou** he's completely mad.

compléter [kɔ̃plete] *verbe*

1. to complete : **compléter la phrase suivante** complete the following sentence
2. to fill in *UK*, to fill out *US* : **n'oubliez pas de compléter le questionnaire** don't forget to fill in the questionnaire.

compliment [kɔ̃plimɑ̃] *nom masculin*

compliment : **il ne me fait jamais de compliments** he never pays me any compliments.

compliqué, e [kɔ̃plike] *adjectif*

complicated : **je ne comprends rien, c'est trop compliqué** I don't understand a thing, it's too complicated.

compliquer [kɔ̃plike] *verbe*

to complicate : **ne complique pas les choses** don't complicate matters

se compliquer *verbe pronominal*

to get complicated : **les choses se compliquent** things are getting complicated.

comportement [kɔ̃pɔrtəmɑ̃] *nom masculin*

behaviour *UK*, behavior *US* : **je n'aime pas son comportement** I don't like his behaviour.

composer [kɔ̃poze] *verbe*

to compose : **qui a composé cette symphonie ?** who composed this symphony?

se composer de *verbe pronominal*

to be made up of : **l'équipe se compose uniquement de filles** the team is made up of girls only.

compositeur, trice [kɔ̃pozitœr, tris] *nom*

masculin, nom féminin
composer : **Mozart est un célèbre compo-**

siteur allemand Mozart is a famous German composer.

composter [kɔ̃pɔste] *verbe*

to date-stamp

COMPOSTER
In France, when you travel on public transport, and especially when travelling by train, you must punch your ticket in a machine (**le composteur**) to validate it for your journey. If you don't validate your ticket before the start of your journey, you risk having to pay a fine.

compote [kɔ̃pɔt] *nom féminin*

➤ **une compote de pommes** stewed apples.

comprendre [kɔ̃prɑ̃dr] *verbe*

1. **to understand : tu as compris l'exercice ?** did you understand the exercise ? ; **je ne comprends pas l'anglais** I don't understand English
2. **to consist of : le concours comprend trois phases** the competition consists of three stages
3. **to include : est-ce que le prix comprend le transport ?** does the price include transport?
➤ **tu comprends** you see : **j'étais énervée, tu comprends** I was annoyed, you see

se comprendre *verbe pronominal*

to understand each other : lui et moi, on se comprend très bien he and I understand each other very well.

compris, e [kɔ̃pri, iz] *participe passé de* comprendre.

compte [kɔ̃t] *nom masculin*

account : compte en banque bank account
➤ **un compte épargne** a savings account
➤ **le compte à rebours** the countdown
➤ **se rendre compte de** to realize : **je ne m'étais pas rendu compte que tu n'étais pas là** I hadn't realized you weren't there
➤ **tenir compte de quelque chose** to take something into account : **il faut tenir compte des erreurs** we must take the errors into account
➤ **tout compte fait** all things considered.

compter [kɔ̃te] *verbe*

to count : le professeur a compté les élèves the teacher counted the pupils

➤ **compter faire quelque chose** to intend to do something : **tu comptes partir à cinq heures ?** do you intend to leave at five?
➤ **compter sur quelqu'un** to count on somebody : **je compte sur vous !** I'm counting on you!

comptoir [kɔ̃twar] *nom masculin*

1. **bar : les consommations sont moins chères au comptoir** drinks are cheaper at the bar
2. **desk : le comptoir d'enregistrement de British Airways** the British Airways' check-in desk.

se concentrer [səkɔ̃sɑ̃tre] *verbe pronominal*

to concentrate : tu vas y arriver si tu te concentres you'll manage if you concentrate.

concerner [kɔ̃sɛrne] *verbe*

to concern : ça ne te concerne pas it doesn't concern you
➤ **en ce qui concerne ...** as far as ... is concerned : **en ce qui concerne la réunion de lundi** as far as Monday's meeting is concerned.

concert [kɔ̃sɛr] *nom masculin*

concert : un concert de rock a rock concert.

conclure [kɔ̃klyr] *verbe*

to conclude : Vincent a conclu son exposé par un poème Vincent concluded his talk with a poem.

conclusion [kɔ̃klyzjɔ̃] *nom féminin*

conclusion : la conclusion de ta rédaction est un peu courte the conclusion of your essay is a bit short.

concombre [kɔ̃kɔ̃br] *nom masculin*

cucumber.

concours [kɔ̃kur] *nom masculin*

competition, competitive examination : Xavier a gagné le concours de photos Xavier won the photography competition ; **Virginie a réussi le concours d'entrée à l'école de commerce** Virginie passed the competitive entrance examination to the business school
➤ **un concours de beauté** a beauty contest.

concret, ète [kɔ̃krɛ, ɛt] *adjectif*

concrete : donne-moi un exemple concret give me a concrete example.

concurrence [kɔ̃kyrɑ̃s] *nom féminin*

competition : il y a beaucoup de concur-

rence dans ce domaine there's a lot of competition in this field.

concurrent, e [kɔ̃kyrɑ̃, ɑ̃t] *nom masculin, nom féminin*

competitor : **leur principal concurrent** their main competitor.

condamner [kɔ̃dane] *verbe*

to sentence : **le criminel a été condamné à dix ans de prison** the criminal was sentenced to ten years in prison.

condition [kɔ̃disjɔ̃] *nom féminin*

condition : **je viens à une condition** I'll come, on one condition
➤ **être en bonne condition physique** to be in good shape
➤ **à condition de** provided : **tu peux rester à condition de ne rien dire** you can stay provided you say nothing
➤ **à condition que** provided : **d'accord, mais à condition que je puisse partir tôt** OK, but provided I can leave early
➤ **les conditions de travail** working conditions.

conditionnel [kɔ̃disjɔnɛl] *nom masculin*

conditional : **ce verbe est au conditionnel** this verb is in the conditional.

conducteur, trice [kɔ̃dyktœr, tris] *nom masculin, nom féminin*

driver : **la conductrice de la voiture ne m'a pas vu** the car driver didn't see me.

conduire [kɔ̃dɥir] *verbe*

to drive : **sais-tu conduire ?** do you know how to drive? ; **elle conduit un autobus** she drives a bus ; **elle n'a jamais conduit en ville** she has never driven in town
➤ **conduire à** to lead to : **ce chemin conduit au gymnase** this path leads to the gym

se conduire *verbe pronominal*

to behave : **Jean-Paul s'est très mal conduit** Jean-Paul behaved very badly.

conduit, e [kɔ̃dɥi, it] *participe passé de* conduire.

conférence [kɔ̃ferɑ̃s] *nom féminin*

conference : **conférence de presse** press conference.

confettis [kɔ̃feti] *nom masculin pluriel*

confetti (*ne s'utilise jamais au pluriel*).

confiance [kɔ̃fjɑ̃s] *nom féminin*

confidence : **avoir confiance en quelqu'un** to have confidence in somebody
➤ **confiance en soi** self-confidence : **Théo manque de confiance en lui** Théo lacks self-confidence
➤ **faire confiance à quelqu'un** to trust somebody : **tu me fais confiance, j'espère ?** I hope you trust me.

confidence [kɔ̃fidɑ̃s] *nom féminin*

➤ **faire des confidences à quelqu'un** to confide in somebody : **Stéphanie m'a fait des confidences** Stéphanie confided in me

⚠️ The French word **confidence** is a false friend, it does not mean 'confidence'.

confier [kɔ̃fje] *verbe*

1. to entrust : **Fabien m'a confié ses clés** Fabien entrusted his keys to me
2. to confide : **elle m'a confié qu'elle était amoureuse de Luc** she confided in me that she was in love with Luc

se confier *verbe pronominal*

se confier à quelqu'un to confide in somebody.

confirmer [kɔ̃firme] *verbe*

to confirm : **le proviseur a confirmé que l'école serait fermée lundi** the headmaster confirmed that the school would be closed on Monday.

confisquer [kɔ̃fiske] *verbe*

to confiscate : **la prof m'a confisqué mon sifflet** the teacher confiscated my whistle.

confiture [kɔ̃fityr] *nom féminin*

jam : **de la confiture de fraises** strawberry jam.

confondre [kɔ̃fɔ̃dr] *verbe*

to mix up, to get mixed up : **elles sont jumelles, je les confonds toujours** they're twins, I always get them mixed up
➤ **confondre quelqu'un avec quelqu'un** to mistake somebody for somebody : **le prof m'a confondu avec mon frère** the teacher mistook me for my brother.

confortable [kɔ̃fɔrtabl] *adjectif*

comfortable : **ce fauteuil est très confortable** this armchair is very comfortable.

congé [kɔ̃ʒe] *nom masculin*

1. **leave** : **congé maladie** sick leave ; **congé de maternité** maternity leave
2. **holiday** *UK*, **vacation** *US* : **il est en congé** he's on holiday *UK* ou he's on vacation *US* ; **j'ai pris une semaine de congé** I took a week off.

congélateur [kɔ̃ʒelatœr] *nom masculin*

    freezer.

congeler [kɔ̃ʒle] *verbe*

    to freeze : **des petits pois congelés** frozen peas.

conjugaison [kɔ̃ʒygɛzɔ̃] *nom féminin*

    conjugation : **la conjugaison anglaise n'est pas difficile** English conjugation isn't difficult.

conjuguer [kɔ̃ʒyge] *verbe*

    to conjugate : **tu sais conjuguer le verbe « to do » ?** can you conjugate the verb "to do"?

connaissance [kɔnɛsɑ̃s] *nom féminin*

> **faire la connaissance de quelqu'un** to meet somebody.

connaître [kɔnɛtr] *verbe*

    to know : **je ne les connais pas** I don't know them ; **connaître quelqu'un de vue** to know somebody by sight

se connaître *verbe pronominal*

    to meet : **on s'est connus l'été dernier** we met last summer ; **vous vous connaissez ?** have you met before?

> **s'y connaître en quelque chose** to know about something : **Clémence s'y connaît en musique** Clémence knows about music.

se connecter [səkɔnɛkte] *verbe pronominal*

    to connect : **je me connecte à l'Internet tous les soirs** I connect to the Internet every evening.

connexion [kɔnɛksjɔ̃] *nom féminin*

    connection : **une connexion Internet** an Internet connection.

connu, e [kɔny] *verbe & adjectif*

▪ *participe passé de* connaître
    ils se sont connus en Italie they met in Italy
▪ *adjectif*

well-known : **un écrivain connu** a well-known writer.

conscience [kɔ̃sjɑ̃s] *nom féminin*

    conscience : **j'ai mauvaise conscience** I have a guilty conscience

> **avoir conscience de quelque chose** to be aware of something : **il n'avait pas conscience du danger** he wasn't aware of the danger.

conscient, e [kɔ̃sjɑ̃, ɑ̃t] *adjectif*

    conscious : **est-ce qu'elle est encore consciente ?** is she still conscious?

> **être conscient de quelque chose** to be aware of something : **je suis conscient de mes défauts** I'm aware of my faults.

conseil [kɔ̃sɛj] *nom masculin*

    advice (*ne s'utilise jamais au pluriel*), **piece of advice** : **j'ai besoin de tes conseils** I need your advice ; **il m'a donné un conseil utile** he gave me a useful piece of advice.

conseiller [kɔ̃seje] *verbe*

1. **to advise** : **Hubert m'a conseillé d'acheter un appareil numérique** Hubert advised me to buy a digital camera
2. **to recommend** : **je te conseille ce dentiste** I recommend this dentist.

conserve [kɔ̃sɛrv] *nom féminin*

    canned food : **ils ne mangent que des conserves** they only eat canned food ; **des petits pois en conserve** canned peas.

conserver [kɔ̃sɛrve] *verbe*

    to keep : **il faut conserver les relevés bancaires** you must keep your bank statements.

considérable [kɔ̃siderabl] *adjectif*

    considerable : **une différence considérable** a considerable difference.

considérer [kɔ̃sidere] *verbe*

    to consider : **je considère Charlotte comme ma meilleure amie** I consider Charlotte as my best friend.

consigne [kɔ̃siɲ] *nom féminin*

1. **left-luggage office** *UK*, **baggage room** *US* : **on va laisser nos valises à la consigne** we're going to leave our suitcases at the left-luggage office
2. **instructions** : **j'ai bien suivi tes consignes** I followed your instructions.

consister [kɔ̃siste] *verbe*

➤ **consister à faire quelque chose** to consist in doing something ; **l'exercice consiste à faire un résumé** the exercise consists in doing a summary

➤ **consister en** to consist of ; **en quoi consiste votre travail ?** what does your job consist of?

console [kɔ̃sɔl] *nom féminin*

console : **une console de jeux** a games console.

consoler [kɔ̃sɔle] *verbe*

to comfort : **Annie a consolé Laure qui pleurait** Annie comforted Laure who was crying.

consommation [kɔ̃sɔmasjɔ̃] *nom féminin*

1. consumption : **consommation d'essence** fuel consumption

2. drink : **c'est quatre euros la consommation** it's four euros for a drink.

consommer [kɔ̃sɔme] *verbe*

to use : **ce radiateur consomme beaucoup d'électricité** this radiator uses a lot of electricity ; **cette voiture ne consomme pas beaucoup** this car doesn't use a lot of fuel.

consonne [kɔ̃sɔn] *nom féminin*

consonant.

constamment [kɔ̃stamɑ̃] *adverbe*

constantly : **il m'interrompt constamment !** he's constantly interrupting me!

constater [kɔ̃state] *verbe*

to notice : **je constate que tu n'as pas fait la vaisselle** I notice that you haven't done the dishes.

construction [kɔ̃stryksjɔ̃] *nom féminin*

la construction de la maison a pris deux ans it took two years to build the house.

construire [kɔ̃strɥir] *verbe*

to build : **il a fallu deux ans pour construire la maison** it took two years to build the house ; **ils ont construit un garage** they built a garage.

construit, e [kɔ̃strɥi, ɥit] *participe passé de* construire.

consulter [kɔ̃sylte] *verbe*

to consult : **consulter un dictionnaire** to consult a dictionary ; **tu devrais consulter un spécialiste** you should consult a specialist.

contact [kɔ̃takt] *nom masculin*

1. contact : **prendre contact avec quelqu'un** to contact somebody OU to get in touch with somebody

2. ignition : **coupe le contact** switch off the ignition.

contacter [kɔ̃takte] *verbe*

to contact, to get in touch with : **je te contacterai la semaine prochaine** I'll contact you next week OU I'll get in touch with you next week.

contagieux, euse [kɔ̃taʒjø, øz] *adjectif*

contagious : **une maladie contagieuse** a contagious disease.

conte [kɔ̃t] *nom masculin*

tale : **un conte de fées** a fairy tale.

contenir [kɔ̃tnir] *verbe*

1. to contain : **cette boisson contient beaucoup de sucre** this drink contains a lot of sugar

2. to hold : **la bouteille contient deux litres** the bottle holds two litres.

content, e [kɔ̃tɑ̃, ɑ̃t] *adjectif*

1. happy : **Dorothée n'a pas l'air content** Dorothée doesn't look happy ; **tu es content de ton cadeau ?** are you happy with your present?

2. glad : **je suis content que ce soit fini** I'm glad that it's finished

➤ **content de** pleased with : **elle est contente d'elle** she's pleased with herself

⚠ The French word **content** is a false friend, it does not mean 'content'.

contenu [kɔ̃tny] *nom masculin*

contents (*s'utilise toujours au pluriel*) : **le contenu de la boîte s'est répandu sur le sol** the contents of the box spilled onto the floor.

continent [kɔ̃tinɑ̃] *nom masculin*

continent : **l'Afrique est un continent** Africa is a continent.

continuer [kɔ̃tinɥe] *verbe*

1. to carry on with : **ils ont continué leur conversation comme si je n'étais pas là** they

carried on with their conversation as if I wasn't there
2. **to go on : la réunion a continué pendant des heures** the meeting went on for hours ; **si tu continues ...** if you go on like this ...
3. **to continue, to carry on : continuer à faire quelque chose** to continue to do something ou to continue doing something ; **il continue à mentir** he continues to lie ; **ils ont continué à chanter** they carried on singing.

contourner [kɔ̃turne] *verbe*

to go round *UK*, to go around *US* : **on a contourné la colline** we went round the hill.

contraire [kɔ̃trɛr] *nom masculin*

opposite : **elle dit toujours le contraire de ce que disent les autres** she always says the opposite of what others say
➤ **au contraire** on the contrary.

contrarier [kɔ̃trarje] *verbe*

to annoy : **ne la contrarie pas, elle pourrait se fâcher** don't annoy her, she might get angry.

contrat [kɔ̃tra] *nom masculin*

contract : **mon père a signé un contrat de deux ans** my father signed a two-year contract.

contravention [kɔ̃travɑ̃sjɔ̃] *nom féminin*

fine : **avoir une contravention** to get fined.

contre [kɔ̃tr] *préposition*

1. against : **ne t'appuie pas contre le mur, la peinture est fraîche** don't lean against the wall, the paint is wet ; **on joue contre Clamart samedi** we're playing against Clamart on Saturday
2. for : **j'ai échangé des magazines contre des timbres** I swapped some magazines for some stamps
➤ **par contre** on the other hand : **il est gentil, par contre il est un peu lent** he's nice, on the other hand he's a bit slow.

contrebasse [kɔ̃trəbas] *nom féminin*

double bass : **David joue de la contrebasse** David plays the double bass.

se contredire [səkɔ̃trədir] *verbe pronominal*

to contradict oneself : **tu te contredis sans arrêt !** you're always contradicting yourself!

contribuer [kɔ̃tribɥe] *verbe*

➤ **contribuer à** to contribute to : **tu veux bien contribuer au cadeau pour Jeanne ?** do you want to contribute to the present for Jeanne?

contrôle [kɔ̃trol] *nom masculin*

1. test : **on a un contrôle d'anglais cet après-midi** we're having an English test this afternoon
2. control : **le contrôle des passeports** passport control
3. check : **un contrôle d'identité** an identity check
4. inspection : **le contrôle des billets** ticket inspection.

contrôler [kɔ̃trole] *verbe*

to check : **il a contrôlé nos billets** he checked our tickets.

contrôleur, euse [kɔ̃trolœr, øz] *nom masculin, nom féminin*

ticket inspector : **est-ce que le contrôleur est passé ?** has the ticket inspector been?

convaincre [kɔ̃vɛ̃kr] *verbe*

1. to persuade : **je n'ai pas réussi à les convaincre** I didn't manage to persuade them ; **convaincre quelqu'un de faire quelque chose** to persuade somebody to do something
2. to convince : **je ne suis pas convaincu** I'm not convinced.

convaincu, e [kɔ̃vɛ̃ky] *participe passé de* convaincre.

convenir [kɔ̃vnir] *verbe*

➤ **convenir à** to suit ; **est-ce que lundi te convient ?** does Monday suit you?

conversation [kɔ̃vɛrsasjɔ̃] *nom féminin*

conversation : **on a eu une longue conversation** we had a long conversation.

convertir [kɔ̃vɛrtir] *verbe*

to convert : **convertir des euros en dollars** to convert euros into dollars.

convoquer [kɔ̃vɔke] *verbe*

1. to summon : **Rachel a été convoquée chez le principal** Rachel has been summoned to the principal's office
2. to notify : **je n'ai pas encore été convoquée pour l'examen** I haven't been notified of the exam yet.

copain *nom & adjectif*

■ *nom masculin*
1. **friend** : Sylvain est venu avec un copain Sylvain came with a friend
2. **boyfriend** : c'est le nouveau copain de Lise he's Lise's new boyfriend
■ *adjectif*
ils sont très **copains** they're great friends.

copie [kɔpi] *nom féminin*
1. **copy** *(pluriel* **copies***)* : fais une copie du fichier make a copy of the file
2. **paper** : le professeur a distribué les copies the teacher handed out the papers.

copier [kɔpje] *verbe*

to copy : tu peux me copier cette disquette ? can you copy this floppy disk for me? ; le prof m'a accusé d'avoir copié sur Benjamin the teacher accused me of copying off Benjamin
➤ **copier-coller** to copy and paste.

copine [kɔpin] *nom & adjectif*

■ *nom féminin*
1. **friend** : Isabelle est venue avec une copine Isabelle came with a friend
2. **girlfriend** : c'est la nouvelle copine d'Éric she's Éric's new girlfriend
■ *adjectif*
elles sont très **copines** they're great friends.

coq [kɔk] *nom masculin*

cockerel, rooster *US* : le coq est l'emblème de la France the cockerel is the emblem of France.

coque [kɔk] *nom féminin*

hull : ils ont réparé la coque du bateau they've repaired the hull of the boat
➤ **un œuf à la coque** a soft-boiled egg.

coquelicot [kɔkliko] *nom masculin*

poppy *(pluriel* **poppies***)*.

coquetier [kɔktje] *nom masculin*

eggcup.

coquillage [kɔkijaʒ] *nom masculin*
1. **shell** : on a ramassé des coquillages sur la plage we collected shells on the beach
2. **shellfish** *(ne s'utilise jamais au pluriel)* : manger des coquillages to eat shellfish.

coquille [kɔkij] *nom féminin*

shell : une coquille d'œuf an eggshell
➤ **des coquilles Saint-Jacques** scallops.

corbeau [kɔrbo] *(pluriel* **corbeaux***) nom masculin*

crow.

corbeille [kɔrbɛj] *nom féminin*

basket : une corbeille de fruits a basket of fruit
➤ **la corbeille à papier** the wastepaper basket OU the wastebasket *US*.

corde [kɔrd] *nom féminin*
1. **rope** : les alpinistes utilisent des cordes mountaineers use ropes
2. **string** : il manque une corde à ta guitare there's a string missing from your guitar
➤ **une corde à linge** a clothesline
➤ **une corde à sauter** a skipping rope *UK* OU a jump rope *US*.

cordonnier, ère [kɔrdɔnje, ɛr] *nom masculin, nom féminin*

shoe repairer : le frère de Pierre est cordonnier Pierre's brother is a shoe repairer.

corne [kɔrn] *nom féminin*

horn : les cornes du taureau the bull's horns.

cornemuse [kɔrnəmyz] *nom féminin*

bagpipes *(s'utilise toujours au pluriel)* : il joue de la cornemuse he plays the bagpipes.

cornet [kɔrnɛ] *nom masculin*
1. **bag** : un cornet de frites a bag of chips *UK* OU a bag of French fries *US*
2. **cone** : un cornet de glace an ice-cream cone.

cornichon [kɔrniʃɔ̃] *nom masculin*

gherkin, pickle *US*.

Cornouailles [kɔrnwaj] *nom féminin*
➤ **la Cornouailles** Cornwall : ma correspondante vit en Cornouailles my penfriend lives in Cornwall ; nous sommes allés en Cornouailles we went to Cornwall.

corps [kɔr] *nom masculin*

body *(pluriel* **bodies***)* : le corps humain the human body.

correct, e [kɔrɛkt] *adjectif*
1. **correct** : la réponse n'est pas correcte the answer isn't correct
2. **decent** : une rédaction correcte a decent essay.

correction [kɔrɛksjɔ̃] *nom féminin*

correction : **les corrections du professeur sont dans la marge** the teacher's corrections are in the margin.

correspondance [kɔrɛspɔ̃dɑ̃s] *nom féminin*

1. correspondence : **il prend des cours par correspondance** he's doing a correspondence course
2. connection : **il a raté sa correspondance** he missed his connection.

correspondant, e [kɔrɛspɔ̃dɑ̃, ɑ̃t] *nom masculin, nom féminin*

pen pal, pen friend *UK* : **ma correspondante s'appelle Pam** my pen pal's name is Pam.

correspondre [kɔrɛspɔ̃dr] *verbe*

correspondre à quelque chose to be equivalent to something ; **un euro correspond à environ 65 pence** one euro is equivalent to 65 pence

➤ **correspondre avec quelqu'un** to write to somebody : **ça fait deux ans que je corresponds avec Stuart** I've been writing to Stuart for two years.

corrigé [kɔriʒe] *nom masculin*

correct version : **tu as le corrigé du problème de maths ?** do you have the correct version of the maths problem?

corriger [kɔriʒe] *verbe*

1. to correct : **j'ai oublié de corriger les fautes dans mon exercice** I forgot to correct the mistakes in my exercise
2. to mark *UK*, to grade *US* : **la prof va corriger les copies pour mardi** the teacher is going to mark the papers for Tuesday.

corsaire [kɔrsɛr] *nom masculin*

pirate : **ils ont été attaqués par des corsaires** they were attacked by pirates.

corse [kɔrs] *adjectif & nom*

▪ *adjectif*
Corsican : **j'aime le fromage corse** I like Corsican cheese
▪ *nom masculin*
Corsican : **les gens du village parlent corse** the village people speak Corsican

Corse

▪ *nom masculin ou féminin*
Corsican : **les Corses** Corsicans

▪ *nom féminin*
➤ **la Corse** Corsica : **ils ont une maison en Corse** they have a house in Corsica ; **je ne suis jamais allée en Corse** I've never been to Corsica.

costume [kɔstym] *nom masculin*

1. suit : **ton costume est très chic** your suit is very smart
2. costume : **le costume traditionnel breton** the traditional Breton costume.

côte [kot] *nom féminin*

1. rib : **il s'est cassé une côte** he broke a rib ; **côte de bœuf** rib of beef
2. chop : **côte de porc** pork chop ; **côte d'agneau** lamb chop
3. hill : **cette côte est très raide** this hill is very steep
4. coast : **on a passé nos vacances sur la côte** we spent our holidays on the coast
➤ **la Côte d'Azur** the French Riviera.

côté [kote] *nom masculin*

side : **les trois côtés d'un triangle** the three sides of a triangle ; **le café se trouve de l'autre côté de la place** the café is on the other side of the square
➤ **à côté** nearby ; **ils habitent juste à côté** they live nearby
➤ **à côté de**
1. next to : **j'étais assise à côté de Mathias** I was sitting next to Mathias
2. compared to : **à côté de sa sœur, elle est vraiment sympa** compared to her sister, she's really nice
➤ **mettre quelque chose de côté** to put something aside : **Marc met de l'argent de côté pour s'acheter un nouveau vélo** Marc has been putting money aside to buy a new bike
➤ **de quel côté est-il parti ?** which way did he go?

côtelette [kotlɛt] *nom féminin*

chop : **côtelette d'agneau** lamb chop.

coton [kɔtɔ̃] *nom masculin*

1. cotton : **un tee-shirt en coton** a cotton T-shirt
2. cotton wool *UK*, absorbent cotton *US* : **elle a mis du coton sur sa coupure** she put some cotton wool on her cut.

cou [ku] *nom masculin*

neck : **j'ai mal au cou** my neck aches ; **elle**

m'a sauté au cou she threw her arms around my neck.

couche [kuʃ] *nom féminin*

1. **coat : deux couches de peinture** two coats of paint
2. **layer : elle porte plusieurs couches de vêtements en hiver** she wears several layers of clothing in winter.

couché, e [kuʃe] *adjectif*

1. **lying : je les ai trouvés couchés dans l'herbe** I found them lying on the grass
2. **in bed : il est huit heures et elle est déjà couchée** it's eight o'clock and she's already in bed.

coucher [kuʃe] *verbe*

1. **to put to bed : Élise a couché le bébé** Élise put the baby to bed
2. **to lay down : les pompiers ont couché le blessé par terre** the firemen laid the injured man down on the ground
3. **to spend the night : j'ai couché chez une copine** I spent the night at a friend's
➤ **coucher avec quelqu'un** *familier* to sleep with somebody

se coucher *verbe pronominal*

1. **to lie down : je vais me coucher sur le canapé deux minutes** I'm going to lie down on the sofa for two minutes
2. **to go to bed : tu te couches déjà ?** are you going to bed already?
3. **to set : le soleil se couche tôt en hiver** the sun sets early in winter

coucher *nom masculin*

➤ **le coucher de soleil** the sunset ; **au coucher du soleil** at sunset.

coucou [kuku] *interjection*

hi! : coucou, ça va ? hi, how are you?

coude [kud] *nom masculin*

elbow : je me suis fait mal au coude I hurt my elbow.

coudre [kudr] *verbe*

to sew on : coudre un bouton to sew a button on.

couette [kwɛt] *nom féminin*

duvet *UK*, **comforter** *US* : **il fait chaud sous la couette** it's warm under the duvet

couettes [kwɛt] *nom féminin pluriel*

bunches *UK*, **pigtails** *US* : **Karine a des couettes** Karine wears her hair in bunches.

couler [kule] *verbe*

1. **to flow : l'eau coule lentement** the water is flowing slowly
2. **to run : tu as le nez qui coule** your nose is running
3. **to sink : le Titanic a coulé après avoir heurté un iceberg** the Titanic sank after hitting an iceberg
➤ **faire couler un bain** to run a bath.

couleur [kulœr] *nom féminin*

colour *UK*, **color** *US* : **quelle est ta couleur préférée ?** what's your favourite colour? *UK* ou what's your favorite color? *US*.

couleuvre [kulœvr] *nom féminin*

grass snake.

couloir [kulwar] *nom masculin*

1. **corridor : attends dans le couloir** wait in the corridor
2. **lane : un couloir d'autobus** a bus lane.

coup [ku] *nom masculin*

1. **blow**

On utilise souvent un verbe en anglais pour traduire « donner un coup » ou « recevoir un coup » :

Sandrine a reçu un coup sur la tête Sandrine received a blow to the head ; **il m'a donné un coup de pied** he kicked me ; **donner un coup de couteau à quelqu'un** to stab somebody ; **donner un coup de poing à quelqu'un** to punch somebody

Lorsque « coup » s'applique à un objet ménager, sa traduction varie selon l'objet. On utilise généralement un verbe pour traduire « donner un coup de ... » ou « passer un coup de ... » :

donne un coup de balai dans la cuisine give the kitchen a sweep ; **je vais passer un coup de chiffon sur la table** I'll give the table a wipe ; **passe un coup d'éponge sur la cuisinière** give the cooker a wipe

2. **knock : on a entendu trois coups à la porte** we heard three knocks at the door ou somebody knocked on the door three times
3. **trick : c'est encore un coup de Nicolas** that's another of Nicolas' tricks ; **ils nous ont**

fait un mauvais coup they played a dirty trick on us

4. *familier* drink : **viens boire un coup avec nous** come and have a drink with us

➤ **un coup de feu** OU **un coup de fusil** a shot OU a gunshot : **j'ai entendu un coup de feu** I heard a shot ; **j'entends des coups de feu** I can hear gunshots

➤ **un coup de fil** *familier* a phone call : **je peux passer un coup de fil ?** can I make a phone call? ; **passer un coup de fil à quelqu'un** to call somebody

➤ **le coup de foudre** love at first sight : **ça a été le coup de foudre entre eux** it was love at first sight

➤ **un coup franc** a free kick

➤ **donner un coup de main à quelqu'un** to give somebody a hand

➤ **jeter un coup d'œil** to have a look : **je vais jeter un coup d'œil dans la cuisine** I'll have a look in the kitchen

➤ **un coup de soleil** a sunburn : **tu as un coup de soleil sur le dos** you got a sunburn on your back ; **prendre un coup de soleil** to get sunburnt

➤ **un coup de téléphone** a phone call : **je peux passer un coup de téléphone ?** can I make a phone call? ; **passer un coup de téléphone à quelqu'un** to phone somebody

➤ **d'un coup** OU **d'un seul coup**
1. in one go : **Jean-Paul a tout avalé d'un coup** Jean-Paul swallowed it all in one go
2. all of a sudden : **elle s'est levée d'un seul coup et elle est partie** she got up all of a sudden and left

➤ **du coup** as a result : **du coup, Marine ne veut plus me parler** as a result, Marine doesn't want to speak to me any more

➤ **du premier coup** first time OU at the first attempt : **je ne réussis jamais du premier coup** I never succeed first time OU I never succeed at the first attempt.

coupable [kupabl] *adjectif & nom*

▪ *adjectif*
guilty : **je me sens coupable** I feel guilty
▪ *nom masculin ou féminin*
culprit : **les coupables n'ont pas été retrouvés** they didn't find the culprits.

coupe [kup] *nom féminin*
1. cup : **la Coupe du monde** the World Cup
2. glass *(pluriel* glasses*)* : **vous prendrez une coupe de champagne ?** would you like a

glass of champagne? ; **une coupe à champagne** a champagne glass
3. cut : **une jolie coupe de cheveux** a nice haircut.

couper [kupe] *verbe*
1. to cut : **je coupe la tarte en huit ?** shall I cut the tart into eight pieces? ; **on peut couper par la rue Montrachet** we can cut through rue Montrachet
2. to cut down : **les bûcherons ont coupé le sapin** the woodcutters cut the fir tree down
3. to cut off : **j'allais répondre, mais Sébastien m'a coupée** I was going to answer, but Sébastien cut me off
➤ **faire un couper-coller** to cut and paste.

se couper *verbe pronominal*
to cut oneself : **Aurélie s'est coupée avec un couteau** Aurélie cut herself with a knife ; **je me suis coupé le doigt** I cut my finger.

couple [kupl] *nom masculin*
couple : **ils font un beau couple** they make a nice couple.

couplet [kuplɛ] *nom masculin*
verse : **une chanson à trois couplets** a song with three verses.

coupure [kupyr] *nom féminin*
cut : **il a mis du désinfectant sur sa coupure** he put some disinfectant on the cut
➤ **une coupure de courant** a power cut.

cour [kur] *nom féminin*
1. courtyard : **la cour du château** the palace courtyard
2. court : **la cour de Louis XIV** the court of Louis XIV
3. playground : **les élèves discutent dans la cour** the pupils are talking in the playground.

courage [kuraʒ] *nom masculin*
1. courage : **il faut du courage pour faire ça** you need courage to do that
2. energy : **je n'ai pas le courage de faire mes devoirs** I don't have the energy to do my homework
➤ **bon courage !** good luck!

courageux, euse [kuraʒø, øz] *adjectif*
brave.

couramment [kuramɑ̃] *adverbe*
fluently : **Jean parle couramment anglais**

Jean speaks English fluently ou Jean speaks fluent English

 Couramment is a false friend, it does not mean 'currently'.

courant ¹, e [kurɑ̃, ɑ̃t] *adjectif*

common : **c'est une expression très courante** it's a very common expression.

courant ² [kurɑ̃] *nom masculin*

current : **je nageais contre le courant** I was swimming against the current
- **courant d'air** draught *UK* ou draft *US*
- **être au courant** to know : **je n'étais pas au courant** I didn't know ; **personne n'est au courant de ce qui s'est passé** nobody knows about what happened

 The French adjective **courant** is a false friend, it does not mean 'current'.

courbatures [kurbatyr] *nom féminin pluriel*
- **avoir des courbatures** to be stiff

courbe [kurb] *nom féminin*

curve : **la rivière décrit une courbe** there's a curve in the river.

coureur, euse [kurœr, øz] *nom masculin, nom féminin*

runner : **coureur de fond** long-distance runner
- **un coureur automobile** a racing driver *UK* ou a race driver *US*
- **un coureur cycliste** a racing cyclist.

courgette [kurʒɛt] *nom féminin*

courgette *UK*, **zucchini** *US*.

courir [kurir] *verbe*

to run : **Stéphanie court très vite** Stéphanie can run very fast
- **courir après quelqu'un** to run after somebody ou to chase after somebody : **le policier a couru après le voleur** the policeman ran after the thief ou the policeman chased after the thief.

couronne [kurɔn] *nom féminin*

crown : **la couronne de la reine** the Queen's crown.

courrier [kurje] *nom masculin*

mail : **il y a du courrier pour moi ?** is there any mail for me?
- **courrier électronique** e-mail

 The French word **courrier** is a false friend, it does not mean 'courier'.

cours [kur] *nom masculin*

1. **class** *(pluriel* **classes)**, **lesson** : **on a cours d'anglais à trois heures** we have an English lesson at three ; **la mère de Camille donne des cours au lycée** Camille's mother teaches at the school
- **au cours de** during : **au cours de la réunion** during the meeting
- **en cours de route** on the way ; **on s'est arrêtés en cours de route** we stopped on the way
2. ➤ CE, CM.

course [kurs] *nom féminin*

1. **race** : **une course cycliste** a cycle race
2. **racing** : **la course automobile** car racing
3. **errand** : **j'ai une course à faire** I've got to run an errand

courses *nom féminin pluriel*

shopping *(s'utilise toujours au singulier)* : **les courses ont coûté cent euros** the shopping cost a hundred euros ; **il est allé faire des courses** he went shopping ; **as-tu fait les courses ?** have you done the shopping?

 The French word **course** is a false friend, it does not mean 'course'.

court, e [kur, kurt] *adjectif*

short : **cette jupe est un peu courte** this skirt is a bit short
- **un court de tennis** a tennis court.

couru, e [kury] *participe passé de* courir.

cousin, e [kuzɛ̃, in] *nom masculin, nom féminin*

cousin : **cousin germain** first cousin ; **Alex est mon cousin germain** Alex is my first cousin.

coussin [kusɛ̃] *nom masculin*

cushion : **le chat dort sur un coussin** the cat is sleeping on a cushion.

cousu, e [kuzy] *participe passé de* coudre.

coût [ku] *nom masculin*

cost : **le coût de la vie** the cost of living.

couteau [kuto] (*pluriel* **couteaux**) *nom masculin*

knife (*pluriel* **knives**).

coûter [kute] *verbe*

to cost : **ça coûte combien ?** how much does it cost? ; **ça coûte vingt euros** it costs twenty euros ; **ça m'a coûté 40 euros** it cost me 40 euros

➤ **coûter cher** to be expensive : **ça coûte trop cher** it's too expensive

➤ **coûter cher à quelqu'un** to cost somebody a lot : **ce voyage leur a coûté cher** this trip cost them a lot.

coutume [kutym] *nom féminin*

custom : **c'est une vieille coutume irlandaise** it's an old Irish custom.

couture [kutyr] *nom féminin*

1. sewing : **je n'aime pas la couture** I don't like sewing ; **faire de la couture** to sew
2. seam : **la couture de mon jean a craqué** the seam on my jeans has burst.

couvercle [kuvɛrkl] *nom masculin*

1. lid : **mets le couvercle pour que ça bouille plus vite** put the lid on so that it boils more quickly
2. top : **où est le couvercle du pot de confiture ?** where's the top to the jam jar?

couvert, e [kuvɛr, ɛrt] *adjectif*

le bébé est bien couvert the baby is well wrapped up ; **une piscine couverte** an indoor swimming pool ; **le ciel est couvert** it has clouded over ou it's overcast

couvert *nom masculin*

➤ **mettre le couvert** to set the table : **c'est à toi de mettre le couvert** it's your turn to set the table

couverts *nom masculin pluriel*

cutlery (*ne s'utilise jamais au pluriel*) : **où est-ce qu'on range les couverts ?** where do you keep the cutlery? ; **les couverts sont en argent** this cutlery is silver.

couverture [kuvɛrtyr] *nom féminin*

blanket : **elle a mis une couverture sur le lit** she put a blanket on the bed.

couvrir [kuvrir] *verbe*

to cover : **j'ai couvert le tableau pour le protéger** I covered the painting to protect it ; **Paul est couvert de bleus** Paul is covered with bruises ; **le parc était couvert de neige** the park was covered in snow

se couvrir *verbe pronominal*

to wrap up : **couvre-toi bien, il fait très froid dehors** wrap up warm, it's very cold outside.

crabe [krab] *nom masculin*

crab : **les crabes ont des pinces** crabs have claws.

cracher [kraʃe] *verbe*

to spit : **il a craché par terre** he spat on the floor.

craindre [krɛ̃dr] *verbe*

to be afraid of : **je crains qu'il ne vienne pas** I'm afraid he won't come ; **il craignait d'être en retard** he was afraid of being late.

craint, e [krɛ̃, ɛ̃t] *participe passé de* craindre.

crampe [krɑ̃p] *nom féminin*

cramp : **j'ai une crampe à la jambe** I have a cramp in my leg.

crâne [kran] *nom masculin*

skull : **le crâne protège le cerveau** the skull protects the brain

 Crâne is a false friend, it does not mean 'crane'.

crapaud [krapo] *nom masculin*

toad.

craquer [krake] *verbe*

1. to split : **mon jean a craqué quand je me suis assis** my jeans split when I sat down
2. to creak : **le plancher craque à cet endroit** the floor creaks here
3. to crack up : **elle a craqué après leur divorce** she cracked up after their divorce
➤ **craquer pour** *familier* to fall for : **Anna a craqué pour Jérôme** Anna has fallen for Jérôme
➤ **plein à craquer** *familier* packed : **le théâtre était plein à craquer hier soir** the theatre was packed last night.

cravate [kravat] *nom féminin*

tie : **il porte une veste et une cravate** he's wearing a jacket and tie.

crawl [krol] *nom masculin*

crawl : **nager le crawl** to do the crawl.

crayon [krɛjɔ̃] *nom masculin*

pencil : **c'est écrit au crayon** it's written in pencil ; **crayon à papier** OU **crayon noir** pencil
> **un crayon de couleur** a coloured pencil *UK* OU a colored pencil *US*.

crèche [krɛʃ] *nom féminin*

crèche *UK*, day-care center *US* : **mon petit frère va à la crèche** my little brother goes to a crèche *UK* OU my little brother goes to a day-care center *US*.

crédit [kredi] *nom masculin*

credit : **acheter quelque chose à crédit** to buy something on credit.

créer [kree] *verbe*

1. to create : **il a créé une nouvelle mode** he created a new fashion ; **ça va créer des problèmes** it will create problems
2. to set up : **elle a créé sa propre entreprise** she set up her own company.

crème [krɛm] *nom féminin*

cream : **des fraises à la crème** strawberries and cream
> **de la crème anglaise** custard
> **une crème caramel** a crème caramel
> **de la crème fraîche** crème fraîche
> **de la crème à raser** shaving cream
> **de la crème solaire** sun cream.

crêpe [krɛp] *nom féminin*

crêpe, pancake *US*.

creux, creuse [krø, øz] *adjectif*

hollow : **un tronc d'arbre creux** a hollow tree trunk

creux *nom masculin*

hole : **il y a un creux dans le rocher** there's a hole in the rock.

crevant, e [krəvɑ̃, ɑ̃t] *adjectif familier*

exhausting.

crevé, e [krəve] *adjectif*

1. *familier* exhausted : **j'étais crevé après la piscine** I was exhausted after swimming

2. punctured, flat *US* : **ma roue arrière est crevée** my back tyre is punctured.

crever [krəve] *verbe*

1. to have a puncture *UK*, to have a flat tire *US* : **c'est la deuxième fois qu'on crève avec cette voiture !** it's the second time this car has had a puncture!
2. *familier* to die : **ma plante a crevé** my plant has died
> **je crève de faim** I'm starving
> **il fait une chaleur à crever** it's boiling hot
> **crever de chaud** to be boiling : **on crève de chaud** it's boiling hot
> **crever de froid** to be freezing : **je crève de froid** I'm freezing.

crevette [krəvɛt] *nom féminin*

crevette rose prawn ; **crevette grise** shrimp.

cri [kri] *nom masculin*

shout, cry : **j'ai entendu un cri** I heard a shout ; **un cri de joie** a cry of joy
> **pousser un cri**
1. to cry out : **il a poussé un cri en se cognant la tête** he cried out when he banged his head
2. to scream : **elle a poussé un cri de douleur** she screamed with pain.

cricket [krikɛt] *nom masculin*

cricket : **jouer au cricket** to play cricket.

crier [krije] *verbe*

1. to shout : **arrête de crier !** stop shouting!
2. cry out : **elle a crié de douleur** she cried out in pain.

crime [krim] *nom masculin*

1. crime : **un crime contre l'humanité** a crime against humanity
2. murder : **il a commis un crime** he committed murder

⚠ The French word **crime** can be used to mean any crime, but it is often used to mean 'murder'.

criminel, elle [kriminɛl] *nom masculin, nom féminin*

criminal : **criminel de guerre** war criminal.

crise [kriz] *nom féminin*

1. crisis : **la crise économique** the economic crisis ; **le pays est en crise** the country is going through a crisis

2. attack : **une crise cardiaque** a heart attack
➤ **piquer une crise** *familier* to have a fit : **il a piqué une crise quand je lui ai dit que je partais** he had a fit when I told him I was leaving.

cristal [kristal] (*pluriel* cristaux [kristo])
nom masculin
crystal : **un verre en cristal** a crystal glass.

critique [kritik] *nom féminin*

1. criticism : **ce n'est pas une critique, juste une remarque** it's not a criticism, just an observation ; **ses critiques m'ont blessé** his criticism hurt me
2. review : **son dernier livre a eu de très bonnes critiques** her last book got very good reviews.

critiquer [kritike] *verbe*
to criticize, to criticise *UK* : **il n'arrête pas de critiquer les autres** he's always criticizing other people.

croche-pied [krɔʃpje] (*pluriel* croche-pieds) *nom masculin*
faire un croche-pied à quelqu'un to trip somebody up ; **il m'a fait un croche-pied** he tripped me up.

crochet [krɔʃɛ] *nom masculin*

1. hook : **j'ai suspendu le miroir au crochet** I hung the mirror on the hook
2. bracket *UK*, parenthesis *US* : **mettre un mot entre crochets** to put a word in brackets *UK* ou to put a word in parentheses *US*.

crocodile [krɔkɔdil] *nom masculin*
crocodile.

croire [krwar] *verbe*

1. to think : **je crois qu'elle est déjà partie** I think she has already left ; **tu crois ?** do you think so? ; **je crois que oui** I think so ; **je crois que non** I don't think so ; **je croyais avoir oublié mes clés** I thought I had forgotten my keys
2. to believe : **je ne te crois pas** I don't believe you ; **il croit en Dieu** he believes in God ; **son frère croit encore au Père Noël** his brother still believes in Father Christmas

se croire *verbe pronominal*
il se croit intelligent he thinks he's intelligent.

croiser [krwaze] *verbe*

1. to meet : **j'ai croisé ta sœur dans la rue** I met your sister in the street
2. to cross : **il a croisé les jambes** he crossed his legs
➤ **croiser les bras** to fold one's arms

se croiser *verbe pronominal*

1. to meet : **nous nous sommes croisés au supermarché** we met at the supermarket ou we bumped into each other at the supermarket
2. to cross, to intersect : **les deux rues se croisent** the two roads cross ou the two roads intersect.

croisière [krwazjɛr] *nom féminin*
cruise : **faire une croisière** to go on a cruise.

croissance [krwasɑ̃s] *nom féminin*
growth : **une mauvaise alimentation peut nuire à la croissance** a poor diet can be harmful to growth.

croix [krwa] *nom féminin*
cross (*pluriel* **crosses**).

croque-monsieur [krɔkməsjø] *nom masculin invariable*
toasted cheese and ham sandwich.

croquer [krɔke] *verbe*
to crunch : **il ne faut pas croquer les bonbons** you shouldn't crunch sweets.

cross [krɔs] *nom masculin*
cross-country running : **faire du cross** to go cross-country running.

croustillant, e [krustijɑ̃, ɑ̃t] *adjectif*
crunchy : **des gâteaux croustillants** crunchy biscuits *UK* ou crunchy cookies *US*.

croûte [krut] *nom féminin*

1. crust : **Léo ne mange que la croûte du pain** Léo only eats the crust
2. rind : **la croûte de ce fromage est dure** the rind on this cheese is hard
3. scab : **j'ai une croûte au genou** I have a scab on my knee.

croûton [krutɔ̃] *nom masculin*

1. crust : **il ne reste plus qu'un croûton de pain** there's only a crust of bread left
2. crouton : **servez la soupe avec des petits croûtons** serve the soup with croutons.

cru ¹, e [kry] *adjectif*

raw : **des carottes crues** raw carrots.

cru ², e [kry] *participe passé de* croire.

crudités [krydite] *nom féminin pluriel*

raw vegetables.

cruel, elle [kryɛl] *adjectif*

cruel : **elle est cruelle avec son frère** she's cruel to her brother.

cueillir [kœjir] *verbe*

to pick : **on a cueilli des fleurs** we picked some flowers.

cuillère [kɥijɛr] *nom féminin*

spoon

> **une cuillère à café** OU **une petite cuillère** a teaspoon

> **une cuillère à soupe** a tablespoon.

cuir [kɥir] *nom masculin*

leather : **une veste en cuir** a leather jacket.

cuire [kɥir] *verbe*

1. to cook : **fais cuire les carottes pendant 20 minutes** cook the carrots for 20 minutes

2. to bake : **faire cuire le gâteau à 200 degrés** bake the cake at 200 degrees.

cuisine [kɥizin] *nom féminin*

1. kitchen : **cette cuisine est trop petite** this kitchen is too small

2. cooking : **la cuisine française** French cooking

> **faire la cuisine** to cook OU to do the cooking ; **est-ce que tu fais souvent la cuisine ?** do you often cook? ; **c'est lui qui fait la cuisine** he does the cooking

> **faire bien la cuisine** to be a good cook : **Mamie fait très bien la cuisine** Granny is a very good cook.

cuisiner [kɥizine] *verbe*

to cook : **j'aime cuisiner** I like cooking ; **elle cuisine bien** she's a good cook.

cuisinier, ère [kɥizinje, ɛr] *nom masculin, nom féminin*

cook : **Marie est cuisinière dans un restaurant** Marie is a cook in a restaurant

cuisinière *nom féminin*

cooker *UK*, stove : **une cuisinière électrique** an electric cooker.

cuisse [kɥis] *nom féminin*

1. thigh : **j'ai mal aux cuisses** my thighs are aching

2. leg : **une cuisse de poulet** a chicken leg.

cuit, e [kɥi, kɥit] *adjectif*

cooked

> **bien cuit** well done

> **pas assez cuit** undercooked

> **trop cuit** overcooked.

cuivre [kɥivr] *nom masculin*

copper : **un bracelet en cuivre** a copper bracelet.

culotte [kylɔt] *nom féminin*

panties, underpants *US* (*s'utilisent toujours au pluriel*) : **une culotte en coton** a pair of cotton underpants.

cultivé, e [kyltive] *adjectif*

well-educated : **c'est quelqu'un de très cultivé** he's very well-educated.

cultiver [kyltive] *verbe*

to grow : **ils cultivent principalement des tomates** they mainly grow tomatoes.

culture [kyltyr] *nom féminin*

1. culture : **il s'intéresse à la culture africaine** he's interested in African culture

2. farming : **la culture biologique** organic farming

> **la culture générale** general knowledge.

curé [kyre] *nom masculin*

priest : **il est curé** he's a priest.

curieux, euse [kyrjø, øz] *adjectif*

1. curious : **Anne est très curieuse, elle pose tout le temps des questions** Anne is very curious, she's always asking questions

2. odd, strange : **c'est curieux, je pensais l'avoir mis là** that's odd, I thought I'd put it there.

curseur [kyrsœr] *nom masculin*

cursor.

cybercafé [sibɛrkafe] *nom masculin*

Internet café.

cycle [sikl] *nom masculin*

cycle : **le cycle des saisons** the cycle of the seasons

⚠ The French word **cycle** is not used to mean a bicycle.

cycliste [siklist] *nom masculin ou féminin*
cyclist.

cygne [siɲ] *nom masculin*
swan.

cymbales [sɛ̃bal] *nom féminin pluriel*
cymbals : **elle joue des cymbales** she plays the cymbals.

d'abord ➤ abord.

d'accord ➤ accord.

daim [dɛ̃] *nom masculin*
1. deer *(pluriel* deer*)* : **le daim est un animal très peureux** deer are very timid animals
2. suede : **des chaussures en daim** suede shoes.

dame [dam] *nom féminin*
1. lady *(pluriel* ladies*)* : **la dame en rouge là-bas, c'est ma tante** the lady in red over there is my aunt
2. queen : **j'ai la dame de trèfle** I have the queen of clubs
➤ **jouer aux dames** to play draughts *UK* ou to play checkers *US*.

danger [dɑ̃ʒe] *nom masculin*
danger : **ils sont en danger** they're in danger ; **vous n'êtes pas en danger ici** you're safe here.

dangereux, euse [dɑ̃ʒrø, øz] *adjectif*
dangerous : **ce virage est dangereux** this is a dangerous bend.

dans [dɑ̃] *préposition*
1. in : **qu'est-ce qu'il y a dans la boîte ?** what's in the box? ; **il n'y a personne dans la rue** there is nobody in the street ; **je reviens dans cinq minutes** I'll be back in five minutes ; **dans les années quatre-vingt-dix** in the 1990s ; **mon père est dans le commerce** my father is in business
2. into : **n'entre pas dans ma chambre !** don't go into my room! ; **Cédric a plongé dans le lac** Cédric dived into the lake
➤ **dans les ...** about ... ou around ... : **ça coûte dans les trente euros** it costs about thirty euros ou it costs around thirty euros ; **il doit être dans les huit heures** it must be about eight ou it must be around eight.

danse [dɑ̃s] *nom féminin*
dancing : **faire de la danse** to go to dancing classes
➤ **la danse classique** ballet : **faire de la danse classique** to go to ballet classes.

danser [dɑ̃se] *verbe*
to dance : **j'apprends à danser le tango** I'm learning to dance the tango.

danseur, euse [dɑ̃sœr, øz] *nom masculin, nom féminin*
dancer : **elle est danseuse** she's a dancer.

date [dat] *nom féminin*
date : **quelle est votre date de naissance ?** what is your date of birth?
➤ **la date limite** the deadline
➤ **date limite de vente** sell-by date
➤ **date limite de consommation** use-by date.

datte [dat] *nom féminin*
date : **il mangeait des dattes** he was eating dates.

dauphin [dofɛ̃] *nom masculin*
dolphin.

davantage [davɑ̃taʒ] *adverbe*
more : **tu devrais travailler davantage** you should work more.

de [də] *préposition & article*
▪ *préposition* (**d'** *devant une voyelle ou un « h » muet*)
1. of : **les monuments de Toulouse** the monuments of Toulouse ; **un verre de vin** a glass of wine ; **une bouteille d'eau** a bottle of water ; **un quart d'heure** a quarter of an hour

d

Dans de nombreux cas, « de » ne se traduit pas :

la porte du salon the living-room door ; les clés de la voiture the car keys ; un billet de dix euros a ten-euro note ; le train de 9 h 30 the 9:30 train ; un enfant de dix ans a ten-year-old child

Lorsqu'il s'agit d'indiquer l'appartenance, on utilise le cas possessif en anglais, indiqué par « 's » lorsque le possesseur est singulier et par une apostrophe seule à la fin du mot lorsque le possesseur est pluriel :

le frère de Pierre Pierre's brother ; le médecin de ma mère my mother's doctor ; la maison de mes cousins my cousins' house
2. from : vous venez de Paris ? do you come from Paris? ; ce café vient de Colombie this coffee comes from Colombia
3. with : il l'a simplement touché du doigt he simply touched it with his finger ; ils sont armés de couteaux they are armed with knives
4. per, a (an devant une voyelle ou un « h » muet) : dix euros de l'heure ten euros per hour OU ten euros an hour

Lorsque « de » indique la cause, il se traduit par différentes prépositions en anglais :

Caro tremble de froid Caro is shivering with cold ; le petit chien sautait de joie the little dog was jumping for joy ; des millions d'enfants meurent de faim millions of children die of hunger
➤ de ... à ...
1. from ... to ... : de Paris à Tokyo from Paris to Tokyo ; de dix heures à midi from ten to twelve
2. between ... and ... : il y avait de dix à quinze personnes there were between ten and fifteen people
■ article partitif
1. Dans les phrases affirmatives some : je voudrais du lait I'd like some milk ; achète des pommes buy some apples
2. Dans les phrases négatives any : ils n'ont pas d'enfants they don't have any children OU they have no children ; je ne veux pas de chocolat I don't want any chocolate
3. Dans les phrases interrogatives any, some

En règle générale, on utilise any dans les interrogations, surtout lorsqu'on ne sait pas si la réponse sera affirmative ou négative :

est-ce que vous avez des devoirs ? do you have any homework? ; est-ce qu'il y a des kangourous en Nouvelle-Zélande ? are there any kangaroos in New Zealand?

Si l'on s'attend à une réponse affirmative, par exemple lorsqu'on demande à quelqu'un s'il veut quelque chose à boire ou à manger, on utilise some :

est-ce que tu veux du thé ? would you like some tea? ; tu as apporté des sandwiches, j'espère ? you've brought some sandwiches, I hope?

« De » ne se traduit pas dans les phrases indiquant une habitude ou une alternative :

elle ne boit jamais de café she never drinks coffee ; je ne mange pas de viande I don't eat meat ; tu veux de l'eau ou du jus d'orange ? do you want water or orange juice?

dé [de] nom masculin

dice (pluriel dice) : c'est à toi de jeter les dés it's your turn to throw the dice.

déballer [debale] verbe

to unpack : je n'ai pas encore déballé ma valise I haven't unpacked my suitcase yet.

débardeur [debardœr] nom masculin

singlet UK, sleeveless T-shirt.

débarquer [debarke] verbe

1. to unload : ils ont débarqué toute la marchandise they unloaded all the goods
2. familier to turn up : elle a débarqué chez moi en pleine nuit she turned up at my place in the middle of the night.

débarrasser [debarase] verbe

to clear up : débarrasse tes affaires clear your things up ; débarrasser la table to clear the table

se débarrasser de verbe pronominal

to get rid of : je voudrais me débarrasser de mon vieux lit I'd like to get rid of my old bed.

débat [deba] nom masculin

debate.

déborder [debɔrde] *verbe*

to overflow : **l'évier a débordé** the sink overflowed.

déboucher [debuʃe] *verbe*

1. to open : **je n'arrive pas à déboucher cette bouteille de vin** I can't open this bottle of wine
2. to unblock : **Martin a réussi à déboucher l'évier** Martin managed to unblock the sink
➤ **déboucher sur** to lead to : **cette rue débouche sur la place** this street leads to the square.

debout [dəbu] *adverbe*

1. standing : **il était debout sur une chaise** he was standing on a chair ; **je préfère être debout** I'd rather stand
2. up : **je suis debout depuis six heures du matin** I've been up since six this morning ; **debout, c'est l'heure !** it's time to get up!
➤ **se mettre debout** to stand up : **mettez-vous debout, s'il vous plaît** stand up, please
➤ **son histoire ne tient pas debout** her story doesn't make sense.

débris [debri] *nom masculin pluriel*

il y a des débris de verre partout there are bits of glass everywhere ou there is glass everywhere.

se débrouiller [sədebruje] *verbe pronominal*

1. to manage : **je me débrouillerai** I'll manage ; **il s'est débrouillé pour partir plus tôt** he managed to leave earlier
2. to get by : **Sandra se débrouille bien en anglais** Sandra gets by in English.

début [deby] *nom masculin*

beginning : **le début du roman est passionnant** the beginning of the novel is exciting ; **au début de l'année** at the beginning of the year
➤ **au début** at first : **au début, je ne comprenais rien** at first, I didn't understand a thing
➤ **dès le début** right from the start : **je savais qu'il mentait dès le début** I knew right from the start he was lying ou I knew all along he was lying.

débutant, e [debytɑ̃, ɑ̃t] *nom masculin, nom féminin*

beginner : **un cours d'anglais pour débutants** an English class for beginners.

décalage [dekalaʒ] *nom masculin*

➤ **décalage horaire**
1. time difference : **n'oublie pas qu'il y a un décalage horaire de deux heures avec la France** don't forget that there is a two-hour time difference with France
2. jet lag : **je suis encore sous l'effet du décalage horaire** I'm still suffering from jet lag.

décaler [dekale] *verbe*

1. *Avancer dans le temps* to bring forward : **est-ce qu'on peut décaler la réunion d'une demi-heure ?** can we bring the meeting forward half an hour?
2. *Reculer dans le temps* to put back : **on pourrait terminer plus tôt si on décale le cours d'une heure** we could finish earlier if we put the lesson back one hour.

décembre [desɑ̃br] *nom masculin*

December : **en décembre** in December
➤ **nous sommes le trois décembre** it's the third of December *UK* ou it's December third *US*

> En anglais, les mois de l'année s'écrivent avec une majuscule.

décès [desɛ] *nom masculin*

death : **on ne connaît pas la cause de son décès** the cause of his death is unknown.

décevoir [desəvwar] *verbe*

to disappoint : **je ne veux pas te décevoir** I don't want to disappoint you ; **elle m'a beaucoup déçu** she really disappointed me

 Décevoir is a false friend, it does not mean 'deceive'.

déchets [deʃɛ] *nom masculin pluriel*

refuse, waste (*ne s'utilisent jamais au pluriel*) : **des déchets radioactifs** radioactive waste.

déchiffrer [deʃifre] *verbe*

to decipher : **Champollion a déchiffré l'écriture égyptienne** Champollion deciphered Egyptian writing ; **son écriture est difficile à déchiffrer** it's hard to read his writing.

déchirer [deʃire] *verbe*

1. to tear up : **il a déchiré le papier** he tore up the piece of paper

2. to tear : **attention, tu vas déchirer ta jupe !** be careful, you'll tear your skirt!

décider [deside] *verbe*

décider : **Bertrand a décidé de partir lundi** Bertrand decided to leave on Monday ; **j'ai décidé que ce n'était pas la peine** I decided that it wasn't worth it

se décider *verbe pronominal*

to make up one's mind : **allez, décide-toi !** come on, make up your mind! ; **Samuel s'est enfin décidé à déménager** Samuel finally made up his mind to move.

décision [desizjɔ̃] *nom féminin*

decision : **c'est une décision difficile à prendre** it's a difficult decision to make.

déclarer [deklare] *verbe*

to declare : **déclarer la guerre à un pays** to declare war on a country ; **rien à déclarer** nothing to declare

se déclarer *verbe pronominal*

to start : **l'incendie s'est déclaré en pleine nuit** the fire started in the middle of the night.

décollage [dekɔlaʒ] *nom masculin*

takeoff : **j'ai toujours un peu peur au décollage** I'm always a little afraid at takeoff.

décoller [dekɔle] *verbe*

1. to get off : **je n'arrive pas à décoller l'étiquette** I can't get the label off
2. to take off : **on a regardé les avions décoller** we watched the planes take off

se décoller *verbe pronominal*

to come off : **le timbre s'est décollé** the stamp came off.

décontracté, e [dekɔ̃trakte] *adjectif*

1. relaxed : **essaie d'être plus décontracté** try to be more relaxed
2. casual : **des vêtements décontractés** casual clothes.

décor [dekɔr] *nom masculin*

1. decor : **le décor du restaurant n'est pas vraiment réussi** the decor in the restaurant isn't great
2. set : **les décors du film sont magnifiques** the film sets are beautiful.

décoration [dekɔrasjɔ̃] *nom féminin*

decoration : **décorations de Noël** Christmas decorations.

décorer [dekɔre] *verbe*

to decorate : **on a décoré la salle avec des dessins** we decorated the room with drawings.

découper [dekupe] *verbe*

1. to cut up : **qui va découper le gâteau ?** who's going to cut the cake up? ; **découpe-le en trois morceaux** cut it into three pieces
2. to cut out : **Paul a découpé des photos de stars dans un magazine** Paul cut some photographs of stars out of a magazine.

décourager [dekuraʒe] *verbe*

to discourage : **ne lui dis pas ça, tu vas le décourager** don't tell him that, you'll discourage him

se décourager *verbe pronominal*

to lose heart : **tu te décourages facilement !** you lose heart easily!

découvert, e [dekuvɛr, ɛrt] *participe passé de* découvrir.

découverte [dekuvɛrt] *nom féminin*

discovery *(pluriel* discoveries*)* : **la découverte de l'Amérique** the discovery of America.

découvrir [dekuvrir] *verbe*

to discover : **ils ont découvert des ruines romaines** they discovered some Roman ruins.

décrire [dekrir] *verbe*

to describe : **tu pourrais me la décrire ?** could you describe her to me?

décrocher [dekrɔʃe] *verbe*

1. to take down : **je vais décrocher ce tableau, il est horrible** I'm going to take that painting down, it's horrible
2. to pick up : **il refuse de décrocher le téléphone** he refuses to pick up the phone.

déçu, e [desy] *adjectif*

disappointed : **Marc est très déçu de ne pas pouvoir aller à Dublin** Marc is very disappointed that he can't go to Dublin.

dedans [dədɑ̃] *adverbe*

inside : **il fait chaud dedans** it's hot inside ;

on ne voit rien de dedans you can't see any-thing from inside.

déduire [dedɥir] *verbe*

1. to deduct : il faut déduire les frais de transport you have to deduct transport costs
2. to deduce : j'en déduis que tu ne veux pas venir I deduce from this that you don't want to come.

défaire [defɛr] *verbe*

1. to undo : je n'arrive pas à défaire le nœud I can't undo the knot
2. to unpack : tu as défait ta valise ? have you unpacked your suitcase?

se défaire *verbe pronominal*

to come undone : tes lacets se sont défaits your laces have come undone.

défaut [defo] *nom masculin*

1. fault : elle a beaucoup de défauts, mais elle est généreuse she has a lot of faults, but she's generous
2. defect : j'ai rapporté le jean au magasin, il avait un défaut I took the jeans back to the shop, they had a defect.

défendre [defɑ̃dr] *verbe*

1. to defend : l'armée défend la ville the army is defending the town ; Paul défend son petit frère Paul sticks up for his little brother
2. to forbid : ma mère m'a défendu de sortir my mother has forbidden me to go out

se défendre *verbe pronominal*

to defend oneself : ne le laisse pas t'accu-ser, défends-toi ! don't let him accuse you, defend yourself!

défense [defɑ̃s] *nom féminin*

1. defence *UK*, defense *US* : le ministère de la Défense the Ministry of Defence
2. tusk : les défenses de l'éléphant the ele-phant's tusks
> **'défense de fumer'** 'no smoking'
> **'défense d'entrer'** 'no entry'
> **prendre la défense de quelqu'un** to stand up for somebody.

défi [defi] *nom masculin*

challenge : c'est un défi ! it's a challenge! ; il m'a lancé un défi he challenged me.

défilé [defile] *nom masculin*

parade : un défilé militaire a military par-ade.

défiler [defile] *verbe*

to march : les soldats ont défilé sur la place the soldiers marched in the square.

défini, e [defini] *adjectif*

precise : il n'a pas de rôle bien défini he doesn't have a precise role.

définir [definir] *verbe*

to define : définissez ce mot define this word.

définitif, ive [definitif, iv] *adjectif*

final : sa décision est définitive her decision is final.

définition [definisjɔ̃] *nom féminin*

definition : quelle est la définition de ce mot ? what is the definition of this word?

définitivement [definitivmɑ̃] *adverbe*

for good : ils se sont séparés définitive-ment they've split up for good

 Définitivement is a false friend, it does not mean 'definitely'.

défoncer [defɔ̃se] *verbe*

to break down : comment ont-ils réussi à défoncer la porte ? how did they manage to break the door down?

se défouler [sədefule] *verbe pronominal*

to let off steam : tu as besoin de te défou-ler you need to let off steam.

dégager [degaʒe] *verbe*

1. to free : les pompiers n'ont pas réussi à le dégager de la voiture the firemen didn't manage to free him from the car
2. to clear : on va dégager la salle pour pou-voir installer les chaises we're going to clear the room so that we can put the chairs in.

dégâts [dega] *nom masculin pluriel*

damage (*ne s'utilise jamais au pluriel*) : l'incendie a fait de gros dégâts the fire caused a lot of damage.

dégonfler [degɔ̃fle] *verbe*

to deflate : j'ai dégonflé le matelas I de-flated the mattress

se dégonfler *verbe pronominal*

to go down : le ballon s'est encore dégonflé the ball has gone down again.

dégourdi, e [degurdi] *adjectif*

clever : elle n'est pas très dégourdie she
isn't very clever.

dégoûtant, e [degutɑ̃, ɑ̃t] *adjectif*

disgusting : arrête, c'est dégoûtant ! stop
it, that's disgusting!

dégoûter [degute] *verbe*

to disgust : ce type me dégoûte that guy
disgusts me

➤ ça m'a dégoûté de faire de la compétition it put me off taking part in competitive
events.

degré [dəgre] *nom masculin*

degree : l'eau bout à 100 degrés Celsius
water boils at 100 degrees Celsius ; il fait
trois degrés it's three degrees.

déguisement [degizmɑ̃] *nom masculin*

1. fancy dress : Bruno a gagné le prix du
meilleur déguisement Bruno won the prize
for the best fancy dress
2. disguise : son déguisement a trompé la
police his disguise fooled the police.

se déguiser [sədegize] *verbe pronominal*

1. to dress up : tu te déguises pour Halloween ? are you dressing up for Hallowe'en? ; se
déguiser en sorcière to dress up as a witch
2. to disguise oneself : ils se sont déguisés
pour pouvoir entrer dans les bureaux they
disguised themselves to get into the offices.

dehors [dəɔr] *adverbe*

outside : il fait froid dehors it's cold outside
➤ mettre quelqu'un dehors
1. to throw somebody out : les videurs les
ont mis dehors the bouncers threw them out
2. to send somebody out : le professeur
d'espagnol a mis Sophie dehors the Spanish
teacher sent Sophie out
➤ en dehors de apart from : en dehors de Lucas, il n'a pas d'amis apart from Lucas, he
hasn't got any friends.

déjà [deʒa] *adverbe*

1. already : Alice a déjà fini Alice has already
finished
2. ever : tu es déjà allé à Oxford ? have you
ever been to Oxford?

déjeuner [deʒœne] *verbe & nom*

■ *verbe*
1. to have breakfast : je déjeune avant de
me doucher I have breakfast before having a
shower
2. to have lunch : on a déjeuné chez Lucie samedi we had lunch at Lucie's on Saturday
■ *nom masculin*
lunch *(pluriel* lunches*)* : le déjeuner était excellent it was an excellent lunch.

délai [delɛ] *nom masculin*

1. time limit : quels sont les délais ? what's
the time limit?
2. deadline : respecter les délais to meet the
deadline
3. extension : j'ai demandé un délai d'une
semaine pour payer mon voyage I asked for
a week's extension to pay the trip

 Délai is a false friend, it does not mean
'delay'.

délavé, e [delave] *adjectif*

faded : un jean délavé a pair of faded jeans.

délégué, e [delege] *nom masculin, nom féminin*

representative : Sophie est notre déléguée
de classe Sophie is our class representative.

délicat, e [delika, at] *adjectif*

1. delicate : un parfum délicat a delicate fragrance
2. difficult, tricky : un problème délicat a
tricky problem.

délicieux, euse [delisjø, øz] *adjectif*

delicious : ce gâteau est délicieux this cake
is delicious.

délinquant, e [delɛ̃kɑ̃, ɑ̃t] *nom masculin, nom
féminin*
delinquent.

délivrer [delivre] *verbe*

to set free : le jeu consiste à délivrer le prisonnier the game consists in setting the prisoner free

 Délivrer is a false friend, it does not mean
'deliver'.

Deltaplane® [dɛltaplan] *nom masculin*

hang-glider
➤ faire du Deltaplane to go hang-gliding.

demain [dəmɛ̃] *adverbe*

tomorrow : **demain matin** tomorrow morning ; **à demain !** see you tomorrow!

demander [dəmɑ̃de] *verbe*

1. to ask for : **demander quelque chose à quelqu'un** to ask somebody for something ; **Denis m'a demandé dix euros** Denis asked me for ten euros ; **Alice m'a demandé si je viens à sa fête** Alice asked me if I was coming to her party
2. to ask : **demander à quelqu'un de faire quelque chose** to ask somebody to do something ; **je t'ai déjà demandé de te taire** I've already asked you to be quiet ; **je lui ai demandé ce qu'il en pensait** I asked him what he thought about it

se demander *verbe pronominal*

to wonder : **elle se demande ce qu'elle va faire** she's wondering what to do ; **je me demande si elle va bien** I wonder if she's all right

> ⚠ Demander is a false friend, it does not mean 'demand'.

démangeaisons [demɑ̃ʒɛzɔ̃] *nom féminin pluriel*

itching (*ne s'utilise jamais au pluriel*) : **ces démangeaisons sont insupportables** this itching is unbearable ; **j'ai des démangeaisons partout** I'm itching all over.

démanger [demɑ̃ʒe] *verbe*

ça me démange I'm itchy OU I'm itching.

démaquillant [demakijɑ̃] *nom masculin*

make-up remover.

se démaquiller [sədemakije] *verbe pronominal*

to remove one's make-up : **on s'est démaquillés après la représentation** we removed our make-up after the show.

démarche [demarʃ] *nom féminin*

walk : **elle a une démarche bizarre** she has a funny walk.

démarrer [demare] *verbe*

1. to start : **la mobylette ne veut pas démarrer** the moped won't start ; **le stage démarre le 13 janvier** the course starts on 13 January
2. to drive off : **il a démarré sans m'attendre** he drove off without waiting for me

> **faire démarrer une voiture** to start a car.

démêler [demɛle] *verbe*

to untangle : **ces fils sont impossibles à démêler** these threads are impossible to untangle ; **brosse-toi les cheveux pour les démêler** brush your hair to get rid of the tangles.

déménagement [demenaʒmɑ̃] *nom masculin*

move : **c'est leur troisième déménagement en deux ans** it's their third move in two years.

déménager [demenaʒe] *verbe*

to move, to move house *UK* : **quand est-ce que vous déménagez ?** when are you moving?

demi, e [dəmi] *adjectif*

half : **un demi-sandwich** half a sandwich ; **un kilo et demi** one and a half kilos ; **il est une heure et demie** it's half past one

demie *nom féminin*

half past : **je te rappelle à la demie** I'll call you back at half past.

demi-finale [dəmifinal] (*pluriel* demi-finales) *nom féminin*

semifinal : **ils sont en demi-finale** they're in the semifinal.

demi-frère [dəmifrɛr] (*pluriel* demi-frères) *nom masculin*

half-brother.

demi-heure [dəmijœr] (*pluriel* demi-heures) *nom féminin*

half an hour : **dans une demi-heure** in half an hour ; **toutes les demi-heures** every half an hour OU every half-hour.

demi-journée [dəmiʒurne] (*pluriel* demi-journées) *nom féminin*

half a day : **une demi-journée de travail** half a day's work OU a half-day's work.

demi-sœur [dəmisœr] (*pluriel* demi-sœurs) *nom féminin*

half-sister.

démissionner [demisjɔne] *verbe*

to resign : **la secrétaire a démissionné** the secretary resigned.

demi-tarif [dəmitarif] (*pluriel* demi-tarifs) *nom masculin*

d

half-price : billet demi-tarif half-price ticket.

demi-tour [dəmitur] (*pluriel* demi-tours) *nom masculin*

> **faire demi-tour** to turn back : **il pleut trop, faisons demi-tour** it's raining too much, let's turn back.

démocrate [demɔkrat] *nom masculin ou féminin*

democrat.

démocratie [demɔkrasi] *nom féminin*

democracy (*pluriel* **democracies**).

démolir [demɔlir] *verbe*

to demolish : **mon père a démoli le mur du jardin** my father demolished the garden wall.

démonstration [demɔ̃strasjɔ̃] *nom féminin*

demonstration : **une démonstration de judo** a judo demonstration.

démonter [demɔ̃te] *verbe*

to take apart : **le garagiste a démonté le moteur** the garage mechanic took the engine apart.

démontrer [demɔ̃tre] *verbe*

to prove : **cette théorie n'a jamais été démontrée** this theory has never been proved.

dénoncer [denɔ̃se] *verbe*

to denounce : **ils l'ont dénoncé à la police** they denounced him to the police.

dense [dɑ̃s] *adjectif*

dense : **un brouillard dense** a dense fog.

dent [dɑ̃] *nom féminin*

tooth (*pluriel* **teeth**) : **Ariel a une dent en or** Ariel's got a gold tooth
> **avoir mal aux dents** to have toothache *UK* ou to have a toothache *US*
> **une dent de sagesse** a wisdom tooth.

dentelle [dɑ̃tɛl] *nom féminin*

lace : **un chemisier en dentelle** a lace blouse.

dentifrice [dɑ̃tifris] *nom masculin*

toothpaste : **un tube de dentifrice** a tube of toothpaste.

dentiste [dɑ̃tist] *nom masculin ou féminin*

dentist : **le père de Daniel est dentiste** Dan-iel's father is a dentist ; **aller chez le dentiste** to go to the dentist's.

déodorant [deɔdɔrɑ̃] *nom masculin*

deodorant : **un déodorant en stick** a stick deodorant.

dépanner [depane] *verbe*

1. to repair : **quelqu'un va venir dépanner la télé** somebody's going to come to repair the TV
2. *familier* to help out : **je n'ai plus d'argent, tu peux me dépanner ?** I haven't got any money left, can you help me out?

départ [depar] *nom masculin*

1. departure : **le hall des départs** the departure lounge
2. start : **le départ de la course** the start of the race
> **au départ** at first : **au départ je l'aimais bien, mais maintenant je le trouve prétentieux** at first I liked him, but now I think he's pretentious.

département [departəmɑ̃] *nom masculin*

department (*territorial and administrative division of France*).

dépasser [depase] *verbe*

1. to overtake *UK*, to pass *US* : **la moto nous a dépassés à 150 à l'heure** the motorbike overtook us at 150 kilometres an hour
2. to be taller than : **Cédric me dépasse de dix centimètres** Cédric is ten centimetres taller than me
3. to go over : **l'exposé ne peut pas dépasser une demi-heure** the talk shouldn't go over a half-hour
4. to go past : **zut, on a dépassé la rue Montpensier !** blast, we've gone past rue Montpensier!
5. to stick out : **la doublure dépasse de ta jupe** the lining is sticking out from under your skirt.

se dépêcher [sədepeʃe] *verbe pronominal*

to hurry up : **dépêche-toi, on est en retard !** hurry up, we're late! ; **dépêchez-vous de mettre vos manteaux** hurry up and put your coats on.

dépendre [depɑ̃dr] *verbe*

to depend : **ça dépend** it depends ; **dépendre de quelque chose** to depend on something ; **ça dépend des professeurs** it depends on the teachers.

dépense [depɑ̃s] *nom féminin*

expense : **c'est une grosse dépense** it's a big expense.

dépenser [depɑ̃se] *verbe*

to spend : **combien tu as dépensé ?** how much did you spend?

déplacer [deplase] *verbe*

to move : **si on déplace la table, il y aura plus de place** if we move the table, there'll be more room

se déplacer *verbe pronominal*

1. to move around : **ma grand-mère a du mal à se déplacer** my grandmother has diffi-culty moving around
2. to travel : **ma mère se déplace beaucoup pour son tavail** my mother travels a lot for her work.

dépliant [deplijɑ̃] *nom masculin*

leaflet
➤ **un dépliant touristique** a tourist bro-chure.

déplier [deplije] *verbe*

to unfold : **déplie le plan pour qu'on voie mieux** unfold the map so we can see it better.

déposer [depoze] *verbe*

1. to put down : **dépose tes bagages là** put your luggage down there
2. to drop : **Isa l'a déposé à la gare** Isa dropped him at the station
3. to deposit : **je vais déposer cet argent à la banque** I'm going to deposit this money in the bank.

dépression [depresjɔ̃] *nom féminin*

depression : **faire de la dépression** to suffer from depression ; **une dépression nerveuse** a nervous breakdown.

déprimé, e [deprime] *adjectif*

depressed : **je me sens un peu déprimé au-jourd'hui** I feel a bit depressed today.

déprimer [deprime] *verbe*

1. to depress : **le film nous a déprimés** the film depressed us
2. *familier* to get depressed : **Audrey déprime facilement** Audrey gets depressed easily.

depuis [dəpɥi] *préposition & adverbe*

◾ *préposition*

1. since : **je ne l'ai pas vu depuis août** I haven't seen him since August
2. for : **Cathy est malade depuis une semaine** Cathy has been ill for a week ; **on se connaît depuis deux ans** we've known each other for two years
3. from : **depuis la route, on pouvait voir la mer** you could see the sea from the road

◾ *adverbe*

since : **nous ne l'avons pas revu depuis** we haven't seen him since
➤ **depuis que** since : **elle n'a pas téléphoné depuis qu'elle a déménagé** she hasn't phoned since she moved
➤ **depuis combien de temps ?** ou **depuis quand ?** how long? : **depuis combien de temps fais-tu du cheval ?** how long have you been riding? ; **depuis quand est-ce que tu le connais ?** how long have you known him?

député, e [depyte] *nom masculin, nom féminin*

member of parliament *UK*, representa-tive *US* : **les députés socialistes** Socialist members of parliament ; **un député euro-péen** a Euro-MP ou a MEP.

déranger [derɑ̃ʒe] *verbe*

to bother, to disturb : **je ne veux pas vous déranger** I don't want to bother you ou I don't want to disturb you
➤ **ça vous dérange si j'ouvre la fenêtre ?** do you mind if I open the window?

se déranger *verbe pronominal*

to bother : **ne te dérange pas, j'irai le chercher moi-même** don't bother, I'll go and get it myself.

déraper [derape] *verbe*

to skid : **attention, tu pourrais déraper** be careful, you might skid.

dernier, ère [dɛrnje, ɛr] *adjectif & nom*

◾ *adjectif*

1. last : **le dernier nom sur la liste** the last name on the list ; **samedi dernier** last Satur-day ; **l'année dernière** last year
2. latest : **tu as entendu la dernière chanson de Steps ?** have you heard the latest Steps song?

◾ *nom masculin, nom féminin*

last one : **tu veux le dernier ?** do you want the last one?

➤ **en dernier** last : **on fera cet exercice en dernier** we'll do this exercise last.

dernièrement [dɛrnjɛrmɑ̃] *adverbe*

lately : **tu as vu Cyril dernièrement ?** have you seen Cyril lately?

dérouler [derule] *verbe*

1. to unwind : **dérouler une pelote de laine** to unwind a ball of wool
2. to unroll : **il a déroulé tout le papier hygiénique !** he unrolled all the toilet paper!

se dérouler *verbe pronominal*

to take place : **l'incident s'est déroulé près d'ici** the incident took place near here.

derrière [dɛrjɛr] *préposition, adverbe & nom*

◾ *préposition & adverbe*
behind : **derrière l'école** behind the school ; **les autres sont restés derrière** the others stayed behind
◾ *nom masculin*
1. back : **le derrière de la maison** the back of the house ; **la porte de derrière** the back door
2. bottom : **une tape sur le derrière** a smack on the bottom.

des [de] *article & préposition*

◾ *article*
1. some : **j'ai acheté des fleurs** I bought some flowers ; **j'ai des frères et sœurs** I've got brothers and sisters
2. any : **est-ce que tu as des cousins ?** have you got any cousins?
◾ *préposition* ➤ de.

dès [dɛ] *préposition*

1. from : **dès demain** from tomorrow ; **dès maintenant** from now on
2. as soon as : **dès son arrivée, il a tout changé** he changed everything, as soon as he arrived
➤ **dès que** as soon as : **j'appellerai dès que j'arriverai** I'll call as soon as I arrive ; **dès que possible** as soon as possible.

désagréable [dezagreabl] *adjectif*

unpleasant : **une impression désagréable** an unpleasant feeling ; **il a été désagréable avec Bernie** he was unpleasant to Bernie OU he wasn't very nice to Bernie.

désastre [dezastr] *nom masculin*

disaster : **la fête était un désastre** the party was a disaster.

descendre [desɑ̃dr] *verbe*

1. to go down : **descends à la cave** go down to the cellar ; **fais attention en descendant la pente** be careful when you go down the hill ; **descendre la rue en courant** to run down the street
2. to come down : **tu peux descendre m'aider, s'il te plaît ?** can you come down and help me, please? ; **je regardais Sam descendre l'escalier** I was watching Sam coming down the stairs
3. to fall : **les températures sont encore descendues** temperatures have fallen again
4. to get off : **tu pourras descendre au feu rouge** you'll be able to get off at the traffic lights ; **descendre du bus** to get off the bus ; **descendre de voiture** to get out of a car.

descente [desɑ̃t] *nom féminin*

la descente a été plus facile que la montée coming down was easier than going up ; **ne va pas trop vite dans la descente** don't go too fast downhill.

description [dɛskripsjɔ̃] *nom féminin*

description : **elle a fait une description détaillée de sa nouvelle maison** she gave a detailed description of her new house.

déséquilibrer [dezekilibre] *verbe*

to throw off balance : **tu dois essayer de déséquilibrer ton adversaire** you have to try to throw your opponent off balance.

désert, e [dezɛr, ɛrt] *adjectif*

1. desert : **une île déserte** a desert island
2. deserted : **les rues sont désertes dès dix-huit heures** the streets are deserted from six o'clock

désert *nom masculin*

desert : **le désert de Gobi** the Gobi desert.

désespéré, e [dezɛspere] *adjectif*

1. desperate : **la pauvre fille est désespérée** the poor girl is desperate ; **un regard désespéré** a desperate look
2. hopeless : **la situation est désespérée** the situation is hopeless.

désespérer [dezɛspere] *verbe*

to despair : **il ne faut pas désespérer** don't despair.

déshabiller [dezabije] *verbe*

to undress : **Lucille a déshabillé sa petite sœur** Lucille undressed her little sister

se déshabiller *verbe pronominal*

to take one's clothes off, to undress : **elle s'est déshabillée et s'est mise au lit** she took her clothes off and got into bed ou she got undressed and got into bed.

se déshydrater [sədezidrate] *verbe pronominal*

to become dehydrated : **bois, sinon tu vas te déshydrater** drink something, or you'll become dehydrated.

désigner [deziɲe] *verbe*

1. to appoint : **il a été désigné comme délégué** he was appointed representative
2. to point at : **désigner quelqu'un du doigt** to point at somebody
3. to refer to : **les mots qui désignent des sentiments** words that refer to feelings.

désinfectant [dezɛ̃fɛktɑ̃] *nom masculin*

disinfectant.

désinfecter [dezɛ̃fɛkte] *verbe*

to disinfect : **il faut désinfecter la plaie** you must disinfect the wound.

se désintégrer [sədezɛ̃tegre] *verbe pronominal*

to break up : **la fusée s'est désintégrée dans l'espace** the rocket broke up in space.

désir [dezir] *nom masculin*

wish (*pluriel* **wishes**) : **ils obéissent à tous ses désirs** they obey all her wishes.

désirer [dezire] *verbe*

to want : **je désire faire une réclamation** I want to make a complaint
➤ **vous désirez ?** can I help you?

désobéir [dezɔbeir] *verbe*

désobéir à quelqu'un to disobey somebody ; **Loïc n'ose pas désobéir à ses parents** Loïc doesn't dare disobey his parents.

désobéissant, e [dezɔbeisɑ̃, ɑ̃t] *adjectif*

disobedient : **il est très désobéissant** he's very disobedient.

désolé, e [dezɔle] *adjectif*

sorry : **je suis désolée, je ne peux pas venir** I'm sorry, I can't come ; **désolé d'être en retard** sorry I'm late.

désordonné, e [dezɔrdɔne] *adjectif*

untidy : **c'est quelqu'un de très désordonné** he's a very untidy person.

désordre [dezɔrdr] *nom masculin*

mess : **quel désordre dans cette chambre !** what a mess it is in this bedroom!

désormais [dezɔrmɛ] *adverbe*

from now on : **désormais tu me demanderas d'abord !** from now on you'll ask me first!

desquels, desquelles [dekɛl] ➤ lequel :

les gens au nom desquels je parle the people on whose behalf I'm speaking.

dessécher [deseʃe] *verbe*

to dry : **le vent dessèche la peau** wind dries the skin

se dessécher *verbe pronominal*

1. to dry out : **ma peau se dessèche en hiver** my skin dries out in winter
2. to wither : **toutes les plantes se sont desséchées** all the plants withered.

dessert [desɛr] *nom masculin*

dessert : **en dessert, je voudrais une mousse au chocolat** I'd like a chocolate mousse for dessert.

dessin [desɛ̃] *nom masculin*

drawing : **Manu a fait un très beau dessin** Manu did a beautiful drawing
➤ **un dessin animé** a cartoon.

dessiner [desine] *verbe*

to draw : **je vais te dessiner un chien** I'll draw you a dog ; **tu dessines très bien** you draw very well.

dessous [dəsu] *adverbe & nom*

▪ *adverbe*

underneath : **il porte un pull sans rien dessous** he's wearing a sweater and nothing underneath

▪ *nom masculin*

underside : **il y a des chewing-gums collés sur le dessous de la table** there is chewing-gum stuck on the underside of the table
➤ **en dessous**

1. underneath : **soulève le classeur, la feuille est en dessous** lift the folder, the piece of paper is underneath

d

2. downstairs : **les gens qui habitent en dessous** the people who live downstairs.

dessus [dəsy] *adverbe & nom*

■ *adverbe*

1. on top : **mon manteau est là, tu peux mettre le tien dessus** my coat is there, you can put yours on top

2. on it : **voici une enveloppe, n'oublie pas d'écrire l'adresse dessus** here's an envelope, don't forget to write the address on it

3. on them : **tes lunettes sont par terre, ne marche pas dessus** your glasses are on the floor, don't step on them

■ *nom masculin*

top : **le dessus de l'armoire est couvert de poussière** the top of the cupboard is covered in dust

➤ **les voisins du dessus** the upstairs neighbours.

destruction [dɛstryksjɔ̃] *nom féminin*

destruction : **l'explosion a provoqué la destruction de la maison** the explosion destroyed the house.

détacher [detaʃe] *verbe*

1. to untie : **je vais détacher le chien** I'm going to untie the dog.

2. to detach : **il faut détacher le coupon et le renvoyer** you have to detach the coupon and send it back

➤ **détacher ses cheveux** to let one's hair down : **elle a détaché ses cheveux** she let her hair down

se détacher *verbe pronominal*

1. to come undone : **comme ça la corde ne se détachera pas** this way the rope won't come undone

2. to come off : **l'un des wagons s'est détaché** one of the carriages came off.

détail [detaj] *nom masculin*

detail : **ce n'est qu'un détail** it's just a detail ; **Simon nous a raconté son voyage en détail** Simon told us about his trip in detail.

détective [detɛktiv] *nom masculin*

detective : **un détective privé** a private detective.

déteindre [detɛ̃dr] *verbe*

to fade : **mon jean a déteint** my jeans have faded

➤ **déteindre au lavage** to run in the wash.

se détendre [sədetɑ̃dr] *verbe pronominal*

1. to relax : **j'écoute de la musique pour me détendre** I listen to music to relax

2. to become more relaxed : **l'ambiance s'est détendue au bout d'un moment** the atmosphere became more relaxed after a while.

détendu, e [detɑ̃dy] *adjectif*

relaxed : **tu as l'air très détendue** you look very relaxed.

détente [detɑ̃t] *nom féminin*

1. relaxation : **une heure de détente** an hour's relaxation

2. trigger : **appuyer sur la détente** to pull the trigger.

se détériorer [sədeterjɔre] *verbe pronominal*

to deteriorate : **la situation s'est détériorée** the situation has deteriorated.

déterminé, e [detɛrmine] *adjectif*

1. given : **une quantité déterminée d'argent** a given amount of money

2. determined : **Rachid est entré d'un air déterminé** Rachid came in looking determined.

détester [detɛste] *verbe*

to hate : **il déteste sa cousine** he hates his cousine ; **je déteste la physique** I hate physics ; **Amélie déteste faire ses devoirs** Amélie hates doing her homework.

détraquer [detrake] *verbe familier*

to break : **arrête, tu vas détraquer la télé !** stop it, you're going to break the TV!

se détraquer *verbe pronominal familier*

to go wrong : **ma montre s'est détraquée** my watch has gone wrong.

détroit [detrwa] *nom masculin*

strait : **le détroit de Gibraltar** the Strait of Gibraltar.

détruire [detrɥir] *verbe*

to destroy : **l'incendie a détruit l'immeuble** the fire destroyed the building.

dette [dɛt] *nom féminin*

debt : **le père de Jackie a des dettes** Jackie's father has debts.

deux [dø] *adjectif numéral & nom masculin*

two : **Karine a deux frères** Karine has two brothers ; **elle a deux ans** she's two

> **nous sommes le deux janvier** it's the second of January *UK* ou it's January second *US*

> **les deux** both : **finalement j'ai acheté les deux** in the end I bought both.

deuxième [døzjɛm] *adjectif numéral & nom*

second : **c'est la deuxième fois que j'essaie** this is the second time I try ; **j'habite au deuxième étage** I live on the second floor *UK* ou I live on the third floor *US* ; **Benoît est arrivé deuxième** Benoît came second.

devant [dəvɑ̃] *préposition, adverbe & nom*

■ *préposition*
in front of : **devant la porte** in front of the door ; **elle a juré devant ses parents** she swore in front of her parents

■ *adverbe*
in front : **passe devant** go in front

■ *nom masculin*
front : **le devant du chemisier est brodé** the front of the blouse is embroidered.

développement [devlɔpmɑ̃] *nom masculin*

1. **development** : **le développement d'un enfant** the development of a child
2. **developing** : **le développement des photos** developing the photographs

> **un pays en développement** a developing country.

développer [devlɔpe] *verbe*

to develop : **la natation développe les muscles** swimming develops the muscles ; **je vais faire développer mes photos** I'm going to get my photos developed

se développer *verbe pronominal*

to develop : **le bébé se développe normalement** the baby is developing normally ; **le pays se développe rapidement** the country is developing rapidly.

devenir [dəvnir] *verbe*

to become : **ils sont devenus très riches** they became very rich

> **qu'est-ce que tu deviens ?** how are you doing?

deviner [dəvine] *verbe*

to guess : **devine ce que j'ai dans la main** guess what I have in my hand

devinette [dəvinɛt] *nom féminin*

riddle : **jouer aux devinettes** to play riddles ; **pose-moi une devinette** ask me a riddle.

devoir[1] [dəvwar] *nom masculin*

duty (*pluriel* **duties**) : **tu dois le faire, c'est ton devoir** you must do it, it's your duty

devoirs *nom masculin pluriel*

homework (*ne s'utilise jamais au pluriel*) : **il est en train de faire ses devoirs** he's doing his homework.

devoir[2] [dəvwar] *verbe*

1. **to owe** : **tu me dois cinq euros** you owe me five euros ; **je crois que je lui dois des excuses** I think you owe her an apology
2. *Indique l'obligation et la nécessité* **must, to have to** : **tu dois te brosser les dents deux fois par jour** you must brush your teeth twice a day ; **Melissa sait qu'elle ne doit pas fumer** Melissa knows that she mustn't smoke ; **je dois y aller** I must go ou I have to go ; **j'ai dû aller avec eux** I had to go with them

> Must indique ce qui est bien du point de vue moral, de la santé, etc., qu'il s'agisse d'une obligation ou d'une recommandation. Must est un verbe modal. Il n'a pas de forme infinitive et ne peut se mettre au passé (« j'ai dû le faire » se traduit par I had to do it). Au présent, il ne prend pas de « s » à la 3ᵉ personne du singulier. Have to indique une obligation imposée par les circonstances.

3. *Au conditionnel* **should** : **tu devrais faire attention** you should be careful ; **vous auriez dû m'en parler** you should have told me about it
4. *Indique la probabilité* **must** : **vous devez avoir faim** you must be hungry
5. *Indique une prévision* **to be due to** : **Alicia doit arriver à six heures** Alicia is due to arrive at six o'clock ou Alicia should arrive at six o'clock.

dévorer [devɔre] *verbe*

to devour : **ils ont dévoré tout ce qu'il y avait dans le frigo** they devoured everything that was in the fridge.

devrai, devras *etc* ➤ **devoir**.

diable [djabl] *nom masculin*

devil : **espèce de petit diable !** you little devil!

diabolo [djabɔlo] *nom masculin*

➤ **un diabolo menthe** a mint cordial and lemonade

➤ **un diabolo fraise** a strawberry cordial and lemonade.

dialogue [djalɔg] *nom masculin*

dialogue : **les dialogues de son dernier film sont très amusants** the dialogue in his last film is very funny.

diamant [djamã] *nom masculin*

diamond : **un collier de diamants** a diamond necklace.

diapositive [djapozitiv] *nom féminin*

slide : **le professeur nous a montré des diapositives** the teacher showed us some slides.

dictée [dikte] *nom féminin*

dictation : **j'ai fait trois fautes à la dictée** I made three mistakes in the dictation.

dictionnaire [diksjɔnɛr] *nom masculin*

dictionary *(pluriel* **dictionaries***)* : **un dictionnaire bilingue** a bilingual dictionary.

dieu [djø] *(pluriel* **dieux***) nom masculin*

god : **les dieux grecs** the Greek gods

Dieu *nom masculin singulier*

mon Dieu ! my God!

différence [diferãs] *nom féminin*

difference : **il y a une grosse différence entre les deux** there's a big difference between the two.

différent, e [diferã, ãt] *adjectif*

different : **ce tableau est très différent de l'autre** this painting is very different from the other one.

difficile [difisil] *adjectif*

difficult, hard : **cet exercice est très difficile** this exercise is very difficult ou this exercise is very hard ; **ne fais pas le difficile** don't be difficult.

difficulté [difikylte] *nom féminin*

difficulty *(pluriel* **difficulties***)* : **mon grand-père a de la difficulté à marcher** my grandfather has difficulty walking ; **Paul a des difficultés en anglais** Paul has difficulties with English.

digérer [diʒere] *verbe*

to digest : **ce plat est difficile à digérer** this dish is difficult to digest.

digestion [diʒɛstjɔ̃] *nom féminin*

digestion.

dimanche [dimɑ̃ʃ] *nom masculin*

Sunday

> En anglais, les jours de la semaine s'écrivent avec une majuscule :

mes copains sont venus dimanche my friends came round on Sunday ; **qu'est-ce que tu fais dimanche matin ?** what are you doing on Sunday morning? ; **Thomas joue au foot le dimanche** Thomas plays football on Sundays ; **dimanche dernier** last Sunday ; **dimanche prochain** next Sunday.

dimension [dimɑ̃sjɔ̃] *nom féminin*

dimension : **quelles sont les dimensions de la pièce ?** what are the dimensions of the room?

diminuer [diminɥe] *verbe*

to decrease : **le nombre d'élèves a diminué** the number of pupils has decreased.

diminutif [diminytif] *nom masculin*

diminutive : **Ben est un diminutif** Ben is a diminutive ; **Pat est le diminutif de Patricia** Pat is short for Patricia.

dinde [dɛ̃d] *nom féminin*

turkey : **on mange de la dinde le jour de Noël** people eat turkey on Christmas Day ; **dinde aux marrons** turkey with chestnuts.

dîner [dine] *verbe & nom*

▪ *verbe*

to have dinner : **mon correspondant anglais dîne à six heures et demie** my English penfriend has dinner at six thirty

▪ *nom masculin*

dinner : **un dîner aux chandelles** a candlelit dinner.

dingue [dɛ̃g] *adjectif familier*

crazy : **il est complètement dingue !** he's completely crazy!

dinosaure [dinozɔr] *nom masculin*

dinosaur : **les dinosaures ont disparu il y a**

65 millions d'années dinosaurs became extinct 65 million years ago.

diplôme [diplom] *nom masculin*

diploma : **un diplôme d'ingénieur** an engineering diploma.

diplômé, e [diplome] *adjectif & nom masculin, nom féminin*

graduate : **Luc est diplômé de l'université de Rennes** Luc is a graduate of Rennes University ; **les diplômés de cette année** this year's graduates.

dire [dir] *verbe*

1. to say : **dis quelque chose !** say something! ; **Louis a dit oui** Louis said yes
2. to tell : **mes parents m'ont dit de ranger ma chambre** my parents told me to tidy my room ; **personne ne m'a dit que le film avait commencé** nobody told me the film had started ; **dis-moi que ce n'est pas vrai !** tell me it isn't true! ; **je ne sais pas s'il dit la vérité** I don't know if he's telling the truth ; **il dit des mensonges** he tells lies

> **SAY ET TELL :**
> Say s'emploie quand on dit quelque chose sans s'adresser à quelqu'un en particulier (he hasn't said anything all evening il n'a rien dit de toute la soirée) ou lorsqu'on rapporte exactement les paroles de quelqu'un.
> Tell s'utilise avec une personne en complément d'objet (to tell somebody) et s'emploie souvent lorsqu'on rapporte les paroles de quelqu'un dans le discours indirect (to tell somebody that ...).

3. to think : **que dis-tu de mon dessin ?** what do you think of my drawing?
> **dis donc** *familier*
1. hey : **dis donc, tu n'aurais pas vu Cédric ?** hey, you haven't seen Cédric, have you?
2. wow : **il y a du monde, dis donc !** wow, there's a lot of people here!
> **on dirait ...**
1. it looks like ... : **on dirait de la soie** it looks like silk
2. it tastes like ... : **on dirait de la menthe** it tastes like mint
3. it smells like ... : **on dirait du chou-fleur** it smells like cauliflower
> **son visage ne me dit rien** I've never seen his face before
> **cette musique me dit quelque chose** I've heard this music before

> **ça te dit d'aller au cinéma ?** do you feel like going to the cinema?
> **ça ne me dit rien** I don't really feel like it

se dire *verbe pronominal*

to think : **je me disais qu'on pourrait appeler Martin** I was thinking that we could call Martin
> **« marteau » se dit « hammer » en anglais** the English for "marteau" is "hammer".

direct, e [dirɛkt] *adjectif*

direct : **un train direct pour Nîmes** a direct train to Nîmes
> **en direct** live : **une émission en direct** a live programme ; **le match a été retransmis en direct** the match was broadcast live.

directement [dirɛktəmã] *adverbe*

straight : **on est rentrés directement à la maison** we went straight home.

directeur, trice [dirɛktœr, tris] *nom masculin, nom féminin*

1. manager : **la directrice du magasin** the shop manager
2. headteacher *UK*, principal *US* : **le directeur de l'école** the headteacher of the school.

direction [dirɛksjɔ̃] *nom féminin*

direction : **ils sont partis dans cette direction** they went in that direction.

directrice ➤ directeur.

diriger [diriʒe] *verbe*

1. to run : **c'est elle qui dirige l'entreprise** she's the one who runs the company
2. to conduct : **qui dirige l'orchestre ce soir ?** who's conducting the orchestra tonight?

se diriger *verbe pronominal*

> **se diriger vers**
1. to go towards, to go toward *US* : **il s'est dirigé vers elle** he went towards her
2. to head for : **ils se sont dirigés vers la sortie** they headed for the exit.

discipline [disiplin] *nom féminin*

discipline : **il y a des problèmes de discipline à l'école** there are discipline problems at the school.

discothèque [diskɔtɛk] *nom féminin*

1. music library *(pluriel* music libraries*)* : **j'ai emprunté ce CD à la discothèque** I borrowed this CD from the music library
2. nightclub : **ils vont en discothèque tous les**

d

samedis soir they go to a nightclub every Saturday night.

discours [diskur] *nom masculin*

speech *(pluriel* speeches*)* : **faire un discours** to make a speech.

discret, ète [diskrɛ, ɛt] *adjectif*

discreet : **Sonia est discrète, elle ne pose pas de questions** Sonia is very discreet, she doesn't ask questions.

discrètement [diskrɛtmã] *adverbe*

il est sorti discrètement he slipped out quietly.

discussion [diskysjɔ̃] *nom féminin*

discussion : **on a eu une discussion très intéressante** we had a very interesting discussion.

discuter [diskyte] *verbe*

1. to talk : **ils ont discuté pendant une heure au téléphone** they talked for an hour on the phone ; **nous avons discuté de nos problèmes** we talked about our problems ou we discussed our problems ; **on a discuté de choses et d'autres** we talked about this and that

2. to argue : **ne discute pas, pose ton livre et viens dîner !** don't argue, put your book down and come and have dinner!

disparaître [disparɛtr] *verbe*

1. to disappear : **Isa a disparu, personne ne sait où elle est** Isa has disappeared, nobody knows where she is.

2. to become extinct : **cette espèce de papillon a disparu** this type of butterfly has become extinct.

disparition [disparisjɔ̃] *nom féminin*

disappearance : **la mystérieuse disparition du ministre** the mysterious disappearance of the minister

➤ **une espèce en voie de disparition** an endangered species

➤ **être en voie de disparition** to become extinct : **cet aigle est en voie de disparition** this eagle is becoming extinct.

disparu, e [dispary] *verbe & nom*

▪ *participe passé de* disparaître

▪ *nom masculin, nom féminin*

missing person : **il y a plusieurs disparus** several people went missing.

dispenser [dispãse] *verbe*

dispenser quelqu'un de quelque chose to

excuse somebody from something ; **être dispensé de gym** to be excused from gym.

se disperser [sədispɛrse] *verbe pronominal*

1. to scatter : **les feuilles se sont dispersées** the leaves scattered

2. to break up : **la foule a fini par se disperser** the crowd eventually broke up.

disponible [disponibl] *adjectif*

available : **il y a encore des places disponibles** there are still some seats available.

disposé, e [dispoze] *adjectif*

être disposé à faire quelque chose to be prepared to do something ; **Benoît est disposé à nous aider** Benoît is prepared to help us.

disposer [dispoze] *verbe*

to arrange : **les chaises étaient disposées en cercle** the chairs were arranged in a circle

➤ **disposer de quelque chose** to have something : **nous disposons de très peu de temps** we have very little time.

disposition [dispozisjɔ̃] *nom féminin*

arrangement : **je n'aime pas la disposition des meubles** I don't like the arrangement of the furniture

➤ **à la disposition de** at the disposal of : **ma voiture est à votre disposition** my car is at your disposal.

dispute [dispyt] *nom féminin*

argument : **ils ont eu une dispute à propos d'argent** they had an argument over money.

se disputer [sədispyte] *verbe pronominal*

to argue : **arrêtez de vous disputer !** stop arguing!

disque [disk] *nom masculin*

1. record : **un magasin de disques** a record shop

2. discus : **le lancer du disque** throwing the discus

➤ **un disque compact** a compact disc

➤ **un disque dur** a hard disk

➤ **un disque laser** a laser disc.

disquette [diskɛt] *nom féminin*

floppy disk : **tu peux me copier le fichier sur disquette ?** can you copy the file onto a floppy disk for me?

dissoudre [disudr] *verbe*

to dissolve

> **faire dissoudre quelque chose** to dissolve something

se dissoudre *verbe pronominal*

to dissolve : **le sucre se dissout dans l'eau** sugar dissolves in water.

distance [distɑ̃s] *nom féminin*

distance : **quelle distance y a-t-il entre Meaux et Senlis ?** what's the distance between Meaux and Senlis? ; **à une distance de 300 mètres** 300 metres away.

distraction [distraksjɔ̃] *nom féminin*

pastime : **sa seule distraction est la philatélie** his only pastime is stamp-collecting
> **par distraction** absent-mindedly ; **il a mis le lait dans le four par distraction** he absent-mindedly put the milk in the oven.

distraire [distrɛr] *verbe*

1. to distract : **on essayait de distraire Laurent pendant qu'il était au tableau** we were trying to distract Laurent while he was at the board
2. to entertain : **ils ont fait venir un magicien pour distraire les enfants** they got a magician to come and entertain the children

se distraire *verbe pronominal*

to keep oneself amused : **il se distrait en lisant des BD** he keeps himself amused reading comics.

distrait, e [distrɛ, ɛt] *adjectif*

absent-minded : **Elsa est très distraite** Elsa is very absent-minded
> **elle est très distraite en classe** she doesn't pay attention in class.

distribuer [distribɥe] *verbe*

1. to hand out, to distribute : **Sarah a distribué des bonbons à tout le monde** Sarah handed out sweets to everybody
2. to deal : **c'est ton tour de distribuer les cartes** it's your turn to deal the cards.

distributeur [distribytœr] *nom masculin*

> **un distributeur automatique de billets** a cash machine, an ATM : **je vais prendre de l'argent au distributeur de billets** I'm going to get some money out of the cash machine
> **un distributeur de boissons** a drinks machine.

dit, e [di, dit] *participe passé de* **dire**.

divers, e [divɛr, ɛrs] *adjectif*

various : **pour diverses raisons** for various reasons.

diviser [divize] *verbe*

to divide : **8 divisé par 4 égalent 2** 8 divided by 4 equals 2.

division [divizjɔ̃] *nom féminin*

division : **je ne sais pas faire cette division** I don't know how to do this division.

divorcé, e [divɔrse] *adjectif*

divorced : **les parents de Lucas sont divorcés** Lucas's parents are divorced.

divorcer [divɔrse] *verbe*

to get divorced : **les Souchet ont divorcé l'année dernière** the Souchets got divorced last year.

dix [dis] *adjectif numéral & nom masculin*

ten : **il y a dix filles dans ma classe** there are ten girls in my class
> **nous sommes le dix juin** it's the tenth of June *UK* ou it's June tenth *US*.

dixième [dizjɛm] *adjectif numéral & nom*

tenth : **le dixième nom sur la liste** the tenth name on the list ; **Anne est arrivée dixième** Anne came tenth ; **un dixième de la somme totale** a tenth of the total sum.

dix-neuf [diznœf] *adjectif numéral & nom masculin*

nineteen : **il y a dix-neuf élèves dans ma classe** there are nineteen pupils in my class
> **nous sommes le dix-neuf décembre** it's the nineteenth of December *UK* ou it's December nineteenth *US*.

dix-neuvième [diznœvjɛm] *adjectif numéral & nom*

nineteenth : **le dix-neuvième nom sur la liste** the nineteenth name on the list ; **Sibylle est arrivée dix-neuvième** Sibylle came nineteenth.

dix-sept [disɛt] *adjectif numéral & nom masculin*

seventeen : **il y a dix-sept élèves dans ma classe** there are seventeen pupils in my class
> **nous sommes le dix-sept avril** it's the seventeenth of April *UK* ou it's April seventeenth *US*.

dix-septième [disɛtjɛm] *adjectif numéral & nom*

seventeenth : **le dix-septième nom sur la liste** the seventeenth name on the list ; **Pierre est arrivé dix-septième** Pierre came seventeenth.

dizaine [dizɛn] *nom féminin*

une dizaine de about ten ; **ça m'a pris une dizaine de minutes** it took me about ten minutes.

docteur [dɔktœr] *nom masculin*

doctor : **je vais chez le docteur à 10 heures** I'm going to the doctor's at 10 o'clock ; **Chloé est chez le docteur** Chloé is at the doctor's.

document [dɔkymɑ̃] *nom masculin*

document.

documentaire [dɔkymɑ̃tɛr] *nom masculin*

documentary (*pluriel* **documentaries**) : **un documentaire sur l'Égypte** a documentary on Egypt.

documentation [dɔkymɑ̃tasjɔ̃] *nom féminin*

information : **je cherche de la documentation sur les volcans** I'm looking for information on volcanos.

se documenter [sədɔkymɑ̃te] *verbe pronominal*

to do some research : **nous nous sommes documentés sur le sujet** we did some research on the subject.

doigt [dwa] *nom masculin*

finger : **j'ai les doigts gelés** my fingers are frozen

➤ **un doigt de pied** a toe
➤ **le petit doigt** the little finger.

dois ➤ devoir.

doive ➤ devoir.

dollar [dɔlar] *nom masculin*

dollar : **ma casquette m'a coûté 5 dollars** my cap cost me 5 dollars.

domaine [dɔmɛn] *nom masculin*

field : **Tom voudrait travailler dans le domaine scientifique** Tom would like to work in the scientific field.

domestique [dɔmɛstik] *adjectif*

les animaux domestiques pets.

domicile [dɔmisil] *nom masculin*

➤ **travailler à domicile** to work from home
➤ **livrer quelque chose à domicile** to deliver something
➤ **sans domicile fixe** homeless.

dominer [dɔmine] *verbe*

1. to dominate : **l'hôtel domine la baie** the hotel dominates the bay
2. to be on top : **notre équipe a dominé pendant tout le match** our team was on top during the whole match.

domino [dɔmino] *nom masculin*

domino (*pluriel* **dominoes**) : **jouer aux dominos** to play dominoes.

dommage [dɔmaʒ] *nom masculin*

quel dommage ! what a shame! ou what a pity! ; **c'est dommage que tu ne puisses pas venir** it's a shame that you can't come ou it's a pity that you can't come.

dompter [dɔ̃te] *verbe*

to tame : **certains animaux sont très difficiles à dompter** some animals are difficult to tame.

DOM-TOM [dɔmtɔm] (*abréviation de* départements d'outre-mer/territoires d'outre-mer) *nom masculin pluriel*
French overseas departments and territories

DOM–TOM
The 'DOM' are French administrative departments which are overseas, such as the islands of Martinique and Guadeloupe. The 'TOM' are French overseas territories, such as the islands of New Caledonia, and French Polynesia. The 'TOM' have more independence than the 'DOM'. The people of the 'DOM–TOM' are all French citizens.

don [dɔ̃] *nom masculin*

gift : **Sandra a un don pour les langues** Sandra has a gift for languages ; **un milliardaire a fait don de ce tableau au musée** a multimillionaire made a gift of this painting to the gallery.

donc [dɔ̃k] *conjonction*

so : **donc tu penses que c'est possible ?** so you think it's possible?

donjon [dɔ̃ʒɔ̃] *nom masculin*

keep : **le donjon, c'est la tour la plus haute d'un château fort** the keep is the tallest tower in a castle.

donné, e [dɔne] *adjectif*

➤ **à un moment donné** at one point
➤ **c'est donné !** it's dirt cheap!
➤ **ce n'est pas donné** it's not cheap.

donner [dɔne] *verbe*

1. to give : **donner quelque chose à quelqu'un** to give somebody something OU to give something to somebody ; **donne-moi le ballon** give me the ball ; **il lui a donné son numéro de téléphone** he gave her his phone number

2. to make : **ça m'a donné soif** it made me thirsty ; **ça m'a donné envie d'y aller** it made me want to go there

➤ **quel âge lui donnes-tu ?** how old do you think he is?
➤ **ça n'a rien donné** it was no good
➤ **donner sur** to look onto : **la chambre donne sur la mer** the room looks onto the sea.

dont [dɔ̃] *pronom relatif*

1. of which : **il y a trois piscines, dont deux sont couvertes** there are three swimming pools, two of which are indoors

2. whose : **j'ai un ami dont les parents sont anglais** I have a friend whose parents are English ; **la fille dont le père est un réalisateur connu** the girl whose father is a famous director

> Notez que **whose** est immédiatement suivi du nom, sans article.

3. of whom : **plusieurs personnes ont appelé, dont ton frère** several people called, one of whom was your brother

➤ **le livre dont je t'ai parlé** the book I told you about
➤ **c'est la fille dont il est amoureux** she's the girl he's in love with OU she's the girl that he's in love with.

doré, e [dɔre] *adjectif*

golden : **une jolie couleur dorée** a nice golden colour.

dorénavant [dɔrenavɑ̃] *adverbe*

from now on : **dorénavant je promets de ne jamais être en retard** from now on I promise never to be late.

dormir [dɔrmir] *verbe*

to sleep : **vous avez bien dormi ?** did you sleep well?

➤ **dormir debout** to be asleep on one's feet : **mais tu dors debout !** but you're asleep on your feet!
➤ **une histoire à dormir debout** an unbelievable story.

dortoir [dɔrtwar] *nom masculin*

dormitory *(pluriel* **dormitories***).*

dos [do] *nom masculin*

back : **j'ai mal au dos** my back hurts ; **au dos de la feuille** on the back of the sheet

➤ **le dos crawlé** backstroke : **nager le dos crawlé** to do backstroke
➤ **de dos** from behind : **je ne l'ai vue que de dos** I only saw her from behind
➤ **tourner le dos à quelqu'un** to turn one's back on somebody : **il m'a tourné le dos** he turned his back on me.

dossier [dosje] *nom masculin*

1. back : **le dossier du fauteuil** the back of the armchair

2. file : **Jérôme a tout un dossier sur les serpents** Jérôme has a whole file on snakes

3. report *UK* : **Alice a un bon dossier scolaire** Alice has a good school report.

douane [dwan] *nom féminin*

customs *(pluriel)* : **passer la douane** to go through customs.

douanier, ère [dwanje, ɛr] *nom masculin, nom féminin*

customs officer : **le frère de Léon est douanier** Léon's brother is a customs officer.

double [dubl] *adjectif & nom*

▪ *adjectif*
double : **double faute** double fault
▪ *nom masculin*

1. double : **trente est le double de quinze** thirty is the double of fifteen

2. copy *(pluriel* **copies***)* : **fais un double du certificat** make a copy of the certificate

3. doubles *(s'utilise toujours au pluriel)* : **le double messieurs** the men's doubles

➤ **j'ai ce timbre en double** I've got two of these stamps.

doubler [duble] *verbe*

1. **to overtake** *UK*, **to pass** *US* : **il est interdit de doubler ici** it's forbidden to overtake here
2. **to double** : **ils ont doublé le nombre de policiers** they've doubled the number of policemen.

douce ➤ doux.

doucement [dusmɑ̃] *adverbe*

1. **gently** : **pose-le doucement sur la table** put it down gently on the table
2. **quietly** : **vous pourriez parler plus doucement ?** could you speak more quietly?
3. **slowly** : **marche plus doucement, je ne peux pas suivre** walk more slowly, I can't keep up.

douche [duʃ] *nom féminin*

shower : **prendre une douche** to have a shower *UK* ou to take a shower *US* .

se doucher [səduʃe] *verbe pronominal*

to have a shower *UK*, **to take a shower** *US* : **je vais me doucher avant de sortir** I'll have a shower before I go out.

doué, e [dwe] *adjectif*

talented : **un chanteur très doué** a very talented singer

➤ **être doué pour quelque chose** to have a gift for something : **Lucie est douée pour les langues** Lucie has a gift for languages.

douleur [dulœr] *nom féminin*

pain : **j'ai une douleur au bras** I've got a pain in my arm.

douloureux, euse [dulurø, øz] *adjectif*

painful : **une opération douloureuse** a painful operation.

doute [dut] *nom masculin*

doubt : **j'ai des doutes sur son honnêteté** I have doubts about his honesty

➤ **sans doute** no doubt : **ils sont sans doute arrivés** they've no doubt arrived.

douter [dute] *verbe*

to doubt : **je doute que ce soit possible** I doubt it's possible ; **ils doutent de son honnêteté** they have doubts about his honesty

se douter *verbe pronominal*

se douter de quelque chose to suspect something ; **personne ne se doutait de ce qui**

allait se passer nobody suspected what was going to happen ; **Émilie se doutait que ce serait difficile** Émilie suspected that it would be difficult

➤ **je m'en doutais** I thought so.

doux, douce [du, dus] *adjectif*

1. **soft** : **un tissu très doux** a very soft material
2. **gentle** : **une voix douce** a gentle voice
3. **mild** : **piment doux** mild pepper.

douzaine [duzɛn] *nom féminin*

1. **dozen** *(pluriel* **dozen***)* : **deux douzaines d'œufs** two dozen eggs
2. **une douzaine** about twelve ; **une douzaine de pages** about twelve pages.

douze [duz] *adjectif numéral & nom masculin*

twelve : **il y avait douze personnes à la réunion** there were twelve people at the meeting

➤ **nous sommes le douze janvier** it's the twelfth of January *UK* ou it's January twelfth *US*.

douzième [duzjɛm] *adjectif numéral & nom*

twelfth : **le douzième nom sur la liste** the twelfth name on the list ; **Aude est arrivée douzième** Aude came twelfth.

dragon [dragɔ̃] *nom masculin*

dragon : **une histoire de chevalier et de dragon** a story about a knight and a dragon.

dramatique [dramatik] *adjectif*

tragic : **la situation est dramatique** the situation is tragic

➤ **ce n'est pas dramatique !** it's not the end of the world!

drame [dram] *nom masculin*

1. **tragedy** *(pluriel* **tragedies***)* : **il y a eu un drame affreux dans leur famille** there was an awful tragedy in their family
2. **drama** : **un drame de Victor Hugo** a drama by Victor Hugo ; **il en a fait tout un drame** he made a drama of it.

drap [dra] *nom masculin*

sheet : **le drap de dessus** the top sheet.

drapeau [drapo] *(pluriel* drapeaux*) nom masculin*

flag : **le drapeau tricolore** the French flag.

dresser [drese] *verbe*

1. **to raise** : **Martin a dressé la tête quand on**

est entrés Martin raised his head when we came in
2. **to train** : **ce chien est bien dressé** this dog is well-trained
➤ **le chien a dressé les oreilles** the dog pricked up its ears

se dresser *verbe pronominal*

to rise up : **les montagnes se dressaient devant nous** the mountains rose up in front of us.

drogue [drɔg] *nom féminin*

drug : **une drogue douce** a soft drug ; **une drogue dure** a hard drug.

se droguer [sədrɔge] *verbe pronominal*

to take drugs : **il paraît qu'il se drogue** apparently he takes drugs.

droit¹ [drwa] *nom masculin*

1. **right** : **les droits de l'homme** human rights
2. **law** : **le droit civil** civil law
3. **fee** : **droits d'inscription** registration fees
➤ **avoir droit à quelque chose** to be entitled to something : **j'ai droit à une réduction avec cette carte** I'm entitled to a reduction with this card
➤ **avoir le droit de faire quelque chose** to be allowed to do something : **nous n'avons pas le droit de sortir** we aren't allowed to go out.

droit², e [drwa, at] *adjectif*

1. **right** : **ta main droite** your right hand
2. **right-hand** : **la maison est sur le côté droit de la rue** the house is on the right-hand side of the street
3. **straight** : **le poster n'est pas droit** the poster isn't straight.

droit *adverbe*

straight : **il ne marche pas droit** he's not walking straight
➤ **tout droit** straight ahead : **allez tout droit** go straight ahead.

droite [drwat] *nom féminin*

right : **l'école est à droite** the school is on the right ; **à droite du bureau** to the right of the desk
➤ **de droite** right-wing : **un gouvernement de droite** a right-wing government.

droitier, ère [drwatje, ɛr] *adjectif*

right-handed : **Lucie est droitière** Lucie is right-handed.

drôle [drol] *adjectif*

1. **funny** : **un film très drôle** a very funny film
2. **strange** : **ce type a l'air drôle** that guy looks strange.

du ➤ de.

dû, due [dy] *participe passé de* devoir.

dur, e [dyr] *adjectif*

1. **hard** : **mon lit est dur** my bed is hard ; **cet exercice est vraiment dur** this exercise is really hard
2. **tough** : **la viande est très dure** the meat is very tough
3. **harsh** : **il est dur avec ses enfants** he's harsh with his children

dur *adverbe*

hard : **travailler dur** to work hard.

durant [dyrã] *préposition*

1. **for** : **ils ont parlé durant des heures** they talked for hours
2. **during** : **ça s'est passé durant la nuit** it happened during the night.

durcir [dyrsir] *verbe*

to harden : **le ciment a durci** the cement has hardened.

durée [dyre] *nom féminin*

quelle est la durée du film ? how long is the film? ; **un séjour d'une durée d'une semaine** a week-long stay ; **pendant toute la durée du vol** throughout the flight.

durer [dyre] *verbe*

1. **to last** : **ça ne durera pas** it won't last
2. **to go on** : **ça fait deux jours que ça dure** it's been going on for two days.

duvet [dyvɛ] *nom masculin*

1. **sleeping bag** : **j'ai dormi dans un duvet** I slept in a sleeping bag
2. **down** : **du duvet de canard** duck down.

dynamique [dinamik] *adjectif*

dynamic : **la prof de gym est très dynamique** the PE teacher is very dynamic.

eau [o] (*pluriel* **eaux**) *nom féminin*

water : **un verre d'eau** a glass of water ; **de l'eau gazeuse** fizzy water
➣ **l'eau douce** freshwater
➣ **l'eau salée** salt water
➣ **l'eau minérale** mineral water
➣ **l'eau de toilette** eau de toilette.

éblouir [ebluir] *verbe*

to dazzle : **j'étais ébloui par les phares de la voiture** I was dazzled by the headlights.

éboueur [ebwœr] *nom masculin*

dustman *UK*, garbage collector *US*.

écaille [ekaj] *nom féminin*

1. scale : **les écailles d'un poisson** the scales of a fish
2. tortoiseshell : **des lunettes en écaille** tortoiseshell glasses.

écart [ekar] *nom masculin*

1. gap : **l'écart entre les deux arbres** the gap between the two trees ; **un écart de trois ans** a three-year gap OU a gap of three years
2. difference : **un grand écart de poids** a big difference in weight
➣ **faire un écart** to swerve : **la voiture a fait un écart** the car swerved
➣ **faire le grand écart** to do the splits
➣ **à l'écart de** away from : **la maison est à l'écart du village** the house is away from the village.

écarter [ekarte] *verbe*

to open : **écartez bien les bras** open your arms wide.

échange [eʃɑ̃ʒ] *nom masculin*

exchange : **je te donne ça en échange** I'll give you this in exchange ; **faire un échange** to swap ; **Pierre et Julien ont fait un échange**

de jeux vidéo Pierre and Julien swapped video games.

échanger [eʃɑ̃ʒe] *verbe*

1. to exchange, to swap : **on a échangé nos adresses** we exchanged addresses ; **je t'échange ce stylo contre ta casquette** I'll swap you this pen for your baseball cap
2. to change : **est-ce que je peux échanger la jupe si ce n'est pas la bonne taille ?** can I change the skirt if it's not the right size?

échapper [eʃape] *verbe*

échapper à quelqu'un to escape from somebody ; **le voleur a réussi à échapper à la police** the thief managed to escape from the police
➣ **son nom m'échappe** his name escapes me
➣ **pardon, ça m'a échappé** sorry, it slipped out

s'échapper *verbe pronominal*

to escape : **ils se sont échappés de prison** they escaped from prison.

écharpe [eʃarp] *nom féminin*

scarf (*pluriel* **scarves**) : **une écharpe en laine** a woollen scarf
➣ **Sylvain a le bras en écharpe** Sylvain has his arm in a sling.

échauffement [eʃofmɑ̃] *nom masculin*

warm-up : **dix minutes d'échauffement** a ten-minute warm-up.

s'échauffer [seʃofe] *verbe pronominal*

to warm up : **on s'échauffe toujours au début du cours de gym** we always warm up at the beginning of the gym class.

échec [eʃɛk] *nom masculin*

failure : **un échec terrible** a terrible failure

échecs *nom masculin pluriel*

chess (*ne s'utilise jamais au pluriel*) : **tu sais jouer aux échecs ?** can you play chess?

échelle [eʃɛl] *nom féminin*

1. ladder : **il est monté sur une échelle pour laver les vitres** he climbed a ladder to clean the windows
2. scale : **quelle est l'échelle de la carte ?** what's the scale of the map?
➣ **faire la courte échelle à quelqu'un** to give somebody a leg up.

écho [eko] *nom masculin*

echo : **il y a de l'écho ici** there's an echo in here.

échouer [eʃwe] *verbe*

to fail : **Aurélie a échoué au permis de conduire** Aurélie failed her driving test

s'échouer *verbe pronominal*

to run aground : **le bateau s'est échoué près d'ici** the boat ran aground near here.

éclabousser [eklabuse] *verbe*

to splash, to spatter : **une voiture m'a éclaboussé** a car splashed me.

éclair [eklɛr] *nom masculin*

flash of lightning : **il y a eu le tonnerre puis un éclair** there was a clap of thunder then a flash of lightning ; **des éclairs illuminaient le ciel** lightning lit up the sky

➤ **un éclair au chocolat** a chocolate eclair.

éclaircir [eklɛrsir] *verbe*

to lighten : **elle veut éclaircir ses cheveux** she wants to lighten her hair

s'éclaircir *verbe pronominal*

1. to brighten up : **le ciel s'éclaircit enfin** the sky is brightening up at last
2. to go lighter : **mes cheveux s'éclaircissent au soleil** my hair goes lighter in the sun
3. to become clearer : **la situation s'éclaircit** the situation is becoming clearer.

éclairer [eklere] *verbe*

to light : **des bougies éclairaient la pièce** the room was lit by candles

s'éclairer *verbe pronominal*

1. to light one's way : **prends la lampe pour t'éclairer** take the torch to light your way
2. to light up : **tout à coup les rues se sont éclairées** suddenly the streets lit up.

éclat [ekla] *nom masculin*

splinter : **des éclats de verre** splinters of glass

➤ **un éclat de rire** a burst of laughter

➤ **rire aux éclats** to burst out laughing ou to roar with laughter.

éclater [eklate] *verbe*

1. to burst : **le ballon a éclaté** the balloon burst

2. to explode : **un obus a éclaté** a shell exploded
3. to break out : **la Première Guerre mondiale a éclaté en 1914** the First World War broke out in 1914

➤ **éclater de rire** to burst out laughing

s'éclater *verbe pronominal familier*

to have a great time : **on s'est éclatés chez Samia** we had a great time at Samia's.

école [ekɔl] *nom féminin*

school : **aller à l'école** to go to school

➤ **l'école maternelle** nursery school

➤ **l'école primaire** primary school *UK* ou grade school *US*

> ÉCOLE
> In France, children can go to nursery school (**école maternelle**) from age 3 to 6. School becomes compulsory at the age of 6, when children go to primary school **école primaire**. They spend 5 years there before starting secondary school.

➤ collège, lycée.

écolier, ère [ekɔlje, ɛr] *nom masculin, nom féminin*

schoolboy *(féminin* schoolgirl*)* : **les écoliers** schoolchildren.

écologique [ekɔlɔʒik] *adjectif*

1. ecological : **l'équilibre écologique** the ecological balance
2. environmentally friendly : **des produits écologiques** environmentally friendly products.

écologiste [ekɔlɔʒist] *adjectif & nom*

▪ *adjectif*
ecological : **le parti écologiste** the green party.

▪ *nom masculin ou féminin*
ecologist.

économie [ekɔnɔmi] *nom féminin*

1. economics : **Raoul fait des études d'économie** Raoul is studying economics
2. economy *(pluriel* economies*)* : **l'économie française** the French economy

économies *nom féminin pluriel*

savings : **elle a dépensé toutes ses écono-**

mies she has spent all her savings ; **faire des économies** to save up.

économique [ekɔnɔmik] *adjectif*

1. **economic : la politique économique du gouvernement** the government's economic policy
2. **economical : ce système de chauffage est très économique** this heating system is very economical
> **classe économique** economy class, coach class *US*.

économiser [ekɔnɔmize] *verbe*

1. **to save : économiser l'électricité** to save electricity
2. **to save up : Tatiana économise pour s'acheter un VTT** Tatiana is saving up to buy a mountain bike.

écorce [ekɔrs] *nom féminin*

1. **bark : l'écorce d'un chêne** the bark of an oak tree
2. **peel : de l'écorce d'orange râpée** grated orange peel.

écossais, e [ekɔsɛ, ɛz] *adjectif*

1. **Scottish : Jane est écossaise** Jane is Scottish
2. **tartan : du tissu écossais** tartan material

Écossais, e *nom masculin, nom féminin*

Scot : les Écossais the Scots.

Écosse [ekɔs] *nom féminin*

> **l'Écosse** Scotland ; **il y a de beaux paysages en Écosse** there is some beautiful scenery in Scotland ; **tu devrais aller en Écosse** you should go to Scotland.

s'écouler [sekule] *verbe pronominal*

1. **to flow : l'eau s'écoule par la gouttière** the water flows through the gutter
2. **to pass : le temps s'écoulait lentement** the time passed slowly.

écouter [ekute] *verbe*

1. **to listen to : j'aime écouter de la musique** I like listening to music
2. **to listen : écoutez, on entend le tonnerre** listen, you can hear thunder ; **écoute, ça suffit maintenant !** listen, that's enough now!

écouteurs [ekutœr] *nom masculin pluriel*

headphones : les écouteurs d'un baladeur the headphones of a personal stereo.

écran [ekrɑ̃] *nom masculin*

screen : j'ai changé l'écran de mon ordinateur I've changed my computer screen.

écraser [ekraze] *verbe*

1. **to crush : tremper les biscuits dans le lait, puis les écraser** dip the biscuits in milk, then crush them
2. **to tread on : aïe, tu m'écrases le pied !** ouch, you're treading on my foot!
> **se faire écraser** to get run over : **elle s'est fait écraser par un camion** she got run over by a lorry

s'écraser *verbe pronominal*

to crash : l'avion s'est écrasé juste après le décollage the plane crashed just after take-off.

écrire [ekrir] *verbe*

to write : tu écris souvent à ton correspondant ? do you often write to your penfriend?

s'écrire *verbe pronominal*

to be spelled : comment s'écrit ce mot ? how do you spell this word?

écrit, e [ekri, it] *adjectif*

written : une épreuve écrite a written exam

écrit *nom masculin*

written exam : Benoît a raté l'écrit Benoît failed the written exam
> **par écrit** in writing : **mets-le par écrit** put it down in writing.

écriture [ekrityr] *nom féminin*

1. **handwriting : ton écriture est illisible** your handwriting is illegible
2. **writing : l'écriture arabe** Arabic writing.

écrivain [ekrivɛ̃] *nom masculin*

writer : un écrivain célèbre a famous writer.

s'écrouler [sekrule] *verbe pronominal*

to collapse : la pile de livres s'est écroulée the pile of books collapsed.

écureuil [ekyrœj] *nom masculin*

squirrel.

écurie [ekyri] *nom féminin*

stable : les chevaux sont à l'écurie the horses are in the stable.

Édimbourg [edēbur] *nom*

Edinburgh : elle habite à Édimbourg she lives in Edinburgh.

éducation [edykasjɔ̃] *nom féminin*

1. **education : le ministère de l'Éducation** the Ministry of Education
2. **upbringing : il a reçu une éducation stricte chez lui** he had a strict upbringing at home
3. **manners : cette fille n'a aucune éducation** this girl has no manners
> **l'éducation physique** physical education
> **l'éducation sexuelle** sex education.

éduquer [edyke] *verbe*

to bring up : un enfant mal éduqué a badly brought up child.

effacer [efase] *verbe*

1. **to erase : efface ce mot, il y a une faute** erase this word, there's a mistake
2. **to delete : Béa a effacé un fichier par erreur** Béa deleted a file by mistake.

effectivement [efɛktivmɑ̃] *adverbe*

indeed : oui, effectivement yes, indeed.

effet [efɛ] *nom masculin*

effect : les cachets ne m'ont fait aucun effet the tablets didn't have any effect on me
> **ça m'a fait un drôle d'effet** it made me feel funny
> **l'effet de serre** the greenhouse effect
> **en effet** indeed : **en effet, tu as raison** indeed you're right
> **en effet, c'est bizarre** it IS strange, isn't it?

efficace [efikas] *adjectif*

1. **effective : une solution efficace** an effective solution
2. **efficient : c'est quelqu'un de très efficace** she's very efficient.

s'effondrer [sefɔ̃dre] *verbe pronominal*

to collapse : le plafond s'est effondré the ceiling collapsed.

effort [efɔr] *nom masculin*

effort : tu pourrais faire un effort ! you could make an effort! ; **il a fait beaucoup d'efforts** he made a really big effort.

effrayer [efreje] *verbe*

to frighten, to scare : le bruit du tonnerre l'effraie the sound of thunder frightens him.

égal, e, aux [egal, o] *adjectif*

equal : en quantités égales in equal quantities
> **ça m'est égal**
1. **I don't mind : tu veux de la viande ou du poisson ? – ça m'est égal** do you want meat or fish? – I don't mind
2. **I don't care : vas-y si tu veux, ça m'est égal** go if you want to, I don't care.

également [egalmɑ̃] *adverbe*

as well, too : ma sœur était là également my sister was there as well ou my sister was there too.

égaliser [egalize] *verbe*

to equalize *UK*, **to tie** *US* : **Arsenal a égalisé trois minutes avant la fin** Arsenal equalized three minutes before the end.

égalité [egalite] *nom féminin*

> **être à égalité** to be equal ou to be tied *US* : **les deux équipes sont à égalité** the two teams are equal.

église [egliz] *nom féminin*

church *(pluriel* **churches***)* : **ils vont à l'église tous les dimanches** they go to church every Sunday.

égoïste [egɔist] *adjectif & nom*

■ *adjectif*
selfish : tu es vraiment égoïste ! you're really selfish!
■ *nom masculin ou féminin*
c'est une égoïste she's selfish.

Égypte [eʒipt] *nom féminin*

> **l'Égypte** Egypt

En anglais, à de rares exceptions près, il n'y a pas d'article devant les noms de pays :

nous avons eu très chaud en Égypte we were very hot in Egypt ; **êtes-vous déjà allé en Égypte ?** have you ever been to Egypt?

égyptien, enne [eʒipsjɛ̃, ɛn] *adjectif*

Egyptian : les temples égyptiens Egyptian temples

En anglais, les adjectifs se rapportant à un pays ou une région s'écrivent avec une majuscule.

Égyptien, enne *nom masculin, nom féminin*

Egyptian.

eh [e] *interjection*

hey! : **eh, toi là-bas !** hey, you over there!
> **eh bien** well
> **eh oui** well, yes.

Eiffel [efɛl] *nom*

la tour Eiffel the Eiffel Tower.
> tour.

élan [elɑ̃] *nom masculin*

1. run-up : **prends ton élan avant de sauter** take a run-up before you jump
2. moose, elk : **l'élan est une sorte de grand cerf** the moose is a type of large deer.

s'élancer [selɑ̃se] *verbe pronominal*

1. to rush : **Matthieu s'est élancé vers nous** Matthieu rushed towards us
2. to start running : **les athlètes se sont élancés sur la piste** the athletes started running.

élargir [elarʒir] *verbe*

to widen : **ils sont en train d'élargir l'avenue** they are widening the avenue

s'élargir *verbe pronominal*

1. to widen : **la route s'élargit ici** the road widens here
2. to stretch : **le pull va s'élargir** the sweater will stretch.

élastique [elastik] *nom masculin*

elastic band *UK*, rubber band *US* : **Dorothée attache ses cheveux avec un élastique** Dorothée ties her hair up with an elastic band.

électeur, trice [elɛktœr, tris] *nom masculin, nom féminin*

voter : **les électeurs vont élire le nouveau président** the voters are going to elect a new president.

élection [elɛksjɔ̃] *nom féminin*

election : **l'élection présidentielle** the presidential elections.

électricien, enne [elɛktrisjɛ̃, ɛn] *nom masculin, nom féminin*

electrician : **le père d'Anne est électricien** Anne's father is an electrician.

électricité [elɛktrisite] *nom féminin*

electricity : **l'électricité a été coupée** the electricity has been cut off.

électrique [elɛktrik] *adjectif*

electric : **un appareil électrique** an electric appliance.

électronique [elɛktrɔnik] *adjectif*

electronic : **circuit électronique** electronic circuit.

élément [elemɑ̃] *nom masculin*

component : **les différents éléments d'une machine** the different components of a machine.

éléphant [elefɑ̃] *nom masculin*

elephant : **l'éléphant d'Afrique** the African elephant.

élevage [ɛlvaʒ] *nom masculin*

1. breeding : **l'élevage du bétail** cattle breeding ; **faire l'élevage de moutons** to breed sheep
2. farm : **il y a un élevage de volaille dans le village** there's a poultry farm in the village.

élève [elɛv] *nom masculin ou féminin*

pupil : **tous les élèves de ma classe** all the pupils in my class.

élevé, e [ɛlve] *adjectif*

high : **des prix élevés** high prices
> **bien élevé** well brought up
> **mal élevé** badly brought up.

élever [ɛlve] *verbe*

1. to bring up : **ce sont ses grands-parents qui l'ont élevé** his grandparents brought him up
2. to breed : **il élève des lapins** he breeds rabbits
3. to put up : **ils ont élevé un mur autour du jardin** they put a wall up around the garden
4. to raise : **élever le niveau de la classe** to raise the standard of the class

s'élever *verbe pronominal*

to rise : **le ballon s'élève dans les airs** the balloon is rising into the air
> **s'élever à** to add up to : **l'addition s'élève à cent euros** the bill adds up to a hundred euros.

éliminer [elimine] *verbe*

1. to eliminate : **ils ont été éliminés en demi-finale** they were eliminated in the semi-final
2. to clean out one's system : **il faut boire de**

l'eau pour éliminer you must drink lots of water to clean out your system.

élire [elir] *verbe*

to elect : **il a été élu président** he was elected president.

elle [εl] *pronom*

1. she : **elle va venir demain** she's coming tomorrow ; **est-ce qu'elle était là ?** was she there?
2. it : **la voiture est au garage, elle est tombée en panne** the car's in the garage, it broke down

> Lorsque « elle » est le sujet de la phrase, il se traduit par **she** s'il s'agit d'une personne ou par **it** s'il s'agit d'une chose ou d'un animal.

3. her : **et elle, tu ne l'as pas vue ?** what about her, didn't you see her? ; **viens avec elle** come with her ; **je ne me souviens pas d'elle** I don't remember her ; **j'ai moins travaillé qu'elle** I worked less than her

> Lorsque « elle » est le complément d'objet de la phrase, il se traduit par **her**.

4. herself : **elle ne pense qu'à elle** she only thinks of herself
> **c'est à elle** it's hers
> **elle-même** herself : **elle a peint sa chambre elle-même** she painted her room herself

elles *pronom pluriel*

1. they ; **elles sont canadiennes** they are Canadian ; **elles sont toutes cassées** they are all broken
2. them : **et elles, tu les as invitées aussi ?** what about them, have you invited them as well? ; **c'est pour elles** it's for them ; **est-ce que tu peux t'occuper d'elles ?** can you look after them? ; **tu chantes mieux qu'elles** you sing better than them
3. themselves : **elles peuvent être fières d'elles** they can be proud of themselves
> **c'est à elles** it's theirs
> **elles-mêmes** themselves : **elles l'ont fait elles-mêmes** they made it themselves.

éloigner [elwaɲe] *verbe*

to move away : **éloigne le verre du bord de la table** move the glass away from the edge of the table

s'éloigner *verbe pronominal*

to move away : **la voiture s'est éloignée lentement** the car moved slowly away.

élu, e [ely] *participe passé de* **élire**.

Élysée [elize] *nom masculin*

the official residence of the French President

> 📖 ÉLYSÉE
> This is the official home of the President of France. It is an eighteenth-century palace near the **Champs-Élysées** in Paris. The **Élysée** has also come to mean the presidency itself, eg. 'The Élysée had no comment to make about the reports'.

e-mail [imεl] (*pluriel* **e-mails**) *nom masculin*

e-mail, email : **Lucas m'a envoyé la photo par e-mail** Lucas sent me the photograph by e-mail.

emballage [ābalaʒ] *nom masculin*

packaging : **garde l'emballage, ça peut être utile** keep the packaging, it may come in handy.

emballer [ābale] *verbe*

to wrap up : **j'ai emballé le cadeau** I wrapped the present up.

embarquement [ābarkəmã] *nom masculin*

boarding : **embarquement immédiat porte 12** immediate boarding gate 12.

embarquer [ābarke] *verbe*

1. to load : **il a fallu trois heures pour embarquer les marchandises** it took three hours to load the goods
2. to board : **les passagers vont embarquer** the passengers are boarding
3. *familier* to take : **qui a embarqué mon livre ?** who took my book?

s'embarquer *verbe pronominal*

to sail : **ils se sont embarqués pour les Antilles** they sailed to the West Indies
> **s'embarquer dans quelque chose** to get involved in something : **Alice s'est encore embarquée dans une histoire bizarre** Alice got involved in some strange business.

embêtant, e [ābεtã, ãt] *adjectif familier*

annoying : **j'ai oublié ma clé, c'est embêtant** that's annoying, I've forgotten my key.

embêter [ɑ̃bɛte] *verbe familier*

to annoy : **arrête d'embêter ton frère !** stop annoying your brother!

s'embêter *verbe pronominal familier*

to be bored : **on peut partir si tu t'embêtes** we can go if you're bored.

embouteillage [ɑ̃butɛjaʒ] *nom masculin*

traffic jam : **on a été pris dans les embouteillages** we were caught in traffic jams.

embrasser [ɑ̃brase] *verbe*

to kiss : **il m'a embrassée sur la joue** he kissed me on the cheek

s'embrasser *verbe pronominal*

to kiss : **je les ai vus s'embrasser** I saw them kissing.

s'embrouiller [sɑ̃bruje] *verbe pronominal*

to get muddled up : **je me suis embrouillé dans les dates** I got the dates muddled up.

émeute [emøt] *nom féminin*

riot : **des émeutes raciales** race riots.

émigré, e [emigre] *nom masculin, nom féminin*

emigrant.

émigrer [emigre] *verbe*

to emigrate : **sa famille a émigré aux États-Unis** his family emigrated to the United States.

émission [emisjɔ̃] *nom féminin*

programme *UK*, program *US* : **une émission sur la mode** a programme on fashion.

emmêler [ɑ̃mele] *verbe*

to tangle up : **tu as emmêlé tous les fils !** you've tangled up all the wires!

s'emmêler *verbe pronominal*

1. to get into a tangle : **les fils se sont emmêlés** the wires have got into a tangle
2. to get mixed up : **je me suis emmêlé dans les dates** I got the dates mixed up.

emménager [ɑ̃menaʒe] *verbe*

to move in : **ils emménagent demain dans leur nouvel appartement** they're moving into their new flat tomorrow.

emmener [ɑ̃mne] *verbe*

to take : **je t'emmène au cinéma** I'm taking you to the cinema.

émotion [emosjɔ̃] *nom féminin*

1. feeling : **je n'ai pas pu cacher mon émotion** I couldn't hide my feelings
2. emotion : **il parlait avec une grande émotion** he was speaking with great emotion
3. fright : **quelle émotion tu m'as faite !** what a fright you gave me!

émouvant, e [emuvɑ̃, ɑ̃t] *adjectif*

moving : **la fin du film est très émouvante** the end of the film is very moving.

émouvoir [emuvwar] *verbe*

to move : **le livre ne m'a pas du tout ému** the book didn't move me at all.

empêchement [ɑ̃pɛʃmɑ̃] *nom masculin*

je ne peux pas venir, j'ai un empêchement I can't come, something has come up.

empêcher [ɑ̃peʃe] *verbe*

to prevent : **empêcher quelqu'un de faire quelque chose** to prevent somebody from doing something ; **mes copains m'ont empêché de lui parler** my friends prevented me from talking to her
➤ **n'empêche que** all the same : **n'empêche que c'est vrai** it's true all the same

s'empêcher *verbe pronominal*

je n'ai pas pu m'empêcher de rire I couldn't help laughing.

empereur [ɑ̃prœr] *nom masculin*

emperor : **l'empereur du Japon** the emperor of Japan.

empiler [ɑ̃pile] *verbe*

to pile up : **Léa a empilé ses livres sur son bureau** Léa piled her books up on her desk.

empire [ɑ̃pir] *nom masculin*

empire : **l'empire romain** the Roman empire.

empirer [ɑ̃pire] *verbe*

to get worse : **la situation empire** the situation is getting worse.

emploi [ɑ̃plwa] *nom masculin*

job : **Bruno a trouvé un emploi** Bruno has found a job
➤ **l'emploi du temps** the timetable *UK* ou the schedule *US*.

employé, e [ãplwaje] *nom masculin, nom féminin*

employee.

employer [ãplwaje] *verbe*

1. to use : **ils ont employé une nouvelle méthode** they used a new method
2. to employ : **l'usine emploie deux cents personnes** the factory employs two hundred people.

empoisonner [ãpwazɔne] *verbe*

to poison : **ils ont été empoisonnés par des champignons vénéneux** they were poisoned by toadstools.

emporter [ãpɔrte] *verbe*

1. to take : **n'oublie pas d'emporter un parapluie** don't forget to take an umbrella
2. to carry away : **la rivière a emporté la barque** the river carried the boat away
> **plats à emporter** takeaway food *UK* ou food to go *US*.

empreinte [ãprɛ̃t] *nom féminin*

print : **des empreintes de pas** footprints
> **empreintes digitales** fingerprints.

emprunt [ãprœ̃] *nom masculin*

loan : **faire un emprunt** to take out a loan.

emprunter [ãprœ̃te] *verbe*

to borrow : **emprunter quelque chose à quelqu'un** to borrow something from somebody ; **Sally m'a emprunté dix euros** Sally borrowed ten euros from me.

ému, e [emy] *adjectif*

moved : **le prof avait l'air ému quand on lui a donné son cadeau** the teacher looked moved when we gave him his present.

en [ã] *préposition, pronom & adverbe*

■ *préposition*

1. in : **en 2002** in 2002 ; **en hiver** in winter ; **en septembre** in September ; **mes amis vivent en Irlande** my friends live in Ireland ; **ça fait combien en dollars ?** how much is it in dollars? ; **dire quelque chose en anglais** to say something in English
2. to : **elle retourne en Australie** she's going back to Australia
3. made of : **cette théière est en porcelaine** this teapot is made of china

Dans certains cas, « en » ne se traduit pas :

une table en métal a metal table ; **une statue en marbre** a marble statue

4. by : **on y va en train** we're going by train ; **c'est plus rapide en avion** it's quicker by plane
5. *Devant un participe présent* **je l'ai vu en sortant** I saw him as I was leaving ; **en arrivant à Paris, on a été pris dans un embouteillage** when we arrived in Paris, we got caught in a traffic jam ; **tu y arriveras en faisant un effort** you'll manage if you make an effort ; **ne parle pas en mangeant !** don't talk while you're eating! ; **il a monté l'escalier en courant** he ran upstairs ; **elle s'est cassé la jambe en tombant** she fell and broke her leg ; **il a réussi son examen en travaillant très dur** by working very hard, he managed to pass his exam

■ *pronom*

1. *Complément*

Lorsque « en » est complément d'un verbe ou d'un adjectif, sa traduction dépend de la structure qui régit ce verbe ou cet adjectif :

je m'en souviens I remember it ; **nous en avons déjà parlé** we've already spoken about it ; **j'en suis très fière** I'm very proud of it

2. *some*

Lorsque « en » indique une quantité, il se traduit par **some** dans les phrases affirmatives ainsi que dans les phrases interrogatives si l'on s'attend à une réponse positive :

il m'en reste I have some left ; **j'ai du chocolat, tu en veux ?** I've got some chocolate, do you want some?

3. *any*

« En » se traduit par **any** dans les phrases négatives ainsi que dans les phrases interrogatives lorsque l'on ignore quelle sera la réponse :

je n'en veux plus, merci I don't want any more, thank you ; **j'ai besoin d'agrafes, tu en as ?** I need some staples, do you have any?

4. *of it, of them*

« En » se traduit par **of it** ou **of them** dans les phrases où il est associé à « plusieurs », « beaucoup », « certains » ou à un chiffre :

il y en a plusieurs there are several of them ; **j'adore le chocolat, j'en mange beaucoup** I love chocolate, I eat a lot of it ; **j'en voudrais deux** I'd like two of them

■ *adverbe*
Indique la provenance **from there : la bibliothèque, j'en viens** the library, I've just come from there.

encadrer [ɑ̃kadre] *verbe*
1. **to frame : tu devrais encadrer ton diplôme** you should frame your diploma
2. **to supervise : les enfants sont bien encadrés dans ce camp** the children are well supervised in this camp.

encaisser [ɑ̃kese] *verbe*
to cash : as-tu encaissé le chèque ? have you cashed the cheque?

enceinte [ɑ̃sɛ̃t] *adjectif & nom*
■ *adjectif féminin*
pregnant : elle est enceinte de 4 mois she is 4 months pregnant
■ *nom féminin*
1. **wall : l'enceinte de la ville** the city wall
2. **speaker : Laurent a changé les enceintes de sa chaîne** Laurent has changed the speakers on his stereo.

enchanté, e [ɑ̃ʃɑ̃te] *adjectif*
1. **delighted : enchanté de faire votre connaissance** delighted to meet you
2. **enchanted : le château enchanté du magicien** the magician's enchanted castle
➤ **enchanté !** pleased to meet you!

encombrant, e [ɑ̃kɔ̃brɑ̃, ɑ̃t] *adjectif*
bulky : des valises encombrantes bulky suitcases.

encombrer [ɑ̃kɔ̃bre] *verbe*
to clutter : la chambre est encombrée de vieilles revues the bedroom is cluttered with old magazines.

encore [ɑ̃kɔr] *adverbe*
1. **still : elle l'aime encore** she still loves him
2. **again : j'ai encore oublié mes clés** I've forgotten my keys again
3. **more : est-ce que tu veux encore des carottes ?** do you want some more carrots? ; **je voudrais encore un peu de sauce** I'd like some more sauce ; **on a encore besoin de deux volontaires** we need two more volunteers
4. **even : c'est encore plus cher** it's even more expensive ; **c'est encore mieux** it's even better

➤ **pas encore** not yet : **je n'ai pas encore terminé** I haven't finished yet

Notez la place de yet en fin de phrase.

➤ **encore une fois** once more ou once again ; **encore une fois, un grand merci !** once again, thank you very much! : **si tu recommences encore une fois, tu seras puni** if you do that once more, you'll be punished
➤ **reste encore un peu** stay a bit longer.

encourager [ɑ̃kuraʒe] *verbe*
to encourage : les parents de Pat l'ont encouragée à faire des études Pat's parents encouraged her to study.

encre [ɑ̃kr] *nom féminin*
ink : écrire à l'encre to write in ink.

encyclopédie [ɑ̃siklɔpedi] *nom féminin*
encyclopedia.

endormi, e [ɑ̃dɔrmi] *adjectif*
asleep : va te coucher, tu es à moitié endormi go to bed, you're half asleep.

endormir [ɑ̃dɔrmir] *verbe*
1. **to send to sleep : cette musique m'endort** this music is sending me to sleep
2. **to put to sleep : on m'a endormie pour l'opération** I was put to sleep for the operation

s'endormir *verbe pronominal*
to fall asleep : on s'est endormis sur le canapé we fell asleep on the sofa.

endroit [ɑ̃drwa] *nom masculin*
place : c'est l'endroit où j'ai rencontré Theresa this is the place where I met Theresa
➤ **à quel endroit ?** where?
➤ **à l'endroit** the right way round *UK* ou the right way around *US* : **remets ton tee-shirt à l'endroit** put your T-shirt the right way round.

énergie [enɛrʒi] *nom féminin*
energy : je suis pleine d'énergie aujourd'hui I'm full of energy today
➤ **l'énergie nucléaire** nuclear energy
➤ **l'énergie solaire** solar energy.

énergique [enɛrʒik] *adjectif*
energetic : ma grand-mère est une femme énergique my grandmother is an energetic woman.

énerver [enɛrve] *verbe*

to annoy : **tu m'énerves avec tes plaisanteries !** you're annoying me with your jokes!

s'énerver *verbe pronominal*

1. to get annoyed : **il s'est énervé contre moi** he got annoyed with me
2. to get worked up : **ne t'énerve pas, tu vas y arriver !** don't get so worked up, you'll manage!

enfance [ɑ̃fɑ̃s] *nom féminin*

childhood : **mon père a habité là dans son enfance** my father lived there in his childhood.

enfant [ɑ̃fɑ̃] *nom masculin ou féminin*

child *(pluriel* **children***)* : **ils ont quatre enfants** they have four children

➤ **attendre un enfant** to be expecting a baby.

enfer [ɑ̃fɛr] *nom masculin*

hell : **le paradis et l'enfer** heaven and hell.

enfermer [ɑ̃fɛrme] *verbe*

to lock in : **Ludo m'a enfermé dans le placard** Ludo locked me in the cupboard

s'enfermer *verbe pronominal*

to lock oneself in : **elle s'est enfermée dans sa chambre** she locked herself in her bedroom.

enfiler [ɑ̃file] *verbe*

1. to thread : **je n'arrive pas à enfiler cette aiguille** I can't thread this needle
2. *familier* to put on : **enfile un pull et descends** put a sweater on and come downstairs.

enfin [ɑ̃fɛ̃] *adverbe*

1. at last : **enfin, vous voilà !** here you are at last!
2. finally : **et enfin, je voudrais remercier tout le monde** and finally, I'd like to thank everybody
3. well : **c'est super, enfin, c'est bien** it's great, well, it's all right.

enfler [ɑ̃fle] *verbe*

to swell up, to swell : **sa cheville a beaucoup enflé** his ankle really swelled up.

enfoncer [ɑ̃fɔ̃se] *verbe*

enfoncer quelque chose dans quelque chose to drive something into something ; **enfon-** cer un clou dans une planche to drive a nail into a plank

➤ **enfoncer une porte** to break a door down

s'enfoncer *verbe pronominal*

to give way : **le sol s'enfonçait sous leurs pas** the ground gave way under their feet

➤ **s'enfoncer dans** to sink into : **la voiture s'est enfoncée dans la boue** the car sank into the mud.

s'enfuir [sɑ̃fɥir] *verbe pronominal*

to run away : **elle s'est enfuie de chez elle** she ran away from home.

énigme [enigm] *nom féminin*

1. mystery *(pluriel* **mysteries***)* : **ce meurtre est une énigme** this murder is a mystery
2. riddle : **j'aime bien les mots croisés et les énigmes** I like crosswords and riddles.

enlever [ɑ̃lve] *verbe*

1. to move, to remove : **enlève tes affaires de là** move your things from there ; **j'essaye d'enlever la tache sur le tapis** I'm trying to remove the stain from the carpet
2. to take off : **j'enlève mon manteau, j'ai trop chaud** I'm taking my coat off, I'm too hot
3. to kidnap : **la femme du ministre a été enlevée** the minister's wife was kidnapped.

ennemi, e [ɛnmi] *nom masculin, nom féminin*

enemy *(pluriel* **enemies***)*.

ennui [ɑ̃nɥi] *nom masculin*

1. boredom : **je meurs d'ennui** I'm dying of boredom
2. problem : **Sylvia a des ennuis** Sylvia has problems OU Sylvia is in trouble

➤ **ce roman est à mourir d'ennui** this book is deadly boring.

ennuyer [ɑ̃nɥije] *verbe*

1. to bother : **ça m'ennuie de la voir si triste** it bothers me to see her so sad
2. to bore : **ses cours m'ennuient** his classes bore me

➤ **ça t'ennuierait de fermer la fenêtre ?** would you mind shutting the window?
➤ **si ça ne t'ennuie pas** if you don't mind

s'ennuyer *verbe pronominal*

to be bored : **je m'ennuie** I'm bored.

ennuyeux, euse [ɑ̃nɥijø, øz] *adjectif*

1. boring : **c'est le film le plus ennuyeux que**

j'aie jamais vu it's the most boring film I've ever seen

2. **annoying : Théo est en retard, c'est ennuyeux** it's annoying, Théo's late.

énorme [enɔrm] *adjectif*

enormous, huge : **un bâtiment énorme** an enormous building.

énormément [enɔrmemɑ̃] *adverbe*

really, enormously : **je regrette énormément de ne pas y être allé** I'm really sorry that I didn't go ; **il me plaît énormément** I like him enormously

➤ **énormément de** a great deal of : **elle a énormément de courage** she has a great deal of courage.

enquête [ɑ̃kɛt] *nom féminin*

1. investigation : **l'enquête de la police n'avance pas** the police investigation isn't making any progress

2. survey : **j'ai répondu à une enquête par téléphone** I took part in a telephone survey.

enquêter [ɑ̃kete] *verbe*

to investigate : **enquêter sur un meurtre** to investigate a murder.

enregistrement [ɑ̃rəʒistrəmɑ̃] *nom masculin*

1. recording : **un enregistrement pirate du concert** a pirate recording of the concert

2. check-in : **enregistrement des bagages** check-in.

enregistrer [ɑ̃rəʒistre] *verbe*

1. to record : **n'oublie pas d'enregistrer le documentaire** don't forget to record the documentary

2. to check in : **il faut enregistrer ses bagages une heure à l'avance** you must check in an hour in advance

3. to store : **enregistrer des données sur disquette** to store data on a floppy disk.

enrhumé, e [ɑ̃ryme] *adjectif*

être enrhumé to have a cold ; **Mathilde est très enrhumée** Mathilde has a bad cold.

s'enrhumer [sɑ̃ryme] *verbe pronominal*

to catch a cold : **couvre-toi, tu vas t'enrhumer** wrap up warm, you'll catch a cold.

s'enrichir [sɑ̃riʃir] *verbe pronominal*

to get rich : **il s'est enrichi en vendant des terrains** he got rich by selling some land.

enrouler [ɑ̃rule] *verbe*

1. to roll up : **on a enroulé le tapis pour bouger les meubles** we rolled the carpet up to move the furniture

2. to wind : **enrouler le fil autour du séchoir à cheveux** to wind the wire around the hairdryer

s'enrouler *verbe pronominal*

s'enrouler autour de quelque chose to wind around something ; **la corde s'est enroulée autour de la branche** the rope wound around the branch.

enseignant, e [ɑ̃sɛɲɑ̃, ɑ̃t] *nom masculin, nom féminin*

teacher : **combien y a-t-il d'enseignants dans cet établissement ?** how many teachers are there in this school?

enseignement [ɑ̃sɛɲmɑ̃] *nom masculin*

1. education : **l'enseignement est obligatoire jusqu'à 16 ans** education is compulsory up to 16 years old ; **l'enseignement primaire** primary education ; **l'enseignement secondaire** secondary education

2. teaching : **l'enseignement est un métier intéressant** teaching is an interesting profession ; **il est dans l'enseignement** he's a teacher.

enseigner [ɑ̃seɲe] *verbe*

to teach : **ma sœur enseigne en maternelle** my sister teaches in nursery school ; **il enseigne l'anglais** he teaches English ; **Marc enseigne l'informatique à des adultes** Marc teaches computing to adults.

ensemble [ɑ̃sɑ̃bl] *adverbe & nom*

▪ *adverbe*

together : **Clémence et Yann sont arrivés ensemble** Clémence and Yann arrived together

▪ *nom masculin*

outfit : **ma mère a un ensemble en soie bleue** my mother has got a blue silk outfit.

ensoleillé, e [ɑ̃sɔleje] *adjectif*

sunny : **une journée ensoleillée** a sunny day.

ensuite [ɑ̃sɥit] *adverbe*

then, next : **et ensuite, que s'est-il passé ?**

what happened then? OU what happened next?

entasser [ɑ̃tase] *verbe*

1. to pile up : **Nicolas a entassé des dictionnaires puis il est monté dessus** Nicolas piled up some dictionaries and then climbed on top of them
2. to squeeze : **j'ai entassé toutes mes affaires dans une valise** I squeezed all my things into one suitcase

s'entasser *verbe pronominal*

1. to pile up : **les vieux magazines s'entassent dans un coin** old magazines are piling up in a corner
2. to squeeze : **on s'est entassés à sept dans la voiture** seven of us squeezed into the car.

entendre [ɑ̃tɑ̃dr] *verbe*

to hear : **tu entends le tonnerre ?** can you hear the thunder? ; **je les ai entendus se disputer** I heard them quarrelling

➤ **entendre dire que ...** to hear that ... : **j'ai entendu dire qu'ils avaient rompu** I heard that they had broken up

➤ **entendre parler de** to hear of : **je n'avais jamais entendu parler de cet auteur** I'd never heard of this author

s'entendre *verbe pronominal*

to get on : **ils s'entendent bien** they get on well ; **Sandrine ne s'entend pas avec ses parents** Sandrine doesn't get on with her parents.

enterrement [ɑ̃tɛrmɑ̃] *nom masculin*

funeral.

enterrer [ɑ̃tere] *verbe*

to bury : **ma grand-mère est enterrée au cimetière du village** my grandmother is buried in the cemetery in the village.

s'entêter [sɑ̃tete] *verbe pronominal*

to persist : **s'entêter à faire quelque chose** to persist in doing something ; **pourquoi tu t'entêtes à travailler avec lui ?** why do you persist in working with him?

enthousiasme [ɑ̃tuzjasm] *nom masculin*

enthusiasm : **il le fait avec beaucoup d'enthousiasme** he does it with great enthusiasm.

entier, ère [ɑ̃tje, ɛr] *adjectif*

whole : **la classe entière** the whole class

➤ **en entier** whole : **j'ai refait la rédaction en entier** I rewrote the whole essay.

entièrement [ɑ̃tjɛrmɑ̃] *adverbe*

completely, entirely : **l'école a été entièrement rénovée** the school was completely renovated ; **tu as entièrement raison** you're completely right.

entorse [ɑ̃tɔrs] *nom féminin*

Christelle s'est fait une entorse à la cheville Christelle sprained her ankle.

entourer [ɑ̃ture] *verbe*

to surround : **les arbres qui entourent la maison** the trees that surround the house.

entracte [ɑ̃trakt] *nom masculin*

interval *UK*, intermission *US* : **on a mangé une glace à l'entracte** we had an ice cream in the interval.

entraînement [ɑ̃trɛnmɑ̃] *nom masculin*

1. training : **j'ai entraînement de badminton ce soir** I have badminton training tonight
2. practise *UK*, practice *US* : **je n'y arrive pas, je manque d'entraînement** I can't do it, I'm out of practise.

entraîner [ɑ̃trene] *verbe*

1. to drag : **Jean m'a entraînée sur la piste de danse** Jean dragged me onto the dance floor
2. to coach : **c'est le cousin d'Anne qui nous entraîne** Anne's cousin is coaching us

s'entraîner *verbe pronominal*

1. to train : **l'équipe de foot s'entraîne le vendredi** the football team trains on Fridays
2. to practise *UK*, to practice *US* : **Simon s'entraîne à jongler avec trois balles** Simon is practising juggling with three balls.

entraîneur, euse [ɑ̃trenœr, øz] *nom masculin, nom féminin*

coach *(pluriel* coaches*)* : **l'entraîneuse de l'équipe de basket** the basketball team's coach.

entre [ɑ̃tr] *préposition*

1. between : **le cinéma est entre la mairie et l'église** the cinema is between the town hall and the church ; **entre nous, ça m'étonnerait** between you and me, I'd be surprised
2. among : **ils se battent entre eux** they fight among themselves

➤ **l'un d'entre nous** one of us

➤ **entre autres**

1. **among other things : il y avait, entre autres, des exercices de calcul** there were, among other things, arithmetic exercises
2. **among others : Alex et Suzanne étaient là, entre autres** Alex and Suzanne were there, among others.

entrecôte [ɑ̃trəkot] *nom féminin*

entrecôte steak, rib steak.

entrée [ɑ̃tre] *nom féminin*

1. **entrance : l'entrée principale du bâtiment** the building's main entrance
2. **hall : attends dans l'entrée** wait in the hall
3. **ticket : j'ai trois entrées pour le spectacle** I have three tickets for the show
4. **starter** UK, **first course** US : **comme entrée, je prendrai la salade** I'll have the salad as a starter.

entrepôt [ɑ̃trəpo] *nom masculin*

warehouse.

entreprise [ɑ̃trəpriz] *nom féminin*

company (*pluriel* **companies**) : **une entreprise de transports** a transport company.

entrer [ɑ̃tre] *verbe*

1. **to go in : entre, moi je reste dehors** go in, I'm staying outside ; **il est entré dans le supermarché** he went into the supermarket
2. **to come in : bonjour, entrez !** hello, come in! ; **il m'a souri quand il est entré dans la pièce** he smiled at me when he came into the room ; **faire entrer quelqu'un** to let somebody in
3. **to enter : il faut entrer son mot de passe pour accéder aux fichiers** you have to enter your password to access the files
➤ **elle entre en troisième en septembre** she's moving up into the fourth year in September.

entre-temps [ɑ̃trətɑ̃] *adverbe*

meanwhile.

entretien [ɑ̃trətjɛ̃] *nom masculin*

1. **maintenance : il est chargé de l'entretien du parc** he's in charge of the park maintenance
2. **interview : un entretien d'embauche** a job interview.

entrouvert, e [ɑ̃truvɛr, ɛrt] *adjectif*

ajar : **la porte était entrouverte** the door was ajar.

envahir [ɑ̃vair] *verbe*

to invade : **les Normands ont envahi l'Europe** the Normans invaded Europe.

enveloppe [ɑ̃vlɔp] *nom féminin*

envelope : **il faut envoyer une enveloppe timbrée** you have to send a stamped addressed envelope.

envelopper [ɑ̃vlɔpe] *verbe*

to wrap : **vous pouvez me l'envelopper, s'il vous plaît ?** can you wrap it for me, please?

envers [ɑ̃vɛr] *nom masculin*

1. **back : c'est écrit sur l'envers de la feuille** it's written on the back of the page
2. **reverse side : l'envers du tissu est uni** the reverse side of the material is plain
➤ **à l'envers**
1. **inside out : tu as mis tes chaussettes à l'envers** you've put your socks on inside out
2. **upside down : le portrait est accroché à l'envers** the portrait is upside down.

envie [ɑ̃vi] *nom féminin*

➤ **avoir envie de quelque chose** to want something : **j'ai envie d'une glace** I want an ice cream
➤ **avoir envie de faire quelque chose** to want to do something OU to feel like doing something : **j'ai envie de l'inviter à danser** I want to ask him to dance ; **elle avait envie de chanter** she felt like singing.

environ [ɑ̃virɔ̃] *adverbe*

about : **il y a environ quinze ans** about fifteen years ago.

environnement [ɑ̃virɔnmɑ̃] *nom masculin*

1. **environment : la protection de l'environnement** the protection of the environment
2. **background : l'environnement familial est très important** family background is very important.

environs [ɑ̃virɔ̃] *nom masculin pluriel*

les environs d'Albi sont très jolis the area around Albi is very pretty
➤ **aux environs de** near : **ils habitent aux environs de Grenoble** they live near Grenoble.

s'envoler [sɑ̃vɔle] *verbe pronominal*

to fly away : **l'aigle s'est envolé** the eagle flew away.

envoyer [ɑ̃vwaje] *verbe*

1. to send : **mes parents m'ont envoyé un co-lis lundi dernier** my parents sent me a parcel last Monday ; **j'ai envoyé mon frère acheter du pain** I sent my brother to buy some bread ; **je lui ai envoyé un e-mail** I sent him an e-mail
2. to throw : **envoie-moi le ballon** throw me the ball.

épais, aisse [epɛ, ɛs] *adjectif*

thick : **une tranche épaisse** a thick slice.

épaisseur [epɛsœr] *nom féminin*

1. thickness : **quelle épaisseur de planche voulez-vous ?** what thickness of plank do you want? ; **quelle est l'épaisseur de la tranche ?** how thick is the slice?
2. layer : **plusieurs épaisseurs de vêtements** several layers of clothes.

épaule [epol] *nom féminin*

shoulder : **j'ai mal à l'épaule** my shoulder hurts.

épave [epav] *nom féminin*

wreck : **les plongeurs ont découvert une épave** the divers discovered a wreck.

épée [epe] *nom féminin*

sword : **les mousquetaires se battaient avec des épées** musketeers fought with swords.

épeler [eple] *verbe*

to spell : **vous pouvez épeler votre nom ?** can you spell your name?

épice [epis] *nom féminin*

spice : **la cannelle et le safran sont des épices** cinnamon and saffron are spices.

épicé, e [epise] *adjectif*

spicy : **j'aime la cuisine épicée** I like spicy food.

épicerie [episri] *nom féminin*

grocer's : **où est l'épicerie la plus proche ?** where is the nearest grocer's?
> **une épicerie fine** a delicatessen.

épicier, ère [episje, ɛr] *nom masculin, nom féminin*

grocer : **la grand-mère de Jeanne était épicière** Jeanne's grandmother was a grocer.

épidémie [epidemi] *nom féminin*

epidemic : **il y a une épidémie de grippe** there's a flu epidemic.

épinards [epinar] *nom masculin pluriel*

spinach (*ne s'utilise jamais au pluriel*) : **ces épinards sont excellents** this spinach is excellent.

épine [epin] *nom féminin*

thorn : **je me suis piqué avec une épine de rose** I pricked myself on a rose thorn.

épingle [epɛ̃gl] *nom féminin*

pin : **une épingle à cheveux** a hairpin ; **une épingle de nourrice** a safety pin.

épisode [epizɔd] *nom masculin*

episode : **j'ai raté le dernier épisode de la série** I missed the last episode in the series.

éplucher [eplyʃe] *verbe*

to peel : **tu n'as pas besoin d'éplucher les courgettes** you don't need to peel the courgettes.

éponge [epɔ̃ʒ] *nom féminin*

sponge : **éponge végétale** vegetable sponge
> **passer un coup d'éponge sur quelque chose** to give something a wipe.

éponger [epɔ̃ʒe] *verbe*

to mop up, to wipe up : **éponge vite le vin !** mop the wine up quickly!

époque [epɔk] *nom féminin*

time : **à l'époque j'habitais Paris** at the time I lived in Paris
> **à l'époque où** when : **à l'époque où j'habitais à Londres** when I lived in London.

épouser [epuze] *verbe*

to marry : **Linda a épousé un peintre** Linda married a painter.

épouvantail [epuvɑ̃taj] *nom masculin*

scarecrow.

épreuve [eprœv] *nom féminin*

1. test : **l'épreuve de maths** the maths test
2. event : **les épreuves d'athlétisme** track events.

éprouver [epruve] *verbe*

1. to feel : il éprouvait une grande tristesse he felt very sad
2. to experience : ils ont éprouvé beaucoup de difficultés they experienced a lot of difficulties.

éprouvette [epruvɛt] *nom féminin*

test tube.

EPS (*abréviation de* éducation physique et sportive) *nom féminin*
PE : nous avons EPS cet après-midi we have PE this afternoon.

épuisé, e [epɥize] *adjectif*

1. exhausted : je suis épuisée, je vais me coucher I'm exhausted, I'm going to bed
2. out of print : le livre est épuisé, je n'ai pas pu l'avoir the book is out of print, I couldn't get it.

équateur [ekwatœr] *nom masculin*

equator : sous l'équateur on the equator.

équerre [ekɛr] *nom féminin*

set square.

équestre [ekɛstr] *adjectif*

➤ un centre équestre a riding school.

équilibre [ekilibr] *nom masculin*

balance : Jonathan a perdu l'équilibre et il est tombé Jonathan lost his balance and fell ; les livres sont en équilibre sur le bord de la table the books are balanced on the edge of the table.

équilibré, e [ekilibre] *adjectif*

well-balanced : un repas équilibré a well-balanced meal.

équipage [ekipaʒ] *nom masculin*

crew : l'équipage de l'avion the plane crew.

équipe [ekip] *nom féminin*

team : l'équipe de hand the handball team ; on a travaillé par équipes we worked in teams

➤ faire équipe avec quelqu'un to team up with somebody.

équipé, e [ekipe] *adjectif*

être équipé de quelque chose to be equipped with something ; le bâtiment est équipé d'un système de sécurité the building is equipped with a security system.

équipement [ekipmɑ̃] *nom masculin*

equipment : n'oublie pas ton équipement d'escalade don't forget your climbing equipment

équipements *nom masculin pluriel*

facilities : équipements sportifs sports facilities.

équitation [ekitasjɔ̃] *nom féminin*

horseriding : faire de l'équitation to go horseriding.

équivalent, e [ekivalɑ̃, ɑ̃t] *adjectif*

equivalent

équivalent *nom masculin*

equivalent : quel est l'équivalent anglais de « jalousie » ? what's the English equivalent of "jalousie"?

ère [ɛr] *nom féminin*

era : l'ère primaire the primary era.

erreur [ɛrœr] *nom féminin*

mistake, error : il y a beaucoup d'erreurs dans son devoir there are a lot of mistakes in his homework ; par erreur by mistake.

éruption [erypsjɔ̃] *nom féminin*

eruption : la dernière éruption de l'Etna the last time Mount Etna erupted.

es ➤ être.

escalade [ɛskalad] *nom féminin*

climbing : faire de l'escalade to go climbing.

escalader [ɛskalade] *verbe*

to climb : on a dû escalader le mur we had to climb the wall.

escale [ɛskal] *nom féminin*

1. port of call : Le Caire est la première escale du bateau Cairo is the boat's first port of call
2. stopover : un vol avec escale à Amsterdam a flight with a stopover in Amsterdam
➤ faire escale à
1. to call at : le paquebot a fait escale à Pointe-à-Pitre the liner called at Pointe-à-Pitre
2. to stop over at : l'avion fera escale à Phi-

ladelphie the plane will stop over in Philadelphia.

escalier [ɛskalje] *nom masculin*

stairs (*pluriel*) : **l'escalier est raide** the stairs are steep ; **monter l'escalier** to go up the stairs ; **descendre l'escalier** to go down the stairs
➤ **un escalier roulant** an escalator.

escargot [ɛskargo] *nom masculin*

snail : **avancer comme un escargot** to go at a snail's pace.

escrime [ɛskrim] *nom féminin*

fencing : **les Français sont doués en escrime** the French are good at fencing ; **faire de l'escrime** to fence.

escroc [ɛskro] *nom masculin*

crook : **ce plombier est un escroc !** that plumber is a crook!

espace [ɛspas] *nom masculin*

space : **un voyage dans l'espace** a journey through space
➤ **les espaces verts** park.

Espagne [ɛspaɲ] *nom féminin*

➤ **l'Espagne** Spain

En anglais, à de rares exceptions près, il n'y a pas d'article devant les noms de pays :

ils vivent en Espagne they live in Spain ; **la dernière fois que je suis allée en Espagne** the last time I went to Spain.

espagnol, e [ɛspaɲɔl] *adjectif*

Spanish : **Mercedes est un prénom espagnol** Mercedes is a Spanish name

espagnol *nom masculin*

Spanish : **Pascale parle bien espagnol** Pascale speaks good Spanish

En anglais, les adjectifs se rapportant à un pays ou une région, ainsi que le nom désignant la langue de ce pays ou de cette région, s'écrivent avec une majuscule.

Espagnol, e *nom masculin, nom féminin*

Spaniard ; **un Espagnol** a Spaniard ; **les Espagnols** the Spanish.

espèce [ɛspɛs] *nom féminin*

1. species (*pluriel* **species**) : **une espèce rare de poisson** a rare species of fish
2. kind : **c'est une espèce d'appareil électronique** it's a kind of electronic device
➤ **espèce d'idiot !** you idiot!

espérer [ɛspere] *verbe*

to hope : **j'espère que tu pourras venir** I hope you'll be able to come ; **ils espèrent déménager en octobre** they're hoping to move in October.

espion, onne [ɛspjɔ̃, ɔn] *nom masculin, nom féminin*

spy (*pluriel* **spies**).

espionnage [ɛspjɔnaʒ] *nom masculin*

spying : **faire de l'espionnage** to spy ; **un roman d'espionnage** a spy novel.

espionner [ɛspjɔne] *verbe*

to spy on : **j'ai l'impression qu'elle m'espionne** I have the impression that she's spying on me.

espoir [ɛspwar] *nom masculin*

hope : **cela m'a donné de l'espoir** it gave me hope
➤ **c'est sans espoir** it's hopeless.

esprit [ɛspri] *nom masculin*

1. mind : **ça ne m'était pas venu à l'esprit** it hadn't crossed my mind
2. spirit : **l'esprit d'équipe** team spirit
3. ghost : **Martine croit aux esprits** Martine believes in ghosts.

essai [ɛsɛ] *nom masculin*

1. attempt : **Mathias a réussi au premier essai** Mathias succeeded at the first attempt
2. test : **essais nucléaires** nuclear tests
3. *Au rugby* try (*pluriel* **tries**) : **marquer un essai** to score a try.

essayer [ɛseje] *verbe*

1. to try : **essaie de finir les mots croisés** try to finish the crossword
2. to try on : **j'ai essayé la robe mais elle ne m'allait pas** I tried the dress on but it didn't fit me.

essence [ɛsɑ̃s] *nom féminin*

petrol *UK*, gas *US* : **on va s'arrêter prendre de l'essence** we'll stop to get petrol.

e

essentiel, elle [esɑ̃sjɛl] *adjectif*

1. **essential** : **c'est essentiel de savoir l'anglais** it's essential to know English
2. **basic** : **apprends au moins le vocabulaire essentiel** learn the basic vocabulary at least

   l'essentiel
1. **the main thing** : **l'essentiel, c'est que tu ne sois pas blessé** the main thing is that you aren't hurt
2. **the essentials** : **n'emportez que l'essentiel** only take the essentials.

essuie-glace [esɥiglas] (*pluriel* **essuie-glaces**) *nom masculin*

   windscreen wiper *UK*, **windshield wiper** *US*.

essuyer [esɥije] *verbe*

1. **to dry** : **c'est ton tour d'essuyer la vaisselle** it's your turn to dry the dishes
2. **to wipe** : **essuie la table, elle est sale** wipe the table, it's dirty

s'essuyer *verbe pronominal*

   to dry oneself : **je n'ai pas eu le temps de m'essuyer après mon bain** I didn't have time to dry myself after my bath ; **essuie-toi les mains** dry your hands.

est¹ [ɛst] *nom & adjectif*

◾ *nom masculin*

   east : **le soleil se lève à l'est** the sun rises in the east ; **à l'est de Nogent** to the east of Nogent

◾ *adjectif invariable*

1. **east** : **la côte est des États-Unis** the east coast of the United States
2. **eastern** : **la banlieue est** the eastern suburbs.

est² [ɛ] ➤ **être**.

est-ce que [ɛskə] *adverbe interrogatif*

   est-ce que ton dessert est bon ? is your dessert good? ; **est-ce que tu aimes le foot ?** do you like football? ; **est-ce que vous avez commencé ?** have you started? ; **est-ce qu'il vivait en France ?** did he live in France? ; **est-ce que tu étais fatigué ?** were you tired? ; **est-ce qu'on ira au British Museum ?** will we go to the British Museum?

estomac [ɛstɔma] *nom masculin*

   stomach : **j'ai mal à l'estomac** I have stomach ache *UK* ou I have a stomach ache *US*
➤ **avoir l'estomac barbouillé** to feel sick.

estrade [ɛstrad] *nom féminin*

   platform : **le bureau est sur l'estrade** the desk is on the platform.

et [e] *conjonction*

1. **and** : **un tee-shirt et une veste** a T-shirt and a jacket ; **et ensuite ...** and then ... ; **il y a deux ans et demi** two and a half years ago

   Lorsqu'il figure dans les nombres et les heures, « et » ne se traduit pas en anglais :

   vingt et un twenty-one ; **trente et un** thirty-one ; **vingt et unième** twenty-first ; **à deux heures et demie** at half past two ; **à trois heures et quart** at a quarter past three

2. *Dans une question* **what about ...?** : **et moi ?** what about me? ; **j'ai envie de rester, et toi ?** I want to stay, what about you?

établissement [etablismɑ̃] *nom masculin*

   establishment : **un établissement très chic** a very smart establishment
➤ **un établissement scolaire** a school.

étage [etaʒ] *nom masculin*

   floor : **au premier étage** on the first floor *UK* ou on the second floor *US* ; **un immeuble de quatre étages** a four-storey building *UK* ou a four-story building *US*
➤ **à l'étage** upstairs.

étagère [etaʒɛr] *nom féminin*

   shelf (*pluriel* **shelves**) : **ton classeur est sur l'étagère du haut** your folder is on the top shelf.

étais, était *etc* ➤ **être**.

étaler [etale] *verbe*

1. **to spread out** : **étale la carte par terre, on verra mieux** spread the map out on the ground, we'll see better
2. **to spread** : **elle a étalé du beurre sur son pain** she spread butter on her bread

s'étaler *verbe pronominal*

   familier **to fall flat on one's face** : **Jérémie s'est étalé au milieu de la cour** Jérémie fell flat on his face in the middle of the playground
➤ **s'étaler sur** to be spread over : **les épreuves s'étalent sur trois jours** the exams are spread over three days.

étang [etɑ̃] *nom masculin*

   pond.

étant [etɑ̃] *participe présent de* être.

étape [etap] *nom féminin*

stage : **on a fait le trajet en trois étapes** we did the journey in three stages
> **on fera étape à Caen** we'll break our journey in Caen.

état [eta] *nom masculin*

state : **dans quel état est la voiture ?** what state is the car in? ; **être en état de faire quelque chose** to be in a fit state to do something ; **être hors d'état de faire quelque chose** to be in no fit state to do something
> **un état d'esprit** a state of mind
> **en bon état** in good condition
> **en mauvais état** in poor condition
> **être dans tous ses états** to be in a state
> **remettre en état** to repair

État *nom masculin*

state : **les États membres de l'Union européenne** the member states of the European Union.

États-Unis [etazyni] *nom masculin pluriel*

> **les États-Unis** the United States : **j'aimerais vivre aux États-Unis** I'd like to live in the United States ; **toute la classe est allée aux États-Unis** the whole class went to the United States.

été[1] [ete] *nom masculin*

summer : **en été** in the summer OU in summer ; **l'été dernier** last summer.

été[2] [ete] *participe passé invariable de* être.

éteindre [etɛ̃dr] *verbe*

1. **to turn off, to switch off** : **Loïc n'a pas voulu éteindre la télé** Loïc didn't want to turn the TV off
2. **to put out** : **ils ont réussi à éteindre l'incendie** they managed to put the fire out

s'éteindre *verbe pronominal*

to go out : **le feu s'est éteint tout seul** the fire went out on its own.

étendre [etɑ̃dr] *verbe*

1. **to spread** : **aide-moi à étendre la nappe** help me to spread the tablecloth
2. **to lay** : **les infirmiers ont étendu le blessé par terre** the nurses laid the injured man on the ground
> **étendre le linge** to hang out the washing

s'étendre *verbe pronominal*

1. **to lie down** : **étendez-vous si vous êtes fatigué** lie down if you're tired
2. **to stretch** : **le village s'étend jusqu'à la forêt** the village stretches as far as the forest
3. **to spread** : **l'épidémie s'est étendue à toute la région** the epidemic spread throughout the region.

étendu, e [etɑ̃dy] *verbe & adjectif*

■ *participe passé de* étendre.
■ *adjectif*
1. **lying** : **Patricia était étendue sur le canapé** Patricia was lying on the sofa
2. **outstretched** : **les bras étendus** with outstretched arms
3. **wide** : **une plaine étendue** a wide plain.

éternité [etɛrnite] *nom féminin*

il y a une éternité que je ne t'ai vu I haven't seen you for ages ; **ça a duré une éternité** it lasted for ages.

éternuer [etɛrnɥe] *verbe*

to sneeze : **ce parfum me fait éternuer** that perfume is making me sneeze.

êtes ➤ être.

étiez, étions *etc* ➤ être.

étincelle [etɛ̃sɛl] *nom féminin*

spark : **le feu faisait des étincelles** the fire was throwing off sparks.

étiquette [etikɛt] *nom féminin*

label : **une étiquette autocollante** a self-adhesive label.

s'étirer [setire] *verbe pronominal*

to stretch : **le chat s'étire près du feu** the cat is stretching by the fire.

étoile [etwal] *nom féminin*

star : **on a regardé les étoiles dans le ciel** we watched the stars in the sky ; **un hôtel trois étoiles** a three-star hotel
> **une étoile filante** a shooting star
> **une étoile de mer** a starfish
> **dormir à la belle étoile** to sleep out in the open.

étonnant, e [etɔnɑ̃, ɑ̃t] *adjectif*

surprising : **c'est étonnant qu'il ne t'ait rien dit** it's surprising that he didn't say anything to you.

étonner [etɔne] *verbe*

to surprise : **ça ne m'étonne pas du tout** it doesn't surprise me at all ; **ça m'étonnerait !** that would surprise me!

étouffant, e [etufɑ̃, ɑ̃t] *adjectif*

stifling : **une chaleur étouffante** stifling heat.

étouffer [etufe] *verbe*

to suffocate : **son agresseur a essayé de l'étouffer** his attacker tried to suffocate him ; **j'étouffe, ouvre la fenêtre** I'm suffocating, open the window

s'étouffer *verbe pronominal*

to choke : **Karine s'est étouffée en mangeant** Karine choked as she was eating.

étourderie [eturdəri] *nom féminin*

careless mistake : **ce n'est pas une faute grave, juste une étourderie** it's nothing serious, just a careless mistake.

étourdi, e [eturdi] *adjectif*

scatterbrained : **elle est étourdie** she's scatterbrained ou she's a scatterbrain.

étrange [etrɑ̃ʒ] *adjectif*

strange : **un bonhomme étrange** a strange fellow.

étranger, ère [etrɑ̃ʒe, ɛr] *adjectif & nom*

■ *adjectif*
foreign : **les pays étrangers** foreign countries

■ *nom masculin, nom féminin*
foreigner : **c'est un étranger** he's a foreigner

➤ **à l'étranger** abroad : **tu es déjà allé à l'étranger ?** have you ever been abroad?

étrangler [etrɑ̃gle] *verbe*

to strangle : **dans le film, le mari étrangle la femme** in the film the husband strangles the wife

s'étrangler *verbe pronominal*

to choke : **j'ai failli m'étrangler avec un os** I almost choked on a bone.

être [ɛtr] *nom & verbe*

■ *nom masculin*
being : **les êtres vivants** living beings ; **les êtres humains** human beings

■ *verbe*

1. to be : **je suis malade** I am ill ; **le père de Jeanne est médecin** Jeanne's father is a doctor ; **Marc est à Cannes en ce moment** Marc is in Cannes at the moment ; **James est de Newcastle** James is from Newcastle ; **quel jour sommes-nous ?** what day is it today? ; **ce blouson est à Jean-Luc** this jacket is Jean-Luc's ; **quelle heure est-il ?** what time is it? ; **il est dix heures dix** it's ten past ten *UK* ou it's ten after ten *US*

> « Être » sert à former le passif : « être » + participe passé en français se traduit par **to be** + participe passé en anglais :

la maison a été vendue the house has been sold

2. *Lorsque « être » signifie aller* to go : **on a été en Martinique l'été dernier** we went to Martinique last summer ; **est-ce que tu as déjà été à Sydney ?** have you ever been to Sydney?

3. *Pour former le passé composé*

> Lorsqu'il sert à former le passé composé, « être » se traduit par **to have** si l'on parle d'une action qui n'est pas encore terminée ou qui se situe de façon imprécise dans le passé :

tu es déjà allé en Chine ? have you ever been to China? ; **il n'est pas encore parti** he hasn't left yet

> « Être » + participe passé se traduit par un prétérit en anglais si l'action est complètement terminée et lorsqu'on précise le moment où l'action a eu lieu :

j'ai attendu mais Romain n'est pas venu I waited but Romain didn't come ; **il est parti il y a une heure** he left an hour ago ; **on est allés au cinéma hier** we went to the cinema yesterday

4. *Pour former d'autres temps* to have : **les filles étaient déjà parties** the girls had already left.

étrennes [etrɛn] *nom féminin pluriel*

1. New Year's Day present : **ma grand-mère nous donne toujours des étrennes** my grandmother always gives us a New Year's Day present

2. Christmas box *UK* : **les étrennes du facteur** the postman's Christmas box.

étroit, e [etrwa, at] *adjectif*

1. narrow : **une rue étroite** a narrow street

2. tight : ce pull est un peu **étroit** this sweater is a bit tight

➤ **être à l'étroit** to be cramped.

étude [etyd] *nom féminin*

1. **study** (*pluriel* **studies**) : **une étude sur le comportement des baleines** a study on the behaviour of whales

2. **study time** *UK*, **study hall** *US* : **j'ai deux heures d'étude entre les cours** I have two hours' study time between classes

études *nom féminin pluriel*

studies : **des études de commerce** business studies

➤ **faire des études** to study : **Sophie fait des études d'informatique** Sophie is studying computing.

étudiant, e [etydjã, ãt] *nom masculin, nom féminin*

student : **des étudiants en droit** law students.

étudier [etydje] *verbe*

to study : **elle étudie le chinois** she's studying Chinese ; **Douglas étudie à Manchester** Douglas is studying in Manchester.

étui [etɥi] *nom masculin*

case : **un étui à lunettes** a glasses case.

eu, eue [y] *participe passé de* **avoir**.

euro [øro] *nom masculin*

euro : **combien ça fait en euros ?** how much is it in euros?

Europe [ørɔp] *nom féminin*

➤ **l'Europe** Europe

En anglais, il n'y a pas d'article devant les noms de continents :

une partie de la Turquie se trouve en Europe part of Turkey is in Europe ; **ils sont venus en Europe pour faire leurs études** they came to Europe to study.

européen, enne [ørɔpeɛ̃, ɛn] *adjectif*

European : **les pays européens** European countries

En anglais, les adjectifs se rapportant à un continent s'écrivent avec une majuscule.

Européen, enne *nom masculin, nom féminin*

European.

eux [ø] *pronom*

1. **them** : **elle a peur d'eux** she's afraid of them ; **j'y suis allé avec eux** I went with them ; **Cyril est plus âgé qu'eux** Cyril is older than them

2. **they** : **ce sont eux qui me l'ont dit** they are the ones who told me ou THEY told me ; **qui veut rester ? – eux** who wants to stay? – they do

3. **themselves** : **ils ne pensent qu'à eux** they only think of themselves

➤ **c'est à eux** it's theirs

➤ **eux-mêmes** themselves : **ils l'ont fait eux-mêmes** they made it themselves.

évacuer [evakɥe] *verbe*

to evacuate : **toute la population a été évacuée** the whole population was evacuated.

s'évader [sevade] *verbe pronominal*

to escape : **deux prisonniers se sont évadés des Baumettes** two prisoners escaped from les Baumettes.

évaluer [evalɥe] *verbe*

1. **to estimate** : **la distance est difficile à évaluer** the distance is difficult to estimate

2. **to value** : **le tableau a été évalué à un million d'euros** the painting was valued at one million euros.

s'évanouir [sevanwir] *verbe pronominal*

to faint : **Lise s'est évanouie au milieu du cours de géo** Lise fainted in the middle of the geography lesson.

évasion [evazjõ] *nom féminin*

escape : **la Grande Évasion** the Great Escape.

événement [evɛnmã] *nom masculin*

event : **c'est un grand événement** it's a big event.

éventail [evãtaj] *nom masculin*

fan : **Thierry m'a rapporté un éventail d'Espagne** Thierry brought me back a fan from Spain.

éventuellement [evɑ̃tɥɛlmɑ̃] *adverbe*

possibly : il viendrait éventuellement avec sa sœur he might possibly come with his sister

 Éventuellement is a false friend, it does not mean 'eventually'.

évidemment [evidamɑ̃] *adverbe*

of course : tu es sûr ? – évidemment ! are you sure? – of course!

évident, e [evidɑ̃, ɑ̃t] *adjectif*

obvious : c'est évident que tu lui plais it's obvious he likes you
> **pas évident** not that easy : cet exercice n'est pas évident this exercise isn't that easy.

évier [evje] *nom masculin*

sink : la vaisselle est dans l'évier the dishes are in the sink.

éviter [evite] *verbe*

1. to avoid : évitez de manger entre les repas avoid eating between meals
2. to save : ça m'évitera de revenir it will save me coming back.

évoluer [evɔlɥe] *verbe*

to evolve : les nouvelles technologies évoluent sans cesse new technologies are constantly evolving.

évoquer [evɔke] *verbe*

to evoke : il évoqua ses souvenirs d'enfance he evoked his childhood memories.

exact, e [ɛgzakt] *adjectif*

exact : vous avez l'heure exacte ? have you got the exact time? OU have you got the right time?
> **c'est exact** that's right.

exactement [ɛgzaktəmɑ̃] *adverbe*

exactly.

ex æquo [ɛgzeko] *adjectif invariable, nom masculin ou féminin invariable & adverbe*

equal : elle est arrivée troisième ex æquo she came in equal third OU she tied for third place.

exagérer [ɛgzaʒere] *verbe*

1. to exaggerate : tu exagères, ce n'était pas si mauvais que ça you're exaggerating, it wasn't that bad
2. to go too far : cette fois, tu exagères ! you're going too far this time!

examen [ɛgzamɛ̃] *nom masculin*

1. exam : on a un examen d'anglais lundi we have an English exam on Monday
2. examination : examen médical medical examination.

examiner [ɛgzamine] *verbe*

to examine : le docteur m'a examiné the doctor examined me.

excellent, e [ɛksɛlɑ̃, ɑ̃t] *adjectif*

excellent : Martha est excellente en anglais Martha is excellent at English.

excentrique [ɛksɑ̃trik] *adjectif*

eccentric.

exception [ɛksɛpsjɔ̃] *nom féminin*

exception : faire une exception to make an exception.

exceptionnel, elle [ɛksɛpsjɔnɛl] *adjectif*

exceptional : dans des circonstances exceptionnelles in exceptional circumstances
> **c'est un cas exceptionnel** it's a special case.

excité, e [ɛksite] *adjectif*

excited.

exclamation [ɛksklamasjɔ̃] *nom féminin*

exclamation : un point d'exclamation an exclamation mark *UK* OU an exclamation point *US*.

s'exclamer [sɛksklame] *verbe pronominal*

to exclaim.

exclure [ɛksklyr] *verbe*

1. to exclude : elle ne voulait pas être exclue de la bande she didn't want to be excluded from the group
2. to expel : Philippe a été exclu de l'école Philippe was expelled from school.

excursion [ɛkskyrsjɔ̃] *nom féminin*

trip : faire une excursion to go on a trip.

excuse [εkskyz] *nom féminin*

excuse : **c'est un peu faible comme excuse !** it's a rather weak excuse!

excuses *nom féminin pluriel*

apology : **tu lui dois des excuses** you owe him an apology ; **faire des excuses à quelqu'un** to apologize to somebody ; **je refuse de lui faire des excuses !** I refuse to apologize to her!

excuser [εkskyze] *verbe*

1. to excuse : **excusez-moi, où est la gare ?** excuse me, where is the station? ; **n'essaie pas de l'excuser** don't try to excuse him
2. to be sorry : **excuse-moi, je ne l'ai pas fait exprès** I'm sorry, I didn't do it on purpose

s'excuser *verbe pronominal*

1. to apologize : **il ne s'est même pas excusé d'être arrivé en retard** he didn't even apologize for arriving late
2. to be sorry : **je m'excuse de ne pas être venu** I'm sorry I didn't come.

exécuter [εgzekyte] *verbe*

to execute : **il a été exécuté** he was executed.

exemplaire [εgzɑ̃plεr] *nom masculin*

copy *(pluriel* copies*)* : **j'ai deux exemplaires de ce livre** I've got two copies of this book.

exemple [εgzɑ̃pl] *nom masculin*

example : **donnez-moi un exemple concret** give me a concrete example
➤ **par exemple** for example OU for instance.

s'exercer [sεgzεrse] *verbe*

to practise *UK*, to practice *US* : **il faut s'exercer tous les jours** you need to practise everyday ; **exerce-toi à chanter en anglais** practise singing in English.

exercice [εgzεrsis] *nom masculin*

exercise : **est-ce que tu as fait tes exercices de chimie ?** have you done your chemistry exercises? ; **je ne fais pas assez d'exercice** I don't get enough exercise.

exiger [εgziʒe] *verbe*

to demand : **le professeur a exigé le silence**

the teacher demanded silence OU the teacher demanded that the pupils be quiet.

exister [εgziste] *verbe*

to exist : **cette coutume n'existe plus** this custom no longer exists
➤ **il existe**
1. there is : **il n'existe pas de traduction exacte** there isn't an exact translation
2. there are : **il existe plusieurs temps du passé** there are several past tenses.

exotique [εgzɔtik] *adjectif*

exotic.

expédier [εkspedje] *verbe*

to send : **j'ai expédié le colis jeudi** I sent the parcel on Thursday.

expéditeur, trice [εkspeditœr, tris] *nom masculin, nom féminin*

sender.

expérience [εksperjɑ̃s] *nom féminin*

1. experience : **avoir de l'expérience** to have experience OU to be experienced ; **est-ce que vous avez de l'expérience en photographie ?** do you have any experience in photography? ; **l'expérience professionnelle** professional experience
2. experiment : **on a fait des expériences en chimie** we did some experiments in the chemistry lesson.

explication [εksplikasjɔ̃] *nom féminin*

explanation : **il ne m'a donné aucune explication** he didn't give me any explanation
➤ **explication de texte** *critical analysis of a text.*

expliquer [εksplike] *verbe*

1. to explain : **explique-moi, je n'ai pas compris** explain it to me, I didn't understand
2. to analyse *UK*, to analyze *US* : **expliquez le texte en une heure** analyse the text in one hour
➤ **explique-moi pourquoi tu as fait ça** tell me why you did it.

exploit [εksplwa] *nom masculin*

feat.

exploiter [εksplwate] *verbe*

to exploit : **il ne reste plus de ressources naturelles à exploiter** there are no more natural resources left to exploit ; **il a l'impres-**

e

sion d'être exploité he thinks he's being exploited.

explorer [ɛksplɔre] *verbe*

to explore : **Champlain a exploré les Grands Lacs nord-américains** Champlain explored the Great Lakes in North America.

exploser [ɛksploze] *verbe*

to explode : **la bombe a explosé** the bomb exploded.

explosif [ɛksplozif] *nom masculin*

explosive.

explosion [ɛksplozjɔ̃] *nom féminin*

explosion : **on a entendu une grande explosion** we heard a loud explosion.

exporter [ɛkspɔrte] *verbe*

to export.

exposé [ɛkspoze] *nom masculin*

talk, presentation : **j'ai fait un exposé sur New York** I gave a talk on New York OU I gave a presentation on New York.

exposer [ɛkspoze] *verbe*

to show : **ils exposaient ses tableaux de jeunesse** they were showing his early paintings

s'exposer *verbe pronominal*

s'exposer au soleil to stay in the sun ; **tu ne devrais pas t'exposer trop longtemps au soleil** you shouldn't stay in the sun too long.

exposition [ɛkspozisjɔ̃] *nom féminin*

exhibition *UK*, exhibit *US* : **on a été voir une exposition de photos** we went to see a photography exhibition.

exprès [ɛksprɛ] *adverbe*

on purpose : **je ne l'ai pas fait exprès** I didn't do it on purpose.

expression [ɛkspresjɔ̃] *nom féminin*

expression : **il a une drôle d'expression sur le visage** he has a funny expression on his face
➤ **une expression idiomatique** an idiom.

exprimer [ɛksprime] *verbe*

to express : **exprimer ses sentiments** to express one's feelings

s'exprimer *verbe pronominal*

to express oneself : **laisse-la s'exprimer** let her express herself.

extensible [ɛkstɑ̃sibl] *adjectif*

stretch : **tissu extensible** stretch fabric.

extérieur, e [ɛksterjœr] *adjectif*

outside : **c'est dans la poche extérieure de ma veste** it's in the outside pocket of my jacket

extérieur *nom masculin*

outside : **l'extérieur de la boîte** the outside of the box
➤ **à l'extérieur** outside : **il fait trop froid pour manger à l'extérieur** it's too cold to eat outside
➤ **à l'extérieur de** outside : **les toilettes sont à l'extérieur de la maison** the toilet is outside the house.

externe [ɛkstɛrn] *adjectif & nom*

■ *adjectif*
outer, external
■ *nom masculin ou féminin*
day pupil : **les externes ne mangent pas à la cantine** day pupils don't have school dinners.

extincteur [ɛkstɛ̃ktœr] *nom masculin*

fire extinguisher.

extraordinaire [ɛkstraɔrdinɛr] *adjectif*

extraordinary.

extraterrestre [ɛkstraterɛstr] *adjectif & nom masculin ou féminin*

alien, extraterrestrial.

extrême [ɛkstrɛm] *adjectif*

extreme : **des sports extrêmes** extreme sports
➤ **l'Extrême-Orient** the Far East.

extrémité [ɛkstremite] *nom féminin*

end : **à l'extrémité de la rue** at the end of the street ; **à l'autre extrémité de la plage** at the other end of the beach.

fabriquer [fabrike] *verbe*

to make : **je l'ai fabriqué moi-même** I made it myself
➤ **fabriqué en France** made in France
➤ **qu'est-ce qu'elle fabrique ?** *familier* what is she up to?

fac [fak] *(abréviation de* faculté*) nom féminin familier*

college : **son frère est en fac** OU **son frère est à la fac** his brother is at college *UK* OU his brother is in college *US*.

façade [fasad] *nom féminin*

facade.

face [fas] *nom féminin*

side : **c'est sur la face B de la cassette** it's on the B-side of the tape
➤ **en face**
1. across the road : **ils habitent en face** they live across the road
2. to somebody's face : **tu aurais pu me le dire en face !** you could have told me to my face!
➤ **en face de**
1. opposite : **Carole habite en face de la gare** Carole lives opposite the station
2. in front of : **regarde en face de toi** look in front of you
➤ **d'en face** opposite : **ils habitaient l'immeuble d'en face** they lived in the building opposite.

fâché, e [faʃe] *adjectif*

angry : **ma mère était très fâchée** my mother was very angry.

se fâcher [səfaʃe] *verbe pronominal*

1. to get angry : **ne te fâche pas** don't get angry
2. to have a row : **il s'est fâché avec sa sœur** he had a row with his sister.

facile [fasil] *adjectif*

easy : **c'est facile à faire** it's easy to do.

facilement [fasilmã] *adverbe*

easily : **il peut le faire très facilement** he can do it very easily.

façon [fasɔ̃] *nom féminin*

way : **il y a différentes façons de le faire** there are different ways of doing it
➤ **de toute façon** anyway OU in any case : **je n'aurais pas pu venir de toute façon** I couldn't have come anyway OU I couldn't have come in any case.

facteur, trice [faktœr, tris] *nom masculin, nom féminin*

postman *(féminin* **postwoman***)*, **mailman** *US*.

facture [faktyr] *nom féminin*

1. bill : **facture de téléphone** phone bill
2. invoice : **je ne retrouve plus la facture du plombier** I can't find the plumber's invoice.

facultatif, ive [fakyltatif, iv] *adjectif*

optional : **une matière facultative** an optional subject.

fade [fad] *adjectif*

bland : **c'est un plat assez fade** it's a rather bland dish.

faible [fɛbl] *adjectif*

weak : **je me sens faible** I feel weak
➤ **elle est très faible en français** she's not very good at French.

faille [faj] ➤ falloir.

faillir [fajir] *verbe*

faillir faire quelque chose to almost do something ; **j'ai failli rater mon train** I almost missed my train.

faillite [fajit] *nom féminin*

bankruptcy
➤ **faire faillite** to go bankrupt : **l'entreprise a fait faillite** the company went bankrupt.

faim [fɛ̃] *nom féminin*

1. **hunger** : **faire une grève de la faim** to go on a hunger strike
2. **starvation** : **tous les jours, des gens meurent de faim** every day, people die of starvation
➤ **avoir faim** to be hungry : **je n'ai pas très faim** I'm not very hungry.

fainéant, e ➤ feignant.

faire [fɛr] *verbe*

Les deux traductions les plus courantes de « faire » au sens de « réaliser » sont do et make. Do s'utilise lorsqu'on ne donne pas de précision sur l'activité ou lorsqu'on parle de tâches ménagères ou de travail en général. Make rend l'idée de création ou de préparation :

1. **to do** : **qu'est-ce que tu fais ?** what are you doing? ; **fais ce que tu veux** do what you like ; **je déteste faire la vaisselle** I hate doing the washing-up ; **qu'est-ce qu'il fait dans la vie ?** what does he do for a living? ; **je lui ai dit de réserver mais il ne l'a pas fait** I told him to book but he didn't do it ; **le train fait du 350 km/h** the train does 350 km/h
2. **to make** : **je fais de la soupe pour dîner** I'm making soup for dinner ; **faisons une carte de la région** let's make a map of the area
3. **to play** : **faire du foot** to play football ; **Alex fait de la clarinette** Alex plays the clarinet
4. **to be** : **ça fait combien ?** how much is it? ; **ça fait trente euros** it's thirty euros ; **la table fait 2 m de long** the table is 2 m long ; **Sylvian fait au moins 80 kilos** Sylvian is at least 80 kilos OU Sylvian weighs at least 80 kilos ; **il fait beau** the weather is fine ; **il fait déjà jour** it's light already ; **il faisait chaud** it was hot ; **2 et 2 font 4** 2 and 2 are 4
5. **to look** : **elle ne fait pas son âge** she doesn't look her age
6. *En parlant de la durée, du moment* **ça fait six mois que je ne l'ai pas vu** I haven't seen him for six months ; **ça fait une heure que Louise a appelé** Louise called an hour ago

FOR ET AGO :
Ago est utilisé pour parler du moment où s'est passé quelque chose (ça fait trois ans qu'ils ont déménagé they moved house three years ago), tandis que for insiste sur la durée écoulée (ça fait une heure que je t'attends I've been waiting for you for an hour).

➤ **ça ne fait rien** it doesn't matter
➤ **fais comme chez toi** make yourself at home
➤ **ne faire que ...** to do nothing but ... : **elle ne fait que bavarder** she does nothing but talk
➤ **faire faire quelque chose** to have something done OU to get something done : **on a fait réparer la voiture** we had the car repaired
➤ **faire faire quelque chose à quelqu'un** to make somebody do something : **le professeur d'anglais nous fait beaucoup travailler** the English teacher makes us work hard

se faire *verbe pronominal*

1. **to make, to make oneself** : **je vais me faire un café** I'm going to make a coffee OU I'm going to make myself a coffee
2. *Avec un infinitif* **Patou s'est fait opérer** Patou had an operation ; **il s'est fait arrêter** he got arrested OU he was arrested ; **où est-ce que tu te fais couper les cheveux ?** where do you have your hair cut?
➤ **ça ne se fait pas** it's not done OU it's not the done thing : **ça ne se fait pas de montrer les gens du doigt** it's not done to point at people OU it's not nice to point at people
➤ **s'en faire** to worry : **ne t'en fais pas, je vais m'en occuper** don't worry, I'll deal with it.

faire-part [fɛrpar] *(pluriel* **faire-part***) nom masculin*

announcement : **un faire-part de mariage** a wedding announcement.

fais, fait *etc* ➤ faire.

faisan [fəzɑ̃] *nom masculin*

pheasant.

faisons ➤ faire.

fait¹, e [fɛ, fɛt] *verbe & adjectif*

■ *participe passé de* faire
tu as fait tes devoirs ? have you done your homework?

■ *adjectif*

made : **c'est fait en bois** it's made of wood
➤ **c'est fait à la main** it's handmade
➤ **c'est bien fait pour lui** it serves him right.

fait² [fɛ] *nom masculin*

fact : **c'est un fait** it's a fact
➤ **faits divers** news in brief : **la rubrique faits divers** the news in brief section
➤ **au fait** by the way : **au fait, est-ce que tu l'as revue ?** by the way, did you see her again?
➤ **en fait** actually OU in fact : **en fait, je ne m'en souviens même pas** actually, I don't even remember
➤ **aller droit au fait** to go straight to the point.

faites ➤ faire.

falaise [falɛz] *nom féminin*

cliff.

falloir [falwar] *verbe (This verb is only used in the third person or in the infinitive)*

1. *Pour dire ce dont on a besoin* **il me faut plus de temps** I need more time ; **il nous faudrait un atlas** we need an atlas ; **il me faudrait deux kilos de pommes, s'il vous plaît** I'd like two kilos of apples, please
2. *Pour dire ce que l'on doit faire* **il faut que je parte** I must go OU I have to go ; **il faut les prévenir si tu arrives tard** you must warn them if you arrive late ; **il faudrait que je leur écrive** I should write to them

> Must indique ce qui est bien du point de vue moral, de la santé, etc., qu'il s'agisse d'une obligation ou d'une recommandation. Have to indique une obligation imposée par les circonstances.

3. *Devant une durée* **il faut deux heures pour aller à Cambridge** it takes two hours to get to Cambridge ; **il m'a fallu trois jours** it took me three days.

fallu [faly] *participe passé invariable de* falloir.

fameux, euse [famø, øz] *adjectif*

1. *famous* : **c'est lui, le fameux Cédric ?** is that the famous Cédric?
2. *familier* **excellent** : **il est fameux ton gâteau** your cake is excellent
➤ **pas fameux** *familier* nothing great : **le CD n'est pas fameux** the CD is nothing great.

familial, e, aux [familjal, o] *adjectif*

family : **une réunion familiale** a family gathering.

familier, ère [familje, ɛr] *adjectif*

informal : **c'est un mot familier** it's an informal word.

famille [famij] *nom féminin*

1. **family** *(pluriel* families*)* : **sa famille a déménagé** his family has moved
2. **relatives** : **j'ai de la famille aux États-Unis** I have relatives in the United States
➤ **une famille d'accueil** a host family : **j'ai passé l'été à Brighton dans une famille d'accueil** I spent the summer in Brighton with a host family
➤ **une famille monoparentale** a single-parent family
➤ **une famille nombreuse** a large family.

fan [fan] *nom masculin ou féminin familier*

fan : **un fan de jazz** a jazz fan.

fané, e [fane] *adjectif*

withered : **les coquelicots sont fanés** the poppies are withered.

fanfare [fɑ̃far] *nom féminin*

brass band : **Kevin fait partie de la fanfare** Kevin is in the brass band.

fantaisie [fɑ̃tezi] *nom féminin*

imagination : **elle manque de fantaisie** she has no imagination
➤ **des bijoux fantaisie** costume jewellery *UK* OU costume jewelery *US*.

fantastique [fɑ̃tastik] *adjectif*

1. **fantastic** : **c'était fantastique !** it was fantastic!
2. **fantasy** : **un roman fantastique** a fantasy novel.

fantôme [fɑ̃tom] *nom masculin*

ghost : **tu crois aux fantômes ?** do you believe in ghosts?

farce [fars] *nom féminin*

1. **practical joke, trick** : **ils ont fait une farce à la prof** they played a practical joke on the teacher OU they played a trick on the teacher
2. **stuffing** : **préparez la farce pour la dinde** prepare the stuffing for the turkey
➤ **un magasin de farces et attrapes** a joke shop *UK* OU a novelty store *US*.

123

farceur, euse [farsœr, øz] *nom masculin, nom féminin*
joker.

farcir [farsir] *verbe*
to stuff : **farcir les tomates avec le mélange** stuff the tomatoes with the mixture.

fard [far] *nom masculin*
make-up
➤ **du fard à joues** blusher
➤ **du fard à paupières** eyeshadow.

farine [farin] *nom féminin*
flour : **de la farine de blé** wheat flour.

fasciner [fasine] *verbe*
to fascinate.

fasse, fassions *etc* ➤ faire.

fast-food [fastfud] *(pluriel **fast-foods**) nom masculin*
fast-food restaurant.

fatigant, e [fatigɑ̃, ɑ̃t] *adjectif*
1. tiring : **j'ai eu une journée fatigante** I had a tiring day
2. tiresome : **il est fatigant avec ses histoires** he's tiresome with his stories.

fatigue [fatig] *nom féminin*
tiredness
➤ **je suis mort de fatigue** I'm dead tired.

fatigué, e [fatige] *adjectif*
tired : **allonge-toi si tu es fatigué** lie down if you're tired.

fatiguer [fatige] *verbe*
to tire : **cette marche l'a fatigué** the walk tired him
➤ **tu me fatigues avec tes questions** you're getting on my nerves with your questions.

faucher [foʃe] *verbe familier*
to steal, to pinch *UK*, to swipe *US* : **on m'a fauché mon vélo** somebody stole my bike.

faucon [fokɔ̃] *nom masculin*
hawk.

faudra ➤ falloir.

se faufiler [səfofile] *verbe pronominal*
j'ai réussi à me faufiler dans la foule I managed to work my way through the crowd ; **il s'est faufilé dans la salle sans qu'on l'aperçoive** he slipped into the room without being seen.

faune [fon] *nom féminin*
fauna : **la faune et la flore** the flora and fauna.

faut ➤ faire.

faute [fot] *nom féminin*
1. mistake : **faire une faute** to make a mistake ; **tu as fait très peu de fautes** you made very few mistakes
2. fault : **ce n'est pas de ma faute** it's not my fault
3. *Au football* foul : **il a commis une faute contre Zidane** he fouled Zidane
4. *Au tennis* fault : **une faute de pied** a foot fault
➤ **une faute de frappe** a keying error
➤ **une faute d'orthographe** a spelling mistake.

fauteuil [fotœj] *nom masculin*
armchair : **un fauteuil en cuir** a leather armchair
➤ **un fauteuil roulant** a wheelchair.

faux, fausse [fo, fos] *adjectif*
1. wrong : **tes calculs sont faux** your calculations are wrong
2. false : **le dauphin est un mammifère, vrai ou faux ?** dolphins are mammals, true or false? ; **une fausse alerte** a false alarm
3. fake : **des faux diamants** fake diamonds
4. forged : **des faux billets** forged banknotes
➤ **faux ami** false friend : **« librairie » et « library » sont des faux amis** "librairie" and "library" are false friends
➤ **chanter faux** to sing out of tune
➤ **jouer faux** to play out of tune
➤ **ce que tu dis est faux** what you're saying isn't true.

faveur [favœr] *nom féminin*
favour *UK*, favor *US* : **ils sont en faveur d'une réforme** they are in favour of a reform.

favorable [favɔrabl] *adjectif*
favourable *UK*, favorable *US* : **des conditions favorables** favourable conditions

> **ils sont favorables à une réforme** they are in favour of a reform.

favori, ite [favɔri, it] *adjectif & nom masculin, nom féminin*

favourite *UK*, favorite *US*.

favoriser [favɔrize] *verbe*

to favour *UK*, to favor *US* : **ils ont toujours favorisé son petit frère** they have always favoured his younger brother.

fax [faks] *nom masculin*

fax : **envoie-moi un fax** send me a fax ; **Thomas vient d'acheter un fax** Thomas has just bought a fax OU Thomas has just bought a fax machine.

faxer [fakse] *verbe*

to fax : **je te faxerai la réponse** I'll fax the answer to you.

féculent [fekylɑ̃] *nom masculin*

starchy food : **évitez les féculents** avoid starchy foods.

fée [fe] *nom féminin*

fairy *(pluriel* **fairies***)* : **un conte de fées** a fairy tale.

feignant, e [fɛɲɑ̃, ɑ̃t] **fainéant, e** [fɛneɑ̃, ɑ̃t] *adjectif & nom*
- *adjectif*
lazy : **elle est très feignante** she's very lazy
- *nom masculin, nom féminin*
lazybones : **c'est un feignant** he's a lazybones.

fêler [fele] *verbe*

to crack : **le vase est fêlé** the vase is cracked.

félicitations [felisitasjɔ̃] *nom féminin pluriel*

congratulations : **toutes mes félicitations !** congratulations!

féliciter [felisite] *verbe*

to congratulate : **ils m'ont félicité** they congratulated me.

félin [felɛ̃] *nom masculin*

big cat.

femelle [fəmɛl] *nom féminin & adjectif*

female : **une femelle éléphant** a female elephant.

féminin, e [feminɛ̃, in] *adjectif*

1. feminine : **un nom féminin** a feminine noun ; **elle est très féminine** she's very feminine
2. women's : **un magazine féminin** a women's magazine

féminin *nom masculin*

feminine : **il n'y a pas de féminin ou de masculin en anglais** there is no feminine or masculine in English.

femme [fam] *nom féminin*

1. woman *(pluriel* **women***)* : **une femme de trente ans** a thirty-year-old woman
2. wife : **je ne connais pas sa femme** I don't know his wife
> **une femme d'affaires** a businesswoman
> **une femme au foyer** a housewife
> **la femme de ménage** the cleaning lady.

fendre [fɑ̃dr] *verbe*

to split : **il a fendu la bûche en deux** he split the log in two

se fendre *verbe pronominal*

to crack : **le vase s'est fendu** the vase cracked.

fenêtre [fənɛtr] *nom féminin*

window : **les voleurs sont entrés par la fenêtre** the burglars got in through the window.

fente [fɑ̃t] *nom féminin*

1. crack : **il y a une fente dans le mur** there's a crack in the wall
2. slot : **mettez une pièce dans la fente** put a coin in the slot.

fer [fɛr] *nom masculin*

iron : **un crochet en fer** an iron hook
> **un fer à cheval** a horseshoe
> **un fer à repasser** an iron.

ferai, feras *etc* ➤ faire.

férié, e [ferje] *adjectif*

demain, c'est férié tomorrow is a public holiday
> **un jour férié** a public holiday *UK* OU a holiday *US* : **le premier mai est un jour férié** the first of May is a public holiday.

ferme¹ [fɛrm] *nom féminin*

farm : **ils vivent dans une ferme** they live on a farm.

ferme² [fɛrm] *adjectif*

firm : **elle s'est montrée très ferme** she was very firm.

fermer [fɛrme] *verbe*

1. to close, to shut : **ferme les yeux** close your eyes OU shut your eyes ; **ferme la porte** close the door OU shut the door ; **le musée ferme à sept heures** the museum closes at seven OU the museum shuts at seven ; **cette fenêtre ferme mal** this window doesn't close properly OU this window doesn't shut properly ; **ça ne ferme pas** it won't shut

2. to turn off, to switch off : **ferme la télé** turn off the TV OU switch off the TV

3. to close down : **la boulangerie a fermé il y a deux ans** the bakery closed down two years ago

➤ **fermer quelque chose à clé** to lock something

se fermer *verbe pronominal*

to close, to shut : **cette boîte se ferme comme ça** the box closes this way OU the box shuts this way.

fermeture [fɛrmətyr] *nom féminin*

1. closing : **heure de fermeture** closing time

2. closure : **ils ont annoncé la fermeture de l'usine** they announced the closure of the factory

➤ **une fermeture Éclair®** a zip *UK* OU a zipper *US*.

fermier, ère [fɛrmje, ɛr] *nom masculin, nom féminin*

farmer : **le père d'Alex est fermier** Alex's father is a farmer.

fermoir [fɛrmwar] *nom masculin*

clasp.

ferry [fɛri] (*pluriel* **ferries**) *nom masculin*

ferry (*pluriel* **ferries**) : **nous pouvons prendre le ferry pour aller sur l'île** we can take the ferry to the island.

fesse [fɛs] *nom féminin*

buttock : **j'ai mal à la fesse gauche** my left buttock hurts

fesses *nom féminin pluriel*

bottom *UK*, buttocks *US* : **un coup de pied aux fesses** a kick up the bottom.

fessée [fese] *nom féminin*

spanking : **donner une fessée à quelqu'un** to give somebody a spanking OU to spank somebody.

festin [fɛstɛ̃] *nom masculin*

feast : **c'était un vrai festin** it was a real feast.

festival [fɛstival] (*pluriel* **festivals**) *nom masculin*

festival : **le festival de Cannes** the Cannes film festival

 FESTIVAL D'AVIGNON

This is a festival of theatre and performing arts. It takes place in July in and around the town of Avignon in southeast France. People come to the festival to see new theatre and dance productions, performed for the first time. They can also watch more informal street performances in the town.

FESTIVAL DE CANNES

Cannes, on the French Riviera, is the home of this world-famous international film festival. Every year in May, Cannes plays host to a huge gathering of actors, film directors, journalists and cinema fans. A distinguished jury awards prizes for the best actor, best actress and best director, as well as for many other categories. The biggest prize of all is the **Palme d'Or**, awarded to the best film at the festival.

fête [fɛt] *nom féminin*

1. party (*pluriel* **parties**) : **Matthieu fait une fête samedi** Matthieu is having a party on Saturday

2. holiday : **les fêtes de fin d'année** the Christmas and New Year holidays ; **le 14 juillet est la fête nationale en France** the 14th of July is France's national holiday

3. saint's day, name day : **je te souhaite une bonne fête** happy saint's day

➤ **une fête foraine** a funfair *UK* OU a carnival *US*

➤ **la fête des Mères** Mother's Day

➤ **la fête de la Musique** annual French music festival

➤ **la fête des Pères** Father's day

➤ **faire la fête** *familier* to party : **ils ont fait la fête toute la nuit** they partied all night

BONNE FÊTE !
In France each day of the year is associated with a particular saint. It is traditional to say **bonne fête** ('Happy Saint's Day') to people whose Christian name is the same as the saint for that day.

 FÊTE DE LA MUSIQUE
Every year on 21 June musicians take to the streets of France to play all kinds of music, from classical and jazz to rock, techno and rap. This public event, open to amateurs and professionals, started in 1982. Its aim is to promote music in France.

fêter [fete] *verbe*

to celebrate : **quand est-ce que tu fêtes ton anniversaire ?** when are you celebrating your birthday?

feu [fø] *(pluriel* **feux***) nom masculin*

1. fire : **au feu !** fire! ; **la maison était en feu** the house was on fire ; **il fait froid, je vais faire du feu** it's cold, I'll make a fire
2. traffic lights : **tournez à droite au feu** turn right at the traffic lights
3. light : **est-ce que tu as du feu ?** have you got a light?
➤ **feu d'artifice** firework : **on a été voir les feux d'artifice** we went to see the fireworks
➤ **le feu rouge** the red light
➤ **le feu vert** the green light
➤ **à feu doux** on a low heat : **faire cuire à feu doux** cook on a low heat
➤ **à feu vif** on a high heat : **faire cuire à feu vif** cook on a high heat
➤ **à petit feu** gently : **faire cuire à petit feu** cook gently
➤ **mettre le feu à** to set fire to : **ils ont mis le feu à la grange** they set fire to the barn
➤ **prendre feu** to catch fire : **la paille a immédiatement pris feu** the straw immediately caught fire.

feuille [fœj] *nom féminin*

1. leaf *(pluriel* **leaves***)* : **une feuille de chêne** an oak leaf
2. sheet of paper : **écris-le sur cette feuille** write it down on this sheet of paper ; **une feuille de papier** a sheet of paper ; **une feuille blanche** a blank sheet ou a blank sheet of paper.

feuilleter [fœjte] *verbe*

to flick through : **j'ai feuilleté quelques magazines** I flicked through a few magazines.

feuilleton [fœjtɔ̃] *nom masculin*

series : **un feuilleton télévisé** a TV series ; **c'est un nouveau feuilleton** it's a new series.

feutre [føtr] *nom masculin*

felt-tip pen : **un feutre vert** a green felt-tip pen.

fève [fɛv] *nom féminin*

1. broad bean : **soupe aux fèves** broad-bean soup
2. *small porcelain figure put in a galette des Rois* ➤ galette des Rois.

février [fevrije] *nom masculin*

February : **en février** in February
➤ **nous sommes le trois février** it's the third of February *UK* ou it's February third *US*

En anglais, les mois de l'année s'écrivent avec une majuscule.

fiable [fjabl] *adjectif*

reliable : **elle n'est pas très fiable** she's not very reliable.

fiançailles [fijɑ̃saj] *nom féminin pluriel*

engagement *(ne s'utilise jamais au pluriel)* : **les fiançailles sont prévues pour décembre** the engagement is planned for December.

fiancé, e [fjɑ̃se] *nom masculin, nom féminin*

fiancé *(féminin* **fiancée***)* : **c'est sa fiancée** she's his fiancée.

se fiancer [səfjɑ̃se] *verbe pronominal*

to get engaged : **ils se sont fiancés en juin** they got engaged in June.

fibre [fibr] *nom féminin*

fibre *UK*, fiber *US*.

ficelle [fisɛl] *nom féminin*

1. string : **est-ce que tu as de la ficelle ?** have you got any string?
2. thin French stick *UK*, thin baguette *US*.

fiche [fiʃ] *nom féminin*

1. index card : **les fiches sont classées par ordre alphabétique** the index cards are in alphabetical order

2. sheet : **fiche de vocabulaire** vocabulary sheet
➤ **une fiche de paie** a pay slip.

ficher [fiʃe] *verbe familier*

to do : **qu'est-ce qu'il fiche ?** what's he doing?
➤ **ficher le camp** *familier* to clear off : **fiche le camp !** clear off!
➤ **ficher la paix à quelqu'un** *familier* to leave somebody alone : **fiche-moi la paix !** leave me alone!

se ficher de *verbe pronominal*

1. to make fun of : **ils se fichent tout le temps de lui** they are always making fun of him
2. not to care : **il se fiche de ce que je pense** he doesn't care about what I think ; **je m'en fiche** I don't care.

fichier [fiʃje] *nom masculin*

file : **n'oublie pas de sauvegarder ton fichier** don't forget to save your file.

fichu, e [fiʃy] *adjectif familier*

➤ **être fichu** to have had it : **la voiture est fichue** the car's had it.

fidèle [fidɛl] *adjectif*

1. faithful : **un mari fidèle** a faithful husband ; **il n'est pas fidèle à sa femme** he's unfaithful to his wife
2. loyal : **il est resté fidèle à son équipe** he remained loyal to his team.

fier, fière [fjɛr] *adjectif*

proud : **je suis fière de toi** I'm proud of you ; **il est fier de participer à la compétition** he's proud to be taking part in the competition.

se fier [səfje] *verbe pronominal*

➤ **se fier à** to trust OU to rely on : **on ne peut pas se fier à lui** you can't trust him OU you can't rely on him.

fierté [fjɛrte] *nom féminin*

pride : **elle regardait son fils avec fierté** she looked at her son with pride.

fièvre [fjɛvr] *nom féminin*

fever, temperature : **avoir de la fièvre** to have a fever OU to have a temperature ; **il a 40 de fièvre** he has a temperature of 105.

figue [fig] *nom féminin*

fig : **des figues sèches** dried figs.

figuier [figje] *nom masculin*

fig tree.

figure [figyr] *nom féminin*

1. face : **elle a une figure toute ronde** she has a round face
2. figure : **voir figure 4, page 21** see figure 4, page 21.

figurer [figyre] *verbe*

to appear : **son nom figure sur la couverture** his name appears on the cover

se figurer *verbe pronominal*

figure-toi qu'il n'a même pas dit bonjour believe it or not, he didn't even say hello ; **s'il se figure que je vais l'aider ...** if he thinks I'm going to help him ...

fil [fil] *nom masculin*

1. thread : **du fil et une aiguille** a needle and thread
2. wire : **fil de fer** wire ; **un fil électrique** an electric wire
➤ **un coup de fil** *familier* a phone call : **passe-moi un coup de fil demain** give me a call tomorrow ; **j'ai reçu un coup de fil de Laura** I got a call from Laura
➤ **au bout du fil** *familier* on the phone : **je viens d'avoir ta sœur au bout du fil** I've just had your sister on the phone
➤ **au fil de** in the course of : **au fil de la conversation** in the course of the conversation.

file [fil] *nom féminin*

1. line : **marcher en file** to walk in line
2. lane : **je roulais sur la file de gauche** I was driving in the left lane
➤ **la file d'attente** the queue *UK* OU the line *US*.

filer [file] *verbe*

1. *familier* to dash : **je suis en retard, il faut que je file** I'm late, I must dash
2. to speed along : **le train filait à toute vitesse** the train was speeding along
3. to ladder *UK*, to run *US* : **mon collant a filé** my tights laddered
4. to spin : **c'est comme ça qu'on filait la laine** that's the way they used to spin wool
➤ **filer quelque chose à quelqu'un** *familier* to give somebody something : **file-moi les clés** give me the keys.

filet [filɛ] *nom masculin*

1. net : **un filet à papillons** a butterfly net
2. fillet, filet *US* : **des filets de sole** fillets of sole.

filière [filjɛr] *nom féminin*

il a choisi la **filière scientifique** he chose science subjects.

fille [fij] *nom féminin*

1. girl : **tu es une grande fille maintenant** you're a big girl now
2. daughter : **ils ont deux filles** they have two daughters.

filleul, e [fijœl] *nom masculin, nom féminin*

godson *(féminin* **goddaughter***)*.

film [film] *nom masculin*

film, movie *US* : **j'ai vu un film génial hier** I saw a great film yesterday
➤ **un film d'horreur** a horror film ou a horror movie *US*
➤ **un film vidéo** a video film.

filmer [filme] *verbe*

to film.

fils [fis] *nom masculin*

son : **ils ont appelé leur fils Antoine** they called their son Antoine.

filtre [filtr] *nom masculin*

filter : **filtre à café** coffee filter.

filtrer [filtre] *verbe*

to filter.

fin¹, e [fɛ̃, fin] *adjectif*

1. thin : **une tranche fine** a thin slice
2. fine : **une plage de sable fin** a beach of fine sand ; **shampooing pour cheveux fins** shampoo for fine hair.

fin² [fɛ̃] *nom féminin*

end : **Thomas viendra fin mars** Thomas is coming at the end of March ; **à la fin de l'histoire, ils se marient** at the end of the story they get married
➤ **en fin de** at the end of : **en fin d'année** at the end of the year
➤ **en fin de compte** in the end : **en fin de compte, il a refusé** in the end he refused.

final, e, als ou **aux** [final, o] *adjectif*

final : **l'examen final** the final exam

finale [final] *nom féminin*

final : **ils ont gagné la finale** they won the final : **nous sommes en finale** we're in the finals.

finalement [finalmɑ̃] *adverbe*

finally : **finalement, ils ont décidé de rester** they finally decided to stay.

financier, ère [finɑ̃sje, ɛr] *adjectif*

financial : **une crise financière** a financial crisis.

finir [finir] *verbe*

1. to finish : **j'ai fini mes devoirs** I've finished my homework ; **j'ai fini de laver la vaisselle** I finished washing the dishes
2. to end : **comment ça finit ?** how does it end?
➤ **finir par faire quelque chose** to end up doing something : **j'ai fini par dire oui** I ended up saying yes ou I eventually said yes.

fissure [fisyr] *nom féminin*

crack : **il y a des fissures dans le mur** there are cracks in the wall.

fixe [fiks] *adjectif*

fixed : **des prix fixes** fixed prices
➤ **un menu à prix fixe** a set menu
➤ **à heures fixes** at set times.

fixement [fiksəmɑ̃] *adverbe*

regarder fixement to stare at ; **elle le regardait fixement** she was staring at him.

fixer [fikse] *verbe*

1. to fix : **fixer une étagère au mur** to fix a shelf to the wall
2. to set : **nous avons fixé une date pour la fête** we set a date for the party
3. to stare at : **il la fixait** he was staring at her

se fixer *verbe pronominal*

se fixer rendez-vous to arrange to meet ; **on s'est fixé rendez-vous à sept heures** we arranged to meet at seven.

flacon [flakɔ̃] *nom masculin*

small bottle : **un flacon de parfum** a small bottle of perfume.

flamme [flam] *nom féminin*

flame

➤ **être en flammes** to be on fire : **la maison est en flammes** the house is on fire.

flan [flɑ̃] *nom masculin*

custard tart *UK*, **custard flan** *US* : **un flan au caramel** a caramel custard tart.

flâner [flane] *verbe*

to stroll : **on a flâné dans le parc** we strolled in the park OU we went for a stroll in the park.

flanquer [flɑ̃ke] *verbe familier*

to give : **le prof m'a flanqué deux heures de colle** the teacher gave me two hours' detention

➤ **flanquer quelqu'un dehors** to kick somebody out

➤ **flanquer une gifle à quelqu'un** to slap somebody in the face

➤ **flanquer quelque chose par terre** to fling something to the ground.

flaque [flak] *nom féminin*

une flaque d'eau a puddle ; **une flaque d'huile** a pool of oil.

flash [flaʃ] *nom masculin*

flash : **prends la photo au flash** take the picture using the flash.

flèche [flɛʃ] *nom féminin*

arrow : **suivez les flèches** follow the arrows.

fléchette [fleʃɛt] *nom féminin*

dart : **jouer aux fléchettes** to play darts.

fléchir [fleʃir] *verbe*

to bend : **fléchissez les bras** bend your arms.

flemmard, e [flemar, ard] *adjectif & nom familier*

▪ *adjectif*

lazy : **il est devenu flemmard** he's become lazy

▪ *nom masculin, nom féminin*

lazybones : **quel flemmard !** what a lazybones!

flemme [flɛm] *nom féminin familier*

j'ai la flemme de sortir I can't be bothered to go out ; **tu viens ? – non, j'ai la flemme** are you coming? – no, I can't be bothered.

fleur [flœr] *nom féminin*

1. **flower** : **un bouquet de fleurs des champs** a bunch of wild flowers

2. **blossom** (*ne s'utilise jamais au pluriel*) : **les fleurs du pommier** the apple blossom

➤ **en fleurs**

1. *Fleurs* **in bloom, in flower** : **les roses sont en fleurs** the roses are in bloom OU the roses are in flower

2. *Arbres* **in blossom** : **les pommiers sont en fleurs** the apple trees are in blossom.

fleuri, e [flœri] *adjectif*

1. **flowery** : **un tissu fleuri** flowery material

2. **full of flowers** : **le parc est très fleuri** the park is full of flowers.

fleurir [flœrir] *verbe*

to flower : **cette plante fleurit au printemps** this plant flowers in the spring.

fleuriste [flœrist] *nom masculin ou féminin*

florist : **je vais chez le fleuriste** I'm going to the florist's.

fleuve [flœv] *nom masculin*

river : **la Loire est le fleuve le plus long de France** the Loire is the longest river in France.

flic [flik] *nom masculin familier*

cop : **les flics sont arrivés tout de suite** the cops arrived straightaway.

flipper [flipœr] *nom masculin*

pinball machine : **jouer au flipper** to play pinball.

flocon [flɔkɔ̃] *nom masculin*

flake : **des flocons d'avoine** porridge oats *UK* OU oatmeal *US*

➤ **un flocon de neige** a snowflake.

flore [flɔr] *nom féminin*

flora.

Floride [flɔrid] *nom féminin*

➤ **la Floride** Florida : **il vit en Floride** he lives in Florida ; **elle est allée en Floride** she went to Florida.

flotter [flɔte] *verbe*

to float : **un sac plastique flottait sur l'eau** a plastic bag was floating on the water

➤ **il flotte** *familier* it's pouring with rain

➤ **je flotte complètement dans ce pantalon** these trousers are far too baggy for me.

flou, e [flu] *adjectif*

blurred : **la photo est floue** the photo is blurred.

fluorescent, e [flyɔresɑ̃, ɑ̃t] *adjectif*
fluorescent.

flûte [flyt] *nom féminin*
1. flute : **une flûte traversière** a flute ; **Lucas joue de la flûte** Lucas plays the flute
2. recorder : **une flûte à bec** a recorder ; **elle joue de la flûte à bec** she plays the recorder
3. thin French stick *UK*, thin baguette *US*
> **une flûte à champagne** a champagne glass.

foi [fwa] *nom féminin*
faith : **avoir la foi** to have faith
> **la bonne foi** sincerity : **être de bonne foi** to be sincere
> **la mauvaise foi** dishonesty : **être de mauvaise foi** to be dishonest.

foie [fwa] *nom masculin*
liver : **du foie de veau** calf's liver
> **du foie gras** foie gras.

foin [fwɛ̃] *nom masculin*
hay *(ne s'utilise jamais au pluriel)* : **le rhume des foins** hay fever.

foire [fwar] *nom féminin*
1. funfair *UK*, amusement park *US* : **j'ai emmené les enfants à la foire** I took the children to the funfair
2. trade fair : **la foire du livre** the book fair.

fois [fwa] *nom féminin*
time : **trois fois** three times ; **c'est trois fois plus long** it's three times as long ; **3 fois 2 égalent 6** 3 times 2 equals 6 ; **chaque fois qu'il vient** every time he comes
> **une fois** once : **une fois par an** once a year ; **une fois que tu auras terminé** once you have finished ; **une fois pour toutes** once and for all ; **pour une fois** for once
> **deux fois** twice : **il est deux fois plus grand** he's twice as big ; **deux fois par an** twice a year
> **à la fois**
1. at the same time : **ils sont tous arrivés à la fois** they all arrived at the same time
2. both : **c'est à la fois bon et mauvais** it's both good and bad
> **des fois** *familier* sometimes : **des fois j'ai envie de tout laisser tomber** sometimes I feel like dropping everything
> **il était une fois une princesse ...** once upon a time there was a princess ...

folie [fɔli] *nom féminin*
madness
> **à la folie** madly : **aimer quelqu'un à la folie** to be madly in love with somebody.

folle ➤ fou.

foncé, e [fɔ̃se] *adjectif*
dark : **bleu foncé** dark blue.

foncer [fɔ̃se] *verbe familier*
to get a move on : **fonce, tu peux encore avoir ton train !** get a move on, you may still catch your train!
> **foncer dans** to crash into : **il a foncé dans un arbre** he crashed into a tree
> **foncer sur** to rush at : **il m'a foncé dessus** he rushed at me.

fonction [fɔ̃ksjɔ̃] *nom féminin*
function : **les différentes fonctions d'un ordinateur** the different functions of a computer
> **en fonction de** according to : **on décidera en fonction du temps** we'll decide according to the weather.

fonctionnaire [fɔ̃ksjɔnɛr] *nom masculin ou féminin*
civil servant.

fonctionner [fɔ̃ksjɔne] *verbe*
to work : **je ne sais pas comment ça fonctionne** I don't know how it works ; **je ne sais pas faire fonctionner cette machine** I don't know how to work this machine ; **je n'arrive pas à faire fonctionner la radio** I can't get the radio to work.

fond [fɔ̃] *nom masculin*
1. bottom : **le fond du puits** the bottom of the well
2. back : **le fond de la pièce** the back of the room
3. background : **sur fond vert** on a green background
> **du fond de teint** foundation cream
> **au fond de**
1. at the bottom of : **c'est au fond de mon sac** it's at the bottom of my bag
2. at the back of : **au fond du tiroir** at the back of the drawer ; **il est assis au fond de la salle** he's sitting at the back of the room
> **à fond** *familier*

1. **at full blast** : il met toujours la musique à **fond** he always puts the music on at full blast
2. **thoroughly** : réviser une matière à **fond** to revise a subject thoroughly.

fondamental, e, aux [fɔ̃damɑ̃tal, o] *adjectif*
basic : une notion **fondamentale** a basic notion.

fondation [fɔ̃dasjɔ̃] *nom féminin*
foundation.

fonder [fɔ̃de] *verbe*
to found : la ville a été **fondée** en 504 the city was founded in 504.

fondre [fɔ̃dr] *verbe*
to melt : la neige a déjà **fondu** the snow has already melted
> **faire fondre quelque chose** to melt something
> **fondre en larmes** to burst into tears.

fondu, e [fɔ̃dy] *participe passé de* fondre.

fondue [fɔ̃dy] *nom féminin*
fondue : **fondue bourguignonne** meat fondue ; **fondue savoyarde** cheese fondue.

font ➤ faire.

fontaine [fɔ̃tɛn] *nom féminin*
fountain.

foot [fut] ➤ football.

football [futbol] *nom masculin*
football UK, soccer US : **jouer au football** to play football
> **le football américain** American football UK ou football US.

footballeur, euse [futbolœr, øz] *nom masculin, nom féminin*
footballer UK, soccer player US.

footing [futiŋ] *nom masculin*
jogging : **faire du footing** to go jogging.

force [fɔrs] *nom féminin*
strength : je n'ai pas la **force** de courir I don't have the strength to run ; **j'ai tiré de toutes mes forces** I pulled with all my strength ; **être à bout de forces** to have no strength left
> **les forces armées** the armed forces

> **les forces de l'ordre** the police
> **à force d'essayer, j'y arriverai bien** if I keep trying, I'll manage in the end
> **de force** by force : **ils me l'ont pris de force** they took it from me by force.

forcément [fɔrsemɑ̃] *adverbe*
elle acceptera **forcément** she's bound to say yes ; **pas forcément** not necessarily.

forcer [fɔrse] *verbe*
to force : ils m'ont **forcé** à y aller they forced me to go

se forcer *verbe pronominal*
to force oneself : je me suis **forcée** à travailler I forced myself to work.

forêt [fɔrɛ] *nom féminin*
forest : une **forêt** de chênes an oak forest ; **la forêt vierge** the virgin forest.

forfait [fɔrfɛ] *nom masculin*
pass : c'est moins cher si tu achètes un **forfait** it's cheaper if you buy a pass.

formater [fɔrmate] *verbe*
to format : il faut d'abord **formater** la disquette you must format the floppy disk first.

formation [fɔrmasjɔ̃] *nom féminin*
1. formation : la **formation** d'un mot the formation of a word
2. training : **formation** professionnelle vocational training.

forme [fɔrm] *nom féminin*
shape : un bijou en **forme** de cœur a jewel in the shape of a heart ou a heart-shaped jewel
> **être en forme** to be in good form : **être en pleine forme** to be on top form.

former [fɔrme] *verbe*
to train : elle **forme** de jeunes professeurs she trains young teachers

se former *verbe pronominal*
to form : de la vapeur se **forme** sur les vitres steam is forming on the windows.

formidable [fɔrmidabl] *adjectif*
great : c'est une fille **formidable** she's a great girl.

formulaire [fɔrmylɛr] *nom masculin*

form : remplissez le formulaire fill in the form *UK* ou fill out the form *US*.

formule [fɔrmyl] *nom féminin*

1. phrase : une formule toute faite a ready-made phrase
2. formula : une formule chimique a chemical formula.

fort, e [fɔr, fɔrt] *adjectif*

1. strong : je ne suis pas assez fort pour le soulever I'm not strong enough to lift it ; il a un fort accent anglais he has a strong English accent.
2. loud : la musique est trop forte the music is too loud

➤ être fort en quelque chose to be good at something : il est très fort en espagnol he's very good at Spanish

fort *adverbe & nom masculin*

■ *adverbe*

1. hard : frapper fort to knock hard
2. loud, loudly : tu parles trop fort you're speaking too loud ou you're speaking too loudly

■ *nom masculin*

1. strong point : l'anglais, ce n'est pas mon fort English is not my strong point
2. fort : il y a un fort à l'entrée de la ville there's a fort at the entrance to the town.

fortifications [fɔrtifikasjɔ̃] *nom féminin pluriel*

fortifications.

fortune [fɔrtyn] *nom féminin*

fortune : faire fortune to make a fortune ; ça vaut une fortune it's worth a fortune.

fossé [fose] *nom masculin*

ditch (*pluriel* ditches) : il s'est retrouvé dans le fossé he ended up in the ditch.

fossette [fosɛt] *nom féminin*

dimple.

fou, folle [fu, fɔl] *adjectif & nom*

■ *adjectif* (**fol** *devant une voyelle ou un « h » muet*)

1. mad : devenir fou to go mad ; il est devenu fou he went mad ; ce bruit va me rendre folle that noise is going to drive me mad
2. huge : avoir un succès fou to be a huge suc-

cess ; il y avait un monde fou there was a huge crowd

➤ fou à lier raving mad ou barking mad *UK*
➤ être fou de quelqu'un to be mad about somebody : il est fou d'elle he's mad about her
➤ être fou de joie to be beside oneself with joy
➤ j'ai eu un mal fou à ouvrir le tiroir I had a lot of trouble opening the drawer

■ *nom masculin, nom féminin*

madman (*féminin* madwoman)
➤ comme un fou ou comme des fous like mad : ils se sont mis à courir comme des fous they started running like mad.

foudre [fudr] *nom féminin*

lightning : la foudre est tombée tout près de la maison lightning struck very near the house.

foudroyer [fudrwaje] *verbe*

être foudroyé to be struck by lightning ; l'arbre a été foudroyé the tree was struck by lightning
➤ foudroyer quelqu'un du regard to glare at somebody : elle m'a foudroyé du regard she glared at me.

fouet [fwɛ] *nom masculin*

1. whip : il l'a menacé d'un fouet he threatened him with a whip
2. whisk : battez les œufs avec un fouet beat the eggs with a whisk
➤ de plein fouet head-on : ils se sont percutés de plein fouet they collided head-on.

fouetter [fwete] *verbe*

1. to whip : il a fouetté son cheval he whipped his horse
2. to whisk : fouettez les œufs whisk the eggs.

fougère [fuʒɛr] *nom féminin*

fern.

fouilles [fuj] *nom féminin pluriel*

excavations : des fouilles archéologiques archeological excavations.

fouiller [fuje] *verbe*

to search : j'ai fouillé partout I searched everywhere
➤ fouiller dans quelque chose to go through something : je me suis permis de fouiller dans tes papiers I took the liberty of going through your papers.

fouillis [fuji] *nom masculin*

mess : quel fouillis dans cette chambre ! what a mess it is in this room!

foulard [fular] *nom masculin*

scarf *(pluriel* **scarves)* : elle a un foulard rouge autour du cou** she has a red scarf round her neck.

foule [ful] *nom féminin*

crowd : je l'ai reconnu dans la foule I recognized him in the crowd.

se fouler [səfule] *verbe pronominal*

1. **to sprain : je me suis foulé la cheville** I sprained my ankle
2. *familier* **to strain oneself : tu ne t'es pas trop foulé !** you didn't exactly strain yourself!

four [fur] *nom masculin*

oven : four électrique electric oven ; **mettre au four 40 minutes** put in the oven for 40 minutes

➤ **un four à micro-ondes** a microwave oven OU a microwave

➤ **faire cuire quelque chose au four** to bake something.

fourchette [furʃɛt] *nom féminin*

fork : des couteaux et des fourchettes knives and forks.

fourgon [furgɔ̃] *nom masculin*

van : fourgon de police police van *UK* OU patrol wagon *US*.

fourmi [furmi] *nom féminin*

ant : des fourmis rouges red ants

➤ **avoir des fourmis** to have pins and needles : **j'ai des fourmis dans les jambes** I have pins and needles in my legs.

fourneau [furno] *(pluriel* fourneaux) *nom masculin*

stove : il y avait un vieux fourneau dans la cuisine there was an old stove in the kitchen.

fournir [furnir] *verbe*

to provide, to supply : l'école fournit les livres the school provides the books OU the school supplies the books ; **c'est elle qui nous fournit tout le matériel** she provides us with all the equipment

fournisseur, euse [furnisœr, øz] *nom masculin, nom féminin*

supplier

➤ **fournisseur d'accès** service provider OU access provider.

fourniture [furnityr] *nom féminin*

supply *(pluriel* **supplies)* : fournitures de bureau** office supplies.

fourré, e [fure] *adjectif*

fur-lined : des bottes fourrées fur-lined boots

➤ **des chocolats fourrés à la fraise** chocolates with strawberry-flavoured centres.

fourrure [furyr] *nom féminin*

fur : un manteau en fourrure OU **un manteau de fourrure** a fur coat ; **une fausse fourrure** a fake fur.

foyer [fwaje] *nom masculin*

1. **home : chacun a regagné son foyer** everybody went home
2. **hostel : un foyer de jeunes travailleurs** a hostel for young workers.

fraction [fraksjɔ̃] *nom féminin*

fraction : il a hésité une fraction de seconde he hesitated for a fraction of a second OU he hesitated for a split second.

fracture [fraktyr] *nom féminin*

fracture : il a une fracture du crâne his skull is fractured OU he has a fractured skull.

fragile [fraʒil] *adjectif*

fragile.

fragment [fragmɑ̃] *nom masculin*

fragment.

frais, fraîche [frɛ, frɛʃ] *adjectif*

1. **fresh : du poisson frais** fresh fish
2. **cool : un vent frais** a cool wind
3. **wet : 'peinture fraîche'** 'wet paint'
➤ **des boissons fraîches** cold drinks

frais *nom masculin*

au frais in a cool place ; **mettre quelque chose au frais** to put something in a cool place ; **mets le champagne au frais** put the champagne to chill

frais *nom masculin pluriel*

expenses, costs : j'ai eu beaucoup de frais ce mois-ci I've had a lot of expenses this month
➤ les frais de scolarité school fees.

frais *adverbe*

il fait frais it's cool ; il commence à faire frais en septembre it starts getting cooler in September.

fraise [frɛz] *nom féminin*

strawberry (*pluriel* strawberries) : une glace à la fraise a strawberry ice cream.

framboise [frɑ̃bwaz] *nom féminin*

raspberry (*pluriel* raspberries) : confiture à la framboise raspberry jam.

franc¹, franche [frɑ̃, frɑ̃ʃ] *adjectif*

frank : il a été très franc avec moi he was very frank with me.

franc² [frɑ̃] *nom masculin*

franc : l'euro a remplacé le franc the euro has replaced the franc ; le franc suisse the Swiss franc.

français, e [frɑ̃sɛ, ɛz] *adjectif*

French : c'est une tradition française it's a French tradition

français *nom masculin*

le français French ; j'apprends le français I'm learning French ; elle parle français ou elle parle le français she speaks French

En anglais, les adjectifs se rapportant à un pays ou une région, ainsi que le nom désignant la langue de ce pays ou de cette région, s'écrivent avec une majuscule.

Français, e *nom masculin, nom féminin*

Frenchman (*féminin* Frenchwoman) : les Français the French.

France [frɑ̃s] *nom féminin*

➤ la France France

En anglais, à de rares exceptions près, il n'y a pas d'article devant les noms de pays :

il habite en France he lives in France ; elle est allée en France she went to France.

franche ➤ franc.

franchement [frɑ̃ʃmɑ̃] *adverbe*

1. frankly : franchement, je ne sais pas frankly I don't know
2. really : c'était franchement génial it was really great.

franchir [frɑ̃ʃir] *verbe*

1. to get over : franchir un obstacle to get over an obstacle
2. to cross : franchir la frontière to cross the border
3. to pass : franchir la barre des dix mille to pass the ten thousand mark.

franchise [frɑ̃ʃiz] *nom féminin*

frankness : j'aime sa franchise I like his frankness.

francophone [frɑ̃kɔfɔn] *adjectif & nom*

■ *adjectif*
French-speaking : les pays francophones French-speaking countries
■ *nom masculin ou féminin*
French speaker.

frange [frɑ̃ʒ] *nom féminin*

fringe *UK*, bangs *US* (*s'utilise toujours au pluriel*) : ma frange est trop longue my fringe is too long *UK* ou my bangs are too long *US*.

frappant, e [frapɑ̃, ɑ̃t] *adjectif*

striking : une ressemblance frappante a striking resemblance.

frapper [frape] *verbe*

1. to hit : c'est lui qui m'a frappé le premier he hit me first
2. to strike : ce qui m'a le plus frappé what struck me most
➤ frapper à la porte to knock on the door ou to knock at the door : quelqu'un frappe à la porte somebody's knocking on the door ou somebody's knocking at the door.

fraude [frod] *nom féminin*

fraud : fraude électorale electoral fraud
➤ passer quelque chose en fraude to smuggle something in.

fredonner [frədɔne] *verbe*

to hum : il fredonnait un air connu he was humming a familiar tune.

freezer [frizœr] *nom masculin*

freezer compartment.

frein [frɛ̃] *nom masculin*

brake : **frein à main** handbrake ; **mets le frein à main** put the handbrake on ; **il a donné un grand coup de frein** he braked sharply.

freiner [frene] *verbe*

to brake : **elle a freiné trop tard** she braked too late.

fréquemment [frekamɑ̃] *adverbe*

frequently : **elle va en Angleterre assez fréquemment** she goes to England quite frequently.

fréquence [frekɑ̃s] *nom féminin*

frequency : **sur quelle fréquence est cette station de radio ?** which frequency is the radio station on?

fréquent, e [frekɑ̃, ɑ̃t] *adjectif*

frequent : **les orages sont fréquents en été** there are frequent storms in the summer.

fréquenté, e [frekɑ̃te] *adjectif*

très fréquenté very busy ; **un bar très fréquenté** a very busy bar.

fréquenter [frekɑ̃te] *verbe*

to mix with : **je n'aime pas les gens que tu fréquentes** I don't like the people you mix with.

frère [frɛr] *nom masculin*

brother : **mon grand frère** my big brother.

friandise [frijɑ̃diz] *nom féminin*

delicacy *(pluriel* delicacies*)*.

fric [frik] *nom masculin familier*

cash : **je n'ai plus de fric** I haven't got any cash left.

Frigidaire® [friʒidɛr] *nom masculin*

fridge *UK*, refrigerator.

frigo [frigo] *nom masculin familier*

fridge *UK* : **mets le poulet au frigo** put the chicken in the fridge.

frileux, euse [frilø, øz] *adjectif*

je suis très frileux I really feel the cold.

frimer [frime] *verbe familier*

to show off : **arrête de frimer !** stop showing off!

frire [frir] *verbe*

to fry : **il a fait frire les pommes de terre** he fried the potatoes ; **des oignons frits** fried onions.

frisé, e [frize] *adjectif*

curly : **il a les cheveux frisés** he has curly hair.

frisson [frisɔ̃] *nom masculin*

shiver : **ça me donne des frissons** it gives me the shivers ; **j'ai des frissons** I'm shivering.

frissonner [frisɔne] *verbe*

to shiver : **il frissonne de froid** he's shivering with cold.

frit, e [fri, frit] *participe passé de* frire.

frite [frit] *nom féminin*

chip *UK*, French fry *(pluriel* French fries*) US* : **des frites** chips *UK* ou French fries *US* ou fries *US*.

froid, e [frwa, frwad] *adjectif*

cold : **de l'eau froide** cold water

froid *adverbe & nom masculin*

◻ *adverbe*
cold : **il fait froid** it's cold
➤ **avoir froid** to be cold : **j'ai froid** I'm cold
◻ *nom masculin*
cold : **cette plante n'aime pas le froid** this plant doesn't like the cold
➤ **il fait un froid de canard** it's freezing cold.

se froisser [səfrwase] *verbe pronominal*

to crease : **cette chemise se froisse facilement** this shirt creases easily.

frôler [frole] *verbe*

to brush against : **je l'ai à peine frôlé** I just brushed against him.

136

fromage [frɔmaʒ] *nom masculin*

cheese : **du fromage de chèvre** goat's cheese

➤ **du fromage blanc** fromage blanc.

froncer [frɔ̃se] *verbe*

froncer les sourcils to frown.

front [frɔ̃] *nom masculin*

1. forehead : **il a un grain de beauté sur le front** he has a mole on his forehead
2. front : **l'ennemi a atteint le front ouest** the enemy has reached the Western front.

frontière [frɔ̃tjɛr] *nom féminin*

border : **ils ont passé la frontière à pied** they crossed the border on foot.

frotter [frɔte] *verbe*

to rub : **tu me frottes le dos ?** can you rub my back?

fruit [frɥi] *nom masculin*

fruit (*ne s'utilise jamais au pluriel*) : **tu veux un fruit ?** do you want a piece of fruit? ; **ces fruits sont excellents** this fruit is excellent ; **fruits secs** dried fruit

➤ **fruits de mer** seafood (*ne s'utilise jamais au pluriel*)

fugue [fyg] *nom féminin*

faire une fugue to run away ; **leur fils a fait une fugue** their son ran away from home.

fui [fɥi] *participe passé invariable de* fuir.

fuir [fɥir] *verbe*

1. to flee : **les voleurs ont déjà fui** the robbers have already fled
2. to leak : **le robinet fuit** the tap is leaking.

fuite [fɥit] *nom féminin*

1. escape, flight : **prendre la fuite** to take flight OU to run away
2. leak : **une fuite de gaz** a gas leak.

fumé, e [fyme] *adjectif*

smoked : **du saumon fumé** smoked salmon.

fumée [fyme] *nom féminin*

smoke : **il y a trop de fumée dans ce pub** there's too much smoke in this pub OU it's too smoky in this pub.

fumer [fyme] *verbe*

to smoke : **Judith fume dix cigarettes par jour** Judith smokes ten cigarettes a day ; **il voudrait arrêter de fumer** he'd like to stop smoking.

fumeur, euse [fymœr, øz] *nom masculin, nom féminin*

smoker : **compartiment fumeurs** smoking compartment.

fur [fyr]

➤ **au fur et à mesure** as you go along : **je règle les problèmes au fur et à mesure** I solve the problems as I go along

➤ **au fur et à mesure que** as : **au fur et à mesure que les gens arrivent, on leur donne un questionnaire** the people are given a questionnaire as they arrive.

furieux, euse [fyrjø, øz] *adjectif*

furious : **il est furieux contre moi** he's furious with me.

fuseau [fyzo] (*pluriel* fuseaux) *nom masculin*

ski-pants : **elle porte un fuseau rouge** she's wearing red ski-pants

➤ **les fuseaux horaires** time zones.

fusée [fyze] *nom féminin*

rocket : **la fusée a décollé** the rocket has taken off.

fusible [fyzibl] *nom masculin*

fuse : **les fusibles ont grillé** the fuses have blown.

fusil [fyzi] *nom masculin*

rifle.

fusiller [fyzije] *verbe*

to shoot : **le prisonnier a été fusillé à l'aube** the prisoner was shot at dawn

➤ **fusiller quelqu'un du regard** to look daggers at somebody : **elle l'a fusillé du regard** she looked daggers at him.

futur, e [fytyr] *adjectif*

future : **sa future femme** his future wife

futur *nom masculin*

future, future tense : **mettre la phrase au futur** put the sentence in the future tense.

gâcher [gaʃe] *verbe*

1. **to waste : je n'aime pas gâcher la nourriture** I don't like wasting food
2. **to spoil : ça a gâché la soirée** it spoiled the evening.

gâchette [gaʃɛt] *nom féminin*

trigger : il a appuyé sur la gâchette he pulled the trigger.

gâchis [gaʃi] *nom masculin*

waste : quel gâchis ! what a waste!

gadget [gadʒɛt] *nom masculin*

gadget : c'est un nouveau gadget it's a new gadget.

gaffe [gaf] *nom féminin familier*

blunder : faire une gaffe to blunder ou to put one's foot in it

➤ **faire gaffe** to be careful : **fais gaffe la prochaine fois** be careful next time ; **fais gaffe aux voitures !** be careful of the cars! ou watch the cars!

gagnant, e [gaɲɑ̃, ɑ̃t] *adjectif & nom*

◼ *adjectif*
winning : l'équipe gagnante the winning team

◼ *nom masculin, nom féminin*
winner : il y a deux gagnants there are two winners.

gagner [gaɲe] *verbe*

1. **to win : qui a gagné le match ?** who won the match?
2. **to earn : il gagne deux mille euros par mois** he earns two thousand euros a month ; **gagner sa vie** to earn one's living

3. **to save : gagner du temps** to save time ; **ça nous fera gagner du temps** it will save us time ; **gagner de la place** to save place.

gai, e [gɛ] *adjectif*

1. **cheerful : c'est quelqu'un de très gai** he's a very cheerful person
2. **bright : des couleurs gaies** bright colours *UK* ou bright colors *US*.

galant, e [galɑ̃, ɑ̃t] *adjectif*

il est très galant he's a gentleman.

galaxie [galaksi] *nom féminin*

galaxy *(pluriel* **galaxies***)*.

galerie [galri] *nom féminin*

gallery *(pluriel* **galleries***)* : **une galerie d'art** an art gallery

➤ **une galerie marchande** ou **une galerie commerciale** a shopping arcade *UK* ou a shopping mall *US*.

galet [galɛ] *nom masculin*

pebble : une plage de galets a pebble beach.

galette [galɛt] *nom féminin*

1. **buckwheat pancake : une galette au fromage** a cheese pancake
2. **biscuit** *UK*, **cookie** *US* : **un paquet de galettes au beurre** a packet of butter biscuits

➤ **la galette des Rois** marzipan tart traditionally eaten on Twelfth Night

GALETTE DES ROIS
This large round pastry is traditionally eaten in France on Twelfth Night, 6 January. It is filled with almond paste and a small porcelain figure (the **fève**) is hidden inside. Whoever finds the **fève** in their slice of cake is crowned king or queen with a cardboard crown.

galipette [galipɛt] *nom féminin*

somersault : faire des galipettes to do somersaults.

Galles [gal] ➤ pays.

gallois, e [galwa, az] *adjectif*

Welsh : le dragon gallois the Welsh dragon

gallois *nom masculin*

Welsh : beaucoup de gens parlent encore le gallois a lot of people still speak Welsh

Gallois, e *nom masculin, nom féminin*

Welshman *(féminin* **Welshwoman***)* : **les Gallois** the Welsh.

galop [galo] *nom masculin*

gallop : **le cheval allait au galop** the horse was galloping.

galoper [galɔpe] *verbe*

1. **to gallop** : **les chevaux galopent dans le champ** the horses are galloping in the field
2. **to charge** : **arrêtez de galoper dans les escaliers !** stop charging up and down the stairs!

gamin, e [gamɛ̃, in] *nom masculin, nom féminin familier*

kid : **un gamin de huit ans** an eight-year-old kid.

gamme [gam] *nom féminin*

1. **range** : **notre nouvelle gamme de parfums** our new range of perfumes
2. **scale** : **faire des gammes au piano** to practise scales on the piano
➤ **bas de gamme** bottom-of-the-range *UK* ou bottom-of-the-line *US* : **un magnétoscope bas de gamme** a bottom-of-the-range videorecorder
➤ **haut de gamme** top-of-the-range *UK* ou top-of-the-line *US* : **un ordinateur haut de gamme** a top-of-the-range computer.

gant [gɑ̃] *nom masculin*

glove : **des gants de boxe** boxing gloves ; **des gants de caoutchouc** rubber gloves
➤ **un gant de toilette** a flannel *UK* ou a washcloth *US*.

garage [garaʒ] *nom masculin*

garage : **j'ai mis la voiture au garage** I put the car in the garage ; **y a-t-il un garage ouvert le dimanche ?** is there a garage open on Sundays?

garagiste [garaʒist] *nom masculin ou féminin*

mechanic, garage mechanic : **il est garagiste** he's a mechanic.

garantie [garɑ̃ti] *nom féminin*

guarantee : **une garantie d'un an** a one-year guarantee.

garantir [garɑ̃tir] *verbe*

1. **to guarantee** : **c'est garanti un an** it's guaranteed for one year

2. **to assure** : **je vous garantis qu'il ne m'a rien dit** I can assure you he didn't tell me anything.

garçon [garsɔ̃] *nom masculin*

1. **boy** : **un petit garçon** a little boy
2. **waiter** : **il est garçon de café** he's a waiter
➤ **un garçon manqué** a tomboy.

garde [gard] *nom*

■ *nom féminin*
guard : **monter la garde** to stand guard
■ *nom masculin*
guard : **un garde du corps** a bodyguard.

garder [garde] *verbe*

1. **to keep** : **je l'ai gardé en souvenir** I kept it as a souvenir
2. **to look after** : **elle garde les enfants tous les week-ends** she looks after the children every weekend

se garder *verbe pronominal*

to keep : **ce gâteau peut se garder longtemps** this cake will keep for a long time.

garderie [gardəri] *nom féminin*

day nursery *UK*, **day-care center** *US*.

garde-robe [gardərɔb] *(pluriel* **garde-robes***) nom féminin*

wardrobe : **ma garde-robe d'hiver** my winter wardrobe.

gardien, enne [gardjɛ̃, ɛn] *nom masculin, nom féminin*

caretaker *UK*, **janitor** *US* : **un gardien d'immeuble** a caretaker
➤ **le gardien de but** the goalkeeper
➤ **le gardien de nuit** the night watchman
➤ **un gardien de prison** a prison warden *UK* ou a prison guard *US*.

gare [gar] *nom & exclamation*

■ *nom féminin*
railway station *UK*, **train station** *US* : **je viendrai te chercher à la gare** I'll come and pick you up at the station
➤ **la gare routière** the bus station ou the coach station *UK*
■ *exclamation*
watch out! : **gare aux voleurs !** watch out for thieves!

g

garer [gaʀe] *verbe*

to park : **où as-tu garé la voiture ?** where did you park the car?

se garer *verbe pronominal*

to park : **il n'y a plus de place pour se garer** there's nowhere to park.

gars [ga] *nom masculin familier*

guy : **c'est un gars plutôt sympa** he's quite a nice guy.

gaspillage [gaspijaʒ] *nom masculin*

waste : **quel gaspillage !** what a waste!

gaspiller [gaspije] *verbe*

to waste : **il gaspille son argent de poche** he wastes his pocket money.

gâteau [gato] (*pluriel* gâteaux) *nom masculin*

cake : **un gâteau d'anniversaire** a birthday cake

➤ **des gâteaux apéritif** savoury biscuits *UK* OU crackers *US*

➤ **des gâteaux secs** OU **des petits gâteaux** biscuits *UK* OU cookies *US*.

gâter [gate] *verbe*

to spoil : **ils nous ont gâtés** they spoiled us

se gâter *verbe pronominal*

1. to go bad : **les fruits se sont gâtés** the fruit has gone bad
2. to change for the worse : **le temps va se gâter dans l'après-midi** the weather will change for the worse in the afternoon.

gauche [goʃ] *nom & adjectif*

■ *nom féminin*

left : **on roule à gauche en Australie** you drive on the left in Australia ; **tournez à gauche** turn left ; **ça sera la deuxième rue à gauche** it's the second street on the left ; **la gauche a gagné les élections** the left won the elections

■ *adjectif*

1. left : **mon pied gauche** my left foot
2. clumsy : **il a toujours été un peu gauche** he's always been a bit clumsy

➤ **de gauche** left-wing : **un gouvernement de gauche** a left-wing government.

gaucher, ère [goʃe, ɛʀ] *adjectif*

left-handed : **Luc est gaucher** Luc is left-handed.

gaufre [gofʀ] *nom féminin*

waffle.

gaufrette [gofʀɛt] *nom féminin*

wafer : **des gaufrettes à la vanille** vanilla wafers.

Gaulois, e [golwa, az] *nom masculin, nom féminin*

Gaul : **les Gaulois** the Gauls.

se gaver [səgave] *verbe pronominal*

to stuff oneself : **ils se sont gavés de gâteaux** they stuffed themselves with cakes.

gaz [gaz] *nom masculin invariable*

gas : **gaz lacrymogène** tear gas

➤ **le gaz carbonique** carbon dioxide

➤ **les gaz d'échappement** exhaust fumes.

gazeux, euse [gazø, øz] *adjectif*

fizzy : **je n'aime pas les boissons gazeuses** I don't like fizzy drinks ; **eau gazeuse** sparkling water.

gazon [gazɔ̃] *nom masculin*

lawn : **tondre le gazon** to mow the lawn

➤ **'défense de marcher sur le gazon'** ' keep off the grass'.

GB, G-B (*abréviation de* Grande-Bretagne) *nom féminin*

GB.

géant, e [ʒeɑ̃, ɑ̃t] *adjectif & nom*

■ *adjectif*

1. giant : **un écran géant** a giant screen
2. gigantic : **une statue géante** a gigantic statue

■ *nom masculin, nom féminin*

giant : **c'est un géant** he's a giant.

gel [ʒɛl] *nom masculin*

1. frost : **le terrain est couvert de gel** the field is covered in frost
2. gel : **du gel pour les cheveux** hair gel.

gelée [ʒəle] *nom féminin*

1. frost : **une gelée matinale** a morning frost
2. jelly : **de la gelée de groseilles** redcurrant jelly.

geler [ʒəle] *verbe*

to freeze : **les récoltes ont gelé** the crops have frozen ; **on gèle dans cette maison !** it's freezing in this house!

se geler *verbe pronominal familier*

je me gèle I'm freezing ; **on s'est gelés à la montagne** we were frozen in the mountains.

Gémeaux [ʒemo] *nom masculin pluriel*

Gemini : **elle est Gémeaux** she's a Gemini.

gênant, e [ʒenã, ãt] *adjectif*

embarrassing : **une situation gênante** an embarrassing situation.

gencive [ʒãsiv] *nom féminin*

gum : **j'ai les gencives qui saignent** my gums are bleeding.

gendarme [ʒãdarm] *nom masculin*

policeman *(pluriel* **policemen***)*.

gendarmerie [ʒãdarməri] *nom féminin*

police station : **ils l'ont emmené à la gendarmerie** they took him to the police station.

gendre [ʒãdr] *nom masculin*

son-in-law.

gêner [ʒene] *verbe*

1. **to embarrass** : **ça me gêne de lui demander** I feel embarrassed asking him
2. **to bother** : **la fumée me gêne** smoke bothers me
> **ça vous gêne si j'ouvre la fenêtre ?** do you mind if I open the window?

se gêner *verbe pronominal*

ne te gêne pas, sers-toi go ahead, help yourself ; **je ne vais pas me gêner pour lui dire ce que je pense !** I won't hesitate to tell her what I think!

général, e, aux [ʒeneral, o] *adjectif*

general : **c'est un terme très général** it's a very general term
> **en général**
1. **generally** : **en général, ça marche** it generally works
2. **in general** : **il n'aime pas l'école en général** he doesn't like school in general

général *nom masculin*

general : **son père est général dans l'armée** his father is a general in the army.

généralement [ʒeneralmã] *adverbe*

generally : **généralement parlant** generally speaking.

génération [ʒenerasjɔ̃] *nom féminin*

generation : **la nouvelle génération** the young generation.

généreux, euse [ʒenerø, øz] *adjectif*

generous : **elle est très généreuse** she's very generous.

générique [ʒenerik] *nom masculin*

credits : **on est arrivés dans la salle pendant le générique** we arrived in the movie theater during the credits.

génétique [ʒenetik] *adjectif*

genetic : **maladie génétique** genetic disease.

génial, e, aux [ʒenjal, o] *adjectif*

familier **great, brilliant** : **c'était génial !** it was great! ou it was brilliant!

génie [ʒeni] *nom masculin*

genius *(pluriel* **geniuses***)* : **Einstein était un génie** Einstein was a genius
> **de génie** **brilliant** : **une idée de génie** a brilliant idea.

genou [ʒənu] *(pluriel* **genoux***) nom masculin*

knee : **il est à genoux** he's on his knees ou he's kneeling
> **se mettre à genoux** to kneel down
> **s'asseoir sur les genoux de quelqu'un** to sit on somebody's lap.

genre [ʒãr] *nom masculin*

1. **kind, type** : **je n'aime pas ce genre de livres** I don't like this kind of book ou I don't like this type of book
2. **gender** : **les noms français s'accordent en genre et en nombre** French nouns agree in gender and number.

gens [ʒã] *nom masculin pluriel*

people : **de nos jours les gens vivent plus longtemps** people live longer nowadays ; **beaucoup de gens ont un téléphone portable** a lot of people have mobile phones.

gentil, ille [ʒãti, ij] *adjectif*

nice, kind : **elle a été très gentille avec eux** she was very nice to them ou she was very kind to them.

gentiment [ʒãtimã] *adverbe*

kindly : **il a gentiment proposé de me prêter l'argent** he kindly offered to lend me the money.

géographie [ʒeɔgrafi] *nom féminin*

geography.

gercé, e [ʒɛrse] *adjectif*

chapped : **j'ai les lèvres gercées** I have chapped lips ou my lips are chapped.

gérer [ʒere] *verbe*

to manage : **il gère une grande entreprise** he manages a large company.

geste [ʒɛst] *nom masculin*

1. gesture : **c'est un beau geste** it's a nice gesture
2. move : **il a fait un geste brusque** he made a sudden move.

gestion [ʒɛstjɔ̃] *nom féminin*

management : **il fait des études de gestion** he's doing management studies.

gibier [ʒibje] *nom masculin*

game : **chasser du gros gibier** to hunt big game.

gicler [ʒikle] *verbe*

to squirt, to spurt : **l'eau a giclé partout** water squirted everywhere.

gifle [ʒifl] *nom féminin*

slap

> **donner une gifle à quelqu'un** to slap somebody : **mon père m'a donné une gifle** my father slapped me.

gifler [ʒifle] *verbe*

to slap : **elle m'a giflé** she slapped me.

gigantesque [ʒigãtɛsk] *adjectif*

gigantic : **une statue gigantesque** a gigantic statue.

gigot [ʒigo] *nom masculin*

leg : **un gigot d'agneau** a leg of lamb.

gilet [ʒilɛ] *nom masculin*

1. cardigan : **elle porte un gilet de laine** she's wearing a wool cardigan
2. waistcoat *UK*, vest *US* : **un costume avec gilet** a suit with a waistcoat
> **un gilet de sauvetage** a life jacket.

girafe [ʒiraf] *nom féminin*

giraffe.

girofle [ʒirɔfl] ➤ clou.

gitan, e [ʒitã, an] *nom masculin, nom féminin*

gipsy *(pluriel* **gipsies***)*.

gîte [ʒit] *nom masculin*

gîte rural *self-catering cottage in the country.*

givre [ʒivr] *nom masculin*

frost : **il y a du givre sur les vitres** there's frost on the windows.

glace [glas] *nom féminin*

1. ice : **la glace fondait au soleil** the ice was melting in the sun
2. ice cream : **de la glace à la fraise** strawberry ice cream ; **il a mangé deux glaces** he ate two ice creams
3. mirror : **elle se regarde dans la glace** she's looking at herself in the mirror
4. window : **à travers la glace de la voiture** through the car window.

glacé, e [glase] *adjectif*

1. freezing : **l'eau est glacée** the water is freezing ou the water is icy cold ; **je suis glacé !** I'm freezing!
2. chilled : **servir glacé** best served chilled.

glacial, e, aux [glasjal, o] *adjectif*

icy : **un vent glacial** an icy wind.

glacier [glasje] *nom masculin*

glacier.

glaçon [glasɔ̃] *nom masculin*

ice cube

> **avec des glaçons** with ice
> **sans glaçons** without ice.

glisser [glise] *verbe*

1. to slip : **j'ai glissé et j'ai failli tomber** I slipped and nearly fell ; **glisse ce papier sous la porte** slip this piece of paper under the door
2. to be slippery ; **attention, ça glisse !** be careful, it's slippery!

globalement [glɔbalmã] *adverbe*

on the whole, overall : **globalement, ça s'est bien passé** on the whole it went well ou overall it went well.

globe [glɔb] *nom masculin*

globe : **le globe terrestre** the globe.

gloire [glwar] *nom féminin*

glory.

glossaire [glɔsɛr] *nom masculin*

glossary (*pluriel* **glossaries**).

gluant, e [glɥɑ̃, ɑ̃t] *adjectif*

sticky : **j'ai les mains gluantes** my hands are sticky ; **du riz gluant** sticky rice.

goal [gol] *nom masculin*

goalkeeper

⚠ In French the word **goal** is not used to mean 'goal'.

gobelet [gɔblɛ] *nom masculin*

tumbler : **un gobelet en métal** a metal tumbler
➤ **un gobelet en plastique** a plastic cup.

golf [gɔlf] *nom masculin*

golf : **jouer au golf** to play golf ; **un terrain de golf** a golf course.

golfe [gɔlf] *nom masculin*

gulf, bay : **le golfe de Gascogne** the Bay of Biscay ; **le golfe du Mexique** the Gulf of Mexico.

gomme [gɔm] *nom féminin*

eraser, rubber *UK* : **prête-moi ta gomme** lend me your eraser.

gommer [gɔme] *verbe*

to erase, to rub out *UK* : **n'oublie pas de gommer mes remarques** don't forget to erase my comments.

gonfler [gɔ̃fle] *verbe*

1. to blow up : **gonfler un pneu** to blow up a tyre **ou** to blow up a tire *US*
2. to swell : **mon poignet commence à gonfler** my wrist is swelling.

gorge [gɔrʒ] *nom féminin*

1. throat : **j'ai mal à la gorge** I have a sore throat

2. gorge : **les gorges du Verdon** the gorges of the Verdon.

gorille [gɔrij] *nom masculin*

gorilla : **il y a des gorilles au zoo** there are gorillas in the zoo.

gosse [gɔs] *nom masculin ou féminin familier*

kid : **ils ont trois gosses** they have three kids.

goulot [gulo] *nom masculin*

neck : **le goulot de la bouteille** the neck of the bottle
➤ **boire au goulot** to drink straight from the bottle.

gourde [gurd] *nom féminin*

water bottle : **je n'ai plus beaucoup d'eau dans ma gourde** I don't have much water left in my water bottle.

gourmand, e [gurmɑ̃, ɑ̃d] *adjectif*

greedy : **Laurent est très gourmand** Laurent is very greedy.

gourmandise [gurmɑ̃diz] *nom féminin*

la gourmandise greed

gousse [gus] *nom féminin*

pod : **une gousse de vanille** a vanilla pod
➤ **une gousse d'ail** a clove of garlic.

goût [gu] *nom masculin*

taste : **la sauce a très bon goût** the sauce tastes very nice ; **on n'a pas les mêmes goûts** we don't have the same tastes
➤ **elle a beaucoup de goût** she has very good taste
➤ **chacun ses goûts** each to his own
➤ **de bon goût** tasteful : **un décor de bon goût** a tasteful decor
➤ **de mauvais goût** tasteless : **une tenue de mauvais goût** tasteless clothes
➤ **avoir un goût** to taste : **ça a bon goût !** it tastes good! ; **ça a un goût de cannelle** it tastes of cinnamon
➤ **ça n'a aucun goût** it's tasteless.

goûter [gute] *verbe & nom*

■ *verbe*
1. to taste : **goûte ça, c'est très bon** taste this, it's very good ; **elle n'a pas voulu goûter à ma soupe** she refused to taste my soup
2. to have an afternoon snack : **est-ce que**

g

vous avez goûté ? have you had your afternoon snack?

■ *nom masculin*

afternoon snack : c'est l'heure du goûter it's time for the children's afternoon snack.

goutte [gut] *nom féminin*

drop : une goutte d'eau a drop of water
➤ ils se ressemblent comme deux gouttes d'eau they are as like as two peas in a pod.

gouttière [gutjɛr] *nom féminin*

gutter.

gouvernement [guvɛrnəmã] *nom masculin*

government.

grâce [gras] *nom féminin*

grace : elle danse avec grâce she danses gracefully
➤ grâce à thanks to : grâce à ton aide thanks to your help.

gradins [gradɛ̃] *nom masculin pluriel*

terraces *UK*, bleachers *US* : les gradins d'un stade the terraces of a stadium.

graffitis [grafiti] *nom masculin pluriel*

graffiti (*ne s'utilise jamais au pluriel*) : il y a des graffitis sur le mur there's graffiti on the wall.

grain [grɛ̃] *nom masculin*

grain : un grain de riz a grain of rice ; des grains de sable grains of sand
➤ un grain de beauté a mole : elle a un grain de beauté sur la joue she has a mole on her cheek
➤ un grain de café a coffee bean
➤ un grain de raisin a grape.

graine [grɛn] *nom féminin*

seed : des graines de tournesol sunflower seeds.

graisse [grɛs] *nom féminin*

fat : enlève la graisse de la viande take the fat off the meat.

grammaire [gramɛr] *nom féminin*

grammar : la grammaire anglaise English grammar.

gramme [gram] *nom masculin*

gram, gramme *UK* : quatre cents grammes de sucre four hundred grams of sugar.

grand, e [grã, grãd] *adjectif*

1. big : une grande maison a big house ; il n'y a pas une grande différence entre eux there isn't a big difference between them ; tu es un grand garçon maintenant you're a big boy now ; tu es assez grand pour le faire tout seul you're old enough to do it by yourself
2. tall : je suis aussi grand que toi I'm as tall as you are
3. great : Gandhi était un grand homme Gandhi was a great man
➤ les grandes personnes grown-ups
➤ un grand frère a big brother OU an older brother
➤ une grande sœur a big sister OU an older sister

⚠ The French word **grand** is a false friend, it does not mean 'grand'.

grand-chose [grãʃoz] *pronom*

pas grand-chose not much ; il ne reste plus grand-chose à manger there's not much left to eat ; je n'ai pas compris grand-chose de ce qu'il a dit I didn't understand much of what he said.

Grande-Bretagne [grãdbrətaɲ] *nom féminin*

➤ la Grande-Bretagne Great Britain

En anglais, à de rares exceptions près, il n'y a pas d'article devant les noms de pays :

j'habite en Grande-Bretagne I live in Great Britain ; je suis allé en Grande-Bretagne I went to Great Britain.

grandeur [grãdœr] *nom féminin*

size : des boîtes de toutes les grandeurs boxes of all sizes
➤ grandeur nature life-size : un portrait grandeur nature a life-size portrait.

grandir [grãdir] *verbe*

1. to grow : sa fille grandit vite her daughter is growing fast ; j'ai grandi de dix centimètres en un an I have grown ten centimetres in the last year
2. to grow up : j'ai grandi en Belgique I grew up in Belgium.

grand-mère [grãmɛr] (*pluriel* grands-mères) *nom féminin*

grandmother.

grand-père [grɑ̃pɛr] (*pluriel* grands-pères) *nom masculin*

grandfather.

grands-parents [grɑ̃parɑ̃] *nom masculin pluriel*

grandparents.

grange [grɑ̃ʒ] *nom féminin*

barn.

graphique [grafik] *nom masculin*

graph : **faire un graphique** to draw a graph.

grappe [grap] *nom féminin*

bunch : **une grappe de raisin** a bunch of grapes.

gras, grasse [gra, gras] *adjectif*

1. fatty : **c'est une viande très grasse** it's very fatty meat
2. greasy : **shampoing pour cheveux gras** shampoo for greasy hair
3. bold : **écrit en caractères gras** written in bold ou written in bold type

gras *nom masculin*

1. fat : **le gras du jambon** the fat of the ham
2. bold : **écrit en gras** written in bold
➤ **faire la grasse matinée** to have a lie-in *UK* ou to sleep late *US*.

gratin [gratɛ̃] *nom masculin*

gratin : **un gratin de fruits de mer** a seafood gratin
➤ **du chou-fleur au gratin** cauliflower cheese.

gratte-ciel [gratsjɛl] (*pluriel* gratte-ciel) *nom masculin*

skyscraper : **il y a de très beaux gratte-ciel à New York** there are some beautiful skyscrapers in New York.

gratter [grate] *verbe*

1. to scratch : **ne gratte pas tes piqûres de moustiques** don't scratch your mosquito bites
2. to be itchy : **ce pull me gratte** this pullover is itchy ; **ça me gratte partout** I'm itching all over

se gratter *verbe pronominal*

to scratch, to scratch oneself : **arrête de te gratter** stop scratching ou stop scratching yourself ; **elle se gratte le menton** she's scratching her chin.

gratuit, e [gratɥi, it] *adjectif*

free : **entrée gratuite** free entry ; **l'entrée est gratuite** it's free to get in.

gratuitement [gratɥitmɑ̃] *adverbe*

for free : **on a voyagé gratuitement** we travelled for free ; **je suis entré gratuitement** I got in free ou I got in for free.

grave [grav] *adjectif*

1. serious : **une maladie grave** a serious illness
2. deep : **elle a une voix grave** she has a deep voice
➤ **ce n'est pas grave** it doesn't matter

⚠ The French word **grave** is a false friend, it does not mean 'grave'.

gravement [gravmɑ̃] *adverbe*

seriously : **il est gravement malade** he is seriously ill.

graver [grave] *verbe*

1. to carve : **il a gravé son nom sur un arbre** he carved his name on a tree.
2. to burn : **graver un CD** to burn a CD.

grec, grecque [grɛk] *adjectif*

Greek : **une tradition grecque** a Greek tradition

grec *nom masculin*

le grec Greek ; **j'apprends le grec** I'm learning Greek ; **le grec ancien** ancient Greek ; **le grec moderne** modern Greek

En anglais, les adjectifs se rapportant à un pays ou à une région, ainsi que le nom désignant la langue de ce pays ou de cette région, s'écrivent avec une majuscule.

Grec, Grecque *nom masculin, nom féminin*

un Grec a Greek ou a Greek man ; **une Grecque** a Greek woman ; **les Grecs** Greeks.

Grèce [grɛs] *nom féminin*

➤ **la Grèce** Greece

En anglais, à de rares exceptions près, il n'y a pas d'article devant les noms de pays :

elle habite en Grèce she lives in Greece ; **je suis allé en Grèce** I went to Greece ; **la Grèce antique** Ancient Greece.

g

grêle [grɛl] *nom féminin*

hail.

grêler [grele] *verbe*

to hail : **il grêle** it's hailing.

grelotter [grəlɔte] *verbe*

to shiver : **elle grelotte de froid** she's shivering with cold.

grenade [grənad] *nom féminin*

1. pomegranate : **j'ai mangé une grenade** I ate a pomegranate
2. grenade : **lancer une grenade** to throw a grenade.

grenier [grənje] *nom masculin*

attic : **le grenier est plein de vieilles malles** the attic is full of old trunks
➤ **le grenier à blé** the granary.

grenouille [grənuj] *nom féminin*

frog : **des cuisses de grenouille** frogs' legs.

grève [grɛv] *nom féminin*

strike : **être en grève** to be on strike ; **faire grève** to go on strike ; **une grève de la faim** a hunger strike.

griffe [grif] *nom féminin*

claw : **les griffes du chat** the cat's claws.

griffer [grife] *verbe*

to scratch : **le chat m'a griffé !** the cat scratched me!

grignoter [griɲɔte] *verbe*

to nibble : **la souris a grignoté le fromage** the mouse nibbled the cheese ou the mouse nibbled at the cheese.

gril [gril] *nom masculin*

grill *UK*, broiler *US* : **faire cuire quelque chose au gril** to grill something *UK* ou to broil something *US*.

grillade [grijad] *nom féminin*

grilled meat : **on a mangé des grillades** we had grilled meat
➤ **faire des grillades** to have a barbecue : **on a fait des grillades dans le jardin** we had a barbecue in the garden.

grillage [grijaʒ] *nom masculin*

wire fence.

grille [grij] *nom féminin*

gate : **la grille du parc est fermée** the park gate is closed.

grille-pain [grijpɛ̃] *(pluriel* **grille-pain***) nom masculin*

toaster.

griller [grije] *verbe*

1. to grill, to broil *US* : **du poisson grillé** grilled fish ; **faites griller la viande** grill the meat
2. to toast : **du pain grillé** toast ; **on a fait griller des tartines** we toasted some bread ou we made some toast
3. to blow : **l'ampoule de l'entrée a grillé** the bulb in the corridor has blown
➤ **griller un feu rouge** to jump the lights ou to go through a red light.

grillon [grijɔ̃] *nom masculin*

cricket : **on entend les grillons chanter** you can hear the crickets.

grimace [grimas] *nom féminin*

➤ **faire une grimace** to pull a face : **il m'a fait une grimace** he pulled a face at me ; **elle n'arrête pas de faire des grimaces** she's always pulling faces.

grimper [grɛ̃pe] *verbe*

to climb : **grimper à un arbre** to climb a tree.

grincer [grɛ̃se] *verbe*

to creak : **la porte grince** the door creaks.

grippe [grip] *nom féminin*

flu *(ne s'utilise jamais au pluriel)* : **Luc a la grippe** Luc has got flu *UK* ou Luc has the flu.

gris, e [gri, griz] *adjectif*

grey *UK*, gray *US* : **un chat gris** a grey cat

gris *nom masculin*

grey *UK*, gray *US* : **je n'aime pas le gris** I don't like grey.

grogner [grɔɲe] *verbe*

to growl : **le chien s'est mis à grogner** the dog started growling.

gronder [grɔ̃de] *verbe*

to tell off : **ma mère m'a grondé** my mother told me off.

gros, grosse [gro, gros] *adjectif*

1. big : **un gros sac** a big bag ; **c'est un gros problème** it's a big problem
2. fat : **leur fils est trop gros** their son is too fat
- **en gros** roughly : **il y aura en gros cinquante personnes** there will be roughly fifty people.

groseille [grozɛj] *nom féminin*

redcurrant
- **des groseilles à maquereau** gooseberries.

grosse [gros] *adjectif* ➤ gros.

grossier, ère [grosje, ɛr] *adjectif*

1. rude : **il s'est montré grossier envers elle** he was rude to her
2. rough : **un croquis grossier** a rough sketch
3. gross : **une erreur grossière** a gross mistake.

grossir [grosir] *verbe*

to put on weight : **j'ai beaucoup grossi** I've put on a lot of weight ; **Sébastien a grossi de trois kilos** Sébastien has put on three kilos.

grotte [grɔt] *nom féminin*

cave : **des grottes préhistoriques** prehistoric caves.

groupe [grup] *nom masculin*

1. group : **un groupe d'élèves** a group of pupils
2. band : **il joue dans un groupe de rock** he plays in a rock band OU he plays in a rock group
- **groupe sanguin** blood group
- **en groupe** in a group OU in groups : **le professeur nous a fait travailler en groupe** the teacher made us work in groups.

se grouper [səgrupe] *verbe pronominal*

to gather : **les élèves se sont groupés autour du professeur** the pupils gathered around the teacher.

grue [gry] *nom féminin*

crane.

guêpe [gɛp] *nom féminin*

wasp.

guère [gɛr] *adverbe*

1. hardly : **nous ne sortons guère** we hardly ever go out

2. barely : **il n'y a guère plus de six ans** it's barely more than six years ago.

guérir [gerir] *verbe*

1. to cure : **le médecin m'a guéri** the doctor cured me
2. to recover : **il a guéri vite** he recovered quickly
3. to heal : **la blessure ne guérit pas** the wound isn't healing.

guerre [gɛr] *nom féminin*

war : **guerre civil** civil war ; **les deux pays sont en guerre depuis deux ans** the two countries have been at war for two years
- **la Première Guerre mondiale** the First World War OU World War One
- **la Seconde Guerre mondiale** the Second World War OU World War Two.

guetter [gete] *verbe*

to watch for : **je vais les guetter au coin de la rue** I'll watch for them on the corner of the street.

gueule [gœl] *nom féminin*

mouth : **la gueule du chien** the dog's mouth.

guichet [giʃɛ] *nom masculin*

1. counter : **payez au guichet** pay at the counter
2. ticket office : **veuillez retirer vos places au guichet** please collect your tickets from the ticket office.

guide [gid] *nom masculin*

1. guide : **il est guide de montagne** he's a mountain guide
2. guidebook : **je cherche un guide sur l'Écosse** I'm looking for a guidebook on Scotland.

guider [gide] *verbe*

to guide : **il nous a guidés dans la ville** he guided us around the town.

guidon [gidɔ̃] *nom masculin*

handlebars (*pluriel*).

guignol [giɲɔl] *nom masculin*

glove puppet.

guillemets [gijmɛ] *nom masculin pluriel*

inverted commas *UK*, quotation marks : **entre guillemets** in inverted commas OU in quotation marks.

g

guirlande [girlãd] *nom féminin*

guirlande de Noël tinsel (*s'utilise toujours au singulier*) : **ils décorent le sapin avec des guirlandes** they are decorating the tree with tinsel.

guitare [gitar] *nom féminin*

guitar : **Simon joue de la guitare** Simon plays the guitar
➤ **une guitare électrique** an electric guitar
➤ **une guitare sèche** an acoustic guitar.

gym [ʒim] *nom féminin*

gym : **aller à la gym** to go to the gym.

gymnastique [ʒimnastik] *nom féminin*

gymnastics (*singulier*) : **faire de la gymnastique** to do exercises.

gynécologue [ʒinekɔlɔg] *nom masculin ou féminin*

gynaecologist *UK*, gynecologist *US* : **son père est gynécologue** her father's a gynaecologist.

habile [abil] *adjectif*

skilful *UK*, skillful *US* : **ce menuisier est très habile** this carpenter is very skilful ; **être très habile de ses mains** to be very clever with one's hands.

habiller [abije] *verbe*

to dress : **je me charge d'habiller les enfants** I'll dress the children

s'habiller *verbe pronominal*

1. to dress, to get dressed : **elle s'est habillée rapidement** she dressed quickly ou she got dressed quickly
2. to dress up : **est-ce qu'il faut s'habiller pour cette soirée ?** do we have to dress up for the party?

habitant, e [abitã, ãt] *nom masculin, nom féminin*

inhabitant : **il y a 59 millions d'habitants en France** there are 59 millions inhabitants in France.

habiter [abite] *verbe*

to live : **où est-ce que tu habites ?** where do you live? ; **j'habite Paris** ou **j'habite à Paris** I live in Paris ; **j'habite en France** I live in France.

habits [abi] *nom masculin pluriel*

clothes : **j'ai besoin de m'acheter de nouveaux habits** I need to buy some new clothes.

habitude [abityd] *nom féminin*

habit : **une mauvaise habitude** a bad habit
➤ **avoir l'habitude de faire quelque chose** to be used to doing something : **j'ai l'habitude de me lever tôt** I'm used to getting up early
➤ **d'habitude** usually : **d'habitude on se retrouve vers cinq heures** usually we meet up around five o'clock
➤ **comme d'habitude** as usual.

habituel, elle [abitɥɛl] *adjectif*

usual : **à l'heure habituelle** at the usual time.

habituer [abitɥe] *verbe*

habituer quelqu'un à faire quelque chose to get somebody used to doing something ; **j'essaie de les habituer à lever le doigt** I'm trying to get them used to putting their hands up
➤ **être habitué à** to be used to : **je ne suis pas habitué à la chaleur** I'm not used to the heat

s'habituer *verbe pronominal*

s'habituer à quelque chose to get used to something ; **il va falloir t'y habituer** you'll have to get used to it ; **s'habituer à faire quelque chose** to get used to doing something ; **je me suis habitué à me lever tôt** I have got used to getting up early.

hache ['aʃ] *nom féminin*

axe, ax *US*.

hacher ['aʃe] *verbe*

1. to chop : **hachez les oignons** chop the onions
2. to mince *UK*, to grind *US* : **hachez la viande** mince the meat *UK* ou grind the meat *US*
> **du steak haché** minced beef *UK*
> **de la viande hachée** minced meat *UK* ou ground meat *US*.

haie ['ɛ] *nom féminin*

1. hedge : **une haie de noisetiers** a hedge of hazel trees
2. hurdle : **400 mètres haies** 400 metres hurdles *UK* ou 400 meters hurdles *US*.

haine ['ɛn] *nom féminin*

hatred.

haïr ['air] *verbe*

to hate : **je la hais** I hate her

se haïr *verbe pronominal*

to hate each other : **ils se haïssent** they hate each other.

haleine [alɛn] *nom féminin*

breath : **il a mauvaise haleine** he's got bad breath ; **je suis hors d'haleine** I'm out of breath.

hall ['ol] *nom masculin*

lobby : **ils se sont retrouvés dans le hall de l'hôtel** they met in the hotel lobby.

halle ['al] *nom féminin*

covered market.

halte ['alt] *nom féminin*

stop : **c'est la dernière halte sur le parcours** it's the last stop on the route
> **faire halte** to stop : **nous avons fait halte à Limoux** we sopped at Limoux.

hamac ['amak] *nom masculin*

hammock : **il dort dans son hamac** he's sleeping in his hammock.

hamburger ['ābœrgœr] *nom masculin*

hamburger.

hameçon [amsɔ̃] *nom masculin*

hook, fish-hook : **j'ai accroché un ver à l'hameçon** I put a worm on the hook.

hamster ['amstɛr] *nom masculin*

hamster.

hanche ['āʃ] *nom féminin*

hip : **elle avait les mains sur les hanches** she had her hands on her hips.

handball ['ādbal] *nom masculin*

handball : **jouer au handball** to play handball.

handicapé, e ['ādikape] *nom masculin, nom féminin*

disabled person : **les handicapés** the disabled
> **un handicapé moteur** a physically disabled person ou a physically handicapped person
> **un handicapé mental** a mentally handicapped person.

hangar ['āgar] *nom masculin*

shed.

hanté, e ['āte] *adjectif*

haunted : **une maison hantée** a haunted house.

harceler ['arsəle] *verbe*

to harass.

hareng ['arā] *nom masculin*

herring
> **hareng saur** ou **hareng fumé** kipper.

haricot ['ariko] *nom masculin*

bean
> **des haricots blancs** haricot beans
> **des haricots rouges** kidney beans
> **des haricots verts** green beans ou string beans *US*.

harmonica [armɔnika] *nom masculin*

harmonica, mouth organ : **Paul joue de l'harmonica** Paul plays the harmonica ou Paul plays the mouth organ.

harpe ['arp] *nom féminin*

harp : **Laure joue de la harpe** Laure plays the harp.

hasard ['azar] *nom masculin*

1. chance : **un jeu de hasard** a game of chance ; **je l'ai rencontrée par hasard** I met her by chance
2. coincidence : **toi ici, quel hasard !** what a coincidence seeing you here!
> **si par hasard tu passes par là ...** if you happen to be passing by ...

h

> **au hasard** at random : **j'en ai pris un au hasard** I took one at random

 Hasard is a false friend, it does not mean 'hazard'.

hausse ['os] *nom féminin*

rise, increase : **une hausse de 20 %** a 20% rise ou a 20% increase

> **être en hausse** to be rising : **le taux de chômage est en hausse** the unemployment rate is rising.

hausser ['ose] *verbe*

to raise : **elle a haussé le ton** she raised her voice

> **hausser les épaules** to shrug : **il a haussé les épaules** he shrugged.

haut, e [o, ot] *adjectif*

1. **high** : **les plafonds sont hauts dans cette maison** the ceilings are high in this house
2. **tall** : **un bâtiment assez haut** quite a tall building

haut *adverbe & nom*

■ *adverbe*
high : **il peut sauter très haut** he can jump very high

■ *nom masculin*
top : **le haut du mur** the top of the wall ; **le tiroir du haut** the top drawer

> **la tour fait 50 mètres de haut** the tower is 50 metres high *UK* ou the tower is 50 meters high *US*

> **en haut** upstairs : **papa est en haut** dad is upstairs

> **en haut de** at the top of : **en haut de la colline** at the top of the hill

> **de haut en bas** from top to bottom

> **tout haut** aloud ou out loud : **j'étais en train de penser tout haut** I was thinking aloud ou I was thinking out loud.

hauteur ['otœr] *nom féminin*

height : **la hauteur de la tour Eiffel** the height of the Eiffel tower

> **quelle est la hauteur du mont Blanc ?** how high is Mont Blanc?

haut-parleur ['oparlœr] (*pluriel* haut-parleurs) *nom masculin*

loudspeaker : **un téléphone avec un haut-parleur intégré** a telephone with a built-in loudspeaker.

hebdomadaire [ɛbdɔmadɛr] *nom masculin & adjectif*

weekly : **une réunion hebdomadaire** a weekly meeting ; **un hebdomadaire d'information** a news weekly ou a weekly news magazine.

hébergement [ebɛrʒəmɑ̃] *nom masculin*

accommodation *UK*, **accommodations** *US* : **le prix comprend l'hébergement** the price includes accommodation *UK* ou the price includes accommodations *US*.

héberger [ebɛrʒe] *verbe*

to put up : **est-ce que tu peux m'héberger cette nuit ?** can you put me up for the night?

hectare [ɛktar] *nom masculin*

hectare : **c'est un champ de deux hectares** this field is two hectares.

hein ['ɛ̃] *exclamation familier*

hein ? qu'est-ce que tu as dit ? what? what did you say? ; **tu ne lui diras pas, hein ?** you won't tell him, will you?

hélas [elas] *exclamation*

unfortunately : **je n'ai pas terminé à temps, hélas !** I didn't finish on time, unfortunately.

hélice [elis] *nom féminin*

propeller : **l'hélice du bateau** the boat's propeller.

hélicoptère [elikɔptɛr] *nom masculin*

helicopter.

hennir ['enir] *verbe*

to neigh : **le cheval hennit** horses neigh.

herbe [ɛrb] *nom féminin*

grass : **marcher pieds nus sur l'herbe** to walk barefoot in the grass

> **des fines herbes** herbs

> **des mauvaises herbes** weeds.

hérisson ['erisɔ̃] *nom masculin*

hedgehog.

héritage [eritaʒ] *nom masculin*

inheritance : **j'ai reçu des bijoux en héritage** I inherited some jewels ; **elle a fait un gros héritage** she came into a big inheritance.

hériter [erite] *verbe*

to inherit : **il a hérité d'une maison** he inherited a house.

héritier, ère [eritje, ɛr] *nom masculin, nom féminin*

heir *(féminin* **heiress***)* : **c'est une riche héritière** she's a wealthy heiress.

héroïne [erɔin] *nom féminin*

1. heroine : **l'héroïne du roman** the heroine of the novel
2. heroin : **l'héroïne est une drogue dure** heroin is a hard drug.

héron ['erɔ̃] *nom masculin*

heron.

héros ['ero] *nom masculin*

hero : **le héros du film est un garçon de 12 ans** the hero of the film is a 12-year-old boy.

hésiter [ezite] *verbe*

to hesitate : **j'hésite entre celle-ci et celle-là** I'm hesitating between this one and that one ; **hésiter à faire quelque chose** to hesitate to do something ; **n'hésite pas à m'appeler** don't hesitate to call me.

hêtre ['ɛtr] *nom masculin*

beech : **une table en hêtre** a beech table.

heure [œr] *nom féminin*

1. hour : **le film dure deux heures** the film lasts two hours
2. time : **quelle heure est-il ?** what time is it? ; **il est deux heures** it's two o'clock ; **demander l'heure à quelqu'un** to ask somebody the time ; **c'est l'heure d'aller à l'école** it's time to go to school
➤ **heure de fermeture** closing time
➤ **heures d'ouverture** opening times
➤ **heures de pointe** rush hour : **évitez les heures de pointe** avoid the rush hour
➤ **à quelle heure ... ?** when ...? ou what time ...? : **à quelle heure commence le spectacle ?** when does the show start? ou what time does the show start?
➤ **être à l'heure** to be on time : **ils ne sont jamais à l'heure** they're never on time
➤ **de bonne heure** early : **je dois me lever de bonne heure** I have to get up early.

heureusement [œrøzmɑ̃] *adverbe*

fortunately : **heureusement, mes parents n'étaient pas là** fortunately, my parents weren't there
➤ **heureusement que ...** it's a good job ... *UK* : **heureusement que tu es venu !** it's a good job you came!

heureux, euse [œrø, øz] *adjectif*

happy : **il a l'air heureux** he looks happy.

heurter ['œrte] *verbe*

to hit : **la voiture a heurté le cycliste** the car hit the cyclist.

hexagone [ɛgzagon] *nom masculin*

hexagon

Hexagone *nom masculin*

l'Hexagone metropolitan France.

hibou ['ibu] *(pluriel* **hiboux***) nom masculin*

owl : **les hiboux chassent la nuit** owls hunt at night.

hier [ijɛr] *adverbe*

yesterday : **hier matin** yesterday morning ; **hier soir** yesterday evening.

hippopotame [ipɔpɔtam] *nom masculin*

hippopotamus, hippo.

hirondelle [irɔ̃dɛl] *nom féminin*

swallow.

histoire [istwar] *nom féminin*

1. history : **nous étudions l'histoire de France** we're studying French history
2. story *(pluriel* **stories***)* : **une histoire d'amour** a love story
➤ **faire des histoires** to make a fuss : **il faut toujours qu'il fasse des histoires !** he always has to make a fuss!

historique [istɔrik] *adjectif*

1. historical : **un roman historique** a historical novel
2. historic : **c'est un événement historique !** it's truly a historic event!

hit-parade ['itparad] *(pluriel* **hit-parades***) nom masculin*

le hit-parade the charts ; **il est premier au hit-parade** he's number one in the charts.

hiver [ivɛr] *nom masculin*

winter : **en hiver** in winter.

h

HLM *(abréviation de* habitation à loyer modéré*) nom masculin & nom féminin*
council flat *UK*, apartment in a public housing unit *US*.

hockey ['ɔkɛ] *nom masculin*
hockey : le hockey hockey ; ils jouent au hockey they're playing hockey ; le hockey sur glace ice hockey *UK* ou hockey *US* ; le hockey sur gazon hockey *UK* ou field hockey *US*.

hold-up ['ɔldœp] *nom masculin invariable*
hold-up.

hollandais, e ['ɔlɑ̃dɛ, ɛz] *adjectif*
Dutch : une tradition hollandaise a Dutch tradition

hollandais *nom masculin*
le hollandais Dutch ; est-ce que tu parles le hollandais ? ou est-ce que tu parles hollandais ? do you speak Dutch?

> En anglais, les adjectifs se rapportant à un pays ou une région, ainsi que le nom désignant la langue de ce pays ou de cette région, s'écrivent avec une majuscule.

Hollandais, e *nom masculin, nom féminin*
Dutchman *(féminin* Dutchwoman*)* : les Hollandais the Dutch.

Hollande ['ɔlɑ̃d] *nom féminin*
> la Hollande Holland.

> En anglais, à de rares exceptions près, il n'y a pas d'article devant les noms de pays :

j'habite en Hollande I live in Holland ; elle est allée en Hollande she went to Holland.

homard ['ɔmar] *nom masculin*
lobster : un casier à homards a lobster pot.

hommage [ɔmaʒ] *nom masculin*
tribute : en hommage à in tribute to ; nous voulons rendre hommage à ce grand pianiste we wish to pay tribute to this great pianist.

homme [ɔm] *nom masculin*
man *(pluriel* men*)* : c'est un homme intelligent he's an intelligent man ; l'homme descend-il du singe ? is man descended from the apes?
> un homme d'affaires a businessman *(pluriel* businessmen*)*

> un homme politique a politician.

homosexuel, elle [ɔmɔsɛksɥɛl] *adjectif & nom masculin, nom féminin*
homosexual.

honnête [ɔnɛt] *adjectif*
honest : il a toujours été honnête avec moi he's always been honest with me.

honnêtement [ɔnɛtmɑ̃] *adverbe*
honestly : honnêtement, je ne pense pas honestly, I don't think so.

honneur [ɔnœr] *nom masculin*
honour *UK*, honor *US*
> en l'honneur de in honour of *UK* ou in honor of *US*.

honte ['ɔ̃t] *nom féminin*
shame
> avoir honte de quelque chose ou quelqu'un to be ashamed of something ou somebody : elle a honte de son accent she's ashamed of her accent.

hôpital [ɔpital] *(pluriel* hôpitaux [ɔpito]*) nom masculin*
hospital : il est à l'hôpital he's in hospital *UK* ou he's in the hospital *US*.

hoquet ['ɔkɛ] *nom masculin*
avoir le hoquet to have hiccups ou to have the hiccups.

horaire [ɔrɛr] *nom masculin*
timetable *UK*, schedule *US* : avez-vous un horaire des trains ? do you have a train timetable?
> les horaires de travail working hours.

horizon [ɔrizɔ̃] *nom masculin*
horizon : à l'horizon on the horizon.

horloge [ɔrlɔʒ] *nom féminin*
clock.

horoscope [ɔrɔskɔp] *nom masculin*
horoscope : elle lit son horoscope dans le journal she's reading her horoscope in the newspaper.

horreur [ɔrœr] *nom féminin*
horror : un film d'horreur a horror film.
> ce tableau est une horreur that painting is horrible

> **avoir horreur de quelque chose** to hate something : **j'ai horreur des épinards** I hate spinach
> **avoir horreur de faire quelque chose** to hate doing something : **j'ai horreur d'arriver en retard** I hate arriving late
> **quelle horreur !** how awful!

horrible [ɔribl] *adjectif*

horrible, awful : **les rideaux sont horribles** the curtains are horrible ou the curtains are awful.

hors-d'œuvre ['ɔrdœvr] *(pluriel* hors-d'œuvre*) nom masculin*

hors-d'œuvre, starter *UK*, appetizer *US*.

hôte, hôtesse [ot, otɛs] *nom masculin, nom féminin*

host : **il a remercié ses hôtes** he thanked his hosts.

hôtel [otɛl] *nom masculin*

hotel : **on a dormi dans un hôtel trois étoiles** we stayed in a three-star hotel
> **l'hôtel de ville** the town hall *UK* ou the city hall *US*.

hôtesse [otɛs] *nom féminin*

hostess
> **une hôtesse d'accueil** a receptionist
> **une hôtesse de l'air** an air hostess *UK* ou a stewardess.

housse ['us] *nom féminin*

cover : **une housse de siège** a seat cover.

houx ['u] *nom masculin*

holly : **les baies de houx sont toxiques** holly berries are poisonous.

huer ['ɥe] *verbe*

to boo : **les spectateurs huaient la chanteuse** the audience booed the singer.

huile [ɥil] *nom féminin*

oil : **de l'huile végétale** vegetable oil ; **de l'huile d'olive** olive oil ; **de l'huile de tournesol** sunflower oil.

huit ['ɥit] *adjectif numéral & nom masculin*

eight : **j'ai huit cousins** I have eight cousins.
> **nous sommes le huit avril** it's the eighth of April *UK* ou it's April eighth *US*.

huitième ['ɥitjɛm] *adjectif numéral & nom*

eighth : **il est arrivé en huitième position**

he came in eighth place ; **il est arrivé huitième** he came eighth
> **nous sommes le huit avril** it's the eighth of April ou it's April eighth.

huître [ɥitr] *nom féminin*

oyster : **j'aime les huîtres** I like oysters.

humain, e [ymɛ̃, ɛn] *adjectif*

human : **un être humain** a human being

humain *nom masculin*

human, human being.

humeur [ymœr] *nom féminin*

mood : **elle est de très bonne humeur** she's in a very good mood ; **il est toujours de mauvaise humeur** he's always in a bad mood.

humide [ymid] *adjectif*

1. damp : **la maison est très humide en hiver** the house is very damp in winter
2. humid : **un climat chaud et humide** a hot and humid climate.

humour [ymur] *nom masculin*

humour *UK*, humor *US* : **le sens de l'humour** a sense of humour *UK* ou a sense of humor *US* ; **elle a de l'humour** ou **elle a le sens de l'humour** she has a good sense of humour *UK* ou she has a good sense of humor *US*.

hurler ['yrle] *verbe*

to howl : **les loups se sont mis à hurler** the wolves started howling.

hutte ['yt] *nom féminin*

hut : **la tribu habite dans des huttes** the tribe lives in huts.

hydratant, e [idratɑ̃, ɑ̃t] *adjectif*

moisturizing
> **une crème hydratante** a moisturizer.

hydroglisseur [idrɔglisœr] *nom masculin*

hovercraft.

hyène [jɛn] *nom féminin*

hyena.

hygiène [iʒjɛn] *nom féminin*

hygiene.

hygiénique [iʒjenik] *adjectif*

hygienic
> **du papier hygiénique** toilet paper
> **une serviette hygiénique** a sanitary towel *UK* ou a sanitary napkin *US*.

h

hymne [imn] *nom masculin*

➤ **l'hymne national** the national anthem.

hypermarché [ipɛrmarʃe] *nom masculin*

hypermarket *UK*, superstore *US*.

hypnotiser [ipnɔtize] *verbe*

to hypnotize.

iceberg [ajsbɛrg] *nom masculin*

iceberg.

ici [isi] *adverbe*

here : **viens ici** come here

➤ **par ici** this way : **venez par ici** come this way

➤ **d'ici là** by then : **d'ici là, je devrais avoir terminé** I should have finished by then.

icône [ikon] *nom féminin*

icon : **cliquez sur l'icône pour lancer le programme** click on the icon to start the program.

idéal, e, als, aux [ideal, o] *adjectif*

ideal : **c'est un endroit idéal pour un pique-nique** it's an ideal place for a picnic

idéal *nom masculin*

➤ **l'idéal, ça serait que tu viennes à huit heures** the best would be if you came at eight.

idée [ide] *nom féminin*

idea : **c'est une bonne idée** that's a good idea ; **je n'en ai pas la moindre idée** I don't have the slightest idea ; **aucune idée !** no idea!

identifier [idɑ̃tifje] *verbe*

to identify : **le témoin a identifié le voleur** the witness identified the thief

s'identifier *verbe pronominal*

to identify : **s'identifier à** to identify with ; **je me suis complètement identifié au personnage** I totally identified with the character.

identité [idɑ̃tite] *nom féminin*

identity : **le policier lui a demandé sa carte d'identité** the policeman asked him for his identity card.

idiot, e [idjo, ɔt] *adjectif & nom*

■ *adjectif*
stupid : **c'est un film complètement idiot** it's a really stupid film

■ *nom masculin, nom féminin*
idiot : **quel idiot !** what an idiot!

➤ **faire l'idiot**

1. to fool around : **ils n'ont pas arrêté de faire les idiots** they kept fooling around

2. to act stupid : **ne fais pas l'idiot, tu sais très bien de quoi je parle** don't act stupid, you know very well what I'm talking about.

ignorant, e [iɲɔrɑ̃, ɑ̃t] *adjectif*

ignorant.

ignorer [iɲɔre] *verbe*

1. not to know : **j'ignorais qu'elle était aussi actrice** I didn't know she was an actress too

2. to ignore : **s'ils essaient de t'embêter, ignore-les** if they try to annoy you, just ignore them.

il [il] *pronom*

> « Il » se traduit par **he** s'il s'agit d'une personne ou par **it** s'il s'agit d'une chose, d'un animal ou s'il est utilisé dans les constructions impersonnelles :

1. he : **il ne m'a rien dit** he didn't tell me anything ; **il s'appelle Harry** he's called Harry

2. it : **je crois qu'il est cassé** I think it's broken ; **il pleut** it's raining ; **quelle heure est-il ?** what time is it?

➤ **il faut faire attention si l'on veut réussir** we must be careful if we want to succeed

➤ **il faut qu'il vienne avec moi** he must come with me

➤ **il te reste deux heures pour terminer** you have two more hours to finish.

il y a *expression impersonnelle*

1. *Suivi d'un nom au singulier* **there is : il y a un problème** there is a problem ; **il y avait beaucoup de bruit** there was a lot of noise
2. *Suivi d'un nom au pluriel* **there are : il y a deux garçons qui t'attendent** there are two boys waiting for you ; **il y aura des centaines de personnes** there will be hundreds of people
3. *En parlant d'un moment du passé* **ago : c'est arrivé il y a trois ans** it happened three years ago ; **il y a longtemps qu'il est parti** he left a long time ago
4. *En parlant d'une durée* **for : il y a une heure que j'attends** I've been waiting for an hour

> N'oubliez pas que l'on utilise la forme progressive (have been + -ing) lorsqu'on parle d'une action toujours en cours.

ils *pronom pluriel*

they : ils sont déjà là they're already here ; **ils sont un peu rayés** they are a bit scratched.

île [il] *nom féminin*

island : une île déserte a desert island
> **les îles Anglo-Normandes** the Channel Islands
> **les îles Britanniques** the British Isles.

illégal, e, aux [ilegal, o] *adjectif*

illegal : tu ne peux pas faire ça, c'est illégal you can't do that, it's illegal.

illisible [ilizibl] *adjectif*

illegible : ton devoir est illisible your homework is illegible.

illusion [ilyzjɔ̃] *nom féminin*

illusion : une illusion d'optique an optical illusion.

illustration [ilystrasjɔ̃] *nom féminin*

illustration : il y a de belles illustrations dans ce livre there are some lovely illustrations in this book.

ils ➤ il.

image [imaʒ] *nom féminin*

picture : un livre avec des images a book with pictures.

imagination [imaʒinasjɔ̃] *nom féminin*

imagination : il manque totalement d'imagination he has absolutely no imagination
> **avoir de l'imagination** to be imaginative : **Samantha a beaucoup d'imagination** Samantha is very imaginative.

imaginer [imaʒine] *verbe*

to imagine : imagine que tu te trouves sur une île déserte imagine that you are on a desert island

s'imaginer *verbe pronominal*

1. **to imagine : imagine-toi une salle de bal immense** imagine a huge ballroom
2. **to think : il s'imagine qu'il peut m'appeler n'importe quand** he thinks he can phone me up whenever he wants.

imbécile [ɛ̃besil] *nom masculin ou féminin*

idiot : quel imbécile ! what an idiot!

imitation [imitasjɔ̃] *nom féminin*

imitation : ce n'est pas un vrai pistolet, c'est une imitation it's not a real pistol, it's an imitation.

immatriculation [imatrikylasjɔ̃] *nom féminin*

registration : numéro d'immatriculation registration number *UK* ou license number *US*.

immédiat, e [imedja, at] *adjectif*

immediate : sa réponse a été immédiate she gave an immediate answer.

immédiatement [imedjatmɑ̃] *adverbe*

immediately : il est venu immédiatement he came immediately.

immense [imɑ̃s] *adjectif*

huge : la Chine est un pays immense China is a huge country.

immeuble [imœbl] *nom masculin*

1. **building : un immeuble du dix-neuvième siècle** a nineteenth-century building
2. **block of flats** *UK*, **apartment block** *US* : **tu habites dans un immeuble ou dans une maison ?** do you live in a block of flats or in a house?

immigré, e [imigre] *adjectif & nom masculin, nom féminin*
immigrant.

immobile [imɔbil] *adjectif*

still : il est resté immobile he remained still.

155

impair, e [ɛ̃pɛr] *adjectif*

odd : **un chiffre impair** an odd number.

impasse [ɛ̃pas] *nom féminin*

dead end : **il faut faire demi-tour, c'est une impasse** we have to turn back, it's a dead end.

impatient, e [ɛ̃pasjɑ̃, ɑ̃t] *adjectif*

impatient : **il était impatient d'ouvrir les cadeaux** he was impatient to open the presents.

s'impatienter [sɛ̃pasjɑ̃te] *verbe pronominal*

to get impatient : **dépêche-toi, il va s'impatienter** hurry up, he's going to get impatient.

impeccable [ɛ̃pekabl] *adjectif*

1. spotless : **sa maison est impeccable** her house is spotless.
2. perfect : **il a rendu un devoir impeccable** he handed in a perfect piece of homework.

impératif [ɛ̃peratif] *nom masculin*

imperative : **mettez les verbes à l'impératif** put the verbs in the imperative.

imperméable [ɛ̃pɛrmeabl] *adjectif & nom*

■ *adjectif*

waterproof : **une veste imperméable** a waterproof jacket

■ *nom masculin*

raincoat.

impliquer [ɛ̃plike] *verbe*

1. to involve : **je ne voulais pas t'impliquer dans tout ça** I didn't want to involve you in all this
2. to mean : **ça implique de venir plus tôt** it means coming earlier.

impoli, e [ɛ̃pɔli] *adjectif*

rude : **Jules a été très impoli avec le professeur** Jules was very rude to the teacher.

importance [ɛ̃pɔrtɑ̃s] *nom féminin*

importance : **j'attache beaucoup d'importance à la présentation** I attach a great deal of importance to presentation

➤ **avoir de l'importance** to be important : **ça n'a pas beaucoup d'importance** it's not very important.

important, e [ɛ̃pɔrtɑ̃, ɑ̃t] *adjectif*

1. important : **c'est une femme très importante** she's a very important woman
2. large : **il a gagné une somme importante** he won a large amount of money.

importer [ɛ̃pɔrte] *verbe*

1. to import : **ils importent des pièces détachées** they import spare parts
2. to matter : **peu importe** it doesn't matter ; **c'est la seule chose qui m'importe** it's the only thing that matters to me

➤ **n'importe comment** any old how : **tu as rangé ta chambre n'importe comment** you've tidied up your room any old how

➤ **n'importe où** anywhere : **tu peux trouver la même n'importe où** you can find the same one anywhere

➤ **n'importe quand** anytime : **tu peux venir n'importe quand** you can come anytime

➤ **n'importe quel** OU **n'importe quelle** any : **n'importe quel étudiant** any student

➤ **n'importe qui** anybody OU anyone : **n'importe qui peut gagner** anyone can win

➤ **n'importe quoi** anything : **il pourrait lui arriver n'importe quoi** anything could happen to her

➤ **raconter n'importe quoi** OU **dire n'importe quoi** to talk nonsense : **tu racontes n'importe quoi !** you're talking nonsense.

imposer [ɛ̃poze] *verbe*

to impose : **ils nous ont imposé plusieurs conditions** they imposed several conditions on us.

impossible [ɛ̃pɔsibl] *adjectif*

impossible : **ce mot est impossible à prononcer** this word is impossible to pronounce ; **impossible de trouver des billets pour le concert !** it's impossible to get tickets for the concert!

impôt [ɛ̃po] *nom masculin*

tax *(pluriel* taxes*)* : **je viens de payer mes impôts** I've just paid my taxes.

impression [ɛ̃presjɔ̃] *nom féminin*

impression : **il a fait bonne impression** he made a good impression ; **j'avais l'impression qu'elle voulait venir** I got the impression that she wanted to come.

impressionner [ɛ̃presjɔne] *verbe*

to impress : **il cherchait à m'impressionner**

he was trying to impress me ; **sa maturité m'a impressionné** I was impressed by her maturity.

imprimante [ɛ̃primɑ̃t] *nom féminin*

printer : **une imprimante laser** a laser printer.

imprimer [ɛ̃prime] *verbe*

to print : **tu peux m'imprimer ce fichier ?** can you print this file for me?

à l'improviste [alɛ̃prɔvist] *adverbe*

unexpectedly, without warning : **il est arrivé à l'improviste** he arrived unexpectedly OU he arrived without warning.

imprudent, e [ɛ̃prydɑ̃, ɑ̃t] *adjectif*

careless : **un conducteur imprudent** a careless driver.

inaperçu, e [inapɛrsy] *adjectif*

> **passer inaperçu** to go unnoticed : **il est passé inaperçu dans la foule** he went unnoticed in the crowd.

inattendu, e [inatɑ̃dy] *adjectif*

unexpected : **une visite inattendue** an unexpected visit.

inattention [inatɑ̃sjɔ̃] *nom féminin*

> **une faute d'inattention** a careless mistake.

inauguration [inogyrasjɔ̃] *nom féminin*

inauguration, opening : **l'inauguration d'une bibliothèque** the inauguration of a library OU the opening of a library.

incapable [ɛ̃kapabl] *adjectif*

incapable : **je suis incapable de faire ça** I'm incapable of doing that.

incendie [ɛ̃sɑ̃di] *nom masculin*

fire : **les pompiers ont réussi à éteindre l'incendie** the firemen managed to put the fire out.

inciter [ɛ̃site] *verbe*

to encourage : **je l'ai incité à lire ce livre** I encouraged him to read this book.

inclure [ɛ̃klyr] *verbe*

to include : **j'ai inclus ton nom dans la liste** I included your name in the list ; **la taxe d'aéroport est incluse** the airport tax is included.

inclus, e [ɛ̃kly, yz] *participe passé* ➤ inclure.

incomplet, ète [ɛ̃kɔ̃plɛ, ɛt] *adjectif*

incomplete : **la liste est incomplète** the list is incomplete.

inconnu, e [ɛ̃kɔny] *adjectif & nom*

▪ *adjectif*
unknown : **la tombe du soldat inconnu** the tomb of the unknown soldier
▪ *nom masculin, nom féminin*
stranger : **n'ouvre pas la porte à des inconnus** don't open the door to strangers.

inconscient, e [ɛ̃kɔ̃sjɑ̃, ɑ̃t] *adjectif*

1. unconscious : **il est encore inconscient** he's still unconscious
2. reckless : **tu es complètement inconscient !** you're totally reckless!

inconvénient [ɛ̃kɔ̃venjɑ̃] *nom masculin*

disadvantage : **les avantages et les inconvénients du projet** the advantages and disadvantages of the plan
> **je n'y vois pas d'inconvénient** I have no objection to this.

incorrect, e [ɛ̃kɔrɛkt] *adjectif*

1. incorrect : **ton raisonnement est incorrect** your reasoning is incorrect
2. rude : **il a été incorrect avec son professeur** he was rude to his teacher.

incroyable [ɛ̃krwajabl] *adjectif*

incredible : **il nous a raconté une histoire incroyable** he told us an incredible story.

Inde [ɛ̃d] *nom féminin*

> **l'Inde** India

En anglais, à de rares exceptions près, il n'y a pas d'article devant les noms de pays :

j'habite en Inde I live in India ; **elle est allée en Inde** she went to India.

indemne [ɛ̃dɛmn] *adjectif*

unharmed : **il est sorti indemne de l'accident** he escaped the accident unharmed.

indémodable [ɛ̃demɔdabl] *adjectif*

la musique de Bob Marley est indémodable Bob Marley's music never goes out of fashion.

indépendance [ɛ̃depɑ̃dɑ̃s] *nom féminin*

independence : **il tient à son indépendan-**

ce he likes his independence ; **le pays a accédé à l'indépendance en 1960** the country gained independence in 1960.

indépendant, e [ɛ̃depɑ̃dɑ̃, ɑ̃t] *adjectif*

independent : **c'est quelqu'un de très indépendant** he's very independent.

index [ɛ̃dɛks] *nom masculin*

1. index finger, forefinger : **l'index est à côté du pouce** the index finger is next to the thumb
2. index *(pluriel* **indexes***)* : **il y a un index à la fin du livre** there's an index at the end of the book.

indicatif [ɛ̃dikatif] *nom masculin*

1. indicative : **le présent de l'indicatif** the present indicative
2. dialling code *UK*, area code *US* : **quel est l'indicatif du Canada ?** what's the dialling code for Canada?

indication [ɛ̃dikasjɔ̃] *nom féminin*

instruction : **suivez les indications du professeur** follow the teacher's instructions.

indice [ɛ̃dis] *nom masculin*

clue : **le détective a trouvé un indice** the detective found a clue.

indien, enne [ɛ̃djɛ̃, ɛn] *adjectif*

Indian

En anglais, les adjectifs se rapportant à un pays ou une région s'écrivent avec une majuscule :

un sari indien an Indian sari

Indien, enne *nom masculin, nom féminin*

Indian : **la majorité des Indiens sont hindous** the majority of Indians are Hindus.

indifférent, e [ɛ̃diferɑ̃, ɑ̃t] *adjectif*

indifferent : **cela m'est complètement indifférent** I'm completely indifferent.

indigestion [ɛ̃diʒɛstjɔ̃] *nom féminin*

indigestion : **avoir une indigestion** to have indigestion.

indigné, e [ɛ̃diɲe] *adjectif*

outraged : **j'ai été indigné par sa réaction** I was outraged by his reaction.

indiquer [ɛ̃dike] *verbe*

1. to tell : **pouvez-vous m'indiquer où se**

trouve le bureau des réclamations ?** can you tell me where the complaints office is?
2. to show : **le plan indique que c'est en face de la gare** the map shows that it's opposite the station ; **il m'a indiqué l'entrée** he showed me where the entrance was ; **un policier m'a indiqué le chemin** a policeman showed me the way
3. to indicate : **la lumière verte indique la sortie** the green light indicates the exit
4. to recommend : **elle m'a indiqué un bon dentiste** she recommended a good dentist to me.

indirect, e [ɛ̃dirɛkt] *adjectif*

indirect : **le complément d'objet indirect** the indirect object.

indiscret, ète [ɛ̃diskrɛ, ɛt] *adjectif*

1. nosy, nosey : **des voisins indiscrets** nosy neighbours
2. indiscreet : **une question indiscrète** an indiscreet question.

indispensable [ɛ̃dispɑ̃sabl] *adjectif*

essential : **il est indispensable que vous soyez là** it is essential that you be there.

individu [ɛ̃dividy] *nom masculin*

person, individual : **deux individus sont venus vers moi** two people came towards me.

individuel, elle [ɛ̃dividɥɛl] *adjectif*

individual : **la liberté individuelle** individual freedom
➤ **une chambre individuelle** a single room.

indulgent, e [ɛ̃dylʒɑ̃, ɑ̃t] *adjectif*

1. indulgent : **elle est indulgente avec sa fille** she's indulgent with her daughter ou she indulges her daughter
2. lenient : **l'examinateur a été indulgent** the examiner was lenient.

industrie [ɛ̃dystri] *nom féminin*

industry *(pluriel* **industries***)* : **l'industrie automobile** the car industry.

industriel, elle [ɛ̃dystrijɛl] *adjectif*

industrial : **une zone industrielle** an industrial park.

inégalité [inegalite] *nom féminin*

inequality *(pluriel* **inequalities***)* : **les inégalités sociales** social inequalities.

inévitable [inevitabl] *adjectif*
inevitable.

infect, e [ɛ̃fɛkt] *adjectif*
revolting : **la nourriture était infecte** the food was revolting.

s'infecter [sɛ̃fɛkte] *verbe pronominal*
to become infected : **la plaie s'est infectée** the wound became infected.

infection [ɛ̃fɛksjɔ̃] *nom féminin*
infection.

inférieur, e [ɛ̃ferjœr] *adjectif*
1. lower : **les étages inférieurs** the lower floors ; **les membres inférieurs** the lower limbs
2. bottom : **le coin inférieur droit** the bottom right-hand corner
3. inferior : **leur dernier album est d'une qualité inférieure** their last album is of inferior quality
➤ **à l'étage inférieur** on the floor below : **son bureau se trouve à l'étage inférieur** his office is on the floor below
➤ **inférieur à**
1. less than : **X est inférieur à Y** X is less than Y
2. below : **les températures sont inférieures à la moyenne** temperatures are below average.

infernal, e, aux [ɛ̃fɛrnal, o] *adjectif*
terrible : **un bruit infernal** a terrible noise.

infini, e [ɛ̃fini] *adjectif*
infinite : **il fait preuve d'une patience infinie** he has infinite patience

infini *nom masculin*
l'infini infinity
➤ **à l'infini** forever : **on pourrait en discuter à l'infini** we could talk about it forever.

infiniment [ɛ̃finimɑ̃] *adverbe*
1. infinitely : **infiniment mieux** infinitely better
2. extremely : **je regrette infiniment** I am extremely sorry
3. so much : **je vous remercie infiniment** thank you so much.

infinitif [ɛ̃finitif] *nom masculin*
infinitive : **mettez le verbe à l'infinitif** put the verb in the infinitive.

infirme [ɛ̃firm] *adjectif & nom*
☐ *adjectif*
disabled
☐ *nom masculin ou féminin*
disabled person.

infirmerie [ɛ̃firməri] *nom féminin*
infirmary *(pluriel* **infirmaries***)* : **l'infirmerie de l'école** the school infirmary ou the sick bay.

infirmier, ère [ɛ̃firmje, ɛr] *nom masculin, nom féminin*
nurse : **Natacha veut être infirmière** Natacha wants to be a nurse.

influence [ɛ̃flyɑ̃s] *nom féminin*
influence : **il a une mauvaise influence sur elle** he is a bad influence on her.

influencer [ɛ̃flyɑ̃se] *verbe*
to influence : **tu te laisses trop facilement influencer** you're too easily influenced.

informaticien, enne [ɛ̃fɔrmatisjɛ̃, ɛn] *nom masculin, nom féminin*
computer scientist : **le frère de Karim est informaticien** Karim's brother is a computer scientist.

information [ɛ̃fɔrmasjɔ̃] *nom féminin*
information *(ne s'utilise jamais au pluriel)* : **des informations** information ; **j'ai besoin d'une information** I need some information ; **je voudrais des informations sur le concert** I'd like some information about the concert

informations *nom féminin pluriel*
les informations the news ; **je l'ai entendu aux informations de 20 heures** I heard it on the eight o'clock news.

informatique [ɛ̃fɔrmatik] *nom & adjectif*
☐ *nom féminin*
computing, computer science : **elle travaille dans l'informatique** she works in computing ; **un cours d'informatique** a computing course ; **son frère s'y connaît en informatique** his brother knows about computers
☐ *adjectif*
computer : **un système informatique** a computer system.

informatiser [ɛ̃fɔrmatize] *verbe*
to computerize.

informer [ɛ̃fɔrme] *verbe*

to inform

s'informer *verbe pronominal*

to ask, to find out : **je m'informerai des horaires** I'll ask about the times OU I'll find out about the times.

infos [ɛ̃fo] (*abréviation de* **informations**) *nom féminin pluriel familier*

news : **est-ce que tu as regardé les infos ?** have you seen the news? ; **les infos passent à 8 heures** the news is on at 8 o'clock.

infusion [ɛ̃fyzjɔ̃] *nom féminin*

herbal tea.

ingénieur [ɛ̃ʒenjœr] *nom masculin*

engineer : **mon père est ingénieur** my father is an engineer.

ingrédient [ɛ̃gredjɑ̃] *nom masculin*

ingredient : **je n'ai pas tous les ingrédients pour cette recette** I don't have all the ingredients for this recipe.

initiale [inisjal] *nom féminin*

initial : **mets tes initiales au bas de la page** put your initials at the bottom of the page.

initiation [inisjasjɔ̃] *nom féminin*

introduction : **une initiation à l'anglais** an introduction to English.

initiative [inisjativ] *nom féminin*

initiative : **ils ont pris l'initiative d'organiser une collecte** they took the initiative to organize a collection.

injure [ɛ̃ʒyr] *nom féminin*

insult : **des injures racistes** racist insults

> ⚠ The French word **injure** is a false friend, it does not mean 'injure' or 'injury'.

injurier [ɛ̃ʒyrje] *verbe*

to insult : **il s'est fait injurier par ses camarades de classe** his classmates insulted him.

injuste [ɛ̃ʒyst] *adjectif*

unfair : **c'est injuste** that's unfair.

innocence [inɔsɑ̃s] *nom féminin*

innocence.

innocent, e [inɔsɑ̃, ɑ̃t] *adjectif*

innocent : **elle a été déclarée innocente** she was found innocent.

inoffensif, ive [inɔfɑ̃sif, iv] *adjectif*

harmless : **la couleuvre est inoffensive** the grass snake is harmless.

inondation [inɔ̃dasjɔ̃] *nom féminin*

flood : **les récoltes ont été détruites par les inondations** the crops were destroyed by floods.

inonder [inɔ̃de] *verbe*

to flood : **le robinet était ouvert et ça a inondé toute la maison** the tap was running and it flooded the whole house.

Inox® [inɔks] *nom masculin invariable*

stainless steel : **un couteau en Inox** a stainless steel knife.

inoxydable [inɔksidabl] *adjectif*

stainless : **de l'acier inoxydable** stainless steel.

inquiet, ète [ɛ̃kjɛ, ɛt] *adjectif*

worried : **elle est très inquiète pour lui** she's very worried about him.

inquiéter [ɛ̃kjete] *verbe*

to worry : **sa maladie inquiète ses parents** his illness worries his parents.

s'inquiéter *verbe pronominal*

1. to worry : **ne t'inquiète pas** don't worry
2. to be worried : **je m'inquiète beaucoup** I'm very worried ; **ils s'inquiètent pour mon avenir** they are worried about my future.

inquiétude [ɛ̃kjetyd] *nom féminin*

worry : **c'est ma seule inquiétude** it's my only worry.

inscription [ɛ̃skripsjɔ̃] *nom féminin*

1. enrolment *UK*, enrollment *US* (*ne s'utilisent jamais au pluriel*) : **les inscriptions débuteront lundi** enrolment will begin on Monday
2. inscription : **une inscription gravée dans la pierre** an inscription engraved on the stone.

inscrire [ɛ̃skrir] *verbe*

1. to enrol *UK*, to enroll *US* : **elle m'a inscrit à l'atelier de 15 heures** she enrolled me in the 3 pm workshop

2. **to write :** inscrivez votre nom en haut de la page write your name at the top of the page

s'inscrire *verbe pronominal*

to enrol *UK*, to enroll *US* : je voudrais m'inscrire au cours d'informatique I'd like to enrol for the computing course

➤ **s'inscrire sur une liste** to put one's name down on a list.

insecte [ε̃sɛkt] *nom masculin*

insect.

insigne [ε̃siɲ] *nom masculin*

badge : il porte l'insigne du club he's wearing the club's badge.

insignifiant, e [ε̃siɲifjɑ̃, ɑ̃t] *adjectif*

insignificant.

insinuer [ε̃sinɥe] *verbe*

to insinuate : qu'est-ce que tu veux insinuer ? what are you trying to insinuate?

insister [ε̃siste] *verbe*

1. **to insist :** il a insisté pour qu'on aille avec lui he insisted that we go with him ou he insisted we go with him
2. **to emphasize :** le prof a insisté sur le dernier chapitre the teacher emphasized the last chapter.

insolation [ε̃sɔlasjɔ̃] *nom féminin*

sunstroke : tu vas attraper une insolation you'll get sunstroke.

insolence [ε̃sɔlɑ̃s] *nom féminin*

cheek : j'en ai assez de ton insolence I've had enough of your cheek.

insolent, e [ε̃sɔlɑ̃, ɑ̃t] *adjectif*

cheeky : ne sois pas insolent ! don't be cheeky!

insomnie [ε̃sɔmni] *nom féminin*

insomnia : avoir des insomnies to suffer from insomnia.

insouciant, e [ε̃susjɑ̃, ɑ̃t] *adjectif*

carefree : c'est une enfant insouciante she's a carefree child.

inspecter [ε̃spɛkte] *verbe*

to inspect : les douaniers ont inspecté nos bagages the customs officers inspected our baggage.

inspecteur, trice [ε̃spɛktœr, tris] *nom masculin, nom féminin*

inspector : un inspecteur de police a police inspector.

inspiration [ε̃spirasjɔ̃] *nom féminin*

inspiration.

inspirer [ε̃spire] *verbe*

1. **to inspire :** ce thème ne m'inspire pas vraiment this topic doesn't exactly inspire me
2. **to breathe in :** inspirez, et maintenant expirez breathe in and now breathe out

s'inspirer *verbe pronominal*

s'inspirer de quelque chose to take one's inspiration from something ; elle s'est inspirée d'un roman célèbre she took her inspiration from a famous novel.

instable [ε̃stabl] *adjectif*

1. **unstable :** la situation dans ce pays est très instable the situation in the country is very unstable
2. **unsettled :** le temps restera instable jusqu'à jeudi the weather will remain unsettled until Thursday.

installation [ε̃stalasjɔ̃] *nom féminin*

l'installation d'un nouveau système coûte cher installing a new system is expensive

➤ **les installations sportives** sports facilities.

installer [ε̃stale] *verbe*

1. **to put up :** mon père m'a installé des étagères my father put some shelves up for me
2. **to install, to instal** *US* : cliquez sur l'icône pour installer le logiciel click on the icon to install the program

s'installer *verbe pronominal*

1. **to move in :** de nouveaux voisins viennent de s'installer new neighbours have just moved in
2. **to sit :** installe-toi dans le grand fauteuil sit in the big armchair
➤ **installez-vous, j'en ai pour une minute** take a seat, I'll be with you in a minute.

instant [ε̃stɑ̃] *nom masculin*

moment, instant : un instant, s'il vous plaît just a moment, please

➤ **à l'instant** a moment ago : il vient de partir à l'instant he left a moment ago

➤ **pour l'instant** for the moment : pour l'ins-

tant, il faut attendre for the moment, we
have to wait.

instantané, e [ɛ̃stɑ̃tane] *adjectif*

instant : **café instantané** instant coffee.

instinct [ɛ̃stɛ̃] *nom masculin*

instinct.

instinctif, ive [ɛ̃stɛ̃ktif, iv] *adjectif*

instinctive : **un geste instinctif** an instinctive move.

institut [ɛ̃stity] *nom masculin*

institute : **l'institut de technologie** the institute of technology
➤ **un institut de beauté** a beauty salon.

instituteur, trice [ɛ̃stitytœr, tris] *nom masculin, nom féminin*

primary-school teacher *UK*, grade-school teacher *US* : **ma mère est institutrice** my mother is a primary-school teacher *UK* ou my mother is a grade-school teacher *US*.

instruction [ɛ̃stryksjɔ̃] *nom féminin*

l'instruction civique civics

instructions *nom féminin pluriel*

instructions : **il m'a donné des instructions précises** he gave me precise instructions ; **lisez bien les instructions** read the instructions carefully.

instruit, e [ɛ̃strɥi, it] *adjectif*

educated : **il est très instruit** he's very well educated.

instrument [ɛ̃strymɑ̃] *nom masculin*

instrument : **tu joues d'un instrument ?** do you play an instrument? ; **un instrument de musique** a musical instrument ; **un instrument à cordes** a stringed instrument ; **un instrument à vent** a wind instrument.

insuffisant, e [ɛ̃syfizɑ̃, ɑ̃t] *adjectif*

1. insufficient : **un nombre insuffisant de professeurs** an insufficient number of teachers
2. unsatisfactory : **travail insuffisant** unsatisfactory work.

insulte [ɛ̃sylt] *nom féminin*

insult : **il hurlait des insultes** he was shouting insults.

insulter [ɛ̃sylte] *verbe*

to insult : **il n'arrête pas de m'insulter** he's always insulting me.

insupportable [ɛ̃sypɔrtabl] *adjectif*

1. impossible : **c'est un enfant insupportable** he's an impossible child
2. unbearable : **des conditions insupportables** unbearable conditions.

intact, e [ɛ̃takt] *adjectif*

intact : **la maison est restée intacte après le tremblement de terre** the house remained intact after the earthquake.

intégré, e [ɛ̃tegre] *adjectif*

built-in : **un appareil photo avec flash intégré** a camera with a built-in flash.

s'intégrer [sɛ̃tegre] *verbe pronominal*

to integrate : **elle s'est bien intégrée dans sa nouvelle classe** she integrated well into her new class.

intellectuel, elle [ɛ̃telɛktɥel] *adjectif & nom masculin, nom féminin*

intellectual.

intelligence [ɛ̃teliʒɑ̃s] *nom féminin*

intelligence : **l'intelligence artificielle** artificial intelligence.

intelligent, e [ɛ̃teliʒɑ̃, ɑ̃t] *adjectif*

intelligent : **c'est une fille très intelligente** she's a very intelligent girl.

intense [ɛ̃tɑ̃s] *adjectif*

intense.

intensif, ive [ɛ̃tɑ̃sif, iv] *adjectif*

intensive : **des cours d'anglais intensifs** an intensive English course.

intention [ɛ̃tɑ̃sjɔ̃] *nom féminin*

intention
➤ **avoir l'intention de faire quelque chose** to intend to do something : **il a l'intention de l'inviter elle aussi** he intends to invite her as well.

interactif, ive [ɛ̃tɛraktif, iv] *adjectif*

interactive : **un jeu vidéo interactif** an interactive video game.

interclasse [ɛ̃tɛrklas] *nom masculin*

je dois voir le directeur pendant l'interclasse I have to see the principal between classes.

162

interdiction [ε̃tεrdiksjɔ̃] *nom féminin*

ban : **l'interdiction de la chasse à la baleine** the ban on whaling
➤ **'interdiction de fumer'** 'no smoking'
➤ **'interdiction de stationner'** 'no parking'.

interdire [ε̃tεrdir] *verbe*

to forbid : **ils m'ont interdit de regarder la télé** they have forbidden me to watch TV.

interdit, e [ε̃tεrdi, it] *verbe & adjectif*

▪ *participe passé de* interdire
▪ *adjectif*
forbidden : **il est interdit de fumer** smoking is forbidden
➤ **'interdit aux mineurs'** 'no children allowed'.

intéressant, e [ε̃tεrεsã, ãt] *adjectif*

interesting : **ce livre est très intéressant** this book is very interesting.

intéressé, e [ε̃tεrese] *adjectif*

1. interested : **il n'avait pas l'air très intéressé par le sujet** he didn't look very interested in the subject
2. self-interested : **une personne intéressée** a person that looks after their own interest.

intéresser [ε̃tεrese] *verbe*

to interest, to be interested : **ça m'intéresse beaucoup** it really interests me OU I'm very interested in it

s'intéresser *verbe pronominal*

s'intéresser à quelque chose to be interested in something ; **elle s'intéresse surtout à la mode** she's mainly interested in fashion.

intérêt [ε̃tεrε] *nom masculin*

interest : **il écoutait avec intérêt** he was listening with interest ; **j'ai agi dans ton intérêt** I acted in your interest ; **ce livre n'a aucun intérêt** this book is of no interest
➤ **on a intérêt à être à l'heure** we'd better be there on time ; **tu as intérêt à me le rendre** you'd better give it back to me
➤ **quel est l'intérêt de faire ça ?**   what's the point of doing that?

intérieur, e [ε̃terjœr] *adjectif*

1. inside : **c'est dans la poche intérieure de ma veste** it's in the inside pocket of my jacket
2. domestic : **l'aérogare pour les vols intérieurs** the terminal for domestic flights

intérieur *nom masculin*

inside : **de l'intérieur** from the inside
➤ **à l'intérieur** inside : **regarde ce qu'il y a à l'intérieur !** look what's inside! ; **les clés sont restées à l'intérieur de la maison** the keys are still inside the house.

intermédiaire [ε̃tεrmedjεr] *nom masculin*

intermediary
➤ **j'ai eu les billets par l'intermédiaire d'un ami** I got the tickets through a friend.

interminable [ε̃tεrminabl] *adjectif*

never-ending.

internat [ε̃tεrna] *nom masculin*

boarding school : **j'ai passé deux ans en internat** I spent two years at boarding school.

international, e, aux [ε̃tεrnasjɔnal, o] *adjectif*

international : **les vols internationaux** international flights.

interne [ε̃tεrn] *nom & adjectif*

▪ *nom masculin ou féminin*
boarder : **il est interne dans cette école** he is a boarder in this school
▪ *adjectif*
internal : **les organes internes** the internal organs.

Internet, internet [ε̃tεrnεt] *nom masculin*

Internet, internet : **l'Internet** the Internet ; **sur Internet** on the Internet.

Interphone® [ε̃tεrfɔn] *nom masculin*

entry phone.

interprète [ε̃tεrprεt] *nom masculin ou féminin*

1. interpreter : **il est interprète aux Nations unies** he's an interpreter at the United Nations
2. performer : **j'ai oublié le nom de l'interprète principal** I've forgotten the name of the main performer.

interpréter [ε̃tεrprete] *verbe*

1. to interpret : **je ne savais pas comment interpréter son comportement** I didn't know how to interpret his behaviour
2. to play the part of : **il interprète Don Juan** he plays the part of Dom Juan
3. to perform, to play : **interpréter un morceau de musique** to perform a piece of music OU to play a piece of music.

interrogation [ɛ̃tɛrɔgasjɔ̃] *nom féminin*

test : **une interrogation écrite** a written test.

interrogatoire [ɛ̃tɛrɔgatwar] *nom masculin*

questioning, interrogation : **on l'a amené au commissariat pour interrogatoire** they took him to the police for questioning.

interroger [ɛ̃tɛrɔʒe] *verbe*

1. to question : **la police l'a interrogé pendant deux heures** the police questioned him for two hours
2. to test : **le professeur va nous interroger sur ce chapitre demain** the teacher is going to test us on this chapter tomorrow.

interrompre [ɛ̃tɛrɔ̃pr] *verbe*

to interrupt : **elle m'a interrompu plusieurs fois** she interrupted me several times

s'interrompre *verbe pronominal*

to stop : **ils ne se sont même pas interrompus pour manger** they didn't even stop to eat.

interrompu, e [ɛ̃tɛrɔ̃py] *participe passé de* interrompre.

interrupteur [ɛ̃tɛryptœr] *nom masculin*

switch, light switch : **l'interrupteur est à droite en entrant** the switch is on the right as you come in.

interruption [ɛ̃tɛrypsjɔ̃] *nom féminin*

break : **il a travaillé toute la journée sans interruption** he worked all day long without a break
➤ **'ouvert de 10 h à 19 h sans interruption'** 'open all day from 10 am to 7 pm'
➤ **interruption volontaire de grossesse** termination of pregnancy.

intersection [ɛ̃tɛrsɛksjɔ̃] *nom féminin*

junction : **tournez à gauche à la prochaine intersection** turn left at the next junction.

intervalle [ɛ̃tɛrval] *nom masculin*

interval : **à intervalles réguliers** at regular intervals
➤ **à six jours d'intervalle** within six days : **il a eu deux accidents à six jours d'intervalle** he had two accidents within six days.

intervenir [ɛ̃tɛrvənir] *verbe*

1. to intervene : **il y a eu une bagarre, mais la**

police est intervenue there was a fight, but the police intervened
2. to speak : **il n'est pas intervenu dans le débat** he didn't speak during the debate.

intervenu, e [ɛ̃tɛrvəny] *participe passé de* intervenir.

interview [ɛ̃tɛrvju] *nom féminin*

interview : **cette star ne donne aucune interview** this star doesn't give interviews.

interviewer [ɛ̃tɛrvjuve] *verbe*

to interview : **elle s'est fait interviewer par un journaliste** she was interviewed by a journalist.

intime [ɛ̃tim] *adjectif*

intimate : **des détails intimes** intimate details
➤ **un ami intime** a close friend.

intimider [ɛ̃timide] *verbe*

to intimidate : **ne te laisse pas intimider** don't be intimidated.

intituler [ɛ̃tityle] *verbe*

to entitle, to call : **il a intitulé son poème « Aurore »** he entitled his poem "Aurore" OU he called his poem "Aurore"

s'intituler *verbe pronominal*

to be entitled, to be called : **comment s'intitule le roman ?** what is the title of the novel? OU what is the novel called?

intoxication [ɛ̃tɔksikasjɔ̃] *nom féminin*

poisoning : **une intoxication alimentaire** food poisoning.

intrigue [ɛ̃trig] *nom féminin*

plot : **l'intrigue est très compliquée** the plot is very complicated.

introduction [ɛ̃trɔdyksjɔ̃] *nom féminin*

introduction : **l'introduction de la dissertation** the introduction to the essay.

introduire [ɛ̃trɔdɥir] *verbe*

1. to insert : **introduire une pièce d'un euro** insert a one-euro coin
2. to introduce : **qui a introduit les pommes de terre en Europe ?** who introduced potatoes to Europe?

introduit, e [ɛ̃trɔdɥi, it] *participe passé de* introduire.

introuvable [ɛ̃truvabl] *adjectif*

nowhere to be found : **les clés sont introuvables** the keys are nowhere to be found.

inutile [inytil] *adjectif*

useless : **un renseignement complètement inutile** a completely useless piece of information

➤ **c'est inutile d'essayer** there's no point in trying.

invalide [ɛ̃valid] *nom masculin ou féminin*

disabled person.

invasion [ɛ̃vazjɔ̃] *nom féminin*

invasion : **une invasion de sauterelles** an invasion of locust.

inventer [ɛ̃vɑ̃te] *verbe*

to invent : **c'est un Écossais qui a inventé le téléphone** it was a Scot who invented the telephone.

inventeur, trice [ɛ̃vɑ̃tœr, tris] *nom masculin, nom féminin*

inventor : **qui a été l'inventeur de la locomotive à vapeur ?** who was the inventor of the steam engine?

invention [ɛ̃vɑ̃sjɔ̃] *nom féminin*

invention.

inverse [ɛ̃vɛrs] *nom & adjectif*

■ *nom masculin*
l'inverse the opposite

■ *adjectif*
1. opposite : **en sens inverse** in the opposite direction
2. reverse : **dans l'ordre inverse** in reverse order.

inverser [ɛ̃vɛrse] *verbe*

to reverse : **inverser les deux mots** reverse the two words.

invisible [ɛ̃vizibl] *adjectif*

invisible.

invitation [ɛ̃vitasjɔ̃] *nom féminin*

invitation : **j'ai reçu une invitation à leur mariage** I got an invitation to their wedding.

invité, e [ɛ̃vite] *nom masculin, nom féminin*

guest : **vous attendez combien d'invités ?** how many guests are you expecting?

inviter [ɛ̃vite] *verbe*

to invite : **ils m'ont invité à dîner** they invited me to dinner.

invraisemblable [ɛ̃vrɛsɑ̃blabl] *adjectif*

1. unlikely, improbable : **une excuse invraisemblable** an unlikely excuse OU an improbable excuse
2. incredible : **une histoire invraisemblable** an incredible story.

irai, iras *etc* ➤ aller.

irlandais, e [irlɑ̃dɛ, ɛz] *adjectif*

Irish

En anglais, les adjectifs se rapportant à un pays ou une région s'écrivent avec une majuscule :

un pub irlandais an Irish pub

irlandais *nom masculin*

Irish : **peu de gens savent encore parler irlandais** few people can still speak Irish

En anglais, les adjectifs se rapportant à un pays ou une région, ainsi que le nom désignant la langue de ce pays ou de cette région, s'écrivent avec une majuscule.

Irlandais, e *nom masculin, nom féminin*

Irishman (*féminin* Irishwoman) ; **les Irlandais** the Irish.

Irlande [irlɑ̃d] *nom féminin*

➤ **l'Irlande** Ireland

En anglais, à de rares exceptions près, il n'y a pas d'article devant les noms de pays :

Cork se trouve en Irlande Cork is in Ireland ; **je suis allé en Irlande cet été** I went to Ireland this summer
➤ **l'Irlande du Nord** Northern Ireland.

irons, iront *etc* ➤ aller.

irrégulier, ère [iregylje, ɛr] *adjectif*

1. irregular : **un verbe irrégulier** an irregular verb
2. uneven : **ses dents sont irrégulières** his teeth are uneven ; **Luc a eu des résultats irréguliers ce trimestre** Luc's results were very uneven this term.

irréparable [ireparabl] *adjectif*

beyond repair : **la radio est irréparable** the radio is beyond repair.

irriter [irite] *verbe*

to irritate : **ce tissu irrite la peau** this fabric irritates the skin.

islamique [islamik] *adjectif*

Islamic

En anglais, les adjectifs et les noms se rapportant à une religion s'écrivent avec une majuscule.

isolé, e [izɔle] *adjectif*

isolated : **un village isolé** an isolated village.

s'isoler [sizɔle] *verbe pronominal*

il s'est isolé dans son bureau pour travailler he shut himself in his office to work.

issue [isy] *nom féminin*

exit : **issue de secours** emergency exit

⚠ The French word **issue** is a false friend, it does not mean 'issue'.

Italie [itali] *nom féminin*

➤ **l'Italie** Italy

En anglais, à de rares exceptions près, il n'y a pas d'article devant les noms de pays :

ma tante vit en Italie my aunt lives in Italy ; **je suis allé en Italie avec ma classe** I went on a school trip to Italy with my class.

italien, enne [italjɛ̃, ɛn] *adjectif*

Italian : **j'aime les glaces italiennes** I like Italian ice cream

italien *nom masculin*

Italian : **tu parles bien italien** you speak good Italian

En anglais, les adjectifs se rapportant à un pays ou une région, ainsi que le nom désignant la langue de ce pays ou de cette région, s'écrivent avec une majuscule.

Italien, enne *nom masculin, nom féminin*

Italian.

italique [italik] *nom masculin*

italic : **en italique** in italics.

itinéraire [itinerɛr] *nom masculin*

route : **ils ont regardé la carte pour choisir leur itinéraire** they looked at the map to choose their route.

ivoire [ivwar] *nom masculin*

ivory : **une statue en ivoire** an ivory statue.

ivre [ivr] *adjectif*

drunk : **après trois verres de vin, il était ivre** after three glasses of wine he was drunk.

j' ➤ je.

jalousie [ʒaluzi] *nom féminin*

jealousy : **il a fait ça par jalousie** he did it out of jealousy.

jaloux, ouse [ʒalu, uz] *adjectif*

jealous : **Éric est jaloux de sa sœur** Éric is jealous of his sister.

jamais [ʒamɛ] *adverbe*

1. *Dans les phrases négatives* never : **il n'est jamais revenu** he never came back ; **il n'est jamais content** he's never happy ; **elle n'en a plus jamais parlé** she never talked about it again

2. *Dans les phrases affirmatives* ever : **plus que jamais** more than ever ; **elle est plus folle que jamais** she's crazier than ever ; **le plus long voyage que j'aie jamais fait** the longest journey I've ever made

➤ **presque jamais** hardly ever : **il ne vient presque jamais** he hardly ever comes

➤ **jamais de la vie !** no way!

> **si jamais tu le vois** if you happen to see him.

jambe [ʒɑ̃b] *nom féminin*

leg : **j'ai mal aux jambes** my legs hurt.

jambon [ʒɑ̃bɔ̃] *nom masculin*

ham : **du jambon fumé** smoked ham ; **du jambon blanc** ham ; **du jambon cru** cured ham

> **un jambon beurre** a ham sandwich.

janvier [ʒɑ̃vje] *nom masculin*

January : **Jonathan est né en janvier** Jonathan was born in January.

En anglais, les mois de l'année s'écrivent avec une majuscule.

Japon [ʒapɔ̃] *nom masculin*

> **le Japon** Japan

En anglais, à de rares exceptions près, il n'y a pas d'article devant les noms de pays :

au Japon, on boit beaucoup de thé vert in Japan people drink a lot of green tea ; **il est allé au Japon l'année dernière** he went to Japan last year.

japonais, e [ʒaponɛ, ɛz] *adjectif*

Japanese : **le sushi est un plat japonais** sushi is a Japanese dish

japonais *nom masculin*

Japanese : **Dan apprend le japonais** Dan is learning Japanese

En anglais, les adjectifs se rapportant à un pays ou une région, ainsi que le nom désignant la langue de ce pays ou de cette région, s'écrivent avec une majuscule.

Japonais, e *nom masculin, nom féminin*

Japanese : **les Japonais** the Japanese.

jardin [ʒardɛ̃] *nom masculin*

garden : **ils ont des arbres dans leur jardin** they have trees in their garden

> **un jardin d'enfants** a kindergarten
> **un jardin public** a park
> **un jardin zoologique** a zoo.

jardinage [ʒardinaʒ] *nom masculin*

gardening : **faire du jardinage** to do some gardening.

jardinier, ère [ʒardinje, ɛr] *nom masculin, nom féminin*

gardener : **le frère de Laurence est jardinier** Laurence's brother is a gardener.

jaune [ʒon] *adjectif & nom masculin*

yellow : **des chaussettes jaunes** yellow socks ; **je n'aime pas le jaune** I don't like yellow

> **jaune citron** lemon yellow
> **un jaune d'œuf** an egg yolk.

jaunir [ʒonir] *verbe*

to turn yellow : **les photos ont jauni** the photographs have turned yellow.

Javel [ʒavɛl] *nom féminin*

de l'eau de Javel bleach.

javelot [ʒavlo] *nom masculin*

javelin : **le lancer du javelot** the javelin.

jazz [dʒaz] *nom masculin*

jazz : **un orchestre de jazz** a jazz band.

je [ʒə] (**j'** *devant une voyelle ou un « h » muet*) *pronom*

I : **je m'appelle François** I'm called François ; **j'habite à Nice** I live in Nice ; **je suis français** I'm French ; **j'ai très faim** I'm very hungry.

jean [dʒin] *nom masculin*

jeans (*pluriel*) : **mon jean est trop petit** my jeans are too small ; **Bruno a un nouveau jean** Bruno has got a new pair of jeans.

jetable [ʒətabl] *adjectif*

disposable : **des rasoirs jetables** disposable razors.

jetée [ʒəte] *nom féminin*

jetty (*pluriel* **jetties**) : **je t'attendrai sur la jetée** I'll wait for you on the jetty.

jeter [ʒəte] *verbe*

1. **to throw** : **je te jette la balle et tu me la renvoies** I'll throw the ball to you and you throw it back ; **jeter quelqu'un dehors** to throw somebody out
2. **to throw away** : **tu peux jeter ces vieux magazines** you can throw those old magazines away

> **jeter un coup d'œil à** to take a look at

se jeter *verbe pronominal*

> **se jeter sur quelqu'un** OU **quelque chose** to pounce on somebody OU something : **le chat s'est jeté sur la souris** the cat pounced on the mouse
> **se jeter dans** to flow into : **l'Adour se jette dans l'Atlantique** the Adour river flows into the Atlantic Ocean.

jeton [ʒətɔ̃] *nom masculin*

counter : **ils comptent les points avec des jetons** they count the points with counters.

jeu [ʒø] (*pluriel* jeux) *nom masculin*

1. game : **c'est un jeu auquel on peut jouer à six** it's a game for six people
2. gambling : **il a perdu tout son argent au jeu** he lost all his money gambling
3. set : **un jeu de clés** a set of keys
4. pack : **un jeu de 52 cartes** a pack of 52 cards
➤ **un jeu de hasard** a game of chance
➤ **un jeu de mots** a play on words OU a pun
➤ **un jeu de société** a parlour game *UK* OU a parlor game *US*
➤ **un jeu télévisé** a game show
➤ **un jeu vidéo** a video game
➤ **les jeux Olympiques** the Olympic Games.

jeudi [ʒødi] *nom masculin*

Thursday

En anglais, les jours de la semaine s'écrivent avec une majuscule.

mes copains sont venus jeudi my friends came on Thursday ; **je pars jeudi matin** I'm leaving on Thursday morning ; **Thomas joue au foot le jeudi** Thomas plays football on Thursdays ; **jeudi dernier** last Thursday ; **jeudi prochain** next Thursday.

à jeun [aʒœ̃] *adverbe*

on an empty stomach : **je dois prendre ces cachets à jeun** I have to take these tablets on an empty stomach.

jeune [ʒœn] *adjectif*

young : **un jeune homme** a young man ; **une jeune femme** a young woman
➤ **une jeune fille** a girl

jeunes *nom masculin pluriel*

les jeunes young people.

jeunesse [ʒœnɛs] *nom féminin*

youth : **mon père a beaucoup voyagé dans sa jeunesse** my father travelled a lot in his youth.

JO (*abréviation de* jeux Olympiques) *nom masculin pluriel*

les JO the Olympic Games.

jogging [dʒɔɡiŋ] *nom masculin*

1. jogging : **faire du jogging** to go jogging
2. tracksuit : **Jane portait un jogging bleu** Jane was wearing a blue tracksuit.

joie [ʒwa] *nom féminin*

joy : **crier de joie** to shout for joy.

joindre [ʒwɛ̃dr] *verbe*

1. to join : **je ne sais pas comment joindre les deux câbles** I don't know how to join the two cables
2. to reach : **tu es arrivée à joindre Alex ?** did you manage to reach Alex?
3. to enclose : **j'ai dû joindre une photocopie de mon passeport au formulaire** I had to enclose a photocopy of my passport with the form
4. to attach : **n'oublie pas de joindre le fichier à ton e-mail** don't forget to attach the file to your e-mail.

joint, e [ʒwɛ̃, ɛ̃t] *adjectif*

sauter à pieds joints to jump
➤ **une pièce jointe**
1. an enclosure
2. *Dans un e-mail* an attachment.

joker [ʒɔkɛr] *nom masculin*

joker.

joli, e [ʒɔli] *adjectif*

pretty : **une jolie fille** a pretty girl.

jongler [ʒɔ̃ɡle] *verbe*

to juggle : **tu sais jongler avec quatre balles ?** can you juggle with four balls?

jongleur, euse [ʒɔ̃ɡlœr, øz] *nom masculin, nom féminin*

juggler : **il y a des jongleurs devant le centre Pompidou** there are jugglers in front of the Pompidou Centre.

jonquille [ʒɔ̃kij] *nom féminin*

daffodil : **la jonquille est l'emblème du pays de Galles** the daffodil is an emblem of Wales.

joue [ʒu] *nom féminin*

cheek : **ce bébé a de grosses joues** this baby has got big cheeks.

jouer [ʒwe] *verbe*

1. to play : **viens jouer avec nous** come and

play with us ; **il joue le rôle de Cyrano** he plays the part of Cyrano
2. **to act : elle joue super bien dans ce film** she acts really well in that film
3. **to gamble : mon oncle joue au casino tous les week-ends** my uncle gambles at the casino every weekend
4. **to bet : on a joué dix euros sur un cheval et on a gagné !** we bet ten euros on a horse and we won!
5. **to put on : ils vont jouer « le Malade imaginaire » à la Comédie-Française** they're going to put on "le Malade imaginaire" at Comédie-Française
➤ **jouer à** to play : **ils jouent au tennis** they're playing tennis ; **on a joué aux cow-boys et aux Indiens** we played cowboys and Indians
➤ **jouer de** to play : **Natacha joue du violon** Natacha plays the violin.

jouet [ʒwɛ] *nom masculin*

toy : **Pierre a énormément de jouets** Pierre has got a lot of toys.

joueur, euse [ʒwœr, øz] *nom masculin, nom féminin*

player : **deux joueurs se sont blessés pendant le match** two players were injured during the match ; **un joueur de foot** a footballer ou a football player
➤ **être mauvais joueur** to be a bad loser.

jour [ʒur] *nom masculin*

1. **day : il reste deux jours avant les vacances** there are two days left before the holidays ; **tous les jours** every day
2. **daylight : on voit le jour à travers les rideaux** you can see daylight through the curtains
➤ **huit jours** a week : **dans huit jours** in a week
➤ **quinze jours** two weeks ou a fortnight *UK* : **dans quinze jours** in two weeks ou in a fortnight *UK*
➤ **le jour de l'An** New Year's Day
➤ **un jour férié** a public holiday *UK* ou a holiday *US*
➤ **de jour** by day : **nous voyagerons de jour** we'll travel by day
➤ **de nos jours** these days ou nowadays
➤ **du jour au lendemain** overnight
➤ **il fait jour** it's light
➤ **mettre quelque chose à jour** to update something

 JOURS FÉRIÉS
There are thirteen annual public holidays in France. On those days, most shops and businesses are closed. May has several public holidays – some years up to four! Public holidays in France include Bastille Day (14 July) and All Saint's Day (1 November).

➤ juillet, Toussaint

journal [ʒurnal] *(pluriel* journaux [ʒurno]*)* *nom masculin*

1. **newspaper : le journal d'aujourd'hui** today's newspaper
2. **diary** *(pluriel* diaries*)* : **Claire écrit tout dans son journal** Claire writes everything down in her diary
➤ **un journal intime** a diary
➤ **le journal télévisé** television news.

journaliste [ʒurnalist] *nom masculin ou féminin*

journalist : **c'est dur de devenir journaliste** it's hard to become a journalist.

journée [ʒurne] *nom féminin*

day : **on a passé la journée à jouer aux échecs** we spent the day playing chess

 Journée is a false friend, it does not mean 'journey'.

joyeux, euse [ʒwajø, øz] *adjectif*

cheerful : **tu as l'air bien joyeux aujourd'hui** you look very cheerful today
➤ **joyeux Noël !** Merry Christmas!

judo [ʒydo] *nom masculin*

judo : **faire du judo** to do judo.

juge [ʒyʒ] *nom masculin*

judge : **le juge l'a condamné à deux ans de prison** the judge sentenced him to two years in prison
➤ **le juge de ligne** the line judge
➤ **le juge de touche** the linesman.

jugement [ʒyʒmã] *nom masculin*

sentence : **le tribunal a prononcé son jugement** the court passed sentence.

juger [ʒyʒe] *verbe*

1. **to judge : tu ne devrais pas juger les gens** you shouldn't judge people
2. **to try : l'accusé sera jugé demain** the accused will be tried tomorrow

3. **to consider :** le proviseur a jugé que ce n'était pas nécessaire the headmaster considered that it wasn't necessary.

juif, juive [ʒɥif, ʒɥiv] *adjectif*

Jewish

En anglais, les adjectifs se rapportant aux religions s'écrivent avec une majuscule.

Juif, Juive *nom masculin, nom féminin*

Jew.

juillet [ʒɥijɛ] *nom masculin*

July

En anglais, les mois de l'année s'écrivent avec une majuscule.

en juillet j'irai à la mer I'm going to the seaside in July

➤ **le 14 juillet** Bastille Day

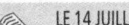 LE 14 JUILLET
The fourteenth of July, or Bastille Day, is France's national holiday. It commemorates the day in 1789 when the Bastille prison in Paris was stormed, marking the beginning of the French revolution. There are celebrations throughout France, often lasting several days, with firework displays and outdoor dances.

juin [ʒɥɛ̃] *nom masculin*

June

En anglais, les mois de l'année s'écrivent avec une majuscule.

mes cousins viennent nous voir en juin my cousins are coming to see us in June.

➤ **nous sommes le cinq juin** it's the fifth of June *UK* ou it's June fifth *US*

jumeau, elle [ʒymo, ɛl] (*pluriel* jumeaux [ʒymo]) *adjectif & nom masculin, nom féminin*

twin : mon frère jumeau my twin brother ; Sabrina a eu des jumelles Sabrina had twins

jumelles *nom féminin pluriel*

binoculars : emporte tes jumelles pour observer les oiseaux take your binoculars to watch the birds.

jumelle ➤ jumeau.

jument [ʒymɑ̃] *nom féminin*

mare : une jument et son poulain a mare and her foal.

jungle [ʒɔ̃gl] *nom féminin*

jungle : « le Livre de la jungle » a été écrit par Rudyard Kipling "The Jungle Book" was written by Rudyard Kipling.

junior [ʒynjɔr] *adjectif & nom masculin ou féminin*

junior : Samia joue dans l'équipe junior Samia plays in the junior team ; les juniors ont gagné contre Reims the juniors won against Reims.

jupe [ʒyp] *nom féminin*

skirt : Sylvie portait une jupe longue Sylvie was wearing a long skirt.

jurer [ʒyre] *verbe*

1. **to swear :** arrête de jurer ! stop swearing! ; Laurent a juré qu'il ne recommencerait plus Laurent swore that he would never do it again ; je te jure que c'est vrai I swear it's true
2. **to clash :** ce jaune jure avec la moquette this yellow clashes with the carpet.

juron [ʒyrɔ̃] *nom masculin*

swearword.

jury [ʒyri] *nom masculin*

1. **jury** (*pluriel* **juries**) **:** le jury a déclaré l'accusé non coupable the jury found the accused not guilty
2. **board of examiners :** le jury a été sympa avec les candidats the examiners were nice to the candidates.

jus [ʒy] *nom masculin*

1. **juice :** du jus d'orange some orange juice
2. **gravy :** tu veux du jus sur ton poulet ? do you want gravy on your chicken?

jusque [ʒysk(ə)]

jusqu'à *préposition*

1. **until, till :** tu peux rester jusqu'à jeudi you can stay until Thursday ou you can stay till Thursday ; jusqu'à présent ou jusqu'ici until now ou so far
2. **as far as :** allez jusqu'à la piscine et tournez à gauche go as far as the swimming pool and turn left ; jusqu'au bout to the end

jusqu'à ce que *conjonction*

until ou **till :** bats les blancs jusqu'à ce qu'ils soient fermes beat the egg whites until they're stiff

jusqu'en préposition

up until : jusqu'en 1999 up until 1999

jusque-là adverbe

1. up to there : l'eau montait jusque-là the water came up to there
2. until then : tout allait bien jusque-là everything was going well until then.

juste [ʒyst] adjectif & adverbe

■ adjectif

1. fair : ce n'est pas juste, c'est toujours moi qui fais la vaisselle ! it's not fair, it's always me that does the dishes!
2. right : la réponse juste the right answer
3. tight : ce jean est un peu juste pour moi these jeans are a bit tight for me

■ adverbe

just : c'est juste ce qu'il me fallait that's just what I needed ; je voulais juste vous poser une question I just wanted to ask you a question

➤ au juste exactly : combien il y en a au juste ? how many are there exactly?

justement [ʒystəmã] adverbe

1. exactly : c'est justement pour ça que tu dois faire attention that's exactly why you have to be careful
2. just : je me disais justement que je devrais t'appeler I was just thinking that I should phone you.

justesse [ʒystɛs] nom féminin

➤ de justesse only just : on a eu notre train de justesse we only just caught our train.

justice [ʒystis] nom féminin

1. justice : il n'y a pas de justice ! there's no justice!
2. law : il a eu des problèmes avec la justice he had problems with the law

➤ passer en justice to stand trial.

justifier [ʒystifje] verbe

to justify : ça ne justifie pas ce qu'elle a fait it doesn't justify what she did

se justifier verbe pronominal

to justify oneself : n'essaie pas de te justifier ! don't try to justify yourself!

juteux, euse [ʒytø, øz] adjectif

juicy : une poire juteuse a juicy pear.

kangourou [kãguru] nom masculin

kangaroo.

karaté [karate] nom masculin

karate : faire du karaté to do karate.

kayak [kajak] nom masculin

canoe : son kayak s'est retourné his canoe capsized ; faire du kayak to go canoeing.

kermesse [kɛrmɛs] nom féminin

fête : la kermesse de l'école the school fête.

ketchup [kɛtʃœp] nom masculin

ketchup, catsup US.

kidnapper [kidnape] verbe

to kidnap.

kilo [kilo] nom masculin

kilo : deux kilos de poires, s'il vous plaît two kilos of pears, please.

kilogramme [kilɔgram] nom masculin

kilogram, kilogramme UK.

kilomètre [kilɔmɛtr] nom masculin

kilometre UK, kilometer US : il faisait du cent cinquante kilomètres à l'heure he was doing a hundred and fifty kilometres an hour.

kilt [kilt] nom masculin

kilt : Andrew porte un kilt pour les grandes occasions Andrew wears a kilt for big occasions.

kiosque [kjɔsk] nom masculin

kiosk : un kiosque à journaux a newspaper kiosk.

kiwi [kiwi] *nom masculin*

kiwi fruit, kiwi : **un kilo de kiwis** one kilo of kiwi fruit.

Klaxon® [klaksɔn] *nom masculin*

horn : **elle a donné un coup de Klaxon** she sounded her horn OU she hooted.

klaxonner [klaksɔne] *verbe*

1. to hoot *UK*, to honk *US* : **pourquoi il klaxonne comme ça ?** why is he hooting like that?

2. to hoot at *UK*, to honk at *US* : **la voiture de derrière nous a klaxonnés** the car behind hooted at us.

K.-O. [kao] *adjectif invariable*

➤ **mettre quelqu'un K.-O.** to knock somebody out : **le boxeur américain a mis son adversaire K.-O.** the American boxer knocked his opponent out

➤ **être K.-O.** *familier* to be exhausted : **je suis K.-O., je vais me coucher** I'm exhausted, I'm going to bed.

l' ➤ **le.**

la¹ [la] (**l'** *devant une voyelle ou un « h » muet*) *article défini* ➤ **le.**

la² [la] (**l'** *devant une voyelle ou un « h » muet*) *pronom*

1. *Représente une personne* her : **tu connais Annelise ? – je la connais bien** do you know Annelise? – I know her well ; **je l'ai vue hier** I saw her yesterday

2. *Représente un objet ou un animal* it : **tu dois avoir la clé, donne-la-moi** you must have the key, give it to me ; **j'ai vu une baleine et je l'ai prise en photo** I saw a whale and took a photograph of it

Lorsqu'il s'agit d'un animal familier, on utilise souvent en anglais le pronom *her*, normalement réservé aux personnes, pour traduire le pronom « la » :

la chienne a envie de sortir, tu veux aller la promener? the dog wants to go out, do you want to take her for a walk?

là [la] *adverbe*

1. *Quand là veut dire "à cet endroit"* there : **à trois kilomètres de là** three kilometres from there ; **allô, est-ce que Guillaume est là ?** hello, is Guillaume there? ; **toc ! toc ! – qui est là ?** knock! knock! – who's there?

2. *Quand là veut dire "ici"* here : **où es-tu ? – je suis là** where are you? – I'm here ; **je les avais posés là** I put them here

3. *Avec un pronom relatif* **c'est là que je prends mes cours de piano** that's where I take my piano classes ; **c'est là que j'ai décidé de ne pas y aller** that's when I decided not to go OU it was then that I decided not to go.

là-bas [laba] *adverbe*

there, over there : **le garçon qui est là-bas, au fond de la salle** the boy that's over there, at the back of the room.

laboratoire [labɔratwar] *nom masculin*

laboratory *(pluriel* **laboratories***)* : **un laboratoire d'analyses** a test laboratory ; **le laboratoire de langues** the language laboratory.

labourer [labure] *verbe*

to plough *UK*, to plow *US* : **le fermier laboure son champ** the farmer is ploughing his field.

labyrinthe [labirɛ̃t] *nom masculin*

maze : **ce village est un vrai labyrinthe** this village is a real maze.

lac [lak] *nom masculin*

lake : **le lac Léman** Lake Geneva.

lacer [lase] *verbe*

to lace up : **mon petit frère ne sait pas lacer ses chaussures** my little brother doesn't know how to lace up his shoes.

lacet [lasɛ] *nom masculin*

lace : **tes lacets sont défaits** your laces are undone

➤ **une route en lacet** a winding road.

lâche [laʃ] *adjectif & nom*

■ *adjectif*

1. **loose** : **le nœud est trop lâche** the knot is too loose
2. **cowardly** : **Clémentine est lâche, elle a laissé accuser son amie** Clémentine is cowardly, she let her friend be accused

■ *nom masculin ou féminin*
   coward : **tu es un lâche !** you're a coward!

lâcher [laʃe] *verbe*

1. **to let go of** : **lâche-moi, tu me fais mal** let go of me, you're hurting me
2. **to drop** : **Andrew a lâché le verre et il s'est cassé** Andrew dropped the glass and it broke
3. **to give way** : **j'espère que la corde ne va pas lâcher** I hope the rope won't give way.

là-dedans [ladədɑ̃] *adverbe*

   in there : **qu'est-ce qu'il y a là-dedans ?** what's in there?

là-dessous [ladsu] *adverbe*

   under there : **le chat se cache là-dessous** the cat is hiding under there.

là-dessus [ladsy] *adverbe*

   on there : **monte là-dessus, tu verras mieux** climb on there, you'll see better.

là-haut [lao] *adverbe*

   up there : **là-haut l'air est pur** the air is pure up there.

laid, e [lɛ, lɛd] *adjectif*

   ugly : **ce bâtiment est vraiment laid** that building is really ugly.

laine [lɛn] *nom féminin*

   wool : **de la laine vierge** pure new wool ; **un pull en laine** a wool sweater OU a woollen sweater
➤ **laine polaire** fleece.

laïque *adjectif*

   secular : **l'école laïque** secular education.

laisse [lɛs] *nom féminin*

   lead *UK*, **leash** *(pluriel* **leashes***)* : **tenir un chien en laisse** to keep a dog on a lead.

laisser [lɛse] *verbe*

   to leave : **laisse-moi un morceau de gâteau** leave a piece of cake for me ; **ils m'ont laissé leur chat pour le week-end** they left their cat with me for the weekend

➤ **laisser quelque chose à quelqu'un** to let somebody have something : **il m'a laissé sa casquette parce qu'elle me plaisait** he let me have his cap because I liked it
➤ **laisser quelqu'un faire quelque chose** to let somebody do something : **les parents de Luc ne le laissent pas sortir** Luc's parents won't let him go out ; **laisse-le faire, il va y arriver** let him do it, he'll manage
➤ **laisser tomber quelque chose** to drop something : **ne laisse pas tomber le vase** don't drop the vase ; **Adrien veut laisser tomber ses études** Adrien wants to drop his studies ; **laisse tomber !** *familier* drop it!
➤ **laisser tomber quelqu'un** to let somebody down : **il m'a laissé tomber au dernier moment** he let me down at the last minute

se laisser *verbe pronominal*

   to let oneself : **ne te laisse pas décourager** don't let yourself be discouraged
➤ **se laisser pousser les cheveux** to let one's hair grow.

lait [lɛ] *nom masculin*

   milk : **du lait de vache** cow's milk
➤ **du lait écrémé** skimmed milk
➤ **du lait entier** whole milk
➤ **du lait en poudre** powdered milk.

laitage [letaʒ] *adjectif*

   dairy product : **vous ne mangez pas assez de laitages** you don't eat enough dairy products.

laitier, ère [letje, ɛr] *adjectif*

   dairy : **des produits laitiers** dairy products.

laitue [lety] *nom féminin*

   lettuce.

lame [lam] *nom féminin*

   blade : **une lame de rasoir** a razor blade.

lamentable [lamɑ̃tabl] *adjectif*

   appalling : **j'ai eu des résultats lamentables ce trimestre** I got appalling results this term.

se lamenter [səlamɑ̃te] *verbe pronominal*

   to complain : **arrête de te lamenter et fais quelque chose !** stop complaining and do something! ; **se lamenter sur quelque chose** to complain about something.

lampadaire [lɑ̃padɛr] *nom masculin*

1. **standard lamp** *UK*, **floor lamp** *US* : **le lampadaire du salon ne marche plus** the standard lamp in the living room doesn't work anymore

2. **street lamp** : **la voiture est rentrée dans un lampadaire** the car crashed into a street lamp.

lampe [lɑ̃p] *nom féminin*

lamp : **allume la lampe** switch the lamp on ; **une lampe de chevet** a bedside lamp
> **une lampe de poche** a torch *UK* ou a flashlight *US*.

lancement [lɑ̃smɑ̃] *nom masculin*

launch : **le lancement de la fusée aura lieu à cinq heures** the rocket launch will take place at five o'clock.

lancer [lɑ̃se] *verbe & nom*

■ *verbe*

1. **to throw** : **lance-moi le ballon** throw me the ball : **ils lui ont lancé des cailloux** they threw stones at him

2. **to drop** : **l'armée lance des bombes sur la ville** the army is dropping bombs on the city

3. **to launch** : **la NASA a lancé une sonde dans l'espace** NASA launched a probe into space

4. **to start** : **comment fait-on pour lancer le programme ?** how do you start the program?

■ *nom masculin*
throwing : **le lancer du disque** throwing the discus

se lancer *verbe pronominal familier*

to take the plunge : **allez, lance-toi, ne sois pas timide** go on, take the plunge, don't be shy.

landau [lɑ̃do] *nom masculin*

pram *UK*, **baby carriage** *US*.

langage [lɑ̃gaʒ] *nom masculin*

language : **le langage des dauphins** the language of dolphins.

langouste [lɑ̃gust] *nom féminin*

crayfish : **on a mangé une langouste entière** we ate a whole crayfish.

langoustine [lɑ̃gustin] *nom féminin*

langoustine, Dublin bay prawn.

langue [lɑ̃g] *nom féminin*

1. **tongue** : **ma petite sœur me tire tout le temps la langue** my little sister is always sticking her tongue out at me

2. **language** : **une langue étrangère** a foreign language ; **les langues vivantes** modern languages
> **ma langue maternelle** my mother tongue
> **une mauvaise langue** a gossip
> **je donne ma langue au chat** I give up.

lanterne [lɑ̃tɛrn] *nom féminin*

lantern : **il y avait des lanternes en papier partout** there were paper lanterns everywhere.

lapin *nom masculin*

rabbit : **ils ont trois lapins dans leur jardin** they have three rabbits in their garden.

laque [lak] *nom féminin*

1. **gloss paint** : **Jean a peint la porte avec de la laque blanche** Jean painted the door with white gloss paint

2. **hair spray** : **j'utilise du gel pour les cheveux, jamais de laque** I use hair gel, never hair spray.

laquelle ➤ **lequel**.

lard [lar] *nom masculin*

bacon : **du lard fumé** smoked bacon.

lardon [lardɔ̃] *nom masculin*

strip of bacon : **de la salade aux lardons** lettuce with strips of bacon.

large [larʒ] *adjectif & nom*

■ *adjectif*
wide : **la route est plus large ici** the road is wider here ; **le jardin est large de cinq mètres** the garden is five metres wide

■ *nom masculin*
la pièce fait quatre mètres de large the room is four metres wide
> **le large** the open sea : **ils pêchent au large** they fish in the open sea
> **au large de** off : **au large des côtes françaises** off the French coast

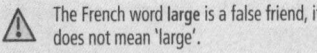
The French word **large** is a false friend, it does not mean 'large'.

largement [larʒəmɑ̃] *adverbe*

easily : **il y aura largement assez de boissons** there'll easily be enough drinks on aura largement le temps we'll have more than enough time.

largeur [larʒœr] *nom féminin*

width : la largeur de la planche n'a pas d'importance the width of the plank isn't important ; **quelle est la largeur du salon ?** how wide is the living room?

larme [larm] *nom féminin*

tear : je l'ai trouvée en larmes dans sa chambre I found her in tears in her bedroom
> fondre en larmes to burst into tears
> il nous a fait rire aux larmes he made us laugh until we cried.

laser [lazɛr] *adjectif invariable & nom masculin*

laser : un disque laser a laser disc.

latin, e [latɛ̃, in] *adjectif & nom masculin*

Latin : les langues latines Latin languages ; je voudrais faire du latin l'année prochaine I'd like to do Latin next year.

latino-américain, e [latinɔamerikɛ̃, ɛn]

(*pluriel* latino-américains, es) *adjectif*
Latin American.

laurier [lɔrje] *nom masculin*

1. laurel : une haie de lauriers a laurel hedge
2. bay leaves : il y a du laurier dans cette sauce there are bay leaves in this sauce.

lavable [lavabl] *adjectif*

washable : lavable en machine machine-washable.

lavabo [lavabo] *nom masculin*

washbasin *UK*, washbowl *US*.

lavande [lavɑ̃d] *nom féminin*

lavender : eau de Cologne à la lavande lavender cologne.

lave-linge [lavlɛ̃ʒ] (*pluriel* lave-linge) *nom masculin*
washing machine.

laver [lave] *verbe*

to wash : est-ce que tu as lavé les verres ? have you washed the glasses?

se laver *verbe pronominal*

to wash : je vais me laver avant de sortir I'm going to wash before I go out ; lave-toi les mains wash your hands.

laverie [lavri] *nom féminin*

laverie automatique launderette *UK* ou Laundromat® *US*.

lave-vaisselle [lavvesɛl] (*pluriel* lave-vaisselle) *nom masculin*
dishwasher.

le¹, la [lə, la] (l' *devant une voyelle ou un « h » muet*) (*pluriel* les [le]) *article défini*

1. the : le lac est gelé the lake is frozen ; tu as fermé la fenêtre ? have you closed the window? ; l'arbre est tombé the tree fell down ; les clés sont sur la table the keys are on the table

> Devant les noms abstraits ou généraux, l'article ne se traduit pas :

la liberté freedom ; les hommes et les femmes men and women ; j'aime le chocolat I like chocolate

> Avec les parties du corps, on utilise les pronoms possessifs en anglais pour traduire l'article défini :

je vais me laver les mains I'm going to wash my hands ; elle se lave les cheveux she's washing her hair ; il s'est cassé le bras he broke his arm

> Lorsqu'on décrit le physique d'une personne, l'article ne se traduit pas :

il a les cheveux blonds he has blond hair ; elle a les yeux bleus she has blue eyes

2. per, a : vingt euros le mètre carré twenty euros per square metre ou twenty euros a square metre ; trois euros la douzaine three euros a dozen

> le lundi on Mondays : j'ai cours de violon le lundi I have violin lessons on Mondays.

le² [lə] (l' *devant une voyelle ou un « h » muet*) *pronom personnel*

1. *Représente une personne* him : tu connais Matthieu ? – je le connais bien do you know Matthieu? – I know him well ; je l'aime I love him
2. *Représente un objet ou un animal* it : ce stylo est à moi, rends-le-moi that pen is mine, give it back to me ; j'ai vu un éléphant et je l'ai pris en photo I saw an elephant and took a photograph of it

175

Lorsqu'il s'agit d'un animal familier, on utilise souvent en anglais le pronom **him**, normalement réservé aux personnes, pour traduire le pronom « le » :

le chien a envie de sortir, tu veux le promener? the dog wants to go out, do you want to take him for a walk?

lécher [leʃe] *verbe*

to lick : le chien m'a léché les mains the dog licked my hands.

leçon [ləsɔ̃] *nom féminin*

lesson : Joanna prend des leçons de conduite Joanna is taking driving lessons ; **des leçons particulières** private lessons

➤ **faire la leçon à quelqu'un** to lecture somebody.

lecteur, trice [lɛktœr, tris] *nom masculin, nom féminin*

1. **reader : beaucoup de lecteurs ont écrit au magazine pour se plaindre** a lot of readers wrote in to the magazine to complain

2. **foreign-language assistant : ma cousine est lectrice aux États-Unis** my cousin is a foreign-language assistant in the United States

lecteur *nom masculin*

player : un lecteur de CD a CD player ; **un lecteur de DVD** a DVD player.

lecture [lɛktyr] *nom féminin*

1. **reading : j'aime la lecture** I like reading

2. **something to read : j'emporte toujours de la lecture en vacances** I always take something to read on holiday

> ⚠ The French word **lecture** is a false friend, it does not mean 'lecture'.

légal, e, aux [legal, o] *adjectif*

legal : ce que j'ai fait était tout à fait légal what I did was perfectly legal.

légende [leʒɑ̃d] *nom féminin*

1. **legend : une ancienne légende indienne** an ancient Indian legend

2. **key : la légende de la carte n'est pas très claire** the map key isn't very clear.

léger, ère [leʒe, ɛr] *adjectif*

1. **light : un repas léger** a light meal

2. **slight : il y a une légère différence entre les deux** there's a slight difference between the two

3. **weak : ce café est trop léger pour moi** this coffee is too weak for me.

légèrement [leʒɛrmɑ̃] *adverbe*

slightly : ce plat est légèrement trop salé this dish is slightly too salty.

légume [legym] *nom masculin*

vegetable : des légumes verts green vegetables.

lendemain [lɑ̃dmɛ̃] *nom masculin*

le lendemain the day after ; **le lendemain matin** the next morning.

lent, e [lɑ̃, lɑ̃t] *adjectif*

slow : ce que tu es lent ! you're so slow!

lentement [lɑ̃tmɑ̃] *adverbe*

slowly : marche plus lentement, je suis fatiguée walk more slowly, I'm tired.

lentille [lɑ̃tij] *nom féminin*

1. **lentil : un plat de lentilles** a lentil dish

2. **lens** *(pluriel* **lenses) : Lionel porte des lentilles de contact** Lionel wears contact lenses.

léopard [leɔpar] *nom masculin*

leopard.

lequel, laquelle [ləkɛl, lakɛl] *(masculin pluriel* **lesquels** [lekɛl], *féminin pluriel* **lesquelles** [lekɛl]) *pronom*

> à + lequel = **auquel**, de + lequel = **duquel**, à + lesquels/lesquelles = **auxquels/auxquelles**, de + lesquels/lesquelles = **desquels/desquelles**. Voir ces mots.

1. **who, whom : la fille avec laquelle Vincent sort** the girl who Vincent is going out with OU the girl Vincent is going out with

2. **which : le crayon avec lequel elle dessine** the pencil which she is drawing with OU the pencil she is drawing with

> Notez qu'en anglais, le pronom relatif est souvent omis.

3. **which one : laquelle tu préfères ?** which one do you prefer?

les [le] *article défini* ➤ **le**.

les [le] *pronom personnel*

them : je les connais bien, ils sont dans ma classe I know them well, they're in my class ;

176

il n'y a plus de bananes, je les ai toutes **mangées** there aren't any bananas left, I ate them all.

lesquels, lesquelles *pluriel de* lequel

je voudrais des gâteaux – lesquels voulez-vous ? I'd like some cakes – which ones would you like? ; j'aime bien ces chaussures – lesquelles ? I like those shoes – which ones?

lessive [lɛsiv] *nom féminin*

1. washing *UK*, laundry *US* : il fait la lessive he's doing the washing
2. wash *(pluriel* washes*) UK* : ma mère fait parfois deux lessives par jour my mother sometimes does two washes a day
3. washing powder *UK*, detergent *US* : une nouvelle marque de lessive a new brand of washing powder.

lettre [lɛtr] *nom féminin*

letter : il manque une lettre dans ce mot there's a letter missing from this word ; une lettre d'amour a love letter

> écrire quelque chose en toutes lettres to write something in full

lettres *nom féminin pluriel*

arts *UK*, humanities *US* : Sandra fait des études de lettres Sandra is studying the arts.

leur [lœr] *pronom & adjectif*

▪ *pronom*

them : je leur en ai parlé I spoke to them about it ; elle leur a donné de l'argent she gave them some money ; je leur ai rapporté des cadeaux I brought some presents back for them ; rends-le-leur give it back to them
▪ *adjectif (pluriel* leurs*)*

their : c'est leur tour it's their turn ; une de leurs amies one of their friends

le leur *(féminin* la leur, *pluriel* les leurs*) pronom*

theirs : mon frère a dix ans, le leur a onze ans my brother is ten, theirs is eleven ; notre voiture est grande, la leur est petite our car is big and theirs is small ; nos parents sont venus, mais pas les leurs our parents came but not theirs.

lever [ləve] *verbe & nom*

▪ *verbe*

to raise : François n'a même pas levé la tête quand je suis entrée François didn't even raise his head when I came in ; si vous êtes

d'accord, levez la main if you agree raise your hands
▪ *nom masculin*

> le lever du jour daybreak : au lever du jour at daybreak
> le lever du soleil sunrise

se lever *verbe pronominal*

1. to get up : à quelle heure tu te lèves ? what time do you get up?
2. to stand up : on se lève quand le proviseur entre we stand up when the headmaster comes in
3. to rise : le soleil se lève à l'est the sun rises in the east
4. to break : le jour se lève tôt en juillet day breaks early in July.

levier [ləvje] *nom masculin*

lever : le levier de vitesses the gear lever *UK* ou the gearshift *US*.

lèvre [lɛvr] *nom féminin*

lip : j'ai les lèvres gercées my lips are chapped.

lexique [lɛksik] *nom masculin*

glossary *(pluriel* glossaries*)* : il y a un lexique à la fin du livre there's a glossary at the end of the book.

lézard [lezar] *nom masculin*

lizard : un lézard vert a green lizard.

libellule [libelyl] *nom féminin*

dragonfly *(pluriel* dragonflies*)*.

libérer [libere] *verbe*

1. to free : les rebelles ont libéré les prisonniers politiques the rebels freed the political prisoners
2. to liberate : le pays a été libéré en 1945 the country was liberated in 1945

se libérer *verbe pronominal*

1. to get away : je vais voir si je peux me libérer mardi I'll see if I can get away on Tuesday
2. to free oneself : il a réussi à se libérer tout seul he managed to free himself.

liberté [libɛrte] *nom féminin*

1. freedom : liberté d'expression freedom of speech
2. free time : le prof nous a laissé deux

177

heures de liberté the teacher gave us two hours' free time

➤ **être en liberté** to be free

➤ **remettre quelqu'un en liberté** to set somebody free.

libraire [librɛr] *nom masculin ou féminin*

bookseller : **la tante de Paul est libraire** Paul's aunt is a bookseller.

librairie [libreri] *nom féminin*

bookshop *UK*, bookstore *US* : **j'ai acheté cette carte à la librairie** I bought this card in the bookshop

 Librairie is a false friend, it does not mean 'library'.

libre [libr] *adjectif*

free : **est-ce que cette place est libre ?** is this seat free? ; **tu es libre de partir si tu veux** you're free to go if you want

➤ **l'école libre** private education.

librement [librəmɑ̃] *adverbe*

freely : **les animaux vont et viennent librement dans la réserve** the animals come and go freely in the reserve.

libre-service [librəservis] *nom masculin*

1. self-service shop : **il y a une épicerie ici ? – oui, il y a un libre-service dans la rue principale** is there a grocer's here? – yes, there's a self-service shop in the main street
2. self-service restaurant : **la cantine de l'école est un libre-service** the school canteen is a self-service restaurant.

licencier [lisɑ̃sje] *verbe*

to lay off : **l'entreprise a licencié vingt salariés** the company laid off twenty employees.

liège [ljɛʒ] *nom masculin*

cork : **des semelles en liège** cork soles ; **un bouchon en liège** a cork.

lien [ljɛ̃] *nom masculin*

1. link : **il n'y a aucun lien entre ces deux événements** there is no link between these two events
2. tie : **ils entretiennent des liens étroits** they have close ties.

lierre [ljɛr] *nom masculin*

ivy : **la maison est couverte de lierre** the house is covered in ivy.

lieu [ljø] (*pluriel* lieux) *nom masculin*

place : **le lieu où se retrouvent les élèves** the place where the pupils meet

➤ **au lieu de** instead of : **au lieu d'aller à la plage, ils sont allés au parc** instead of going to the beach, they went to the park

➤ **avoir lieu** to take place : **la cérémonie aura lieu sur la place** the ceremony will take place in the square.

lièvre [ljɛvr] *nom masculin*

hare.

ligne [liɲ] *nom féminin*

line : **la première ligne n'est pas lisible** the first line is illegible ; **la ligne est occupée** the line is busy

➤ **la ligne d'arrivée** the finishing line *UK* ou the finish line *US*

➤ **en ligne** on line : **j'ai acheté ce CD en ligne** I bought this CD on line.

ligoter [ligɔte] *verbe*

to tie up : **les policiers l'ont retrouvé ligoté** the police found him tied up ; **ligoter quelqu'un à une chaise** to tie somebody to a chair.

lilas [lila] *nom masculin & adjectif invariable*

lilac.

limace [limas] *nom féminin*

slug.

lime [lim] *nom féminin*

file : **une lime à ongles** a nail file.

limer [lime] *verbe*

to file through : **le prisonnier a limé les barreaux pour s'évader** the prisoner filed through the bars to escape

se limer *verbe pronominal*

se limer les ongles to file one's nails.

limitation [limitasjɔ̃] *nom féminin*

limitation de vitesse speed limit.

limite [limit] *nom & adjectif*

■ *nom féminin*

1. limite : **n'exagère pas, il y a des limites !** don't go too far, there are limits!
2. deadline : **la limite pour les inscriptions est le 13 juin** the deadline for enrolments is 13 June

➤ **à la limite** if necessary : **à la limite, je pour-**

rais te prêter de l'argent if necessary, I could lend you some money

■ *adjectif*

maximum : **quel est l'âge limite ?** what's the maximum age? OU what's the age limit?

limiter [limite] *verbe*

to limit : **ils ont limité le nombre de billets à deux par personnes** they've limited the number of tickets to two per person

se limiter *verbe pronominal*

se limiter à quelque chose to limit oneself to something ; **Christian se limite à deux gâteaux par jour** Christian limits himself to two cakes a day.

limonade [limɔnad] *nom féminin*

lemonade : **un verre de limonade** a glass of lemonade.

lin [lɛ̃] *nom masculin*

linen : **un costume en lin** a linen suit.

linge [lɛ̃ʒ] *nom masculin*

washing : **étendre le linge** to hang out the washing.

lion *nom masculin*

lion : **le lion rugissait** the lion roared

Lion *nom masculin*

Leo : **Agnès est Lion** Agnès is a Leo.

liquide [likid] *nom & adjectif*

■ *nom masculin*

1. liquid : **un liquide épais** a thick liquid
2. cash : **je préfère payer en liquide** I prefer to pay cash

■ *adjectif*

watery : **cette sauce est trop liquide** this sauce is too watery
➤ **des aliments liquides** liquids.

lire [lir] *verbe*

to read : **est-ce que tu as lu le dernier Harry Potter ?** have you read the latest Harry Potter? ; **Matthieu ne sait pas encore lire** Matthieu can't read yet.

lis, lys [lis] *nom masculin*

lily *(pluriel* **lilies***)*.

lisible [lizibl] *adjectif*

legible : **une écriture lisible** a legible handwriting.

lisse [lis] *adjectif*

smooth : **elle a de beaux cheveux lisses** she has beautiful smooth hair.

liste [list] *nom féminin*

liste : **la liste des courses** the shopping list ; **le professeur a fait une liste de textes à étudier** the teacher made a list of texts to study
➤ **être sur liste d'attente** to be on the waiting list
➤ **être sur liste rouge** to be ex-directory *UK* OU to have an unlisted number *US*.

lit [li] *nom masculin*

bed : **Amélie va au lit très tôt** Amélie goes to bed very early ; **est-ce que tu as fait ton lit ?** have you made your bed?
➤ **un lit à une place** a single bed
➤ **un lit à deux places** OU **un grand lit** a double bed
➤ **un lit de camp** a camp bed
➤ **des lits jumeaux** twin beds
➤ **des lits superposés** bunk beds.

litre [litr] *nom masculin*

litre *UK*, liter *US* : **deux litres d'eau** two litres of water.

littéraire [literɛr] *adjectif*

literary : **faire des études littéraires** to study literature.

littérature [literatyr] *nom féminin*

literature : **la littérature anglaise** English literature.

livraison [livrɛzɔ̃] *nom féminin*

delivery *(pluriel* **deliveries***)* : **livraison à domicile** home delivery.

livre [livr] *nom*

■ *nom masculin*

book : **tu as lu de bons livres récemment ?** have you read any good books recently?
➤ **un livre de cuisine** a cookery book *UK* OU a cookbook *US*
➤ **un livre de poche** a paperback

■ *nom féminin*

1. pound : **la livre sterling est la monnaie britannique** the pound sterling is the British currency
2. half a kilo : **une livre de raisins** half a kilo of grapes.

livrer [livre] *verbe*

1. to deliver : **ils m'ont livré l'ordinateur le**

lendemain matin they delivered the computer the next day

2. **to hand over : ses complices l'ont livré à la police** his accomplices handed him over to the police

se livrer *verbe pronominal*

to give oneself up : **elle a choisi de se livrer à la police** she chose to give herself up to the police.

livret [livrɛ] *nom masculin*

passbook : **un livret de caisse d'épargne** a savings bank passbook

> **livret de famille** *official family record book, given by a registrar to newlyweds*

> **livret scolaire** school report *UK*, report card *US*.

local, e, aux [lɔkal, o] *adjectif*

local : **une radio locale** a local radio

local *nom masculin*

premises (*s'utilise toujours au pluriel*) : **nous cherchons un local pour monter un club** we're looking for premises to set up a club.

locataire [lɔkatɛr] *nom masculin ou féminin*

tenant : **le locataire du premier s'appelle Alex** the tenant on the first floor is called Alex.

location [lɔkasjɔ̃] *nom féminin*

1. renting : **la location de chambres aux étudiants est très rentable** renting rooms to students is very profitable ou letting rooms to students is very profitable

2. hire *UK*, rental *US* : **un magasin de location de vélos** a bicycle hire shop.

locomotive [lɔkɔmɔtiv] *nom féminin*

locomotive : **la locomotive est tombée en panne** the locomotive broke down.

loft [lɔft] *nom masculin*

loft conversion, loft : **ils vivent dans un loft immense** they live in a huge loft.

loge [lɔʒ] *nom féminin*

1. lodge : **la loge de la concierge** the concierge's lodge

2. dressing room : **il est interdit d'entrer dans la loge des acteurs** it's forbidden to go into the actors' dressing room.

logement [lɔʒmɑ̃] *nom masculin*

1. apartment, flat *UK* : **ils ont trouvé un lo-**

gement dans un immeuble ancien they found an apartment in an old building

2. house : **un logement avec jardin** a house with a garden.

loger [lɔʒe] *verbe*

1. to stay : **nous avons logé à l'hôtel** we stayed in a hotel

2. to put up : **Luc et Sarah n'ont pas pu nous loger** Luc and Sarah couldn't put us up.

logiciel [lɔʒisjɛl] *nom masculin*

software : **un logiciel de traitement de texte** a word-processing software

> **logiciel de navigation** browser.

logique [lɔʒik] *adjectif & nom*

◻ *adjectif*

logical : **ce que tu dis n'est pas logique** what you're saying isn't logical

◻ *nom féminin*

logic : **il n'y a aucune logique dans son raisonnement** there's no logic in his argument.

logiquement [lɔʒikmɑ̃] *adverbe*

if all goes well : **logiquement, tu devrais le recevoir demain** if all goes well, you should get it tomorrow.

loi [lwa] *nom féminin*

law : **c'est interdit, c'est la loi** it's forbidden, that's the law.

loin [lwɛ̃] *adverbe*

1. far, far away : **c'est loin, la mer ?** is the sea far away? ou is it far to the sea?

2. a long time ago : **l'école primaire, ça me semble loin maintenant** primary school seems a long time ago now

3. a long way off : **Noël est encore loin** Christmas is still a long way off

> **de loin**

1. from a distance : **je vois mal de loin** I can't see properly from a distance

2. by far : **Noureddine est de loin le meilleur élève de la classe** Noureddine is by far the best pupil in the class

> **loin de** far from : **tu habites loin de l'école ?** do you live far from school? ; **non, loin de là !** no, far from it!

> **pas loin de** nearly : **il n'est pas loin de 9 heures** it's nearly 9 o'clock

> **plus loin** farther ou further.

loisir [lwazir] *nom masculin*

1. **leisure : pendant ses heures de loisir** during his leisure time
2. **leisure activity : nous n'avons plus beaucoup de temps pour les loisirs** we don't have much time for leisure activities.

Londonien, enne [lɔ̃dɔnjɛ̃, ɛn] *nom masculin, nom féminin*
Londoner.

Londres [lɔ̃dr] *nom*

London : **ils habitent à Londres** they live in London.

long, longue [lɔ̃, lɔ̃g] *adjectif*

long : **un long morceau de tissu** a long piece of material ; **le voyage m'a paru long** the trip seemed long to me

long *nom masculin*

➤ **faire 4 mètres de long** to be 4 metres long

➤ **marcher de long en large** to walk up and down

➤ **le long** along : **on s'est promenés le long de la rivière** we walked along the river.

longer [lɔ̃ʒe] *verbe*

1. **to walk along : nous avons longé la route** we walked along the road
2. **to run along : le mur qui longe le jardin** the wall that runs along the garden.

longtemps [lɔ̃tɑ̃] *adverbe*

a long time : **j'ai attendu longtemps** I waited for a long time ; **Cécile habite là depuis longtemps** Cécile has been living there a long time ; **tu as mis longtemps à te préparer** you took a long time to get ready

➤ **je n'en ai pas pour longtemps** I won't be long

➤ **il y a longtemps que ça s'est passé** it happened a long time ago

➤ **il y a longtemps que je n'ai pas vu Pierre** I haven't seen Pierre for a long time.

longue ➤ long.

longueur [lɔ̃gœr] *nom féminin*

length : **la longueur de la planche n'a pas d'importance** the length of the plank isn't important

➤ **quelle est la longueur des rideaux ?** how long are the curtains?

➤ **longueur d'onde** wavelength : **nous sommes sur la même longueur d'onde** we are on the same wavelength.

look [luk] *nom masculin*

look : **j'aime bien son look** I like his look.

lorsque [lɔrsk(ə)] *conjonction*

when : **appelle-nous lorsque tu seras prêt** call us when you are ready.

losange [lɔzɑ̃ʒ] *nom masculin*

diamond.

lot [lo] *nom masculin*

prize : **il y avait des lots intéressants à la tombola** there were some interesting prizes in the raffle

➤ **le gros lot** the jackpot.

loterie [lɔtri] *nom féminin*

lottery *(pluriel* lotteries*)* : **la Loterie nationale** the National Lottery.

lotion [lɔsjɔ̃] *nom féminin*

lotion : **lotion après-rasage** aftershave lotion.

lotissement [lɔtismɑ̃] *nom masculin*

housing development : **ils habitent dans un lotissement** they live in a housing development.

Loto [lɔto] *nom masculin*

le Loto the French National Lottery ; **le Loto sportif** the pools *UK*.

louche [luʃ] *adjectif*

1. **suspicious : un individu louche** a suspicious individual
2. **sleazy : un bar louche** a sleazy bar.

loucher [luʃe] *verbe*

to squint : **c'est dommage, elle est jolie mais elle louche un peu** it's a shame, she's pretty but she squints a little.

louer [lwe] *verbe*

1. **to rent : on a loué un gîte pour les vacances** we rented a gîte for the holidays
2. **to book : je peux louer les places pour vous** I can book the seats for you.

loup [lu] *nom masculin*

wolf *(pluriel* wolves*)* : **il y a encore des loups en Roumanie** there are still wolves in Romania.

loupe [lup] *nom féminin*

magnifying glass *(pluriel* **magnifying glasses***)* : **regarder quelque chose à la loupe** to look at something with a magnifying glass.

louper [lupe] *verbe familier*

1. to miss : **vite, on va louper le bus !** quick, we're going to miss the bus!
2. to make a mess of : **j'ai complètement loupé la tarte** I made a complete mess of the tart.

lourd, e [lur, lurd] *adjectif*

heavy : **ton sac à dos est très lourd** your rucksack is very heavy

➤ **il fait lourd** it's close today.

Louvre [luvr] *nom*

➤ **le Louvre** the Louvre

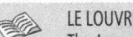
LE LOUVRE
The Louvre, which was once a royal palace, is one of the largest museums in the world, with a huge collection of antiques, sculptures and paintings. The items on display range from Egyptian mummies to the portrait of Mona Lisa (**la Joconde**). The glass pyramid that was built in the main courtyard of the Louvre in 1989 amid much controversy is now the main entrance to the museum.

loyer [lwaje] *nom masculin*

rent : **le loyer n'est pas cher** the rent isn't expensive.

LP *(abréviation de* lycée professionnel*) nom masculin*
secondary school for vocational training.

lu, e [ly] *participe passé de* lire.

lucarne [lykarn] *nom féminin*

1. skylight : **le soleil entre par la lucarne** the sun comes in through the skylight
2. top corner of the net : **le ballon est entré pile dans la lucarne** the ball went right into the top corner of the net.

luge [lyʒ] *nom féminin*

toboggan : **faire de la luge** to go tobogganning.

lui [lɥi] *pronom*

1. *Complément d'objet, s'il s'agit d'un homme* him : **je lui ai parlé** I talked to him ; **sans lui, je n'y serais pas arrivé** I wouldn't have managed without him ; **tous ces CD sont à lui** all these CDs are his ; **elle est plus jeune**

que lui she's younger than him ; **rends-le-lui** give it back to him ; **et lui, tu le connais ?** what about him, do you know him?
2. *Complément d'objet, s'il s'agit d'une femme* her : **je lui ai parlé** I talked to her ; **rends-le-lui** give it back to her
3. *Complément d'objet, s'il s'agit d'un animal ou d'une chose* it : **je lui ai donné à manger des croquettes** I gave it some dry food to eat
4. *Sujet* he : **lui, il dit que c'est vrai** he says it's true **et lui, qu'est-ce qu'il en pense ?** what does he think about it?
5. himself : **il est content de lui** he's pleased with himself
➤ **lui-même** himself : **il l'a décoré lui-même** he decorated it himself.

luisant, e [lɥizɑ̃, ɑ̃t] *adjectif*

1. gleaming : **les yeux luisants de colère** eyes gleaming with anger
2. glossy : **mon chien a le poil luisant** my dog has a glossy coat.

lumière [lymjɛr] *nom féminin*

light : **allume la lumière** put the light on.

lumineux, euse [lyminø, øz] *adjectif*

1. luminous : **un cadran lumineux** a luminous dial
2. crystal-clear : **son explication était lumineuse** his explanation was crystal-clear
3. light : **cette pièce est très lumineuse** this room is very light
➤ **une enseigne lumineuse** a neon sign.

lundi [lœ̃di] *nom masculin*

Monday

En anglais, les jours de la semaine s'écrivent avec une majuscule.

mes copains sont venus lundi my friends came on Monday ; **Thomas joue au tennis le lundi** Thomas plays tennis on Mondays ; **elle part lundi matin** she's leaving on Monday morning ; **lundi dernier** last Monday ; **lundi prochain** next Monday
➤ **le lundi de Pâques** Easter Monday.

lune [lyn] *nom féminin*

moon : **aujourd'hui c'est la pleine lune** it's full moon today
➤ **lune de miel** honeymoon
➤ **être dans la lune** to have one's head in the clouds : **elle est dans la lune** she's got her head in the clouds.

lunettes [lynɛt] *nom féminin pluriel*

glasses : **des lunettes noires** dark glasses
➤ **des lunettes de soleil** sunglasses.

lustre [lystr] *nom masculin*

chandelier : **un lustre en cristal** a crystal chandelier.

lutte [lyt] *nom féminin*

1. fight : **la lutte contre le racisme** the fight against racism
2. wrestling : **mon père aime regarder la lutte à la télé** my father likes watching wrestling on TV.

lutter [lyte] *verbe*

to fight : **le gouvernement lutte contre la pauvreté** the government is fighting against poverty.

luxe [lyks] *nom masculin*

luxury : **des boutiques de luxe** luxury boutiques
➤ **de luxe** luxury : **un hôtel de luxe** a luxury hotel.

luxueux, euse [lyksɥø, øz] *adjectif*

luxurious : **une chambre d'hôtel luxueuse** a luxurious hotel room.

lycée [lise] *nom masculin*

secondary school *UK*, high school *US* : **Arthur entre au lycée en septembre** Arthur is going to secondary school in September
➤ **un lycée professionnel** a training college

📖   LYCÉE
At 15 schoolchildren leave **collège** and can go on to a **lycée** to study for the baccalauréat exam. The three years they spend here are called **seconde** (15-16 yrs), **première** (16-17 yrs) and **terminale** (17-18 yrs).

➤ école, collège.

lycéen, enne [liseɛ̃, ɛn] *nom masculin, nom féminin*

secondary-school pupil *UK*, high-school student *US*.

M (*abréviation de* Monsieur) [ɛm]
Mr.

m' ➤ me.

ma ➤ mon.

macaronis [makarɔni] *nom masculin pluriel*

macaroni (*ne s'utilise jamais au pluriel*) : **ces macaronis sont excellents** this macaroni is excellent.

mâcher [maʃe] *verbe*

to chew : **ne mâche pas si bruyamment** don't chew so noisily.

machin [maʃɛ̃] *nom masculin familier*

thing : **c'est quoi, ce machin ?** what's this thing?

Machin, e [maʃɛ̃, in] *nom masculin, nom féminin familier*

what's-his-name (*féminin* **what's-her-name**) : **Machin est venu, tu sais, ton copain écossais** what's-his-name came, you know, your Scottish friend ; **c'est Machine, la sœur de Bruno** that's what's-her-name, Bruno's sister.

machinal, e, aux [maʃinal, o] *adjectif*

mechanical : **un geste machinal** a mechanical gesture.

machine [maʃin] *nom féminin*

machine
➤ **une machine à coudre** a sewing machine
➤ **une machine à écrire** a typewriter
➤ **une machine à laver** a washing machine
➤ **une machine à sous** a fruit machine *UK* ou a slot machine *US*.

mâchoire [maʃwar] *nom féminin*

jaw : **la mâchoire supérieure** the upper jaw.

madame [madam] (*pluriel* mesdames [me-dam]) *nom féminin*

1. Mrs : **madame Dutronc ne nous a pas donné de devoirs** Mrs Dutronc didn't give us any homework ; **bonjour, madame !** good morning! ; **bonjour, mesdames !** good morning!
2. Miss : **Madame, je peux sortir, s'il vous plaît ?** can I leave the classroom, Miss?
3. madam : **vous oubliez votre sac, madame !** you've forgotten your bag, madam!

mademoiselle [madmwazɛl] (*pluriel* mesdemoiselles [medmwazɛl]) *nom féminin*
Miss : **demande à mademoiselle Lainé** ask Miss Lainé ; **Mademoiselle, je peux sortir, s'il vous plaît ?** can I leave the classroom, Miss? ; **bonjour, mademoiselle !** good morning! ; **bonjour, mesdemoiselles !** good morning!

magasin [magazɛ̃] *nom masculin*
shop *UK*, store *US* : **un magasin de meubles** a furniture shop *UK* ou a furniture store *US* ; **faire les magasins** to go round the shops
➤ **les grands magasins** department stores.

magazine [magazin] *nom masculin*
magazine : **Lydie est abonnée à un magazine pour les jeunes** Lydie has a subscription to a youth magazine.

mage [maʒ] *nom masculin*
les Rois mages the Three Wise Men.

magicien, enne [maʒisjɛ̃, ɛn] *nom masculin, nom féminin*
magician.

magie [maʒi] *nom féminin*
magic : **c'est de la magie !** it's magic! ; **comme par magie** as if by magic.

magique [maʒik] *adjectif*
magic : **la baguette magique de la fée** the fairy's magic wand.

magnétique [maɲetik] *adjectif*
magnetic : **bande magnétique** magnetic tape.

magnétophone [maɲetɔfɔn] *nom masculin*
tape recorder.

magnétoscope [maɲetɔskɔp] *nom masculin*
videorecorder : **enregistrer un film au magnétoscope** to video a film.

magnifique [maɲifik] *adjectif*
great, magnificent : **tu es magnifique avec ce costume** you look great in that suit.

mai [mɛ] *nom masculin*
May

> En anglais, les mois de l'année s'écrivent avec une majuscule.

vous viendrez en mai ? will you come in May?
➤ **nous sommes le dix-huit mai** it's the eighteenth of May *UK* ou it's May eighteenth *US*
➤ **le premier mai** May Day.

maigre [mɛgr] *adjectif*

1. thin : **je trouve David trop maigre** I think David looks too thin ; **maigre comme un clou** *familier* as thin as a rake
2. low-fat : **des yaourts maigres** low-fat yoghurts.

maigrir [megrir] *verbe*
to lose weight : **Dorothée voudrait maigrir** Dorothée would like to lose weight ; **maigrir de trois kilos** to lose three kilos.

maillot [majo] *nom masculin*
shirt : **un maillot de rugby** a rugby shirt
➤ **maillot de bain**
1. *De fille* swimsuit : **Suzanne a un joli maillot de bain** Suzanne has a pretty swimsuit
2. *De garçon* swimming trunks (*s'utilise toujours au pluriel*) : **le maillot de bain de Renaud est un peu petit** Renaud's swimming trunks are a bit small
➤ **un maillot de corps** a vest *UK* ou an undershirt *US*.

main [mɛ̃] *nom féminin*
hand : **donne-moi la main pour traverser** give me your hand to cross the road ; **ils se tenaient par la main** they were holding hands ; **qu'est-ce que tu tiens à la main ?** what have you got in your hand?

> **faire quelque chose à la main** to do something by hand
> **fait main** handmade
> **la main dans la main** hand in hand
> **serrer la main à quelqu'un** to shake somebody's hand
> **se serrer la main** to shake hands.

maintenant [mɛ̃tnɑ̃] *adverbe*

now : **et maintenant, qu'est-ce qu'on fait ?** and now what do we do? ; **maintenant que tu la connais, tu peux lui demander de t'aider** now that you know her, you can ask her to help you.

maintenir [mɛ̃tnir] *verbe*

1. to support : **les piliers qui maintiennent la voûte** the pillars that support the vault
2. to claim, to maintain : **Loïc maintient que ce n'est pas sa faute** Loïc claims that it isn't his fault.

maire [mɛr] *nom masculin*

mayor.

mairie [meri] *nom féminin*

town hall *UK*, city hall *US* : **j'habite près de la mairie** I live near the town hall.

mais [mɛ] *conjonction*

but : **j'ai des devoirs mais j'ai quand même envie de sortir** I've got homework but I still want to go out ; **mais bien sûr !** but of course!
> **mais non !** of course not!

maïs [mais] *nom masculin*

1. maize *UK*, corn *US* : **des champs de maïs** maize fields
2. sweetcorn : **du maïs en boîte** canned sweetcorn.

maison [mɛzɔ̃] *nom féminin*

1. house : **ils louent une maison en Ardèche** they're renting a house in the Ardèche
2. homemade : **des confitures maison** homemade jams
> **à la maison**
1. at home : **je suis restée à la maison toute la journée** I stayed at home all day
2. home : **je rentre à la maison** I'm going home
> **une maison de campagne** a house in the country.

maître, maîtresse [mɛtr, mɛtrɛs] *nom masculin, nom féminin*

1. teacher : **le maître que j'avais en maternelle était très gentil** the teacher I had at nursery school was very nice ; **une maîtresse d'école** a school teacher
2. owner : **ce chien a perdu son maître** that dog has lost its owner
> **un maître nageur** a swimming instructor.

maîtriser [metrize] *verbe*

1. to control : **il ne sait pas maîtriser ses élèves** he can't control his pupils ; **apprends à maîtriser tes émotions** learn to control your emotions
2. to master : **c'est une langue difficile à maîtriser** it's a difficult language to master

se maîtriser *verbe pronominal*

to control oneself : **maîtrise-toi un peu !** control yourself!

majeur, e [maʒœr] *adjectif*

1. major : **un événement majeur** a major event
2. of age : **il est majeur, il peut faire ce qu'il veut** he's of age, he can do what he wants

majeur *nom masculin*

middle finger : **Anne porte une bague au majeur** Anne wears a ring on her middle finger.

majorette [maʒɔrɛt] *nom féminin*

majorette.

majorité [maʒɔrite] *nom féminin*

majority : **la majorité des gens** the majority of people
> **atteindre sa majorité** to come of age.

majuscule [maʒyskyl] *nom féminin & adjectif*

capital : **en majuscules** in capitals ; **E majuscule** capital E.

mal [mal] (*pluriel* maux [mo]) *nom masculin*

1. ache : **j'ai mal partout** I'm aching all over : **j'ai mal à la tête** my head aches ou I have a headache **avoir mal au dents** to have toothache *UK* ou to have a toothache *US* ; **avoir mal au dos** to have backache *UK* ou to have a backache *US* ; **avoir mal à la gorge** to have a sore throat ; **avoir mal au ventre** to have stomachache *UK* ou to have a stomachache *US* ; **j'ai mal au bras** my arm hurts
2. evil : **le bien et le mal** good and evil
> **avoir mal au cœur** to feel sick

➤ **avoir le mal de mer** to be seasick
➤ **avoir du mal à faire quelque chose** to have trouble doing something : **j'ai eu du mal à trouver une place libre** I had trouble finding a free seat
➤ **faire mal à quelqu'un** to hurt somebody : **aïe, tu m'as fait mal !** ouch, you hurt me! ; **ça fait mal** that hurts ; **tu t'es fait mal ?** did you hurt yourself?

mal *adverbe*

badly : **Noureddine chante vraiment mal** Noureddine sings really badly
➤ **aller mal**
1. **not to be well** : **elle va mal, elle a besoin qu'on l'aide** she isn't well, she needs help
2. **to go wrong** : **tout va mal en ce moment !** everything's going wrong at the moment!
➤ **se sentir mal** to feel ill
➤ **pas mal**
1. **not bad** : **il n'est pas mal pour son âge** he isn't bad for his age
2. **not badly** : **Alice ne joue pas mal du piano** Alice doesn't play the piano badly
➤ **pas mal de** quite a lot of : **il y avait pas mal de gens à la réunion** there were quite a lot of people at the meeting.

malade [malad] *adjectif & nom*

▨ *adjectif*
1. **ill, sick** : **Édouard est absent, il est malade** Édouard is absent, he's ill ; **tomber malade** to fall ill ou to fall sick
2. *familier* **crazy** : **tu es malade ou quoi ?** **tu as failli me tuer !** are you crazy or what? you almost killed me!
▨ *nom masculin ou féminin*
patient : **le médecin passe voir les malades à l'hôpital** the doctor visits the patients in hospital.

maladie [maladi] *nom féminin*

illness (*pluriel* **illnesses**), **disease** : **une maladie grave** a serious illness ; **la maladie d'Alzheimer** Alzheimer's disease ; **la maladie de la vache folle** mad-cow disease.

maladroit, e [maladrwa, at] *adjectif*

clumsy : **ce que tu es maladroit !** you're so clumsy!

malaise [malɛz] *nom masculin*

unease : **on sentait qu'il y avait un malaise entre eux** you could feel a certain unease between them

➤ **avoir un malaise** to feel faint.

malchance [malʃɑ̃s] *nom féminin*

bad luck.

mâle [mal] *adjectif & nom masculin*

male : **un éléphant mâle** a male elephant ; **c'est un mâle ou une femelle ?** is it a male or a female?

malentendu [malɑ̃tɑ̃dy] *nom masculin*

misunderstanding : **il y a eu un malentendu** there was a misunderstanding.

malgré [malgre] *préposition*

in spite of : **malgré tous ses défauts, je l'aime bien** in spite of all his faults, I like him
➤ **malgré tout**
1. **in spite of everything** : **elle a réussi malgré tout** she managed in spite of everything
2. **even so** : **c'était un bon film, mais malgré tout je me suis ennuyé** it was a good film but even so I got bored.

malheur [malœr] *nom masculin*

misfortune (*ne s'utilise jamais au pluriel*) : **ils n'ont eu que des malheurs** they've had nothing but misfortune
➤ **porter malheur à quelqu'un** to bring somebody bad luck : **ne dis pas ça, tu vas me porter malheur !** don't say that, you'll bring me bad luck!

malheureusement [malœrøzmɑ̃] *adverbe*

unfortunately : **malheureusement je ne vais pas pouvoir venir** unfortunately I won't be able to come.

malheureux, euse [malœrø, øz] *adjectif*

unhappy : **pauvre Amélie, elle a l'air malheureuse** poor Amélie, she looks unhappy.

malhonnête [malɔnɛt] *adjectif*

dishonest : **un homme d'affaires malhonnête** a dishonest businessman.

malhonnêteté [malɔnɛtte] *nom féminin*

dishonesty : **je ne supporte pas la malhonnêteté** I can't stand dishonesty.

malice [malis] *nom féminin*

mischief : **un regard plein de malice** a look full of mischief.

malicieux, euse [malisjø, øz] *adjectif*

mischievous : **un petit garçon malicieux** a mischievous little boy.

malin, igne [malɛ̃, iɲ] *adjectif*

1. crafty : **il est malin, il va trouver un moyen pour ne pas faire ses devoirs** he's crafty, he'll find a way to get out of doing his homework
2. clever : **tu te crois malin ?** do you think you're clever? ; **c'est malin !** that's clever!

malle [mal] *nom féminin*

trunk : **Samantha voyage avec deux énormes malles** Samantha travels with two enormous trunks.

mallette [malɛt] *nom féminin*

briefcase : **le professeur a oublié sa mallette dans la salle** the teacher left her briefcase in the classroom.

maman [mamɑ̃] *nom féminin*

mum *UK*, mom *US* : **oui, maman** yes, mum ; **la maman de Jean** Jean's mum.

mamie [mami] *nom féminin*

granny, grandma : **bonjour, mamie !** hello, granny! OU hello, grandma! : **la mamie de Raphaëlle** Raphaëlle's granny OU Raphaëlle's grandma.

mammifère [mamifɛr] *nom masculin*

mammal : **le chien est un mammifère** dogs are mammals.

mammouth [mamut] *nom masculin*

mammoth.

manche [mɑ̃ʃ] *nom*

■ *nom féminin*

1. sleeve : **les manches sont trop courtes** the sleeves are too short ; **un tee-shirt à manches longues** a long-sleeved T-shirt ; **un tee-shirt à manches courtes** a short-sleeved T-shirt
2. round : **c'est un jeu en trois manches** it's a game in three rounds
3. *Au tennis* set : **Sampras a remporté la première manche** Sampras won the first set

■ *nom masculin*

handle : **le manche du couteau est en ivoire** the handle of the knife is made of ivory.

Manche [mɑ̃ʃ] *nom féminin*

> **la Manche** the Channel OU the English Chan-

nel ; **on a traversé la Manche à Calais** we crossed the Channel at Calais.

mandarine [mɑ̃darin] *nom féminin*

mandarin.

manège [manɛʒ] *nom masculin*

1. merry-go-round : **un tour de manège coûte deux euros** a go on the merry-go-round costs two euros
2. riding school : **Élodie va dans un manège pour apprendre à monter à cheval** Élodie goes to a riding school to learn how to ride.

manette [manɛt] *nom féminin*

lever : **appuie sur la manette** push the lever
> **une manette de jeux** a joystick.

mangeable [mɑ̃ʒabl] *adjectif*

edible.

manger [mɑ̃ʒe] *verbe*

to eat : **les garçons ont mangé tout le pain** the boys have eaten all the bread ; **mange, ça va refroidir** eat or it'll get cold.

mangue [mɑ̃g] *nom féminin*

mango.

maniaque [manjak] *adjectif*

fussy : **il reste une tache là – ce que tu es maniaque !** there's a stain left – you're so fussy!

manie [mani] *nom féminin*

habit : **elle a ses petites manies** she has her little habits ; **Christophe a la manie d'allumer toutes les lumières** Christophe has a habit of switching all the lights on.

manier [manje] *verbe*

to handle : **un outil facile à manier** a tool that's easy to handle.

manière [manjɛr] *nom féminin*

way : **de quelle manière avez-vous résolu le problème ?** how did you solve the problem?
> **de manière à** in order to : **nous partirons tôt de manière à éviter les embouteillages** we'll leave early in order to avoid the traffic jams
> **de toute manière** anyway : **de toute manière, il m'énerve** he gets on my nerves anyway
> **faire des manières** to pussyfoot around : **ne fais pas de manières, accepte** don't pussyfoot around, say yes

manières nom féminin pluriel

manners : **les bonnes manières** good manners.

manif [manif] nom féminin familier

demo UK : **une manif contre la guerre** an anti-war demo.

manifestant, e [manifɛstã, ãt] nom masculin, nom féminin
demonstrator.

manifestation [manifɛstasjɔ̃] nom féminin

demonstration : **une manifestation de soutien aux ouvriers** a demonstration in support of the wrokers.

manifester [manifɛste] verbe

to demonstrate : **les étudiants ont manifesté contre l'augmentation des droits d'inscription** the students demonstrated against the increase in enrolment fees.

manipuler [manipyle] verbe

1. to handle : **c'est dangereux de manipuler des explosifs** handling explosives is dangerous
2. to manipulate : **il a l'impression d'avoir été manipulé** he feels that he has been manipulated.

mannequin [mankɛ̃] nom masculin

1. dummy (pluriel **dummies**) : **on regardait les mannequins dans la vitrine** we were looking at the dummies in the shop window
2. model : **Céline rêve d'être mannequin** Céline dreams of being a model.

manœuvre [manœvr] nom féminin

manoeuvre UK, maneuver US : **une manœuvre difficile** a difficult manoeuvre : **faire une manœuvre pour se garer** to manoeuvre into a parking place.

manœuvrer [manœvre] verbe

to operate : **cette machine est facile à manœuvrer** this machine is easy to operate.

manque [mãk] nom masculin

lack : **le manque de sommeil le rendait grincheux** lack of sleep made him grumpy.

manqué, e [mãke] adjectif

1. failed : **après plusieurs essais manqués** after several failed attempts
2. missed : **encore une occasion manquée !** another missed opportunity!

manquer [mãke] verbe

to miss : **je n'ai jamais manqué un seul cours** I've never missed a single lesson ; **manquer le bus** to miss the bus
➤ **il manque quelqu'un** somebody is missing
➤ **il me manque un euro** I'm one euro short
➤ **tu me manques** I miss you ; **il me manque** I miss him
➤ **manquer de**
1. to lack : **Dorothée manque d'imagination** Dorothée lacks imagination
2. to be short of : **on manque de pain** we're short of bread.

manteau [mãto] (pluriel **manteaux**) nom masculin

coat : **un manteau en laine** a wool coat.

manuel, elle [manɥɛl] adjectif

manual : **un métier manuel** a manual job

manuel nom masculin

manual : **un manuel d'utilisation** an instruction manual.

manuscrit, e [manyskri, it] adjectif

handwritten : **une lettre manuscrite** a handwritten letter

manuscrit nom masculin

manuscript : **le département des manuscrits anciens** the ancient-manuscript department.

mappemonde [mapmɔ̃d] nom féminin

map of the world.

maquereau [makro] (pluriel **maquereaux**) nom masculin
mackerel.

maquette [makɛt] nom féminin

model : **une maquette d'avion** a model plane.

maquillage [makijaʒ] nom masculin

make-up : **des produits de maquillage** make-up.

se maquiller [səmakije] *verbe pronominal*

to put on one's make-up : **il lui faut une heure pour se maquiller** it takes her an hour to put on her make-up.

marais [marɛ] *nom masculin*

marsh *(pluriel* **marshes***)* : **marais salant** salt marsh.

marathon [maratɔ̃] *nom masculin*

marathon : **Noémie s'entraîne à courir le marathon** Noémie is training to run the marathon.

marbre [marbr] *nom masculin*

marble : **une salle de bains en marbre** a marble bathroom.

marchand, e [marʃɑ̃, ɑ̃d] *nom masculin, nom féminin*

stallholder *UK* : **il y a au moins deux cents marchands à la foire** there are at least two hundred stallholders at the fair
➤ **un marchand de fleurs** a florist
➤ **le marchand de journaux** the newsagent *UK* ou the newsdealer *US*.

marchander [marʃɑ̃de] *verbe*

to haggle : **je n'ai pas osé marchander** I didn't dare haggle.

marchandise [marʃɑ̃diz] *nom féminin*

goods *(pluriel)* : **la marchandise est de mauvaise qualité** the goods are poor quality.

marche [marʃ] *nom féminin*

1. step : **attention à la marche** mind the step
2. walking : **la marche est un excellent exercice** walking is excellent exercise ; **faire de la marche** to go walking
3. walk : **on a fait une longue marche** we went for a long walk ; **à deux heures de marche du village** two hours' walk from the village
➤ **marche arrière** reverse : **en marche arrière** in reverse ; **faire marche arrière** to reverse
➤ **la marche à pied** walking
➤ **être en marche**
1. to be on : **est-ce que l'imprimante est en marche ?** is the printer on?
2. to be running : **le moteur est en marche** the engine is running
➤ **mettre quelque chose en marche** to start something up.

marché [marʃe] *nom masculin*

market : **ma mère va au marché tous les samedis** my mother goes to the market every Saturday
➤ **le marché aux puces** the flea market
➤ **bon marché** cheap ; **meilleur marché** cheaper.

marcher [marʃe] *verbe*

1. to walk : **on a marché pendant des heures** we walked for hours
2. to work : **hélas, son idée n'a pas marché** unfortunately his idea didn't work
3. to be going well : **et l'école, ça marche ?** is school going well?
➤ **marcher sur quelque chose** to tread on something : **ne marche pas sur mes lunettes** don't tread on my glasses
➤ **tu me fais marcher !** *familier* you're pulling my leg!

mardi [mardi] *nom masculin*

Tuesday

> En anglais, les jours de la semaine s'écrivent avec une majuscule.

mes copains sont venus mardi my friends came on Tuesday ; **Thomas joue au foot le mardi** Thomas plays football on Tuesdays ; **je pars mardi matin** I'm leaving on Tuesday morning ; **mardi dernier** last Tuesday ; **mardi prochain** next Tuesday

> MARDI GRAS
> **Mardi Gras**, Shrove Tuesday, is carnival time. It is the towns on the Côte d'Azur, such as Nice, which put on the biggest shows these days. The carnival in Nice has a different theme each year and huge floats covered in flowers are always a feature.

mare [mar] *nom féminin*

pond : **la mare aux canards** the duck pond.

marécage [mareka3] *nom masculin*

marsh *(pluriel* **marshes***)*.

marée [mare] *nom féminin*

tide ; **à marée haute** at high tide ; **à marée basse** at low tide
➤ **une marée noire** an oil slick.

margarine [margarin] *nom féminin*

margarine.

marge [mar3] *nom féminin*

margin : **les corrections sont dans la marge** the corrections are in the margin.

marguerite [margərit] *nom féminin*

daisy *(pluriel* daisies*)* : **un bouquet de marguerites** a bunch of daisies.

mari [mari] *nom masculin*

husband : **le mari de madame Berger est professeur** Mrs Berger's husband is a teacher.

mariage [marjaʒ] *nom masculin*

1. marriage : **Adeline ne croit pas au mariage** Adeline doesn't believe in marriage
2. wedding : **nous sommes invités au mariage de ma cousine** we've been invited to my cousin's wedding.

marié, e [marje] *adjectif & nom*

▪ *adjectif*

married : **est-ce que Sacha est marié ?** is Sacha married?

▪ *nom masculin, nom féminin*

groom *(féminin* bride*)* : **le marié et la mariée sont venus nous remercier** the bride and groom came to thank us.

se marier [səmarje] *verbe pronominal*

to get married : **Anne et Jean-Luc se marient samedi** Anne and Jean-Luc are getting married on Saturday ; **se marier avec quelqu'un** to marry somebody.

marin, e [marɛ̃, in] *adjectif*

sea : **l'air marin** the sea air

marin *nom masculin*

sailor : **Yann veut devenir marin** Yann wants to become a sailor

marine *nom féminin*

navy : **mon grand frère est dans la marine** my big brother is in the navy.

marionnette [marjɔnɛt] *nom féminin*

puppet : **un spectacle de marionnettes** a puppet show.

marmelade [marmalad] *nom féminin*

de la marmelade d'oranges marmalade ; **les brocolis étaient en marmelade** the broccoli was cooked to a pulp.

marmite [marmit] *nom féminin*

cooking pot.

marque [mark] *nom féminin*

1. mark : **il y a des marques partout sur les vitres** there are marks all over the windows
2. make, brand : **de quelle marque sont tes chaussures ?** what make are your shoes?

➤ **de marque** designer : **des vêtements de marque** designer clothes

➤ **à vos marques, prêts, partez !** ready, steady, go!

marquer [marke] *verbe*

1. to mark : **les sites intéressants sont marqués d'une croix** the interesting sites are marked with a cross
2. to write : **je vais marquer l'adresse sur ce bout de papier** I'll write the address on this piece of paper
3. to leave its mark on : **la guerre a beaucoup marqué mon grand-père** the war left its mark on my grandfather
4. to score : **qui a marqué le premier but ?** who scored the first goal?

marqueur [markœr] *nom masculin*

marker pen : **prête-moi ton marqueur fluo** lend me your fluorescent marker pen.

marraine [marɛn] *nom féminin*

godmother : **ma marraine m'envoie toujours un cadeau de Noël** my godmother always sends me a Christmas present.

marrant, e [marɑ̃, ɑ̃t] *adjectif familier*

funny : **Hubert nous a raconté une histoire marrante** Hubert told us a funny story.

se marrer [səmare] *verbe pronominal familier*

to have a good laugh : **on s'est marrés à la soirée de Kamel** we had a good laugh at Kamel's party.

marron [marɔ̃] *nom & adjectif*

▪ *nom masculin*

1. chestnut : **des marrons chauds** roast chestnuts ; **des marrons glacés** candied chestnuts
2. brown : **je n'aime pas le marron** I don't like brown

▪ *adjectif invariable*

brown : **des chaussures marron** brown shoes.

marronnier [marɔnje] *nom masculin*

chestnut tree.

mars [mars] *nom masculin*

March

> En anglais, les mois de l'année s'écrivent avec une majuscule.

l'anniversaire de Louis est en mars Louis's birthday is in March.

> **nous sommes le dix mars** it's the tenth of March *UK* ou it's March tenth *US*

marteau [marto] (*pluriel* marteaux) *nom masculin*

hammer : **Olivier s'est donné un coup de marteau sur les doigts** Olivier hit his fingers with a hammer
> **un marteau piqueur** a pneumatic drill *UK* ou a jackhammer *US*.

martien, enne [marsjɛ̃, ɛn] *nom masculin, nom féminin*
Martian.

masculin, e [maskylɛ̃, in] *adjectif*

1. masculine : **« magasin » est un nom masculin** "magasin" is a masculine noun
2. male : **le sexe masculin** the male sex

masculin *nom masculin*
masculine.

masque [mask] *nom masculin*

mask : **les acteurs portaient des masques** the actors were wearing masks ; **un masque à gaz** a gas mask ; **un masque de plongée** a diving mask.

massage [masaʒ] *nom masculin*

massage : **tu peux me faire un massage ?** can you give me a massage?

masse [mas] *nom féminin*

mass (*pluriel* masses) : **on voyait vaguement une masse noire** we could vaguely see a black mass
> **une masse de** ou **des masses de** *familier* masses of : **Bertrand a des masses de BD** Bertrand has got masses of comics.

masser [mase] *verbe*

to massage : **j'aime quand tu me masses le dos** I like it when you massage my back.

massif, ive [masif, iv] *adjectif*

solid : **c'est de l'or massif** it's solid gold

massif *nom masculin*

massif : **le massif enneigé se dressait devant nous** the snow-covered massif rose in front of us
> **le Massif central** the Massif Central.

mat, e [mat] *adjectif*

1. matt *UK*, matte *US* : **de la peinture mate** matt paint

2. dark : **elle a le teint mat** she has a dark complexion.

mât [ma] *nom masculin*

mast : **le voilier a perdu un de ses mâts** the sailing boat lost one of its masts.

match [matʃ] (*pluriel* matches ou matchs) *nom masculin*

match (*pluriel* matches) : **un match de foot** a football match
> **un match nul** a draw *UK* ou a tie *US* : **Manchester et Liverpool ont fait match nul** Manchester and Liverpool drew.

matelas [matla] *nom masculin invariable*

mattress (*pluriel* mattresses) : **ce matelas est trop mou** this mattress is too soft
> **un matelas pneumatique** an airbed.

matériau [materjo] (*pluriel* matériaux) *nom masculin*

material : **des matériaux de construction** building materials.

matériel [materjɛl] *nom masculin*

1. equipment : **nous manquons de matériel pour faire des expériences** we're short of equipment to do experiments
2. hardware : **c'est un problème de matériel ou de logiciel ?** is it a hardware problem or a software problem?

maternelle [matɛrnɛl] *nom féminin*

nursery school : **ma petite sœur est encore en maternelle** my little sister is still at nursery school.

mathématiques [matematik] *nom féminin pluriel*

mathematics (*singulier*) : **les mathématiques sont ma matière préférée** mathematics is my favourite subject.

maths [mat] *nom féminin pluriel familier*

maths *UK* (*singulier*), math *US* : **les maths sont ma matière préférée** maths is my favourite subject.

matière [matjɛr] *nom féminin*

1. subject : **quelle est ta matière préférée ?** what's your favourite subject?
2. material : **des matières premières** raw materials

➤ **matière grasse** fat.

Matignon [matiɲɔ̃] *nom*

building in Paris which houses the offices of the Prime Minister

> MATIGNON
> Since 1935, the French Prime Minister's official residence has been the Hôtel Matignon in Paris. **Matignon** is often used to mean the Prime Minister and his or her staff, for example 'Matignon received the delegation'.

matin [matɛ̃] *nom masculin*

morning : **je prends toujours ma douche le matin** I always have a shower in the morning ; **il faisait froid ce matin** it was cold this morning ; **à trois heures du matin** at three o'clock in the morning.

matinée [matine] *nom féminin*

morning : **on a passé la matinée à lire des BD** we spent the morning reading comics.

matraque [matrak] *nom féminin*

truncheon.

mauvais, e [movɛ, ɛz] *adjectif*

1. bad : **ce couscous n'est pas mauvais** this couscous isn't bad ; **j'ai eu de mauvais résultats ce trimestre** I had bad results this term
2. wrong : **c'est la mauvaise réponse** it's the wrong answer

mauvais *adverbe*

il fait mauvais the weather is bad.

mauve [mov] *nom masculin & adjectif*

mauve : **une jupe mauve** a mauve skirt ; **le mauve est la couleur préférée d'Anne** mauve is Anne's favourite colour.

maux ➤ **mal.**

maximum [maksimɔm] (*pluriel* maximums *ou* maxima [maksima]) *adjectif & nom*

▪ *adjectif*
maximum : **la vitesse maximum** the maximum speed.

▪ *nom masculin*
➤ **au maximum** at the most : **j'aurai douze sur vingt au maximum** I'll get twelve out of twenty at the most ; **je te donne dix minutes au maximum** I'm giving you ten minutes at the most

➤ **faire le maximum** to do one's best : **Sylvain a fait le maximum pour se rendre utile** Sylvain did his best to make himself useful.

mayonnaise [majɔnɛz] *nom féminin*

mayonnaise.

me [mə] (**m'***devant une voyelle ou un « h » muet*) *pronom*

1. me, to me : **Fred m'a invité à sa soirée** Fred invited me to his party ; **ne me pousse pas** don't push me ; **elle me l'a donné** she gave it to me
2. *Dans les verbes pronominaux*

> Pour les verbes qui ne sont que pronominaux, c'est-à-dire qui ne s'utilisent qu'avec un pronom, « me » ne se traduit pas en anglais :

je me souviens maintenant I remember now ; je me suis évanouie I fainted

> Lorsque « me » a une valeur réfléchie, il se traduit par **myself** ou bien il ne se traduit pas :

je m'habille I'm getting dressed ; je me suis fait mal I hurt myself ; je me suis lavé les cheveux I washed my hair

> Notez qu'en anglais on utilise les adjectifs possessifs avec les parties du corps.

➤ **me voilà !** here I am!

mec [mɛk] *nom masculin familier*

guy : **il y a un mec qui attend devant la porte** there's a guy waiting at the door.

mécanicien, enne [mekanisjɛ̃, ɛn] *nom masculin, nom féminin*

mechanic : **le père de Laure est mécanicien** Laure's father is a garage mechanic.

mécanique [mekanik] *adjectif*

mechanical : **un problème mécanique** a mechanical problem.

mécanisme [mekanism] *nom masculin*

mechanism.

méchanceté [meʃɑ̃ste] *nom féminin*

1. nastiness : **son plus grand défaut, c'est sa méchanceté** his biggest fault is his nastiness
2. nasty thing : **dire des méchancetés à quelqu'un** to say nasty things to someboy.

méchant, e [meʃɑ̃, ɑ̃t] *adjectif*

1. **nasty : Charles est méchant avec sa copine** Charles is nasty to his girlfriend
2. **naughty : si tu es méchant, je le dirai à papa** I'll tell dad if you're naughty.

mèche [mɛʃ] *nom féminin*

1. **wick : la mèche de la bougie** the candle wick
2. **fuse : la mèche d'une bombe** the fuse of a bomb
3. **lock : elle garde une mèche de cheveux de son mari** she keeps a lock of her husband's hair.

médaille [medaj] *nom féminin*

1. **medallion : elle porte une médaille** she's wearing a medallion
2. **medal : mon grand-père a des médailles de guerre** my grandfather has got some war medals
3. **tag : le chien a perdu sa médaille** the dog has lost its tag.

médaillon [medajɔ̃] *nom masculin*

locket : Sandra porte un médaillon en or Sandra wears a gold locket.

médecin [medsɛ̃] *nom masculin*

doctor : mon père est médecin my father is a doctor.

médecine [medsin] *nom féminin*

medicine : Anaïs voudrait faire des études de médecine plus tard Anaïs would like to study medicine later.

médias [medja] *nom masculin pluriel*

media : l'information a été diffusée dans tous les médias the news was broadcast by all the media.

médiathèque [medjatɛk] *nom féminin*

media library *(pluriel* **media libraries***)* **: j'ai emprunté cette cassette à la médiathèque** I borrowed this video from the media library.

médical, e, aux [medikal o] *adjectif*

medical : un examen médical a medical exam.

médicament [medikamɑ̃] *nom masculin*

medicine : un médicament contre les allergies a medicine against allergies ; **n'oublie pas de prendre tes médicaments** don't forget to take your medicine.

médiéval, e [medjeval] *(pluriel* médiévaux [medjevo]) *adjectif*
medieval.

médiocre [medjɔkr] *adjectif*

mediocre : des résultats scolaires médiocres mediocre school results.

médire [medir] *verbe*

to gossip : elles adorent médire they love to gossip.

Méditerranée [mediterane] *nom féminin*

la Méditerranée the Mediterranean ou the Mediterranean Sea.

méduse [medyz] *nom féminin*

jellyfish : il s'est fait piquer par une méduse he was stung by a jellyfish.

méfiant, e [mefjɑ̃, ɑ̃t] *adjectif*

suspicious : elle m'a jeté un regard méfiant she gave me a suspicious look.

se méfier [sə mefje] *verbe pronominal*

to be careful : méfie-toi, c'est un escroc be careful, he's a crook
➤ **se méfier de quelqu'un** to distrust somebody : **je me suis toujours méfié d'elle** I've always distrusted her.

mégaoctet [megaɔktɛ] *nom masculin*

megabyte.

meilleur, e [mɛjœr] *adjectif & nom*

▪ *adjectif*
1. **better : Karim est meilleur que moi en français** Karim is better than me at French ; **qui est la meilleure cuisinière des deux ?** who's the better cook of the two?
2. **best : c'est le meilleur joueur de foot anglais** he's the best English football player
▪ *nom masculin, nom féminin*
➤ **le meilleur** ou **la meilleure**
1. **the better : Chloé est la meilleure des deux** Chloé is the better of the two
2. **the best : c'est le meilleur de tous** he's the best of all.

mélange [melɑ̃ʒ] *nom masculin*

mixture : un mélange de jus d'orange et de limonade a mixture of orange juice and lemonade.

mélanger [melɑ̃ʒe] *verbe*

1. **to mix** : **mélange bien les œufs et le sucre** mix the eggs and the sugar well
2. **to get mixed up** : **mais non, tu mélanges tout !** no, you're getting everything mixed up!

se mélanger

to mix : **les couleurs se sont mélangées** the colours mixed.

mêlée [mele] *nom féminin*

scrum : **ils ont récupéré le ballon après la mêlée** they got the ball back after the scrum.

mêler [mele]

se mêler à | *verbe pronominal*

to join : **Alex n'a pas voulu se mêler au groupe** Alex didn't want to join the group

se mêler de | *verbe pronominal*

to get mixed up in : **elle aime se mêler des affaires des autres** she likes to get mixed up in other people's business

➤ **de quoi je me mêle !** OU **mêle-toi de ce qui te regarde !** mind your business

mélodie [melɔdi] *nom féminin*

melody *(pluriel* **melodies***).*

melon [məlɔ̃] *nom masculin*

melon : **un melon bien mûr** a ripe melon

➤ **un chapeau melon** a bowler hat : **il porte un chapeau melon** he's wearing a bowler hat.

membre [mɑ̃br] *nom & adjectif*

■ *nom masculin*

1. **limb** : **les membres supérieurs et les membres inférieurs** the upper and lower limbs
2. **member** : **Aurélie est membre du club d'échecs** Aurélie is a member of the chess club

■ *adjectif*

member : **les pays membres de l'Union européenne** the member countries of the European Union.

même [mɛm] *adjectif, pronom & adverbe*

■ *adjectif*

same : **il a le même âge que moi** he's the same age as me ; **nous avons eu les mêmes résultats** we got the same results

■ *pronom*

➤ **le même, la même** the same one : **les mêmes** the same ones ; **j'ai les mêmes que toi** I have the same ones as you

■ *adverbe*

even : **même moi je peux le faire** even I can do it ; **tu n'as même pas essayé** you didn't even try

➤ **aujourd'hui même** this very day

➤ **ici même** right here

➤ **même si** even if : **j'irai même s'il ne fait pas beau** I'll go even if the weather's bad

➤ **quand même** all the same OU still : **il veut quand même venir** he wants to come all the same OU he still wants to come ; **quand même, tu aurais pu me prévenir !** you could have told me all the same! OU still, you could have told me!

mémé [meme] *nom féminin familier*

grandma, granny : **oui, mémé** yes, grandma OU yes, granny ; **la mémé de Cathy** Cathy's grandma OU Cathy's granny.

mémoire [memwar] *nom féminin*

memory *(pluriel* **memories***)* : **Ludo a une bonne mémoire** OU **Ludo a de la mémoire** Ludo has a good memory ; **j'ai une mauvaise mémoire** OU **je n'ai pas de mémoire** I have a bad memory.

menaçant, e [mənasɑ̃, ɑ̃t] *adjectif*

threatening : **de gros nuages menaçants** big threatening clouds.

menace [mənas] *nom féminin*

threat : **c'est une menace pour la paix mondiale** it's a threat to world peace.

menacer [mənase] *verbe*

to threaten : **ils m'ont menacé** they threatened me.

ménage [menaʒ] *nom masculin*

faire le ménage to do housework.

ménager, ère [menaʒe, ɛr] *adjectif*

household : **des appareils ménagers** household appliances.

mendiant, e [mɑ̃djɑ̃, ɑ̃t] *nom masculin, nom féminin*

beggar : **il y a beaucoup de mendiants dans la ville** there are a lot of beggars in the city.

mendier [mɑ̃dje] *verbe*

to beg : **ils doivent mendier pour survivre** they have to beg in order to survive.

mener [məne] *verbe*

to lead : **qui mène l'enquête ?** who's leading the investigation? ; **elle mène une vie in-téressante** she leads an interesting life ; **Li-moges mène 80 à 64** Limoges is leading 80 to 64 ; **ce chemin mène à l'église** this path leads to the church.

menottes [mənɔt] *nom féminin pluriel*

handcuffs : **passer les menottes à quelqu'un** to handcuff somebody.

mensonge [mãsɔ̃ʒ] *nom masculin*

lie : **Corentin ne peut pas s'empêcher de dire des mensonges** Corentin can't help telling lies.

mensuel, elle [mãsɥɛl] *adjectif & nom masculin*

monthly : **les résultats mensuels** the monthly results ; **je suis abonné à un mensuel d'information** I subscribe to a news monthly.

mental, e, aux [mãtal o] *adjectif*

mental : **le calcul mental** mental arithmetic.

menteur, euse [mãtœr, øz] *nom masculin, nom féminin*

liar : **espèce de menteuse !** you liar!

menthe [mãt] *nom féminin*

mint : **du thé à la menthe** mint tea
> **une menthe à l'eau** a peppermint cordial UK.

mentir [mãtir] *verbe*

to lie : **il ment sans arrêt** he's always lying ; **mentir à quelqu'un** to lie to somebody ; **ne me mens pas, je sais où tu étais** don't lie to me, I know where you were.

menton [mãtɔ̃] *nom masculin*

chin : **elle a un grain de beauté sur le menton** she has a mole on her chin.

menu¹, e [məny] *adjectif*

1. slight : **Aïcha est menue mais elle est douée en sport** Aïcha is slight but she's good at sport
2. tiny : **couper en menus morceaux** to cut into tiny pieces.

menu² [məny] *nom masculin*

1. menu : **ils ont un menu très varié dans ce restaurant** they have a very varied menu in this restaurant ; **le menu à dix euros** the ten-euro menu
2. set menu : **je vais prendre un menu** I'll have the set menu.

menuisier [mənɥizje] *nom masculin*

joiner UK, carpenter US : **mon grand-père était menuisier** my grandfather was a joiner.

mépris [mepri] *nom masculin*

contempt : **un regard plein de mépris** a look full of contempt
> **avoir du mépris pour quelqu'un** to despise somebody.

méprisant, e [meprizã, ãt] *adjectif*

contemptuous : **un sourire méprisant** a contemptuous smile.

mépriser [meprize] *verbe*

to despise : **je sais qu'il me méprise** I know that he despises me.

mer [mɛr] *nom féminin*

1. sea : **la mer est calme aujourd'hui** the sea is calm today
2. seaside : **aller en vacances à la mer** to go on holidays to the seaside
> **la mer du Nord** the North Sea.

mercerie [mɛrsəri] *nom féminin*

haberdasher's shop UK, notions store US : **il y a une mercerie au coin de la rue** there's a haberdasher's shop on the corner of the street.

merci [mɛrsi] *interjection*

thank you! : **merci beaucoup !** thank you very much! ; **dire merci à quelqu'un** to thank somebody ; **il ne m'a même pas dit merci** he didn't even thank me.

mercredi [mɛrkrədi] *nom masculin*

Wednesday

> En anglais, les jours de la semaine s'écrivent avec une majuscule.

mes copains sont venus mercredi my friends came on Wednesday ; **Thomas joue au foot le mercredi** Thomas plays football on Wednesdays ; **il part mercredi matin** he's leaving on Wednesday morning ; **mercredi dernier** last Wednesday ; **mercredi prochain** next Wednesday.

mère [mɛr] *nom féminin*

mother : **comment s'appelle ta mère ?** what's your mother's name?
> **une mère célibataire** a single mother.

merguez [mɛrgɛz] *nom féminin invariable*

North African spiced sausage.

meringue [mərɛ̃g] *nom féminin*

meringue.

mérite [merit] *nom masculin*

credit : **il a du mérite de faire ses études tout en travaillant** it is to his credit that he studies and works at the same time.

mériter [merite] *verbe*

to deserve : **bravo, tu mérites une récompense !** well done, you deserve a reward! ; **Sam mérite d'être puni** Sam deserves to be punished.

merle [mɛrl] *nom masculin*

blackbird.

merveille [mɛrvɛj] *nom féminin*

wonder : **les sept merveilles du monde** the seven wonders of the world ; **ce tableau est une merveille** this painting is wonderful.

merveilleux, euse [mɛrvɛjø, øz] *adjectif*

1. wonderful : **Prague est une ville merveilleuse** Prague is a wonderful city
2. magic : **le monde merveilleux des contes de fées** the magic world of fairy tales.

mes ➤ mon.

mesdames ➤ madame.

mesdemoiselles ➤ mademoiselle.

message [mɛsaʒ] *nom masculin*

message : **est-ce que je peux lui laisser un message ?** can I leave a message for her?
➤ **un message électronique** an e-mail.

messagerie [mɛsaʒri] *nom féminin*

➤ **la messagerie électronique** e-mail
➤ **la messagerie vocale** voice mail.

messe [mɛs] *nom féminin*

mass *(pluriel* masses*)* : **aller à la messe** to go to mass : **la messe de minuit** midnight mass.

messieurs ➤ monsieur.

mesure [məzyr] *nom féminin*

1. measurement : **quelles sont les mesures de la pièce ?** what are the measurements of the room? ; **prendre les mesures de quelque chose** to measure something
2. measure : **le proviseur a dû prendre des mesures d'urgence** the headmaster had to take emergency measures

➤ **battre la mesure** to beat time
➤ **un costume sur mesure** a made-to-measure suit.

mesurer [məzyre] *verbe*

to measure : **je vais mesurer la hauteur de la porte** I'm going to measure the height of the door
➤ **Karin mesure 1,50 mètre** Karin is 1.5 metres tall
➤ **la table mesure 1,50 mètre** the table is 1.5 metres long.

métal [metal] *(pluriel* métaux [meto]*) nom masculin*

metal : **un briquet en métal** a metal lighter.

métallique [metalik] *adjectif*

metallic : **un objet métallique** a metallic object.

météo [meteo] *nom féminin*

weather forecast : **tu as écouté la météo aujourd'hui ?** have you heard the weather forecast today?

météore [meteɔr] *nom masculin*

meteor.

météorite [meteɔrit] *nom féminin*

meteorite.

méthode [metɔd] *nom féminin*

1. method : **une méthode efficace pour apprendre par cœur** an efficient method for learning by heart
2. primer : **une méthode d'anglais en cent leçons** an English primer in a hundred lessons.

méticuleux, euse [metikylø, øz] *adjectif*

meticulous : **Lucas est très méticuleux dans son travail** Lucas is very meticulous in his work.

métier [metje] *nom masculin*

job, occupation : **quel est votre métier ?** ou **qu'est-ce que vous faites comme métier ?** what's your job ou what's your occupation?
➤ **un métier à tisser** a loom.

métis, isse [metis] *nom masculin, nom féminin*

person of mixed race.

mètre [mɛtr] *nom masculin*

metre *UK*, meter *US* : **le lit fait deux mètres de long** the bed is two metres long ;

mètre carré square metre ; **mètre cube** cubic metre.

métro [metro] *nom masculin*

underground *UK*, subway *US*

> MÉTRO
> The first line of the Paris **métro** was opened in 1900. Today, trains run on fifteen lines across the whole city between 5:30 am and 1 am, carrying over 5 million passengers every day. The entrances to the stations are known as **bouches de métro**. Some are extremely decorative and were designed in the Art Nouveau style in the early 1900s. Many metro stations have themes. For example, the elegant station at the Louvre contains replicas of the statues to be found in the museum above.

metteur en scène [metœr ɑ̃sɛn] *nom masculin*

director.

mettre [mɛtr] *verbe*

1. **to put** : **mets tes affaires là** put your things over there ; **je ne sais pas quoi mettre sur la carte postale** I don't know what to put on the postcard
2. **to put on** : **je mets un pull et j'arrive** I'll put a sweater on and I'm coming ; **mets la radio, on va écouter les infos** put the radio on, we'll listen to the news
3. **to wear** : **je ne mets plus ma robe noire** I don't wear my black dress anymore
4. **to take** : **Rachida a mis une heure à se préparer** Rachida took an hour to get ready ; **mettre longtemps à faire quelque chose** to take a long time to do something
> **faire mettre le chauffage** to have the heating put in
> **faire mettre de la moquette** to have a carpet fitted

se mettre *verbe pronominal*

1. **to go** : **où est-ce que ça se met ?** where does it go?
2. **to get** : **se mettre en colère** to get angry
3. **to sit** : **mets-toi au premier rang** sit in the front row
4. **to stand** : **les plus grands se sont mis derrière sur la photo** the tallest people stood at the back in the photograph ; **se mettre debout** to stand up
5. **to put on** : **mets-toi une veste** put a jacket on

6. **to wear** : **je n'ai rien à me mettre** I haven't got anything to wear
> **se mettre à faire quelque chose** to start doing something : **Charlotte s'est mise à pleurer tout d'un coup** Charlotte suddenly started crying
> **se mettre au lit** to go to bed.

meubles [mœbl] *nom masculin pluriel*

furniture *(ne s'utilise jamais au pluriel)* : **ces meubles sont très lourds** this furniture is very heavy ; **des meubles de jardin** garden furniture.

meublé, e [mœble] *adjectif*

furnished : **ils louent un appartement meublé** they're renting a furnished apartment.

meuf [mœf] *nom féminin familier*

woman *(pluriel* **women***).*
> verlan.

meugler [møgle] *verbe*

to moo.

meule [møl] *nom féminin*

une meule de foin a haystack.

meurtre [mœrtr] *nom masculin*

murder : **il est accusé de meurtre** he has been accused of murder.

mi- [mi] *préfixe*

mid- : **à la mi-juin** in mid-June
> **à mi-chemin** halfway there : **on s'est arrêtés à mi-chemin** we stopped halfway there.

miauler [mjole] *verbe*

to miaow *UK*, to meow *US*.

micro [mikro] *nom masculin*

mike : **parlez dans le micro** speak into the mike.

microbe [mikrɔb] *nom masculin*

microbe, germ : **tu vas attraper tous ses microbes** you're going to catch all her germs.

micro-ondes [mikrɔ̃d] *nom masculin invariable & nom féminin pluriel*

un micro-ondes OU **un four à micro-ondes** a microwave OU a microwave oven.

micro-ordinateur [mikrɔɔrdinatœr] *(pluriel* **micro-ordinateurs***) nom masculin*

microcomputer.

microphone [mikrɔfɔn] *nom masculin*
microphone.

microprocesseur [mikrɔprɔsesœr] *nom masculin*
microprocessor.

microscope [mikrɔskɔp] *nom masculin*
microscope : **regarder quelque chose au microscope** to look at something through a microscope.

midi [midi] *nom masculin*
1. midday, twelve o'clock : **il est midi** it's midday ou it's twelve o'clock
2. lunchtime : **est-ce que tu restes à l'école à midi ?** do you stay in school at lunchtime?
3. South : **ils partent en vacances dans le Midi** they are going on holidays to the South.

mie [mi] *nom féminin*
Pat n'aime pas la croûte du pain, seulement la mie Pat doesn't like the crust of the bread, only the soft part.

miel [mjɛl] *nom masculin*
honey : **du miel liquide** clear honey.

le mien, la mienne [ləmjɛ̃, lamjɛn] (*masculin pluriel* **les miens** [lemjɛ̃], *féminin pluriel* **les miennes** [lemjɛn]) *pronom*
mine : **Sabine a un chat comme le mien** Sabine has a cat like mine ; **leur sœur a deux ans de plus que la mienne** their sister is two years older than mine ; **tes gants sont plus chauds que les miens** your gloves are warmer than mine ; **ses yeux sont bleus, les miens sont marron** her eyes are blue, mine are brown ; **leurs parents sont plus sévères que les miens** their parents are stricter than mine.

miette [mjɛt] *nom féminin*
crumb : **il y a des miettes partout sur le tapis** there are crumbs all over the carpet ; **des miettes de pain** breadcrumbs
➤ **être en miettes** to be in pieces : **mettre quelque chose en miettes** to smash something to pieces.

mieux [mjø] *adverbe, adjectif & nom*

■ *adverbe & adjectif*
better : **Jack joue mieux au foot que Scott** Jack plays football better than Scott ; **vous vous sentez mieux ?** are you feeling better? ; **Sandra est mieux que sa sœur** Sandra is better-looking than her sister
➤ **tu ferais mieux de partir** you'd better go ou you had better go ; **nous ferions mieux d'attendre** we'd better wait ou we had better wait
➤ **classe-les le mieux possible** file them as best as you can
➤ **de mieux en mieux** better and better : **elle va de mieux en mieux** she's getting better and better
■ *nom masculin*
➤ **le mieux, la mieux, les mieux**
1. the better : **c'est lui qui chante le mieux des deux** he's the one who sings the better of the two ; **David est le mieux des deux** David is the better-looking of the two
2. the best : **c'est Karim qui joue le mieux de toute l'équipe** Karim is the best player in the team ; **la mieux de toutes les filles de la classe** the best-looking of all the girls in the class
➤ **le mieux, c'est de rester ici** it's best to stay here
➤ **j'ai fait de mon mieux** I've done my best.

mignon, onne [miɲɔ̃, ɔn] *adjectif*
sweet : **ce garçon est mignon comme tout** that boy is really sweet ; **sois mignonne, va me chercher mes lunettes** be a sweety and get my glasses.

migraine [migrɛn] *nom féminin*
migraine : **j'ai la migraine** I have a migraine.

mijoter [miʒɔte] *verbe*
1. to simmer : **la viande doit mijoter pendant deux heures** the meat has to simmer for two hours ; **faire mijoter quelque chose** to simmer something
2. to make, to prepare : **je vais te mijoter une bonne soupe** I'll make some nice soup for you
3. *familier* to cook up : **qu'est-ce qu'ils mijotent encore, ces deux-là ?** what are those two cooking up now?

milieu [miljø] (*pluriel* **milieux**) *nom masculin*
1. middle : **au milieu de la chambre** in the middle of the bedroom ; **en plein milieu du film** right in the middle of the film

2. background : **le milieu familial est très important** family background is very important
➤ **un milieu de terrain** a midfielder.

militaire [militɛr] *nom & adjectif*

◻ *nom masculin*
soldier : il est militaire de carrière he is a professional soldier
◻ *adjectif*
military : une école militaire a military school.

mille [mil] *nom masculin invariable & adjectif invariable*
a thousand, one thousand : **il y avait plus de mille spectateurs** there were more than a thousand spectators ; **trois mille cinq cents** three thousand five hundred.

mille-feuille [milfœj] (*pluriel* mille-feuilles) *nom masculin*
vanilla slice *UK*, **napoleon** *US*.

millénaire [milenɛr] *nom masculin*
millennium : au début du troisième millénaire at the beginning of the third millennium.

mille-pattes [milpat] (*pluriel* mille-pattes) *nom masculin*
centipede, millipede.

milliard [miljar] *nom masculin*
billion : il y a plus d'un milliard d'habitants en Inde there are more than a billion inhabitants in India ; **il y a six milliards d'habitants sur Terre** there are six billion inhabitants on Earth ; **des milliards d'insectes** billions of insects.

milliardaire [miljardɛr] *adjectif & nom masculin ou féminin*
billionaire : un milliardaire saoudien a Saudi billionaire ; **elle est milliardaire** she's a billionaire.

millier [milje] *nom masculin*
1. **thousand : des milliers de gens** thousands of people ; **des oiseaux par milliers** birds in their thousands
2. **about a thousand : ça coûte un millier d'euros** it costs about a thousand euros.

millimètre [milimɛtr] *nom masculin*
millimetre *UK*, **millimeter** *US*.

million [miljɔ̃] *nom masculin*
million : dix million d'euros ten million euros ; **des millions de gens** millions of people.

millionnaire [miljɔnɛr] *adjectif & nom masculin ou féminin*
millionaire : un millionnaire argentin an Argentinian millionaire ; **elle est millionnaire** she's a millionaire.

mime [mim] *nom masculin*
mime.

mimer [mime] *verbe*
to mime.

minable [minabl] *adjectif & nom familier*
◻ *adjectif*
pathetic : j'ai eu des notes minables ce trimestre I got pathetic marks this term
◻ *nom masculin ou féminin*
loser : espèce de minable ! you loser!

mince [mɛ̃s] *adjectif & exclamation*
◻ *adjectif*
1. **slim : elle est toute mince** she's really slim
2. **thin : une mince couche de sucre** a thin layer of sugar
◻ *exclamation*
blast! *UK*, **damn!** *US* : **mince, j'ai oublié mon classeur de géo !** blast, I've forgotten my geography folder!

mincir [mɛ̃sir] *verbe*
to lose weight : tu as minci, non ? you've lost weight, haven't you?

mine [min] *nom féminin*
1. **mine : une mine de charbon** a coal mine ; **une mine d'or** a gold mine ; **la mine a explosé** the mine exploded
2. **lead : un crayon à mine dure** a pencil with a hard lead
➤ **avoir bonne mine** to look well : **tu as très bonne mine ces temps-ci** you're looking very well these days
➤ **avoir mauvaise mine** to look ill : **la prof de maths a mauvaise mine** the maths teacher looks ill.

minéral, e, aux [mineral, o] *adjectif & nom masculin*
◻ *adjectif*

n

mineral : de l'eau minérale mineral water ;
un minéral rare a rare mineral.

■ nom masculin
mineral

mineur, e [minœr] adjectif & nom

■ adjectif
minor : Simon est encore mineur Simon is
still a minor

■ nom masculin, nom féminin
les mineurs doivent être accompagnés
d'un adulte minors must be accompanied by
an adult

miniature [minjatyr] adjectif
miniature : un train miniature a miniature
train.

minichaîne [miniʃɛn] nom féminin
portable hi-fi.

MiniDisc® [minidisk] nom masculin
MiniDisc.

minijupe [miniʒyp] nom féminin
miniskirt : elle porte une minijupe she's
wearing a miniskirt.

minime [minim] nom & adjectif

■ nom masculin ou féminin
junior : Léa est dans l'équipe des minimes
Léa is in the junior team

■ adjectif
minimal : des conséquences minimes minimal consequences.

minimum [minimɔm] adjectif & nom

■ adjectif
minimum : la température minimum the
minimum temperature

■ nom masculin
minimum
➤ le strict minimum the bare minimum
➤ au minimum at least : il y avait cinquante
personnes au minimum there were fifty
people at least.

ministère [ministɛr] nom masculin
department : le ministère de l'Agriculture
the Ministry of Agriculture.

ministre [ministr] nom masculin
secretary (pluriel secretaries), minister
UK : la ministre de l'Éducation the Minister
of Education.

Minitel® [minitɛl] nom masculin
teletext system.

minorité [minɔrite] nom féminin
minority (féminin minorities) : malheureusement nous sommes en minorité unfortunately we're in the minority ; les minorités
ethniques ethnic minorities.

minuit [minɥi] nom masculin
midnight : le film finit à minuit the film finishes at midnight.

minuscule [minyskyl] adjectif & nom

■ adjectif
1. tiny : une chambre minuscule a tiny bedroom
2. small : b minuscule small b
■ nom féminin
small letter : mets tout en minuscules put
everything in small letters.

minute [minyt] nom féminin
minute : on a encore cinq minutes avant
de remettre les copies we still have five minutes before we have to hand the papers in ;
attends deux minutes wait a minute
➤ d'une minute à l'autre any minute now :
le professeur peut revenir d'une minute à
l'autre the teacher may come back any minute now.

minuter [minyte] verbe
to time : chaque étape est minutée each
stage is timed.

minutieux, euse [minysjø, øz] adjectif
meticulous : c'est une élève très minutieuse she's a very meticulous pupil.

miracle [mirakl] nom masculin
miracle : je ne peux pas faire de miracles I
can't work miracles ; Arnaud a survécu par
miracle by some miracle Arnaud survived.

miroir [mirwar] nom masculin
mirror : se regarder dans le miroir to look at
oneself in the mirror ; un miroir déformant a
distorting mirror.

mis, mise [mi, miz] participe passé de mettre.

mise [miz] nom féminin
➤ la mise en page ou la mise en pages the
layout
➤ mise au point

1. **focusing :** la mise au point est facile avec cet appareil it's easy to focus with this camera
2. **clarification :** je voudrais faire une petite mise au point I'd like to make a small clarification
> **mise en scène** direction : la mise en scène est de Jean Dutertre the direction is by Jean Dutertre.

misérable [mizerabl] *adjectif*

poor : un quartier misérable a poor area

 Misérable is a false friend, it does not mean 'miserable'.

misère [mizɛr] *nom féminin*

poverty : ils vivent dans une grande misère they live in great poverty

 Misère is a false friend, it does not mean 'misery'.

missile [misil] *nom masculin*

missile : un missile antichar an antitank missile.

mission [misjɔ̃] *nom féminin*

mission : j'ai pour mission de convaincre Daniel my mission is to convince Daniel.

mitaines [mitɛn] *nom féminin pluriel*

fingerless gloves : il porte des mitaines he's wearing fingerless gloves.

mi-temps [mitã] (*pluriel* mi-temps) *nom féminin*

half : la première mi-temps était plus intéressante que la seconde the first half was more interesting than the second
> **à la mi-temps** at half-time : on est allés acheter une glace à la mi-temps we went to buy an ice cream at half-time
> **à mi-temps** part-time : un travail à mi-temps a part-time job ; travailler à mi-temps to work part-time.

mitrailleuse [mitrajøz] *nom féminin*

machine gun.

mixer¹, mixeur [miksœr] *nom masculin*

food mixer : mettez tous les ingrédients dans le mixer put all the ingredients in the food mixer.

mixer² [mikse] *verbe*

to blend : mixe bien les ingrédients blend the ingredients well.

Mlle (*abréviation de* Mademoiselle)

Miss.

MM (*abréviation de* Messieurs)

Messrs.

Mme (*abréviation de* Madame)

Mrs.

mobile [mɔbil] *nom masculin*

mobile : il y a un mobile au-dessus du lit du bébé there's a mobile above the baby's bed.

mobilier, ère [mɔbilje, ɛr] *adjectif*

furniture : un magasin de mobilier de bureau an office furniture shop.

mocassins [mɔkasɛ̃] *nom masculin pluriel*

mocassins.

moche [mɔʃ] *adjectif familier*

ugly : ce tableau est vraiment moche this painting is really ugly.

mode [mɔd] *nom*

▪ *nom féminin*
fashion : Dorothée suit la mode de très près Dorothée follows fashion very closely ; lancer une mode to start a fashion
> **à la mode** fashionable
▪ *nom masculin*
form : il y a plusieurs modes de paiement possibles several forms of payment are possible
> **le mode d'emploi** the instructions : où est le mode d'emploi ? where are the instructions?

modèle [mɔdɛl] *nom masculin*

model : le prof nous a donné un modèle à suivre the teacher gave us a model to follow
> **un modèle réduit** a scale model.

modélisme [mɔdelism] *nom masculin*

scale-model making.

modem [mɔdɛm] *nom masculin*

modem : un modem fax a fax modem.

modéré, e [mɔdere] *adjectif*

moderate.

moderne [mɔdɛrn] *adjectif*

modern : **l'architecture moderne** modern architecture.

moderniser [mɔdɛrnize] *verbe*

to modernize : **ils ont décidé de moderniser l'entreprise** they've decided to modernize the factory

se moderniser *verbe pronominal*

to become more modernized : **le pays s'est modernisé dans les années 1970** the country became more modernized in the 1970s.

modeste [mɔdɛst] *adjectif*

modest : **ne sois pas si modeste !** don't be so modest! ; **un salaire modeste** a modest salary.

modestie [mɔdɛsti] *nom féminin*

modesty : **c'est de la fausse modestie** it's false modesty.

modification [mɔdifikasjõ] *nom féminin*

modification : **apporter une modification à quelque chose** to modify something.

modifier [mɔdifje] *verbe*

to modify : **tu devrais modifier la conclusion** you should modify the conclusion.

moelle [mwal] *nom féminin*

marrow : **la moelle osseuse** bone marrow
➤ **la moelle épinière** the spinal cord.

moelleux, euse [mwalø, øz] *adjectif*

1. soft : **un canapé moelleux** a soft canapé
2. moist : **un bon gâteau moelleux** a nice moist cake.

moi [mwa] *pronom*

1. me : **c'est pour moi ?** is that for me? ; **il est arrivé après moi** he arrived after me ; **elle est plus âgée que moi** she's older than me ; **aide-moi** help me ; **donne-le-moi** give it to me ; **et moi, tu m'as oublié ?** what about me, have you forgotten me? ; **j'ai sommeil – moi aussi** I'm sleepy – so am I ; **qui est là ? – c'est moi** who's there? – it's me
2. I : **moi je crois qu'il a tort** I think he's wrong ; **qui veut venir ? – moi** who wants to come? – me ou who wants to come? – I do ; **c'est moi qui leur ai dit** I told them
3. myself : **je suis fière de moi** I'm proud of myself

➤ **c'est à moi** it's mine : **ces CD sont à moi** these CDs are mine

moi-même *pronom*

myself : **je l'ai fait moi-même** I made it myself.

moindre [mwɛ̃dr] *adjectif superlatif*

le moindre, la moindre the slightest ; **sans la moindre difficulté** without the slightest difficulty ; **je n'ai pas la moindre idée** I haven't got the slightest idea
➤ **dans les moindres détails** in the smallest detail
➤ **merci de m'avoir aidé – c'est la moindre des choses** thank you for helping me – it's the least I could do.

moine [mwan] *nom masculin*

monk.

moineau [mwano] (*pluriel* **moineaux**) *nom masculin*

sparrow.

moins [mwɛ̃] *adverbe & préposition*

■ *adverbe*

less : **elle est moins sympa que Cécile** she's less nice than Cécile ou she's not as nice as Cécile ; **tu devrais manger moins** you should eat less ; **ils habitent moins loin que toi** they don't live as far away as you
➤ **moins de**
1. *Suivi d'un nom singulier* less : **j'ai moins de courage que toi** I have less courage than you ou I'm not as brave as you
2. *Suivi d'un nom pluriel* fewer : **il y a moins de gens que la dernière fois** there are fewer people than last time
3. *Suivi d'un chiffre* less than : **ça va me prendre moins de dix minutes** it'll take me less than ten minutes
➤ **le moins** ou **la moins** ou **les moins** the least : **c'est lui qui travaille le moins** he works the least ou he does the least work ; **la fille la moins égoïste que je connaisse** the least selfish girl I know ; **c'est le moins grand de tous** it's the smallest of all

■ *préposition*

1. minus : **dix moins huit font deux** ten minus eight is two ; **il fait moins vingt degrés** it's minus twenty degrees
2. *Pour dire l'heure* **il est trois heures moins vingt** it's twenty to three ; **il est moins dix** it's ten to

> **à moins de** ou **à moins que** unless : **on n'y arrivera jamais, à moins de demander de l'aide** we'll never manage unless we ask for help ; **on peut aller au cinéma, à moins que tu ne préfères le théâtre** we can go to the cinema, unless you prefer the theatre
> **au moins** at least : **il fait au moins trente degrés** it's at least thirty degrees ; **tu pourrais au moins dire bonjour !** you could at least say hello!
> **celui-ci coûte dix euros de moins que l'autre** this one costs ten euros less than the other
> **j'ai un an de moins que Justine** I'm a year younger than Justine
> **de moins en moins**
> 1. less and less : **de moins en moins d'argent** less and less money
> 2. fewer and fewer : **de moins en moins d'élèves** fewer and fewer pupils
> **en moins** missing : **il y a une personne en moins** there's a person missing
> **le moins possible** as little as possible.

mois [mwa] *nom masculin*

month : **Benjamin a passé trois mois en Floride** Benjamin spent three months in Florida.

moisi, e [mwazi] *adjectif*

mouldy *UK*, moldy *US*
> **ça a un goût de moisi** it tastes mouldy
> **ça sent le moisi** it smells musty.

moisir [mwazir] *verbe*

to go mouldy *UK*, to go moldy *US* : **les biscuits ont moisi** the biscuits have gone mouldy.

moisissure [mwazisyr] *nom féminin*

mould *UK*, mold *US*.

moisson [mwasɔ̃] *nom féminin*

harvest : **la moisson a été bonne cette année** the harvest was good this year ; **ils font la moisson en août** they harvest in August.

moissonner [mwasɔne] *verbe*

to harvest : **ils ont déjà moissonné le blé** they've already harvested the wheat.

moite [mwat] *adjectif*

1. clammy : **tu as les mains moites** your hands are all clammy
2. moist : **une chaleur moite** a moist heat.

moitié [mwatje] *nom féminin*

half : **tu peux manger la moitié de mon sandwich** you can have half my sandwich ; **la moitié du temps** half the time ; **moitié rouge, moitié bleu** half red, half blue
> **à moitié vide** half-empty
> **faire quelque chose à moitié** to half-do something.

moka [mɔka] *nom masculin*

coffee cake : **ma mère a fait un moka pour mon anniversaire** my mother made a coffee cake for my birthday.

molaire [mɔlɛr] *nom féminin*

molar : **le dentiste m'a enlevé une molaire** the dentist pulled out one of my molars.

Molière *nom*

Molière

> MOLIÈRE
> Molière was a seventeenth-century playwright and to this day is a key figure in French literary culture. Molière made comedy a respected art form at the theatre and he specialised in social satire. One of his plays, 'Tartuffe', the story of a religious hypocrite, was originally banned as immoral. Other plays include 'le Misanthrope' and 'l'Avare'.

molle ➤ mou.

mollet [mɔlɛ] *nom masculin*

calf *(pluriel calves)* : **j'ai mal aux mollets** my calves hurt.

moment [mɔmɑ̃] *nom masculin*

1. moment : **j'arrive dans un moment** I'll be there in a moment
2. while : **ça nous a pris un moment** it took us a while
3. time : **on a passé de bons moments ensemble** we had some good times together ; **ce n'est pas le moment de plaisanter !** this is no time for joking!
> **au moment de**
> 1. when : **au moment de l'accident** when the accident happened
> 2. just as : **au moment de partir, je me suis aperçu que je n'avais pas mon portefeuille** just as I was leaving, I realized I didn't have my wallet
> **au moment où** just as : **au moment où le film commençait** just as the film was starting

m

➤ **du moment que** since : **du moment que tu es d'accord, il n'y a pas de problème** since you agree, there's no problem
➤ **en ce moment** at the moment
➤ **par moments** at times
➤ **pour le moment** for the moment.

momie [mɔmi] *nom féminin*

mummy (*pluriel* **mummies**).

mon [mɔ̃] (*féminin* **ma** [ma], *pluriel* **mes** [me]) *adjectif*

my : **mon vélo** my bike ; **ma jupe rouge** my red skirt ; **je n'ai pas fini mon histoire** I haven't finished my story ; **un de mes meilleurs amis** one of my best friends.

monarchie [mɔnarʃi] *nom féminin*

monarchy (*pluriel* **monarchies**) : **le Royaume-Uni est une monarchie parlementaire** the United Kingdom is a parliamentary monarchy.

monastère [mɔnastɛr] *nom masculin*

monastery (*pluriel* **monasteries**).

monde [mɔ̃d] *nom masculin*

1. world : **des jeunes du monde entier** young people from all over the world ; **l'homme le plus riche du monde** the richest man in the world ; **dans le monde de l'art** in the art world
2. people : **il y a beaucoup de monde ici** there are a lot people here
➤ **tout le monde** everybody ou everyone : **tout le monde est là** everybody is here.

mondial, e, aux [mɔ̃djal, o] *adjectif*

world : **l'économie mondiale** the world economy.

moniteur, trice [mɔnitœr, tris] *nom masculin, nom féminin*

1. instructor : **moniteur d'auto-école** driving instructor ; **moniteur de ski** ski instructor
2. supervisor *UK*, counselor *US* : **les moniteurs du camp de vacances étaient super sympas** the holiday camp supervisors were really nice

moniteur *nom masculin*

monitor : **le moniteur d'un ordinateur** the monitor of a computer.

monnaie [mɔnɛ] *nom féminin*

1. currency (*pluriel* **currencies**) : **la monnaie unique** the single currency : **la livre sterling est la monnaie britannique** the pound sterling is the British currency
2. change : **tu as de la monnaie pour le bus ?** do you have change for the bus? ; **vous avez la monnaie de dix euros ?** do you have change for ten euros? ; **je vais faire la monnaie** I'm going to get some change ; **elle a oublié de me rendre la monnaie** she forgot to give me my change.

monsieur [məsjø] (*pluriel* **messieurs** [mesjø]) *nom masculin*

1. Mr : **monsieur Lacroix est très sévère** Mr Lacroix is very strict
2. sir : **monsieur, je peux sortir, s'il vous plaît ?** can I leave the classroom, sir?
3. gentleman (*pluriel* **gentlemen**) : **un monsieur demande à te parler** a gentleman is asking to talk to you
➤ **messieurs dames, votre attention, s'il vous plaît** ladies and gentlemen, your attention, please
➤ **bonjour, monsieur !** good morning! ; **bonjour, messieurs !** good morning!

monstre [mɔ̃str] *nom & adjectif*

▪ *nom masculin*
monster : **un monstre imaginaire** an imaginary monster
▪ *adjectif familier*
colossal : **j'ai fait une erreur monstre** I made a colossal mistake.

monstrueux, euse [mɔ̃stryø, øz] *adjectif*

1. monstrous : **une vague monstrueuse** a monstrous wave
2. terrible : **une erreur monstrueuse** a terrible mistake.

mont [mɔ̃] *nom masculin*

mount : **le mont Everest** Mount Everest ; **le mont Blanc est le plus haut sommet des Alpes** Mont Blanc is the highest mountain in the Alps.

montage [mɔ̃taʒ] *nom masculin*

photomontage : **ce n'est pas vraiment elle, c'est un montage** it's not really her, it's a photomontage.

montagne [mɔ̃taɲ] *nom féminin*

mountain : **on voit les montagnes là-bas**

you can see the mountains over there ; **aller en vacances à la montagne** to go to the mountains on holiday ; **une montagne de vieux journaux** a mountain of old newspapers

➤ **des montagnes russes** a roller coaster

➤ **faire de la montagne** to go mountain climbing.

montant [mɔ̃tɑ̃] *nom masculin*

amount : écris le montant sur cette ligne write the amount on this line

➤ **d'un montant de** for : **une facture d'un montant de deux cents euros** an invoice for two hundred euros.

montée [mɔ̃te] *nom féminin*

1. **climb** : la montée était longue et difficile the climb was long and hard

2. **slope** : attends-moi en haut de la montée wait for me at the top of the slope.

monter [mɔ̃te] *verbe*

1. **to go up** : monte me chercher mes lunettes, s'il te plaît go up and fetch my glasses, please ; **fais attention en montant l'escalier** be careful when you go up the stairs **ou** be careful when you go upstairs

2. **to come up** : montez, je suis en haut come up, I'm upstairs ; **j'étais au premier et je les regardais monter l'escalier** I was on the first floor and I was watching them come up the stairs

3. **to take up** : vous pouvez monter ces valises, s'il vous plaît ? can you take these suitcases up, please?

4. **to bring up** : monte-moi le journal bring the newspaper up for me

> Notez la différence de traduction selon que la personne qui parle se trouve en bas, traduction to go up, to take up, ou déjà en haut, traduction to come up, to bring up.

5. **to climb** : la route monte à cet endroit the road climbs at this point ; **Claire est montée sur un tabouret** Claire climbed onto a stool

6. **to get in, to get into** : montez vite dans la voiture ! get in the car quick! **ou** get into the car quick!

7. **to get on** : plusieurs passagers sont montés à la station Saint-Sulpice several passengers got on at Saint-Sulpice station

8. **to rise** : les prix montent toujours prices are still rising ; **la température monte** the temperature is rising

9. **to turn up** : qui a monté le son ? who turned the sound up?

10. **to assemble** : ce sont des étagères qu'on monte soi-même these are shelves that you assemble yourself

11. **to put up** : on a monté la tente en dix minutes we put the tent up in ten minutes

➤ **la marée monte** the tide is coming in

➤ **monter à cheval** to ride **ou** to ride a horse : **tu sais monter à cheval ?** can you ride a horse?

➤ **monter en courant** to run up.

montre [mɔ̃tr] *nom féminin*

watch *(pluriel watches)* : **une montre à quartz** a quartz watch

➤ **une épreuve contre la montre** a time trial.

montrer [mɔ̃tre] *verbe*

to show : **montrer quelque chose à quelqu'un** to show somebody something **ou** to show something to somebody ; **montre-moi ta rédaction** show me your essay

➤ **montrer du doigt** to point at : **c'est impoli de montrer les gens du doigt** it's rude to point at people

se montrer *verbe pronominal*

to show oneself : **Karl n'ose pas se montrer** Karl doesn't dare show himself.

monture [mɔ̃tyr] *nom féminin*

frames : **une monture de lunettes en plastique** plastic glasses frames.

monument [mɔnymɑ̃] *nom masculin*

monument : **les monuments de Dublin** the monuments of Dublin

➤ **le monument aux morts** the war memorial.

monumental, e, aux [mɔnymɑ̃tal, o], *adjectif*

monumental : **une erreur monumentale** a monumental mistake.

se moquer [sə mɔke] *verbe pronominal*

➤ **se moquer de**

1. **to laugh at, to make fun of** : **ne te moque pas de moi** don't laugh at me

2. **not to care about** : **Yasmine se moque de ce que les gens peuvent penser d'elle** Yasmine doesn't care about what people think of her.

m

moquette [mɔkɛt] *nom féminin*

fitted carpet *UK*, **wall-to-wall carpet** : **faire mettre de la moquette** to have a carpet fitted.

moral, e, aux [mɔral, o] *adjectif*

moral : **les valeurs morales** moral values

moral *nom masculin*

morale : **c'est bon pour le moral** it's good for morale
> **avoir le moral** to be in good spirits
> **ne pas avoir le moral** to be depressed
> **remonter le moral à quelqu'un** to cheer somebody up

morale *nom féminin*

moral : **quelle est la morale de l'histoire ?** what's the moral of the story?
> **faire la morale à quelqu'un** to lecture somebody.

morceau [mɔrso] (*pluriel* morceaux) *nom masculin*

1. **piece** : **un morceau de pain** a piece of bread ; **couper en morceaux** to cut into pieces
2. **passage** : **la prof nous a lu un morceau du poème** the teacher read us a passage from the poem
> **un morceau de sucre** a lump of sugar
> **manger un morceau** to have a bite to eat.

mordre [mɔrdr] *verbe*

1. **to bite** : **le chien a mordu le facteur** the dog bit the postman ; **se faire mordre** to get bitten
2. **to step over** : **il a mordu la ligne de départ** he stepped over the starting line
> **ça mord ?** are the fish biting?
> **mordre dans quelque chose** to bite into something : **Zoé s'est cassée une dent en mordant dans une pomme** Zoé broke a tooth as she bit into an apple.

mordu, e [mɔrdy] *participe passé de* mordre.

morse [mɔrs] *nom masculin*

1. **walrus** (*pluriel* walruses OU walrus) : **les morses ont des défenses** walrusses have tusks
2. **Morse code** : **un message en morse** a message in Morse code.

morsure [mɔrsyr] *nom féminin*

bite : **les morsures de serpent peuvent être mortelles** snake bites can be fatal.

mort, e [mɔr, mɔrt] *adjectif*

dead : **un chien mort** a dead dog
> **mort de fatigue** dead tired
> **mort de peur** scared to death

mort

■ *nom masculin*
fatality (*pluriel* fatalities) : **il y a eu trois morts et dix blessés** there were three fatalities and ten people injured
■ *nom féminin*
death : **avoir peur de la mort** to be frightened of death
> **elle m'en veut à mort** she hates my guts
> **freiner à mort** to slam the brakes on.

mortel, elle [mɔrtɛl] *adjectif*

1. **fatal** : **une maladie mortelle** a fatal illness
2. **dead boring** : **le cours de chimie était mortel** the chemistry lesson was dead boring.

morue [mɔry] *nom féminin*

cod : **de la morue salée** salt cod.

mosaïque [mɔzaik] *nom féminin*

mosaic.

mosquée [mɔske] *nom féminin*

mosque.

mot [mo] *nom masculin*

1. **word** : **j'ai appris un nouveau mot en anglais** I've learned a new word in English
2. **note** : **Jonathan m'a laissé un mot pour dire où il était** Jonathan left me a note to say where he was
> **un gros mot** a swearword
> **le mot de passe** the password
> **les mots croisés** crossword
> **mot à mot** word for word
> **avoir le dernier mot** to have the last word
> **j'ai deux mots à te dire** I want to have a word with you.

motard [mɔtar] *nom masculin*

1. **motorcyclist** : **un club de motards** a motorcyclists' club
2. **motorcycle policeman** (*pluriel* motorcycle policemen) : **la voiture était poursuivie par des motards** the car was chased by motorcycle policemen.

moteur [mɔtœr] *nom masculin*

engine : **un moteur à réaction** a jet engine
> **un moteur de recherche** a search engine.

motif [mɔtif] *nom masculin*

1. raison : **personne ne connaît le motif de son absence** nobody knows the reason for his absence
2. pattern : **un tissu à motifs bleus** a material with a blue pattern.

motiver [mɔtive] *verbe*

to motivate : **un système de récompense pour motiver les élèves** a reward system to motivate the pupils.

moto [mɔto] *nom féminin*

motorbike *UK*, motorcycle *US* : **ils sont arrivés à moto** they came on a motorbike ; **faire de la moto** to ride a motorbike.

motocross [mɔtɔkrɔs] *nom masculin*

motocross.

mou, molle [mu, mɔl] *adjectif*

1. soft : **ce matelas est trop mou** this mattress is too soft
2. apathetic : **ce que tu es mou !** you're so apathetic!

mouche [muʃ] *nom féminin*

fly *(pluriel* **flies)** : **il y a des mouches partout dans la maison** there are flies all over the house.

se moucher [səmuʃe] *verbe pronominal*

to blow one's nose : **Rose fait un bruit terrible quand elle se mouche** Rose makes a terrific noise when she blows her nose.

mouchoir [muʃwar] *nom masculin*

handkerchief *(pluriel* **handkerchiefs** ou **handkerchieves)**
> **un mouchoir en papier** a tissue.

moudre [mudr] *verbe*

to grind.

moue [mu] *nom féminin*

faire la moue to pout ; **Denis a fait une moue de dégoût** Denis screwed his face up in disgust.

mouette [mwɛt] *nom féminin*

seagull.

moufles [mufl] *nom féminin pluriel*

mittens.

mouillé, e [muje] *adjectif*

wet : **tu as les cheveux mouillés** your hair is wet.

mouiller [muje] *verbe*

to wet : **tu dois d'abord mouiller le papier** you must wet the paper first ; **se faire mouiller** to get wet

se mouiller *verbe pronominal*

1. to get wet : **on s'est mouillés en rentrant de l'école** we got wet coming back from school
2. to wet : **mouille-toi les cheveux** wet your hair.

moule [mul] *nom*

■ *nom masculin*
mould *UK*, mold *US* : **la pâte à modeler est difficile à sortir du moule** the modelling clay is hard to get out of the mould
> **un moule à gâteau** a cake tin *UK* ou a cake pan *US*
> **un moule à tarte** a flan dish *UK*, a pie dish *US*
■ *nom féminin*
mussel : **les moules frites sont une spécialité belge** mussels served with chips is a Belgian speciality.

moulin [mulɛ̃] *nom masculin*

mill : **an ancien moulin à eau** an old water mill
> **un moulin à café** a coffee grinder
> **un moulin à vent** a windmill.

moulu, e [muly] *adjectif*

ground : **du café moulu** ground coffee.

mourant, e [murɑ̃, ɑ̃t] *adjectif*

dying : **il est mourant** he's dying.

mourir [murir] *verbe*

to die : **on peut mourir du paludisme** you can die of malaria
> **mourir d'envie de faire quelque chose** to be dying to do something : **je meurs d'envie de lui parler** I'm dying to talk to him
> **mourir de faim** to be starving
> **mourir de soif** to be dying of thirst
> **s'ennuyer à mourir** to be bored to death
> **c'est à mourir de rire** it's a scream.

mousse [mus] *nom féminin*

1. moss : **la mousse sur les arbres** the moss on the trees

m

2. **foam** : **la mousse du matelas** the foam in the mattress
3. **mousse** : **une délicieuse mousse au chocolat** a delicious chocolate mousse.

mousser [muse] *verbe*

1. **to lather** : **ce savon mousse bien** this soap lathers well
2. **to be fizzy, to sparkle** : **ce champagne ne mousse pas beaucoup** this champagne isn't very fizzy.

moustache [mustaʃ] *nom féminin*

moustache *UK*, **mustache** *US* : **mon oncle porte la moustache** my uncle has a moustache

moustaches *nom féminin pluriel*

whiskers : **les moustaches du chat** the cat's whiskers.

moustachu, e [mustaʃy] *adjectif*

with a moustache *UK*, **with a mustache** *US* : **un homme moustachu** a man with a moustache.

moustique [mustik] *nom masculin*

mosquito *(pluriel* **mosquitoes** ou **mosquitos)* : **Lise s'est fait piquer par les moustiques** Lise got bitten by mosquitoes.

moutarde [mutard] *nom féminin*

mustard : **de la moutarde forte** strong mustard.

mouton [mutɔ̃] *nom masculin*

1. **sheep** *(pluriel* **sheep)* : **un troupeau de soixante moutons** a flock of sixty sheep
2. **mutton** : **nous avons mangé un ragoût de mouton** we had mutton stew.

mouvement [muvmɑ̃] *nom masculin*

movement : **ne faites pas de mouvements brusques** don't make any sudden movements.

moyen¹, enne [mwajɛ̃, ɛn] *adjectif*

1. **medium** : **c'est une grande taille ou une taille moyenne ?** is it a big size or a medium size?
2. **average** : **la température moyenne au mois de mars** the average temperature in March.

moyen² [mwajɛ̃] *nom masculin*

way, means *(singulier)* : **Pascal a trouvé un**

moyen d'entrer sans payer Pascal has found a way of getting in without paying

> **les moyens de communication** means of communication
> **les moyens de transport** means of transport
> **au moyen de** with : **Cathy a tout traduit au moyen d'un dictionnaire** Cathy translated everything with a dictionary
> **employer les grands moyens** to take drastic steps
> **avoir les moyens** to be well-off : **laisse-le payer, il a les moyens** let him pay, he's well-off
> **avoir les moyens d'acheter quelque chose** to be able to afford something : **je n'ai pas les moyens de m'acheter une console de jeux** I can't afford a games console.

Moyen Âge [mwajɛnaʒ] *nom masculin*

le Moyen Âge the Middle Ages ; **au Moyen Âge** in the Middle Ages.

moyenne [mwajɛn] *nom féminin*

1. **average** : **ma moyenne de l'année est de douze sur vingt** my average for the year is twelve out of twenty
2. **pass mark** : **ouf, j'ai la moyenne !** phew, I got the pass mark!

muet, muette [mɥɛ, ɛt] *adjectif & nom*

▪ *adjectif*

1. **speech-impaired** : **elle est muette, mais elle se fait comprendre** she's speech-impaired but she makes herself understood
2. **silent** : **un h muet** a silent h ; **les films muets** silent films
▪ *nom masculin, nom féminin*
> **les muets communiquent par signes** speech-impaired people communicate by signs.

mugir [myʒir] *verbe*

to moo : **la vache mugit** cows moo.

muguet [mygɛ] *nom masculin*

lily of the valley : **un brin de muguet** a sprig of lily of the valley

MUGUET
On May Day, 1 May, people in France traditionally buy bunches of lily of the valley. They give them to other people as presents. The flowers are supposed to bring good luck.

mulet [mylɛ] *nom masculin*

mule : **les mulets portent les provisions** mules are carrying the supplies.

multicolore [myltikɔlɔr] *adjectif*

multicoloured *UK*, multicolored *US*.

multiplication [myltiplikasjɔ̃] *nom féminin*

multiplication : **ils apprennent à faire les multiplications** they are learning to do multiplications.

multiplier [myltiplije] *verbe*

to multiply : **multiplie le prix du menu par le nombre de personnes** multiply the price of the menu by the number of people ; **3 multiplié par 8 égale 24** 3 multiplied by 8 equals 24.

municipal, e, aux [mynisipal, o] *adjectif*

public, municipal : **la bibliothèque municipale** the public library.

munitions [mynisjɔ̃] *nom féminin pluriel*

ammunition *(ne s'utilise jamais au pluriel)* : **les munitions sont stockées là** the ammunition is stocked there.

mur [myr] *nom masculin*

wall : **ne t'appuie pas contre le mur** don't lean on the wall
franchir le mur du son to break the sound barrier.

mûr, e [myr] *adjectif*

ripe : **les poires ne sont pas encore mûres** the pears aren't ripe yet
mature : **Laurie est très mûre pour son âge** Laurie is very mature for her age.

muraille [myraj] *nom féminin*

wall : **les murailles du château fort** the walls of the castle.

mûre *nom féminin*

blackberry *(pluriel* blackberries*)* : **on a ramassé des mûres pour faire de la confiture** we picked some blackberries to make jam.

mûrir [myrir] *verbe*

to ripen : **laisse mûrir les bananes, elles sont vertes** leave the bananas to ripen, they're green
to mature : **Alex a beaucoup mûri depuis l'année dernière** Alex has matured a lot since last year.

murmurer [myrmyre] *verbe*

to murmur : **tu n'as pas besoin de murmurer comme ça** you don't need to murmur like that.

muscade [myskad] *nom féminin*

la noix de muscade nutmeg.

muscle [myskl] *nom masculin*

muscle : **un exercice pour développer les muscles des cuisses** an exercise to develop your thigh muscles.

musclé, e [myskle] *adjectif*

muscular : **Roland est très musclé** Roland is very muscular.

musculation [myskylasjɔ̃] *nom féminin*

body-building : **faire de la musculation** to do body-building.

museau [myzo] *(pluriel* museaux*)* *nom masculin*

muzzle : **le museau du chien est humide** the dog's muzzle is damp.

musée [myze] *nom masculin*

1. museum : **le musée d'histoire naturelle** the natural history museum
2. art gallery *(pluriel* art galleries*)* : **ce tableau est dans un musée londonien** this painting is in a London art gallery.

musical, e, aux [myzikal, o] *adjectif*

musical : **un spectacle musical** a musical.

musicien, enne [myzisjɛ̃, ɛn] *nom & adjectif*
nom masculin, nom féminin
musician : **Sophie rêve de devenir musicienne** Sophie dreams of becoming a musician
■ *adjectif*
je ne suis pas très musicien I'm not very musical.

musique [myzik] *nom féminin*

music : **j'écoute beaucoup de musique** I listen to a lot of music
➤ **la musique de chambre** chamber music
➤ **une musique de film** a film score *UK* ou a movie score *US*.

musulman, e [myzylmɑ̃, an] *adjectif & nom*
masculin, nom féminin
Muslim

m

En anglais, les adjectifs et les noms se rapportant à une religion s'écrivent avec une majuscule :

les élèves musulmans Muslim pupils ; **Rachida est musulmane** Rachida is a Muslim ; **les musulmans** Muslims.

myope [mjɔp] *adjectif*

shortsighted *UK*, nearsighted *US* : **Anita porte des lunettes parce qu'elle est myope** Anita wears glasses because she's shortsighted.

myrtille [mirtij] *nom féminin*

bilberry *(pluriel* bilberries*) UK*, blueberry *(pluriel* blueberries*) US*.

mystère [mistɛr] *nom masculin*

mystery *(pluriel* mysteries*)* : **personne ne comprend, c'est un mystère** nobody understands, it's a mystery

➤ **faire des mystères** to be mysterious : **arrête de faire des mystères** stop being mysterious.

mystérieux, euse [misterjø, øz] *adjectif*

mysterious.

mythologie [mitɔlɔʒi] *nom féminin*

mythology : **la mythologie grecque** Greek mythology.

n' ➤ ne.

nacre [nakr] *nom féminin*

mother-of-pearl : **une chemise avec des boutons de nacre** a shirt with mother-of-pearl buttons.

nage [naʒ] *nom féminin*

swimming : **la nage est un bon exercice** swimming is good exercise.

nageoire [naʒwar] *nom féminin*

1. fin : **ces poissons ont des nageoires très longues** these fish have very long fins

2. flipper : **les phoques ont des nageoir**
seals have flippers.

nager [naʒe] *verbe*

to swim : **j'ai nagé un quart d'heure** I swa
for a quarter of an hour.

nageur, euse [naʒœr, øz] *nom masculin, no*
féminin

swimmer : **c'est un bon nageur** he's a goo
swimmer.

nain, e [nɛ̃, nɛn] *nom masculin, nom féminin*

dwarf *(pluriel* dwarves*)* : **Blanche-Neige**
les sept nains Snow White and the seve
dwarves.

naissance [nɛsɑ̃s] *nom féminin*

birth : **quelle est votre date de naissance**
what is your date of birth?

naître [nɛtr] *verbe*

to be born : **je suis né à Paris en 1990** I wa
born in Paris in 1990.

nana [nana] *nom féminin familier*

1. girl : **deux nanas et trois mecs** two girls ar
three guys

2. girlfriend : **tu as vu sa nouvelle nana**
have you seen his new girlfriend?

nappe [nap] *nom féminin*

tablecloth : **mets une nappe propre sur**
table put a clean tablecloth on the table.

narine [narin] *nom féminin*

nostril.

natal, e, als [natal] *adjectif*

native : **Dublin est sa ville natale** Dublin
his native city.

natation [natasjɔ̃] *nom féminin*

swimming : **cours de natation** swimmin
class ; **faire de la natation** to go swimming
je fais de la natation tous les jeudis I g
swimming every Thursday.

nation [nasjɔ̃] *nom féminin*

nation

➤ **les Nations unies** the United Nations.

national, e, aux [nasjɔnal, o] *adjectif*

national : **l'hymne national** the national a
them.

nationale [nasjɔnal] *nom féminin*

A road *UK*, state highway *US*.

nationalité [nasjɔnalite] *nom féminin*

nationality (*pluriel* **nationalities**) : **vous êtes de quelle nationalité ?** what nationality are you?
il est de nationalité canadienne he's Canadian.

natte [nat] *nom féminin*

plait *UK*, **braid** *US* : **elle a des nattes** she wears plaits *UK* OU she wears braids *US*.

nature [natyr] *nom & adjectif*

nom féminin

nature : **la protection de la nature** nature conservation ; **la nature humaine** human nature
countryside : **le dimanche on va se promener dans la nature** we're going for a walk in the countryside on Sundays
disparaître dans la nature to disappear into thin air
une nature morte a still life
adjectif invariable
plain : **yaourt nature** plain yoghurt.

naturel, elle [natyrɛl] *adjectif*

natural : **c'est tout à fait naturel** it's only natural.

naturellement [natyrɛlmã] *adverbe*

naturally : **ça lui vient naturellement** it comes naturally to him ; **tu vas à la fête ? – naturellement !** are you going to the party? – of course!

naufrage [nofraʒ] *nom masculin*

sinking : **le naufrage du Titanic** the sinking of the Titanic
faire naufrage to be wrecked : **plusieurs bateaux ont fait naufrage** several boats were wrecked.

nausée [noze] *nom féminin*

avoir la nausée to feel sick *UK* OU to feel nauseous *US* : **j'ai la nausée** I feel sick
donner la nausée à quelqu'un to make somebody feel sick *UK* OU to make somebody nauseous *US* : **ça me donne la nausée** it makes me feel sick.

navet [navɛ] *nom masculin*

turnip : **faites cuire les navets séparément** cook the turnips separately

2. *familier* **ce film est un navet** it's a really bad film OU the film is a turkey *US*.

navette [navɛt] *nom féminin*

shuttle : **il y a une navette pour aller à l'aéroport** there's a shuttle service to the airport ; **une navette spatiale** a space shuttle
▸ **faire la navette** to commute : **elle fait la navette entre Paris et Rouen tous les jours** she commutes between Paris and Rouen every day.

navigateur, trice [navigatœr, tris] *nom masculin, nom féminin*

navigator
▸ **un navigateur solitaire** a single-handed yachtsman

navigateur *nom masculin*

browser : **il faut un navigateur pour accéder à Internet** you need a browser to access the Internet.

naviguer [navige] *verbe*

1. **to sail** : **nous avons navigué toute la nuit** we sailed through the night
2. **to browse** : **j'ai trouvé ça en naviguant sur le Net** I found this while browsing on the Net.

navire [navir] *nom masculin*

ship : **un navire de guerre** a warship.

ne [nə] (**n'** *devant une voyelle ou un « h » muet*) *adverbe*

1. *Dans une négation*

« Ne » est toujours suivi de « jamais », « pas », « personne », « plus », « que », « rien », « aucun » (voir ces mots pour savoir comment se traduisent ces différentes constructions) pour former des phrases négatives :

il ne peut pas y aller he can't go ; **je n'ai vu personne** I didn't see anyone
2. *Dans une comparaison*

« Ne » ne se traduit pas lorsqu'il fait partie d'une comparaison :

il est plus grand que je ne croyais he's taller than I imagined.

né, e [ne] *participe passé de* **naître**

Ludovic est né en 1991 Ludovic was born in 1991 ; **elle est née le 17 juin** she was born on the 17th of June *UK* OU she was born on June 17th *US*.

n

nécessaire [neseser] *adjectif & nom*

■ *adjectif*

necessary : **si nécessaire je vous envoie les documents par e-mail** if necessary I'll send you the documents by e-mail

■ *nom masculin*

> **le strict nécessaire** the bare essentials.

nectarine [nɛktarin] *nom féminin*

nectarine.

néerlandais, e [neɛrlɑ̃dɛ, ɛz] *adjectif*

Dutch : **le parlement néerlandais** the Dutch parliament

néerlandais *nom masculin*

Dutch : **tu parles bien néerlandais** you speak good Dutch

En anglais, les adjectifs se rapportant à un pays ou une région, ainsi que le nom désignant la langue de ce pays ou de cette région, s'écrivent avec une majuscule.

Néerlandais, e *nom masculin, nom féminin*

un Néerlandais a Dutchman ; **une Néerlandaise** a Dutchwoman ; **les Néerlandais** the Dutch.

négatif, ive [negatif, iv] *adjectif*

negative : **une réponse négative** a negative answer

négatif *nom masculin*

negative : **j'ai perdu le négatif de cette photo** I've lost the negative of this photo.

négligé, e [negliʒe] *adjectif*

scruffy : **une tenue négligée** scruffy clothes.

négligent, e [negliʒɑ̃, ɑ̃t] *adjectif*

careless : **il s'est montré négligent** he was careless.

négliger [negliʒe] *verbe*

to neglect : **elle néglige son travail** she's neglecting her work

se négliger *verbe pronominal*

not to look after oneself : **tu te négliges en ce moment** you're not looking after yourself these days.

négociation [negɔsjasjɔ̃] *nom féminin*

negotiation : **des négociations de paix** peace negotiations.

négocier [negɔsje] *verbe*

to negotiate.

neige [nɛʒ] *nom féminin*

snow : **de la neige artificielle** artificial sno⟨w⟩

neiger [neʒe] *verbe*

to snow : **il neige** it's snowing ; **il a neigé⟨ la⟩ nuit dernière** it snowed last night.

néon [neɔ̃] *nom masculin*

neon light : **les néons de Piccadilly Circ⟨us⟩** the neon lights in Piccadilly Circus.

néo-zélandais, e [neɔzelɑ̃dɛ, ɛz] *(masc⟨ulin⟩ pluriel* néo-zélandais, *féminin pluriel* né⟨o-⟩ zélandaises) *adjectif*

New Zealand : **l'équipe de rugby né⟨o-⟩ zélandaise** the New Zealand rugby team

En anglais, les adjectifs se rapportant à un pay⟨s⟩ ou une région s'écrivent avec une majuscule.

Néo-Zélandais, e *nom masculin, nom fémin⟨in⟩*

New Zealander.

nerf [nɛr] *nom masculin*

nerve : **elle me tape sur les nerfs** she's g⟨et⟩ting on my nerves

> **être à bout de nerfs** to be at the end ⟨of⟩ one's tether.

nerveux, euse [nɛrvø, øz] *adjectif*

nervous : **tu me rends nerveux** you're ma⟨k⟩ing me nervous.

n'est-ce pas [nɛspa] *adverbe*

c'est délicieux, n'est-ce pas ? it's delicio⟨us⟩ isn't it? ; **vous vous êtes bien amusés, n'e⟨st-⟩ce pas ?** you enjoyed yourselves, didn't you⟨ ;⟩ **tu as un frère, n'est-ce pas ?** you've go⟨t a⟩ brother, haven't you?

net, nette [nɛt] *adjectif & adverbe*

■ *adjectif*

1. clear : **la photo est bien nette** the phot⟨o is⟩ very clear : **une nette amélioration** a cle⟨ar⟩ improvement

2. net : **le poids net** the net weight

■ *adverbe*

> **s'arrêter net** to stop dead

> **se casser net** to snap.

Net [nɛt] *nom masculin*

le Net the Net : **j'ai trouvé un site là-des⟨sus⟩ sur le Net** I found a website about it on ⟨the⟩ Net.

nettement [nɛtmɑ̃] *adverbe*

1. **clearly** : **on voit nettement les Alpes d'ici** you can see the Alps clearly from here
2. **much** : **c'est nettement mieux** it's much better ; **nettement plus** much more ; **nettement moins** much less.

nettoyage [netwajaʒ] *nom masculin*

cleaning
➤ **le nettoyage à sec** dry cleaning.

nettoyer [netwaje] *verbe*

to clean : **je dois nettoyer le four** I must clean the oven.

neuf¹, neuve [nœf, nœv] *adjectif*

new : **il est neuf, ton manteau ?** is that a new coat?
➤ **tout neuf** OU **flambant neuf** brand new : **un vélo tout neuf** OU **un vélo flambant neuf** a brand new bike
➤ **quoi de neuf ?** what's new?

neuf² [nœf] *adjectif numéral & nom masculin*

nine : **il y a neuf garçons dans ma classe** there are nine boys in my class ; **nous sommes le neuf novembre** it's the ninth of November *UK* OU it's November ninth *US*.

neutre [nøtr] *adjectif*

neutral : **la Suisse est un pays neutre** Switzerland is a neutral country.

neuve ➤ **neuf¹**.

neuvième [nœvjɛm] *adjectif numéral, nom masculin & nom masculin ou féminin*

ninth : **c'est la neuvième fois que je vois ce film** it's the ninth time I've seen this film ; **Anne est arrivée neuvième** Anne came ninth ; **un neuvième de la somme totale** a ninth of the total sum.

neveu [nəvø] (*pluriel* neveux) *nom masculin*

nephew.

nez [ne] *nom masculin*

nose : **elle a un petit nez retroussé** she has a small turned-up nose
➤ **nez à nez** face to face : **je me suis retrouvé nez à nez avec le prof** I found myself face to face with the teacher.

ni [ni] *conjonction*

➤ **ni ... ni** neither ... nor : **ni Kevin ni son frère n'ont voulu jouer** neither Kevin nor his brother wanted to play
➤ **ni lui ni moi** neither of us
➤ **ni l'un ni l'autre n'a parlé** neither of them spoke
➤ **je ne les aime ni l'un ni l'autre** I don't like either of them.

niche [niʃ] *nom féminin*

kennel *UK*, **doghouse** *US* : **le chien est dans sa niche** the dog is in its kennel.

nid [ni] *nom masculin*

nest : **un nid d'oiseau** a bird's nest.

nièce [njɛs] *nom féminin*

niece.

nier [nje] *verbe*

to deny : **il a tout nié** he denied it all.

n'importe ➤ importer.

niveau [nivo] (*pluriel* niveaux) *nom masculin*

1. **level** : **le niveau de l'eau est monté** the water level has risen
2. **standard** : **le niveau de vie** the standard of living
➤ **il a un bon niveau en anglais** his English is good.

noces [nɔs] *nom féminin pluriel*

wedding : **une photo prise le jour de leurs noces** a photograph taken on their wedding day ; **ils fêtent leurs noces d'argent** they're celebrating their silver wedding anniversary.

Noël [nɔɛl] *nom masculin*

Christmas : **à Noël** at Christmas ; **joyeux Noël !** Happy Christmas! OU Merry Christmas!

> **NOËL**
> Christmas in France begins on Christmas Eve. Traditionally, families sit down to a supper of turkey with chestnuts followed by a **bûche de Noël** or Yule log. Children used to leave their shoes by the fireplace for Father Christmas to fill with presents. These days, presents are usually put under the Christmas tree and opened on Christmas Eve.

nœud [nø] *nom masculin*

knot : **faire un nœud** to make a knot OU to tie a knot
➤ **un nœud papillon** a bow tie.

noir, e [nwar] *adjectif*

1. black : **il porte des chaussures noires** he's wearing black shoes
2. dark : **il fait déjà noir** it's already dark

Noir, e *nom masculin, nom féminin*

black man *(féminin* **black woman***)* : **les Noirs** Black people
➤ **un Noir américain** an African American

noir *nom masculin*

1. black : **le noir ne me va pas** black doesn't suit me
2. dark : **on ne voyait rien dans le noir** we couldn't see anything in the dark
➤ **le travail au noir** moonlighting.

noisette [nwazɛt] *nom féminin*

hazelnut.

noix [nwa] *nom féminin*

walnut : **un gâteau aux noix** a walnut cake
➤ **les noix de cajou** cashew nuts OU cashews
➤ **une noix de coco** a coconut
➤ **de la noix de muscade** nutmeg.

nom [nɔ̃] *nom masculin*

1. name : **pouvez-vous épeler votre nom, s'il vous plaît ?** can you spell your name, please?
2. noun : **un nom commun** a common noun ; **un nom propre** a proper noun
➤ **nom de famille** surname : **quel est votre nom de famille ?** what is your surname?
➤ **nom de jeune fille** maiden name.

nombre [nɔ̃br] *nom masculin*

number : **un nombre impair** an odd number ; **un nombre pair** an even number
➤ **un grand nombre de** many OU a lot of : **j'ai trouvé un grand nombre de fautes** I found many mistakes OU I found a lot of mistakes.

nombreux, euse [nɔ̃brø, øz] *adjectif*

1. large : **une famille nombreuse** a large family
2. a lot of, many : **ils ont de nombreux enfants** they have a lot of children OU they have many children
➤ **peu nombreux** not many OU few : **ils étaient peu nombreux** there weren't many of them OU there were few of them.

nombril [nɔ̃bril] *nom masculin*

navel, belly button.

nommer [nɔme] *verbe*

1. to name : **nommez ces animaux en anglais** name these animals in English
2. to appoint : **il a été nommé président de l'association** he was appointed president of the association

se nommer *verbe pronominal*

to be called : **elle se nomme Agathe** she's called Agathe.

non [nɔ̃] *adverbe*

1. no : **elle a dit non** she said no
2. not : **non seulement il ment, mais en plus ça le fait rire** not only is he lying, but he also thinks it's funny
➤ **c'est une bonne idée, non ?** it's a good idea, isn't it?
➤ **moi non plus** : **il n'a pas faim, moi non plus** he isn't hungry and neither am I ; **elle n'a pas de vélo, moi non plus** she doesn't have a bike, and neither do I ; **il ne voulait pas y aller et moi non plus** he didn't want to go and neither did I.

nonante [nɔnɑ̃t] *adjectif numéral*

Belgique & Suisse ninety : **il y a nonante garçons dans mon école** there are ninety boys in my school.

non-fumeur, euse [nɔ̃fymœr, øz] *nom masculin, nom féminin*

non-smoker : **cette partie du restaurant est réservée aux non-fumeurs** this part of the restaurant is for non-smokers only
➤ **une zone non-fumeur** a non-smoking area.

nord [nɔr] *nom & adjectif*

▪ *nom masculin*
north : **au nord** in the north ; **au nord de Montréal** north of Montreal
➤ **l'Amérique du Nord** North America
▪ *adjectif invariable*
1. north : **la côte nord** the north coast
2. northern : **la banlieue nord** the northern suburbs.

nord-est [nɔrɛst] *nom masculin & adjectif invariable*

northeast.

nord-ouest [nɔrwɛst] *nom masculin & adjectif invariable*

northwest.

normal, e, aux [nɔrmal, o] *adjectif*

normal : **en temps normal** in normal circumstances ; **ce n'est pas normal, ils ne sont pas encore arrivés** there's something wrong ; they haven't arrived yet

c'est tout à fait normal it's only natural.

normalement [nɔrmalmã] *adverbe*

normally, usually : **normalement il vient déjeuner le mercredi** he normally comes for lunch on Wednesday ou he usually comes for lunch on Wednesday

> **normalement, il devrait déjà être ici** he should be here by now.

Normandie [nɔrmãdi] *nom féminin*

> **la Normandie** Normandy : **Rouen est en Normandie** Rouen is in Normandy : **j'aimerais aller en Normandie** I'd like to go to Normandy.

nos ➤ notre.

notaire [nɔtɛr] *nom masculin*

notary public, solicitor UK.

note [nɔt] *nom féminin*

1. **note** : **prendre des notes** to take notes ; **les notes de musique** musical note
2. **mark** UK, **grade** US : **j'ai eu une bonne note** I got a good mark ; **elle a eu une mauvaise note** she got a bad mark.

noter [nɔte] *verbe*

1. **to note down, to write down** : **est-ce que tu as noté la date ?** have you noted down the date? ou have you written the date down?
2. **to mark** UK, **to grade** US : **le devoir est noté sur 20** the homework is marked out of 20 UK ou the homework is graded out of 20 US.

notice [nɔtis] *nom féminin*

instructions (*s'utilise toujours au pluriel*) : **lis bien la notice** read the instructions carefully.

notion [nɔsjõ] *nom féminin*

> **avoir des notions de quelque chose** to have a basic knowledge of something : **j'ai seulement quelques notions d'allemand** I only have a basic knowledge of German.

notre [nɔtr] (*pluriel* **nos** [no]) *adjectif*

our : **dans notre classe** in our class ; **c'est l'une de nos matières préférées** it's one of our favourite subjects.

le nôtre, la nôtre [lənotr, lanotr] (*pluriel* **les nôtres** [lenotr]) *pronom*

ours : **c'est votre chien ? – non, le nôtre est plus petit** is this your dog? – no, ours is smaller ; **s'il n'a pas de place, nous lui laisserons la nôtre** if he doesn't have a seat, we'll let him have ours ; **nos parents n'ont pas voulu – les nôtres non plus** our parents refused – so did ours.

nougat [nuga] *nom masculin*

nougat.

nouilles [nuj] *nom féminin pluriel*

noodles (*s'utilise toujours au pluriel*).

nourrir [nurir] *verbe*

to feed : **il nourrit son chien deux fois par jour** he feeds his dog twice a day

se nourrir *verbe pronominal*

to eat : **ce serpent se nourrit de rongeurs** this snake eats rodents.

nourriture [nurityr] *nom féminin*

food : **la nourriture est délicieuse à la cantine** the food in the canteen is delicious.

nous [nu] *pronom*

1. **we** : **nous avons une autre sœur** we have another sister ; **c'est nous qui y sommes allés finalement** we went in the end
2. **us, to us** : **ils nous ont invités** they invited us ; **il nous a regardés bizarrement** he looked at us strangely ; **elle nous parle uniquement en anglais** she only speaks English to us ; **tu en as eu plus que nous** you had more than us ; **rends-le-nous** give it back to us ; **et nous, tu nous as comptés ?** what about us, did you count us in?
3. **ourselves** : **nous sommes fières de nous** we're proud of ourselves
4. *Dans les verbes pronominaux*

   Pour les verbes qui ne sont que pronominaux, c'est-à-dire qui ne s'utilisent qu'avec un pronom, « nous » ne se traduit pas :

   nous nous souvenons we remember

   Lorsque « nous » a une valeur réfléchie, soit il se traduit par **ourselves**, soit il ne se traduit pas :

   nous nous sommes fait mal we hurt ourselves ; **nous nous sommes habillés** we got

n

dressed ; **nous sommes allés nous promener** we went for a walk

5. *Dans les verbes pronominaux à l'impératif* **let's** : **dépêchons-nous** let's hurry up

> Lorsque « nous » a une valeur réciproque, soit il se traduit par **each other**, soit il ne se traduit pas :

nous nous appelons tous les jours we call each other every day ; **nous nous battons** we fight

➤ **nous voilà !** here we are!
➤ **c'est à nous** it's ours

nous-mêmes *pronom personnel*

ourselves : **nous l'avons fait nous-mêmes** we did it ourselves.

nouveau, elle, x [nuvo, ɛl, o] (**nouvel**

devant un nom masculin commençant par une voyelle ou un « h » muet) adjectif & nom

■ *adjectif*
new : **Samir a un nouveau VTT** Samir has a new mountain bike ; **il a un nouvel appartement** he has a new flat

➤ **le Nouvel An** the New Year

■ *nom masculin, nom féminin*
new boy (*féminin* new girl) : **il y a une nouvelle dans notre classe** there's a new girl in our class

➤ **à nouveau** OU **de nouveau** again : **il faut refaire ce travail à nouveau** the work will have to be done again ; **elle est de nouveau en retard** she's late again.

nouvelle [nuvɛl] *nom féminin*

1. news : **c'est une bonne nouvelle !** that's good news!

2. short story (*pluriel* short stories) : **un recueil de nouvelles de Maupassant** a collection of short stories by Maupassant

nouvelles *nom féminin pluriel*

news (*singulier*) : **les nouvelles** the news ; **les nouvelles sont à vingt heures** the news is at eight o'clock

➤ **avoir des nouvelles de quelqu'un** to hear from somebody : **est-ce que tu as eu de leurs nouvelles récemment ?** have you heard from them recently?

➤ **demander des nouvelles de quelqu'un** to ask after somebody : **elle a demandé de tes nouvelles** she asked after you.

nouvel ➤ nouveau.

Nouvelle-Calédonie [nuvɛlkaledɔni]
nom féminin

➤ **la Nouvelle-Calédonie** New Caledonia
Peter est en Nouvelle-Calédonie depuis janvier Peter has been in New Caledonia since January ; **Elsa aimerait aller en Nouvelle-Calédonie** Elsa would like to go to New Caledonia.

Nouvelle-Zélande [nuvɛlzelãd] *nom féminin*

➤ **la Nouvelle-Zélande** New Zealand

> En anglais, à de rares exceptions près, il n'y a pas d'article devant les noms de pays :

Christchurch est en Nouvelle-Zélande Christchurch is in New Zealand ; **ils sont partis en Nouvelle-Zélande** they have gone to New Zealand.

novembre [nɔvãbr] *nom masculin*

November

> En anglais, les mois de l'année s'écrivent avec une majuscule :

je vais à Londres en novembre I'm going to London in November

➤ **nous sommes le trois novembre** it's the third of November *UK* OU it's November third *US*

noyau [nwajo] (*pluriel* noyaux) *nom masculin*

stone *UK*, pit *US* : **des noyaux de pêche** peach stones *UK* OU peach pits *US*.

se noyer [sənwaje] *verbe pronominal*

to drown : **j'ai failli me noyer** I nearly drowned.

nu, e [ny] *adjectif*

naked ; **elle était nue** she was naked ; **il est tout nu** he's completely naked OU he's stark naked

➤ **pieds nus** barefoot : **j'aime marcher pieds nus** I like walking barefoot.

nuage [nɥaʒ] *nom masculin*

cloud : **un gros nuage noir** a big black cloud

➤ **être dans les nuages** to have one's head in the clouds.

nuageux, euse [nɥaʒø, øz] *adjectif*

cloudy : **le temps est nuageux** it's cloudy.

nuance [nɥãs] *nom féminin*

1. difference : **je ne comprends pas la nuan-**

ce entre les deux I don't understand the difference between the two

2. **shade** : **des nuances de bleu** shades of blue.

nucléaire [nyklɛɛr] *adjectif*

nuclear : **l'énergie nucléaire** nuclear energy OU nuclear power.

nuit [nɥi] *nom féminin*

night : **les nuits sont longues en hiver** the nights are long in winter

➤ **cette nuit**

1. **last night** : **j'ai mal dormi cette nuit** I didn't sleep well last night

2. **tonight** : **je vais bien dormir cette nuit** I'm going to sleep well tonight

➤ **une nuit blanche** a sleepless night : **j'ai passé une nuit blanche** I had a sleepless night

➤ **il fait nuit** it's dark.

nul, nulle [nyl] *adjectif*

1. **bad** : **le film était nul** the film was rubbish OU it was really a bad film

2. **useless, hopeless** : **je suis nulle en français** I'm useless at French OU I'm hopeless at French

➤ **faire match nul** to draw *UK* OU to tie *US* : **les deux équipes ont fait match nul** the two teams drew

nulle part *adverbe*

1. **nowhere** : **il n'a nulle part où aller** he has nowhere to go OU he doesn't have anywhere to go

2. **anywhere** : **je ne le trouve nulle part** I can't find it anywhere.

numérique [nymerik] *adjectif*

digital : **un appareil photo numérique** a digital camera.

numéro [nymero] *nom masculin*

number : **quel est votre numéro de téléphone ?** what is your phone number? ; **Flora habite au numéro 12** Flora lives at number 12.

nuque [nyk] *nom féminin*

back of the neck : **il a pris un coup de soleil sur la nuque** he got sunburnt on the back of his neck.

Nylon® [nilɔ̃] *nom masculin*

nylon : **une chemise de nuit en Nylon** a nylon nightdress.

obéir [ɔbeir] *verbe*

to obey : **obéir à quelqu'un** to obey somebody ; **le chien refuse d'obéir à son maître** the dog won't obey its owner.

obéissant, e [ɔbeisɑ̃, ɑ̃t] *adjectif*

obedient : **des élèves obéissants** obedient pupils.

objectif, ive [ɔbʒɛktif, iv] *adjectif*

objective : **il faut rester objectif** you must be objective

objectif *nom masculin*

1. **goal, objective** : **il s'est fixé un objectif** he set himself a goal

2. **lens** *(pluriel* **lenses***)* : **l'objectif d'un appareil photo** a camera lens.

objection [ɔbʒɛksjɔ̃] *nom féminin*

objection : **personne n'a fait d'objections** nobody made any objections.

objet [ɔbʒɛ] *nom masculin*

1. **object** : **ça sert à quoi, cet objet bizarre ?** what's this strange object for?

2. **subject** : **cela fera l'objet d'une émission spéciale** this will be the subject of a special programme

➤ **des objets de valeur** valuables.

obligation [ɔbligasjɔ̃] *nom féminin*

obligation : **un père de famille a des obligations** a father has obligations ; **tu peux y aller, mais ce n'est pas une obligation** you can go, but you're not obliged to.

obligatoire [ɔbligatwar] *adjectif*

compulsory : **une matière obligatoire** a compulsory subject.

obliger [ɔbliʒe] *verbe*

➤ **obliger quelqu'un à faire quelque chose** to force somebody to do something : **je**

O

ne peux pas t'obliger à y aller I can't force you to go
➤ **être obligé de faire quelque chose** to have to do something : **je suis obligé de terminer mes devoirs d'abord** I have to finish my homework first.

obscur, e [ɔpskyr] *adjectif*

dark : **une pièce obscure** a dark room.

obscurité [ɔpskyrite] *nom féminin*

darkness : **la maison était plongée dans l'obscurité** the house was in darkness.

obsédé, e [ɔpsede] *adjectif & nom*

◼ *adjectif*
obsessed : **il est obsédé par cette idée** he's obsessed with the idea
◼ *nom masculin, nom féminin*
un obsédé sexuel a sex maniac.

observateur, trice [ɔpsɛrvatœr, tris] *adjectif*
observant : **elle est très observatrice** she's very observant.

observation [ɔpsɛrvasjɔ̃] *nom féminin*

1. comment : **note tes observations dans la marge** write your comments in the margin
2. observation : **le malade est en observation** the patient is under observation
➤ **il n'a pas un bon sens de l'observation** he's not very observant.

observer [ɔpsɛrve] *verbe*

to watch, to observe : **j'observais son expression** I watched her expression ou I observed her expression.

obstacle [ɔpstakl] *nom masculin*

1. obstacle : **le plus grand obstacle, c'est l'argent** money is the biggest obstacle
2. jump : **le cheval est tombé au dernier obstacle** the horse fell at the last jump.

obstiné, e [ɔpstine] *adjectif*

obstinate : **c'est un enfant obstiné** he's an obstinate child.

s'obstiner [sɔpstine] *verbe pronominal*

➤ **s'obstiner à faire quelque chose** to persist in doing something : **il s'obstine à vouloir le faire tout seul** he persists in wanting to do it himself ; **elle s'obstine à ne pas écouter** she refuses to listen ou she just won't listen.

obtenir [ɔptənir] *verbe*

to get : **il a obtenu le premier prix au festival** he got the first prize at the festival.

obus [ɔby] *nom masculin*

shell : **un obus est tombé sur la maison** a shell hit the house.

occasion [ɔkazjɔ̃] *nom féminin*

opportunity : **tu as manqué une bonne occasion** you've missed a good opportunity
➤ **d'occasion** second-hand : **un vélo d'occasion** a second-hand bike.

Occident [ɔksidɑ̃] *nom masculin*

l'Occident the West.

occidental, e, aux [ɔksidɑ̃tal, o] *adjectif*

Western : **les pays occidentaux** Western countries

Occidental, e, aux *nom masculin, nom féminin*
Westerner.

occupation [ɔkypasjɔ̃] *nom féminin*

occupation
➤ **il a de nombreuses occupations** he does a lot of different things.
➤ **pendant l'Occupation** during the occupation of France

occupé, e [ɔkype] *adjectif*

1. busy : **elle est occupée à faire ses devoirs** she's busy doing her homework
2. engaged *UK*, busy *US* : **ça sonne occupé** it's engaged *UK* ou it's busy *US*.

occuper [ɔkype] *verbe*

1. to occupy : **l'armée a occupé la capitale** the army has occupied the capital
2. to keep busy : **essaie d'occuper les enfants** try to keep the children busy

s'occuper *verbe pronominal*

➤ **s'occuper de quelqu'un** to take care of somebody ou to look after somebody : **elle s'occupe des enfants** she takes care of the children ou she looks after the children
➤ **s'occuper de quelque chose**
1. to take care of something : **je m'occupe de la vaisselle** I'll take care of the washing-up
2. to look after : **je m'occupe de ses plantes quand elle n'est pas là** I look after her plants when she's not there
➤ **je m'en occupe** I'll do it ou I'll take care of it

> **occupe-toi de tes affaires !** mind your own business!
> **je m'occupe en lisant** I spend my time reading
> **elle arrive à s'occuper** she manages to keep herself busy.

océan [ɔseã] *nom masculin*

ocean
> **l'océan Atlantique** the Atlantic Ocean
> **l'océan Pacifique** the Pacific Ocean.

octante [ɔktãt] *adjectif numéral Belgique & Suisse*

eighty : **il y a octante élèves dans mon école** there are eighty pupils in my school.

octobre [ɔktɔbr] *nom masculin*

October

En anglais, les mois de l'année s'écrivent avec une majuscule :

mon anniversaire est en octobre my birthday is in October
> **nous sommes le cinq octobre** it's the fifth of October *UK* OU it's October fifth *US*

odeur [ɔdœr] *nom féminin*

smell : **quelle bonne odeur !** what a nice smell!

odorat [ɔdɔra] *nom masculin*

sense of smell : **avoir un bon odorat** to have a good sense of smell.

œil [œj] *(pluriel* yeux [jø]) *nom masculin*

eye : **elle a les yeux bleus** she has blue eyes
> **un œil au beurre noir** a black eye
> **mon œil !** *familier* my foot!
> **à l'œil** *familier* for free : **on a eu deux places à l'œil** we got two seats for free.

œuf [œf, *pluriel* ø] *nom masculin*

egg
> **des œufs brouillés** scrambled eggs
> **un œuf à la coque** a boiled egg
> **un œuf dur** a hard-boiled egg
> **un œuf de Pâques** an Easter egg
> **un œuf au plat** OU **un œuf sur le plat** a fried egg
> **un œuf poché** a poached egg.

œuvre [œvr] *nom féminin*

work : **une œuvre d'art** a work of art.

office [ɔfis] *nom masculin*

l'office du tourisme the tourist office.

officiel, elle [ɔfisjɛl] *adjectif*

official : **est-ce que la nouvelle est officielle ?** is the news official?

officier [ɔfisje] *nom masculin*

officer : **il est officier dans l'armée** he's an officer in the army.

offre [ɔfr] *nom féminin*

offer : **une offre d'emploi** a job offer ; **offre spéciale !** special offer!

offrir [ɔfrir] *verbe*

1. to give : **ils m'ont offert des rollers pour mon anniversaire** they gave me rollerblades for my birthday
2. to offer : **il a offert ses services** he offered his services

s'offrir *verbe pronominal*

to treat oneself to : **on s'est offert un week-end à Dublin** we treated ourselves to a weekend in Dublin.

oie [wa] *nom féminin*

goose *(pluriel* geese).

oignon [ɔɲɔ̃] *nom masculin*

onion : **soupe à l'oignon** onion soup ; **une tarte aux oignons** an onion tart
> **mêle-toi de tes oignons** *familier* mind your own business.

oiseau [wazo] *(pluriel* oiseaux) *nom masculin*

bird : **un oiseau de proie** a bird of prey.

O.K. [ɔke] *adjectif & adverbe*

OK : **O.K., j'arrive !** OK, I'm coming!

olive [ɔliv] *nom féminin*

olive : **des olives noires** black olives ; **des olives vertes** green olives.

olivier [ɔlivje] *nom masculin*

olive tree.

olympique [ɔlɛ̃pik] *adjectif*

Olympic : **les jeux Olympiques** the Olympic Games OU the Olympics.

ombre [ɔ̃br] *nom féminin*

1. shade : **asseyons-nous à l'ombre** let's sit in the shade
2. shadow : **l'ombre de l'arbre sur le mur** the shadow of the tree on the wall.

O

omelette [ɔmlɛt] *nom féminin*

omelette, omelet *US* : **une omelette aux champignons** a mushroom omelette.

omnibus [ɔmnibys] *nom masculin*

stopping train *UK*, **local train** *US*.

omnisports [ɔmnispɔr] *adjectif invariable*

sports : **salle omnisports** sports centre.

on [ɔ̃] *pronom*

1. **we : on y va ?** shall we go? ; **on est arrivés trop tard** it was too late when we got there
2. **somebody, someone : on t'a appelé au téléphone ce matin** somebody called for you this morning OU someone called for you this morning OU there was a call for you this morning

> Lorsque « on » est utilisé pour désigner quelqu'un dont on ne veut pas ou ne peut pas spécifier l'identité, « on » se traduit souvent en anglais par un passif :

on m'a volé ma calculatrice somebody has stolen my calculator OU my calculator's been stolen

3. **people : on me dit souvent que je ressemble à mon père** people often say I look like my father ; **on vit de plus en plus vieux en Europe** people in Europe are living longer and longer
4. **you : on n'a pas le droit de jouer au foot ici** you're not allowed to play football here
> **on ne sait jamais** one never knows.

oncle [ɔ̃kl] *nom masculin*

uncle.

onctueux, euse [ɔ̃ktɥø, øz] *adjectif*

creamy : **un yaourt onctueux** a creamy yogurt.

ongle [ɔ̃gl] *nom masculin*

nail : **arrête de te ronger les ongles** stop biting your nails.

ont ➤ avoir.

ONU, Onu [ɔny] *(abréviation de* Organisation des Nations unies) *nom féminin*
> **l'ONU** the UN.

onze [ɔ̃z] *adjectif & nom masculin*

eleven : **j'ai onze ans** I am eleven years old
> **nous sommes le onze juillet** it's the eleventh of July *UK* OU it's July eleventh *US*.

onzième [ɔ̃zjɛm] *adjectif, nom masculin & nom masculin ou féminin*

eleventh : **c'est ma onzième médaille** this is my eleventh medal ; **Dimitri est arrivé onzième** Dimitri came eleventh ; **un onzième de la somme totale** an eleventh of the total sum.

opéra [ɔpera] *nom masculin*

opera : **on va à l'opéra samedi** we're going to the opera on Saturday ; **un opéra de Puccini** an opera by Puccini.

opération [ɔperasjɔ̃] *nom féminin*

1. **operation : j'ai eu une opération au genou** I had an operation on my knee
2. **calculation : tu as fait une erreur dans ton opération** you made a mistake in your calculation.

opérer [ɔpere] *verbe*

to operate on : **ils l'ont opérée mardi dernier** they operated on her last Tuesday
> **se faire opérer** to have an operation : **je me suis fait opérer du genou** I had a knee operation.

opinion [ɔpinjɔ̃] *nom féminin*

opinion : **l'opinion publique** public opinion.

opposé, e [ɔpoze] *adjectif*

opposite : **dans la direction opposée** in the opposite direction
> **être opposé à quelque chose** to be opposed to something.

opposer [ɔpoze] *verbe*

un match qui opposera la France à l'Angleterre a match between France and England

s'opposer *verbe pronominal*

s'opposer à quelque chose to be opposed to something ; **ils s'opposent à cette réforme** they're against this reform.

opposition [ɔpozisjɔ̃] *nom féminin*

opposition : **l'opposition a voté contre** the opposition voted against
> **par opposition à** as opposed to.

opticien, enne [ɔptisjɛ̃, ɛn] *nom masculin, nom féminin*

optician : **mon père est opticien** my father is an optician ; **je dois aller chez l'opticien** I need to go to the optician's.

optimiste [ɔptimist] *nom & adjectif*

- *nom masculin ou féminin*
  optimist : **c'est une optimiste** she's an optimist
- *adjectif*
  optimistic : **tu es bien optimiste !** you're very optimistic!

option [ɔpsjɔ̃] *nom féminin*

1. **optional subject** : **j'ai pris latin en option** I took Latin as an optional subject
2. **optional extra** : **l'airbag est en option** the airbag is an optional extra.

or[1] [ɔr] *nom masculin*

gold : **une bague en or** a gold ring.

or[2] [ɔr] *conjonction*

but : **je pensais que c'était facile, or ce n'était pas le cas** I thought it would be easy, but it wasn't the case.

orage [ɔraʒ] *nom masculin*

storm : **l'orage va éclater** there's going to be a storm.

orageux, euse [ɔraʒø, øz] *adjectif*

stormy : **le temps est orageux** it's stormy.

oral, e, aux [ɔral, o] *adjectif*

oral : **une épreuve orale** an oral exam

oral *nom masculin*

oral : **Suzanne passe l'oral demain** Suzanne is taking her oral tomorrow

➤ **à l'oral** : **il est meilleur à l'oral qu'à l'écrit** his oral work is better than his written work.

orange [ɔrɑ̃ʒ] *nom & adjectif*

- *nom féminin*
  orange : **un kilo d'oranges** a kilo of oranges ; **un jus d'orange** an orange juice
  ➤ **une orange pressée** a freshly squeezed orange juice
- *nom masculin & adjectif invariable*
  orange : **l'orange ne me va pas** orange doesn't suit me ; **Luc porte des chaussures orange** Luc is wearing orange shoes.

orangeade [ɔrɑ̃ʒad] *nom féminin*

orangeade.

oranger [ɔrɑ̃ʒe] *nom masculin*

orange tree.

orbite [ɔrbit] *nom féminin*

1. **orbit** : **le nouveau satellite est sur orbite** the new satellite is in orbit
2. **socket** : **l'orbite de l'œil** the eye socket.

orchestre [ɔrkɛstr] *nom masculin*

1. **orchestra** : **un orchestre symphonique** a symphony orchestra
2. **band** : **un orchestre de jazz** a jazz band.

orchidée [ɔrkide] *nom féminin*

orchid.

ordinaire [ɔrdinɛr] *adjectif & nom*

- *adjectif*
  ordinary : **un repas tout à fait ordinaire** a very ordinary meal
  ➤ **de l'essence ordinaire** two-star petrol *UK* ou regular gas *US*
- *nom masculin*
  ➤ **ça sort de l'ordinaire** it's out of the ordinary.

ordinateur [ɔrdinatœr] *nom masculin*

computer : **il s'est acheté un nouvel ordinateur** he bought himself a new computer
➤ **un ordinateur portable** a laptop.

ordonnance [ɔrdɔnɑ̃s] *nom féminin*

prescription : **le médecin m'a fait une ordonnance** the doctor gave me a prescription.

ordonné, e [ɔrdɔne] *adjectif*

tidy : **Rémi est très ordonné** Rémi is very tidy.

ordonner [ɔrdɔne] *verbe*

to order : **ordonner à quelqu'un de faire quelque chose** to order somebody to do something ; **je t'ordonne d'arrêter ça tout de suite !** I order you to stop this immediately!

ordre [ɔrdr] *nom masculin*

order : **par ordre alphabétique** in alphabetical order ; **remets les mots dans l'ordre pour faire une phrase** put the words in order to make a sentence ; **il aime bien donner des ordres** he likes giving orders
➤ **être en ordre** to be tidy : **ma chambre est en ordre** my room is tidy
➤ **mettre de l'ordre dans quelque chose** to tidy something up : **il faut que je mette de l'ordre dans ma chambre** I need to tidy up my room.

ordures [ɔrdyr] *nom féminin pluriel*

rubbish *UK* (*ne s'utilise jamais au pluriel*), **garbage** *US* (*ne s'utilise jamais au pluriel*) : **ils ramassent les ordures tous les matins** they collect the rubbish every morning *UK* ou they collect the garbage every morning *US*.

oreille [ɔrɛj] *nom féminin*

ear : **les lapins ont de longues oreilles** rabbits have long ears ; **avoir de l'oreille** to have a good ear for music

➤ **j'ai mal aux oreilles** I've got earache *UK* ou I've got an earache *US*.

oreiller [ɔreje] *nom masculin*
pillow.

oreillons [ɔrejɔ̃] *nom masculin pluriel*

mumps (*malgré le* **s** *final, ce mot s'utilise au singulier*) : **avoir les oreillons** to have mumps.

organe [ɔrgan] *nom masculin*

organ : **les organes internes** the internal organs.

organisé, e [ɔrganize] *adjectif*

organized, organised *UK* : **c'est quelqu'un de très organisé** he's a very organized person ou he's very organized.

organiser [ɔrganize] *verbe*

1. **to organize, to organise** *UK* : **il a organisé le colloque** he organized the conference
2. **to have** : **Laura organise une soirée samedi prochain** Laura is having a party next Saturday

s'organiser *verbe pronominal*

to get organized : **il va falloir qu'on s'organise** we need to get organized.

organisme [ɔrganism] *nom masculin*

1. **organization, organisation** *UK* : **un organisme international** an international organization
2. **organism** : **organisme génétiquement modifié** genetically modified organism.

orgue [ɔrg] *nom masculin*

organ : **Pierre joue de l'orgue à l'église** Pierre plays the organ in the church.

orgueilleux, euse [ɔrgœjø, øz] *adjectif*

proud : **c'est quelqu'un de très orgueilleux** he's very proud.

Orient [ɔrjɑ̃] *nom masculin*

➤ **l'Orient** the East : **en Orient** in the East.

oriental, e, aux [ɔrjɑ̃tal, o] *adjectif*

1. **eastern** : **la côte orientale de la Grèce** the eastern coast of Greece
2. **oriental** : **les langues orientales** oriental languages.

orientation [ɔrjɑ̃tasjɔ̃] *nom féminin*

course of study : **qu'est-ce que vous avez choisi comme orientation ?** what subjects have you chosen to study?

➤ **avoir le sens de l'orientation** to have a good sense of direction : **je n'ai aucun sens de l'orientation** I have no sense of direction

➤ **la course d'orientation** orienteering.

originaire [ɔriʒinɛr] *adjectif*

être originaire de to be from ; **ses parents sont originaires de Madagascar** her parents are from Madagascar.

original, e, aux [ɔriʒinal, o] *adjectif*

original : **une idée très originale** a very original idea

original (*pluriel* originaux) *nom masculin*

original : **le tableau est un original** the painting is an original.

origine [ɔriʒin] *nom féminin*

origin : **d'origine écossaise** of Scottish origin

➤ **à l'origine** originally.

orphelin, e [ɔrfəlɛ̃, in] *adjectif & nom masculin, nom féminin*
orphan : **il est orphelin** he's an orphan.

orphelinat [ɔrfəlina] *nom masculin*

orphanage : **il a grandi dans un orphelinat** he grew up in an orphanage.

orteil [ɔrtɛj] *nom masculin*

toe : **le gros orteil** the big toe.

orthographe [ɔrtɔgraf] *nom féminin*

spelling : **une faute d'orthographe** a spelling mistake.

ortie [ɔrti] *nom féminin*
nettle.

os [ɔs, *pluriel* o] *nom masculin*

bone : **le chien a enterré son os** the dog buried its bone.

oser [oze] *verbe*

to dare : **oser faire quelque chose** to dare to do something ; **je n'ose pas l'appeler** I don't dare to phone him OU I daren't phone him *UK* ; **je n'ai pas osé lui dire** I didn't dare to tell him OU I didn't dare tell him.

otage [ɔtaʒ] *nom masculin*

hostage : **deux journalistes ont été pris en otage** two journalists have been taken hostage.

otarie [ɔtari] *nom féminin*

sea lion.

ôter [ote] *verbe*

to take off : **ôtez votre manteau** take off your coat.

otite [ɔtit] *nom féminin*

ear infection : **avoir une otite** to have an ear infection.

ou [u] *conjonction*

or : **tu préfères le grand ou le petit ?** do you prefer the big one or the small one? ; **est-ce qu'il est anglais ou américain ?** is he English or American? ; **arrête ou je te frappe !** stop it or I'll hit you! OU stop it or else I'll hit you!

➤ **ou ... ou ...** OU **ou bien ... ou bien ...** either ... or ... : **ou tu travailles, ou tu joues, tu ne peux pas faire les deux !** either you work or you play, you can't do both!

où [u] *pronom & adverbe*

■ *pronom*

« Où » se traduit par where ou that suivant qu'il désigne un lieu ou un moment, ou bien ne se traduit pas :

1. where : **le village où j'habite** the village where I live ; **elle ne savait pas par où commencer** she didn't know where to start ; **la région d'où je viens** the region where I come from OU the region I come from

2. that : **le jour où je suis venu** the day I came OU the day that I came

➤ **au prix où c'est** at that price

➤ **dans l'état où elle est** in the state she is

■ *adverbe*

Avec valeur interrogative where : **où vas-tu ?** where are you going? ; **d'où est-elle ?** where is she from? ; **dites-moi où il est allé** tell me where he's gone ; **va où tu veux** go where you like

➤ **où que** wherever : **ce sera pareil où que tu sois** it'll be the same wherever you are

oublier [ublije] *verbe*

1. to forget : **oublier de faire quelque chose** to forget to do something ; **j'ai oublié de lui dire** I forgot to tell him ; **j'avais complètement oublié !** I'd completely forgotten!

2. to leave : **j'ai dû oublier mon portable chez Lucie** I must have left my mobile at Lucie's.

ouest [wɛst] *nom & adjectif*

■ *nom masculin*

west : **le soleil se couche à l'ouest** the sun sets in the west ; **le village se trouve à l'ouest de Dublin** the village is west of Dublin

■ *adjectif invariable*

west : **la côte ouest des États-Unis** the west coast of the United States.

oui [wi] *adverbe & nom masculin invariable*

yes : **tu parles anglais ? – oui** do you speak English? – yes, I do ; **bien sûr que oui** yes, of course

➤ **je crois que oui** I think so

➤ **tu viens, oui ou non ?** are you coming or not?

➤ **pour un oui ou pour un non** for no apparent reason.

ouïe [wi] *nom féminin*

hearing : **elle a l'ouïe très fine** her hearing is very sharp

ouïes *nom féminin pluriel*

gills : **les poissons respirent par les ouïes** fish breathe through their gills.

ouragan [uragɑ̃] *nom masculin*

hurricane.

ourlet [urlɛ] *nom masculin*

hem : **l'ourlet est défait** the hem has come undone.

ours [urs] *nom masculin*

bear : **un ours en peluche** a teddy bear ; **un ours polaire** a polar bear.

o

oursin [ursɛ̃] *nom masculin*
sea urchin.

ourson [ursɔ̃] *nom masculin*
bear cub.

outil [uti] *nom masculin*
tool : **une boîte à outils** a toolbox.

outre-mer [utrəmɛr] *adverbe*
overseas : **les départements d'outre-mer** France's overseas departments ; **les territoires d'outre-mer** France's overseas territories.

ouvert, e [uvɛr, ɛrt] *verbe & adjectif*
◼ *participe passé de* ouvrir
le magasin a ouvert à neuf heures the shop opened at nine o'clock
◼ *adjectif*
ı. open : **la fenêtre est grande ouverte** the window is wide open ; **les magasins sont ouverts de 9 heures à 19 heures** the shops are open from 9 a.m. to 7 p.m.
2. open-minded : **ce n'est pas quelqu'un de très ouvert** he's not very open-minded.

ouverture [uvɛrtyr] *nom féminin*
opening : **quelles sont les heures d'ouverture ?** what are the opening times?
➢ **ouverture d'esprit** open-mindedness.

ouvrage [uvraʒ] *nom masculin*
book : **un ouvrage de référence** a reference book.

ouvre-boîtes [uvrəbwat] (*pluriel* ouvre-boîtes) *nom masculin*
can opener, tin opener *UK*.

ouvre-bouteilles [uvrəbutɛj] (*pluriel* ouvre-bouteilles) *nom masculin*
bottle opener.

ouvrier, ère [uvrije, ɛr] *adjectif & nom*
◼ *adjectif*
working-class : **un quartier ouvrier** a working-class area
◼ *nom masculin, nom féminin*
worker : **les ouvriers sont en grève** the workers are on strike.

ouvrir [uvrir] *verbe*
ı. to open : **ouvre la porte !** open the door! ; **le magasin ouvre à neuf heures** the shop opens at nine

2. to turn on : **ouvrir le robinet** to turn on the tap

s'ouvrir *verbe pronominal*
to open : **les fleurs commencent à s'ouvrir** the flowers are beginning to open.

ovale [ɔval] *adjectif & nom masculin*
oval : **une table ovale** an oval table ; **un rond et un ovale** a circle and an oval.

OVNI, ovni [ɔvni] (*abréviation de* objet volant non identifié) *nom masculin*
UFO (*pluriel* UFOs) : **tu as déjà vu un ovni ?** have you already seen a UFO?

oxygène [ɔksiʒɛn] *nom masculin*
oxygen.

ozone [ozon] *nom masculin*
ozone : **la couche d'ozone** the ozone layer.

pacifique [pasifik] *adjectif*
peaceful : **une manifestation pacifique** a peaceful demonstration

Pacifique *nom masculin*
➢ **le Pacifique** the Pacific ou the Pacific Ocean.

pagaille, pagaïe [pagaj] *nom féminin familier*
mess : **quelle pagaille ici !** what a mess it is in here! ; **ils ont mis la pagaille dans la maison** they made a real mess of the house.

page [paʒ] *nom féminin*
page : **ouvrez vos livres, page ı3** open your books at page 13
➢ **la page d'accueil** the home page
➢ **les pages jaunes** the Yellow Pages®.

paie [pɛ], **paye** [pɛj] nom féminin

pay : **toucher sa paie** to be paid.

paiement [pɛmã] nom masculin

payment.

paillasson [pajasɔ̃] nom masculin

doormat : **essuyez vos pieds sur le paillasson** wipe your feet on the doormat.

paille [paj] nom féminin

straw : **il boit toujours son lait avec une paille** he always drinks his milk through a straw.

paillettes [pajɛt] nom féminin pluriel

sequin : **un haut à paillettes** a top with sequins OU a sequined top.

pain [pɛ̃] nom masculin

bread (ne s'utilise jamais au pluriel) : **il ne reste plus de pain** there isn't any bread left
➤ **un pain** a loaf OU a loaf of bread
➤ **un petit pain** a roll OU a bread roll
➤ **un pain au chocolat** a sweet flaky pastry with chocolate filling
➤ **du pain complet** wholemeal bread UK OU wholewheat bread US
➤ **du pain d'épice** gingerbread
➤ **un pain au lait** a sweet roll
➤ **du pain de mie** sliced bread OU white bread US

> PAIN
> The French eat bread with every meal and buy it in a **boulangerie**. The basic French loaf is a long stick known as a **baguette** but there are also other types : a **ficelle** (long and thin), and a **pain** (long and thick).

pair, e [pɛr] adjectif

even : **un nombre pair** an even number

au pair adverbe

au pair : **une jeune fille au pair** an au pair girl.

paire [pɛr] nom féminin

pair : **une paire de chaussures** a pair of shoes ; **une paire de ciseaux** a pair of scissors.

paix [pɛ] nom féminin

peace : **un traité de paix** a peace treaty ; **faire la paix** to make peace
➤ **j'ai enfin la paix !** peace and quiet at last!
➤ **fiche-moi la paix** familier leave me alone.

palace [palas] nom masculin

luxury hotel.

palais [palɛ] nom masculin

1. palace : **le palais de la reine** the queen's palace
2. roof of the mouth : **je me suis brûlé le palais** I burnt the roof of my mouth.

pâle [pal] adjectif

pale : **tu es tout pâle** you're very pale.

palier [palje] nom masculin

landing : **les toilettes sont sur le palier** the toilets are on the landing.

pâlir [palir] verbe

to turn pale : **elle a pâli quand elle a vu Lucas** she turned pale when she saw Lucas.

palme [palm] nom féminin

flipper : **nager avec des palmes** to swim with flippers OU to swim with fins US
➤ **la Palme d'Or** award given to the best film at the Cannes Film Festival.

➤ festival.

palmier [palmje] nom masculin

palm tree.

pamplemousse [pɑ̃pləmus] nom masculin

grapefruit.

pan [pɑ̃] interjection

bang!

panaché [panaʃe] nom masculin

shandy UK (pluriel **shandies**) : **un panaché, s'il vous plaît** a shandy, please.

pancarte [pɑ̃kart] nom féminin

sign : **il y a une pancarte sur la porte du magasin** there's a sign on the shop door.

pané, e [pane] adjectif

breaded : **du poisson pané** breaded fish OU fish in breadcrumbs.

panier [panje] nom masculin

basket : **un panier en osier** a wicker basket ; **marquer un panier** to score a basket.

panique [panik] nom féminin

panic : **pas de panique !** don't panic!

paniquer [panike] verbe

to panic : **ne paniquez pas !** don't panic!

panne [pan] *nom féminin*

➤ **une panne d'électricité** a power failure OU a power cut OU a power outage *US*

➤ **être en panne** to be out of order : **l'ascenseur est en panne** the lift is out of order *UK* OU the elevator is out of order *US*

➤ **tomber en panne** to break down : **on est tombés en panne en chemin** we broke down on the way

➤ **tomber en panne d'essence** to run out of petrol *UK* OU to run out of gas *US*.

panneau [pano] (*pluriel* **panneaux**) *nom masculin*

sign : **on a raté le panneau pour Chartres** we missed the sign for Chartres ; **panneau de signalisation** road sign

➤ **panneau d'affichage** noticeboard *UK* OU bulletin board *US*.

panoplie [panɔpli] *nom féminin*

outfit : **une panoplie de Batman** a Batman outfit.

panorama [panɔrama] *nom masculin*

view : **d'ici le panorama est magnifique** the view is magnificent from here.

pansement [pɑ̃smɑ̃] *nom masculin*

plaster *UK*, Band-Aid® *US*.

pantalon [pɑ̃talɔ̃] *nom masculin*

trousers *UK*, pants *US* (*s'utilisent toujours au pluriel*) : **un pantalon** a pair of trousers *UK* OU a pair of pants *US* ; **mon pantalon est trop serré** my trousers are too tight *UK* OU my pants are too tight *US*.

pantin [pɑ̃tɛ̃] *nom masculin*

puppet.

pantoufle [pɑ̃tufl] *nom féminin*

slipper : **une paire de pantoufles** a pair of slippers.

paon [pɑ̃] *nom masculin*

peacock : **le paon faisait la roue** the peacock spread its tail.

papa [papa] *nom masculin*

dad, daddy.

pape [pap] *nom masculin*

pope.

papeterie [papɛtri] *nom féminin*

stationer's *UK*, stationery store *US* : **je vais à la papeterie** I'm going to the stationer's.

papier [papje] *nom masculin*

paper : **un bout de papier** a piece of paper ; **l'imprimante n'a plus de papier** the printer has run out of paper

➤ **papier aluminium** OU *familier* **papier alu** tinfoil

➤ **papier d'emballage** wrapping paper

➤ **papier à lettres** writing paper

➤ **papier peint** wallpaper

➤ **papier hygiénique** OU **papier toilette** toilet paper

papiers *nom masculin pluriel*

papers : **papiers d'identité** identity papers.

papillon [papijɔ̃] *nom masculin*

butterfly (*pluriel* **butterflies**)

➤ **la brasse papillon** butterfly stroke.

paquebot [pakbo] *nom masculin*

liner.

pâquerette [pakrɛt] *nom féminin*

daisy (*pluriel* **daisies**).

Pâques [pak] *nom féminin pluriel*

Easter : **à Pâques** at Easter ; **joyeuses Pâques** Happy Easter.

paquet [pakɛ] *nom masculin*

1. packet *UK*, package *US*, pack *US* : **un paquet de chewing-gum** a packet of chewing gum

2. parcel *UK*, package *US* : **j'ai deux paquets à envoyer** I have two parcels to send.

par [par] *préposition*

1. by : **par bateau** by boat ; **par avion** by plane ; **il la tenait par la main** he was holding her by the hand ; **André a été puni par le prof d'espagnol** André was punished by the Spanish teacher

2. per, a : **une heure par jour** an hour per day OU an hour a day ; **cent euros par personne** a hundred euros per person

3. out of : **je l'ai fait uniquement par pitié** I did it purely out of pity ; **regarder par la fenêtre** to look out of the window

4. with : **le spectacle s'est terminé par un feu d'artifice** the show ended with a firework display

5. through : **vous devrez passer par Reims**

you'll have to go through Reims ; **les voleurs sont entrés par la fenêtre** the burglars came in through the window

➤ **travailler deux par deux** to work in twos

➤ **par-ci, par-là** here and there : **il y a quelques erreurs par-ci, par-là** there are a few errors here and there

➤ **par endroits** in places

➤ **par ici**

1. this way : **venez par ici** come this way

2. around here : **mon cousin habite par ici** my cousin lives around here

➤ **par là**

1. that way : **on est passés par là** we went that way

2. around there : **Yacine habite quelque part par là** Yacine lives somewhere around there.

parachute [paraʃyt] *nom masculin*

parachute : **sauter en parachute** to do a parachute jump.

paradis [paradi] *nom masculin*

1. paradise : **c'est le paradis ici !** it's paradise here!

2. heaven : **l'enfer et le paradis** Heaven and Hell.

parages [paraʒ] *nom masculin pluriel*

viens me voir si tu es dans les parages come and see me if you're around.

paragraphe [paragraf] *nom masculin*

paragraph.

paraître [parɛtr] *verbe*

1. to look, to seem : **elle paraît très sûre d'elle** she looks very sure of herself ou she seems very sure of herself

2. to come out : **son dernier roman est paru le mois dernier** his last novel was published last month

➤ **il paraît que ...** apparently ... : **il paraît qu'Amélie sort avec Nicolas** apparently Amélie is going out with Nicolas.

parallèle [paralɛl] *adjectif*

parallel : **deux lignes parallèles** two parallel lines.

paralysé, e [paralize] *adjectif*

paralysed *UK*, paralyzed *US*.

parapente [parapɑ̃t] *nom masculin*

paragliding : **faire du parapente** to go paragliding.

parapluie [paraplɥi] *nom masculin*

umbrella : **il a ouvert son parapluie** he put his umbrella up.

parasite [parazit] *nom masculin*

parasite : **les puces sont des parasites** fleas are parasites

parasites *nom masculin pluriel*

interference : **le son n'est pas bon, il y a des parasites** the sound isn't good, there's interference.

parasol [parasɔl] *nom masculin*

beach umbrella.

parc [park] *nom masculin*

park : **un parc d'attractions** an amusement park ; **un parc à thème** a theme park.

parce que [parsk(ə)] *conjonction*

because : **elle n'est pas venue parce qu'elle avait du travail** she didn't come because she had work to do ; **pourquoi ? – parce que !** why? – because!

parcmètre [parkmɛtr] *nom masculin*

parking meter.

parcourir [parkurir] *verbe*

1. to cover : **il a parcouru tout le chemin en une heure** he covered the whole distance in an hour

2. to skim through : **je n'ai fait que parcourir le journal** I only skimmed through the paper.

parcours [parkur] *nom masculin*

route : **le parcours du bus** the bus route.

parcouru, e [parkury] *participe passé de* parcourir.

par-derrière [pardɛrjɛr] *adverbe*

round the back *UK*, around the back *US* : **passez par-derrière** go round the back.

par-dessous [pardəsu] *préposition & adverbe*

■ *préposition*

under, underneath : **passe par-dessous la barrière** go under the fence ou go underneath the fence

p

adverbe
underneath : il est passé par-dessous he went underneath.

par-dessus [pardəsy] *préposition & adverbe*

■ *préposition*
over : ils sont passés par-dessus le mur they went over the wall
■ *adverbe*
over it : passe par-dessus go over it.

par-devant [pardəvã] *adverbe*

round the front *UK*, **around the front** *US* : passe par-devant go round the front.

pardon [pardɔ̃] *interjection & nom*

■ *interjection*
1. **sorry** : pardon, je vous ai fait mal ? sorry, did I hurt you?
2. **excuse me** : pardon, où sont les toilettes ? excuse me, where are the toilets, please?
➤ **pardon ?** sorry? *UK* ou pardon? : **pardon ? qu'est-ce que tu dis ?** sorry, what did you say? ou pardon, what did you say?
■ *nom masculin*
➤ **demander pardon à quelqu'un** to apologize to somebody : **tu dois lui demander pardon** you must apologize to him.

pardonner [pardɔne] *verbe*

to forgive : pardonner quelque chose à quelqu'un to forgive somebody for something ; **je ne lui pardonnerai jamais ce qu'elle a dit** I will never forgive her for what she said ; **elle ne lui a pas pardonné de lui avoir rayé son CD préféré** she didn't forgive him for scratching her favourite CD.

pare-brise [parbriz] (*pluriel* pare-brise)

nom masculin
windscreen *UK*, **windshield** *US*.

pare-chocs [parʃɔk] (*pluriel* pare-chocs)

nom masculin
bumper.

pareil, eille [parɛj] *adjectif*

the same : ce n'est pas pareil it's not the same
➤ **pareil que** the same as : **mes chaussures sont exactement pareilles que les tiennes** my shoes are exactly the same as yours
➤ **je n'ai jamais vu une chose pareille** I've never seen anything like it

pareil *adverbe*

the same : elles s'habillent pareil they dress the same.

parent, e [parã, ãt] *adjectif & nom*

■ *adjectif*
related : ils sont parents they are related
■ *nom masculin, nom féminin*
relative : un parent éloigné a distant relative

parents | *nom masculin pluriel*

parents : mes parents ont le même âge my parents are the same age.

parenthèse [parãtɛz] *nom féminin*

bracket *UK*, **parenthesis** *US* : entre parenthèses in brackets *UK* ou in parentheses *US*.

paresseux, euse [parɛsø, øz] *adjectif & nom*

■ *adjectif*
lazy : mon père est très paresseux my dad is really lazy
■ *nom masculin, nom féminin*
lazy person : quel paresseux tu fais ! you're so lazy!

parfait, e [parfɛ, ɛt] *adjectif*

perfect : ça va comme ça ? – c'est parfait ! is it OK like this? – it's perfect!

parfois [parfwa] *adverbe*

sometimes : on va parfois à la campagne le week-end we sometimes go to the countryside at weekends.

parfum [parfœ̃] *nom masculin*

1. **perfume** : je ne mets pas de parfum I don't wear perfume
2. **fragrance, scent** : ces roses n'ont aucun parfum these roses have no fragrance ou these roses have no scent
3. **flavour** *UK*, **flavor** *US* : tu veux une glace à quel parfum ? what flavour ice cream do you want?

parfumé, e [parfyme] *adjectif*

1. **perfumed** : du savon parfumé perfumed soap
2. **flavoured** *UK*, **flavored** *US* : un dessert parfumé à la vanille a vanilla-flavoured dessert.

se parfumer [sə parfyme] *verbe pronominal*

to put perfume on : je me suis parfumée I put some perfume on.

parfumerie [parfymri] *nom féminin*

perfume shop *UK*, **perfume store** *US*.

pari [paʀi] *nom masculin*

bet : **on fait un pari ?** shall we make a bet?

parier [paʀje] *verbe*

to bet : **je te parie qu'il ne viendra pas** I bet you he won't come.

Paris [paʀi] *nom*

Paris : **j'habite Paris** OU **j'habite à Paris** I live in Paris ; **je voudrais aller à Paris** I would like to go to Paris.

parisien, enne [paʀizjɛ̃, ɛn] *adjectif*

1. Parisian : **les théâtres parisiens** the Parisian theatres
2. Paris : **dans la banlieue parisienne** in the Paris suburbs

Parisien, enne *nom masculin, nom féminin*

Parisian : **c'est une Parisienne** she's a Parisian.

parking [paʀkiŋ] *nom masculin*

car park *UK*, parking lot *US*

⚠ In French the word **parking** is never used to mean the action of **parking**.

parlement [paʀləmã] *nom masculin*

parliament : **le parlement écossais** the Scottish parliament.

parler [paʀle] *verbe*

1. to talk : **nous avons parlé de nos projets pour le week-end** we talked about our plans for the weekend ; **j'étais en train de parler avec Anna** I was talking to Anna ; **est-ce que tu as parlé de la soirée à Jérôme ?** did you talk to Jérôme about the party?
2. to speak : **pouvez-vous parler plus fort ?** can you speak louder? ; **elle parle anglais** she speaks English ; **ils parlaient en chinois** they were speaking Chinese
➤ **ça parle de quoi ?** what is it about?

se parler *verbe pronominal*

to speak to each other : **ils ne se parlent plus depuis leur dispute** they haven't been speaking to each other since their argument.

parmi [paʀmi] *préposition*

among : **il ne compte pas parmi les meilleurs** he is not among the best.

parole [paʀɔl] *nom féminin*

word : **des paroles rassurantes** reassuring words

➤ **adresser la parole à quelqu'un** to speak to somebody : **elle ne m'adresse plus la parole** she isn't speaking to me anymore
➤ **couper la parole à quelqu'un** to interrupt somebody : **tu me coupes tout le temps la parole !** you're always interrupting me!
➤ **tenir parole** to keep one's word : **il a tenu parole** he kept his word
➤ **donner sa parole** to give one's word : **je te donne ma parole que je ne lui ai rien dit !** I give you my word that I haven't told him anything!

paroles *nom féminin pluriel*

lyrics, words : **je ne me souviens plus des paroles de la chanson** I can't remember the lyrics OU I can't remember the words to the song.

parquet [paʀkɛ] *nom masculin*

wooden floor, parquet.

parrain [paʀɛ̃] *nom masculin*

godfather.

part [paʀ] *nom féminin*

piece, slice : **une part de gâteau** a piece of cake OU a slice of cake
➤ **de la part de quelqu'un**
1. from somebody : **c'est un cadeau de la part de Daniel** it's a present from Daniel
2. on behalf of somebody : **je vous appelle de la part de Guillaume** I'm calling on behalf of Guillaume
➤ **c'est de la part de qui ?** who's speaking, please?
➤ **à part**
1. apart from : **à part ça, il va bien** apart from that, he's OK
2. separately : **il faut cuire la viande et les légumes à part** you must cook the meat and vegetables separately
➤ **autre part** somewhere else OU someplace else *US*
➤ **d'une part ..., d'autre part** on the one hand ..., on the other hand.

partager [paʀtaʒe] *verbe*

1. to share : **partage le croissant avec ton frère** share the croissant with your brother
2. to divide : **on peut le partager en deux** we can divide it in two

se partager *verbe pronominal*

to share : **ils se sont partagé le gâteau** they shared the cake between them.

partenaire [partənɛr] *nom masculin ou féminin*

partner : **son partenaire de double** her doubles partner.

parti¹, e [parti] *participe passé de* partir.

parti² [parti] *nom masculin*

party *(pluriel* **parties***)* : **le parti démocrate** the Democratic party.

participer [partisipe] *verbe*

1. to take part : **l'important c'est de participer** it's taking part that counts
2. to contribute : **on fait un cadeau à Fabien, tu veux participer ?** we're buying a present for Fabien, do you want to contribute?
➤ **participer à quelque chose** to take part in something : **les élèves ont participé au projet** the pupils took an active part in the project.

particulier, ère [partikylje, ɛr] *adjectif*

1. private : **cours particuliers** private lessons
2. particular : **sans raison particulière** for no particular reason
3. distinctive, special : **ce thé a un arôme très particulier** this tea has a very distinctive aroma ; **qu'est-ce que tu as fait hier ? – rien de particulier** what did you do yesterday? – nothing special
➤ **en particulier** in particular : **je ne pensais pas à lui en particulier** I wasn't thinking of him in particular.

particulièrement [partikyljɛrmã] *adverbe*

particularly : **une idée particulièrement stupide** a particularly stupid idea ; **ça te plaît ? – pas particulièrement** do you like it? – not particularly.

partie [parti] *nom féminin*

1. part : **la première partie du film est très drôle** the first part of the film is very funny
2. game : **qui veut faire une partie de cartes ?** who wants to have a game of cards?
➤ **faire partie de**
1. to be in : **il fait partie de la chorale** he's in the choir
2. to be part of : **ça ne fait pas partie de mon travail** that's not part of my job
➤ **ça fait partie du jeu** it's part of the game

➤ **en partie** partly : **c'est en partie vrai** it's partly true.

partir [partir] *verbe*

1. to go, to leave : **elle est déjà partie** she has already gone OU she has already left
2. to come out : **est-ce que la tache est partie ?** has the stain come out?
➤ **partir de**
1. to leave : **il part du travail à 19 heures** he leaves work at 7 o'clock
2. to start from : **le sentier part de ce moulin** the path starts from this mill
➤ **partir à** to go to : **je pars à Londres demain** I'm going to London tomorrow
➤ **à partir de** from : **à partir de lundi** from Monday ; **à partir de maintenant** from now on.

partisan, e [partizã, an] *adjectif*

être partisan de quelque chose to be in favour of something *UK* OU to be in favor of something *US*.

partition [partisjɔ̃] *nom féminin*

score : **une partition de violon** a violin score.

partout [partu] *adverbe*

everywhere : **j'ai cherché partout** I looked everywhere
➤ **partout dans la maison** all over the house
➤ **j'ai mal partout** I'm aching all over
➤ **trente partout** *au tennis* thirty all.

paru, e [pary] *participe passé de* paraître.

pas¹ [pa] *nom masculin*

1. step : **fais un pas en avant** take a step forward
2. pace : **ils marchaient d'un pas rapide** they were walking at a quick pace
➤ **faire les cent pas** to pace up and down
➤ **c'est à deux pas d'ici** it's just around the corner
➤ **le pas de la porte** the doorstep.

pas² [pa] *adverbe*

not : **tu l'as vu ou pas ?** have you seen him or not? ; **qui veut de la soupe ? – pas moi !** who wants soup? – not me! ; **il a décidé de ne pas y aller** he decided not to go ; **pas encore** not yet

Avec le verbe **to be**, la négation se forme en ajoutant simplement **not** ou la forme contractée **n't** après le verbe :

ce n'est pas drôle ! it's not funny! OU it isn't funny ; **ces gants ne sont pas à moi** these gloves aren't mine

Avec les autres verbes au présent, il faut utiliser l'auxiliaire **do** à la forme négative (**do not, does not,** ou **don't, doesn't**) :

Luc n'aime pas l'ail Luc does not like garlic OU Luc doesn't like garlic ; **ne fais pas attention à lui** don't pay any attention to him

Aux temps autres que le présent, c'est aussi l'auxiliaire qui se met à la forme négative :

tu n'as pas terminé ? haven't you finished? ; **je ne l'ai pas revue** I didn't see her again ; **le film ne finira pas avant dix heures** the film will not finish until ten OU the film won't finish until ten
➤ **pas de ...** not any ... OU no ...

Pas de se traduit le plus souvent par la forme négative suivie de **any** ; on peut aussi utiliser la forme affirmative suivie de **no** :

je n'ai pas de devoirs pour demain I don't have any homework for tomorrow OU I have no homework for tomorrow

passage [pasaʒ] *nom masculin*

1. **way :** il y a un **passage** dans les buissons there is a way through the bushes ; **'céder le passage'** 'give way'
2. **passage :** on a lu un **passage** de Hamlet we read a passage from Hamlet
➤ **un passage piétons** a pedestrian crossing *UK* OU a crosswalk *US*
➤ **je suis juste de passage** I'm just passing through
➤ **elle est de passage à Lille pour deux jours** she's in Lille for a couple of days
➤ **un passage souterrain** a subway *UK* OU an underpass *US*.

passager, ère [pasaʒe, ɛr] *nom masculin, nom féminin*

passenger : les **passagers** à destination de New York passengers to New York.

passant, e [pasã, ãt] *nom masculin, nom féminin*
passer-by *(pluriel* **passers-by***).*

passe [pas] *nom féminin*

pass : il ne fait jamais de **passes** he never passes the ball
➤ **traverser une mauvaise passe** to be going through a bad patch.

passé¹, e [pase] *adjectif*

last : la **semaine passée** last week
➤ **il est huit heures passées** it's after eight.

passé² [pase] *nom masculin*

past : mettre les verbes au **passé** put the verbs in the past.

passeport [paspɔr] *nom masculin*

passport : mon **passeport** n'est plus valide my passport is no longer valid.

passer [pase] *verbe*

1. **to get through :** il y a trop de monde, on ne **passera** pas there are too many people, we won't get through ; laissez-moi **passer !** let me go through!
2. **to go past :** on a regardé **passer** les coureurs we watched the cyclists go past ; le bus **passe** devant la maison the bus goes past the house ; quand vous **passerez** le pont when you go past the bridge
3. **to go :** vous devrez **passer** par Annecy you'll have to go through Annecy ; est-ce que ton mal de tête est **passé ?** has your headache gone?
4. **to get in :** l'eau **passe** par les fentes the water gets in through the cracks
5. **to move up :** je **passe** en cinquième I'm moving up to year eight
6. **to pass, to go by :** le temps est **passé** vite time passed quickly OU time went by quickly
7. **to be on :** ça **passe** à la télé en ce moment it's on TV at the moment ; qu'est-ce qui **passe** au cinéma ce soir ? what's on the cinema tonight?
8. **to spend :** nous avons **passé** deux semaines en Grèce we spent two weeks in Greece ; je vais **passer** Noël chez mes parents I'm going to spend Christmas with my parents ; ils ont **passé** leurs vacances en Espagne they spent their holidays in Spain
9. **to give :** **passe**-moi ton cahier give me your exercise book
10. **to put :** Lucien a **passé** le bras par la fenêtre Lucien put his arm through the window
11. **to take :** mon frère **passe** son examen aujourd'hui my brother is taking his exam today

⚠ 'Passer un examen' ne se traduit pas par to pass an exam.

12. **to have** : **je dois passer un scanner** I'm due to have a scan

13. **au téléphone** : **je te passe Camille** here's Camille ; **tu peux me passer Fred ?** can you put Fred on?

➤ **le facteur n'est pas encore passé** the postman hasn't been yet *UK* OU the mailman hasn't been by yet *US*

➤ **je suis passée chez Lucille** I called on Lucille

➤ **je passerai ce soir** I'll call in tonight *UK* OU I'll come and see you tonight

➤ **on passera te prendre** we'll come and pick you up OU we'll come and fetch you

se passer *verbe pronominal*

1. **to happen** : **qu'est-ce qui s'est passé ?** what happened?

2. **to go** : **comment ça s'est passé ?** how did it go? ; **ça s'est bien passé** it went well

➤ **en passant**

1. **in passing** : **Loïc m'a dit ça en passant** Loïc told me that in passing

2. **on one's way past** : **arrête-toi en passant** stop on your way past

➤ **se passer de** to do without : **tu devras te passer de dessert** you'll have to do without a dessert.

passerelle [pasʀɛl] *nom féminin*
footbridge.

passe-temps [pastɑ̃] (*pluriel* passe-temps) *nom masculin*
pastime : **la lecture est mon passe-temps favori** reading is my favourite pastime.

passion [pasjɔ̃] *nom féminin*
passion : **il a une réelle passion pour les arts martiaux** he has a real passion for martial arts.

passionnant, e [pasjɔnɑ̃, ɑ̃t] *adjectif*

1. **exciting** : **le match était passionnant** the match was exciting

2. **gripping** : **un documentaire passionnant** a gripping documentary.

passionné, e [pasjɔne] *adjectif*
elle est passionnée de mythologie grecque she has a passion for Greek mythology.

se passionner [səpasjɔne] *verbe pronominal*

➤ **se passionner pour quelque chose** to have a passion for something : **il se passionne pour la guitare** he has a passion for the guitar.

passoire [paswaʀ] *nom féminin*
colander : **égouttez les légumes dans la passoire** strain the vegetables in the colander.

pastèque [pastɛk] *nom féminin*
watermelon.

pastille [pastij] *nom féminin*
lozenge : **des pastilles pour la toux** cough lozenges.

patate [patat] *nom féminin familier*
potato (*pluriel* **potatoes**)

➤ **une patate douce** a sweet potato.

pataugeoire [patoʒwaʀ] *nom féminin*
paddling pool *UK*, wading pool *US*.

patauger [patoʒe] *verbe*
to splash about : **ils pataugeaient dans l'eau** they were splashing about in the water.

pâte [pat] *nom féminin*

1. **pastry** : **de la pâte brisée** shortcrust pastry *UK* OU shortpaste *US* ; **de la pâte feuilletée** puff pastry ; **de la pâte sablée** rich shortcrust pastry *UK* OU sugarcrust *US*

2. **dough** : **elle fait sa propre pâte à pain** she makes her own bread dough

➤ **de la pâte d'amandes** marzipan

➤ **de la pâte à modeler** modelling clay *UK* OU modeling clay *US*

pâtes *nom féminin pluriel*
pasta (*ne s'utilise jamais au pluriel*) : **ces pâtes sont très bonnes** this pasta is very good.

pâté [pate] *nom masculin*
pâté : **un sandwich au pâté** a pâté sandwich

➤ **un pâté de maisons** a block OU a block of houses : **on a fait le tour du pâté de maisons** we walked around the block.

patience [pasjɑ̃s] *nom féminin*
patience : **elle n'a aucune patience** she has no patience.

patient, e [pasjɑ̃, ɑ̃t] *adjectif & nom*

■ *adjectif*
patient : **sois patiente !** be patient!

■ *nom masculin, nom féminin*
les patients du docteur Frêne Dr Frêne's patients.

patin [patɛ̃] *nom masculin*

skate : des patins à glace ice-skates ; faire du patin à glace to go ice-skating ; des patins à roulettes roller skates ; faire du patin à roulettes to go roller-skating.

patinage [patinaʒ] *nom masculin*

ice-skating : le patinage artistique figure skating.

patiner [patine] *verbe*

to skate : tu sais patiner ? can you skate?

patinoire [patinwar] *nom féminin*

ice rink, skating rink.

pâtisserie [patisri] *nom féminin*

1. cake : elle mange trop de pâtisseries she eats too many cakes
2. cake shop *UK*, bakery *US* : il y a une nouvelle pâtisserie au coin de la rue there's a new cake shop on the corner.

patron, onne [patrɔ̃, ɔn] *nom masculin, nom féminin*

boss *(pluriel bosses)* : elle ne s'entend pas avec son patron she doesn't get on with her boss.

patte [pat] *nom féminin*

1. paw : les pattes du chien the dog's paws
2. leg : les araignées ont huit pattes spiders have eight legs
➤ un pantalon pattes d'éph *familier* flares
➤ se mettre à quatre pattes to get down on all fours.

paume [pom] *nom féminin*

palm : ça tient dans la paume de la main you can hold it in the palm of your hand.

paupière [popjɛr] *nom féminin*

eyelid.

pause [poz] *nom féminin*

break : on va faire une pause de dix minutes we'll have a ten-minute break.

pauvre [povr] *adjectif & nom*

■ *adjectif*
poor : ils sont très pauvres they're very poor ; pauvre Anaïs ! poor Anaïs!
■ *nom masculin ou féminin*
les pauvres the poor

pauvreté [povrəte] *nom féminin*

poverty.

pavé, e [pave] *adjectif*

cobbled : une rue pavée a cobbled street.

pavé [pave] *nom masculin*

cobblestone
➤ un pavé numérique a numeric keypad.

payant, e [pɛjɑ̃, ɑ̃t] *adjectif*

est-ce que l'entrée est payante ? is there an admission charge?

paye ➤ paie.

payer [peje] *verbe*

1. to pay : je n'ai pas encore payé I haven't paid yet
2. to pay for : elle a payé son ordinateur très cher she paid a lot of money for her computer
➤ faire payer
1. to charge : ils m'ont fait payer vingt euros they charged me twenty euros
2. to charge for : ils ne font pas payer la livraison they don't charge for delivery.

pays [pei] *nom masculin*

country *(pluriel countries)* : l'Australie est un grand pays Australia is a big country
➤ le pays de Galles Wales : elle habite au pays de Galles she lives in Wales ; j'aimerais aller au pays de Galles I would like to go to Wales.

paysage [peizaʒ] *nom masculin*

landscape : un paysage rural a rural landscape
➤ de beaux paysages beautiful scenery.

paysan, anne [peizɑ̃, an] *nom masculin, nom féminin*

small farmer.

Pays-Bas [peiba] *nom masculin pluriel*

➤ les Pays-Bas the Netherlands : je suis restée un mois aux Pays-Bas I stayed one month in the Netherlands ; mes parents vont aller aux Pays-Bas my parents are going to the Netherlands.

PC [pese] *(abréviation de* personal computer*)* *nom masculin* PC.

péage [peaʒ] *nom masculin*

toll : tu as de la monnaie pour le péage ? have you got change for the toll?

p

peau [po] *nom féminin*

1. skin : **elle a la peau très douce** she has very soft skin
2. peel : **enlevez la peau de la pomme** remove the peel from the apple ou peel the apple
➤ **elle se sent bien dans sa peau** she's at ease with herself
➤ **il se sent mal dans sa peau** he's not a happy person.

pêche¹ [pɛʃ] *nom féminin*

peach (*pluriel* **peaches**) : **j'adore les pêches** I love peaches
➤ **avoir la pêche** *familier* to be full of beans *UK* ou to be full of pep *US*.

pêche² [pɛʃ] *nom féminin*

fishing : **aller à la pêche** to go fishing.

pêcher [peʃe] *verbe*

1. to fish : **il va pêcher tous les dimanches** he goes fishing every Sunday
2. to catch : **je n'ai pêché que deux petits poissons** I only caught two small fish.

pêcheur [peʃœr] *nom masculin*

fisherman (*pluriel* **fishermen**) : **Loïc est pêcheur** Loïc is a fisherman.

pédale [pedal] *nom féminin*

pedal : **la pédale d'accélérateur** the accelerator pedal *UK* ou the gas pedal *US*.

pédaler [pedale] *verbe*

to pedal : **il pédalait aussi vite qu'il pouvait** he was pedalling as fast as he could.

Pédalo® [pedalo] *nom masculin*

pedal boat, pedalo *UK*.

peigne [pɛɲ] *nom masculin*

comb : **un peigne en ivoire** an ivory comb ; **donne-toi un coup de peigne** give your hair a comb.

peigner [peɲe] *verbe*

to comb : **elle aime peigner sa fille** she likes combing her daughter's hair

se peigner *verbe pronominal*

to comb one's hair : **je ne me suis pas peigné** I haven't combed my hair.

peignoir [peɲwar] *nom masculin*

bathrobe.

peindre [pɛ̃dr] *verbe*

to paint : **j'ai peint ma chambre en violet** I painted my room purple.

peine [pɛn] *nom féminin*

➤ **avoir de la peine** to be upset
➤ **faire de la peine à quelqu'un** to upset somebody : **ça lui a fait beaucoup de peine** it really upset him
➤ **ce n'est pas la peine** it's not worth it : **ce n'est pas la peine d'y aller** it's not worth going there
➤ **ça vaut la peine** it's worth it : **ça ne vaut pas la peine** it's not worth it
➤ **la peine de mort** the death penalty
➤ **à peine** hardly ou barely : **je l'ai à peine reconnu** I hardly recognized him ou I barely recognized him.

peint, e [pɛ̃, pɛ̃t] *participe passé de* peindre.

peintre [pɛ̃tr] *nom masculin*

painter : **Renoir est un célèbre peintre français** Renoir is a famous French painter.

peinture [pɛ̃tyr] *nom féminin*

1. painting : **une peinture de Picasso** a painting by Picasso
2. paint : **'peinture fraîche'** 'wet paint'.

peler [pəle] *verbe*

to peel : **peler une orange** to peel an orange ; **j'ai le nez qui pèle** my nose is peeling.

pélican [pelikɑ̃] *nom masculin*

pelican.

pelle [pɛl] *nom féminin*

1. shovel : **une pelle à charbon** a coal shovel
2. spade : **sa mère lui a acheté un seau et une pelle** his mother bought him a bucket and a spade
3. dustpan : **utilise le balai et la pelle qui sont derrière la porte** use the broom and the dustpan which are behind the door.

pellicule [pelikyl] *nom féminin*

film : **une pellicule 24 poses** a 24-exposure film

pellicules *nom féminin pluriel*

dandruff (*ne s'utilise jamais au pluriel*) : **avoir des pellicules** to have dandruff.

pelote [pəlɔt] *nom féminin*

ball : **une pelote de laine** a ball of wool.

pelouse [pəluz] *nom féminin*

lawn : **il tond la pelouse** he's mowing the lawn.

peluche [pəlyʃ] *nom féminin*

cuddly toy : **j'ai eu une peluche pour Noël** I got a cuddly toy for Christmas.

penalty [penalti] (*pluriel* penaltys ou penalties) *nom masculin*

penalty (*pluriel* **penalties**) : **l'arbitre a sifflé un penalty** the referee blew his whistle for a penalty.

pencher [pɑ̃ʃe] *verbe*

to bend : **elle a penché la tête en avant** she bent her head forward

se pencher *verbe pronominal*

1. to lean : **ne te penche pas à la fenêtre** don't lean out of the window
2. to bend down : **il s'est penché pour ramasser un caillou** he bent down to pick up a pebble.

pendant [pɑ̃dɑ̃] *préposition*

1. during : **je serai à la maison pendant la journée** I'll be at home during the day ; **pendant la guerre** during the war
2. for : **j'ai habité au Canada pendant deux ans** I lived in Canada for two years

> DURING et FOR :
> On utilise **during** pour indiquer que quelque chose se passe dans une période donnée et on emploie **for** lorsqu'on parle d'une durée.

➤ **pendant que** while : **il me dérange tout le temps pendant que je fais mes devoirs** he keeps disturbing me while I'm doing my homework

⚠ The French word **pendant** is a false friend, it does not mean 'pendant'.

pendentif [pɑ̃dɑ̃tif] *nom masculin*

pendant : **elle porte un pendentif en jade** she's wearing a jade pendant.

penderie [pɑ̃dri] *nom féminin*

wardrobe *UK*, closet *US*.

pendre [pɑ̃dr] *verbe*

to hang : **le rideau pend jusqu'au sol** the curtain hangs down to the floor ; **j'ai pendu mon manteau** I hanged my coat

se pendre *verbe pronominal*

to hang oneself : **il s'est pendu** he hanged himself.

pendule [pɑ̃dyl] *nom féminin*

clock : **la pendule retarde** the clock is slow.

pénétrer [penetre] *verbe*

pénétrer dans to enter ; **il a pénétré dans la maison sans bruit** he entered the house without a sound.

pénible [penibl] *adjectif*

1. difficult, hard : **le voyage a été vraiment pénible** the journey was really difficult
2. painful : **des souvenirs pénibles** painful memories
➤ **il est vraiment pénible !** *familier* he's a real pain!

péniche [peniʃ] *nom féminin*

barge.

pénis [penis] *nom masculin*

penis.

penser [pɑ̃se] *verbe*

to think : **je pense qu'elle est déjà rentrée** I think she has come back already ; **je pense que oui** I think so ; **je pense que non** I don't think so
➤ **penser à quelqu'un** ou **à quelque chose** to think about somebody ou something : **je pensais justement à toi** I was just thinking about you
➤ **penser à faire quelque chose** to remember to do something : **pense à acheter du pain** remember to buy some bread
➤ **fais-moi penser à prendre les clés** remind me to take the keys
➤ **penser faire quelque chose** to be planning to do something : **je pensais y aller directement** I was planning to go straight there
➤ **qu'est-ce que tu en penses ?** what do you think?

pension [pɑ̃sjɔ̃] *nom féminin*

boarding school : **être en pension** to be at boarding school
➤ **une pension alimentaire** maintenance allowance *UK* ou alimony *US*.

pensionnaire [pɑ̃sjɔnɛr] *nom masculin ou féminin*

boarder.

pente [pɑ̃t] *nom féminin*

slope : **la pente est raide** it's a steep slope
> **le chemin est en pente** the path goes uphill.

Pentecôte [pɑ̃tkot] *nom féminin*

Whitsun.

pépin [pepɛ̃] *nom masculin*

pip : **cette orange est pleine de pépins** there are a lot of pips in this orange.

percer [pɛrse] *verbe*

1. to pierce : **je me suis fait percer les oreilles** I had my ears pierced
2. to drill : **il a fallu percer un trou dans le mur** we had to drill a hole in the wall.

perceuse [pɛrsøz] *nom féminin*

drill.

perche [pɛrʃ] *nom féminin*

pole : **le saut à la perche** the pole vault.

percuter [pɛrkyte] *verbe*

to crash into : **leur voiture a percuté un arbre** their car crashed into a tree.

perdant, e [pɛrdɑ̃, ɑ̃t] *adjectif & nom*

■ *adjectif*
losing : **l'équipe perdante** the losing team
■ *nom masculin, nom féminin*
loser : **il est mauvais perdant** he's a bad loser ; **les perdants** the losers.

perdre [pɛrdr] *verbe*

1. to lose : **j'ai perdu mes lunettes** I've lost my glasses
2. to waste : **perdre du temps et de l'argent** to waste time and money

se perdre *verbe pronominal*

1. to get lost : **je me suis perdu** I got lost
2. to die out : **certaines traditions se perdent** some traditions are dying out.

perdu, e [pɛrdy] *verbe & adjectif*

■ *participe passé de* perdre
■ *adjectif*
lost : **je me sens perdu sans elle** I'm lost without her.

père [pɛr] *nom masculin*

father : **le père de Jean est médecin** Jean's father is a doctor

> **le Père Noël** Santa Claus ou Father Christmas *UK*.

perfectionner [pɛrfɛksjɔne] *verbe*

to improve : **Sandrine est allée à Londres pour perfectionner son anglais** Sandrine went to London to improve her English

se perfectionner *verbe pronominal*

to improve : **il a besoin de se perfectionner en allemand** he needs to improve his German.

performance [pɛrfɔrmɑ̃s] *nom féminin*

performance (*singulier*) : **les performances d'un athlète** an athlete's performance

⚠ In French the word **performance** is only used to talk about the performance of a person or a machine.

périmé, e [perime] *adjectif*

past the use-by date : **le lait est périmé** the milk is past its use-by date
> **mon passeport est périmé** my passport is out-of-date.

périmètre [perimetr] *nom masculin*

perimeter.

période [perjɔd] *nom féminin*

period : **pendant toute cette période** throughout this period.

périphérique [periferik] *nom masculin*

ring road *UK*, beltway *US* : **on va prendre le périphérique** we'll take the ringroad *UK* ou we'll take the beltway *US*.

perle [pɛrl] *nom féminin*

1. pearl : **un collier de perles** a pearl necklace
2. bead : **des perles de verre** glass beads.

permanence [pɛrmanɑ̃s] *nom féminin*

study room *UK*, study hall *US*
> **j'ai deux heures de permanence** I have a two-hour study period
> **en permanence** permanently : **il pleut en permanence** it's permanently raining.

permanent, e [pɛrmanɑ̃, ɑ̃t] *adjectif*

permanent : **j'ai une douleur permanente au dos** I have a permanent pain in my back.

permanente [pɛrmanɑ̃t] *nom féminin*

perm, permanent US : **elle s'est fait faire une permanente** she's had a perm.

permettre [pɛrmɛtr] *verbe*

1. to allow : **je ne te permets pas de me parler sur ce ton** I won't allow you to speak to me like that ; **ce n'est pas permis** it's not allowed
2. to enable : **cet argent te permettra d'acheter les livres dont tu as besoin** this money will enable you to buy the books you need

se permettre *verbe pronominal*

1. **se permettre de faire quelque chose** to take the liberty of doing something : **je me suis permis de regarder tes photos** I took the liberty of looking at your photos
2. to afford : **je ne peux pas me permettre de dîner au restaurant** I can't afford to eat out.

permis¹, e [pɛrmi, iz] *participe passé de* **permettre.**

permis² [pɛrmi] *nom masculin*

permit : **un permis de travail** a work permit
> **un permis de conduire** a driving licence *UK* OU a driver's license *US*.

permission [pɛrmisjɔ̃] *nom féminin*

permission : **est-ce que tu as demandé la permission d'y aller ?** did you ask permission to go?

perpendiculaire [pɛrpɑ̃dikylɛr] *adjectif*

perpendicular : **perpendiculaire à** perpendicular to.

perroquet [pɛrɔkɛ] *nom masculin*

parrot.

perruche [pɛryʃ] *nom féminin*

budgerigar *UK*, parakeet *US*.

perruque [pɛryk] *nom féminin*

wig : **il porte une perruque** he wears a wig.

persil [pɛrsi] *nom masculin*

parsley.

persister [pɛrsiste] *verbe*

to persist : **pourquoi persistes-tu à dire des mensonges ?** why do you persist in telling lies?

personnage [pɛrsɔnaʒ] *nom masculin*

character : **le personnage principal dans le roman** the main character in the novel.

personnalité [pɛrsɔnalite] *nom féminin*

personality : **elle a une personnalité très forte** she has a very strong personality.

personne [pɛrsɔn] *nom & pronom*

■ *nom féminin*

person *(pluriel* **people***)* : **c'est une personne très gentille** she's a very kind person ; **deux personnes ont appelé** two people phoned ; **les personnes âgées** old people OU the elderly
> **une grande personne** a grown-up : **les grandes personnes** the grown-ups
> **en personne** in person : **il est venu me voir en personne** he came to see me in person
■ *pronom*

1. nobody, no one : **personne n'est venu** nobody came OU no one came ; **personne d'autre** nobody else OU no one else
2. anybody, anyone : **je n'ai vu personne** I didn't see anybody OU I didn't see anyone.

personnel, elle [pɛrsɔnɛl] *adjectif*

personal : **une lettre personnelle** a personal letter

personnel *nom masculin*

staff : **le personnel de l'entreprise** the company's staff.

personnellement [pɛrsɔnɛlmɑ̃] *adverbe*

personally.

persuader [pɛrsɥade] *verbe*

to persuade : **je l'ai finalement persuadé de venir** I eventually persuaded him to come
> **être persuadé que** to be convinced that : **je suis persuadé qu'il ne l'a pas fait exprès** I'm convinced he didn't do it on purpose.

perte [pɛrt] *nom féminin*

loss *(pluriel* **losses***)* : **perte de poids** weight loss
> **une perte de temps** a waste of time.

perturber [pɛrtyrbe] *verbe*

1. to disrupt : **il perturbe tout le temps la classe** he's always disrupting the class
2. to disturb : **cet incident l'a profondément perturbé** this incident disturbed him deeply.

pèse-personne [pɛzpɛrsɔn] *(pluriel* **pèse-personne** ou **pèse-personnes***) nom masculin*

scales *(pluriel)* : **le pèse-personne est détraqué** the scales are broken.

p

peser [pəze] *verbe*

to weigh : je pèse quarante kilos I weigh forty kilos ; pèse la farine d'abord weigh the flour first

➤ **peser lourd** to be heavy : ça pèse lourd it's heavy

se peser *verbe pronominal*

to weigh oneself : je ne me pèse pas souvent I don't weigh myself often.

pessimiste [pesimist] *adjectif & nom*

◼ *adjectif*
pessimistic : ne sois pas pessimiste don't be pessimistic

◼ *nom masculin ou féminin*
pessimist : c'est un pessimiste he's a pessimist.

pétale [petal] *nom masculin*

petal : des pétales de rose rose petals.

pétanque [petɑ̃k] *nom féminin*

kind of bowls played with steel balls

> PÉTANQUE
> Although it originated in the south of France, **pétanque** is a very popular game throughout the country. It is played with steel balls (**boules**) which the players throw or roll along the ground in an attempt to bring them as near as possible to the **cochonnet**, the jack. Pétanque is played on all kinds of terrains (including **boulodromes** which are special gravel-covered areas) and groups of people playing **pétanque** are a common sight in city squares and parks.

pétard [petar] *nom masculin*

firecracker : ils ont tiré des pétards toute la nuit they let off firecrackers all night.

pétiller [petije] *verbe*

1. to sparkle : ses yeux pétillaient de joie her eyes were sparkling with joy
2. to fizz : de l'eau qui pétille fizzy water.

petit, e [pəti, it] *adjectif & nom*

◼ *adjectif*
1. small : une petite quantité a small quantity ; un petit carnet a small notebook ; il est petit pour son âge he's small for his age ; il est plus petit que toi he's smaller than you ; ce jean est trop petit these jeans are too small
2. little : une petite fille et un petit garçon a little girl and a little boy ; une jolie petite maison a nice little house ; quand j'étais petite when I was little

➤ **un petit frère** a little brother OU a younger brother

➤ **une petite sœur** a little sister OU a younger sister

➤ **son petit ami** her boyfriend

➤ **sa petite amie** his girlfriend

➤ **des petits pois** peas

➤ **les petites annonces** small ads *UK* OU classified ads *US*

➤ **petit à petit** little by little

➤ **petit déjeuner** breakfast : je n'ai pas encore pris mon petit déjeuner I haven't had breakfast yet

◼ *nom masculin, nom féminin*
mon petit est malade my little boy is ill ; la pauvre petite ! poor little thing!

petite-fille [p(ə)titfij] (*pluriel* petites-filles) *nom féminin*

granddaughter.

petit-fils [p(ə)tifis] (*pluriel* petits-fils) *nom masculin*

grandson.

petits-enfants [p(ə)tizɑ̃fɑ̃] *nom masculin pluriel*

grandchildren.

petit-suisse [p(ə)tisɥis] *nom masculin*

thick fromage frais sold in small individual portions.

pétrole [petrɔl] *nom masculin*

oil, petroleum : un puits de pétrole an oil well

⚠ Pétrole is a false friend, it does not mean 'petrol'.

peu [pø] *adverbe*

1. *Avec un verbe* not much : j'ai peu dormi I didn't sleep much ; Isa mange très peu Isa doesn't eat much at all OU Isa eats very little
2. *Avec un adjectif* not very : il est peu soigneux he isn't very tidy

➤ **peu de**

1. *Avec un nom singulier* not much : nous avons peu de travail we haven't got much work
2. *Avec un nom pluriel* not many : il reste peu de jours there aren't many days left

> **un peu** a little OU a bit : **j'ai un peu faim** I'm
a little hungry OU I'm a bit hungry ; **tu veux du
gâteau ? – juste un peu** do you want some
cake? – just a little

> **un peu de** a little OU a bit : **donne-moi un
peu de pain** give me a little bread OU give me
a bit of bread

> **peu à peu** little by little OU gradually : **tu
t'amélioreras peu à peu** you'll improve little
by little OU you'll improve gradually.

peuple [pœpl] *nom masculin*

people : **le peuple français** the French
people.

peur [pœr] *nom féminin*

fear : **c'est la peur qui l'a fait agir** it was
fear that made him act

> **avoir peur de quelque chose** to be afraid
of something : **j'ai peur du noir** I'm afraid of
the dark

> **avoir peur de faire quelque chose** to be
afraid of doing something : **j'ai peur de plonger** I'm afraid of diving

> **j'ai peur qu'il ne vienne pas** I'm afraid
he won't come

> **faire peur à quelqu'un** to frighten some-
body : **tu m'as fait peur !** you frightened me!

peut ➤ pouvoir.

peut-être [pøtɛtr] *adverbe*

perhaps, maybe : **il n'a peut-être pas
compris** perhaps he didn't understand OU
maybe he didn't understand.

peux ➤ pouvoir.

phare [far] *nom masculin*

1. lighthouse : **un gardien de phare** a lighthouse keeper

2. headlight : **allumez vos phares** put your
headlights on.

pharmacie [farmasi] *nom féminin*

chemist's *UK*, pharmacy *US*, drugstore
US : **je dois aller à la pharmacie** I need to go
to the chemist's *UK* OU I need to go to the
pharmacy *US*.

pharmacien, enne [farmasjɛ̃, ɛn] *nom
masculin, nom féminin*

chemist *UK*, druggist *US* : **ma mère est
pharmacienne** my mother is a chemist.

phénomène [fenɔmɛn] *nom masculin*

phenomenon *(pluriel* **phenomena***)*.

philatélie [filateli] *nom féminin*

stamp-collecting.

philosophe [filɔzɔf] *nom masculin ou féminin*

philosopher : **Socrate était philosophe** Soc-
rates was a philosopher.

philosophie [filɔzɔfi] *nom féminin*

philosophy : **un cours de philosophie** a philosophy class.

phoque [fɔk] *nom masculin*

seal : **les phoques sont des mammifères**
seals are mammals.

photo [foto] *nom féminin*

photo, picture : **je n'ai pas pris beaucoup de
photos** I didn't take many photos ; **je voulais
les prendre en photo** I wanted to take a photo
of them OU I wanted to take a picture of them

> **une photo d'identité** a passport photo.

photocopie [fotokɔpi] *nom féminin*

photocopy *(pluriel* **photocopies***)* : **je vais
faire une photocopie de l'article** I'm going
to make a photocopy of the article.

photocopier [fotokɔpje] *verbe*

to photocopy : **il a photocopié la carte** he
photocopied the map.

photocopieur [fotokɔpjœr] *nom masculin*

photocopieuse [fotokɔpjøz] *nom féminin*
photocopier.

photographe [fotɔgraf] *nom masculin ou féminin*

photographer : **il est photographe de
mode** he's a fashion photographer

 Photographe is a false friend, it does not
mean 'photograph'.

photographie [fotɔgrafi] *nom féminin*

1. photograph : **une photographie de mon
frère à trois ans** a photograph of my brother
at three years old

2. photography : **elle est douée en photographie** she has a gift for photography.

photographier [fotɔgrafje] *verbe*

to photograph.

p

Photomaton® [fɔtɔmatɔ̃] *nom masculin*

photo booth.

phrase [fraz] *nom féminin*

sentence : **cette phrase n'a pas de verbe** this sentence doesn't have a verb.

physique [fizik] *adjectif & nom féminin*

■ *adjectif*
physical : **de l'exercice physique** physical exercise

■ *nom féminin*
physics *(singulier)* : **la physique est ma matière préférée** physics is my favourite subject.

pianiste [pjanist] *nom masculin ou féminin*

pianist : **Philippe est pianiste** Philippe is a pianist.

piano [pjano] *nom masculin*

piano : **jouer du piano** OU **faire du piano** to play the piano
➤ **un piano à queue** a grand piano.

pic [pik] *nom masculin*

peak : **les pics enneigés** the snowy peaks
➤ **tomber à pic** to come just at the right moment
➤ **le bateau a coulé à pic** the boat went straight down.

pichet [piʃɛ] *nom masculin*

jug *UK*, pitcher *US* : **un pichet d'eau** a jug of water.

pickpocket [pikpɔkɛt] *nom masculin*

pickpocket : **'attention aux pickpockets'** 'beware of pickpockets'.

pièce [pjɛs] *nom féminin*

1. coin : **une pièce de monnaie** a coin
2. room : **il y a des radiateurs dans toutes les pièces** there are radiators in every room
3. play : **une pièce de théâtre** a play.

pied [pje] *nom masculin*

foot *(pluriel* **feet)** : **elle a de grands pieds** she has big feet
➤ **à pied** on foot : **nous sommes venus à pied** we came on foot OU we walked here ; **je vais à l'école à pied** I walk to school
➤ **casser les pieds à quelqu'un** *familier* to get on somebody's nerves : **il me casse les pieds avec ses problèmes** he's getting on my nerves with his problems.

piège [pjɛʒ] *nom masculin*

trap : **attention, c'est un piège !** be careful, it's a trap! ; **ils étaient pris au piège** they were trapped.

pierre [pjɛr] *nom féminin*

stone : **une pierre précieuse** a precious stone ; **un pont en pierre** a stone bridge.

piéton, onne [pjetɔ̃, ɔn] *nom masculin, nom féminin & adjectif*

pedestrian : **une rue piétonne** a pedestrian street.

piétonnier, ère [pjetɔnje, ɛr] *adjectif*

pedestrian : **une rue piétonnière** a pedestrian street.

pieuvre [pjœvr] *nom féminin*

octopus *(pluriel* **octopuses)**.

pigeon [piʒɔ̃] *nom masculin*

pigeon.

pile [pil] *nom & adverbe*

■ *nom féminin*
1. pile : **une pile de magazines** a pile of magazines
2. battery *(pluriel* **batteries)** : **ça marche avec des piles** it works off batteries
➤ **on tire à pile ou face ?** shall we toss for it?
➤ **pile ou face ?** heads or tails?
■ *adverbe familier*
right : **tu tombes pile !** you've come at just the right time!
➤ **à deux heures pile** at two o'clock on the dot.

pilier [pilje] *nom masculin*

pillar : **des piliers en pierre** stone pillars.

pilote [pilɔt] *nom masculin*

pilot : **son père est pilote** his father is a pilot.

pilule [pilyl] *nom féminin*

pill : **prendre la pilule** to be on the pill.

piment [pimɑ̃] *nom masculin*

chilli, chili : **piment rouge** red chilli pepper.

pin [pɛ̃] *nom masculin*

pine : **une table en pin** a pine table.

pince [pɛ̃s] *nom féminin*

pincer : **les pinces d'un crabe** a crab's pincers
➤ **une pince à épiler** tweezers *(pluriel)*

➤ **une pince à linge** a clothes peg *UK* ou a clothespin *US*.

pinceau [pɛ̃so] *(pluriel* pinceaux*) nom masculin*

paintbrush *(pluriel* **paintbrushes***)*.

pincée [pɛ̃se] *nom féminin*

pinch : une pincée de sel a pinch of salt.

pincer [pɛ̃se] *verbe*

to pinch : il m'a pincé au bras he pinched my arm ou he pinched me on the arm.

pingouin [pɛ̃gwɛ̃] *nom masculin*

penguin.

ping-pong [piŋpɔ̃g] *nom masculin*

table tennis : jouer au ping-pong to play table tennis.

pioche [pjɔʃ] *nom féminin*

1. **pick : il creuse le sol avec une pioche** he's breaking up the ground with a pick
2. **pile : Sophie a pris une carte dans la pioche** Sophie took a card from the pile.

pion, pionne [pjɔ̃, pjɔn] *nom masculin, nom féminin familier*

person paid to supervise pupils during breaks and study periods

pion *nom masculin*

1. **piece : avance ton pion de trois cases** move your piece forward three squares
2. *Aux échecs* **pawn : combien de pions est-ce qu'il y a dans un jeu d'échecs ?** how many pawns are there in a game of chess?

pipe [pip] *nom féminin*

pipe : son père fume la pipe his father smokes a pipe.

pipi [pipi] *nom masculin familier*

pee : j'ai besoin de faire pipi I need to have a pee.

piquant, e [pikɑ̃, ɑ̃t] *adjectif*

hot, spicy : une sauce piquante a hot sauce ou a spicy sauce.

pique [pik] *nom masculin*

spades : la dame de pique the queen of spades.

pique-nique [piknik] *(pluriel* pique-niques*) nom masculin*

picnic : nous allons faire un pique-nique au parc we're going to have a picnic in the park.

piquer [pike] *verbe*

1. **to sting : je me suis fait piquer par une guêpe** I got stung by a wasp
2. **to bite : je me suis fait piquer par un moustique** I got bitten by a mosquito
3. *familier* **to steal, to pinch** *UK* : **qui m'a piqué mon stylo ?** who stole my pen?

piqûre [pikyr] *nom féminin*

1. **injection : l'infirmière m'a fait une piqûre** the nurse gave me an injection
2. **sting : une piqûre de guêpe** a wasp sting
3. **bite : une piqûre de moustique** a mosquito bite.

pirate [pirat] *nom masculin*

pirate : un navire de pirates a pirate ship
➤ **un pirate de l'air** a hijacker.

pire [pir] *adjectif & nom*

▢ *adjectif*

1. **worse : c'est pire que ce que je pensais** it's worse than I thought
2. **worst : c'est le pire livre que j'aie jamais lu** it's the worst book I've ever read ; **la pire chose qui puisse arriver** the worst thing that could happen

▢ *nom masculin*

le pire the worst ; **le pire, c'est que je n'ai pas fini mes devoirs** the worst is that I haven't finished my homework

▢ *nom masculin, nom féminin*

le pire ou **la pire** the worst ; **parmi tous les élèves, c'est la pire** out of all the pupils, she's the worst.

piscine [pisin] *nom féminin*

swimming pool : on va à la piscine ? shall we go to the swimming pool?

pistache [pistaʃ] *nom féminin*

pistachio : une glace à la pistache a pistachio ice cream.

piste [pist] *nom féminin*

track, trail : la police est sur la piste des voleurs the police are on the thieves' trail
➤ **une piste d'atterrissage** a runway
➤ **une piste cyclable** a cycle path *UK* ou a bike path *US*
➤ **une piste de danse** a dance floor
➤ **une piste de ski** a ski run.

p

pistolet [pistɔlɛ] *nom masculin*

gun : **il a sorti son pistolet** he pulled out his gun.

pitié [pitje] *nom féminin*

pity : **je ne veux pas de ta pitié** I don't want your pity

> **avoir pitié de quelqu'un** to feel sorry for somebody

> **il me fait pitié** I feel sorry for him.

pitre [pitr] *nom masculin*

clown : **il n'arrête pas de faire le pitre** he's always clowning.

pittoresque [pitɔrɛsk] *adjectif*

picturesque : **la Dordogne est une région très pittoresque** Dordogne is a very picturesque region.

pizza [pidza] *nom féminin*

pizza : **une pizza aux champignons et aux olives** a mushroom and olive pizza.

placard [plakar] *nom masculin*

cupboard : **range les verres dans le placard** put the glasses in the cupboard.

place [plas] *nom féminin*

I. place : **ce livre n'est pas à sa place** that book isn't in the right place

2. room, space : **est-ce qu'il y a assez de place ?** is there enough room? ; **ça prend trop de place** it takes up too much room ou it takes up too much space

3. seat : **est-ce qu'il reste des places pour demain soir ?** are there any seats left for tomorrow night?

4. square : **la place des Vosges est une des plus anciennes places de Paris** the Place des Vosges is one of the oldest squares in Paris

> **à ta place** if I were you : **à ta place, je ne l'inviterais pas** if I were you, I wouldn't invite him

> **ne pas se sentir à sa place** to feel out of place

> **il ne tient pas en place** he won't keep still.

placer [plase] *verbe*

I. to put, to place : **elle a placé le vase sur la table** she put the vase on the table ou she placed the vase on the table

2. to seat : **je ne sais pas où placer les invités** I don't know where to seat the guests.

plafond [plafɔ̃] *nom masculin*

ceiling.

plage [plaʒ] *nom féminin*

beach *(pluriel* **beaches***)* : **ils vont à la plage** they're going to the beach ; **nous avons passé la journée à la plage** we spent the day on the beach.

plaie [plɛ] *nom féminin*

wound : **la plaie s'est infectée** the wound became infected.

plaindre [plɛ̃dr] *verbe*

to pity : **je la plains** I pity her

se plaindre *verbe pronominal*

to complain : **il n'arrête pas de se plaindre** he's always complaining ; **elle se plaint de son nouveau travail** she complains about her new job ; **il s'est plaint au prof** he complained to the teacher.

plaine [plɛn] *nom féminin*

plain : **une plaine entourée de montagnes** a plain surrounded by mountains.

plaint, e [plɛ̃, plɛ̃t] *participe passé de* plaindre.

plainte [plɛ̃t] *nom féminin*

complaint : **porter plainte** to make a complaint.

plaire [plɛr] *verbe*

ça me plaît I like it ; **elle lui plaît beaucoup** he really likes her ; **c'est un modèle qui plaît beaucoup** it's a very popular model

> **s'il te plaît** ou **s'il vous plaît** please.

plaisanter [plɛzɑ̃te] *verbe*

to joke : **arrête de plaisanter !** stop joking!

plaisanterie [plɛzɑ̃tri] *nom féminin*

joke : **faire des plaisanteries** to tell jokes.

plaisir [plezir] *nom masculin*

pleasure : **il fait ça pour son plaisir** ou **il fait ça par plaisir** he does it for pleasure ; **avec plaisir** with pleasure

> **ça me fait plaisir que tu sois là** I'm glad you're here

> **quel plaisir de te revoir !** what a pleasure it is to see you again! ou how nice it is to see you again!

plan [plɑ̃] *nom masculin*

1. **map : un plan de la ville** a map of the city
2. **plan : voilà le plan de la maison** here's the plan of the house ; **le plan d'un devoir** an essay plan
➤ **à l'arrière-plan** in the background
➤ **au premier plan** in the foreground.

planche [plɑ̃ʃ] *nom féminin*

plank : il y a des planches clouées en travers de la porte there are planks nailed across the door
➤ **une planche à dessin** a drawing board
➤ **une planche à repasser** an ironing board
➤ **une planche à voile** a sailboard : **faire de la planche à voile** to go windsurfing
➤ **faire la planche** to float.

plancher [plɑ̃ʃe] *nom masculin*

floor : le plancher n'est pas très solide the floor isn't very solid.

planer [plane] *verbe*

1. **to glide : un aigle plane dans le ciel** an eagle is gliding in the sky
2. *familier* **to live in a dream world : il plane complètement** he lives in a dream world.

planète [planɛt] *nom féminin*

planet : il y a neuf planètes dans notre système solaire there are nine planets in our solar system.

plante [plɑ̃t] *nom féminin*

plant : une plante verte a house plant
➤ **la plante des pieds** the soles of the feet.

planter [plɑ̃te] *verbe*

1. **to plant : mon père a planté un sapin dans le jardin** my father planted a fir tree in the garden
2. **to hammer in : il suffit de planter un clou dans le mur** all you have to do is hammer a nail into the wall
3. **to drive in : planter un piquet dans le sol** to drive a stake into the ground
4. **to pitch : on pourrait planter la tente ici** we could pitch the tent here
5. **to crash : mon ordinateur a planté** my computer has crashed
➤ **être planté devant la télévision** to be glued to the television

se planter *verbe pronominal familier*

1. **to get it wrong : tu t'es planté, ce n'est pas ici** you've got it wrong, it's not here

2. **to fail : je me suis planté en géographie** I failed in geography.

plaque [plak] *nom féminin*

1. **sheet : une plaque de verre** a sheet of glass
2. **plaque : le nom du médecin est sur la plaque** the doctor's name is on the plaque
3. **patch** *(pluriel* **patches)** : **Léa a des plaques rouges sur le visage** Léa has red patches on her face
➤ **une plaque chauffante** a hotplate
➤ **la plaque d'immatriculation** the number plate *UK* ou the license plate *US*.

plaqué, e [plake] *adjectif*

un bracelet plaqué or a gold-plated bracelet ; **des boucles d'oreille plaquées argent** silver-plated earrings.

plaquette [plakɛt] *nom féminin*

➤ **une plaquette de beurre** a pack of butter
➤ **une plaquette de chocolat** a bar of chocolate.

plastique [plastik] *nom masculin*

plastic : un jouet en plastique a plastic toy.

plat, e [pla, plat] *adjectif*

flat : le paysage est très plat en Belgique the landscape is very flat in Belgium ; **des chaussures plates** flat shoes
➤ **de l'eau plate** still water

plat *nom masculin*

1. **dish** *(pluriel* **dishes)** : **mets les pâtes dans un grand plat** put the pasta in a large dish ; **un plat thaïlandais à base de poisson** a fish-based Thai dish
2. **course : le plat principal** the main course
➤ **un plat cuisiné** a ready-cooked dish
➤ **le plat du jour** today's special
➤ **à plat**
1. **flat : mets la carte à plat sur la table** put the map flat on the table ; **le pneu est à plat** the tyre is flat
2. *familier* **exhausted : je suis à plat, je vais me coucher** I'm exhausted, I'm going to bed
➤ **faire un plat** to do a belly-flop : **Bruno a fait un plat, il ne sait pas plonger** Bruno did a belly-flop, he can't dive
➤ **n'en fais pas tout un plat !** *familier* don't make a song and dance about it!

plateau [plato] *(pluriel* **plateaux)** *nom masculin*

p

1. **tray : je lui ai apporté son petit-déjeuner sur un plateau** I took him breakfast on a tray
2. **plateau : du plateau, on a une belle vue** you get a good view from the plateau
3. **set : un plateau de télévision** a TV set
➤ **un plateau de fromages** a cheese board.

plate-forme [platfɔrm] (*pluriel* plates-formes) *nom féminin*
➤ **une plate-forme pétrolière** an oil rig.

platine [platin]
▢ *nom masculin*
platinum : une montre en platine a platinum watch
▢ *nom féminin*
deck : une platine cassettes a cassette deck
➤ **une platine laser** a CD player.

plâtre [platr] *nom masculin*
plaster : Ludo a le bras dans le plâtre Ludo has his arm in plaster ; **il y a du plâtre qui tombe du plafond** there's plaster falling off the ceiling.

play-back [plɛbak] *nom masculin invariable*
chanter en play-back to mime.

plein, e [plɛ̃, plɛn] *adjectif*
full : la bouteille est presque pleine the bottle is almost full
➤ **plein à craquer** full to bursting : **ma valise est pleine à craquer** my suitcase is full to bursting
➤ **en plein air** in the open air : **manger en plein air** to eat in the open air
➤ **un marché en plein air** an open-air market
➤ **en plein jour** in broad daylight
➤ **en pleine nuit** in the middle of the night
➤ **en plein** right : **en plein dans la figure** right in the face ; **en plein sur la tête** right on the head
➤ **plein de** *familier* lots of ou a lot of : **Anne a plein d'amis** Anne has lots of friends

plein *nom masculin*
faire le plein to fill up ; **le plein, s'il vous plaît** fill her up, please.

pleurer [plœre] *verbe*
to cry : ma petite sœur pleure tout le temps my little sister cries all the time
➤ **pleurer de joie** to weep for joy.

pleurnicher [plœrniʃe] *verbe*
to whine : arrête de pleurnicher, c'est agaçant ! stop whining, it's irritating!

pleuvoir [pløvwar] *verbe*
to rain : il pleut it's raining ; **il pleuvait** it was raining.

pli [pli] *nom masculin*
crease : la jupe est pleine de plis the skirt is all creased.

pliant, e [plijã, ãt] *adjectif*
folding : une chaise pliante a folding chair.

plier [plije] *verbe*
1. **to fold : tu n'as pas bien plié les tee-shirts** you haven't folded the T-shirts properly
2. **to fold up : on a dû plier le parasol à toute vitesse** we had to fold up the parasol double quick
3. **to bend : plie les genoux, sinon tu vas te faire mal au dos** bend your knees, or you'll hurt your back ; **la branche a plié mais ne s'est pas cassée** the branch bent but didn't break.

plissé, e [plise] *adjectif*
pleated : une jupe plissée a pleated skirt.

plomb [plɔ̃] *nom masculin*
1. **lead : le plomb est un métal très lourd** lead is a very heavy metal ; **une gouttière en plomb** a lead gutter
2. **fuse : les plombs ont sauté** the fuses have blown.

plombage [plɔ̃baʒ] *nom masculin*
filling : le dentiste m'a fait un plombage the dentist gave me a filling.

plombier [plɔ̃bje] *nom masculin*
plumber : le père de Mathias est plombier Mathias's father is a plumber.

plongée [plɔ̃ʒe] *nom féminin*
diving : un stage de plongée a diving course ; **faire de la plongée** to go diving
➤ **la plongée sous-marine** scuba diving.

plongeoir [plɔ̃ʒwar] *nom masculin*
diving board.

plongeon [plɔ̃ʒɔ̃] *nom masculin*
dive : quel beau plongeon ! what a beautiful dive! ; **faire un plongeon** to dive.

plonger [plɔ̃ʒe] *verbe*

to dive : **le maître nageur nous apprend à plonger** the swimming instructor is teaching us to dive.

plu [ply] *verbe*

- *participe passé invariable de* **plaire**
  le film t'a plu ? did you like the film?
- *participe passé invariable de* **pleuvoir**
  il a plu toute la semaine it rained all week.

pluie [plɥi] *nom féminin*

rain : **ne restez pas sous la pluie** don't stay out in the rain.

plume [plym] *nom féminin*

1. **feather** : **une plume d'oiseau** a bird feather : **un oreiller en plume** a feather pillow
2. **nib** : **la plume de mon stylo est abîmée** the nib of my pen is damaged.

plumer [plyme] *verbe*

to pluck : **plumer un poulet** to pluck a chicken.

plupart [plypar] *nom féminin*

➤ **la plupart de** most of : **la plupart des élèves** most of the pupils ; **la plupart du temps** most of the time.

pluriel [plyrjɛl] *nom masculin*

plural : **ce verbe est au pluriel** this verb is in the plural.

plus [ply(z)] *adverbe & préposition*

- *adverbe*

1. *Dans les comparatifs et les superlatifs* (**plus** *se prononce* [ply] *lorsqu'il est suivi d'une consonne ou* [plyz] *lorsqu'il est suivi d'une voyelle ou d'un 'h' muet*) **more** : **c'est un joueur plus expérimenté** he's a more experienced player : **c'est plus difficile qu'avant** it's more difficult than before

> La formation du comparatif de supériorité en anglais dépend de la longueur de l'adjectif qui suit : avec un adjectif de plus de deux syllabes : **more + adjectif** (plus difficile = **more difficult** ; plus confortable = **more comfortable**) ; avec un adjectif de deux syllabes maximum : **adjectif + terminaison -er** (plus grand = **taller** ; plus court = **shorter**). Pour former le comparatif d'un adjectif se terminant par « y », on n'utilise pas **more**.

elle est bien plus paresseuse que lui she's much lazier than him ; **c'est plus court par là** it's quicker that way ; **un peu plus loin** a bit further

➤ **plus ou moins** more or less

➤ **le plus** ou **la plus** ou **les plus** the most : **le cours le plus intéressant** the most interesting lesson of all

> La formation du superlatif de supériorité en anglais dépend de la longueur de l'adjectif qui suit : avec un adjectif de plus de deux syllabes : **the most + adjectif** (le plus intéressant = **the most interesting** ; le plus difficile = **the most difficult**) ; avec un adjectif de deux syllabes maximum : **adjectif + terminaison -est** (le plus sympa = **the nicest** ; le plus facile = **the easiest**). Pour former le superlatif d'un adjectif se terminant par « y », on n'utilise pas **most**. Notez que le « y » final (easy ; lazy) devient « i » (easiest ; laziest) :

la fille la plus sympa the nicest girl ; **il est l'homme le plus heureux du monde** he's the happiest man in the world

2. *Dans une phrase à la forme négative avec ne* (**plus** *se prononce* [ply]) **not ... any more** : **Karim ne vient plus nous voir** Karim doesn't come to see us any more

3. *Modifiant un verbe* (**plus** *se prononce* [plys]) **more** : **tu devrais travailler plus** you should work more

➤ **plus de**

1. **more** : **Lucas a plus de jeux vidéo que moi** Lucas has got more video games than me
2. **more than** : **il y a plus de 15 ans** more than 15 years ago

➤ **de plus** more : **celui-ci coûte dix euros de plus que l'autre** this one costs ten euros more than the other ; **j'ai un an de plus que Justine** I'm a year older than Justine

➤ **en plus**

1. **extra** : **les boissons sont en plus** drinks are extra
2. **what's more** : **il est gentil, et en plus il est rigolo** he's nice and what's more, he's funny

➤ **en plus de** as well as ou in addition to : **j'ai eu un CD en plus des livres** I got a CD as well as some books

➤ **le plus possible** as much as possible

➤ **de plus en plus** more and more : **de plus en plus de gens** more and more people

- *préposition*

plus : **trois plus trois font six** three plus three is six.

p

plusieurs [plyzjœr] *adjectif pluriel & pronom pluriel*

several : **plusieurs BD** several comic books ; **plusieurs d'entre eux** several of them.

plutôt [plyto] *adverbe*

1. rather : **elle est plutôt sympa** she's rather nice
2. instead : **prends plutôt une bière** have a beer instead
➤ **plutôt que** instead of OU rather than : **je prendrai un chocolat plutôt qu'un café** I'll have a hot chocolate instead of a coffee OU I'll have a hot chocolate rather than a coffee ; **viens avec nous plutôt que de rester là** come with us rather than stay here.

pneu [pnø] *nom masculin*

tyre *UK*, tire *US* : **les pneus avant** the front tyres.

pneumonie [pnømɔni] *nom féminin*

pneumonia : **avoir une pneumonie** to have pneumonia.

poche [pɔʃ] *nom féminin*

1. pocket : **Marc a mis le billet dans sa poche** Marc put the note in his pocket
2. bag : **elle a des poches sous les yeux** she has bags under her eyes
➤ **de poche** pocket : **un couteau de poche** a pocket knife ; **de l'argent de poche** pocket money
➤ **un livre de poche** a paperback.

pochette [pɔʃɛt] *nom féminin*

1. sleeve : **où est la pochette du disque ?** where's the record sleeve?
2. wallet : **je mets mes photocopies dans des pochettes en plastique** I put my photocopies in plastic wallets.

poêle [pwal] *nom féminin*

pan : **une poêle à frire** a frying pan.

poème [pɔɛm] *nom masculin*

poem.

poésie [pɔezi] *nom féminin*

1. poetry : **Patricia écrit de la poésie** Patricia writes poetry
2. poem : **une poésie de Prévert** a poem by Prévert.

poète [pɔɛt] *nom masculin*

poet : **les grands poètes romantiques** the great Romantic poets.

poids [pwa] *nom masculin*

1. weight : **perdre du poids** to lose weight ; **prendre du poids** to put on weight ; **quel poids fais-tu ?** how much do you weigh?
2. shot : **le lancer du poids** shot put
➤ **un poids lourd** a heavy goods vehicle *UK* OU a truck *US*.

poignard [pwaɲar] *nom masculin*

dagger.

poignée [pwaɲe] *nom féminin*

1. handle : **la poignée de la valise me fait mal** the handle of the suitcase is hurting me
2. handful : **une poignée de bonbons** a handful of sweets
➤ **une poignée de main** a handshake : **échanger une poignée de mains** to shake hands.

poignet [pwaɲɛ] *nom masculin*

wrist : **Sylvia a les poignets fins** Sylvia has thin wrists.

poil [pwal] *nom masculin*

1. hair : **il y a des poils de chat partout dans la maison** there are cat's hairs all over the house
2. bristle : **les poils du pinceau** the bristles of the brush
➤ **à poil** *familier* naked OU starkers *UK* : **il était à poil quand on est entrés** he was naked when we came in
➤ **à un poil près** *familier* almost : **à un poil près on ratait le train** we almost missed the train.

poilu, e [pwaly] *adjectif*

hairy : **des jambes poilues** hairy legs.

poinçonner [pwɛ̃sɔne] *verbe*

to punch : **n'oubliez pas de poinçonner vos billets** don't forget to punch your tickets.

poing [pwɛ̃] *nom masculin*

fist : **les poings serrés** with clenched fists
➤ **dormir à poings fermés** to sleep like a log.

point [pwɛ̃] *nom masculin*

1. dot : **il manque le point sur le i** the dot is missing from the i
2. full stop *UK*, period *US* : **mets un point à la fin de la phrase** put a full stop at the end of the sentence
3. stitch *(pluriel stitches)* : **tu peux me faire un**

point à la manche ? can you put a stitch in my sleeve?

4. **point : Bertrand a marqué trois points** Bertrand scored three points
➤ **les points cardinaux** cardinal points OU points of compass
➤ **un point de côté** a stitch : **aïe, j'ai un point de côté** ouch, I have a stitch
➤ **un point d'exclamation** an exclamation mark *UK* OU an exclamation point *US*
➤ **un point faible** a weak point
➤ **un point fort** a strong point
➤ **un point d'interrogation** a question mark
➤ **un point noir** a blackhead
➤ **point de repère**
1. reference point : **mon point de repère, c'est 1789** my reference point is 1789
2. landmark : **la tour Eiffel est un excellent point de repère** the Eiffel Tower is an excellent landmark
➤ **points de suspension** suspension points
➤ **le médecin m'a fait trois points de suture** the doctor gave me three stitches
➤ **point de vue**
1. viewpoint : **il y a un beau point de vue d'ici** there's a beautiful view from here
2. point of view : **quel est ton point de vue sur ce sujet ?** what's your point of view on this subject?
➤ **à point**
1. just right : **le gâteau est à point** OU **le gâteau est cuit à point** the cake is just right
2. medium : **comment voulez-vous votre steak ? – à point** how do you want your steak? – medium
3. just at the right time : **tu tombes à point** you've come just at the right time
➤ **à ce point** that : **tu es fatigué à ce point ?** are you that tired?
➤ **au point mort** in neutral : **laisse la voiture au point mort** leave the car in neutral
➤ **avoir des points communs avec quelqu'un** to have things in common with somebody
➤ **être sur le point de faire quelque chose** to be about to do something : **j'étais justement sur le point de t'appeler** I was just about to call you
➤ **faire le point** to take stock : **bon, faisons le point avant de continuer** right, let's take stock before carrying on.

pointe [pwɛ̃t] *nom féminin*

point : la pointe du couteau the point of the knife

➤ **de pointe**
1. leading : **une industrie de pointe** a leading industry
2. cutting-edge : **une technique de pointe** a cutting-edge technique
➤ **une pointe de** a touch of : **il a dit ça avec une pointe d'ironie** he said that with a touch of irony
➤ **sur la pointe des pieds** on tiptoe.

pointillé [pwɛ̃tije] *nom masculin*

dotted line : **écris ton nom sur le pointillé** write your name on the dotted line ; **tracer une ligne en pointillé** to draw a dotted line.

pointu, e [pwɛ̃ty] *adjectif*

pointed : **un bâton pointu** a pointed stick.

pointure [pwɛ̃tyr] *nom féminin*

shoe size : **quelle est votre pointure ?** what's your shoe size?

point-virgule [pwɛ̃virgyl] (*pluriel* **points-virgules**) *nom masculin*
semi-colon.

poire [pwar] *nom féminin*

pear : **un kilo de poires** a kilo of pears.

poireau [pwaro] (*pluriel* **poireaux**) *nom masculin*

leek : **des poireaux vinaigrette** leeks with vinaigrette dressing.

poirier [pwarje] *nom masculin*

pear tree : **nous avons un poirier dans le jardin** we have a pear tree in the garden
➤ **faire le poirier** to do a headstand.

pois [pwa] *nom masculin*

dot : **un chemisier rouge à pois blancs** a red blouse with white dots
➤ **des pois chiches** chickpeas
➤ **des petits pois** peas OU garden peas.

poison [pwazɔ̃] *nom masculin*

poison.

poisson [pwasɔ̃] *nom masculin*

fish : **il y a du poisson à la cantine aujourd'hui** there's fish at the canteen today ; **un poisson rouge** a goldfish ; **un poisson volant** a flying fish
➤ **poisson d'avril !** April fool!
➤ **être comme un poisson dans l'eau** to be in one's element

p

Poissons *nom masculin pluriel*

Pisces : **je suis Poissons** I'm Pisces

 POISSON D'AVRIL
Look out for April Fool's tricks (poisson d'avril) on 1st April. In France, a popular practical joke to play on people is to try to stick a coloured paper fish on someone's back without their noticing it. Why a fish? Because traditionally this is the season for catching and eating fish.

poissonnerie [pwasɔnri] *nom féminin*

fish shop, fishmonger's *UK* : **je vais à la poissonnerie acheter des huîtres** I'm going to the fish shop to buy oysters.

poitrine [pwatrin] *nom féminin*

1. chest : **il l'a frappé en pleine poitrine** he hit him right in the chest
2. *d'une fille* breast.

poivre [pwavr] *nom masculin*

pepper : **du poivre noir** black pepper.

poivron [pwavrɔ̃] *nom masculin*

pepper : **des poivrons rouges** red peppers.

pôle [pol] *nom masculin*

pole : **le pôle Nord** the North Pole ; **le pôle Sud** the South Pole.

poli, e [pɔli] *adjectif*

polite : **tu pourrais au moins être poli !** you could at least be polite!

police [pɔlis] *nom féminin*

police *(pluriel)* : **la police est déjà là** the police are already there ; **le frère d'Ahmed est dans la police** Ahmed's brother is a policeman ou Ahmed's brother is in the police force.

policier, ère [pɔlisje, ɛr] *adjectif*

1. police : **une enquête policière** a police investigation
2. detective : **un film policier** a detective film ; **un roman policier** a detective novel

policier *nom masculin*

police officer, policeman : **Charles voudrait devenir policier** Charles would like to be a police officer ou Charles would like to be a policeman.

politesse [pɔlitɛs] *nom féminin*

politeness : **M. Lopez accorde beaucoup d'importance à la politesse** Mr Lopez attaches great importance to politeness.

politique [pɔlitik] *nom & adjectif*

◻ *nom féminin*
1. politics *(singulier)* : **je ne m'intéresse pas à la politique** I'm not interested in politics.
2. policy *(pluriel* policies*)* : **la politique étrangère du gouvernement** the government's foreign policy
◻ *adjectif*
political : **le pouvoir politique** political power.

pollué, e [pɔlɥe] *adjectif*

polluted : **cette rivière est très polluée** this river is very polluted.

polluer [pɔlɥe] *verbe*

to pollute.

pollution [pɔlysjɔ̃] *nom féminin*

pollution : **il faut réduire la pollution** we must reduce pollution.

polo [pɔlo] *nom masculin*

1. polo shirt : **Patrice porte un polo rouge** Patrice is wearing a red polo shirt
2. polo : **jouer au polo** to play polo.

pommade [pɔmad] *nom féminin*

ointment : **je vais me passer de la pommade sur le genou** I'm going to rub some ointment on my knee.

pomme [pɔm] *nom féminin*

apple : **un kilo de pommes** a kilo of apples
➤ **une pomme de pin** a pine cone
➤ **des pommes frites** chips *UK* ou French fries ou fries *US*
➤ **des pommes vapeur** steamed potatoes.

pomme de terre [pɔmdətɛr] *nom féminin*

potato *(pluriel* potatoes*)* : **des pommes de terre à l'eau** boiled potatoes ; **des pommes de terre frites** chips *UK* ou French fries ou fries *US*.

pommette [pɔmɛt] *nom féminin*

cheekbone : **avoir les pommettes saillantes** to have high cheekbones.

pommier [pɔmje] *nom masculin*

apple tree.

pompe [pɔ̃p] *nom féminin*

1. pump : est-ce que tu as une pompe à vélo ? do you have a bicycle pump?
2. *familier* shoe : j'ai de nouvelles pompes I have new shoes

➤ **une pompe à essence** a petrol pump *UK* ou a gas pump *US*
➤ **une pompe à incendie** a fire engine ou a fire truck *US*
➤ **les pompes funèbres** the undertaker's.

pomper [pɔ̃pe] *verbe*

to pump : on a dû pomper toute l'eau du bateau we had to pump all the water out of the boat.

pompier [pɔ̃pje] *nom masculin*

fireman *(pluriel* firemen*)*, firefighter *US* : Fred est pompier Fred's a fireman.

ponctuation [pɔ̃ktɥasjɔ̃] *nom féminin*

punctuation : des signes de ponctuation punctuation marks.

pondre [pɔ̃dr] *verbe*

to lay : ces poules pondent beaucoup d'œufs these hens lay a lot of eggs.

pondu, e [pɔ̃dy] *participe passé de* pondre.

poney [pɔnɛ] *nom masculin*

pony *(pluriel* ponies*)*.

pont [pɔ̃] *nom masculin*

1. bridge : on a traversé le pont we crossed the bridge ou we went over the bridge
2. deck : les passagers du bateau sont sur le pont the boat's passengers are on the deck
➤ **faire le pont** to have a long weekend.

pop [pɔp] *nom féminin & adjectif*

pop : la musique pop pop music ; la pop française French pop music.

pop-corn [pɔpkɔrn] *(pluriel* pop-corn*) nom masculin*

popcorn : ils mangent du pop-corn they're eating popcorn.

populaire [pɔpylɛr] *adjectif*

1. working-class : un quartier populaire de Paris a working-class area of Paris
2. popular : Adam est très populaire auprès des filles Adam is very popular with the girls.

population [pɔpylasjɔ̃] *nom féminin*

population : la population mondiale est de 6 milliards environ the population of the world is about 6 billion.

porc [pɔr] *nom masculin*

1. pig : ils élèvent des porcs they breed pigs
2. pork : une côte de porc a pork chop.

porcelaine [pɔrsəlɛn] *nom féminin*

china : des petits objets en porcelaine small china objects.

porche [pɔrʃ] *nom masculin*

porch *(pluriel* porches*)* : sous le porche de l'église in the church porch.

port [pɔr] *nom masculin*

1. harbour *UK*, harbor *US* : on s'est promenés près du port we went for a walk near the harbour
2. port : Toulon est un grand port Toulon is a large port.

portable [pɔrtabl] *adjectif & nom*

■ *adjectif*
1. portable, laptop : un ordinateur portable a portable computer
2. mobile : un téléphone portable a mobile phone
■ *nom masculin*
1. laptop : j'emporte mon portable pour travailler dans le train I'm taking my laptop to work on the train
2. mobile, mobile phone : tu peux m'appeler sur mon portable you can call me on my mobile.

portail [pɔrtaj] *nom masculin*

gates *(pluriel)* : il est descendu de la voiture pour ouvrir le portail he got out of the car to open the gates.

porte [pɔrt] *nom féminin*

1. door : je n'arrive pas à ouvrir la porte I can't open the door ; Loïc m'a claqué la porte au nez Loïc slammed the door in my face
2. gate : les portes de la ville the city gates
➤ **la porte d'embarquement** the departure gate
➤ **la porte d'entrée** the front door
➤ **mettre quelqu'un à la porte** to throw somebody out.

porte-bagages [pɔrtbagaʒ] *(pluriel* porte-bagages*) nom masculin*

rack : je mets mon sac à dos sur le porte-bagages du vélo I put my rucksack on the bike rack.

p

porte-bonheur [pɔrtbɔnœr] (*pluriel* porte-bonheur) *nom masculin*

lucky charm.

porte-clefs, porte-clés [pɔrtəkle] (*pluriel* porte-clefs ou porte-clés) *nom masculin*
keyring.

porte-fenêtre [pɔrtfənɛtr] (*pluriel* portes-fenêtres) *nom féminin*
French window.

portefeuille [pɔrtəfœj] *nom masculin*

wallet : **Samuel s'est fait voler son porte-feuille** Samuel had his wallet stolen.

portemanteau [pɔrtmɑ̃to] (*pluriel* porte-manteaux) *nom masculin*

coat rack : **mets ta veste sur le portemanteau** hang your jacket on the coat rack.

porte-monnaie [pɔrtmɔnɛ] (*pluriel* porte-monnaie) *nom masculin*

purse *UK*, change purse *US*.

porter [pɔrte] *verbe*

1. **to carry** : **aide-moi à porter les bagages** help me carry the luggage
2. **to wear** : **Camille porte un jean noir** Camille is wearing black jeans
3. **to bear** : **le certificat porte le nom de l'élève et de l'école** the certificate bears the name of the pupil and of the school

se porter *verbe pronominal*

to be : **Antoine se porte mieux maintenant** Antoine is better now.

portière [pɔrtjɛr] *nom féminin*

door : **tu as mal fermé la portière** you haven't shut the door properly.

portillon [pɔrtijɔ̃] *nom masculin*

barrier : **ils ont sauté par-dessus le portillon du métro** they jumped over the ticket barrier in the metro.

portion [pɔrsjɔ̃] *nom féminin*

portion : **ils servent de grosses portions dans ce restaurant** they serve big portions at that restaurant.

portrait [pɔrtrɛ] *nom masculin*

portrait : **Rembrandt a fait le portrait de nombreuses femmes** Rembrandt painted a lot of portraits of women

➤ **c'est tout le portrait de sa mère** he's the spitting image of his mother.

portugais, e [pɔrtygɛ, ɛz] *adjectif*

Portuguese : **Fernando Pessoa est un poète portugais** Fernando Pessoa is a Portuguese poet

portugais *nom masculin*

Portuguese : **Béa apprend le portugais** Béa is learning Portuguese

> En anglais, les adjectifs se rapportant à un pays ou une région, ainsi que le nom désignant la langue de ce pays ou de cette région, s'écrivent avec une majuscule.

Portugais, e *nom masculin, nom féminin*

Portuguese : **les Portugais** the Portuguese.

Portugal [pɔrtygal] *nom masculin*

➤ **le Portugal** Portugal

> En anglais, à de rares exceptions près, il n'y a pas d'article devant les noms de pays :

beaucoup de gens parlent français au Portugal a lot of people speak French in Portugal ; **Nazaré va toujours au Portugal en vacances** Nazaré always goes to Portugal on holiday.

poser [poze] *verbe*

1. **to put** : **j'ai posé mes livres sur la table** I put my books on the table
2. **to put down** : **pose ton livre et viens manger** put your book down and come and have dinner
3. **to put up** : **poser du papier peint** to put up wallpaper
4. **to lay** *UK*, **to fit** : **poser une moquette** to lay a carpet
5. **to pose** : **poser pour une photo** to pose for a photo
➤ **poser une question à quelqu'un** to ask somebody a question

se poser *verbe pronominal*

1. **to land** : **l'avion s'est posé sur l'aéroport de Chicago** the plane landed at Chicago airport ; **la pie s'est posée sur la branche** the magpie landed on the branch
2. **to come up** : **un nouveau problème se pose aujourd'hui** a new problem has come up today.

positif, ive [pozitif, iv] *adjectif*

positive : **une réponse positive** a positive answer : **soyons positifs !** let's be positive!

position [pozisjɔ̃] *nom féminin*

position : **l'équipe de l'école est en troisième position** the school team is in third position ou the school team is in third place ; **il change constamment de position** he keeps changing position.

posséder [pɔsede] *verbe*

1. to own : **il possède plusieurs maisons** he owns several houses
2. to have : **posséder des connaissances en informatique** to have a knowledge of computing.

possessif, ive [pɔsesif, iv] *adjectif*

possessive : **c'est quelqu'un de très possessif** she's a very possessive person ; **« son » est un adjectif possessif** "son" is a possessive adjective.

possibilité [pɔsibilite] *nom féminin*

1. possibility *(pluriel* possibilities*)* : **il y a plusieurs possibilités** there are several possibilities
2. opportunity *(pluriel* opportunities*)* : **cette bourse va lui donner la possibilité d'aller à l'université** this grant will give him the opportunity to go to university.

possible [pɔsibl] *adjectif*

possible : **je regrette, ce n'est pas possible** I'm sorry, it's not possible ; **dès que possible** as soon as possible ; **le plus d'élèves possible** as many pupils as possible

➤ **c'est pas possible !** *familier* I can't believe it!

➤ **faire tout son possible** to do one's very best ; **on fera tout notre possible pour t'aider** we'll do our very best to help you.

poste [pɔst] *nom*

■ *nom féminin*

1. mail, post *UK* : **j'ai envoyé les photos par la poste** I sent the photos by mail ou I sent the photos by post
2. post office : **je vais à la poste** I'm going to the post office

➤ **poste aérienne** airmail

■ *nom masculin*

1. job, post : **un poste d'ingénieur** an engineering job ou an engineering post.

2. set : **un poste de radio** a radio set ; **un poste de télé** a TV set
3. extension : **passez-moi le poste 316, s'il vous plaît** put me through to extension 316, please

➤ **le poste de police** the police station.

poster¹ [pɔstɛr] *nom masculin*

poster : **mettre un poster au mur** to put a poster on the wall.

poster² [pɔste] *verbe*

to post *UK*, to mail *US* : **j'ai oublié de poster la lettre** I forgot to post the letter.

postiche [pɔstiʃ] *adjectif*

false : **une barbe postiche** a false beard.

postier, ère [pɔstje, ɛr] *nom masculin, nom féminin*

post-office worker : **Marie est postière à Paris** Marie is a post-office worker in Paris.

pot [po] *nom masculin*

1. pot : **un pot de yaourt** a pot of yoghurt
2. jar : **un pot de confiture** a jar of jam
3. *familier* drink : **on va prendre un pot, tu viens ?** we're going to have a drink, are you coming?
4. *familier* drinks party *UK* : **les profs ont organisé un pot pour la retraite de M. Lambert** the teachers have organized a drinks party for Mr Lambert's retirement

➤ **le pot d'échappement** the exhaust pipe ou the exhaust

➤ **un pot de fleurs** a flowerpot.

potable [pɔtabl] *adjectif*

1. **eau potable** drinking water ; **cette eau n'est pas potable** this water isn't suitable for drinking
2. *familier* acceptable : **la rédaction de Matthieu est potable, sans plus** Matthieu's essay is just about acceptable, no more than that.

potage [pɔtaʒ] *nom masculin*

soup : **un potage aux légumes** vegetable soup.

pot-au-feu [pɔtofø] *nom masculin invariable*

beef stew.

poteau [pɔto] *(pluriel* poteaux*)* *nom masculin*

post : **les poteaux de but** the goalposts ; **un poteau de bois** a wooden post

➤ **un poteau indicateur** a signpost.

poterie [pɔtri] *nom féminin*

1. **pottery : Anna fait un stage de poterie** Anna is doing a pottery course
2. **piece of pottery : une ancienne poterie inca** a piece of ancient Inca pottery.

potiron [pɔtirɔ̃] *nom masculin*

pumpkin : de la soupe au potiron pumpkin soup.

poubelle [pubɛl] *nom féminin*

dustbin *UK*, **trashcan** *US* : **mettre quelque chose à la poubelle** to put something in the dustbin.

pouce [pus] *nom masculin*

1. **thumb : tu es trop grande pour sucer ton pouce** you're too old to suck your thumb
2. **inch** *(pluriel* **inches)** : **un écran de 14 pouces** a 14-inch screen.

poudre [pudr] *nom féminin*

powder : de la poudre à éternuer sneezing powder

➤ **en poudre** powdered : **du lait en poudre** powdered milk.

poulain [pulɛ̃] *nom masculin*

foal : la jument et son poulain the mare and her foal.

poule [pul] *nom féminin*

hen : ces poules pondent beaucoup d'œufs these hens lay a lot of eggs.

poulet [pulɛ] *nom masculin*

chicken : on a mangé du poulet rôti we ate roast chicken.

pouls [pu] *nom masculin*

pulse : le médecin m'a pris le pouls the doctor took my pulse.

poumon [pumɔ̃] *nom masculin*

lung.

poupée [pupe] *nom féminin*

doll : ma petite sœur adore jouer à la poupée my little sister loves playing with dolls.

pour [pur] *préposition & adverbe*

■ *préposition*

1. **for : tiens, c'est pour toi** here, this is for you ; **un billet pour Rouen, s'il vous plaît** a ticket for Rouen, please ; **Roland a été puni pour avoir triché** Roland was punished for cheating

2. **to : je suis venu pour vous voir** I've come to see you
3. **so as : j'ai fait ça pour ne pas les déranger** I did that so as not to disturb them

■ *adverbe*

in favour *UK*, **in favor** *US* : **qui est pour ?** who's in favour?

➤ **pour moi** as far as I'm concerned : **pour moi, il n'y a pas de problème** as far as I'm concerned, there's no problem

➤ **pour que** so that : **ils se sacrifient pour que leurs enfants puissent faire des études** they make sacrifices so that their children can study.

pourboire [purbwar] *nom masculin*

tip : trois euros de pourboire a three-euro tip

POURBOIRE

In France, you don't have to leave a tip (**pourboire**) in a café or a restaurant. A certain percentage of the bill is automatically set aside to pay for table service. However, if you like, you can leave an extra tip. In this case it is always left in cash.

pourquoi [purkwa] *adverbe*

why : pourquoi est-ce qu'elle est triste ? why is she sad? ; **pourquoi tu ne veux pas venir ?** why don't you want to come? ; **je ne comprends pas pourquoi** I don't understand why ; **pourquoi pas ?** why not?

➤ **c'est pourquoi ...** that's why ...

pourri, e [puri] *adjectif*

rotten : cette pomme est pourrie this apple is rotten ; **il a fait un temps pourri** *familier* the weather was awful ou the weather was rotten.

pourrir [purir] *verbe*

to rot, to go rotten : le bois a pourri très vite the wood rotted very quickly ; **les fruits ont pourri dans le placard** the fruit has got rotten in the cupboard.

poursuite [pursɥit] *nom féminin*

chase : une poursuite en voiture a car chase

➤ **se lancer à la poursuite de quelqu'un** to chase after somebody ou to start chasing somebody.

poursuivi, e [pursɥivi] *participe passé de* poursuivre.

poursuivre [pursɥivr] *verbe*

1. **to chase : la police a poursuivi les voleurs** the police chased the thieves
2. **to carry on with : le prof a poursuivi son cours comme si rien ne s'était passé** the teacher carried on with his class as if nothing had happened
3. **to prosecute : ils sont poursuivis pour fraude** they're being prosecuted for fraud
4. **to sue : leur voisine les a poursuivis parce que le chien l'a mordue** their neighbour sued them because the dog bit her.

pourtant [purtɑ̃] *adverbe*

yet : et pourtant il avait dit qu'il le ferait and yet he said that he would do it.

pourvu que [purvy] *conjonction*

1. **provided : mes parents me laissent sortir pourvu que je rentre avant minuit** my parents let me go out provided I come back before midnight
2. **let's hope that : pourvu qu'ils n'aient pas de problèmes !** let's hope that they don't have any problems!

pousser [puse] *verbe*

1. **to push : Éric l'a poussé et il est tombé** Éric pushed him and he fell over ; **vas-y, pousse !** go on, push!
2. **to give : Aurélie a poussé un gros soupir** Aurélie gave a big sigh
3. **to grow : cette plante pousse vite** this plant is growing quickly ; **tu te laisses pousser les cheveux ?** are you letting your hair grow? OU are you growing your hair?

➤ **pousser quelqu'un à faire quelque chose** to urge somebody to do something : **ses parents le poussent à faire des études** his parents are urging him to go to university

se pousser *verbe pronominal*

to move over : pousse-toi, je veux m'asseoir là move over, I want to sit there.

poussette [puset] *nom féminin*

pushchair *UK*, **stroller** *US*.

poussière [pusjɛr] *nom féminin*

dust : il y a de la poussière partout there's dust everywhere

➤ **faire la poussière** to dust OU to do the dusting

➤ **et des poussières** *familier* and a bit : **cin-**

quante euros et des poussières fifty euros and a bit.

poussiéreux, euse [pusjerø, øz] *adjectif*

dusty : des meubles poussiéreux dusty furniture.

poussin [pusɛ̃] *nom masculin*

chick : la poule et ses poussins the hen and her chicks.

poutre [putr] *nom féminin*

beam : des poutres en bois wooden beams.

pouvoir [puvwar] *nom & verbe*

■ *nom masculin*

power : la sorcière a des pouvoirs magiques the witch has magical powers ; **qui est au pouvoir dans ce pays ?** who is in power in this country?

■ *verbe*

1. *Pour exprimer la possibilité de faire quelque chose* **can, to be able to : tu peux m'aider ?** can you help me? ; **finalement elle a pu y aller** in the end she was able to go ; **pourriez-vous me dire l'heure, s'il vous plaît ?** could you give me the time, please? ; **tu aurais pu me le dire !** you could have told me! ; **je te donnerai son numéro pour que tu puisses l'appeler** I'll give you his number so that you can call him

> Can n'a que deux formes : can et could. Could peut être le passé ou le conditionnel. On forme les autres temps à partir de l'expression to be able to.

2. *Pour exprimer la permission de faire quelque chose* **can, may : je peux prendre la voiture ?** can I take the car OU may I take the car?

> May et can ont tous deux la même signification dans ce contexte, mais may appartient à la langue plus soutenue.

3. *Au conditionnel, pour exprimer l'éventualité* **might, could : attention, vous pourriez rater votre train** be careful, you might miss your train OU be careful, you could miss your train

se pouvoir *verbe pronominal impersonnel*

➤ **ça se peut** OU **ça se pourrait** that's quite possible

➤ **il se peut qu'ils arrivent aujourd'hui** they may arrive today OU maybe they'll arrive today.

prairie [preri] *nom féminin*

meadow.

pratique [pratik] *nom & adjectif*

■ *nom féminin*

practice : **tu manques de pratique** you don't get enough practice ; **mettre ses idées en pratique** to put one's ideas into practice

■ *adjectif*

practical : **ce sac est très pratique** this bag is very practical.

pratiquement [pratikmã] *adverbe*

practically : **il n'y a pratiquement pas eu de neige** there has been practically no snow OU there has been hardly any snow.

pratiquer [pratike] *verbe*

I. to do : **est-ce que tu pratiques un sport ?** do you do a sport?

2. to practise *UK*, to practice *US* : **elle voudrait pratiquer son anglais** she'd like to practise her English.

pré [pre] *nom masculin*

meadow.

préau [preo] (*pluriel* **préaux**) *nom masculin*

covered play area : **quand il pleut, on reste dans le préau** when it rains we stay in the covered play area.

précaution [prekosjõ] *nom féminin*

precaution : **prendre des précautions** to take precautions.

précédent, e [presedã, ãt] *adjectif*

previous : **l'année précédente** the previous year.

précéder [presede] *verbe*

I. to precede, to come before : **le roi qui a précédé Charlemagne** the king that preceded Charlemagne OU the king that came before Charlemagne

2. to precede, to go ahead of : **le guide nous a précédés dans la cathédrale** the guide preceded us into the cathedral OU the guide went ahead of us into the cathedral

précieux, euse [presjø, øz] *adjectif*

precious : **des antiquités précieuses** precious antiques.

se précipiter [səpresipite] *verbe pronominal*

I. to throw oneself : **il s'est précipité dans le vide** he threw himself into space

2. to rush : **ils se sont précipités vers moi pour m'embrasser** they rushed towards me to kiss me.

précis, e [presi, iz] *adjectif*

I. precise : **ta description n'est pas très précise** your description isn't very precise

2. specific : **il a fait ça pour une raison précise ?** did he do that for a specific reason?

précisément [presizemã] *adverbe*

precisely : **c'est précisément ce dont on parlait** that's precisely what we were talking about.

préciser [presize] *verbe*

I. to specify : **Benoît n'a pas précisé l'heure** Benoît didn't specify a time

2. to make clearer : **pourriez-vous préciser votre argument ?** could you make your argument clearer?

se préciser *verbe pronominal*

to become clearer : **les choses se précisent enfin** things are becoming clearer at last.

précision [presizjõ] *nom féminin*

I. precision : **décrire quelque chose avec précision** to describe something precisely OU to describe something exactly

2. detail : **tu pourrais nous donner des précisions ?** could you give us some details?

prédire [predir] *verbe*

to predict : **la voyante m'a prédit que j'aurais beaucoup d'enfants** the clairvoyant predicted that I would have a lot of children.

prédit, e [predi, it] *participe passé de* **prédire**.

préface [prefas] *nom féminin*

preface, foreword : **la préface de son dernier roman** the preface to his latest novel.

préféré, e [prefere] *adjectif & nom masculin, nom féminin*

favourite *UK*, favorite *US* : **quelle est ta matière préférée ?** what's your favourite subject? ; **elle a ses préférés** she has her favourites.

préférence [preferɑ̃s] *nom féminin*

preference : **je n'ai pas de préférence** I have no particular preference
➤ **de préférence** preferably : **nous viendrions de préférence samedi** we would come on Saturday preferably.

préférer [prefere] *verbe*

to prefer : **je préfère le thé au café** I prefer tea to coffee
➤ **je préfère rentrer** I'd rather go home ; **je préfèrerais que tu viennes** I'd rather you came.

préhistorique [preistɔrik] *adjectif*

prehistoric : **des animaux préhistoriques** prehistoric animals.

préjugé [preʒyʒe] *nom masculin*

prejudice : **avoir des préjugés** to be prejudiced.

premier, ère [prəmje, ɛr] *adjectif & nom*

■ *adjectif*
first : **c'est la première fois que je la vois** it's the first time I've ever seen her ; **prenez la première rue à droite** take the first street on the right
■ *nom masculin, nom féminin*
1. first one : **je préfère la première, celle qui est bleue** I prefer the first one, the blue one
2. first : **Loïc a terminé premier** Loïc finished first
➤ **le premier de l'An** New Year's Day
➤ **en premier** first : **qu'est-ce qu'on va faire en premier ?** what shall we do first?

première *nom féminin*

1. year twelve *UK*, eleventh grade *US* : **ma grande sœur est en première** my older sister is in year twelve
2. first class : **ils préfèrent voyager en première** they prefer to travel first class
3. first gear : **on a dû monter la côte en première** we had to go up the hill in first gear.

premièrement [prəmjɛrmɑ̃] *adverbe*

first, firstly.

prendre [prɑ̃dr] *verbe*

1. to take : **prends ça, c'est pour toi** take this, it's for you ; **il doit prendre des médicaments** he has to take some medicine ; **prendre l'avion** to take the plane ; **prenez la première à gauche** take the first street on the

left ; **ça nous a pris des heures** it took us hours
2. to get : **prends du pain en rentrant** get some bread on your way home
3. to have : **prends un peu de gâteau** have some cake ; **vous prendrez quelque chose à boire ?** will you have something to drink? ; **prendre une douche** to have a shower ; **prendre son petit déjeuner** to have breakfast
➤ **prendre quelqu'un pour** to mistake somebody for : **il m'a prise pour ma sœur** he mistook me for my sister
➤ **qu'est-ce qui te prend ?** what's wrong with you?
➤ **se faire prendre** to get caught : **Marie s'est fait prendre à fouiller dans les tiroirs** Marie got caught going through the drawers

se prendre *verbe pronominal*

pour qui il se prend ? who does he think he is? ; **elle se prend pour une top model** she thinks she's a top model.

prénom [prenɔ̃] *nom masculin*

first name : **quel est son prénom ?** what is his first name?

préoccuper [preɔkype] *verbe*

to worry : **l'examen le préoccupe beaucoup** he's very worried about the exam

se préoccuper de *verbe pronominal*

to care about : **Simon ne se préoccupe pas des autres** Simon doesn't care about other people.

préparer [prepare] *verbe*

1. to prepare : **Fanny a préparé son exposé très soigneusement** Fanny prepared her talk very carefully
2. to make : **je vais te préparer du café** I'll make you some coffee ; **elle prépare le dîner** she's making dinner ou she's getting dinner ready

se préparer *verbe pronominal*

1. to get ready : **elle met toujours des heures à se préparer** she always takes hours to get ready ; **on se préparait à partir quand il est arrivé** we were just getting ready to leave when he arrived
2. to prepare : **tu t'es préparé pour l'interro ?** have you prepared for the test?

près [prɛ] *adverbe*

nearby : **j'habite tout près** I live very nearby

➤ **près de**

1. **near** OU **close to : l'école est près du stade** the school is near the stadium OU the school is close to the stadium

2. **close to : mon anniversaire est près de Noël** my birthday is close to Christmas

3. **nearly** OU **almost : il y a près de cent ans** nearly a hundred years ago OU almost a hundred years ago

➤ **à peu près** about OU around : **il est à peu près cinq heures** it's about five o'clock OU it's around five o'clock

➤ **de près**

1. **closely : regarder quelque chose de près** to watch something closely

2. **close up : je n'y vois pas bien de près** I can't see very well close up.

prescrire [prɛskrir] *verbe*

to prescribe : **le médecin m'a prescrit des antibiotiques** the doctor prescribed some antibiotics for me.

présence [prezɑ̃s] *nom féminin*

presence : **en ma présence** in my presence.

présent, e [prezɑ̃, ɑ̃t] *adjectif*

present : **les élèves présents au cours** the pupils present at the lesson ; **la situation présente** the present situation

présent *nom masculin*

1. **present : tu dois penser au présent, pas au passé** you must think of the present, not of the past

2. **present tense : mettez le verbe au présent** put the verb in the present tense

➤ **à présent** now : **tu peux rentrer à présent** you can come in now ; **jusqu'à présent** until now.

présentateur, trice [prezɑ̃tatœr, tris] *nom masculin, nom féminin*

presenter *UK* : **Noémie veut devenir présentatrice de télévision** Noémie wants to be a TV presenter.

présentation [prezɑ̃tasjɔ̃] *nom féminin*

presentation : **le prof donne aussi une note pour la présentation** the teacher also gives a mark for presentation

➤ **faire les présentations** to do the introductions : **venez, je vais faire les présentations** come along, I'll do the introductions.

présenter [prezɑ̃te] *verbe*

1. **to introduce : je vais te présenter ma sœur** I'll introduce you to my sister

2. **to present : Camille doit présenter son exposé devant toute la classe** Camille has to present her project in front of the whole class

3. **to offer : il nous a présenté ses excuses** he offered us his apologies

➤ **je vous présente mon ami Raoul** this is my friend Raoul

➤ **présenter sa démission** to hand in one's resignation

se présenter *verbe pronominal*

1. **to introduce oneself : je me présente, je m'appelle Rachel** let me introduce myself, my name is Rachel

2. **to come up, to arise : si l'occasion se présente** if the opportunity comes up

➤ **se présenter aux élections** to stand for election *UK* OU to run in the election *US*

➤ **ça se présente bien** things are looking good.

préservatif [prezɛrvatif] *nom masculin*

condom.

président, e [prezidɑ̃, ɑ̃t] *nom masculin, nom féminin*

1. **president : le président de la République** the President of the Republic

2. **chairman** *(féminin* **chairwoman***)* **: le président du club de foot** the chairman of the football club.

présider [prezide] *verbe*

to chair : **présider une réunion** to chair a meeting.

presque [prɛsk] *adverbe*

1. **almost, nearly : Hakim a presque quinze ans** Hakim is almost fifteen OU Hakim is nearly fifteen

2. **hardly : on n'a presque pas travaillé aujourd'hui** we hardly did any work today.

presse [prɛs] *nom féminin*

press : **la presse nationale** the national press

➤ **la presse à sensation** the tabloids.

pressé, e [prese] *adjectif*

in a hurry : **je dois y aller, je suis pressé** I must go, I'm in a hurry.

presser [prese] *verbe*

1. **to squeeze** : **une orange pressée** a freshly squeezed orange juice.
2. **to press** : **presse le bouton vert** press the green button

se presser *verbe pronominal*

to hurry : **il ne se presse jamais pour aller à l'école** he never hurries to school.

pressing [presiŋ] *nom masculin*

dry cleaner's : **ton pantalon est au pressing** your trousers are at the dry cleaner's.

pression [presjɔ̃] *nom féminin*

1. **pressure** : **la pression atmosphérique** atmospheric pressure ; **faire pression sur quelqu'un** to put pressure on somebody
2. **press stud** *UK*, **snap fastener** *US* : **ce gilet se ferme avec des pressions** this cardigan fastens with press studs
3. **glass of beer** : **une pression et un café, s'il vous plaît** a glass of beer and a coffee, please.

prestidigitateur, trice [prɛstidiʒitatœr, tris] *nom masculin, nom féminin*
conjurer.

présumer [prezyme] *verbe*

to presume : **je présume que tu as l'intention de venir ?** I presume you intend to come?

prêt, e [prɛ, prɛt] *adjectif*

ready : **tu es prêt ?** are you ready? ; **ils sont prêts à nous aider** they're ready to help us
> **prêts ? partez !** ready, steady, go!

prêt *nom masculin*

loan : **la banque leur a accordé un prêt** the bank gave them a loan.

prétendre [pretɑ̃dr] *verbe*

to claim : **Chloé prétend que Stéphane lui a demandé de sortir avec lui** Chloé claims that Stéphane asked her to go out with him

⚠ Prétendre is a false friend, it does not mean 'pretend'.

prétendu, e [pretɑ̃dy] *participe passé de* **prétendre**.

prétentieux, euse [pretɑ̃sjø, øz] *adjectif & nom*

■ *adjectif*
pretentious : **il est vraiment prétentieux** he's really pretentious
■ *nom masculin, nom féminin*
poser : **quelle prétentieuse !** what a poser!

prêter [prete] *verbe*

to lend : **prêter quelque chose à quelqu'un** to lend somebody something ; **tu peux me prêter deux euros ?** can you lend me two euros?

prétexte [pretɛkst] *nom masculin*

excuse : **ça c'est un prétexte pour ne pas t'aider** that's an excuse for not helping you
> **sous aucun prétexte** on no account.

prêtre [prɛtr] *nom masculin*

priest : **il est prêtre** he's a priest.

preuve [prœv] *nom féminin*

1. **proof** (*ne s'utilise jamais au pluriel*) : **c'est la preuve qu'il ne l'a pas fait exprès** this is proof that he didn't do it on purpose
2. **evidence** (*ne s'utilise jamais au pluriel*) : **la police a besoin de preuves** the police need evidence
> **faire preuve de quelque chose** to show something : **Mathias a fait preuve de courage** Mathias showed courage.

prévenir [prevnir] *verbe*

1. **to warn** : **je te préviens, ne refais jamais ça !** I'm warning you, don't ever do that again!
2. **to let know** : **préviens-moi quand tu auras terminé** let me know when you've finished
3. **to call** : **on devrait prévenir la police** we should call the police.

prévenu, e [prevny] *participe passé de* **prévenir**.

prévision [previzjɔ̃] *nom féminin*

forecast : **les prévisions météorologiques** the weather forecast.

prévoir [prevwar]

1. **to anticipate** : **nous n'avions pas prévu ça** we hadn't anticipated that
2. **to predict** : **les experts prévoient une augmentation de la température** experts predict a rise in temperatures
3. **to plan** : **je prévois une grande fête pour mon anniversaire** I'm planning a big party for my birthday ; **comme prévu** as planned
4. **to allow** : **prévoyez vingt euros par personne** allow twenty euros per person.

prévu, e [prevy] *participe passé de* prévoir.

prier [prije] *verbe*

1. to pray : **Lucas est entré dans l'église pour prier** Lucas went into the church to pray
2. to request : **vous êtes priés de ne pas fumer** you are requested not to smoke
➤ **je te prie** OU **je vous prie** please : **je te prie de me pardonner** please forgive me
➤ **je t'en prie** OU **je vous en prie** : **je peux m'asseoir ici ? – je vous en prie** can I sit here? – please do ; **merci – je vous en prie** thank you – don't mention it.

prière [prijɛr] *nom féminin*

prayer : **Quentin fait ses prières tous les soirs** Quentin says his prayers every night
➤ **prière de ...** please ... : **prière de frapper avant d'entrer** please knock before entering.

primaire [primɛr] *adjectif & nom*

◼ *adjectif*
primary : **les couleurs primaires** the primary colours *UK* OU the primary colors *US* ; **l'enseignement primaire** primary education
◼ *nom masculin*
primary school *UK*, grade school *US*, elementary school *US* : **mon petit frère est encore en primaire** my little brother is still at primary school.

prime [prim] *nom féminin*

1. bonus *(pluriel* bonuses*)* : **les employés reçoivent une prime à Noël** employees get a bonus at Christmas
2. allowance : **il y a une prime de transport en plus du salaire** there's a transport allowance in addition to the salary.

prince [prɛ̃s] *nom masculin*

prince : **le Prince Charmant** Prince Charming.

princesse [prɛ̃sɛs] *nom féminin*

princess *(pluriel* princesses*)* : **la princesse Anne** Princess Anne.

principal, e, aux [prɛ̃sipal, o] *adjectif*

main : **les principales villes de la région** the main cities in the region

principal *nom masculin*

headteacher *UK*, principal *US* : **comment s'appelle le principal de votre collège ?** what's the name of your headteacher?
➤ **le principal** the main thing : **le principal,** **c'est que tu sois là** the main thing is that you're here.

principalement [prɛ̃sipalmɑ̃] *adverbe*

mainly.

principe [prɛ̃sip] *nom masculin*

principle : **cet appareil fonctionne selon un principe très simple** this device works according to a very simple principle
➤ **en principe**
1. all being well : **en principe, on devrait arriver vers vingt heures** all being well, we should arrive around eight o'clock
2. as a rule : **en principe, il se réveille tôt** as a rule he gets up early
➤ **par principe** on principle : **j'ai refusé par principe** I refused on principle.

printemps [prɛ̃tɑ̃] *nom masculin*

spring : **au printemps** in spring OU in the spring.

priorité [prijɔrite] *nom féminin*

1. priority *(pluriel* priorities*)* : **pour lui c'est une priorité absolue** for him it's an absolute priority
2. right of way : **sur cette route tu as la priorité** on this road you have the right of way ; **il y a priorité à droite** you must give way to traffic coming from the right.

pris, e [pri, priz] *verbe & adjectif*

◼ *participe passé de* prendre
tu as pris ton maillot de bain ? have you taken your swimming trunks?
◼ *adjectif*
1. taken : **désolée, cette place est prise** sorry, this seat is taken
2. busy : **si tu n'es pas pris mardi** if you're not busy on Tuesday

prise *nom féminin*

➤ **prise de courant** OU **prise**
1. plug : **la prise de l'ordinateur** the plug of the computer
2. socket : **il y a plusieurs prises au mur** there are several sockets on the wall
➤ **une prise de sang** a blood test : **on m'a fait une prise de sang** I had a blood test.

prison [prizɔ̃] *nom féminin*

prison, jail : **son frère est en prison** her brother is in prison OU her brother is in jail ; **elle a été condamnée à dix ans de prison** she was sentenced to ten years in prison OU she was sentenced to ten years in jail ; **il a fait de la prison** he has been to prison.

prisonnier, ère [prizɔnje, ɛr] *nom masculin, nom féminin*

prisoner : **plusieurs prisonniers se sont échappés** several prisoners escaped ; **faire prisonnier quelqu'un** to take somebody prisoner.

privé, e [prive] *adjectif*

private : **une plage privée** a private beach
➤ **en privé** in private.

priver [prive] *verbe*

mes parents m'ont privé de télé my parents made me go without TV

se priver *verbe pronominal*

to make sacrifices : **ils se privent toute l'année pour pouvoir partir en vacances** they make sacrifices all year long to be able to go on holiday.

privilégié, e [privileʒje] *adjectif*

privileged : **nous sommes privilégiés par rapport à d'autres** we are privileged compared to others.

prix [pri] *nom masculin*

1. price : **le prix de l'essence a encore augmenté** the price of petrol has gone up again
2. prize : **Esther a gagné le premier prix** Esther won the first prize OU Esther won first prize ; **le prix Nobel de littérature** the Nobel Prize for literature
➤ **à tout prix** at all cost : **tu dois à tout prix réussir** you must succeed at all cost
➤ **hors de prix** ridiculously expensive.

probable [prɔbabl] *adjectif*

likely : **il est probable qu'il pleuvra** it's likely to rain OU it will probably rain.

probablement [prɔbabləmɑ̃] *adverbe*

probably : **j'irai probablement** I'll probably go.

problème [prɔblɛm] *nom masculin*

problem : **Antoine a beaucoup de problèmes** Antoine has a lot of problems ; **un problème de maths** a maths problem *UK* OU a math problem *US* ; **d'accord, pas de problème !** OK, no problem!

procès [prɔsɛ] *nom masculin*

trial : **le procès des kidnappeurs commen-** ce demain the kidnappers' trial starts tomorrow
➤ **intenter un procès à quelqu'un** to sue somebody.

prochain, e [prɔʃɛ̃, ɛn] *adjectif*

next : **je descends à la prochaine station** I'm getting off at the next stop ; **l'été prochain** next summer
➤ **à la prochaine !** *familier* see you!

proche [prɔʃ] *adjectif*

1. near : **où est l'arrêt de bus le plus proche ?** where is the nearest bus stop? ; **la bibliothèque est proche de l'école** the library is near the school
2. close : **ce sont des amis proches** they are close friends.

procurer [prɔkyre] *verbe*

procurer quelque chose à quelqu'un to get something for somebody ; **je peux te procurer des places de cinéma** I can get cinema tickets for you

se procurer *verbe pronominal*

to get : **comment est-ce que tu t'es procuré ce livre ?** how did you get this book?

producteur, trice [prɔdyktœr, tris] *nom masculin, nom féminin*

producer : **les producteurs de céréales** grain producers.

production [prɔdyksjɔ̃] *nom féminin*

production : **l'usine va augmenter sa production** the factory is going to increase its production.

produire [prɔdɥir] *verbe*

to produce : **cette entreprise produit des composants électroniques** this factory produces electronic components

se produire *verbe pronominal*

1. to take place : **des événements étranges se sont produits dans cette région** some strange events have taken place in this region
2. to appear : **le groupe se produira à Toulouse samedi** the band will appear in Toulouse on Saturday.

produit, e [prɔdɥi, ɥit] *participe passé de* produire

produit *nom masculin*

product : **les produits de beauté** beauty products

p

➤ **les produits agricoles** agricultural produce
➤ **des produits chimiques** chemicals.

prof [prɔfɛsœr] *(abréviation de* professeur*)* *nom masculin ou féminin familier*
teacher : **la prof de français** the French teacher ; **je voudrais être prof** I would like to be a teacher.

professeur [prɔfɛsœr] *nom masculin*
teacher : **le professeur d'anglais** the English teacher ; **Isabelle fait des études pour être professeur** Isabelle is studying to be a teacher
➤ **un professeur des écoles** a primary-school teacher *UK* ou a grade-school teacher *US*
➤ **un professeur d'université** a university professor.

profession [prɔfɛsjɔ̃] *nom féminin*
profession : **quelle est votre profession ?** what is your profession?
➤ **sans profession** unemployed.

professionnel, elle [prɔfɛsjɔnɛl] *adjectif & nom*
■ *adjectif*
1. professional : **un photographe professionnel** a professional photographer
2. vocational : **l'enseignement professionnel** vocational education ; **un lycée professionnel** a vocational school
■ *nom masculin, nom féminin*
professional : **c'est du travail de professionnel** it's the work of a professional.

profil [prɔfil] *nom masculin*
profile : **Carmen a un joli profil** Carmen has a nice profile ; **je vais te peindre de profil** I'm going to paint you in profile.

profit [prɔfi] *nom masculin*
profit : **l'entreprise a fait de gros profits** the company has made large profits ou the company has made a big profit
➤ **tirer profit de** to benefit from : **Jacob a bien tiré profit de son année en Angleterre** Jacob has benefited a lot from his year in England.

profiter [prɔfite]
➤ **profiter de**
1. to enjoy : **profite bien de tes vacances !** enjoy your holiday!

2. to take advantage of : **tu ne vois pas qu'il profite de toi ?** don't you see that he's taking advantage of you? ; **ils ont profité de la situation** they took advantage of the situation
➤ **profiter de l'occasion pour faire quelque chose** to take the opportunity to do something : **on a profité de l'occasion pour passer une journée à la plage** we took the opportunity to spend a day on the beach
➤ **en profiter** to make the most of it : **profites-en !** make the most of it!

profond, e [prɔfɔ̃, ɔ̃d] *adjectif*
deep : **le trou est assez profond** the hole is quite deep
➤ **peu profond** shallow : **l'eau est peu profonde** the water is shallow.

profondément [prɔfɔ̃demã] *adverbe*
deeply : **respirer profondément** to breathe deeply
➤ **dormir profondément** to be fast asleep.

profondeur [prɔfɔ̃dœr] *nom féminin*
depth : **mesure d'abord la profondeur** measure the depth first ; **quelle est la profondeur du trou ?** how deep is the hole? ; **un puits de trois mètres de profondeur** a well three-metres deep
➤ **en profondeur** in depth.

programme [prɔgram] *nom masculin*
1. programme *UK*, program *US* : **le programme du festival est intéressant** the festival programme is interesting ; **les programmes valent sept euros** the programmes cost seven euros
2. syllabus *(pluriel* syllabuses*)* : **le programme scolaire** the school syllabus
3. schedule : **j'ai un programme chargé aujourd'hui** I have a busy schedule today
4. program : **un programme de traitement de texte** a word-processing program
➤ **le programme de télévision** the TV guide.

programmer [prɔgrame] *verbe*
1. to plan : **qu'est-ce que tu as programmé pour ce soir ?** what have you got planned for this evening?
2. to set : **tu sais comment programmer le magnétoscope ?** do you know how to set the video?
3. to program : **programmer un ordinateur** to program a computer.

progrès [prɔgrɛ] *nom masculin*

progress (*ne s'utilise jamais au pluriel*) **: faire des progrès** to make progress ; **être en progrès** to be making progress.

progresser [prɔgrese] *verbe*

1. **to make progress : Sylvie a bien progressé en anglais ce trimestre** Sylvie has made good progress in English this term ; **l'enquête progresse** the investigation is making progress
2. **to spread : l'épidémie progresse rapidement** the epidemic is spreading rapidly.

proie [prwa] *nom féminin*

prey : le lion a partagé sa proie avec ses petits the lion shared its prey with its cubs ; **un oiseau de proie** a bird of prey.

projecteur [prɔʒɛktœr] *nom masculin*

1. **spotlight : les projecteurs du théâtre** the theatre spotlights
2. **projector : un projecteur de diapositives** a slide projector.

projet [prɔʒɛ] *nom masculin*

1. **plan : vous avez des projets pour les vacances ?** do you have any plans for the holidays?
2. **project : un projet de réaménagement du quartier** a project to redevelop the area.

projeter [prɔʒte] *verbe*

1. **to show : le prof nous a projeté des diapositives** the teacher showed us some slides
2. **to plan : nous projetons un voyage en Sicile** we're planning a trip to Sicily.

prolongations [prɔlɔ̃gasjɔ̃] *nom féminin pluriel*

extra time *UK*, **overtime** *US* **: il a fallu jouer les prolongations** they had to go into extra time.

prolonger [prɔlɔ̃ʒe] *verbe*

to extend : j'aurais aimé prolonger mes vacances I would have liked to extend my holidays ; **la réunion a été prolongée d'une demi-heure** the meeting was extended by half an hour ; **ils vont prolonger la route de plusieurs kilomètres** they're going to extend the road by several kilometres

se prolonger *verbe pronominal*

to go on : la soirée s'est prolongée jusqu'à trois heures du matin the party went on until three in the morning.

promenade [prɔmnad] *nom féminin*

1. **walk : faire une promenade** to go for a walk ; **on va faire une promenade en forêt ?** shall we go for a walk in the forest?
2. **promenade : la promenade longe le front de mer** the promenade runs along the seafront
➤ **une promenade à vélo** a bike ride **: on va faire une promenade à vélo** we're going for a bike ride
➤ **une promenade en voiture** a drive **: ils sont allés faire une promenade en voiture** they went for a drive.

promener [prɔmne] *verbe*

to take for a walk : je vais promener le chien I'm going to take the dog for a walk

se promener *verbe pronominal*

to go for a walk : on pourrait se promener le long du canal we could go for a walk along the canal
➤ **se promener à vélo** to go for a bike ride
➤ **se promener en voiture** to go for a drive.

promesse [prɔmɛs] *nom féminin*

promise : tu n'as pas tenu ta promesse you didn't keep your promise.

promettre [prɔmɛtr] *verbe*

to promise : mes parents m'ont promis une console de jeux pour Noël my parents have promised me a games console for Christmas ; **tu promets de ne pas recommencer ?** do you promise not to do it again? ; **je te promets que je vais faire un effort** I promise you that I'll make an effort.

promis, e [prɔmi, iz] *participe passé de* **promettre.**

promotion [prɔmɔsjɔ̃] *nom féminin*

1. **promotion : il a fait une soirée pour fêter sa promotion** he had a party to celebrate his promotion
2. **special offer : il y a plein de promotions au supermarché** there are lots of special offers at the supermarket ; **en promotion** on special offer.

prononcer [prɔnɔ̃se] *verbe*

to pronounce : je n'arrive pas à prononcer ce mot I can't pronounce this word

se prononcer *verbe pronominal*

1. **to be pronounced : comment ça se prononce ?** how is it pronounced?

p

2. to give one's opinion : **Lucas a refusé de se prononcer** Lucas refused to give his opinion.

prononciation [prɔnɔ̃sjasjɔ̃] *nom féminin*

pronunciation : **Aurélie a une bonne prononciation en anglais** Aurélie's English pronunciation is good.

pronostic [prɔnɔstik] *nom masculin*

forecast : **tu as écouté les pronostics du tiercé ?** did you hear the horseracing forecast?

propice [prɔpis] *adjectif*

right, suitable : **attendre le moment propice** to wait for the right moment.

propos [prɔpo] *nom masculin pluriel*

tenir des propos racistes to say racist things

➤ **à propos** by the way : **à propos, tu as revu Camille ?** by the way, have you seen Camille again?

➤ **c'est à quel propos ?** what is it about?

➤ **à propos de** about : **je vous appelle à propos de l'annonce** I'm phoning about the ad ; **à propos de devoirs, tu as fini ta rédaction ?** talking about homework, have you finished your essay?

proposer [prɔpoze] *verbe*

1. to offer : **Baptiste m'a proposé son vélo pour aller à l'école** Baptiste offered me his bike to go to school ; **ils ont proposé de nous aider** they offered to help us

2. to suggest : **je propose de faire les courses maintenant** I suggest we do the shopping now ; **je propose qu'on parte tout de suite** I suggest we leave at once ; **il a proposé de faire une promenade** he suggested going for a walk.

proposition [prɔpozisjɔ̃] *nom féminin*

1. offer : **ils lui ont fait une proposition intéressante mais il a refusé** they made him an attractive offer but he refused

2. suggestion : **ce n'est qu'une proposition** it's only a suggestion.

propre [prɔpr] *adjectif*

1. clean : **ce verre n'est pas très propre** this glass isn't very clean

2. own : **chacun doit apporter son propre repas** everybody must bring their own meal

➤ **recopier quelque chose au propre** to make a fair copy of something

⚠ **Propre** is a false friend, it does not mean 'proper'.

proprement [prɔprəmɑ̃] *adverbe*

➤ **mange proprement!** don't make such a mess when you're eating! ou eat properly!

➤ **proprement dit** actual : **l'école proprement dite** the actual school ou the school itself

➤ **à proprement parler** strictly speaking.

propreté [prɔprəte] *nom féminin*

cleanliness : **la maison est d'une propreté éclatante** the house is sparkling clean.

propriétaire [prɔprijetɛr] *nom masculin ou féminin*

1. owner : **qui est le propriétaire de cette voiture ?** who is the owner of this car?

2. landlord *(feminine* **landlady)** : **la propriétaire a encore augmenté le loyer** the landlady has increased the rent again.

propriété [prɔprijete] *nom féminin*

property *(pluriel* **properties)** : **c'est une propriété privée** it's private property : **ils ont une grande propriété à la campagne** they have a large property in the country.

prose [proz] *nom féminin*

prose : **un poème en prose** a poem in prose.

prospectus [prɔspɛktys] *nom masculin*

advertising leaflet : **il y a tout le temps des prospectus dans la boîte aux lettres** the letterbox is always full of advertising leaflets.

protection [prɔtɛksjɔ̃] *nom féminin*

protection : **la protection de l'environnement** protection of the environment.

protéger [prɔteʒe] *verbe*

to protect : **ça protège la peau contre les coups de soleil** it protects the skin against sunburn.

protestant, e [prɔtɛstɑ̃, ɑ̃t] *adjectif & nom masculin, nom féminin*

Protestant : **Thomas est protestant** Thomas is a Protestant : **les protestants** Protestants.

protester [prɔtɛste] *verbe*

to protest : **nous avons protesté contre la**

modification de l'emploi du temps we pro-
tested against the changes in the timetable.

prouver [pʀuve] *verbe*

to prove : **tu ne peux rien prouver** you can't
prove anything ; **ça prouve que c'est faisa-
ble** that proves that it can be done

Provence [pʀɔvɑ̃s] *nom féminin*

> **la Provence** Provence : **ils ont une villa en
Provence** they have a villa in Provence ; **nous
allons en Provence tous les étés** we go to
Provence every summer.

provenir [pʀɔvniʀ] *verbe*

> **provenir de**

1. to come from : **ces produits proviennent
d'Espagne** these products come from Spain
2. to be due to : **le problème provient d'un
malentendu** the problem is due to a misunderstanding.

proverbe [pʀɔvɛʀb] *nom masculin*

proverb.

province [pʀɔvɛ̃s] *nom féminin*

1. province : **une province canadienne** a
Canadian province
2. provinces (*pluriel*) : **ils habitent en province**
they live in the provinces.

proviseur [pʀɔvizœʀ] *nom masculin*

headteacher *UK*, principal *US*.

provision [pʀɔvizjɔ̃] *nom féminin*

stock : **on a toute une provision de bois** we
have a large stock of wood

provisions *nom féminin pluriel*

shopping : **on a mis les provisions dans le
coffre** we put the shopping in the boot ; **faire
des provisions** to do the shopping.

provisoire [pʀɔvizwaʀ] *adjectif*

temporary : **c'est une solution provisoire**
it's a temporary solution.

provoquer [pʀɔvɔke] *verbe*

1. to cause : **qu'est-ce qui a provoqué l'accident ?** what caused the accident?
2. to provoke : **si tu me provoques, je vais
me fâcher** if you provoke me, I'm going to get
angry.

prudence [pʀydɑ̃s] *nom féminin*

care, caution

> **avec prudence** carefully : **elle conduit**

avec beaucoup de prudence she drives very
carefully

> **prudence !** be careful! : **la piste est dange-
reuse, alors prudence !** the slope is dangerous, so be careful!

prudent, e [pʀydɑ̃, ɑ̃t] *adjectif*

careful : **sois prudent !** be careful!

prune [pʀyn] *nom féminin*

plum : **de la confiture de prunes** plum jam

 Prune is a false friend, it does not mean
'prune'.

pruneau [pʀyno] (*pluriel* **pruneaux**) *nom
masculin*

prune.

psychiatre [psikjatʀ] *nom masculin ou féminin*

psychiatrist : **Hervé voudrait être psychiatre** Hervé would like to be a psychiatrist.

psychologue [psikɔlɔg] *nom & adjectif*

◾ *nom masculin ou féminin*
psychologist : **le copain de Valérie est
psychologue** Valérie's boyfriend is a psychologist
◾ *adjectif*
perceptive : **tu n'es pas très psychologue !**
you're not very perceptive!

pu [py] *participe passé de* **pouvoir**.

puant, e [pɥɑ̃, ɑ̃t] *adjectif*

smelly : **un camembert puant** a smelly Camembert.

puanteur [pɥɑ̃tœʀ] *nom féminin*

stink : **quelle puanteur !** what a stink!

pub [pyb] *nom féminin familier*

1. ad : **tu as vu la pub pour cette voiture ?**
have you seen the ad for that car?
2. advertising : **ma mère travaille dans la
pub** my mother works in advertising

 The French word **pub** is a false friend, it
does not mean 'pub'.

public, ique [pyblik] *adjectif*

1. public : **dans un lieu public** in a public place
2. state *UK*, public *US* : **les écoles publiques**
state schools *UK* ou public schools *US*.

public *nom masculin*

audience : le public a beaucoup applaudi the audience clapped a lot
➤ **en public** in public.

publicitaire [pyblisitɛr] *adjectif*

advertising : une campagne publicitaire an advertising campaign.

publicité [pyblisite] *nom féminin*

1. advert *UK*, commercial : il y a une publicité très rigolote à la télé en ce moment there's a very funny advert on TV at the moment
2. advertising : il travaille dans la publicité he works in advertising.

publier [pyblije] *verbe*

to publish : quand ce livre a-t-il été publié ? when was this book published?

puce [pys] *nom féminin*

1. flea : le chien a des puces the dog has fleas
2. chip : une puce électronique an electronic chip
➤ **ma puce** sweetheart.

puer [pɥe] *verbe*

1. to stink : ça pue ici ! it stinks in here!
2. to stink of : ça pue le fromage it stinks of cheese.

puis [pɥi] *adverbe*

then : tournez à gauche puis à droite turn left then right
➤ **et puis**
1. and then : on a pique-niqué et puis on a fait la sieste we had a picnic and then we had a nap
2. and besides : c'est trop cher et puis je n'en ai pas vraiment besoin it's too expensive and besides I don't really need it.

puiser [pɥize] *verbe*

to draw : puiser de l'eau au puits to draw water from the well ; ils ont dû puiser dans leurs économies they had to draw on their savings.

puisque [pɥiskə] *conjonction*

since : puisqu'il reste deux jours, je n'ai pas besoin de me dépêcher since there are two days left, I don't need to hurry
➤ **puisque c'est comme ça** if that's the way it is : puisque c'est comme ça, fais-le tout seul ! if that's the way it is, do it on your own!

puissance [pɥisãs] *nom féminin*

power : la puissance du moteur the engine power ; les grandes puissances the major powers.

puissant, e [pɥisã, ãt] *adjectif*

powerful : il a une puissante musculature he has powerful muscles ; c'est une femme riche et puissante she's a rich and powerful woman.

puisse, puisses *etc* ➤ pouvoir.

puits [pɥi] *nom masculin*

well : allons chercher de l'eau au puits let's go and get some water from the well
➤ **un puits de pétrole** an oil well.

pull [pyl], **pull-over** [pylɔvɛr] (*pluriel* pull-overs) *nom masculin*

sweater, jumper *UK* : un pull en laine a wool sweater ou a woollen sweater.

pulpe [pylp] *nom féminin*

pulp : de la pulpe d'orange orange pulp.

pulvériser [pylverize] *verbe*

to spray : pulvériser de l'eau sur une plante to spray water on a plant.

punaise [pynɛz] *nom féminin*

drawing pin *UK*, thumbtack *US* : ils ont accroché le poster avec des punaises they put the poster up with drawing pins.

punir [pynir] *verbe*

to punish : le prof de géo a puni Roland the geography teacher punished Roland ; il s'est fait punir he was punished.

punition [pynisjõ] *nom féminin*

punishment : c'est une punition sévère it's a harsh punishment : la prof m'a donné une punition the teacher punished me.

pur, e [pyr] *adjectif*

1. pure : l'air est pur ici the air is pure here : pure laine vierge pure new wool
2. straight, neat : un whisky pur a straight whisky ou a neat whisky
➤ **pur et simple** pure and simple : c'est de l'ignorance pure et simple it's ignorance pure and simple.

purée [pyre] *nom féminin*

1. mashed potatoes (*pluriel*) : on a mangé de

la purée à midi we had mashed potatoes for lunch

2. **purée : de la purée de tomates** tomato purée
➤ **de la purée de pommes de terre** mashed potatoes (*s'utilise toujours au pluriel*)

puzzle [pœzl] *nom masculin*

jigsaw puzzle, jigsaw : on a passé l'après-midi à faire ce puzzle we spent the afternoon doing this jigsaw puzzle.

P-V [peve] *nom masculin (abréviation de* procès-verbal*)*

ticket : Alex a encore eu un P-V Alex got another ticket ; **elle m'a mis un P-V** she gave me a ticket.

pyjama [piʒama] *nom masculin*

pyjamas *UK*, **pajamas** *US* (*s'utilisent toujours au pluriel*) : **Caro est en pyjama** Caro is in her pyjamas ou Caro is wearing pyjamas.

pylône [pilon] *nom masculin*

pylon : un pylône électrique an electricity pylon.

pyramide [piramid] *nom féminin*

pyramid.

Pyrénées [pirene] *nom féminin pluriel*

les Pyrénées the Pyrenees.

qu' ➤ que.

quai [kɛ] *nom masculin*

1. **platform : le train part du quai 3** the train leaves from platform 3

2. **quay : on est allés sur les quais pour regarder les bateaux** we went to the quays to see the boats

3. **bank : on peut pique-niquer sur les quais de la Loire** you can have a picnic on the banks of the Loire.

qualification [kalifikasjɔ̃] *nom féminin*

qualification : il n'a pas les qualifications nécessaires he doesn't have the necessary qualifications.

qualifié, e [kalifje] *adjectif*

qualified : est-ce qu'elle est qualifiée pour faire ce travail ? is she qualified to do this job?

qualifier [kalifje] *verbe*

qualifier de quelque chose to describe as something ; **je le qualifierais d'hypocrite** I'd describe him as a hypocrite

se qualifier *verbe pronominal*

to qualify : l'équipe de l'école s'est qualifiée the school team has qualified.

qualité [kalite] *nom féminin*

quality (*pluriel* **qualities**) : **Séréna a beaucoup de qualités** Séréna has many qualities ; **un produit de bonne qualité** a quality product ; **du tissu de mauvaise qualité** poor-quality material.

quand [kɑ̃] *conjonction & adverbe*

when : il arrive toujours quand nous sommes à table he always comes when we are eating ; **quand tu le verras, demande-lui de m'appeler** when you see him, ask him to call me ; **quand est-ce que tu pars ?** when are you leaving? ; **je ne me rappelle plus quand je l'ai vu** I don't remember when I saw him

> Lorsque la proposition subordonnée est au futur en français (**quand tu le verras**), elle est au présent en anglais (**when you see him**).

➤ **depuis quand** how long : **depuis quand êtes-vous là ?** how long have you been here?
➤ **quand même**
1. **all the same : mes parents me l'ont interdit, mais j'irai quand même** my parents have forbidden me to go, but I'll go all the same
2. **really : quand même, tu exagères !** you really go too far !

quantité [kɑ̃tite] *nom féminin*

quantity (*pluriel* **quantities**) : **quelle quantité de farine faut-il ?** what quantity of flour do you need? ou how much flour do you need? ; **en grande quantité** in large quantities
➤ **une quantité de** ou **des quantités de** a

q

lot of : **ils ont des quantités de livres** they have a lot of books.

quarante [karɑ̃t] *adjectif numéral & nom masculin*

forty : il y avait quarante élèves au voyage scolaire there were forty pupils on the school trip.

quarantième [karɑ̃tjɛm] *adjectif numéral & nom*

fortieth : c'est le quarantième nom sur la liste it's the fortieth name on the list ; **il est arrivé quarantième** he came fortieth.

quart [kar] *nom masculin*

quarter : quel est le quart de 160 ? what's a quarter of 160? ; **un quart d'heure** a quarter of an hour ; **il est deux heures moins le quart** it's a quarter to two OU it's a quarter of two *US* ; **il est deux heures et quart** it's a quarter past two : **il est moins le quart** it's a quarter to OU it's a quarter of *US*
➤ **les quarts de finale** the quarterfinals.

quartier [kartje] *nom masculin*

area : un quartier résidentiel a residential area ; **les beaux quartiers** the smart areas.

quartz [kwarts] *nom masculin*

quartz : une montre à quartz a quartz watch.

quatorze [katɔrz] *adjectif numéral & nom masculin*

fourteen : Ludovic a quatorze ans Ludovic is fourteen years old OU Ludovic is fourteen
➤ **nous sommes le quatorze mai** it's the fourteenth of May *UK* OU it's May fourteenth *US*.

quatorzième [katɔrzjɛm] *adjectif numéral & nom*

fourteenth : au quatorzième siècle in the fourteenth century ; **Manon est arrivée quatorzième** Manon came fourteenth.

quatre [katr] *adjectif numéral & nom masculin*

four : j'ai quatre frères et sœurs I have four brothers and sisters ; **il a quatre ans** he's four years old OU he's four
➤ **nous sommes le quatre juin** it's the fourth of June *UK* OU it's June fourth *US*
➤ **se mettre en quatre pour quelqu'un** to bend over backwards for somebody

➤ **monter l'escalier quatre à quatre** to race up the stairs
➤ **un de ces quatre** *familier* one of these days.

quatre-vingt ➤ quatre-vingts.

quatre-vingt-dix [katrəvɛ̃dis] *adjectif numéral & nom masculin*

ninety : mon arrière-grand-père a quatre-vingt-dix ans my great-grandfather is ninety years old.

quatre-vingts, quatre-vingt [katrə-vɛ̃] *adjectif numéral & nom masculin*

eighty : ma grand-mère a quatre-vingts ans my grandmother is eighty years old ; **quatre-vingt-quatre** eighty-four
➤ **quatre-vingt-dix** ninety
➤ **quatre-vingt-onze** ninety-one
➤ **quatre-vingt-douze** ninety-two.

quatrième [katrijɛm] *adjectif & nom*

▪ *adjectif numéral & nom*
fourth : c'est la quatrième fois que je te le dis ! that's the fourth time I've told you! ; **Anne est arrivée quatrième** Anne came fourth

▪ *nom féminin*
year nine *UK*, **eighth grade** *US* ; **Bertrand est en quatrième** Bertrand is in year nine.

que [kə] *conjonction & pronom*

▪ *conjonction*
1. that

> La conjonction « que » ou « qu' » introduisant une subordonnée se traduit par **that** ou ne se traduit pas :

j'espère que tu vas bien I hope you're all right OU I hope that you're all right ; **Pierre a dit qu'il viendrait** Pierre said he would come OU Pierre said that he would come

> Notez la structure dans les exemples suivants avec des verbes exprimant le souhait ou la volonté (**want, like**, etc) :

j'aimerais que tu m'aides I'd like you to help me ; **je veux qu'ils viennent** I want them to come

2. *Dans les comparatifs de supériorité ou d'infériorité* **than : tu es plus jeune que moi** you're younger than me ; **c'est moins difficile qu'hier** it's less difficult than yesterday

3. *Dans les comparatifs d'égalité* **as : Pat a la même robe que moi** Pat has the same dress as me ; **tu es aussi grand que Marc** you're as tall as Marc

■ *pronom*

1. **that, whom**

> Lorsque « que » représente une personne, il se traduit par **that** ou **whom** ou bien il ne se traduit pas :

> **le garçon que tu vois là-bas** the boy that you can see over there OU the boy whom you can see over there OU the boy you can see over there

2. **that, which**

> Lorsque « que » représente une chose, il se traduit par **which** ou **that** ou bien il ne se traduit pas :

> **le livre que tu m'as prêté** the book which you lent me OU the book that you lent me OU the book you lent me

■ *pronom interrogatif*

  what : que savez-vous au juste ? what do you know exactly?

➤ **ne … que** only : **il ne reste que deux euros** there are only two euros left

■ *adverbe exclamatif*

➤ **qu'est-ce que**

1. *Dans les questions* **what : qu'est-ce que tu veux ?** what do you want?

2. *Dans les exclamations* **qu'est-ce que c'était rigolo !** it was so funny! ; **qu'est-ce que tu as changé !** you've changed so much!

➤ **qu'est-ce qui se passe ?** what is going on?

Québec [kebɛk] *nom masculin*

➤ **le Québec** Quebec ; **j'ai des cousins au Québec** I have cousins in Quebec ; **mon père va souvent au Québec pour son travail** my father often goes to Quebec on business.

québécois, e [kebekwa, az] *adjectif*

1. **of Quebec : le gouvernement québécois** the government of Quebec

2. **from Quebec : Lucie est québécoise** Lucie is from Quebec

Québécois, e *nom masculin, nom féminin*

Quebecker, Québécois : les Québécois ont un accent charmant Quebeckers have a charming accent OU the Québécois have a charming accent.

---

quel, quelle [kɛl] (*masculin pluriel* **quels,** *féminin pluriel* **quelles**) *adjectif & pronom*

■ *adjectif interrogatif*

1. *En parlant d'une personne* **which, who : quel élève a eu la meilleure note ?** which pupil got the best mark? ; **quelle est ton actrice préférée ?** who is your favourite actress?

2. *En parlant d'une chose* **what, which : je ne sais pas quels sont ses projets** I don't know what his plans are ; **quelle heure est-il ?** what time is it?

> On emploie **which** plutôt que **what** ou **who** lorsqu'on se réfère à un choix entre des choses ou des personnes bien précises :

> **quel livre est-ce que tu veux ?** which book do you want? ; **quelle jupe tu préfères ?** which skirt do you prefer? ; **quelle est la capitale du Japon ?** what is the capital of Japan?

■ *adjectif exclamatif*

what : quelle imbécile ! what an idiot! ; **quel mauvais temps !** what terrible weather!

> N'oubliez pas l'article **a** ou **an** devant le nom (**what an idiot !**, **what a beautiful house !**) lorsque celui-ci est un nom singulier dénombrable.

■ *pronom interrogatif*

which one, which : de vous trois, quel est le plus jeune ? which one of you three is the youngest?

➤ **quel que soit …** whatever … : **quel que soit le nombre de candidats** whatever the number of candidates.

quelconque [kɛlkɔ̃k] *adjectif*

1. **any : si pour une raison quelconque vous ne pouviez pas venir** if for any reason you can't come

2. **average : comment était le film ? – quelconque** what was the film like? – average.

quelque [kɛlk(ə)] *adjectif indéfini*

some : il a l'air fatigué depuis quelque temps he has looked tired for some time

➤ **quelques** a few OU some : **il me reste quelques timbres** I have a few stamps left OU I have some stamps left

➤ **et quelques**

1. **just over : cent euros et quelques** just over a hundred euros

2. **just after : midi et quelques** just after midday.

q

quelque chose [kɛlkəʃoz] *pronom*

> Lorsqu'on pose une question, « quelque chose » se traduit en règle générale par **anything**. Quand on fait une proposition ou quand on anticipe une réponse affirmative, la traduction de « quelque chose » est **something**.

1. **something** : **j'ai acheté quelque chose pour toi** I've bought you something ; **tu veux boire quelque chose ?** would you like something to drink? ; **quelque chose d'autre** something else
2. **anything** : **je descends au marché, veux-tu quelque chose ?** I'm going to the market, do you want anything?
> **ça m'a fait quelque chose** I really felt it

quelquefois [kɛlkəfwa] *adverbe*

> **sometimes** : **je vais quelquefois à la piscine avec mon frère** I sometimes go to the swimming pool with my brother.

quelque part [kɛlkəpar] *adverbe*

1. **somewhere** : **ces lunettes doivent bien être quelque part** those glasses must be somewhere
2. **anywhere** : **tu vas quelque part ce week-end ?** are you going anywhere this weekend?

quelques-uns, quelques-unes [kɛlkəzœ̃, kɛlkəzyn] *pronom*

> **some** : **quelques-uns d'entre eux ont refusé** some of them refused **des cartes postales ? – j'en ai quelques-unes** postcards? – I have some.

quelqu'un [kɛlkœ̃] *pronom*

1. **somebody, someone** : **quelqu'un a téléphoné pour toi** somebody phoned for you
2. **anybody, anyone** : **il y a quelqu'un ?** is anybody in?
> **c'est quelqu'un de sympathique** he's a nice person.

qu'est-ce que [kɛskə] ➤ **que.**

qu'est-ce qui [kɛski] ➤ **que.**

question [kɛstjɔ̃] *nom féminin*

> **question** : **poser une question à quelqu'un** to ask somebody a question ; **je peux vous poser une question ?** can I ask you a question?

> **il est question de construire une piscine** they're talking about building a swimming pool
> **il n'en est pas question** that's out of the question
> **pas question !** *familier* no way!

questionnaire [kɛstjɔnɛr] *nom masculin*

> **questionnaire** : **tu as répondu au questionnaire ?** have you answered the questionnaire?

quête [kɛt] *nom féminin*

> **faire la quête** to take a collection.

queue [kø] *nom féminin*

1. **tail** : **le chien remue la queue** the dog is wagging its tail
2. **stalk** : **enlève la queue des cerises** remove the cherry stalks
3. **queue** *UK*, **line** *US* : **il y avait au moins cent personnes dans la queue** there were at least a hundred people in the queue
4. **rear, back** : **nous étions en queue de train** we were at the rear of the train
> **faire la queue** to queue *UK* ou to stand in line *US*
> **à la queue leu leu** in single file.

queue-de-cheval [kødʃəval] (*pluriel* queues-de-cheval) *nom féminin*

> **ponytail** : **Laëtitia se fait souvent des queues-de-cheval** Laëtitia always wears her hair in a ponytail.

qui [ki] *pronom*

■ *pronom relatif*

1. *Représente une personne* **who, that** : **la fille qui me parlait** the girl who was talking to me ou the girl that was talking to me
2. *Représente une chose ou un animal* **that, which** : **le chien qui aboie** the dog that is barking ou the dog which is barking
3. *Après une préposition* **whom** : **la personne à qui tu parlais** the person you were talking to ou the person to whom you were talking ; **la copine pour qui j'ai enregistré ce CD** the friend I taped this CD for ou the friend for whom I taped this CD

> **Whom** appartient à la langue écrite ou soutenue ; dans la langue courante « qui » ne se traduit pas.

■ *pronom interrogatif*

1. **who** : **qui a fait ça ?** who did this? ; **dis-moi qui sera là** tell me who will be there ; **qui**

voulez-vous voir ? who do you want to see? ;
à qui tu vas le donner ? who are you going to
give it to? OU to whom are you going to give it?
2. whose : à qui est ce manteau ? whose coat is
this? ; c'est à qui de jouer ? whose turn is it?

quiche [kiʃ] *nom féminin*

quiche : une quiche aux poireaux a leek quiche ; une quiche lorraine a quiche lorraine.

quille [kij] *nom féminin*

keel : la quille du bateau est abîmée the
keel of the boat is damaged

quilles *nom féminin pluriel*

skittles *UK* : jouer aux quilles to play skittles.

quincaillerie [kɛ̃kajri] *nom féminin*

hardware shop : tu trouveras ce genre de
clous à la quincaillerie you'll find this type of
nails at the hardware shop.

quinzaine [kɛ̃zɛn] *nom féminin*

une quinzaine de about fifteen ; ça va durer
une quinzaine de minutes it'll last about fifteen minutes ; une quinzaine de jours two
weeks OU a fortnight *UK*.

quinze [kɛ̃z] *adjectif numéral & nom masculin*

fifteen : Alice a quinze ans Alice is fifteen
years old

➤ nous sommes le quinze août it's the fifteenth of August *UK* OU it's August fifteenth
US

➤ quinze jours two weeks : reviens dans
quinze jours come back in two weeks.

quinzième [kɛ̃zjɛm] *adjectif numéral & nom*

fifteenth : la quinzième ligne à partir du
haut the fifteenth line from the top ; Isabelle
est arrivée quinzième Isabelle came fifteenth.

quitter [kite] *verbe*

to leave : il a quitté la maison à 7 heures he
left home at 7 o'clock ; son copain l'a quittée
her boyfriend left her
➤ ne quittez pas ! hold the line, please!

se quitter *verbe pronominal*

to part : on était tristes quand on s'est
quittés we were sad when we parted.

quoi [kwa] *pronom interrogatif*

what : c'est quoi ? what's that? ; tu lis
quoi ? what are you reading? ; à quoi tu
penses ? what are you thinking about? ; je ne

sais pas quoi dire I don't know what to say ;
quoi ? qu'est-ce que tu dis ? what? what
did you say?

➤ de quoi

1. something : tu as de quoi écrire ? have you
got something to write with? ; emportez de
quoi boire take something to drink

2. enough : il y a de quoi nourrir cinquante
personnes there's enough to feed fifty people

➤ merci ! - il n'y a pas de quoi thank you!
– don't mention it

➤ quoi que whatever : quoi qu'on fasse
whatever we do.

quoique [kwakə] *conjonction*

although : je vais y aller quoique je n'en
aie pas très envie I'm going although I don't
really want to ; on pourrait aller au bowling
... quoique le cinéma ça ne serait pas mal
non plus we could go to the bowling alley ...
although cinema wouldn't be bad either.

quotidien, enne [kɔtidjɛ̃, ɛn] *adjectif*

daily : les tâches quotidiennes the daily
tasks

quotidien *nom masculin*

daily newspaper : quel quotidien est-ce
que vous lisez ? which daily newspaper do
you read?

r

rabais [rabɛ] *nom masculin*

discount : un rabais de dix pour cent a ten-
percent discount : faire un rabais à quelqu'un to give somebody a discount.

rabat [raba] *nom masculin*

flap : le rabat de la poche est déchiré the
flap of your pocket is torn.

rabattre [rabatr] *verbe*

to put down : il oublie toujours de rabattre
le siège des W.-C. he always forgets to put
the toilet seat down.

rabattu, e [rabaty] *participe passé de* **rabat-tre**.

rabbin [rabɛ̃] *nom masculin*

rabbi : **il est rabbin** he's a rabbi.

raccommoder [rakɔmɔde] *verbe*

to mend : **tu peux me raccommoder la manche ?** can you mend the sleeve for me?

raccompagner [rakɔ̃paɲe] *verbe*

1. to take : **le père de Sandra m'a raccompagné chez moi** Sandra's father took me home
2. to walk : **je te raccompagne jusqu'au bout de la rue** I'll walk you to the end of the street.

raccourci [rakursi] *nom masculin*

shortcut : **on va prendre un raccourci** we'll take a shortcut.

raccourcir [rakursir] *verbe*

1. to shorten : **ma mère a dû raccourcir ma jupe** my mother had to shorten my skirt
2. to get shorter : **les jours raccourcissent** the days are getting shorter.

raccrocher [rakrɔʃe] *verbe*

to hang up : **Sandrine m'a raccroché au nez** Sandrine hung up on me.

race [ras] *nom féminin*

1. race : **la race humaine** the human race
2. breed : **c'est une race de chat très rare** it's a very rare breed of cat
➤ **de race** pedigree : **un chien de race** a pedigree dog.

racheter [raʃte] *verbe*

1. to buy another : **tu vas devoir racheter un stylo** you'll have to buy another pen
2. to buy some more : **rachète du pain, sinon on va en manquer** buy some more bread, otherwise we won't have enough
3. to buy : **racheter quelque chose à quelqu'un** to buy something from somebody ; **je te rachète ton VTT cent euros** I'll buy your moutain bike from you for a hundred euros
4. to buy up : **l'usine a été rachetée par une société américaine** the factory was bought up by an American company

se racheter *verbe pronominal*

to make amends, to make up for it : **pour se racheter, il m'a offert des fleurs** to make amends, he bought me some flowers.

racine [rasin] *nom féminin*

root : **les racines de l'arbre** the roots of the tree : **quelle est la racine carrée de neuf ?** what is the square root of nine?

racisme [rasism] *nom masculin*

racism.

raciste [rasist] *nom masculin ou féminin & adjectif*

racist.

racler [rakle] *verbe*

to scrape : **racle le fond de la casserole** scrape the bottom of the pan

se racler *verbe pronominal*

se racler la gorge to clear one's throat ; **il se racle tout le temps la gorge, c'est agaçant** he's always clearing his throat, it's irritating.

raconter [rakɔ̃te] *verbe*

1. to tell : **Sophie nous a raconté une histoire super marrante** Sophie told us a really funny story
2. to tell about : **raconte-nous ton week-end** tell us about your weekend.

radiateur [radjatœr] *nom masculin*

radiator : **un radiateur électrique** an electric radiator.

radin, e [radɛ̃, in] *adjectif & nom familier*

■ *adjectif*
stingy : **elle est vraiment radine !** she's really stingy!

■ *nom masculin, nom féminin*
skinflint : **quel radin !** what a skinflint!

radio [radjo] *nom féminin*

1. radio : **allume la radio** switch on the radio ou put the radio on ; **je l'ai entendu à la radio** I heard it on the radio
2. X-ray : **passer une radio** to have an X-ray.

radio-réveil [radjorevɛj] (*pluriel* **radios-réveils**) *nom masculin*
radio alarm.

radis [radi] *nom masculin*

radish (*pluriel* **radishes**).

raffoler [rafɔle] *verbe*

raffoler de quelque chose to really love something ; **je raffole de la mousse au chocolat** I really love chocolate mousse.

rafraîchir [rafrɛʃir] *verbe*

to refresh : **ça va te rafraîchir la mémoire** it'll refresh your memory

se rafraîchir *verbe pronominal*

1. **to get colder** : le temps se rafraîchit it's getting colder OU the weather is getting colder
2. **to have a drink** : venez vous rafraîchir, vous devez avoir soif come and have a drink, you must be thirsty.

rafraîchissant, e [rafrɛʃisɑ̃, ɑ̃t] *adjectif*

refreshing : une boisson rafraîchissante a refreshing drink.

rafting [raftiŋ] *nom masculin*

whitewater rafting : on a fait du rafting dans les Pyrénées we went whitewater rafting in the Pyrenees.

rage [raʒ] *nom féminin*

1. **rage** : il était fou de rage he was mad with rage
2. **rabies** (*singulier*) : un renard qui a la rage a fox with rabies
➤ **il a une rage de dents terrible** he has terrible toothache *UK* OU he has a terrible toothache *US*.

ragots [rago] *nom masculin pluriel*

gossip (*ne s'utilise jamais au pluriel*) : ce ne sont que des ragots it's just gossip.

ragoût [ragu] *nom masculin*

stew : un ragoût d'agneau a lamb stew.

raide [rɛd] *adjectif*

1. **straight** : Mélanie a les cheveux raides Mélanie has straight hair
2. **stiff** : aïe, j'ai les jambes raides ouch, my legs are stiff ; elle n'est pas très bonne en gym, elle est trop raide she isn't very good at gymnastics, she's too stiff
3. **steep** : une pente raide a steep slope
➤ **tomber raide mort** to fall down dead.

raie [rɛ] *nom féminin*

1. **stripe** : une chemise blanche à raies bleues a white shirt with blue stripes
2. **parting** *UK*, **part** *US* : Simon porte la raie à gauche Simon has a left parting
3. **skate** : de la raie au beurre noir skate in brown butter sauce.

rail [raj] *nom masculin*

rail : le train est sorti des rails the train went off the rails OU the train derailed.

raisin [rɛzɛ̃] *nom masculin*

grapes (*s'utilise toujours au pluriel*) : manger du raisin to eat grapes : j'aime le raisin noir I like black grapes

⚠ The French word **raisin** is a false friend, it does not mean 'raisin'.

➤ **des raisins secs** raisins.

raison [rɛzɔ̃] *nom féminin*

reason : tu n'as aucune raison de t'inquiéter you have no reason to worry ; ce n'est pas une raison pour me parler comme ça that's no reason for you to talk to me like that
➤ **avoir raison** to be right : tu vois, j'avais raison ! you see, I was right! ; tu as eu raison de lui demander des explications you were right to ask him for an explanation.

raisonnable [rɛzɔnabl] *adjectif*

1. **reasonable** : des prix très raisonnables very reasonable prices
2. **sensible** : elle est très raisonnable pour son âge she's very sensible for her age.

raisonnement [rɛzɔnmɑ̃] *nom masculin*

argument : je ne comprends pas ton raisonnement I don't understand your argument.

raisonner [rɛzɔne] *verbe*

to reason with : on a essayé de la raisonner we tried to reason with her.

rajeunir [raʒœnir] *verbe*

rajeunir quelqu'un to make somebody look younger ; cette coupe de cheveux te rajeunit this haircut makes you look younger.

rajouter [raʒute] *verbe*

to add : rajoute un peu de sel add a bit of salt
➤ **en rajouter** *familier* to exaggerate : ce n'était pas si terrible, tu en rajoutes ! it wasn't that terrible, you're exaggerating!

ralenti [ralɑ̃ti] *nom masculin*

slow motion : une scène filmée au ralenti a scene filmed in slow motion.

ralentir [ralɑ̃tir] *verbe*

to slow down : ralentis, tu vas trop vite ! slow down, you're going too fast!

râler [rale] *verbe familier*

to moan : arrête de râler ! stop moaning!

r

rallonge [ralɔ̃ʒ] *nom féminin*

extension : **une table à rallonge** a table with an extension ; **il me faut une rallonge pour brancher l'ordinateur** I need an extension to connect the computer.

rallonger [ralɔ̃ʒe] *verbe*

1. **to extend : on a pu rallonger notre séjour d'une semaine** we were able to extend our stay by a week
2. **to get longer : les jours rallongent** the days are getting longer.

rallye [rali] *nom masculin*

rally (*pluriel* **rallies**) : **un rallye moto** a motorbike rally.

ramassage [ramasaʒ] *nom masculin*

le ramassage scolaire the school bus service.

ramasser [ramase] *verbe*

1. **to pick : tu viens ramasser les champignons avec moi ?** are you coming to pick mushrooms with me?
2. **to collect : le professeur a commencé à ramasser les copies** the teacher started collecting the papers
3. **to pick up : Sébastien a refusé de ramasser le papier qu'il avait fait tomber** Sébastien refused to pick up the piece of paper he'd dropped
4. *familier* **to get : si tu continues, tu vas ramasser une claque !** if you carry on, you're going to get a slap!

rame [ram] *nom féminin*

1. **oar : j'ai laissé tomber la rame dans l'eau** I dropped the oar in the water
2. **train : la dernière rame de métro** the last metro train.

ramener [ramne] *verbe*

1. **to bring back : tu peux ramener les enfants ici ce soir ?** can you bring the children back here tonight?
2. **to take back : je peux te ramener à l'école si tu veux** I can take you back to school if you want.

ramer [rame] *verbe*

to row : rame plus vite ! row faster!

ramollir [ramɔlir] *verbe*

to go soft : il fait chaud, le beurre a ramolli it's hot, the butter has gone soft.

rampe [rɑ̃p] *nom féminin*

1. **banister : accroche-toi à la rampe** hold on to the banister
2. **ramp : il y a une rampe pour les fauteuils roulants** there is a ramp for wheelchairs
➤ **une rampe de lancement** a launch pad.

ramper [rɑ̃pe] *verbe*

to crawl : il a rampé sous la clôture he crawled under the fence.

rancune [rɑ̃kyn] *nom féminin*

➤ **sans rancune !** no hard feelings!

rancunier, ère [rɑ̃kynje, ɛr] *adjectif*

être rancunier to bear grudges ; tu as de la chance, je ne suis pas rancunière ! you're lucky, I don't bear grudges!

randonnée [rɑ̃dɔne] *nom féminin*

1. **hike : faire une randonnée** to go for a hike
2. **hiking : faire de la randonnée** to go hiking
➤ **une randonnée à vélo** a bike ride.

rang [rɑ̃] *nom masculin*

row : on était assis au premier rang we were sitting in the front row ; **au dernier rang** in the back row
➤ **se mettre en rang** to line up

rangée [rɑ̃ʒe] *nom féminin*

row : une rangée de maisons a row of houses.

ranger [rɑ̃ʒe] *verbe*

1. **to tidy : je dois ranger ma chambre avant de sortir** I have to tidy my bedroom before I go out
2. **to put away : j'ai rangé mon agenda, maintenant je ne sais plus où il est** I put my diary away and now I don't know where it is
3. **to arrange : les dossiers sont rangés par ordre alphabétique** the files are arranged in alphabetical order.

rap [rap] *nom masculin*

rap : j'aime le rap I like rap music ; **un chanteur de rap** a rap singer.

rapace [rapas] *nom masculin*

bird of prey : l'aigle est un rapace the eagle is a bird of prey.

râpé, e [rape] *adjectif*

grated : du fromage râpé grated cheese.

rapide [rapid] *adjectif & nom*

■ *adjectif*

1. **fast : un coureur très rapide** a very fast runner
2. **rapid : Benoît a fait des progrès rapides** Benoît made rapid progress
   nom masculin
   rapid : les rapides du Congo the rapids on the Congo river.

rapidement [rapidmɑ̃] *adverbe*

quickly : nous devons réagir rapidement we must react quickly.

rapiécé, e [rapjese] *adjectif*

patched : son jean est rapiécé her jeans are patched.

rappel [rapɛl] *nom masculin*

1. **reminder : on a reçu un rappel pour la facture du gaz** we got a reminder for the gas bill
2. **booster : le médecin m'a fait le rappel du tétanos** the doctor gave me a booster for tetanus
3. **encore : il y a eu deux rappels, puis ils ont chanté une dernière chanson** there were two encores, then they sang a last song
   la descente en rappel abseiling *UK* ou rappelling *US*
   descendre en rappel to abseil down *UK* ou to rappel *US*.

rappeler [raple] *verbe*

to call back : je rappellerai cet après-midi I'll call back this afternoon
rappeler quelque chose à quelqu'un to remind somebody of something : **ça me rappelle mon village** it reminds me of my village ; **rappelle-moi d'acheter du pain** remind me to buy some bread

se rappeler *verbe pronominal*

to remember : tu te rappelles la date de son anniversaire ? do you remember when his birthday is?

rapport [rapɔr] *nom masculin*

1. **connection : il n'y a aucun rapport entre les deux** there's no connection between the two ; **je ne vois pas le rapport** I don't see the connection
2. **report : un rapport sur les activités du groupe** a report on the group's activities
   le rapport qualité-prix value for money
   par rapport à compared with ou compared

to : **par rapport à son frère, c'est un génie !** compared with his brother, he's a genius!

rapports *nom masculin pluriel*

relations : nous avons de bons rapports avec nos voisins we have good relations with our neighbours
➤ **avoir des rapports sexuels avec quelqu'un** to have sex with somebody.

rapporter [rapɔrte] *verbe*

1. **to bring back : tu m'as rapporté quelque chose de ton voyage ?** have you brought me something back from your trip?
2. **to take back : n'oublie pas de rapporter les livres à la bibliothèque** don't forget to take the books back to the library.

rapprocher [raprɔʃe] *verbe*

1. **to bring nearer, to bring closer : rapproche ta chaise, tu verras mieux** bring your chair nearer, you'll see better ou bring your chair closer, you'll see better
2. **to move closer : il a rapproché sa chaise du feu** he moved his chair closer to the fire
3. **to bring together : cette tragédie les a rapprochés** this tragedy has brought them together

se rapprocher *verbe pronominal*

1. **to come closer : rapproche-toi, que je te voie mieux** come closer so that I can see you better
2. **to become closer : nous nous sommes rapprochés après cette aventure** we became closer after this adventure.

raquette [rakɛt] *nom féminin*

1. **racket : une raquette de tennis** a tennis racket
2. **bat** *UK*, **paddle** *US* : **une raquette de ping-pong** a table-tennis bat
3. **snowshoe : marcher dans la neige avec des raquettes** to walk in the snow with snowshoes.

rare [rar] *adjectif*

1. **rare : un objet rare** a rare object
2. **few : les rares personnes qu'ils fréquentent** the few people they see.

rarement [rarmɑ̃] *adverbe*

rarely : je vois rarement Anaïs I rarely see Anaïs.

r

ras *adverbe*

short : ses cheveux sont coupés **ras** his hair is cut short

➤ **au ras de** level with : **au ras de l'eau** level with the water

➤ **à ras bord** to the brim : **ne remplis pas ton verre à ras bord** don't fill your glass to the brim

➤ **en avoir ras le bol** *familier* to be fed up : **en avoir ras le bol de** to be fed up with ; **j'en ai ras le bol de ses mensonges !** I'm fed up with his lies!

raser [raze] *verbe*

1. **to shave off :** Sam a **rasé** sa barbe Sam shaved his beard off

2. **to fly low over :** l'avion a **rasé** le toit des maisons the plane flew low over the houses

3. **to raze :** l'immeuble a été **rasé** the building was razed to the ground

se raser *verbe pronominal*

to shave : il se **rase** deux fois par semaine he shaves twice a week ; **se raser les jambes** to shave one's legs.

rasoir [razwar] *nom & adjectif*

■ *nom masculin*
razor : des **rasoirs** jetables disposable razors
➤ **un rasoir électrique** an electric shaver

■ *adjectif invariable familier*
boring : le cours d'histoire était vraiment **rasoir** the history lesson was really boring.

rassembler [rasãble] *verbe*

to gather : le proviseur a **rassemblé** les élèves dans la cour the headmaster gathered the pupils in the playground ; **il a rassemblé ses papiers** he gathered his papers together

se rassembler *verbe pronominal*

1. **to assemble :** les manifestants se sont **rassemblés** sur la place the demonstrators assembled on the square

2. **to get together :** toute la famille se **rassemble** pour Noël the whole family is getting together for Christmas.

se rasseoir [səraswar] *verbe pronominal*

to sit down again : **rasseyez-vous**, la projection n'est pas finie sit down again, the screening isn't over.

rassis, e [rasi, iz] *adjectif*

stale : du pain **rassis** et de l'eau stale bread and water.

rassurer [rasyre] *verbe*

to reassure : il a essayé de la **rassurer** he tried to reassure her

➤ **rassure-toi, ça ne va pas durer** don't worry, it won't last for long.

rat [ra] *nom masculin*

rat : un **rat** blanc a white rat.

raté, e [rate] *adjectif*

failed : une tentative **ratée** a failed attempt ; **oh non, le gâteau est complètement raté !** oh no, the cake is a complete failure!

➤ **une occasion ratée** a missed opportunity

➤ **raté !** you missed!

rater [rate] *verbe*

1. **to mess up, to make a mess of :** j'ai **raté** la photo I messed up the photograph ou I made a mess of the photograph

2. **to miss :** vite, on va **rater** le train ! quick we're going to miss the train! ; **rater une occasion** to miss an opportunity

3. **to fail :** Stéphanie a **raté** son permis de conduire Stéphanie failed her driving test

4. **to go wrong :** tout a **raté** à cause de toi everything went wrong because of you.

rattrapage [ratrapaʒ] *nom masculin*

j'étais malade et j'ai été obligé de prendre des cours de **rattrapage** I was ill and I had to take extra classes to catch up.

rattraper [ratrape] *verbe*

1. **to catch up with :** on part, ils nous **rattraperont** we're leaving, they'll catch up with us

2. **to catch :** Élise a **rattrapé** le vase de justesse Élise caught the vase just in time

3. **to catch up on :** comment est-ce que je vais **rattraper** les cours que j'ai ratés ? how am I going to catch up on the lessons I missed?

➤ **rattraper le temps perdu** to make up for lost time

se rattraper *verbe pronominal*

se rattraper à quelque chose to catch hold of something ; **heureusement qu'il s'est rattrapé à la rambarde** luckily he caught hold of the banister.

rauque [rok] *adjectif*

1. hoarse : **j'ai trop crié, j'ai la voix rauque** I've shouted too much, my voice is hoarse
2. husky : **une chanteuse à la voix rauque** a singer with a husky voice.

ravi, e [ravi] *adjectif*

delighted : **le prof est ravi de nos résultats** the teacher is delighted with our results ; **je suis ravi de l'avoir trouvé** I'm delighted to have found it ; **je suis ravi qu'il soit venu** I'm delighted that he has come

➤ **ravi de vous connaître** pleased to meet you.

ravin [ravɛ̃] *nom masculin*

ravine.

raviolis [ravjɔli] *nom masculin pluriel*

ravioli (*ne s'utilise jamais au pluriel*) : **ces raviolis sont très bons** this ravioli is very good.

ravitailler [ravitaje] *verbe*

to refuel : **ravitailler un avion en vol** to refuel a plane in flight

se ravitailler *verbe pronominal*

1. to get supplies : **on se ravitaille au village le plus proche** we get supplies from the nearest village
2. to refuel : **l'avion s'est posé à Séoul pour se ravitailler** the plane landed in Seoul to refuel.

rayé, e [rɛje] *adjectif*

1. striped : **une chemise rayée** a striped shirt
2. scratched : **le disque est rayé** the record is scratched.

rayer [rɛje] *verbe*

1. to scratch : **j'ai rayé mes lunettes** I've scratched my glasses
2. to cross out, to delete : **pourquoi tu as rayé ce mot ?** why did you cross this word out? ou why did you delete this word? ; **ton nom a été rayé de la liste** your name has been crossed off the list.

rayon [rɛjɔ̃] *nom masculin*

1. ray : **les rayons du soleil** the sun's rays ; **rayons X** X-rays
2. beam : **un rayon laser** a laser beam
3. department : **le rayon enfant** the children's department
4. radius (*pluriel* radii) : **un cercle d'un rayon de 5 cm** a circle with a radius of 5 cm

5. spoke : **les rayons d'une roue de bicyclette** the spokes of a bicycle wheel.

rayure [rɛjyr] *nom féminin*

1. stripe : **du tissu blanc à rayures vertes** white material with green stripes
2. scratch (*pluriel* **scratches**) : **il y a des rayures sur le piano** there are scratches on the piano.

raz de marée [radmare] *nom masculin*

tidal wave : **le raz de marée a tout emporté** the tidal wave carried everything along with it.

réaction [reaksjɔ̃] *nom féminin*

reaction : **quelle a été sa réaction ?** what was his reaction?

réagir [reaʒir] *verbe*

1. to react : **comment est-ce qu'elle a réagi ?** how did she react?
2. to respond : **il réagit bien au traitement** he's responding well to the treatment.

réalisateur, trice [realizatœr, tris] *nom masculin, nom féminin*

director : **un grand réalisateur français** a great French director.

réaliser [realize] *verbe*

1. to carry out : **ce projet sera difficile à réaliser** this plan will be difficult to carry out
2. to realize, to realise *UK* : **il n'a jamais réalisé son rêve** he never realized his dream ; **tu réalises qu'on est déjà en décembre ?** do you realize it's already December? ou do you realize that it's already December?
3. to produce : **un film entièrement réalisé par les élèves** a film produced entirely by the pupils
4. to direct : **c'est Chabrol qui a réalisé ce film** it was Chabrol who directed this film

se réaliser *verbe pronominal*

to come true : **mon rêve s'est enfin réalisé !** my dream has come true at last!

réaliste [realist] *adjectif*

realistic : **soyons réalistes** let's be realistic.

réalité [realite] *nom féminin*

reality : **c'est la triste réalité** that's the sad reality

➤ **en réalité** in reality.

r

rebondir [rəbõdir] *verbe*

to bounce : **le ballon a rebondi très haut** the ball bounced very high

➤ **faire rebondir quelque chose** to bounce something : **il faisait rebondir une balle de tennis contre le mur** he was bouncing a tennis ball against the wall.

rebord [rəbɔr] *nom masculin*

sill, ledge : **le rebord de la fenêtre** the window sill OU the window ledge.

reboucher [rəbuʃe] *verbe*

to fill in : **reboucher un trou** to fill in a hole.

récemment [resamã] *adverbe*

recently : **tu as vu Lisa récemment ?** have you seen Lisa recently?

récent, e [resã, ãt] *adjectif*

recent : **c'est un modèle tout récent** it's a very recent model.

réception [resɛpsjõ] *nom féminin*

1. reception, reception desk : **je vais demander à la réception** I'll ask at reception
2. receipt : **payable à la réception** payable on receipt
3. reception, party : **donner une réception** to hold a reception.

réceptionniste [resɛpsjɔnist] *nom masculin ou féminin*

receptionist : **Claude est réceptionniste** Claude is a receptionist.

recette [rəsɛt] *nom féminin*

recipe : **la recette du bœuf bourguignon** the recipe for beef bourguignon.

recevoir [rəsəvwar] *verbe*

1. to get, to receive : **j'ai reçu une lettre de Charles** I got a letter from Charles OU I received a letter from Charles ; **il a reçu un coup sur la tête** he was hit on the head OU he got a blow on the head
2. to have around *UK*, to have over *US* : **recevoir des amis à dîner** to have friends around for dinner

➤ **être bien reçu** to be given a warm welcome : **nous avons été très bien reçus en Irlande** we were given a warm welcome in Ireland

➤ **être reçu à un examen** to pass an exam.

rechange [rəʃãʒ] *adjectif*

➤ **de rechange** spare : **des vêtements de rechange** spare clothes.

réchaud [reʃo] *nom masculin*

stove : **un réchaud de camping** a camping stove.

réchauffer [reʃofe] *verbe*

1. to reheat : **faire réchauffer quelque chose** to reheat something ; **je réchauffe la soupe** I'm reheating the soup
2. to warm up : **bois ce chocolat, ça te réchauffera** drink this chocolate, it'll warm you up

se réchauffer *verbe pronominal*

1. to warm up : **essaie de te réchauffer près du feu** try to warm up by the fire ; **je n'arrive pas à me réchauffer les pieds** I can't get my feet warm
2. to get warmer : **le temps se réchauffe** the weather is getting warmer.

recherche [rəʃɛrʃ] *nom féminin*

1. search (*ne s'utilise jamais au pluriel*) : **faire une recherche sur Internet** to do a search on the Internet
2. research (*ne s'utilise jamais au pluriel*) : **le père de Mathieu fait de la recherche médicale** Mathieu's father does medical research ; **j'ai fait des recherches en bibliothèque pour mon exposé** I did some research in the library for my project

➤ **être à la recherche de quelque chose** to be looking for something OU to be in search of something : **il est parti à sa recherche** he has gone looking for her

➤ **avec recherche** elegantly : **elle s'habille avec recherche** she dresses elegantly.

récif [resif] *nom masculin*

reef : **un récif de corail** a coral reef.

réciproque [resiprɔk] *adjectif*

mutual : **elle m'énerve et je sais que c'est réciproque** she gets on my nerves and I know it's mutual.

réciter [resite] *verbe*

to recite : **il a récité un poème devant la classe** he recited a poem in front of the class.

réclamation [reklamasjɔ̃] *nom féminin*

complaint : **faire une réclamation** to make a complaint.

réclamer [reklame] *verbe*

to ask for, to keep asking for : **je réclame des baskets à ma mère depuis trois mois** I've been asking my mother for trainers for three months ; **je suis toujours obligé de lui réclamer l'argent qu'il me doit** I have to keep asking him for the money he owes me.

se recoiffer [sərəkwafe] *verbe pronominal*

to do one's hair : **je me recoiffe et j'arrive** I'll just do my hair and I'll be right with you.

recoller [rəkɔle] *verbe*

to stick back together : **ça va me prendre des heures de recoller les morceaux du vase** it'll take me hours to stick the pieces of the vase back together.

récolte [rekɔlt] *nom féminin*

harvest : **la récolte a été bonne cette année** there was a good harvest this year.

récolter [rekɔlte] *verbe*

to harvest : **ils récoltent des tonnes de blé** they harvest tons of wheat
to pick : **on les a aidés à récolter les pommes de terre** we helped them to pick the potatoes.

recommandé, e [rəkɔmɑ̃de] *adjectif & nom*

adjectif
registered : **une lettre recommandée** a registered letter
advisable : **ce n'est pas très recommandé** it's not very advisable
nom masculin
envoyer quelque chose en recommandé to send something by registered post *UK* ou to send something by registered mail *US*.

recommander [rəkɔmɑ̃de] *verbe*

to recommend : **tu peux me recommander un bon dentiste ?** can you recommend a good dentist?
to advise : **je vous recommande de réserver à l'avance** I advise you to book in advance.

recommencer [rəkɔmɑ̃se] *verbe*

1. to start again : **tu ne vas pas recommencer à pleurer !** you're not going to start crying again!
2. to do again : **je recommence l'introduction, elle est nulle** I'm doing the introduction again, it's useless ; **ne recommence pas !** don't do it again!

récompense [rekɔ̃pɑ̃s] *nom féminin*

reward : **qu'est-ce qu'ils t'ont donné en récompense ?** what did they give you as a reward?

récompenser [rekɔ̃pɑ̃se] *verbe*

to reward : **tu seras récompensé de ta générosité** you'll be rewarded for your generosity.

se réconcilier [sərekɔ̃silje] *verbe pronominal*

to make up : **j'espère que vous allez vous réconcilier** I hope you two are going to make up.

reconnaissant, e [rəkɔnɛsɑ̃, ɑ̃t] *adjectif*

grateful : **je vous en suis très reconnaissant** I'm very grateful to you : **je vous serais reconnaissant de m'aider** I would be grateful if you would help me.

reconnaître [rəkɔnɛtr] *verbe*

1. to recognize : **je ne t'avais pas reconnu, tu as changé !** I didn't recognize you, you've changed!
2. to admit : **reconnais que tu as tort** admit that you're wrong.

reconnu, e [rəkɔny] *participe passé de* reconnaître.

recopier [rəkɔpje] *verbe*

to copy out : **le prof veut qu'on recopie tout le texte** the teacher wants us to copy the whole text out
➤ **recopier quelque chose au propre** to make a fair copy of something.

record [rəkɔr] *nom masculin & adjectif invariable*

record : **battre un record** to break a record ; **il a battu le record du monde** he broke the world record ; **en un temps record** in record time.

se recoucher [sərəkuʃe] *verbe pronominal*

to go back to bed : **recouche-toi, il n'est**

que six heures go back to bed, it's only six o'clock.

recoudre [rəkudr] *verbe*

1. to sew back on : Aurélien ne sait même pas recoudre un bouton Aurélien can't even sew a button back on again
2. to sew up again : tu peux me recoudre l'ourlet, s'il te plaît ? can you please sew the hem up again for me?

recouvert, e [rəkuvɛr, ɛrt] *participe passé de* recouvrir.

recouvrir [rəkuvrir] *verbe*

to cover : il a recouvert sa voiture d'une bâche en plastique he covered his car with a plastic sheet ; les champs sont recouverts de neige the fields are covered in snow.

récréation [rekreasjɔ̃] *nom féminin*

break *UK*, recess *US* : on se retrouve à la récréation we'll meet up during the break.

récrire [rekrir] *verbe* ➤ réécrire.

rectangle [rɛktɑ̃gl] *nom masculin*

rectangle.

recto [rɛkto] *nom masculin*

front : au recto on the front ; recto verso on both sides.

reçu¹, e [rəsy] *participe passé de* recevoir.

reçu² [rəsy] *nom masculin*

receipt : tu as gardé le reçu ? did you keep the receipt?

recueil [rəkœj] *nom masculin*

collection : un recueil de poèmes de René Char a collection of poems by René Char.

recueillir [rəkœjir] *verbe*

1. to take in : ils ont recueilli un sans-abri they've taken in a homeless person
2. to collect : recueillir des renseignements to collect information

se recueillir *verbe pronominal*

to meditate : se recueillir sur la tombe de quelqu'un to meditate at somebody's graveside.

recul [rəkyl] *nom masculin*

➤ avoir un mouvement de recul to recoil : elle a eu un mouvement de recul quand elle

a vu l'araignée she recoiled when she sa the spider

➤ **prendre du recul** to stand back : il fat prendre du recul pour juger plus objective ment you have to stand back in order to judg more objectively.

reculer [rəkyle] *verbe*

1. to move back : reculez, laissez-les passer move back, let them through! ; recule un pe ton fauteuil move your armchair back a bit
2. to reverse : le bus est rentré dans le porta en reculant the bus crashed into the gate as was reversing
3. to put back : est-ce qu'on pourrait recule la date de la réunion ? could we put back th date of the meeting?

reculons [rəkylɔ̃] *adverbe*

➤ à reculons backwards : marcher à reculon to walk backwards.

récupérer [rekypere] *verbe*

1. to get back : tu ne récupéreras jamais to argent you'll never get your money back
2. to salvage : j'ai récupéré un vieux fauteu dans la rue I salvaged an old armchair off th street
3. to recover : on n'a qu'une minute pour re cupérer entre chaque sprint you only hav one minute to recover between sprints.

recycler [rəsikle] *verbe*

to recycle : est-ce que vous recyclez l vieux journaux ? do you recycle old new papers?

rédaction [redaksjɔ̃] *nom féminin*

essay : on a une rédaction à faire pour de main we have an essay to write for tomorrow

redemander [rədəmɑ̃de] *verbe*

1. to ask for again : j'ai dû lui redemand mon stylo I had to ask him for my pen agai
2. to ask for more : je n'ai pas osé redema der du gâteau I didn't dare ask for more cak

redescendre [rədesɑ̃dr] *verbe*

to go back down : tu peux redescendre la cave ? can you go back down to the cell again?

rediffusion [rədifyzjɔ̃] *nom féminin*

repeat, rerun : il y a tout le temps des r diffusions à la télé there are repeats all th time on TV.

rédiger [rediʒe] *verbe*

to write : on doit rédiger une page sur la **Révolution** we have to write one page on the Revolution.

redire [rədir] *verbe*

to repeat : j'ai dû le lui redire trois fois I had to repeat it to him three times

> **trouver à redire à quelque chose** to find fault with something : **Amélie trouve à redire à tout** Amélie finds fault with everything.

redit, e [rədi, it] *participe passé de* redire.

redonner [rədɔne] *verbe*

1. **to give back** : tu me redonnes mon classeur ? can you give me back my folder?
2. **to give some more** : je te redonne de la soupe si tu veux I'll give you some more soup if you want
3. **to restore** : ça m'a redonné du courage it restored my courage.

redoubler [rəduble] *verbe*

to repeat a year : Sylvain va redoubler s'il ne travaille pas Sylvain will have to repeat a year if he doesn't work.

redresser [rədrɛse] *verbe*

to straighten : redresser une barre tordue to straighten a bent bar

se redresser *verbe pronominal*

to straighten up : redresse-toi, tu te tiens mal ! straighten up, your posture is bad!

réduction [redyksjɔ̃] *nom féminin*

reduction : il y a 20% de réduction there's a 20% reduction.

réduire [redɥir] *verbe*

1. **to cut back on** : on devrait réduire nos dépenses we should cut back on our expenses
2. **to reduce** : il faut réduire sa vitesse par mauvais temps you must reduce speed in bad weather.

réduit, e [redɥi, ɥit] *verbe & adjectif*

■ *participe passé de* réduire
■ *adjectif*
1. **small** : un nombre réduit d'élèves a small number of pupils
2. **reduced** : des tarifs réduits reduced rates.

réécrire [reekrir], **récrire** [rekrir] *verbe*

to rewrite : je ne vais pas réécrire tout le texte ! I'm not going to rewrite the whole text!

réel, réelle [reɛl] *adjectif*

real : elle a une réelle passion pour la physique she has a real passion for physics.

réellement [reɛlmɑ̃] *adverbe*

really : il ne m'a pas réellement convaincu he didn't really convince me.

réessayer [reeseje] *verbe*

to try again : tu veux réessayer ? do you want to try again?

refaire [rəfɛr] *verbe*

Les deux traductions les plus courantes de « refaire » au sens de « réaliser à nouveau » sont **do again** et **make again**.
Do again s'utilise lorsqu'on parle de tâches ménagères, de sport ou de travail en général.
Make again rend l'idée de création ou de préparation.
Make again s'utilise également dans les situations où l'on oblige une personne à effectuer une action

1. **to do again** : je refuse de refaire la vaisselle ! I refuse to do the washing-up again! ; j'ai dû refaire mes devoirs I had to do my homework again
2. **to make again** : tu refais de la soupe ? are you making soup again? ; nous avons dû refaire une carte de la région we had to make a plan of the area again ; le prof d'anglais nous a refait traduire le texte the English teacher made us translate the text again
3. *En parlant du temps, du climat* il refait beau the weather is fine again ; il refait chaud it's hot again
> **refaire la peinture** to repaint OU to redo the paintwork
> **se faire refaire le nez** to have a nose job

se refaire *verbe pronominal*

1. *Préparer à nouveau* je vais me refaire un café I'm going to make myself another coffee ; refais-toi du thé si tu veux make yourself some more tea if you like
2. *Avec un infinitif familier* Hugo s'est refait opérer Hugo had another operation ; ils se sont refait arrêter they got arrested again.

refait, e [rəfɛ, ɛt] *participe passé de* refaire.

r

réfectoire [refɛktwar] *nom masculin*

dining hall, canteen *UK*, cafeteria *US* : **le réfectoire de l'école** the school dining hall ou the school canteen *UK* ou the school cafeteria *US*.

référence [referɑ̃s] *nom féminin*

reference : **tu as noté la référence du livre ?** have you noted down the book reference?
> **faire référence à** to refer to.

refermer [rəfɛrme] *verbe*

to close, to shut : **refermez vos livres et écoutez la cassette** close your books and listen to the tape

se refermer *verbe pronominal*

to close, to shut : **la porte s'est refermée brusquement** the door closed abruptly ou the door shut abruptly.

réfléchir [refleʃir] *verbe*

to think : **réfléchis bien** think carefully ; **réfléchis avant de dire des bêtises !** think before you talk nonsense! ; **réfléchir à quelque chose** to think about something ; **j'ai réfléchi à ce que tu m'as dit** I've been thinking about what you told me.

reflet [rəflɛ] *nom masculin*

reflection : **Narcisse admirait son reflet dans l'eau** Narcissus was admiring his reflection in the water.

refléter [rəflete] *verbe*

to reflect : **ce poème reflète la mélancolie de l'auteur** this poem reflects the author's melancholy

se refléter *verbe pronominal*

to be reflected : **son image se reflète dans le lac** his image is reflected in the lake.

réflexe [reflɛks] *nom masculin*

1. reflex *(pluriel* **reflexes***)* : **il a de bons réflexes** he has good reflexes
2. reaction : **mon premier réflexe a été de crier** my first reaction was to shout.

réflexion [reflɛksjɔ̃] *nom féminin*

1. remark : **une réflexion désagréable** an unpleasant remark
2. thought : **c'est un travail de réflexion** it's work that needs some thought
> **réflexion faite** ou **à la réflexion** on reflection.

réforme [refɔrm] *nom féminin*

reform.

refrain [rəfrɛ̃] *nom masculin*

chorus *(pluriel* **choruses***)* : **tout le monde a chanté le refrain** everybody sang the chorus.

réfrigérateur [refriʒeratœr] *nom masculin*

refrigerator, fridge *UK* : **remets le lait au réfrigérateur** put the milk back in the fridge.

refroidir [rəfrwadir] *verbe*

1. to cool down : **laisse refroidir la soupe** leave the soup to cool down
2. to get cold : **mon thé a refroidi, il n'est pas bon** my tea has got cold, it doesn't taste nice

se refroidir *verbe pronominal*

to get cooler : **le temps se refroidit** it's getting cooler.

refuge [rəfyʒ] *nom masculin*

1. refuge : **chercher refuge** to seek refuge
2. hut : **un refuge de montagne** a mountain hut.

réfugié, e [refyʒje] *nom masculin, nom féminin*

refugee : **un camp de réfugiés** a refugee camp.

se réfugier [sərefyʒje] *verbe pronominal*

1. to take shelter : **on s'est réfugiés sous un arbre** we took shelter under a tree
2. to take refuge : **ils se sont réfugiés à l'ambassade** they took refuge in the embassy.

refus [rəfy] *nom masculin*

refusal : **un refus catégorique** a blunt refusal
> **ce n'est pas de refus** I wouldn't say no.

refuser [rəfyze] *verbe*

1. to refuse : **Martin a refusé mon offre** Martin refused my offer ou Martin turned down my offer ; **Adeline refuse de parler à Marc** Adeline refuses to speak to Marc ou Adeline won't speak to Marc
2. to turn away : **ils ont dû refuser du monde** they had to turn some people away
> **être refusé à un examen** to fail an exam.

régal [regal] *(pluriel* **régals***) nom masculin*

treat : **ce repas est un vrai régal** this meal is a real treat.

se régaler [səregale] *verbe pronominal*

quand mamie fait la cuisine on se régale it's

a real treat when granny cooks : **on s'est régalé** it was a real treat.

regard [rəgar] *nom masculin*

look : Audrey m'a lancé un regard furieux Audrey gave me a furious look

> **fusiller quelqu'un du regard** OU **foudroyer quelqu'un du regard** to glare at somebody

⚠ The French word **regard** is a false friend, it does not mean 'regard'.

regarder [rəgarde] *verbe*

1. **to look at : regarde Jean, il a l'air tout triste** look at Jean, he looks very sad
2. **to look : regardez, un aigle !** look, an eagle!
3. **to watch : vous avez regardé le match de foot ?** did you watch the football match? ; **il m'a regardée travailler toute l'après-midi** he watched me work all afternoon

> **ça ne te regarde pas** it's none of your business.

reggae [rege] *nom masculin*

reggae : j'aime bien le reggae I like reggae.

régime [reʒim] *nom masculin*

1. **diet : Suzanne est au régime** Suzanne is on a diet ; **se mettre au régime** to go on a diet ; **un régime amincissant** a slimming diet
2. **regime : ce pays est sous un régime militaire** this country is under a military regime
3. **bunch** (*pluriel* **bunches**) **: un régime de bananes** a bunch of bananas.

régiment [reʒimã] *nom masculin*

regiment : un régiment de cavalerie a cavalry regiment.

région [reʒjɔ̃] *nom féminin*

region, area : c'est une région très riche it's a very rich region OU it's a very rich area ; **la région parisienne** the Paris area OU the Paris region

  RÉGIONS
Mainland France is divided into 21 administrative regions, with the island of Corsica bringing the number up to 22. France also has four overseas regions. Each region is made up of several **départements** and elects a regional council with responsibilities in education, culture, land-use and planning.

régional, e, aux [reʒjɔnal, o] *adjectif*

regional.

registre [rəʒistr] *nom masculin*

register : la secrétaire a inscrit leurs noms dans le registre the secretary wrote their names in the register.

réglage [reglaʒ] *nom masculin*

1. **tuning : le moteur marche bien, il faut juste un petit réglage** the engine is working well, it just needs a bit of tuning
2. **setting : le réglage du thermostat** setting the thermostat.

règle [regl] *nom féminin*

1. **rule : les règles du jeu** the rules of the game
2. **ruler : sers-toi d'une règle pour souligner** use a ruler to underline

> **en règle** in order : **mes papiers sont en règle** OU **je suis en règle** my papers are in order

> **en règle générale** as a rule

règles *nom féminin pluriel*

period : j'ai mes règles I have my period.

règlement [regləmã] *nom masculin*

1. **rules** (*pluriel*), **regulations** (*pluriel*) **: c'est interdit par le règlement de l'école** it's forbidden by the school rules
2. **payment : acceptez-vous les règlements par chèque ?** do you accept payments by cheque?

réglementation [regləmãtasjɔ̃] *nom féminin*

rules (*pluriel*), **regulations** (*pluriel*) **: c'est contraire à la réglementation** it's against the rules OU it's against the regulations.

régler [regle] *verbe*

1. **to sort out : le problème va être vite réglé** the problem will soon be sorted out
2. **to adjust : le chauffage est mal réglé** the heating isn't adjusted properly
3. **to tune : le garagiste a réglé le moteur** the garage mechanic tuned the engine
4. **to pay : qui va régler l'addition ?** who is going to pay the bill? ; **n'oublie pas de régler la femme de ménage** don't forget to pay the cleaning lady.

réglisse [reglis] *nom féminin*

liquorice *UK*, **licorice** *US* **: des bonbons à**

r

la réglisse liquorice sweets *UK* ou licorice candy *US*.

règne [rɛɲ] *nom masculin*

reign : **sous le règne d'Henri IV** in the reign of Henry IV.

regret [rəgrɛ] *nom masculin*

regret : **je n'ai aucun regret** I have no regrets ; **nous avons le regret de vous informer que votre candidature n'a pas été retenue** we regret to inform you that your application was unsuccessful.

regretter [rəgrɛte] *verbe*

1. to miss : **Jacques regrette son ancienne école** Jacques misses his old school ; **on te regrettera quand tu seras partie** we'll miss you when you've gone
2. to be sorry : **je regrette de ne pas pouvoir venir** I'm sorry I can't come ; **je regrette de lui avoir fait confiance** I'm sorry I trusted him ; **non, je regrette, je ne peux pas** no, I'm sorry, I can't.

regrouper [rəgrupe] *verbe*

to group together : **on a eu du mal à regrouper tout le monde** we had difficulty grouping everybody together

se regrouper *verbe pronominal*

to gather : **les manifestants se sont regroupés sur la place** the demonstrators gathered on the square.

régulier, ère [regylje, ɛr] *adjectif*

1. regular : **manger à des heures régulières** to eat at regular times ; **à intervalles réguliers** at regular intervals
2. steady : **une augmentation régulière des prix** a steady increase in prices
3. consistent : **les résultats de Jérémie sont plus réguliers qu'avant** Jérémie's results are more consistent than before
4. legal : **ce n'est pas très régulier comme méthode** this method isn't really legal.

régulièrement [regyljɛrmã] *adverbe*

regularly : **mes grand-parents viennent régulièrement nous voir** my grandparents come and visit us regularly.

rein [rɛ̃] *nom masculin*

kidney : **on l'a opéré d'un rein** he had a kidney operation.

reins [rɛ̃] *nom masculin pluriel*

back : **avoir mal aux reins** to have backache *UK* ou to have a backache *US*.

reine [rɛn] *nom féminin*

queen : **la reine d'Angleterre** the Queen of England ; **la reine Élisabeth** Queen Elizabeth ; **la reine de carreau** the queen of diamonds.

rejeter [rəʒte] *verbe*

to reject : **rejeter une offre** to reject an offer.

rejoindre [rəʒwɛ̃dr] *verbe*

1. to join : **rejoins-nous quand tu auras fini** join us when you've finished
2. to catch up with : **l'athlète nigériane a rejoint ses concurrentes** the Nigerian athlete caught up with her competitors

se rejoindre *verbe pronominal*

to meet : **on se rejoint à 8 heures au café** we'll meet at 8 o'clock at the café ou I'll see you at 8 o'clock at the café.

rejoint, e [rəʒwɛ̃, ɛ̃t] *participe passé de* rejoindre.

relâcher [rəlaʃe] *verbe*

to release : **les otages ont été relâchés** the hostages have been released.

se relâcher *verbe pronominal*

1. to loosen : **la corde s'est relâchée** the rope loosened
2. to slacken off : **la prof m'a dit de ne pas me relâcher** the teacher told me not to slacken off.

relais [rəlɛ] *nom masculin*

relay : **le relais 4 × 100 mètres** the 4 × 100 metres relay
➤ **un relais routier** a transport café *UK*, a truck stop *US*.
➤ **passer le relais à quelqu'un** to hand over to somebody : **je suis fatigué, je te passe le relais** I'm tired, I'm handing over to you
➤ **prendre le relais** to take over : **je prendrai le relais à cinq heures** I'll take over at five o'clock.

relatif, ive [rəlatif, iv] *adjectif*

relative : **tout est relatif** everything is relative.

relation [rəlasjɔ̃] *nom féminin*

relationship : **il n'y a aucune relation entre ces deux phénomènes** there's no relationship between these two phenomena ; **ils ont une relation très tendue** they have a very tense relationship ; **ils ont de bonnes relations** they have a good relationship OU they get on well

➤ **mettre quelqu'un en relation avec quelqu'un** to put somebody in touch with somebody

➤ **relations sexuelles** sexual intercourse : **avoir des relations sexuelles avec quelqu'un** to have sexual intercourse with somebody

➤ **avoir des relations** to have connections : **c'est un homme important qui a des relations** he is an important man who has connections.

relative ➤ relatif.

relativement [rəlativmɑ̃] *adverbe*

relatively : **relativement facile** relatively easy.

relaxation [rəlaksasjɔ̃] *nom féminin*

relaxation : **des exercices de relaxation** relaxation exercises.

relayer [rəlɛje] *verbe*

to take over from : **tu veux que je te relaie ?** do you want me to take over from you?

se relayer *verbe pronominal*

to take turns : **on s'est relayés pour compter les points** we took turns at counting the points.

relevé, e [rəlve] *adjectif*

spicy : **cette sauce est très relevée** this sauce is very spicy

relevé *nom masculin*

➤ **un relevé de compte** a bank statement.

relève [rəlɛv] *nom féminin*

prendre la relève to take over : **je prends la relève de Mathias à deux heures** I'm taking over from Mathias at two o'clock.

relever [rəlve] *verbe*

1. to raise : **il n'a même pas relevé la tête quand je suis entrée** he didn't even raise his head when I came in

2. to roll up : **relève tes manches, sinon tu vas les mouiller** roll your sleeves up or you'll get them wet

3. to collect, to take in : **le prof commence à**

relever les copies the teacher is starting to collect the papers OU the teacher is starting to take in the papers

4. to note down : **tu as relevé le numéro d'immatriculation ?** did you note the registration number down?

se relever *verbe pronominal*

to stand up : **la pauvre dame n'arrivait pas à se relever** the poor lady couldn't stand up.

relief [rəljɛf] *nom masculin*

relief : **nous étudions le relief de la région** we're studying the relief of the region

➤ **des motifs en relief** a raised pattern

 The French word relief is a false friend, it does not mean 'relief'.

relier [rəlje] *verbe*

1. to connect : **l'imprimante est reliée à l'ordinateur** the printer is connected to the computer

2. to join : **reliez les deux points par un trait** join the two points with a line.

religieux, euse [rəliʒjø, øz] *adjectif*

religious : **les croyances religieuses** religious beliefs.

religieuse *nom féminin*

nun : **ma tante est religieuse** my aunt is a nun

➤ **une religieuse au chocolat** a chocolate cream puff.

religion [rəliʒjɔ̃] *nom féminin*

religion.

relire [rəlir] *verbe*

1. to reread : **j'ai relu l'article pour être sûr d'avoir tout compris** I reread the article to make sure I had understood everything

2. to read over : **est-ce que tu peux relire ma rédaction, s'il te plaît ?** can you read over my essay, please?

se relire *verbe pronominal*

to read over what one has written : **n'oublie pas de te relire** don't forget to read over what you've written.

relu, e [rəly] *participe passé de* relire.

r

se remarier [sərəmarje] *verbe pronominal*

to remarry : **mon père ne s'est jamais re-marié** my father never remarried.

remarquable [rəmarkabl] *adjectif*

remarkable : **il a fait des progrès remarquables** he has made remarkable progress.

remarque [rəmark] *nom féminin*

1. comment, remark : **est-ce que quelqu'un a des remarques à faire ?** has anybody got any comments to make? ; **j'en ai assez de tes remarques !** I've had enough of your remarks!
2. note : **j'ai oublié de lire les remarques en fin de chapitre** I forgot to read the notes at the end of the chapter.

remarquer [rəmarke] *verbe*

to notice : **tu as remarqué comme Nathalie a changé ?** have you noticed how Nathalie has changed?

➤ **faire remarquer quelque chose à quelqu'un** to point something out to somebody : **c'est Quentin qui m'a fait remarquer la différence** it's Quentin who pointed the difference out to me

➤ **se faire remarquer** to draw attention to oneself : **elle aime se faire remarquer** she likes to draw attention to herself.

rembobiner [rãbɔbine] *verbe*

to rewind : **n'oublie pas de rembobiner la cassette** don't forget to rewind the tape.

rembourser [rãburse] *verbe*

1. to pay back : **Léon a remboursé tout ce qu'il devait** Léon paid back everything he owed ; **jamais elle ne me remboursera** she'll never pay me back
2. to refund : **ils m'ont remboursé mon billet de train** they refunded me for the train ticket
➤ **se faire rembourser** to get a refund.

remerciement [rəmɛrsimã] *nom masculin*

thanks (*pluriel*) : **une lettre de remerciement** a letter of thanks ; **avec tous mes remerciements** with all my thanks.

remercier [rəmɛrsje] *verbe*

to thank : **j'ai voulu les remercier de leur aide** I wanted to thank them for their help ; **je vous remercie** thank you.

remettre [rəmɛtr] *verbe*

1. to put back on : **elle a remis son manteau** she put her coat back on
2. to put back : **il a remis le livre dans le tiroir** he put the book back in the drawer
➤ **remettre à** to put off until : **la réunion a été remise à lundi** the meeting was put off until Monday

se remettre *verbe pronominal*

to recover from : **il s'est remis de sa maladie** he recovered from his illness
➤ **se remettre à faire quelque chose** to start doing something again : **il s'est remis à travailler** he started working again ; **il s'est remis à pleuvoir** it started raining again.

remis, e [rəmi, iz] *participe passé de* remettre.

remise [rəmiz] *nom féminin*

1. discount : **la vendeuse nous a fait une remise de dix euros** the sales assistant gave us a ten-euro discount
2. shed : **la tondeuse est dans la remise** the lawnmower is in the shed.

remonte-pente [rəmõtpãt] (*pluriel* remonte-pentes) *nom masculin*
ski-tow.

remonter [rəmõte] *verbe*

1. to go back up, to come back up : **il est remonté nous chercher** he came back up to fetch us ; **remonte, je t'attends dehors** go back up, I'll wait for you outside ; **j'ai dû remonter l'escalier** I had to go back up the stairs
2. to take back up, to bring back up : **il faut que je remonte les clés** I've got to take the keys back up

> Notez la différence de traduction selon que la personne qui parle se trouve en bas (**to go back up**) ou en haut (**to come back up**).

3. to get back into : **remonte dans la voiture !** get back into the car!
4. to rise again : **les prix remontent** prices are rising again
5. to pull up : **remonte tes chaussettes !** pull up your socks!
6. to put together again : **j'ai démonté le moteur mais je n'arrive pas à le remonter** I've stripped the engine down but I can't put it together again

➤ **cela remonte à plusieurs années** this goes back several years.

remords [rəmɔr] *nom masculin*

remorse (*ne s'utilise jamais au pluriel*) : **avoir des remords** to be full of remorse ; **je n'ai aucun remords** I have no remorse.

remorque [rəmɔrk] *nom féminin*

trailer : **la remorque s'est détachée** the trailer came off.

remorquer [rəmɔrke] *verbe*

to tow : **le garagiste nous a remorqués jusqu'au garage** the mechanic towed us to the garage.

remplaçant, e [rãplasã, ãt] *nom masculin, nom féminin*

1. substitute : **le remplaçant du gardien de but** the goalkeeper's substitute

2. supply teacher *UK*, substitute teacher *US* : **on a eu un remplaçant en histoire** we had a supply teacher for history.

remplacer [rãplase] *verbe*

1. to replace : **j'ai remplacé toutes les ampoules par des neuves** I've replaced all the bulbs with new ones

2. to stand in for : **madame Lambert remplace notre prof de maths** Mrs Lambert is standing in for our maths teacher

3. to substitute : **Sénéchal a remplacé Petit à la trentième minute du match** Sénéchal substituted Petit in the thirtieth minute of the match.

rempli, e [rãpli] *adjectif*

full : **un saladier rempli d'eau** a bowl full of water

➤ **une journée bien remplie** a very busy day.

remplir [rãplir] *verbe*

1. to fill : **qui a rempli mon verre ?** who filled my glass? ; **Loïc a rempli la marge de petits dessins** Loïc filled the margin with little drawings

2. to fill in, to fill out : **on doit remplir ce questionnaire** we have to fill in this questionnaire

se remplir *verbe pronominal*

to fill : **va chercher ton pyjama pendant que la baignoire se remplit** go and get your pyjamas while the bath is filling.

remporter [rãpɔrte] *verbe*

1. to take away : **tu peux remporter ton échelle, je n'en ai plus besoin** you can take your ladder away, I don't need it any more

2. to win : **Metz a remporté le championnat** Metz won the championship.

remuer [rəmɥe] *verbe*

1. to move : **il y a quelque chose qui remue derrière le buisson** there's something moving behind the bush ; **arrête de remuer les jambes** stop moving your legs

2. to wag : **le chien remue la queue** the dog is wagging its tail

3. to stir : **remue bien ton café** stir your coffee well

se remuer *verbe pronominal*

familier to get a move on : **remue-toi un peu !** get a move on!

renard [rənar] *nom masculin*

fox (*pluriel* **foxes**).

rencontre [rãkɔ̃tr] *nom féminin*

meeting : **une rencontre d'athlétisme** an athletics meeting

➤ **aller à la rencontre de quelqu'un** to go towards somebody ; **je suis allée à sa rencontre** I went towards him.

rencontrer [rãkɔ̃tre] *verbe*

1. to meet : **j'ai rencontré ton frère au bowling** I met your brother at the bowling alley

2. to meet with : **nous avons rencontré plusieurs problèmes** we met with several problems

se rencontrer *verbe pronominal*

to meet : **nous nous sommes rencontrés à la gare** we met at the station.

rendez-vous [rãdevu] (*pluriel* **rendez-vous**) *nom masculin*

1. appointment : **j'ai rendez-vous chez le dentiste** I have an appointment with the dentist OU I have an appointment at the dentist's ; **on a tous rendez-vous au café** we're all meeting at the café ; **prendre rendez-vous avec quelqu'un** to make an appointment with somebody

2. date : **c'est son premier rendez-vous avec une fille** it's his first date

➤ **donner rendez-vous à quelqu'un** to arrange to meet somebody : **se donner rendez-vous** to arrange to meet.

se rendormir [sərɑ̃dɔrmir] *verbe pronominal*

to go back to sleep : **je n'arrive pas à me rendormir** I can't go back to sleep.

rendre [rɑ̃dr] *verbe*

1. to give back : **il m'a rendu mon CD** he gave me my CD back ou he gave me back my CD ; **rends-moi mon ballon !** give my ball back to me! ou give me my ball back!
2. to return : **je dois rendre mes livres à la bibliothèque** I must return my books to the library
3. to hand in : **je n'ai pas rendu mon devoir** I haven't handed in my homework
4. to make : **ce film m'a rendu triste** this film made me sad ; **ça rendra les choses plus faciles** that will make things easier

➤ **rendre quelqu'un fou** to drive somebody mad : **ce chien me rend fou !** that dog is driving me mad!

se rendre *verbe pronominal*

1. to surrender : **les rebelles se sont rendus** the rebels surrendered
2. to make oneself : **je voudrais me rendre utile** I'd like to make myself useful ; **arrête de manger, tu vas te rendre malade** stop eating, you'll make yourself ill

➤ **se rendre à** to go to : **ils se sont rendus à la mairie** they went to the town hall.

renifler [rənifle] *verbe*

to sniff.

renne [rɛn] *nom masculin*

reindeer *(pluriel* **reindeer***)*.

renommé, e [rənɔme] *adjectif*

renowned : **la Brie est renommée pour son fromage** the Brie area is renowned for its cheese

renommée *nom féminin*

➤ **un artiste de renommée internationale** a world-famous artist.

renoncer [rənɔ̃se] *verbe*

to give up : **c'est trop dur, je renonce !** it's too dur, I give up! ; **il a définitivement renoncé au tabac** he's given up smoking for good.

renouveler [rənuvle] *verbe*

to renew : **je dois renouveler mon abonnement** I have to renew my subscription.

rénovation [renɔvasjɔ̃] *nom féminin*

renovation : **les travaux de rénovation ont commencé** the renovation work has started.

rénover [renɔve] *verbe*

to renovate : **le quartier sera rénové peu à peu** the area will be renovated little by little.

renseignement [rɑ̃sɛɲəmɑ̃] *nom masculin*

piece of information, information : **un renseignement utile** a useful piece of information ; **merci du renseignement** thank you for that information ; **je cherche des renseignements sur la Grande Barrière** I'm looking for information about the Great Barrier Reef

➤ **les renseignements** directory enquiries *UK* ou information *US*

➤ **le bureau des renseignements** the information desk.

renseigner [rɑ̃sɛɲe] *verbe*

to give information to : **vous pourriez me renseigner sur les horaires de bus ?** could you give me some information about bus times?

se renseigner *verbe pronominal*

1. to get some information : **je me suis renseigné sur les vols pour Londres** I got some information on flights to London
2. to find out : **attendez ici, je vais me renseigner** wait here, I'll go and find out.

rentable [rɑ̃tabl] *adjectif*

profitable : **une affaire rentable** a profitable business.

rentrée [rɑ̃tre] *nom féminin*

la rentrée des classes ou **la rentrée** the start of the new school year.

rentrer [rɑ̃tre] *verbe*

1. to get back : **il est rentré à 3 heures du matin** he got back at 3 o'clock in the morning ; **il n'est pas encore rentré** he's not back yet
2. to get in : **je n'ai pas pu rentrer** I couldn't get in
3. to go back in, to come back in : **je l'ai vu rentrer** I saw him go back in ; **rentrez tout de suite en classe !** come back in the classroom at once!

286

Suivant que la personne qui parle se trouve ou non à l'endroit en question, on emploiera to come back in ou to go back in.

4. **to bring in** : n'oublie pas de rentrer le linge don't forget to bring the washing in
➤ **rentrer chez soi** to go home : je rentre chez moi I'm going home
➤ **rentre ton ventre** pull your stomach in
➤ **rentrer dans**
1. **to fit into** : mes affaires ne rentrent pas dans la valise my things don't fit into the suitcase
2. **to crash into** : la voiture est rentrée dans l'arbre the car crashed into the tree ; la camionnette nous est rentrée dedans the van crashed into us.

renverser [rɑ̃vɛrse] *verbe*

1. **to knock over** : j'ai renversé le vase I knocked the vase over
2. **to run over** : la voiture a renversé un piéton the car ran a pedestrian over
3. **to spill** : Thomas a renversé de l'eau partout Thomas spilled water everywhere

se renverser | *verbe pronominal*

to overturn : le camion s'est renversé au milieu de la route the lorry overturned in the middle of the road.

renvoyer [rɑ̃vwaje] *verbe*

1. **to send back** : est-ce que je peux renvoyer les livres si je n'en veux pas ? can I send the books back if I don't want them?
2. **to throw back** : renvoie-moi la balle throw the ball back to me
3. **to expel** : Lise a été renvoyée du collège Lise was expelled from school.

répandu, e [repɑ̃dy] *adjectif*

widespread : c'est une maladie très répandue it's a very widespread disease.

réparation [reparasjɔ̃] *nom féminin*

repair : la réparation coûte cinquante euros the repair costs fifty euros.

réparer [repare] *verbe*

to repair : qui va réparer la télé ? who is going to repair the TV? ; je vais faire réparer ma montre I'm going to get my watch repaired.

repartir [rəpartir] *verbe*

1. **to go back** : il veut repartir dans son pays he wants to go back to his country

2. **to set off again** : on s'est arrêtés sur l'autoroute pour déjeuner, puis on est repartis we stopped on the motorway for lunch, then we set off again
3. **to start again** : finalement, le moteur est reparti the engine eventually started again.

répartir [repartir] *verbe*

1. **to share out** : elle a réparti le travail entre les trois groupes she shared out the work among the three groups
2. **to split up** : les élèves sont répartis en quatre niveaux différents the pupils are split up into four different levels

se répartir | *verbe pronominal*

to share : ils se répartissent les tâches ménagères they share the housework.

repas [rəpa] *nom masculin*

meal : ils ne font que deux repas par jour they only have two meals a day
➤ **un repas d'affaires** a business lunch
➤ **le repas de midi** lunch
➤ **le repas du soir** dinner.

repassage [rəpasaʒ] *nom masculin*

ironing : je déteste faire le repassage I hate doing the ironing.

repasser [rəpase] *verbe*

1. **to iron** : j'ai une pile de linge à repasser I have a pile of washing to iron
2.

Lorsqu'il s'agit d'un verbe, la notion de « à nouveau », exprimée en français par le préfixe re-, est souvent rendue en anglais par l'adverbe again (refaire = to do again, to make again ; redire = to say again ; reprendre = to take again). Le préfixe re- est parfois employé en anglais (voir sens 6 ci-dessous), mais il est nettement plus rare qu'en français.

to go past again : les coureurs vont repasser the cyclists will go past again ; l'homme est repassé devant la maison the man went past the house again
3. **to go again** : on devra repasser par Clermont we'll have to go through Clermont again
4. *A la télé, au cinéma* ça repasse à la télé en ce moment it's on TV again at the moment ; ils repassent Toy Story au cinéma they're showing Toy Story again at the cinema

5. **to give again : repasse-moi ton cahier** give me your exercise book again
6. **to retake : mon frère repasse son examen aujourd'hui** my brother is retaking his exam today
7. **to have another : je dois repasser un scanner** I have to have another scan
8. *Au téléphone* **je te repasse Camille** here's Camille again ; **tu peux me repasser Fred ?** can you put Fred on again?

repère [rəpɛr] *nom masculin*

1. **mark : fais un repère sur le mur pour savoir où percer** make a mark on the wall so that you know where to drill
2. **landmark : la tour Montparnasse est un bon repère** the Montparnasse tower is a good landmark.

repérer [rəpere] *verbe*

1. **to locate : repérons le village sur la carte avant de partir** let's locate the village on the map before leaving
2. **to spot : j'ai repéré Anaïs dès que je suis arrivée** I spotted Anaïs as soon as I arrived

se repérer *verbe pronominal*

to get one's bearings : je ne me repère pas du tout dans cette ville I can't get my bearings at all in this city.

répertoire [rəpɛrtwar] *nom masculin*

1. **thumb-indexed notebook : j'ai un répertoire où je note le vocabulaire anglais** I have a thumb-indexed notebook in which I write my English vocabulary
2. **repertoire : ils ont un répertoire de chansons assez réduit** they have quite a small repertoire of songs.

répéter [repete] *verbe*

1. **to repeat : on apprend la prononciation en répétant les mots après le professeur** we learn pronunciation by repeating the words after the teacher
2. **to rehearse : le groupe de théâtre répète tous les mardis** the theatre group rehearses every Tuesday.

répétition [repetisjɔ̃] *nom féminin*

1. **rehearsal : on a une répétition tous les lundis soirs** we have a rehearsal every Monday night
2. **repetition : le professeur a dit qu'il y avait des répétitions dans ma rédaction** the

teacher said there were repetitions in my essay.

répliquer [replike] *verbe*

to reply : elle m'a répliqué que ça ne me regardait pas she replied that it was none of my business.

répondeur [repɔ̃dœr] *nom masculin*

answering machine.

répondre [repɔ̃dr] *verbe*

1. **to answer : pourquoi tu ne réponds pas ?** why aren't you answering? ; **réponds-moi !** answer me! ; **as-tu répondu à toutes les questions ?** did you answer all the questions? ; **répondre au téléphone** to answer the phone ; **ça ne répond pas** there's no answer
2. **to reply : Jean m'a répondu que ça ne l'intéressait pas** Jean replied that he wasn't interested
3. **to answer back : Anne a été punie pour avoir répondu à un professeur** Anne was punished for answering a teacher back.

répondu, e [repɔ̃dy] *participe passé de* **répondre.**

réponse [repɔ̃s] *nom féminin*

1. **answer : ce n'était pas la bonne réponse** it wasn't the right answer
2. **response : la réponse du gouvernement a été immédiate** the government's response was immediate.

reportage [rəpɔrtaʒ] *nom masculin*

report : un reportage sur l'Irlande a report on Ireland.

reporter [rəpɔrtɛr] *nom masculin*

reporter : il est reporter à la radio he's a radio reporter.

reporter [rəpɔrte] *verbe*

to postpone : la réunion est reportée à mercredi the meeting is postponed until Wednesday.

repos [rəpo] *nom masculin*

rest : il te faut du repos you need rest ou you need some rest.

reposer [rəpoze] *verbe*

1. **to put back : repose-le où tu l'as trouvé** put it back where you found it
2. **to put down again : j'ai dû reposer mon li-**

vre pour les aider I had to put my book down again to help them

3. **to rest** : **je m'allonge pour reposer mes jambes** I'm lying down to rest my legs

> **reposer une question à quelqu'un** to ask somebody a question again

se reposer *verbe pronominal*

to rest : **allez vous reposer** go and rest.

repousser [rəpuse] *verbe*

1. **to grow back** : **l'herbe a repoussé** the grass has grown back

2. **to push away** : **elle a repoussé Jérémie qui essayait de l'embrasser** she pushed Jérémie away as he was trying to kiss her

3. **to postpone** : **nous devrons repousser notre départ** we'll have to postpone our departure ; **la réunion est repoussée à la semaine prochaine** the meeting is postponed until next week.

reprendre [rəprãdr] *verbe*

1. **to have some more, to have another** : **je vais reprendre de la soupe** I'll have some more soup ; **je vais reprendre une huître** I'll have another oyster

2. **to regain** : **il a repris conscience** he regained consciousness ; **elle a repris confiance** she regained her confidence

3. **to take up again** : **il a décidé de reprendre ses études** he decided to take up his studies again

4. **to start again** : **les cours reprennent début septembre** classes start again at the beginning of September

> **les affaires reprennent** business is picking up.

représentant, e [rəprezãtã, ãt] *nom masculin, nom féminin*

representative : **son père est représentant de commerce** his father is a sales representative.

représentation [rəprezãtasjõ] *nom féminin*

performance : **la représentation commence à vingt heures** the performance starts at eight o'clock.

représenter [rəprezãte] *verbe*

to represent : **que représente ce dessin ?** what does this drawing represent? ; **Cédric nous représente aux conseils de classe** Cédric represents us at staff meetings.

repris, e [rəpri, iz] *participe passé de* reprendre.

reprise [rəpriz] *nom féminin*

> **à plusieurs reprises** on several occasions.

reproche [rəprɔʃ] *nom masculin*

reproach *(pluriel* reproaches) : **il m'a fait des reproches** he reproached me.

reprocher [rəprɔʃe] *verbe*

1. **to reproach** : **il m'a reproché de ne pas être venu** he reproached me for not coming

2. **to blame** : **il m'a reproché d'avoir cassé le vase** he blamed me for breaking the vase

se reprocher *verbe pronominal*

se reprocher d'avoir fait quelque chose to blame oneself for doing something ; **je me reproche de l'avoir laissé partir** I blame myself for letting him go.

reproduction [rəprɔdyksjõ] *nom féminin*

reproduction : **une reproduction de Chagall** a Chagall reproduction ; **la reproduction animale** animal reproduction.

reproduire [rəprɔdɥir] *verbe*

to reproduce : **reproduire un son** to reproduce a sound

se reproduire *verbe pronominal*

1. **to breed** : **les pandas se reproduisent difficilement en captivité** pandas have difficulty breeding in captivity

2. **to recur** : **cette erreur se reproduit plusieurs fois dans le texte** this mistake recurs several times in the text

> **et que ça ne se reproduise plus !** and don't let it happen again!

reptile [rɛptil] *nom masculin*

reptile : **les lézards sont des reptiles** lizards are reptiles.

république [repyblik] *nom féminin*

republic : **la République française** the French Republic.

répugnant, e [repyɲã, ãt] *adjectif*

revolting, disgusting.

réputation [repytasjõ] *nom féminin*

reputation : **il a bonne réputation** he has a good reputation ; **Samir a la réputation**

r

d'être généreux Samir has a reputation for being generous.

réputé, e [repyte] *adjectif*

famous : cette région est réputée pour ses vins this region is famous for its wine.

requin [rəkɛ̃] *nom masculin*

shark.

RER [ɛrəɛr] *(abréviation de* réseau express régional) *nom masculin*

train service between central Paris and the suburbs and airports.

réseau [rezo] *nom masculin*

network : le réseau routier the road network.

réservation [rezɛrvasjɔ̃] *nom féminin*

reservation, booking *UK* **:** vous avez une réservation ? do you have a reservation?

réserve [rezɛrv] *nom féminin*

1. **reserve :** les réserves d'énergie s'épuisent energy reserves are running out
2. **reservation :** une réserve indienne an Indian reservation
> une réserve naturelle a natural reserve
> faire des réserves de quelque chose to lay in supplies of something.

réservé, e [rezɛrve] *adjectif*

reserved : c'est quelqu'un de très réservé he's very reserved ; est-ce que cette table est réservée ? is this table reserved?

réserver [rezɛrve] *verbe*

1. **to reserve, to book :** j'ai réservé trois places pour le concert I've reserved three tickets for the concert OU I've booked three tickets for the concert ; je vous réserve une table ? shall I reserve a table for you?
2. **to keep, to save :** je réserve ça pour plus tard I'm keeping it for later OU I'm saving it for later

se réserver *verbe pronominal*

to save oneself : je me réserve pour le dessert I'm saving myself for dessert
> se réserver quelque chose to keep something for oneself : Sylvie s'est réservé le meilleur morceau Sylvie has kept the best piece for herself.

réservoir [rezɛrvwar] *nom masculin*

1. **tank :** le réservoir d'essence the fuel tank

2. **reservoir :** on peut se baigner dans le réservoir you can swim in the reservoir.

résidence [rezidɑ̃s] *nom féminin*

1. **residence :** leur résidence principale their main residence
2. **block of luxury flats** *UK*, **luxury apartment building** *US* **:** ils habitent dans une résidence en banlieue they live in a block of luxury flats in the suburbs
> une résidence secondaire a second home
> résidence universitaire hall of residence *UK* OU dormitory *US*.

résidentiel, elle [rezidɑ̃sjɛl] *adjectif*

residential : les quartiers résidentiels residential areas.

se résigner [səreziɲe] *verbe pronominal*

to resign oneself : je ne peux pas me résigner à ne plus la voir I can't resign myself to not seeing her anymore.

résistance [rezistɑ̃s] *nom féminin*

resistance : il s'est laissé arrêter sans résistance he let himself be arrested without putting up any resistance ; elle était dans la Résistance she was in the Resistance.

résistant, e [rezistɑ̃, ɑ̃t] *adjectif*

tough, resilient : c'est une fille très résistante she's a very tough girl.

résister [reziste] *verbe*

to resist : je n'ai pas pu résister I couldn't resist
> résister à
1. **to resist :** Isa n'a pas pu résister à la tentation Isa couldn't resist the temptation
2. **to withstand :** le toit a bien résisté à la tempête the roof withstood the storm.

résolu, e [rezɔly] *verbe & adjectif*

▪ *participe passé de* résoudre
le problème est résolu the problem is solved
▪ *adjectif*
determined : il a l'air très résolu he looks very determined ; elle est résolue à travailler sérieusement she's determined to work hard.

résolution [rezɔlysjɔ̃] *nom féminin*

resolution : on a pris la résolution de travailler plus we made a resolution to work more.

résoudre [rezudr] *verbe*

to solve : **je n'ai pas réussi à résoudre le problème** I couldn't solve the problem ; **le problème sera vite résolu** the problem will soon be solved.

respect [rɛspɛ] *nom masculin*

respect : **les élèves ont beaucoup de respect pour ce professeur** the pupils have a lot of respect for this teacher.

respecter [rɛspɛkte] *verbe*

to respect : **tous les élèves le respectent** all the pupils respect him ; **respecter la loi** to respect the law OU to obey the law.

respiration [rɛspirasjɔ̃] *nom féminin*

1. breathing : **sa respiration est bruyante** his breathing is loud
2. breath : **retenir sa respiration** to hold one's breath.

respirer [rɛspire] *verbe*

to breathe : **il a du mal à respirer** he has difficulty breathing ; **respirez profondément** breathe deeply.

responsabilité [rɛspɔ̃sabilite] *nom féminin*

responsibility *(pluriel* **responsibilities***)* : **il refuse de prendre ses responsabilités** he refuses to face up to his responsibilities.

responsable [rɛspɔ̃sabl] *adjectif & nom*

■ *adjectif*
responsible : **qui est responsable de ce désastre ?** who is responsible for this disaster?
■ *nom masculin ou féminin*

1. person responsible *(pluriel* **people responsible***)* : **les responsables de l'attentat** the people responsible for the terrorist attack
2. official : **les responsables syndicaux** the union officials
3. person in charge : **je veux parler au responsable** I want to talk to the person in charge.

ressembler [rəsɑ̃ble] *verbe*

➤ **ressembler à quelqu'un** to look like somebody : **tu ne ressembles pas du tout à ton frère** you don't look at all like your brother OU you don't look anything like your brother
➤ **ça ne lui ressemble pas d'être en retard** it's not like him to be late

se ressembler *verbe pronominal*

to look alike : **les deux sœurs se ressemblent beaucoup** the two sisters look very alike.

ressentir [rəsɑ̃tir] *verbe*

to feel : **j'ai ressenti beaucoup d'angoisse** I felt a great deal of anxiety.

resserrer [rəsere] *verbe*

to tighten : **tu devrais resserrer un peu le nœud** you should tighten the knot a bit

se resserrer *verbe pronominal*

to narrow : **la route se resserre à cet endroit** the road narrows in this spot.

resservir [rəsɛrvir] *verbe*

1. to give another helping to : **Sarah nous a resservi du poulet** Sarah gave us another helping of chicken
2. to be used again : **garde-le, ça peut resservir** keep it, it can be used again

se resservir *verbe pronominal*

1. to have another helping : **je peux me resservir ?** can I have another helping? ; **on s'est tous resservi du gâteau** we all had another helping of cake OU we all helped ourselves to more cake
2. to use again : **je ne me suis jamais resservi de l'agenda** I never used the diary again.

ressort [rəsɔr] *nom masculin*

spring : **les ressorts du canapé sont abîmés** the springs in the sofa are damaged.

ressortir [rəsɔrtir] *verbe*

1. to go out again : **il faut que je ressorte, j'ai oublié le pain** I've got to go out again, I've forgotten the bread
2. to come out again : **tu peux ressortir deux minutes ? je veux te montrer un truc** can you come out again for two minutes? I want to show you something

> Notez la différence de traduction selon que la personne qui parle se trouve à l'intérieur (sens 1, traduction **to go out again**) ou déjà dehors (sens 2, traduction **to come out again**).

3. to get out : **les voleurs sont ressortis par la fenêtre** the burglars got out through the window

r

4. to take out again : **Manu a dû ressortir son vélo du garage** Manu had to take his bike out of the garage again
5. to stand out : **le tableau ressort bien sur le mur blanc** the painting stands out well against the white wall
➤ **faire ressortir** to bring out : **ce pull fait ressortir le bleu de tes yeux** this pullover brings out the blue of your eyes.

ressources [rəsurs] *nom féminin pluriel*

resources : **les ressources naturelles** natural resources.

restaurant [rɛstɔrɑ̃] *nom masculin*

restaurant : **un restaurant indien** an Indian restaurant : **nous sommes allés manger au restaurant** we went to a restaurant OU we ate out
➤ **le restaurant universitaire** the university cafeteria.

reste [rɛst] *nom masculin*

rest : **je ferai le reste de l'exercice demain** I'll do the rest of the exercise tomorrow

restes *nom masculin pluriel*

leftovers : **ce soir on mange des restes** we're having leftovers tonight.

rester [rɛste] *verbe*

1. to stay : **reste là, j'ai besoin de toi** stay here, I need you ; **restez calmes !** stay calm! ; **ils sont restés trois jours** they stayed three days OU they stayed for three days
2. to be left : **c'est tout ce qui reste** this is all that's left ; **il en reste un peu** there's a bit left ; **il te reste de l'argent ?** do you have any money left?

resto [rɛsto] *nom masculin familier*

restaurant : **un resto grec** a Greek restaurant
➤ **le resto U** the university cafeteria.

résultat [rezylta] *nom masculin*

result : **les résultats des examens sont affichés sur le panneau** the exam results are on the noticeboard.

résumé [rezyme] *nom masculin*

summary *(pluriel* **summaries***)* : **on doit faire un résumé du texte pour demain** we have to write a summary of the text for tomorrow
➤ **en résumé** to sum up.

résumer [rezyme] *verbe*

to summarize : **est-ce que tu peux résumer l'histoire ?** can you summarize the story?

 Résumer is a false friend, it does not mean 'to resume'.

rétablir [retablir] *verbe*

to restore : **la paix est maintenant rétablie** peace is now restored

se rétablir *verbe pronominal*

to recover : **elle s'est vite rétablie** she soon recovered.

retard [rətar] *nom masculin*

delay : **un retard d'une demi-heure** a half-hour delay
➤ **être en retard** OU **avoir du retard** to be late : **vous êtes encore en retard !** you're late again! ; **être en retard de vingt minutes** to be twenty minutes late
➤ **rattraper son retard** to make up for lost time.

retarder [rətarde] *verbe*

1. to delay : **désolée, j'ai été retardée** I'm sorry, I was delayed
2. to put back, to postpone : **nous envisageons de retarder notre départ** we're considering putting back our departure OU we're considering postponing our departure
3. to be slow : **ma montre retarde** my watch is slow ; **tu retardes de trois minutes** your watch is three minutes slow.

retenir [rətnir] *verbe*

1. to hold back : **retiens-moi ou je fais un malheur !** hold me back or I'll hurt somebody!
2. to reserve, to book : **je voudrais retenir une chambre** I'd like to reserve a room OU I'd like to book a room
3. to remember : **je n'arrive pas à retenir ce poème** I can't remember this poem
4. to keep : **vous êtes en retard, qu'est-ce qui vous a retenus ?** you're late, what kept you?
➤ **retenir son souffle** to hold one's breath
➤ **je pose 7 et je retiens 3** I put down 7 and carry 3.

retenu, e [rətny] *participe passé de* retenir.

retirer [rətire] *verbe*

1. to take off : **tu peux retirer ta cravate** you can take your tie off

2. **to withdraw : je vais retirer de l'argent** I'm going to withdraw some money ; **les voisins ont retiré leur plainte** the neighbours have withdrawn their complaint

➤ **retirer quelque chose à quelqu'un** to take something away from somebody : **la police lui a retiré son permis** the police took his driving licence away from him.

retomber [rətɔ̃be] *verbe*

to land : il est retombé sur le dos he landed on his back.

retour [rətur] *nom masculin*

1. **return : tout le monde attend leur retour** everybody is waiting for their return ; **retour à l'envoyeur** return to sender

2. **return journey : le retour m'a paru plus court que l'aller** the return journey seemed quicker than the outward journey

➤ **à mon retour** when I get back : **je t'appellerai à mon retour** I'll phone you when I get back

➤ **être de retour** to be back : **il est de retour à Paris** he's back in Paris.

retourner [rəturne] *verbe*

1. **to turn over : aide-moi à retourner le matelas** help me to turn the mattress over

2. **to go back, to return : elle est retournée au bureau** she returned to the office ; **tu es retourné à Londres depuis l'année dernière ?** have you been back to London since last year? ; **retourner chez soi** to go back home

➤ **retourner en arrière** to turn back : **on a dû retourner en arrière** we had to turn back

se retourner *verbe pronominal*

1. **to turn around, to turn round** *UK* : **ne te retourne pas, il est juste derrière nous** don't turn around, he's just behind us

2. **to capsize : le bateau s'est retourné** the boat capsized.

retrait [rətrɛ] *nom masculin*

withdrawal : tous les retraits figurent sur le relevé all the withdrawals appear on the statement

➤ **retrait des bagages** baggage reclaim

➤ **rester en retrait** to stand back.

retraite [rətrɛt] *nom féminin*

1. **retirement : retraite anticipée** early retirement

2. **pension : mes grands-parents touchent**

une **bonne retraite** my grandparents get a good pension

➤ **être à la retraite** to be retired

➤ **prendre sa retraite** to retire.

retraité, e [rətrete] *adjectif & nom*

■ *adjectif*

retired : ma grand-mère est retraitée my grandmother is retired

■ *nom masculin, nom féminin*

pensioner *UK*, **retiree** *US* : **il y a beaucoup de retraités dans cette association** there are a lot of pensioners in this association.

rétrécir [retresir] *verbe*

to shrink : mon tee-shirt a rétréci au lavage my T-shirt has shrunk in the wash.

retrousser [rətruse] *verbe*

to roll up : je vais retrousser mon pantalon pour ne pas le mouiller I'll roll up my trousers so as not to get them wet.

retrouver [rətruve] *verbe*

1. **to find : tu as retrouvé ton portable ?** have you found your mobile phone?

2. **to meet : j'ai retrouvé mes copains pour jouer au foot** I met my friends to play football

se retrouver *verbe pronominal*

1. **to meet up : on se retrouve à 7 heures devant le cinéma** we'll meet up at 7 o'clock in front of the cinema ou I'll see you at 7 o'clock in front of the cinema

2. **to end up : je ne sais pas comment on s'est retrouvés là** I don't know how we ended up there

➤ **je ne m'y retrouve pas, c'est trop compliqué** I'm completely lost, it's too complicated.

rétroviseur [retrɔvizœr] *nom masculin*

rear-view mirror.

réunion [reynjɔ̃] *nom féminin*

meeting : ma mère a une réunion ce soir my mother has a meeting tonight

➤ **une réunion de famille** a family reunion

➤ **une réunion parents-professeurs** a parent-teacher evening.

réunir [reynir] *verbe*

to bring together : on essaie de réunir le plus de gens possible we are trying to bring together as many people as possible

se réunir *verbe pronominal*

to meet : **on se réunit tous les samedis après-midi** we meet every Saturday afternoon.

réussi, e [reysi] *adjectif*

successful : **une soirée très réussie** a very successful party.

réussir [reysir] *verbe*

1. to succeed : **bravo, tu as réussi !** well done, you've succeeded! ; **réussir à faire quelque chose** to manage to do something OU to succeed in doing something ; **il a réussi à me convaincre** he managed to persuade me
2. to make a success of : **tu as très bien réussi le curry** you've made a real success of the curry
3. to pass : **mon frère a réussi son permis de conduire** my brother passed his driving test
➤ **ça ne me réussit pas** it doesn't agree with me.

réussite [reysit] *nom féminin*

1. success : **c'est une belle réussite** it's a great success
2. patience *UK*, solitaire *US* : **je m'ennuyais, alors j'ai fait une réussite** I was bored, so I played a game of patience.

revanche [rəvɑ̃ʃ] *nom féminin*

1. revenge : **prendre sa revanche** to take one's revenge OU to get one's own back ; **Patou a juré de prendre sa revanche** Patou swore she would take her revenge OU Patou swore she would get her own back
2. return game : **on fait la revanche ?** shall we have a return game?
➤ **en revanche** on the other hand.

rêve [rɛv] *nom masculin*

dream : **j'ai fait un rêve bizarre** I had a strange dream ; **fais de beaux rêves !** sweet dreams!
➤ **de rêve** dream : **ils ont une maison de rêve** they have a dream house.

réveil [revɛj] *nom masculin*

1. waking up : **le réveil est toujours difficile** waking up is always hard OU it's always hard to wake up
2. alarm clock : **mets le réveil à sonner pour 7 heures** set the alarm clock for 7 o'clock.

réveiller [reveje] *verbe*

to wake up : **vous pouvez me réveiller à 8 heures ?** can you wake me up at 8 o'clock?

se réveiller *verbe pronominal*

to wake up : **réveille-toi, il est neuf heures !** wake up, it's nine o'clock!

réveillon [revejɔ̃] *nom masculin*

meal eaten on Christmas Eve or on New Year's Eve.

révéler [revele] *verbe*

to reveal : **elle a refusé de révéler ses projets** she refused to reveal her plans

se révéler *verbe pronominal*

to turn out to be, to prove to be : **ce médicament s'est révélé très efficace** this medicine turned out to be very effective OU this medicine proved to be very effective.

revenir [rəvnir] *verbe*

to come back : **reviens !** come back! ; **Roland est revenu du Canada** Roland has come back from Canada ; **tout d'un coup son nom m'est revenu** all of a sudden his name came back to me
➤ **revenir à** to cost : **ça nous est revenu à cent euros** it cost us a hundred euro
➤ **revenir cher** to be expensive
➤ **ça revient au même** it amounts to the same thing
➤ **il n'en revenait pas** he couldn't get over it
➤ **faire revenir** to brown : **faites revenir les oignons** brown the onions.

revenu [rəvny] *nom masculin*

income : **l'impôt sur le revenu** income tax.

rêver [rɛve] *verbe*

1. to dream : **j'ai rêvé que mes parents m'achetaient une moto** I dreamt that my parents were buying me a motorbike ; **j'ai rêvé de toi** I dreamt of you OU I dreamt about you ; **je rêve de partir en voyage** I dream of going on a trip
2. to daydream : **aide-nous au lieu de rêver** help us instead of daydreaming.

réverbère [reverbɛr] *nom masculin*

street lamp.

revers [rəver] *nom masculin*

1. lapel : **Lionel porte une rose sur le revers de sa veste** Lionel is wearing a rose on the lapel of his jacket

2. **backhand** : elle joue bien au tennis mais son revers n'est pas très bon she plays tennis well but her backhand isn't very good.

rêveur, euse [rɛvœr, øz] *adjectif & nom*

■ *adjectif*
dreamy : un regard rêveur a dreamy look
■ *nom masculin, nom féminin*
dreamer : Alice est une rêveuse Alice is a dreamer.

réviser [revize] *verbe*

1. **to revise** *UK*, **to review** *US* : tu as révisé ta géo pour demain ? have you revised your geography for tomorrow? ; j'ai passé toute la journée à réviser I spent all day revising
2. **to service** : mon père a fait réviser la voiture my father had the car serviced.

révision [revizjɔ̃] *nom féminin*

1. **revision** *UK*, **review** *US* (*ne s'emploient jamais au pluriel*) : les révisions avant l'examen the revision before the exam
2. **service** : la voiture est au garage pour une révision the car is in the garage for a service.

revoir [rəvwar] *verbe*

1. **to see again** : tu as revu Caro depuis la soirée chez Luc ? have you seen Caro again since the party at Luc's?
2. **to revise** *UK*, **to review** *US* : le prof a dit que je devais revoir la première partie du devoir the teacher said I should revise the first part of the paper

se revoir *verbe pronominal*

to see each other again, to meet again : on ne s'est jamais revus we never saw each other again OU we never met again
➤ **au revoir !** goodbye!

révolter [revɔlte] *verbe*

to disgust : leur attitude me révolte their attitude disgusts me

se révolter *verbe pronominal*

to revolt, to rebel : les paysans se sont révoltés contre le pouvoir militaire the peasants revolted against the military regime OU the peasants rebelled against the military regime.

révolution [revɔlysjɔ̃] *nom féminin*

revolution : la Révolution française the French Revolution.

revolver [revɔlvɛr] *nom masculin*

revolver.

revue [rəvy] *nom féminin*

magazine : une revue de mode a fashion magazine
➤ **passer quelque chose en revue** to review something.

rez-de-chaussée [redʃose] (*pluriel* rez-de-chaussée) *nom masculin*

ground floor *UK*, **first floor** *US* : on habite au rez-de-chaussée we live on the ground floor *UK* OU we live on the first floor *US*.

Rhin [rɛ̃] *nom masculin*

le Rhin the Rhine.

rhinocéros [rinoserɔs] *nom masculin*

rhinoceros (*pluriel* rhinoceroses), **rhino**.

Rhône [ron] *nom masculin*

le Rhône the Rhône river.

rhubarbe [rybarb] *nom féminin*

rhubarb : une tarte à la rhubarbe a rhubarb tart.

rhum [rɔm] *nom masculin*

rum : du rhum blanc white rum.

rhume [rym] *nom masculin*

cold : attraper un rhume to catch a cold
➤ **rhume des foins** hay fever.

ri [ri] *participe passé invariable de* **rire**.

ricaner [rikane] *verbe*

to snigger.

riche [riʃ] *adjectif & nom*

■ *adjectif*
rich : les gens riches rich people ; une céréale riche en vitamines a cereal that is rich in vitamins ; une région riche en pétrole an area with a lot of oil
■ *nom masculin ou féminin*
les riches the rich.

richesse [riʃɛs] *nom féminin*

1. **wealth** : ils aiment étaler leur richesse they like to parade their wealth
2. **abundance** : la richesse de la faune the abundance of wildlife

richesses *nom féminin pluriel*

resources : **d'énormes richesses minières** huge mining resources.

ricocher [rikɔʃe] *verbe*

to ricochet : **les balles ricochaient sur le mur** the bullets ricochet off the wall.

ride [rid] *nom féminin*

wrinkle : **elle a déjà des rides** she already has wrinkles.

rideau [rido] (*pluriel* **rideaux**) *nom masculin*

curtain, drape *US* : **tu as fermé les rideaux ?** have you drawn the curtains? ; **un rideau de douche** a shower curtain.

ridicule [ridikyl] *adjectif*

ridiculous : **quelle idée ridicule !** what a ridiculous idea!

rien [rjɛ̃] *pronom indéfini*

ı. nothing : **qu'est-ce que tu fais ? – rien** what are you doing? – nothing ; **il n'y a rien de nouveau depuis hier** there's nothing new since yesterday ; **rien d'autre ne convient** nothing else is suitable ; **je l'ai eu pour rien** I got it for nothing ; **on a fait tout ça pour rien** we did all that for nothing

2. anything : **Lise est partie sans rien dire** Lise left without saying anything

3. *Au tennis* love : **quarante à rien** forty love

➤ **ne ... rien** nothing ou not ... anything : **ne dis rien** say nothing ou don't say anything ; **il n'y a plus rien dans le frigo** there's nothing left in the fridge ou there isn't anything left in the fridge ; **je ne veux rien du tout** I don't want anything at all

➤ **merci ! – de rien !** thank you! – you're welcome!

➤ **rien que** just : **rien que de penser à l'interro, je suis déprimée** just thinking about the test depresses me.

rigide [riʒid] *adjectif*

ı. stiff : **du carton rigide** stiff cardboard

2. rigid : **une discipline rigide** rigid discipline.

rigoler [rigɔle] *verbe familier*

ı. to laugh : **je ne pouvais plus m'arrêter de rigoler** I couldn't stop laughing

2. to have fun, to have a good time : **on a bien rigolé chez Martha** we had fun at Martha's ou we had a good time at Martha's

3. to joke : **ce n'est pas le moment de rigoler** this is no time for joking ; **c'est pas vrai, tu rigoles !** it's not true, you're joking! ; **je disais ça pour rigoler** I was joking.

rigolo, ote [rigɔlo, ɔt] *adjectif familier*

funny : **une histoire très rigolote** a very funny story.

rigueur [rigœr] *nom féminin*

➤ **à la rigueur** if necessary : **à la rigueur, on pourrait revenir demain** if necessary, we could come back tomorrow.

rime [rim] *nom féminin*

rhyme.

rimer [rime] *verbe*

to rhyme : **« amour » rime avec « toujours »** 'amour' rhymes with 'toujours'.

rincer [rɛ̃se] *verbe*

to rinse : **elle rince les verres** she's rinsing the glasses

se rincer *verbe pronominal*

il se rince les cheveux he's rinsing his hair.

rire [rir] *nom & verbe*

■ *nom masculin*

laugh : **elle a un rire contagieux** she has an infectious laugh

➤ **j'entendais des rires** I could hear laughter

■ *verbe*

to laugh : **ne me fais pas rire !** don't make me laugh!

risque [risk] *nom masculin*

risk : **prendre des risques** to take risks.

risqué, e [riske] *adjectif*

risky : **c'est une entreprise risquée** it's a risky business.

risquer [riske] *verbe*

to risk : **il a risqué sa vie** he risked his life

➤ **risquer de faire quelque chose** to be likely to do something : **tu risques d'être en retard** you're likely to be late.

rivage [rivaʒ] *nom masculin*

shore : **nous nous sommes promenés sur le rivage** we walked along the shore.

rive [riv] *nom féminin*

bank : **les rives du fleuve** the banks of the river

➤ **la rive droite** *the right bank of the Seine in Paris*

la rive gauche the left bank of the Seine in Paris.

rivière [rivjɛr] nom féminin

river : **l'Oise est une rivière** the Oise is a river.

riz [ri] nom masculin

rice : **manger du riz** to eat rice
➤ **du riz au lait** rice pudding.

robe [rɔb] nom féminin

dress (pluriel dresses) : **Émilie porte une robe verte** Émilie is wearing a green dress
➤ **une robe de chambre** a dressing gown UK ou a robe US.

robinet [rɔbinɛ] nom masculin

tap UK, faucet US : **il a ouvert le robinet** he turned the tap on ; **ferme le robinet** turn the tap off.

robot [rɔbo] nom masculin

robot.

roc [rɔk] nom masculin

rock : **les marches sont taillées dans le roc** the steps are cut into the rock.

roche [rɔʃ] nom féminin

rock : **une sculpture taillée dans la roche** a sculpture carved out of the rock.

rocher [rɔʃe] nom masculin

rock : **il y a un tas de rochers sur la plage** there's a pile of rocks on the beach.

Rocheuses [rɔʃøz] nom féminin pluriel

les Rocheuses the Rockies.

rocheux, euse [rɔʃø, øz] adjectif

rocky
➤ **les montagnes Rocheuses** the Rocky Mountains.

rock [rɔk] nom masculin

rock : **un groupe de rock** a rock group.

roi [rwa] nom masculin

king : **le Roi Louis XIV** King Louis XIV
➤ **la fête des Rois** Twelfth Night.

Roland-Garros [rɔlãgaros] nom

tennis stadium in Paris where the French Open is held

📖 ROLAND-GARROS
This is the name of the tennis stadium outside Paris and its biggest tournament, the French Open. The French Open is one of the four 'grand slams' and one of the world's biggest sporting events - broadcast in over 150 countries. You can also watch live tennis action on the Roland-Garros website.

rôle [rol] nom masculin

role, part : **qui joue le rôle de Hamlet ?** who's playing the role of Hamlet?

roller [rɔllœr] nom masculin

Rollerblade® : **Denis a des rollers neufs** Denis has got a new pair of Rollerblades
➤ **faire du roller** to go rollerblading

⚠ In French the word **roller** is a false friend, it does not mean 'roller'.

romain, e [rɔmɛ̃, ɛn] adjectif

Roman

En anglais, les adjectifs se rapportant à un pays ou une région s'écrivent avec une majuscule :

l'empire romain the Roman empire

Romain, e nom masculin, nom féminin

Roman : **les Romains** the Romans.

roman [rɔmã] nom masculin

novel : **un roman policier** a detective novel
➤ **un roman noir** a thriller.

romantique [rɔmãtik] adjectif

romantic : **une soirée romantique** a romantic evening : **c'est une fille très romantique** she's very romantic.

rompre [rɔ̃pr] verbe

to break
➤ **rompre avec quelqu'un** to break up with somebody : **Céline a rompu avec Timothée** Céline has broken up with Timothée.

rond, e [rɔ̃, rɔ̃d] adjectif

round : **un visage tout rond** a round face ; **en chiffres ronds** in round figures

rond nom masculin

circle : **en rond** in a circle.

r

rondelle [rɔ̃dɛl] *nom féminin*

slice : **elle a coupé le citron en rondelles** she cut the lemon into slices.

rond-point [rɔ̃pwɛ̃] (*pluriel* ronds-points) *nom masculin*

roundabout *UK*, **traffic circle** *US*.

ronfler [rɔ̃fle] *verbe*

to snore : mon frère ronfle my brother snores.

se ronger [sərɔ̃ʒe] *verbe pronominal*

se ronger les ongles to bite one's nails ; **arrête de te ronger les ongles !** stop biting your nails!

ronronner [rɔ̃rɔne] *verbe*

to purr : le chat ronronne the cat's purring.

rosbif [rɔsbif] *nom masculin*

roast beef : nous avons mangé du rosbif à midi we had roast beef for lunch.

rose [roz] *nom & adjectif*

- *nom féminin*
  rose : un bouquet de roses a bunch of roses
- *nom masculin*
  pink : j'aime le rose I like pink
- *adjectif*
  pink : un foulard rose a pink scarf.

rosier [rozje] *nom masculin*

rosebush (*pluriel* **rosebushes**).

rossignol [rɔsiɲɔl] *nom masculin*

nightingale.

roter [rɔte] *verbe familier*

to burp.

rôti [roti] *nom masculin*

roast : du rôti de porc roast pork.

roue [ru] *nom féminin*

wheel : la roue arrière the back wheel
➤ **une roue de secours** a spare wheel
➤ **faire la roue** to do a cartwheel.

rouge [ruʒ] *nom & adjectif*

- *nom masculin*
  red : le rouge te va bien red suits you
➤ **du rouge à lèvres** lipstick
- *adjectif*
  red : une jupe rouge a red skirt.

rouge-gorge [ruʒgɔrʒ] (*pluriel* rouges-gorges) *nom masculin*

robin.

rougeole [ruʒɔl] *nom féminin*

measles (*singulier*) **: avoir la rougeole** to have measles.

rougir [ruʒir] *verbe*

to blush : tu me fais rougir you're making me blush.

rouille [ruj] *nom féminin*

rust : mon vélo est couvert de rouille my bike is covered in rust.

rouillé, e [ruje] *adjectif*

rusty : mes clés sont rouillées my keys are rusty.

rouiller [ruje] *verbe*

to go rusty, to rust : les outils ont rouillé the tools have gone rusty.

rouleau [rulo] (*pluriel* rouleaux) *nom masculin*

roll : un rouleau de papier peint a roll of wallpaper
➤ **un rouleau à pâtisserie** a rolling pin.

rouler [rule] *verbe*

1. **to drive : on a roulé pendant deux heures** we drove for two hours
2. **to go : la voiture roulait trop vite** the car was going too fast
3. **to roll up : ils ont roulé le tapis** they rolled the carpet up
4. **to roll : elle roule les « r »** she rolls her 'r's ; **la bille a roulé sous la table** the marble rolled under the table.

roulette [rulɛt] *nom féminin*

wheel : une table à roulettes a table on wheels.

roulotte [rulɔt] *nom féminin*

caravan *UK*, **trailer** *US*.

rouquin, e [rukɛ̃, in] *adjectif & nom familier*

- *adjectif*
  red-haired : un garçon rouquin a red-haired boy
- *nom masculin, nom féminin*
  redhead : une petite rouquine a redhead ou a red-haired girl.

rousse ➤ roux.

route [rut] *nom féminin*

1. **road : prenez la première route à droite** take the first road on the right
2. **way : c'est sur ma route** it's on my way ; **nous nous sommes arrêtés en route** we stopped on the way
> **en route !** let's go!
> **mettre le moteur en route** to start the engine
> **se mettre en route** to set off : **elle s'est mise en route tôt le matin** she set off early in the morning.

routier, ère [rutje, ɛr] *adjectif*

road : une carte routière a road map.

routine [rutin] *nom féminin*

routine : je ne supporte pas la routine I can't stand routine.

roux, rousse [ru, rus] *adjectif & nom*

■ *adjectif*

1. **red : elle a les cheveux roux** OU **elle est rousse** she has red hair
2. **red-haired : une jeune fille rousse** a red-haired girl

■ *nom masculin, nom féminin*

redhead : sa fille est une rousse her daughter's a redhead.

royal, e, aux [rwajal, o] *adjectif*

royal : la famille royale the royal family.

royaume [rwajom] *nom masculin*

kingdom.

Royaume-Uni [rwajomyni] *nom masculin*

> **le Royaume-Uni** the United Kingdom : **sa sœur travaille au Royaume-Uni** her sister works in the United Kingdom ; **je vais aller au Royaume-Uni en août** I'm going to the United Kingdom in August.

ruban [rybã] *nom masculin*

ribbon : elle attache ses cheveux avec un ruban she ties her hair up with a ribbon
> **du ruban adhésif** sticky tape *UK* OU adhesive tape *US*.

rubéole [rybeɔl] *nom féminin*

German measles : Macha a la rubéole Macha has German measles.

rubrique [rybrik] *nom féminin*

column, section : la rubrique des sports the sports column OU the sports section.

ruche [ryʃ] *nom féminin*

hive, beehive.

rue [ry] *nom féminin*

street : une rue piétonne a pedestrian street.

ruelle [rɥɛl] *nom féminin*

alley.

se ruer [sərɥe] *verbe pronominal*

se ruer sur to pounce on ; **il s'est rué sur lui** he pounced on him ; **ils se sont rués sur le gâteau** they pounced on the cake ; **se ruer vers** to rush towards ; **il s'est rué vers la sortie** he rushed towards the exit.

rugby [rygbi] *nom masculin*

rugby : jouer au rugby to play rugby.

rugir [ryʒir] *verbe*

to roar : le lion rugissait the lion roared.

rugueux, euse [rygø, øz] *adjectif*

rough : une peau rugueuse rough skin.

ruine [rɥin] *nom féminin*

ruin : le château est en ruine the castle is in ruins ; **tomber en ruine** to fall into ruin.

ruiner [rɥine] *verbe*

to ruin : toutes ces dépenses me ruinent all these expenses are ruining me

se ruiner *verbe pronominal*

to spend a fortune : je me suis ruinée en jeux vidéos I spent a fortune on video games.

ruisseau [rɥiso] (*pluriel* ruisseaux) *nom masculin*

stream.

rumeur [rymœr] *nom féminin*

rumour *UK*, **rumor** *US* : **ce n'est qu'une rumeur** it's just a rumour.

ruse [ryz] *nom féminin*

trick.

rusé, e [ryze] *adjectif*

crafty : elle est très rusée she's very crafty.

russe [rys] *adjectif*

Russian : une tradition russe a Russian tradition

r

russe *nom masculin*

Russian : ils parlent le russe ou **ils parlent russe** they speak Russian

> En anglais, les adjectifs se rapportant à un pays ou une région, ainsi que le nom désignant la langue de ce pays ou de cette région, s'écrivent avec une majuscule.

Russe *nom masculin ou féminin*

Russian : les Russes the Russians.

Russie [rysi] *nom féminin*

➤ **la Russie** Russia

> En anglais, à de rares exceptions près, il n'y a pas d'article devant les noms de pays :

la Russie est un pays immense Russia is a huge country ; **Saint-Pétersbourg est en Russie** St Petersburg is in Russia ; **tu es déjà allé en Russie ?** have you already been to Russia?

rythme [ritm] *nom masculin*

1. **rhythm : elle a le sens du rythme** she has a good sense of rhythm
2. **pace : travaille à ton rythme** work at your own pace
3. **rate : au rythme d'une page par heure** at the rate of one page an hour.

s' ➤ se, si.

sa ➤ son.

sable [sabl] *nom masculin*

sand
➤ **une plage de sable** a sandy beach.

sablé [sable] *nom masculin*

shortbread biscuit *UK*, **shortbread cookie** *US*.

sabot [sabo] *nom masculin*

1. **clog : elle porte des sabots** she's wearing clogs
2. **hoof** *(pluriel* **hoofs** ou **hooves***)* : **les sabots d'un cheval** a horse's hoofs ou a horse's hooves.

sac [sak] *nom masculin*

bag ; un sac de couchage a sleeping bag ; **un sac en plastique** ou **un sac plastique** a plastic bag
➤ **un sac à dos** a rucksack
➤ **un sac à main** a handbag ou a purse *US*.

sachant *participe présent de* **savoir**.

sache, saches ➤ **savoir**.

sachet [saʃɛ] *nom masculin*

sachet : un sachet de sucre a sachet of sugar
➤ **un sachet de thé** a teabag.

sacoche [sakɔʃ] *nom féminin*

bag
➤ **une sacoche de vélo** a saddlebag.

sac-poubelle [sakpubɛl] *(pluriel* **sacs-poubelle***) nom masculin*

bin liner *UK*, **garbage bag** *US*.

sacré, e [sakre] *adjectif*

sacred : un objet sacré a sacred object
➤ **sacrée Marie !** good old Marie!

safari [safari] *nom masculin*

safari : faire un safari to go on a safari.

sage [saʒ] *adjectif*

good : sois sage be good.

sagement [saʒmɑ̃] *adverbe*

quietly : les enfants jouaient sagement the children were playing quietly.

Sagittaire [saʒitɛr] *nom masculin*

Sagittarius : Paul est Sagittaire Paul's a Sagittarius.

saignant, e [sɛɲɑ̃, ɑ̃t] *adjectif*

rare : vous préférez votre bifteck saignant ou bien cuit ? do you like your steak rare or well done?

saigner [seɲe] *verbe*

to bleed
➤ **je saigne du nez** my nose is bleeding ou I've got a nosebleed.

sain, e [sɛ̃, sɛn] *adjectif*

healthy : ce climat est très sain it's a very healthy climate : **il mène une vie saine** he leads a healthy life
➤ **sain et sauf** safe and sound.

saint, e [sɛ̃, sɛ̃t] *adjectif & nom*

■ *adjectif*
holy : un livre saint a holy book
■ *nom masculin, nom féminin*
Saint : saint François Saint Francis OU St Francis
➤ **la Saint-Sylvestre** the New Year's Eve.

sais, sait ➤ savoir.

saisir [sezir] *verbe*

1. **to grab, to grasp : il m'a saisi par le poignet** he grabbed me by the wrist ; **je n'ai pas bien saisi la différence** I didn't quite grasp the difference
2. **to seize : tu devrais saisir cette occasion** you should seize this opportunity.

saison [sɛzɔ̃] *nom féminin*

season : les quatre saisons the four seasons.

salade [salad] *nom féminin*

1. **salad : j'ai fait une salade de riz** I made a rice salad ; **une salade de fruits** a fruit salad
2. **lettuce : lavez bien la salade** wash the lettuce carefully.

saladier [saladje] *nom masculin*

salad bowl.

salaire [salɛr] *nom masculin*

salary, wage.

salarié, e [salarje] *nom masculin, nom féminin*

employee.

sale [sal] *adjectif*

1. **dirty : j'ai les mains sales** my hands are dirty
2. *familier* **rotten : elle a un sale caractère** she has a rotten temper ; **quel sale temps !** what rotten weather!

salé, e [sale] *adjectif*

1. **salted : des cacahuètes salées** salted peanuts
2. **salty : un goût salé** a salty taste ; **l'eau de mer est salée** seawater is salty ; **c'est trop salé** it's too salty.

saler [sale] *verbe*

to put salt in : as-tu salé la soupe ? did you put salt in the soup?

saleté [salte] *nom féminin*

il y a des saletés dans l'eau the water is dirty ; **sa cave est d'une saleté inimaginable** her cellar is incredibly dirty
➤ **faire des saletés** to make a mess.

salir [salir] *verbe*

to get something dirty : attention, tu vas salir la nappe be careful or you'll get the tablecloth dirty

se salir *verbe pronominal*

to get dirty, to get oneself dirty : tu vas te salir you'll get dirty OU you'll get yourself dirty.

salive [saliv] *nom féminin*

saliva.

salle [sal] *nom féminin*

room
➤ **la salle d'attente** the waiting room
➤ **la salle de bains** the bathroom
➤ **une salle de cinéma** a screen OU a movie theater *US* : **le film passe en salle 2** the film is showing on screen 2
➤ **la salle de classe** the classroom
➤ **une salle de concert** a concert hall
➤ **la salle d'embarquement** the departure lounge
➤ **la salle à manger** the dining room.

salon [salɔ̃] *nom masculin*

1. **living room, lounge** *UK* : **on a pris le thé au salon** we had tea in the living room
2. **show, fair : le Salon de l'Agriculture** the agricultural show ; **le Salon du Livre** the Book Fair
➤ **un salon de coiffure** a hairdressing salon OU a hairdresser's
➤ **un salon de beauté** a beauty salon.

salopette [salɔpɛt] *nom féminin*

dungarees *UK*, **overalls** *US* (*s'utilisent toujours au pluriel*) : **ma salopette est sale** my dungarees are dirty.

saluer [salɥe] *verbe*

1. **to say hello to : elle ne m'a même pas salué** she didn't even say hello to me
2. **to say goodbye to : elle m'a salué et elle est partie** she said goodbye to me and she left

S

> **il m'a salué de la main** he waved to me.

salut [saly] *interjection familier*

1. hi! : **salut, ça va ?** hi, how are you doing?
2. bye!, see you! : **allez, salut !** OK, bye! OU OK, see you!

samedi [samdi] *nom masculin*

Saturday

> En anglais, les jours de la semaine s'écrivent avec une majuscule :

Aude va à la piscine le samedi Aude goes to the swimming pool on Saturdays ; **samedi dernier** last Saturday ; **samedi prochain** next Saturday.

SAMU, Samu [samy] *(abréviation de* Service d'aide médicale d'urgence*) nom masculin* French ambulance service.

sandale [sãdal] *nom féminin*

sandal : **Jean porte des sandales** Jean is wearing sandals.

sandwich [sãdwitʃ] *(pluriel* sandwiches OU sandwichs*) nom masculin* sandwich *(pluriel* **sandwiches**) : **un sandwich au poulet** a chicken sandwich.

sang [sã] *nom masculin*

blood : **en sang** covered in blood
> **se faire du mauvais sang** to get really worried.

sanglier [sãglije] *nom masculin*

wild boar.

sanglot [sãglo] *nom masculin*

> **éclater en sanglots** to burst into tears.

sanguin, e [sãgɛ̃, in] *adjectif*

blood : **groupe sanguin** blood group.

Sanisette® [sanizɛt] *nom féminin*

automatic public toilet.

sans [sã] *préposition*

without : **j'ai réussi sans aucune aide** I managed without any help ; **il va falloir faire sans** we'll have to do without it ; **sans rien dire** without saying anything

sans que *conjonction*

sans qu'il s'en rende compte without him realizing.

sans-abri [sãzabri] *nom masculin ou féminin invariable*

homeless person : **les sans-abri** the homeless.

santé [sãte] *nom féminin*

health : **elle est en bonne santé** she's in good health ; **est-ce que c'est bon ou mauvais pour la santé ?** is it good or bad for your health?
> **à ta santé !** OU **à votre santé !** cheers!

saoul ➤ soûl.

saouler ➤ soûler.

sapin [sapɛ̃] *nom masculin*

fir, fir tree
> **un sapin de Noël** a Christmas tree.

sardine [sardin] *nom féminin*

sardine : **une boîte de sardines** a tin of sardines.

satellite [satelit] *nom masculin*

satellite : **la télévision par satellite** satellite TV.

satin [satɛ̃] *nom masculin*

satin : **une robe en satin** a satin dress.

satisfaisant, e [satisfəzã, ãt] *adjectif*

satisfactory : **ce n'est pas une excuse satisfaisante** it's not a satisfactory excuse.

satisfait, e [satisfɛ, ɛt] *adjectif*

satisfied : **je ne suis pas satisfaite de tes résultats** I'm not satisfied with your results.

sauce [sos] *nom féminin*

sauce : **de la sauce tomate** tomato sauce.

saucisse [sosis] *nom féminin*

sausage
> **des saucisses de Francfort** frankfurters.

saucisson [sosisɔ̃] *nom masculin*

salami.

sauf [sof] *préposition*

except : **ils étaient tous là sauf Matthieu** they were all there except Matthieu.

saule [sol] *nom masculin*

willow : **saule pleureur** weeping willow.

saumon [somɔ̃] *nom masculin*

salmon : **du saumon fumé** smoked salmon.

sauna [sona] *nom masculin*

sauna : **aller au sauna** to have a sauna.

saurai, sauras ➤ savoir.

saut [so] *nom masculin*

jump : **faire un saut** to jump
➤ **le saut en hauteur** the high jump
➤ **le saut en longueur** the long jump ou the broad jump *US*.

saute-mouton [sotmutɔ̃] *nom masculin invariable*

jouer à saute-mouton to play leapfrog.

sauter [sote] *verbe*

1. **to jump** : **saute par dessus la barrière** jump over the gate
2. **to skip** : **il a sauté une classe** he skipped a year ; **j'ai sauté une dizaine de pages** I skipped about ten pages ; **tu ne devrais pas sauter de repas** you shouldn't skip any meals
➤ **sauter de joie** to jump for joy
➤ **faire sauter quelque chose** to blow something up : **ils ont fait sauter le pont** they blew up the bridge
➤ **les plombs ont sauté** the fuses have blown.

sauterelle [sotrɛl] *nom féminin*

grasshopper.

sautiller [sotije] *verbe*

to hop.

sauvage [sovaʒ] *adjectif*

1. **wild** : **une bête sauvage** a wild animal
2. **shy** : **sa petite sœur est plutôt sauvage** her little sister is quite shy.

sauvegarder [sovgarde] *verbe*

to save : **j'ai oublié de sauvegarder le fichier** I forgot to save the file.

sauver [sove] *verbe*

to save : **il m'a sauvé la vie** he saved my life

se sauver *verbe pronominal*

1. **to run away** : **il s'est sauvé à toute vitesse** he ran away as fast as he could
2. *familier* **to be off** : **bon, je me sauve** right, I'm off.

savant [savɑ̃] *nom masculin*

scientist.

savoir [savwar] *verbe*

to know : **je ne sais pas comment ça marche** I don't know how it works ; **il sait ce qu'il fait** he knows what he's doing ; **est-ce que tu sais qui était Galilée ?** do you know who Galileo was? ; **il savait tout** he knew everything ; **je le saurai demain** I'll know tomorrow
➤ **est-ce que tu sais jouer aux échecs ?** can you play chess?
➤ **il ne sait pas nager** he can't swim
➤ **je n'en sais rien** I have no idea.

savon [savɔ̃] *nom masculin*

soap : **du savon parfumé** perfumed soap
➤ **un savon** a bar of soap.

savonnette [savɔnɛt] *nom féminin*

bar of soap.

saxophone [saksɔfɔn] *nom masculin*

saxophone : **Sidney joue du saxophone** Sidney plays the saxophone.

scandale [skɑ̃dal] *nom masculin*

scandal : **son dernier film a fait scandale** his latest film caused a scandal
➤ **c'est un scandale !** it's outrageous!

scanner¹ [skane] *verbe*

to scan : **tu peux me scanner cette photo ?** can you scan this photo for me?

scanner² [skanɛr] *nom masculin*

1. **scanner** : **un ordinateur avec scanner** a computer with a scanner
2. **scan** : **passer un scanner** to have a scan.

scarabée [skarabe] *nom masculin*

beetle.

scène [sɛn] *nom féminin*

1. **scene** : **acte III, scène 5** act three, scene five ; **Valentine a fait une scène hier soir** Valentine made a scene last night
2. **stage** : **le groupe est entré en scène** the group came on stage
➤ **mettre une pièce en scène** to direct a play.

schéma [ʃema] *nom masculin*

diagram : **j'ai fait un schéma** I drew a diagram.

S

scie [si] *nom féminin*

saw.

science [sjɑ̃s] *nom féminin*

science : **la science moderne** modern science

> **les sciences naturelles** natural sciences.

science-fiction [sjɑ̃sfiksjɔ̃] *nom féminin*

science fiction : **un livre de science-fiction** a science-fiction book.

scientifique [sjɑ̃tifik] *adjectif & nom*

■ *adjectif*
scientific : **une expérience scientifique** a scientific experiment
■ *nom masculin ou féminin*
scientist : **des scientifiques ont découvert un nouveau vaccin** scientists have discovered a new vaccine.

scier [sje] *verbe*

to saw : **le menuisier a scié la planche en deux** the carpenter sawed the plank in half.

scolaire [skɔlɛr] *adjectif*

school : **les vacances scolaires** the school holidays *UK* OU the school vacation *US*.

scooter [skutœr] *nom masculin*

scooter : **elle est trop jeune pour faire du scooter** she's too young to ride a scooter

> **un scooter des neiges** a snowmobile.

score [skɔr] *nom masculin*

score : **quel est le score final ?** what's the final score?

scorpion [skɔrpjɔ̃] *nom masculin*

scorpion : **il s'est fait piquer par un scorpion** he was stung by a scorpion

Scorpion *nom masculin*

Scorpio : **Richard est Scorpion** Richard is a Scorpio.

Scotch® [skɔtʃ] *nom masculin*

Sellotape® *UK*, Scotch tape® *US*.

scotcher [skɔtʃe] *verbe*

to sellotape *UK*, to scotchtape *US*.

scout [skut] *nom masculin*

scout : **Luc est scout** Luc's a scout.

sculpteur [skyltœr] *nom masculin*

sculptor : **Bourdelle était sculpteur** Bourdelle was a sculptor.

sculpture [skyltyr] *nom féminin*

sculpture : **une sculpture en marbre** a marble sculpture.

SDF [ɛsdeɛf] *(abréviation de* sans domicile fixe*) nom masculin ou féminin*
homeless person : **les SDF** the homeless.

se [sə] (**s'** *devant une voyelle ou un « h » muet*) *pronom*

1. *Dans les verbes pronominaux*

> Pour les verbes qui ne sont que pronominaux, c'est-à-dire qui ne s'utilisent qu'avec le pronom « se », « se » ne se traduit pas en anglais :

il s'est évanoui he fainted ; **il se souvient** he remembers

2. *Dans les verbes pronominaux réfléchis* himself

> Lorsque « se » représente une personne, il se traduit par himself (féminin herself, pluriel themselves) ou bien il ne se traduit pas :

il s'est fait mal he hurt himself ; **elle se regardait dans le miroir** she was looking at herself in the mirror ; **ils se sont coupés** they cut themselves ; **elles se sont présentées au reste de la classe** they introduced themselves to the rest of the class ; **elle se lève tôt** she gets up early ; **il se rase tous les jours** he shaves everyday

> Lorsque « se » représente une chose ou un animal, il se traduit par itself ou bien il ne se traduit pas :

cette espèce se reproduit très vite this species reproduces very quickly ; **le cheval s'est fait mal** the horse hurt itself

> Notez qu'en anglais, on utilise l'adjectif possessif avec les parties du corps :

ils doivent d'abord se laver les mains they have to wash their hands first ; **Patrick s'est coupé le doigt** Patrick cut his finger ; **elle se ronge tout le temps les ongles** she's always biting her nails

> Lorsque le verbe est à l'infinitif et que « se » représente une personne indéfinie, soit il se traduit par oneself, soit il ne se traduit pas :

se faire mal to hurt oneself ; **se coucher** to go to bed

3. *Dans les verbes pronominaux réciproques*

> Lorsque « se » a une valeur réciproque, il se traduit par **each other** ou bien il ne se traduit pas :

elles se sont rencontrées dans la rue they bumped into each other in the street ; **ils se battent tout le temps** they never stop fighting

4. *Avec un sens passif* **ce modèle se vend partout** this model is sold everywhere ou you can buy this model everywhere ; **ça se boit frais** you drink it cold.

séance [seɑ̃s] *nom féminin*

performance : **j'irai à la séance de 18 heures** I'm going to the 6 o'clock performance.

seau [so] *(pluriel* **seaux***) nom masculin*

bucket : **un seau d'eau** a bucket of water.

sec, sèche [sɛk, sɛʃ] *adjectif*

1. dry : **j'ai la peau sèche** I have dry skin ; **mon jean n'est pas encore sec** my jeans aren't dry yet
2. dried : **fruits secs** dried fruit.

sèche-cheveux [sɛʃʃəvø] *(pluriel* **sèche-cheveux***) nom masculin*
hairdryer.

sécher [seʃe] *verbe*

to dry : **j'ai mis le linge à sécher** I put the washing out to dry ; **sèche tes larmes** dry your tears ou dry your eyes ; **je me suis séché les cheveux** I dried my hair
> **sécher un cours** *familier* to skip a class.

sécheresse [sɛʃrɛs] *nom féminin*

drought : **la sécheresse a duré pendant des mois** the drought lasted for months.

séchoir [seʃwar] *nom masculin*

dryer : **une machine à laver et un séchoir** a washing machine and a dryer.

second, e [səgɔ̃, ɔ̃d] *adjectif & nom*

■ *adjectif numéral*
second : **le second tome du roman** the second volume of the novel
■ *nom masculin, nom féminin*
second : **le second recevra un prix de consolation** the runner-up will get a consolation prize.

secondaire [səgɔ̃dɛr] *adjectif*

secondary : **l'enseignement secondaire** secondary education.

seconde [səgɔ̃d] *nom féminin*

1. second : **une seconde !** just a second!
2. year eleven *UK,* tenth grade *US* : **ma sœur est en seconde** my sister is in year eleven
> **voyager en seconde** ou **voyager en seconde classe** to travel second class.

secouer [səkwe] *verbe*

to shake : **secouez la bouteille avant l'emploi** shake the bottle before use ; **il m'a secoué** he shook me.

secours [səkur] *nom masculin*

help : **va chercher du secours** go and get help ; **au secours !** help!
> **les premiers secours** first aid
> **une sortie de secours** an emergency exit.

secret, ète [səkrɛ, ɛt] *adjectif*

secret : **un code secret** a secret code

secret *nom masculin*

secret : **je vais te confier un secret** I'm going to tell you a secret ; **sais-tu garder un secret ?** can you keep a secret?

secrétaire [səkretɛr] *nom masculin ou féminin*

secretary *(pluriel* **secretaries***) :* **elle est secrétaire** she's a secretary.

sécurité [sekyrite] *nom féminin*

1. safety : **la sécurité routière** road safety
2. security : **des mesures de sécurité** security measures
> **la Sécurité sociale** the French social security system
> **être en sécurité** to be safe : **nous sommes en sécurité ici** we're safe here.

séduisant, e [sedɥizɑ̃, ɑ̃t] *adjectif*

attractive : **elle est très séduisante** she's very attractive.

seigle [sɛgl] *nom masculin*

rye : **du pain de seigle** rye bread.

sein [sɛ̃] *nom masculin*

breast

au sein de *préposition*

within.

S

Seine [sɛn] *nom féminin*

la Seine the Seine OU the River Seine.

seize [sɛz] *adjectif numéral & nom masculin*

sixteen : **il y avait seize personnes à mon anniversaire** there were sixteen people at my birthday party

> **nous sommes le seize février** it's the sixteenth of February *UK* OU it's February sixteenth *US*.

seizième [sɛzjɛm] *adjectif numéral & nom*

sixteenth : **Carole est arrivée seizième** Carole came sixteenth ; **le seizième arrondissement** the sixteenth arrondissement.

séjour [seʒur] *nom masculin*

stay : **bon séjour !** enjoy your stay!

> **un séjour linguistique** a stay abroad to learn the language : **il fait un séjour linguistique au Canada** he's staying in Canada to learn the language.

sel [sɛl] *nom masculin*

salt : **passez-moi le sel** pass me the salt ; **le sel et le poivre** the salt and pepper ; **gros sel** coarse salt.

sélectionner [selɛksjɔne] *verbe*

to select.

self-service [sɛlfsɛrvis] (*pluriel* self-services) *nom masculin*

a self-service cafeteria.

selle [sɛl] *nom féminin*

saddle : **il s'est mis en selle** he got on his horse.

selon [səlɔ̃] *préposition*

according to : **selon lui** according to him ; **selon moi** in my opinion.

semaine [səmɛn] *nom féminin*

week : **je travaille en semaine** I work during the week ; **je pars dans une semaine** I'm leaving in a week's time ; **la semaine dernière** last week ; **la semaine prochaine** next week.

semblable [sɑ̃blabl] *adjectif*

similar : **ta veste est semblable à la mienne** your jacket is similar to mine.

semblant [sɑ̃blɑ̃] *nom masculin*

> **faire semblant de faire quelque chose** to pretend to do something.

sembler [sɑ̃ble] *verbe*

to seem : **elle semblait assez contente** she seemed quite happy ; **il semble qu'il soit en retard** it seems that he's late OU he seems to be late.

semelle [səmɛl] *nom féminin*

sole : **les semelles de mes bottes sont trouées** the soles of my boots have got holes in them.

semestre [səmɛstr] *nom masculin*

semester.

sénat [sena] *nom masculin*

Senate.

sens [sɑ̃s] *nom masculin*

1. sense : **les cinq sens** the five senses
2. meaning, sense : **le sens d'un mot** the meaning of a word OU the sense of a word
3. direction : **dans le sens inverse** in the opposite direction

> **sens interdit** OU **sens unique** one-way street

> **avoir le sens de l'humour** to have a sense of humour *UK* OU to have a sense of humor *US*

> **avoir le sens de l'orientation** to have a good sense of direction.

sensation [sɑ̃sasjɔ̃] *nom féminin*

feeling, sensation : **il avait la sensation d'être suivi** he had the feeling he was being followed.

sensationnel, elle [sɑ̃sasjɔnɛl] *adjectif*

fantastic.

sensible [sɑ̃sibl] *adjectif*

1. sensitive : **Julien est très sensible** Julien is very sensitive
2. noticeable : **une amélioration sensible** noticeable improvement

> **je suis très sensible au froid** I really feel the cold

 The French word **sensible** is a false friend, it does not mean 'sensible'.

sentier [sɑ̃tje] *nom masculin*

path : **un sentier mène à la rivière** a path leads to the river.

sentiment [sɑ̃timɑ̃] *nom masculin*

feeling : **un sentiment de bonheur** a feeling of happiness.

sentimental, e, aux [sɑ̃timɑ̃tal, o] *adjectif*

sentimental : **ça a une valeur sentimentale** it has sentimental value.

sentir [sɑ̃tir] *verbe*

1. to feel : **je n'ai rien senti** I didn't feel anything
2. to smell : **ça sent bon** it smells good ; **j'ai senti une odeur de brûlé** I could smell burning
3. to smell of : **ça sent la cannelle** it smells of cinnamon

se sentir *verbe pronominal*

to feel : **se sentir bien** to feel good ; **se sentir mal** to feel ill ; **se sentir en sécurité** to feel safe.

séparé, e [separe] *adjectif*

1. separate : **ils dorment dans des chambres séparées** they sleep in separate rooms
2. separated : **mes parents sont séparés** my parents are separated.

séparer [separe] *verbe*

to separate : **elle a voulu séparer les garçons qui se battaient** she tried to separate the boys that were fighting
➤ **séparer en** to divide into : **on peut le séparer en deux** we can divide it into two

se séparer *verbe pronominal*

to split up, to separate : **mes parents se sont séparés il y a deux ans** my parents split up two years ago
➤ **se séparer de** to split up with : **elle s'est séparée de Pierre** she split up with Pierre.

sept [sɛt] *adjectif numéral & nom masculin*

seven : **j'ai sept cousins** I have seven cousins
➤ **nous sommes le sept janvier** it's the seventh of January *UK* ou it's January seventh *US*.

septembre [sɛptɑ̃br] *nom masculin*

September

En anglais, les mois de l'année s'écrivent avec une majuscule.

l'école recommence en septembre school starts again in September
➤ **nous sommes le trois septembre** it's the third of September *UK* ou it's September third *US*

septième [sɛtjɛm] *adjectif numéral & nom*

seventh : **je suis arrivé septième** I came sev-

enth ; **le septième arrondissement** the seventh arrondissement.

serai, seras *etc* ➤ **être**.

série [seri] *nom féminin*

series *(pluriel* series*)* : **une série de questions** a series of questions ; **il y a une nouvelle série à la télé** there's a new series on TV
➤ **une série télé** a TV series.

sérieusement [serjøzmɑ̃] *adverbe*

seriously : **il est sérieusement atteint** he's seriously injured
➤ **je parle sérieusement** I'm serious ou I'm being serious.

sérieux, euse [serjø, øz] *adjectif*

serious : **il a l'air très sérieux** he looks very serious ; **elle est sérieuse dans son travail** she's serious about her work

sérieux *nom masculin*

➤ **prendre quelque chose au sérieux** to take something seriously
➤ **prendre quelqu'un au sérieux** to take somebody seriously : **il se prend trop au sérieux** he takes himself too seriously
➤ **garder son sérieux** to keep a straight face.

serpent [sɛrpɑ̃] *nom masculin*

snake
➤ **un serpent à sonnette** a rattlesnake.

serpillière [sɛrpijɛr] *nom féminin*

floorcloth *UK*, mop *US*.

serre [sɛr] *nom féminin*

greenhouse : **des fleurs cultivées sous serre** flowers grown in a greenhouse
➤ **l'effet de serre** the greenhouse effect.

serré, e [sere] *adjectif*

tight : **cette robe est trop serrée pour moi** this dress is too tight for me.

serrer [sere] *verbe*

1. to grip : **elle serre la poignée de son sac** she's gripping the handle of her bag
2. to be too tight : **mes nouvelles chaussures me serrent** my new shoes are too tight
➤ **serrer la main à quelqu'un** to shake somebody's hand : **il m'a serré la main** he shook my hand
➤ **serrer quelqu'un dans ses bras** to hug somebody ou to give somebody a hug

S

se serrer *verbe pronominal*

to squeeze up *UK*, to squeeze together *US* : **serrez-vous un peu** squeeze up a bit
➤ **se serrer la main** to shake hands : **on s'est serré la main** we shook hands.

serre-tête [sɛrtɛt] (*pluriel* serre-tête) *nom masculin*

headband.

serrure [seryr] *nom féminin*

lock.

serveur, euse [sɛrvœr, øz] *nom masculin, nom féminin*

waiter *(féminin* waitress*)* : **Patou est serveuse** Patou is a waitress.

serviable [sɛrvjabl] *adjectif*

helpful : **il est très serviable** he's very helpful.

service [sɛrvis] *nom masculin*

1. favour *UK*, favor *US* : **je peux te demander un service ?** can I ask you a favour?
2. service : **le service est compris** service is included
3. department : **il travaille au service informatique** he works in the IT department
4. *Au tennis* serve : **il a un bon service** he has a good serve
➤ **rendre service à quelqu'un** to do somebody a favour *UK* ou to do somebody a favor *US*
➤ **hors service** out of order.

serviette [sɛrvjɛt] *nom féminin*

1. napkin : **une serviette en papier** a paper napkin
2. towel : **une serviette de bain** a bath towel
➤ **une serviette hygiénique** a sanitary towel *UK* ou a sanitary napkin *US*.

servir [sɛrvir] *verbe*

1. to be useful : **ce guide m'a bien servi** this guidebook has been very useful
2. to serve : **je n'ai pas été servi** I haven't been served yet
➤ **à quoi ça sert ?** what's this for?
➤ **servir à faire quelque chose** to be used to do something : **le caoutchouc servait à fabriquer des pneus** rubber was used to make tyres
➤ **ça ne sert à rien** it's useless : **ça ne sert à rien d'y aller** it's pointless going

se servir *verbe pronominal*

to help oneself : **sers-toi un peu plus de viande** help yourself to some more meat
➤ **se servir de quelque chose** to use something : **je me suis servi de ton stylo** I used your pen.

ses ➤ son.

set [sɛt] *nom masculin*

Au tennis set : **il a gagné en trois sets** he won in three sets
➤ **un set de table** a table mat.

seul, e [sœl] *adjectif & nom*

■ *adjectif*

1. alone, on one's own : **elle vit seule** she lives alone ou she lives on her own
2. lonely : **se sentir seul** to feel lonely ou to be lonely ; **il se sent seul** he feels lonely ou he's lonely
➤ **tout seul** by oneself : **j'ai réussi à le faire toute seule** I managed to do it by myself
■ *nom masculin, nom féminin*
c'est le seul que j'ai it's the only one I've got ; **ce sont les seuls qui restent** they are the only ones left ; **il n'en reste qu'un seul** there's only one left.

seulement [sœlmã] *adverbe*

only : **il en reste deux seulement** there are only two left ; **non seulement il est bête mais en plus il est méchant !** not only is he stupid, he's also nasty!

sévère [sever] *adjectif*

strict : **ses parents sont sévères avec lui** his parents are strict with him.

sexe [sɛks] *nom masculin*

sex : **des jeunes gens des deux sexes** young people of both sexes.

sexiste [sɛksist] *adjectif*

sexist.

sexy [sɛksi] *adjectif invariable familier*

sexy.

shampooing [ʃãpwɛ̃] *nom masculin*

shampoo : **du shampooing pour cheveux secs** shampoo for dry hair
➤ **se faire faire un shampooing et une coupe** to get a wash and a cut.

shopping [ʃɔpiŋ] *nom masculin*

shopping : je vais faire du shopping avec Leïla I'm going shopping with Leïla.

short [ʃɔrt] *nom masculin*

shorts : Roland porte un short bleu Roland is wearing blue shorts OU Roland is wearing a pair of blue shorts.

si [si] *adverbe & conjonction*

■ *adverbe*

1. **so : c'est si beau !** it's so beautiful! ; **il roulait si vite qu'il a eu un accident** he was driving so fast that he had an accident

2. **as : ce n'est pas si facile que ça** it's not as easy as that

3. *Dans les questions à la forme négative* **yes : tu n'aimes pas le rap ? – si** don't you like rap? – yes, I do

➤ **je n'y arriverai jamais – mais si !** I'll never manage – of course you will!

■ *conjonction*

if : si tu triches, je ne joue plus if you cheat, I'm not playing any more ; **si je pouvais, j'irais vivre en Amérique** if I could, I would go and live in America ; **si seulement tu me l'avais dit avant !** if only you had told me earlier! ; **dis-moi si c'est possible** tell me if it's possible OU tell me whether it's possible.

SIDA, Sida [sida] *(abréviation de* syndrome immunodéficitaire acquis*) nom masculin*
AIDS : la lutte contre le SIDA the fight against AIDS.

siècle [sjɛkl] *nom masculin*

century *(pluriel* centuries*)* **: le vingt-et-unième siècle** the twenty-first century.

siège [sjɛʒ] *nom masculin*

seat : le siège avant the front seat.

le sien, la sienne [ləsjɛ̃, lasjɛn] *(masculin pluriel* les siens [lesjɛ̃], *féminin pluriel* les siennes [lesjɛn]) pronom*

1. *Lorsque le possesseur est un homme* **his : j'ai oublié mon stylo alors il m'a prêté le sien** I forgot my pen so he lent me his ; **Mickaël m'a dit que cette bicyclette était la sienne** Mickaël told me this bike was his ; **Jérôme aussi a les yeux bleus – non, les siens sont verts** Jérôme has blue eyes too – no, his are green

2. *Lorsque le possesseur est une femme* **hers : j'ai perdu mon stylo alors elle m'a**

prêté le sien I lost my pen so she lent me hers ; **Laura m'a dit que cette bicyclette était la sienne** Laura told me this bike was hers ; **Fanny aussi a les yeux bleus – non, les siens sont verts** Fanny has blue eyes too – no, hers are green.

les siens, les siennes ➤ le sien.

sieste [sjɛst] *nom féminin*

nap : faire la sieste to have a nap.

siffler [sifle] *verbe*

1. **to whistle : sais-tu siffler ?** do you know how to whistle?

2. **to boo : le public a sifflé les acteurs** the audience booed the actors.

sifflet [siflɛ] *nom masculin*

whistle : l'arbitre a donné un coup de sifflet the referee blew his whistle.

signal [siɲal] *(pluriel* signaux [siɲo]*) nom masculin*

signal : il a donné le signal du départ he gave the signal to start.

signaler [siɲale] *verbe*

to point out : je te signale que c'est moi qui ai gagné I'd like to point out that I'm the one that won

➤ **il n'y a rien à signaler** there's nothing to report.

signature [siɲatyr] *nom féminin*

signature : ta signature est illisible your signature is illegible.

signe [siɲ] *nom masculin*

sign : les signes du zodiaque the signs of the zodiac ; **c'est bon signe** it's a good sign

➤ **faire un signe à quelqu'un** to signal to somebody : **il m'a fait signe de quitter la pièce** he signalled to me to leave the room

➤ **faire un signe de tête** to nod : **elle m'a fait un signe de tête** she nodded at me.

signer [siɲe] *verbe*

to sign : signez en bas de la page sign at the bottom of the page.

signifier [siɲifje] *verbe*

to mean : que signifie ce mot ? what does this word mean?

S

silence [silɑ̃s] *nom masculin*

silence : **j'ai besoin de silence pour travailler** I need silence to work
➤ **sortez en silence** leave quietly
➤ **silence !** be quiet!

silencieux, euse [silɑ̃sjø, øz] *adjectif*

silent, quiet.

silhouette [silwɛt] *nom féminin*

figure : **je voyais une silhouette sombre** I could see a dark figure.

simple [sɛ̃pl] *adjectif*

simple : **une question simple** a simple question ou an easy question
➤ **un aller simple** a single ticket *UK* ou a one-way ticket *US*.

sincère [sɛ̃sɛr] *adjectif*

sincere : **tu crois qu'il était sincère ?** do you think he was being sincere?

sincèrement [sɛ̃sɛrmɑ̃] *adverbe*

honestly : **sincèrement, je ne sais pas** honestly, I don't know.

singe [sɛ̃ʒ] *nom masculin*

monkey
➤ **faire le singe** to clown around : **arrête de faire le singe** stop clowning around.

singulier [sɛ̃gylje] *nom masculin*

singular : **mettre les noms au singulier** put the nouns in the singular.

sinistre [sinistr] *adjectif*

grim : **un endroit sinistre** a grim place.

sinon [sinɔ̃] *conjonction*

otherwise, or else : **je dois y aller maintenant sinon je vais être en retard** I must go now, otherwise I'll be late.

sirène [sirɛn] *nom féminin*

siren.

sirop [siro] *nom masculin*

syrup *UK*, sirop *US* : **du sirop d'érable** maple syrup ; **un sirop contre la toux** cough syrup.

site [sit] *nom masculin*

site : **un site Web** a website.

situation [sitɥasjɔ̃] *nom féminin*

1. situation : **c'est une situation difficile** it's a difficult situation

2. job : **elle a une bonne situation** she has a good job.

situer [sitɥe] *verbe*

la maison est située à deux minutes de la gare the house is two minutes from the station ou the house is located two minutes from the station

se situer *verbe pronominal*

1. to be set : **l'action se situe dans un pays imaginaire** the action is set in an imaginary country

2. to be, to be located : **Valence se situe au sud de Lyon** Valence is south of Lyons.

six [sis *en fin de phrase*, si *devant une consonne ou un* « h » *aspiré*, siz *devant une voyelle ou un* « h » *muet*] *adjectif numéral & nom masculin invariable*

six : **il reste six bonbons** there are six sweets left ; **nous étions six** there were six of us
➤ **nous sommes le six mars** it's the sixth of March *UK* ou it's March sixth *US*.

sixième [sizjɛm] *adjectif & nom*

■ *adjectif numéral & nom masculin ou féminin*
sixth : **c'est la sixième fois que j'y vais** it's the sixth time I've been ; **je suis arrivé sixième** I came sixth
■ *nom féminin*
year seven *UK*, sixth grade *US* : **Anaïs est en sixième** Anaïs is in year seven *UK* ou Anaïs is in sixth grade *US*.

skateboard [skɛtbɔrd] *nom masculin*

skateboard : **faire du skateboard** to go skateboarding.

sketch [skɛtʃ] *(pluriel* sketches*) nom masculin*

sketch *(pluriel* sketches*)* : **le sketch le plus connu du comique** the comedian's most famous sketch.

ski [ski] *nom masculin*

1. ski : **j'ai loué une paire de skis** I hired a pair of skis

2. skiing : **le ski alpin** Alpine skiing ; **le ski de fond** cross-country skiing ; **le ski nautique** water-skiing
➤ **faire du ski** to go skiing.

skier [skje] *verbe*

to ski : **j'apprends à skier** I'm learning to ski.

slip [slip] *nom masculin*

briefs, underpants *(s'utilisent toujours au pluriel)*

> **un slip de bain** swimming trunks (*s'utilise toujours au pluriel*)

smiley [smaɪlɪ] *nom masculin*

smiley.

smoking [smɔkiŋ] *nom masculin*

dinner jacket *UK*, tuxedo *US*.

SNCF (*abréviation de* Société nationale des chemins de fer français) *nom féminin*
French national railway company.

snob [snɔb] *nom & adjectif*

■ *nom masculin ou féminin*
snob : **espèce de snob !** you snob!
■ *adjectif*
snobbish : **elle est vraiment snob** she's very snobbish ou she's a real snob.

sociable [sɔsjabl] *adjectif*

sociable.

social, e, aux [sɔsjal, o] *adjectif*

social : **les services sociaux** the social services.

société [sɔsjete] *nom féminin*

1. society : **la société française** French society
2. company, firm : **mon père travaille dans une société informatique** my father works in a computer company ou my father works in a computer firm.

socquette [sɔkɛt] *nom féminin*

ankle sock : **elle porte des socquettes** she's wearing ankle socks.

sœur [sœr] *nom féminin*

sister : **ma grande sœur** my big sister ; **ma petite sœur** my little sister.

soi [swa] *pronom personnel*

oneself : **ne penser qu'à soi** to always think about oneself

soi-même *pronom personnel*

oneself : **se connaître soi-même** to know oneself.

soi-disant [swadizã] *adjectif & adverbe*

▦ *adjectif invariable*
so-called : **un soi-disant champion de natation** a so-called swimming champion

■ *adverbe*
supposedly : **elle est soi-disant mannequin** she's supposedly a model.

soie [swa] *nom féminin*

silk : **un foulard en soie** a silk scarf.

soif [swaf] *nom féminin*

thirst : **je meurs de soif** I'm dying of thirst ; **pour étancher ta soif** to quench your thirst
> **avoir soif** to be thirsty : **j'ai soif** I'm thirsty
> **donner soif à quelqu'un** to make somebody thirsty : **ça m'a donné soif** it made me thirsty.

soigné, e [swaɲe] *adjectif*

careful, neat : **un travail soigné** careful work ou neat work.

soigner [swaɲe] *verbe*

1. to treat : **il l'a bien soigné** he treated him well
2. to take care over : **soignez la présentation** take care over the presentation

se soigner *verbe pronominal*

to take care of oneself, to look after oneself : **soigne-toi bien** take care of yourself ou look after yourself.

soigneusement [swaɲøzmã] *adverbe*

carefully.

soigneux, euse [swaɲø, øz] *adjectif*

careful : **il est très soigneux, il range bien ses affaires** he's very tidy, he puts his things away ; **un élève soigneux** a careful student.

soin [swɛ̃] *nom masculin*

care : **prendre soin de quelque chose** to take care of something ; **prends bien soin des plantes** take good care of the plants
> **avec soin** carefully

soins *nom masculin pluriel*

care (*ne s'utilise jamais au pluriel*) : **les soins médicaux sont gratuits** medical care is free.

soir [swar] *nom masculin*

evening : **le soir** in the evening
> **ce soir** this evening ou tonight
> **demain soir** tomorrow evening ou tomorrow night
> **hier soir** yesterday evening ou last night
> **à onze heures du soir** at eleven in the evening ou at eleven at night
> **à ce soir !** see you tonight!

S

soirée [sware] *nom féminin*

1. evening : **il a passé toute la soirée devant la télé** he spent the whole evening watching TV
2. party *(pluriel* **parties***)* : **il y a une soirée chez Jérôme samedi** there's a party at Jérôme's on Saturday.

sois, soit *etc* ➤ être.

soit [swa] *conjonction*

➤ **soit ... soit** either ... or ... : **viens chez moi soit mardi soit jeudi** come round to my place either on Tuesday or Thursday.

soixante [swasɑ̃t] *adjectif numéral & nom masculin*

sixty : **ça coûte soixante euros** it costs sixty euros ; **nous étions soixante en tout** there were sixty of us altogether
➤ **les années soixante** the sixties.

soixante-dix [swasɑ̃tdis] *adjectif numéral & nom masculin*

seventy : **il y avait soixante-dix invités** there were seventy guests ; **il en reste soixante-dix** there are seventy left
➤ **les années soixante-dix** the seventies.

soja [sɔʒa] *nom masculin*

soya
➤ **de la sauce de soja** soy sauce.

sol [sɔl] *nom masculin*

1. floor : **le sol de la maison n'est pas régulier** the floor of the house is not even
2. ground : **il était étendu sur le sol, à côté de son vélo** he was lying on the ground, by his bike
3. soil : **sur le sol français** on French soil.

solaire [sɔlɛr] *adjectif*

1. solar : **le système solaire** the solar system
2. sun : **de la crème solaire** sun cream.

soldat [sɔlda] *nom masculin*

soldier.

solde [sɔld] *nom masculin*

en solde in the sale *UK* ou on sale *US* : **j'ai acheté ce manteau en solde** I bought this coat in the sale

soldes *nom masculin pluriel*

sales : **faire les soldes** to go round the sales.

soleil [sɔlɛj] *nom masculin*

sun : **au soleil** in the sun.

solide [sɔlid] *adjectif*

1. solid : **le pont est très solide** the bridge is very solid
2. strong : **c'est un garçon solide** he's strong.

solitude [sɔlityd] *nom féminin*

1. loneliness : **beaucoup de personnes âgées souffrent de la solitude** a lot of old people suffer from loneliness
2. solitude : **j'aime la solitude** I like solitude.

solo [sɔlo] *nom masculin*

solo : **un solo de guitare** a guitar solo ; **jouer en solo** to play a solo.

solution [sɔlysjɔ̃] *nom féminin*

solution : **elle a trouvé la solution au problème** she found the solution to the problem.

sombre [sɔ̃br] *adjectif*

dark : **la pièce est très sombre** the room is very dark ; **il porte un costume sombre** he's wearing a dark suit.

sommaire [sɔmɛr] *nom masculin*

list of contents, table of contents.

somme [sɔm] *nom féminin*

sum : **une grosse somme** a large sum.

sommeil [sɔmɛj] *nom masculin*

sleep : **j'ai besoin de neuf heures de sommeil** I need nine hours' sleep
➤ **avoir sommeil** to be sleepy ou to feel sleepy.

sommes ➤ être.

sommet [sɔmɛ] *nom masculin*

summit : **ils ont atteint le sommet** they reached the summit
➤ **au sommet de la montagne** at the top of the mountain.

somnambule [sɔmnɑ̃byl] *adjectif*

être somnambule to be a sleepwalker.

somnifère [sɔmnifɛr] *nom masculin*

sleeping pill.

son¹, sa [sɔ̃, sa] *(pluriel* **ses** [se]*) adjectif*

1. *Lorsque le possesseur est un homme* his : **il s'entend bien avec son frère** he gets on well with his brother ; **sa femme l'a quitté**

his wife left him ; **Théo m'a prêté quelques-uns de ses jeux vidéo** Théo lent me some of his video games

2. *Lorsque le possesseur est une femme* her : **son petit frère est déjà plus grand qu'elle** her younger brother is already taller than her ; **Julia et sa sœur sont jumelles** Julia and her sister are twins ; **elle est venue avec ses parents** she came with her parents

3. *Lorsque le possesseur est un animal ou une chose* its : **la ville a perdu de son charme** the town has lost some of its charm ; **on a séparé le chaton de sa mère** the kitten was taken away from its mother.

son² [sɔ̃] *nom masculin*

sound : **le son de ma voix** the sound of my voice.

son³ [sɔ̃] *nom masculin*

bran : **un pain au son** a bran loaf.

sondage [sɔ̃daʒ] *nom masculin*

poll, survey : **faire un sondage** to carry out a poll ou to carry out a survey.

sonner [sɔne] *verbe*

1. to ring : **je crois que le téléphone sonne** I think that the phone's ringing ; **quelqu'un a sonné à la porte** somebody rang the doorbell

2. to go off : **mon réveil n'a pas sonné** the alarm didn't go off.

sonnerie [sɔnri] *nom féminin*

la sonnerie de la porte the doorbell

➤ **je n'ai pas entendu la sonnerie du téléphone** I didn't hear the phone ringing ou I didn't hear the phone ring

➤ **je n'ai pas entendu la sonnerie du réveil** I didn't hear the alarm go off.

sonnette [sɔnɛt] *nom féminin*

doorbell.

sono [sɔno] *nom féminin*

sound system.

sont ➤ être.

sorbet [sɔrbɛ] *nom masculin*

sorbet *UK*, sherbet *US* : **un sorbet au citron** a lemon sorbet.

sorcier, ère [sɔrsje, ɛr] *nom masculin, nom féminin*

wizard *(féminin* **witch***)*.

sort [sɔr] *nom masculin*

fate : **je me demande ce que le sort nous réserve** I wonder what fate has in store for us

➤ **tirer au sort** to draw lots.

sorte [sɔrt] *nom féminin*

sort, kind : **une sorte de gros lézard** a sort of big lizard ou a kind of big lizard

➤ **en quelque sorte** in a way.

sortie [sɔrti] *nom féminin*

1. exit, way out : **la sortie de secours** the emergency exit ; **je suis tombée sur Fabien à la sortie** I bumped into Fabien on the way out ; **on se retrouve à la sortie de l'école** I'll see you after school

2. release : **la sortie du film est prévue en mars** the film is due for release in March ou the film is due out in March ; **ils ont célébré la sortie de leur nouvel album** they celebrated the release of their new album

3. publication : **la sortie de ce livre a provoqué un scandale** the publication of this book caused a scandal

4. outing : **il y a une sortie au musée organisée par l'école** there's a school outing to the museum.

sortir [sɔrtir] *verbe*

1. to go out : **ne sors pas, il fait trop froid dehors** don't go out, it's too cold outside ; **on pourrait sortir ce soir** we could go out tonight ; **Camille sort avec Hubert** Camille is going out with Hubert

2. to come out : **sors, je veux te dire quelque chose** come out, I want to tell you something ; **quand sort son dernier film ?** when is her latest film coming out?

> Notez la différence de traduction selon que la personne qui parle se trouve à l'intérieur (premier exemple du sens 1, traduction **to go out**) ou déjà dehors (premier exemple du sens 2, traduction **to come out**).

3. to get out : **ils sont sortis par la fenêtre** they got out through the window ; **sors de là !** get out of here!

4. to take out : **elle a sorti un stylo de sa poche** she took a pen out of her pocket

5. to put out : **n'oubliez pas de sortir la poubelle** don't forget to put the bin out

6. to bring out : **ils viennent de sortir un nouvel album** they've just brought out a new album

➤ **sortir de table** to leave the table

S

s'en sortir *verbe pronominal*

1. **to manage : tu t'en sors ou tu veux que je t'aide ?** can you manage, or do you want some help?
2. **to pull through : il est grièvement blessé, mais il s'en sortira** he's seriously injured, but he'll pull through
3. **to escape : Michaël s'en est sorti avec juste quelques bleus** Michaël escaped with just a few bruises.

sosie [sɔzi] *nom masculin*

double : c'est le sosie de son frère he's his brother's double ou he's the spitting image of his brother.

sottise [sɔtiz] *nom féminin*

dire une sottise to say something stupid ; **faire une sottise** to do something stupid.

sou [su] *(pluriel* **sous)** *nom masculin*

money *(ne s'utilise jamais au pluriel)* **: je n'ai plus un sou** I haven't got any money left.

souci [susi] *nom masculin*

worry *(pluriel* **worries)* **: nous avons bien des soucis** we have a lot of worries
➤ **se faire du souci** to worry : **ne te fais pas de souci !** don't worry!
➤ **se faire du souci pour quelqu'un**   to worry about somebody ou to be worried about somebody : **je me fais du souci pour Linda** I'm worried about Linda.

soucoupe [sukup] *nom féminin*

saucer
➤ **une soucoupe volante** a flying saucer.

soudain, e [sudɛ̃, ɛn] *adjectif*

sudden : un changement soudain a sudden change

soudain *adverbe*

suddenly, all of sudden : soudain la lumière s'est éteinte suddenly the light went out ou all of a sudden the light went out.

souffert, e [sufɛr, ɛrt] *participe passé de* **souffrir.**

souffle [sufl] *nom masculin*

breath : je suis à bout de souffle I'm out of breath ; **retiens ton souffle pendant vingt secondes** hold your breath for twenty seconds ; **il n'y a pas un souffle de vent** there isn't a breath of air.

souffler [sufle] *verbe*

1. **to blow : le vent souffle fort** the wind is blowing hard
2. **to blow out : vas-y, souffle tes bougies !** go on, blow the candles out!
➤ **souffler quelque chose à quelqu'un** to whisper something to somebody : **elle m'a soufflé la réponse** she whispered the answer to me.

souffrir [sufrir] *verbe*

to suffer : il souffre de rhumatismes he suffers from rheumatism.

souhait [swɛ] *nom masculin*

wish *(pluriel* **wishes)* **: fais un souhait** make a wish
➤ **à tes souhaits !** ou **à vos souhaits !** bless you!

souhaiter [swete] *verbe*

1. **to wish : j'ai oublié de te souhaiter un joyeux anniversaire** I forgot to wish you a happy birthday
2. **to hope : je te souhaite de réussir** I hope that you succeed.

soûl, e ; saoul, e [su, sul] *adjectif*

drunk.

soulagé, e [sulaʒe] *adjectif*

relieved : je me sens soulagé I feel relieved.

se soûler, se saouler [səsule] *verbe pronominal*

to get drunk.

soulever [sulve] *verbe*

to lift : je n'arrive même pas à soulever cette valise I can't even lift this suitcase.

souligner [suliɲe] *verbe*

to underline : soulignez tous les verbes underline all the verbs.

soupçon [supsɔ̃] *nom masculin*

suspicion.

soupçonner [supsɔne] *verbe*

to suspect : je le soupçonne de mentir I suspect him of lying.

soupe [sup] *nom féminin*

soup : un bol de soupe à la tomate a bowl of tomato soup.

soupir [supir] *nom masculin*

sigh : **pousser un soupir** to give a sigh.

soupirer [supire] *verbe*

to sigh.

souple [supl] *adjectif*

1. supple : **je ne suis pas très souple** I'm not very supple

2. soft : **une brosse à dents souple** a soft toothbrush.

source [surs] *nom féminin*

1. source : **une source d'information** a source of information

2. spring : **eau de source** spring water.

sourcil [sursi] *nom masculin*

eyebrow

➤ **froncer les sourcils** to frown.

sourd, e [sur, surd] *adjectif & nom*

■ *adjectif*
deaf : **il est sourd** he's deaf

■ *nom masculin, nom féminin*
deaf person

➤ **les sourds** the deaf.

sourd-muet, sourde-muette [sur-mɥɛ, surdmɥɛt], (*pluriel* sourds-muets, sourdes-muettes) *nom masculin, nom féminin*
deaf-mute, deaf and dumb person.

souriant, e [surjɑ̃, ɑ̃t] *adjectif*

cheerful : **elle est souriante** she's cheerful.

sourire [surir] *verbe & nom*

■ *verbe*
to smile : **sourire à quelqu'un** to smile at somebody ; **il m'a souri** he smiled at me

■ *nom masculin*
smile : **il avait un grand sourire** he had a big smile on his face

➤ **faire un sourire à quelqu'un** to smile at somebody : **elle m'a fait un sourire** she smiled at me.

souris [suri] *nom féminin*

mouse (*pluriel* **mice**).

sous [su] *préposition*

under : **le chat est sous le lit** the cat is under the bed ; **elle porte un tee-shirt sous son pull** she's wearing a T-shirt under her sweater

➤ **nager sous l'eau** to swim underwater

➤ **sous la pluie** in the rain : **nous avons marché sous la pluie** we walked in the rain.

sous-marin [sumarɛ̃] (*pluriel* sous-marins) *nom masculin*
submarine.

sous-sol [susɔl] (*pluriel* sous-sols) *nom masculin*
basement : **au sous-sol** in the basement.

sous-titre [sutitr] (*pluriel* sous-titres) *nom masculin*
subtitle : **je lis toujours les sous-titres** I always read the subtitles.

soustraire [sustrɛr] *verbe*

to subtract : **tu dois soustraire 13 de 47** you must subtract 13 from 47.

sous-vêtements [suvɛtmɑ̃] *nom masculin pluriel*
underwear (*ne s'utilise jamais au pluriel*) : **ces sous-vêtements sont en coton** this underwear is made of cotton.

soutenir [sutnir] *verbe*

1. to support : **ils ont tous soutenu le projet** they all supported the plan

2. to maintain : **elle soutient que ce n'est pas elle** she maintains that it wasn't her.

souterrain, e [sutɛrɛ̃, ɛn] *adjectif*

underground : **un parking souterrain** an underground car park *UK* ou an underground parking lot *US*

souterrain *nom masculin*

underground passage.

soutien-gorge [sutjɛ̃gɔrʒ] (*pluriel* soutiens-gorge) *nom masculin*
bra.

souvenir [suvnir] *nom masculin*

1. memory (*pluriel* **memories**) : **un souvenir d'enfance** a childhood memory

2. souvenir : **Sandra m'a rapporté un souvenir de Londres** Sandra brought me a souvenir from London

se souvenir *verbe pronominal*

to remember : **je ne me souviens pas de la fin de l'histoire** I can't remember the end of the story ; **est-ce que tu te souviens d'elle ?** do you remember her?

souvent [suvɑ̃] *adverbe*

often : **ils font souvent des fêtes** they often have parties.

S

souvenu, e [suvny] *participe passé de* souvenir.

soyez ➤ être.

spaghettis [spageti] *nom masculin pluriel*

spaghetti *(ne s'utilise jamais au pluriel)* : **ces
spaghettis sont délicieux** this spaghetti is
delicious.

sparadrap [sparadra] *nom masculin*

plaster *UK*, Band-Aid® *US*.

spatial, e, aux [spasjal, o] *adjectif*

➤ **un vaisseau spatial** a spaceship.

spécial, e, aux [spesjal, o] *adjectif*

1. special : **une offre spéciale** a special offer
2. particular, odd : **il a un style un peu spécial** his style is quite particular ou he has a
rather odd style.

spécialiste [spesjalist] *nom masculin ou féminin*

specialist : **un spécialiste des arts martiaux** a specialist in martial arts.

spécialité [spesjalite] *nom féminin*

speciality *UK (pluriel* **specialities**), specialty *US (pluriel* **specialties**).

spectacle [spɛktakl] *nom masculin*

show : **nous allons voir un spectacle** we're
going to see a show ; **le spectacle commence
à 20 heures** the show starts at 8 o'clock.

spectaculaire [spɛktakylɛr] *adjectif*

spectacular : **un feu d'artifice spectaculaire** a spectacular fireworks display.

spectateur, trice [spɛktatœr, tris] *nom
masculin, nom féminin*

spectator.

spirale [spiral] *nom féminin*

spiral : **un escalier en spirale** a spiral staircase.

splendide [splɑ̃did] *adjectif*

magnificent, splendid : **la vue du sommet
était splendide** the view from the summit
was magnificent.

sport [spɔr] *nom & adjectif*

◼ *nom masculin*
sport : **faire du sport** to do sport ; **Sophie ne**

fait pas assez de sport Sophie doesn't get
enough exercise

➤ **les sports d'hiver** winter sports : **aller aux
sports d'hiver** to go on a skiing holiday
➤ **des vêtements de sport** sportswear
◼ *adjectif invariable*
casual : **elle a un style plutôt sport** she
dresses casually.

sportif, ive [spɔrtif, iv] *adjectif & nom*

◼ *adjectif*
1. sporty : **elle est très sportive** she's very
sporty
2. sports : **un commentateur sportif** a sports
commentator
◼ *nom masculin, nom féminin*
sportsman *(féminin* **sportswoman***)*.

spot [spɔt] *nom masculin*

spotlight : **on a mis des spots dans la salle
de bains** we put spotlights in the bathroom
➤ **un spot publicitaire** a commercial ou an
advert *UK*.

square [skwar] *nom masculin*

small public garden.

squash [skwaʃ] *nom masculin*

squash : **faire du squash** ou **jouer au
squash** to play squash.

squelette [skəlɛt] *nom masculin*

skeleton.

St *(abréviation de* saint*)*

St : **St Georges** St George.

stable [stabl] *adjectif*

1. steady : **la table n'est pas stable** the table
isn't steady ; **un travail stable** a steady job
2. stable : **un pays politiquement stable** a politically stable country.

stade [stad] *nom masculin*

1. stadium : **ils ont construit un nouveau stade** they've built a new stadium
2. stage : **un stade décisif** a crucial stage.

stage [staʒ] *nom masculin*

1. training course : **j'ai fait un stage d'informatique** I went on a computer training course
2. lessons : **je voudrais faire un stage de voile**
I'd like to have sailing lessons

 The French word **stage** is a false friend, it
does not mean 'stage'.

stagiaire [staʒjɛr] *nom masculin ou féminin*
trainee, intern *US*.

stand [stɑ̃d] *nom masculin*

1. **stand** : **un stand d'exposition** an exhibition stand
2. **stall** : **elle tient un stand à la kermesse** she has a stall at the fête.

standard [stɑ̃dar] *adjectif & nom*

■ *adjectif invariable*
standard : **le modèle standard** the standard model

■ *nom masculin*
switchboard : **quel est le numéro du standard téléphonique ?** what's the number of the switchboard?

standardiste [stɑ̃dardist] *nom masculin ou féminin*
switchboard operator.

star [star] *nom féminin*
star : **une star de rock** a rock star.

station [stasjɔ̃] *nom féminin*

1. **station** : **une station de métro** a metro station ; **une station de radio** a radio station ; **une station essence** a petrol station *UK* ou a gas station *US*
2. **resort** : **une station de sports d'hiver** a ski resort.

stationner [stasjɔne] *verbe*
to park : **'défense de stationner'** 'no parking'.

station-service [stasjɔ̃sɛrvis] (*pluriel* **stations-service**) *nom féminin*
petrol station *UK*, gas station *US*.

statistique [statistik] *nom féminin*
statistic.

statue [staty] *nom féminin*
statue : **une statue en marbre** a marble statue ; **la statue de la Liberté** the Statue of Liberty.

Ste (*abréviation de* **sainte**)
St : **Ste Anne** St Ann.

steak [stɛk] *nom masculin*
steak : **j'ai mangé un steak à midi** I had a steak for lunch
➤ **du steak haché** minced beef *UK* ou ground beef *US*.

stéréo [stereo] *adjectif invariable & nom féminin*
stereo : **le son stéréo** stereo sound ; **en stéréo** in stereo.

steward [stiwart] *nom masculin*
steward : **il est steward chez British Airways** he's a steward with British Airways.

stop [stɔp] *interjection & nom*

■ *interjection*
stop ! stop!
■ *nom masculin*
➤ **faire du stop** to hitchhike ou to hitch
➤ **on y est allés en stop** we hitchhiked there ou we hitched there.

store [stɔr] *nom masculin*
blind : **baisse le store** put the blind down.

stress [strɛs] *nom masculin*
stress : **mes maux de tête sont dûs au stress** my headaches are due to stress.

strict, e [strikt] *adjectif*
strict : **il est très strict avec ses élèves** he's very strict with his pupils.

strophe [strɔf] *nom féminin*
stanza, verse : **le poème a cinq strophes** the poem has five verses.

structure [stryktyr] *nom féminin*
structure.

studio [stydjo] *nom masculin*

1. **studio** : **un studio d'enregistrement** a recording studio
2. **studio flat** *UK*, **studio apartment** *US* : **ma sœur vit dans un studio** my sister lives in a studio flat *UK* ou my sister lives in a studio apartment *US*.

stupéfait, e [stypefɛ, ɛt] *adjectif*
astonished.

stupide [stypid] *adjectif*
stupid : **ne sois pas stupide !** don't be stupid!

style [stil] *nom masculin*
style : **j'aime leur style** I like their style.

stylo [stilo] *nom masculin*
pen : **un stylo à bille** ou **un stylo bille** a ballpoint pen ou a Biro® *UK* ; **un stylo à plume** ou **un stylo plume** a fountain pen.

stylo-feutre [stiloføtr] (*pluriel* stylos-feutres) *nom masculin*
felt-tip pen.

su, e [sy] *participe passé de* savoir.

subir [sybir] *verbe*
to suffer : **l'armée a subi de grosses pertes** the army suffered major losses
➤ **subir une opération** to have an operation.

subjonctif [sybʒɔ̃ktif] *nom masculin*
subjunctive : **au subjonctif** in the subjunctive.

substance [sypstɑ̃s] *nom féminin*
substance : **une substance nocive** a harmful substance.

subtil, e [syptil] *adjectif*
subtle : **ses plaisanteries ne sont pas très subtiles** his jokes aren't very subtle.

subventionner [sybvɑ̃sjɔne] *verbe*
to subsidize.

succès [syksɛ] *nom masculin*
success : **ça a été un grand succès** it was a great success
➤ **avoir du succès** to be successful : **ça n'a pas eu beaucoup de succès** it wasn't very successful.

sucer [syse] *verbe*
to suck : **il suce encore son pouce** he still sucks his thumb.

sucette [sysɛt] *nom féminin*
lollipop : **une sucette à la fraise** a strawberry lollipop.

sucre [sykr] *nom masculin*
sugar : **tu mets du sucre dans ton thé ?** do you take sugar in your tea?
➤ **du sucre roux** brown sugar
➤ **du sucre en poudre** caster sugar *UK* OU granulated sugar *US*.

sucré, e [sykre] *adjectif*
sweet : **ces cerises sont très sucrées** these cherries are very sweet.

sucrer [sykre] *verbe*
to put sugar in : **je ne sucre pas mon café** I don't take sugar in my coffee.

sucreries [sykrəri] *nom féminin pluriel*
sweets *UK*, candy *US* : **tu manges trop de sucreries** you eat too many sweets *UK* OU you eat too much candy *US*.

sud [syd] *nom & adjectif*
■ *nom masculin invariable*
south : **au sud** in the south ; **au sud de Paris** to the south of Paris
■ *adjectif invariable*
1. south : **la côte sud de l'île** the south coast of the island
2. southern : **la banlieue sud** the southern suburbs.

sud-africain, e [sydafrikɛ̃, ɛn] (*pluriel* sud-africains, sud-africaines) *adjectif*
South African

En anglais, les adjectifs se rapportant à un pays ou une région s'écrivent avec une majuscule :

le climat sud-africain the South African climate

Sud-Africain, e *nom masculin, nom féminin*
South African.

sud-américain, e [sydamerikɛ̃, ɛn] (*pluriel* sud-américains, sud-américaines) *adjectif*
South American

En anglais, les adjectifs se rapportant à un pays ou une région s'écrivent avec une majuscule :

la musique sud-américaine South American music

Sud-Américain, e *nom masculin, nom féminin*
South American.

sud-est [sydɛst] *nom masculin & adjectif invariable*
southeast.

sud-ouest [sydwɛst] *nom masculin & adjectif invariable*
southwest.

suer [sɥe] *verbe*
to sweat : **elle sue à grosses gouttes** she's dripping with sweat.

sueur [sɥœr] *nom féminin*
sweat : **mon tee-shirt est trempé de sueur** my T-shirt is soaked in sweat

➤ **en sueur** in a sweat : **elle est en sueur** she's in a sweat ou she's sweating.

suffire [syfir] *verbe*

to be enough : **ça suffit !** that's enough!
➤ **il suffit de tourner ce bouton** all you need to do is turn this knob ; **il suffisait de me le demander** you only needed to ask.

suffisamment [syfizamã] *adverbe*

enough : **je n'ai pas suffisamment travaillé** I haven't done enough work
➤ **suffisamment de** enough : **est-ce que tu as suffisamment de chaises ?** do you have enough chairs?

suffisant, e [syfizã, ãt] *adjectif*

sufficient : **une quantité suffisante de nourriture** a sufficient quantity of food.

suggérer [sygʒere] *verbe*

to suggest : **c'est lui qui m'a suggéré de lire ce livre** he suggested that I read this book.

suggestion [sygʒestjɔ̃] *nom féminin*

suggestion : **faire une suggestion** to make a suggestion.

suicide [sɥisid] *nom masculin*

suicide.

se suicider [səsɥiside] *verbe pronominal*

to commit suicide : **elle s'est suicidée** she commited suicide.

suis ➤ être.

suisse [sɥis] *adjectif*

Swiss

En anglais, les adjectifs se rapportant à un pays ou une région s'écrivent avec une majuscule :

j'aime le chocolat suisse I like Swiss chocolate

Suisse *nom*

▪ *nom féminin*
➤ **la Suisse** Switzerland

En anglais, à de rares exceptions près, il n'y a pas d'article devant les noms de pays :

j'habite en Suisse I live in Switzerland ; **on est allé en Suisse à Noël** we went to Switzerland at Christmas
▪ *nom masculin ou féminin*
les Suisses the Swiss.

suite [sɥit] *nom féminin*

1. **rest** : **je n'ai pas écouté la suite** I didn't listen to the rest
2. **sequel** : **ils vont bientôt sortir la suite du film** they're bringing out the sequel of the film soon
➤ **de suite** one after another : **il a mangé trois gâteaux de suite** he ate three cakes one after the other.

suivant, e [sɥivã, ãt] *adjectif & nom*

▪ *adjectif*
next, following : **le jour suivant** the next day ou the following day
▪ *nom masculin, nom féminin*
next one : **le premier cours était ennuyeux, le suivant plus intéressant** the first lesson was boring, the next one was more interesting ; **au suivant !** next!

suivi, e [sɥivi] *participe passé de* suivre.

suivre [sɥivr] *verbe*

1. **to follow** : **suis-moi** follow me
2. **to keep up** : **Léo a du mal à suivre en classe** Léo's finding it difficult to keep up in class.

sujet [syʒɛ] *nom masculin*

subject : **le sujet de la phrase** the subject of the sentence
➤ **c'est à quel sujet ?** what is it about?
➤ **au sujet de** about : **je voulais te parler au sujet du voyage** I wanted to talk to you about the trip.

super [syper] *adjectif invariable familier*

great : **le concert était super** the concert was great.

superbe [syperb] *adjectif*

superb : **il a fait un temps superbe** the weather was superb.

supérieur, e [syperjœr] *adjectif*

1. **upper, top** : **les étages supérieurs** the upper floors ou the top floors
2. **superior** : **qualité supérieure** superior quality
➤ **à l'étage supérieur** on the floor above.

supermarché [sypermarʃe] *nom masculin*

supermarket : **je vais au supermarché** I'm going to the supermarket.

superstitieux, euse [syperstisjø, øz] *adjectif*

superstitious : **Ben est très superstitieux** Ben is very superstitious.

supplément [syplemã] *nom masculin*

extra charge : **il y a un supplément à payer** there's an extra charge.

supplémentaire [syplemãtɛr] *adjectif*

extra, additional : **des classes supplémentaires** extra classes.

supplier [syplije] *verbe*

to beg : **je t'en supplie** I beg you

⚠️ Supplier is a false friend, it does not mean 'supplier'.

supporter [syporte] *verbe*

to stand, to bear : **il ne supporte pas qu'on le contredise** he can't stand being contradicted ou he can't bear being contradicted ; **je ne peux pas la supporter** I can't stand her ou I can't bear her.

supporter [syporter] *nom masculin*

supporter : **les supporters agitent des drapeaux** the supporters are waving flags.

supposer [sypoze] *verbe*

to suppose : **je suppose que tu n'as toujours pas fait tes devoirs** I suppose you still haven't done your homework.

suppositoire [sypozitwar] *nom masculin*

suppository *(pluriel* **suppositories***)*.

supprimer [syprime] *verbe*

1. to delete : **il a supprimé plusieurs phrases** he deleted several sentences
2. to kill : **ils ont supprimé le témoin** they killed the witness.

sur [syr] *préposition*

1. on : **tes lunettes sont sur la table** your glasses are on the table ; **il y a des crocodiles sur l'île** there are crocodiles on the island ; **la cathédrale est sur votre gauche** the cathedral is on your left ; **un livre sur le Japon** a book on Japan ou a book about Japan
2. over : **mets un pull sur ton tee-shirt** put a jumper over your T-shirt
3. out of : **neuf élèves sur dix ont choisi le premier sujet** nine pupils out of ten chose the first subject ; **j'ai eu 14 sur 20** I got 14 out of 20

4. by : **la chambre fait trois mètres sur quatre** the bedroom is three metres by four
5. for : **il y a des travaux sur dix kilomètres** there are works for ten kilometres
➤ **un jour sur deux** every other day
➤ **une personne sur deux** one person in two.

sûr, e [syr] *adjectif*

1. sure : **est-ce que tu es sûr ?** are you sure? ; **je suis sûre de t'avoir donné les clés** I'm sure I gave you the keys ; **elle est très sûre d'elle** she's very sure of herself
2. safe : **dans un endroit sûr** in a safe place
➤ **sûr et certain** absolutely certain : **j'en suis sûre et certaine** I'm absolutely certain.

surdoué, e [syrdwe] *adjectif*

gifted : **les enfants surdoués** gifted children.

sûrement [syrmã] *adverbe*

probably : **il m'a dit qu'il viendrait sûrement** he told me he would probably come.

surf [sœrf] *nom masculin*

1. surfing : **faire du surf** to go surfing
2. surfboard : **j'emmène mon surf** I'm taking my surfboard
3. snowboard : **il s'est acheté un nouveau surf** he bought himself a new snowboard
➤ **le surf des neiges** snowboarding : **faire du surf des neiges** to go snowboarding.

surface [syrfas] *nom féminin*

surface : **la surface du lac est gelée** the surface of the lake is frozen
➤ **une grande surface** a hypermarket.

surfer [sœrfe] *verbe*

to surf : **surfer sur Internet** to surf the Net.

surgelé, e [syrʒəle] *adjectif*

frozen : **des petits pois surgelés** frozen peas

surgelés *nom masculin pluriel*

frozen food : **il ne mange que des surgelés** he only eats frozen food.

surgir [syrʒir] *verbe*

to appear suddenly : **un animal a surgi devant eux** an animal appeared suddenly in front of them.

surligner [syrliɲe] *verbe*

to highlight : **les mots importants sont surlignés en jaune** the important words are highlighted in yellow.

surligneur [syrliɲœr] *nom masculin*

highlighter, highlighter pen : **un surligneur jaune** a yellow highlighter.

surnom [syrnɔ̃] *nom masculin*

nickname : **son surnom, c'est Tintin** his nickname is Tintin

 Surnom is a false friend, it does not mean 'surname'.

surnommer [syrnɔme] *verbe*

to nickname : **ses copains l'ont surnommé « crevette »** his friends nicknamed him "crevette".

surprenant, e [syrprənã, ãt] *adjectif*

surprising : **Alex est en retard, c'est surprenant** Alex is late, that's surprising.

surprendre [syrprãdr] *verbe*

1. to surprise : **sa réaction a surpris tout le monde** his reaction surprised everybody
2. to catch : **Sabine a surpris sa sœur en train de fouiller dans ses affaires** Sabine caught her sister going through her things.

surpris, e [syrpri, iz] *participe passé de* surprendre.

surprise [syrpriz] *nom féminin*

surprise : **quelle bonne surprise !** what a nice surprise! ; **faire une surprise à quelqu'un** to give somebody a surprise OU to surprise somebody.

sursaut [syrso] *nom masculin*

➤ **en sursaut** with a start : **je me suis réveillée en sursaut** I woke up with a start.

sursauter [syrsote] *verbe*

to start, to jump : **Patrick a sursauté quand on est entrés** Patrick started when we came in OU Patrick jumped when we came in.

surtout [syrtu] *adverbe*

1. above all : **il est sympa, rigolo et surtout généreux** he's nice, funny and above all generous
2. especially : **j'aime le chocolat, surtout le chocolat noir** I like chocolate, especially dark chocolate.
3. whatever you do : **surtout ne leur dis rien !** whatever you do, don't tell them anything!

survécu [syrveky] *participe passé invariable de* survivre.

surveillant, e [syrvejã, ãt] *nom masculin, nom féminin*

supervisor : **les surveillants sont sympas dans l'ensemble** the supervisors are nice on the whole.

surveiller [syrveje] *verbe*

1. to watch : **surveille le bébé pendant que je vais à la poste** watch the baby while I go to the post office ; **je dois surveiller mon poids** I must watch my weight
2. to invigilate *UK* : **deux professeurs surveillent l'examen** there are two teachers invigilating the exam.

survêtement [syrvɛtmã] *nom masculin*

tracksuit : **elle porte un survêtement bleu** she's wearing a blue tracksuit.

survivant, e [syrvivã, ãt] *nom masculin, nom féminin*

survivor : **il n'y a aucun survivant** there are no survivors.

survivre [syrvivr] *verbe*

to survive : **trois personnes ont survécu à l'accident** three people survived the accident.

susceptible [sysɛptibl] *adjectif*

touchy : **ne sois pas si susceptible !** don't be so touchy!

➤ **être susceptible de** to be likely to : **mes projets sont susceptibles de changer** my plans are likely to change OU my plans might change.

suspect, e [syspɛ, ɛkt] *adjectif & nom*

■ *adjectif*

suspicious : **il a encore eu la meilleure note, c'est suspect** he got the best mark again, that's suspicious

■ *nom masculin, nom féminin*

suspect : **le suspect sera interrogé par la police** the suspect will be interrogated by the police.

suspendre [syspãdr] *verbe*

to hang : **où vas-tu suspendre le lustre ?** where are you going to hang the chandelier? ; **il y a un mobile suspendu au plafond** there is a mobile hanging from the ceiling

se suspendre *verbe pronominal*

to hang : **le singe s'est suspendu à une branche** the monkey hung from a branch.

suspendu, e [syspɑ̃dy] *participe passé de* suspendre.

suspense [syspɛns] *nom masculin*

suspense : **un livre plein de suspense** a book full of suspense
➤ **un film à suspense** a thriller.

SVP *(abréviation de* s'il vous plaît*)* please.

sweat-shirt [switʃœrt] *(pluriel* sweat-shirts) *nom masculin*

sweatshirt : **Chloé porte un sweat-shirt rouge** Chloé is wearing a red sweatshirt.

syllabe [silab] *nom féminin*

syllable : **« magasin » a trois syllabes** "magasin" has three syllables.

symbole [sɛ̃bɔl] *nom masculin*

symbol : **la colombe est le symbole de la paix** the dove is a symbol of peace.

sympa [sɛ̃pa] *(abréviation de* sympathique)
adjectif familier

nice : **Charles est super sympa** Charles is really nice ; **c'est un endroit sympa** it's a nice place.

sympathie [sɛ̃pati] *nom féminin*

avoir de la sympathie pour quelqu'un to like somebody ; **je n'ai aucune sympathie pour elle** I don't like her at all

 Sympathie is a false friend, it doesn't mean 'sympathy'.

sympathique [sɛ̃patik] *adjectif*

nice : **c'est un garçon sympathique** he's a nice boy ; **un café très sympathique** a very nice café

 Sympathique is a false friend, it does not mean 'sympathetic'.

sympathiser [sɛ̃patize] *verbe*

to get on well : **on a tout de suite sympathisé** we got on well right away.

synagogue [sinagɔg] *nom féminin*

synagogue.

syndicat [sɛ̃dika] *nom masculin*

union : **le syndicat des enseignants** the teachers' union
➤ **le syndicat d'initiative** the tourist office.

synonyme [sinɔnim] *nom & adjectif*

■ *nom masculin*
synonym : **donne-moi un synonyme de « joli »** give me a synonym for "pretty"
■ *adjectif*
synonymous : **« maison » et « logement » ne sont pas synonymes** "house" and "housing" aren't synonymous.

synthèse [sɛ̃tɛz] *nom féminin*

summary *(pluriel* summaries*)* : **c'est une bonne synthèse du problème** it's a good summary of the problem ; **faire la synthèse de quelque chose** to summarize something.

systématique [sistematik] *adjectif*

systematic.

système [sistɛm] *nom masculin*

1. system : **le système nerveux** the nervous system
2. way : **je connais un système pour payer moins cher** I know a way of paying less
➤ **le système d'exploitation** the operating system
➤ **le système solaire** the solar system.

t' ➤ te.

ta ➤ ton.

tabac [taba] *nom masculin*

1. tobacco : **du tabac blond** mild tobacco
2. tobacconist's *UK* : **tu peux acheter tes tickets de métro au tabac** you can buy your metro tickets at the tobacconist's.

table [tabl] *nom féminin*

table : **le journal est sur la table** the newspaper is on the table ; **mettre la table** to lay the table *UK* ou to set the table ; **une table de billard** a billiard table

> **une table basse** a coffee table
> **une table de chevet** OU **une table de nuit** a bedside table
> **table des matières** contents (*s'utilise toujours au pluriel*)
> **les tables de multiplication** multiplication tables
> **à table !** *au déjeuner* lunch is ready!

tableau [tablo] (*pluriel* tableaux) *nom masculin*

1. painting : **un tableau de Seurat** a painting by Seurat
2. blackboard : **la prof m'a encore envoyé au tableau** the teacher sent me up to the blackboard again
3. table : **il y a des tableaux de conjugaison à la fin du dictionnaire** there are conjugation tables at the back of the dictionary
> **un tableau d'affichage** a noticeboard *UK* OU a bulletin board *US*
> **tableau de bord**
1. dashboard : **la Jaguar a un tableau de bord en bois** the Jaguar has a wooden dashboard
2. instrument panel : **le tableau de bord de l'avion** the instrument panel of the plane.

tablette [tablɛt] *nom féminin*

1. bar : **une tablette de chocolat aux noisettes** a bar of chocolate with hazelnuts
2. stick : **une tablette de chewing-gum** a stick of chewing-gum.

tablier [tablije] *nom masculin*

apron : **il ne met jamais de tablier pour faire la cuisine** he never wears an apron for cooking.

tabouret [taburɛ] *nom masculin*

stool : **un tabouret de piano** a piano stool.

tache [taʃ] *nom féminin*

1. stain : **ton jean est plein de taches** your jeans are covered in stains ; **une tache d'encre** an ink stain
2. marking : **un chien noir avec des taches blanches** a black dog with white markings
3. mark : **elle a des taches rouges sur les joues** she has red marks on her cheeks
> **des taches de rousseur** freckles.

tâche [taʃ] *nom féminin*

task : **les tâches administratives** administrative tasks
> **les tâches ménagères** household chores OU housework.

tacher [taʃe] *verbe*

to stain : **attention à ne pas tacher ton chemisier** be careful not to stain your blouse.

tâcher [taʃe] *verbe*

tâcher de faire quelque chose to try to do something ; **tâchez de la convaincre** try to convince her.

tact [takt] *nom masculin*

tact : **il faut un minimum de tact** you need a minimum of tact
> **avoir du tact** to be tactful
> **manquer de tact** to be tactless.

tactique [taktik] *nom féminin*

tactics (*pluriel*) : **ta tactique est assez inhabituelle** your tactics are quite unusual.

taie [tɛ] *nom féminin*

une taie d'oreiller a pillowcase.

taille [taj] *nom féminin*

1. size : **quelle est la taille de la pièce ?** what size is the room? OU how big is the room? ; **ils n'avaient pas ma taille en bleu** they didn't have my size in blue ; **vous faites quelle taille ?** what size are you? OU what size do you take? ; **de taille moyenne** medium-sized
2. height : **il faut une taille minimum pour être hôtesse de l'air** you need to have a minimum height to become an air hostess
3. waist : **c'est trop serré à la taille** it's too tight at the waist.

taille-crayon [tajkrɛjɔ̃] (*pluriel* taille-crayons) *nom masculin*
pencil sharpener.

tailler [taje] *verbe*

1. to cut : **ils taillent des diamants pour en faire des bijoux** they cut diamonds to make jewels
2. to prune : **mon père a taillé la haie le week-end dernier** my father pruned the hedge last weekend
3. to sharpen : **ce crayon est mal taillé** this pencil isn't sharpened properly
4. to cut out : **tailler une jupe dans du tissu** to cut a skirt out of some material.

tailleur [tajœr] *nom masculin*

1. tailor : **le père de Lucas est tailleur** Lucas's father is a tailor
2. suit : **un tailleur pantalon** a trouser suit
> **s'asseoir en tailleur** to sit cross-legged.

t

se taire [sətɛr] *verbe pronominal*

1. **to stop talking** : **tout d'un coup tout le monde s'est tu** all of a sudden everybody stopped talking
2. **to keep silent** : **je préfère me taire** I'd rather keep silent ou I'd rather not say anything
➤ **taisez-vous !** be quiet!

talc [talk] *nom masculin*

talcum powder.

talent [talɑ̃] *nom masculin*

talent : **ce chanteur a beaucoup de talent** this singer has a lot of talent ou this singer is very talented.

talon [talɔ̃] *nom masculin*

heel : **j'ai mal aux talons** my heels hurt
➤ **le talon d'Achille** Achilles' heel
➤ **des talons aiguilles** stiletto heels
➤ **des talons hauts** high heels : **elle porte des talons hauts** she's wearing high heels.

tambour [tɑ̃bur] *nom masculin*

drum : **jouer du tambour** to play the drum.

Tamise [tamiz] *nom féminin*

la Tamise the Thames ou the River Thames.

tampon [tɑ̃pɔ̃] *nom masculin*

stamp : **une lettre portant le tampon de l'école** a letter that bears the school's stamp
➤ **des tampons hygiéniques** tampons
➤ **un tampon à récurer** a scourer.

tamponner [tɑ̃pɔne] *verbe*

to stamp : **ils ont oublié de tamponner le certificat** they've forgotten to stamp the certificate.

tandem [tɑ̃dɛm] *nom masculin*

tandem : **ils se promènent en tandem** they ride around on a tandem.

tandis que [tɑ̃dikə] *conjonction*

1. **whereas** : **il fait beau à Manchester tandis qu'ici il pleut** the weather's nice in Manchester whereas it's raining here
2. **while** : **Jean attendait dans la voiture tandis que je faisais les courses** Jean was waiting in the car while I was doing the shopping.

tant [tɑ̃] *adverbe*

so much : **il me manque tant !** I miss him so much! ; **j'ai tant mangé que j'ai été malade** I ate so much that I was sick

➤ **tant de**

1. *Suivi d'un nom singulier* **so much** : **j'ai tant de travail que je ne sais pas par où commencer** I've got so much work that I don't know where to start
2. *Suivi d'un nom pluriel* **so many** : **si nous n'avions pas eu tant de problèmes ...** if we hadn't had so many problems ...

➤ **tant que**

1. **as much** : **mange tant que tu veux** eat as much as you want
2. **while** : **on devrait sortir tant qu'il ne pleut pas** we should go out while it isn't raining

➤ **tant mieux** **good** : **finalement je peux venir – tant mieux !** I can come after all – good! ; **tant mieux pour elle** good for her

➤ **tant pis** **never mind** : **il n'y a plus de pommes – tant pis, je prendrai une orange** there aren't any apples left – never mind, I'll have an orange

➤ **tant pis pour toi** **too bad** : **tant pis pour toi, tu n'avais qu'à faire plus d'efforts !** too bad, you should have tried harder!

➤ **en tant que** **as** : **ils lui ont demandé son avis en tant qu'expert** they asked for his opinion as an expert.

tante [tɑ̃t] *nom féminin*

aunt : **tante Agathe** aunt Agathe.

tantôt [tɑ̃to] *adverbe*

sometimes : **on se voit tantôt le mercredi, tantôt le samedi** we sometimes see each other on Wednesday, sometimes on Saturday.

tape [tap] *nom féminin*

slap : **donner une tape à quelqu'un** to give somebody a slap

 The French word **tape** is a false friend, it does not mean 'tape'.

taper [tape] *verbe*

1. **to bang** : **les volets tapent contre le mur** the shutters are banging against the wall ; **il tapait du poing sur la table** he was banging his fist on the table
2. **to type** : **tu pourrais me taper cette lettre ?** could you type this letter for me? ; **Sandra tape très vite** Sandra types very fast
➤ **taper sur** **to hit** : **j'ai tapé sur la planche de toutes mes forces** I hit the plank with all my strength.

tapis [tapi] *nom masculin*

1. carpet, rug : **un tapis d'Orient** an Oriental rug
2. mat : **un tapis de gymnastique** a gym mat
> **un tapis roulant** a travolator
> **un tapis de souris** a mouse mat *UK* ou a mouse pad *US*.

tapisserie [tapisri] *nom féminin*

tapestry *(pluriel* **tapestries***)* : **la tapisserie de Bayeux** the Bayeux tapestry.

taquiner [takine] *verbe*

to tease : **arrête de taquiner ce pauvre Kevin !** stop teasing poor Kevin!

tard [tar] *adverbe*

late : **il est tard, je rentre** it's late, I'm going home ; **je finirai plus tard** I'll finish later ; **lundi au plus tard** Monday at the latest.

tarder [tarde] *verbe*

tarder à faire quelque chose to take a long time to do something ; **ils tardent à répondre** they're taking a long time to answer ; **elle ne devrait plus tarder maintenant** she should be here any time now ; **il ne va pas tarder** he won't be long.

tarif [tarif] *nom masculin*

1. price : **les tarifs hôteliers sont élevés à Londres** hotel prices are high in London ; **payer plein tarif** to pay full price
2. price list : **le tarif est affiché en vitrine** the price list is displayed in the window
> **tarif réduit** concession *UK* ou reduced price.

tarte [tart] *nom féminin*

tart *UK*, pie *US* : **une tarte aux pommes** an apple tart.

tartine [tartin] *nom féminin*

piece of bread and butter : **un café au lait et des tartines** a white coffee with bread and butter ; **une tartine de confiture** a piece of bread and jam
> **une tartine grillée** a piece of toast.

tartiner [tartine] *verbe*

to spread : **il a tartiné son pain de beurre** he spread some butter on his bread
> **du chocolat à tartiner** chocolate spread
> **du fromage à tartiner** cheese spread.

tas [ta] *nom masculin*

pile : **un tas de livres** a pile of books

> **un tas de** ou **des tas de** *familier* a lot of ou lots of : **il a un tas de problèmes** he has a lot of problems.

tasse [tas] *nom féminin*

cup : **une tasse de café** a cup of coffee ; **une tasse à café** a coffee cup.

tasser [tase] *verbe*

to pack down : **tasse bien la terre** pack the earth down well

se tasser *verbe pronominal*

1. to settle : **le sol s'est tassé peu à peu** the ground gradually settled
2. to squeeze : **on s'est tous tassés dans la voiture** we all squeezed into the car
3. *familier* to settle down : **les choses se sont enfin tassées** things have finally settled down.

tâter [tate] *verbe*

to feel : **tâte les kiwis pour voir s'ils sont mûrs** feel the kiwis to see whether they're ripe.

tatouage [tatwaʒ] *nom masculin*

tattoo : **se faire faire un tatouage** to get a tattoo.

tatouer [tatwe] *verbe*

to tattoo : **il a les bras tatoués** his arms are tattooed ; **se faire tatouer** to get a tattoo.

taupe [top] *nom féminin*

mole
> **myope comme une taupe** as blind as a bat.

taureau [toro] *(pluriel* **taureaux***) nom masculin*

bull : **le taureau nous a foncé dessus** the bull rushed at us
> **prendre le taureau par les cornes** to take the bull by the horns

Taureau *nom masculin*

Taurus : **je suis Taureau** I'm a Taurus.

taux [to] *nom masculin*

1. rate : **le taux de change** the exchange rate ; **les taux d'intérêts** interest rates
2. level : **le taux d'alcool dans le sang** the level of alcohol in the blood.

taxe [taks] *nom féminin*

tax *(pluriel* **taxes***)* : **la taxe sur la valeur ajoutée** value-added tax

➤ **une boutique hors-taxes**   a   duty-free shop.

taxi [taksi] *nom masculin*

taxi : on prend un taxi ? shall we take a taxi?

te [tə] (**t'** *devant une voyelle ou un « h » muet*) *pronom*

1. you : je t'entends mal I can't hear you ; **qui te l'a offert ?** who gave it to you? ; **te voilà enfin !** here you are at last!

2. *Dans les verbes pronominaux*

> Dans les verbes qui ne sont que pronominaux, c'est-à-dire qui ne s'utilisent qu'avec un pronom, « te » ne se traduit pas en anglais :

tu te souviens ? do you remember?

> Lorsque « te » a une valeur réfléchie, soit il ne se traduit pas, soit il se traduit par **yourself** :

va t'habiller go and get dressed ; **tu t'es lavé les mains ?** did you wash your hands? ; **est-ce que tu t'es fait mal ?** did you hurt yourself?

➤ **te voilà !** here you are!

technique [tɛknik] *adjectif & nom*

◼ *adjectif*
technical : c'est trop technique pour moi it's too technical for me ; **un lycée technique** a technical school

◼ *nom féminin*
technique : une technique moderne a modern technique.

techno [tɛkno] *adjectif & nom féminin*

techno : Lionel n'écoute que de la techno Lionel only listens to techno.

technologie [tɛknɔlɔʒi] *nom féminin*

technology (*ne s'utilise jamais au pluriel*) **: des technologies de pointe** state-of-the-art technology.

tee-shirt, T-shirt [tiʃœrt] (*pluriel* tee-shirts *ou* T-shirts) *nom masculin*

T-shirt : un tee-shirt à manches longues a long-sleeved T-shirt.

teindre [tɛ̃dr] *verbe*

to dye : j'ai envie de teindre mon jean en noir I want to dye my jeans black ; **ma grand-mère se fait teindre les cheveux** my grandmother has her hair dyed

se teindre *verbe pronominal*

se teindre les cheveux ou **se teindre** to dye one's hair : **Isabelle s'est teint en roux** Isabelle dyed her hair red.

teint, e [tɛ̃, ɛ̃t] *participe passé de* teindre

teint *nom masculin*

complexion : elle a un joli teint pâle she has a nice pale complexion

teinte *nom féminin*

colour *UK,* **color** *US* **: une belle teinte vive** a lovely bright colour.

teinté, e [tɛ̃te] *adjectif*

tinted : des verres teintés tinted glasses.

teinture [tɛ̃tyr] *nom féminin*

dye : une teinture naturelle a natural dye.

teinturerie [tɛ̃tyrri] *nom féminin*

dry cleaner's : je porte ton blouson à la teinturerie I'm taking your jacket to the dry cleaner's.

tel, telle [tɛl] (*masculin pluriel* tels, *féminin pluriel* telles) *adjectif*

such : un tel homme such a man ; **un tel bonheur** such happiness ; **de telles habitudes** such habits

➤ **tel que** such as ou like **: les matières telles que l'histoire et la géographie** subjects such as history and geography ou subjects like history and geography

➤ **tel quel** as it is **: apporte-le-moi tel quel** bring it to me as it is ; **je te les rends tels quels** I'm giving them back to you as they are

➤ **à tel point que** to such an extent that

➤ **de telle sorte que** so that **: ils sont arrivés tôt, de telle sorte qu'on a pu bavarder** they arrived early, so that we were able to chat.

tél. (*abréviation de* téléphone)

tel.

télé [tele] *nom féminin familier*

TV, telly *UK* **: une télé à écran plat** a TV with a flat screen ; **regarder la télé** to watch TV ; **qu'est-ce qu'il y a ce soir à la télé ?** what's on TV tonight?

➤ **la télé par câble** cable TV.

télécharger [teleʃarge] *verbe*

to download : j'ai mis une heure à télé-

charger ce programme it took me an hour to download this programme.

télécommande [telekɔmɑ̃d] *nom féminin*

remote control : **où est la télécommande de la télé ?** where's the remote control for the TV?

télécopie [telekɔpi] *nom féminin*

fax : **numéro de télécopie** fax number ; **envoyer un document à quelqu'un par télécopie** to fax a document to somebody.

télécopieur [telekɔpjœr] *nom masculin*

fax, fax machine.

téléfilm [telefilm] *nom masculin*

TV movie.

téléphérique [teleferik] *nom masculin*

cable car.

téléphone [telefɔn] *nom masculin*

1. phone, telephone : **le téléphone sonne** the phone is ringing ; **ils n'ont pas le téléphone** they haven't got a phone OU they're not on the phone *UK*
2. *familier* telephone number : **tu as noté mon téléphone ?** have you written down my telephone number?
   ➤ **un téléphone à carte** a cardphone
   ➤ **un téléphone sans fil** a cordless phone OU a cordless telephone
   ➤ **un téléphone portable** a mobile phone.

téléphoner [telefɔne] *verbe*

1. to phone : **téléphone-moi vers cinq heures** phone me around five o'clock
2. to make a phone call : **je peux téléphoner ?** can I make a phone call?

télescope [teleskɔp] *nom masculin*

telescope : **regarde dans le télescope** look through the telescope.

télésiège [telesjɛʒ] *nom masculin*

chairlift.

téléski [teleski] *nom masculin*

ski tow.

téléspectateur, trice [telespɛktatœr, tris] *nom masculin, nom féminin*
TV viewer.

téléviseur [televizœr] *nom masculin*

television set.

télévision [televizjɔ̃] *nom féminin*

television : **une télévision à écran plat** a television with a flat screen ; **regarder la télévision** to watch television ; **qu'est-ce qu'il y a ce soir à la télévision ?** what's on television tonight?
➤ **la télévision par câble** cable television
➤ **la télévision numérique** digital television
➤ **la télévision par satellite** satellite television.

tellement [tɛlmɑ̃] *adverbe*

1. so : **il est tellement beau !** he's so good-looking! ; **je ne comprends rien tellement il parle vite** he talks so quickly that I can't understand a word ; **personne ne le prend au sérieux tellement il est jeune** he's so young that nobody takes him seriously
2. so much : **tellement plus long** so much longer : **tellement mieux** so much better ; **elle a tellement changé !** she's changed so much! ; **j'ai tellement marché que je ne sens plus mes jambes** I've walked so much that I can't feel my legs anymore
➤ **tellement de**
1. so much : **ils ont tellement de meubles qu'ils ne savent pas quoi en faire** they have so much furniture that they don't know what to do with it
2. so many : **Anne a tellement d'amis qu'elle ne peut pas tous les inviter** Anne has so many friends that she can't invite them all
➤ **pas tellement** not particularly : **Alain n'est pas tellement sympa** Alain isn't particularly nice.

témoignage [temwaɲaʒ] *nom masculin*

1. testimony *(pluriel* testimonies*)* : **son témoignage est particulièrement important pour la police** his testimony is particularly important for the police.
2. account : **un témoignage sur la France de l'après-guerre** an account of post-war France.

témoigner [temwaɲe] *verbe*

to testify : **la police a demandé à Lucille de témoigner** the police asked Lucille to testify ; **j'ai dû témoigner qu'il était avec moi ce soir-là** I had to testify that he was with me that night.

témoin [temwɛ̃] *nom masculin*

1. witness *(pluriel* witnesses*)* : **la police inter-**

roge les témoins the police are interrogating witnesses
➤ **être témoin d'un accident** to witness an accident
2. **baton : passer le témoin à un autre coureur** to hand over the baton to another runner.

température [tɑ̃peratyr] *nom féminin*

temperature : **la température est basse pour la saison** the temperature is low for this time of year ; **Carole a de la température** Carole has a temperature ; **tu as pris ta température ?** have you taken your temperature?

tempête [tɑ̃pɛt] *nom féminin*

storm : **la tempête a fait beaucoup de dégâts** the storm did a lot of damage
➤ **une tempête de neige** a snowstorm
➤ **une tempête de sable** a sandstorm.

temple [tɑ̃pl] *nom masculin*

1. temple : **un temple grec** a Greek temple
2. church (*pluriel* **churches**) : **un temple protestant** a Protestant church ; **aller au temple** to go to church.

temporaire [tɑ̃pɔrɛr] *adjectif*

temporary : **un emploi temporaire** a temporary job.

temps [tɑ̃] *nom masculin*

1. time : **est-ce qu'on aura le temps de manger ?** will we have time to eat? ; **il est temps de partir** it's time to leave ; **pour gagner du temps** to save time ; **ma mère n'a pas beaucoup de temps libre** my mother hasn't got much free time
2. weather : **il fait un temps affreux** the weather's awful ; **quel temps fait-il à Paris ?** what's the weather like in Paris?
3. tense : **les temps du passé** the past tenses
➤ **à temps** in time : **vous arrivez juste à temps !** you've got here just in time!
➤ **à plein temps** full-time : **il travaille à plein temps** he works full-time OU he has a full-time job
➤ **à temps partiel** part-time : **elle travaille à temps partiel** she works part-time OU she has a part-time job
➤ **ces derniers temps** lately OU recently
➤ **ces temps-ci** these days : **je ne sors pas beaucoup ces temps-ci** I don't go out much these days
➤ **de temps en temps** from time to time
➤ **du temps de** in the days of : **du temps de**

la Révolution in the days of the French Revolution
➤ **en même temps** at the same time
➤ **pendant ce temps** meanwhile : **pendant ce temps, je parlais à Paul** meanwhile I was talking to Paul
➤ **tout le temps** all the time : **elle rit tout le temps** she laughs all the time
➤ **il était temps !** about time too!

tendance [tɑ̃dɑ̃s] *nom féminin*

trend : **les dernières tendances de la mode** the latest fashion trends
➤ **avoir tendance à faire quelque chose** to have a tendency to do something OU to tend to do something : **Roland a tendance à mentir** Roland has a tendency to lie.

tendre [tɑ̃dr] *adjectif*

tender : **un geste tendre** a tender gesture ; **cette viande est très tendre** this meat is very tender.

tendre [tɑ̃dr] *verbe*

1. to tighten : **tends bien la corde** tighten the rope
2. to stretch : **on a tendu la corde à linge entre deux arbres** we stretched the clothesline between two trees
➤ **tendre quelque chose à quelqu'un** to hold something out to somebody : **elle lui a tendu la clé** she held the key out to him ; **je lui ai tendu la main** I held out my hand to him
➤ **tendre un piège à quelqu'un** to set a trap for somebody.

tendu, e [tɑ̃dy] *verbe & adjectif*

■ *participe passé de* tendre
■ *adjectif*

1. tight : **les cordes de la guitare ne sont pas assez tendues** the guitar strings aren't tight enough
2. tense : **j'étais tendue avant l'examen** I felt tense before the test
3. strained : **une atmosphère tendue** a strained atmosphere.

tenir [tənir] *verbe*

1. to hold : **qu'est-ce que tu tiens à la main ?** what are you holding in your hand? ; **elle tenait le bébé dans ses bras** she was holding the baby in her arms ; **utilise des agrafes, sinon ça ne tiendra pas** use staples, otherwise it won't hold
➤ **tu n'as pas tenu ta promesse** you didn't keep your promise

2. to fit : **ça ne tiendra jamais dans la valise** it will never fit in the suitcase ; **on tient à six dans la voiture** you can fit six people in the car

3. to run : **la mère de Jean tient un restaurant** Jean's mother runs a restaurant

➤ **tenir à** to be very fond of : **on voit qu'il tient à elle** you can tell he's very fond of her ; **je tiens beaucoup à ce collier** I'm very fond of this necklace

➤ **tenir à faire quelque chose** to insist on doing something : **si tu tiens vraiment à y aller ...** if you really insist on going ...

➤ **tenir le coup** *familier* to take it : **j'étais trop fatiguée, je n'ai pas tenu le coup** I was too tired, I couldn't take it

➤ **tiens !** ou **tenez !** here! : **tenez, c'est pour vous** here, this is for you

➤ **tenir de quelqu'un** to take after somebody : **elle tient de sa mère** she takes after her mother

➤ **tiens, tiens !** well, well!

se tenir *verbe pronominal*

1. to hold on : **tiens-toi bien pour ne pas tomber** hold on tight so that you don't fall ; **tenez-vous à la rampe** hold on to the banister

2. to stand : **ils se tenaient derrière nous** they were standing behind us

➤ **bien se tenir** to behave : **tu as intérêt à bien te tenir quand les invités seront là !** you'd better behave yourself when the guests are here!

➤ **se tenir droit**

1. *assis* to sit up straight : **tiens-toi droite !** sit up straight!

2. *debout* to stand up straight : **il se tient très droit** he stands up very straight

➤ **se tenir par la main** to hold hands : **je les ai vus qui se tenaient par la main** I saw them holding hands.

tennis [tenis] *nom*

■ *nom masculin*
tennis : **tu sais jouer au tennis ?** can you play tennis?

■ *nom masculin pluriel*
tennis shoes : **des tennis en cuir blanc** white leather tennis shoes

➤ **le tennis de table** table tennis.

tension [tãsjõ] *nom féminin*

1. blood pressure : **mon père a de la tension, il doit prendre des médicaments** my father

has high blood pressure, he has to take medicine

2. **tension** (*ne s'utilise jamais au pluriel*) : **il y a des tensions entre eux** there's some tension between them

3. voltage : **une ligne à haute tension** a high-voltage line.

tentation [tãtasjõ] *nom féminin*

temptation : **je n'ai pas pu résister à la tentation** I couldn't resist the temptation.

tentative [tãtativ] *nom féminin*

attempt : **une tentative de suicide** a suicide attempt.

tente [tãt] *nom féminin*

tent : **on a monté la tente en dix minutes** we put up the tent in ten minutes.

tenter [tãte] *verbe*

to tempt : **l'offre ne te tente pas ?** doesn't the offer tempt you? ; **je suis tentée d'accepter** I'm tempted to accept

➤ **tenter de faire quelque chose** to try to do something : **les prisonniers ont tenté de s'évader** the prisoners tried to escape

➤ **tenter le coup** to have a go ou to have a try.

tenu, e [təny] *participe passé de* tenir.

tenue [təny] *nom féminin*

outfit, clothes (*s'utilise toujours au pluriel*) : **Adèle porte une tenue extravagante** Adèle is wearing an outrageous outfit ; **une tenue d'été** summer clothes

➤ **tenue de soirée** evening dress.

terme [tɛrm] *nom masculin*

term : **un terme technique** a technical term ; **un projet à court terme** a short-term project ; **des prévisions à long terme** long-term predictions

➤ **en d'autres termes** in other words.

terminal [tɛrminal] (*pluriel* terminaux [tɛrmino]) *nom masculin*
terminal : **le vol part du terminal 3** the flight leaves from terminal 3.

terminale [tɛrminal] *nom féminin*

year thirteen *UK*, twelfth grade *US* : **Marion est en terminale** Marion is in year thirteen.

t

terminer [tɛrmine] *verbe*

to finish : **tu as terminé ton petit déjeuner ?** have you finished your breakfast?

se terminer *verbe pronominal*

to end : **la fête s'est terminée vers trois heures** the party ended around three o'clock ; **le spectacle se termine par un feu d'artifice** the show ends with a firework display.

terminus [tɛrminys] *nom masculin*

terminus : **le terminus de l'Eurostar à Londres** the London terminus of the Eurostar
➤ **il faut qu'on aille jusqu'au terminus** we've got to ride all the way to the end of the line.

terrain [tɛrɛ̃] *nom masculin*

1. **piece of land : la maison est vendue avec le terrain** the house is sold with the piece of land
2. **pitch** *UK (pluriel* **pitches**)**, field** *US* : **un terrain de football** a football pitch ; **un terrain de rugby** a rugby pitch
➤ **un terrain de camping** a campsite
➤ **un terrain vague** a piece of waste ground *UK*, a vacant lot *US*.

terre [tɛr] *nom féminin*

1. **soil : la terre est fertile dans cette région** the soil is fertile in this region
2. **ground : la terre est couverte de neige** the ground is covered in snow
3. **land : ils possèdent des terres en Bourgogne** they own land in Burgundy ; **sur la terre ferme** on dry land
➤ **la Terre** the Earth : **la Terre tourne autour du Soleil** the Earth revolves around the sun
➤ **terre cuite** terracotta
➤ **par terre**
1. **on the ground : on s'est assis par terre pour pique-niquer** we sat on the ground to have a picnic
2. **on the floor : pose les courses par terre** put the shopping on the floor
➤ **sous terre** underground
➤ **terre à terre** down-to-earth.

terreur [tɛrœr] *nom féminin*

terror.

terrible [tɛribl] *adjectif*

terrible : **un accident terrible** a terrible accident ; **ils font un bruit terrible** they make a terrible noise

➤ **ce n'est pas terrible** *familier* it's not very good.

terrifier [tɛrifje] *verbe*

to terrify.

territoire [tɛritwar] *nom masculin*

territory *(pluriel* **territories***)* : **un territoire d'outre-mer** an overseas territory.

terrorisme [tɛrɔrism] *nom masculin*

terrorism.

terroriste [tɛrɔrist] *adjectif & nom masculin ou féminin*

terrorist : **un attentat terroriste** a terrorist attack.

tes ➤ ton.

test [tɛst] *nom masculin*

test : **un test de grossesse** a pregnancy test.

testament [tɛstamɑ̃] *nom masculin*

will : **vous avez fait votre testament ?** have you made your will?

tête [tɛt] *nom féminin*

1. **head : ce bébé a une grosse tête** this baby has a big head ; **de la tête aux pieds** from head to toe ; **la tête la première** head-first ; **calculer quelque chose de tête** to calculate something in one's head
2. **face : cette fille a une drôle de tête** that girl has a strange face ; **pourquoi tu fais cette tête ?** why are you making such a long face?
➤ **être en tête** to be in the lead : **c'est le coureur espagnol qui est en tête** the Spanish cyclist is in the lead
➤ **en tête de**
1. **at the front of : on est en tête de train** we're at the front of the train
2. **leading : le Parti républicain est en tête des sondages** the Republican Party is leading in the polls
➤ **avoir la grosse tête** *familier* to be big-headed
➤ **être tête en l'air** to have one's head in the clouds
➤ **faire la tête** to sulk : **arrête de faire la tête** stop sulking.

têtu, e [tety] *adjectif*

stubborn : **ne sois pas si têtue !** don't be so stubborn!

texte [tɛkst] *nom masculin*

1. **text : on doit faire le commentaire de ce texte pour demain** we have to do a commentary on this text for tomorrow
2. **lyrics** (*s'utilise toujours au pluriel*) **: les textes de ses chansons sont intéressants** the lyrics to his songs are interesting.

texto [tɛksto] *nom masculin*

text-message : je t'ai envoyé un texto I sent you a text-message.

TGV (*abréviation de* train à grande vitesse)

nom masculin
French high-speed train

> TGV
> The TGV, or train à grande vitesse (high-speed train), can reach speeds of 270 to 300 km per hour. It connects Paris to France's other major cities, such as Lyons, Marseilles, and Lille, as well as to 8 other European cities, such as London, Brussels and Amsterdam. Over 200 million passengers a year travel on the TGV.

thé [te] *nom masculin*

tea : je vais prendre une tasse de thé I'll have a cup of tea ; **un thé au citron** tea with lemon ; **un thé au lait** tea with milk ; **un thé nature** tea without milk.

théâtre [teatr] *nom masculin*

theatre *UK*, **theater** *US* **: on va au théâtre jeudi avec l'école** we're going to the theatre on Thursday with the school.

théière [tejɛr] *nom féminin*

teapot.

thème [tɛm] *nom masculin*

1. **theme : quel est le thème du débat ?** what's the theme of the debate? ou what's the subject of the debate?
2. **prose translation, translation into a foreign language : ma sœur est bonne en thème** my sister is good at prose translation.

théorie [teɔri] *nom féminin*

theory (*pluriel* **theories**) **: ma théorie, c'est que ...** my theory is that ... ; **en théorie** in theory ou theoretically.

thermomètre [tɛrmɔmɛtr] *nom masculin*

thermometer : le thermomètre indique 29° the thermometer says 29°.

thon [tɔ̃] *nom masculin*

tuna : du thon à l'huile tuna in oil.

tibia [tibja] *nom masculin*

1. **tibia : Corentin s'est cassé le tibia** Corentin broke his tibia
2. **shin : il m'a donné un coup de pied dans les tibias !** he kicked me in the shins!

ticket [tikɛ] *nom masculin*

ticket : un carnet de tickets de métro a book of metro tickets
> **un ticket de caisse** a receipt ou a till receipt.

tiède [tjɛd] *adjectif*

1. **lukewarm : ce thé est tiède** this tea is lukewarm
2. **warm : une bonne brise tiède** a nice warm breeze.

le tien, la tienne [lətjɛ̃, latjɛn] (*masculin pluriel* les tiens [letjɛ̃], *féminin pluriel* les tiennes [letjɛn]) *pronom*

yours : j'aime bien son collier mais je préfère le tien I like her necklace but I like yours more ; **je ne trouve plus ma calculatrice, est-ce je peux emprunter la tienne ?** I can't find my calculator, can I borrow yours? ; **mes parents ne peuvent pas venir, et les tiens ?** my parents can't come, what about yours? ; **j'aimerais avoir des chaussures comme les tiennes** I'd like to have some shoes like yours
> **à la tienne !** cheers!

tiers [tjɛr] *nom masculin*

third : un tiers de la somme totale a third of the total sum.

tiers-monde [tjɛrmɔ̃d] *nom masculin*

le tiers-monde the Third World.

tige [tiʒ] *nom féminin*

1. **stem, stalk : les tiges des tulipes sont cassées** the stems of the tulips are broken
2. **rod : une tige en métal** a metal rod.

tigre [tigr] *nom masculin*

tiger.

timbre [tɛ̃br] *nom masculin*

stamp : colle le timbre sur l'enveloppe stick the stamp on the envelope.

timbrer [tɛ̃bre] *verbe*

to stamp : n'oublie pas de timbrer la lettre don't forget to stamp the letter.

timide [timid] *adjectif*

shy : **c'est une fille très timide** she's a very shy girl.

tir [tir] *nom masculin*

1. **shooting** : **ils font du tir à la carabine** they go rifle-shooting
2. **shot** : **un magnifique tir de Beckham** a beautiful shot by Beckham
➤ **le tir à l'arc** archery
➤ **les tirs au but** the penalty shoot-out.

tire-bouchon [tirbuʃɔ̃] (*pluriel* tire-bouchons) *nom masculin*

corkscrew
➤ **queue en tire-bouchon** corkscrew tail.

tirelire [tirlir] *nom féminin*

piggybank, moneybox *UK* (*pluriel* **moneyboxes**).

tirer [tire] *verbe*

1. **to pull** : **aidez-moi à tirer la table au milieu de la pièce** help me to pull the table to the centre of the room : **ne tire pas trop fort sur la poignée** don't pull on the handle too hard
2. **to draw** : **tirer les rideaux** to draw the curtains : **tirer un trait** to draw a line : **j'ai tiré le numéro gagnant** I drew the winning number
3. **to fire** : **le soldat a tiré sa dernière balle** the soldier fired his last bullet
4. **to shoot** : **ne tirez pas !** don't shoot!
➤ **tirer la langue à quelqu'un** to stick one's tongue out at somebody : **elle m'a tiré la langue !** she stuck her tongue out at me!

se tirer *verbe pronominal*

➤ **se tirer de quelque chose** to get out of something : **comment est-ce qu'on va se tirer de cette situation ?** how are we going to get out of this situation?
➤ **s'en tirer** *familier* to manage : **tu vas t'en tirer, ce n'est pas si difficile** you'll manage, it isn't that difficult.

tiroir [tirwar] *nom masculin*

drawer : **les chaussettes sont dans le tiroir du haut** the socks are in the top drawer.

tisane [tizan] *nom féminin*

herbal tea.

tisser [tise] *verbe*

1. **to weave** : **Charlotte apprend à tisser la laine** Charlotte is learning to weave wool

2. **to spin** : **l'araignée tisse sa toile** the spider is spinning its web.

tissu [tisy] *nom masculin*

fabric, material : **du tissu à carreaux** checked fabric ou checked material.

titre [titr] *nom masculin*

1. **title** : **j'ai oublié le titre du livre** I've forgotten the title of the book
2. **headline** : **je ne lis que les titres du journal** I only read the newspaper headlines
➤ **un titre de transport** a ticket.

toboggan [tɔbɔgã] *nom masculin*

slide : **le toboggan de l'aire de jeux** the slide in the playground.

toi [twa] *pronom*

1. **you** : **tiens, c'est pour toi** take this, it's for you ; **elle parle tout le temps de toi** she's always talking about you ; **j'en ai eu moins que toi** I had less than you ; **toi non plus, tu ne joues pas ?** aren't you playing either? ; **et toi, tu veux venir ?** what about you, do you want to come? ; **et toi, il t'a invité ?** what about you, did he invite you? ; **qui est le plus âgé ? – toi** who's the oldest? – you ou who's the oldest? – you are ; **c'est toi qui me l'as dit** you told me so
2. **yourself** : **tu ne penses qu'à toi** you only think of yourself
3. *Dans les verbes pronominaux à l'impératif* **dépêche-toi** hurry up ; **assieds-toi** sit down ; **amuse-toi bien** enjoy yourself
➤ **toi-même** yourself : **est-ce que tu l'as préparé toi-même ?** did you make it yourself?
➤ **ce livre est à toi** this book is yours.

toile [twal] *nom féminin*

1. **cloth, canvas** : **de la toile de coton** cotton cloth ; **des chaussures en toile** canvas shoes
2. **painting** : **une toile du Greco** a painting by El Greco
➤ **une jupe de toile** a cotton skirt
➤ **un sac en toile** a canvas bag
➤ **la Toile** the Web : **surfer sur la Toile** to surf on the Web
➤ **une toile d'araignée** a spider's web.

toilette [twalɛt] *nom féminin*

➤ **faire sa toilette** to wash ou to have a wash *UK* ou to wash up *US*

toilettes *nom féminin pluriel*

toilet *UK*, **restroom** *US* : **où sont les toi-**

lettes ? where are the toilets? *UK* OU where is the restroom? *US* ; je dois aller aux toilettes I need to go to the toilet.

toit [twa] *nom masculin*

roof : **un toit en tuiles** a tiled roof
➤ **un toit ouvrant** a sunroof.

tolérant, e [tɔlerã, ãt] *adjectif*

tolerant : **il faut être tolérant et ne pas juger les autres** you must be tolerant and not judge other people.

tolérer [tɔlere] *verbe*

to tolerate : **je ne tolérerai pas que tu me parles comme ça !** I won't tolerate you speaking to me like this!

tomate [tɔmat] *nom féminin*

tomato *(pluriel* tomatoes*)* : **un kilo de tomates** a kilo of tomatoes ; **de la soupe à la tomate** tomato soup.

tombe [tɔ̃b] *nom féminin*

grave : **nous sommes allés sur la tombe de mon grand-père** we visited my grandfather's grave.

tombée [tɔ̃be] *nom féminin*

à la tombée de la nuit at nightfall.

tomber [tɔ̃be] *verbe*

1. to fall : **attention, tu vas tomber !** watch out, you're going to fall! ; **la nuit tombe** night is falling ; **mon anniversaire tombe un jeudi** my birthday falls on a Thursday OU my birthday is on a Thursday
2. to fall off : **Adèle est tombée de sa chaise** Adèle fell off her chair ; **l'ouvrier est tombé du toit** the workman fell off the roof
3. to drop, to fall : **la température est encore tombée** the temperature has fallen again OU the temperature has dropped again
➤ **faire tomber quelqu'un** OU **quelque chose** to knock somebody OU something over
➤ **tomber bien** to come at the right time : **tu tombes bien, j'ai besoin d'aide** you've come at the right time, I need help
➤ **être bien tombé** to be lucky : **je suis bien tombé, ce steak est excellent** I was lucky, this steak is excellent
➤ **être mal tombé** to be unlucky : **j'ai choisi un film au hasard mais je suis mal tombé** I chose a film at random but I was unlucky
➤ **tomber amoureux** to fall in love
➤ **tomber malade** to fall ill

➤ **tomber sur quelque chose** to come across something : **Richard est tombé sur une photo de son oncle dans un magazine** Richard came across a photograph of his uncle in a magazine.

tombola [tɔ̃bɔla] *nom féminin*

raffle : **les billets de tombola valent un euro** the raffle tickets cost one euro.

tome [tɔm] *nom masculin*

volume : **un roman en trois tomes** a novel in three volumes.

ton¹ [tɔ̃] *nom masculin*

1. tone : **Asim m'a parlé d'un ton amical** Asim spoke to me in a friendly tone ; **ne me parle pas sur ce ton !** don't use that tone of voice with me! OU don't speak to me like that!
➤ **hausser le ton** to raise one's voice
2. shade : **un joli ton de vert** a nice shade of green.

ton², ta [tɔ̃, ta] *(pluriel* tes [te]*)* *adjectif*

your : **ton ordinateur** your computer ; **quelle est ton actrice préférée ?** who is your favourite actress? ; **tu n'as pas fini ta rédaction** you haven't finished your essay ; **un de tes meilleurs amis** one of your best friends.

tonne [tɔn] *nom féminin*

ton, tonne : **deux tonnes de blé** two tons of wheat OU two tonnes of wheat
➤ **des tonnes de** *familier* tons of : **Betty a des tonnes de BD chez elle** Betty has tons of comic books at home.

tonneau [tɔno] *(pluriel* tonneaux*)* *nom masculin*

barrel, cask : **un tonneau de vin** a barrel of wine OU a cask of wine
➤ **faire un tonneau** to roll over : **la voiture a fait trois tonneaux** the car rolled over three times.

tonnerre [tɔnɛr] *nom masculin*

thunder : **tu entends le tonnerre ?** can you hear the thunder? ; **un coup de tonnerre** a thunderclap OU a clap of thunder.

tonus [tɔnys] *nom masculin*

energy : **je n'ai aucun tonus ces temps-ci** I have no energy these days.

torche [tɔrʃ] *nom féminin*

torch *(pluriel* torches*)* : **une torche électrique** an electric torch *UK* OU a flashlight *US*.

t

torchon [tɔrʃɔ̃] *nom masculin*

1. cloth : **ce torchon sert à essuyer la vaisselle** this cloth is for drying the dishes
2. *familier* mess : **tu ne vas pas rendre ce torchon au prof ?** you're not going to give the teacher this mess?

tordre [tɔrdr] *verbe*

to twist : **Paul m'a tordu le bras** Paul twisted my arm.

se tordre *verbe pronominal*

to twist : **se tordre la cheville** to twist one's ankle : **mon père s'est tordu la cheville en jouant au squash** my father twisted his ankle playing squash

➤ **se tordre de douleur** to be doubled up with pain
➤ **se tordre de rire** *familier* to be in stitches OU to be doubled up with laughter.

tordu, e [tɔrdy] *participe passé de* **tordre**.

tornade [tɔrnad] *nom féminin*

tornado.

torrent [tɔrɑ̃] *nom masculin*

mountain stream
➤ **il pleut à torrents** it's pouring down OU it's pouring with rain.

torse [tɔrs] *nom masculin*

chest : **regarde comme il bombe le torse** look how he throws out his chest
➤ **torse nu** bare-chested.

tort [tɔr] *nom masculin*

➤ **avoir tort** to be wrong : **tu as tort** you're wrong ; **Jean ne veut pas reconnaître qu'il a tort** Jean won't admit that he's wrong ; **tu as eu tort de me parler comme ça** you were wrong to talk to me like that
➤ **à tort** wrongly : **Agnès a été accusée à tort** Agnès was wrongly accused
➤ **faire du tort à quelqu'un** to wrong somebody.

torticolis [tɔrtikɔli] *nom masculin*

stiff neck : **j'ai un torticolis** I have a stiff neck.

tortiller [tɔrtije] *verbe*

to twist : **elle tortillait nerveusement une mèche de cheveux** she was nervously twisting a lock of her hair

se tortiller *verbe pronominal*

1. to wriggle : **arrête de te tortiller sur ta chaise** stop wriggling on your chair
2. to squirm : **Natacha se tortillait parce qu'elle était gênée** Natacha was squirming with embarrassment.

tortue [tɔrty] *nom féminin*

tortoise *UK*, **turtle** *US* : **elle a une tortue à la maison** she has a pet tortoise
➤ **une tortue marine** a turtle.

tôt [to] *adverbe*

early : **c'est un peu tôt pour partir** it's a bit early to leave
➤ **tôt ou tard** sooner or later
➤ **ce n'est pas trop tôt !** about time too!

total, e, aux [tɔtal, o] *adjectif*

total : **la somme totale** the total sum

total *nom masculin*

total : **à combien s'élève le total ?** how much is the total? OU what is the total?

totalement [tɔtalmɑ̃] *adverbe*

totally, completely : **la ville est totalement détruite** the town has been completely destroyed.

touchant, e [tuʃɑ̃, ɑ̃t] *adjectif*

touching : **un geste touchant** a touching gesture.

touche [tuʃ] *nom féminin*

1. key : **appuie sur la touche « Retour »** press the "Return" key
2. touch : **une touche de maquillage** a touch of make-up ; **la ligne de touche** the touchline ; **envoyer le ballon en touche** to kick the ball into touch.

toucher [tuʃe] *verbe*

1. to touch : **ne touche pas le radiateur** don't touch the radiator ; **tu n'as pas touché à ton repas, tu es malade ?** you haven't touched your meal, are you ill? ; **leur accueil nous a beaucoup touchés** we were very touched by their welcome
2. to get : **Sandrine touche dix euros de l'heure** Sandrine gets ten euros an hour
3. to cash : **il n'a pas encore touché son chèque** he hasn't cashed his cheque yet
4. to be next to, to be adjacent to : **leur maison touche la nôtre** their house is next to ours

5. to affect : **ce changement ne touche pas tous les élèves** this change doesn't affect all pupils

➤ **toucher le gros lot** to win the jackpot.

toujours [tuʒur] *adverbe*

1. always : **Mathias est toujours en retard** Mathias is always late ; **on peut toujours demander aux renseignements** we can always ask directory enquiries

2. still : **tu es toujours fâché ?** are you still angry?

➤ **pour toujours** forever : **elle est partie pour toujours** she has gone forever.

tour¹ [tur] *nom masculin*

1. turn : **c'est ton tour maintenant** it's your turn now

2. trick : **jouer un mauvais tour à quelqu'un** to play a dirty trick on somebody

➤ **le tour de taille** the waist measurement

➤ **faire le tour de quelque chose** to go round something : **le chien a fait trois fois le tour du jardin** the dog went round the garden three times

➤ **faire un tour** to go for a walk : **j'aimerais faire un tour mais il pleut** I'd like to go for a walk but it's raining

➤ **faire un tour en voiture** to go for a drive

➤ **faire un tour à vélo** to go for a bike ride

➤ **tour de piste** lap : **les athlètes ont refait un tour de piste** the athletes did another lap

➤ **faire quelque chose à tour de rôle** to take it in turns to do something : **on fait la vaisselle à tour de rôle** we do the washing-up in turn OU we take it in turns to do the washing-up

➤ **fermer quelque chose à double-tour** to double-lock something

TOUR DE FRANCE
This is a world-famous cycle race which takes place in France every summer. Almost 200 cyclists take part in the race, which is divided into several legs. Competitors enter the race as part of a team. During the **Tour**, the cyclist who is overall leader wears the yellow jersey. This is then awarded to the winner at the end of the race which always finishes at the **Arc de Triomphe** at the end of the **avenue des Champs Élysées** in Paris.

tour² [tur] *nom féminin*

1. tower : **la tour Eiffel** the Eiffel Tower ; **la tour de contrôle** the control tower

2. high-rise building : **les tours de New York** the high-rise buildings in New York

3. tower block *UK*, high-rise *US* : **Chris habite dans une tour en banlieue** Chris lives in a tower block in the suburbs *UK* OU Chris lives in a high-rise in the suburbs *US*

4. *Aux échecs* rook, castle : **la tour avance en ligne droite** the rook moves in a straight line OU the castle moves in a straight line

TOUR EIFFEL
The Eiffel tower, the symbol of Paris, was built in 1889 by Gustave Eiffel amid much controversy. The 320-metre tower was the tallest building in the world at the time. Visitors can take a lift to the very top of the tower or, if they are feeling particularly energetic, can climb some of the 1665 steps to the first or second floor. On a clear day there are panoramic views of Paris and beyond.

tourisme [turism] *nom masculin*

tourism : **le tourisme est la première industrie de la région** tourism is the primary industry in the region

➤ **faire du tourisme** to go sightseeing.

touriste [turist] *nom masculin ou féminin*

tourist.

touristique [turistik] *adjectif*

1. tourist : **une brochure touristique** a tourist brochure

2. popular with tourists : **cette ville est très touristique** this town is very popular with tourists

3. touristy : **malheureusement ce quartier est devenu très touristique** unfortunately, this area has become very touristy.

tournant [turnã] *nom masculin*

bend : **attention au tournant, il est mauvais** watch the bend, it's dangerous.

tournée [turne] *nom féminin*

1. tour : **le groupe part en tournée** the band is going on tour

2. round : **le facteur fait sa tournée** the postman is doing his round ; **je paie une tournée !** *familier* it's my round!

tourner [turne] *verbe*

1. to turn : **tournez à droite, puis à gauche** turn right, then left ; **tourne le bouton vers la droite** turn the knob to the right

2. to revolve : **la Terre tourne autour du soleil** the Earth revolves around the sun

3. to shoot : **le film sera tourné en Italie** the film will be shot in Italy

4. to go off *UK*, to go bad *US* : **le lait a tourné** the milk has gone off

se tourner *verbe pronominal*

to turn around, to turn round *UK* : **tourne-toi pendant que je me change** turn around while I get changed ; **se tourner vers** to turn towards ; **Marie s'est tournée vers moi** Marie turned towards me.

tournesol [turnəsɔl] *nom masculin*

sunflower : **de l'huile de tournesol** sunflower oil.

tournevis [turnəvis] *nom masculin*

screwdriver.

tournoi [turnwa] *nom masculin*

tournament : **notre collège a gagné le tournoi** our school won the tournament.

tous ➤ tout.

Toussaint [tusɛ̃] *nom féminin*

la Toussaint All Saint's Day

📖 TOUSSAINT
All Saints' Day, 1 November, is a special day for remembering people who have died. Flowers, especially chrysanthemums, are placed on the graves of family members. Often, people travel long distances to meet up with their families at the gravesides or tombs of their relatives.

tousser [tuse] *verbe*

to cough.

tout, toute [tu, tut] (*masculin pluriel* tous [tus], *féminin pluriel* toutes [tut]) *adjectif, pronom & adverbe*

■ *adjectif*

all : **c'est toi qui as fait tout ce travail ?** did you do all this work? ; **toute ma famille était là** all my family was there ou my whole family was there ; **tout ça m'a fait réfléchir** all that made me think.

➤ **tout le, toute la** the whole ou all the : **vous avez mangé tout le gâteau ?** have you eaten the whole cake? ou have you eaten all the cake? ; **ils ont bu toute la limonade** they drank all the lemonade

➤ **tous les, toutes les**

1. all the ou every : **tous les garçons de la**

classe portent des jeans all the boys in the class are wearing jeans ou every boy in the class is wearing jeans

2. all : **tous les hommes sont égaux** all men are equal

3. every : **j'ai un cours de dessin tous les mardis** I have an art class every Tuesday ; **tous les jours** every day ; **tous les deux ans** every two years

All et every s'utilisent différemment :
all peut s'utiliser avec des noms au pluriel (all men) ou des noms singuliers indénombrables (all the money) ; every, en revanche, ne peut s'utiliser qu'avec des noms dénombrables au singulier (every town in the country).

Notez que all the s'emploie lorsqu'on parle de la totalité d'un groupe défini (all the boys in the class = les garçons de la classe et non pas tous les garçons du monde), alors que all s'emploie seul lorsqu'on parle d'un groupe indéfini (all men = tous les hommes du monde).

➤ **tous les deux, toutes les deux** both : **elle nous a parlé à tous les deux** she talked to us both ou she talked to both of us ; **vous êtes toutes les deux responsables** you are both responsible ou both of you are responsible ; **ils sont venus tous les deux** they both came ou both of them came

■ *pronom*

1. everything : **je t'ai tout dit** I've told you everything ; **tout ou rien** everything or nothing

2. all : **tout est bien qui finit bien** all is well that ends well ; **ils ont tous accepté ma proposition** they all accepted my suggestion ; **une fois pour toutes** once and for all

➤ **c'est tout** that's all : **bon, c'est tout pour aujourd'hui** right, that's all for today

➤ **en tout** in all : **en tout, il y a 850 élèves dans notre lycée** in all, there are 850 pupils in our school

■ *adverbe*

1. very : **il est tout jeune** he's very young ; **c'est tout près d'ici** it's very near here

2. right : **tout en haut du placard** right at the top of the cupboard ; **tout au début** right at the beginning

➤ **tout seul** all alone : **Paul est tout seul** Paul is all alone

➤ **tout en** while : **elle sifflait tout en travaillant** she whistled while she worked

➤ **pas du tout** not at all : **ça ne me plaît pas du tout** I don't like it at all ; **je vous** dérange ? – non, pas du tout ! am I disturbing you? – no, not at all!

> **tout à fait**

1. **quite : ce n'est pas tout à fait fini** it's not quite finished ; **tu as tout à fait raison** you're quite right
2. **absolutely : tu es d'accord ? – tout à fait !** do you agree? – absolutely!
3. **exactly : c'est tout à fait ce que je voulais** it's exactly what I wanted

> **tout à l'heure**

1. **later : je t'appelle tout à l'heure** I'll call you later ; **à tout à l'heure !** see you later!
2. **a little while ago : j'ai vu Patrice tout à l'heure** I saw Patrice a little while ago

> **tout de suite** straightaway OU at once : **je vais le faire tout de suite** I'll do it straightaway OU I'll do it at once.

toux [tu] *nom féminin*

> **cough : un sirop contre la toux** a cough syrup
une quinte de toux a coughing fit.

trac [trak] *nom masculin*

> **avoir le trac**

1. **to get nervous : j'ai toujours le trac avant les interros** I always get nervous before tests
2. **to get stage fright : certains acteurs n'ont jamais le trac** some actors never get stage fright.

trace [tras] *nom féminin*

1. **mark : il y a des traces de brûlure sur le canapé** there are burn marks on the sofa ; **des traces de doigt** finger marks
2. **trail, track : les chiens suivent la trace du renard** the dogs are following the fox's trail
3. **trace : elle a une légère trace d'accent anglais** she has a slight trace of an English accent

> **des traces de pas** footprints.

tracer [trase] *verbe*

> **to draw : trace un trait là** draw a line there.

tracteur [traktœr] *nom masculin*

> **tractor**.

tradition [tradisjɔ̃] *nom féminin*

> **tradition : c'est une vieille tradition écossaise** it's an old Scottish tradition.

traditionnel, elle [tradisjɔnɛl] *adjectif*

> **traditional : des chants traditionnels irlandais** traditional Irish songs.

traducteur, trice [tradyktœr, tris] *nom masculin, nom féminin*

> **translator : la mère de Louis est traductrice** Louis' mother is a translator.

traduction [tradyksjɔ̃] *nom féminin*

> **translation : une traduction de l'anglais vers le français** a translation from English into French.

traduire [traduir] *verbe*

> **to translate : on doit traduire cette phrase en anglais** we have to translate this sentence into English.

trafic [trafik] *nom masculin*

1. **trafficking : le trafic de drogue** drug trafficking
2. **traffic : il y a trop de trafic sur cette route** there's too much traffic on this road.

tragédie [traʒedi] *nom féminin*

> **tragedy** *(pluriel* **tragedies***) :* **c'est une véritable tragédie** it's a real tragedy.

tragique [traʒik] *adjectif*

> **tragic : un événement tragique** a tragic event.

trahir [trair] *verbe*

1. **to betray : trahir son pays** to betray one's country ; **trahir la confiance de quelqu'un** to betray somebody's trust
2. **to give away : ton sourire t'a trahi !** your smile gave you away!

se trahir *verbe pronominal*

> **to give oneself away : en riant, tu t'es trahie** you gave yourself away by laughing.

train [trɛ̃] *nom masculin*

> **train : le train à grande vitesse** the high-speed train ; **le train de 14 h** the two o'clock train ; **voyager en train** to travel by train
> **être en train de faire quelque chose** to be doing something : **tu ne vois pas que je suis en train de lire ?** can't you see that I'm reading?

traîneau [treno] *(pluriel* **traîneaux***) nom masculin*

> **sledge** *UK,* **sled** *US :* **les chiens ont du mal à tirer le traîneau** the dogs are having difficulty pulling the sledge.

t

traîner [trene] *verbe*

1. **to drag : ne traîne pas les pieds comme ça** don't drag your feet like that ; **ils m'ont traîné au cinéma alors que j'avais la grippe** they dragged me to the cinema even though I had the flu
2. **to lie around : leurs affaires traînent partout dans la maison** their things are lying around all over the house
3. **to hang around : il traîne dans la rue avec ses copains** he hangs around the streets with his friends
4. **to dawdle : ne traînez pas, on est en retard !** stop dawdling, we're late!
5. **to drag on : cette histoire traîne depuis des mois** this business has been dragging on for months.

traire [trɛr] *verbe*

to milk : le fermier trait les vaches tous les matins the farmer milks the cows every morning.

trait [trɛ] *nom masculin*

line : tire un trait sous ce paragraphe draw a line under this paragraph
➤ **un trait d'union** a hyphen
➤ **boire quelque chose d'un trait** to drink something in one go

traits *nom masculin pluriel*

features : il a les traits fins pour un garçon he's got fine features for a boy.

traitement [trɛtmã] *nom masculin*

treatment : mon père est sous traitement pour son cœur my father is having treatment for his heart
➤ **traitement de texte** word processing.

traiter [trete] *verbe*

1. **to treat : tu n'as pas honte de traiter ta sœur comme ça ?** aren't you ashamed of treating your sister like that? ; **Albin se fait traiter à l'hôpital Broussard** Albin is being treated at Broussard hospital
2. **il m'a traitée d'imbécile !** he called me an imbecile!
➤ **traiter de quelque chose** to deal with something : **de quoi traite ce livre ?** what does this book deal with? ou what is this book about?

traître, esse [trɛtr, ɛs] *nom masculin, nom féminin*

traitor.

trajet [traʒɛ] *nom masculin*

1. **journey : j'ai une heure de trajet pour aller à l'école** the journey to school takes me an hour ; **le trajet m'a semblé long** the journey seemed long
2. **route : sur le trajet du bus** on the bus route.

trampoline [trãpɔlin] *nom masculin*

trampoline.

tramway [tram(wɛ)] *nom masculin*

tram *UK*, streetcar *US* : **venez, on va prendre le tramway** come, we'll take the tram.

tranchant, e [trãʃã, ãt] *adjectif*

sharp : avec un instrument tranchant with a sharp instrument.

tranche [trãʃ] *nom féminin*

slice : deux tranches de jambon two slices of ham ; **couper en tranches** to cut into slices.

tranquille [trãkil] *adjectif*

quiet : un endroit tranquille a quiet place ; **restez tranquilles !** keep quiet!
➤ **laisser tranquille** to leave alone : **laisse ton petit frère tranquille !** leave your little brother alone! ; **laisse ces allumettes tranquilles !** leave those matches alone!
➤ **soyez tranquille, il ne leur arrivera rien** don't worry, nothing will happen to them.

tranquillement [trãkilmã] *adverbe*

quietly : on jouait tranquillement dans un coin we were playing quietly in a corner.

tranquillité [trãkilite] *nom féminin*

1. **peacefulness, quietness : la tranquillité du quartier est un avantage** the peacefulness of the area is an advantage ou the quietness of the area is an advantage
2. **peace and quiet : j'ai besoin d'un peu de tranquillité pour travailler** I need a bit of peace and quiet to work.

transférer [trãsfere] *verbe*

to transfer.

transformation [trãsfɔrmasjɔ̃] *nom féminin*

transformation : quelle transformation depuis la dernière fois ! what a transformation since last time!

transformer [trãsfɔrme] *verbe*

1. **to transform, to change : ils veulent com-**

plètement transformer la bibliothèque they
want to completely transform the library ; **la
sorcière a transformé le prince en grenouille** the witch changed the prince into a frog ou
the witch turned the prince into a frog

2. to convert : **on va transformer le grenier
en bureau** we're going to convert the attic
into an office

se transformer *verbe pronominal*

to change : **ce quartier s'est transformé en
l'espace de quelques années** this area has
changed in the space of a few years ; **la citrouille s'est transformée en carrosse** the
pumpkin turned into a coach.

transfusion [trãsfyzjɔ̃] *nom féminin*

transfusion sanguine blood transfusion : **on
lui a fait une transfusion** he was given a
transfusion.

transgénique [trãsʒenik] *adjectif*

genetically modified : **du soja transgénique** genetically modified soya.

transit [trãzit] *nom masculin*

transit : **les passagers en transit** passengers
in transit.

transmettre [trãsmɛtr] *verbe*

to pass on : **tu transmettras le message à
Audrey** pass the message on to Audrey ou
pass on the message to Audrey.

transmis, e [trãsmi, iz] *participe passé de*
transmettre.

transparent, e [trãsparã, ãt] *adjectif*

transparent : **une feuille de plastique
transparent** a sheet of transparent plastic.

transpercer [trãspɛrse] *verbe*

to pierce : **attention à ne pas transpercer le
carton** be careful not to pierce the cardboard.

transpiration [trãspirasjɔ̃] *nom féminin*

sweat, perspiration.

transpirer [trãspire] *verbe*

to sweat, to perspire : **je transpire beaucoup quand je cours** I sweat a lot when I run.

transport [trãspɔr] *nom masculin*

transport, transportation *US (ne s'utilisent
jamais au pluriel)* : **le transport aérien** air transport : **les moyens de transport** means of

transport ; **les transports en commun** ou **les
transports collectifs** public transport.

transporter [trãspɔrte] *verbe*

to transport : **les marchandises sont trans-
portées par train** the goods are transported
by train.

trapèze [trapɛz] *nom masculin*

trapeze : **un numéro de trapèze éblouis-
sant** a dazzling trapeze act.

trapéziste [trapezist] *nom masculin ou féminin*

trapeze artist : **Marie rêve d'être trapéziste** Marie dreams of being a trapeze artist.

trapu, e [trapy] *adjectif*

stocky : **un petit bonhomme trapu** a stocky
little guy.

traumatiser [tromatize] *verbe*

to traumatize : **l'accident l'a complètement traumatisée** the accident completely
traumatized her.

travail [travaj] *nom masculin*

1. work : **on a beaucoup de travail en quatrième** we have a lot of work in third year

2. job : **c'est un travail difficile** it's a difficult
job ; **ma mère a trouvé un travail à temps
partiel** my mother's found a part-time job
> **au travail !** get to work!
> **se mettre au travail** to get down to work.

travaux *nom masculin pluriel*

1. work *(singulier)* : **ils font faire des travaux
dans leur maison** they're having work done
in their house ; **les travaux dirigés** class
work ; **les travaux manuels** arts and crafts ;
les travaux pratiques practical work

2. roadworks *UK*, roadwork *US* : **il y a des
travaux près du rond-point** there are roadworks near the roundabout

travailler [travaje] *verbe*

1. to work : **mon cousin travaille dans l'informatique** my cousin works in computing ; **Simon travaille bien à l'école** Simon works
hard at school

2. to work at, to work on : **la prof m'a conseillé de travailler mon algèbre** the teacher
advised me to work at my algebra ou the
teacher advised me to work on my algebra

3. to practise *UK*, to practice *US* : **Suzanne
travaille son piano une heure par jour** Su-

t

zanne practises her piano for an hour every day.

travailleur, euse [travajœr, øz] *adjectif & nom*

■ *adjectif*

hard-working : Romain n'est pas très travailleur Romain isn't very hard-working

■ *nom masculin, nom féminin*

worker : **les travailleurs immigrés** immigrant workers.

travers [travɛr]

à travers *préposition*

through : on voit le ciel à travers la lucarne you can see the sky through the skylight ; **les murs sont minces, on entend à travers** the walls are thin, you can hear through them

de travers *adverbe*

crooked : ta casquette est de travers your cap is crooked

➤ **aller de travers** to go wrong : **tout va de travers** everything is going wrong

➤ **comprendre de travers** to misunderstand : **il comprend toujours tout de travers** he always misunderstands everything

➤ **regarder quelqu'un de travers** to look askance at somebody

en travers *adverbe*

crosswise : plie la feuille en travers fold the sheet crosswise

en travers de *préposition*

across : **l'arbre est tombé en travers de la route** the tree fell across the road.

traversée [travɛrse] *nom féminin*

crossing : la traversée est longue the crossing is long.

traverser [travɛrse] *verbe*

1. **to cross** : fais attention en traversant la rue be careful when you cross the street ; **il a traversé la rue en courant** he ran across the street

2. **to go through** : on est obligé de traverser Toulouse you have to go through Toulouse ; **Muriel traverse une période difficile** Muriel is going through a difficult period ; **la balle a traversé la cloison** the bullet went through the partition.

trébucher [trebyʃe] *verbe*

to stumble : **Sandra a trébuché sur une branche** Sandra stumbled over a branch.

trèfle [trɛfl] *nom masculin*

1. **clover** : **un trèfle à quatre feuilles** a four-leaf clover

2. **clubs** : **le roi de trèfle** the king of clubs.

treize [trɛz] *adjectif numéral & nom masculin*

thirteen : il y a treize garçons dans ma classe there are thirteen boys in my class ; **le treize juin** the thirteenth of June *UK* ou June thirteenth *US*.

treizième [trɛzjɛm] *adjectif numéral & nom*

thirteenth : le treizième nom sur la liste the thirteenth name on the list ; **Théo est arrivé treizième** Théo came thirteenth.

tréma [trema] *nom masculin*

diaeresis *UK*, **dieresis** *US* : **e tréma** e diaeresis.

tremblement [trɑ̃bləmɑ̃] *nom masculin*

être pris de tremblements to start to shake ou to start shaking.

➤ **tremblement de terre** earthquake.

trembler [trɑ̃ble] *verbe*

1. **to shiver** : tu trembles de froid, rentre vite ! you're shivering with cold, go in quick!

2. **to tremble, to shake** : trembler de peur to tremble with fear ou to shake with fear

3. **to quaver** : sa voix tremblait d'émotion his voice was quavering with emotion

4. **to shake** : le bâtiment entier a tremblé the whole building shook.

trempé, e [trɑ̃pe] *adjectif*

soaked : vous êtes trempés, venez vous sécher you're soaked, come and dry yourselves.

tremper [trɑ̃pe] *verbe*

to soak : le linge trempe depuis trois heures the washing has been soaking for three hours

➤ **tremper quelque chose dans** to dip something into : **Nicolas trempe son pain dans son café** Nicolas dips his bread into his coffee

➤ **faire tremper quelque chose** to soak something

➤ **se faire tremper** to get soaked.

tremplin [trɑ̃plɛ̃] *nom masculin*

springboard.

trente [trɑ̃t] *adjectif numéral & nom masculin*

thirty : **il y avait trente élèves pour le voyage scolaire** there were thirty pupils for the school trip

➤ **nous sommes le trente septembre** it's the thirtieth of September *UK* ou it's September thirtieth *US*.

trente et un [trɑ̃teœ̃] *adjectif numéral & nom masculin*

thirty-one : **il y a trente et un jours en janvier** January has thirty-one days

➤ **nous sommes le trente et un décembre** it's the thirty-first of December *UK* ou it's December thirty-first *UK*.

trentième [trɑ̃tjɛm] *adjectif numéral & nom*

thirtieth : **le trentième nom sur la liste** the thirtieth name on the list : **Paul est arrivé trentième** Paul came thirtieth.

très [trɛ] *adverbe*

very : **Andrew est très beau** Andrew is very handsome ; **je ne me sens pas très bien** I don't feel very well ; **j'ai très faim** I'm very hungry.

trésor [trezɔr] *nom masculin*

treasure : **le trésor est enterré ici** the treasure is buried here

➤ **mon trésor** my precious.

tresse [trɛs] *nom féminin*

plait, braid *US* : **Céline porte des tresses** Céline has plaits.

triangle [trijɑ̃gl] *nom masculin*

triangle : **un triangle rectangle** a right-angled triangle.

triangulaire [trijɑ̃gylɛr] *adjectif*

triangular.

tribu [triby] *nom féminin*

tribe.

tribunal [tribynal] (*pluriel* tribunaux [tribyno]) *nom masculin*

court : **le tribunal correctionnel** the criminal court.

tribunes [tribyn] *nom féminin pluriel*

stands : **les tribunes du stade étaient bondées** the stands of the stadium were packed.

tricher [triʃe] *verbe*

to cheat : **tu as triché, je t'ai vu !** you've cheated, I saw you!

tricheur, euse [triʃœr, øz] *nom masculin, nom féminin*

cheat : **espèce de tricheuse !** you cheat!

tricolore [trikɔlɔr] *adjectif*

three-coloured *UK*, three-colored *US* : **un drapeau tricolore** a three-coloured flag ou a tricolour.

tricot [triko] *nom masculin*

knitting : **ma grand-mère emporte son tricot partout** my grandmother takes her knitting everywhere

➤ **faire du tricot** to knit.

tricoter [trikɔte] *verbe*

to knit : **ma grand-mère m'a tricoté une écharpe** my grandmother knitted me a scarf.

trier [trije] *verbe*

to sort out : **je dois trier mes affaires avant de partir** I have to sort out my things before I leave.

trimestre [trimɛstr] *nom masculin*

term *UK*, trimester *US*, quarter *US* : **les notes du premier trimestre** the marks for the first term.

trimestriel, elle [trimɛstrijɛl] *adjectif*

1. quarterly : **un magazine trimestriel** a quarterly magazine
2. end-of-term *UK* : **le bulletin trimestriel** the end-of-term report.

trinquer [trɛ̃ke] *verbe*

trinquer à to drink to : **trinquons aux jeunes mariés !** let's drink to the newlyweds!

triomphe [trijɔ̃f] *nom masculin*

1. triumph : **ils ont fêté leur triomphe au championnat du monde** they celebrated their triumph in the world championship
2. great success : **le spectacle fait un triomphe** the show is a great success.

triple [tripl] *adjectif & nom*

■ *adjectif*
triple : **le triple saut** the triple jump
■ *nom masculin*
le triple (de) three times as much (as) : **celui-ci coûte le triple de celui-là** this one costs three times as much as that one

t

triste [trist] *adjectif*

sad : ne sois pas triste, elle va revenir don't be sad, she'll be back ; je suis triste de devoir partir I'm sad that I have to leave.

tristesse [tristɛs] *nom féminin*

sadness : un regard plein de tristesse a look full of sadness.

trois [trwa] *adjectif numéral & nom masculin*

three : Joanna a trois frères Joanna has three brothers ; le trois mars the third of March *UK* OU March third *US*
➤ **trois fois rien** nothing at all.

troisième [trwazjɛm] *adjectif & nom*

▪ *adjectif numéral & nom masculin ou féminin*
third : c'est la troisième fois que je te le dis ! this is the third time I've told you! : Anne est arrivée troisième Anne came third
▪ *nom féminin*
1. year ten *UK*, ninth grade *US* : Loïc est en troisième Loïc is in year ten
2. third gear : tu peux passer la troisième maintenant you can go into third gear now.

trombone [trɔ̃bɔn] *nom masculin*

1. paper clip : les feuilles sont attachées par un trombone the sheets are fastened with a paper clip
2. trombone : Alex joue du trombone Alex plays the trombone.

trompe [trɔ̃p] *nom féminin*

trunk : la trompe de l'éléphant the elephant's trunk.

tromper [trɔ̃pe] *verbe*

1. to deceive, to fool : il a trompé tout le monde avec son air calme he deceived everybody with his quiet manner OU he fooled everybody with his quiet manner
2. to be unfaithful to : elle trompe son mari she's unfaithful to her husband

se tromper *verbe pronominal*

1. to make a mistake : je me suis trompé, je recommence I made a mistake, I'll start again
2. to be wrong : non, tu te trompes, c'est en 1999 qu'elle est partie no, you're wrong, she left in 1999 ; se tromper d'adresse to get the wrong address ; je me suis trompé de numéro I got the wrong number.

trompette [trɔ̃pɛt] *nom féminin*

trumpet : Emmanuelle joue de la trompette Emmanuelle plays the trumpet.

tronc [trɔ̃] *nom masculin*

trunk : ils ont gravé leurs initiales sur le tronc de l'arbre they carved their initials on the tree trunk
➤ **un tronc commun** a core syllabus : il y a un tronc commun à toutes les classes de lycée there's a core syllabus for all high-school classes.

trône [tron] *nom masculin*

throne.

trop [tro] *adverbe*

1. too : il est trop vieux he's too old ; c'est trop loin it's too far ; j'ai trop chaud I'm too hot
2. too much : il mange trop he eats too much
➤ **trop de**
1. too much : on a trop de travail cette année we have too much work this year
2. too many : il y a trop d'élèves dans ma classe there are too many pupils in my class
➤ **en trop** OU **de trop**
1. too much : un euro de trop OU un euro en trop one euro too much
2. too many : une personne de trop OU une personne en trop one person too many
➤ **se sentir de trop** to feel unwelcome OU to feel that one is in the way
➤ **pas trop**
1. not much : je n'aime pas trop le chocolat I don't like chocolate very much
2. not really : je ne sais pas trop I don't really know.

tropical, e, aux [trɔpikal, o] *adjectif*

tropical : les forêts tropicales tropical rain forests.

tropique [trɔpik] *nom masculin*

tropic : le tropique du Cancer the Tropic of Cancer ; sous les tropiques in the tropics.

trotter [trɔte] *verbe*

to trot : les chevaux trottent dans le champ the horses are trotting in the field.

trottoir [trɔtwar] *nom masculin*

pavement *UK*, sidewalk *US*
➤ **un trottoir roulant** a travolator.

trou [tru] *nom masculin*

1. hole : **tu as un trou dans ton jean** you've got a hole in your jeans
2. gap : **j'ai un trou de deux à trois, on peut se voir si tu veux** I have a gap between two and three, we can meet up if you want
> **j'ai un trou de mémoire** I can't remember OU my mind has gone blank
> **le trou de la serrure** the keyhole : **regarder par le trou de la serrure** to look through the keyhole
> **habiter un trou perdu** *familier* to live in the middle of nowhere OU to live in the back of beyond.

trouble [trubl] *adjectif*

cloudy : **l'eau est trouble** the water is cloudy.

trouer [true] *verbe*

to make a hole in : **j'ai troué mon collant** I've made a hole in my tights.

troupe [trup] *nom féminin*

troop : **les troupes sont arrivées dans la ville** the troops have arrived in the town
> **une troupe de théâtre** a theatre company *UK* OU a theater company *US*.

troupeau [trupo] (*pluriel* troupeaux) *nom masculin*

1. herd : **un troupeau de vaches** a herd of cows
2. flock : **un troupeau de moutons** a flock of sheep.

trousse [trus] *nom féminin*

pencil case : **j'ai oublié ma trousse, tu peux me prêter un stylo ?** I've forgotten my pencil case, can you lend me a pen?
> **une trousse de maquillage** a make-up bag
> **une trousse à outils** a tool kit
> **une trousse de toilette** a toilet bag.

trouver [truve] *verbe*

1. to find : **j'ai trouvé exactement les bottes que je voulais** I found just the boots I wanted ; **tu as trouvé quelque chose à faire ?** have you found something to do?
2. to think : **je trouve Lucas sympa** I think Lucas is nice ; **tu ne trouves pas que c'est trop cher ?** don't you think it's too expensive?

se trouver *verbe pronominal*

1. to be : **où se trouve le lycée ?** where is the school?
2. to think : **il se trouve beau** he thinks he's handsome
> **se trouver mal** to feel faint
> **il se trouve que ...** the fact is that ... : **il se trouve que je n'ai pas envie d'y aller** the fact is that I don't feel like going.

truc [tryk] *nom masculin*

1. *familier* thing : **c'est quoi ce truc ?** what's this thing? ; **le rap ce n'est pas mon truc** rap isn't my thing
2. trick : **les magiciens ne révèlent jamais leurs trucs** magicians never reveal their tricks.

trucage ➤ truquage.

truite [tryit] *nom féminin*

trout.

truquage, trucage [trykaʒ] *nom masculin*

special effect : **ce n'est pas une vraie araignée, c'est un truquage** it's not a real spider, it's a special effect.

tu¹, e [ty] *participe passé de* taire.

tu² [ty] *pronom*

you : **tu viens ?** are you coming? ; **tu aurais dû me prévenir** you should have told me ; **comment vas-tu ?** how are you?

« Tu » et « vous » se traduisent tous les deux par le même pronom en anglais : **you**.

TU
In French, there are two forms of the word 'you'. Tu is the informal form. It is used between close friends and family; adults use tu when they talk to children; children and young people use it amongst themselves; animals are addressed as tu.

➤ vous

tuba [tyba] *nom masculin*

1. snorkel : **un masque et un tuba** a diving mask and a snorkel ; **explorer le récif avec un masque et un tuba** to go snorkelling on the reef
2. tuba : **Samuel joue du tuba** Samuel plays the tuba.

tube [tyb] *nom masculin*

1. tube : **un tube de peinture** a tube of paint.
2. *familier* hit : **le tube de l'été** this summer's hit
> **le tube digestif** the digestive tract
> **un tube de rouge à lèvres** a lipstick.

t

tuer [tɥe] *verbe*

to kill : **il a été tué dans l'accident** he was killed in the accident

se tuer *verbe pronominal*

1. to die, to be killed : **ils se sont tués dans un accident de voiture** they died ou they were killed in a car crash
2. to kill oneself : **elle s'est tuée par désespoir** she killed herself out of despair.

tueur, euse [tɥœr, øz] *nom masculin, nom féminin*

killer : **le tueur est toujours en liberté** the killer is still at large

➤ **un tueur en série** a serial killer.

tuile [tɥil] *nom féminin*

1. tile : **une tuile est tombée du toit** a tile fell off the roof ; **un toit en tuiles** a tiled roof
2. *familier* nuisance : **j'ai perdu mon portefeuille — quelle tuile !** I've lost my wallet — what a nuisance!

tulipe [tylip] *nom féminin*

tulip.

tunnel [tynɛl] *nom masculin*

tunnel : **le tunnel sous la Manche** the Channel Tunnel

turbulent, e [tyrbylɑ̃, ɑ̃t] *adjectif*

rowdy : **certains élèves de cette classe sont turbulents** some of the pupils in this class are a bit rowdy.

tutoyer [tytwaje] *verbe*

to call 'tu' : **tu peux me tutoyer** you can call me 'tu'.

se tutoyer *verbe pronominal*

to call each other 'tu' : **on se tutoie ?** shall we call each other 'tu'?

tuyau [tɥijo] (*pluriel* tuyaux) *nom masculin*

1. pipe : **les tuyaux du gaz** the gas pipes
2. *familier* tip : **je vais te donner un tuyau pour l'interro** I'll give you a tip for the test
➤ **le tuyau d'arrosage** the hosepipe.

tympan [tɛ̃pɑ̃] *nom masculin*

eardrum : **j'ai mal aux tympans en avion** my eardrums hurt when I take the plane.

type [tip] *nom masculin*

1. type : **plusieurs types de raquettes** several types of rackets ; **Arnaud ne te plaît pas ? —**

non, ce n'est pas mon type don't you like Arnaud? – no, he's not my type
2. *familier* guy : **c'est qui ce type ?** who's that guy?
3. features : **elle a le type nordique** she has Nordic features.

typique [tipik] *adjectif*

typical : **un exemple typique d'architecture gothique** a typical example of Gothic architecture.

UE (*abréviation de* Union européenne) *nom féminin*

l'UE the EU.

un, une [œ̃, yn] *article, pronom, adjectif & nom*

■ *article indéfini*

a, an (*devant une voyelle ou un 'h' muet*) : **il y a un magasin au coin** there is a shop on the corner ; **une pomme** an apple ; **une heure** an hour

➤ des

■ *pronom indéfini*

one : **un de mes amis** one of my friends ; **l'une des plus grandes actrices françaises** one of the greatest French actresses

➤ **un par un** one by one

■ *adjectif numéral*

one : **j'ai un frère et deux sœurs** I have one brother and two sisters

■ *nom masculin*

one : **un plus trois égale quatre** one plus three equals four.

unanimité [ynanimite] *nom féminin*

à l'unanimité unanimously : **les délégués de classe ont été élus à l'unanimité** the class representatives were elected unanimously.

uni, e [yni] *adjectif*

1. plain : **du tissu uni** plain material ; **elle porte une robe unie** she's wearing a plain dress
2. close : **c'est une famille très unie** they're a very close family.

uniforme [ynifɔrm] *nom masculin*

uniform : **le pilote porte un uniforme** ou **le pilote est en uniforme** the pilot is wearing a uniform
➤ **un policier en uniforme** a uniformed policeman.

union [ynjɔ̃] *nom féminin*

union : **l'union monétaire** monetary union
➤ **l'Union européenne** the European Union.

unique [ynik] *adjectif*

1. only : **Patrice a mangé l'unique bonbon qui restait** Patrice ate the only sweet that was left ; **elle est fille unique** she's an only child
2. single : **la monnaie unique** the single currency.

uniquement [ynikmã] *adverbe*

only : **je viens uniquement pour te faire plaisir** I'm only coming to please you.

unir [ynir] *verbe*

to unite : **ils veulent unir les deux partis** they want to unite the two parties

s'unir *verbe pronominal*

to unite : **s'unir pour faire quelque chose** to unite to do something ; **jeunes de tous les pays, unissez-vous !** young people of all countries, unite!

unité [ynite] *nom féminin*

unit : **les unités de mesure** units of measurement
➤ **l'unité centrale** the central processing unit
➤ **vendu à l'unité** sold singly.

univers [ynivɛr] *nom masculin*

1. universe : **l'astronomie étudie l'univers** astronomy is the study of the universe
2. world : **l'univers de la mode** the world of fashion.

université [ynivɛrsite] *nom féminin*

university *(pluriel* **universities)** : **Cécile voudrait aller à l'université** Cécile would like to go to university *UK* ou Cécile would like to go to college *US*.

urbain, e [yrbɛ̃, ɛn] *adjectif*

urban : **les transports urbains** the urban transport system.

urgence [yrʒãs] *nom féminin*

emergency *(pluriel* **emergencies)** : **en cas**

d'urgence in case of emergency ou in the event of an emergency
➤ **les urgences** casualty *UK* ou the casualty department *UK* ou the emergency room *US* : **on a dû emmener Cyril aux urgences** we had to take Cyril to casualty ou we had to take Cyril to the casualty department
➤ **d'urgence**
1. emergency : **ils ont pris des mesures d'urgence** they took emergency measures
2. immediately : **vous devez venir d'urgence** you must come immediately.

urgent, e [yrʒã, ãt] *adjectif*

urgent : **prends ton temps, ce n'est pas urgent** take your time, it's not urgent.

USA *(abréviation de* United States of America) *nom masculin pluriel*

les USA the USA ; **les Européens qui vivent aux USA** Europeans who live in the USA ; **ils rêvent d'émigrer aux USA** they dream of emigrating to the USA.

usé, e [yze] *adjectif*

worn out : **ce manteau est très usé** this coat is very worn out.

user [yze] *verbe*

to wear out : **tu vas user ton jean très vite si tu continues à faire ça** you'll wear your jeans out very quickly if you go on doing that

s'user *verbe pronominal*

to wear out : **ces chaussures se sont usées très vite** these shoes have worn out very quickly
➤ **s'user les yeux** to strain one's eyes.

usine [yzin] *nom féminin*

factory *(pluriel* **factories)** : **une usine de chaussures** a shoe factory ; **le père de Laure travaille à l'usine** Laure's father works in a factory.

ustensile [ystãsil] *nom masculin*

implement : **un ustensile très pratique pour laver les vitres** a very practical implement for cleaning the windows
➤ **les ustensiles de cuisine** kitchen utensils.

utile [ytil] *adjectif*

useful : **un outil très utile** a very useful tool ; **essaie de te rendre utile** try to make yourself

u

useful ; **ces conseils nous ont été très utiles** this advice was very useful to us

➤ **il n'est pas utile d'en parler à Camille** there's no need to tell Camille about it.

utiliser [ytilize] *verbe*

to use : j'utilise beaucoup le dictionnaire I use the dictionary a lot.

vacances [vakɑ̃s] *nom féminin pluriel*

holiday *UK*, **vacation** *US* (*s'utilisent toujours au singulier*) **: les vacances sont presque finies** the holiday is almost over ; **les grandes vacances** the summer holidays

➤ **bonnes vacances !** have a good holiday!

➤ **être en vacances** to be on holiday

➤ **partir en vacances** to go on holiday

> 📖 VACANCES SCOLAIRES
> The main school holiday is of course in the summer. During these two months business and politics slow down too. Other school holidays include one week at the beginning of November, two weeks at Christmas, two weeks in February or March, and two weeks in April or May.

vaccin [vaksɛ̃] *nom masculin*

vaccine : le vaccin contre la grippe the flu vaccine.

vacciner [vaksine] *verbe*

to vaccinate : se faire vacciner to get vaccinated.

vache [vaʃ] *nom & adjectif*

■ *nom féminin*
cow : un troupeau de vaches a herd of cows
■ *adjectif*
familier **mean : la prof a été vraiment vache avec toi** the teacher was really mean to you.

vachement [vaʃmɑ̃] *adverbe familier*

1. **dead** *UK*, **real** *US* **: il est vachement mignon** he's dead cute

2. **really : j'ai vachement travaillé pour cette interro** I worked really hard for this test.

vague [vag] *adjectif & nom*

■ *adjectif*
vague : ce n'est qu'un projet très vague it's only a very vague plan
■ *nom féminin*
wave : j'adore plonger dans les vagues I love diving into the waves
➤ **une vague de chaleur** a heatwave
➤ **une vague de froid** a cold spell.

vaguement [vagmɑ̃] *adverbe*

vaguely : tu t'en souviens ? – vaguement do you remember? – vaguely.

vaincre [vɛ̃kr] *verbe*

1. **to defeat : les Gaulois ont été vaincus par César** the Gauls were defeated by Cesar

2. **to overcome : l'actrice a réussi à vaincre son trac** the actress succeeded in overcoming her stage fright.

vaincu, e [vɛ̃ky] *participe passé de* vaincre.

vainqueur [vɛ̃kœr] *nom masculin*

winner : le vainqueur du 100 m the winner of the 100 m.

vais ➤ aller.

vaisseau [vɛso] (*pluriel* vaisseaux) *nom masculin*

vessel : les vaisseaux sanguins blood vessels
➤ **un vaisseau spatial** a spaceship.

vaisselle [vɛsɛl] *nom féminin*

crockery : ma mère a sorti la vaisselle du dimanche my mother took out the best crockery
➤ **faire la vaisselle** to do the dishes OU to do the washing-up *UK*
➤ **du liquide vaisselle** washing-up liquid *UK* OU dishwashing liquid *US*.

valable [valabl] *adjectif*

valid : ton passeport n'est plus valable your passport isn't valid anymore.

valet [valɛ] *nom masculin*

1. servant : **le valet du comte** the count's servant
2. jack, knave : **le valet de cœur** the jack of hearts OU the knave of hearts.

valeur [valœr] *nom féminin*

value : **personne ne connaît la valeur de ce tableau** nobody knows the value of this painting ; **les actions ont pris de la valeur** the shares have gone up in value
> **avoir de la valeur** to be valuable : **ce bijou a beaucoup de valeur** this jewel is very valuable
> **vos objets de valeur** your valuables
> **mettre en valeur** to highlight : **tu devrais mettre tes qualités en valeur** you should highlight your qualities.

valise [valiz] *nom féminin*

suitcase : **tu peux m'aider à porter mes valises ?** can you help me to carry my suitcases?
> **faire ses valises** to pack one's bags.

vallée [vale] *nom féminin*

valley : **la vallée de la Loire** the Loire valley.

valoir [valwar] *verbe*

1. to be worth : **cette voiture doit valoir une fortune** that car must be worth a fortune ; **cette bague ne vaut rien** this ring is worthless OU this ring isn't worth anything
2. to cost : **ça vaut combien ?** how much does it cost? ; **ça vaut cent euros** it costs a hundred euros
> **ça vaut cher** it's expensive
> **valoir la peine** to be worth it : **ça ne vaut pas la peine** it's not worth it
> **ça vaut mieux comme ça** it's best this way
> **il vaut mieux que je parte** I'd better leave
> **il vaudrait mieux que tu lui en parle** it woul be better if you told him.

valu [valy] *participe passé invariable de* valoir.

vampire [vɑ̃pir] *nom masculin*

vampire : **un film de vampires** a vampire film.

vanille [vanij] *nom féminin*

vanilla : **de la glace à la vanille** vanilla ice cream.

se vanter [səvɑ̃te] *verbe pronominal*

to boast, to brag : **arrête de te vanter** stop boasting OU stop bragging ; **Andrew se vante d'être sorti avec Céline** Andrew boasts about going out with Céline OU Andrew brags about going out with Céline.

vapeur [vapœr] *nom féminin*

steam : **on ne voit rien avec toute cette vapeur** you can't see anything with all this steam
> **à la vapeur** steamed : **des pommes de terre à la vapeur** steamed potatoes
> **à vapeur** steam : **une locomotive à vapeur** a steam engine
> **un bateau à vapeur** a steamboat OU a steamer.

varappe [varap] *nom féminin*

rock climbing : **on va faire de la varappe cet été** we're going to go rock climbing this summer.

varicelle [varisɛl] *nom féminin*

chickenpox : **Thomas est absent parce qu'il a la varicelle** Thomas is absent because he's got chickenpox.

varié, e [varje] *adjectif*

varied : **les menus de la cantine sont variés** the menus at the canteen are varied.

varier [varje] *verbe*

to vary : **les températures varient en cette saison** temperatures vary at this time of year.

variété [varjete] *nom féminin*

1. variety *(pluriel* **varieties***)* : **le menu manque de variété** the menu lacks variety ; **plusieurs variétés de chocolat** several varieties of chocolate
2. easy-listening music : **la variété française** French easy-listening music
> **une émission de variétés** OU **des variétés** a variety show.

vas ➤ aller.

vase [vaz] *nom masculin*

vase : **un vase en porcelaine** a china vase.

vaudrait ➤ valoir.

vaut ➤ valoir.

vautour [votur] *nom masculin*

vulture.

V

veau [vo] (*pluriel* **veaux**) *nom masculin*

1. calf (*pluriel* **calves**) : **la vache et son veau** the cow and her calf

2. veal : **une escalope de veau** a veal escalope.

vécu, e [veky] *verbe & adjectif*

■ *participe passé de* **vivre**
il a vécu au dix-huitième siècle he lived in the eighteenth century

■ *adjectif*
true : **c'est une histoire vécue** it's a true story.

végétal, e [veʒetal] (*pluriel* **végétaux** [veʒeto]) *adjectif & nom*

■ *adjectif*

1. vegetable : **de l'huile végétale** vegetable oil

2. plant : **des fibres végétales** plant fibres

■ *nom masculin*
plant : **un végétal exotique** an exotic plant.

végétarien, enne [veʒetarjɛ̃, ɛn] *adjectif & nom masculin, nom féminin*

vegetarian : **le menu végétarien** the vegetarian menu ; **Caro est végétarienne** Caro is a vegetarian.

véhicule [veikyl] *nom masculin*

vehicle.

veille [vɛj] *nom féminin*

day before : **ça s'est passé la veille de mon anniversaire** it happened the day before my birthday ; **la veille au soir** the previous evening ou the evening before
➤ **la veille de Noël** Christmas Eve.

veiller [veje] *verbe*

to stay up : **on a veillé jusqu'à trois heures du matin** we stayed up until three in the morning
➤ **veiller à** to make sure ; **veillez à ne pas être en retard** make sure you're not late : **je veillerai à ce que Dan t'appelle** I'll make sure Dan calls you.

veinard, e [vɛnar, ard] *nom masculin, nom féminin familier*

lucky devil : **quelle veinarde !** you lucky devil!

veine [vɛn] *nom féminin*

1. vein : **les veines de mes jambes sont gonflées** the veins in my legs are swollen

2. *familier* luck : **ce n'est pas du talent, c'est**
de la veine it's not talent, it's luck ; **avoir de la veine** to be lucky ; **mon pauvre, tu n'as pas eu de veine !** poor thing, you've been unlucky!

vélo [velo] *nom masculin*

bike : **Lionel ne sait pas encore faire du vélo** Lionel can't ride a bike yet ; **tu veux qu'on fasse du vélo ?** do you want to go for a bike ride? ou do you want to go cycling? ; **je vais à l'école à vélo** I cycle to school
➤ **un vélo d'appartement** an exercise bike
➤ **un vélo de course** a racing bike
➤ **un vélo tout-terrain** a mountain bike.

velours [vəlur] *nom masculin*

velvet : **des coussins en velours** velvet cushions
➤ **du velours côtelé** corduroy : **un jean en velours côtelé** corduroy jeans.

vendeur, euse [vɑ̃dœr, øz] *nom masculin, nom féminin*

sales assistant *UK*, sales clerk *US* : **les vendeuses ne sont pas très aimables dans ce magasin** the sales assistants aren't very nice in this shop
➤ **un vendeur de journaux** a newsvendor *UK* ou a newsdealer *US*.

vendre [vɑ̃dr] *verbe*

to sell : **ils veulent vendre leur voiture** they want to sell their car : **cette maison est à vendre** this house is for sale.

vendredi [vɑ̃drədi] *nom masculin*

Friday

En anglais les jours de la semaine s'écrivent avec une majuscule :

mes copains sont venus vendredi my friends came on Friday ; **Thomas joue au foot le vendredi** Thomas plays football on Fridays ; **je t'appelle vendredi matin** I'll call you on Friday morning ; **vendredi dernier** last Friday ; **vendredi prochain** next Friday.

vendu, e [vɑ̃dy] *participe passé de* **vendre**.

vénéneux, euse [venenø, øz] *adjectif*

poisonous : **un champignon vénéneux** a poisonous mushroom.

se venger [səvɑ̃ʒe] *verbe pronominal*

to get one's revenge : **je me vengerai !** I'll get my revenge!

se venger de quelqu'un to take ones' revenge on somebody : **Anaïs s'est vengée de Martin en lui volant sa casquette** Anaïs took her revenge on Martin by stealing his cap

venimeux, euse [vənimø, øz] *adjectif*

poisonous : **un serpent venimeux** a poisonous snake.

venir [vənir] *verbe*

to come : **tu viens avec moi à la piscine ?** are you coming to the swimming pool with me? ; **venez me chercher à quatre heures** come and get me at four o'clock ; **Cédric est venu me voir** Cédric came to see me : **Paul vient du Mali** Paul comes from Mali

➤ **je viens de la voir** I've just seen her
➤ **il vient d'arriver** he has just arrived
➤ **faire venir quelqu'un** to call somebody : **vous avez fait venir le docteur ?** did you call the doctor?
➤ **où veux-tu en venir ?** what are you getting at?

vent [vã] *nom masculin*

wind : **le vent vient du nord** the wind is coming from the north
➤ **il y a du vent** it's windy.

vente [vãt] *nom féminin*

sale : **ils ont organisé la vente de la maison** they have organized the sale of the house ; **en vente** on sale
➤ **une vente de charité** a charity bazaar
➤ **la vente par correspondance** mail order
➤ **une vente aux enchères** an auction.

ventilateur [vãtilatœr] *nom masculin*

fan : **mets le ventilateur, il fait trop chaud** put the fan on, it's too hot.

ventre [vãtr] *nom masculin*

stomach : **j'ai mal au ventre** I have got stomach ache *UK* ou I have a stomach ache *US*
➤ **avoir du ventre** to have a paunch ou to have a big stomach
➤ **à plat ventre** flat on one's stomach : **mettez-vous à plat ventre** lie flat on your stomach.

venu, e [vəny] *participe passé de* venir.

ver [vɛr] *nom masculin*

1. worm : **les oiseaux mangent des vers** birds eat worms

2. maggot : **il y a un ver dans cette pomme** there's a maggot in this apple
➤ **un ver luisant** a glowworm
➤ **un ver à soie** a silkworm
➤ **un ver de terre** an earthworm.

verbe [vɛrb] *nom masculin*

verb : **les verbes irréguliers** irregular verbs.

verglas [vɛrgla] *nom masculin*

black ice, glaze *US* : **des plaques de verglas** patches of black ice.

vérifier [verifje] *verbe*

to check : **vérifie que la porte est fermée** check that the door is locked.

véritable [veritabl] *adjectif*

real : **du cuir véritable** real leather ou genuine leather.

vérité [verite] *nom féminin*

truth : **je crois qu'il dit la vérité** I think he's telling the truth ; **c'est la vérité, je te le jure !** it's true, I swear!
➤ **dire ses quatre vérités à quelqu'un** *familier* to tell somebody a few home truths.

verlan [vɛrlã] *nom masculin*

back slang

VERLAN
This is a form of slang, which is popular among young people. To make a word into its verlan form, you invert the syllables. The term verlan is formed itself from **'l'envers'**, meaning the other way around. Well-known examples of verlan are **laisse béton!** (laisse tomber! – forget it!), **meuf** (femme-woman) and **zarbi** (bizarre-strange).

verni, e [vɛrni] *adjectif*

1. varnished : **une commode vernie** a varnished chest of drawers
2. patent leather : **des chaussures vernies** patent leather shoes.

vernis [vɛrni] *nom masculin*

varnish : **le vernis de la table est abîmé** the varnish on the table is damaged
➤ **du vernis à ongles** nail polish ou nail varnish : **tu te mets souvent du vernis à ongles ?** do you often wear nail polish?

V

verre [vɛr] *nom masculin*

1. glass *(pluriel* **glasses***)* : **des verres à vin** wine glasses ; **un verre de lait** a glass of milk
2. drink : **boire un verre** OU **prendre un verre** to have a drink

verrou [vɛru] *nom masculin*

bolt : **mettre le verrou** to bolt the door
➤ **être sous les verrous** to be behind bars : **mettre quelqu'un sous les verrous** to put somebody behind bars.

verrue [vɛry] *nom féminin*

wart : **Hugo a une verrue sur la main** Hugo has a wart on his hand
➤ **des verrues plantaires** verrucas.

vers ¹ [vɛr] *nom*

▪ *nom masculin*
line : **je n'arrive pas à me rappeler le troi-sième vers du poème** I can't remember the third line of the poem

▪ *nom masculin pluriel*
verse : **un poème en vers** a poem in verse ; **des vers libres** free verse.

vers ² [vɛr] *préposition*

1. towards, toward *US* : **Peter s'est tourné vers moi** Peter turned towards me
2. around : **on arrive à Paris vers le 30 juillet** we arrive in Paris around 30 July.

Versailles [vɛrsaj] *nom*

Versailles

> ✎ VERSAILLES
> Louis XIV had this magnificent palace built in the middle of the 17th century. The palace, whose façade measures 670 metres in length, contains 500 rooms and has a total of 2143 windows. It is famous for the **Galerie des Glaces** or 'Hall of Mirrors'. Today the palace and its gardens are open to the public and every weekend from March to September the fountains, or **Grandes Eaux de Versailles**, are switched on.

à verse [avɛrs] *adverbe*

il pleut à verse it's pouring down OU it's pouring with rain.

Verseau [vɛrso] *nom masculin*

Aquarius : **je suis Verseau** I'm an Aquarius.

verser [vɛrse] *verbe*

1. to pour : **fais attention en versant l'eau** be careful when you pour the water ; **verse-moi à boire, s'il te plaît** pour me a drink, please ; **il a versé le vin dans un verre** he poured the wine in a glass
2. to pay : **je vais verser cet argent sur mon compte** I'm going to pay this money into my account.

version [vɛrsjɔ̃] *nom féminin*

1. version : **c'est ta version des événements** that's your version of events
2. translation : **une version anglaise** a translation from English into French : **Bérénice a eu 17 en version anglaise** Bérénice got 17 for her English-French translation
➤ **un film en version originale** a film in the original language.

verso [vɛrso] *nom masculin*

back : **c'est écrit au verso** it's written on the back.

vert, e [vɛr, vɛrt] *adjectif & nom masculin*

green : **des chaussettes vertes** green socks ; **je n'aime pas le vert** I don't like green ; **vert bouteille** bottle green ; **vert émeraude** emerald green ; **vert pomme** apple green
➤ **les Verts** the Greens OU the Green party.

vertical, e, aux [vɛrtikal, o] *adjectif*

vertical.

vertige [vɛrtiʒ] *nom masculin*

1. vertigo : **Suzanne ne peut pas faire d'esca-lade, elle a le vertige** Suzanne can't go climb-ing, she suffers from vertigo
2. dizzy spell : **tu as souvent des vertiges ?** do you often have dizzy spells? ; **je ne peux pas continuer, j'ai le vertige** I can't carry on, I feel dizzy ; **ça me donne le vertige** it makes me dizzy OU it makes me feel dizzy.

veste [vɛst] *nom féminin*

jacket : **il porte une veste à carreaux** he's wearing a checked jacket.

vestiaire [vɛstjɛr] *nom masculin*

1. cloakroom : **on peut laisser nos affaires au vestiaire pendant qu'on visite** we can leave our things in the cloakroom while we're visit-ing
2. changing room *UK*, locker room *US* : **les vestiaires du stade** the changing rooms in the stadium.

vêtements [vɛtmɑ̃] *nom masculin pluriel*

clothes : **emportez des vêtements chauds** take some warm clothes with you
> **des vêtements de sport** sportswear.

vétérinaire [veterinɛr] *nom masculin ou féminin*

vet, veterinarian *US* : **Fabrice veut devenir vétérinaire** Fabrice wants to be a vet.

veuf, veuve [vœf, vœv] *nom masculin, nom féminin*

widower *(feminine* **widow***)* : **elle est veuve** she's a widow.

veuille ➤ vouloir.

veut ➤ vouloir.

veuve ➤ veuf.

veux ➤ vouloir.

vexé, e [vɛkse] *adjectif*

upset : **tu crois que Lisa est vexée ?** do you think Lisa is upset?

vexer [vɛkse] *verbe*

to offend, to upset : **j'espère que je ne t'ai pas vexé** I hope I haven't offended you ou I hope I haven't upset you.

se vexer *verbe pronominal*

to take offence *UK*, to take offense *US* : **ne te vexe pas** don't take offence.

viande [vjɑ̃d] *nom féminin*

meat : **de la viande rouge** red meat.

vicieux, euse [visjø, øz] *adjectif*

perverted

⚠ Vicieux is a false friend, it does not mean 'vicious'.

victime [viktim] *nom féminin*

1. victim : **les victimes du tueur en série** the serial killer's victims
2. casualty *(pluriel* **casualties***)* : **l'accident a fait cinq victimes** there were five casualties in the accident.

victoire [viktwar] *nom féminin*

victory *(pluriel* **victories***)* : **c'est la troisième victoire de l'équipe bordelaise** it's the Bordeaux team's third victory.

vide [vid] *adjectif & nom*

■ *adjectif*
empty : **la bouteille est déjà vide** the bottle is already empty
■ *nom masculin*
vacuum : **conditionné sous vide** vacuum-packed
> **avoir peur du vide** to be afraid of heights.

vidéo [video] *nom féminin & adjectif invariable*

video : **la vidéo du mariage** the wedding video ; **une cassette vidéo** a video cassette.

vide-ordures [vidɔrdyr] *(pluriel* **vide-ordures***) nom masculin*
rubbish chute *UK*, garbage chute *US*.

vider [vide] *verbe*

1. to empty : **tu peux m'aider à vider le placard ?** can you help me to empty the cupboard?
2. *familier* to chuck out : **ils se sont fait vider de la boîte** they were thrown out of the club

se vider *verbe pronominal*

to empty : **le pub se vide vers onze heures** the pub empties around eleven.

vie [vi] *nom féminin*

life *(pluriel* **lives***)* : **tu m'as sauvé la vie !** you saved my life! ; **la vie privée des stars** the stars' private lives
> **c'est la vie !** that's life!
> **à vie** for life : **emprisonné à vie** in prison for life
> **en vie** alive : **est-ce qu'il est encore en vie ?** is he still alive?

vieil ➤ vieux.

vieille ➤ vieux.

vieillesse [vjɛjɛs] *nom féminin*

old age : **elle est morte de vieillesse** she died of old age.

vieillir [vjejir] *verbe*

to grow old : **il y a des gens qui ont peur de vieillir** there are people who are afraid of growing old
> **cette coiffure te vieillit** that haircut makes you look older.

vierge [vjɛrʒ] *nom & adjectif*

■ *nom féminin*
virgin : **la Vierge** the Virgin Mary

V

■ *adjectif*

1. **virgin : elle est vierge** she's a virgin
2. **blank : une cassette vierge** a blank tape

Vierge *nom féminin*

Virgo : **je suis Vierge** I'm a Virgo.

vieux, vieille [vjø, vjɛj] *adjectif & nom*

■ *adjectif* (**vieil** *devant un mot commençant par une voyelle ou un « h »*)
old : **Catherine est plus vieille que toi** Catherine is older than you ; **on se fait vieux** we're getting old ; **un vieil homme** an old man

■ *nom masculin, nom féminin*
familier old man *(feminine* old woman*) (pluriel* old men, old women*) :* **un vieux de quatre-vingts ans** an old man of eighty ; **les vieux** old people

➤ **mon vieux** *familier* mate *UK* ou buddy *US* : **bon courage, mon vieux !** good luck, mate!

➤ **ma vieille** *familier* darling : **vas-y, ma vieille !** come on, darling!

vif, vive [vif, viv] *adjectif*

1. **bright : des couleurs vives** bright colours ; **rouge vif** bright red
2. **sharp ; elle n'est pas très vive** she isn't very sharp : **une vive douleur à la jambe** a sharp pain in the leg

vigne [viɲ] *nom féminin*

vine : **les vignes poussent bien ici** vines grow well here

vilain, e [vilɛ̃, ɛn] *adjectif*

1. **ugly : ce bâtiment est vraiment vilain** this building is really ugly
2. **naughty : ne sois pas vilain, ton papa va revenir bientôt** don't be naughty, your father will be back soon
3. **nasty : c'est une vilaine blessure que tu as là** it's a nasty wound you've got there.

village [vilaʒ] *nom masculin*

village : **je vais au village chercher du pain** I'm going to the village to buy some bread

ville [vil] *nom féminin*

1. **town : une petite ville de cinq mille habitants** a small town with five thousand inhabitants
2. **city** *(pluriel* cities*) :* **les grandes villes** big cities

➤ **en ville**
1. **in town : Mathieu habite en ville** Mathieu lives in town

2. **into town : on va en ville cet après-midi ?** are we going into town this afternoon?

Villette [vilɛt] *nom*

➤ **la Villette** *cultural complex in north Paris (including a science museum, theatre and park).*

PARC DE LA VILLETTE
This is an ultra-modern music, arts and science complex set in a large park in north Paris. It includes the **Cité des sciences et de l'industrie**, a high-tech interactive science museum, and the **Cité de la musique** which contains a concert hall as well as a school and a museum of music. The **Grande Halle** is an enormous exhibition space. Outside the complex, the spherical **Géode** cinema shows 180-degree films.

vin [vɛ̃] *nom masculin*

wine : **du vin blanc** white wine ; **du vin rouge** red wine ; **une bouteille de vin** a bottle of wine.

vinaigre [vinɛgr] *nom masculin*

vinegar : **du vinaigre de vin** wine vinegar.

vinaigrette [vinɛgrɛt] *nom féminin*

vinaigrette, French dressing.

vingt [vɛ̃] *adjectif numéral & nom masculin*

twenty : **Marine a au moins vingt paires de chaussures** Marine has got at least twenty pairs of shoes ; **il a vingt ans** he's twenty ou he's twenty years old

➤ **nous sommes le vingt janvier** it's the twentieth of January *UK* ou it's January twentieth *US*.

vingtaine [vɛ̃tɛn] *nom féminin*

une vingtaine about twenty ; **j'ai invité une vingtaine de copains** I've invited about twenty friends.

vingt et un [vɛ̃teɛ̃] *adjectif numéral & nom masculin*

twenty-one : **il y a vingt et un ans** twenty-one years ago

➤ **nous sommes le vingt et un avril** it's the twenty-first of April *UK* ou it's April the twenty-first *US*.

vingtième [vɛ̃tjɛm] *adjectif numéral & nom*

twentieth : **le vingtième nom sur la liste** the twentieth name on the list ; **Anne est arrivée vingtième** Anne came twentieth.

violence [vjɔlɑ̃s] *nom féminin*

violence.

violent, e [vjɔlɑ̃, ɑ̃t] *adjectif*

1. violent : Nathan a un tempérament violent
Nathan has a violent temperament
2. acute : une violente douleur dans les côtes
an acute pain in the ribs.

violet, ette [vjɔlɛ, ɛt] *adjectif*

purple : des petites fleurs violettes little
purple flowers

violet *nom masculin*

purple : le violet est la couleur préférée de
Samantha purple is Samantha's favourite colour.

violon [vjɔlɔ̃] *nom masculin*

violin : Tarik apprend à jouer du violon
Tarik is learning to play the violin.

violoncelle [vjɔlɔ̃sɛl] *nom masculin*

cello : Clémence joue du violoncelle dans
un orchestre Clémence plays the cello in an
orchestra.

violoniste [vjɔlɔnist] *nom masculin ou féminin*

violinist : elle est violoniste she's a violinist.

vipère [vipɛr] *nom féminin*

viper : Jules s'est fait mordre par une vipère Jules was bitten by a viper.

virage [viraʒ] *nom masculin*

bend : attention, ce virage est dangereux
be careful, this bend is dangerous.

virer [vire] *verbe familier*

to fire : ils ont été virés they got fired
➤ se faire virer du collège to be expelled
from school.

virgule [virgyl] *nom féminin*

1. comma : tu as oublié la virgule you've forgotten the comma
2. point : cinq virgule quatre five point four

> En anglais, les décimales s'écrivent avec un point
> et non avec une virgule : 5,4 s'écrit 5.4 et se lit
> five point four.

virus [virys] *nom masculin*

virus : le virus de la grippe the flu virus ; un
virus informatique a computer virus.

vis [vis] *nom féminin*

screw.

visa [viza] *nom masculin*

visa : on a fait une demande de visa pour la
Russie we applied for a visa for Russia.

visage [vizaʒ] *nom masculin*

face : une crème pour le visage a face
cream.

visé, e [vize] *adjectif*

je me suis senti visé quand il a fait cette remarque I felt I was being got at when he
made that remark.

viser [vize] *verbe*

1. to aim at : il visait la cible he was aiming at
the target ; cette remarque ne visait personne en particulier this remark wasn't aimed at
anybody in particular
2. to aim : j'ai mal visé I didn't aim properly

visière [vizjɛr] *nom féminin*

1. visor : la visière d'un casque the visor of a
helmet
2. peak : la visière d'une casquette the peak
of a baseball cap
3. eyeshade : Dorothée porte une visière
pour jouer au tennis Dorothée wears an eyeshade when she plays tennis.

visite [vizit] *nom féminin*

1. visit : nous avons eu la visite de mes cousins we had a visit from my cousins ; rendre
visite à quelqu'un to pay somebody a visit ou
to visit somebody
2. tour : la visite du château dure environ
une heure the tour of the château takes about
an hour
➤ une visite guidée a guided tour
➤ une visite médicale a medical examination : on doit tous passer une visite médicale à l'école we all must have a medical examination at school
➤ avoir de la visite to have visitors : tu attends de la visite ? are you expecting visitors?

visiter [vizite] *verbe*

to visit : on a visité Bourges dimanche dernier we visited Bourges last Sunday.

visser [vise] *verbe*

to screw on : tu as mal vissé le couvercle
you haven't screwed the lid on properly.

V

vitamine [vitamin] *nom féminin*

vitamin : **il prend de la vitamine C** he takes vitamin C.

vite [vit] *adverbe*

quickly, fast : **ne marche pas si vite** don't walk so quickly ou don't walk so fast ; **vite, le prof arrive !** quick, the teacher's coming!
➤ **fais vite !** hurry up!

vitesse [vitɛs] *nom féminin*

1. speed : **à quelle vitesse vous alliez ?** what speed were you doing? ; **les coureurs prennent de la vitesse** the cyclists are picking up speed

2. gear : **un vélo à dix vitesses** a ten-gear bike ou a bike with ten gears ; **changer de vitesse** to change gear
➤ **à toute vitesse** at top speed
➤ **en vitesse** quickly : **je fais mes devoirs en vitesse et je viens te voir** I'll do my homework quickly and I'll come and see you.

vitre [vitr] *nom féminin*

window : **les enfants ont cassé une vitre** the children broke a window ; **tu peux m'aider à faire les vitres ?** can you help me to clean the windows? ; **baisse la vitre, il fait chaud** wind the window down, it's hot.

vitrine [vitrin] *nom féminin*

shop window, window : **la jupe qui est en vitrine** the skirt that's in the shop window
➤ **faire les vitrines** to go window-shopping.

vivant, e [vivɑ̃, ɑ̃t] *adjectif*

1. alive : **le moineau était encore vivant** the sparrow was still alive

2. lively : **c'est un quartier très vivant** it's a very lively area.

vive [viv] *interjection*

long live : **vive la France !** long live France!

vivement [vivmɑ̃] *interjection*

vivement les vacances ! roll on the holidays! *UK* : **vivement que l'été arrive !** I'll be glad when the summer comes!

vivre [vivr] *verbe*

1. to live : **le frère de Benoît vit au Canada** Benoît's brother lives in Canada ; **de quoi est-ce qu'ils vivent ?** what do they live on?

2. to go through : **Isabelle a vécu des moments difficiles** Isabelle has been through some hard times

vocabulaire [vɔkabylɛr] *nom masculin*

vocabulary : **Audrey lit beaucoup pour enrichir son vocabulaire** Audrey reads a lot to build up her vocabulary.

vœu [vø] (*pluriel* **vœux**) *nom masculin*

wish (*pluriel* **wishes**) : **une étoile filante, fais un vœu !** a shooting star, make a wish!

vœux *nom masculin pluriel*

best wishes : **tous nos vœux de bonheur** our best wishes for your future happiness
➤ **Meilleurs Vœux** Season's Greetings.

voici [vwasi] *préposition*

1. here is, here's : **voici l'argent que je te dois** here's the money I owe you ; **le voici !** here he is!

2. here are : **voici les magazines que tu m'as demandés** here are the magazines you asked me for ; **les voici enfin !** here they are at last!

3. this is : **voici ce qui s'est passé** this is what happened.

voie [vwa] *nom féminin*

1. road : **c'est une voie privée** it's a private road

2. lane : **mets-toi sur la voie de gauche** move into the left-hand lane ; **une route à trois voies** a three-lane road

3. railway track *UK*, railroad track *US* : **ne traverse pas les voies, c'est dangereux** don't cross the railway tracks, it's dangerous

4. platform : **le train part de la voie six** the train leaves from platform six
➤ **la voie ferrée** the railway line *UK* ou the railroad line *US*
➤ **les pays en voie de développement** developing countries
➤ **tu es sur la bonne voie** you're on the right track.

voilà [vwala] *préposition*

1. there is, there's : **voilà la fille dont je te parlais** there's the girl I was telling you about ; **le voilà !** there he is!

2. there are : **voilà tes lunettes de soleil** there are your sunglasses ; **les voilà enfin !** there they are at last!

3. that's : **voilà comment ça s'est passé** that's how it happened.

voile [vwal] *nom féminin*

1. sail : **l'une des voiles est déchirée** one of the sails is torn

2. sailing : **faire de la voile** to go sailing

voile[2] *nom masculin*

veil : **elle porte le voile** she's wearing a veil.

voilier [vwalje] *nom masculin*

sailing boat *UK*, sailboat *US*.

voir [vwar] *verbe*

to see : **Adrien voit souvent ses copains de Clamart** Adrien often sees his friends from Clamart ; **tu vois la maison là-bas ?** can you see the house over there? ; **on ne voit rien ici** you can't see anything in here ; **je l'ai vu tomber** I saw him fall

➤ **faire voir quelque chose à quelqu'un** to show somebody something : **fais-moi voir ton bouquin** show me your book

➤ **ça n'a rien à voir** that has nothing to do with it

➤ **voyons ...** let's see ...

➤ **faites attention, voyons !** be careful, will you!

se voir *verbe pronominal*

1. to see oneself : **je me suis vu dans la vitrine** I saw myself in the shop window

2. to see each other : **vous vous voyez souvent ?** do you see each other often?

3. to show : **la tache ne se voit presque pas** the stain hardly shows.

voisin, e [vwazɛ̃, in] *nom & adjectif*

▪ *nom masculin, nom féminin*
neighbour *UK*, neighbor *US* : **nos voisins sont sympa** our neighbours are nice

▪ *adjectif*
neighbouring *UK*, neighboring *US* : **les pays voisins** the neighbouring countries

➤ **le voisin de palier** the next-door neighbour *UK* ou the next-door neighbor *US*.

voiture [vwatyr] *nom féminin*

1. car : **mes parents ont deux voitures** my parents have two cars

2. carriage *UK*, car *US* : **nos places sont dans la voiture de queue** our seats are in the rear carriage

➤ **une voiture de location** a hire car *UK* ou a rental car *US*

➤ **une voiture de sport** a sports car.

voix [vwa] *nom féminin*

1. voice : **David a la voix grave** David has a deep voice

2. vote : **Natacha a obtenu vingt voix** Natacha got twenty votes

➤ **à voix basse** in a low voice

➤ **à voix haute**

1. aloud : **le professeur m'a fait lire à voix haute** the teacher made me read aloud

2. in a loud voice : **parler à voix haute** to speak in a loud voice.

vol [vɔl] *nom masculin*

1. flight : **le vol BM356 pour Paris** flight BM356 to Paris.

2. theft, robbery *(pluriel* **robberies***)* : **il y a beaucoup de vols dans ce quartier** there are a lot of robberies in this area ou there are a lot of burglaries in this area ; **les vols de voitures** car thefts

➤ **vol à main armée** armed robbery

➤ **à vol d'oiseau** as the crow flies.

volant [vɔlɑ̃] *nom masculin*

steering wheel : **ne lâche pas le volant !** don't let go of the steering wheel!

volcan [vɔlkɑ̃] *nom masculin*

volcano *(pluriel* **volcanoes** ou **volcanos***)* : **un volcan en activité** a live volcano.

voler [vɔle] *verbe*

1. to fly : **les autruches ne volent pas** ostriches don't fly

2. to steal : **quelqu'un m'a volé mon porte-clés** somebody stole my key ring

3. to rob : **ils se sont encore fait voler** they've been robbed again.

volet [vɔlɛ] *nom masculin*

shutter : **tu as fermé les volets ?** have you closed the shutters?

voleur, euse [vɔlœr, øz] *nom masculin, nom féminin*

thief *(pluriel* **thieves***)* : **la police a arrêté les voleurs** the police arrested the thieves

➤ **au voleur !** stop, thief!

volley-ball [vɔlɛbol] *(pluriel* volley-balls*)* *nom masculin*

volleyball : **Quentin joue au volley-ball le samedi** Quentin plays volleyball on Saturdays.

volontaire [vɔlɔ̃tɛr] *adjectif & nom*

▪ *adjectif*
intentional, deliberate : **je suis désolé, ce n'était pas volontaire** I'm sorry, it wasn't intentional

V

■ *nom masculin ou féminin*

volunteer : j'ai besoin de trois volontaires I need three volunteers

➤ **se porter volontaire pour faire quelque chose** to volunteer to do something.

volonté [vɔlɔ̃te] *nom féminin*

willpower : tu n'as aucune volonté ! you have no willpower!

➤ **la bonne volonté** good will : **être plein de bonne volonté** to be full of good will.

volontiers [vɔlɔ̃tje] *adverbe*

gladly : je le ferai volontiers I'll gladly do it ou I'll be happy to do it.

volume [vɔlym] *nom masculin*

volume : le premier volume de l'encyclopédie the first volume of the encyclopedia ; **on peut régler le volume avec ce bouton** you can adjust the volume with this button.

vomir [vɔmir] *verbe*

to be sick *UK*, **to vomit : Sandrine a vomi sur le bateau** Sandrine was sick on the boat ; **j'ai envie de vomir** I feel sick.

vont ➤ aller.

vos ➤ votre.

vote [vɔt] *nom masculin*

vote : je propose d'organiser un vote I propose a vote.

voter [vɔte] *verbe*

to vote : on ne peut pas voter avant dix-huit ans you can't vote until you're eighteen ; **pour qui as-tu voté ?** who did you vote for?

votre [vɔtr] (*pluriel* **vos** [vo]) *adjectif*

your : elle est dans votre classe she's in your class ; **quels sont vos groupes préférés ?** which are your favourite bands?

le vôtre, la vôtre [ləvotr, lavotr] (*pluriel* **les vôtres** [levotr]) *pronom*

yours : mon ordinateur ne marche plus, est-ce que je peux utiliser le vôtre ? my computer's not working anymore, can I use yours? ; **notre voiture est là, où est la vôtre ?** our car is there, where is yours? ; **tous mes amis sont invités, et les vôtres aussi** all my friends are invited and so are yours

➤ **à la vôtre !** cheers!

vouloir [vulwar] *verbe*

1. **to want : je veux partir** I want to leave ; **tu**
veux du chocolat ? do you want some chocolate? ; **elle ne veut plus de ces vieilles affaires** she doesn't want those old things anymore ; **je veux que tu m'aides** I want you to help me ; **il voudrait que ses parents soient plus patients** he would like his parents to be more patient

2. *Au conditionnel et dans les demandes polies* **would like : Sandra voudrait un nouveau manteau** Sandra would like a new coat : **voulez-vous boire quelque chose ?** would you like something to drink?

➤ **comme tu veux** ou **comme vous voulez** as you like : **fais comme tu veux** do as you like

➤ **si tu veux** ou **si vous voulez** if you like ou if you want

➤ **sans le vouloir** without meaning to : **j'ai vexé Thomas sans le vouloir** I offended Thomas without meaning to

➤ **oui, je veux bien** yes, please : **un peu plus de gâteau ? – oui, je veux bien** a bit more cake? – yes, please

➤ **bien vouloir faire quelque chose** to be prepared to do something ou to be quite happy to do something : **tu veux bien lui parler ?** are you prepared to talk to him? ; **je veux bien t'aider** I'll be quite happy to help you

➤ **veuillez vous asseoir** please sit down

➤ **vouloir dire** to mean : **que veut dire « storm » ?** what does 'storm' mean? ; **qu'est-ce que tu veux dire ?** what do you mean?

➤ **en vouloir à quelqu'un** to have a grudge against somebody : **j'ai l'impression qu'elle m'en veut** I get the feeling she has a grudge against me

➤ **s'en vouloir** to be cross with oneself : **je m'en veux d'avoir cédé** I'm cross with myself for giving in.

voulu, e [vuly] *adjectif*

intentional : je ne crois pas que ce soit voulu I don't think it is intentional.

vous [vu] *pronom personnel*

1. **you : vous êtes arrivés à quelle heure ?** at what time did you arrive? ; **Mme Dupont, vous avez oublié vos lunettes** Mrs Dupont, you forgot your glasses ; **je vous cherchais** I was looking for you ; **je vous l'ai envoyé hier** I sent it to you yesterday ; **c'est pour vous** it's for you ; **c'est vous qui avez tout payé** you paid it all : **et vous, qu'est-ce que vous faites ?** what about you, what are you doing? ; **vous, on vous appellera plus tard** as for you, we'll call you later ; **vous voilà enfin !** here you are at last!

➤ **à vous** yours : **est-ce que ces lunettes sont à vous ?** are these glasses yours?

> « Vous » et « tu » se traduisent par le même pronom en anglais : **you**.

2. **yourself** : **vous ne pensez qu'à vous** you only think about yourself

3. **yourselves** : **vous ne pensez qu'à vous** you only think about yourselves

> Lorsque « vous » a une valeur réfléchie, il se traduit par **yourself**, si « vous » représente une personne, ou par **yourselves**, si « vous » représente plusieurs personnes, ou bien il ne se traduit pas :

4. *Dans les verbes pronominaux*

> Pour les verbes qui ne sont que pronominaux, c'est-à-dire qui ne s'utilisent qu'avec un pronom, « vous » ne se traduit pas en anglais :

vous vous souvenez ? do you remember? ; **vous vous êtes fait mal ?** did you hurt yourself? ou did you hurt yourselves? ; **vous vous êtes habillés ?** did you get dressed? ; **vous vous êtes lavé les mains ?** did you wash your hands?

> Notez qu'avec les parties du corps, on utilise l'adjectif possessif en anglais.

> Lorsque « vous » a une valeur réciproque, il se traduit par **each other** ou bien il ne se traduit pas :

est-ce que vous vous voyez souvent ? do you see each other often? ; **vous vous battez ?** are you fighting?

5. *Dans les verbes pronominaux, à l'impératif* **dépêchez-vous** hurry up ; **détendez-vous** relax

➤ **vous-même** yourself : **vous l'avez fait vous-même ?** did you do it yourself?

➤ **vous-mêmes** yourselves : **vous l'avez fait vous-mêmes ?** did you do it yourselves?

> VOUS
> In French, there are two forms of the word 'you'. Vous is the more formal or polite form. It is used when people have just met or when they don't know each other very well. It is also used between work colleagues, especially when they are of different levels.

➤ tu.

vouvoyer [vuvwaje] *verbe*

to call "vous" : **le prof d'histoire nous vouvoie** the history teacher calls us "vous"

se vouvoyer *verbe pronominal*

to call each other 'vous' : **mes parents se vouvoient** my parents call each other 'vous'.

voyage [vwajaʒ] *nom masculin*

journey, trip : **le voyage a été long** it was a long journey ; **comment s'est passé votre voyage en Australie ?** how did your trip to Australia go?

➤ **un voyage d'affaires** a business trip
➤ **le voyage de noces** the honeymoon
➤ **un voyage organisé** a package tour
➤ **bon voyage !** have a good journey! ou have a good trip!
➤ **partir en voyage** to go on a trip.

voyager [vwajaʒe] *verbe*

to travel : **j'adore voyager** I love travelling ; **voyager en première classe** to travel first class.

voyageur, euse [vwajaʒœr, øz] *nom masculin, nom féminin*

traveller *UK*, traveler *US*.

voyant, e [vwajɑ̃, ɑ̃t] *adjectif & nom*

■ *adjectif*
loud : **des couleurs voyantes** loud colours

■ *nom masculin, nom féminin*
clairvoyant : **Mélanie est allée consulter une voyante** Mélanie went to see a clairvoyant

voyant *nom masculin*

warning light : **le voyant d'essence est allumé** the petrol warning light is on.

voyelle [vwajɛl] *nom féminin*

vowel : **il y a six voyelles en français** there are six vowels in French.

voyou [vwaju] *nom masculin*

yob *UK*, lout : **les voyous qui traînent dans le centre commercial** the yobs who hang around in the shopping centre.

vrai, e [vrɛ] *adjectif*

1. true : **une histoire vraie** a true story ; **ce n'est pas vrai !** it's not true!

2. real : **ce n'est pas son vrai nom** it's not his real name.

vraiment [vrɛmɑ̃] *adverbe*

really : **merci, c'est vraiment sympa** thanks, that's really nice of you ; **ce n'est pas vraiment mon genre** he's not really my type ;

ce n'est vraiment pas rigolo ! it really isn't
funny!

VTT (abréviation de vélo tout-terrain) nom masculin
mountain bike : je fais du VTT avec mes
copains I go mountain-bike riding with my
friends.

vu, e [vy] verbe & adjectif
■ participe passé de voir.
■ adjectif
c'est bien vu d'apporter un petit cadeau
it's good form to take a little present ; c'est
mal vu de fumer smoking is disapproved of.

vu [vy] préposition
given : vu tes notes habituelles ... given
your usual marks ...
➤ vu que seeing that : tu pourrais nous aider,
vu que tu n'as rien à faire you could help us,
seeing that you haven't got anything to do.

vue [vy] nom féminin
1. sight, eyesight : Paul a des problèmes de
vue Paul has problems with his eyesight
2. view : la vue est magnifique d'ici the view
is beautiful from here
➤ à première vue at first sight
➤ à vue de nez familier at a rough guess
➤ avoir quelque chose en vue to have
something in mind : on a un appartement en
vue we have an apartment in mind
➤ connaître quelqu'un de vue to know
somebody by sight.

vulgaire [vylgɛr] adjectif
vulgar : ne sois pas si vulgaire ! don't be so
vulgar!

➤ un wagon de marchandises a goods
wagon UK ou a goods truck UK ou a freight
car US.

wagon-lit [vagɔli] (pluriel wagons-lits)
nom masculin
sleeping car, sleeper.

wagon-restaurant [vagɔrɛstɔrɑ̃] (pluriel
wagons-restaurants) nom masculin
restaurant car UK, dining car US.

Walkman® [wɔkman] nom masculin
personal stereo, Walkman®.

W.-C. [vese] (abréviation de water closet) nom
masculin pluriel
WC UK (ne s'utilise jamais au pluriel), toilets : où
sont les W.-C. ? where is the WC? ou where
are the toilets? ou where is the bathroom
US?.

Web [wɛb] nom masculin
le Web the Web.

week-end [wikɛnd] (pluriel week-ends)
nom masculin
weekend : bon week-end ! have a nice
weekend! ; on part en week-end we're
going away for the weekend.

wagon [vagɔ̃] nom masculin
carriage UK, car US : un wagon fumeurs a
smoking carriage

xylophone [gsilɔfɔn] nom masculin
xylophone : Danny joue du xylophone
Danny plays the xylophone.

y [i] *pronom*

1. *Représente un lieu* **there : j'y vais demain** I'm going there tomorrow ; **on y est restés longtemps** we stayed there for a long time
2. *Représente une chose* **it : penses-y** think about it ; **mets-y du sel** put some salt in it ; **n'y comptez pas** don't count on it.

yaourt [jaurt], **yogourt, yoghourt** [jɔgurt] *nom masculin*
yoghurt, yogurt : **un yaourt aux fruits** a fruit yoghurt ; **des yaourts nature** plain yoghurts.

yeux ➤ œil.

yoga [jɔga] *nom masculin*
yoga : **ma mère fait du yoga** my mother does yoga.

yoghourt, yogourt ➤ yaourt.

zapper [zape] *verbe*
to channel-hop.

zèbre [zɛbr] *nom masculin*
zebra.

zéro [zero] *nom & adjectif*

■ *nom masculin*
1. zero, nought *UK* : **un nombre à trois zéros** a number with three zeroes OU a number with three noughts ; **Aurélie a eu zéro en anglais** Aurélie got a zero in English ; **il fait au-dessous de zéro** it's below zero
2. O *UK* [ou], zero *US* : **mon numéro de téléphone est le 06 41 15 12 34** my phone numer is O six, four one, one five, one two, three four
3. *Au football* nil *UK* : **deux buts à zéro** two nil
4. *Au tennis* love : **trente à zéro pour Agassi** thirty love for Agassi
➤ **repartir de zéro** to start again from scratch
■ *adjectif*
zéro fautes no mistakes : **zéro degré** zero degrees.

zigzag [zigzag] *nom masculin*
zigzag
➤ **marcher en zigzag** to zigzag along
➤ **une route en zigzag** a winding road.

zodiaque [zɔdjak] *nom masculin*
zodiac : **les douze signes du zodiaque** the twelve signs of the zodiac.

zone [zon] *nom féminin*
zone, area : **la zone euro** the euro zone
➤ **zone bleue** restricted parking area
➤ **une zone commerciale** a retail park
➤ **une zone industrielle** an industrial estate *UK* OU an industrial park *US*
➤ **une zone piétonne** OU **une zone piétonnière** a pedestrian precinct *UK* OU a pedestrian zone *US*.

zoo [zo(o)] *nom masculin*
zoo : **j'emmène mon petit frère au zoo mercredi** I'm taking my little brother to the zoo on Wednesday.

zut [zyt] *exclamation familier*
damn.

z

Planches thématiques en couleurs

Themed colour plates

Sommaire

 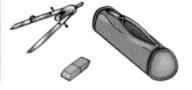

Index

La maison

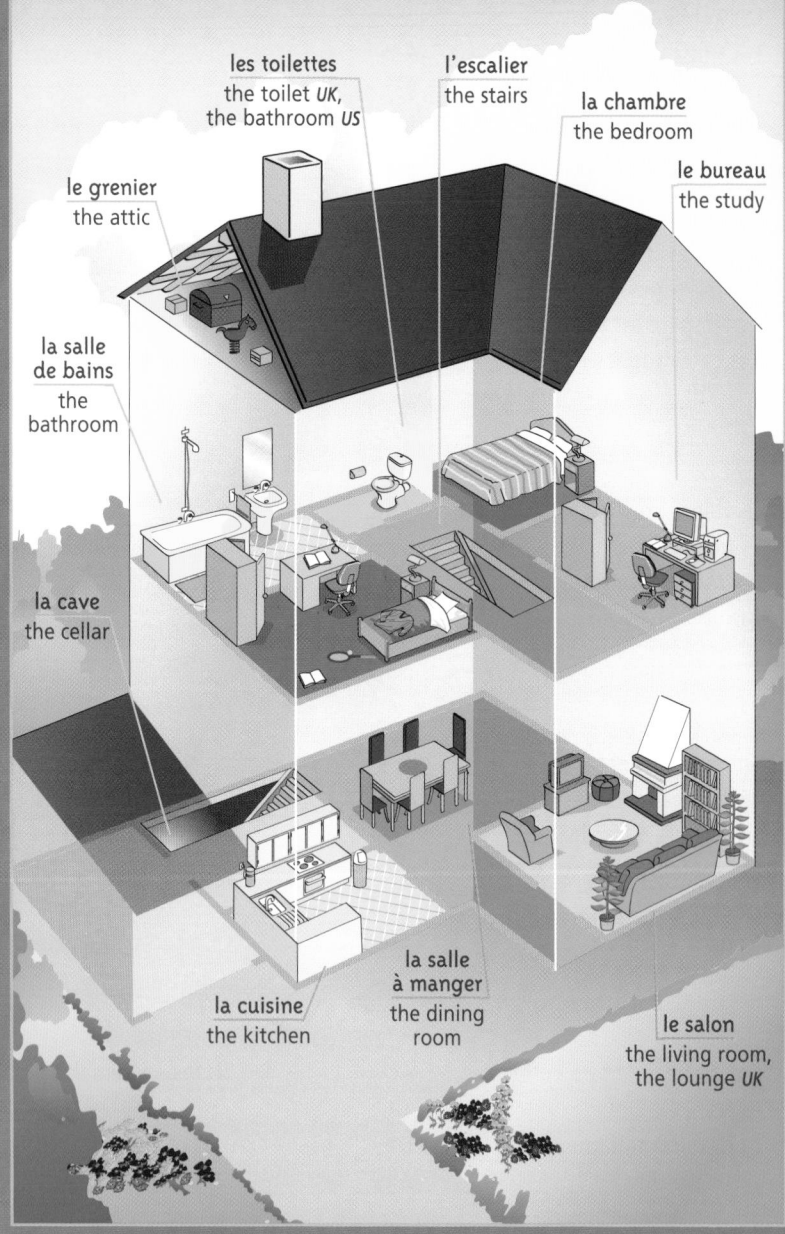

les toilettes
the toilet *UK*,
the bathroom *US*

l'escalier
the stairs

la chambre
the bedroom

le bureau
the study

le grenier
the attic

**la salle
de bains**
the
bathroom

la cave
the cellar

la cuisine
the kitchen

**la salle
à manger**
the dining
room

le salon
the living room,
the lounge *UK*

4

The house

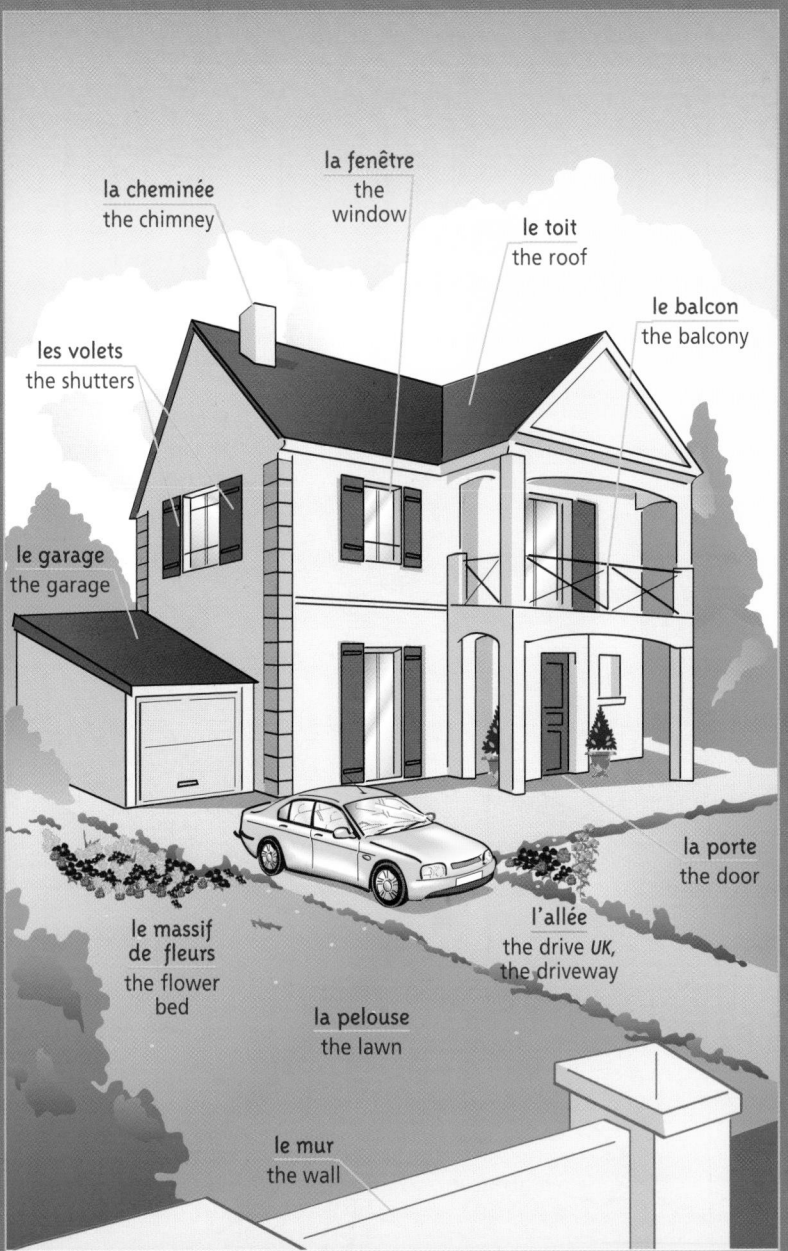

la cheminée
the chimney

la fenêtre
the window

le toit
the roof

le balcon
the balcony

les volets
the shutters

le garage
the garage

la porte
the door

le massif
de fleurs
the flower
bed

l'allée
the drive *UK*,
the driveway

la pelouse
the lawn

le mur
the wall

la vaisselle
plates

le placard
the cupboard

la hotte
the extractor hood

la bouilloire
the kettle

la table de cuisson
the hob

le grille-pain
the toaster

le robinet
the tap

l'évier
the sink

la casserole
the pan

le torchon
the tea towel

la poubelle
the bin *UK*, the garbage can *US*

le lave-vaisselle
the dishwasher

le tiroir
the drawer

le four
the oven

le réfrigérateur
the fridge

le tableau
the painting

les rideaux
the curtains

la télévision
the television

le canapé
the sofa

le vase
the vase

la table basse
the coffee table

le buffet
the side-
board

la table
the
table

la
fourchette
the fork

le couteau
the knife

la serviette
the napkin

le banc
the bench

la chaise
the chair

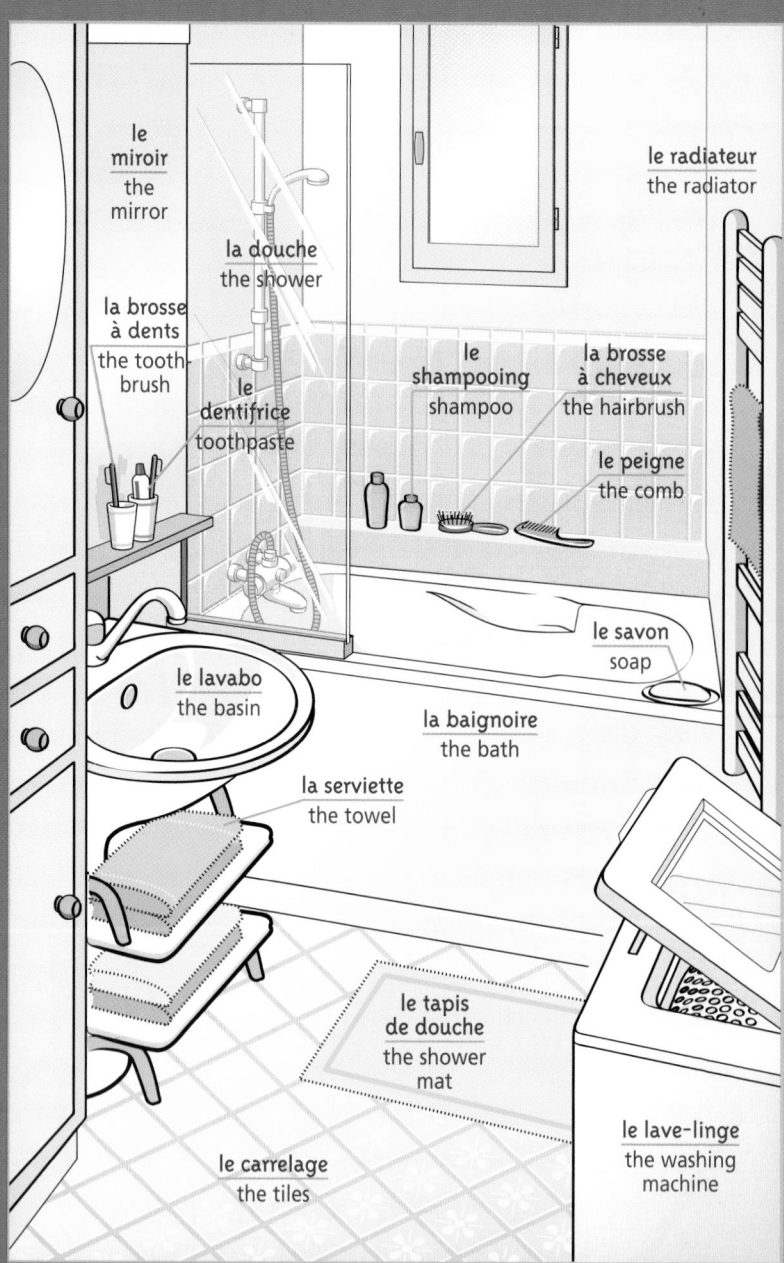

le miroir
the mirror

la douche
the shower

la brosse
à dents
the tooth-
brush

le
dentifrice
toothpaste

le
shampooing
shampoo

la brosse
à cheveux
the hairbrush

le peigne
the comb

le radiateur
the radiator

le savon
soap

le lavabo
the basin

la baignoire
the bath

la serviette
the towel

le tapis
de douche
the shower
mat

le carrelage
the tiles

le lave-linge
the washing
machine

le poster
the poster

les étagères
the shelves

l'armoire
the wardrobe

le poisson rouge
the goldfish

la lampe
the lamp

le lit
the bed

l'oreiller
the pillow

la couette
the duvet *UK*,
the comforter *US*

le réveil
the alarm clock

la commode
the chest of drawers

la table de chevet
the bedside table

le tapis
the rug

le bureau
the desk

le baladeur
the walkman

la chaise
the chair

une batterie
drums

une cymbale
a cymbal

un xylophone
a xylophone

un tambourin
a tambourine

des maracas
maracas

une flûte
traversière
a flute

un trombone
a trombone

une trompette
a trumpet

un saxophone
a saxophone

une
clarinette
a clarinet

un harmonica
a harmonica

un piano
a piano

une contrebasse
a double
bass

une
guitare
a guitar

un violon
a violin

arrière-grand-mère
great-grandmother

arrière-grand-père
great-grandfather

grand-mère
grandmother

grand-père
grandfather

mère
mother

père
father

tante
aunt

oncle
uncle

fille, sœur
daughter, sister

fils, frère
son, brother

cousine
cousin

cousin
cousin

Les sentiments

Léa est contente,
elle sourit
Lea is happy,
she's smiling

Aude est en colère,
elle crie
Aude is angry,
she's shouting

Pierre est triste,
il pleure
Pierre is sad,
he's crying

Oscar a peur,
il tremble
Oscar is afraid,
he's trembling

Arthur est fatigué,
il bâille
Arthur is tired,
he's yawning

Marie est timide,
elle rougit
Marie is shy,
she's blushing

Hugo est surpris,
il a sursauté
Hugo is surprised,
he jumped

Elsa est amoureuse,
elle rêve
Elsa is in love,
she's daydreaming

Vincent est contrarié,
il fronce les sourcils

Vincent is annoyed,
he's frowning

Victor s'en fiche,
il hausse les épaules

Victor doesn't care,
he's shrugging his
shoulders

Chloé est vexée,
elle fait la tête

Chloé is hurt,
she's sulking

Benjamin n'est
pas d'accord,
il fait non de la tête

Benjamin disagrees,
he's shaking his head

Marion s'amuse,
elle rit

Marion is enjoying herself,
she's laughing

Audrey est d'accord,
elle fait oui de la tête

Audrey agrees,
she's nodding

Thomas s'ennuie,
il soupire

Thomas is bored,
he's sighing

Alice n'aime pas les épinards,
elle fait la grimace

Alice doesn't like spinach,
she's pulling a face

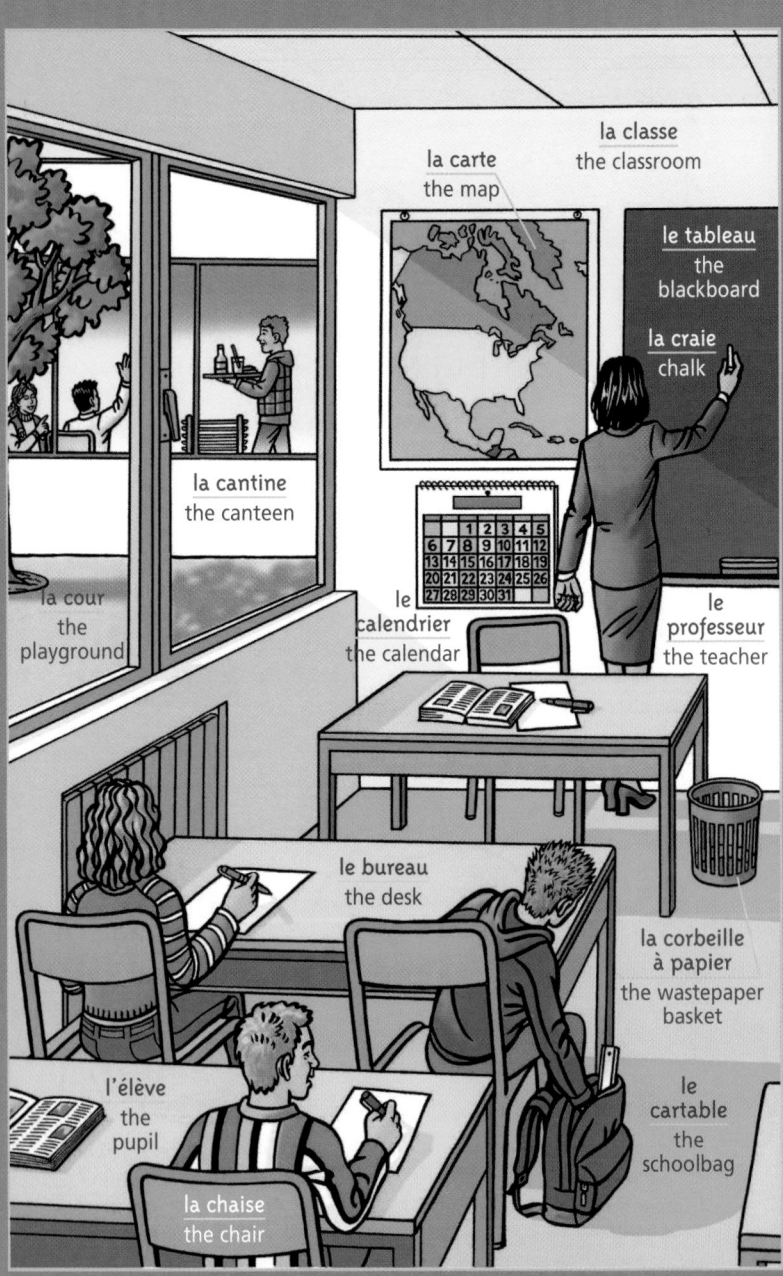

la classe
the classroom

la carte
the map

le tableau
the blackboard

la craie
chalk

la cantine
the canteen

la cour
the playground

le calendrier
the calendar

le professeur
the teacher

le bureau
the desk

la corbeille à papier
the wastepaper basket

l'élève
the pupil

le cartable
the schoolbag

la chaise
the chair

En classe In the classroom

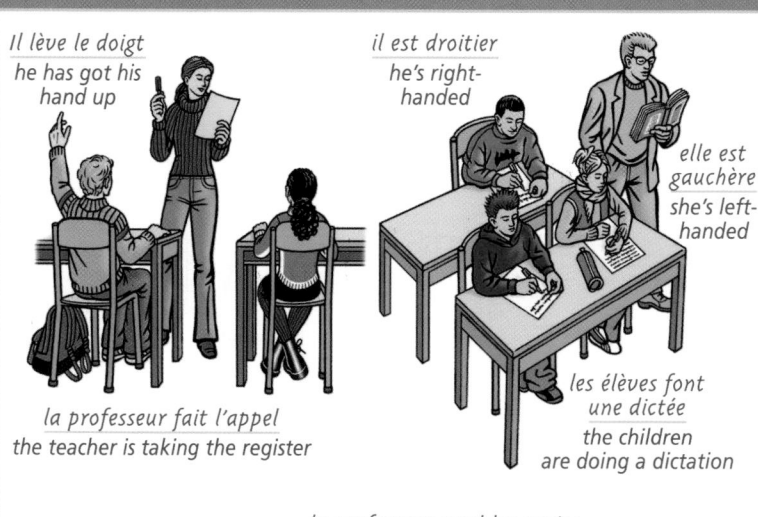

Il lève le doigt
he has got his hand up
la professeur fait l'appel
the teacher is taking the register
il est droitier
he's right-handed
elle est gauchère
she's left-handed
les élèves font une dictée
the children are doing a dictation
la professeur rend les copies
the teacher is handing back the work
le professeur interroge un élève
the teacher is testing a student
la professeur surveille
the teacher is watching the students
il cherche un mot dans le dictionnaire
he's looking a word up in the dictionary
les élèves font un devoir
the students are doing their homework

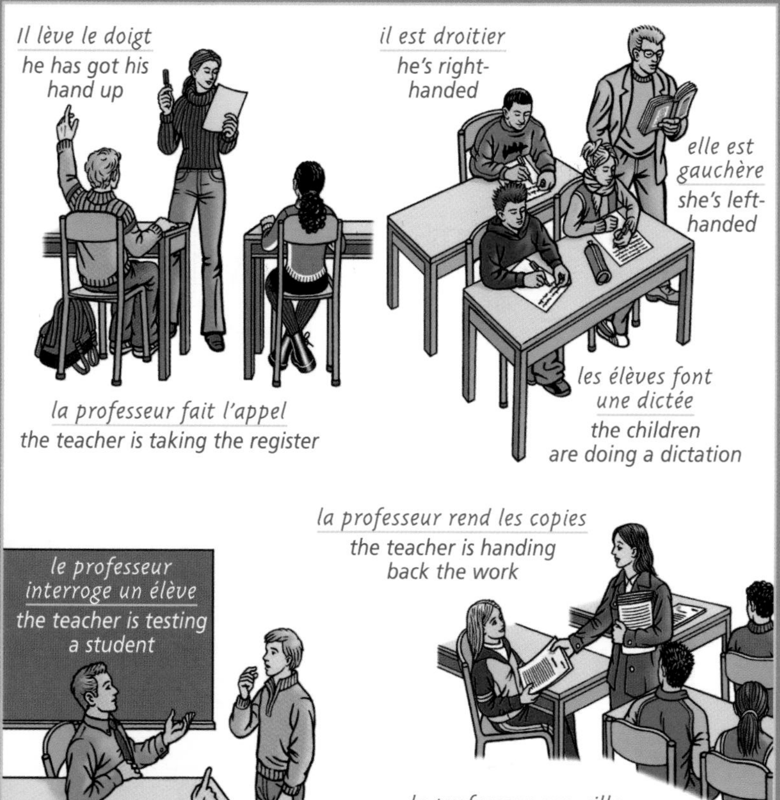

l'entrée
the starter

le dessert
dessert

le plat
the main course

des légumes
vegetables

de la viande
meat

le plateau
the tray

une assiette
a plate

la carafe d'eau
the water jug

le yaourt
yoghurt

un gâteau
a cake

le verre
the glass

du fromage
cheese

les couverts
the cutlery

le pain
bread

des crudités
raw vegetables

Le bureau   The desk

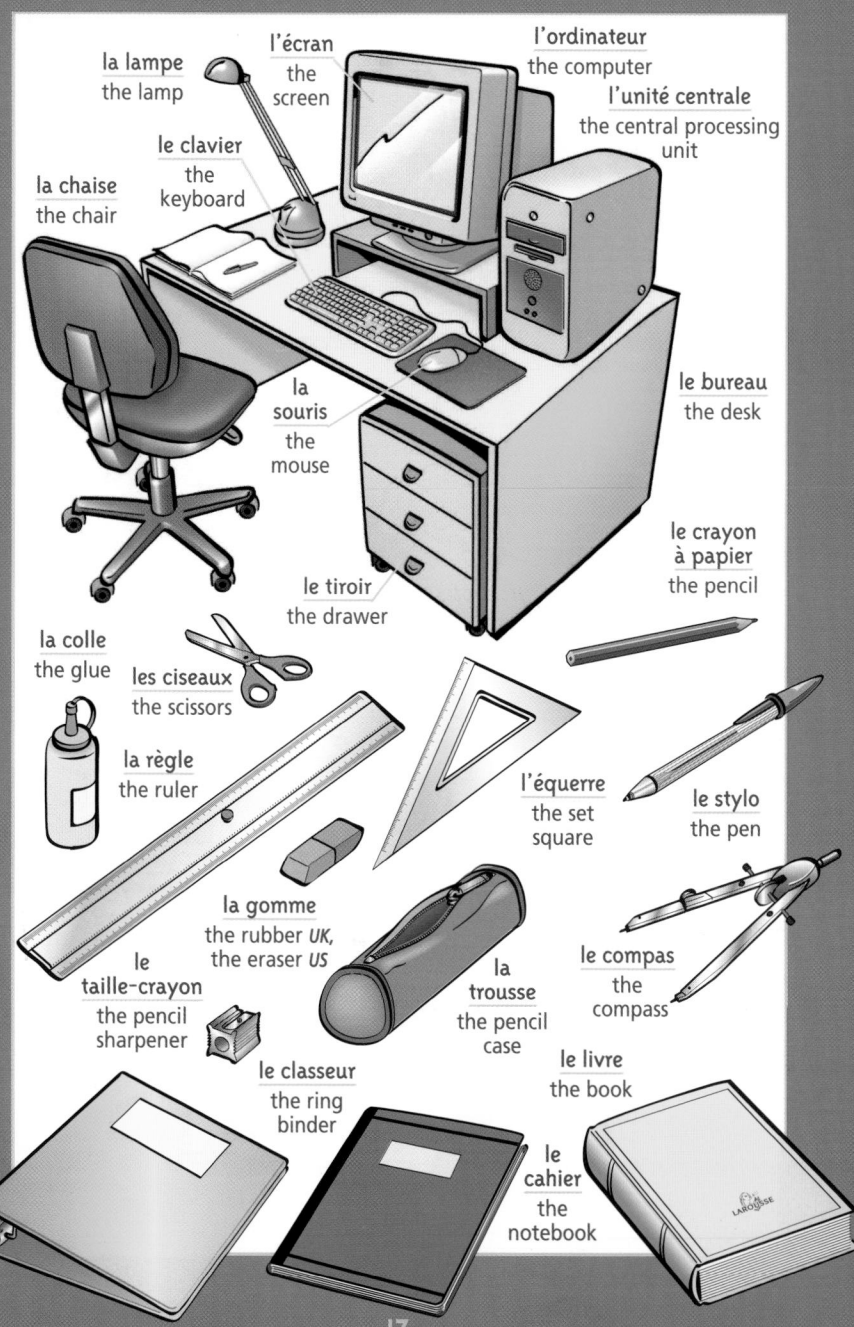

la lampe
the lamp

l'écran
the screen

l'ordinateur
the computer

l'unité centrale
the central processing
unit

le clavier
the keyboard

la chaise
the chair

le bureau
the desk

la souris
the mouse

le crayon
à papier
the pencil

le tiroir
the drawer

la colle
the glue

les ciseaux
the scissors

la règle
the ruler

l'équerre
the set
square

le stylo
the pen

la gomme
the rubber *UK*,
the eraser *US*

le compas
the compass

le
taille-crayon
the pencil
sharpener

la trousse
the pencil
case

le livre
the book

le classeur
the ring
binder

le cahier
the notebook

il est pompier
he's a fireman,
he's a
firefighter US

elle est médecin
she's a doctor

elle est chimiste
she's a chemist

il est professeur
he's a teacher

elle est journaliste
she's a journalist

il est pilote
he's a pilot

il est mécanicien
he's a mechanic

il est facteur
he's
a postman,
he's
a mailman US

elle est policière
she's a policewoman

elle est avocate
she's a lawyer

il est banquier
he's a banker

elle est architecte
she's an architect

il est ingénieur
he's an engineer

il est informaticien
he's a computer scientist

elle est artiste peintre
she's a painter

elle est actrice
she's an actress

elle est photographe
she's a photographer

elle est coiffeuse
she's a hairdresser

elle est vendeuse
she's a sales assistant UK,
she's a sales clerk US

il est styliste
he's a
designer

Le corps humain

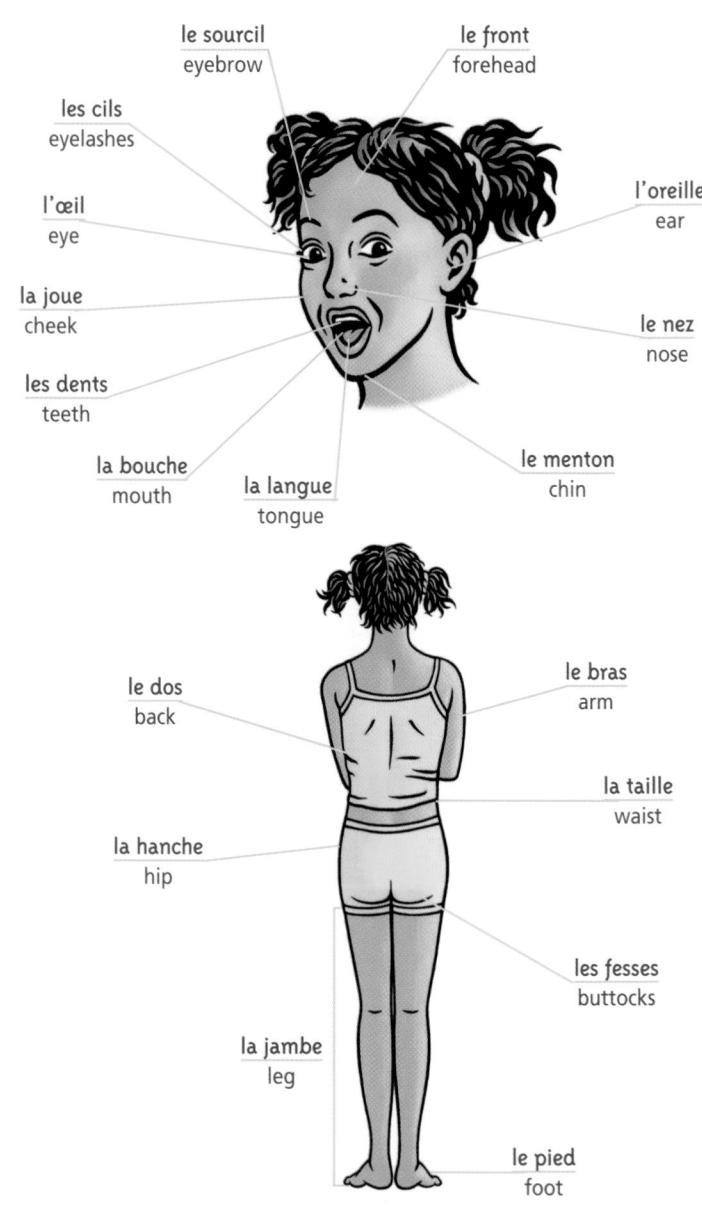

le sourcil
eyebrow

le front
forehead

les cils
eyelashes

l'œil
eye

la joue
cheek

les dents
teeth

la bouche
mouth

la langue
tongue

l'oreille
ear

le nez
nose

le menton
chin

le dos
back

le bras
arm

la taille
waist

la hanche
hip

les fesses
buttocks

la jambe
leg

le pied
foot

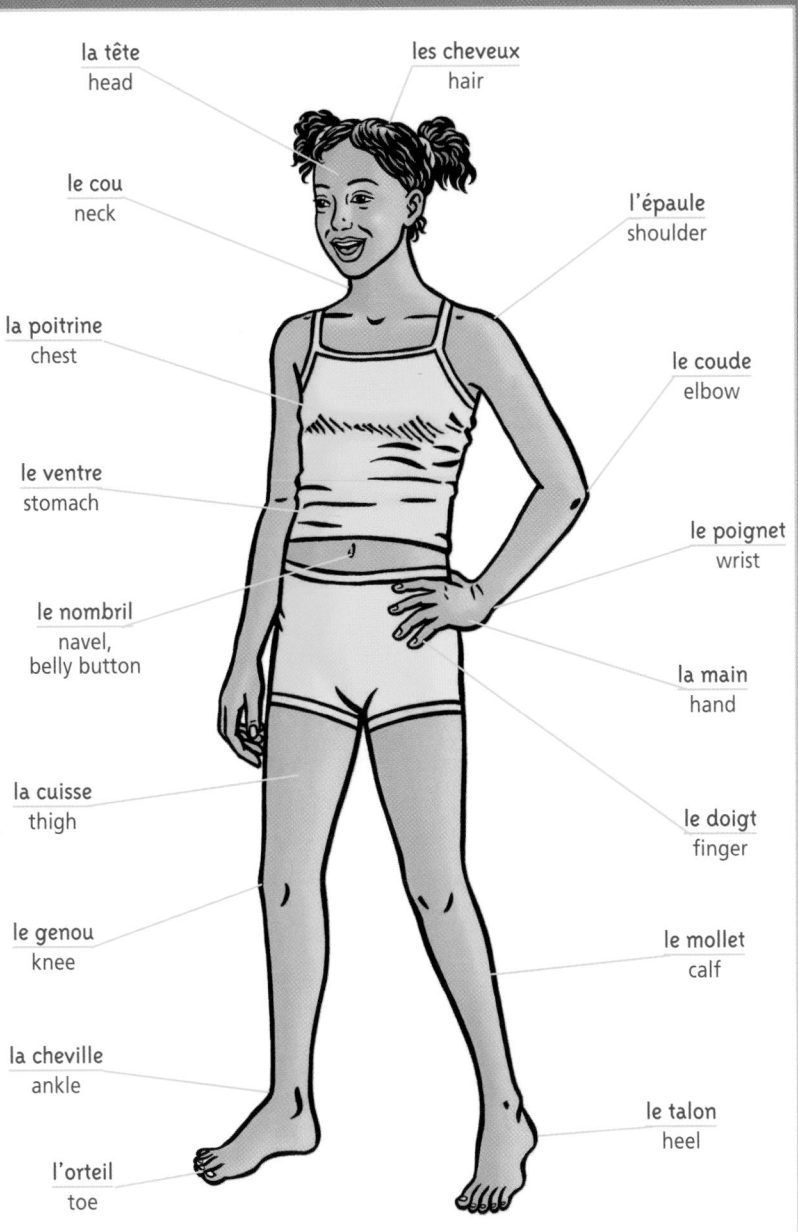

la tête
head

les cheveux
hair

le cou
neck

l'épaule
shoulder

la poitrine
chest

le coude
elbow

le ventre
stomach

le poignet
wrist

le nombril
navel,
belly button

la main
hand

la cuisse
thigh

le doigt
finger

le genou
knee

le mollet
calf

la cheville
ankle

le talon
heel

l'orteil
toe

le hockey sur glace
ice hockey *UK*,
hockey *US*

le basket-ball
basketball

le rugby
rugby

le volley-ball
volleyball

le football
football *UK*,
soccer *US*

le base-ball
baseball

le football
américain
American
football

le tennis
tennis

la natation
swimming

le ski
skiing

l'équitation
riding

le golf
golf

le judo
judo

la voile
sailing

le patinage
skating

l'escrime
fencing

la planche à voile
windsurfing

le canoë
canoeing

la course
running

Le mouvement - La position

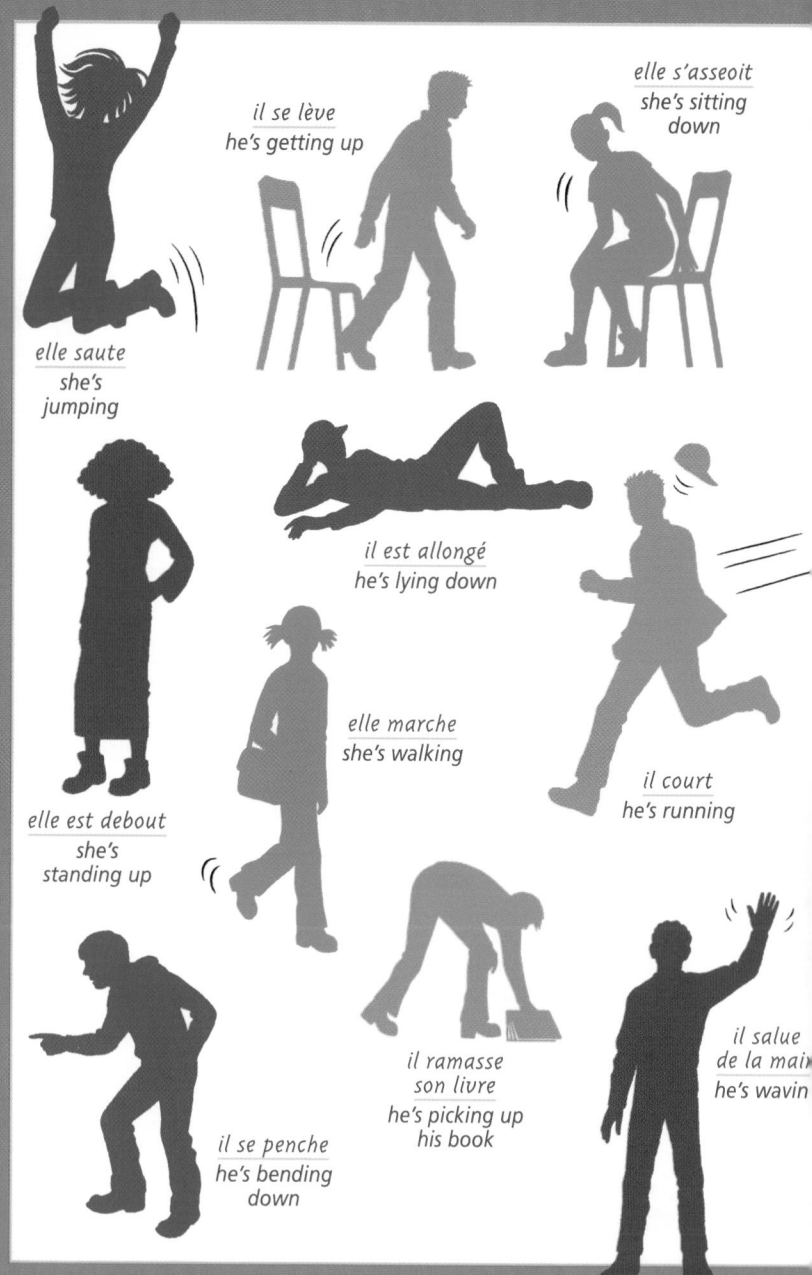

elle saute
she's jumping

il se lève
he's getting up

elle s'asseoit
she's sitting down

il est allongé
he's lying down

elle est debout
she's standing up

elle marche
she's walking

il court
he's running

il se penche
he's bending down

il ramasse son livre
he's picking up his book

il salue de la main
he's wavin

*elle est assise
en tailleur*
she's sitting
cross-legged

il tombe
he's falling

il est accroupi
he's squatting
down

*elle marche sur la
pointe des pieds*
she's walking
on tiptoes

*il est assis
jambes croisées*
he is sitting
with his legs
crossed

*il est accoudé
à la table*
he's resting his
elbows on
the table

elle danse
she's dancing

*elle est adossée
au mur*
she's leaning
against the wall

*elle est recroquevillée
dans un fauteuil*
she's curled up
in an armchair

*elle est
à genoux*
she's kneeling

25

Décrire une personne

Marion est rousse,
elle a les cheveux courts
et des tâches de rousseur

Marion is a redhead,
she has short hair
and freckles

Alice a les cheveux
attachés et porte des
boucles d'oreille

Alice is wearing her
hair up and has
earrings on

Oscar a les cheveux
courts et une cicatrice
sur le menton

Oscar has short hair
and a scar on his chin

Vincent a les cheveux
en brosse et des boutons
sur les joues

Vincent has a crew cut and
spots on his cheeks

Thomas a un épi
dans les cheveux
et les sourcils épais

Thomas' hair
sticks up and he
has thick eyebrows

Elsa a les cheveux longs
et porte un bandeau

Elsa has long hair and is
wearing a headband

Pierre est châtain
et a les yeux bleus

Pierre has brown hair
and blue eyes

Léa est blonde
aux yeux verts

Léa is blonde with
green eyes

*Aude a des cheveux
bruns au carré
avec la raie au milieu*

Aude has brown hair cut in a
bob with a middle parting UK /
part US

*Victor a les cheveux
frisés et un grain
de beauté sur la joue*

Victor has curly hair
and a mole on
his cheek

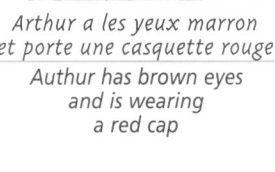

*Arthur a les yeux marron
et porte une casquette rouge*

Authur has brown eyes
and is wearing
a red cap

*Audrey a le nez retroussé
et une queue de cheval*

Audrey has a turned-up nose
and a ponytail

*Marie a les cheveux frisés
et porte un collier*

Marie has curly hair and
is wearing a necklace

*Benjamin porte
des lunettes et la raie
sur le côté*

Benjamin is wearing glasses
and has a side parting UK
or part US

*Hugo
a le bras cassé*

Hugo has a broken arm

*Chloé a une frange
et une tresse*

Chloé has a fringe and
a plait / braid US

Les vêtements

un
soutien-gorge
a bra

une
culotte
panties

un collant
tights *UK*,
pantyhose *US*

une chemise
de nuit
a nightie

un peignoir
en éponge
a towelling robe

des lunettes
de soleil
sunglasses

une robe
à pois
a dress with
dots on

une robe
à fleurs
a flowery
dress

une mini-jupe
a mini skirt

des sandales
sandals

un maillot
de bain
a swimming
costume *UK*
a bathing su

une robe un
a dress

une veste en laine
a wool jacket

un bonnet
a woolly hat *UK*,
a wooly hat *US*

un
manteau
a coat

des gants
gloves

une
écharpe
a scarf

un pull à col en V
a V-neck sweater,
a V-neck jumper *UK*

un pull
à col roulé
a polo neck *UK*,
a turtle neck
sweater *US*

un gilet
a cardigan

un chemisier
a blouse

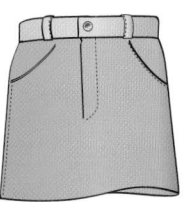

une jupe
a skirt

une jupe
évasée
a flared
skirt

des
bottes
boots

Les vêtements

un pyjama
pyjamas

un slip
underpants

des
chaussettes
socks

des
pantoufles
slippers

une robe de chambre
en laine polaire
a fleece dressing gown

un tee-shirt shirt
à manches courtes
a short-sleeved
T-shirt

un tee-shirt
à manches longues
a long-sleeved T-shirt

un tee-shirt
à rayures
a striped T-shirt

un
survêtement
a tracksuit UK,
a sweatsuit US

un short
shorts

des tennis
trainers UK,
sneakers US

un blouson en cuir
a leather jacket

une veste
a jacket

un impermeable
a raincoat

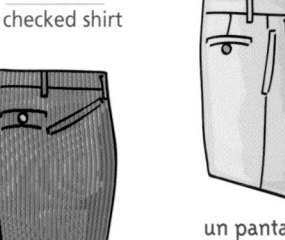

une chemise à carreaux
a checked shirt

une chemise
a shirt

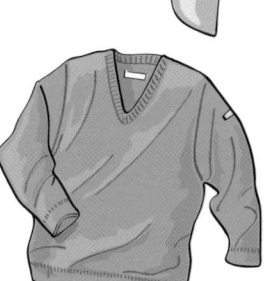

un pull
a sweater,
a jumper *UK*

un pantalon en velours côtelé
corduroy trousers *UK* /
corduroy pants *US*

un pantalon à pinces
pleated trousers *UK* /
pleated pants *US*

un pantalon taille basse
trousers *UK* / pants *US*
with a low waist

un jean
jeans

des chaussures
shoes

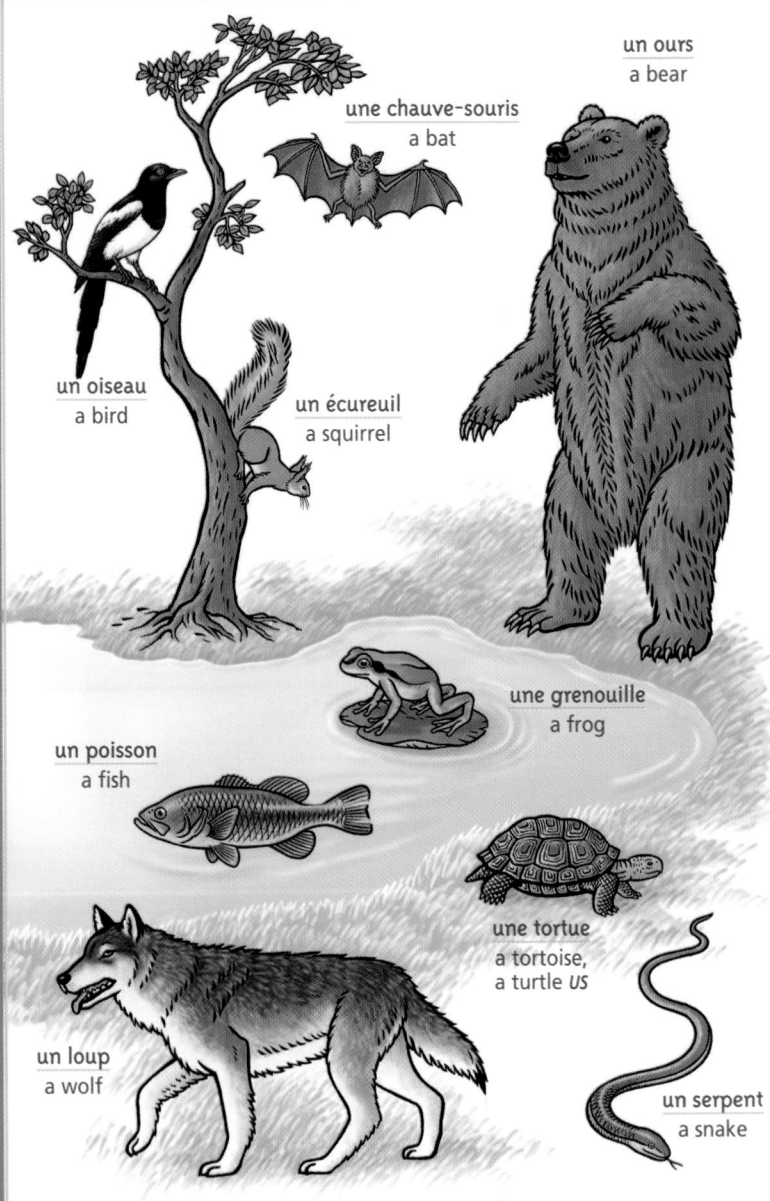

un ours
a bear

une chauve-souris
a bat

un oiseau
a bird

un écureuil
a squirrel

une grenouille
a frog

un poisson
a fish

une tortue
a tortoise,
a turtle *US*

un loup
a wolf

un serpent
a snake

un canard
a duck

une souris
a mouse

un mouton
a sheep

un chat
a cat

un chien
a dog

un lapin
a rabbit

une vache
a cow

une poule
a hen

un cheval
a horse

un cochon
a pig

un perroquet
a parrot

un lion
a lion

un singe
a monkey

une girafe
a giraffe

un éléphant
an elephant

un zèbre
a zebra

un rhinocéros
a rhinoceros

un hippopotame
a hippopotamus

un dauphin
a dolphin

un pingouin
a penguin

une baleine
a whale

un requin
a shark

ne tortue
marine
a turtle

un lama
a llama

un kangourou
a kangaroo

un crocodile
a crocodile

Les fruits

du raisin
grapes

des groseilles
redcurrants

des myrtilles
blueberries

des airelles
cranberries

des cassis
blackcurrants

une framboise
a raspberry

une mûre
a blackberry

des cerises
cherries

des prunes
plums

une fraise
a strawberry

un abricot
an apricot

une poire
a pear

une pomme
an apple

une pêche
a peach

un melon
a melon

une pastèque
a watermelon

un fruit
de la passion
a passion fruit

une figue
a fig

un citron
a lemon

une banane
a banana

un citron vert
a lime

un kiwi
a kiwi

une orange
an orange

une grenade
a pomegranate

un avocat
an avocado

un ananas
a pineapple

une
goyave
a guava

une noix
de coco
a coconut

une mangue
a mango

Les légumes

de l'ail
garlic

un oignon
an onion

une laitue
a lettuce

des champignons
mushrooms

un poireau
a leek

des épinards
spinach

une courgette
a courgette *UK*,
a zucchini *US*

des poivrons
rouge et vert
red and green
peppers

une aubergine
an aubergine *UK*,
an eggplant *US*

une tomate
a tomato

un potiron
a pumpkin

un concombre
a cucumber

une pomme
de terre
a potato

une patate
douce
a sweet
potato

une carotte
a carrot

du céleri
celery

des haricots verts
green beans,
string beans US

des petits pois
peas

des haricots rouges
kidney beans

un navet
a turnip

une betterave
a beetroot UK,
a beet US

des radis
radishes

des germes de soja
beansprouts

des asperges
asparagus

un artichaut
an artichoke

des choux de Bruxelles
brussels sprouts

un chou-fleur
a cauliflower

du maïs
sweetcorn UK,
corn US

du brocoli
broccoli

un pin
a pine

un chêne
an oak tree

un sapin
a fir tree

un olivier
an olive tree

un érable
a maple

un platane
a plane
tree

un palmier
a palm tree

un hêtre
a beech tree

un
<u>œillet</u>
a carnation

du
<u>muguet</u>
lily of the
valley

une
<u>rose</u>
a rose

une
<u>marguerite</u>
a daisy

des
<u>violettes</u>
violets

un chardon
a thistle

des
<u>géraniums</u>
geraniums

une
<u>orchidée</u>
an orchid

un
<u>coquelicot</u>
a poppy

une
<u>tulipe</u>
a tulip

du
<u>lilas</u>
lilac

<u>un iris</u>
an iris

un
<u>tournesol</u>
a sunflower

les montagnes
the mountains

les collines
the hills

la vallée
the valley

la rivière
the river

la forêt
the forest

le volcan
the volcano

la mer
the sea

la ferme
the farm

la falaise
the cliff

la plage
the beach

la campagne
the countryside

l'île
the island

Le temps – Les saisons   The weather – The seasons

le soleil
the sun

les nuages
the clouds

l'orage
the storm

les éclairs
lightning

la grêle
hail

le printemps
spring

l'été
summer

le vent
wind

la neige
snow

la pluie
rain

le brouillard
fog

l'automne
autumn / fall US

l'hiver
winter

Les catastrophes naturelles

une éruption volcanique
a volcanic eruption

un volcan
a volcano

un cratère
a crater

une coulée de lave
a lava flow

un raz de marée
a tidal wave

une vague
a wave

le rivage
the shore

une inondation
a flood

les secours
the rescuers

un glissement de terrain
a landslide

la crue d'une rivière
the flooding of a river

un cyclone
a cyclone

un tourbillon
a whirlwind

un tremblement de terre
an earthquake

la faille
the fault line

les dégâts matériels
material damage

une maison immergée
a flooded house

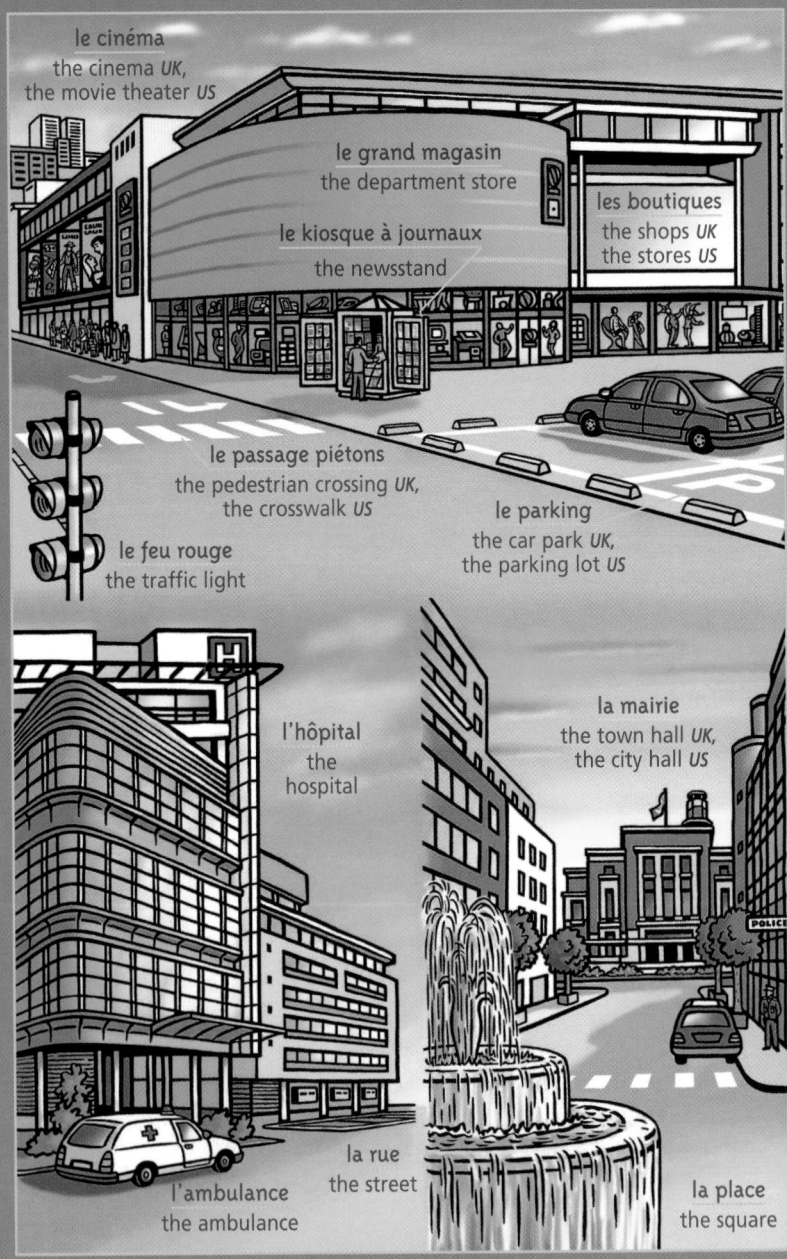

le cinéma
the cinema *UK*,
the movie theater *US*

le grand magasin
the department store

les boutiques
the shops *UK*
the stores *US*

le kiosque à journaux
the newsstand

le passage piétons
the pedestrian crossing *UK*,
the crosswalk *US*

le parking
the car park *UK*,
the parking lot *US*

le feu rouge
the traffic light

l'hôpital
the
hospital

la mairie
the town hall *UK*,
the city hall *US*

la rue
the street

l'ambulance
the ambulance

la place
the square

il essaye une veste
he's trying on a jacket

la cabine d'essayage
the fitting room

l'escalier roulant
the escalator

le portant
the rack

la vendeuse
the sales assistant *UK*, the sales clerk *US*

le mannequin
the dummy

la caissière rend la monnaie à la cliente
the cashier is giving the customer her change

des billets
banknotes

un cintre
a clothes hanger

des pièces
coins

le présentoir
the display shelf

un porte-monnaie
a purse *UK*, a wallet *US*

la caisse
the cash desk

une cliente
a customer

des clés
keys

un sac à dos
a rucksack

un téléphone portable
a mobile phone

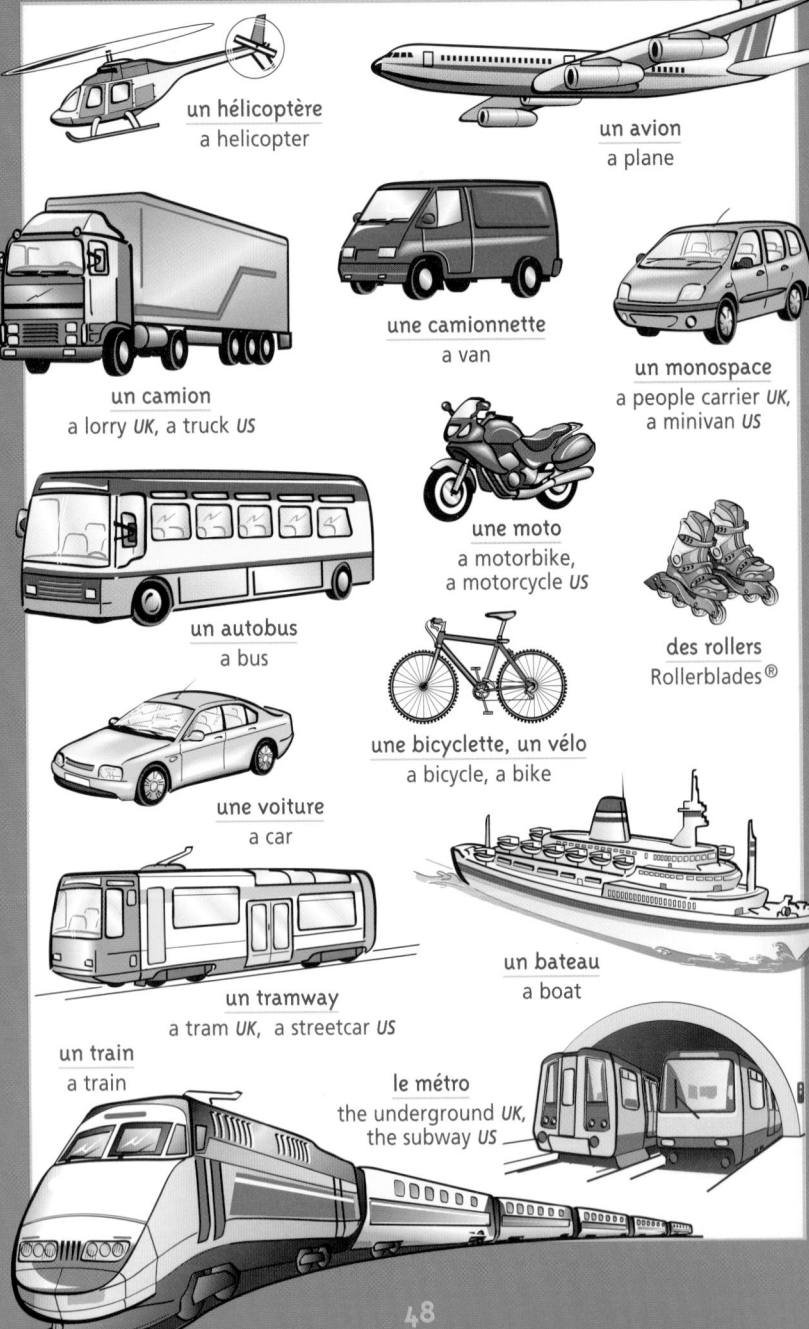

un hélicoptère
a helicopter

un avion
a plane

une camionnette
a van

un monospace
a people carrier *UK*,
a minivan *US*

un camion
a lorry *UK*, a truck *US*

une moto
a motorbike,
a motorcycle *US*

un autobus
a bus

des rollers
Rollerblades ®

une voiture
a car

une bicyclette, un vélo
a bicycle, a bike

un bateau
a boat

un tramway
a tram *UK*, a streetcar *US*

un train
a train

le métro
the underground *UK*,
the subway *US*

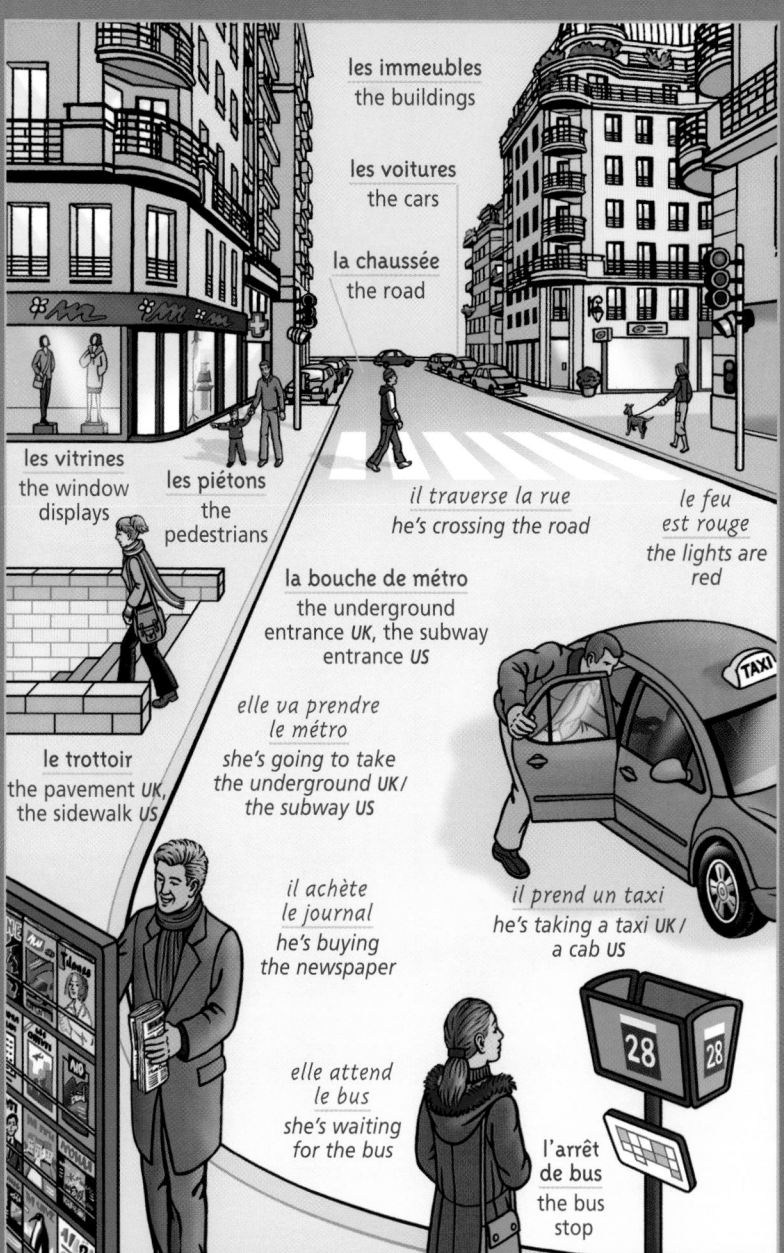

les immeubles
the buildings

les voitures
the cars

la chaussée
the road

les vitrines
the window displays

les piétons
the pedestrians

il traverse la rue
he's crossing the road

le feu est rouge
the lights are red

la bouche de métro
the underground entrance *UK*, the subway entrance *US*

elle va prendre le métro
she's going to take the underground UK / the subway US

le trottoir
the pavement *UK*, the sidewalk *US*

il achète le journal
he's buying the newspaper

il prend un taxi
he's taking a taxi UK / a cab US

elle attend le bus
she's waiting for the bus

l'arrêt de bus
the bus stop

Situer dans l'espace

*elle va **chez** son amie*
she's going **to** her
friend's house

*le chapeau
est accroché
au portemanteau*
the hat
is hanging **on**
the peg

*il va **à** la plage*
he's going **to**
the beach

*elle est **à** la bibliothèque*
she's **in** the library

*il est **chez** lui*
he's **at** home

*Léo marche **sur** la pelouse,
Emma est assise **sous** le parasol*
Léo is walking **on** the grass,
Emma is sitting **under** a parasol

*la voiture passe **sur** le pont,
le bateau passe **sous** le pont*
the car is going **over** the bridge,
the boat is going **under** the bridge

l'hélicoptère vole
au-dessus *de la ville*
the helicopter is flying
over the town

il accroche le tableau
au-dessus *de la cheminée*
he's hanging the picture
above the fireplace

le chien saute
par-dessus *la barrière*
the dog is jumping
over the fence

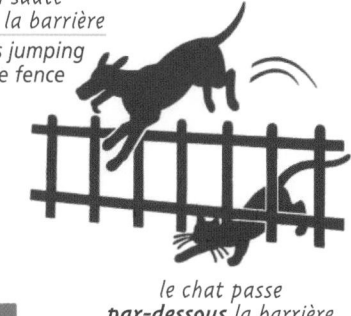

elle porte une veste
avec un col roulé **dessous**
she's wearing a jacket with
a polo neck UK/
turtleneck US **underneath**

le chat passe
par-dessous *la barrière*
the cat is going
under the fence

le lit est
contre *le mur*
the bed is **against**
the wall

il pose l'échelle
contre *le mur*
he's leaning
the ladder **against**
the wall

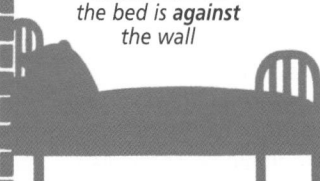

Romain est **à droite** de Marie, mais il est **à gauche** de Lucas

Romain is **on Marie's right**, but he is **on Lucas' left**

Lucas est assis **devant** Marie, Marie est assise **derrière** Lucas

Lucas is sitting **in front of** Marie, Marie is sitting **behind** Lucas

Jules est assis **à côté de** Paul

Jules is sitting **next to** Paul

Tom est **au centre**, il est **entre** Gabriel et Julie

Tom is **in the middle**, he is **between** Gabriel and Julie

Paul est **en haut de** l'escalier, Zoé est **en bas de** l'escalier

Paul's **at the top of** the stairs, Zoé's **at the bottom of** the stairs

Tom est assis **en face de** Léa

Tom is sitting **opposite** Léa

la **clef** est
dans la serrure

the key is
in the lock

elle met le sucre
dans le placard

she's putting
the sugar
in the cupboard

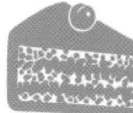

une part de gâteau
avec une cerise
dessus

a slice of cake with
a cherry **on top**

de la fenêtre **au** lit
il y a un mètre

it is one metre UK
or meter US **from** the
window **to** the bed

il doit courir
jusqu'à
la ligne d'arrivée

he must run
to the finishing line

le chien court **vers** Tom

the dog is running
towards Tom

il est **tombé
par terre**

he **fell down**

Les contraires

la voiture est rapide,
la trottinette est lente

the car is fast,
the scooter is slow

la route est large,
le chemin est étroit

the road is wide,
the path is narrow

le vélo rouge est
grand, le bleu est pe

the red bike is big,
the blue one is sma

le miroir est droit,
le tableau est penché

the mirror is straight,
the painting is crooked

l'immeuble est haut,
la maison est basse

the building is tall,
the house is small

le paysage est beau,
le tableau est laid

the scenery is beautiful,
the painting is ugly

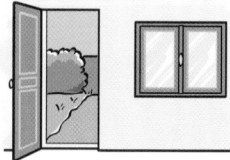

la porte est ouverte,
la fenêtre est fermée

the door is open, the
window is closed

le vase est transparent,
la vitre est opaque

the vase is transparent,
the window pane
is opaque

le tee-shirt est sale,
le short est propre
the T-shirt is dirty,
the shorts are clean

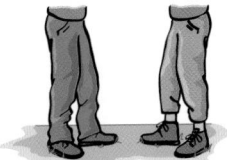

le pantalon vert est long,
le marron est court
the green trousers UK / pants US
are long, the brown ones
are short

Paul est gros,
Pierre est mince
Paul is fat,
Pierre is thin

le livre est épais,
le cahier est mince
the book is thick,
the exercise book is thin

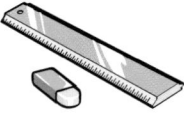

la gomme est souple,
la règle est rigide
the rubber is flexible,
the ruler is rigid

le poids est lourd,
la plume est légère
the weight is heavy,
the feather is light

la bouteille est pleine,
le verre est vide
the bottle is full,
the glass is empty

la glace est froide,
la soupe est chaude
the ice cream is cold,
the soup is hot

les bouts des ciseaux
sont arrondis, la lame du
couteau est pointue
the ends of the scissors
are rounded, the blade of
the knife is sharp

le morceau de sucre est dur,
le beurre est mou
the sugar lump is hard,
the butter is soft

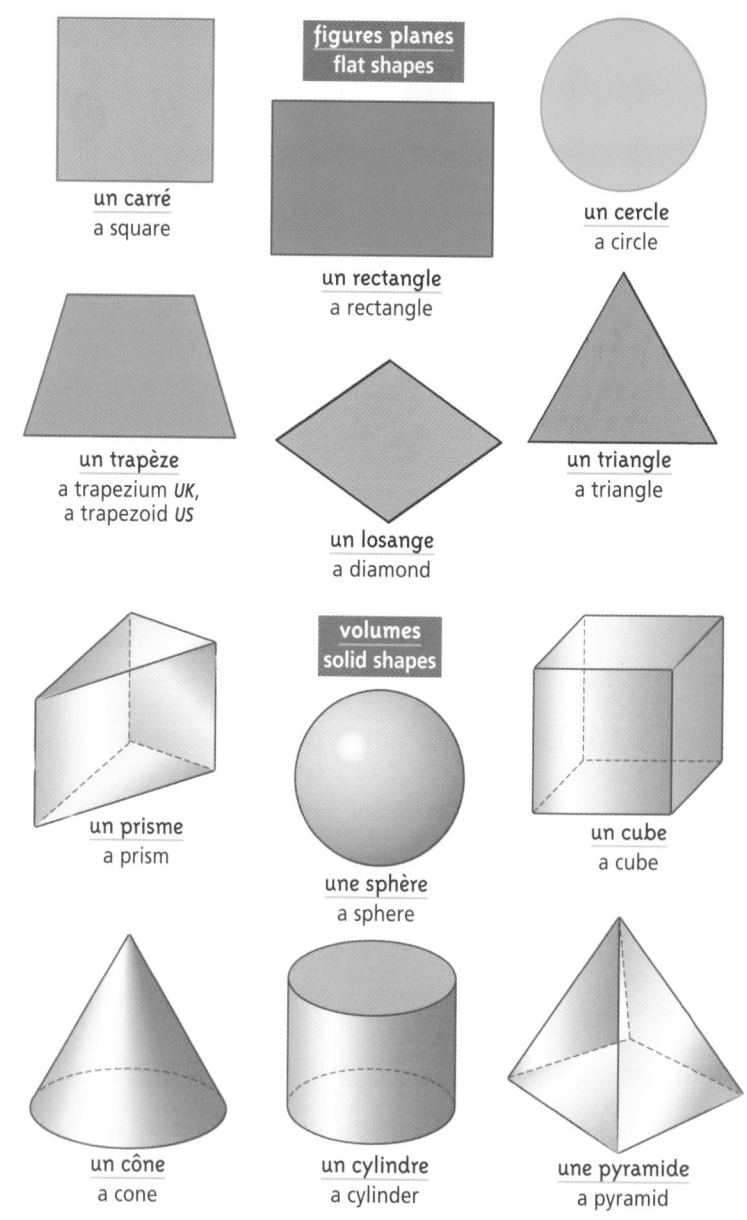

figures planes
flat shapes

un carré
a square

un rectangle
a rectangle

un cercle
a circle

un trapèze
a trapezium *UK*,
a trapezoid *US*

un losange
a diamond

un triangle
a triangle

volumes
solid shapes

un prisme
a prism

une sphère
a sphere

un cube
a cube

un cône
a cone

un cylindre
a cylinder

une pyramide
a pyramid

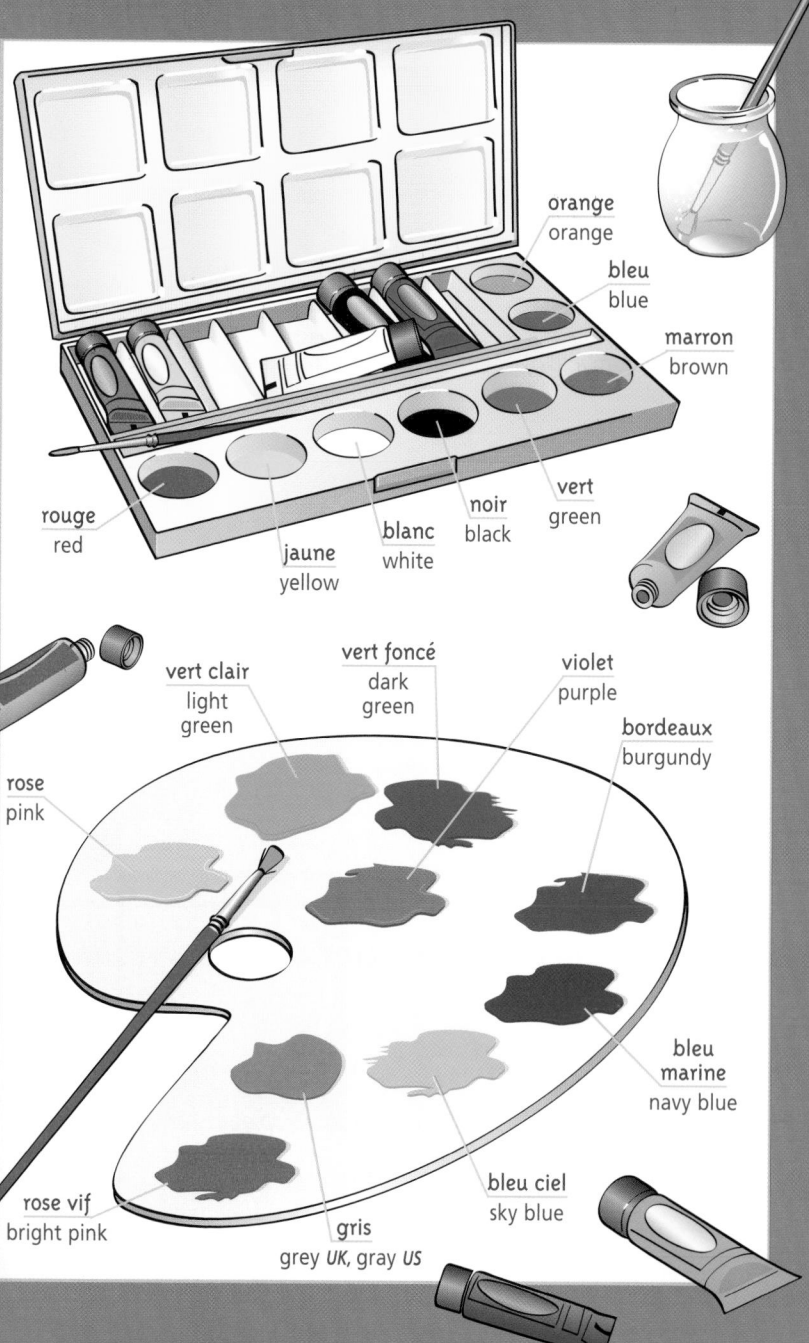

orange
orange

bleu
blue

marron
brown

vert
green

noir
black

rouge
red

blanc
white

jaune
yellow

vert clair
light
green

vert foncé
dark
green

violet
purple

bordeaux
burgundy

rose
pink

bleu
marine
navy blue

rose vif
bright pink

gris
grey *UK*, gray *US*

bleu ciel
sky blue

*il est
quatre heures dix*

it's ten past four
it's ten after four US

*il est quatre heures
et quart*

it's (a) quarter past
four / it's a quarter
after four US

*il est quatre heures
et demie*

it's half past four

*il est cinq heures
moins le quart*

it's (a) quarter to five
it's a quarter of five US

*il est cinq heures
moins dix*

it's ten to five
it's ten of five US

*il est cinq
heures*

it's five o'clock

il est midi
it's midday

il est minuit
it's midnight

Janvier

Janvier		
		January

Agathe est née le 6 juin
Agathe was born
on 6th June

*les vacances de Pâques
commencent le 23 avril*
the Easter holidays start on
23rd April UK ,
the Easter vacation starts
on 23rd April US

*le contrôle de maths
est dans une semaine*
the maths test is
in one week's time

*aujourd'hui,
nous sommes
le 16 janvier*
it is 16th January
today

*cette année, le 1ᵉʳ novembre
tombe un mardi*
this year 1st November
is on a Tuesday

*l'anniversaire
de Thomas
est le 7 février*
Thomas' birthday
is on 7th February

1	Samedi	Saturday
2	Dimanche	Sunday
3	Lundi	Monday
4	Mardi	Tuesday ☾
5	Mercredi	Wednesday
6	Jeudi	Thursday
7	Vendredi	Friday
8	Samedi	Saturday
9	Dimanche	Sunday
10	Lundi	Monday
11	Mardi	Tuesday ●
12	Mercredi	Wednesday
13	Jeudi	Thursday
14	Vendredi	Friday
15	Samedi	Saturday
16	Dimanche	Sunday
17	Lundi	Monday
18	Mardi	Tuesday ☽
19	Mercredi	Wednesday
20	Jeudi	Thursday
21	Vendredi	Friday
22	Samedi	Saturday
23	Dimanche	Sunday
24	Lundi	Monday
25	Mardi	Tuesday ○
26	Mercredi	Wednesday
27	Jeudi	Thursday
28	Vendredi	Friday
29	Samedi	Saturday
30	Dimanche	Sunday
31	Lundi	Monday

Janvier	January
Février	February
Mars	March
Avril	April
Mai	May
Juin	June
Juillet	July
Août	August
Septembre	September
Octobre	October
Novembre	November
Décembre	December

Les drapeaux et les emblèmes   Flags and emblems

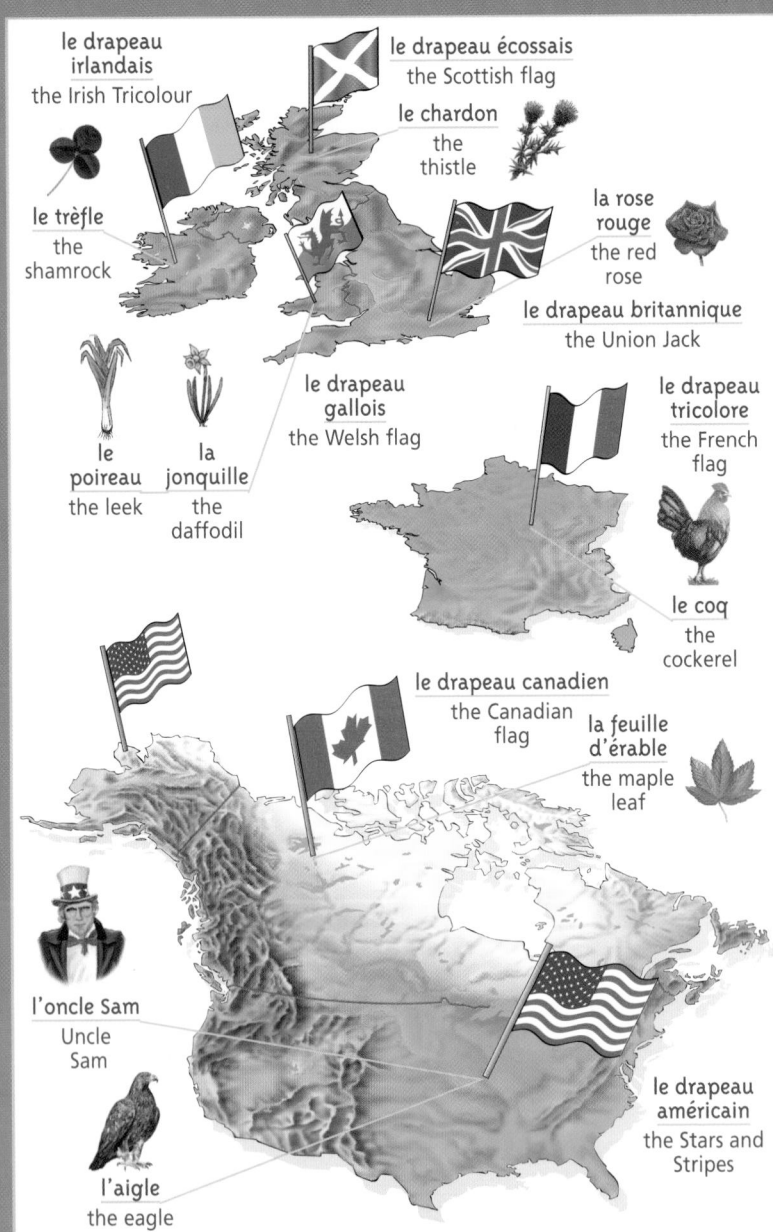

le drapeau
irlandais
the Irish Tricolour

le drapeau écossais
the Scottish flag

le chardon
the
thistle

le trèfle
the
shamrock

la rose
rouge
the red
rose

le drapeau britannique
the Union Jack

le drapeau
gallois
the Welsh flag

le
poireau
the leek

la
jonquille
the
daffodil

le drapeau
tricolore
the French
flag

le coq
the
cockerel

le drapeau canadien
the Canadian
flag

la feuille
d'érable
the maple
leaf

l'oncle Sam
Uncle
Sam

le drapeau
américain
the Stars and
Stripes

l'aigle
the eagle

La France

France

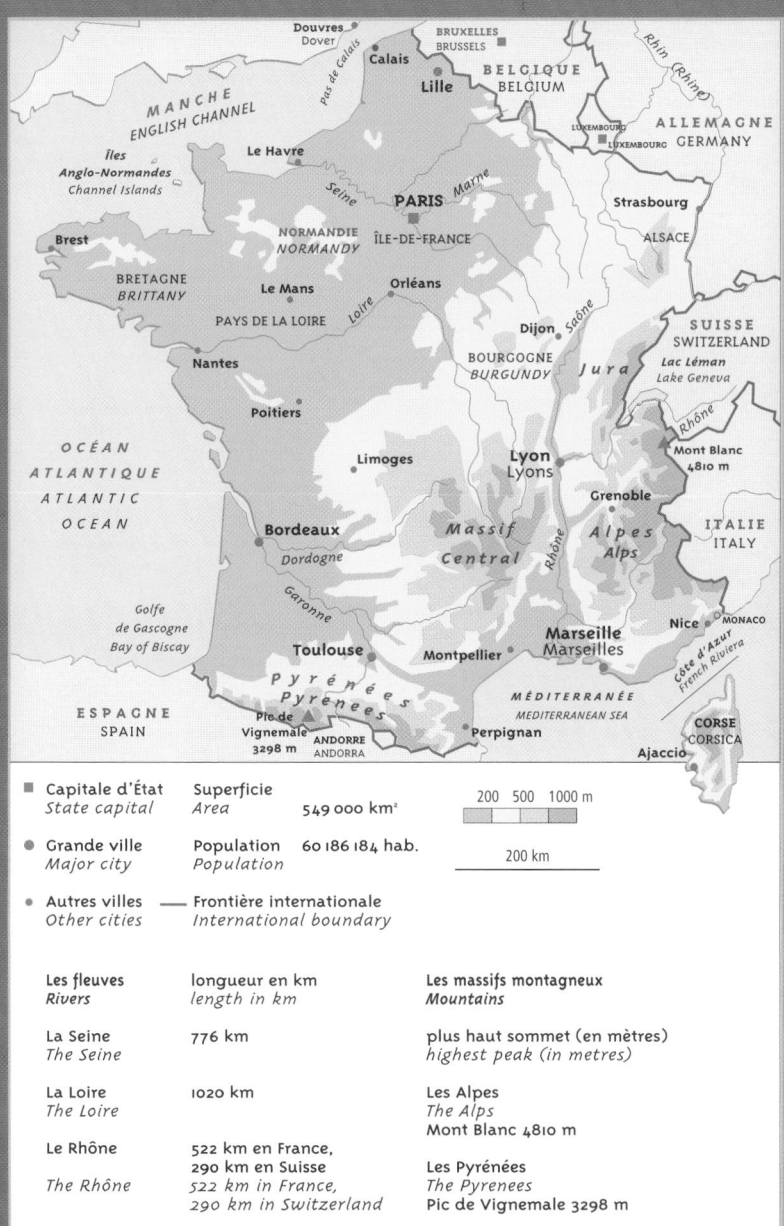

Douvres
Dover
MANCHE
ENGLISH CHANNEL
Pas de Calais
Calais
BRUXELLES
BRUSSELS
BELGIQUE
BELGIUM
Lille
Rhin (Rhine)
ALLEMAGNE
GERMANY
LUXEMBOURG
Îles
Anglo-Normandes
Channel Islands
Le Havre
Seine
Marne
PARIS
Strasbourg
NORMANDIE
NORMANDY
ÎLE-DE-FRANCE
ALSACE
Brest
BRETAGNE
BRITTANY
Le Mans
Orléans
Loire
Saône
Dijon
SUISSE
SWITZERLAND
Nantes
BOURGOGNE
BURGUNDY
Jura
Lac Léman
Lake Geneva
Poitiers
Rhône
OCÉAN
ATLANTIQUE
ATLANTIC
OCEAN
Limoges
Lyon
Lyons
Mont Blanc
4810 m
Grenoble
Bordeaux
Massif
Central
Alpes
Alps
ITALIE
ITALY
Dordogne
Rhône
Garonne
Golfe
de Gascogne
Bay of Biscay
Toulouse
Montpellier
Marseille
Marseilles
Nice
MONACO
Côte d'Azur
French Riviera
Pyrénées
Pyrénées
MÉDITERRANÉE
MEDITERRANEAN SEA
CORSE
CORSICA
ESPAGNE
SPAIN
Pic de
Vignemale
3298 m
ANDORRE
ANDORRA
Perpignan
Ajaccio

		200 500 1000 m
■ Capitale d'État *State capital*	**Superficie** *Area*	549 000 km²
● Grande ville *Major city*	**Population** *Population*	60 186 184 hab.

200 km

● Autres villes
Other cities

—— **Frontière internationale**
International boundary

Les fleuves *Rivers*	**longueur en km** *length in km*	**Les massifs montagneux** *Mountains*
La Seine *The Seine*	776 km	**plus haut sommet (en mètres)** *highest peak (in metres)*
La Loire *The Loire*	1020 km	**Les Alpes** *The Alps* Mont Blanc 4810 m
Le Rhône *The Rhône*	522 km en France, 290 km en Suisse *522 km in France,* *290 km in Switzerland*	**Les Pyrénées** *The Pyrenees* Pic de Vignemale 3298 m

La Grande-Bretagne   Great Britain

ORKNEY ISLANDS
Îles Orcades

SHETLAND ISLANDS
Îles Shetland

WESTERN
ISLES

Scotland
Écosse

NORTH SEA
MER DU NORD

Ben Nevis
4406 ft
1344 m

ATLANTIC OCEAN
OCÉAN ATLANTIQUE

Edinburgh
Édimbourg

Glasgow

UNITED KINGDOM
ROYAUME-UNI

*Northern
Ireland*
Irlande du Nord

Ulster

IRELAND
IRLANDE

Belfast

Isle of Man
Île de Man

England
Angleterre

Leeds

Irish Sea
Mer d'Irlande

Manchester

Liverpool   Sheffield

DUBLIN

Wales
*Pays
de Galles*

Birmingham

Limerick

Cambridge

Cork

Oxford

Cardiff   Bristol

Thames
Tamise

LONDON
Londres

St. George's Channel

CORNWALL
Cornouailles

ISLE OF WIGHT
Île de Wight

ENGLISH CHANNEL
MANCHE

ISLES OF SCILLY
Îles Sorlingues

Shannon

■	Capitale d'État *State capital*	100 km	200 500 m
●	Grande ville *Major city*	Superficie 253 500 km² *Area*	
●	Autres villes *Other cities*	Population 58 400 000 hab. *Population*	

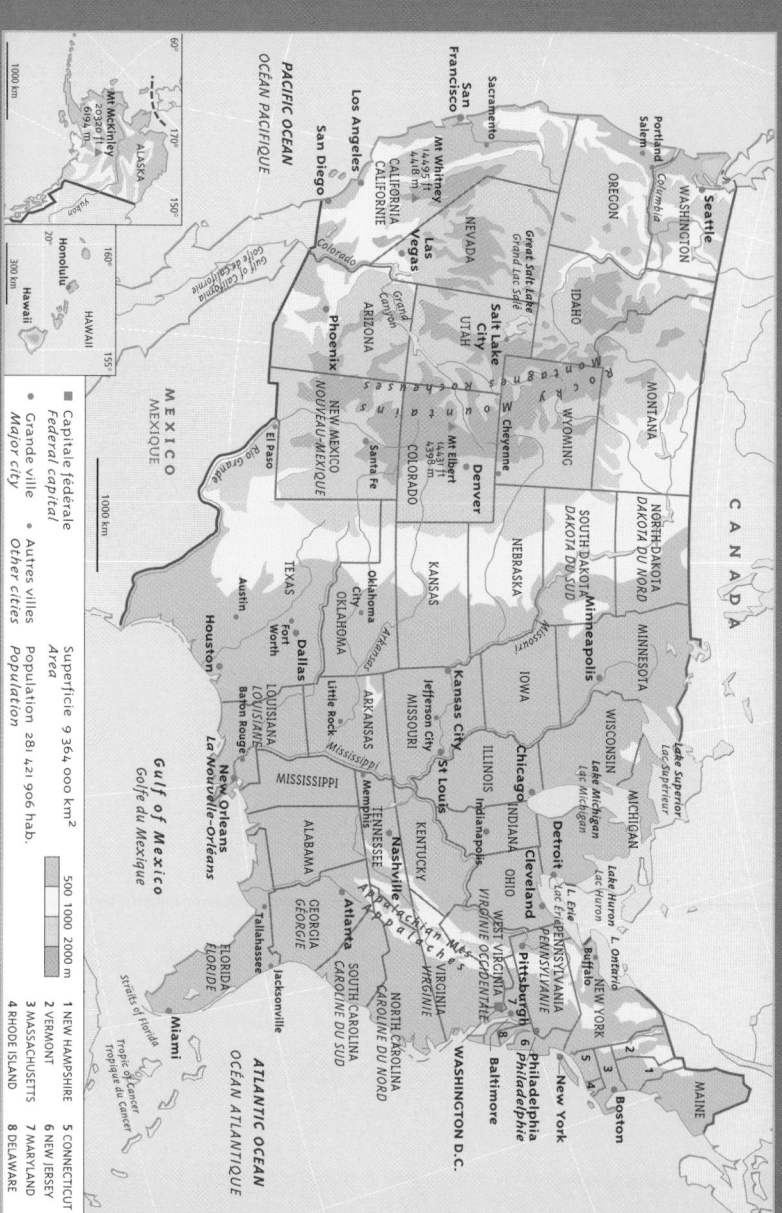

Les États-Unis — The United States

Capitale fédérale
Federal capital

Grande ville
Major city

Autres villes
Other cities

Superficie 9 364 000 km²
Area

Population 281 421 906 hab.
Population

500 1000 2000 m

1 NEW HAMPSHIRE
2 VERMONT
3 MASSACHUSETTS
4 RHODE ISLAND
5 CONNECTICUT
6 NEW JERSEY
7 MARYLAND
8 DELAWARE

English-French
Anglais-Français

a [eɪ, ə] *indefinite article* (**an** [ən] *devant une voyelle*)

1. **un** *(masculine)*, **une** *(feminine)* : **is it a bird or a plane?** c'est un oiseau ou un avion ? ; **it's an ostrich** c'est une autruche
2. *When talking about somebody's job*

> The indefinite article is not translated in French when you say what somebody's profession or trade is:

he's an air steward il est steward ; **she's a doctor** elle est médecin

3. *When talking about prices, quantities and rates* **it costs 2 euros a kilo** ça coûte 2 euros le kilo ; **50 miles an hour** 80 kilomètres à l'heure ; **$10 an hour** 10 dollars de l'heure ; **£7 a head** 7 livres par tête ; **twice a week** deux fois par semaine.

abbey ['æbɪ] *noun*

abbaye *(feminine)*.

abbreviation [ə,briːvɪ'eɪʃn] *noun*

abréviation *(feminine)*.

ability [ə'bɪlətɪ] *noun*

capacité *(feminine)* : **children of different abilities** des enfants ayant des capacités différentes.

able ['eɪbl] *adjective*

> **to be able to do something**
1. **pouvoir faire quelque chose** : **I'm sure I'll be able to come** je suis sûr que je pourrai venir
2. **savoir faire quelque chose** : **I'd like to be able to swim** j'aimerais bien savoir nager.

about [ə'baʊt] *preposition & adverb*

■ *preposition*
1. **au sujet de, sur** : **his parents worry about him** ses parents s'inquiètent à son sujet ; **I'm**
reading a book about magic je lis un livre sur la magie
2. **dans, partout dans** : **they walked about the town** ils se sont promenés dans la ville ; **his things are lying about the room** ses affaires traînent partout dans la chambre

■ *adverb*
1. **environ, à peu près** : **there were about 50 people** il y avait environ 50 personnes
2. **vers** : **they'll get here about 5 o'clock** ils vont arriver vers 17 heures
3. **dans les parages** : **she's somewhere about** elle est dans les parages
4. **partout** : **he left his books lying about** il a laissé traîner ses livres partout

> **what's it about?** de quoi s'agit-il ? : **what are you talking about?** de quoi parlez-vous ?
> **just about** presque : **I'm just about ready** je suis presque prêt
> **to be about to do something** être sur le point de faire quelque chose : **he was about to leave, when the phone rang** il était sur le point de partir quand le téléphone a sonné
> **how about ...?** OR **what about ...?** et si ... ? : **how about going to the beach?** et si on allait à la plage ?

above [ə'bʌv] *preposition & adverb*

■ *preposition*
1. **au-dessus de** : **the sun is shining above the clouds** le soleil brille au-dessus des nuages
2. **plus de** : **temperatures above 45 degrees** des températures de plus de 45 degrés

■ *adverb*
1. **au-dessus** : **put it on the shelf above** mets-le sur l'étagère au-dessus
2. **plus** : **a score of 70 or above** un score de 70 ou plus

> **above all** surtout : **above all, remember to drive on the left!** surtout, souvenez-vous de conduire à gauche !

abroad [ə'brɔːd] *adverb*

à l'étranger : **Mary is going abroad** Mary va à l'étranger.

abseiling *UK* ['æbseɪlɪŋ] *noun*

rappel *(masculine)* : **to go abseiling** faire du rappel.

absent ['æbsənt] *adjective*

absent : **Fred is absent from school** Fred est absent de l'école.

1

absolutely ['æbsə'luːtlɪ] *adverb*

tout à fait : **she's absolutely right** elle a tout à fait raison.

accelerate [ək'seləreɪt] *verb*

accélérer : **the train is accelerating** le train accélère.

accent ['æksent] *noun*

accent *(masculine)* : **she has an English accent** elle a l'accent anglais.

accept [ək'sept] *verb*

accepter : **I accept your offer** j'accepte votre offre.

access ['ækses] *noun*

accès *(masculine)* : **to have access to something** avoir accès à quelque chose.

accessory [ək'sesərɪ] *noun*

accessoire *(masculine)* : **fashion accessories** des accessoires de mode.

accident ['æksɪdənt] *noun*

accident *(masculine)* : **he had an accident** il a eu un accident

➤ **by accident** par hasard : **I met her by accident** je l'ai rencontrée par hasard.

accommodation *UK* [ə͵kɒmə'deɪʃn] *uncountable noun*, **accommodations** *US* [ə͵kɒmə'deɪʃns] *plural noun*

logement *(masculine)* : **many students live in rented accommodation** beaucoup d'étudiants louent des logements.

accord [ə'kɔːd] *noun*

➤ **to do something of one's own accord** faire quelque chose de son propre chef : **I did it of my own accord** je l'ai fait de mon propre chef.

according to [ə'kɔːdɪŋtuː] *preposition*

d'après, selon : **according to her** d'après elle ; **according to the rules** d'après les règles

➤ **everything went according to plan** tout s'est passé comme prévu.

account [ə'kaʊnt] *noun*

1. compte *(masculine)* : **a bank account** un compte bancaire OR un compte en banque
2. compte rendu *(masculine)* : **he gave us an account of his adventures** il nous a fait le compte rendu de ses aventures

➤ **to take something into account** prendre quelque chose en compte.

accountant [ə'kaʊntənt] *noun*

comptable *(masculine or feminine)* : **Tanya's father is an accountant** le père de Tanya est comptable.

accurate ['ækjʊrət] *adjective*

exact : **it's an accurate description** c'est une description exacte.

accuse [ə'kjuːz] *verb*

accuser : **she accused him of lying** elle l'a accusé d'avoir menti ; **they accused him of murder** ils l'ont accusé de meurtre.

ace [eɪs] *noun*

as *(masculine)* : **the ace of clubs** l'as de trèfle.

ache [eɪk] *noun & verb*

■ *noun*
douleur *(feminine)* : **aches and pains** des douleurs

■ *verb*
my head aches j'ai mal à la tête.

achieve [ə'tʃiːv] *verb*

1. réaliser : **she achieved her ambition** elle a réalisé son ambition
2. obtenir : **he achieved success** il a obtenu du succès

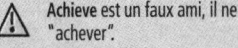 Achieve est un faux ami, il ne signifie pas "achever".

achievement [ə'tʃiːvmənt] *noun*

réussite *(feminine)* : **it's a real achievement** c'est une vraie réussite.

acid ['æsɪd] *noun*

acide *(masculine)*.

acne ['æknɪ] *uncountable noun*

acné *(feminine)* : **Myrtle has acne** Myrtle a de l'acné.

acquainted [ə'kweɪntɪd] *adjective*

to be acquainted with somebody connaître quelqu'un.

acrobat ['ækrəbæt] *noun*

acrobate *(masculine or feminine)*.

across [ə'krɒs] *preposition & adverb*

■ *preposition*

there's a bridge across the river il y a un pont sur la rivière ; **the house across the road** la maison d'en face

> When 'across' is used with a verb of movement (to walk across, to run across), you can use a verb alone in French to translate it:

I walked across the street j'ai traversé la rue ; **don't run across the road** ne traverse pas la route en courant
■ *adverb*
the river is 2 km across la rivière fait 2 km de large ; **he ran across** il a traversé en courant.

act [ækt] *noun & verb*
■ *noun*
1. **acte** *(masculine)* : **the ghost appears in the second act** le fantôme apparaît dans le deuxième acte
2. **numéro** *(masculine)* : **a circus act** un numéro de cirque
■ *verb*
1. **agir** : **we must act quickly** il faut agir vite
2. **jouer** : **have you ever acted in a play?** as-tu déjà joué dans une pièce de théâtre ?

action ['ækʃn] *noun*
action *(feminine)* : **we must take action** il faut agir ; **a film with lots of action** un film avec beaucoup d'action
➤ **an action movie** un film d'action.

active ['æktɪv] *adjective*
actif *(feminine* **active)** : **he's very active** il est très actif
➤ **an active volcano** un volcan en activité.

activity [æk'tɪvətɪ] *noun*
activité *(feminine)* : **the club offers many outdoor activities** le club propose de nombreuses activités de plein air.

actor ['æktər] *noun*
acteur *(masculine)* : **he's an actor** il est acteur.

actress ['æktrɪs] *noun*
actrice *(feminine)* : **she's an actress** elle est actrice.

actual ['æktʃʊəl] *adjective*
réel *(feminine* **réelle)** : **what are your actual reasons?** quelles sont vos raisons réelles ? ; **the actual ceremony starts at ten** la cérémonie proprement dite commence à dix heures

> ⚠ Actual est un faux ami, il ne signifie pas "actuel".

actually ['æktʃʊəlɪ] *adverb*
1. **vraiment** : **it's not actually raining** il ne pleut pas vraiment
2. **en fait** : **actually I do know the answer** en fait, je connais la réponse

> ⚠ Actually est un faux ami, il ne signifie pas "actuellement".

acute [ə'kjuːt] *adjective*
aigu *(feminine* **aiguë)** : **an acute pain** une douleur aiguë ; **an e acute** un e accent aigu.

ad [æd] *(abbreviation of* advertisement) *noun informal*
1. **annonce** *(feminine)* : **a newspaper ad** une annonce dans le journal
2. **pub** *(feminine)* : **he likes TV ads** il aime bien les pubs à la télé

AD [eɪdiː] *(abbreviation of* Anno Domini)
apr. J.-C. : **in 2000 AD** en 2000 apr. J.-C.

adapt [ə'dæpt] *verb*
s'adapter : **he has adapted well to his new school** il s'est bien adapté à sa nouvelle école.

add [æd] *verb*
1. **ajouter** : **add some sugar to the mixture** ajoutez du sucre au mélange
2. **additionner** : **she added the numbers together** elle a additionné les chiffres

add up *phrasal verb*
additionner : **add the numbers up** additionnez les chiffres.

adder ['ædər] *noun*
vipère *(feminine)*.

addict ['ædɪkt] *noun*
he's a drug addict c'est un drogué OR c'est un toxicomane ; **she's a TV addict** c'est une mordue de la télé.

addicted [ə'dɪktɪd] *adjective*
to be addicted to drugs être drogué OR être toxicomane ; **he's addicted to jogging** c'est un mordu de jogging.

addition [ə'dɪʃn] *noun*
addition *(feminine)*

> **in addition to** en plus de : **there are some extras to pay in addition to the price** il y a des suppléments à payer en plus du prix.

additive ['ædɪtɪv] *noun*

additif *(masculine)* : **food additives** des additifs alimentaires.

address [ə'dres] *noun*

adresse *(feminine)* : **what's your address?** quelle est votre adresse ?

> **an address book** un carnet d'adresses.

adjective ['ædʒɪktɪv] *noun*

adjectif *(masculine)* : **'happy' and 'sad' are adjectives** les mots « heureux » et « triste » sont des adjectifs.

adjust [ə'dʒʌst] *verb*

1. **ajuster, régler** : **he adjusted the volume** il a réglé le volume
2. **s'adapter** : **I adjusted to the new situation** je me suis adapté à la nouvelle situation.

administration [əd͵mɪnɪ'streɪʃn] *noun*

1. **administration** *(feminine)* : **the administration of a company** l'administration d'une entreprise
2. **gouvernement** *(masculine)* : **the Clinton administration** le gouvernement Clinton.

admire [əd'maɪər] *verb*

admirer : **he admires his teacher** il admire son professeur.

admission [əd'mɪʃn] *noun*

entrée *(feminine)* : **admission to the museum is free** l'entrée du musée est gratuite.

admit [əd'mɪt] *verb*

1. **reconnaître** : **I admit that I'm wrong** je reconnais que j'ai tort
2. **avouer** : **the accused admits stealing the car** l'accusé avoue avoir volé la voiture
> **to be admitted to hospital** être admis à l'hôpital.

adolescent [͵ædə'lesnt] *noun*

adolescent *(masculine)*, **adolescente** *(feminine)*.

adopt [ə'dɒpt] *verb*

adopter : **he was adopted** il a été adopté.

adore [ə'dɔːr] *verb*

adorer : **I adore chocolate** j'adore le chocolat.

adult ['ædʌlt] *noun*

adulte *(masculine or feminine)* : **he's an adult** c'est un adulte.

advance [*UK* əd'vɑːns, *US* əd'væns] *noun & verb*

■ *noun*

1. **avancée** *(feminine)* : **the enemy's advance** l'avancée de l'ennemi
2. **progrès** *(masculine)* : **there have been great advances in technology** il y a eu de grands progrès dans le domaine de la technologie
> **in advance** à l'avance : **we reserved our seats in advance** nous avons réservé nos places à l'avance

■ *verb*

avancer : **the soldiers are advancing** les soldats avancent.

advanced [*UK* əd'vɑːnst, *US* əd'vænst] *adjective*

an advanced course in computing un cours de niveau supérieur en informatique.

advantage [*UK* əd'vɑːntɪdʒ, *US* əd'væntɪdʒ] *noun*

avantage *(masculine)* : **what are the advantages?** quels sont les avantages ?

> **to take advantage of something** profiter de quelque chose.

adventure [əd'ventʃər] *noun*

aventure *(feminine)*

> **an adventure playground** *UK* une aire de jeux.

adverb ['ædvɜːb] *noun*

adverbe *(masculine)* : **"quickly" is an adverb** « vite » est un adverbe.

advert *UK* ['ædvɜːt] *noun*

1. **annonce** *(feminine)* : **he put an advert in the newspaper** il a mis une annonce dans le journal
2. **pub** *(feminine)* : **I like watching adverts on the TV** j'aime regarder les pubs à la télé.

advertise ['ædvətaɪz] *verb*

1. **faire de la publicité** : **they advertise on TV** ils font de la publicité à la télé
2. **faire de la publicité pour** : **a lot of companies advertise their products on the Internet** de nombreuses entreprises font de la publicité pour leurs produits sur Internet.

advertisement [UK əd'vɜːtɪsmənt, US ædvər'taɪzmənt] noun

1. **annonce** (feminine) : **he put an advertisement in the newspaper** il a passé une annonce dans le journal
2. **publicité** (feminine) : **a TV advertisement** une publicité à la télévision.

advice [əd'vaɪs] uncountable noun

conseils (masculine plural) : **can you give me some advice?** peux-tu me donner des conseils ?
> **a piece of advice** un conseil : **it was a good piece of advice** c'était un bon conseil.

advise [əd'vaɪz] verb

conseiller : **to advise somebody to do something** conseiller à quelqu'un de faire quelque chose ; **he advised me to wait** il m'a conseillé d'attendre ; **he advised me not to go** il m'a conseillé de ne pas y aller.

adviser UK, **advisor** US [əd'vaɪzər] noun

conseiller (masculine), **conseillère** (feminine).

aerial UK ['eərɪəl] noun

antenne (feminine) : **a television aerial** une antenne de télévision.

aerobics [eə'rəʊbɪks] noun

aérobic (masculine) : **she does aerobics** elle fait de l'aérobic.

aeroplane UK ['eərəpleɪn] noun

avion (masculine).

aerosol ['eərəsɒl] noun

aérosol (masculine)
> **an aerosol can** une bombe aérosol.

affect [ə'fekt] verb

1. **avoir un effet sur** : **pollution affects the environment** la pollution a un effet sur l'environnement
2. **toucher** : **these problems affect a lot of people** ces problèmes touchent un grand nombre de personnes.

affectionate [ə'fekʃənət] adjective

affectueux (feminine **affectueuse**).

afford [ə'fɔːd] verb

> **to be able to afford something** avoir les moyens d'acheter quelque chose : **I can't afford a new car** je n'ai pas les moyens d'acheter une nouvelle voiture ; **I can't afford the time** je n'ai pas le temps.

afraid [ə'freɪd] adjective

> **to be afraid**
1. **avoir peur** : **I'm afraid of the dark** j'ai peur du noir ; **she's afraid of going out alone** elle a peur de sortir seule ; **I'm afraid so** j'ai bien peur que oui
2. **regretter** : **I'm afraid I can't come** je regrette de ne pas pouvoir venir.

Africa ['æfrɪkə] noun

l'Afrique (feminine)

In French the names of continents are used with the definite article l', except when they follow the preposition en:

Africa is a continent l'Afrique est un continent ; **the Sahara is in Africa** le Sahara est en Afrique ; **she's going to Africa** elle va en Afrique.

African ['æfrɪkən] adjective & noun

■ adjective
africain

The French adjective does not start with a capital letter:

the African bush la brousse africaine
■ noun
Africain (masculine), **Africaine** (feminine).

after [UK 'ɑːftər, US 'æftər] preposition, conjunction & adverb

■ preposition
après : **after you!** après vous ! ; **we'll leave after breakfast** nous partirons après le petit déjeuner
> **it's twenty after three** US il est trois heures vingt
■ conjunction
après que : **after I had spoken to him I left** après lui avoir parlé, je suis parti
■ adverb
après : **that comes after** ça vient après ; **the day after** le jour d'après
> **after all** après tout : **it doesn't really matter after all** après tout, ça n'a pas beaucoup d'importance.

afternoon [UK ɑːftə'nuːn, US æftə'nuːn] noun

après-midi (masculine) [plural **après-midi**] :

5

what are you doing tomorrow afternoon? que fais-tu demain après-midi ? ; **they went for a walk in the afternoon** ils sont allés se promener l'après-midi ; **I'll see you on Tuesday afternoon** je te verrai mardi après-midi

➤ **good afternoon!** bonjour !

afterwards *UK* ['ɑːftəwədz], **afterward** *US* ['æftərwərd] *adverb*

après : **they went home afterwards** ils sont rentrés chez eux après.

again [ə'gen] *adverb*

encore, encore une fois : **try calling him again** essaie de le rappeler encore ; **tell me again!** dis-le-moi encore une fois !

> Again is often translated in French by adding re- to the beginning of a verb:

she began again elle a recommencé ; **don't do it again!** ne recommence pas ! ; **I'd like to see you again** j'aimerais te revoir ; **can you read that again, please?** pouvez-vous le relire, s'il vous plaît ?

➤ **again and again** à plusieurs reprises : **he tried again and again** il a essayé à plusieurs reprises.

against [ə'genst] *preposition*

contre : **she was leaning against the wall** elle était appuyée contre le mur

➤ **it's against the rules** c'est contraire au règlement.

age [eɪdʒ] *noun*

1. âge *(masculine)* : **you can leave school at the age of 16** on peut quitter l'école à l'âge de 16 ans
2. **it took ages to download** cela a pris des heures pour télécharger ; **I haven't seen him for ages** je ne l'ai pas vu depuis une éternité

> 📖 AGE
> Comme en France, on peut voter aux États-Unis et en Grande-Bretagne à partir de 18 ans. En revanche, on peut conduire dès l'âge de 17 ans en Grande-Bretagne et de 16 ans aux États-Unis. Il faut avoir au moins 16 ans en Grande-Bretagne et 21 ans aux États-Unis pour avoir le droit de boire de l'alcool dans un bar.

agency ['eɪdʒənsɪ] *noun*

agence *(feminine)* : **a travel agency** une agence

de voyages ; **an employment agency** un bureau de placement.

aggressive [ə'gresɪv] *adjective*

agressif *(feminine* **aggressive***)*.

ago [ə'gəʊ] *adverb*

il y a : **it was a long time ago** c'était il y a longtemps ; **she left three years ago** elle est partie il y a trois ans.

agree [ə'griː] *verb*

1. être d'accord : **I agree with you** je suis d'accord avec vous ; **I don't agree** je ne suis pas d'accord
2. accepter : **Gary agreed to go** Gary a accepté d'y aller
3. se mettre d'accord : **they agreed to share the costs** ils se sont mis d'accord pour partager les frais.

agreement [ə'griːmənt] *noun*

accord *(masculine)* : **we've reached an agreement** nous sommes parvenus à un accord.

ahead [ə'hed] *adverb*

1. devant : **look straight ahead** regarde droit devant ; **he was ahead of me** il était devant moi
2. en avant : **they sent him on ahead** on l'a envoyé en avant
3. en avance : **the work is ahead of schedule** le travail est en avance sur le planning ; **Scotland are ahead by two goals to one** l'Écosse mène par deux buts à un
4. à l'avance : **we have to book ahead** il faut réserver à l'avance.

aid [eɪd] *noun*

aide *(feminine)* : **the refugees received aid from the government** les réfugiés ont reçu une aide du gouvernement.

AIDS, Aids [eɪdz] *(abbreviation of* acquired immune deficiency syndrome*) noun*

SIDA *(masculine)*, sida *(masculine)* : **he has AIDS** il a le sida.

aim [eɪm] *noun & verb*

■ *noun*
but *(masculine)* : **I did it with the aim of saving him** je l'ai fait dans le but de le sauver

➤ **to take aim** viser
■ *verb*
braquer : **to aim a gun at somebody** braquer un pistolet sur quelqu'un

> **to aim at somebody** viser quelqu'un : **she aimed at me** elle m'a visé
> **to aim to do something** avoir l'intention de faire quelque chose : **I aim to help him** j'ai l'intention de l'aider.

air [eə^r] *noun*

   air *(masculine)* : **he threw the ball into the air** il a jeté la balle en l'air
> **by air** en avion : **to travel by air** voyager en avion
> **the air force** l'armée de l'air
> **an air hostess** *UK* une hôtesse de l'air : **she's an air hostess** elle est hôtesse de l'air
> **an air raid** un raid aérien
> **an air steward** un steward : **he's an air steward** il est steward
> **an air terminal** une aérogare.

air-conditioning [eə^rkən'dıʃnıŋ] *noun*

   climatisation *(feminine)*.

airline ['eəlaɪn] *noun*

   compagnie *(feminine)* aérienne.

airmail ['eəmeɪl] *noun*

   poste *(feminine)* aérienne : **by airmail** par avion.

airplane *US* ['eəpleɪn] *noun*

   avion *(masculine)*.

airport ['eəpɔːt] *noun*

   aéroport *(masculine)* : **they met me at the airport** ils m'attendaient à l'aéroport.

aisle [aɪl] *noun*

1. **allée** *(feminine)* : **a supermarket aisle** une allée de supermarché
2. **couloir** *(masculine)* : **an aisle seat in a plane** une place côté couloir dans un avion.

ajar [ə'dʒɑː^r] *adjective*

   entrouvert : **the door is ajar** la porte est entrouverte.

alarm [ə'lɑːm] *noun*

   alarme *(feminine)* : **I raised the alarm** j'ai donné l'alarme ; **a fire alarm** une sirène d'incendie
> **an alarm clock** un réveil : **I'll set the alarm for 7 a.m.** je vais mettre le réveil pour 7 heures du matin.

album ['ælbəm] *noun*

   album *(masculine)* : **Garbage's new album** le nouvel album de Garbage.

alcohol ['ælkəhɒl] *noun*

   alcool *(masculine)*.

A level ['eɪlevl] *(abbreviation of* Advanced level*) noun*
   examen de fin d'études secondaires en Angleterre, au pays de Galles et en Irlande, équivalant au baccalauréat français.

alien ['eɪljən] *noun*

1. extraterrestre *(masculine or feminine)* : **an alien from outer space** un extraterrestre, une extraterrestre
2. étranger *(masculine)*, étrangère *(feminine)* : **illegal aliens** des étrangers en situation irrégulière.

alike [ə'laɪk] *adverb*

> **to look alike** OR **to be alike** se ressembler : **they really look alike** ils se ressemblent beaucoup.

alive [ə'laɪv] *adjective*

   vivant : **is he still alive?** est-il encore vivant ?

all [ɔːl] *adjective, pronoun & adverb*

   ▪ *adjective & pronoun*
   tout *(feminine* **toute***, masculine plural* **tous***, feminine plural* **toutes***)*

   > Remember that French adjectives must agree in gender (**masculine** or **feminine**) and number (**singular** or **plural**) with the noun they refer to:

   she laughs all the time elle rit tout le temps ; **they danced all night** ils ont dansé toute la nuit ; **he lost all his money** il a perdu tout son argent ; **all of the girls were laughing** toutes les filles riaient ; **we all want to help** nous voulons tous aider ; **I've invited all of them** je les ai tous invités
   ▪ *adverb*
1. **tout** : **he was all wet** il était tout mouillé ; **tell me all about it** raconte-moi tout ; **all you need is love!** tout ce qu'il te faut, c'est de l'amour ! ; **that was all he said** c'est tout ce qu'il a dit
2. **partout** : **the score was 3 all** on en était à 3 partout
> **all alone** tout seul : **the boys are all alone**

les garçons sont tout seuls ; **she was all alone** elle était toute seule

➤ **not at all** pas du tout : **I didn't like the film at all** je n'ai pas du tout aimé le film

➤ **all the more** d'autant plus : **it's all the more difficult** c'est d'autant plus difficile.

allergic [ə'lɜːdʒɪk] *adjective*

allergique : **he's allergic to antibiotics** il est allergique aux antibiotiques.

allergy ['ælədʒɪ] *noun*

allergie *(feminine)*.

alley ['ælɪ], **alleyway** ['ælɪweɪ] *noun*

ruelle *(feminine)*.

alligator ['ælɪgeɪtər] *noun*

alligator *(masculine)*.

allow [ə'laʊ] *verb*

permettre, autoriser : **to allow someone to do something** autoriser quelqu'un à faire quelque chose OR permettre à quelqu'un de faire quelque chose ; **are you allowed to go out alone?** es-tu autorisé à sortir seul ?

all right ['ɔːlraɪt] *adverb*

1. bien : **it works all right** ça marche bien ; **are you all right?** tu te sens bien ? OR ça va ?

2. sain et sauf *(feminine* saine et sauve*)* : **she had an accident but she's all right** elle a eu un accident mais elle est saine et sauve

3. d'accord : **shall we go? – all right!** on y va ? – d'accord !

4. pas mal : **did you like the film ? – it was all right** as-tu aimé le film ? – c'était pas mal

5. sorry – **that's all right** excusez-moi – ce n'est pas grave.

almond ['ɑːmənd] *noun*

amande *(feminine)*.

almost ['ɔːlməʊst] *adverb*

presque : **I've almost finished** j'ai presque terminé

➤ **I almost missed the bus** j'ai failli rater le bus.

alone [ə'ləʊn] *adjective & adverb*

seul : **he's all alone** il est tout seul ; **she went out alone** elle est sortie seule

➤ **leave me alone!** laisse-moi tranquille !

➤ **leave my things alone!** ne touche pas à mes affaires !

along [ə'lɒŋ] *adverb & preposition*

■ *adverb*

to walk along se promener ; **to move along** avancer ; **can I come along with you?** est-ce que je peux venir avec vous ?

➤ **all along** depuis le début : **he was in his room all along** il était dans sa chambre depuis le début

■ *preposition*

le long de : **I walked along the beach** je me suis promené le long de la plage.

aloud [ə'laʊd] *adverb*

à voix haute : **he was reading aloud** il lisait à voix haute.

alphabet ['ælfəbet] *noun*

alphabet *(masculine)*.

alphabetical [ˌælfə'betɪkl] *adjective*

alphabétique : **they're in alphabetical order** ils sont dans l'ordre alphabétique.

Alps [ælps] *plural noun*

the Alps les Alpes *(feminine plural)* .

already [ɔːl'redɪ] *adverb*

déjà : **he has already left** il est déjà parti.

alright ➤ all right.

Alsatian *UK* [æl'seɪʃn] *noun*

berger *(masculine)* allemand.

also ['ɔːlsəʊ] *adverb*

aussi : **he also speaks Spanish** il parle aussi espagnol.

alternate [*UK* ɔːl'tɜːnət, *US* 'ɔːltərnət] *adjective*

on alternate days tous les deux jours.

alternative [ɔːl'tɜːnətɪv] *adjective & noun*

■ *adjective*

autre : **there's an alternative route** il y a une autre route

➤ **alternative medicine** médecine *(feminine)* parallèle OR médecine *(feminine)* douce

■ *noun*

choix *(masculine)* : **I have no alternative** je n'ai pas le choix.

although [ɔːl'ðəʊ] *conjunction*

bien que : **she has gone to school although she is ill** elle est allée à l'école bien qu'elle soit malade

The conjunction **bien que** is followed by a verb in the subjunctive.

altogether [ˌɔːltə'geðər] *adverb*

1. **tout à fait : that's not altogether true** ce n'est pas tout à fait juste
2. **en tout : how much is it altogether?** c'est combien en tout ?

aluminium *UK* [ˌæljʊ'mɪnɪəm], **aluminum** *US* [ə'luːmɪnəm] *noun*

aluminium *(masculine)*
> **aluminium foil** papier *(masculine)* alu.

always ['ɔːlweɪz] *adverb*

toujours : **she's always late** elle est toujours en retard.

am [æm] ➤ **be**

I am tired je suis fatigué ; **I am reading** je lis.

a.m. [eɪem]
> **at 3 a.m.** à 3 heures du matin.

amazed [ə'meɪzd] *adjective*

stupéfait : **I was amazed to see her** j'étais stupéfait de la voir.

amazing [ə'meɪzɪŋ] *adjective*

1. **étonnant : it's an amazing story** c'est une histoire étonnante
2. **excellent : he's an amazing player** c'est un excellent joueur.

amber ['æmbər] *noun & adjective*

ambre *(masculine)* : **an amber ring** une bague en ambre
> **an amber light** *UK* un feu orange.

ambition [æm'bɪʃn] *noun*

ambition *(feminine)* : **her ambition is to be an astronaut** son ambition est d'être astronaute.

ambitious [æm'bɪʃəs] *adjective*

ambitieux *(feminine* ambitieuse*)* : **John is very ambitious** John est très ambitieux.

ambulance ['æmbjʊləns] *noun*

ambulance *(feminine)*.

America [ə'merɪkə] *noun*

l'Amérique *(feminine)*

In French the names of continents are used with the definite article **l'**, except when they follow the preposition **en**:

America is a continent l'Amérique est un continent ; **I'm going to America** je vais en Amérique ; **Las Vegas is in America** Las Vegas est en Amérique

> AMERICA
Pour parler des États-Unis d'Amérique **(the United States of America)**, on se contente souvent de dire **America**. Cependant, le terme **America** évoque aussi le continent américain qui comprend l'Amérique du Nord (c'est-à-dire les États-Unis d'Amérique, le Canada et le Mexique) et toute l'Amérique latine. Le mot **America** vient du prénom de l'explorateur Amerigo Vespucci qui, en 1499, fut le premier à affirmer que l'Amérique était un continent.

American [ə'merɪkn] *adjective & noun*

■ *adjective*
américain

The French adjective does not start with a capital letter:

he has an American accent il a un accent américain
> **the American Revolution** la guerre d'Indépendance
■ *noun*
Américain *(masculine)*, **Américaine** *(feminine)* ; ➤ **Civil War**

> THE AMERICAN REVOLUTION
On désigne ainsi la guerre qui opposa les Américains aux Anglais de 1775 à 1783. Les Américains voulaient être indépendants, notamment pour ne plus avoir à payer d'impôts à l'Angleterre. Le 4 juillet 1776, Thomas Jefferson, futur président, signa la Déclaration d'indépendance, mais l'Angleterre la refusa et la guerre continua. George Washington, aidé de soldats français, menait les troupes américaines, et en 1783 la paix fut signée : les États-Unis d'Amérique étaient nés.

among [ə'mʌŋ] *preposition*

parmi : **there are children among the crowd** il y a des enfants parmi la foule.

amount [ə'maʊnt] *noun*

1. quantité *(feminine)* : **there was a large**

amount of cream il y avait une grande quantité de crème

2. somme (feminine) : **he has a large amount of money** il a une grosse somme d'argent.

amp [æmp] noun

1. ampli (masculine) : **'amp' is short for amplifier** « amp » est l'abréviation de « amplifier »

2. ampère (masculine) : **a thirteen-amp fuse** un fusible de treize ampères.

amuse [ə'mju:z] verb

amuser : **the joke amused him** la plaisanterie l'a amusé.

amusement arcade UK [ə'mju:zmənt-ɑː'keɪd] noun

galerie (feminine) **de jeux**.

amusement park [ə'mju:zməntpɑːk] noun

parc (masculine) **d'attractions**.

an indefinite article ➤ a.

anaesthetic UK, **anesthetic** US [ˌænɪs-'θetɪk] noun

anesthésie (feminine) : **he's under anaesthetic** il est sous anesthésie.

analyse UK, **analyze** US ['ænəlaɪz] verb

analyser.

ancestor ['ænsestər] noun

ancêtre (masculine or feminine).

anchor ['æŋkər] noun

ancre (feminine) : **they dropped anchor** ils ont jeté l'ancre.

ancient ['eɪnʃənt] adjective

ancien (feminine **ancienne**) : **it's an ancient monument** c'est un monument ancien.

and [ænd, ənd] conjunction

et : **your father and mother** ton père et ta mère ; **six and a half years** six ans et demi

When giving numbers with 'a hundred' and 'a thousand', the 'and' is not translated in French:

one hundred and twenty cent vingt ; **two thousand and ten** deux mille dix

➤ **come and see!** viens voir ! ; **try and come** essaie de venir

➤ **and so on, and so forth** et ainsi de suite.

anesthetic US ➤ anaesthetic.

angel ['eɪndʒəl] noun

ange (masculine).

anger ['æŋgər] noun

colère (feminine) : **he's shaking with anger** il tremble de colère.

angle ['æŋgl] noun

angle (masculine) : **a triangle has three angles** un triangle a trois angles.

angry ['æŋgrɪ] adjective

en colère : **I'm angry with him** je suis en colère contre lui

➤ **to get angry** se mettre en colère OR se fâcher : **she got angry** elle s'est mise en colère OR elle s'est fâchée.

animal ['ænɪml] noun

animal (masculine) [plural **animaux**] : **wild animals** des animaux sauvages.

ankle ['æŋkl] noun

cheville (feminine) : **he has twisted his ankle** il s'est foulé la cheville.

anniversary [ˌænɪ'vɜːsərɪ] noun

anniversaire (masculine) : **it's their wedding anniversary** c'est leur anniversaire de mariage.

announce [ə'naʊns] verb

annoncer : **they announced the news** ils ont annoncé la nouvelle.

announcement [ə'naʊnsmənt] noun

annonce (feminine) : **the president made an announcement** le président a fait une annonce.

annoy [ə'nɔɪ] verb

agacer : **you're annoying me!** tu m'agaces !

annoyed [ə'nɔɪd] adjective

fâché : **he's annoyed with me** il est fâché contre moi ; **I got annoyed with her** je me suis fâché avec elle.

annoying [ə'nɔɪɪŋ] adjective

agaçant : **it's very annoying** c'est très agaçant.

annual ['ænjʊəl] adjective

annuel (feminine **annuelle**).

anonymous [ə'nɒnɪməs] adjective

anonyme.

another [ə'nʌðəʳ] *adjective & pronoun*

1. encore un, un autre : **would you like another drink?** voulez-vous encore un verre ? ; **he ate another apple** il a mangé une autre pomme ; **can I have another?** est-ce que je peux en avoir un autre ?
2. un autre : **he's looking for another job** il cherche un autre travail
➣ **one another** l'un l'autre ; **they love one another** ils s'aiment.

answer [*UK* 'ɑːnsəʳ, *US* 'ænsəʳ] *noun & verb*

◼ *noun*
1. réponse *(feminine)* : **I'm waiting for an answer** j'attends une réponse
2. solution *(feminine)* : **there's no answer to the problem** il n'y a pas de solution au problème
◼ *verb*
répondre : **she didn't answer** elle n'a pas répondu ; **can you answer the phone?** pouvez-vous répondre au téléphone ?
➣ **to answer the door** aller ouvrir la porte.

answering machine [*UK* 'ɑːnsərɪŋ mə'ʃiːn, *US* 'ænsərɪŋ mə'ʃiːn] *noun*
répondeur *(masculine)*.

ant [ænt] *noun*
fourmi *(feminine)*.

Antarctic [æn'tɑːktɪk] *noun*
the Antarctic l'Antarctique *(masculine)* .

anthem ['ænθəm] *noun*
hymne *(masculine)* : **the national anthem** l'hymne national.

antibiotic [ˌæntɪbaɪ'ɒtɪk] *noun*
antibiotique *(masculine)* : **I'm on antibiotics** je suis sous antibiotiques.

anticlockwise *UK* [ˌæntɪ'klɒkwaɪz] *adjective & adverb*
dans le sens inverse des aiguilles d'une montre.

antique [æn'tiːk] *adjective*
objet *(masculine)* ancien : **it's an antique** c'est un objet ancien
➣ **an antique shop** un magasin d'antiquités.

antiseptic [ˌæntɪ'septɪk] *noun*
antiseptique *(masculine)*.

anxious ['æŋkʃəs] *adjective*
très inquiet *(feminine* très inquiète*)* : **I'm very anxious about the exam** je suis très inquiet à propos de l'examen
➣ **to be anxious to do something**   tenir beaucoup à faire quelque chose : **I'm anxious to meet him** je tiens beaucoup à le rencontrer.

any ['enɪ] *adjective, pronoun & adverb*

◼ *adjective*
1. *In questions or conditional sentences* du *(before a vowel* de l'*) (feminine* de la*)* : **have you got any bread?** est-ce que tu as du pain ? ; **do you want any cream?** voulez-vous de la crème ? ; **is there any water?** est-ce qu'il y a de l'eau ? ; **are there any famous people here?** est-ce qu'il y a des gens célèbres ici ? ; **call me if you want any help** appelle-moi si tu veux de l'aide
2. *In negative sentences* de *(d' before a vowel)* : **there isn't any ice cream** il n'y a pas de glace ; **I haven't got any money** je n'ai pas d'argent
3. *When 'any' means 'whichever'* n'importe quel *(feminine* n'importe quelle*)* : **any glass will do** n'importe quel verre fera l'affaire ; **you can listen to any station you like** tu peux écouter n'importe quelle radio
◼ *pronoun*
en : **is there any left?** est-ce qu'il en reste ? ; **I don't want any of it** je n'en veux pas ; **I don't have any** je n'en ai pas
◼ *adverb*
is he any better? est-ce qu'il va mieux ? ; **I can't go any faster** je ne peux pas aller plus vite
➣ **any more** : **is there any more?** est-ce qu'il en reste ? ; **do you want any more?** tu en veux encore ? ; **I don't want any more** je n'en veux plus ; **she doesn't live here any more** elle n'habite plus ici

⚠ En anglais britannique, any more s'écrit habituellement en deux mots. En anglais américain, il s'écrit souvent en un seul mot : she doesn't live here anymore "elle n'habite plus ici".

anybody ['enɪˌbɒdɪ], **anyone** ['enɪwʌn] *pronoun*
1. personne : **I can't see anybody** je ne vois personne
2. quelqu'un : **is there anybody there?** y a-t-il quelqu'un ?
3. n'importe qui : **anybody can do it** n'importe qui peut le faire.

anyhow *adverb* ➣ anyway.

anymore US ['enɪmɔːr] adverb ➤ any.

anyone pronoun ➤ anybody.

anyplace US ➤ anywhere.

anything ['enɪθɪŋ] pronoun
1. **rien** : I can't see anything je ne vois rien
2. **quelque chose** : can I do anything? est-ce que je peux faire quelque chose ?
3. **n'importe quoi** : anything can happen il peut arriver n'importe quoi.

anyway ['enɪweɪ], **anyhow** ['enɪhaʊ] adverb
de toute façon : I don't want to go, and anyway it's too late je ne veux pas y aller, et de toute façon, il est trop tard.

anywhere ['enɪweər], **anyplace** US ['enɪpleɪs] adverb
1. **nulle part** : I can't find him anywhere je ne le trouve nulle part
2. **quelque part** : have you seen him anywhere? est-ce que tu l'as vu quelque part ?
3. **n'importe où** : put it down anywhere pose-le n'importe où.

apart [ə'pɑːt] adverb
we kept them apart nous les avions séparés ; **they are two metres apart** ils sont séparés l'un de l'autre par une distance de deux mètres
➤ **apart from** à part : apart from that, you're right à part ça, tu as raison.

apartment [ə'pɑːtmənt] noun
appartement (masculine) : she lives in an apartment elle habite un appartement
➤ **an apartment building** un immeuble d'habitation.

apologize, apologise UK [ə'pɒlədʒaɪz] verb
s'excuser : he apologized il s'est excusé ; she apologized for being late elle s'est excusée d'être en retard ; they apologized to me ils m'ont présenté leurs excuses.

apology [ə'pɒlədʒɪ] noun
excuses (feminine plural) : she made an apology elle a fait ses excuses.

apostrophe [ə'pɒstrəfɪ] noun
apostrophe (feminine).

apparatus [UK ˌæpə'reɪtəs, US ˌæpə-'rætəs] noun
agrès (masculine plural) : the children are playing on the apparatus les enfants jouent sur les agrès.

apparently [ə'pærəntlɪ] adverb
apparemment : apparently she doesn't live here anymore apparemment, elle n'habite plus ici.

appeal [ə'piːl] verb
1. **to appeal to somebody** plaire à quelqu'un ; it appeals to me ça me plaît
2. **they appealed for help** ils ont lancé un appel au secours.

appear [ə'pɪər] verb
1. **apparaître** : he suddenly appeared il est apparu soudain
2. **sembler, paraître** : she appears to be sleeping elle semble dormir.

appearance [ə'pɪərəns] noun
apparence (feminine) : don't judge by appearances ne vous fiez pas aux apparences.

appetite ['æpɪtaɪt] noun
appétit (masculine) : Dudley has a big appetite Dudley a un gros appétit.

applaud [ə'plɔːd] verb
applaudir : everyone applauded tout le monde applaudissait.

applause [ə'plɔːz] uncountable noun
applaudissements (masculine plural) : the singer was greeted by loud applause le chanteur a reçu beaucoup d'applaudissements.

apple ['æpl] noun
pomme (feminine)
➤ **an apple pie** une tarte aux pommes
➤ **an apple tree** un pommier.

appliance [ə'plaɪəns] noun
appareil (masculine) : domestic appliances des appareils ménagers.

application [ˌæplɪ'keɪʃn] noun
demande (feminine) : he made an applica-

tion for a job il a fait une demande d'emploi OR il a posé sa candidature pour un poste
➤ **an application form** un dossier de candidature.

apply [ə'plaɪ] *verb*

1. faire une demande : **I applied for a job** j'ai fait une demande d'emploi OR j'ai posé ma candidature pour un poste
2. s'appliquer : **this rule applies to everybody** ce règlement s'applique à tout le monde.

appointment [ə'pɔɪntmənt] *noun*

rendez-vous *(masculine)* [plural **rendez-vous**] : **I made an appointment with Mr Jones** j'ai pris rendez-vous avec M. Jones ; **he has an appointment with the dentist** il a un rendez-vous chez le dentiste.

approach [ə'prəʊtʃ] *verb*

1. s'approcher : **the enemy is approaching** l'ennemi s'approche
2. s'approcher de : **we approached the summit** nous nous sommes approchés du sommet
3. aborder : **we must approach the problem in a different way** nous devons aborder le problème d'une autre façon.

appropriate [ə'prəʊprɪət] *adjective*

approprié : **those shoes aren't appropriate for climbing** ces chaussures ne sont pas appropriées pour l'escalade.

approve [ə'pruːv] *verb*

approuver
➤ **to approve of something** approuver quelque chose : **I don't approve of his ideas** je n'approuve pas ses idées.

approximately [ə'prɒksɪmətlɪ] *adverb*

à peu près : **it costs approximately twenty euros** ça coûte à peu près vingt euros.

apricot ['eɪprɪkɒt] *noun*

abricot *(masculine)*.

April ['eɪprəl] *noun*

avril *(masculine)* : **in April** en avril ; **on April 17th** le 17 avril ; **next April** en avril prochain ; **last April** en avril dernier

In French the months of the year do not start with a capital letter:

➤ **April Fool's Day** le 1er avril

 APRIL FOOL'S DAY
En Grande-Bretagne et aux États-Unis, le 1er avril, les gens se font des farces. Même la radio et les journaux diffusent des canulars. En revanche, la tradition du poisson d'avril n'existe pas.

apron ['eɪprən] *noun*

tablier *(masculine)* : **the cook is wearing an apron** le cuisinier porte un tablier.

aquarium [ə'kweərɪəm] *noun*

aquarium *(masculine)*.

Aquarius [ə'kweərɪəs] *noun*

Verseau *(masculine)* : **I'm an Aquarius** je suis Verseau.

aquarobics [ˌækwə'rəʊbɪks] *noun*

aquagym *(feminine)*.

Arab ['ærəb] *adjective & noun*

■ *adjective*
arabe

The French adjective does not start with a capital letter:

the Arab countries les pays arabes
■ *noun*
Arabe *(masculine or feminine)* : **the Arabs** les Arabes.

Arabic ['ærəbɪk] *adjective & noun*

■ *adjective*
arabe : **Arabic numerals** les chiffres arabes
■ *noun*
arabe : **she speaks Arabic** elle parle arabe

Remember not to use a capital letter for the adjective and the language in French.

arcade [ɑː'keɪd] *noun*

galerie *(feminine)* : **a shopping arcade** une galerie marchande
➤ **an arcade game** un jeu d'arcade.

archaeologist , **archeologist**   US
[ˌɑːkɪ'ɒlədʒɪst] *noun*
archéologue *(masculine or feminine)* : **Paul is an archaeologist** Paul est archéologue.

archaeology , **archeology**   US
[ˌɑːkɪ'ɒlədʒɪ] *noun*
archéologie *(feminine)*.

a

architect ['ɑːkɪtekt] *noun*

architecte *(masculine or feminine)* : **Marion is an architect** Marion est architecte.

architecture ['ɑːkɪtektʃəʳ] *noun*

architecture *(feminine)*.

Arctic ['ɑːktɪk] *noun*

the Arctic l'Arctique *(masculine)* .

are [əʳ, ɑːʳ] ➤ be

where are you going? où vas-tu ? ; **we are very happy** nous sommes très heureux ; **they are my friends** ils sont mes amis.

area ['eərɪə] *noun*

1. région *(feminine)* : **he lives in the London area** il vit dans la région de Londres
2. quartier *(masculine)* : **I like this area of town** j'aime bien ce quartier
3. superficie *(feminine)* : **the room has an area of 20 m²** la pièce a une superficie de 20 m²
➤ **the area code** l'indicatif de zone : **the area code for Paris is 1** l'indicatif de zone pour Paris est 1.

aren't [ɑːnt] = are not

you aren't too late tu n'es pas trop en retard ; **we aren't coming** nous ne venons pas ; **they aren't here** ils ne sont pas là.

argue ['ɑːgjuː] *verb*

se disputer : **they're always arguing** ils se disputent tout le temps.

argument ['ɑːgjʊmənt] *noun*

dispute *(feminine)*
➤ **to have an argument** se disputer : **they had an argument** ils se sont disputés.

Aries ['eəriːz] *noun*

Bélier *(masculine)* : **I'm an Aries** je suis Bélier.

arm [ɑːm] *noun*

bras *(masculine)* : **he put his arm around her** il a passé son bras autour de ses épaules.

armchair ['ɑːmtʃeəʳ] *noun*

fauteuil *(masculine)* : **she's sitting in an armchair** elle est assise dans un fauteuil.

armour UK, **armor** US ['ɑːməʳ] *noun*

armure *(feminine)* : **a knight in armour** un chevalier revêtu de son armure.

army ['ɑːmɪ] *noun*

armée *(feminine)* : **he's in the army** il est dans l'armée.

around [ə'raʊnd] *preposition & adverb*

■ *preposition*
1. autour de : **she put her arm around his neck** elle a passé son bras autour de son cou ; **they walked around the lake** ils se sont promenés autour du lac OR ils ont fait le tour du lac
2. dans, partout dans : **we walked around the town** nous nous sommes promenés dans la ville ; **her things are lying around the room** ses affaires traînent partout dans la chambre
■ *adverb*
1. environ : **it's around 5 miles away** c'est à environ 8 kilomètres d'ici
2. vers : **I'll see you around 9 o'clock** je te verrai vers 9 heures
3. autour : **a yard with a fence all around** une cour avec une clôture tout autour
4. dans les parages : **he's somewhere around** il est dans les parages ; **he lives around here** il habite par ici
5. partout : **his clothes were lying around** ses vêtements traînaient partout.

arrange [ə'reɪndʒ] *verb*

1. disposer : **she arranged the chairs around the table** elle a disposé les chaises autour de la table
2. organiser : **they've arranged a meeting for Monday** ils ont organisé une réunion pour lundi
➤ **to arrange to do something** convenir de faire quelque chose : **we've arranged to meet at the park** nous avons convenu de nous retrouver au parc.

arrangements [ə'reɪndʒmənts] *plural noun*

dispositions *(feminine plural)* : **to make arrangements** prendre des dispositions ; **we've made arrangements to go to Spain** nous avons pris nos dispositions pour aller en Espagne.

arrest [ə'rest] *noun & verb*

■ *noun*
arrestation *(feminine)* : **you're under arrest** vous êtes en état d'arrestation
■ *verb*
arrêter : **the police arrested the thief** la police a arrêté le voleur.

arrival [əˈraɪvl] *noun*

arrivée *(feminine)* : **what's the arrival time?** quelle est l'heure d'arrivée ?

arrive [əˈraɪv] *verb*

arriver : **Uncle Tony has just arrived** l'oncle Tony vient d'arriver.

arrow [ˈærəʊ] *noun*

flèche *(feminine)*
> **the arrow key** la touche de direction.

art [ɑːt] *noun*

art *(masculine)* : **modern art** l'art moderne ; **it's a work of art** c'est une œuvre d'art.

artichoke [ˈɑːtɪtʃəʊk] *noun*

artichaut *(masculine)*.

article [ˈɑːtɪkl] *noun*

article *(masculine)*.

artificial [ˌɑːtɪˈfɪʃl] *adjective*

artificiel *(feminine* **artificielle***)* : **it's an artificial lake** c'est un lac artificiel.

artist [ˈɑːtɪst] *noun*

artiste *(masculine or feminine)* : **Tracey is an artist** Tracey est artiste.

as [əz, æz] *conjunction & adverb*

1. **au moment où** : **as he walked into the room everyone started clapping** au moment où il est entré dans la pièce, tout le monde s'est mis à applaudir
2. **comme** : **as you can see I'm very busy** comme tu le vois, je suis très occupé ; **he's late as usual** comme d'habitude, il est en retard
3. **puisque** : **as he was out, I left a message** puisqu'il n'était pas là, j'ai laissé un message
> **as ... as** aussi ... que : **he's as tall as his father** il est aussi grand que son père
> **as much as** autant que : **she doesn't earn as much as I do** elle ne gagne pas autant que moi
> **as many as** autant que : **you can have as many as you like** tu peux en prendre autant que tu veux
> **as soon as possible** dès que possible : **I'll come as soon as possible** je viendrai dès que possible
> **as if** OR **as though** comme si : **he acted as if nothing had happened** il a fait comme si rien ne s'était passé.

a.s.a.p. *(abbreviation of* as soon as possible*)*

dès que possible.

ash [æʃ] *noun*

cendre *(feminine)*.

ashamed [əˈʃeɪmd] *adjective*

to be ashamed avoir honte ; **you should be ashamed of yourself!** tu devrais avoir honte !

ashtray [ˈæʃtreɪ] *noun*

cendrier *(masculine)*.

Asia [*UK* ˈeɪʃə, *US* ˈeɪʒə] *noun*

l'Asie *(feminine)*

In French the names of continents are used with the definite article l', except when they follow the preposition en:

Asia is a continent l'Asie est un continent ; **Indonesia is in Asia** l'Indonésie se trouve en Asie.

Asian [*UK* ˈeɪʃn, *US* ˈeɪʒn] *adjective & noun*

■ *adjective*
1. **asiatique**
2. *UK* **indo-pakistanais**

The French adjective does not start with a capital letter.

■ *noun*
1. **Asiatique** *(masculine or feminine)*
2. *UK* **Indo-pakistanais** *(masculine)*, **Indo-pakistanaise** *(feminine)*

📖 ASIAN
En anglais britannique, **Asian** désigne le plus souvent les habitants de l'Inde et des pays limitrophes. Lorsqu'on parle de la **Asian community** en Grande-Bretagne, on fait référence à la communauté indo-pakistanaise.

aside [əˈsaɪd] *adverb*

de côté : **I put it aside** je l'ai mis de côté.

ask [*UK* ɑːsk, *US* æsk] *verb*

1. **demander** : **he asked me my name** il m'a demandé mon nom
2. **inviter** : **he asked me to the party** il m'a invité à la soirée
> **to ask for something** demander quelque chose : **Fiona asked for help** Fiona a demandé de l'aide
> **to ask somebody to do something** de-

mander à quelqu'un de faire quelque chose ; **I asked her to wait** je lui ai demandé d'attendre

▶ **to ask somebody a question** poser une question à quelqu'un.

asleep [ə'sliːp] *adjective*

▶ **to be asleep** dormir : **he's fast asleep** il dort profondément

▶ **to fall asleep** s'endormir : **she fell asleep** elle s'est endormie.

asparagus [ə'spærəgəs] *uncountable noun*

asperges *(feminine plural)*.

aspirin ['æsprɪn] *noun*

aspirine *(feminine)*.

asset ['æset] *noun*

atout *(masculine)* : **Fred is an asset to the team** Fred est un atout pour l'équipe.

assignment [ə'saɪnmənt] *noun*

devoir *(masculine)* : **he handed in his assignment** il a rendu son devoir.

assistant [ə'sɪstənt] *noun*

assistant *(masculine)*, assistante *(feminine)* : **he's my assistant** c'est mon assistant

▶ **a shop assistant** UK un vendeur, une vendeuse.

assume [UK ə'sjuːm, US ə'suːm] *verb*

supposer : **I assume you're coming too** je suppose que tu viens aussi.

assure [ə'ʃʊəʳ] *verb*

assurer : **I assure you I'm not lying** je t'assure que je ne mens pas.

asterisk ['æstərɪsk] *noun*

astérisque *(masculine)*.

asthma [UK 'æsmə, US 'æzmə] *noun*

asthme *(masculine)* : **she has asthma** elle a de l'asthme.

astonished [ə'stɒnɪʃt] *adjective*

étonné : **I was astonished to hear the news** j'ai été étonné d'apprendre cette nouvelle.

astrology [ə'strɒlədʒɪ] *noun*

astrologie *(feminine)*.

astronaut ['æstrənɔːt] *noun*

astronaute *(masculine or feminine)* : **she's an astronaut** elle est astronaute.

astronomy [ə'strɒnəmɪ] *noun*

astronomie *(feminine)*.

at [ət, æt] *preposition*

1. *Indicating a place, a time or a speed* à

Remember that à + le = au and à + les = aux:

they're at school ils sont à l'école ; **John's at work** John est au travail ; **we arrived late at the airport** nous sommes arrivés en retard à l'aéroport ; **the film starts at 8 o'clock** le film commence à 8 heures ; **she left the party at midnight** elle a quitté la fête à minuit ; **at Christmas** à Noël ; **she was driving at 100 miles an hour** elle conduisait à 160 km à l'heure

2. *Talking about somebody's home or shop* chez : **I was at home last night** j'étais chez moi hier soir ; **we stayed at home** nous sommes restés chez nous ; **he's at the doctor's** il est chez le médecin

▶ **at night** la nuit : **owls hunt at night** les hiboux chassent la nuit

▶ **at the weekend** UK le week-end : **what did you do at the weekend?** qu'est-ce que tu as fait ce week-end ?

ate [UK et, US eɪt] *past tense of* eat

I ate all my carrots j'ai mangé toutes mes carottes.

athlete ['æθliːt] *noun*

athlète *(masculine or feminine)*.

Atlantic [ət'læntɪk] *adjective & noun*

■ *adjective*
atlantique : **the Atlantic coast** la côte atlantique

■ *noun*
the Atlantic l'Atlantique *(masculine)* .

atlas ['ætləs] *noun*

atlas *(masculine)* : **a world atlas** un atlas du monde.

ATM [eɪtiː'em] *noun*

distributeur *(masculine)* automatique de billets, DAB : **I'll get some money from the ATM** je vais prendre de l'argent au distributeur.

atmosphere ['ætmə͵sfɪəʳ] *noun*

1. atmosphère *(feminine)* : **the earth's atmosphere** l'atmosphère terrestre

2. ambiance *(feminine)* : **the atmosphere is good in school** il y a une bonne ambiance à l'école.

atom ['ætəm] *noun*

atome *(masculine)*
➤ **the atom bomb** la bombe atomique.

atomic [ə'tɒmɪk] *adjective*

atomique.

attach [ə'tætʃ] *verb*

1. **mettre, attacher : he attached the label to his luggage** il a mis l'étiquette sur ses bagages ; **she attached the rope round the tree** elle a attaché la corde autour de l'arbre
2. **joindre : I'll attach the file to the e-mail** je vais joindre le fichier à l'e-mail.

attack [ə'tæk] *noun & verb*

■ *noun*
1. **attaque** *(feminine)* **: they launched an attack against the enemy** ils ont lancé une attaque contre l'ennemi
2. **crise** *(feminine)* **: a heart attack** une crise cardiaque
■ *verb*
attaquer : the army attacked the fort l'armée a attaqué le fort.

attempt [ə'tempt] *noun & verb*

■ *noun*
tentative *(feminine)* **: she made a final attempt** elle a fait une dernière tentative
■ *verb*
tenter : to attempt to do something tenter de faire quelque chose.

attend [ə'tend] *verb*

1. **aller à : he attends the local school** il va à l'école du quartier
2. **assister à : he attended the meeting** il a assisté à la réunion

> ⚠️ Attend est un faux ami, il ne signifie pas "attendre".

attention [ə'tenʃn] *uncountable noun*

attention *(feminine)* **: I was trying to catch her attention** j'essayais d'attirer son attention
➤ **pay attention!** écoute !
➤ **to stand to attention** se mettre au garde-à-vous.

attic ['ætɪk] *noun*

grenier *(masculine)* **: the picture is up in the attic** le tableau est au grenier.

attitude [*UK* 'ætɪtjuːd, *US* 'ætɪtuːd] *noun*

attitude *(feminine)* **: I don't like her attitude** je n'aime pas son attitude.

attorney *US* [ə'tɜːnɪ] *noun*

avocat *(masculine)*, **avocate** *(feminine)* **: he's an attorney** il est avocat.

attract [ə'trækt] *verb*

attirer : magnets attract iron l'aimant attire le fer
➤ **to be attracted to somebody** être attiré par quelqu'un.

attraction [ə'trækʃn] *noun*

attraction *(feminine)* **: tourist attractions** des attractions touristiques.

attractive [ə'træktɪv] *adjective*

séduisant : she's a very attractive girl c'est une fille très séduisante.

aubergine *UK* ['əʊbəʒiːn] *noun*

aubergine *(feminine)*.

audience ['ɔːdjəns] *uncountable noun*

spectateurs *(masculine plural)* **: the audience started clapping** les spectateurs ont commencé à applaudir.

August ['ɔːgəst] *noun*

août *(masculine)* **: in August** en août ; **next August** en août prochain ; **last August** en août dernier

> In French the months of the year do not start with a capital letter.

aunt [*UK* 'ɑːnt, *US* 'ænt] *noun*

tante *(feminine)* **: aunt Emily** tante Emily.

auntie, aunty [*UK* ɑːntɪ, *US* æntɪ] *noun*

tantine *(feminine)* **: auntie Ann** tantine Ann.

Australia [ɒ'streɪljə] *noun*

l'Australie *(feminine)*

> In French the names of countries are used with the definite article (le, la or l'), except when they follow the preposition en:

Australia is a huge country l'Australie est un pays gigantesque ; **I'm going to Australia** je vais en Australie ; **she lives in Australia** elle vit en Australie.

Australian [ɒ'streɪljən] *adjective & noun*

■ *adjective*
australien *(feminine* **australienne***)*

The French adjective does not start with a capital letter:

the Australian bush le bush australien
■ *noun*
Australien *(masculine)*, **Australienne** *(feminine)*.

author ['ɔːθəʳ] *noun*

auteur *(masculine)* : **J.K. Rowling is a famous author** J.K. Rowling est un auteur célèbre.

autograph ['ɔːtəgrɑːf] *noun*

autographe *(masculine)* : **I've got Mick Jagger's autograph** j'ai un autographe de Mick Jagger.

automatic [ˌɔːtə'mætɪk] *adjective*

automatique.

automatically [ˌɔːtə'mætɪklɪ] *adverb*

automatiquement : **the door opens automatically** la porte s'ouvre automatiquement.

automobile *US* ['ɔːtəməbiːl] *noun*

automobile *(feminine)*.

autumn ['ɔːtəm] *noun*

automne *(masculine)* : **in autumn** en automne.

available [ə'veɪləbl] *adjective*

disponible : **this book is available everywhere** ce livre est disponible partout.

avalanche ['ævəlɑːnʃ] *noun*

avalanche *(feminine)*.

avenue [*UK* 'ævənjuː, *US* 'ævənuː] *noun*

avenue *(feminine)*.

average ['ævərɪdʒ] *adjective & noun*

■ *adjective*
moyen *(feminine* **moyenne***)* : **that's the average price** c'est le prix moyen
■ *noun*
moyenne *(feminine)* : **on average** en moyenne.

avocado [ˌævə'kɑːdəʊ] *noun*

avocat *(masculine)* : **she's eating an avocado** elle mange un avocat.

avoid [ə'vɔɪd] *verb*

éviter : **I avoid cycling through the city centre** j'évite de rouler à vélo dans le centre-ville.

awake [ə'weɪk] *adjective*

réveillé : **he's wide awake** il est complètement réveillé.

award [ə'wɔːd] *noun*

prix *(masculine)* : **she won an award** elle a remporté un prix ; **the award for best film** le prix du meilleur film.

aware [ə'weəʳ] *adjective*

➤ **to be aware of something** être conscient de quelque chose : **he wasn't aware of the danger** il n'était pas conscient du danger.

away [ə'weɪ] *adverb*

1. **absent** : **I'll be away for two weeks** je serai absent deux semaines
2. *Talking about distances* **is the beach far away?** est-ce que la plage est loin ? ; **it's two kilometres away** c'est à deux kilomètres d'ici.

awful ['ɔːfʊl] *adjective*

affreux *(feminine* **affreuse***)* : **the weather is awful** il fait un temps affreux
➤ **an awful lot of** énormément de : **there were an awful lot of people there** il y avait là énormément de gens.

awfully ['ɔːflɪ] *adverb*

vraiment : **I'm awfully sorry** je suis vraiment désolé ; **it's awfully cold** il fait vraiment froid.

awkward ['ɔːkwəd] *adjective*

1. **maladroit** : **he's a rather awkward child** c'est un enfant un peu maladroit
2. **délicat** : **the situation is a bit awkward** la situation est assez délicate
3. **mal à l'aise** : **I felt awkward** je me sentais mal à l'aise.

axe *UK*, **ax** *US* [æks] *noun*

hache *(feminine)*.

baby ['beɪbɪ] *noun*

bébé *(masculine)*.

baby-sit ['beɪbɪsɪt] *verb*

faire du baby-sitting : **Laura is baby-sitting for the neighbours** Laura fait du baby-sitting pour les voisins.

baby-sitter ['beɪbɪˌsɪtə'] *noun*

baby-sitter *(masculine or feminine)*.

bachelor ['bætʃələ'] *noun*

célibataire *(masculine or feminine)* : **he's a bachelor** il est célibataire.

back [bæk] *noun, adjective, adverb & verb*

■ *noun*

1. dos *(masculine)* : **he's lying on his back** il est allongé sur le dos ; **write the address on the back of the envelope** écris l'adresse au dos de l'enveloppe

2. arrière *(masculine)* : **she sat in the back of the car** elle s'est assise à l'arrière de la voiture

3. fond *(masculine)* : **he was sitting at the back of the room** il était assis au fond de la salle ; **it's right at the back of the cupboard** c'est tout au fond du placard

➤ **back to front** à l'envers : **you've got your jumper on back to front** tu as mis ton pull à l'envers

■ *adjective*

1. arrière : **the map's on the back seat** la carte est sur le siège arrière

2. de derrière : **the back door** la porte de derrière

■ *adverb*

1. en arrière : **she took a step back** elle a fait un pas en arrière

2. de retour : **I'll be back at 8** je serai de retour à 8 heures

➤ **to get back** rentrer : **we got back late** nous sommes rentrés tard

➤ **to go back** retourner : **I went back to the shop** je suis retourné au magasin

➤ **to give something back** rendre quelque chose : **he gave me my book back** il m'a rendu mon livre

➤ **to put something back** remettre quelque chose : **she put the bottle back in the fridge** elle a remis la bouteille dans le réfrigérateur

■ *verb*

1. soutenir : **he backed the government** il a soutenu le gouvernement

2. parier sur : **I backed the winning horse** j'ai parié sur le cheval gagnant

back up *phrasal verb*

1. soutenir : **I'll back you up** je te soutiendrai

2. sauvegarder : **he backed up his files** il a sauvegardé ses fichiers.

backache ['bækeɪk] *noun*

to have backache *UK* OR to have a backache *US* avoir mal au dos.

background ['bækgraʊnd] *noun*

1. arrière-plan *(masculine)* : **in the background** à l'arrière-plan

2. milieu *(masculine)* [*plural* milieux] : **he comes from a modest background** il vient d'un milieu modeste.

backpack ['bækpæk] *noun*

sac *(masculine)* à dos.

backstroke ['bækstrəʊk] *noun*

dos *(masculine)* crawlé : **he's swimming backstroke** il nage le dos crawlé.

backwards *UK* ['bækwədz], **backward** *US* ['bækwərd] *adverb*

1. en arrière : **to take a step backwards** faire un pas en arrière

2. à reculons : **to walk backwards** marcher à reculons

➤ **to walk backwards and forwards** aller et venir.

backyard *US* [ˌbæk'jɑːd] *noun*

jardin situé à l'arrière de la maison.

bacon ['beɪkən] *noun*

bacon *(masculine)* : **bacon and eggs** des œufs au bacon.

bacteria [bæk'tɪərɪə] *plural noun*

bactéries *(feminine plural)*.

bad [bæd] (*comparative* worse, *superlative* worst) *adjective*

1. **mauvais : it's a bad example** c'est un mauvais exemple ; **she's in a bad mood** elle est de mauvaise humeur ; **I'm bad at history** je suis mauvais en histoire
2. **méchant : he's a bad boy** c'est un garçon méchant
> **a bad cold** un gros rhume
> **I have a bad leg** j'ai mal à la jambe
> **it's not bad** ce n'est pas mal
> **too bad!** dommage !
> **to go bad** se gâter : **this apple has gone bad** cette pomme s'est gâtée.

badge [bædʒ] *noun*

badge *(masculine)*.

badger [ˈbædʒəʳ] *noun*

blaireau *(masculine)*.

badly [ˈbædlɪ] (*comparative* worse, *superlative* worst) *adverb*

1. **mal : he plays very badly** il joue très mal
2. **grièvement : he's badly wounded** il est grièvement blessé
> **she's badly in need of help** elle a vraiment besoin d'aide.

badminton [ˈbædmɪntən] *noun*

badminton *(masculine)* : **they're playing badminton** ils jouent au badminton.

bag [bæg] *noun*

1. **sac** *(masculine)* : **a paper bag** un sac en papier
2. **valise** *(feminine)* : **I'm packing my bags** je fais mes valises.

baggage [ˈbægɪdʒ] *uncountable noun*

bagages *(masculine plural)* : **he has a lot of baggage** il a beaucoup de bagages.

baggy [ˈbægɪ] *adjective*

très large : **a baggy jumper** un pull-over très large.

bagpipes [ˈbægpaɪps] *plural noun*

cornemuse *(feminine)* : **she plays the bagpipes** elle joue de la cornemuse.

bake [beɪk] *verb*

faire cuire au four : **I'm baking a cake** je fais cuire un gâteau au four
> **baked beans** haricots blancs à la sauce tomate
> **a baked potato** une pomme de terre en robe des champs.

baker [ˈbeɪkəʳ] *noun*

boulanger *(masculine)*, **boulangère** *(feminine)* : **at the baker's** chez le boulanger
> **the baker's shop** la boulangerie.

bakery [ˈbeɪkərɪ] (*plural* bakeries) *noun*

boulangerie *(feminine)*.

balaclava [ˌbæləˈklɑːvə] *noun*

cagoule *(feminine)* : **he's wearing a balaclava** il porte une cagoule.

balance [ˈbæləns] *noun & verb*

■ *noun*
équilibre *(masculine)* : **I lost my balance** j'ai perdu l'équilibre

■ *verb*
se tenir en équilibre : **he is balancing on one foot** il se tient en équilibre sur un pied.

balcony [ˈbælkənɪ] (*plural* balconies) *noun*

balcon *(masculine)*.

bald [bɔːld] *adjective*

chauve : **he's going bald** il devient chauve OR il perd ses cheveux.

ball [bɔːl] *noun*

1. **balle** *(feminine)* : **a tennis ball** une balle de tennis
2. **ballon** *(masculine)* : **the footballer kicked the ball** le footballeur a donné un coup de pied dans le ballon
3. **boule** *(feminine)* : **it's in the shape of a ball** c'est en forme de boule
4. **bal** *(masculine)* : **Cinderella went to the ball** Cendrillon est allée au bal.

ballerina [ˌbæləˈriːnə] *noun*

ballerine *(feminine)* : **she's a ballerina** elle est ballerine.

ballet [ˈbæleɪ] *noun*

ballet *(masculine)* : **we went to a ballet** nous avons assisté à un ballet
> **a ballet dancer** un danseur classique *(masculine)*, une danseuse classique *(feminine)*.

balloon [bəˈluːn] *noun*

ballon *(masculine)* : **the children are blowing up the balloons** les enfants gonflent les ballons.

ballpoint pen [ˈbɔːlpɔɪntpen] *noun*

stylo *(masculine)* à bille.

banana [UK bə'nɑːnə, US bə'nænə] noun

banane (feminine) : **a bunch of bananas** un régime de bananes.

band [bænd] noun

1. groupe (masculine) : **a rock band** un groupe de rock
2. fanfare (feminine) : **a military band** une fanfare militaire
3. orchestre (masculine) : **a jazz band** un orchestre de jazz.

bandage ['bændɪdʒ] noun

bandage (masculine) : **he has a bandage round his head** il a un bandage autour de la tête.

Band-Aid® US ['bændeɪd] noun

pansement (masculine) adhésif.

bang [bæŋ] noun & verb

■ noun

1. détonation (feminine) : **I heard a bang** j'ai entendu une détonation
2. coup (masculine) : **she got a bang on her head** elle a reçu un coup sur la tête

■ verb

1. frapper : **somebody's banging on the door** on frappe à la porte
2. se cogner : **I banged my head** je me suis cogné la tête
3. claquer : **don't bang the door** ne claque pas la porte.

bangle ['bæŋgl] noun

bracelet (masculine).

bangs US [bæŋz] plural noun

frange (feminine) : **she wears bangs** elle porte une frange.

bank [bæŋk] noun

1. banque (feminine) : **she has money in the bank** elle a de l'argent à la banque
2. rive (feminine) : **the right bank of the river** la rive droite du fleuve
➤ **a bank account** un compte bancaire OR un compte en banque
➤ **a bank holiday** UK un jour férié
➤ **a bank note** un billet de banque.

banker ['bæŋkər] noun

banquier (masculine), banquière (feminine) : **he's a banker** il est banquier.

banned [bænt] adjective

interdit : **smoking is banned** il est interdit de fumer.

bar [bɑr] noun

1. barre (feminine) : **an iron bar** une barre de fer
2. bar (masculine) : **the hotel bar** le bar de l'hôtel
➤ **a bar of chocolate** une tablette de chocolat
➤ **a bar of soap** une savonnette.

barbecue ['bɑːbɪkjuː] noun

barbecue (masculine) : **we're having a barbecue** nous faisons un barbecue.

barbed wire UK ['bɑːbdwaɪər], **barbwire** US ['bɑːrbwaɪər] noun

fil (masculine) de fer barbelé.

barber ['bɑːbər] noun

coiffeur (masculine) : **he went to the barber** il est allé chez le coiffeur
➤ **a barber's shop** un salon de coiffure.

bare [beər] adjective

nu : **his feet were bare** il avait les pieds nus.

barefoot [‚beə'fʊt] adjective & adverb

■ adjective

he was barefoot il était pieds nus

■ adverb

I was walking barefoot je marchais pieds nus OR je marchais nu-pieds.

barely ['beəlɪ] adverb

à peine : **I barely have enough time** j'ai à peine le temps.

bargain ['bɑːgɪn] noun

affaire (feminine) : **it's a real bargain** c'est une véritable affaire.

barge [bɑːdʒ] noun

péniche (feminine).

bark [bɑːk] noun & verb

■ noun

écorce (feminine) : **the bark of a tree** l'écorce d'un arbre

■ verb

aboyer : **the dog barked at the boy** le chien a aboyé après le garçon.

barmaid ['bɑːmeɪd] noun

barmaid (feminine) : **she's a barmaid** elle est barmaid.

barman *UK* ['bɑːmən] (*plural* barmen ['bɑːmən]) *noun*
barman *(masculine)* : **he's a barman** il est barman.

barn [bɑːn] *noun*
grange *(feminine)*.

bartender *US* ['bɑːtendəʳ] *noun*
barman *(masculine)* : **he's a bartender** il est barman.

base [beɪs] *noun*
base *(feminine)* : **an air base** une base aérienne.

baseball ['beɪsbɔːl] *noun*
base-ball *(masculine)* : **he plays baseball** il joue au base-ball
➤ **a baseball cap** une casquette de base-ball

> BASEBALL
> Le base-ball est le sport le plus populaire aux États-Unis. Il y a neuf joueurs dans chacune des deux équipes. On joue avec une longue batte en bois (**bat**), une petite balle (**baseball**) et de larges gants en cuir. Le championnat de baseball s'appelle **the World Series**. Ce sont les **New York Yankees** qui ont gagné ce championnat le plus grand nombre de fois. Parmi les autres équipes connues, on peut citer les **Boston Red Sox**, les **Cleveland Indians** et les **Detroit Tigers**.

basement ['beɪsmənt] *noun*
sous-sol *(masculine)* : **she went down to the basement** elle est descendue au sous-sol.

basic ['beɪsɪk] *adjective*
1. **fondamental** : **what are the basic principles?** quels sont les principes fondamentaux ?
2. **de base** : **a basic knowledge of French** des connaissances de base en français.

basically ['beɪsɪklɪ] *adverb*
au fond : **basically, he's a fool** au fond, c'est un idiot.

basics ['beɪsɪks] *plural noun*
the basics l'essentiel *(masculine singular)*.

basil ['bæzl] *noun*
basilic *(masculine)*.

basin *UK* ['beɪsn] *noun*
lavabo *(masculine)* : **she's washing her hands in the basin** elle se lave les mains dans le lavabo.

basis ['beɪsɪs] (*plural* bases ['beɪsiːz]) *noun*
on a regular basis régulièrement ; **on a monthly basis** tous les mois.

basket ['bɑːskɪt] *noun*
1. **panier** *(masculine)* : **a shopping basket** un panier à provisions
2. **corbeille** *(feminine)* : **a wastepaper basket** une corbeille à papier

⚠ Basket est un faux ami, il ne signifie pas "chaussure de sport".

basketball ['bɑːskɪtbɔːl] *noun*
basket-ball *(masculine)*, **basket** *(masculine)* : **they're playing basketball** ils jouent au basket.

bass [beɪs] *noun*
basse *(feminine)* : **a bass guitar** une guitare basse ; **he plays the bass** il joue de la basse
➤ **a double bass** une contrebasse.

bat [bæt] *noun*
1. **batte** *(feminine)* : **a baseball bat** une batte de base-ball
2. **chauve-souris** *(feminine)* : **bats come out at night** les chauves-souris sortent la nuit.

bath [bɑːθ] *noun*
1. **bain** *(masculine)* : **to have a bath** prendre un bain ; **I'm going to have a bath** je vais prendre un bain
2. **baignoire** *(feminine)* : **he's sitting in the bath** il est assis dans sa baignoire
➤ **a bath towel** une serviette de bain.

bathe [beɪð] *verb*
1. *UK* **se baigner** : **she was bathing in the river** elle se baignait dans la rivière
2. *US* **prendre un bain** : **I'm going to bathe** je vais prendre un bain.

bathrobe *US* ['bɑːθrəʊb] *noun*
peignoir *(masculine)*.

bathroom ['bɑːθrʊm] *noun*
1. **salle** *(feminine)* **de bains** : **the bathroom's upstairs** la salle de bains est à l'étage
2. *US* **toilettes** *(feminine plural)* : **where's the bathroom?** où sont les toilettes ?

bathtub ['bɑːθtʌb] *noun*
  baignoire *(feminine)*.

battery ['bætərɪ] *(plural* batteries*) noun*
1. **pile** *(feminine)* : **a radio battery** une pile pour radio
2. **batterie** *(feminine)* : **a car battery** une batterie de voiture.

battle ['bætl] *noun*
1. **bataille** *(feminine)* : **the battle of Hastings took place in 1066** la bataille de Hastings a eu lieu en 1066
2. **lutte** *(feminine)* : **the battle against cancer** la lutte contre le cancer.

bay [beɪ] *noun*
  baie *(feminine)* : **they are swimming in the bay** ils nagent dans la baie.

BBC [,biːbiː'siː] *(abbreviation of* British Broadcasting Corporation*) noun*
  Office national britannique de radiodiffusion

> 📖   BBC
> La **BBC** regroupe les grandes stations de radio et chaînes de télévision publiques du Royaume-Uni. On a longtemps considéré la prononciation des présentateurs de la **BBC** (surnommée le **BBC English**) comme étant la plus correcte, mais à l'heure actuelle, on entend différents accents sur la **BBC**.

BC [biː'siː] *(abbreviation of* before Christ*)*
  av. J.-C. : in 200 BC en l'an 200 av. J.-C.

be [biː] *(past tense* was OR were, *past participle* been*) verb*
1. **être** : **I'm very happy** je suis très heureux ; **you're late** tu es en retard ; **Anne is French** Anne est française ; **he wants to be a pilot** il veut être pilote ; **the soup is cold** la soupe est froide ; **we are alone** nous sommes seuls ; **they are in Brighton** ils sont à Brighton ; **it's midnight** il est minuit
2. *Describing physical sensations* **avoir**

> With certain adjectives that describe how you feel, like 'cold', 'hot', hungry' or 'thirsty', you use the verb avoir in French:

  I'm cold j'ai froid ; **my hands are cold** j'ai les mains froides ; **I'm too hot** j'ai trop chaud ; **are you hungry?** as-tu faim ? ; **he's thirsty** il a soif

3. *Saying how old somebody is* **avoir : how old are you?** quel âge as-tu ? ; **I'm thirteen years old** j'ai treize ans
4. *To talk about the weather* **faire : it's cold today** il fait froid aujourd'hui ; **it's very hot** il fait très chaud
5. *To talk about health and say how somebody is* **aller : how are you?** comment allez-vous ? ; **I'm very well, thank you** je vais très bien, merci ; **she isn't very well** elle ne va pas très bien ; **Sam is much better** Sam va beaucoup mieux
6. *In question tags* **n'est-ce pas : Strasbourg is in France, isn't it?** Strasbourg est en France, n'est-ce pas ? ; **you're Jane's friend, aren't you?** tu es l'amie de Jane, n'est-ce pas ?
7. *In the continuous tense*

> The present continuous is usually translated by the simple present tense in French:

  I'm working je travaille ; **what are you doing?** qu'est-ce que tu fais ? ; **Dan isn't coming** Dan ne vient pas ; **it's raining** il pleut

> The past continuous is translated by the imperfect tense in French:

  I was doing my homework je faisais mes devoirs ; **Sarah was cleaning the car** Sarah lavait la voiture

> If you want to emphasize that someone is in the middle of doing something you can use être + en train de + infinitive:

  be quiet! I'm watching a film tais-toi ! je suis en train de regarder un film ; **I was reading when you phoned** j'étais en train de lire quand tu as appelé

8. *The passive*

> The passive is formed in the same way in French and in English: être (to be) + past participle. Remember that in French the past participle must agree in gender (masculine & feminine) and number (singular & plural) with the subject of the verb:

  this method is used by many people cette méthode est utilisée par beaucoup de gens ; **I was hit in the arm by a bullet** j'ai été touché au bras par une balle

> Sometimes the passive form in English is translated by an active form in French using on:

I was told to leave on m'a dit de partir ; **my bag has been stolen** on m'a volé mon sac ➤ been.

beach [biːtʃ] *noun*

plage *(feminine)* : **shall we go to the beach?** on va à la plage ? ; **they're playing on the beach** ils jouent sur la plage.

bead [biːd] *noun*

perle *(feminine)* : **a necklace made of glass beads** un collier en perles de verre.

beak [biːk] *noun*

bec *(masculine)* : **the pelican has a big beak** les pélicans ont un grand bec.

beam [biːm] *noun*

1. rayon *(masculine)* : **a laser beam** un rayon laser
2. poutre *(feminine)* : **wooden beams** des poutres en bois.

bean [biːn] *noun*

haricot *(masculine)*
➤ **green beans** haricots verts.

beansprouts ['biːnsprauts] *plural noun*

germes *(masculine plural)* **de soja**.

bear [beəʳ] *noun & verb*

◾ *noun*
ours *(masculine)* : **a polar bear** un ours polaire
◾ *verb (past tense* bore, *past participle* borne)
supporter : **I can't bear him** je ne le supporte pas.

beard [bɪəd] *noun*

barbe *(feminine)* : **my uncle has a beard** mon oncle porte la barbe.

beat [biːt] *noun & verb*

◾ *noun*
rythme *(masculine)* : **this music has a strong beat** cette musique a un rythme marqué
◾ *verb (past tense* beat, *past participle* beaten)
battre : **our team beat them 4-2** notre équipe les a battus 4 à 2

beat up *phrasal verb*

rouer de coups : **he was beaten up** il a été roué de coups.

beaten ['biːtn] *past participle of* beat

we've beaten the French team again nous avons encore battu l'équipe française.

beautiful ['bjuːtɪfʊl] *adjective*

beau *(feminine* belle*)* : **a beautiful girl** une

belle fille ; **he has beautiful eyes** il a de beaux yeux.

beauty ['bjuːtɪ] *noun*

beauté *(feminine)*
➤ **a beauty parlour** OR **a beauty salon** un institut de beauté.

became [bɪ'keɪm] *past tense of* become

he became an actor il est devenu acteur.

because [bɪ'kɒz] *conjunction*

parce que : **he has gone to bed early because he has to get up at 6** il s'est couché tôt parce qu'il doit se lever à 6 heures
➤ **because of** à cause de : **I can't sleep because of the noise** je n'arrive pas à dormir à cause du bruit.

become [bɪ'kʌm] *(past tense* became, *past participle* become*) verb*

devenir : **she became famous** elle est devenue célèbre ; **what has become of them?** que sont-ils devenus ?

bed [bed] *noun*

lit *(masculine)* : **he's in bed** il est au lit OR il est couché
➤ **to go to bed** se coucher OR aller se coucher : **I went to bed at 9 pm** je me suis couché à 9 heures ; **I'm going to bed** je vais me coucher
➤ **to get out of bed** se lever
➤ **a bed and breakfast** une chambre d'hôte.

bedroom ['bedrʊm] *noun*

chambre *(feminine)* **à coucher** : **he's in his bedroom** il est dans sa chambre.

bee [biː] *noun*

abeille *(feminine)* : **she was stung by a bee** elle s'est fait piquer par une abeille.

beef [biːf] *noun*

bœuf *(masculine)*
➤ **roast beef** rosbif *(masculine)*.

beefburger ['biːf͵bɜːgəʳ] *noun*

hamburger *(masculine)*.

Beefeater ['biːf͵iːtəʳ] *noun*

surnom des gardiens de la Tour de Londres
➤ Tower of London.

been [biːn, *US* bɪn] *past participle of* be

I have been in this country for three years

je suis dans ce pays depuis trois ans ; **he has always been clever** il a toujours été intelligent

> When 'has been' or 'have been' is used as a past participle of go, use a conjugated form of **aller** to translate it:

I have been there once j'y suis allé une fois ; **have you ever been to Boston?** es-tu déjà allé à Boston ?

beer [bɪə^r] *noun*

bière *(feminine)* : **a pint of beer** une pinte de bière.

beet *US* [biːt] *noun*

betterave *(feminine)*.

beetle ['biːtl] *noun*

scarabée *(masculine)* : **beetles are insects** le scarabée est un insecte.

beetroot *UK* ['biːtruːt] *noun*

betterave *(feminine)*.

before [bɪ'fɔː^r] *preposition, adverb & conjunction*

■ *preposition*
avant : **I'll be back before midnight** je serai de retour avant minuit ; **he arrived before me** il est arrivé avant moi

■ *adverb*
1. avant : **you should have told me before** tu aurais dû me le dire avant
2. déjà : **I have met him before** je l'ai déjà rencontré

■ *conjunction*
avant de, avant que : **she phoned me before she left** elle m'a appelé avant de partir ; **I'll cook dinner before they arrive** je vais préparer le dîner avant qu'ils arrivent.

beg [beg] *(past tense & past participle* begged*)* *verb*

mendier : **he was begging in the street** il mendiait dans la rue
> **to beg somebody to do something** supplier quelqu'un de faire quelque chose
> **I beg your pardon?** pardon ?

began [bɪ'gæn] *past tense of* begin

he began to sing il a commencé à chanter.

beggar ['begə^r] *noun*

mendiant *(masculine)*, mendiante *(feminine)*.

begin [bɪ'gɪn] *(past tense* began, *past participle* begun*)* *verb*

commencer : **when does the film begin?** à quelle heure commence le film ?
> **to begin doing something** OR **to begin to do something** commencer à faire quelque chose : **she began to play** elle a commencé à jouer
> **it began to rain** il s'est mis à pleuvoir.

beginner [bɪ'gɪnə^r] *noun*

débutant *(masculine)*, débutante *(feminine)*.

beginning [bɪ'gɪnɪŋ] *noun*

début *(masculine)* : **in the beginning** au début.

begun [bɪ'gʌn] *past participle of* begin

the film has begun le film a commencé.

behalf [*UK* bɪ'hɑːf, *US* bɪ'hæf] *noun*

> **on behalf of somebody** *UK* OR **in behalf of somebody** *US*
1. au nom de quelqu'un, de la part de quelqu'un : **I'm speaking on behalf of all the class** je parle au nom de toute la classe
2. pour quelqu'un : **he did it on my behalf** il l'a fait pour moi.

behave [bɪ'heɪv] *verb*

se conduire : **he behaves badly** il se conduit mal ; **the children are behaving themselves** les enfants se conduisent bien.

behaviour *UK*, **behavior** *US* [bɪ'heɪvjə^r] *noun*

conduite *(feminine)*, comportement *(masculine)*.

behind [bɪ'haɪnd] *preposition, adverb & noun*

■ *preposition*
derrière : **he's behind you** il est derrière toi ; **the switch is behind the door** l'interrupteur est derrière la porte

■ *adverb*
en retard : **he's behind with his work** il est en retard dans son travail
> **to leave something behind** oublier quelque chose : **I left my umbrella behind** j'ai oublié mon parapluie

■ *noun*
derrière *(masculine)* : **he was sitting on his behind** il était assis sur son derrière.

being ['biːɪŋ] *noun*

être : **we are human beings** nous sommes des êtres humains.

Belgian ['beldʒən] *adjective & noun*

■ *adjective*
belge

> The French adjective does not start with a capital letter:

I love Belgian chocolates j'adore les chocolats belges

■ *noun*
Belge *(masculine or feminine)* : **the Belgians** les Belges.

Belgium ['beldʒəm] *noun*

la Belgique

> In French the names of countries are used with the definite article (**le, la** or **l'**), except when they follow the preposition **en**:

Belgium has two official languages la Belgique a deux langues officielles ; **I'm going to Belgium** je vais en Belgique ; **he lives in Belgium** il habite en Belgique.

believe [bɪ'liːv] *verb*

croire : **I believe you** je te crois
➤ **to believe in something** croire à quelque chose : **do you believe in ghosts?** tu crois aux fantômes ?
➤ **to believe in God** croire en Dieu.

bell [bel] *noun*

1. **sonnette** *(feminine)* : **where's the bell?** où est la sonnette ? ; **somebody rang the bell** on a sonné
2. **cloche** *(feminine)* : **the church bells** les cloches de l'église
3. **clochette** *(feminine)* : **the cow has a bell on its neck** la vache a une clochette autour du cou.

belly ['belɪ] *(plural* **bellies**) *noun*

ventre *(masculine)*
➤ **the belly button** le nombril.

belong [bɪ'lɒŋ] *verb*

➤ **to belong to**
1. **appartenir à** : **this pen belongs to me** ce stylo m'appartient OR ce stylo est à moi
2. **être membre de** : **he belongs to a tennis club** il est membre d'un club de tennis
➤ **put it back where it belongs** remets-le à sa place.

belongings [bɪ'lɒŋɪŋz] *plural noun*

affaires *(feminine plural)* : **my personal belongings** mes affaires personnelles.

below [bɪ'ləʊ] *preposition & adverb*

■ *preposition*
1. **au-dessous de** : **her dress came to below the knee** sa robe était au-dessous du genou
2. **moins de** : **it's below freezing** il fait moins de zéro
■ *adverb*
en dessous : **they live on the floor below** ils habitent l'étage en dessous.

belt [belt] *noun*

ceinture *(feminine)* : **he's wearing a belt** il porte une ceinture ; **a safety belt** une ceinture de sécurité.

bench [bentʃ] *noun*

banc *(masculine)* : **she's sitting on the bench** elle est assise sur le banc.

bend [bend] *noun & verb*

■ *noun*
virage *(masculine)* : **there's a bend in the road** il y a un virage sur la route
■ *verb (past tense & past participle* **bent**)
1. **plier** : **I can't bend my arm** je n'arrive pas à plier le bras
2. **tordre** : **I bent the wire** j'ai tordu le fil de fer

bend down *phrasal verb*

se baisser : **he bent down to pick up his book** il s'est baissé pour ramasser son livre

bend over *phrasal verb*

se pencher : **she bent over to have a closer look** elle s'est penchée pour mieux voir.

bent [bent] *adjective & verb form*

■ *adjective*
tordu : **a bent nail** un clou tordu
■ *past tense & past participle of* **bend**
he bent over il s'est penché.

beret ['bereɪ] *noun*

béret *(masculine)* : **she's wearing a beret** elle porte un béret.

berry ['berɪ] *(plural* **berries**) *noun*

baie *(feminine)* : **holly has red berries** le houx a des baies rouges.

beside [bɪ'saɪd] *preposition*

à côté de : **come and sit beside me** viens t'asseoir à côté de moi
➤ **he's beside himself with anger** il est hors de lui
➤ **she's beside herself with joy** elle est folle de joie.

besides [bɪ'saɪdz] *adverb & preposition*

◾ *adverb*
en plus : **besides, I think you're wrong** en plus, je pense que tu as tort
◾ *preposition*
en plus de : **besides this book I bought two other ones** en plus de ce livre, j'en ai acheté deux autres.

best [best] *adjective, adverb & noun*

◾ *adjective (superlative of good)*
meilleur : **he's the best student in the class** c'est le meilleur élève de la classe ; **she's my best friend** c'est ma meilleure amie
➤ **the best man** le garçon d'honneur
◾ *adverb (superlative of well)*
le mieux : **Jim plays best** c'est Jim qui joue le mieux
◾ *noun*
➤ **the best**
1. le meilleur, la meilleure : **of all the players I know, you're the best** de tous les joueurs que je connais, c'est toi le meilleur
2. le mieux : **I'll do my best** je ferai de mon mieux.

bestseller [best'selər] *noun*

best-seller *(masculine)*.

bet [bet] *noun & verb*

◾ *noun*
pari *(masculine)* : **let's make a bet** faisons un pari
◾ *verb (past tense & past participle bet OR betted, present participle betting)*
parier : **I bet you can't do it** je parie que tu ne peux pas le faire.

better ['betər] *adjective & adverb*

◾ *adjective (comparative of good)*
meilleur : **this method is better than the other** cette méthode est meilleure que l'autre
◾ *adverb (comparative of well)*
mieux : **she sings better than I do** elle chante mieux que moi ; **I feel much better now** je me sens beaucoup mieux maintenant

➤ **to get better**
1. s'améliorer : **the weather is getting better** le temps s'améliore
2. se remettre : **he's getting better after his operation** il se remet après son opération
➤ **I'd better go home** je ferais mieux de rentrer
➤ **you'd better leave** tu ferais mieux de partir

⚠️ Dans la phrase **I'd better go home**, I'd better = I had better et dans la phrase **you'd better leave**, you'd better = you had better.

between [bɪ'twiːn] *preposition & adverb*

◾ *preposition*
entre : **he's sitting between Graham and Anne** il est assis entre Graham et Anne
◾ *adverb*
au milieu
➤ **in between** au milieu : **John's sitting in between** John est assis au milieu.

beware [bɪ'weər] *verb*

prendre garde : **beware of pickpockets!** attention aux pickpockets ! ; **'beware of the dog!'** 'attention, chien méchant !'

⚠️ Beware s'emploie uniquement à l'infinitif et à l'impératif.

beyond [bɪ'jɒnd] *preposition*

au-delà de : **don't go beyond the gate** ne va pas au-delà de la barrière
➤ **it's beyond me!** ça me dépasse !

bicycle ['baɪsɪkl] *noun*

vélo *(masculine)*, bicyclette *(feminine)* : **can you ride a bicycle?** tu sais faire du vélo ? ; **he goes to school on his bicycle** il va à l'école à vélo
➤ **a bicycle path** une piste cyclable
➤ **a bicycle pump** une pompe à vélo.

big [bɪg] *(comparative* bigger, *superlative* biggest) *adjective*
1. grand : **a big tree** un grand arbre ; **my big brother** mon grand frère
2. gros *(feminine* grosse) : **a big book** un gros livre ; **a big parcel** un gros colis
➤ **the Big Apple** New York

➤ **Big Ben** Big Ben
➤ **the big wheel** *UK* la grande roue

> 📖 **BIG APPLE**
> **The Big Apple**, qui signifie la Grosse Pomme, est le surnom de la ville de New York. Ce nom fut utilisé pour la première fois par les jazzmen des années vingt en référence au succès qu'ils pouvaient rencontrer dans cette ville. D'autres villes américaines comme Chicago et Detroit ont également un surnom : **the Windy City** pour la première, à cause des vents forts qui y soufflent, et **Motown** pour la seconde, car c'est la ville de l'automobile.

> 📖 **BIG BEN**
> **Big Ben** est le surnom de la cloche de la tour des **Houses of Parliament** à Londres. Le son de cette cloche est très connu car il annonce souvent les nouvelles à la radio et à la télévision. Beaucoup de gens pensent à tort que **Big Ben** est le nom de l'horloge ou de la tour elle-même.

bigheaded [ˌbɪɡˈhedɪd] *adjective informal*

crâneur *(feminine* crâneuse*)*.

bike [baɪk] *noun*

vélo *(masculine)* : **she goes to work by bike** elle va au travail en vélo.

bikini [bɪˈkiːnɪ] *noun*

Bikini® *(masculine)* : **she's wearing a bikini** elle porte un Bikini.

bilingual [baɪˈlɪŋɡwəl] *adjective*

bilingue : **she's bilingual** elle est bilingue.

bill [bɪl] *noun*

1. facture *(feminine)* : **a telephone bill** une facture de téléphone
2. addition *(feminine)* : **can I have the bill, please?** l'addition, s'il vous plaît !
3. *US* billet *(masculine)* de banque : **a ten-dollar bill** un billet de dix dollars.

billiards [ˈbɪljədz] *noun*

billard *(masculine)* : **they're playing billiards** ils jouent au billard.

billion [ˈbɪljən] *noun*

milliard *(masculine)*.

bin *UK* [bɪn] *noun*

poubelle *(feminine)* : **throw the empty packet in the bin** jette le paquet vide à la poubelle.

binoculars [bɪˈnɒkjʊləz] *plural noun*

jumelles *(feminine plural)* : **a pair of binoculars** des jumelles.

biology [baɪˈɒlədʒɪ] *noun*

biologie *(feminine)*.

bird [bɜːd] *noun*

oiseau *(masculine)* [*plural* oiseaux] : **eagles are birds of prey** les aigles sont des oiseaux de proie.

Biro® *UK* [ˈbaɪərəʊ] *noun*

stylo *(masculine)* à bille.

birth [bɜːθ] *noun*

naissance *(feminine)* : **what's your date of birth?** quelle est votre date de naissance ?
➤ **a birth certificate** un acte de naissance.

birthday [ˈbɜːθdeɪ] *noun*

anniversaire *(masculine)* : **when is your birthday?** c'est quand ton anniversaire ? ; **Gary's birthday is on February 6ᵗʰ** l'anniversaire de Gary est le 6 février
➤ **happy birthday!** joyeux anniversaire !

biscuit *UK* [ˈbɪskɪt] *noun*

biscuit *(masculine)* : **a chocolate biscuit** un biscuit au chocolat.

bishop [ˈbɪʃəp] *noun*

évêque *(masculine)*.

bison [ˈbaɪsn] *noun*

bison *(masculine)*.

bit [bɪt] *noun & verb form*

■ *noun*
morceau *(masculine)*, bout *(masculine)* : **a bit of cheese** un morceau de fromage ; **a bit of paper** un bout de papier
➤ **a bit** un peu : **I'm a bit tired** je suis un peu fatigué
➤ **a bit of** un peu de : **he has a bit of money** il a un peu d'argent
➤ **bit by bit** petit à petit
➤ **for a bit** pendant quelque temps : **he didn't say anything for a bit** il n'a rien dit pendant quelque temps
■ *past tense of* bite
the dog bit the postman le chien a mordu le facteur.

bite [baɪt] *noun & verb*

■ *noun*
1. **piqûre** *(feminine)* : **an insect bite** une piqûre d'insecte
2. **morsure** *(feminine)* : **a snake bite** une morsure de serpent
➤ **to have a bite to eat** manger un morceau : **do you want a bite to eat?** tu veux manger un morceau ?

■ *verb* (*past tense* **bit**, *past participle* **bitten**)
1. **mordre** : **the dog bit me** le chien m'a mordu ; **I bit into the apple** j'ai mordu dans la pomme
2. **piquer** : **I've been bitten by mosquitoes** j'ai été piqué par des moustiques
➤ **to bite one's nails** se ronger les ongles : **he bites his nails** il se ronge les ongles.

bitten ['bɪtn] *past participle of* bite

he was bitten by a dog il a été mordu par un chien.

bitter ['bɪtər] *adjective*
1. **amer** *(feminine* **amère***)* : **it has a bitter taste** cela a un goût amer
2. **glacial** : **there's a bitter wind** il y a un vent glacial.

black [blæk] *adjective*

noir : **black ink** de l'encre noire ; **he's black** il est noir
➤ **a black eye** un œil poché OR un œil au beurre noir : **he has a black eye** il a un œil poché
➤ **black pudding** *UK* boudin *(masculine)* noir.

blackberry ['blækbərɪ] (*plural* black-berries) *noun*

mûre *(feminine)* : **to go blackberry picking** aller cueillir des mûres.

blackbird ['blækbɜːd] *noun*

merle *(masculine)*.

blackboard ['blækbɔːd] *noun*

tableau *(masculine)* : **the teacher is writing on the blackboard** le professeur écrit au tableau.

blackcurrant [ˌblæk'kʌrənt] *noun*

cassis *(masculine)*.

blade [bleɪd] *noun*

lame *(feminine)* : **a razor blade** une lame de rasoir.

blame [bleɪm] *verb*
➤ **to blame somebody for something** reprocher quelque chose à quelqu'un : **he blames me for these problems** c'est à moi qu'il reproche ces problèmes
➤ **who's to blame?** à qui la faute ? : **he's to blame** c'est de sa faute.

blank [blæŋk] *adjective*
1. **blanc** *(feminine* **blanche***)* : **a blank sheet of paper** une feuille blanche
2. **vierge** : **a blank cassette** une cassette vierge
➤ **my mind went blank** j'ai eu un trou de mémoire.

blanket ['blæŋkɪt] *noun*

couverture *(feminine)* : **she put a blanket on the bed** elle a mis une couverture sur le lit.

blast [blɑːst] *noun*

explosion *(feminine)* : **a bomb blast** une explosion.

bleach [bliːtʃ] *noun*

eau *(feminine)* **de Javel**.

bleached [bliːtʃt] *adjective*

décoloré : **she has bleached hair** elle a les cheveux décolorés.

bleed [bliːd] (*past tense & past participle* bled [bled]) *verb*

saigner : **my nose is bleeding** je saigne du nez.

bless [bles] (*past tense & past participle* blessed) *verb*

bénir : **the priest blessed him** le prêtre l'a béni
➤ **bless you!** à vos souhaits !

blew [bluː] *past tense of* blow

she blew the candles out elle a soufflé les bougies.

blind [blaɪnd] *adjective & noun*

■ *adjective*
aveugle : **he's blind** il est aveugle
■ *noun*
store *(masculine)* : **pull down the blind** baisse le store.

blindfold ['blaɪndfəʊld] *noun & verb*

■ *noun*
bandeau *(masculine)* : **they put a blindfold on me** ils m'ont mis un bandeau

verb

bander les yeux à : they blindfolded me ils m'ont bandé les yeux.

blink [blɪŋk] *verb*

cligner des yeux : he was blinking il clignait des yeux.

blister ['blɪstər] *noun*

ampoule *(feminine)* : I have a blister on my ankle j'ai une ampoule à la cheville.

block [blɒk] *noun & verb*

■ *noun*

1. **bloc** *(masculine)* : a block of ice un bloc de glace
2. *UK* **immeuble** *(masculine)* : an office block un immeuble de bureaux ; a block of flats un immeuble
3. *US* **pâté** *(masculine)* **de maisons** : I'll walk around the block je ferai le tour du pâté de maisons ; it's five blocks from here c'est à cinq rues d'ici

➤ **block capitals** OR **block letters** capitales *(feminine plural)* d'imprimerie ; write your name in block capitals écrivez votre nom en majuscules

■ *verb*

1. **bloquer** : a fallen tree is blocking the road un arbre qui est tombé bloque la rue
2. **boucher** : the pipe is blocked le tuyau est bouché.

bloke *UK* [bləʊk] *noun*

informal **type** *(masculine)* : he's a nice bloke c'est un type sympa.

blond, blonde [blɒnd] *adjective & noun*

■ *adjective*

blond : he has blond hair il a les cheveux blonds

■ *noun*

blond *(masculine)*, **blonde** *(feminine)* : Anne's a blonde Anne est une blonde.

blood [blʌd] *noun*

sang *(masculine)* : he's covered in blood il est couvert de sang

➤ **blood group** groupe *(masculine)* sanguin
➤ **blood pressure** tension *(feminine)* artérielle
➤ **a blood test** une prise de sang
➤ **a blood transfusion** une transfusion sanguine.

blouse [*UK* blaʊz, *US* blaʊs] *noun*

chemisier *(masculine)* : she's wearing a pretty blouse elle porte un joli chemisier.

blow [bləʊ] (*past tense* blew, *past participle* blown) *verb*

souffler : the wind is blowing le vent souffle

➤ **to blow a whistle** donner un coup de sifflet : the referee blew his whistle l'arbitre a donné un coup de sifflet

➤ **to blow one's nose** se moucher : I blew my nose je me suis mouché

blow out *phrasal verb*

souffler : blow the candles out souffle les bougies

blow up *phrasal verb*

1. **gonfler** : I'm going to blow up some balloons for the party je vais gonfler des ballons pour la fête
2. **faire sauter** : they have blown up the bridge ils ont fait sauter le pont
3. **sauter** : the whole building blew up tout l'immeuble a sauté.

blow-dry ['bləʊdraɪ] *noun*

Brushing® *(masculine)* : a cut and a blow-dry une coupe avec Brushing.

blown [bləʊn] *past participle of* blow

I've blown up the balloons j'ai gonflé les ballons.

blue [bluː] *adjective*

bleu : Cathy has blue eyes Cathy a les yeux bleus ; she's wearing a blue dress elle porte une robe bleue.

bluebell ['bluːbel] *noun*

jacinthe *(feminine)* **des bois**.

blueberry ['bluːbərɪ] (*plural* blueberries) *noun*

myrtille *(feminine)* : a blueberry pie une tarte aux myrtilles.

blunder ['blʌndər] *noun*

gaffe *(feminine)* : I've made a blunder j'ai fait une gaffe.

blunt [blʌnt] *adjective*

1. **émoussé** : the knife is blunt le couteau est émoussé

2. **mal taillé** : **my pencil is blunt** mon crayon est mal taillé
3. **direct** : **he's very blunt** c'est quelqu'un de très direct.

blurred [blɜːʳd] *adjective*

flou : **the photo is blurred** la photo est floue.

blush [blʌʃ] *verb*

rougir : **you're blushing** tu rougis ; **she blushed** elle a rougi.

board [bɔːd] *noun*

1. **planche** *(feminine)* : **a bread board** une planche à pain
2. **tableau** *(masculine)* : **write the sentence on the board** écris la phrase au tableau
3. **panneau** *(masculine)* **d'affichage** : **there are a lot of notices on the board** il y a beaucoup d'affiches sur le panneau
4. **tableau** *(masculine)* **de jeu** : **put the pieces on the board** mettez les jetons sur le tableau de jeu
5. **conseil** *(masculine)* : **Mr Owen is on the board of directors** M. Owen est membre du conseil d'administration
➤ **board games** jeux *(masculine plural)* de société
➤ **full board** pension *(feminine)* complète
➤ **half board** demi-pension *(feminine)*
➤ **on board** à bord : **I went on board** je suis monté à bord ; **on board the ship** à bord du bateau.

boarding card [ˈbɔːdɪŋkɑːd] *noun*

carte *(feminine)* **d'embarquement**.

boarding school [ˈbɔːdɪŋskuːl] *noun*

pensionnat *(masculine)* : **he goes to boarding school** il est interne OR il est en pension.

boast [bəʊst] *verb*

se vanter : **she's boasting about her exam results** elle se vante de ses résultats à l'examen.

boat [bəʊt] *noun*

bateau *(masculine)* [*plural* **bateaux**] : **we're going to Dublin by boat** nous allons à Dublin en bateau.

body [ˈbɒdɪ] *(plural* **bodies**) *noun*

corps *(masculine)* : **the human body** le corps humain
➤ **a dead body** un cadavre.

bodyguard [ˈbɒdɪgɑːd] *noun*

garde *(masculine)* **du corps** : **he's the president's bodyguard** c'est le garde du corps du président.

boil [bɔɪl] *verb & noun*
▪ *verb*
1. **faire bouillir** : **I'll boil the kettle for a cup of tea** je vais faire bouillir de l'eau pour le thé
2. **bouillir** : **the water is boiling** l'eau bout
▪ *noun*
furoncle *(masculine)* : **he has a boil on his nose** il a un furoncle sur le nez.

boiled [ˈbɔɪld] *adjective*

a boiled egg un œuf à la coque ; **boiled potatoes** des pommes de terre à l'eau.

boiler [ˈbɔɪləʳ] *noun*

chaudière *(feminine)*.

boiling [ˈbɔɪlɪŋ] *adjective*

extrêmement chaud : **it's boiling hot today** il fait extrêmement chaud aujourd'hui.

bold [bəʊld] *adjective*
1. **audacieux** *(feminine* **audacieuse**) : **it's a bold venture** c'est une entreprise audacieuse
2. **gras** : **bold type** des caractères gras ; **in bold** en gras.

bolt [bəʊlt] *noun & verb*
▪ *noun*
1. **boulon** *(masculine)* : **nuts and bolts** des écrous et des boulons
2. **verrou** *(masculine)* : **there's a bolt on the door** il y a un verrou sur la porte
▪ *verb*
verrouiller : **have you bolted the door?** as-tu verrouillé la porte ?

bomb [bɒm] *noun & verb*
▪ *noun*
bombe *(feminine)* : **a bomb scare** une alerte à la bombe
▪ *verb*
bombarder : **London was bombed in the Second World War** Londres a été bombardé pendant la Seconde Guerre mondiale.

bone [bəʊn] *noun*
1. **os** *(masculine)* : **he gave the dog a bone** il a donné un os au chien
2. **arête** *(feminine)* : **a fish bone** une arête de poisson.

bonfire ['bɒnˌfaɪəʳ] *noun*

feu *(masculine)* de joie : **she lit a bonfire in her garden** elle a allumé un feu de joie dans son jardin.

Bonfire Night *UK* ['bɒnˌfaɪəʳnaɪt] *noun*

fête célébrée le 5 novembre en Grande-Bretagne avec des feux de joie et des feux d'artifice ➤ Guy Fawkes Night.

bonnet ['bɒnɪt] *noun*

1. *UK* capot *(masculine)* : **he lifted the bonnet of the car** il a soulevé le capot de la voiture
2. bonnet *(masculine)* : **a baby's bonnet** un bonnet de bébé.

boo [buː] *noun & verb*

■ *noun*
huée *(feminine)*

■ *verb*
huer : **the audience booed** le public a hué
➤ **boo!** hou !

book [bʊk] *noun & verb*

■ *noun*
1. livre *(masculine)* : **Brian is reading a book** Brian lit un livre
2. carnet *(masculine)* : **a book of tickets** un carnet de tickets

■ *verb*
réserver : **I want to book two tickets to Pittsburgh** je veux réserver deux billets pour Pittsburgh.

bookcase ['bʊkkeɪs] *noun*

bibliothèque *(feminine)* : **there's a bookcase in the office** il y a une bibliothèque dans le bureau.

booklet ['bʊklɪt] *noun*

brochure *(feminine)*.

bookmark ['bʊkmɑːk] *noun*

marque-page *(masculine)*, signet *(masculine)*.

bookshelf ['bʊkʃelf] *(plural* bookshelves ['bʊkʃelvz]) *noun*

étagère *(feminine)* à livres.

bookshop *UK* ['bʊkʃɒp], **bookstore** *US* ['bʊkstɔːʳ] *noun*

librairie *(feminine)* : **is there a bookshop near here?** est-ce qu'il y a une librairie près d'ici ?

boot [buːt] *noun*

1. botte *(feminine)* : **she's wearing yellow boots** elle porte des bottes jaunes
2. chaussure *(feminine)* : **football boots** des chaussures de football ; **walking boots** des chaussures de marche
3. *UK* coffre *(masculine)* : **the shopping is in the boot of the car** les courses sont dans le coffre de la voiture
➤ **ankle boots** bottines *(feminine plural)*.

border ['bɔːdəʳ] *noun*

frontière *(feminine)* : **the border between the USA and Mexico** la frontière entre les États-Unis et le Mexique.

bore [bɔːʳ] *verb*

ennuyer : **you really bore me!** tu m'ennuies vraiment !

bored [bɔːd] *adjective*

to be bored s'ennuyer ; **I'm very bored** je m'ennuie beaucoup ; **I'm bored with this book** ce livre m'ennuie
➤ **I'm bored to tears** OR **I'm bored to death** je meurs d'ennui.

boredom ['bɔːdəm] *noun*

ennui *(masculine)*.

boring ['bɔːrɪŋ] *adjective*

ennuyeux *(feminine* ennuyeuse*)* : **what a boring film!** quel film ennuyeux !

born [bɔːn] *adjective*

➤ to be born naître : **where were you born?** où es-tu né ? ; **I was born in 1990** je suis né en 1990.

borrow ['bɒrəʊ] *verb*

emprunter : **can I borrow your pen?** je peux t'emprunter ton stylo ? ; **he borrowed some money from a friend** il a emprunté de l'argent à un ami.

boss [bɒs] *noun*

patron *(masculine)*, patronne *(feminine)*, chef *(masculine or feminine)* : **she's my boss** c'est ma patronne OR c'est ma chef.

bossy ['bɒsɪ] *adjective*

autoritaire : **his sister is very bossy** sa sœur est très autoritaire.

both [bəʊθ] *adjective & pronoun*

les deux, tous les deux *(feminine* toutes les

b

deux) : **both of the girls are Spanish** OR **both girls are Spanish** les deux filles sont espagnoles ; **both his cars are old** ses voitures sont vieilles toutes les deux ; **both of them are coming** ils viennent tous les deux ; **the girls were both hungry** les filles avaient faim toutes les deux.

bother ['bɒðə^r] *verb*

1. **déranger : I'm sorry to bother you** excusez-moi de vous déranger

2. **inquiéter : something is bothering her** quelque chose l'inquiète ; **don't bother about me** ne vous inquiétez pas pour moi

➤ **to bother to do something** se donner la peine de faire quelque chose : **he didn't bother to get up** il ne s'est pas donné la peine de se lever

➤ **don't bother!** ce n'est pas la peine !

➤ **I can't be bothered** j'ai la flemme : **I can't be bothered to go out** j'ai la flemme de sortir.

bottle ['bɒtl] *noun*

bouteille *(feminine)* : **a bottle of milk** une bouteille de lait.

bottle-opener ['bɒtl'əʊpnə^r] *noun*

ouvre-bouteille *(masculine)* [*plural* ouvre-bouteilles].

bottom ['bɒtəm] *noun & adjective*

■ *noun*

1. **fond** *(masculine)* : **at the bottom of the lake** au fond du lac

2. **bas** *(masculine)* : **at the bottom of the page** au bas de la page

3. **pied** *(masculine)* : **at the bottom of the hill** au pied de la colline

4. **derrière** *(masculine)* : **he was sitting on his bottom** il était assis sur son derrière

■ *adjective*

1. **du bas : the bottom shelf** l'étagère du bas

2. *UK* **dernier** *(feminine* **dernière***)* : **he's bottom in the class** il est le dernier de la classe.

bought [bɔ:t] *past tense & past participle of* buy

he bought a new bicycle il a acheté un nouveau vélo ; **my aunt has bought me a watch** ma tante m'a acheté une montre.

bounce [baʊns] *verb*

1. **rebondir : the ball bounced twice** la balle a rebondi deux fois

2. **faire rebondir : she was bouncing the ball against the wall** elle faisait rebondir la balle sur le mur.

bound [baʊnd] *adjective*

he's bound to win il va sûrement gagner ; **it was bound to happen** c'était à prévoir.

bow *noun & verb*

■ *noun* [bəʊ]

1. **arc** *(masculine)* : **a bow and arrows** un arc et des flèches

2. **nœud** *(masculine)* : **she tied the ribbon in a bow** elle a fait un nœud dans le ruban

➤ **a bow tie** un nœud papillon

■ *verb* [baʊ]

saluer : the actors bowed les acteurs ont salué.

bowl [bəʊl] *noun*

1. **bol** *(masculine)* : **a bowl of milk** un bol de lait ; **a salad bowl** un saladier

2. **bassine** *(feminine)* : **a washing-up bowl** une bassine pour faire la vaisselle.

bowler hat ['bəʊlə^r hæt] *noun*

chapeau *(masculine)* **melon.**

bowling ['bəʊlɪŋ] *uncountable noun*

bowling *(masculine)* : **she goes bowling every Friday** elle joue au bowling tous les vendredis

➤ **a bowling alley** un bowling.

bowls *UK* [bəʊlz] *plural noun*

boules *(feminine plural)* : **they're playing bowls** ils jouent aux boules.

box [bɒks] *noun*

boîte *(feminine)* : **a box of chocolates** une boîte de chocolats.

boxer ['bɒksə^r] *noun*

boxeur *(masculine)* : **he's a boxer** il est boxeur.

boxer shorts ['bɒksə^rʃɔ:ts] *plural noun*

caleçon *(masculine singular)* : **a pair of boxer shorts** un caleçon.

boxing ['bɒksɪŋ] *uncountable noun*

boxe *(feminine)* : **he likes boxing** il aime la boxe

➤ **a boxing match** un match de boxe.

Boxing Day ['bɒksɪŋdeɪ] *noun*

le lendemain de Noël

BOXING DAY
Le 26 décembre, jour férié en Grande-Bretagne, s'appelle **Boxing Day**. Ce nom vient de la **Christmas box** (la boîte de Noël), petit cadeau ou somme d'argent que les maîtres de maison

donnaient traditionnellement à leurs domestiques ce jour-là. De nos jours, au moment des fêtes de Noël, on donne de l'argent ou un petit cadeau au facteur, au livreur de lait ou aux éboueurs.

boy [bɔɪ] noun

garçon (masculine) : **a young boy** un petit garçon

➤ **a boy band** un boys band.

boyfriend ['bɔɪfrend] noun

copain (masculine), **petit ami** (masculine).

bra [brɑː] noun

soutien-gorge (masculine) [plural **soutiens-gorge**].

brace UK [breɪs], **braces** US [breɪsɪz] noun

appareil (masculine) **dentaire** : **he wears a brace** UK OR **he wears braces** US il porte un appareil dentaire.

bracelet ['breɪslɪt] noun

bracelet (masculine) : **she's wearing a silver bracelet** elle porte un bracelet en argent.

brackets UK ['brækɪts] plural noun

parenthèses (feminine plural)

➤ **in brackets** entre parenthèses.

brag [bræg] verb

se vanter : **he's always bragging about his rich father** il se vante toujours d'avoir un père riche.

brain [breɪn] noun

cerveau (masculine) : **the human brain** le cerveau humain

➤ **he's got brains** il est intelligent.

brainy ['breɪnɪ] adjective

intelligent.

brake [breɪk] noun & verb

▢ noun
frein (masculine) : **he put on the brakes** il a freiné

▢ verb
freiner.

branch [brɑːntʃ] noun

1. **branche** (feminine) : **the monkey was swinging from branch to branch** le singe se balançait de branche en branche

2. **agence** (feminine) : **the bank has a branch in Paris** la banque a une agence à Paris.

brand [brænd] noun

marque (feminine) : **it's a well-known brand of clothing** c'est une marque de vêtements très connue

➤ **a brand name** une marque.

brand-new [UK 'brændnjuː, US 'brændnuː] adjective

tout neuf (feminine **toute neuve**) : **I've bought a brand-new computer** j'ai acheté un ordinateur tout neuf.

brass [brɑːs] noun

cuivre (masculine) : **it's made of brass** c'est en cuivre

➤ **a brass band** une fanfare.

brave [breɪv] adjective

courageux (feminine **courageuse**) : **he's very brave** il est très courageux.

bread [bred] uncountable noun

pain (masculine)

➤ **a loaf of bread** un pain.

break [breɪk] noun & verb

▢ noun
1. **pause** (feminine) : **they took a break** ils ont fait une pause

2. UK **récréation** (feminine) : **some pupils play sports during the lunch break** certains élèves font du sport pendant la récréation de midi

▢ verb (past tense **broke**, past participle **broken**)
1. **casser** : **I've broken the radio** j'ai cassé la radio

2. **se casser** : **the glass broke** le verre s'est cassé ; **he broke his arm** il s'est cassé le bras ; **she has broken her leg** elle s'est cassé la jambe

➤ **to break the law** enfreindre la loi : **she broke the law** elle a enfreint la loi

➤ **to break a promise** manquer à une promesse : **Tom broke his promise** Tom a manqué à sa promesse

➤ **to break a record** battre un record : **he broke the world record** il a battu le record du monde

break down phrasal verb

1. **tomber en panne** : **their car broke down** leur voiture est tombée en panne

2. **enfoncer** : **the police broke the door down** la police a enfoncé la porte

b

break in | *phrasal verb*

entrer par effraction : a burglar broke in through the window un cambrioleur est entré par la fenêtre

break up | *phrasal verb*

1. **rompre** : he broke up with his girlfriend il a rompu avec sa copine
2. **se terminer** : the meeting broke up at lunchtime la réunion s'est terminée à midi.

breakdown ['breɪkdaʊn] *noun*

panne *(feminine)* : we had a breakdown on the motorway nous sommes tombés en panne sur l'autoroute

➤ **a nervous breakdown** une dépression nerveuse.

breakfast ['brekfəst] *noun*

petit déjeuner *(masculine)* : they had toast for breakfast ils ont mangé du pain grillé au petit déjeuner.

breast [brest] *noun*

sein *(masculine)*

➤ **a chicken breast** un blanc de poulet.

breaststroke ['breststrəʊk] *noun*

brasse *(feminine)* : he's swimming breaststroke il nage la brasse.

breath [breθ] *noun*

souffle *(masculine)* : hold your breath retiens ton souffle ; I need to get my breath back je dois reprendre mon souffle ; he took a deep breath il a respiré profondément

➤ **out of breath** essoufflé OR à bout de souffle : I'm out of breath je suis essoufflée OR je suis à bout de souffle.

breathe [briːð] *verb*

respirer : breathe deeply respirez profondément

breathe in | *phrasal verb*

inspirer

breathe out | *phrasal verb*

expirer

breed [briːd] *verb & noun*

■ *verb* (*past tense & past participle* bred)

1. **élever** : he breeds ostriches il élève des autruches
2. **se reproduire** : rabbits breed very fast les lapins se reproduisent vite

■ *noun*

race *(feminine)*, **espèce** *(feminine)* : what breed is that dog? quelle race de chien est-ce ?

breeze [briːz] *noun*

brise *(feminine)* : there's a breeze il y a une brise.

brick [brɪk] *noun*

brique *(feminine)* : a brick wall un mur en briques.

bride [braɪd] *noun*

mariée *(feminine)* : the bride and groom les mariés.

bridegroom ['braɪdgrʊm] *noun*

marié *(masculine)*.

bridesmaid ['braɪdzmeɪd] *noun*

demoiselle *(feminine)* **d'honneur**.

bridge [brɪdʒ] *noun*

pont *(masculine)* : she walked across the bridge elle a traversé le pont.

bridle path ['braɪdlpɑːθ], **bridleway** ['braɪdlweɪ] *noun*

piste *(feminine)* **cavalière**.

brief [briːf] *adjective*

bref *(feminine* **brève***)* : his speech was very brief son discours a été très bref.

briefcase ['briːfkeɪs] *noun*

porte-documents *(masculine)* [*plural* **porte-documents**] : the papers are in his briefcase les papiers sont dans son porte-documents.

briefs [briːfs] *plural noun*

slip *(masculine)* : a pair of briefs un slip.

bright [braɪt] *adjective*

1. **vif** *(feminine* **vive***)* : I like bright colours j'aime les couleurs vives ; her dress is bright pink sa robe est rose vif ; she has bright eyes elle a un regard vif
2. **clair** : the room is very bright la chambre est très claire
3. **intelligent** : she's very bright elle est très intelligente.

brilliant ['brɪljənt] *adjective*

1. **brillant** : he's a brilliant student c'est un étudiant brillant

2. *informal* **super** *(invariable)*, **génial** : the film was brilliant! le film était super !

bring [brɪŋ] *(past tense & past participle* brought) *verb*

1. **apporter** : **I've brought you some flowers** je t'ai apporté des fleurs ; **can you bring me a cup of tea?** peux-tu m'apporter une tasse de thé ?
2. **amener** : **you can bring a friend** tu peux amener un ami

bring back *phrasal verb*

1. **rapporter** : **he brought a T-shirt back from Rome** il a rapporté un tee-shirt de Rome
2. **ramener** : **she brought him back home** elle l'a ramené chez lui

bring up *phrasal verb*

1. **élever** : **he was brought up by his grandparents** il a été élevé par ses grands-parents
2. **soulever** : **he brought the question up at the meeting** il a soulevé la question à la réunion.

Britain ['brɪtn] *noun*

la Grande-Bretagne

In French the names of countries are used with the definite article (**le, la** or **l'**), except when they follow the preposition **en**:

I'm going to Britain je vais en Grande-Bretagne ; **she lives in Britain** elle vit en Grande-Bretagne
➤ Great Britain.

British ['brɪtɪʃ] *adjective & noun*

■ *adjective*
britannique

The French adjective does not start with a capital letter:

he's a British actor c'est un acteur britannique
■ *noun*
➤ **the British** les Britanniques *(masculine plural)*
➤ **the British Isles** les îles *(feminine plural)* Britanniques.

Brittany ['brɪtənɪ] *noun*

la Bretagne : **St Malo is in Brittany** Saint-Malo est en Bretagne.

broad [brɔːd] *adjective*

large : **he has broad shoulders** il a les épaules larges
➤ **in broad daylight** en plein jour

➤ **broad beans** fèves *(feminine plural)*.

broadcast ['brɔːdkɑːst] *(past tense & past participle* broadcast) *noun & verb*

■ *noun*
émission *(feminine)* : **a live TV broadcast** une émission de télévision en direct
■ *verb*
1. **radiodiffuser** : **the programme is broadcast on the radio** le programme est radiodiffusé
2. **diffuser** : **the programme is broadcast on TV** le programme est diffusé à la télévision.

Broadway ['brɔːdweɪ] *noun*

nom d'une rue de New York

BROADWAY
Broadway est le nom d'une rue de New York, dans Manhattan, où se trouvent de nombreux théâtres. Centre de la création théâtrale américaine, Broadway est notamment connu pour ses comédies musicales.

broccoli ['brɒkəlɪ] *uncountable noun*

brocolis *(masculine plural)* : **I like broccoli** j'aime les brocolis ou j'aime le brocoli.

broil *US* [brɔɪl] *verb*

griller.

broke [brəʊk] *adjective & verb form*

■ *adjective*
informal **fauché** : **he's broke** il est fauché
■ *past tense of* **break**
he broke the glass il a cassé le verre.

broken ['brəʊkn] *adjective & verb form*

■ *adjective*
cassé : **the cup is broken** la tasse est cassée
■ *past participle of* **break**
he has broken his leg il s'est cassé la jambe.

bronze [brɒnz] *noun*

bronze *(masculine)* : **he got the bronze medal** il a eu la médaille de bronze ; **a bronze statue** une statue en bronze.

brooch [brəʊtʃ] *noun*

broche *(feminine)* : **she's wearing a ruby brooch** elle porte une broche en rubis.

broom [bruːm] *noun*

balai *(masculine)*.

brother ['brʌðər] *noun*

frère *(masculine)* : **she has two brothers** elle a deux frères.

brother-in-law ['brʌðərɪnlɔ:] *noun*

beau-frère *(masculine)* [*plural* **beaux-frères**].

brought [brɔ:t] *past tense & past participle of* bring

he brought a friend with him il a amené un ami avec lui ; **have you brought the map?** as-tu apporté la carte ?

brown [braʊn] *adjective*

1. brun *(feminine* **brune**), marron *(invariable)* : **he has brown hair** il a les cheveux bruns ; **brown shoes** des chaussures marron
2. bronzé : **he was very brown after his holiday** il était très bronzé après ses vacances
➤ **brown bread** pain *(masculine)* complet
➤ **brown sugar** sucre *(masculine)* roux.

brownie ['braʊnɪ] *noun*

brownie *(masculine)* : **he had a brownie for lunch** il a mangé un brownie à midi.

Brownie ['braʊnɪ] *noun*

jeannette *(feminine)* : **she's a Brownie** elle est jeannette.

browse [braʊz] *verb*

1. regarder : **he's browsing through a magazine** il regarde un magazine
2. naviguer : **she's browsing the Net** elle navigue sur le Net.

browser ['braʊzər] *noun*

navigateur *(masculine)* : **an Internet browser** un navigateur d'Internet.

bruise [bru:z] *noun & verb*

■ *noun*
bleu *(masculine)* : **he's covered in bruises** il est couvert de bleus
■ *verb*
he bruised his knee il s'est fait un bleu au genou.

brunch [brʌntʃ] *noun*

brunch *(masculine)* : **we had brunch** nous avons brunché.

brush [brʌʃ] *noun & verb*

■ *noun*
1. brosse *(feminine)* : **a hairbrush** une brosse à cheveux

2. pinceau *(masculine)* : **a paintbrush** un pinceau
■ *verb*
1. brosser : **she brushed the little girl's hair** elle a brossé les cheveux de la petite fille ; **she's brushing her hair** elle se brosse les cheveux ; **don't forget to brush your teeth!** n'oublie pas de te brosser les dents !
2. frôler : **she brushed against the table** elle a frôlé la table.

Brussels ['brʌslz] *noun*

Bruxelles : **she lives in Brussels** elle vit à Bruxelles ; **I'm going to Brussels** je vais à Bruxelles
➤ **Brussels sprouts** choux *(masculine plural)* de Bruxelles.

bubble ['bʌbl] *noun & verb*

■ *noun*
bulle *(feminine)* : **she was blowing bubbles through a straw** elle faisait des bulles avec une paille
■ *verb*
bouillonner : **the water is beginning to bubble** l'eau commence à bouillonner.

buck *US* [bʌk] *noun informal*

dollar *(masculine)* : **it costs ten bucks** ça coûte dix dollars.

bucket ['bʌkɪt] *noun*

seau *(masculine)* : **a bucket of water** un seau d'eau.

Buckingham Palace ['bʌkɪŋəm'pælɪs] *noun*

le palais de Buckingham

> BUCKINGHAM PALACE
> Le palais de Buckingham, dans le centre de Londres, est la résidence officielle de la famille royale britannique. Chaque jour, les gardes se relèvent pour monter la garde du palais. De nombreux touristes s'arrêtent pour regarder cette cérémonie de la relève de la garde (**the Changing of the Guard**).

buckle ['bʌkl] *noun*

boucle *(feminine)* : **my belt buckle is broken** la boucle de ma ceinture est cassée.

buddy ['bʌdɪ] *(plural* **buddies**) *noun informal*
copain *(masculine)*, copine *(feminine)*.

b

budgerigar UK ['bʌdʒərɪgɑːʳ] noun
perruche (feminine).

buffalo ['bʌfələʊ] noun
buffle (masculine).

bug [bʌg] noun & verb
■ noun
1. insecte (masculine) : **a bug flew in through the window** un insecte est entré par la fenêtre
2. microbe (masculine) : **he's caught a bug** il a attrapé un microbe
3. bogue (masculine) : **there's a bug in the program** le programme est bogué
■ verb informal
embêter : **stop bugging me!** arrête de m'embêter !

build [bɪld] (past tense & past participle built) verb
construire : **they're building houses next to the school** ils construisent des maisons à côté de l'école.

building ['bɪldɪŋ] noun
bâtiment (masculine).
➤ **an apartment building** un immeuble
➤ **a building site** un chantier.

built [bɪlt] past tense & past participle of build
he built a wall around the garden il a construit un mur autour du jardin ; **they have built some new houses** ils ont construit de nouvelles maisons.

bulb [bʌlb] noun
ampoule (feminine) : **a light bulb** une ampoule électrique.

bull [bʊl] noun
taureau (masculine) [plural taureaux].

bullet ['bʊlɪt] noun
balle (feminine) : **he put a bullet in the gun** il a mis une balle dans son revolver.

bull's-eye ['bʊlzaɪ] noun
mille (masculine), centre (masculine) de la cible : **bull's-eye!** dans le mille ! ; **she hit the bull's-eye!** elle a mis dans le mille !

bully ['bʊlɪ] noun & verb
■ noun (plural bullies)
tyran (masculine) : **he's a real bully** c'est un vrai tyran
■ verb
tyranniser : **she bullies the whole class** elle tyrannise toute la classe.

bump [bʌmp] noun & verb
■ noun
1. bosse (feminine) : **I've got a bump on my forehead** j'ai une bosse au front
2. choc (masculine) : **she felt a bump when the car hit the post** elle a senti un choc quand la voiture a touché le poteau
■ verb
cogner : **I bumped my head** je me suis cogné la tête

bump into phrasal verb
1. rentrer dans : **they bumped into the wall** ils sont rentrés dans le mur
2. rencontrer par hasard : **I bumped into my old teacher** j'ai rencontré mon ancien professeur par hasard.

bumper ['bʌmpəʳ] noun
pare-chocs (masculine) [plural pare-chocs].

bumpy ['bʌmpɪ] adjective
1. cahoteux (feminine cahoteuse) : **the road is bumpy** la route est cahoteuse
2. agité : **we had a bumpy flight** nous avons eu un vol agité.

bun [bʌn] noun
1. petit pain (masculine) au lait : **Alan ate a currant bun** Alan a mangé un petit pain aux raisins
2. chignon (masculine) : **Susie wears her hair in a bun** Susie porte un chignon.

bunch [bʌntʃ] noun
a bunch of flowers un bouquet de fleurs ; **a bunch of grapes** une grappe de raisin ; **a bunch of bananas** un régime de bananes ; **a bunch of keys** un trousseau de clés.

bungalow ['bʌŋgələʊ] noun
maison (feminine) à un étage.

bunk beds ['bʌŋk'bedz] plural noun
lits (masculine plural) superposés : **they sleep in bunk beds** ils dorment dans des lits superposés.

burger ['bɜːgəʳ] noun
hamburger (masculine).

burglar ['bɜːglər] *noun*
cambrioleur *(masculine)*
➤ **a burglar alarm** un système d'alarme.

burgundy ['bɜːgəndɪ] *adjective & noun*
◼ *adjective*
bordeaux *(invariable)* : **a burgundy scarf** une écharpe bordeaux
◼ *noun*
➤ **Burgundy** la Bourgogne : **Mary lives in Burgundy** Marie habite en Bourgogne
➤ **a bottle of Burgundy** une bouteille de Bourgogne.

buried ['berɪd] *past tense & past participle of* bury
the dog buried the bone le chien a enterré l'os.

burn [bɜːn] *verb & noun*
◼ *verb* (*past tense & past participle* burnt OR burned)
brûler : the house is burning la maison brûle ; **I've burnt myself** je me suis brûlé ; **I've burnt my hand** je me suis brûlé la main
◼ *noun*
brûlure *(feminine)* : **she has a burn on her arm** elle a une brûlure au bras.

burnt [bɜːnt] *past tense & past participle of* burn
he burnt the letter il a brûlé la lettre ; **have you burnt yourself?** tu t'es brûlé ?

burp [bɜːp] *verb*
informal **roter.**

burst [bɜːst] (*past tense & past participle* burst)
verb
1. **éclater : the tyre burst** le pneu a éclaté
2. **faire éclater : he burst the balloon** il a fait éclater le ballon
➤ **to burst into tears** fondre en larmes : **the little boy burst into tears** le petit garçon a fondu en larmes
➤ **to burst out laughing** éclater de rire : **they all burst out laughing** ils ont tous éclaté de rire.

bury ['berɪ] (*past tense & past participle* buried)
verb
enterrer : my grandmother is buried in Turville ma grand-mère est enterrée à Turville.

bus [bʌs] (*plural* buses) *noun*
bus *(masculine)* : **we took the bus into town** nous avons pris le bus pour aller en ville
➤ **a bus stop** un arrêt de bus : **we get off at the next bus stop** nous descendons au prochain arrêt.

bush [buʃ] (*plural* bushes) *noun*
buisson *(masculine)*
➤ **the African bush** la brousse africaine
➤ **the Australian bush** le bush australien.

business ['bɪznɪs] *noun*
1. (*uncountable*) **affaires** *(feminine plural)* : **business is good** les affaires vont bien ; **a business meeting** un rendez-vous d'affaires
2. (*plural* businesses) **entreprise** *(feminine)* : **he has a small business** il a une petite entreprise
➤ **mind your own business!** occupe-toi de tes affaires !

businessman ['bɪznɪsmæn] (*plural* businessmen ['bɪznɪsmen]) *noun*
homme *(masculine)* **d'affaires.**

businesswoman ['bɪznɪsˌwʊmən] (*plural* businesswomen ['bɪznɪsˌwɪmɪn]) *noun*
femme *(feminine)* **d'affaires.**

busker *UK* ['bʌskər] *noun*
musicien *(masculine)* **des rues, musicienne** *(feminine)* **des rues.**

bust [bʌst] *noun*
poitrine *(feminine)*.

busy ['bɪzɪ] *adjective*
1. **occupé : I'm very busy** je suis très occupé ; **Harry is busy reading** Harry est occupé à lire
2. **chargé : I have a busy week** j'ai une semaine chargée
3. **animé : Brighton is a busy town** Brighton est une ville animée
➤ **I got the busy signal** *US* ça sonnait occupé.

but [bʌt] *conjunction*
mais : I phoned him but he wasn't there je l'ai appelé mais il n'était pas là.

butcher ['butʃər] *noun*
boucher *(masculine)* : **I'm going to the butcher's** je vais chez le boucher
➤ **the butcher's shop** la boucherie.

b

butter ['bʌtəʳ] *noun*

beurre *(masculine)* : **would you like some butter?** voulez-vous du beurre ?

buttercup ['bʌtəkʌp] *noun*

bouton *(masculine)* **d'or**.

butterfly ['bʌtəflaɪ] *(plural* butterflies) *noun*

papillon *(masculine)*.

buttocks ['bʌtəks] *plural noun*

fesses *(feminine plural)*.

button ['bʌtn] *noun*

1. bouton *(masculine)* : **he did up his shirt buttons** il a boutonné sa chemise ; **click on the left mouse button** cliquez sur le bouton gauche de la souris
2. *US* pin's *(masculine)* : **he's wearing a button with a big smiley face on it** il porte un pin's avec un grand visage souriant.

buy [baɪ] *(past tense & past participle* bought) *verb*

acheter : **I'm going to buy some bread** je vais acheter du pain ; **she bought him a present** OR **she bought a present for him** elle lui a acheté un cadeau.

buzz [bʌz] *verb*

bourdonner : **the bees were buzzing** les abeilles bourdonnaient.

buzzer ['bʌzəʳ] *noun*

sonnette *(feminine)* : **I rang the buzzer** j'ai sonné.

by [baɪ] *preposition*

1. par : **this temple was built by the Romans** ce temple a été construit par les Romains ; **he paid by cheque** il a payé par chèque ; **I locked the door by mistake** j'ai fermé la porte à clé par erreur
2. de : **a book by Roald Dahl** un livre de Roald Dahl ; **a painting by Turner** un tableau de Turner
3. en : **we went there by bus** nous y sommes allés en bus ; **he always travels by train** il voyage toujours en train
4. près de : **he was sitting by the fire** il était assis près du feu ; **come and sit by me** viens t'asseoir près de moi
5. avant : **I'll be there by eight** je serai là avant huit heures ; **he must finish his work by next week** il doit finir son travail avant la semaine prochaine

➤ **by oneself** tout seul : **she was all by herself** elle était toute seule ; **I did it all by myself** je l'ai fait tout seul

➤ **by the way** à propos : **by the way, are you coming tonight?** à propos, tu viens ce soir ?

bye [baɪ], **bye-bye** [ˌbaɪ'baɪ, bə'baɪ] *exclamation*

au revoir !, salut ! : **bye, see you next week!** au revoir, à la semaine prochaine !

cab [kæb] *noun*

taxi *(masculine)* : **I'll take a cab** je vais prendre un taxi.

cabbage ['kæbɪdʒ] *noun*

chou *(masculine)*.

cabin ['kæbɪn] *noun*

1. cabine *(feminine)* : **her cabin is on the top deck** sa cabine est sur le pont supérieur
2. cabane *(feminine)* : **he lives in a log cabin** il habite une cabane en rondins.

cabinet ['kæbɪnɪt] *noun*

1. **a bathroom cabinet** une armoire de salle de bains
2. cabinet *(masculine)* : **he was in Tony Blair's cabinet** il faisait partie du cabinet de Tony Blair

⚠ Cabinet est un faux ami, il ne couvre pas les sens de "cabinet de toilette" et de "cabinet médical".

cable ['keɪbl] *noun*

câble *(masculine)*

➤ **a cable car** un téléphérique

➤ **cable television** OR **cable TV** la télévision par câble OR le câble : **we have cable television** nous sommes câblés OR nous avons le câble.

cafe, café ['kæfeɪ] *noun*

café *(masculine)* : **we had ice cream in a café** nous avons mangé une glace dans un café.

cafeteria [ˌkæfɪ'tɪərɪə] *noun*

cantine *(feminine)* : **we had lunch at the cafeteria** nous avons déjeuné à la cantine.

cage [keɪdʒ] *noun*

cage *(feminine)*.

cagoule *UK* [kə'guːl] *noun*

K-way® *(masculine)*

⚠ Le mot anglais **cagoule** est un faux ami, il ne signifie pas "cagoule".

cake [keɪk] *noun*

gâteau *(masculine)* [*plural* gâteaux] : **she's making a chocolate cake** elle fait un gâteau au chocolat

➤ **a cake shop** une pâtisserie.

calculator ['kælkjʊleɪtər] *noun*

calculette *(feminine)* : **a pocket calculator** une calculette.

calendar ['kælɪndər] *noun*

calendrier *(masculine)* : **mark the date on the calendar** coche la date sur le calendrier.

calf [kɑːf] (*plural* calves [kɑːvz]) *noun*

1. veau *(masculine)* [*plural* veaux] : **a cow and her calf** une vache et son veau
2. mollet *(masculine)* : **I've got a pain in my calf** j'ai mal au mollet.

California [ˌkælɪ'fɔːnjə] *noun*

la Californie : **Hollywood is in California** Hollywood est en Californie.

call [kɔːl] *noun & verb*

■ *noun*

appel *(masculine)* : **there's a call for you** il y a un appel pour toi ; **I'll give you a call** je t'appellerai

➤ **a call box** *UK* une cabine téléphonique

■ *verb*

1. appeler : **we called the police** nous avons appelé la police ; **everyone calls her Sassy** tout le monde l'appelle Sassy
2. traiter de : **he called me a liar** il m'a traité de menteur

➤ **to be called** s'appeler : **what is he called?**

comment s'appelle-t-il ? ; **what's this called?** comment ça s'appelle ?

➤ **who's calling?** qui est à l'appareil ?

call back *phrasal verb*

rappeler : **I'll call back later** je rappellerai plus tard

call off *phrasal verb*

annuler : **they called off the meeting** ils ont annulé la réunion

call on *phrasal verb*

rendre visite à : **they called on us yesterday** ils nous ont rendu visite hier

call round *UK phrasal verb*

passer : **I'll call round this afternoon** je passerai cet après-midi.

calm [kɑːm] *adjective & verb*

calme : **the sea is calm** la mer est calme ; **she tried to keep calm** elle a essayé de garder son calme

calm down *phrasal verb*

se calmer : **calm down!** calmez-vous !

calves *plural of* calf.

camcorder ['kæmˌkɔːdər] *noun*

Caméscope® *(masculine)*.

came [keɪm] *past tense of* come

he came to see me il est venu me voir.

camel ['kæml] *noun*

chameau *(masculine)* [*plural* chameaux].

camera ['kæmərə] *noun*

1. appareil photo *(masculine)* : **a digital camera** un appareil photo numérique
2. caméra *(feminine)* : **a video camera** une caméra vidéo.

camp [kæmp] *noun & verb*

■ *noun*

camp *(masculine)* : **we set up camp near the river** nous avons établi un camp près de la rivière

➤ **a camp bed** un lit de camp

➤ **a camp site** un terrain de camping OR un camping

■ *verb*
camper : we camped on the beach nous avons campé sur la plage.

camper [ˈkæmpəʳ] *noun*

campeur *(masculine)*, **campeuse** *(feminine)* : **there are campers near the river** il y a des campeurs près de la rivière
➤ **a camper van** un camping-car.

camping [ˈkæmpɪŋ] *uncountable noun*

camping *(masculine)* : **they go camping every summer** ils font du camping tous les étés

⚠ En anglais, le mot **camping** est un faux ami, il ne signifie pas "terrain de camping".

can *verb & noun*

■ *verb* [kən, kæn]
1. (*negative* **can't** *or* **cannot**) **pouvoir** : **can I help you?** je peux t'aider ? ; **Peter can't come on Friday** Peter ne peut pas venir vendredi ; **can I speak to Rachel, please?** est-ce que je peux parler à Rachel ?

When **can** is used with a verb of perception (like **see, hear, feel, understand**) it is not translated at all:

I can't see je ne vois pas ; **can you hear me?** tu m'entends ? ; **I can't feel anything** je ne sens rien ; **he can't understand what you are saying** il ne comprend pas ce que tu dis

2. *When 'can' means 'know how to'* **savoir** : **can you swim?** tu sais nager ? ; **she can speak Italian** elle sait parler italien ; **I can't drive** je ne sais pas conduire
■ *noun* [kæn]
boîte *(feminine)* : **a can of beans** une boîte de haricots
➤ **a can opener** un ouvre-boîtes.

Canada [ˈkænədə] *noun*

le Canada

In French the names of countries are used with the definite article (**le, la** or **l'**). Remember that the French preposition **à** combines with **le** to become **au**:

Canada is a big country with a small population le Canada est un grand pays peu peuplé ; **I'm going to Canada** je vais au Canada ; **Henry lives in Canada** Henry vit au Canada.

Canadian [kəˈneɪdjən] *adjective & noun*

■ *adjective*
canadien *(feminine* **canadienne***)*

The French adjective does not start with a capital letter:

there is a maple leaf on the Canadian flag il y a une feuille d'érable sur le drapeau canadien
■ *noun*
Canadien *(masculine)*, **Canadienne** *(feminine)*.

canal [kəˈnæl] *noun*

canal *(masculine)* [*plural* **canaux**].

cancel [ˈkænsl] *verb*

annuler : **they cancelled the meeting** ils ont annulé la réunion ; **the flight has been cancelled** le vol a été annulé.

cancer [ˈkænsəʳ] *noun*

1. **cancer** *(masculine)* : **she has cancer** elle a un cancer
2. **Cancer** *(masculine)* : **he's a Cancer** il est Cancer.

candidate [ˈkændɪdət, *US* ˈkændɪdeɪt] *noun*

candidat *(masculine)*, **candidate** *(feminine)* : **he's a candidate in the elections** il est candidat aux élections.

candies [ˈkændɪz] *plural of* candy.

candle [ˈkændl] *noun*

bougie *(feminine)* : **she blew out the candle** elle a soufflé la bougie.

candlestick [ˈkændlstɪk] *noun*

bougeoir *(masculine)*.

candy *US* [ˈkændɪ] *noun*

1. (*plural* **candies**) **bonbon** *(masculine)* : **do you want a candy?** tu veux un bonbon ?
2. (*uncountable*) **bonbons** *(masculine plural)* : **he likes candy** il aime les bonbons
➤ **a candy store** une confiserie.

candyfloss *UK* [ˈkændɪflɒs] *uncountable noun*

barbe *(feminine)* **à papa**.

canned [kænd] *adjective*

en boîte, en conserve : canned sardines des sardines en boîte.

cannot ['kænɒt] *negative of* can

you cannot leave the classroom vous ne pouvez pas quitter la salle de classe

La forme **cannot** est surtout employée dans la langue écrite. Dans la langue parlée ou plus familière, **cannot** devient **can't**.

canoe [kə'nuː] *noun*

canoë *(masculine)*.

canoeing [kə'nuːɪŋ] *uncountable noun*

canoë-kayak *(masculine)* **: to go canoeing** faire du canoë-kayak ; **she likes canoeing** elle aime faire du canoë-kayak.

can't [kɑːnt] = cannot

I can't come to the party je ne peux pas venir à la fête ; **she can't swim** elle ne sait pas nager.

canteen UK [kæn'tiːn] *noun*

cantine *(feminine)* **: we eat in the canteen** nous mangeons à la cantine.

canvas ['kænvəs] *noun*

toile *(feminine)* **: canvas shoes** des chaussures en toile.

cap [kæp] *noun*

1. casquette *(feminine)* **: he wears his baseball cap back to front** il porte sa casquette à l'envers

2. capsule *(feminine)* **: take the cap off the bottle** enlevez la capsule de la bouteille.

capable ['keɪpəbl] *adjective*

capable **: I'm quite capable of doing it by myself** je suis tout à fait capable de le faire tout seul.

capital ['kæpɪtl] *noun*

1. capitale *(feminine)* **: Edinburgh is the capital of Scotland** Édimbourg est la capitale de l'Écosse

2. majuscule *(feminine)* **: write your name in capitals** écrivez votre nom en majuscules
➤ **a capital city** une capitale
➤ **in capital letters** en majuscules.

Capricorn ['kæprɪkɔːn] *noun*

Capricorne *(masculine)* **: she's a Capricorn** elle est Capricorne.

capsize [kæp'saɪz, US 'kæpsaɪz] *verb*

chavirer **: the boat capsized** le bateau a chaviré.

captain ['kæptɪn] *noun*

capitaine *(masculine)* **: he's the captain of our team** c'est le capitaine de notre équipe.

car [kɑːʳ] *noun*

1. voiture *(feminine)* **: can you drive a car?** tu sais conduire une voiture ? ; **we're going by car** nous y allons en voiture

2. US wagon *(masculine)* **: this train has ten cars** ce train a dix wagons
➤ **a car crash** un accident de voiture
➤ **a car park** UK un parking **: my car is in the car park** ma voiture est au parking.

caravan UK ['kærəvæn] *noun*

caravane *(feminine)*
➤ **a caravan site** un camping pour caravanes.

card [kɑːd] *noun*

carte *(feminine)* **: a birthday card** une carte d'anniversaire ; **a game of cards** un jeu de cartes ; **they're playing cards** ils jouent aux cartes.

cardboard ['kɑːdbɔːd] *noun*

carton *(masculine)* **: a cardboard box** une boîte en carton.

cardigan ['kɑːdɪgən] *noun*

gilet *(masculine)* **: Janet is wearing a woollen cardigan** Janet porte un gilet en laine.

care [keəʳ] *noun & verb*

▪ *uncountable noun*
soin *(masculine)* **: skin care** des soins pour la peau
➤ **to take care of**
1. s'occuper de **: he takes care of the children** il s'occupe des enfants
2. prendre soin de **: you must take care of your books** il faut prendre soin de tes livres ; **take care!** prends bien soin de toi !
▪ *verb*
I don't care ça m'est égal ; **who cares?** qu'est-ce que ça peut faire ?

care about *phrasal verb*

se soucier de **: she doesn't care about her appearance** elle ne se soucie pas de son apparence

care for *phrasal verb*

1. **s'occuper de** : she cares for her elderly parents elle s'occupe de ses parents âgés
2. **aimer** : I don't care for his new friends je n'aime pas trop ses nouveaux amis.

career [kə'rɪəʳ] *noun*

carrière *(feminine)* : a career in medicine une carrière de médecin.

careful ['keəfʊl] *adjective*

prudent : he's always very careful il est toujours très prudent ; I'm always careful not to make a noise je fais toujours attention à ne pas faire de bruit
➤ **be careful!** fais attention !

carefully ['keəfəlɪ] *adverb*

1. **prudemment** : he drives carefully il conduit prudemment
2. **soigneusement** : she did the work carefully elle a fait le travail soigneusement.

careless ['keəlɪs] *adjective*

1. **négligent** : Mary is very careless Mary est très négligente
2. **peu soigné** : his work is careless son travail est peu soigné
➤ **a careless mistake** une faute d'inattention.

caretaker UK ['keəˌteɪkəʳ] *noun*

gardien *(masculine)*, gardienne *(feminine)* : he's the caretaker of the building c'est le gardien de l'immeuble.

Caribbean [UK kærɪ'biːən, US kə'rɪbɪən]

noun & adjective

◼ *noun*
the Carribean les Caraïbes *(feminine plural)* ; they live in the Caribbean ils vivent dans les Caraïbes ; she's going to the Caribbean elle va aux Caraïbes

◼ *adjective*
antillais

> The French adjective does not start with a capital letter:

I like Caribbean music j'aime la musique antillaise
➤ **the Caribbean Sea** la mer des Caraïbes.

carnival ['kɑːnɪvl] *noun*

carnaval *(masculine)*.

carol ['kærəl] *noun*

chant *(masculine)* : a Christmas carol un chant de Noël.

carpet ['kɑːpɪt] *noun*

1. **tapis** *(masculine)* : a Turkish carpet un tapis turc
2. **moquette** *(feminine)* : wall-to-wall carpet une moquette.

carriage UK ['kærɪdʒ] *noun*

voiture *(feminine)* : the train has six carriages le train a six voitures.

carried ['kærɪd] *past tense & past participle of* carry
I carried the box into the house j'ai porté le carton jusque dans la maison.

carrier bag UK ['kærɪəʳ ˌbæg] *noun*

sac *(masculine)* en plastique.

carrot ['kærət] *noun*

carotte *(feminine)*.

carry ['kærɪ] *verb*

1. **porter** : she's carrying a large bag elle porte un grand sac
2. **transporter** : the bus can carry fifty passengers le bus peut transporter cinquante passagers

carry on *phrasal verb*

continuer : he carried on working il a continué à travailler.

cart ['kɑːt] *noun*

1. **charrette** *(feminine)* : the horse was pulling the cart le cheval tirait la charrette
2. *US* **chariot** *(masculine)*, **Caddie®** *(masculine)* : a shopping cart un chariot OR un Caddie.

carton ['kɑːtn] *noun*

carton *(masculine)* : my books are in a large carton mes livres sont dans un grand carton
➤ **a carton of yoghurt** un pot de yaourt
➤ **a carton of milk** une brique de lait.

cartoon [kɑː'tuːn] *noun*

1. **dessin** *(masculine)* **humoristique** : she likes the cartoons in the newspapers elle aime les dessins humoristiques dans les journaux
2. **dessin** *(masculine)* **animé** : there's a cartoon on TV il y a un dessin animé à la télé
3. **bande** *(feminine)* **dessinée** : a cartoon strip une bande dessinée.

cartwheel ['kɑːtwiːl] *noun*

to do a cartwheel faire la roue.

carve [kɑːv] *verb*

1. sculpter : he carved a statue out of wood il a sculpté une statue en bois
2. graver : Kilroy carved his name on the bench Kilroy a gravé son nom sur le banc
3. découper : she's carving the turkey elle découpe la dinde.

case [keɪs] *noun*

1. valise *(feminine)* : I've packed my case j'ai fait ma valise
2. étui *(masculine)* : she put her glasses in their case elle a mis ses lunettes dans leur étui
3. cas *(masculine)* : in that case I'm not coming dans ce cas-là je ne viens pas ; a serious case of flu un grave cas de grippe
> in any case de toute façon
> in case au cas où : come early just in case viens tôt au cas où ; take your coat in case it rains prends ton manteau au cas où il pleuvrait.

cash [kæʃ] *uncountable noun*

espèces *(feminine plural)*, argent *(masculine)* liquide : I have no cash on me je n'ai pas d'argent sur moi ; a hundred dollars in cash cent dollars en espèces OR cent dollars en liquide
> to pay cash payer comptant OR payer en espèces
> a cash dispenser *UK* OR a cash machine un distributeur automatique de billets.

cashew nut ['kæʃuːnʌt] *noun*

noix *(feminine)* de cajou.

cashier [kæ'ʃɪəʳ] *noun*

caissier *(masculine)*, caissière *(feminine)* : she's a cashier elle est caissière.

casserole *UK* ['kæsərəʊl] *noun*

ragoût *(masculine)* : she made a lamb casserole elle a préparé un ragoût d'agneau
> a casserole dish une cocotte

⚠️ Casserole est un faux ami, il ne signifie pas "casserole" au sens de "ustensile de cuisine".

cassette [kæ'set] *noun*

cassette *(feminine)*
> a cassette player un lecteur de cassettes
> a cassette recorder un magnétophone à cassettes.

castle ['kɑːsl] *noun*

château *(masculine)* [plural châteaux].

casual ['kæʒʊəl] *adjective*

1. décontracté : they were wearing casual clothes ils avaient une tenue décontractée
2. désinvolte : he's very casual il est très désinvolte.

casualty ['kæʒjʊəltɪ], **casualty department** ['kæʒjʊəltɪdɪ'pɑːtmənt] *noun*

service *(masculine)* des urgences.

cat [kæt] *noun*

chat *(masculine)*, chatte *(feminine)* : they have a cat called Kieth ils ont un chat qui s'appelle Kieth ; my cat has had kittens ma chatte a eu des petits.

catalogue *UK*, **catalog** *US* ['kætəlɒg] *noun*

catalogue *(masculine)*.

catch [kætʃ] *(past tense & past participle* caught) *verb*

1. attraper : he caught a fish il a attrapé un poisson ; she has caught a cold elle a attrapé un rhume
2. prendre : Fred is catching the 6 o'clock train Fred prend le train de 6 heures
3. surprendre : I caught him smoking je l'ai surpris en train de fumer
4. saisir : I didn't catch what you said je n'ai pas saisi ce que tu as dit
5. I caught my finger in the door je me suis pris le doigt dans la porte

catch up *phrasal verb*

rattraper : you go on and I'll catch you up continue, je te rattraperai ; I was away yesterday so I'll have to catch up j'étais absent hier, donc je dois rattraper mon retard.

catching ['kætʃɪŋ] *adjective*

contagieux *(feminine* contagieuse) : this disease isn't catching cette maladie n'est pas contagieuse.

category ['kætəgərɪ] *noun*

catégorie *(feminine)*.

caterpillar ['kætəpɪləʳ] *noun*

chenille *(feminine)* : caterpillars turn into butterflies la chenille se transforme en papillon.

C

cathedral [kə'θiːdrəl] *noun*

cathédrale *(feminine)* : **St Paul's Cathedral is in London** la cathédrale Saint-Paul se trouve à Londres.

Catholic ['kæθlɪk] *adjective & noun*

catholique.

catsup *US noun* ➤ ketchup.

cattle ['kætl] *plural noun*

bétail *(masculine)* : **the cattle are in the field** le bétail est dans le champ.

caught [kɔːt] *past tense & past participle of* catch

he caught a large fish il a attrapé un gros poisson ; **I've caught a cold** j'ai attrapé un rhume.

cauliflower ['kɒlɪ,flaʊəʳ] *noun*

chou-fleur *(masculine)* [*plural* choux-fleurs].

cause [kɔːz] *noun & verb*

■ *noun*

cause *(feminine)* : **we don't know the cause of the accident** nous ignorons la cause de l'accident

■ *verb*

causer, provoquer : **the storm caused a lot of damage** la tempête a causé de graves dégâts ; **what caused the accident?** qu'est-ce qui a provoqué l'accident ?

cautious ['kɔːʃəs] *adjective*

prudent : **Mr Jones is very cautious** M. Jones est très prudent.

cave [keɪv] *noun*

grotte *(feminine)*, **caverne** *(feminine)*

⚠ Le mot anglais **cave** est un faux ami, il ne signifie pas "cave".

CD [,siː'diː] *(abbreviation of* compact disc*) noun*

CD *(masculine)* : **have you heard his new CD?** tu as écouté son dernier CD ?
➤ **a CD player** un lecteur de CD.

CD-ROM [,siːdiː'rɒm] *(abbreviation of* compact disc read-only memory*) noun*
CD-ROM *(masculine)*.

ceiling ['siːlɪŋ] *noun*

plafond *(masculine)*.

celebrate ['selɪbreɪt] *verb*

1. fêter : **we're going to celebrate my birthday** nous allons fêter mon anniversaire
2. faire la fête : **people are celebrating in the streets** les gens font la fête dans la rue.

celebration [,selɪ'breɪʃn] *noun*

fête *(feminine)*.

celebrity [sɪ'lebrətɪ] *noun*

célébrité *(feminine)* : **he's a celebrity** c'est une célébrité.

celery ['selərɪ] *noun*

céleri *(masculine)* : **a stick of celery** une branche de céleri.

cell [sel] *noun*

cellule *(feminine)*.

cellar ['seləʳ] *noun*

cave *(feminine)* : **I'm going down to the cellar** je descends à la cave.

cello ['tʃeləʊ] *noun*

violoncelle *(masculine)* : **she plays the cello** elle joue du violoncelle.

cemetery ['semɪtrɪ] *(plural* cemeteries*) noun*

cimetière *(masculine)*.

cent [sent] *noun*

cent *(masculine)* : **that's five dollars and twenty cents** ça fait cinq dollars et vingt cents.

center *US* ➤ centre *UK*.

centigrade ['sentɪgreɪd] *adjective*

centigrade *(masculine)* : **it's 20 degrees centigrade** il fait 20 degrés.

centimetre *UK*, **centimeter** *US* ['sentɪ,miːtəʳ] *noun*

centimètre *(masculine)* : **the table is 50 centimetres wide** la table fait 50 centimètres de large.

central ['sentrəl] *adjective*

central : **central processing unit** unité centrale.

centre *UK*, **center** *US* ['sentəʳ] *noun*

centre *(masculine)* : **there's a statue in the centre of the room** il y a une statue au centre de la pièce

> **in the centre of town** dans le centre-ville.

century ['sentʃʊrɪ] (plural **centuries**) noun

siècle (masculine) : **in the twentieth century** au vingtième siècle.

cereal ['sɪərɪəl] noun

céréales (feminine plural) : **I have cereal for breakfast** je mange des céréales au petit déjeuner.

ceremony ['serɪmənɪ] (plural **ceremonies**) noun

cérémonie (feminine).

certain ['sɜːtn] adjective

certain : **I'm certain that it's her** je suis certain que c'est elle ; **I'm certain of it** j'en suis certain ; **certain people think he's guilty** certaines personnes croient qu'il est coupable
> **to make certain of something** s'assurer de quelque chose : **he made certain the window was closed** il s'est assuré que la fenêtre était fermée.

certainly ['sɜːtnlɪ] adverb

certainement, bien sûr : **certainly not!** certainement pas ! ; **are you coming too? – I certainly am!** tu viens, toi aussi ? – bien sûr que oui !

certificate [sə'tɪfɪkət] noun

certificat (masculine).

chain [tʃeɪn] noun

chaîne (feminine) : **Elsa is wearing a silver chain** Elsa porte une chaîne en argent
> **to pull the chain** tirer la chasse.

chair [tʃeəʳ] noun

1. chaise (feminine) : **a table and four chairs** une table et quatre chaises
2. fauteuil (masculine) : **there was a comfortable chair by the fire** il y avait un fauteuil confortable au coin du feu.

chairman ['tʃeəmən] (plural **chairmen** ['tʃeəmən]) noun
président (masculine).

chairperson ['tʃeə,pɜːsn] noun
président (masculine), présidente (feminine).

chairwoman ['tʃeə,wʊmən] (plural **chairwomen** ['tʃeə,wɪmɪn]) noun
présidente (feminine).

chalk [tʃɔːk] uncountable noun

craie (feminine) : **a piece of chalk** un morceau de craie.

challenge ['tʃælɪndʒ] noun & verb

■ noun
défi (masculine)
■ verb
he challenged me to a game of tennis il m'a proposé de faire une partie de tennis.

champagne [,ʃæm'peɪn] noun

champagne (masculine) : **they're drinking champagne** ils boivent du champagne.

champion ['tʃæmpjən] noun

champion (masculine), championne (feminine) : **she's the world champion** elle est championne du monde.

championship ['tʃæmpjənʃɪp] noun

championnat (masculine) : **he's playing in the championship** il joue dans le championnat.

chance [tʃɑːns] noun

1. chance (feminine) : **she doesn't have a chance** elle n'a aucune chance ; **he has a good chance of winning** il a de fortes chances de gagner
2. occasion (feminine) : **it gave me a chance to explore the city** ça m'a donné l'occasion d'explorer la ville
3. hasard (masculine) : **I met him by chance** je l'ai rencontré par hasard
4. risque (masculine) : **he took a chance** il a pris un risque.

change [tʃeɪndʒ] noun & verb

■ noun
1. changement (masculine) : **there's been a change of plan** il y a eu un changement de programme
2. monnaie (feminine) : **do you have any change?** vous avez de la monnaie ?
> **a change of clothes** des vêtements de rechange
> **that makes a change** ça change
> **for a change** pour changer : **let's go dancing for a change** allons danser, pour changer
■ verb
1. changer : **he really has changed** il a vraiment changé ; **I want to change 200 dollars into euros** je veux changer 200 dollars en euros

C

2. changer de : **we have to change trains** nous devons changer de train ; **he changed into another pair of trousers** il a changé de pantalon ; **she changed gear** elle a changé de vitesse

3. se changer : **she changed before going out** elle s'est changée avant de sortir

4. échanger : **you can change the skirt if it doesn't fit** vous pouvez échanger cette jupe si ce n'est pas la bonne taille

➤ **to change one's mind** changer d'avis : **Richard changed his mind** Richard a changé d'avis

➤ **to get changed** se changer : **I'm going to get changed** je vais me changer.

changing room ['tʃeɪndʒɪŋ ˌruːm] noun

1. UK vestiaire (masculin) : **the football team is in the changing room** l'équipe de football est dans le vestiaire

2. cabine (feminine) d'essayage : **the store has no changing rooms** le magasin n'a pas de cabine d'essayage.

channel ['tʃænl] noun

chaîne (feminine) : **can you change the channel?** peux-tu changer de chaîne ?

➤ **the Channel** OR **the English Channel** la Manche

➤ **the Channel Islands** les îles (feminine plural) Anglo-Normandes

➤ **the Channel Tunnel** le tunnel sous la Manche.

chapter ['tʃæptər] noun

chapitre (masculine) : **the hero dies in chapter three** le héros meurt au chapitre trois.

character ['kærəktər] noun

1. caractère (masculine) : **Jennifer has a very gentle character** Jennifer a un caractère très doux

2. personnage (masculine) : **I like the character played by Johnny Depp** j'aime bien le personnage joué par Johnny Depp.

charge [tʃɑːdʒ] noun & verb

◼ noun

1. frais (masculine plural) : **there's a delivery charge** il y a des frais de livraison

2. accusation (feminine) : **he denies the charges** il rejette les accusations

➤ **there's a charge for admission** l'entrée est payante

➤ **it's free of charge** c'est gratuit

➤ **to be in charge** être responsable : **Mrs Duncan is in charge** la responsable c'est Mme Duncan ; **I'm in charge of the department** je suis responsable du service

◼ verb

1. faire payer : **they charged me five dollars** ils m'ont fait payer cinq dollars

2. prendre : **how much do you charge?** vous prenez combien ?

3. inculper, accuser : **he has been charged with murder** il a été inculpé de meurtre

⚠ Le mot anglais **charge** est un faux ami. Le verbe ne signifie pas "charger" et le nom n'a pas le sens de "charge".

charity ['tʃærətɪ] (plural **charities**) noun

1. association (feminine) caritative : **Oxfam is a charity** Oxfam est une association caritative

2. charité (feminine) : **I helped him out of charity** je l'ai aidé par charité

➤ **for charity** pour les bonnes œuvres : **we raised £100 for charity** nous avons collecté 100 livres pour les bonnes œuvres.

charm [tʃɑːm] noun

charme (masculine).

charming ['tʃɑːmɪŋ] adjective

charmant : **he's very charming** il est tout à fait charmant.

chart [tʃɑːt] noun

tableau (masculine) : **the chart shows average temperatures** le tableau indique les températures moyennes

➤ **the charts** le hit-parade : **her new song is number two in the charts** sa nouvelle chanson est numéro deux au hit-parade.

chase [tʃeɪs] noun & verb

◼ noun

poursuite (feminine) : **a car chase** une poursuite en voiture

◼ verb

poursuivre : **somebody is chasing me** quelqu'un me poursuit

chase after phrasal verb

courir après : **the dog was chasing after me** le chien courait après moi

chase away phrasal verb

chasser : **he chased the intruder away** il a chassé l'intrus.

chat [tʃæt] *noun & verb*

■ *noun*

1. **conversation** *(feminine)* **: we were having a chat** nous parlions de choses et d'autres
2. **discussion** *(feminine)*, **chat** *(masculine)* **: on-line chat** discussion en ligne
➤ **a chat room** un forum de discussion OR un chat

■ *verb*

1. **bavarder, parler : he was chatting with a friend** il bavardait avec un ami
2. **bavarder, dialoguer : to chat live** bavarder en direct OR dialoguer en direct.

chatterbox ['tʃætəbɒks] *noun*

moulin *(masculine)* **à paroles : Tommy's a real chatterbox** Tommy est un vrai moulin à paroles.

cheap [tʃiːp] *adjective*

pas cher *(feminine* **pas chère)* : **it's a cheap dress** c'est une robe pas chère.

cheaper ['tʃiːpər] *(comparative of* cheap) *adjective*

moins cher *(feminine* **moins chère)* : **this coat is cheaper than the other** ce manteau est moins cher que l'autre.

cheapest ['tʃiːpəst] *(superlative of* cheap) *adjective*

le moins cher *(feminine* **la moins chère)* : **it's the cheapest shop in town** c'est le magasin le moins cher de la ville.

cheat [tʃiːt] *noun & verb*

■ *noun*

tricheur *(masculine)*, **tricheuse** *(feminine)* **: he's a cheat** c'est un tricheur

■ *verb*

tricher : he cheats at cards il triche aux cartes.

cheater *US* ['tʃiːtər] *noun* ➤ cheat.

check [tʃek] *noun & verb*

■ *noun*

1. **contrôle** *(masculine)* **: an identity check** un contrôle d'identité
2. *US* **addition** *(feminine)* **: can I have the check, please?** l'addition, s'il vous plaît !
3. *US* **chèque** *(masculine)* **: he paid by check** il a payé par chèque
➤ **a check shirt** une chemise à carreaux

■ *verb*

1. **vérifier : the accountant checked the figures** le comptable a vérifié les chiffres
2. **contrôler : they checked our passports** ils ont contrôlé nos passeports

check in *phrasal verb*

1. **se présenter à l'enregistrement : they checked in for their flight to Rome** ils se sont présentés à l'enregistrement de leur vol pour Rome
2. **se présenter à la réception : we checked in at the hotel** en arrivant, nous nous sommes présentés à la réception de l'hôtel

check out *phrasal verb*

1. **régler sa note : they checked out from the hotel** ils ont réglé leur note d'hôtel
2. *informal* **regarder : check this out!** regarde-moi ça !

checkbook *US noun* ➤ chequebook *UK*.

checked [tʃekt] *adjective*

à carreaux : a checked shirt une chemise à carreaux.

checkers *US* ['tʃekəz] *noun*

jeu *(masculine)* **de dames : they're playing checkers** ils jouent aux dames.

check-in [tʃekɪn] *noun*

enregistrement *(masculine)* **: check-in is at 6 o'clock** l'enregistrement est à 6 heures.

checkout ['tʃekaut] *noun*

caisse *(feminine)* **: a supermarket checkout** une caisse de supermarché.

checkroom *US* ['tʃekruːm] *noun*

consigne *(feminine)* **: leave your bag in the checkroom** laisse ta valise à la consigne.

checkup ['tʃekʌp] *noun*

1. **bilan** *(masculine)* **de santé : he went to the hospital for a checkup** il est allé à l'hôpital pour un bilan de santé
2. **examen** *(masculine)* **de routine : he's going to the dentist for a checkup** il va chez le dentiste pour un examen de routine.

cheek [tʃiːk] *noun*

1. **joue** *(feminine)* **: she kissed him on the cheek** elle l'a embrassé sur la joue
2. *UK* **culot** *(masculine)* **: what a cheek!** quel culot !

cheeky UK ['tʃiːkɪ] adjective

effronté : **a cheeky little girl** une petite effrontée

➤ **to be cheeky** avoir du culot : **Tony's very cheeky!** Tony a un sacré culot !

cheer [tʃɪəʳ] noun & verb

■ noun

acclamation (feminine) : **there were cheers when he came on stage** il y a eu des acclamations quand il est monté sur scène

➤ **three cheers for Harry!** hourra pour Harry !

➤ **cheers!**

1. santé ! : **here's to you, cheers!** à ta santé !
2. UK salut ! : **I'm off, cheers!** je pars, salut !

■ verb

applaudir : **everyone was cheering** tout le monde applaudissait

cheer up phrasal verb

1. remonter le moral à : **I tried to cheer him up** j'ai essayé de lui remonter le moral
2. retrouver le moral : **he cheered up when his friends came to see him** il a retrouvé le moral quand ses amis sont venus le voir ; **cheer up!** allez, un petit sourire !

cheerful ['tʃɪəfʊl] adjective

gai : **Ellen is very cheerful** Ellen est très gaie.

cheese [tʃiːz] noun

fromage (masculine) : **a cheese sandwich** un sandwich au fromage.

cheeseburger ['tʃiːz,bɜːgəʳ] noun

cheeseburger (masculine).

cheesecake ['tʃiːzkeɪk] noun

gâteau (masculine) au fromage blanc, cheesecake (masculine) : **a strawberry cheesecake** un cheesecake à la fraise.

chef [ʃef] noun

chef (masculine) : **he's a chef in an Indian restaurant** il est chef dans un restaurant indien.

chemical ['kemɪkl] noun

produit (masculine) chimique.

chemist UK ['kemɪst] noun

1. pharmacien (masculine), pharmacienne (feminine) : **he's a chemist** il est pharmacien
2. pharmacie (feminine) : **is there a chemist near here?** y a-t-il une pharmacie près d'ici ? ; **at the chemist's** à la pharmacie.

chemistry ['kemɪstrɪ] noun

chimie (feminine) : **a chemistry lesson** un cours de chimie.

cheque UK, **check** US [tʃek] noun

chèque (masculine) : **she paid by cheque** elle a payé par chèque.

chequebook UK, **checkbook** US ['tʃekbʊk] noun

chéquier (masculine).

cherry ['tʃerɪ] (plural cherries) noun

cerise (feminine)

➤ **a cherry tree** un cerisier.

chess [tʃes] noun

échecs (masculine plural) : **they're playing chess** ils jouent aux échecs.

chessboard ['tʃesbɔːd] noun

échiquier (masculine).

chest [tʃest] noun

1. poitrine (feminine) : **he has a pain in his chest** il a une douleur dans la poitrine
2. coffre (masculine) : **there's a big chest under the bed** il y a un gros coffre sous le lit
➤ **a chest of drawers** une commode.

chestnut ['tʃesnʌt] noun

châtaigne (feminine)

➤ **a chestnut tree** un châtaignier.

chew [tʃuː] verb

mâcher.

chewing gum ['tʃuːɪŋgʌm] noun

chewing-gum (masculine) : **a stick of chewing gum** un chewing-gum.

chicken ['tʃɪkɪn] noun

poulet (masculine) : **a roast chicken** un poulet rôti.

chickenpox ['tʃɪkɪnpɒks] noun

varicelle (feminine) : **he has chickenpox** il a la varicelle.

chief [tʃiːf] noun & adjective

■ noun

chef (masculine) : **he's the chief of an Indian tribe** c'est le chef d'une tribu indienne

■ adjective

principal : **that's the chief problem** c'est le problème principal.

child [tʃaɪld] (*plural* children ['tʃɪldrən])

noun

enfant *(masculine or feminine)* : **she's just a child** c'est une enfante ; **the children's department in a store** le rayon enfant dans un magasin.

childhood ['tʃaɪldhʊd] *noun*

enfance *(feminine)* : **it happened in her childhood** ça s'est passé dans son enfance.

children *plural of* child.

chili, chilli ['tʃɪlɪ] (*plural* chilies OR chillies)

noun

piment *(masculine)*.

chill [tʃɪl] *noun & verb*

■ *noun*

she caught a chill elle a pris froid ; **there's a chill in the air** il fait un peu froid

■ *verb*

mettre au frais : **you should chill the champagne** il faut mettre le champagne au frais.

chilli *noun* ➤ chili.

chilly ['tʃɪlɪ] *adjective*

froid : **I feel chilly** j'ai froid ; **it's chilly** il fait froid.

chimney ['tʃɪmnɪ] *noun*

cheminée *(feminine)*.

chimpanzee [tʃɪmpən'zi:] *noun*

chimpanzé *(masculine)*.

chin [tʃɪn] *noun*

menton *(masculine)* : **he has a scar on his chin** il a une cicatrice au menton.

china ['tʃaɪnə] *uncountable noun*

porcelaine *(feminine)* : **a china cup** une tasse en porcelaine.

China ['tʃaɪnə] *noun*

la Chine

In French the names of countries are used with the definite article (**le**, **la** or **l'**), except when they follow the preposition **en**:

China is in Asia la Chine est en Asie ; **I'm going to China** je vais en Chine ; **Robert lives in China** Robert vit en Chine.

Chinese [ˌtʃaɪ'ni:z] *adjective & noun*

■ *adjective*

chinois : **Chinese medicine** la médecine chinoise

■ *noun*

chinois : **she speaks Chinese** elle parle chinois

➤ **the Chinese** les Chinois

Remember not to use a capital letter for the adjective and the language in French. Only use a capital letter for the inhabitants.

chip [tʃɪp] *noun*

1. *UK* **frite** *(feminine)* : **fish and chips** poisson frit avec des frites ; **a chip shop** une friterie
2. *US* **chips** *(feminine plural)* : **a packet of chips** un paquet de chips
3. **puce** *(feminine)* : **a computer chip** une puce d'ordinateur

⚠ En anglais britannique, **chips** ne signifie pas "des chips", alors qu'en anglais américain ce mot a le même sens qu'en français.

chocolate ['tʃɒkələt] *noun*

chocolat *(masculine)* : **he's eating chocolate** il mange du chocolat

➤ **a bar of chocolate** une tablette de chocolat

➤ **a chocolate cake** un gâteau au chocolat.

choice [tʃɔɪs] *noun*

choix *(masculine)* : **you have a choice between meat or fish** tu as le choix entre de la viande et du poisson ; **we have no choice** nous n'avons pas le choix.

choir ['kwaɪər] *noun*

chorale *(feminine)* : **David sings in the choir** David fait partie de la chorale.

choke [tʃəʊk] *verb*

s'étrangler : **he's choking** il s'étrangle.

choose [tʃu:z] (*past tense* chose, *past participle* chosen) *verb*

choisir : **it's hard to choose between the two** il est difficile de choisir entre les deux.

chop [tʃɒp] *noun & verb*

■ *noun*

côtelette *(feminine)* : **a pork chop** une côtelette de porc

51

■ *verb*

1. **couper : he's chopping wood** il coupe du bois
2. **hacher : you have to chop the vegetables** il faut hacher les légumes

chop down *phrasal verb*

abattre : they chopped the tree down ils ont abattu l'arbre.

chopsticks ['tʃɒpstɪks] *plural noun*

baguettes *(feminine plural)* **: can you eat with chopsticks?** tu sais manger avec des baguettes ?

chose [tʃəʊz] *past tense of* choose

Patricia chose the red dress Patricia a choisi la robe rouge.

chosen ['tʃəʊzn] *past participle of* choose

George hasn't chosen yet George n'a pas encore choisi.

christening ['krɪsnɪŋ] *noun*

baptême *(masculine)*.

Christian ['krɪstʃən] *adjective & noun*

chrétien *(feminine* **chrétienne***)* **: she's a Christian** elle est chrétienne.

Christmas ['krɪsməs] *noun*

Noël *(masculine)* **: what are you doing at Christmas?** qu'est-ce que tu fais à Noël ?
➤ **Happy Christmas!** OR **Merry Christmas!** Joyeux Noël !
➤ **a Christmas card** une carte de Noël
➤ **Christmas Day** le jour de Noël
➤ **Christmas Eve** la veille de Noël
➤ **Christmas pudding** *gâteau à base de fruits secs et de fruits confits qu'on mange au repas de Noël*
➤ **a Christmas tree** un sapin de Noël OR un arbre de Noël

CHRISTMAS
Le 25 décembre en Grande-Bretagne et aux États-Unis, le repas traditionnel se compose de dinde accompagnée de légumes puis d'un **Christmas pudding**, un gâteau consistant servi avec une sauce sucrée à base de cognac ou de whisky. Pendant la période de Noël, les gens envoient des **Christmas cards** (cartes de vœux) à leur famille et à leurs amis.

chubby ['tʃʌbɪ] *adjective*

potelé : the baby is chubby le bébé est potelé
➤ **she's got chubby cheeks** elle est joufflue.

chunk [tʃʌŋk] *noun*

gros morceau *(masculine)* **: a chunk of cheese** un gros morceau de fromage.

church [tʃɜːtʃ] *(plural* churches ['tʃɜːtʃɪz]*)* *noun*

église : we go to church on Sundays nous allons à l'église le dimanche.

cider ['saɪdər] *noun*

cidre *(masculine)*.

cigar [sɪˈgɑːr] *noun*

cigare *(masculine)* **: he's smoking a cigar** il fume un cigare.

cigarette [ˌsɪgəˈret] *noun*

cigarette *(feminine)* **: she's smoking a cigarette** elle fume une cigarette.

cinema *UK* ['sɪnəmə] *noun*

cinéma *(masculine)* **: what's on at the cinema?** qu'est-ce qui passe au cinéma ? ; **we're going to the cinema** nous allons au cinéma.

cinnamon ['sɪnəmən] *noun*

cannelle *(feminine)*.

circle ['sɜːkl] *noun*

cercle *(masculine)* **: the stones stand in a circle** les pierres forment un cercle.

circulate ['sɜːkjʊleɪt] *verb*

circuler : blood circulates around the body le sang circule dans le corps.

circumflex ['sɜːkəmfleks] *noun*

accent *(masculine)* **circonflexe**.

circumstances ['sɜːkəmstənsɪz] *plural noun*

circonstances *(feminine plural)* **: under the circumstances** étant donné les circonstances.

circus ['sɜːkəs] *noun*

cirque *(masculine)* **: we're going to the circus** nous allons au cirque.

citizen ['sɪtɪzn] *noun*

citoyen *(masculine)*, **citoyenne** *(feminine)* **: he's a French citizen** c'est un citoyen français.

city ['sɪtɪ] (*plural* cities) *noun*

ville (*feminine*)
> **the city centre** le centre-ville : **they live in the city centre** ils habitent dans le centre-ville
> **the city hall** *US* la mairie
> **the City** la City : **the City is the financial district of London** la City est le quartier financier de Londres.

civil war ['sɪvlwɔːʳ] *noun*

guerre (*feminine*) civile
> **the American Civil War** la guerre de Sécession

> THE AMERICAN CIVIL WAR
> La guerre de Sécession opposa entre 1861 et 1865 les États du Sud, à l'économie agricole fondée sur l'esclavage, et les États plus industriels du Nord, partisans de l'abolition de l'esclavage. Les États du Nord, qui avaient plus de soldats et d'armes, gagnèrent finalement la guerre et abolirent l'esclavage.

claim [kleɪm] *verb & noun*

□ *verb*
1. **prétendre** : **he claims to be famous** il prétend qu'il est célèbre
2. **réclamer** : **he claimed compensation** il a réclamé un dédommagement
3. **toucher** : **she claims unemployment benefits** elle touche les allocations chômage
□ *noun*
demande (*feminine*).

clap [klæp] *verb*

applaudir : **everyone clapped** tout le monde a applaudi.

clapping ['klæpɪŋ] *uncountable noun*

applaudissements (*masculine plural*) : **the clapping was loud** les applaudissements étaient très forts.

clarinet [ˌklærə'net] *noun*

clarinette (*feminine*) : **she plays the clarinet** elle joue de la clarinette.

clash [klæʃ] *verb*

1. **tomber le même jour** : **the concert clashes with Dexter's party** le concert tombe le même jour que la fête de Dexter
2. **jurer** : **those pink shoes clash with the yellow trousers** ces chaussures roses jurent avec le pantalon jaune.

class [klɑːs] *noun*

1. **classe** (*feminine*) : **she's in my class** elle est dans ma classe ; **we travelled first class** nous avons voyagé en première classe
2. **cours** (*masculine*) : **I have a Spanish class at 11 o'clock** j'ai un cours d'espagnol à 11 heures.

classic ['klæsɪk] *adjective & noun*

□ *adjective*
classique : **it's a classic design** c'est un modèle classique
□ *noun*
classique (*masculine*) : **this film is a classic** ce film est un classique.

classical ['klæsɪkl] *adjective*

classique : **classical music** la musique classique.

classroom ['klɑːsrʊm] *noun*

classe (*feminine*), **salle** (*feminine*) **de classe**.

claw [klɔː] *noun*

1. **griffe** (*feminine*) : **cats have sharp claws** les chats ont des griffes acérées
2. **pince** (*feminine*) : **crab claws** des pinces de crabe.

clean [kliːn] *adjective & verb*

□ *adjective*
propre : **my hands are clean** j'ai les mains propres
□ *verb*
1. **nettoyer** : **clean the table before you set it** nettoie la table avant de mettre le couvert
2. **laver** : **Tom's cleaning the car** Tom lave la voiture
> **to clean the windows** laver les fenêtres
> **to clean one's teeth** se laver les dents : **she's cleaning her teeth** elle se lave les dents

clean up *phrasal verb*

nettoyer : **don't forget to clean up before you go** n'oublie pas de nettoyer avant de partir.

cleaner ['kliːnəʳ] *noun*

1. **femme** (*feminine*) **de ménage** : **she's a cleaner** elle est femme de ménage
2. **teinturier** (*masculine*) : **I took my clothes to the cleaner's** j'ai apporté mes vêtements chez le teinturier.

C

cleaning ['kli:nɪŋ] *uncountable noun*

ménage *(masculine)* : **she's doing the cleaning** elle fait le ménage.

clear [klɪəʳ] *adjective & verb*

■ *adjective*
1. **clair** : **the instructions are clear** les instructions sont claires ; **it's clear he has made a mistake** il est clair qu'il a fait une erreur
2. **transparent** : **it's clear glass** c'est du verre transparent
3. **net** *(feminine* **nette)** : **there's a clear difference between the two** il y a une nette différence entre les deux
4. **dégagé** : **the road is clear** la route est dégagée

■ *verb*
1. **dégager** : **they're clearing the road** ils sont en train de dégager la route
2. **débarrasser** : **can you clear the table?** tu peux débarrasser ?
3. **se dissiper** : **the fog is beginning to clear** le brouillard commence à se dissiper

clear out *phrasal verb*

vider : **I'm going to clear out the cupboards** je vais vider les placards

clear up *phrasal verb*
1. **ranger** : **he cleared up the house after the party** il a rangé la maison après la fête
2. **s'éclaircir** : **it's clearing up** ça s'éclaircit.

clearly ['klɪəlɪ] *adverb*
1. **clairement** : **you've explained it clearly** tu l'as expliqué clairement
2. **manifestement** : **he's clearly wrong** il a manifestement tort
3. **distinctement** : **she doesn't speak very clearly** elle ne parle pas très distinctement.

clementine ['kleməntaɪn] *noun*

clémentine *(feminine)*.

clerk [*UK* klɑːk, *US* klɜːrk] *noun*
1. *US* **vendeur** *(masculine)*, **vendeuse** *(feminine)* : **he's a clerk in the toy department** il est vendeur au rayon jouets
2. **employé** *(masculine)* **de bureau**, **employée** *(feminine)* **de bureau** : **he's an office clerk** il est employé de bureau
➤ **a hotel clerk** *US* un réceptionniste, une réceptionniste.

clever ['klevəʳ] *adjective*
1. **intelligent** : **Stephen's a clever boy** Stephen est un garçon intelligent
2. **astucieux** *(feminine* **astucieuse)** : **it's a clever gadget** c'est un gadget astucieux
3. **habile** : **he's clever with his hands** il est habile de ses mains.

click [klɪk] *verb*
1. **cliquer** : **click on the icon** cliquez sur l'icône
2. **faire claquer** : **he clicked his fingers** il a fait claquer ses doigts.

client ['klaɪənt] *noun*

client *(masculine)*, **cliente** *(feminine)*.

cliff [klɪf] *noun*

falaise *(feminine)*.

climate ['klaɪmɪt] *noun*

climat *(masculine)*.

climb [klaɪm] *verb*
1. **monter** : **she climbed the stairs** elle a monté l'escalier
2. **escalader** : **they climbed Everest** ils ont escaladé l'Everest
➤ **to climb a ladder** monter sur une échelle
➤ **to climb a tree** grimper à un arbre

climb down *phrasal verb*

descendre : **he climbed down the ladder** il est descendu de l'échelle

climb over *phrasal verb*

passer par-dessus : **he climbed over the fence** il est passé par-dessus la barrière

climb up *phrasal verb*

monter : **he climbed up the stairs** il a monté l'escalier.

climbing ['klaɪmɪŋ] *uncountable noun*

escalade *(feminine)* : **he goes climbing in Wales** il fait de l'escalade au pays de Galles.

cling [klɪŋ] *(past tense & past participle* clung*) verb*

s'accrocher : **she was clinging to the rope** elle s'accrochait à la corde.

clingfilm *UK* ['klɪŋfɪlm] *noun*

film *(masculine)* **alimentaire**.

clip [klɪp] *noun*
1. **trombone** *(masculine)* : **I need a clip for these**

papers j'ai besoin d'un trombone pour ces papiers
2. **pince** *(feminine)* : **she's looking for a clip for her hair** elle cherche une pince pour ses cheveux.

cloakroom ['kləʊkrʊm] *noun*

1. **vestiaire** *(masculine)* : **put your coat in the cloakroom** mets ton manteau au vestiaire
2. *UK* **toilettes** *(feminine plural)* : **where is the ladies' cloakroom?** où sont les toilettes pour dames ?

clock [klɒk] *noun*

1. **pendule** *(feminine)* : **the clock on my desk is fast** la pendule sur mon bureau avance
2. **horloge** *(feminine)* : **the church clock struck midnight** l'horloge de l'église a sonné minuit
> **round the clock** 24 heures sur 24 : **this supermarket is open round the clock** ce supermarché est ouvert 24 heures sur 24.

clockwise ['klɒkwaɪz] *adverb*

dans le sens des aiguilles d'une montre.

clog [klɒg] *noun*

sabot *(masculine)*.

close *verb, adjective & adverb*

▪ *verb* [kləʊz]

1. **fermer** : **he closed his eyes** il a fermé les yeux ; **the shops close at six o'clock** les magasins ferment à six heures
2. **se fermer** : **the door closed behind him** la porte s'est fermée derrière lui

▪ *adjective* [kləʊs]

1. **près** *(invariable)*, **proche** : **the school's close to the station** l'école est près de la gare ; **the station and the pub are very close to each other** la gare et le pub sont proches l'un de l'autre
2. **proche** : **she's very close to her brother** elle est très proche de son frère
3. **lourd** : **it's very close today** il fait très lourd aujourd'hui
4. **serré** : **it's a close contest** la lutte est serrée

▪ *adverb* [kləʊs]

près : **I looked at it close up** je l'ai regardé de près
> **close by** tout près : **they live close by** ils habitent tout près d'ici
> **come closer** rapproche-toi
> **close to** près de : **I live close to the park** j'habite près du parc.

closed [kləʊzd] *adjective*

fermé : **the museum is closed** le musée est fermé.

closely ['kləʊslɪ] *adverb*

de près : **he looked at it closely** il l'a regardé de près.

closet *US* ['klɒzɪt] *noun*

placard *(masculine)*.

cloth [klɒθ] *noun*

1. **chiffon** *(masculine)* : **she wiped the table with a cloth** elle a essuyé la table avec un chiffon
2. **tissu** *(masculine)* : **I like this cloth** j'aime bien ce tissu.

clothes [kləʊðz] *plural noun*

vêtements *(masculine plural)* : **I'm going to buy some new clothes** je vais m'acheter de nouveaux vêtements ; **she put her clothes on** elle s'est habillée ; **he took his clothes off** il s'est déshabillé.

clothes peg *UK* ['kləʊðzpeg], **clothespin** *US* ['kləʊðzpɪn] *noun*

pince *(feminine)* **à linge.**

cloud [klaʊd] *noun*

nuage *(masculine)* : **there isn't a cloud in the sky** il n'y a pas un nuage.

cloudy ['klaʊdɪ] *adjective*

nuageux *(feminine* **nuageuse)** : **it's cloudy today** c'est nuageux aujourd'hui.

clown [klaʊn] *noun*

clown *(masculine)*.

club [klʌb] *noun*

1. **club** *(masculine)* : **she's a member of the chess club** elle est membre du club d'échecs
2. **boîte** *(feminine)* : **we went to a club last night** nous sommes allés en boîte hier soir
3. **massue** *(feminine)* : **he hit him with a club** il lui a donné un coup de massue
> **a golf club** un club de golf.

clue [kluː] *noun*

indice *(masculine)* : **the police are looking for clues** la police cherche des indices
> **give me a clue!** aide-moi un peu !

clumsy ['klʌmzɪ] *adjective*

gauche, maladroit.

clung [klʌŋ] *past tense & past participle of* cling

he clung to the branch il s'est accroché à la branche.

cm *(abbreviation of* centimetre) *noun*

cm.

coach [kəʊtʃ] *noun*

1. **entraîneur** *(masculine)*, **entraîneuse** *(feminine)* : **the team needs a new coach** l'équipe a besoin d'un nouvel entraîneur

2. **voiture** *(feminine)* : **the train has seventeen coaches** le train a dix-sept voitures

3. **carrosse** *(masculine)* : **Cinderella's coach** le carrosse de Cendrillon

4. *UK* **car** *(masculine)*, **autocar** *(masculine)* : **we went to Manchester by coach** nous sommes allés à Manchester en car

➤ **the coach station** *UK* la gare routière.

coal [kəʊl] *noun*

charbon *(masculine)*.

coast [kəʊst] *noun*

côte *(feminine)* : **Marseille is on the coast** Marseille est sur la côte.

coastguard ['kəʊstɡɑːd] *noun*

garde-côte *(masculine)* [*plural* gardes-côtes].

coat [kəʊt] *noun*

1. **manteau** *(masculine)* [*plural* manteaux] : **put your coat on** mets ton manteau

2. **couche** *(feminine)* : **a coat of paint** une couche de peinture

➤ **a coat hanger** un cintre : **your jacket's on the coat hanger** ta veste est sur le cintre.

cobweb ['kɒbweb] *noun*

toile *(feminine)* d'araignée.

Coca-Cola® [kəʊkə'kəʊlə], **Coke**® [kəʊk] *noun*

Coca® *(masculine)* : **a can of Coke** une canette de Coca.

cockerel ['kɒkrəl] *noun*

coq *(masculine)* : **the cockerel is a symbol of France** le coq est l'un des symboles de la France.

Cockney ['kɒknɪ] *noun*

Cockney *(masculine or feminine)*
➤ East End

cockroach ['kɒkrəʊtʃ] *noun*

cafard *(masculine)*.

cocoa ['kəʊkəʊ] *noun*

cacao *(masculine)* : **cocoa is used to make chocolate** le cacao sert à fabriquer le chocolat
➤ **a cup of cocoa** une tasse de chocolat.

coconut ['kəʊkənʌt] *noun*

noix *(feminine)* de coco.

cod [kɒd] *(plural* cod) *noun*

morue *(feminine)*.

code [kəʊd] *noun*

code *(masculine)* : **a secret code** un code secret ; **the message is in code** ce message est codé.

coffee ['kɒfɪ] *noun*

café *(masculine)* : **I'll have a coffee** je vais prendre un café ; **a cup of coffee** une tasse de café
➤ **a coffee bar** *UK* un café
➤ **a coffee pot** une cafetière
➤ **a coffee shop** un café.

coffin ['kɒfɪn] *noun*

cercueil *(masculine)*.

coin [kɔɪn] *noun*

pièce *(feminine)* de monnaie : **a one-pound coin** une pièce d'une livre ; **a 50-cent coin** une pièce de 50 cents

⚠ Le mot anglais **coin** est un faux ami, il ne signifie pas "coin".

cold [kəʊld] *adjective & noun*

■ *adjective*
froid
➤ **to be cold** avoir froid : **I'm cold** j'ai froid ; **my hands are cold** j'ai les mains froides
➤ **it's cold outside** il fait froid dehors

■ *noun*

1. **rhume** *(masculine)* : **he caught a cold** il a attrapé un rhume
2. **froid** *(masculine)* : **she doesn't like the cold** elle n'aime pas le froid.

coleslaw ['kəʊlslɔː] *noun*

salade à base de chou et de carottes crus.

collapse [kə'læps] *verb*

s'effondrer : **the whole building collapsed** tout l'immeuble s'est effondré.

collar ['kɒləʳ] *noun*

1. **col** *(masculine)* : **his shirt collar is dirty** le col de sa chemise est sale
2. **collier** *(masculine)* : **the dog is wearing a collar** le chien porte un collier.

collect [kə'lekt] *verb*

1. **ramasser** : **they're collecting seashells** ils ramassent des coquillages
2. **collectionner** : **he collects stamps** il collectionne les timbres
3. **aller chercher** : **she collected the children from school** elle est allée chercher les enfants à l'école

➤ **a collect call** *US* un appel en PCV : **I'd like to make a collect call** je voudrais appeler en PCV.

collection [kə'lekʃn] *noun*

1. **collection** *(feminine)* : **his stamp collection** sa collection de timbres
2. **quête** *(feminine)* : **they took up a collection for the refugees** ils ont fait une quête pour les réfugiés.

college ['kɒlɪdʒ] *noun*

1. *UK* **établissement** *(masculine)* **d'enseignement supérieur** : **he goes to college** il fait des études supérieures
2. *US* **université** *(feminine)* : **she's in college** elle est à l'université
➤ School

⚠ College est un faux ami, il ne signifie pas "collège".

collide [kə'laɪd] *verb*

entrer en collision : **his bicycle collided with a truck** son vélo est entré en collision avec un camion.

colon ['kəʊlən] *noun*

deux-points *(masculine)* : **you use a colon to introduce a list** on utilise le deux-points pour introduire une liste.

colonel ['kɜːnl] *noun*

colonel *(masculine)* : **he's a colonel** il est colonel.

colour *UK*, **color** *US* ['kʌləʳ] *noun*

couleur *(feminine)* : **what colour is it?** c'est de quelle couleur ? ; **the film is in colour** le film est en couleurs
➤ **a colour photo** une photo en couleurs
➤ **a colour television** un téléviseur couleur.

colourful *UK*, **colorful** *US* ['kʌləfʊl] *adjective*

coloré : **a colourful dress** une robe colorée.

column ['kɒləm] *noun*

1. **colonne** *(feminine)* : **the columns of a Greek temple** les colonnes d'un temple grec
2. **rubrique** *(feminine)* : **the sports column in the newspaper** la rubrique sport dans le journal.

comb [kəʊm] *noun & verb*

■ *noun*
peigne *(masculine)*
■ *verb*
peigner : **to comb one's hair** se peigner ; **he combed his hair** il s'est peigné.

come [kʌm] (*past tense* came, *past participle* come) *verb*

1. **venir** : **come and look!** viens voir ! ; **he's coming to the match with us** il vient au match avec nous ; **we came by bike** nous sommes venus à vélo ; **Donald came to see me** Donald est venu me voir ; **where do you come from?** d'où venez-vous ? ; **I come from Birmingham** je viens de Birmingham

> If you say which country a person comes from, use the verb être with an adjective in French:
>
> **Andy comes from England** Andy est anglais ; **Moira comes from Scotland** Moira est écossaise.

2. **arriver** : **I'm coming!** j'arrive ! ; **the bus is coming** le bus arrive
➤ **come on!** allez ! : **come on, hurry up!** allez ! dépêche-toi !
➤ **to come true** se réaliser : **her dream came true** son rêve s'est réalisé

come around *US* ➤ come round *UK*

come back *phrasal verb*

revenir : **come back soon!** reviens vite ! ; **I'll come back later** je reviendrai plus tard

come down *phrasal verb*

1. descendre : **he came down to say goodbye** il est descendu dire au revoir
2. baisser : **prices have come down** les prix ont baissé

come in *phrasal verb*

entrer : **come in!** entrez ! ; **she came in through the kitchen window** elle est entrée par la fenêtre de la cuisine

come off *phrasal verb*

se détacher : **one of my buttons has come off** un de mes boutons s'est détaché

come out *phrasal verb*

1. sortir : **come out with your hands up!** sortez les mains en l'air ! ; **their new album is coming out in May** leur nouvel album sort en mai
2. partir : **this mark won't come out** cette tache ne part pas

come over *phrasal verb*

venir : **come over this evening** viens chez nous ce soir

come round *UK*, **come around** *US* *phrasal verb*

1. venir : **Janet is coming round tonight** Janet vient ce soir
2. reprendre connaissance : **he's starting to come round** il commence à reprendre connaissance

come to *phrasal verb*

reprendre connaissance

come up *phrasal verb*

1. monter : **come up here!** monte !
2. se lever : **the sun has come up** le soleil s'est levé
3. être soulevé : **the problem came up in class** le problème a été soulevé en classe

come up to *phrasal verb*

1. arriver à : **the mud came up to our knees** la boue nous arrivait jusqu'aux genoux
2. s'approcher de : **he came up to me and** shook my hand il s'est approché de moi et m'a serré la main.

comedian [kə'miːdjən] *noun*

comique *(masculine)* : **he's a comedian** c'est un comique

 Comedian est un faux ami, il ne signifie pas "comédien".

comedy ['kɒmədɪ] *noun*

comédie *(feminine)*.

comfort ['kʌmfət] *noun & verb*

◼ *noun*
1. confort *(masculine)* : **he likes comfort** il aime bien le confort
2. réconfort *(masculine)* : **you've been a great comfort to me** tu as été pour moi d'un grand réconfort

◼ *verb*
réconforter : **the policeman comforted the crying girl** le policier a réconforté la fille qui pleurait.

comfortable ['kʌmftəbl] *adjective*
1. confortable : **it's a very comfortable bed** c'est un lit très confortable
2. à l'aise : **are you comfortable?** êtes-vous à l'aise ? ; **make yourself comfortable** mettez-vous à l'aise.

comic ['kɒmɪk] *noun*

bande *(feminine)* dessinée : **a lot of newspapers have comic strips** beaucoup de journaux ont des bandes dessinées ; **a comic book** une bande dessinée.

comma ['kɒmə] *noun*

virgule *(feminine)*.

command [kə'mɑːnd] *noun & verb*

◼ *noun*
ordre *(masculine)* : **the captain gave a command** le capitaine a donné un ordre

◼ *verb*
ordonner : **the king commanded him to leave** le roi lui a ordonné de partir.

comment ['kɒment] *noun & verb*

◼ *noun*
commentaire *(masculine)* : **he made some comments on my work** il a fait quelques commentaires sur mon travail

◼ *verb*
faire des commentaires : **she commented**

58

on the news elle a fait des commentaires sur cette nouvelle

> ⚠ Le mot anglais **comment** est un faux ami, il ne signifie pas "comment".

commercial [kə'mɜːʃl] *adjective & noun*

■ *adjective*
commercial : the film is a commercial success le film est un succès commercial

■ *noun*
publicité *(feminine)* : **he doesn't like TV commercials** il n'aime pas les publicités à la télé.

commit [kə'mɪt] *verb*

commettre : he has committed many crimes il a commis beaucoup de crimes
> **to commit suicide** se suicider.

committee [kə'mɪtɪ] *noun*

comité *(masculine)*.

common ['kɒmən] *adjective*

1. **courant : it's a common expression** c'est une expression courante
2. **commun : the English and the Americans share a common language** les Anglais et les Américains ont une langue commune
> **in common** en commun : **we have a lot in common** nous avons beaucoup de choses en commun
> **common sense** bon sens *(masculine)* : **she has a lot of common sense** elle a du bon sens
> **the Commons** *UK* les Communes : **the House of Commons** la Chambre des communes
> ➤ The Houses of Parliament.

communicate [kə'mjuːnɪkeɪt] *verb*

communiquer : we communicate by e-mail nous communiquons par e-mail.

communication [kə,mjuːnɪ'keɪʃn] *noun*

communication *(feminine)*.

community [kə'mjuːnətɪ] *(plural communities) noun*

communauté *(feminine)* : **there is a large French community in London** il y a une grande communauté française à Londres.

compact disc *UK*, **compact disk** *US*

[,kɒmpækt'dɪsk] *noun*
disque *(masculine)* **compact**.

companion [kəm'pænjən] *noun*

compagnon *(masculine)*, **compagne** *(feminine)* :

my travelling companions mes compagnons de voyage.

company ['kʌmpənɪ] *(plural companies) noun*

société *(feminine)* : **she works for an Irish company** elle travaille pour une société irlandaise
> **an insurance company** une compagnie d'assurances
> **an airline company** une compagnie aérienne
> **to keep somebody company** tenir compagnie à quelqu'un.

compare [kəm'peər] *verb*

comparer
> **compared with** OR **compared to** comparé à ; **she's very clever compared to her brother:** comparée à son frère, elle est très intelligente.

comparison [kəm'pærɪsn] *noun*

comparaison *(feminine)* : **France is small in comparison with Australia** la France est un petit pays en comparaison avec l'Australie.

compass ['kʌmpəs] *noun*

1. **boussole** *(feminine)* : **we used a compass to find our way** nous avons utilisé une boussole pour trouver notre chemin
2. **compas** *(masculine)* : **a pair of compasses** un compas.

compete [kəm'piːt] *verb*

participer : there are ten runners competing in the race dix coureurs participent à la course
> **to compete against somebody** être en compétition avec quelqu'un
> **to compete for something** se disputer quelque chose : **they're competing for the gold medal** ils se disputent la médaille d'or.

competition [,kɒmpɪ'tɪʃn] *noun*

concours *(masculine)* : **she entered a beauty competition** elle a participé à un concours de beauté.

competitor [kəm'petɪtər] *noun*

concurrent *(masculine)*, **concurrente** *(feminine)*.

complain [kəm'pleɪn] *verb*

se plaindre : don't complain! ne te plains pas ! ; **he complained about the cold** il s'est plaint du froid ; **I complained to the manager** je me suis plaint au directeur.

complaint [kəm'pleɪnt] *noun*

plainte *(feminine)* : **they received a lot of complaints** ils ont reçu beaucoup de plaintes
> **to make a complaint** se plaindre : **I'm going to make a complaint** je vais me plaindre.

complete [kəm'pliːt] *adjective & verb*

■ *adjective*
1. complet *(feminine* **complète***)* : **a complete deck of cards** un jeu complet de cartes ; **the complete works of Roald Dahl** l'œuvre complète de Roald Dahl ; **I feel like a complete idiot** je me sens complètement idiot
2. achevé : **work on the building is complete** les travaux de l'immeuble sont achevés
■ *verb*
1. compléter : **can you complete this sentence?** pouvez-vous compléter cette phrase ?
2. achever : **I've completed my work** j'ai achevé mon travail.

completely [kəm'pliːtlɪ] *adverb*

complètement : **he's completely crazy** il est complètement fou.

complexion [kəm'plekʃn] *noun*

teint *(masculine)* : **he has a very light complexion** il a le teint très clair.

complicated ['kɒmplɪkeɪtɪd] *adjective*

compliqué.

compliment ['kɒmplɪmənt] *noun*

compliment *(masculine)* : **she paid me a compliment** elle m'a fait un compliment.

composer [kəm'pəʊzər] *noun*

compositeur *(masculine)*, compositrice *(feminine)* : **Gershwin is a famous American composer** Gershwin est un célèbre compositeur américain.

comprehensive school *UK* [ˌkɒmprɪ'hensɪvskuːl] *noun*
établissement secondaire d'enseignement général
➤ School.

compulsory [kəm'pʌlsərɪ] *adjective*

obligatoire : **English and maths are compulsory** l'anglais et les maths sont obligatoires.

computer [kəm'pjuːtər] *noun*

ordinateur *(masculine)* : **he's working on the computer** il travaille sur l'ordinateur
> **a portable computer** OR **a laptop computer** un ordinateur portable
> **computer games** jeux *(masculine plural)* électroniques
> **computer science** l'informatique *(feminine)*.

computing [kəm'pjuːtɪŋ] *uncountable noun*

informatique *(feminine)* : **he works in computing** il travaille dans l'informatique.

concentrate ['kɒnsəntreɪt] *verb*

se concentrer : **I can't concentrate** je n'arrive pas à me concentrer ; **concentrate on what you're doing** concentre-toi sur ce que tu fais.

concentration [ˌkɒnsən'treɪʃn] *noun*

concentration *(feminine)* : **it needs a lot of concentration** cela demande beaucoup de concentration.

concern [kən'sɜːn] *verb*

concerner : **this concerns us all** ceci nous concerne tous
> **as far as I'm concerned** en ce qui me concerne
> **to be concerned** s'inquiéter : **I'm concerned about him** je m'inquiète à son sujet.

concert ['kɒnsət] *noun*

concert *(masculine)* : **they're going to a concert** ils vont à un concert.

concrete ['kɒŋkriːt] *noun*

béton *(masculine)* : **a concrete wall** un mur en béton.

condition [kən'dɪʃn] *noun*

1. condition *(feminine)* : **he will come with us, but on one condition** il viendra avec nous, mais à une condition
2. état *(masculine)* : **it's in good condition** c'est en bon état.

conditioner [kən'dɪʃnər] *noun*

après-shampooing *(masculine)*.

condo *US* ['kɒndəʊ] *noun*

appartement *(masculine)* : **her father lives in a condo in Florida** son père vit dans un appartement en Floride.

condom [ˈkɒndəm] *noun*

préservatif *(masculine)*.

conductor [kənˈdʌktəʳ] *noun*

1. chef *(masculine)* **d'orchestre : an orchestra conductor** un chef d'orchestre
2. chef *(masculine)* **de train : a conductor of a train** un chef de train.

cone [kəʊn] *noun*

cornet *(masculine)* **: an ice-cream cone** un cornet de glace.

confess [kənˈfes] *verb*

avouer : **he confessed to the murder** il a avoué le meurtre.

confetti [kənˈfetɪ] *noun*

confettis *(masculine plural)* **: they threw confetti over the bride and groom** ils ont jeté des confettis sur les jeunes mariés.

confidence [ˈkɒnfɪdəns] *noun*

1. assurance *(feminine)* **: he has no confidence** il manque d'assurance
2. confiance *(feminine)* **: I have confidence in you** j'ai confiance en toi

> ⚠ Le mot anglais **confidence** est un faux ami, il n'a pas le sens de "confidence".

confident [ˈkɒnfɪdənt] *adjective*

sûr **: I'm confident you'll win** je suis sûr que tu vas gagner ; **she's very confident** elle est très sûre d'elle.

confirm [kənˈfɜːm] *verb*

confirmer : **you must confirm your flight** vous devez confirmer votre vol.

confuse [kənˈfjuːz] *verb*

1. embrouiller : **don't confuse me!** ne m'embrouille pas les idées !
2. confondre : **he confused me with my brother** il m'a confondu avec mon frère.

confused [kənˈfjuːzd] *adjective*

désorienté : **he looked confused** il avait l'air désorienté ; **I'm confused, can you say all that again?** je n'y suis plus, tu peux tout répéter ?

> ⚠ **Confused** est un faux ami, il ne signifie pas "confus" au sens de "gêné" ou "embarrassé".

confusing [kənˈfjuːzɪŋ] *adjective*

pas clair : it's very confusing ce n'est pas du tout clair.

confusion [kənˈfjuːʒn] *noun*

confusion *(feminine)* **: there's some confusion over the dates** il y a une petite confusion à propos des dates.

congratulate [kənˈgrætʃʊleɪt] *verb*

féliciter : **they congratulated me on winning the prize** ils m'ont félicité d'avoir remporté le prix.

congratulations [kənˌgrætʃʊˈleɪʃənz] *plural noun*

félicitations *(feminine plural)* **: congratulations on your success!** félicitations pour votre succès !

Congress [ˈkɒŋgres] *noun*

le Congrès.

connect [kəˈnekt] *verb*

1. relier : **the bridge connects the two parts of the town** le pont relie les deux parties de la ville
2. connecter : **I can't connect to Internet** je n'arrive pas à me connecter à Internet.

connection [kəˈnekʃn] *noun*

1. rapport *(masculine)* **: there's no connection between the two events** il n'y a aucun rapport entre les deux événements
2. correspondance *(feminine)* **: I don't want to miss my connection** je ne veux pas rater ma correspondance
3. connexion *(feminine)* **: an Internet connection** une connexion Internet.

conscience [ˈkɒnʃəns] *noun*

conscience *(feminine)* **: he has a guilty conscience** il a mauvaise conscience.

conscious [ˈkɒnʃəs] *adjective*

conscient **: I wasn't conscious of what I was doing** je n'étais pas conscient de ce que je faisais.

consciousness [ˈkɒnʃəsnɪs] *noun*

connaissance *(feminine)* **: he lost consciousness** il a perdu connaissance.

Conservative [kənˈsɜːvətɪv] *adjective & noun*

conservateur *(masculine)*, **conservatrice** *(femi-*

nine) : **the Conservative Party** *UK* le parti conservateur.

consider [kən'sɪdəʳ] *verb*

1. **considérer** : **I consider him my friend** je le considère comme mon ami
2. **envisager** : **she's considering leaving her job** elle envisage de quitter son travail
3. **prendre en compte** : **you must consider the risks** il faut prendre en compte les risques.

considerate [kən'sɪdərət] *adjective*

prévenant : **she's always considerate to others** elle est toujours prévenante envers les autres.

consideration [kən͵sɪdə'reɪʃn] *noun*

➤ **to take something into consideration** prendre quelque chose en compte : **I'll take that into consideration** je prendrai cela en compte.

consist [kən'sɪst] *verb*

consister : **our job consists in helping others** notre travail consiste à aider les autres
➤ **to consist of** être composé de : **our team consists of ten players** notre équipe est composé de dix joueurs.

consonant ['kɒnsənənt] *noun*

consonne *(feminine)*.

constant ['kɒnstənt] *adjective*

continuel *(feminine* **continuelle)** : **constant criticism** des critiques continuelles.

constantly ['kɒnstəntlɪ] *adverb*

constamment : **fashion is constantly changing** la mode change constamment.

constipated ['kɒnstɪpeɪtɪd] *adjective*

constipé : **he's constipated** il est constipé.

consumer [*UK* kən'sjuːməʳ, *US* kən-'suːməʳ] *noun*

consommateur *(masculine)*, **consommatrice** *(feminine)*.

contact ['kɒntækt] *noun & verb*

■ *noun*

contact *(masculine)* : **we've lost contact with her** nous ne sommes plus en contact avec elle
➤ **contact lenses** verres *(masculine plural)* de contact OR lentilles *(feminine plural)* : **he wears contact lenses** il porte des verres de contact OR il porte des lentilles

■ *verb*

contacter : **I couldn't contact him** je n'ai pas pu le contacter.

contain [kən'teɪn] *verb*

contenir : **milk contains calcium** le lait contient du calcium.

container [kən'teɪnəʳ] *noun*

récipient *(masculine)* : **I need a bigger container** il me faut un récipient plus grand.

contents ['kɒntents] *plural noun*

1. **contenu** *(masculine)* : **he emptied the contents of the box onto the floor** il a vidé le contenu de la boîte par terre
2. **table** *(feminine)* **des matières** : **the contents are at the front of the book** la table des matières est au début du livre.

contest ['kɒntest] *noun*

concours *(masculine)* : **a beauty contest** un concours de beauté.

contestant [kən'testənt] *noun*

concurrent *(masculine)*, **concurrente** *(feminine)*.

continent ['kɒntɪnənt] *noun*

continent *(masculine)* : **there are five continents** il y a cinq continents
➤ **the Continent** *UK* l'Europe *(feminine)*.

continental breakfast [͵kɒntɪ'nentl-'brekfɪst] *noun*

petit déjeuner *(masculine)* **continental**.

continue [kən'tɪnjuː] *verb*

1. **continuer** : **they continued playing** ils ont continué à jouer ; **he continued with his work** il a continué son travail
2. **reprendre** : **let's stop now and continue later** on va arrêter maintenant et reprendre plus tard.

contraceptive [͵kɒntrə'septɪv] *noun*

contraceptif *(masculine)*.

contract ['kɒntrækt] *noun*

contrat *(masculine)* : **he signed the contract** il a signé le contrat.

contrary ['kɒntrərɪ] *noun*

contraire *(masculine)*
➤ **on the contrary** au contraire.

contrast ['kɒntrɑːst] *noun*

contraste *(masculine)* : **there's a big contrast**

between life in England and life in France il
y a un grand contraste entre la vie en Angleterre et la vie en France.

contribute [kən'trɪbjuːt] *verb*

1. **contribuer : he contributed to the success
of the project** il a contribué au succès du projet
2. **donner : he contributed a lot of money** il a
donné beaucoup d'argent.

control [kən'trəʊl] *noun & verb*

■ *noun*
contrôle *(masculine)* : **we're in control of the
situation** nous avons le contrôle de la situation ; **she lost control of her car** OR **her car
went out of control** elle a perdu le contrôle
de sa voiture
➤ **everything's under control** nous avons
la situation en main
■ *verb*
1. **diriger : who controls the company?** qui dirige l'entreprise ?
2. **contenir : the police can't control the
crowd** la police n'arrive pas à contenir la foule
3. **maîtriser : he can't control his anger** il ne
peut pas maîtriser sa colère
➤ **to control oneself** se contrôler.

controls [kən'trəʊls] *plural noun*
commandes *(feminine plural)* : **the pilot is at
the controls** le pilote est aux commandes.

convenience store [kən'viːnjənsstɔːʳ]
noun
petit magasin d'alimentation.

convenient [kən'viːnjənt] *adjective*

1. **pratique : it's a convenient place to meet**
c'est un endroit pratique pour se retrouver
2. **bien situé : the hotel is convenient for the
shops** l'hôtel est bien situé, il est proche des
commerces
➤ **to be convenient for somebody** convenir à quelqu'un : **is Monday convenient for
you?** est-ce que lundi vous convient ?

conversation [ˌkɒnvə'seɪʃn] *noun*
conversation *(feminine)* : **I had a long conversation with her** j'ai eu une longue conversation avec elle.

convince [kən'vɪns] *verb*
convaincre : he convinced me to wait il
m'a convaincu d'attendre.

cook [kʊk] *noun & verb*

■ *noun*
cuisinier *(masculine)*, **cuisinière** *(feminine)* :
he's a good cook il est bon cuisinier
1. **faire la cuisine : she likes cooking** elle aime
bien faire la cuisine
2. **préparer : I'm cooking breakfast** je prépare
le petit déjeuner
3. **faire cuire : cook the potatoes for thirty
minutes** faites cuire les pommes de terre pendant trente minutes
4. **cuire : the vegetables are cooking** les légumes sont en train de cuire.

cookbook *US* ['kʊkbʊk] *noun*
livre *(masculine)* **de cuisine.**

cooker *UK* ['kʊkəʳ] *noun*
cuisinière *(feminine)* : **we have an electric
cooker** nous avons une cuisinière électrique.

cookery ['kʊkərɪ] *noun*
cuisine *(feminine)* : **a cookery book** *UK* un livre de cuisine.

cookie *US* ['kʊkɪ] *noun*
biscuit *(masculine)* : **he's eating a cookie** il
mange un biscuit.

cooking ['kʊkɪŋ] *uncountable noun*
cuisine *(feminine)* : **I like English cooking** j'aime bien la cuisine anglaise ; **I do the cooking**
c'est moi qui fais la cuisine.

cool [kuːl] *adjective & verb*

■ *adjective*
1. **frais** *(feminine* **fraîche)* : **the water's cool** l'eau
est fraîche ; **it's cool tonight** il fait frais ce soir
2. **calme : he stayed cool** il a gardé son calme
3. *informal* **cool, génial : what a cool computer!** il est cool, ton ordinateur !
■ *verb*
refroidir : leave it to cool laisse-le refroidir

cool down *phrasal verb*

1. **refroidir : the water has cooled down** l'eau
a refroidi
2. **rafraîchir : this drink will cool you down**
cette boisson va te rafraîchir.

cope [kəʊp] *verb*
s'en sortir : I can't cope je ne m'en sors pas
➤ **to cope with something** faire face à quelque chose : **he has to cope with lots of pro-**

blems il doit faire face à beaucoup de problèmes.

copied ['kɒpɪd] *past tense & past participle of*
copy
he copied the file il a copié le fichier.

copper ['kɒpəʳ] *noun*
cuivre *(masculine)* : **a copper bracelet** un bracelet en cuivre.

copy ['kɒpɪ] *noun & verb*
■ *noun (plural* **copies***)*
1. **copie** *(feminine)* : **make a copy of the disk** faites une copie de la disquette
2. **exemplaire** *(masculine)* : **they've sold a thousand copies of the book** ils ont vendu mille exemplaires du livre
■ *verb*
copier : **he copied the picture from the book** il a copié le dessin du livre
➤ **to copy and paste** faire un copier-coller : **he copied and pasted the text** il a fait un copier-coller du texte.

corduroy ['kɔːdərɔɪ] *noun*
velours *(masculine)* **côtelé** : **a corduroy shirt** une chemise en velours côtelé.

cork [kɔːk] *noun*
bouchon *(masculine)* : **take the cork out of the bottle** enlève le bouchon de la bouteille.

corkscrew ['kɔːkskruː] *noun*
tire-bouchon *(masculine)*.

corn [kɔːn] *uncountable noun*
1. *UK* **blé** *(masculine)* : **corn fields** des champs de blé
2. *US* **maïs** *(masculine)*
➤ **a corn on the cob** un épi de maïs.

corner ['kɔːnəʳ] *noun*
1. **coin** *(masculine)* : **Ron is sitting in a corner** Ron est assis dans un coin ; **she lives at the corner of the street** elle habite au coin de la rue
2. **corner** *(masculine)* : **Beckham took a corner** Beckham a tiré un corner
3. **virage** *(masculine)* : **the car took the corner too quickly** la voiture a pris le virage trop vite
➤ **the shop's just around the corner** le magasin est à deux pas d'ici.

cornflakes ['kɔːnfleɪks] *plural noun*
corn flakes *(masculine plural)*.

Cornwall ['kɔːnwɔːl] *noun*
la Cornouailles : **Cornwall is a county in the southwest of England** la Cornouailles est un comté situé au sud-ouest de l'Angleterre.

corpse [kɔːps] *noun*
corps *(masculine)*, **cadavre** *(masculine)* : **the police have found a corpse** la police a découvert un corps.

correct [kə'rekt] *adjective & verb*
■ *adjective*
1. **exact** : **that's correct** c'est exact
2. **bon** *(feminine* **bonne***)* : **that's the correct answer** c'est la bonne réponse ; **you've made the correct decision** tu as pris la bonne décision
■ *verb*
corriger : **I corrected the mistake** j'ai corrigé l'erreur.

correction [kə'rekʃn] *noun*
correction *(feminine)* : **the corrections are in red** les corrections sont en rouge.

corridor ['kɒrɪdɔːʳ] *noun*
couloir *(masculine)* : **my bedroom is at the end of the corridor** ma chambre est au bout du couloir.

cosmetics [kɒz'metɪks] *plural noun*
produits *(masculine plural)* **de beauté**.

cost [kɒst] *verb & noun*
■ *verb (past tense & past participle* cost*)*
coûter : **how much does it cost?** combien ça coûte ? ; **it costs twenty pounds** ça coûte vingt livres ; **it costs a lot of money** ça coûte beaucoup d'argent
■ *noun*
coût *(masculine)* : **the cost of living** le coût de la vie.

costume [*UK* 'kɒstjuːm, *US* 'kɒstuːm] *noun*
1. **costume** *(masculine)* : **he's wearing the national costume** il porte le costume de son pays
2. *UK* **maillot** *(masculine)* **de bain** : **a swimming costume** un maillot de bain.

cosy *UK*, **cozy** *US* ['kəʊzɪ] *adjective*
douillet *(feminine* **douillette***)* : **a cosy bedroom** une chambre douillette
➤ **it's cosy in here** on est bien ici.

cottage ['kɒtɪdʒ] *noun*

cottage *(masculine)* : **a thatched cottage** un cottage au toit de chaume.

cotton ['kɒtn] *uncountable noun*

coton *(masculine)* : **a cotton T-shirt** un tee-shirt en coton

> **cotton candy** *US* barbe *(feminine)* à papa
> **cotton wool** *UK* coton *(masculine)* hydrophile.

couch [kaʊtʃ] *(plural* couches ['kaʊtʃɪz]*)*

noun

canapé *(masculine)* : **the dog's lying on the couch** le chien est allongé sur le canapé.

cough [kɒf] *noun & verb*

■ *noun*

toux *(feminine)*

> **to have a cough** tousser : **I've got a cough** je tousse

■ *verb*

tousser : **the smoke's making me cough** la fumée me fait tousser.

could [kʊd] *(negative* couldn't*) verb*

I. pouvoir : **he couldn't come to the party** il ne pouvait pas venir à la fête ; **they couldn't stay for dinner** ils ne pouvaient pas rester pour dîner

> When you make a polite request, an offer or a suggestion, 'could' is translated by the French verb **pouvoir** in the conditional tense:

could I speak to Scott, please? est-ce que je pourrais parler à Scott, s'il vous plaît ? ; **could you help me, please?** pourriez-vous m'aider, s'il vous plaît ? ; **you could wait for him** tu pourrais l'attendre ; **don't touch it, it could be dangerous** ne le touche pas, ça pourrait être dangereux

> When 'could' is used with a verb of perception (see, hear, feel, understand) it is not translated at all:

I couldn't see anything je ne voyais rien ; **she couldn't hear me** elle ne m'entendait pas ; **we could understand what they were saying** nous avons compris ce qu'ils disaient

2. *When 'could' means 'knew how to'* savoir : **she couldn't swim** elle ne savait pas nager ; **they couldn't speak English** ils ne savaient pas parler anglais.

couldn't ['kʊdnt] = could not **I couldn't do it** je ne pouvais pas le faire ; **she couldn't see anything** elle ne voyait rien.

could've ['kʊdəv] = could have **I could've done it for you** j'aurais pu le faire pour toi.

council ['kaʊnsl] *noun*

I. conseil : **the Council of Europe** le Conseil de l'Europe

2. *UK* conseil *(masculine)* municipal, municipalité *(feminine)* : **he sent a letter to the council** il a envoyé une lettre au conseil municipal

> **a council estate** *UK* une cité
> **a council house** *UK* un HLM.

count [kaʊnt] *verb*

compter : **count up to a hundred** comptez jusqu'à cent ; **he counted sheep to get to sleep** il a compté les moutons pour s'endormir

> **to count on somebody** compter sur quelqu'un : **you can count on me** tu peux compter sur moi.

counter ['kaʊntər] *noun*

I. comptoir *(masculine)* : **the barman is behind the counter** le barman est derrière le comptoir

2. jeton *(masculine)* : **each player has ten counters** chaque joueur a dix jetons.

counterclockwise *US* [ˌkaʊntərˈklɒk-waɪz] *adverb*

dans le sens inverse des aiguilles d'une montre.

country ['kʌntrɪ] *(plural* countries*) noun*

I. pays *(masculine)* : **it's interesting to visit foreign countries** c'est intéressant de visiter des pays étrangers

2. campagne *(feminine)* : **we live in the country** nous habitons à la campagne.

countryside ['kʌntrɪsaɪd] *noun*

campagne *(feminine)* : **she loves the countryside** elle adore la campagne.

county ['kaʊntɪ] *(plural* counties*) noun*

comté *(masculine)* : **Kent is a county in the south of England** le Kent est un comté du sud de l'Angleterre.

couple ['kʌpl] *noun*

couple *(masculine)* : **a young couple** un jeune couple

C

➤ **a couple of** deux ou trois OR quelques ; **I waited a couple of hours** j'ai attendu deux ou trois heures ; **he left a couple of years later** il est parti quelques années plus tard.

courage ['kʌrɪdʒ] *noun*

    courage *(masculine)* : **he plucked up the courage to go in** il a trouvé le courage d'entrer.

courgette *UK* [kɔː'ʒet] *noun*

    courgette *(feminine)*.

course [kɔːs] *noun*

1. **cours** *(masculine plural)* : **he's taking a Spanish course** il suit des cours d'espagnol
2. **plat** *(masculine)* : **the main course of the meal** le plat principal du repas ; **the first course** l'entrée ; **a five-course meal** un repas composé de cinq plats
3. **terrain** *(masculine)* : **a golf course** un terrain de golf
➤ **of course** bien sûr
➤ **of course not** bien sûr que non

> ⚠ Le mot anglais **course** est un faux ami, il ne signifie pas "course".

court [kɔːt] *noun*

1. **tribunal** *(masculine)* : **he appeared in court** il est passé devant le tribunal
2. **court** *(masculine)* : **a tennis court** un court de tennis
3. **terrain** *(masculine)* : **a basketball court** un terrain de basket.

courthouse *US* ['kɔːthaʊs, *plural* 'kɔːthaʊ- zɪz] *noun*

    tribunal *(masculine)*.

courtyard ['kɔːtjɑːd] *noun*

    cour *(feminine)* : **the building has a courtyard** l'immeuble a une cour.

cousin ['kʌzn] *noun*

    cousin *(masculine)*, **cousine** *(feminine)*.

Covent Garden [ˌkɒvənt'gɑːdn] *noun*

    quartier du centre de Londres

> 📖 COVENT GARDEN
> Situé au centre de Londres, **Covent Garden** était autrefois un marché aux fruits et légumes. Le quartier a été rénové et désormais on y trouve une galerie marchande et de nombreux cafés et boutiques. C'est un endroit très fréquen-

té où l'on peut assister à des spectacles de rue avant de se rendre à la **Royal Opera House**, l'Opéra, qui se trouve à côté.

cover ['kʌvər] *noun & verb*

■ *noun*
1. **couvercle** *(masculine)* : **put the cover on the saucepan** mets le couvercle sur la casserole
2. **couverture** *(feminine)* : **there's a dragon on the cover of the book** il y a un dragon sur la couverture du livre ; **she put two covers on the bed** elle a mis deux couvertures sur le lit
➤ **to take cover** se mettre à l'abri : **they're coming, let's take cover** ils arrivent, mettons-nous à l'abri
➤ **under cover** à l'abri : **they're all under cover** ils sont tous à l'abri
■ *verb*
1. **couvrir** : **Tom is covered with bruises** Tom est couvert de bleus
2. **recouvrir** : **she covered the chair with a sheet** elle a recouvert la chaise d'un drap.

cow [kaʊ] *noun*

    vache *(feminine)*.

coward ['kaʊəd] *noun*

    lâche *(masculine or feminine)* : **he's a coward** il est lâche.

cowboy ['kaʊbɔɪ] *noun*

    cow-boy *(masculine)* : **Randy's a cowboy** Randy est cow-boy.

cozy *US adjective* ➤ **cosy** *UK*.

crab [kræb] *noun*

    crabe *(masculine)*.

crack [kræk] *noun & verb*

■ *noun*
1. **fêlure** *(feminine)* : **there's a crack in the plate** cette assiette est fêlée
2. **fissure** *(feminine)* : **there are cracks in the wall** il y a des fissures dans ce mur
■ *verb*
1. **fêler** : **I've cracked the glass** j'ai fêlé le verre
2. **casser** : **you have to crack the egg first** il faut d'abord casser l'œuf
3. **se fêler, se fissurer** : **the mirror cracked** le miroir s'est fêlé ; **the ice cracked** la glace s'est fissurée
➤ **to crack a code** déchiffrer un code : **they managed to crack the code** ils ont réussi à déchiffrer le code

➤ **to crack a joke** faire une plaisanterie : **Lynne cracked a joke** Lynne a fait une plaisanterie.

cracked [krækt] *adjective*

1. fêlé : **the glass is cracked but not broken** le verre est fêlé mais pas cassé
2. fissuré : **the ground is cracked** le sol est fissuré.

cracker ['krækə'] *noun*

cracker *(masculine)* : **he's eating a cracker** il mange un cracker

 CRACKERS

En Grande-Bretagne, on trouve traditionnellement sur la table de Noël des **Christmas crackers**. Ces petits rouleaux en carton recouverts de papier cadeau brillant doivent être ouverts par deux personnes, chacune d'elle tirant sur un bout, ce qui déclenche un pétard. À l'intérieur se trouvent un petit jouet, une blague et un chapeau en papier.

craftsman ['krɑːftsmən] *(plural* craftsmen ['krɑːftsmən])* noun*
artisan *(masculine)*.

crafty ['krɑːftɪ] *adjective*

rusé : **he's very crafty** il est très rusé.

cranberry ['krænbərɪ] *(plural* cranberries)*
adjective
airelle *(feminine)* : **cranberry sauce** sauce aux airelles
➤ Thanksgiving.

crane [kreɪn] *noun*

grue *(feminine)* : **there's a crane on the building site** il y a une grue sur le chantier

⚠ Crane est un faux ami, il ne signifie pas "crâne".

crash [kræʃ] *noun & verb*

▣ *noun*

1. accident *(masculine)* : **he was injured in a car crash** il a été blessé dans un accident de voiture
2. fracas *(masculine)* : **I heard a loud crash** j'ai entendu un grand fracas OR j'ai entendu un grand bruit
➤ **a crash helmet** un casque : **the motorcyclist is wearing a crash helmet** le conducteur de la moto porte un casque

▣ *verb*

1. avoir un accident : **I'm driving carefully, I don't want to crash** je conduis prudemment, je ne veux pas avoir d'accident ; **he crashed his car** il a eu un accident avec sa voiture
2. s'écraser : **the plane crashed** l'avion s'est écrasé
3. se percuter : **the two trains crashed into each other** les deux trains se sont percutés
➤ **to crash into something** rentrer dans quelque chose : **they crashed into a wall** ils sont rentrés dans un mur.

crawl [krɔːl] *verb & noun*

▣ *verb*

1. marcher à quatre pattes : **the baby is crawling** le bébé marche à quatre pattes
2. ramper : **the snake crawled along the tree trunk** le serpent rampait le long du tronc

▣ *noun*
crawl *(masculine)* : **he's doing the crawl** il nage le crawl.

crayon ['kreɪɒn] *noun*

crayon *(masculine)* de couleur.

crazy ['kreɪzɪ] *adjective informal*

fou *(feminine* folle*)* : **you're completely crazy!** t'es complètement fou ! ; **that noise is driving me crazy** ce bruit me rend fou.

cream [kriːm] *noun*

crème *(feminine)* : **strawberries and cream** des fraises à la crème
➤ **a cream cake** un gâteau à la crème.

crease [kriːs] *noun & verb*

▣ *noun*
pli *(masculine)*
▣ *verb*
froisser : **try not to crease your dress** essaie de ne pas froisser ta robe.

create [kriːˈeɪt] *verb*

créer : **he created a new company** il a créé une nouvelle société ; **to create a file** créer un fichier.

creature ['kriːtʃə'] *noun*

créature *(feminine)* : **creatures from outer space** des créatures de l'espace.

credit ['kredɪt] *noun*

crédit *(masculine)*
➤ **a credit card** une carte de crédit.

creep [kri:p] (*past tense & past participle* crept)
verb
se glisser : **he crept into the room** il s'est glissé dans la chambre.

creeps [kri:ps] *plural noun*
➤ **to give somebody the creeps** donner la chair de poule à quelqu'un : **the graveyard gives me the creeps** le cimetière me donne la chair de poule.

crept [krept] *past tense & past participle of* creep
I crept into bed je me suis glissé dans le lit.

crew [kru:] *noun*
1. **équipage** (*masculine*) : **the ship's crew** l'équipage du navire
2. **équipe** (*feminine*) : **a film crew** une équipe de tournage.

cricket ['krɪkɪt] *noun*
1. **cricket** (*masculine*) : **they're playing cricket** ils jouent au cricket
2. **grillon** (*masculine*) : **I can hear the crickets** j'entends les grillons

> CRICKET
> Pratiqué en été, le cricket est un sport très apprécié des Anglais. Les onze joueurs de chaque équipe, habillés tout en blanc, jouent avec une batte en bois (**cricket bat**) et une petite balle dure recouverte de cuir. Les joueurs doivent marquer des points en frappant la balle et en courant entre deux séries de piquets plantés sur le terrain. Les règles du jeu sont très complexes et une partie peut durer plusieurs jours. Ce sport est également très populaire dans d'autres pays tels que l'Australie, la Nouvelle-Zélande ou l'Inde.

cried [kraɪd] *past tense & past participle of* cry
she cried all night elle a pleuré toute la nuit.

crime [kraɪm] *noun*
crime (*masculine*) : **theft is a crime** le vol est un crime

⚠ Le mot anglais **crime** est utilisé uniquement au sens de "délit" et de "criminalité" et non au sens de "meurtre".

criminal ['krɪmɪnl] *noun*
criminel (*feminine* **criminelle**) : **he's a criminal** c'est un criminel

➤ **to have a criminal record** avoir un casier judiciaire.

crisis ['kraɪsɪs] (*plural* crises ['kraɪsi:z]) *noun*
crise (*feminine*) : **there's an economic crisis** il y a une crise économique.

crisps *UK* [krɪsps] *plural noun*
chips (*feminine plural*) : **a packet of crisps** un paquet de chips.

critic ['krɪtɪk] *noun*
critique (*masculine or feminine*) : **she's a film critic** elle est critique de cinéma.

criticism ['krɪtɪsɪzm] *noun*
critique (*feminine*) : **he doesn't like criticism** il n'aime pas la critique.

criticize , **criticise** *UK* ['krɪtɪsaɪz] *verb*
critiquer : **she's always criticizing me** elle est tout le temps en train de me critiquer.

crocodile ['krɒkədaɪl] *noun*
crocodile (*masculine*) : **crododiles are reptiles** les crocodiles sont des reptiles.

crook [krʊk] *noun*
escroc (*masculine*) : **he's a crook** c'est un escroc.

crooked ['krʊkɪd] *adjective*
1. **de travers** : **the picture's crooked** le tableau est de travers
2. **crochu** : **he has a crooked nose** il a le nez crochu.

crop [krɒp] *noun*
1. **culture** (*feminine*) : **they grow many different crops in this region** ils ont beaucoup de cultures différentes dans cette région
2. **récolte** (*feminine*) : **we had a good crop of cherries this year** on a eu une bonne récolte de cerises cette année.

cross [krɒs] *adjective, noun & verb*
■ *adjective*
fâché : **he's very cross with you** il est très fâché contre toi
■ *noun*
croix (*feminine*) : **the hotel's marked with a cross on the map** l'hôtel est marqué d'une croix sur le plan

■ *verb*
1. **traverser : he crossed the road** il a traversé la rue
2. **croiser : she crossed her legs** elle a croisé les jambes ; **let's cross our fingers** croisons les doigts

cross off *phrasal verb*

rayer : he crossed my name off the list il a rayé mon nom de la liste

cross out *phrasal verb*

barrer : she crossed out the word elle a barré le mot

cross over *phrasal verb*

traverser : I crossed over the road j'ai traversé la rue.

crossing ['krɒsɪŋ] *noun*
1. **UK passage** *(masculine)* **pour piétons : you must cross the road on the crossing** il faut traverser la rue au passage pour piétons
2. **traversée** *(feminine)* **: the crossing to Calais took two hours** la traversée jusqu'à Calais a duré deux heures.

crossroads *UK* ['krɒsrəʊdz] *(plural* crossroads*) noun*

carrefour *(masculine)* **: turn left at the crossroads** tournez à gauche au carrefour.

crosswalk *US* ['krɒswɔːk] *noun*

passage *(masculine)* **pour piétons**.

crossword *UK* ['krɒswɜːd], **crossword puzzle** *US* ['krɒswɜːd'pʌzl] *noun*

mots *(masculine plural)* **croisés : he's doing a crossword** il fait des mots croisés.

crow [krəʊ] *noun*

corbeau *(masculine)* [*plural* **corbeaux**].

crowd [kraʊd] *noun*

foule *(feminine)* **: there's a huge crowd** il y a une foule immense.

crowded ['kraʊdɪd] *adjective*
1. **bondé : the train is crowded** le train est bondé
2. **plein de monde : the streets are crowded** les rues sont pleines de monde.

crown [kraʊn] *noun*

couronne *(feminine)* **: the queen is wearing a crown** la reine porte une couronne

➤ **the crown jewels** les joyaux de la Couronne ➤ Tower of London.

cruel [krʊəl] *adjective*

cruel *(feminine* **cruelle***)* **: he's very cruel to his sister** il est très cruel avec sa sœur.

cruise [kruːz] *noun*

croisière *(feminine)* **: she's going on a Caribbean cruise** elle va faire une croisière aux Caraïbes.

crumb [krʌm] *noun*

miette *(feminine)* **: there are lots of crumbs on the table** il y a beaucoup de miettes sur la table.

crush [krʌʃ] *verb & noun*

■ *verb*

écraser : he crushed a fly il a écrasé une mouche

■ *noun informal*

➤ **to have a crush on somebody** craquer pour quelqu'un **: he's got a crush on my sister** il craque pour ma sœur.

crust [krʌst] *noun*

croûte *(feminine)*.

cry [kraɪ] *(past tense & past participle* cried*) verb*
1. **pleurer : don't cry!** ne pleure pas !
2. **crier : 'help!' she cried** « au secours ! » cria-t-elle

cry out *phrasal verb*

pousser un cri : he cried out in pain il a poussé un cri de douleur.

cube [kjuːb] *noun*

cube *(masculine)* **: a dice is a cube** un dé est un cube.

cuckoo ['kʊkuː] *noun*

coucou *(masculine)*.

cucumber ['kjuːkʌmbəʳ] *noun*

concombre *(masculine)*.

cuddle ['kʌdl] *noun & verb*

■ *noun*

câlin *(masculine)* **: she gave him a cuddle** elle lui a fait un câlin

■ *verb*

câliner : she's cuddling the baby elle câline le bébé.

C

cuddly toy [ˈkʌdlɪtɔɪ] *noun*

jouet *(masculine)* **en peluche**.

culprit [ˈkʌlprɪt] *noun*

coupable *(masculine or feminine)* : **who is the culprit?** qui est le coupable ?

culture [ˈkʌltʃər] *noun*

culture *(feminine)* : **London is a city with many different cultures** Londres est une ville où se mélangent beaucoup de cultures différentes.

cunning [ˈkʌnɪŋ] *adjective*

1. **rusé : he's very cunning** il est très rusé
2. **astucieux** *(feminine* **astucieuse)** : **it's a cunning idea** c'est une idée astucieuse.

cup [kʌp] *noun*

1. **tasse** *(feminine)* : **she's drinking a cup of tea** elle boit une tasse de thé
2. **coupe** *(feminine)* : **France won the cup last year** la France a gagné la coupe l'année dernière.

cupboard *UK* [ˈkʌbəd] *noun*

placard *(masculine)* : **put it in the cupboard** mets-le dans le placard.

curb *US* [kɜːb] *noun*

bord *(masculine)* **du trottoir : he was sitting on the curb** il était assis sur le bord du trottoir.

cure [kjʊər] *noun & verb*

■ *noun*

remède *(masculine)* : **it's a cure for flu** c'est un remède contre la grippe

■ *verb*

guérir : **the doctor cured him** le médecin l'a guéri.

curious [ˈkjʊərɪəs] *adjective*

curieux *(feminine* **curieuse)** : **he's curious to know what happened** il est curieux de savoir ce qui s'est passé ; **that's a curious story** c'est une histoire curieuse.

curly [ˈkɜːlɪ] *adjective*

1. **bouclé : she has long curly hair** elle a de longs cheveux bouclés
2. **frisé : she has very curly hair** elle a les cheveux frisés.

currant [ˈkʌrənt] *noun*

raisin *(masculine)* **de Corinthe**.

currency [ˈkʌrənsɪ] *(plural* **currencies)** *noun*

monnaie *(feminine)* : **the pound is the currency of the United Kingdom** la livre sterling est la monnaie du Royaume-Uni.

current [ˈkʌrənt] *adjective & noun*

■ *adjective*

actuel *(feminine* **actuelle)** : **the current fashion** la mode actuelle

➤ **current affairs** l'actualité *(feminine)* : **he is interested in current affairs** il s'intéresse à l'actualité

 L'adjectif **current** est un faux ami, il ne signifie pas "courant".

■ *noun*

courant *(masculine)* : **electric current** courant électrique ; **he was swimming against the current** il nageait à contre-courant.

curry [ˈkʌrɪ] *(plural* **curries)** *noun*

curry *(masculine)* : **a chicken curry** un curry de poulet.

cursor [ˈkɜːsər] *noun*

curseur *(masculine)* : **put the cursor in the box** mets ton curseur sur la boîte.

curtain [ˈkɜːtn] *noun*

rideau *(masculine)* : **draw the curtains, it's getting dark** tire les rideaux, il commence à faire nuit.

curve [kɜːv] *noun*

courbe *(feminine)* : **there's a curve in the river** la rivière décrit une courbe.

cushion [ˈkʊʃn] *noun*

coussin *(masculine)* : **the cat is sitting on a cushion** le chat est assis sur un coussin.

custard [ˈkʌstəd] *noun*

crème *(feminine)* **anglaise : apple pie and custard** tourte aux pommes à la crème anglaise.

custom [ˈkʌstəm] *noun*

coutume *(feminine)* : **it's an old English custom** c'est une vieille coutume anglaise.

customer [ˈkʌstəmər] *noun*

client *(masculine)*, **cliente** *(feminine)* : **the customer is always right** le client a toujours raison.

customs ['kʌstəmz] *plural noun*

douane *(feminine)* : **we went through customs** nous avons passé la douane.

cut [kʌt] *noun & verb*

■ *noun*

1. **coupure** *(feminine)* : **I've got a cut on my arm** je me suis fait une coupure au bras
2. **coupe** *(feminine)* : **a cut and blow-dry** une coupe-Brushing
3. **réduction** *(feminine)* : **a cut in prices** une réduction des prix

■ *verb (past tense & past participle* cut*)*

couper : **he cut the cake into four slices** il a coupé le gâteau en quatre ; **he cut his finger** il s'est coupé le doigt

cut off | *phrasal verb*

couper : **he cut off another slice** il a coupé une autre tranche ; **the phone has been cut off** le téléphone a été coupé

cut out | *phrasal verb*

découper : **I cut out the article** j'ai découpé l'article.

cute [kjuːt] *adjective*

mignon *(feminine* **mignonne***)* : **the baby's really cute** ce bébé est vraiment mignon.

cutlery ['kʌtləri] *uncountable noun*

couverts *(masculine plural)*.

cyberspace ['saɪbəspeɪs] *noun*

cyberespace *(masculine)*.

cycle ['saɪkl] *noun & verb*

■ *noun*

1. **vélo** *(masculine)* : **let's go for a cycle ride** allons faire un tour à vélo
2. **cycle** *(masculine)* : **the cycle of the seasons** le cycle des saisons

■ *verb*

faire du vélo : **she likes cycling** elle aime bien faire du vélo ; **they cycle to school** ils vont à l'école à vélo.

cycling ['saɪklɪŋ] *noun*

cyclisme *(masculine)* : **cycling is a popular sport** le cyclisme est un sport populaire

➤ **to go cycling** faire du vélo : **I go cycling on Sundays** je fais du vélo le dimanche.

cyclist ['saɪklɪst] *noun*

cycliste *(masculine or feminine)*.

cymbals ['sɪmblz] *plural noun*

cymbales *(feminine plural)* : **she plays the cymbals** elle joue des cymbales.

dad [dæd], **daddy** ['dædi] *noun*

1. **papa** *(masculine)* : **hello, dad** bonjour, papa
2. **père** *(masculine)* : **my dad's a baker** mon père est boulanger.

daffodil ['dæfədɪl] *noun*

jonquille *(feminine)* : **the daffodil is a national emblem of Wales** la jonquille est l'un des emblèmes nationaux du pays de Galles.

daily ['deɪli] *adjective & adverb*

■ *adjective*

quotidien *(feminine* **quotidienne***)* : **a daily newspaper** un quotidien

■ *adverb*

tous les jours : **open daily from 8 till 6** ouvert tous les jours de 8 heures à 18 heures.

dairy ['deəri] *adjective*

laitier *(feminine* **laitière***)* : **dairy products** des produits laitiers.

daisy ['deɪzi] *(plural* daisies*)* *noun*

pâquerette *(feminine)*.

dam [dæm] *noun*

barrage *(masculine)* : **there's a dam across the river** il y a un barrage sur le fleuve.

damage ['dæmɪdʒ] *noun & verb*

■ *uncountable noun*

dégâts *(masculine plural)* : **the rain caused a lot of damage** la pluie a fait beaucoup de dégâts

■ *verb*

1. **endommager** : **the computer was badly damaged** l'ordinateur a été très endommagé

2. abîmer : **you'll damage your eyes** tu vas t'abîmer les yeux.

damp [dæmp] adjective

humide : **my clothes are still damp** mes vêtements sont toujours humides.

dance [dɑːns] noun & verb

■ noun

1. danse (feminine) : **the rumba is a Cuban dance** la rumba est une danse cubaine

2. bal (masculine) : **he invited her to the dance** il l'a invitée au bal

■ verb

danser : **can you dance?** tu sais danser ?

dancer ['dɑːnsər] noun

danseur (masculine), danseuse (feminine) : **he's a dancer** il est danseur.

dancing ['dɑːnsɪŋ] uncountable noun

danse (feminine) : **he has dancing lessons** il suit des cours de danse

➤ **to go dancing** aller danser : **he goes dancing every Tuesday** il va danser tous les mardis.

dandruff ['dændrʌf] uncountable noun

pellicules (feminine plural) : **she has dandruff** elle a des pellicules.

danger ['deɪndʒər] noun

danger (masculine) : **we're in danger** nous sommes en danger ; **you're out of danger now** tu es hors de danger maintenant

➤ **to be in danger of doing something** risquer de faire quelque chose : **he's in danger of losing all his money** il risque de perdre tout son argent.

dangerous ['deɪndʒərəs] adjective

dangereux (feminine dangereuse) : **skydiving can be dangerous** le parachutisme en chute libre peut être dangereux.

dare [deər] verb

1. oser : **to dare to do something** oser faire quelque chose ; **I daren't tell him** je n'ose pas le lui dire ; **I didn't dare to do it** OR **I didn't dare do it** je n'ai pas osé le faire

2. défier : **I dare you to take it** je te défie de le prendre.

daring ['deərɪŋ] adjective

audacieux (feminine audacieuse) : **you're very daring** tu es très audacieux.

dark [dɑːk] adjective & noun

■ adjective

1. sombre : **it's dark in here** il fait sombre ici

2. foncé : **dark blue trousers** un pantalon bleu foncé

3. brun : **he has dark hair** il a les cheveux bruns

■ noun

the dark le noir ; **she is afraid of the dark** elle a peur du noir

➤ **it's getting dark** il commence à faire nuit

➤ **it's dark ouside** il fait nuit dehors

➤ **after dark** après la tombée de la nuit : **he never goes out after dark** il ne sort jamais après la tombée de la nuit.

darling ['dɑːlɪŋ] noun

chéri (masculine), chérie (feminine) : **hello, darling!** bonjour, chéri !

dart [dɑːt] noun

fléchette (feminine) : **he's playing darts** il joue aux fléchettes.

dash [dæʃ] verb

se précipiter : **he dashed into the room** il s'est précipité dans la pièce.

data ['deɪtə, 'dætə] uncountable noun

données (feminine plural) : **the data is stored on computer** les données sont stockées sur ordinateur.

database ['deɪtəbeɪs, 'dætəbeɪs] noun

base (feminine) de données.

date [deɪt] noun

1. date (feminine) : **what's your date of birth?** quelle est votre date de naissance ? ; **what's the date today?** quel jour sommes-nous ?

2. rendez-vous (masculine) [plural **rendez-vous**] : **let's make a date for lunch** prenons rendez-vous pour déjeuner

3. datte (feminine) : **I like dates** j'aime les dattes

➤ **to have a date with somebody** sortir avec quelqu'un : **she has a date with Ken tonight** elle sort avec Ken ce soir.

daughter ['dɔːtər] noun

fille (feminine) : **they have two daughters** ils ont deux filles.

daughter-in-law ['dɔːtərɪnlɔː] noun

belle-fille (feminine) [plural **belles-filles**].

dawn [dɔːn] noun

aube (feminine) : **I got up at dawn** je me suis levé à l'aube.

day [deɪ] *noun*

1. **jour** *(masculine)* : **he took two days off** il a pris deux jours de congé ; **she comes to see him every day** elle vient le voir tous les jours
2. **journée** *(feminine)* : **he spent the whole day working** il a passé toute la journée à travailler
> **the day before** la veille
> **the day after** le lendemain
> **the day before yesterday** avant-hier
> **the day after tomorrow** après-demain.

daylight ['deɪlaɪt] *noun*
> **it's daylight** il fait jour.

daytime ['deɪtaɪm] *noun*

journée *(feminine)* : **it happened in the daytime** cela s'est passé pendant la journée.

dead [ded] *adjective & adverb*

■ *adjective*
mort : **he's dead** il est mort.
■ *adverb*
> **I'm dead against it** je suis absolument contre
> **dead on time** pile à l'heure : **she arrived dead on time** elle est arrivée pile à l'heure
> **to stop dead** s'arrêter net : **she stopped dead** elle s'est arrêtée net.

deaf [def] *adjective*

sourd : **he's deaf** il est sourd.

deal [diːl] *noun & verb*

■ *noun*
marché *(masculine)* : **I'll make a deal with you** je te propose un marché ; **it's a deal!** marché conclu !
> **a good deal** OR **a great deal** beaucoup : **I don't have a great deal of time** je n'ai pas beaucoup de temps
■ *verb* (*past tense & past participle* dealt)
distribuer : **to deal the cards** distribuer les cartes

deal with *phrasal verb*

1. **s'occuper de** : **I'll deal with it** je vais m'en occuper
2. **traiter de** : **we'll deal with that subject in the next chapter** nous allons traiter de ce sujet dans le chapitre suivant.

dealt [delt] *past tense & past participle of* deal

he has dealt with it il s'en est occupé.

dear [dɪəʳ] *adjective & exclamation*

■ *adjective*
cher *(feminine* **chère)** : **he's a dear friend** c'est un ami qui m'est cher ; **Dear Mr Jones** Cher Monsieur Jones
■ *exclamation*
oh dear! mon Dieu ! ; **oh dear, what happened?** mon Dieu, qu'est-ce qui s'est passé ?

death [deθ] *noun*

mort *(feminine)* : **it's the tenth anniversary of his death** c'est le dixième anniversaire de sa mort
> **I was bored to death** je m'ennuyais à mourir
> **I was scared to death** j'avais une peur bleue.

debate [dɪ'beɪt] *noun*

débat *(masculine)*.

debt [det] *noun*

dette *(feminine)* : **they are in debt** ils ont des dettes.

decade ['dekeɪd] *noun*

décennie *(feminine)* : **for decades** depuis des décennies.

deceive [dɪ'siːv] *verb*

tromper : **he deceived his family** il a trompé sa famille

 Deceive est un faux ami, il ne signifie pas "décevoir".

December [dɪ'sembəʳ] *noun*

décembre *(masculine)* : **in December** en décembre ; **next December** en décembre prochain ; **last December** en décembre dernier

In French the months of the year do not start with a capital letter.

decent ['diːsnt] *adjective*

1. **correct** : **they gave us a decent meal** ils nous ont servi un repas correct
2. **bien** *(invariable)* : **he's a decent man** c'est un type bien
3. **décent** : **put on something more decent** mets quelque chose de plus décent.

d

decide [dɪˈsaɪd] *verb*

1. **décider : I decided to help him** j'ai décidé de l'aider ; **she decided not to go** elle a décidé de ne pas y aller
2. **se décider : I can't decide** je n'arrive pas à me décider.

decimal [ˈdesɪml] *adjective*

décimal : the decimal system le système décimal

➤ **a decimal point** une virgule : **don't forget the decimal point when you write the sum** n'oublie pas la virgule quand tu fais le calcul.

decision [dɪˈsɪʒn] *noun*

décision *(feminine)* : **I've made a decision** j'ai pris une décision.

deck [dek] *noun*

1. **pont** *(masculine)* : **they were on the deck of the ship** ils étaient sur le pont du navire
2. **jeu** *(masculine)* : **he bought a deck of cards** il a acheté un jeu de cartes.

deckchair [ˈdektʃeər] *noun*

chaise *(feminine)* **longue : he's sitting on a deckchair** il est assis sur une chaise longue.

declare [dɪˈkleər] *verb*

déclarer : do you have anything to declare? avez-vous quelque chose à déclarer ?

decorate [ˈdekəreɪt] *verb*

1. **décorer : they decorated the Christmas tree** ils ont décoré le sapin de Noël
2. *UK* **peindre : we are decorating the kitchen** nous sommes en train de peindre la cuisine.

decoration [ˌdekəˈreɪʃn] *noun*

décoration *(feminine)* : **they are putting up the Christmas decorations** ils mettent les décorations de Noël.

decrease *noun & verb*

◼ *noun* [ˈdiːkriːs]
diminution *(feminine)*, **baisse** *(feminine)* : **there's been a decrease in sales** il y a eu une diminution des ventes

◼ *verb* [dɪˈkriːs]
diminuer, baisser : the number of students has decreased le nombre d'étudiants a diminué.

deep [diːp] *adjective*

1. **profond : the hole is deep** le trou est pro-

fond ; **how deep is the river?** quelle est la profondeur du fleuve ?
2. **grave : he has a deep voice** il a une voix grave.

deeply [ˈdiːplɪ] *adverb*

profondément : he deeply regrets it il le regrette profondément.

deer [dɪər] *(plural* deer*) noun*

cerf *(masculine)* : **male deer have antlers** les cerfs mâles ont des bois.

defeat [dɪˈfiːt] *noun & verb*

◼ *noun*
défaite *(feminine)* : **Napoleon suffered a defeat at Waterloo** Napoléon a subi une défaite à Waterloo

◼ *verb*
battre, vaincre : our team was defeated by two goals to nil notre équipe a été battue par deux buts à zéro.

defence *UK*, **defense** *US* [dɪˈfens] *noun*

défense *(feminine)* : **he came to my defence** il a pris ma défense ; **he plays in defence** il joue en défense.

defend [dɪˈfend] *verb*

défendre : she tried to defend herself elle a essayé de se défendre.

defense *US noun* ➤ defence *UK*.

definite [ˈdefɪnɪt] *adjective*

1. **sûr : is it definite that he's coming?** c'est sûr qu'il vient ? ; **we want a definite answer** nous voulons une réponse sûre
2. **catégorique : she was quite definite about it** elle était catégorique là-dessus
3. **précis : I haven't made any definite plans** je n'ai pas de projets précis
4. **net** *(feminine* nette*)* : **there's a definite improvement** il y a une nette amélioration.

definitely [ˈdefɪnɪtlɪ] *adverb*

sans faute : I will definitely come je viendrai sans faute

➤ **definitely not!** certainement pas !

 Definitely est un faux ami, il ne signifie pas "définitivement".

degree [dɪˈgriː] *noun*

1. **degré** *(masculine)* : **it's 30 degrees in the shade** il fait 30 degrés à l'ombre

2. **licence** *(feminine)* : **she has a degree in English** elle a une licence d'anglais
➤ **to a certain degree** jusqu'à un certain point.

delay [dɪ'leɪ] *noun & verb*

■ *noun*
retard *(masculine)* : **there's a two-hour delay** il y a deux heures de retard
➤ **without delay** sans tarder

 Delay est un faux ami, il ne signifie pas "délai".

■ *verb*
retarder : **he delayed his departure** il a retardé son départ.

delayed [dɪ'leɪd] *adjective*
retardé : **our flight has been delayed** notre vol a été retardé.

delete [dɪ'liːt] *verb*
effacer, supprimer : **the delete key** la touche d'effacement.

deliberate [dɪ'lɪbərət] *adjective*
voulu, délibéré : **that was deliberate!** c'était voulu ! or c'était délibéré !

deliberately [dɪ'lɪbərətlɪ] *adverb*
exprès, délibérément : **he did it deliberately** il l'a fait exprès.

delicate ['delɪkət] *adjective*
délicat : **she has delicate features** elle a des traits délicats.

delicatessen [ˌdelɪkə'tesn] *noun*
épicerie *(feminine)* **fine, traiteur** *(masculine)*.

delicious [dɪ'lɪʃəs] *adjective*
délicieux *(feminine* **délicieuse)** : **this soup is delicious** cette soupe est délicieuse.

delighted [dɪ'laɪtɪd] *adjective*
ravi : **I'm delighted to see you** je suis ravi de te voir.

deliver [dɪ'lɪvəʳ] *verb*
livrer : **when can you deliver the order?** quand pouvez-vous livrer la commande ?

➤ **to deliver a speech** prononcer un discours

 Deliver est un faux ami, il ne signifie pas "délivrer".

delivery [dɪ'lɪvərɪ] *(plural* **deliveries)** *noun*
livraison *(feminine)* : **they do free deliveries** chez eux, la livraison est gratuite ; **you pay on delivery** vous payez à la livraison.

demand [dɪ'mɑːnd] *verb & noun*

■ *verb*
exiger : **I demand an explanation** j'exige une explication

 Demand est un faux ami, il ne signifie pas "demander".

■ *noun*
1. **exigence** *(feminine)* : **they won't meet their demands** ils ne veulent pas satisfaire à leurs exigences
2. **demande** *(feminine)* : **there's a lot of demand for organic produce** il y a une forte demande en produits biologiques.

demo ['dɪməʊ] *noun informal*
1. **démo** *(feminine)* : **a video game demo** une démo de jeu vidéo
2. *UK* **manif** *(feminine)* : **a peace demo** une manif pour la paix.

democracy [dɪ'mɒkrəsɪ] *(plural* **democracies)** *noun*
démocratie *(feminine)* : **France is a democracy** la France est une démocratie.

Democrat *US* ['deməkræt] *noun*
démocrate *(masculine or feminine)*
➤ Political parties.

democratic [ˌdemə'krætɪk] *adjective*
démocratique
➤ **the Democratic Party** *US* le parti démocrate
➤ Political parties.

demonstrate ['demənstreɪt] *verb*
1. **manifester** : **students are demonstrating in the street** les étudiants manifestent dans la rue
2. **faire une démonstration de** : **he demonstrated how to use the vacuum cleaner** il a fait une démonstration du fonctionnement de l'aspirateur.

d

demonstration [demən'streɪʃn] *noun*

1. **manifestation** *(feminine)* : **she went on an anti-war demonstration** elle a participé à une manifestation contre la guerre
2. **démonstration** *(feminine)* : **he gave us a demonstration of the computer's functions** il nous a fait une démonstration des fonctions de l'ordinateur.

denied [dɪ'naɪd] *past tense & past participle of* deny
he denied it il l'a nié.

denim ['denɪm] *adjective*

en jean : **a denim jacket** un blouson en jean.

denims ['denɪmz] *plural noun*

jean *(masculine)* : **he's wearing denims** il porte un jean.

dense [dens] *adjective*

1. **dense** : **a dense crowd** une foule dense
2. **épais** : **a dense fog** un brouillard épais.

dentist ['dentɪst] *noun*

dentiste *(masculine or feminine)* : **I'm going to the dentist** je vais chez le dentiste.

deny [dɪ'naɪ] (*past tense & past participle* denied) *verb*

nier : **don't deny it!** ne le nie pas ! ; **he denied taking the money** il a nié avoir pris l'argent.

deodorant [di:'əʊdərənt] *noun*

déodorant *(masculine)*.

depart [dɪ'pɑːt] *verb*

partir : **the train is now departing** le train part.

department [dɪ'pɑːtmənt] *noun*

1. **service** *(masculine)* : **the complaints department** le service des réclamations
2. **rayon** *(masculine)* : **the food department** le rayon alimentation
3. **département** *(masculine)* : **the Spanish department at the university** le département d'espagnol de l'université
> **a department store** un grand magasin.

departure [dɪ'pɑːtʃər] *noun*

départ *(masculine)* : **the train's departure was delayed** le départ du train a été retardé
> **the airport departure lounge** la salle d'embarquement à l'aéroport.

depend [dɪ'pend] *verb*

dépendre : **it depends on you** cela dépend de vous ; **it all depends** cela dépend.

deposit [dɪ'pɒzɪt] *noun*

1. **caution** *(feminine)* : **you will get your deposit back when you return the keys** on vous remboursera la caution quand vous aurez rendu les clés
2. **acompte** *(masculine)* : **you pay a deposit now and the rest later** vous payez un acompte maintenant et le solde plus tard
> **to make a deposit** déposer de l'argent : **he made a deposit at the bank** il a déposé de l'argent à la banque.

depressed [dɪ'prest] *adjective*

déprimé : **she's very depressed** elle est très déprimée.

depression [dɪ'preʃn] *noun*

dépression *(feminine)* : **he's suffering from depression** il fait une dépression.

depth [depθ] *noun*

profondeur *(feminine)* : **what is the depth of the river?** quelle est la profondeur du fleuve ?
> **I'm out of my depth** je n'ai plus pied.

deputy ['depjʊtɪ] *adjective*

adjoint : **he's the deputy mayor** c'est le maire adjoint.

describe [dɪ'skraɪb] *verb*

décrire : **describe your room** décris ta chambre.

description [dɪ'skrɪpʃn] *noun*

description *(feminine)* : **she gave a detailed description of the thief** elle a donné une description détaillée du voleur.

desert ['dezət] *noun*

désert *(masculine)* : **camels live in the desert** les chameaux vivent dans le désert
> **a desert island** une île déserte.

deserve [dɪ'zɜːv] *verb*

mériter : **he got what he deserved** il a eu ce qu'il méritait ; **she doesn't deserve to succeed** elle ne mérite pas de réussir.

design [dɪ'zaɪn] *noun & verb*

■ *noun*

1. **conception** *(feminine)* : **it's a car with a com-**

pletely new design c'est une voiture d'une conception nouvelle

2. **plan** (masculine) : **I like the designs for the new house** j'aime bien le plan de la maison

3. **motif** (masculine) : **a carpet with a floral design** un tapis à motif floral

■ verb

concevoir, créer : **he designed this bicycle for young children** il a conçu cette bicyclette pour les jeunes enfants ; **she designs jewellery** elle crée des bijoux.

designer [dɪ'zaɪnər] noun

styliste (masculine or feminine) : **he's a big fashion designer** c'est un grand styliste

➤ **designer clothes** vêtements (masculine plural) griffés.

desk [desk] noun

1. bureau (masculine) : **he's sitting at his desk** il est assis à son bureau

2. réception (feminine) : **leave your key at the desk** laissez votre clé à la réception.

desktop ['desktɒp] noun

bureau (masculine) : **the icon is on the desktop of the computer** l'icône se trouve sur le bureau de l'ordinateur

➤ **a desktop computer** un ordinateur de bureau.

desperate ['despərət] adjective

désespéré : **the situation is desperate** la situation est désespérée

➤ **to be desperate to do something** vouloir faire quelque chose à tout prix : **I was desperate to leave** je voulais partir à tout prix.

despite [dɪ'spaɪt] preposition

malgré : **despite the rain he went out** il est sorti malgré la pluie.

dessert [dɪ'zɜːt] noun

dessert (masculine) : **what's for dessert?** qu'est-ce qu'il y a au dessert ?

destroy [dɪ'strɔɪ] verb

détruire : **the bomb destroyed the village** la bombe a détruit le village.

detached house UK [dɪ'tætʃthaʊs] noun

maison (feminine) individuelle : **they live in a detached house** ils habitent une maison individuelle.

detail ['diːteɪl] noun

détail (masculine) : **I don't want to go into details** je ne veux pas entrer dans les détails

➤ **in detail** en détail : **he described the island in detail** il a décrit l'île en détail.

detective [dɪ'tektɪv] noun

1. inspecteur (masculine) de police : **the detective in charge of the investigation** l'inspecteur responsable de l'enquête

2. détective (masculine) : **he's a private detective** c'est un détective privé

➤ **a detective story** un roman policier.

determined [dɪ'tɜːmɪnd] adjective

déterminé : **he's determined to go back to England** il est déterminé à rentrer en Angleterre.

develop [dɪ'veləp] verb

1. développer : **they're trying to develop the business** ils essaient de développer leur société ; **I got my photos developed** j'ai fait développer mes photos

2. se développer : **babies develop very fast** les bébés se développent très vite

➤ **to develop into** devenir : **he developed into a charming young man** il est devenu un jeune homme charmant.

device [dɪ'vaɪs] noun

appareil (masculine) : **a device for opening cans** un appareil pour ouvrir les boîtes de conserve.

devil ['devl] noun

diable (masculine) : **little devil!** petit diable !

devote [dɪ'vəʊt] verb

consacrer : **he devoted himself to his studies** il s'est consacré à ses études.

diagram ['daɪəgræm] noun

schéma (masculine) : **I drew a diagram** j'ai fait un schéma.

dial ['daɪəl] verb & noun

■ verb

(past tense & past participle dialled UK, dialed US)
composer : **she dialled the number** elle a composé le numéro

■ noun

cadran (masculine) : **a watch with a luminous dial** une montre à cadran lumineux.

dial tone US ➤ dialling tone.

dialling code UK ['daɪəlɪŋkəʊd] noun
indicatif (masculine).

dialling tone UK ['daɪəlɪŋtəʊn], **dial tone** US ['daɪəltəʊn] noun
tonalité (feminine) : **there's no dialling tone** il n'y a pas de tonalité.

dialogue UK, **dialog** US ['daɪəlɒg] noun
dialogue (masculine) : **the dialogue box** la boîte de dialogue.

diamond ['daɪəmənd] noun
1. diamant (masculine) : **a diamond ring** une bague en diamant
2. carreau (masculine) : **the ace of diamonds** l'as de carreau.

diaper US ['daɪəpər] noun
couche (feminine) : **he put a diaper on the baby** il a mis une couche au bébé.

diary ['daɪərɪ] (plural diaries) noun
1. agenda (masculine) : **I wrote down the time of the meeting in my diary** j'ai noté l'heure de la réunion sur mon agenda
2. journal (masculine) : **she keeps a diary** elle tient un journal.

dice [daɪs] (plural dice) noun
dé (masculine) : **he rolled the dice** il a lancé les dés.

dictation [dɪk'teɪʃn] noun
dictée (feminine).

dictionary ['dɪkʃənrɪ] (plural dictionaries) noun
dictionnaire (masculine) : **look it up in the dictionary** cherche-le dans le dictionnaire.

did [dɪd] past tense of do
I did it je l'ai fait ; **did you water the plants?** as-tu arrosé les plantes ?

didn't ['dɪdnt] = did not
I didn't do it je ne l'ai pas fait.

die [daɪ] (present participle dying) verb
mourir : **he died last year** il est mort l'année dernière
➤ **to be dying to do something** mourir d'envie de faire quelque chose : **I'm dying to see you** je meurs d'envie de te voir
➤ **to be dying for something** avoir une envie folle de quelque chose : **I'm dying for a**
drink j'ai une envie folle de boire quelque chose.

diet ['daɪət] noun
1. alimentation (feminine) : **it is important to have a balanced diet** il est important d'avoir une alimentation équilibrée
2. régime (masculine) : **she's on a diet** elle est au régime ; **he went on a diet** il s'est mis au régime.

difference ['dɪfrəns] noun
différence (feminine) : **there's a big difference between the two of them** il y a une grande différence entre les deux
➤ **it makes no difference** ça ne change rien.

different ['dɪfrənt] adjective
différent : **London is different from New York** Londres est différent de New York
➤ **you look different** tu as changé.

difficult ['dɪfɪkəlt] adjective
difficile : **it's a difficult problem** c'est un problème difficile ; **it's difficult to say** c'est difficile à dire.

difficulty ['dɪfɪkəltɪ] (plural difficulties) noun
difficulté (feminine) : **she did it without any difficulty** elle l'a fait sans aucune difficulté
➤ **to have difficulty doing something** avoir du mal à faire quelque chose : **I had difficulty persuading him** j'ai eu du mal à le persuader.

dig [dɪg] (past tense & past participle dug) verb
1. creuser : **he's digging a hole** il creuse un trou ; **they're digging for gold** ils creusent pour trouver de l'or
2. enfoncer : **he dug his hand into the sand** il a enfoncé sa main dans le sable ; **your elbow is digging into my ribs** tu enfonces ton coude dans mes côtes

dig up phrasal verb
déterrer : **the dog dug some bones up** le chien a déterré des os.

digital ['dɪdʒɪtl] adjective
numérique
➤ **a digital camera** un appareil photo numérique
➤ **digital television** la télévision numérique
➤ **a digital watch** une montre à affichage numérique.

dilute [daɪ'luːt] *verb*

> diluer : **you dilute the juice with water** tu dilues le jus avec de l'eau.

dim [dɪm] *adjective*

> faible : **the light's a bit dim** la lumière est un peu faible.

dime *US* [daɪm] *noun*

> dix cents *(masculine plural)* : **he put a dime in the machine** il a introduit une pièce de dix cents dans la machine.

diner *US* ['daɪnər] *noun*

> petit restaurant *(masculine)*.

dinghy ['dɪŋgɪ] *(plural* dinghies) *noun*

> - **a sailing dinghy** un dériveur
> - **a rubber dinghy** un canot.

dining room ['daɪnɪŋruːm] *noun*

> salle *(feminine)* **à manger**.

dinner ['dɪnər] *noun*

> dîner *(masculine)* : **he's cooking dinner** il prépare le dîner
> - **Christmas dinner** le repas de Noël
> - **school dinners** *UK* déjeuners servis à la cantine de l'école.

dinnertime ['dɪnətaɪm] *noun*

> heure *(feminine)* **du dîner** : **it's dinnertime** c'est l'heure du dîner.

dinosaur ['daɪnəsɔːr] *noun*

> dinosaure *(masculine)* : **dinosaurs became extinct millions of years ago** les dinosaures ont disparu il y a des millions d'années.

dip [dɪp] *(past tense & past participle* dipped) *verb*

> tremper : **she dipped her bread into the soup** elle a trempé son pain dans la soupe.

diploma [dɪ'pləʊmə] *noun*

> diplôme *(masculine)* : **he has a diploma in sociology** il a un diplôme de sociologie.

direct [dɪ'rekt] *adjective & verb*

■ *adjective*

> direct : **a direct flight between Paris and Athens** un vol direct entre Paris et Athènes

■ *verb*

1. diriger : **he directs the company** il dirige l'entreprise
2. réaliser : **Spielberg directed the film** Spielberg a réalisé ce film

3. indiquer le chemin à : **he directed me to the station** il m'a indiqué le chemin de la gare.

direction [dɪ'rekʃn] *noun*

> direction *(feminine)* : **we're going in the wrong direction** nous allons dans la mauvaise direction ; **we went in the opposite direction** nous sommes allés dans la direction opposée
> - **to ask for directions** demander son chemin : **she asked me for directions** elle m'a demandé son chemin
> - **directions for use** mode *(masculine)* d'emploi : **read the directions** lisez le mode d'emploi.

directly [dɪ'rektlɪ] *adverb*

1. directement : **I went directly to the station** je suis allé directement à la gare
2. juste : **he was directly behind me** il était juste derrière moi.

director [dɪ'rektər] *noun*

1. directeur *(masculine)*, directrice *(feminine)* : **he's the director of a big firm** c'est le directeur d'une grande entreprise
2. réalisateur *(masculine)*, réalisatrice *(feminine)* : **who's the director of this film?** qui est le réalisateur de ce film ?

directory [dɪ'rektərɪ] *(plural* directories) *noun*

> annuaire *(masculine)* : **the telephone directory** l'annuaire
> - **directory enquiries** *UK* les renseignements *(masculine plural)* : **I phoned directory enquiries** j'ai appelé les renseignements.

dirt [dɜːt] *uncountable noun*

1. saleté *(feminine)* : **it's covered in dirt** c'est très sale
2. *US* terre *(feminine)* : **put some dirt in the flower pot** mets de la terre dans le pot de fleurs.

dirty ['dɜːtɪ] *adjective*

> sale : **my jeans are dirty** mon jean est sale
> - **to get something dirty** salir quelque chose : **I got my shoes dirty** j'ai sali mes chaussures.

disabled [dɪs'eɪbld] *adjective*

> handicapé : **she's disabled** elle est handicapée.

d

disadvantage [ˌdɪsəd'vɑːntɪdʒ] *noun*

inconvénient *(masculine)* : **the plan has several disadvantages** le projet présente plusieurs inconvénients.

disagree [ˌdɪsə'griː] *verb*

ne pas être d'accord : **I disagree with you** je ne suis pas d'accord avec vous.

disappear [ˌdɪsə'pɪər] *verb*

disparaître : **the fox disappeared** le renard a disparu.

disappoint [ˌdɪsə'pɔɪnt] *verb*

décevoir : **he really disappointed me** il m'a vraiment déçu.

disappointed [ˌdɪsə'pɔɪntɪd] *adjective*

déçu : **I was disappointed in the film** j'étais déçu par le film.

disappointment [ˌdɪsə'pɔɪntmənt] *noun*

déception *(feminine)* : **what a disappointment!** quelle déception !

disapprove [ˌdɪsə'pruːv] *verb*

être tout à fait contre : **she disapproves of smoking** elle est tout à fait contre le tabac.

disaster [dɪ'zɑːstər] *noun*

catastrophe *(feminine)*, **désastre** *(masculine)* : **an air disaster** une catastrophe aérienne ; **a natural disaster** une catastrophe naturelle ; **the meeting was a disaster** la réunion a été un désastre.

disc *UK*, **disk** *US* [dɪsk] *noun*

disque *(masculine)* : **a compact disc** un disque compact

➤ **a disc jockey** un disc-jokey : **he's a disc jokey** il est disc-jokey.

discipline ['dɪsɪplɪn] *noun*

discipline *(feminine)*.

disco ['dɪskəʊ] *(abbreviation of discotheque) noun*

boîte *(feminine)*, **discothèque** *(feminine)* : **they go to a disco on Saturdays** ils vont en boîte le samedi.

discount ['dɪskaʊnt] *noun*

remise *(feminine)*, **réduction** *(feminine)* : **I got a 20 % discount on it** on m'a fait une remise de 20%.

discover [dɪ'skʌvər] *verb*

découvrir : **Christopher Columbus discovered America in 1492** Christophe Colomb a découvert l'Amérique en 1492.

discovery [dɪ'skʌvərɪ] *(plural discoveries) noun*

découverte : **they've made some new discoveries** ils ont fait de nouvelles découvertes.

discrimination [dɪˌskrɪmɪ'neɪʃn] *noun*

discrimination *(feminine)* : **racial discrimination** la discrimination raciale.

discuss [dɪ'skʌs] *verb*

discuter de : **she discussed the problem with him** elle a discuté du problème avec lui.

discussion [dɪ'skʌʃn] *noun*

discussion *(feminine)* : **they had a long discussion** ils ont eu une longue discussion ; **we had a discussion about politics** nous avons discuté de politique.

disease [dɪ'ziːz] *noun*

maladie *(feminine)* : **she caught a rare disease** elle a attrapé une maladie rare.

disguise [dɪs'gaɪz] *verb & noun*

■ *verb*

déguiser : **she's disguised as a witch** elle est déguisée en sorcière

■ *noun*

➤ **in disguise** deguisé : **everyone was in disguise** tout le monde était déguisé.

disgusting [dɪs'gʌstɪŋ] *adjective*

dégoûtant : **that smell is disgusting** cette odeur est dégoûtante.

dish [dɪʃ] *(plural dishes) noun*

plat *(masculine)* : **paella is a Spanish dish** la paella est un plat espagnol

➤ **the dishes** la vaisselle : **he's doing the dishes** OR **he's washing the dishes** il fait la vaisselle.

dishonest [dɪs'ɒnɪst] *adjective*

malhonnête.

dishtowel *US* [dɪʃ'taʊəl] *noun*

torchon *(masculine)* : **I need the dishtowel to dry the dishes** j'ai besoin du torchon pour essuyer la vaisselle.

dishwasher ['dɪʃˌwɒʃəʳ] *noun*

lave-vaisselle *(masculine)* [*plural* lave-vaisselle].

disinfectant [ˌdɪsɪn'fektənt] *noun*

désinfectant *(masculine)*.

disk [dɪsk] *noun*

1. disque *(masculine)* : **the hard disk is full** le disque dur est plein
2. disquette *(feminine)* : **save the file on a disk** sauvegardez le fichier sur une disquette
3. *US* ➤ disc *UK*.

diskette [dɪs'ket] *noun*

disquette *(feminine)*.

dismiss [dɪs'mɪs] *verb*

renvoyer : **she was dismissed from her job** elle a été renvoyée.

disorganized [dɪs'ɔːgənaɪzd] *adjective*

désorganisé : **they are very disorganized** ils sont très désorganisés.

display [dɪ'spleɪ] *noun & verb*

■ *noun*
1. exposition *(feminine)* : **an art display** une exposition d'art
2. spectacle *(masculine)* : **an acrobatics display** un spectacle d'acrobates
➤ **on display** exposé : **his paintings are on display** ses tableaux sont exposés
■ *verb*
1. exposer : **the goods are displayed in the shop window** les marchandises sont exposées dans la vitrine du magasin
2. faire preuve de : **he displayed great courage** il a fait preuve d'un grand courage
3. afficher : **the information is displayed on the screen** l'information est affichée à l'écran.

disposable [dɪ'spəʊzəbl] *adjective*

jetable : **a disposable camera** un appareil photo jetable.

distance ['dɪstəns] *noun*

distance *(feminine)* : **what's the distance between the two towns?** quelle est la distance entre les deux villes ?
➤ **in the distance** au loin : **I could see her in the distance** je la voyais au loin
➤ **it's within walking distance** on peut y aller à pied.

distant ['dɪstənt] *adjective*

lointain : **in the distant future** dans un avenir lointain.

distinguish [dɪ'stɪŋgwɪʃ] *verb*

distinguer : **he can't distinguish between red and green** il n'arrive pas à distinguer le rouge du vert.

distort [dɪ'stɔːt] *verb*

déformer : **this mirror distorts your face** ce miroir déforme le visage.

distract [dɪ'strakt] *verb*

distraire : **you're distracting me from work** tu me distrais de mon travail.

distribute [dɪ'strɪbjuːt] *verb*

distribuer : **students were distributing leaflets** les étudiants distribuaient des tracts.

district ['dɪstrɪkt] *noun*

1. quartier *(masculine)* : **the City is the financial district of London** la City est le quartier financier à Londres
2. région *(feminine)* : **the Lake District** la région des lacs.

disturb [dɪ'stɜːb] *verb*

déranger : **sorry to disturb you** désolé de vous déranger.

dive [daɪv] *(past tense* dived *OR* dove *US, past participle* dived*) verb*

plonger : **he dived into the water** il a plongé dans l'eau.

diver ['daɪvəʳ] *noun*

plongeur *(masculine)*, plongeuse *(feminine)*.

divide [dɪ'vaɪd] *verb*

1. diviser : **she divided the cake into three equal parts** elle a divisé le gâteau en trois parts égales ; **14 divided by 2 is 7** 14 divisé par 2 égale 7
2. séparer : **a partition divides the room in two** une cloison sépare la pièce en deux
3. partager : **they divided the money between them** ils se sont partagé l'argent.

diving ['daɪvɪŋ] *noun*

plongée *(feminine)* : **he goes diving** il fait de la plongée
➤ **a diving board** un plongeoir.

divorced [dɪ'vɔːst] *adjective*

divorcé : his parents are divorced ses parents sont divorcés ; **they're getting divorced** ils sont en train de divorcer.

DIY *UK* [ˌdiːaɪ'waɪ] *(abbreviation of* do-it-yourself*) noun*

bricolage *(masculine)* : **a DIY store** un magasin de bricolage.

dizzy ['dɪzɪ] *adjective*

➤ **to feel dizzy** avoir la tête qui tourne : **I'm feeling a bit dizzy** j'ai la tête qui tourne.

DJ ['diːdʒeɪ] *(abbreviation of* disc jockey*) noun*

DJ *(masculine or feminine)* : **he's a DJ** il est DJ.

do [duː] *(past tense* did*, past participle* done*) verb*

1. **faire : what are you doing?** qu'est-ce que tu fais ? ; **I'm doing my homework** je fais mes devoirs ; **I've got a lot to do** j'ai beaucoup à faire ; **that walk has done me good** cette promenade m'a fait du bien ; **do as you're told!** fais ce qu'on te dit !

2. **suffire : will 10 euros do?** est-ce que 10 euros suffiront ? ; **that'll do now!** ça suffit maintenant !

3. **aller : how are you doing?** comment ça va ? ; **I'm doing well** je vais bien

4. *In questions*

> In French you form a question by putting **est-ce que** in front of the subject and the verb, or, if the subject is a pronoun (**tu, il, elle,** etc), you can reverse the order of the subject and the verb and put a hyphen in between (**es-tu, as-tu,** etc). In the spoken language you will often hear an affirmative statement made into a question simply by using an inquiring tone:

do you speak English? est-ce que vous parlez anglais ? OR parlez-vous anglais ? ; **do you know Valerie?** tu connais Valerie ? ; **did Tom phone?** est-ce que Tom a appelé ?

5. *In negatives*

> To form a negative in French you put **ne ... pas** on either side of the verb:

I don't want to come je ne veux pas venir ; **he doesn't eat meat** il ne mange pas de viande ; **we didn't go out last night** nous ne sommes pas sortis hier soir

6. *In short answers*

> 'Do' is not translated when it is used to take the place of another verb:

I like reggae – so do I j'aime bien le reggae – moi aussi ; **do you know how to ski? – no, I don't** sais-tu faire du ski ? – non

7. *In question tags*

> When a question tag is in the affirmative, use **n'est-ce pas?** as a translation. When a question tag is in the negative, use **si?** as a translation:

you know Fran, don't you? tu connais Fran, n'est-ce pas ? ; **he doesn't like garlic, does he?** il n'aime pas l'ail, si ?

8. *In emphatic sentences* **I DO like him, but I don't want to marry him** je l'aime bien, mais je ne veux pas me marier avec lui ; **I DO want to go** je veux bien y aller

9. *In polite requests* **je vous en prie : do sit down!** asseyez-vous, je vous en prie

➤ **how do you do?** enchanté !

➤ **to do well** s'en sortir bien : **he's doing well at school** il s'en sort bien à l'école

➤ **to do one's hair** se coiffer

do up *phrasal verb*

1. **fermer : he did up his jacket** il a fermé sa veste

2. **attacher : do your laces up** attache tes lacets

3. **boutonner : do up your shirt buttons** boutonne ta chemise

4. **retaper : they're doing up an old farmhouse** ils retapent une vieille ferme

do without *phrasal verb*

se passer de : they did without bread ils se sont passé de pain.

doctor ['dɒktər] *noun*

médecin *(masculine)* : **I went to the doctor** je suis allé chez le médecin ; **she's a doctor** elle est médecin.

document ['dɒkjʊmənt] *noun*

document *(masculine)*.

documentary [ˌdɒkjʊ'mentərɪ] *(plural* documentaries*) noun*

documentaire *(masculine)* : **there's a documentary about sharks on TV** il y a un documentaire sur les requins à la télé.

does [dəz, dʌz] ➤ do

he **does** yoga il fait du yoga ; **does** she like football? est-ce qu'elle aime le football ?

doesn't ['dʌznt] = does not

it **doesn't** matter ça ne fait rien ; he **doesn't** read much il ne lit pas beaucoup.

dog [dɒg] noun

chien (masculine), chienne (feminine) : we have a **dog** called Cassius nous avons un chien qui s'appelle Cassius.

do-it-yourself [duːɪtjɔːˈself] noun

bricolage (masculine) : a **do-it-yourself** shop un magasin de bricolage.

doll [dɒl] noun

poupée (feminine).

dollar ['dɒlər] noun

dollar (masculine) : it costs twenty **dollars** ça coûte vingt dollars
➤ a **dollar bill** un billet d'un dollar.

dolphin ['dɒlfɪn] noun

dauphin (masculine) : **dolphins** are mammals les dauphins sont des mammifères.

dominoes ['dɒmɪnəʊz] noun

dominos (masculine plural) : they're playing **dominoes** ils jouent aux dominos.

donate [dəˈneɪt] verb

faire don de : he **donated** a hundred pounds to charity il a fait don de cent livres aux œuvres de bienfaisance
➤ to **donate blood** donner son sang OR faire un don de sang.

done [dʌn] adjective & verb form

■ adjective
1. fini : I'm nearly **done** j'ai presque fini
2. cuit : the potatoes aren't **done** les pommes de terre ne sont pas cuites
■ past participle of do
I haven't **done** it yet je ne l'ai pas encore fait.

donkey ['dɒŋkɪ] noun

âne (masculine).

don't [dəʊnt] = do not

they **don't** play tennis ils ne jouent pas au tennis ; I **don't** know what to do je ne sais pas quoi faire.

donut US noun ➤ doughnut.

door [dɔːr] noun

1. porte (feminine) : close the **door** fermez la porte
2. portière (feminine) : the car **door** is dented la portière de la voiture est cabossée.

doorbell ['dɔːbel] noun

sonnette (feminine)
➤ to ring the **doorbell** sonner : somebody rang the **doorbell** on a sonné.

doormat ['dɔːmæt] noun

paillasson (masculine) : wipe your feet on the **doormat** essuie tes pieds sur le paillasson.

doorstep ['dɔːstep] noun

pas (masculine) de la porte : she's sitting on the **doorstep** elle est assise sur le pas de la porte.

dormitory ['dɔːmətrɪ] (plural dormitories) noun

dortoir (masculine) : the boys' **dormitory** has fifteen beds in it il y a quinze lits dans le dortoir des garçons.

dot [dɒt] noun

point (masculine) : don't forget the **dot** on the "i" n'oublie pas de mettre le point sur le « i »
➤ on the **dot** à l'heure pile : at 6 o'clock on the **dot** à 6 heures pile.

dotted line ['dɒtɪdlaɪn] noun

pointillés (masculine plural) : cut along the **dotted line** coupez suivant les pointillés.

double ['dʌbl] adjective, adverb, noun & verb

■ adjective
1. double : she had a **double** helping of ice cream elle a mangé une double portion de glace
2. deux : "address" is spelt with a **double** "d" « address » s'écrit avec deux « d »
3. In phone numbers **double** two three five vingt-deux, trente-cinq
➤ the **double bass** la contrebasse : she plays the **double bass** elle joue de la contrebasse
➤ a **double bed** un grand lit

d

> **double cream** *UK* crème *(feminine)* fraîche épaisse
> **a double room** une chambre pour deux personnes
■ *adverb*
1. **le double : those tickets cost double** ces billets coûtent le double
2. **en deux : he was bent double** il était plié en deux
■ *noun*
1. **double** *(masculine)* **: the men's doubles** le double messieurs
2. **sosie** *(masculine)* **: she's my double** c'est mon sosie
■ *verb*
doubler : prices have doubled les prix ont doublé.

double-click ['dʌblklɪk] *verb*

double-cliquer, cliquer deux fois : double-click on the icon double-cliquez sur l'icône.

double-decker *UK* ['dʌbl'dekəʳ] *noun*

autobus *(masculine)* **à impériale.**

doubt [daʊt] *noun & verb*

■ *noun*
doute *(masculine)* **: there is no doubt about it** il n'y a aucun doute là-dessus
> **without doubt** sans aucun doute **: he's without doubt the champion** il est sans aucun doute le champion
> **to be in doubt** ne pas être sûr **: if you're in doubt ask your parents** si tu n'es pas sûr, demande à tes parents
■ *verb*
douter : I doubt it j'en doute **; I doubt he'll come** je doute qu'il vienne.

dough [dəʊ] *uncountable noun*

pâte *(feminine)* **: bread is made from dough** on fabrique le pain avec de la pâte.

doughnut , donut *US* ['dəʊnʌt] *noun*

beignet *(masculine)* **: she likes jam doughnuts** elle aime les beignets à la confiture.

dove *noun & verb form*

■ *noun* [dʌv]
colombe *(feminine)* **: the dove is a symbol of peace** la colombe est un symbole de la paix
■ *past tense* [dəʊv] *of* dive *US*
he dove into the pool il a plongé dans la piscine.

down [daʊn] *adverb, preposition & adjective*

■ *adverb*
1. *With a verb of movement*

> When 'down' is used with a verb of movement in English (to come down, to go down, etc), you often use a verb alone in French to translate it:

are you coming down? tu descends ? **; she cycled all the way down** elle est descendue à vélo **; we're going down south** nous descendons vers le sud **; I'm going down to the shops** je vais aux magasins **; he travelled down to London** il est descendu à Londres **; prices have come down** les prix ont baissé
2. **en bas : down below** en bas **; she's down in the street** elle est en bas dans la rue
3. **par terre : I fell down** je suis tombé par terre **; he threw the book down** il a jeté le livre par terre
> **down there** là-bas **: can you see that man down there?** tu vois cet homme là-bas ?
■ *preposition*
1. *With a verb of movement*

> When 'down' is used with a verb of movement in English (to come down, to go down, etc), you often use a verb alone in French to translate it:

we walked down the street nous avons descendu la rue **; they ran down the hill** ils ont descendu la colline en courant
2. **en bas de : the bathroom is down the stairs** la salle de bains est en bas de l'escalier
> **further down** plus bas **: they live further down the street** ils habitent plus bas dans la rue
■ *adjective*
informal **déprimé : I feel a bit down** je me sens un peu déprimé.

downhill [daʊn'hɪl] *adjective*

> **to go downhill** descendre **: the road goes downhill** la rue descend **; we ran downhill** nous avons descendu la pente en courant.

Downing Street ['daʊnɪŋstriːt] *noun*

nom d'une rue de Londres

> DOWNING STREET
> C'est au numéro 10 de cette rue que se trouve la résidence officielle du Premier ministre britannnique. Le ministre des Finances réside au numéro 11. Le terme **Downing Street** est souvent employé dans la presse pour désigner le Premier ministre ou le gouvernement eux-mêmes.

download [ˌdaʊnˈləʊd] *verb*

télécharger : he downloaded the attached file il a téléchargé la pièce jointe.

downstairs [ˌdaʊnˈsteəz] *adjective & adverb*

■ *adjective*
1. du dessous : our downstairs neighbours nos voisins du dessous
2. du bas : the downstairs rooms les pièces du bas
■ *adverb*
en bas : wait for me downstairs attends-moi en bas
➤ to come downstairs OR to go down-stairs descendre OR descendre l'escalier : he went downstairs to answer the phone il est descendu pour répondre au téléphone ; she ran downstairs elle a descendu l'escalier en courant.

downtown *US* [ˌdaʊnˈtaʊn] *adjective & adverb*

■ *adjective*
they live in downtown Chicago ils habitent dans le centre de Chicago
■ *adverb*
dans le centre-ville : tomorrow we're going downtown demain nous irons dans le centre-ville.

downwards [ˈdaʊnwədz] *adverb*

vers le bas : he looked downwards il a regardé vers le bas.

dozen [ˈdʌzn] *noun*

douzaine *(feminine)* : they cost 50p a dozen ils coûtent 50 pence la douzaine ; she bought a dozen eggs elle a acheté une douzaine d'œufs.

Dr *(abbreviation of Doctor)*

Dr : Dr Watson Dr Watson.

draft *US noun* ➤ draught *UK*.

drafty *US adjective* ➤ draughty *UK*.

drag [dræg] *(past tense & past participle dragged) verb*

traîner : he's dragging his bag along the ground il traîne son sac par terre ; she dragged the chair over to the window elle a traîné la chaise jusqu'à la fenêtre.

dragon [ˈdrægən] *noun*

dragon *(masculine)* : the dragon is a national emblem of Wales le dragon est l'un des emblèmes nationaux du pays de Galles.

drain [dreɪn] *noun & verb*

■ *noun*
égout *(masculine)* : the drains are blocked les égouts sont bouchés
■ *verb*
égoutter : you have to drain the vegetables first il faut d'abord égoutter les légumes.

draining board *UK* [ˈdreɪnɪŋbɔːrd], **drainboard** *US* [ˈdreɪnbɔːrd] *noun*

égouttoir *(masculine)* : put the dishes on the draining board mets la vaisselle dans l'égouttoir.

drama [ˈdrɑːmə] *noun*

1. art *(masculine)* dramatique : he teaches drama il enseigne l'art dramatique
2. drame *(masculine)* : the play is a drama la pièce est un drame.

dramatic [drəˈmætɪk] *adjective*

spectaculaire : the end of the film was very dramatic la fin du film était spectaculaire.

drank [dræŋk] *past tense of* drink

she drank a glass of water elle a bu un verre d'eau.

drapes *US* [dreɪps] *plural noun*

rideaux *(masculine plural)* : close the drapes ferme les rideaux.

draught *UK* [drɑːft], **draft** *US* [dræft] *noun*

courant *(masculine)* d'air : there's a draught from the window il y a un courant d'air qui vient de la fenêtre.

draughts *UK* [drɑːfts] *plural noun*

jeu *(masculine)* de dames : they're playing draughts ils jouent aux dames.

draughty *UK* [ˈdrɑːftɪ], **drafty** *US* [ˈdræftɪ] *adjective*

plein de courants d'air : this room is draughty cette pièce est pleine de courants d'air.

draw [drɔː] *verb & noun*

■ *verb (past tense* drew, *past participle* drawn*)*
1. dessiner : she drew a picture elle a fait un dessin ; he drew a picture of a dinosaur il a dessiné un dinosaure

2. tirer : she drew she curtains elle a tiré les rideaux

3. attirer : we tried to draw his attention nous avons essayé d'attirer son attention

4. faire match nul : the two teams drew les deux équipes ont fait match nul

➤ **let's draw lots** on va tirer au sort

◼ *noun*

1. match *(masculine)* **nul :** the game ended in a draw ils ont fait match nul

2. tirage *(masculine)* **:** the lottery draw is tonight le tirage du loto a lieu ce soir.

drawer [drɔːʳ] *noun*

tiroir *(masculine)* **:** she took the knife out of the drawer elle a pris le couteau dans le tiroir.

drawing ['drɔːɪŋ] *noun*

dessin *(masculine)* **:** she did a drawing of a whale elle a dessiné une baleine

➤ **a drawing pin** *UK* une punaise **:** they put the poster up with drawing pins ils ont fixé l'affiche avec des punaises.

drawn [drɔːn] *past participle of* draw

I've drawn a picture of a horse j'ai dessiné un cheval.

dreadful ['dredfʊl] *adjective*

affreux *(feminine* affreuse) **:** the weather is dreadful il fait un temps affreux

➤ **to feel dreadful** ne pas se sentir bien **: I feel dreadful** je ne me sens pas bien du tout

➤ **to look dreadful**

1. être affreux : you look dreadful in that hat tu es affreux avec ce chapeau

2. avoir très mauvaise mine : you look dreadful, you should go and lie down tu as très mauvaise mine, tu devrais aller te coucher.

dream [driːm] *noun & verb*

◼ *noun*

rêve *(masculine)* **: I had a strange dream** j'ai fait un rêve bizarre

◼ *verb*

(*past tense & past participle* dreamed OR dreamt) **rêver : I dreamt about you last night** j'ai rêvé de toi cette nuit **; he dreamed he was a prince** il a rêvé qu'il était un prince.

dreamt [dremt] *past tense & past participle of* dream

she dreamt she was flying elle a rêvé qu'elle volait.

drenched [drentʃt] *adjective*

trempé **: I'm completely drenched** je suis complètement trempé.

dress [dres] *noun & verb*

◼ *noun*

robe *(feminine)* **: Joy's wearing a summer dress** Joy porte une robe d'été

◼ *verb*

1. s'habiller : she dresses very smartly elle s'habille avec beaucoup d'élégance

2. habiller : she's dressing the children elle habille les enfants **; they were dressed in black** ils étaient habillés en noir

➤ **to get dressed** s'habiller **: I got dressed and went out** je me suis habillé et je suis sorti

dress up *phrasal verb*

1. se déguiser : she dressed up as a witch elle s'est déguisée en sorcière

2. s'habiller, se mettre sur son trente et un : she always dresses up to go out elle se met toujours sur son trente et un pour sortir.

dressing gown ['dresɪŋɡaʊn] *noun*

robe *(feminine)* de chambre **:** she's wearing a dressing gown elle porte une robe de chambre.

dressing table ['dresɪŋ'teɪbl] *noun*

coiffeuse *(feminine)* **:** she's sitting at her dressing table elle est assise à sa coiffeuse.

drew [druː] *past tense of* draw

she drew a beautiful picture elle a fait un beau dessin.

dried [draɪd] *adjective & verb*

◼ *adjective*

séché **: dried flowers** des fleurs séchées

◼ *past tense & past participle of* dry

she dried her hair elle s'est séché les cheveux **; has the paint dried?** est-ce que la peinture a séché ?

drill [drɪl] *noun & verb*

◼ *noun*

perceuse *(feminine)*

◼ *verb*

percer **:** he's drilling a hole il est en train de percer un trou.

drink [drɪŋk] *noun & verb*

■ *noun*

1. **boisson** *(feminine)* : **a cold drink** une boisson fraîche
2. **verre** *(masculine)* : **we went out for a drink** nous sommes sortis prendre un verre
➤ **would you like a drink?** vous voulez boire quelque chose ?

■ *verb*
(*past tense* drank, *past participle* drunk) **boire** : **he's drinking coffee** il boit du café ; **they've been drinking** ils ont bu.

drinking water ['drɪŋkɪŋ'wɔːtər] *noun*

eau *(feminine)* **potable**.

drive [draɪv] *noun & verb*

■ *noun*

1. **promenade** *(feminine)* **en voiture** : **we went for a drive** nous avons fait une promenade en voiture
2. **trajet** *(masculine)* : **it's a long drive** le trajet est long
3. **allée** *(feminine)* : **we walked up the drive to the house** nous avons remonté l'allée vers la maison
4. **lecteur** *(masculine)* : **the disk drive** le lecteur de disquettes

■ *verb* (*past tense* drove, *past participle* driven)

1. **conduire** : **can you drive?** sais-tu conduire ? ; **he was driving a sports car** il conduisait une voiture de sport ; **she drove me to the airport** elle m'a conduit à l'aéroport
2. **aller en voiture** : **I don't want to drive, I'll take the bus** je ne veux pas y aller en voiture, je vais prendre le bus
3. **rouler** : **they drive on the left in the UK** on roule à gauche au Royaume-Uni
➤ **to drive somebody mad** rendre quelqu'un fou : **you're driving me mad!** tu me rends fou !

driven ['drɪvn] *past participle of* drive

have you ever driven a truck? as-tu déjà conduit un camion ?

driver ['draɪvər] *noun*

1. **conducteur** *(masculine)*, **conductrice** *(feminine)* : **he's a good driver** c'est un bon conducteur
2. **chauffeur** *(masculine)* : **he's a taxi driver** il est chauffeur de taxi
➤ **a driver's license** *US* un permis de con-

duire : **he has a driver's license** il a le permis de conduire OR il a son permis.

driving ['draɪvɪŋ] *noun*

conduite *(feminine)*
➤ **a driving lesson** une leçon de conduite
➤ **a driving licence** *UK* un permis de conduire : **he has a driving licence** il a le permis de conduire OR il a le permis
➤ **a driving test** un examen de conduite ; **he's taking his driving test** il va passer son permis ; **he passed his driving test** il a eu son permis.

drop [drɒp] *noun & verb*

■ *noun*

1. **goutte** *(feminine)* : **a few drops of water** quelques gouttes d'eau
2. **baisse** *(feminine)* : **there's been a drop in the temperature** il y a eu une baisse de température

■ *verb* (*past tense & past participle* dropped)

1. **laisser tomber** : **I dropped the plate** j'ai laissé tomber l'assiette
2. **déposer** : **can you drop me at the station?** tu peux me déposer à la gare ?
3. **baisser** : **temperatures have dropped** les températures ont baissé

drop by *phrasal verb*

passer : **can you drop by tomorrow?** tu peux passer demain ?

drought [draʊt] *noun*

sécheresse *(feminine)*.

drove [drəʊv] *past tense of* drive

we drove here nous sommes venus en voiture.

drown [draʊn] *verb*

se noyer : **he drowned in the lake** il s'est noyé dans le lac.

drug [drʌg] *noun*

1. **médicament** *(masculine)* : **the doctor prescribed drugs** le médecin a prescrit des médicaments
2. **drogue** *(feminine)* : **opium is a drug** l'opium est une drogue
➤ **a drug addict** un drogué, une droguée.

druggist *US* ['drʌgɪst] *noun*

pharmacien *(masculine)*, **pharmacienne** *(feminine)*.

d

drugstore US ['drʌgstɔːr] *noun*

pharmacie *(feminine)* : **you can get it at the drugstore** tu peux l'acheter à la pharmacie.

drum [drʌm] *noun*

tambour *(masculine)* : **he's beating a drum** il bat du tambour

➤ **the drums** la batterie : **she plays the drums** elle joue de la batterie.

drummer ['drʌmər] *noun*

batteur *(masculine)*, **batteuse** *(feminine)*.

drunk [drʌŋk] *adjective & verb form*

■ *adjective*
ivre : **you're drunk** tu es ivre
➤ **to get drunk** se soûler : **he got drunk** il s'est soûlé
■ *past participle of* drink
have you drunk your milk? as-tu bu ton lait ?

dry [draɪ] *adjective & verb*

■ *adjective*
1. **sec** *(feminine* **sèche***)* : **the ink is dry** l'encre est sèche
2. **sans pluie** : **it'll be dry tomorrow** on aura une journée sans pluie demain
➤ **the dry cleaner** OR **the dry cleaner's** la teinturerie : **he took his coat to the dry cleaner** il a porté son manteau à la teinturerie
■ *verb (past tense & past participle* dried*)*
1. **sécher** : **he put the washing out to dry** il a mis le linge à sécher dehors
2. **se sécher** : **dry yourself** sèche-toi ; **she dried her hair** elle s'est séché les cheveux
3. **faire sécher** : **we need to dry the clothes** il faut faire sécher les vêtements
4. **essuyer** : **he's drying the dishes** il est en train d'essuyer la vaisselle.

dryer ['draɪər] *noun*

sèche-linge *(masculine)* [*plural* **sèche-linge**] : **put the clothes in the dryer** mets les vêtements dans le sèche-linge.

dubbed [dʌbd] *adjective*

doublé : **the film is dubbed into English** le film est doublé en anglais.

duck [dʌk]

■ *noun*
canard *(masculine)* : **there are some ducks on the river** il y a des canards sur la rivière
■ *verb*

se baisser : **he ducked as he went through the door** il s'est baissé en passant par la porte.

due [*UK* djuː, *US* duː] *adjective*

when is the train due? à quelle heure le train doit-il arriver ? ; **she's due back soon** elle doit revenir bientôt
➤ **due to** à cause de : **he arrived late due to the bad weather** il est arrivé en retard à cause du mauvais temps.

dug [dʌg] *past tense & past participle of* dig

he dug a hole il a creusé un trou ; **the dog has dug a hole in the lawn** le chien a fait un trou dans la pelouse.

dull [dʌl] *adjective*

1. **ennuyeux** *(feminine* **ennuyeuse***)* : **the film is very dull** le film est très ennuyeux
2. **maussade** : **it's a dull day** le temps est maussade aujourd'hui.

dumb [dʌm] *adjective*

1. **muet** *(feminine* **muette***)* : **he was struck dumb** il est resté muet
2. **idiot** : **that was a dumb thing to do** c'était idiot de faire ça.

dump [dʌmp] *noun*

décharge *(feminine)* : **we took the rubbish to the dump** on a déposé les ordures à la décharge.

dungarees [ˌdʌŋgəˈriːz] *plural noun*

salopette *(feminine)* : **Katie's wearing dungarees** Katie porte une salopette.

during ['djʊərɪŋ] *preposition*

pendant : **it happened during the night** cela s'est passé pendant la nuit.

dusk [dʌsk] *noun*

crépuscule *(masculine)* : **we went home at dusk** nous sommes rentrés au crépuscule.

dust [dʌst] *noun & verb*

■ *noun*
poussière *(feminine)* : **there's a layer of dust on the table** il y a une couche de poussière sur la table
■ *verb*
1. **épousseter** : **he dusted the sideboard** il a épousseté le buffet
2. **faire les poussières** : **I'm dusting** je fais les poussières.

dustbin *UK* ['dʌstbɪn] *noun*

poubelle *(feminine)* : **they've emptied the dustbins** ils ont vidé les poubelles.

duster ['dʌstər] *noun*

chiffon *(masculine)* **à poussière**.

dustman *UK* ['dʌstmən] (*plural* dustmen ['dʌstmən]) *noun*

éboueur *(masculine)* : **he's a dustman** il est éboueur.

dusty ['dʌstɪ] *adjective*

poussiéreux *(feminine* **poussiéreuse***)* : **the piano is very dusty** le piano est couvert de poussière.

Dutch [dʌtʃ]

◾ *adjective*
néerlandais, hollandais : **Edam is a Dutch cheese** l'édam est un fromage hollandais

◾ *noun*
hollandais *(masculine)* : **I speak Dutch** je parle hollandais
➤ **the Dutch** les Néerlandais OR les Hollandais

Remember not to use a capital letter for the adjective and the language in French. Only use a capital letter for the inhabitants.

duty [*UK* 'djuːtɪ, *US* 'duːtɪ] (*plural* duties)
noun
devoir *(masculine)* : **he's doing his duty** il fait son devoir
➤ **on duty**
1. **de garde** : **Dr Jones is on duty** le Dr Jones est de garde
2. **de service** : **go and get the policeman on duty** va chercher le policier de service.

duty-free [*UK* 'djuːtɪ'friː, *US* 'duːtɪ'friː]
adjective
hors taxes : **a duty-free shop** une boutique hors taxes.

duvet *UK* ['duːveɪ] *noun*
couette *(feminine)* : **a duvet cover** une housse de couette.

DVD [diːviːˈdiː] (*abbreviation of* Digital Video Disc OR Digital Versatile Disc) *noun*
DVD *(masculine)* : **I watched the film on DVD** j'ai vu le film en DVD.

dwarf [dwɔːf] (*plural* dwarfs OR dwarves [dwɔːvz]) *noun*
nain *(masculine)*, **naine** *(feminine)*.

dye [daɪ] *noun & verb*

◾ *noun*
teinture *(feminine)*
◾ *verb*
teindre : **I'm going to dye my jeans** je vais teindre mon jean
➤ **to dye one's hair** se teindre les cheveux : **she dyed her hair pink** elle s'est teint les cheveux en rose.

dying ['daɪɪŋ] *present participle of* die.

each [iːtʃ] *adjective & pronoun*

◾ *adjective*
chaque : **each time I see that film, I cry** chaque fois que je vois ce film, je pleure ; **each child has their own computer** chaque enfant a son propre ordinateur
◾ *pronoun*
1. **chacun** : **they each have their own room** ils ont chacun leur chambre ; **the answers are worth 10 points each** les réponses valent dix points chacune ; **each of us had a dessert** chacun de nous a pris un dessert OR chacun d'entre nous a pris un dessert
2. **la pièce** : **melons cost 90 cents each** les melons coûtent 90 cents la pièce
➤ **each other**

A reflexive pronoun (se, s', nous or vous) is normally used in French to translate 'each other':

they love each other ils s'aiment ; **we write to each other** nous nous écrivons ; **do you know each other?** vous vous connaissez ?

eager ['iːgər] *adjective*
➤ **to be eager to do something** avoir très envie de faire quelque chose : **she's eager to learn French** elle a très envie d'apprendre le français.

eagle ['iːgl] *noun*
aigle *(masculine)* : **the eagle is a symbol of the**

United States of America l'aigle est l'un des symboles des États-Unis.

ear [ɪəʳ] *noun*

oreille *(feminine)* : **rabbits have long ears** les lapins ont de longues oreilles.

earache ['ɪəreɪk] *noun*

➤ **to have earache** *UK* OR **to have an earache** *US* avoir mal à l'oreille OR avoir mal aux oreilles : **she has an earache** elle a mal à l'oreille.

earlier ['ɜːlɪəʳ] *(comparative of* early*) adverb & adjective*

▣ *adverb*

I. plus tôt : **I got up earlier than usual** je me suis levé plus tôt que d'habitude

2. tout à l'heure : **I saw them earlier** je les ai vus tout à l'heure

▣ *adjective*

I took an earlier train j'ai pris un train plus tôt.

earliest ['ɜːlɪəst] *(superlative* early*) adjective & noun*

▣ *adjective*

premier *(feminine* première*)* : **what is your earliest delivery date?** quelle est votre première date de livraison possible ?

▣ *noun*

at the earliest au plus tôt ; **I can come at seven o'clock at the earliest** je peux venir à sept heures au plus tôt.

early ['ɜːlɪ] *adverb & adjective*

▣ *adverb*

I. tôt, de bonne heure : **I got up early** je me suis levé tôt OR je me suis levé de bonne heure

2. en avance : **you're early** tu es en avance ; **he's ten minutes early** il a dix minutes d'avance

▣ *adjective*

he had an early night il s'est couché tôt ; **she made an early start** elle est partie de bonne heure ; **in early spring** au début du printemps.

earn [ɜːn] *verb*

gagner : **how much does he earn?** il gagne combien ? ; **she earns 40 dollars an hour** elle gagne 40 dollars de l'heure.

earphones ['ɪəfəʊnz] *plural noun*

casque *(masculine)* : **put on your earphones**

to listen to the CD mets ton casque pour écouter le CD.

earring ['ɪərɪŋ] *noun*

boucle *(feminine)* d'oreille : **she's wearing gold earrings** elle porte des boucles d'oreille en or.

earth [ɜːθ] *noun*

terre *(feminine)* : **the moon goes round the earth** la Lune tourne autour de la Terre ; **the box was covered with earth** la boîte était couverte de terre

➤ **what on earth is that?** mais qu'est-ce que c'est que ça ?

In French **Terre** is written with a capital letter when it means the planet earth.

earthquake ['ɜːθkweɪk] *noun*

tremblement *(masculine)* de terre : **there was an earthquake in California** il y a eu un tremblement de terre en Californie.

ease [iːz] *noun & verb*

▣ *uncountable noun*

facilité *(feminine)*

➤ **with ease** sans difficultés : **he passed the exam with ease** il a réussi l'examen sans difficultés

➤ **at ease** à l'aise : **she felt at ease with them** elle se sentait à l'aise avec eux

▣ *verb*

calmer : **this ointment will ease the pain** cette pommade va calmer la douleur.

easier *comparative of* easy.

easiest *superlative of* easy.

easily ['iːzɪlɪ] *adverb*

I. facilement : **I'll easily finish it tonight** j'aurai facilement fini ce soir

2. de loin : **that's easily the best film I've ever seen** c'est de loin le meilleur film que j'aie jamais vu.

east [iːst] *noun, adjective & adverb*

▣ *noun*

est *(masculine)* : **the sun rises in the east** le soleil se lève à l'est

▣ *adjective*

est *(invariable)* : **Norfolk is on the east coast of England** Norfolk est sur la côte est de l'Angleterre

■ adverb

vers l'est : we went east nous sommes allés vers l'est

➤ **east of** à l'est de : **Manchester is east of Liverpool** Manchester est à l'est de Liverpool

➤ **the East End** les quartiers est de Londres

 THE EAST END

Le **East End** est un quartier situé dans l'est de Londres, connu pour ses docks (où l'on charge et décharge les bateaux). Ses habitants sont appelés les **Cockneys**. Ces dernières années, avec la construction de nombreux logements, cet ancien quartier ouvrier a complètement changé.

➤ Cockney.

Easter ['i:stər] noun

Pâques (feminine plural) : **I went to see her at Easter** je suis allé la voir à Pâques

➤ **an Easter egg** un œuf de Pâques.

eastern ['i:stən] adjective

de l'est : Eastern Europe l'Europe de l'Est.

easy ['i:zi] (comparative **easier** ['i:ziər], superlative **easiest** ['i:ziəst]) adjective

facile : an easy job un travail facile ; **it's easy to install this software** il est facile d'installer ce logiciel

➤ **as easy as pie** simple comme bonjour.

eat [i:t] (past tense **ate**, past participle **eaten**) verb

manger : she's eating a sandwich elle mange un sandwich ; **there's nothing to eat** il n'y a rien à manger.

eaten ['i:tn] past participle of **eat**

I haven't eaten anything je n'ai rien mangé.

echo ['ekəʊ] (plural **echoes**) noun

écho (masculine) : **there's an echo in this cave** il y a de l'écho dans cette grotte.

eclipse [ɪ'klɪps] noun

éclipse (feminine) : **there was an eclipse of the sun** il y a eu une éclipse de Soleil.

ecological [ˌi:kə'lɒdʒɪkl] adjective

écologique.

ecology [ɪ'kɒlədʒɪ] noun

écologie (feminine).

economic [ˌi:kə'nɒmɪk] adjective

économique : an economic crisis une crise économique.

economical [ˌi:kə'nɒmɪkl] adjective

économique : their car is very economical leur voiture est très économique.

economics [ˌi:kə'nɒmɪks] uncountable noun

économie (feminine) : **she's studying economics** elle fait des études d'économie.

economy [ɪ'kɒnəmɪ] (plural **economies**) noun

économie (feminine) : **the country's economy is strong** l'économie du pays se porte bien.

edge [edʒ] noun

bord (masculine) : **he's standing on the edge of the cliff** il est au bord de la falaise.

Edinburgh ['edɪnbrə] noun

Édimbourg : she lives in Edinburgh elle habite à Édimbourg ; **we went to Edinburgh** nous sommes allés à Édimbourg.

edition [ɪ'dɪʃn] noun

édition (feminine) : **a new edition of the dictionary** une nouvelle édition du dictionnaire.

educated [ˌedʒʊ'keɪtɪd] adjective

cultivé : he's not very well educated il n'est pas très cultivé ; **he was educated at Oxford** il a fait ses études à Oxford.

education [ˌedʒʊ'keɪʃn] noun

éducation (feminine), **enseignement** (masculine) : **the Ministry of Education** le ministère de l'Éducation ; **she works in education** elle travaille dans l'enseignement.

effect [ɪ'fekt] noun

effet (masculine) : **the drug had no effect on him** le médicament n'a eu aucun effet sur lui

➤ **special effects** effets (masculine plural) spéciaux.

effective [ɪ'fektɪv] adjective

efficace : the treatment is very effective le traitement est très efficace.

efficient [ɪ'fɪʃənt] adjective

efficace : our secretary is very efficient notre secrétaire est très efficace.

effort ['efət] noun

effort (masculine) : **make an effort!** fais un effort !

egg [eg] *noun*

œuf *(masculine)* : **fried eggs** des œufs sur le plat ; **a boiled egg** un œuf à la coque ; **egg yolk** jaune d'œuf.

eggcup ['egkʌp] *noun*

coquetier *(masculine)*.

eggplant *US* ['egplænt] *noun*

aubergine *(feminine)*.

Egypt ['iːdʒɪpt] *noun*

l'Égypte *(feminine)*

> In French the names of countries are used with the definite article (le, la or l'), except when they follow the preposition en:

Egypt is in Africa l'Égypte est en Afrique ; **she lives in Egypt** elle habite en Égypte ; **we're going to Egypt** nous allons en Égypte.

Egyptian [ɪ'dʒɪpʃn] *adjective & noun*

■ *adjective*
égyptien *(feminine* égyptienne)

> The French adjective does not start with a capital letter:

Cleopatra was an Egyptian queen Cléopâtre était une reine égyptienne

■ *noun*
Égyptien *(masculine)*, Égyptienne *(feminine)*.

eight [eɪt] *number*

huit : **there are eight boys in the group** il y a huit garçons dans le groupe ; **she's eight** elle a huit ans ; **the film starts at eight** le film commence à huit heures.

eighteen [ˌeɪ'tiːn] *number*

dix-huit : **she's eighteen** elle a dix-huit ans.

eighteenth [ˌeɪ'tiːnθ] *number*

dix-huitième : **it's her eighteenth birthday** c'est son dix-huitième anniversaire
> **it's the eighteenth of May** *UK* OR **it's May eighteenth** *US* nous sommes le dix-huit mai.

eighth [eɪtθ] *number*

huitième : **on the eighth floor** au huitième étage
> **it's the eighth of November** *UK* OR **it's November eighth** *US* nous sommes le huit novembre.

eighty ['eɪtɪ] *number*

quatre-vingts : **she's eighty** elle a quatre-vingts ans
> **eighty-one** quatre-vingt-un
> **eighty-two** quatre-vingt-deux.

Eire ['eərə] *noun*

la République d'Irlande.

either ['aɪðər, 'iːðər] *adverb, adjective & pronoun*

■ *adverb*
non plus : **I don't want to go and he doesn't either** je ne veux pas y aller et lui non plus ; **I haven't had anything to eat – I haven't either** je n'ai rien mangé – moi non plus

■ *adjective*
1. l'un ou l'autre : **either team could win** l'une ou l'autre des équipes pourrait gagner
2. chaque : **there are trees on either side of the road** il y a des arbres de chaque côté de la route

■ *pronoun*
l'un ou l'autre : **you can have either of the photos** tu peux prendre l'une ou l'autre des photos ; **I don't like either of them** je n'aime ni l'un ni l'autre
> **either ... or ...** soit ... soit ... OR ou ... ou ... : **you can pay in either euros or dollars** on peut payer soit en euros, soit en dollars ; **either you be quiet, or I'll go home** ou tu te tais, ou je rentre chez moi.

elastic [ɪ'læstɪk] *adjective*

élastique *(masculine)*
> **an elastic band** un élastique.

elbow ['elbəʊ] *noun*

coude *(masculine)*.

elder ['eldər] *adjective*

aîné : **he's my elder brother** c'est mon frère aîné.

elderly ['eldəlɪ] *adjective*

âgé : **she looks after her elderly parents** elle s'occupe de ses parents âgés.

eldest ['eldɪst] *adjective*

aîné : **she's my eldest sister** c'est ma sœur aînée.

elect [ɪ'lekt] *verb*

élire : **he was elected president** il a été élu président.

election [ɪ'lekʃn] *noun*

élection *(feminine)* : **he won the election** il a gagné les élections

> ELECTIONS
> Aux États-Unis, les élections présidentielles ont lieu tous les quatre ans. Les électeurs élisent d'abord les représentants d'un collège électoral, qui à son tour élit pour quatre ans le Président. Les élections sont organisées le lendemain du premier lundi de novembre. Les Britanniques, quant à eux, élisent au suffrage direct et pour cinq ans leur Premier ministre ainsi que les députés de la Chambre des communes (généralement appelés **MPs**).

electric [ɪ'lektrɪk] *adjective*

électrique : **an electric light** une lumière électrique
> **an electric blanket** une couverture chauffante
> **an electric shock** une décharge électrique : **I got an electric shock** j'ai reçu une décharge électrique.

electrical [ɪ'lektrɪkl] *adjective*

électrique : **an electrical appliance** un appareil électrique.

electrician [ˌɪlek'trɪʃn] *noun*

électricien *(masculine)*, **électricienne** *(feminine)* : **he's an electrician** il est électricien.

electricity [ˌɪlek'trɪsətɪ] *noun*

électricité *(feminine)*.

electronic [ˌɪlek'trɒnɪk] *adjective*

électronique : **electronic mail** courrier électronique.

elegant ['elɪɡənt] *adjective*

élégant : **she looks very elegant** elle est très élégante.

elementary school *US* [ˌelɪ'mentərɪ-skuːl] *noun*

école *(feminine)* **primaire**.

elephant ['elɪfənt] *noun*

éléphant : **the Indian elephant is smaller than the African elephant** l'éléphant d'Asie est plus petit que l'éléphant d'Afrique.

elevator *US* ['elɪveɪtər] *noun*

ascenseur *(masculine)* : **he took the elevator** il a pris l'ascenseur.

eleven [ɪ'levn] *number*

onze : **there are eleven glasses** il y a onze verres ; **he's eleven** il a onze ans ; **I went out at eleven** je suis sorti à onze heures.

eleventh [ɪ'levnθ] *number*

onzième : **it's his eleventh birthday** c'est son onzième anniversaire
> **it's the eleventh of January** *UK* OR **it's January eleventh** *US* nous sommes le onze janvier.

else [els] *adverb*

d'autre : **what else?** quoi d'autre ? ; **somebody else** quelqu'un d'autre ; **nothing else** rien d'autre ; **I don't want anything else** je ne veux rien d'autre
> **everyone else** tous les autres ; **everyone else has left** tous les autres sont partis
> **something else** autre chose
> **or else** sinon ; **hurry up or else we'll be late** dépêche-toi, sinon on va être en retard.

e-mail, email ['iːmeɪl] *noun & verb*

■ *noun*
e-mail *(masculine)*, **courrier** *(masculine)* **électronique** : **I'll send you an e-mail** je vais t'envoyer un e-mail
■ *verb*
> **to e-mail somebody** envoyer un e-mail à quelqu'un : **he e-mailed me** il m'a envoyé un e-mail
> **to e-mail something** envoyer quelque chose par e-mail : **he e-mailed the file to me** il m'a envoyé le fichier par e-mail
> **an e-mail address** une adresse électronique.

embarrassed [ɪm'bærəst] *adjective*

embarrassé, gêné : **Laura's very embarrassed** Laura est très gênée.

embarrassing [ɪm'bærəsɪŋ] *adjective*

gênant : **it's very embarrassing** c'est très gênant.

embassy ['embəsɪ] (*plural* embassies) *noun*

ambassade *(feminine)* : **the British embassy** l'ambassade britannique.

emblem ['embləm] *noun*

emblème *(masculine)*.

emerald ['emərəld] *noun*

émeraude *(feminine)* : **an emerald necklace** un collier en émeraude.

emergency [ɪ'mɜːdʒənsɪ] (*plural* emergencies) *noun & adjective*

■ *noun*
urgence *(feminine)* : **this is an emergency!** c'est une urgence !

➤ **in an emergency** en cas d'urgence : **in an emergency call the police** en cas d'urgence, appelez la police

■ *adjective*
d'urgence : **the emergency services** les services d'urgence

➤ **an emergency exit** une sortie de secours.

emotion [ɪ'məʊʃn] *noun*

émotion *(feminine)*.

emperor ['empərəʳ] *noun*

empereur *(masculine)* : **Julius Caesar was a Roman emperor** Jules César était un empereur romain.

emphasize , **emphasise** *UK* ['emfəsaɪz] *verb*

insister sur : **he emphasized the importance of physical exercise** il a insisté sur l'importance de faire de l'exercice physique.

empire ['empaɪəʳ] *noun*

empire *(masculine)* : **the Roman empire** l'empire romain.

employ [ɪm'plɔɪ] *verb*

employer : **the firm employs 100 people** l'entreprise emploie 100 personnes.

employee [ɪm'plɔɪiː] *noun*

employé *(masculine)*, **employée** *(feminine)* : **Ted's an employee in the company** Ted est un employé de l'entreprise.

employer [ɪm'plɔɪəʳ] *noun*

employeur *(masculine)*, **employeuse** *(feminine)* : **they are good employers** ce sont de bons employeurs.

employment [ɪm'plɔɪmənt] *noun*

emploi *(masculine)* : **the employment ministry** le ministère de l'emploi.

empty ['emptɪ] *adjective & verb*

■ *adjective*
vide : **the bottle is empty** la bouteille est vide
■ *verb*
(*past tense & past participle* emptied) vider : **he emptied his pockets** il a vidé ses poches.

encourage [ɪn'kʌrɪdʒ] *verb*

encourager
➤ **to encourage somebody to do something** encourager quelqu'un à faire quelque chose : **he encouraged me to work harder** il m'a encouragé à travailler davantage.

encyclopedia , **encyclopaedia** *UK* [ɪn,saɪklə'piːdjə] *noun*

encyclopédie *(feminine)* : **look it up in the encyclopedia** cherche-le dans l'encyclopédie.

end [end] *noun & verb*

■ *noun*
1. fin *(feminine)* : **she dies at the end of the film** elle meurt à la fin du film ; **I'm leaving at the end of the week** je pars à la fin de la semaine
2. bout *(masculine)* : **the shop's at the end of the street** le magasin est au bout de la rue
➤ **in the end** finalement : **in the end she said yes** finalement, elle a dit oui
■ *verb*
1. finir, se terminer : **the show ends at 11 o'clock** le spectacle finit à 11 heures ; **how does the story end?** comment se termine l'histoire ?
2. mettre fin à : **this ended our friendship** cela a mis fin à notre amitié

end up *phrasal verb*

1. finir : **he ended up doing all the work himself** il a fini par faire tout le travail lui-même
2. se retrouver : **he ended up in Spain** il s'est retrouvé en Espagne.

ending ['endɪŋ] *noun*

fin *(feminine)* : **the ending is very sad** la fin est très triste ; **the film has a happy ending** le film finit bien.

enemy ['enɪmɪ] (*plural* enemies) *noun*

ennemi *(masculine)*, **ennemie** *(feminine)* : **he has many enemies** il a beaucoup d'ennemis.

energetic [ˌenəˈdʒetɪk] *adjective*

énergique : **she's very energetic** elle est très énergique.

energy [ˈenədʒɪ] *uncountable noun*

énergie *(feminine)* : **I don't have any energy** je suis sans énergie ; **we should try and save energy** nous devrions essayer de faire des économies d'énergie.

engaged [ɪnˈgeɪdʒd] *adjective*

1. fiancé : **they are engaged** ils sont fiancés
2. *UK* occupé : **the line is engaged** c'est occupé
➤ **to get engaged** se fiancer : **they have just got engaged** ils viennent de se fiancer

 Engaged est un faux ami, il ne signifie pas "engagé".

engagement [ɪnˈgeɪdʒmənt] *noun*

fiançailles *(feminine plural)* : **an engagement ring** une bague de fiançailles.

engine [ˈendʒɪn] *noun*

1. moteur *(masculine)* : **their car has a powerful engine** leur voiture a un moteur puissant
2. locomotive *(feminine)* : **a steam engine** une locomotive à vapeur.

engineer [ˌendʒɪˈnɪəʳ] *noun*

1. ingénieur *(masculine)* : **the engineer that designed the bridge** l'ingénieur qui a conçu le pont
2. mécanicien *(masculine)* : **the engineer repaired the engine** le mécanicien a réparé le moteur.

England [ˈɪŋglənd] *noun*

l'Angleterre *(feminine)*

In French the names of countries are used with the definite article (le, la or l'), except when they follow the preposition en:

England is part of the United Kingdom l'Angleterre fait partie du Royaume-Uni ; **we live in England** nous habitons en Angleterre ; **they went to England for the weekend** ils sont allés en Angleterre pour le week-end.

English [ˈɪŋglɪʃ] *adjective & noun*

◼ *adjective*
anglais : **the English countryside** la campagne anglaise

➤ **the English Channel** la Manche

◼ *noun*
anglais *(masculine)* : **do you speak English?** parlez-vous anglais ?

➤ **the English** les Anglais

Remember not to use a capital letter for the adjective and the language in French. Only use a capital letter for the inhabitants.

 ENGLISH

Il existe un certain nombre de différences entre l'anglais britannique et l'anglais américain, non seulement en matière d'accent mais aussi dans le vocabulaire. Ainsi, en anglais britannique, « pantalon » se dit **trousers** et « frites » se dit **chips**, mais aux États-Unis, on parle de **pants** et de **fries**. L'orthographe varie également d'une langue à l'autre : par exemple, les mots qui en anglais britannique se terminent par **-our** et **-re** (**colour** ou **centre**), s'écrivent en anglais américain avec **-or** et **-er** (**color** ou **center**).
Dans l'ensemble, l'anglais américain est une langue plus directe et certaines tournures britanniques sont considérées aux États-Unis comme trop soutenues ou peu naturelles.

Englishman [ˈɪŋglɪʃmən] *(plural* Englishmen [ˈɪŋglɪʃmən]) *noun*
Anglais *(masculine)*.

Englishwoman [ˈɪŋglɪʃˌwʊmən] *(plural* Englishwomen [ˈɪŋglɪʃˌwɪmɪn]) *noun*
Anglaise *(feminine)*.

enjoy [ɪnˈdʒɔɪ] *verb*

aimer : **she enjoyed the book** elle a aimé le livre ; **I enjoy listening to music** j'aime bien écouter de la musique

➤ **to enjoy oneself** s'amuser : **I really enjoyed myself at the party** je me suis vraiment amusé à la fête ; **are you enjoying yourself?** tu t'amuses ?

enormous [ɪˈnɔːməs] *adjective*

énorme : **what an enormous dog!** quel chien énorme !

enough [ɪˈnʌf] *adjective, adverb & pronoun*

◼ *adjective*
assez de : **have you got enough money?** est-ce que tu as assez d'argent ? ; **there isn't enough room** il n'y a pas assez de place

■ *adverb & pronoun*

assez : **have you had enough to eat?** est-ce que tu as assez mangé ? ; **would you like some more or do you have enough?** est-ce que tu en veux encore ou est-ce que tu en as assez ? ; **I've had enough of him!** j'en ai assez de lui !

➤ **that's enough!** ça suffit !

enquire *UK* [ɪnˈkwaɪərʳ] *verb*

se renseigner

➤ **to enquire about something** se renseigner sur quelque chose : **he enquired about the departure time** il s'est renseigné sur l'heure du départ.

enquiry [ɪnˈkwaɪrɪ] (*plural* **enquiries**) *noun*

demande *(feminine)* **de renseignements**

➤ **to make enquiries** se renseigner.

enter [ˈentəʳ] *verb*

1. **entrer** : **he knocked on the door and entered** il a frappé à la porte et il est entré
2. **entrer dans** : **everyone looked at her when she entered the room** tout le monde l'a regardée quand elle est entrée dans la pièce
3. **s'inscrire à** : **I entered a competition** je me suis inscrit à une compétition
4. **taper, entrer** : **enter your password and click on OK** tapez votre mot de passe et cliquez sur OK

➤ **the enter key** la touche « entrée ».

entertainment [ˌentəˈteɪnmənt] *noun*

divertissement *(masculine)* : **this film is good family entertainment** ce film est un divertissement pour toute la famille

➤ **the entertainment business** l'industrie du spectacle.

enthusiasm [ɪnˈθjuːzɪæzm] *noun*

enthousiasme *(masculine)* : **the pupils showed great enthusiasm** les élèves ont montré beaucoup d'enthousiasme OR les élèves se sont montrés très enthousiastes.

enthusiastic [ɪnˌθjuːzɪˈæstɪk] *adjective*

enthousiaste : **she's very enthusiastic** elle est très enthousiaste.

entire [ɪnˈtaɪəʳ] *adjective*

entier *(feminine* **entière***)* : **he ate an entire chicken** il a mangé un poulet tout entier.

entirely [ɪnˈtaɪəlɪ] *adverb*

entièrement : **it's entirely my fault** c'est entièrement de ma faute.

entrance [ˈentrəns] *noun*

entrée *(feminine)* : **wait for me at the school entrance** attends-moi à l'entrée de l'école

➤ **an entrance exam** un examen d'entrée.

entry [ˈentrɪ] *noun*

entrée *(feminine)*

➤ **'no entry'** 'défense d'entrer'

➤ **an entry phone** un Interphone®.

envelope [ˈenvələʊp] *noun*

enveloppe *(feminine)* : **he put the letter in the envelope** il a mis la lettre dans l'enveloppe.

environment [ɪnˈvaɪərənmənt] *noun*

environnement *(masculine)* : **we must look after the environment** il faut essayer de protéger l'environnement.

episode [ˈepɪsəʊd] *noun*

épisode *(masculine)* : **the first episode is on TV tonight** le premier épisode passe à la télé ce soir.

equal [ˈiːkwəl] *adjective & verb*

■ *adjective*

égal [*plural* **égaux**] : **I divided the cake into two equal parts** j'ai coupé le gâteau en deux parts égales

➤ **the two teams are equal** les deux équipes sont à égalité

➤ **equal opportunities** l'égalité *(feminine)* des chances

■ *verb*

égaler : **4 plus 5 equals 9** 4 plus 5 égalent 9.

equator [ɪˈkweɪtəʳ] *noun*

équateur *(masculine)* : **Mount Kilimanjaro is practically on the equator** le Kilimandjaro est pratiquement sur l'équateur.

equipment [ɪˈkwɪpmənt] *uncountable noun*

1. **équipement** *(masculine)* : **diving equipment** équipement de plongée
2. **matériel** *(masculine)* : **camping equipment** matériel de camping.

equivalent [ɪˈkwɪvələnt] *adjective & noun*

■ *adjective*

équivalent

➤ **to be equivalent to something** équivaloir à quelque chose : **this is equivalent to 5 euros** cela équivaut à 5 euros

■ *noun*
équivalent *(masculine)* : **it costs the equivalent of £50** cela coûte l'équivalent de 50 livres.

eraser [ɪ'reɪzə^r] *noun*

gomme *(feminine)*.

error ['erə^r] *noun*

erreur *(feminine)* : **he made a serious error** il a fait une grave erreur
➤ **a typing error** une faute de frappe.

erupt [ɪ'rʌpt] *verb*

entrer en éruption : **the volcano erupted** le volcan est entré en éruption.

escalator ['eskəleɪtə^r] *noun*

escalier *(masculine)* **roulant, Escalator®** *(masculine)*.

escape [ɪ'skeɪp] *noun & verb*

■ *noun*
évasion *(feminine)* : **the Great Escape** la Grande Évasion
➤ **he had a lucky escape** il l'a échappé belle
■ *verb*
1. **s'échapper** : **a monkey escaped from the zoo** un singe s'est échappé du zoo
2. **s'évader** : **he escaped from prison** il s'est évadé de prison.

especially [ɪ'speʃəlɪ] *adverb*

surtout : **I like all animals, especially horses** j'aime tous les animaux, surtout les chevaux.

essay ['eseɪ] *noun*

dissertation *(feminine)* : **she wrote an essay on the environment** elle a écrit une dissertation sur l'environnement.

estate [ɪ'steɪt] *noun*

1. **propriété** *(feminine)*, **domaine** *(masculine)* : **the house is in a large estate** la maison est dans une grande propriété
2. *UK* **cité** *(feminine)* : **they live in a housing estate** ils habitent une cité
➤ **an estate agent** *UK* un agent immobilier
➤ **an estate car** *UK* un break.

estimate ['estɪmeɪt] *verb*

estimer : **he estimated the price at 500 dollars** il a estimé le prix à 500 dollars.

EU ['iː'juː] *(abbreviation of* European Union*)* *noun*

UE *(feminine)* : **how many countries are there in the EU?** combien de pays font partie de l'UE ?

euro ['jʊərəʊ] *(plural* euro OR euros*)* *noun*

euro *(masculine)* : **it costs 50 euros** ça coûte 50 euros.

Europe ['jʊərəp] *noun*

l'Europe *(feminine)*

> In French the names of continents are used with the definite article (**le, la** or **l'**), except when they follow the preposition **en**:

Europe is a continent l'Europe est un continent ; **Greece is in Europe** la Grèce est en Europe ; **we're going to Europe** nous allons en Europe.

European [ˌjʊərə'piːən] *adjective & noun*

■ *adjective*
européen *(feminine* **européenne***)*

> The French adjective does not start with a capital letter:

the European continent le continent européen
➤ **the European Union** l'Union européenne
■ *noun*
Européen *(masculine)*, **Européenne** *(feminine)*.

eve [iːv] *noun*

veille *(feminine)*
➤ **Christmas Eve** la veille de Noël
➤ **New Year's Eve** la Saint-Sylvestre.

even ['iːvn] *adjective & adverb*

■ *adjective*
1. **régulier** *(feminine* **régulière***)* : **the surface is even** la surface est régulière
2. **égal** : **their chances are about even** leurs chances sont à peu près égales ; **the teams are even** les équipes sont à égalité
3. **pair** : **four is an even number** quatre est un nombre pair
➤ **to get even with somebody** se venger de quelqu'un
■ *adverb*
1. **même** : **he can't even sing** il ne sait même pas chanter

2. **encore** : **it's even better now** c'est encore mieux maintenant ; **it's even more difficult** c'est encore plus difficile

➤ **even if** même si : **even if he comes it won't make any difference** même s'il vient, ça ne changera rien

➤ **even though** bien que : **I think she's wrong even though she's my sister** je pense qu'elle a tort, bien qu'elle soit ma sœur.

evening ['iːvnɪŋ] noun

1. **soir** (masculine) : **I'm staying at home this evening** je reste chez moi ce soir ; **she relaxes in the evening** elle se détend le soir ; **at seven in the evening** à sept heures du soir

2. **soirée** (feminine) : **we had a lovely evening** nous avons passé une très bonne soirée ; **I waited all evening** j'ai attendu toute la soirée

➤ **yesterday evening** hier soir

➤ **evening classes** cours (masculine plural) du soir.

event [ɪ'vent] noun

1. **événement** (masculine) : **it's an important event** c'est un événement important

2. **épreuve** (feminine) : **a sporting event** une épreuve sportive.

eventually [ɪ'ventʃʊəlɪ] adverb

finalement : **he left eventually** finalement, il est parti

⚠ Eventually est un faux ami, il ne signifie pas "éventuellement".

ever ['evər] adverb

1. **jamais** : **nothing ever happens** il ne se passe jamais rien ; **I hardly ever watch television** je ne regarde presque jamais la télévision ; **it's the best film I've ever seen** c'est le meilleur film que j'aie jamais vu

2. **déjà** : **have you ever been to China?** est-ce que tu es déjà allé en Chine ? ; **have you ever seen an eclipse?** est-ce que tu as déjà vu une éclipse ?

3. **toujours** : **she's as cheerful as ever** elle est toujours aussi gaie ; **he left for ever** il est parti pour toujours

➤ **ever since** depuis que OR depuis : **it's been raining ever since I arrived** il pleut depuis que je suis arrivé OR il pleut depuis mon arrivée

➤ **ever so** UK vraiment : **I'm ever so hungry** j'ai vraiment faim.

every ['evrɪ] adjective

tous les (feminine **toutes les**)

'Every' + singular noun is usually translated by **tous les** or **toutes les** + plural noun in French. You can also use **chaque** + singular noun, if you want to emphasize that you mean 'every single one':

every pupil in the class passed the exam tous les élèves de la classe ont réussi l'examen ; **every house in the street has a garden** toutes les maisons de la rue ont un jardin ; **every pupil read out a different poem** chaque élève a lu un poème différent

➤ **every day** tous les jours

➤ **every other day** tous les deux jours

➤ **every time**

1. **à chaque fois** : **he wins every time** il gagne à chaque fois

2. **chaque fois que** : **every time I go to London, I visit my uncle** chaque fois que je vais à Londres, je rends visite à mon oncle.

everybody ['evrɪˌbɒdɪ], **everyone** ['evrɪwʌn] pronoun

tout le monde : **everybody knows him** tout le monde le connaît ; **everyone was enjoying themselves** tout le monde s'amusait.

everyplace US adverb ➤ everywhere.

everything ['evrɪθɪŋ] pronoun

tout : **do you have everything?** est-ce que tu as tout ? ; **I've told you everything I know** je t'ai dit tout ce que je savais.

everywhere ['evrɪweər], **everyplace** US ['evrɪˌpleɪs] adverb

partout : **I've looked for it everywhere** je l'ai cherché partout ; **she follows me everywhere I go** elle me suit partout où je vais.

evidence ['evɪdəns] uncountable noun

1. **preuve** (feminine) : **there's no evidence that he killed her** il n'y a pas de preuve qu'il l'ait tuée

2. **témoignage** (masculine) : **his evidence was very important in the case** son témoignage était très important dans cette affaire

⚠ Evidence est un faux ami, il ne signifie pas "évidence".

evil [ˈiːvl] *adjective & noun*

- *adjective*
  méchant, mauvais : **he's an evil man** c'est un homme méchant
- *noun*
  mal *(masculine)* : **to tell good from evil** distinguer le bien du mal.

exact [ɪgˈzækt] *adjective*

exact : **what is the exact time?** quelle est l'heure exacte ?

exactly [ɪgˈzæktlɪ] *adverb*

exactement : **that's exactly what I mean** c'est exactement ce que je veux dire
➤ **it's exactly 6 o'clock** il est 6 heures pile.

exaggerate [ɪgˈzædʒəreɪt] *verb*

exagérer : **don't exaggerate!** n'exagère pas !

exam [ɪgˈzæm], **examination** [ɪgˌzæ-mɪˈneɪʃn] *noun*

examen *(masculine)* : **he took the exam yesterday** il a passé l'examen hier ; **I passed my English exam** j'ai réussi mon examen d'anglais.

examine [ɪgˈzæmɪn] *verb*

examiner : **he examined the fly through the microscope** il a examiné la mouche au microscope.

example [ɪgˈzɑːmpl] *noun*

exemple *(masculine)*
➤ **for example** par exemple.

excellent [ˈeksələnt] *adjective*

excellent : **he's an excellent teacher** c'est un excellent professeur.

except [ɪkˈsept] *preposition & conjunction*

sauf : **everyone can swim except me** tout le monde sait nager sauf moi
➤ **except for** sauf : **everybody came except for Lisa** tout le monde est venu sauf Lisa
➤ **except that** sauf que : **I don't remember anything except that I was scared** je ne me souviens de rien, sauf que j'avais peur.

exception [ɪkˈsepʃn] *noun*

exception *(feminine)* : **it's an exception to the rule** c'est une exception à la règle
➤ **to make an exception** faire une exception : **I'll make an exception for you** je vais faire une exception pour vous.

exchange [ɪksˈtʃeɪndʒ] *verb & noun*

- *verb*
  échanger : **she exchanged the CD for a book** elle a échangé le CD contre un livre
- *noun*
  échange *(masculine)* : **I gave him a pen in exchange for a watch** je lui ai donné un stylo en échange d'une montre
➤ **the exchange rate** le taux de change.

excited [ɪkˈsaɪtɪd] *adjective*

excité : **the children are excited** les enfants sont excités.

exciting [ɪkˈsaɪtɪŋ] *adjective*

passionnant : **it was a very exciting film** c'était un film passionnant.

exclamation mark *UK* [ˌekskləˈmeɪʃn-mɑːk], **exclamation point** *US* [ˌekskləˈmeɪʃnpɔɪnt] *noun*
point *(masculine)* **d'exclamation.**

excuse *noun & verb*

- *noun* [ɪkˈskjuːs]
  excuse *(feminine)* : **that's just an excuse!** ce n'est qu'une excuse !
- *verb* [ɪkˈskjuːz]
  excuser : **excuse-me!** excusez-moi !

exercise [ˈeksəsaɪz] *noun*

exercice *(masculine)* : **he doesn't get enough exercise** il ne fait pas assez d'exercice
➤ **an exercise book** *UK* un cahier : **she wrote the answers in her exercise book** elle a noté les réponses sur son cahier.

exhausted [ɪgˈzɔːstɪd] *adjective*

épuisé : **I'm exhausted** je suis épuisé.

exhaust fumes [ɪgˈzɔːstfjuːms] *plural noun*

gaz *(masculine)* **d'échappement.**

exhausting [ɪgˈzɔːstɪŋ] *adjective*

épuisant : **the work is exhausting** le travail est épuisant.

exhaust pipe [ɪgˈzɔːstpaɪp] *noun*

tuyau *(masculine)* **d'échappement.**

e

99

exhibit *US* [ɪɡ'zɪbɪt] *noun*

exposition *(feminine)* : **there's a big exhibit in New York** il y a une grande exposition à New York.

exhibition *UK* [ˌeksɪ'bɪʃn] *noun*

exposition *(feminine)* : **I went to an exhibition of modern art** je suis allé à une exposition d'art moderne.

exist [ɪɡ'zɪst] *verb*

exister : **that doesn't exist anymore** ça n'existe plus.

exit ['eksɪt] *noun*

sortie *(feminine)*.

exotic [ɪɡ'zɒtɪk] *adjective*

exotique.

expect [ɪk'spekt] *verb*

1. s'attendre à : **I wasn't expecting his visit** je ne m'attendais pas à sa visite ; **I was expecting him to be here** je m'attendais à ce qu'il soit là
2. attendre : **I'm expecting a letter** j'attends une lettre ; **she's expecting a baby** elle attend un enfant
3. supposer, penser : **I expect he has left the country** je suppose qu'il a quitté le pays ; **I expect so** je suppose que oui.

expel [ɪk'spel] *(past tense & past participle* expelled) *verb*

renvoyer : **Fred got expelled from school** Fred s'est fait renvoyer de l'école.

expenses [ɪk'spensəz] *plural noun*

frais *(masculine plural)* : **our expenses are very high** nos frais sont très élevés.

expensive [ɪk'spensɪv] *adjective*

cher *(feminine* chère*)* : **this dress is too expensive** cette robe est trop chère.

experience [ɪk'spɪərɪəns] *noun*

expérience *(feminine)* : **he has a lot of experience** il a beaucoup d'expérience.

experiment [ɪk'sperɪmənt] *noun & verb*

◻ *noun*
expérience *(feminine)* : **they did an experiment in the laboratory** ils ont fait une expérience au laboratoire

◻ *verb*
faire une expérience, faire des expériences.

expert ['ekspɜːt] *noun*

spécialiste *(masculine or feminine)* : **he's a computer expert** c'est un spécialiste en informatique.

explain [ɪk'spleɪn] *verb*

expliquer : **can you explain what happened?** peux-tu expliquer ce qui s'est passé ?

explanation [ˌeksplə'neɪʃn] *noun*

explication *(feminine)* : **I'd like an explanation** j'aimerais des explications.

explode [ɪk'spləʊd] *verb*

1. exploser : **the bomb exploded** la bombe a explosé
2. faire exploser : **the police exploded the bomb** la police a fait exploser la bombe.

exploit *noun & verb*

◻ *noun* ['eksplɔɪt]
exploit *(masculine)* : **he told us about his exploits in the jungle** il nous a raconté ses exploits dans la jungle
◻ *verb* [ɪk'splɔɪt]
exploiter.

explore [ɪk'splɔːʳ] *verb*

explorer : **they explored the ruins** ils ont exploré les ruines.

explorer [ɪk'splɔːrəʳ] *noun*

explorateur *(masculine)*, exploratrice *(feminine)* : **David Livingstone was a Scottish explorer** David Livingstone était un explorateur écossais.

explosion [ɪk'spləʊʒn] *noun*

explosion *(feminine)*.

export [ɪk'spɔːt] *verb*

exporter : **Brazil exports coffee** le Brésil exporte du café.

express [ɪk'spres] *adjective & verb*

◻ *adjective*
express : **an express train** un train express
◻ *verb*
exprimer : **she expressed her feelings** elle a exprimé ses sentiments
➤ **to express oneself** s'exprimer : **he ex-**

presses himself well in Spanish il s'exprime bien en espagnol.

expression [ɪk'spreʃn] *noun*

expression *(feminine)* : **it's a common expression** c'est une expression courante ; **she had a funny expression on her face** elle avait une drôle d'expression sur le visage.

expressway *US* [ɪk'spresweɪ] *noun*

voie *(feminine)* **express**.

extend [ɪk'stend] *verb*

1. prolonger : **I'm going to extend my stay** je vais prolonger mon séjour
2. étendre : **he extended his hand** il a étendu la main
3. s'étendre : **the plain extends to the mountain** la plaine s'étend jusqu'à la montagne.

extension [ɪk'stenʃn] *noun*

1. annexe *(feminine)* : **we've built an extension** nous avons construit une annexe
2. poste *(masculine)* : **you can reach me on extension 429** tu peux me joindre au poste 429.

extent [ɪk'stent] *noun*

> to a certain extent jusqu'à un certain point : **to a certain extent you're right** tu as raison jusqu'à un certain point.

exterior [ɪk'stɪərɪər] *adjective*

extérieur : **an exterior wall** un mur extérieur.

extinct [ɪk'stɪŋkt] *adjective*

> to be extinct avoir disparu : **dinosaurs are extinct** les dinosaures ont disparu
> these bears are becoming extinct ces ours sont en voie de disparition.

extra ['ekstrə] *adjective, adverb & noun*

■ *adjective*
1. supplémentaire : **he's taking extra lessons** il prend des cours supplémentaires
2. autre : **I have an extra pen** j'ai un autre stylo
■ *adverb*
to pay extra payer un supplément ; **do you have to pay extra?** est-ce qu'il faut payer un supplément ? ; **I paid ten pounds extra** j'ai payé dix livres de supplément
■ *noun*
1. supplément *(masculine)* : **the price is fixed and there are no extras** le prix est fixe et il n'y a pas de supplément

2. figurant *(masculine)*, figurante *(feminine)* : **he's an extra in the film** il est figurant dans le film.

extraordinary [ɪk'strɔːdnrɪ] *adjective*

extraordinaire.

extravagant [ɪk'strævəgənt] *adjective*

1. dépensier *(feminine* dépensière*)* : **he's very extravagant with his money** il est très dépensier
2. extravagant : **he wears very extravagant outfits** il porte des tenues très extravagantes.

extreme [ɪk'striːm] *adjective & noun*

■ *adjective*
extrême : **extreme sports** les sports extrêmes
■ *noun*
extrême *(masculine)* : **she goes from one extreme to another** elle va d'un extrême à l'autre.

extremely [ɪk'striːmlɪ] *adverb*

extrêmement : **it's an extremely interesting book** c'est un livre extrêmement intéressant.

eye [aɪ] *noun*

œil *(masculine)* [*plural* yeux] : **she has green eyes** elle a les yeux verts
> to keep an eye on something surveiller quelque chose : **can you keep an eye on my luggage?** vous pouvez surveiller mes bagages ?

eyebrow ['aɪbraʊ] *noun*

sourcil *(masculine)*.

eyedrops ['aɪdrɒps] *plural noun*

gouttes *(feminine plural)* **pour les yeux, collyre** *(masculine)*.

eyelash ['aɪlæʃ] *(plural* eyelashes*)* *noun*

cil *(masculine)* : **she has long eyelashes** elle a de longs cils.

eyelid ['aɪlɪd] *noun*

paupière *(feminine)*.

eyesight ['aɪsaɪt] *noun*

vue *(feminine)* : **he has good eyesight** il a une bonne vue.

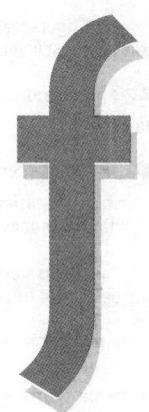

fabric ['fæbrɪk] *noun*

tissu *(masculine)* : **cotton fabric** du tissu en coton

⚠ Fabric est un faux ami, il ne signifie pas "fabrique".

fabulous ['fæbjʊləs] *adjective*

sensationnel *(feminine* **sensationnelle***)* : **we had a fabulous evening** nous avons passé une soirée sensationnelle.

face [feɪs] *noun & verb*

■ *noun*

1. **visage** *(masculine)* : **she has a beautiful face** elle a un très beau visage
2. **grimace** *(feminine)* : **he made a face** il a fait une grimace
3. **cadran** *(masculine)* : **the clock face is broken** le cadran de la pendule est cassé
➤ **face to face** face à face

■ *verb*

1. **faire face à** : **he turned and faced me** il s'est retourné et m'a fait face ; **we must face these problems** nous devons faire face à ces problèmes
2. **donner sur** : **our house faces the sea** notre maison donne sur la mer
➤ **to be facing somebody** OR **something** être en face de quelqu'un OR quelque chose : **I was facing him** j'étais en face de lui ; **there's a church facing the school** il y a une église en face de l'école

face up to *phrasal verb*

faire face à : **he faced up to the problem** il a fait face au problème.

facilities [fə'sɪlətɪz] *plural noun*

installations *(feminine plural)* : **the school has good sports facilities** l'école a de bonnes installations sportives

⚠ Facilities est un faux ami, il n'a pas le sens de "facilité" en français.

fact [fækt] *noun*

1. **fait** *(masculine)* : **that's a fact** c'est un fait
2. *(uncountable noun)* **réalité** *(feminine)* : **fact and fiction** la réalité et la fiction
➤ **in fact** en fait
➤ **a fact sheet** une fiche d'informations.

factory ['fæktərɪ] *(plural* **factories***)* *noun*

usine *(feminine)* : **a car factory** une usine d'automobiles.

fade [feɪd] *verb*

1. **se décolorer** : **my jeans are beginning to fade** mon jean commence à se décolorer
2. **passer** : **the colour has faded** la couleur a passé
3. **baisser** : **the light is fading** la lumière baisse
4. **diminuer** : **the sound gradually faded** le bruit a diminué peu à peu.

fail [feɪl] *verb*

1. **rater, échouer à** : **he failed the exam** il a raté l'examen
2. **échouer** : **two students failed** deux étudiants ont échoué
3. **ne pas réussir** : **I tried to persuade him but I failed** j'ai essayé de le convaincre mais je n'ai pas réussi
4. **lâcher** : **the brakes failed** les freins ont lâché
➤ **to fail to do something**
1. **ne pas arriver à faire quelque chose** : **I failed to convince him** je ne suis pas arrivé à le convaincre
2. **ne pas faire quelque chose** : **the letter failed to arrive** la lettre n'est pas arrivée.

failure ['feɪljər] *noun*

1. **échec** *(masculine)* : **it ended in failure** ça s'est terminé par un échec
2. **raté** *(masculine)*, **ratée** *(feminine)* : **she's a failure** c'est une ratée
➤ **a power failure** une panne d'électricité.

faint [feɪnt] *adjective & verb*

■ *adjective*

1. **léger** *(feminine* **légère***)* : **there's a faint smell of smoke** il y a une légère odeur de fumée
2. **faible** : **a faint light** une faible lumière

to feel faint se sentir mal : **he suddenly felt faint** soudain, il s'est senti mal

■ verb
s'évanouir : **she fainted** elle s'est évanouie.

fair [feə'] adjective & verb

■ adjective
1. **juste** : **that's not fair!** ce n'est pas juste !
2. **assez bon** (feminine **assez bonne**) : **she has a fair chance of winning** elle a d'assez bonnes chances de gagner
3. **blond** : **Clive has fair hair** Clive a les cheveux blonds
4. **clair** : **Carol has a fair skin** Carol a la peau claire
5. **beau** (feminine **belle**) : **the weather is fair** il fait beau

■ noun
1. *UK* **fête** (feminine) **foraine** : **the children are going to the fair** les enfants vont aller à la fête foraine
2. **foire** (feminine) : **we went to the book fair** nous sommes allés à la foire du livre.

fairly ['feəlɪ] adverb
1. **assez** : **it's fairly late** il est assez tard
2. **équitablement** : **they divided the money fairly** ils ont réparti l'argent équitablement.

fairy ['feərɪ] (plural **fairies**) noun
fée (feminine)
➤ **a fairy tale** un conte de fées.

faith [feɪθ] noun
1. **confiance** (feminine) : **I've lost faith in him** j'ai perdu confiance en lui
2. **foi** (feminine) : **the Christian faith** la foi chrétienne.

faithful ['feɪθfʊl] adjective
fidèle.

fake [feɪk] adjective & noun

■ adjective
faux (feminine **fausse**) : **these pearls are fake** ces perles sont fausses

■ noun
faux (masculine) : **this painting is a fake** ce tableau est un faux.

fall [fɔ:l] noun & verb

■ noun
1. **chute** (feminine) : **I had a fall** j'ai fait une chute
2. *US* **automne** (masculine) : **in the fall** en automne

■ verb (past tense **fell**, past participle **fallen**)

1. **tomber** : **I slipped and fell** j'ai glissé et je suis tombé
2. **baisser** : **the temperature has fallen** la température a baissé
➤ **to fall asleep** s'endormir : **she fell asleep** elle s'est endormie
➤ **to fall in love** tomber amoureux : **he fell in love with Britney** il est tombé amoureux de Britney

fall down phrasal verb
tomber : **the little girl fell down** la petite fille est tombée

fall off phrasal verb
tomber : **he fell off his bicycle** il est tombé de son vélo

fall out phrasal verb
1. **tomber** : **the keys fell out of my pocket** les clés sont tombées de ma poche
2. **se brouiller** : **he's fallen out with his best friend** il s'est brouillé avec son meilleur ami

fall over phrasal verb
1. **tomber** : **the vase fell over** le vase est tombé
2. **trébucher sur** : **he fell over a log** il a trébuché sur une bûche.

fallen ['fɔ:ln] past participle of **fall**
he's fallen in the water il est tombé dans l'eau.

false [fɔ:ls] adjective
faux (feminine **fausse**) : **it was a false alarm** c'était une fausse alerte
➤ **false teeth** un dentier : **he has false teeth** il porte un dentier.

fame [feɪm] noun
célébrité (feminine).

familiar [fə'mɪljə'] adjective
familier (feminine **familière**) : **she has a familiar face** son visage m'est familier.

family ['fæmlɪ] (plural **families**) noun
famille (feminine) : **he's one of the family** il fait partie de la famille ; **the Sedgwick family** la famille Sedgwick.

famous ['feɪməs] adjective
célèbre : **she's a famous artist** c'est une artiste célèbre.

f

fan [fæn] *noun*

1. **éventail** *(masculine)* : **she was holding a fan** elle tenait un éventail
2. **ventilateur** *(masculine)* : **an electric fan** un ventilateur
3. **fan** *(masculine or feminine)* : **she's a fan of the Beatles** elle est fan des Beatles
4. **supporter** *(masculine or feminine)* : **football fans** des supporters de football.

fancy ['fænsɪ] *adjective & verb*

■ *adjective*
1. **extravagant** : **she's wearing a fancy hat** elle porte un chapeau extravagant
2. **chic, de luxe** : **they went to a fancy restaurant** ils sont allés dans un restaurant chic
➤ **fancy dress** déguisement *(masculine)* : **she was in fancy dress** elle portait un déguisement
➤ **a fancy-dress party** un bal costumé
■ *verb UK informal*
1. **avoir envie de** : **I fancy a cup of tea** j'ai envie d'une tasse de thé ; **do you fancy going to see a film?** est-ce que tu as envie d'aller voir un film ?
2. **s'enticher de** : **he fancies the girl next door** il s'est entiché de sa voisine.

fantastic [fæn'tæstɪk] *adjective*

formidable, fantastique : **we had a fantastic evening** nous avons passé une soirée formidable.

far [fɑːʳ] *(comparative* **farther** OR **further**, *superlative* **farthest** OR **furthest**) *adverb & adjective*
■ *adverb*
1. **loin** : **is it far?** c'est loin ? ; **it's not far** OR **it's not far away** ce n'est pas loin ; **Oxford isn't far from London** Oxford n'est pas loin de Londres
2. **beaucoup** : **that's far too much** c'est beaucoup trop ; **I feel far better** je me sens beaucoup mieux
➤ **how far is it?** c'est à quelle distance ? OR c'est à combien d'ici ? : **how far is it to Boston?** il y a combien de kilomètres jusqu'à Boston ? OR Boston est à combien d'ici ?
➤ **as far as I know** pour autant que je sache
➤ **so far** jusqu'ici : **so far so good** jusqu'ici ça va
■ *adjective*
1. **extrême** : **the far left** l'extrême gauche
2. **autre** : **at the far end of the road** à l'autre bout de la rue
➤ **the Far East** l'Extrême-Orient *(masculine)*

➤ **in the far north** tout au nord.

fare [feəʳ] *noun*

prix *(masculine)* **du billet** : **the train fare to Paris** le prix du billet de train pour Paris
➤ **half fare** demi-tarif *(masculine)*
➤ **full fare** plein tarif *(masculine)* : **I paid full fare** j'ai payé plein tarif.

farm [fɑːm] *noun*

ferme *(feminine)* : **he works on a farm** il travaille dans une ferme.

farmer ['fɑːməʳ] *noun*

fermier *(masculine)*, **fermière** *(feminine)* : **Nicola's father is a farmer** le père de Nicola est fermier.

farmhouse ['fɑːmhaʊs, *plural* 'fɑːmhaʊzɪz] *noun*

ferme *(feminine)* : **they live in a farmhouse** ils habitent une ferme.

farming ['fɑːmɪŋ] *noun*

agriculture *(feminine)*.

farther ['fɑːðəʳ] *(comparative of* **far**) *adverb & adjective*
■ *adverb*
plus loin : **we have to walk a bit farther** il faut aller un peu plus loin
■ *adjective*
on the farther side of the room de l'autre côté de la pièce.

farthest ['fɑːðəst] *(superlative of* **far**) *adverb & adjective*
■ *adverb*
le plus loin : **he went the farthest** c'est lui qui est allé le plus loin
■ *adjective*
le plus éloigné : **the farthest tree from the house** l'arbre le plus éloigné de la maison.

fascinating ['fæsɪneɪtɪŋ] *adjective*

fascinant : **it's a fascinating book** c'est un livre fascinant.

fashion ['fæʃn] *noun*

mode *(feminine)* : **it's the latest fashion** c'est la dernière mode
➤ **in fashion** à la mode : **this coat is in fashion** ce manteau est à la mode
➤ **it has gone out of fashion** c'est démodé : **that hairstyle has gone out of fashion** cette coiffure est démodée

> **a fashion show** un défilé de mode.

fashionable ['fæʃnəbl] *adjective*

à la mode : **she likes to buy fashionable clothes** elle aime bien s'acheter des vêtements à la mode.

fast [*UK* fɑːst, *US* fæst] *adjective & adverb*

■ *adjective*
rapide : **this train is very fast** ce train est très rapide

> **my watch is fast** ma montre avance : **the clock is ten minutes fast** l'horloge avance de dix minutes

> **fast food** la restauration rapide

> **a fast-food restaurant** un fast-food

■ *adverb*
vite : **he works fast** il travaille vite

> **to be fast asleep** dormir profondément : **the baby is fast asleep** le bébé dort profondément.

fasten [*UK* 'fɑːsn, *US* 'fæsn] *verb*

1. attacher : **fasten your seat belts** attachez vos ceintures
2. fermer : **she fastened her bag** elle a fermé son sac.

fat [fæt] *adjective & noun*

■ *adjective*
gros *(feminine* grosse*)* : **he's very fat** il est très gros

> **to get fat** grossir : **she doesn't want to get fat** elle ne veut pas grossir

■ *noun*
1. gras *(masculine)* : **there's too much fat on this ham** ce jambon a trop de gras
2. matière *(feminine)* grasse : **this yoghurt has no fat in it** ce yaourt ne contient pas de matières grasses.

fatal ['feɪtl] *adjective*

1. mortel *(feminine* mortelle*)* : **he had a fatal accident** il a eu un accident mortel
2. fatal : **it was a fatal mistake** c'était une erreur fatale.

father ['fɑːðəʳ] *noun*

père *(masculine)*
> **Father's Day** la fête des pères.

father-in-law ['fɑːðərɪnlɔː] *noun*

beau-père *(masculine)* [*plural* beaux-pères].

fattening ['fætnɪŋ] *adjective*

to be fattening faire grossir ; **cakes are fattening** les gâteaux font grossir.

faucet *US* ['fɔːsit] *noun* robinet *(masculine)*.

fault ['fɔːlt] *noun*

1. faute *(feminine)* : **whose fault is it?** à qui la faute ? ; **it's my fault** c'est de ma faute
2. défaut *(masculine)* : **he has many faults** il a beaucoup de défauts.

favour *UK*, **favor** *US* ['feɪvəʳ] *noun*

service *(masculine)* : **to do somebody a favour** rendre service à quelqu'un ; **can you do me a favour?** peux-tu me rendre un service ?

> **to be in favour of something** être pour quelque chose : **we're all in favour of world peace** nous sommes tous pour la paix mondiale.

favourite *UK*, **favorite** *US* ['feɪvrɪt] *adjective & noun*

■ *adjective*
préféré : **purple is my favourite colour** le violet est ma couleur préférée

■ *noun*
préféré *(masculine)*, préférée *(feminine)* : **let's listen to this CD, it's my favourite** écoutons ce CD, c'est mon préféré.

fax [fæks] *noun & verb*

■ *noun* *(plural* **faxes***)*
fax *(masculine)* : **he sent me a fax** il m'a envoyé un fax

> **a fax machine** un fax

■ *verb*
1. envoyer un fax : **I faxed him** je lui ai envoyé un fax
2. faxer : **I faxed the letter** j'ai faxé la lettre.

fear [fɪəʳ] *noun & verb*

■ *noun*
peur *(feminine)* : **have no fear!** n'ayez pas peur !

■ *verb*
craindre, avoir peur de : **she has nothing to fear** elle n'a rien à craindre.

feast [fiːst] *noun*

festin *(masculine)*.

feather ['feðəʳ] *noun*

plume *(feminine)*.

feature ['fiːtʃəʳ] *noun*

1. caractéristique *(feminine)* : **an interesting**

feature of the landscape une caractéristique intéressante du paysage

2. **trait** *(masculine)* **: she has fine features** elle a des traits fins.

February [ˈfebrʊərɪ] *noun*

février *(masculine)* **: in February** en février ; **next February** en février prochain ; **last February** en février dernier

> In French the months of the year do not start with a capital letter.

fed [fed] *past tense & past participle of* **feed**

I've fed the dog j'ai donné à manger au chien.

fed up [ˈfedʌp] *adjective informal*

➢ **to be fed up** en avoir marre **: I'm fed up!** j'en ai marre !

➢ **to be fed up with something** en avoir marre de quelque chose **: I'm fed up with waiting** j'en ai marre d'attendre.

feed [fiːd] *(past tense & past participle* **fed***) verb*

1. **donner à manger à : she's feeding the dogs** elle donne à manger aux chiens

2. **nourrir : he needs to feed his family** il doit nourrir sa famille.

feel [fiːl] *(past tense & past participle* **felt***) verb*

1. **se sentir : how do you feel?** comment te sens-tu ? ; **I don't feel very well** je ne me sens pas très bien ; **he felt very stupid** il se sentait très bête

> When 'feel' is used with certain adjectives (cold, hot, hungry or thirsty), you should translate it with the French verb **avoir** (**avoir froid**, **avoir chaud**, **avoir faim** and **avoir soif**):

I feel cold j'ai froid ; **my hands feel cold** j'ai froid aux mains ; **do you feel hungry?** est-ce que tu as faim ?

> When you are describing how something feels to the touch, you should use the verb **être** in French:

this bed feels very hard ce lit est très dur ; **the water feels cold** l'eau est froide

2. **sentir : I felt the ground shake** j'ai senti la terre trembler ; **I can't feel anything in my fingers** je ne sens plus mes doigts

3. **tâter : he felt his pockets** il a tâté ses poches

➢ **to feel as if** OR **to feel as though** avoir l'impression que **: I feel as if I'm going to faint** j'ai l'impression que je vais m'évanouir

➢ **to feel like doing something** avoir envie de faire quelque chose **: I feel like going to bed** j'ai envie de me coucher.

feeling [ˈfiːlɪŋ] *noun*

1. **sentiment** *(masculine)* **: a feeling of sadness** un sentiment de tristesse

2. **sensation** *(feminine)* **: I have a funny feeling in my leg** j'ai une sensation étrange dans la jambe.

feet *plural of* **foot**.

fell [fel] *past tense of* **fall**

he fell down il est tombé.

fellow [ˈfeləʊ] *noun*

homme *(masculine)* **: he's a very nice fellow** c'est un brave homme

➢ **a fellow passenger** un compagnon de voyage

➢ **a fellow student** un camarade de classe, une camarade de classe.

felt [felt] *past tense & past participle of* **feel**

he felt tired il se sentait fatigué.

felt-tip pen [ˈfelttɪppen] *noun*

feutre *(masculine)*, **stylo-feutre** *(masculine)*.

female [ˈfiːmeɪl] *noun & adjective*

▢ *noun*
femelle *(feminine)*

▢ *adjective*

1. **femelle : a female kangaroo** une femelle kangourou

2. **féminin : I heard a female voice** j'ai entendu une voix féminine

➢ **a female student** une étudiante.

feminine [ˈfemɪnɪn] *adjective*

féminin.

fence [fens] *noun*

clôture *(feminine)* **: there is a fence around the field** une clôture entoure le champ.

ferris wheel [ˈferɪswiːl] *noun*

grande roue *(feminine)* **: let's have a ride on the ferris wheel** allons faire un tour sur la grande roue.

ferry [ˈferɪ] *(plural* **ferries***) noun*

ferry *(masculine)* **: we took the ferry to France** nous avons pris le ferry pour aller en France.

festival ['festəvl] *noun*

festival *(masculine)* : **there's a film festival in Leeds next week** il y a un festival de cinéma à Leeds la semaine prochaine.

fetch [fetʃ] *verb*

aller chercher : **fetch my slippers** va me chercher mes pantoufles ; **he went to fetch the doctor** il est allé chercher le médecin.

fever ['fiːvəʳ] *noun*

fièvre *(feminine)* : **Chris has a fever** Chris a de la fièvre.

few [fjuː] *adjective & pronoun*

■ *adjective*
peu de : **few people come here** peu de gens viennent ici

➤ **a few** quelques : **I need a few books** j'ai besoin de quelques livres

■ *pronoun*
peu : **few of them agree** peu d'entre eux sont d'accord

➤ **a few** quelques-uns, quelques-unes : **would you like some cherries? – just a few** tu veux des cerises ? – juste quelques-unes ; **a few of them are wearing hats** quelques-uns d'entre eux portent des chapeaux.

fewer ['fjuːəʳ] *adjective & pronoun*

■ *adjective*
moins de : **we have fewer problems than last year** nous avons moins de problèmes que l'an dernier

■ *pronoun*
moins : **I have a lot fewer than you** j'en ai beaucoup moins que toi.

fewest ['fjuːəst] *adjective & pronoun*

■ *adjective*
moins de : **the fewest mistakes possible** le moins d'erreurs possible

■ *pronoun*
moins : **I have the fewest** c'est moi qui en ai le moins.

fiancé [fɪ'ɒnseɪ] *noun*

fiancé *(masculine)*.

fiancée [fɪ'ɒnseɪ] *noun*

fiancée *(feminine)*.

fiction ['fɪkʃn] *uncountable noun*

1. **fiction** *(feminine)* : **fact and fiction** la réalité et la fiction

2. **romans** *(masculine plural)* : **he reads a lot of fiction** il lit beaucoup de romans.

fidget ['fɪdʒɪt] *verb*

gigoter : **stop fidgeting!** arrête de gigoter !

field [fiːld] *noun*

1. **champ** *(masculine)* : **there are cows in the field** il y a des vaches dans le champ

2. **terrain** *(masculine)* : **they're playing on the football field** ils jouent sur le terrain de football

3. **domaine** *(masculine)* : **she's an expert in that field** elle est spécialiste en ce domaine.

fierce [fɪəs] *adjective*

1. **féroce** : **a fierce dog** un chien féroce

2. **violent** : **it was a fierce battle** la bataille a été violente.

fifteen [fɪf'tiːn] *number*

quinze : **fifteen people came to the party** quinze personnes sont venues à la fête ; **she's fifteen** elle a quinze ans.

fifteenth [fɪf'tiːnθ] *number*

quinzième

➤ **it's the fifteenth of May** *UK* OR **it's May fifteenth** *US* nous sommes le quinze mai.

fifth [fɪfθ] *number*

cinquième : **he came fifth** il est arrivé cinquième

➤ **it's the fifth of November** *UK* OR **it's November fifth** *US* nous sommes le cinq novembre.

fifty ['fɪftɪ] *number*

cinquante : **she's fifty** elle a cinquante ans

➤ **fifty-one** cinquante et un

➤ **fifty-two** cinquante-deux.

fig [fɪg] *noun*

figue *(feminine)*.

fight [faɪt] *noun & verb*

■ *noun*

1. **bagarre** *(feminine)* : **there was a fight in the street** il y a eu une bagarre dans la rue

2. **lutte** *(feminine)* : **the fight against disease** la lutte contre la maladie

3. **dispute** *(feminine)* : **to have a fight** se disputer ; **he had a fight with his wife** il s'est disputé avec sa femme

■ *verb (past tense & past participle* fought*)*

1. **se battre : they were fighting in the street** ils se battaient dans la rue
2. **combattre : we must fight the enemy** nous devons combattre l'ennemi
3. **lutter contre : we must fight this disease** il faut lutter contre cette maladie.

figure [UK 'fɪgə', US 'fɪgjər] noun & verb

■ noun
1. **chiffre** (masculine) **: I added up the figures** j'ai additionné les chiffres
2. **personnalité** (feminine) **: he's a well-known figure in politics** c'est une personnalité politique
3. **silhouette** (feminine) **: I could see a tall dark figure** je voyais une grande silhouette sombre
4. **ligne** (feminine) **: she's worried about her figure** elle s'inquiète pour sa ligne ; **she has a nice figure** elle est bien faite
■ verb US
penser : I figure he'll be late je pense qu'il sera en retard

figure out phrasal verb
1. **comprendre : I can't figure out why** je ne comprends pas pourquoi
2. **calculer : I tried to figure out the total** j'ai essayé de calculer le total.

file [faɪl] noun & verb

■ noun
1. **dossier** (masculine) **: the police have a file on him** la police a un dossier sur lui
2. **fichier** (masculine) **: there are twenty files on the disk** il y a vingt fichiers sur la disquette
3. **classeur** (masculine) **: I put my notes in a red file** je range mes notes dans un classeur rouge
4. **lime** (feminine) **: a nail file** une lime à ongles
➤ **in single file** en file indienne : **we walked in single file** nous marchions en file indienne
■ verb
1. **classer : she's filing her papers** elle classe ses papiers
2. **limer : she's filing her nails** elle se lime les ongles.

fill [fɪl] verb
remplir : I filled the bottle with water j'ai rempli la bouteille d'eau

fill in phrasal verb
1. **remplir : I filled in the form** j'ai rempli le formulaire
2. **boucher : he filled in the hole** il a bouché le trou

fill out phrasal verb
remplir : she filled out the form elle a rempli le formulaire

fill up phrasal verb
remplir : he filled the tank up with water il a rempli le réservoir d'eau.

fillet UK, **filet** US ['fɪlɪt] noun
filet (masculine) **: a fillet steak** un filet de bœuf.

filling ['fɪlɪŋ] adjective & noun

■ adjective
bourratif (feminine **bourrative**) **: the meal was filling** le repas était bourratif
■ noun
plombage (masculine) **: the dentist gave me a filling** le dentiste m'a fait un plombage.

film [fɪlm] noun
1. **film** (masculine) **: there's a good film on television** il y a un bon film à la télévision
2. **pellicule** (feminine) **: I need some more film for my camera** j'ai besoin d'une nouvelle pellicule pour mon appareil photo
➤ **a film star** une vedette de cinéma : **he's a film star** c'est une vedette de cinéma.

filthy ['fɪlθɪ] adjective
très sale : the plates are filthy les assiettes sont très sales.

fin [fɪn] noun
1. **nageoire** (feminine) **: fish have fins** les poissons ont des nageoires
2. **palme** (feminine) **: the diver is wearing fins** le plongeur porte des palmes.

final ['faɪnl] adjective & noun

■ adjective
1. **dernier** (feminine **dernière**) **: this is my final lesson** c'est ma dernière leçon
2. **définitif** (feminine **définitive**) **: that's my final decision** c'est ma décision définitive
■ noun
finale (feminine) **: England are in the final** l'Angleterre est en finale.

finally ['faɪnəlɪ] adverb
enfin : he has finally arrived il est enfin arrivé.

financial [fɪ'nænʃl] adjective
financier (feminine **financière**) **: they have fi-**

nancial problems ils ont des problèmes financiers.

find [faɪnd] (*past tense & past participle* found)
verb
trouver : **I can't find my address book** je ne trouve pas mon carnet d'adresses

find out | *phrasal verb*
1. se renseigner : **I'm going to find out about the concert** je vais me renseigner sur le concert
2. découvrir : **he found out the truth** il a découvert la vérité.

fine [faɪn] *adjective, adverb, noun & verb*
■ *adjective*
1. excellent : **he did a fine job** il a fait un excellent travail
2. très bien : **how are you? – I'm fine!** comment vas-tu ? – très bien !
3. fin : **she has fine features** elle a les traits fins
4. beau (*feminine* belle) : **it's a fine day** il fait beau ; **the fine arts** les beaux-arts
■ *adverb*
très bien : **he feels fine** il se sent très bien ; **I want to go – fine!** je veux partir – très bien !
■ *noun*
amende (*feminine*) : **he got a twenty-pound fine** il a eu une amende de vingt livres
■ *verb*
condamner à une amende : **they fined him twenty pounds** on l'a condamné à une amende de vingt livres.

finger [ˈfɪŋgər] *noun*
doigt (*masculine*) : **she has a big ring on her finger** elle a une grosse bague au doigt.

fingernail [ˈfɪŋgəneɪl] *noun*
ongle (*masculine*).

fingerprint [ˈfɪŋgəprɪnt] *noun*
empreinte (*feminine*) **digitale** : **the police took his fingerprints** la police a pris ses empreintes.

finish [ˈfɪnɪʃ] *verb & noun*
■ *verb*
1. finir, terminer : **she has finished her letter** elle a fini sa lettre OR elle a terminé sa lettre
2. finir, se terminer : **the film finishes at 11 o'clock** le film finit à 11 heures OR le film se termine à 11 heures

➤ **to finish doing something** finir de faire quelque chose : **I've finished eating** j'ai fini de manger
■ *noun*
1. fin (*feminine*) : **from start to finish** du début à la fin
2. arrivée (*feminine*) : **we watched the finish of the race** nous avons regardé l'arrivée de la course.

Finnish [ˈfɪnɪʃ] *adjective & noun*
■ *adjective*
finlandais, finnois
■ *noun*
finnois (*masculine*) : **he speaks Finnish** il parle finnois
➤ **the Finnish** les Finlandais

> Remember not to use a capital letter for the adjective and the language in French. Only use a capital letter for the inhabitants.

fir [fɜːr] *noun*
sapin (*masculine*)
➤ **a fir tree** un sapin.

fire [ˈfaɪər] *noun & verb*
■ *noun*
1. feu (*masculine*) : **he lit a fire** il a fait du feu
2. incendie (*masculine*) : **they are trying to put out the fire** ils essaient d'éteindre l'incendie
3. *UK* radiateur (*masculine*) : **can you put the fire on?** tu peux allumer le radiateur ?
➤ **on fire** en feu : **the house is on fire** la maison est en feu
➤ **to catch fire** prendre feu : **my papers caught fire** mes papiers ont pris feu
➤ **to set fire to something** mettre le feu à quelque chose : **they set fire to the house** ils ont mis le feu à la maison
➤ **a fire alarm** une alarme incendie
➤ **the fire brigade** *UK* OR **the fire department** *US* les pompiers OR les sapeurs-pompiers
➤ **a fire engine** une voiture de pompiers
➤ **a fire escape** un escalier de secours
➤ **a fire extinguisher** un extincteur
➤ **the fire station** la caserne de pompiers
■ *verb*
1. tirer : **they fired at him** ils ont tiré sur lui ; **she fired the gun** elle a tiré un coup de feu
2. renvoyer : **he fired the secretary** il a renvoyé la secrétaire.

f

fireman ['faɪəmən] (*plural* **firemen** ['faɪə-mən]), **firefighter** *US* ['faɪə'faɪtər] *noun*
pompier *(masculine)* : **he's a fireman** il est pompier.

fireplace ['faɪəpleɪs] *noun*
cheminée *(feminine)*.

fireworks ['faɪəwɜːks] *plural noun*
feu *(masculine)* **d'artifice** : **we're going to see the fireworks** nous allons voir le feu d'artifice.

firm [fɜːm] *adjective & noun*

■ *adjective*
ferme : **the cushion is firm** le coussin est ferme ; **he was firm with me** il a été ferme avec moi

■ *noun*
entreprise *(feminine)* : **she works for a firm in Scotland** elle travaille pour une entreprise en Écosse.

first [fɜːst] *adjective, adverb & noun*

■ *adjective*
premier *(feminine* **première***)* : **it's the first time I've seen him** c'est la première fois que je le vois ; **it's the first of May** *UK* OR **it's May first** *US* nous sommes le premier mai

■ *adverb*
1. le premier *(feminine* **la première***)* : **I saw it first** c'est moi qui l'ai vu le premier ; **he came first in the race** il est arrivé premier dans la course
2. d'abord : **I want to have something to eat first** je veux d'abord manger quelque chose

■ *noun*
premier *(masculine)*, **première** *(feminine)* : **she was the first to leave** elle était la première à partir

➤ **first of all** tout d'abord : **first of all tell me your name** tout d'abord, dites-moi votre nom

➤ **at first** d'abord : **at first I thought he was mad** j'ai d'abord cru qu'il était fou

➤ **first aid** premiers secours *(masculine plural)* : **a first-aid kit** une trousse de premiers secours

➤ **the first floor**
1. *UK* le premier étage
2. *US* le rez-de-chaussée

➤ **first name** prénom *(masculine)* : **what is your first name?** quel est ton prénom ?

first-class [*UK* 'fɜːst̩klɑːs, *US* 'fɜːst̩klæs] *adjective*
1. de première classe : **I bought a first-class**

ticket j'ai acheté un billet de première classe
2. **excellent** : **the service was first-class** le service était excellent.

fish [fɪʃ] *noun & verb*

■ *noun (plural* **fish***)*
poisson *(masculine)* : **there are lots of fish in the lake** il y a beaucoup de poissons dans le lac ; **he doesn't like fish** il n'aime pas le poisson

■ *verb*
pêcher : **he was fishing in the river** il pêchait dans la rivière

➤ **fish and chips** *UK* poisson frit accompagné de frites ; **fish-and-chip shop** magasin où l'on vend du poisson frit et des frites

> FISH AND CHIPS
> Le **fish and chips** est un plat bon marché typiquement britannique, composé de poisson pané frit et de frites. On l'achète dans un fish-and-chip shop et on l'emporte emballé dans du papier pour le manger chez soi ou dans la rue. Les Britanniques le consomment salé et arrosé de vinaigre.

fishing ['fɪʃɪŋ] *uncountable noun*
pêche *(feminine)* : **to go fishing** aller à la pêche

➤ **a fishing boat** un bateau de pêche

➤ **a fishing rod** une canne à pêche.

fishmonger *UK* ['fɪʃ̩mʌŋgər] *noun*
poissonnier *(masculine)*, **poissonnière** *(feminine)*

➤ **the fishmonger's** la poissonnerie.

fist [fɪst] *noun*
poing *(masculine)*.

fit [fɪt] *adjective, noun & verb*

■ *adjective*
en forme : **she's very fit** elle est très en forme ; **he tries to keep fit** il essaie de se maintenir en forme

■ *noun*
1. crise *(feminine)* : **an epileptic fit** une crise d'épilepsie ; **my mother had a fit when she saw the mess** ma mère a piqué une crise quand elle a vu le désordre
2. accès *(masculine)* : **a fit of anger** un accès de colère

■ *verb (past tense* fitted OR fit *US, past participle* fitted)*
1. être à la bonne taille : **these trousers**

don't fit ce pantalon n'est pas à la bonne taille ; **this coat fits me perfectly** ce manteau me va parfaitement
2. **tenir : the clothes don't fit in the case** les vêtements ne tiennent pas dans la valise
3. **introduire : he fitted the key into the lock** il a introduit la clé dans la serrure
4. **installer : he fitted a radio in his car** il a installé une radio dans sa voiture.

fitting room ['fɪtɪŋruːm] *noun*

cabine *(feminine)* d'essayage.

five [faɪv] *number*

cinq : **there are five pieces of cake** il y a cinq morceaux de gâteau ; **she's five** elle a cinq ans ; **I went out at five** je suis sorti à cinq heures.

fix [fɪks] *verb*

1. **fixer : I fixed the mirror to the wall** j'ai fixé le miroir au mur ; **can we fix a date?** on peut fixer une date ?
2. **réparer : he's trying to fix the TV** il essaie de réparer la télé
3. **préparer : she's fixing a meal for us** elle nous prépare un repas.

fizzy ['fɪzɪ] *adjective*

gazeux *(feminine* gazeuse*)* : **she likes fizzy drinks** elle aime les boissons gazeuses.

flag [flæg] *noun*

drapeau *(masculine)* [*plural* drapeaux] : **the children were waving flags** les enfants agitaient des drapeaux.

flame [fleɪm] *noun*

flamme *(feminine)* : **the house was in flames** la maison était en flammes.

flan [flæn] *noun*

1. *UK* tarte *(feminine)* : **a strawberry flan** une tarte aux fraises
2. **quiche** *(feminine)* : **a cheese flan** une quiche au fromage.

flannel *UK* ['flænl] *noun*

gant *(masculine)* de toilette.

flap [flæp] (*past tense & past participle* flapped)

verb

battre : **the bird flapped its wings** l'oiseau battait des ailes.

flash [flæʃ] *noun & verb*

■ *noun*
1. **éclat** *(masculine)* : **I saw a flash of light** j'ai vu un éclat de lumière
2. **flash** *(masculine)* : **this camera has a flash** cet appareil photo a un flash
➤ **a flash of lightning** un éclair
➤ **as quick as a flash** rapide comme l'éclair
■ *verb*
clignoter : **all the lights are flashing** toutes les lumières clignotent
➤ **to flash one's headlights** faire un appel de phares.

flashlight *US* ['flæʃlaɪt] *noun*

lampe *(feminine)* de poche.

flat [flæt] *adjective & noun*

■ *adjective*
1. **plat : the countryside is flat around our town** la campagne est plate autour de notre ville ; **flat shoes** des chaussures plates
2. **crevé : a flat tyre** un pneu crevé
■ *noun*
UK appartement *(masculine)* : **they live in a flat** ils habitent un appartement.

flavour *UK*, **flavor** *US* ['fleɪvəʳ] *noun*

1. **goût** *(masculine)* : **this soup doesn't have much flavour** ce potage n'a pas beaucoup de goût
2. **parfum** *(masculine)* : **which flavour ice cream do you want?** ta glace, à quel parfum la veux-tu ?

flea [fliː] *noun*

puce *(feminine)*
➤ **the flea market** le marché aux puces OR les puces.

fleece [fliːs] *noun*

1. **laine** *(feminine)* **polaire : a fleece jacket** une veste en laine polaire
2. **polaire** *(masculine)* : **he was wearing a fleece** il portait un polaire
3. **toison** *(feminine)* : **the sheep's fleece keeps it warm** la toison du mouton lui tient chaud.

Flemish ['flemɪʃ] *adjective & noun*

■ *adjective*
flamand
■ *noun*
flamand *(masculine)* : **she speaks Flemish** elle parle flamand
➤ **the Flemish** les Flamands

Remember not to use a capital letter for the adjective and the language in French. Only use a capital letter for the inhabitants.

flew [flu:] *past tense of* fly

the bird flew away l'oiseau s'est envolé ; we flew to Italy nous avons pris l'avion pour l'Italie.

flick [flɪk] *verb*

appuyer sur : I flicked the TV switch j'ai appuyé sur le bouton de la télé

flick off *phrasal verb*

éteindre : he flicked the TV off il a éteint la télé

flick on *phrasal verb*

allumer : flick the light on allume la lumière

flick through *phrasal verb*

feuilleter : she flicked through the magazine elle a feuilleté la revue.

flies *UK* [flaɪz] *plural noun*

braguette *(feminine)* : your flies are undone ta braguette est ouverte ➤ fly.

flight [flaɪt] *noun*

vol *(masculine)* : the flight to Rome is at two o'clock le vol pour Rome est à deux heures
➤ a flight of stairs un escalier.

fling [flɪŋ] *(past tense & past participle* flung*) verb*

jeter : he flung his coat on the floor il a jeté son manteau par terre.

flip-flop *UK* ['flɪpflɒp] *noun*

tong *(feminine)* : she's wearing flip-flops elle porte des tongs.

flipper ['flɪpəʳ] *noun*

1. nageoire *(feminine)* : seals have flippers les phoques ont des nageoires
2. palme *(feminine)* : the diver's wearing flippers le plongeur porte des palmes.

float [fləʊt] *verb*

flotter : there's a bottle floating on the water il y a une bouteille qui flotte sur l'eau.

flock [flɒk] *noun*

➤ a flock of birds un vol d'oiseau
➤ a flock of sheep un troupeau de moutons.

flood [flʌd] *noun & verb*

◻ *noun*

1. inondation *(feminine)* : there have been floods in this area il y a eu des inondations dans cette région
2. déluge *(masculine)* : we got a flood of letters nous avons reçu un déluge de lettres

◻ *verb*

inonder : the fields are flooded les champs sont inondés.

floor [flɔːʳ] *noun*

1. sol *(masculine)* : the floor's wet le sol est mouillé
2. étage *(masculine)* : which floor do you live on? vous habitez à quel étage ?
➤ on the ground floor au rez-de-chaussée
➤ on the first floor
1. *UK* au premier étage OR au premier
2. *US* au rez-de-chaussée
➤ on the floor par terre : she's sitting on the floor elle est assise par terre.

floppy disk ['flɒpɪdɪsk] *noun*

disquette *(feminine)* : put the floppy disk into the drive mets la disquette dans le lecteur.

Florida ['flɒrɪdə] *noun*

la Floride : Miami is in Florida Miami est en Floride.

florist ['flɒrɪst] *noun*

fleuriste *(masculine or feminine)* : at the florist's chez le fleuriste.

flour ['flaʊəʳ] *noun*

farine *(feminine)*.

flow [fləʊ] *verb*

couler : the water flows along the pipe l'eau coule dans le tuyau.

flower ['flaʊəʳ] *noun & verb*

◻ *noun*

fleur *(feminine)* : a bunch of flowers un bouquet de fleurs ; she picked some flowers elle a cueilli des fleurs

◻ *verb*

fleurir : these roses are about to flower ces roses vont bientôt fleurir.

flowerpot ['flaʊəpɒt] *noun*

pot *(masculine)* de fleurs.

flown [fləʊn] *past participle of* fly

the bird has flown away l'oiseau s'est envolé.

flu [fluː] *uncountable noun*

grippe *(feminine)* : she has flu *UK* OR she has the flu *US* elle a la grippe.

fluent ['fluːənt] *adjective*

she's fluent in Spanish OR she speaks fluent Spanish elle parle espagnol couramment.

flung [flʌŋ] *past tense & past participle of* fling

she flung her gloves on the floor elle a jeté ses gants par terre.

flush [flʌʃ] *verb*

to flush the toilet tirer la chasse.

flute [fluːt] *noun*

flûte *(feminine)* : he plays the flute il joue de la flûte.

fly [flaɪ] *noun & verb*

◾ *noun (plural* **flies)**

1. mouche *(feminine)* : there's a fly in my soup il y a une mouche dans ma soupe

2. *US* braguette *(feminine)* : your fly is undone ta braguette est ouverte

◾ *verb (past tense* flew, *past participle* flown)

1. voler : the birds were flying above us les oiseaux volaient au-dessus de nos têtes

2. faire voler : he's flying a kite il fait voler un cerf-volant

3. voyager en avion, prendre l'avion : he flies all the time il voyage sans cesse en avion ; I'm afraid of flying j'ai peur de prendre l'avion

4. aller en avion : we flew to Paris nous sommes allés à Paris en avion

5. piloter : can you fly a plane? sais-tu piloter un avion ?

fly away *phrasal verb*

s'envoler : the bird flew away l'oiseau s'est envolé.

focus ['fəʊkəs] *noun & verb*

◾ *noun*

➤ out of focus flou : the picture is out of focus la photo est floue

◾ *verb*

to focus on something se concentrer sur quelque chose.

fog [fɒg] *noun*

brouillard *(masculine)*.

foggy ['fɒgɪ] *adjective*

it's foggy il y a du brouillard ; it was a foggy day il y avait du brouillard ce jour-là.

foil [fɔɪl] *uncountable noun*

papier *(masculine)* d'alu.

fold [fəʊld] *verb*

plier : I folded the paper in half j'ai plié le papier en deux

➤ to fold one's arms croiser les bras : she folded her arms elle a croisé les bras.

folder ['fəʊldər] *noun*

1. chemise *(feminine)* : I put my papers in the folder j'ai rangé mes papiers dans la chemise

2. dossier *(masculine)* : you can store computer files in a folder tu peux stocker des fichiers informatiques dans un dossier.

folding ['fəʊldɪŋ] *adjective*

pliant : a folding bed un lit pliant.

follow ['fɒləʊ] *verb*

suivre : she was following me elle me suivait ; follow me! suivez-moi !

following ['fɒləʊɪŋ] *adjective*

suivant : it happened the following month cela s'est passé le mois suivant

➤ the following day le lendemain.

fond [fɒnd] *adjective*

➤ to be fond of somebody OR something aimer beaucoup quelqu'un OR quelque chose : he's very fond of chocolate il aime beaucoup le chocolat.

food [fuːd] *uncountable noun*

nourriture *(feminine)* : there's enough food for everyone il y a assez de nourriture pour tout le monde OR il y a assez à manger pour tout le monde.

fool [fuːl] *noun*

idiot *(masculine)*, idiote *(feminine)* : what a fool! quel idiot !

foolish ['fuːlɪʃ] *adjective*

stupide, idiot.

foot [fʊt] *(plural* feet [fiːt]) *noun*

1. pied *(masculine)* : I've hurt my foot je me suis fait mal au pied ; let's go on foot allons-y à pied

f

2. = 30,48 cm : **he's six foot tall** il mesure un mètre quatre-vingts.

football ['fʊtbɔːl] *noun*

1. *UK* **football** *(masculine)*, **foot** *(masculine)* : **they're playing football** ils jouent au football
2. *US* **football** *(masculine)* **américain**
3. **ballon** *(masculine)* **de football** : **he kicked the football** il a donné un coup de pied dans le ballon
> **a football team** une équipe de football.

footballer *UK* ['fʊtbɔːlər] *noun*

joueur *(masculine)* **de football**, **joueuse** *(feminine)* **de football** : **he's a footballer** il est joueur de football.

footpath ['fʊtpɑːθ, *plural* 'fʊtpɑːðz] *noun*

sentier *(masculine)*.

footprint ['fʊtprɪnt] *noun*

trace *(feminine)* **de pas** : **we saw footprints in the snow** nous avons vu des traces de pas dans la neige.

footstep ['fʊtstep] *noun*

bruit *(masculine)* **de pas** : **I can hear footsteps** j'entends des bruits de pas.

for [fɔːr] *preposition*

1. **pour** : **this is for you** c'est pour toi ; **a knife for cutting bread** un couteau pour le pain ; **the train for London** le train pour Londres ; **can you type this letter for me?** tu peux taper cette lettre pour moi ? ; **he bought the car for 200 dollars** il a acheté la voiture pour 200 dollars
2. *In time expressions*

When you are talking about a period of time that started in the past and is still going on, you use a verb in the present tense + **depuis** in French:

he has lived in France for five years il vit en France depuis cinq ans ; **I've been waiting for two hours** j'attends depuis deux heures

When you are talking about completed actions in the past, you should use a verb in the past tense + **pendant**:

she lived in Spain for two years elle a vécu en Espagne pendant deux ans

When you are talking about future actions, you should use a verb in the present or the future tense + **pour**:

I'm going to the Seychelles for two weeks je vais aux Seychelles pour deux semaines ; **we are going away for the weekend** nous partons pour le week-end

3. *With distances* **pendant** : **we walked for miles** nous avons marché pendant des kilomètres

4. **comme** : **T for Tony** T comme Tony
> **for sale** à vendre
> **what's the French for "horse"?** comment dit-on « horse » en français ?
> **what for?** pour quoi faire ? : **I need some money – what for?** j'ai besoin d'argent – pour quoi faire ?
> **what's it for?** c'est pour quoi faire ?

forbid [fə'bɪd] (*past tense* **forbade**, *past participle* **forbidden**) *verb*

interdire : **I forbid you to smoke** je t'interdis de fumer.

forbidden [fə'bɪdn] *adjective*

interdit : **smoking is forbidden** OR **it's forbidden to smoke** il est interdit de fumer.

force [fɔːs] *noun & verb*

■ *noun*
force *(feminine)* : **they took him away by force** ils l'ont emmené de force
■ *verb*
forcer : **he forced me to tell the truth** il m'a forcé à dire la vérité
> **to force one's way into something** entrer de force dans quelque chose : **he forced his way into the office** il est entré de force dans le bureau.

forecast [*UK* 'fɔːkɑːst, *US* 'fɔːkæst] *noun*

prévisions *(feminine plural)*
> **the weather forecast** la météo : **what's the weather forecast for tomorrow?** que dit la météo pour demain ?

forehead ['fɔːhed] *noun*

front *(masculine)*.

foreign ['fɒrən] *adjective*

étranger *(feminine* **étrangère)** : **foreign languages** les langues étrangères ; **she lives in a foreign country** elle vit à l'étranger.

foreigner ['fɒrənə'] *noun*

étranger *(masculine)*, **étrangère** *(feminine)* : he's a foreigner c'est un étranger.

forest ['fɒrɪst] *noun*

forêt *(feminine)* : she got lost in the forest elle s'est perdue dans la forêt.

forever [fə'revə'] *adverb*

pour toujours : he's gone forever il est parti pour toujours

➤ it won't last forever ça ne peut pas durer éternellement.

forgave [fə'geɪv] *past tense of* forgive

I forgave him je lui ai pardonné.

forge [fɔːdʒ] *verb*

contrefaire : she forged her mother's signature elle a contrefait la signature de sa mère.

forged [fɔːdʒd] *adjective*

faux *(feminine* fausse*)* : it's a forged passport c'est un faux passeport.

forget [fə'get] *(past tense* forgot, *past participle* forgotten) *verb*

oublier : I've forgotten your address j'ai oublié ton adresse ; don't forget to phone! n'oublie pas d'appeler ! ; she forgot to take her passport elle a oublié de prendre son passeport.

forgive [fə'gɪv] *(past tense* forgave, *past participle* forgiven [fə'gɪvən]) *verb*

pardonner : I forgive you je te pardonne ; I forgave him for not telling the truth je lui ai pardonné de ne pas avoir dit la vérité.

forgot [fə'gɒt] *past tense of* forget

he forgot to come il a oublié de venir.

forgotten [fə'gɒtn] *past participle of* forget

I've forgotten his name j'ai oublié son nom.

fork [fɔːk] *noun*

1. fourchette *(feminine)* : a knife and fork un couteau et une fourchette
2. fourche *(feminine)* : she's digging up the weeds with a fork elle arrache les mauvaises herbes avec une fourche.

form [fɔːm] *noun & verb*

■ *noun*

1. forme *(feminine)* : there are different forms

of life on the planet il y a différentes formes de vie sur cette planète
2. formulaire *(masculine)* : I filled in the form j'ai rempli le formulaire
3. *UK* classe *(feminine)* : what form are you in? tu es dans quelle classe ?

■ *verb*

former : the children formed a circle les enfants ont formé un cercle.

formal ['fɔːml] *adjective*

officiel *(feminine* officielle*)* : they made a formal announcement ils ont fait une annonce officielle

➤ formal language langage *(masculine)* soutenu.

former ['fɔːmə'] *adjective*

ancien *(feminine* ancienne*)* : he's a former pupil c'est un ancien élève.

fort [fɔːt] *noun*

fort *(masculine)*.

fortnight *UK* ['fɔːtnaɪt] *noun*

quinze jours *(masculine plural)* : I'll be away for a fortnight je serai absent pendant quinze jours ; it happened a fortnight ago ça s'est passé il y a quinze jours ; I see him once a fortnight je le vois tous les quinze jours.

fortunately ['fɔːtʃnətlɪ] *adverb*

heureusement : fortunately, you didn't fall heureusement, tu n'es pas tombé.

fortune ['fɔːtʃuːn] *noun*

fortune *(feminine)* : he earns a fortune il gagne une fortune

➤ to tell somebody's fortune dire la bonne aventure à quelqu'un.

forty ['fɔːtɪ] *number*

quarante : he's forty il a quarante ans
➤ forty-one quarante et un
➤ forty-two quarante-deux.

forward ['fɔːwəd], **forwards** ['fɔːwədz] *adverb*

en avant : he leaned forward il s'est penché en avant

➤ to move forward avancer : the army is moving forward l'armée avance ; we have to move the clocks forward il faut avancer les pendules.

fought [fɔːt] *past tense & past participle of* fight

the two boys **fought** in the street les deux garçons se sont battus dans la rue ; he has **fought** in two wars il s'est battu dans deux guerres.

foul [faʊl] *adjective & noun*

■ *adjective*
infect : what a **foul** taste! quel goût infect !

■ *noun*
faute *(feminine)* : Beckham committed a **foul** Beckham a fait une faute.

found [faʊnd] *past tense & past participle of* find

I **found** my keys j'ai trouvé mes clés ; have you **found** the address? as-tu trouvé l'adresse ?

fountain [ˈfaʊntɪn] *noun*

fontaine *(feminine)*
➤ a **fountain** pen un stylo à plume.

four [fɔːʳ] *number*

quatre : they have **four** children ils ont quatre enfants ; she's **four** elle a quatre ans ; we went out at **four** nous sommes sortis à quatre heures.

fourteen [ˌfɔːˈtiːn] *number*

quatorze : he's **fourteen** il a quatorze ans.

fourth [fɔːθ] *number*

quatrième : he came **fourth** il est arrivé quatrième
➤ it's the **fourth** of March *UK* OR it's March **fourth** *US* nous sommes le quatre mars
➤ the **Fourth** of July *le 4 juillet*

> THE FOURTH OF JULY
> Le 4 juillet est le jour de la fête nationale américaine, jour où l'on célèbre la déclaration d'indépendance des États-Unis par de nombreux défilés et des feux d'artifice. On l'appelle **Independence Day** ou **The Fourth of July**. Les gens mettent un drapeau américain à l'entrée de leur maison et organisent des pique-niques.

fox [fɒks] *(plural* foxes [ˈfɒksɪz]*) noun*

renard *(masculine)*.

fraction [ˈfrækʃn] *noun*

fraction *(feminine)*.

fragile [ˈfrædʒaɪl] *adjective*

fragile.

frame [freɪm] *noun*

cadre *(masculine)* : I put the photo in a **frame** j'ai mis la photo dans un cadre.

France [*UK* frɑːns, *US* fræns] *noun*

la France

> In French the names of countries are used with the definite article (le, la or l'), except when they follow the preposition en:

I like **France** j'aime la France ; do you live in **France?** est-ce que tu habites en France ? ; we are going to **France** next week nous allons en France la semaine prochaine.

freckle [ˈfrekl] *noun*

tache *(feminine)* de rousseur : Rachel has **freckles** Rachel a des taches de rousseur.

free [friː] *adjective & verb*

■ *adjective*
1. libre : are you **free** this evening? tu es libre ce soir ? ; is this seat **free?** est-ce que cette place est libre ? ; you're **free** to go vous êtes libre de partir
2. gratuit : the tickets are **free** les billets sont gratuits ; it's **free** of charge c'est gratuit
➤ a **free** gift un cadeau
➤ a **free** kick un coup franc

■ *verb*
libérer : they **freed** the prisoner ils ont libéré le prisonnier.

freedom [ˈfriːdəm] *noun*

liberté *(feminine)* : **freedom** of speech la liberté d'expression.

freeway *US* [ˈfriːweɪ] *noun*

autoroute *(feminine)*.

freeze [friːz] *(past tense* froze, *past participle* frozen) *verb*
1. geler : the water has **frozen** l'eau a gelé
2. congeler : I've **frozen** the chicken j'ai congelé le poulet.

freezer [ˈfriːzəʳ] *noun*

congélateur *(masculine)* : she put the chicken in the **freezer** elle a mis le poulet au congélateur.

freezing ['fri:zɪŋ] *adjective*

gelé : **your hands are freezing** tu as les mains gelées
> **I'm freezing** je suis gelé
> **it's freezing today** il fait un froid glacial aujourd'hui.

French [frentʃ] *adjective & noun*

■ *adjective*
français : **I like French cooking** j'aime la cuisine française
> **French fries** frites *(feminine plural)*
■ *noun*
français *(masculine)* : **he speaks French** il parle français
> **the French** les Français

> Remember not to use a capital letter for the adjective and the language in French. Only use a capital letter for the inhabitants.

Frenchman ['frentʃmən] *(plural* Frenchmen ['frentʃmən]) *noun*
Français *(masculine)*.

Frenchwoman ['frentʃ,wʊmən] *(plural* Frenchwomen ['frentʃ,wɪmɪn]) *noun*
Française *(feminine)*.

frequent ['fri:kwənt] *adjective*

fréquent : **accidents are frequent here** les accidents sont fréquents ici.

frequently ['fri:kwəntlɪ] *adverb*

fréquemment.

fresh [freʃ] *adjective*

1. frais *(feminine* fraîche*)* : **fresh bread** du pain frais
2. nouveau *(feminine* nouvelle*)* : **start a fresh page** prenez une nouvelle page ; **he wants to make a fresh start** il veut prendre un nouveau départ
> **fresh air** de l'air frais : **let's go and get some fresh air** allons prendre l'air.

freshen up ['freʃnʌp] *phrasal verb*

faire un brin de toilette : **I'm just going to freshen up** je vais juste faire un brin de toilette.

fret [fret] *(past tense & past participle* fretted) *verb*

s'inquiéter : **don't fret!** ne t'inquiète pas !

Friday ['fraɪdɪ] *noun*

vendredi *(masculine)* : **it's Friday today** nous sommes vendredi ; **next Friday** vendredi prochain ; **last Friday** vendredi dernier
> **on Friday** vendredi : **I'll see you on Friday** je te reverrai vendredi
> **on Fridays** le vendredi : **Sam goes swimming on Fridays** Sam va à la piscine le vendredi

> In French the days of the week do not start with a capital letter.

fridge *UK* [frɪdʒ] *noun*

réfrigérateur *(masculine)* : **put the butter in the fridge** mets le beurre dans le réfrigérateur.

fried [fraɪd] *adjective*

frit : **fried fish** du poisson frit
> **a fried egg** un œuf sur le plat
> **fried rice** riz *(masculine)* cantonais.

friend [frend] *noun*

ami *(masculine)*, amie *(feminine)* : **we're friends** nous sommes amis ; **I'm friends with him** je suis ami avec lui
> **to make friends**
1. se faire des amis : **she has trouble making friends** elle a du mal à se faire des amis
2. devenir amis : **the two children made friends** les deux enfants sont devenus amis.

friendly ['frendlɪ] *adjective*

1. gentil *(feminine* gentille*)* : **he's very friendly** il est très gentil
2. chaleureux *(feminine* chaleureuse*)* : **she got a friendly welcome** elle a reçu un accueil chaleureux.

friendship ['frendʃɪp] *noun*

amitié *(feminine)*.

fries [fraɪz] *plural noun*

frites *(feminine plural)* : **she ordered a hamburger with fries** elle a commandé un hamburger avec des frites.

fright [fraɪt] *noun*

> **to give somebody a fright** faire peur à quelqu'un : **she gave me a fright** elle m'a fait peur
> **to get a fright** avoir peur : **I got a fright** j'ai eu peur.

frighten [ˈfraɪtn] verb

faire peur à : **you frightened me** tu m'as fait peur.

frightened [ˈfraɪtnd] adjective

➤ **to be frightened** avoir peur : **she's frightened of snakes** elle a peur des serpents ; **I'm frightened of walking home in the dark** j'ai peur de rentrer chez moi à pied quand il fait nuit.

frightening [ˈfraɪtnɪŋ] adjective

effrayant : **she told us a frightening story** elle nous a raconté une histoire effrayante.

fringe UK [frɪndʒ] noun

frange (feminine) : **Julia has a fringe** Julia a une frange.

frog [frɒg] noun

grenouille (feminine)

➤ **frog's legs** cuisses (feminine plural) de grenouilles

➤ **to have a frog in one's throat** avoir un chat dans la gorge.

from [frəm, frɒm] preposition

1. **de** (**d'** before a vowel or mute "h") : **I got a letter from my brother** j'ai reçu une lettre de mon frère ; **where do you come from?** d'où venez-vous ? ; **I come from Chicago** je viens de Chicago ; **the house is 5 miles from the sea** la maison est à 8 kilomètres de la mer

> Remember that de + le = du, and de + les = des:

there's a good view from the bridge on a une très belle vue du pont ; **wine from the United States** du vin des États-Unis

> When you say which country a person is from, you should use an adjective to give the person's nationality in French:

she's from America elle est américaine ; **Keith's from Canada** Keith est canadien

2. **à partir de** : **from Monday, I'll be having school dinners** à partir de lundi, je mangerai à la cantine ; **from now on** à partir de maintenant

➤ **from ... to ...** de ... à ... : **we took the train from Paris to London** nous avons pris le train de Paris à Londres ; **the bank's open from 9 am to 4 pm** la banque est ouverte de 9 heures à 16 heures.

front [frʌnt] noun & adjective

■ noun

1. **devant** (masculine) : **the front of your shirt is dirty** le devant de ta chemise est sale

2. **avant** (masculine) : **the front of the car is dented** l'avant de la voiture est tout cabossé ; **she's sitting in the front of the car** elle est assise à l'avant de la voiture

■ adjective

1. **de devant** (invariable) : **they are playing in the front garden** ils jouent dans le jardin de devant

2. **avant** (invariable) : **the front seat of the car** le siège avant de la voiture

3. **premier** (feminine **première**) : **we were sitting in the front row** nous étions assis au premier rang ; **the front page** la première page ; **his photo was on the front page** sa photo était en première page

➤ **in front** devant : **Bob is walking in front** Bob marche devant

➤ **in front of** devant : **George is standing in front of the house** George se trouve debout devant la maison

➤ **the front door** la porte d'entrée.

frontier [ˈfrʌnˌtɪər] noun

frontière (feminine).

frost [frɒst] noun

gel (masculine)

➤ **there's a frost** il gèle.

frosty [ˈfrɒstɪ] adjective

➤ **it's frosty** il gèle.

frown [fraʊn] verb

froncer les sourcils : **she frowned** elle a froncé les sourcils.

froze [frəʊz] past tense of freeze

the lake froze le lac a gelé.

frozen [ˈfrəʊzn] adjective & verb form

■ adjective

1. **gelé** : **my hands are frozen** j'ai les mains gelées

2. **surgelé** : **she bought some frozen vegetables** elle a acheté des légumes surgelés

■ past participle of freeze

the water has frozen l'eau a gelé.

fruit [fruːt] uncountable noun

fruit (masculine) : **fruit is good for you** les

fruits sont bons pour la santé ; **a piece of fruit** un fruit

➤ **a fruit juice** un jus de fruits

➤ **a fruit salad** une salade de fruits.

fruitcake ['fruːtkeɪk] *noun*

cake *(masculine)* : **do you want some fruitcake?** tu veux du cake ?

fry [fraɪ] *(past tense & past participle* fried) *verb*

faire frire : **he's frying some fish** il fait frire du poisson.

frying pan ['fraɪɪŋˌpæn] *noun*

poêle *(feminine)* **à frire**.

ft *(abbreviation of* foot OR feet)

he's 6 ft tall il mesure 1 m 80.

fuel ['fjʊəl] *noun*

carburant *(masculine)* : **we need some more fuel for the car** il nous faut du carburant pour la voiture.

full [fʊl] *adjective*

1. **plein** : **the glass is full of water** le verre est plein d'eau

2. **complet** *(feminine* **complète**) : **the hotel is full** l'hôtel est complet

3. **chargé** : **I've had a full day** j'ai eu une journée chargée

➤ **I'm full** OR **I'm full up** je n'ai plus faim

➤ **the full moon** la pleine lune : **it's a full moon** c'est la pleine lune

➤ **your full name** vos nom et prénoms

➤ **at full speed** à toute vitesse

➤ **a full stop** *UK* un point : **you put a full stop at the end of a sentence** on met un point à la fin d'une phrase.

full-time ['fʊltaɪm] *adjective & adverb*

◼ *adjective*
à plein temps : **he has a full-time job** il a un travail à plein temps

◼ *adverb*
à plein temps : **he works full-time** il travaille à plein temps.

fully ['fʊlɪ] *adverb*

complètement : **she has fully recovered** elle s'est complètement remise.

fun [fʌn] *uncountable noun*

➤ **to have fun** s'amuser : **they're having fun** ils s'amusent ; **have fun!** amuse-toi bien !

➤ **to be fun** être amusant : **this game is great fun** ce jeu est très amusant

➤ **to make fun of somebody** se moquer de quelqu'un : **don't make fun of your brother** ne te moque pas de ton frère.

funeral ['fjuːnərəl] *noun*

enterrement *(masculine)*.

funfair *UK* ['fʌnfeəʳ] *noun*

fête *(feminine)* **foraine**.

funnies *US* ['fʌnɪz] *plural noun*

bandes *(feminine plural)* **dessinées**.

funny ['fʌnɪ] *adjective*

1. **drôle** : **the film's very funny** le film est très drôle

2. **bizarre** : **what a funny smell!** quelle odeur bizarre !

fur [fɜːʳ] *noun*

1. **pelage** *(masculine)* : **he was stroking the cat's fur** il caressait le pelage du chat

2. **fourrure** *(feminine)* : **she's wearing a fur** elle porte une fourrure

➤ **a fur coat** un manteau de fourrure.

furious ['fjʊərɪəs] *adjective*

furieux *(feminine* **furieuse**) : **he's furious with me** il est furieux contre moi.

furniture ['fɜːnɪtʃəʳ] *uncountable noun*

meubles *(masculine plural)* : **the furniture is very modern** les meubles sont très modernes ; **a piece of furniture** un meuble.

further ['fɜːðəʳ] *(comparative of* **far**) *adverb & adjective*

◼ *adverb*
plus loin : **they went a bit further** ils sont allés un peu plus loin ; **is it much further?** c'est encore loin ?

◼ *adjective*
do you have any further questions? est-ce que vous avez d'autres questions ?

➤ **until further notice** jusqu'à nouvel ordre.

furthest ['fɜːðɪst] *(superlative of* **far**) *adverb & adjective*

◼ *adverb*
le plus loin : **he walked furthest** c'est lui qui a marché le plus loin

◼ *adjective*
le plus éloigné : **the furthest house** la maison la plus éloignée.

f

fuse [fjuːz] *noun*

fusible *(masculine)* : **the fuse has blown** le fusible a sauté.

fuss [fʌs] *uncountable noun*

agitation *(feminine)* : **there's a lot of fuss outside in the street** il y a beaucoup d'agitation dans la rue

➤ **to make a fuss** faire des histoires : **don't make a fuss** ne fais pas d'histoires.

fussy ['fʌsɪ] *adjective*

difficile : **don't be so fussy** ne fais pas le difficile.

future ['fjuːtʃər] *noun*

1. **avenir** *(masculine)* : **we can't predict the future** on ne peut pas prédire l'avenir ; **I won't help you in future** je ne t'aiderai pas à l'avenir

2. **futur** *(masculine)* : **put this verb into the future** mettez ce verbe au futur.

gadget ['gædʒɪt] *noun*

gadget *(masculine)*.

gale [geɪl] *noun*

grand vent *(masculine)* : **there's a gale blowing** il y a un grand vent.

gallery ['gælərɪ] *(plural* galleries*) noun*

1. **musée** *(masculine)* : **we visited an art gallery** nous avons visité un musée d'art

2. **galerie** *(feminine)* : **he bought a painting from a gallery** il a acheté un tableau dans une galerie.

gallon ['gælən] *noun*

1. *UK* = 4,546 litres

2. *US* = 3,785 litres.

gallop ['gæləp] *noun & verb*

■ *noun*
galop *(masculine)*

■ *verb*
galoper : **the horses galloped along the beach** les chevaux galopaient sur la plage.

gamble ['gæmbl] *verb*

jouer (pour de l'argent) : **she gambled 100 pounds** elle a joué 100 livres ; **he never gambles** il ne joue jamais pour de l'argent.

gambling ['gæmblɪŋ] *uncountable noun*

jeu *(masculine)*, **jeux** *(masculine plural)* **d'argent** : **she doesn't like gambling** elle n'aime pas le jeu.

game [geɪm] *noun*

1. **jeu** *(masculine)* *[plural* jeux*]* : **they're playing a card game** ils jouent à un jeu de cartes

2. **match** *(masculine)* : **what time is the football game?** il est à quelle heure, le match de foot ?

3. **partie** *(masculine)* : **they're having a game of chess** ils font une partie d'échecs.

gang [gæŋ] *noun*

bande *(feminine)*.

gap [gæp] *noun*

1. **trou** *(masculine)* : **they went through a gap in the fence** ils sont passés par un trou dans la clôture

2. **espace** *(masculine)* : **leave a gap between your car and the next** laissez un espace entre votre voiture et celle de devant

3. **lacune** *(feminine)* : **there are big gaps in his knowledge** il a de grosses lacunes

4. **écart** *(masculine)* : **the gap between the rich and the poor** l'écart entre les riches et les pauvres.

garage [*UK* 'gærɑːʒ, *UK* 'gærɪdʒ, *US* 'gərɑːʒ] *noun*

garage *(masculine)* : **the car's in the garage** la voiture est au garage.

garbage *US* ['gɑːbɪdʒ] *uncountable noun*

ordures *(feminine plural)*

➤ **a garbage can** une poubelle

➤ **a garbage truck** un camion-poubelle.

garden ['gɑːdn] *noun*

jardin *(masculine)*.

gardener ['gɑːdnər] *noun*

jardinier *(masculine)*, **jardinière** *(feminine)* : **he's a gardener** il est jardinier.

gardening [ˈgɑːdnɪŋ] *uncountable noun*

jardinage *(masculine)* : **to do the gardening** faire du jardinage.

garlic [ˈgɑːlɪk] *uncountable noun*

ail *(masculine)*
➤ **garlic bread** pain *(masculine)* à l'ail.

garment [ˈgɑːmənt] *noun*

vêtement *(masculine)*.

gas [gæs] *noun*

1. gaz *(masculine)* : **a gas cooker** une cuisinière à gaz ; **a gas mask** un masque à gaz
2. *US* essence *(feminine)* : **he filled up with gas** il a fait le plein.
➤ **a gas station** une station-service.

gasoline *US* [ˈgæsəliːn] *uncountable noun*

essence *(feminine)* : **he filled up with gasoline** il a fait le plein.

gate [geɪt] *noun*

1. barrière *(feminine)* : **I opened the gate and went into the field** j'ai ouvert la barrière et je suis entré dans le champ
2. grille *(feminine)* : **they tried to climb over the park gate** ils ont essayé d'escalader la grille du parc
3. porte *(feminine)* : **boarding is at gate number 4** l'embarquement se fait porte numéro 4.

gather [ˈgæðəʳ] *verb*

1. se rassembler : **people are gathering in front of the embassy** les gens se rassemblent devant l'ambassade
2. cueillir : **she's gathering blackberries** elle cueille des mûres
➤ **to gather speed** prendre de la vitesse : **the train is gathering speed** le train prend de la vitesse.

gave [geɪv] *past tense of* give

my aunt gave me a nice present ma tante m'a offert un joli cadeau.

gaze [geɪz] *verb*

regarder : **she's gazing out of the window** elle regarde par la fenêtre.

GB [ˌdʒiːˈbiː] *(abbreviation of* Great Britain*)* *noun*

G-B *(feminine)*.

GCSE [ˌdʒiːsiːesˈiː] *(abbreviation of* General Certificate of Secondary Education*)* *noun*

premier examen de fin de scolarité en Grande-Bretagne.

gear [gɪəʳ] *noun*

1. vitesse *(feminine)* : **my bike has ten gears** mon vélo a dix vitesses ; **he changed gear** il a changé de vitesse
2. matériel *(masculine)* : **he had all his fishing gear** il avait tout son matériel de pêche
3. tenue *(feminine)* : **she's in her tennis gear** elle est en tenue de tennis.

geese *plural of* goose.

gel [dʒel] *noun*

gel *(masculine)* : **hair gel** gel pour les cheveux.

gem [dʒem] *noun*

pierre *(feminine)* précieuse : **diamonds, rubies and other gems** des diamants, des rubis et d'autres pierres précieuses.

Gemini [ˈdʒemɪnaɪ] *noun*

Gémeaux : **he's a Gemini** OR **he's Gemini** il est Gémeaux.

gene [dʒiːn] *noun*

gène *(masculine)*.

general [ˈdʒenərəl] *adjective & noun*

▪ *adjective*
général : **it's a general question** c'est une question générale
➤ **a general election** *UK* élections *(feminine plural)* législatives
➤ **general knowledge** culture *(feminine)* générale
➤ **the general public** le grand public
▪ *noun*
général *(masculine)* : **he's a general in the army** il est général dans l'armée
➤ **in general** en général.

generally [ˈdʒenərəlɪ] *adverb*

généralement : **generally they go to school at 8 o'clock** généralement, ils vont à l'école à 8 heures.

generation [ˌdʒenəˈreɪʃn] *noun*

génération *(feminine)* : **the younger generation** la nouvelle génération.

generous ['dʒenərəs] *adjective*

généreux *(feminine* **généreuse***)* **: he's very generous** il est très généreux.

genius ['dʒiːnjəs] *noun*

génie *(masculine)* **: she's a genius** c'est un génie.

gentle ['dʒentl] *adjective*

1. **doux** *(feminine* **douce***)* **: she's a gentle woman** c'est une femme douce ; **as gentle as a lamb** doux comme un agneau
2. **léger** *(feminine* **légère***)* **: there's a gentle breeze** il y a une brise légère.

gentleman ['dʒentlmən] *(plural* **gentlemen** ['dʒentlmən]*)* *noun*

monsieur *(masculine)* **: come in, gentlemen!** entrez, messieurs !

gents *UK* ['dʒents] *noun*

toilettes *(feminine plural)* **pour hommes : where's the gents?** où sont les toilettes pour hommes ?

genuine ['dʒenjʊɪn] *adjective*

1. **véritable : it's genuine gold** c'est de l'or véritable
2. **vrai : a genuine Van Gogh** un vrai Van Gogh
3. **sincère : she's very genuine** elle est très sincère.

geography [dʒɪ'ɒgrəfɪ] *noun*

géographie *(feminine)*.

germ [dʒɜːm] *noun*

microbe *(masculine)*.

German ['dʒɜːmən] *adjective & noun*

■ *adjective*
allemand : Dieter is a German name Dieter est un prénom allemand
■ *noun*
1. **allemand** *(masculine)* **: she speaks German** elle parle allemand
2. **Allemand** *(masculine)*, **Allemande** *(feminine)* **: the Germans** les Allemands

> Remember not to use a capital letter for the adjective and the language in French. Only use a capital letter for the inhabitants.

Germany ['dʒɜːmənɪ] *noun*

l'Allemagne *(feminine)*

> In French the names of countries are used with the definite article (**le**, **la** or **l'**), except when they follow the preposition **en**:

Germany won the World Cup last year l'Allemagne a gagné la Coupe du Monde l'année dernière ; **she lives in Germany** elle habite en Allemagne ; **she's going to Germany** elle va en Allemagne.

gesture ['dʒestʃər] *noun*

geste *(masculine)*.

get [get] *(past tense* **got***, past participle* **got***, US* **gotten***) verb*

1. *When get means 'receive'* **recevoir, avoir : I got a letter from my brother** j'ai reçu une lettre de mon frère ; **what presents did you get?** qu'est-ce que tu as reçu comme cadeaux ? OR qu'est-ce que tu as eu comme cadeaux ? ; **she gets good grades** elle a de bonnes notes ; **I got a shock when I saw him** j'ai eu un choc en le voyant
2. *When 'get' means 'find'* **trouver : where did you get that book?** où est-ce que tu as trouvé ce livre ?
3. *When 'get' means 'buy'* **acheter : I'm going to the shop to get some milk** je vais au magasin acheter du lait ; **I don't know what to get Harry for his birthday** je ne sais pas quoi acheter à Harry pour son anniversaire
4. *When 'get' means 'fetch'* **chercher : go and get the doctor** va chercher le médecin ; **can you get my slippers?** tu peux aller me chercher mes pantoufles ?
5. *When 'get' means 'catch'* **attraper : he got the flu** il a attrapé la grippe ; **did they get the thief?** est-ce qu'ils ont attrapé le voleur ?
6. *When 'get' means 'take'* **prendre : I got the bus into town** j'ai pris le bus pour aller en ville ; **let's get a taxi to the station** prenons un taxi jusqu'à la gare
7. *When 'get' means 'become'*

> When 'get' means 'become' and is followed by an adjective, it can sometimes be translated by **devenir** + adjective. You will often find there is a single verb in French that can replace **devenir** + adjective (to get old = **vieillir**, from the adjective **vieux**):

he gets jealous easily il devient facilement jaloux ; **she's getting old** elle vieillit ; **he got angry** il s'est fâché ; **he got married last June**

il s'est marié en juin dernier ; **it's getting dark** il commence à faire nuit

8. *When 'get' means 'arrive'* **arriver** : **when did you get here?** quand es-tu arrivé ?

9. *When 'get' means 'go'* **aller** : **how do you get to the station?** comment fait-on pour aller à la gare ?

10. *When 'get' means 'understand'* **comprendre** : **I didn't get the joke** je n'ai pas compris la blague

➤ **to get something ready** préparer quelque chose : **he's getting dinner ready** il prépare le dîner

➤ **to get something done** faire faire quelque chose : **I must get the car cleaned** je dois faire nettoyer la voiture ; **he's going to get his hair cut** il va se faire couper les cheveux

➤ **to get somebody to do something** faire faire quelque chose à quelqu'un : **I got him to clean the car** je lui ai fait nettoyer la voiture

➤ have

get away *phrasal verb*

s'échapper : **the thief got away** le voleur s'est échappé

get back *phrasal verb*

1. **rentrer** : **I got back late** je suis rentré tard
2. **récupérer** : **did you get your money back?** tu as récupéré ton argent ?

get down *phrasal verb*

descendre : **he got down from the tree** il est descendu de l'arbre

get in *phrasal verb*

1. **entrer** : **they got in through the window** ils sont entrés par la fenêtre
2. **monter dans** : **get in the car!** monte dans la voiture !

get off *phrasal verb*

1. **descendre de** : **he got off the bus** il est descendu du bus
2. **descendre** : **where do we get off?** où est-ce qu'on descend ?

get on *phrasal verb*

1. **monter dans** : **they got on the train** ils sont montés dans le train
2. **s'entendre** : **they get on well** ils s'entendent bien

get out *phrasal verb*

1. **sortir** : **get out!** sortez ! ; **he managed to get out of the building** il a réussi à sortir du bâtiment

2. **descendre** : **she got out of the taxi** elle est descendue du taxi

get up *phrasal verb*

se lever : **what time did you get up?** à quelle heure tu t'es levé ? ; **Sam gets up at dawn** Sam se lève à l'aube.

ghost [gəʊst] *noun*

fantôme *(masculine)* : **do you believe in ghosts?** tu crois aux fantômes ?

giant ['dʒaɪənt] *noun*

géant *(masculine)*.

giddy ['gɪdɪ] *adjective*

to feel giddy avoir la tête qui tourne ; **I feel giddy** j'ai la tête qui tourne.

gift [gɪft] *noun*

1. **cadeau** *(masculine)* [*plural* **cadeaux**] : **I gave her a gift** je lui ai fait un cadeau ; **a gift shop** une boutique de cadeaux

2. **don** *(masculine)* : **she has a gift for languages** elle a un don pour les langues.

gifted ['gɪftɪd] *adjective*

doué : **his son is gifted** son fils est doué.

gigantic [dʒaɪ'gæntɪk] *adjective*

gigantesque : **they live in a gigantic house** ils habitent une maison gigantesque.

giggle ['gɪgl] *verb*

rire bêtement : **the girls were giggling** les filles riaient bêtement.

ginger ['dʒɪndʒəʳ] *noun & adjective*

▢ *noun*
gingembre *(masculine)* : **it tastes of ginger** cela a un goût de gingembre

▢ *adjective UK*
roux *(feminine* **rousse***)* : **she has ginger hair** elle a les cheveux roux.

gipsy ['dʒɪpsɪ] *(plural* gipsies ['dʒɪpsiːz]*)* *noun*

gitan *(masculine)*, gitane *(feminine)*.

giraffe [*UK* dʒɪ'rɑːf, *US* dʒɪ'ræf] *noun*

girafe *(feminine)*.

girl [gɜːl] *noun*

fille *(feminine)* : **a little girl** une petite fille

➤ **a girl guide** *UK* OR **a girl scout** *US* une éclaireuse OR une guide.

g

girlfriend ['gɜːlfrend] *noun*

1. **copine** *(feminine)*, **petite amie** *(feminine)* : **Robin has a girlfriend** Robin a une copine OR Robin a une petite amie
2. **amie** *(feminine)* : **she has lots of girlfriends** elle a beaucoup d'amies.

give [gɪv] *(past tense* gave, *past participle* given*) verb*

1. **donner** : **to give something to somebody** donner quelque chose à quelqu'un ; **give me the book** donne-moi le livre ; **give it to me!** donne-le-moi ! ; **he gave them some money** il leur a donné de l'argent
2. **offrir** : **she gave him a CD for his birthday** elle lui a offert un CD pour son anniversaire
➤ **to give somebody a present** faire un cadeau à quelqu'un
➤ **to give something back to somebody** rendre quelque chose à quelqu'un : **he gave the book back to me** il m'a rendu le livre

give in *phrasal verb*

céder : **his mother gave in and let him go out** sa mère a cédé et l'a laissé sortir
➤ **I give in, tell me!** je donne ma langue au chat, dis-le-moi !

give out *phrasal verb*

distribuer : **the teacher gave out the exam papers** le professeur a distribué les copies d'examen

give up *phrasal verb*

1. **abandonner** : **it's too hard, I give up** c'est trop dur, j'abandonne
2. **arrêter** : **he gave up smoking** il a arrêté de fumer.

given ['gɪvn] *past participle of* give

he has given me his watch il m'a donné sa montre.

glad [glæd] *adjective*

content : **I'm glad you've come** je suis content que tu sois venu ; **I'm glad about it** j'en suis content.

glamor *US* ➤ glamour *UK*.

glamorous ['glæmərəs] *adjective*

1. **glamour** *(invariable)* : **she's very glamorous** elle est très glamour
2. **prestigieux** *(feminine* prestigieuse*)* : **she has a glamorous job** elle a un travail prestigieux.

glamour *UK*, **glamor** *US* ['glæmər] *noun*

glamour *(masculine)* : **the glamour of Hollywood** le glamour d'Hollywood

⚠ En anglais, le mot "glamour" n'est pas un adjectif.

glance [*UK* glɑːns, *US* glæns] *noun & verb*

■ *noun*
coup d'œil : **at first glance** au premier coup d'œil
■ *verb*
to glance at something jeter un coup d'œil à quelque chose ; **he glanced at his watch** il a jeté un coup d'œil à sa montre.

glass [*UK* glɑːs, *US* glæs] *noun*

verre *(masculine)* : **can I have a glass of water?** est-ce que je peux avoir un verre d'eau ? ; **it's made out of glass** c'est en verre.

glasses [*UK* 'glɑːsɪz, *US* 'glæsɪz] *plural noun*

lunettes *(feminine plural)* : **Sandra wears glasses** Sandra porte des lunettes.

glider ['glaɪdər] *noun*

planeur *(masculine)*.

glitter ['glɪtər] *verb & noun*

■ *verb*
scintiller : **the diamond glittered in the sun** le diamant scintillait au soleil
■ *uncountable noun*
paillettes *(feminine plural)* : **the children put glitter on their pictures** les enfants mettaient des paillettes sur leurs dessins.

global ['gləʊbl] *adjective*

mondial : **a global problem** un problème mondial
➤ **global warming** le réchauffement de la planète.

globe [gləʊb] *noun*

globe *(masculine)*.

gloomy ['gluːmɪ] *adjective*

1. **triste** : **you're looking gloomy today** tu as l'air triste aujourd'hui
2. **lugubre** : **this house is gloomy** cette maison est lugubre.

glorious ['glɔːrɪəs] *adjective*

magnifique.

glove [glʌv] *noun*

gant *(masculine)* : **he's wearing gloves** il porte des gants.

glow [gləʊ] *noun & verb*

▨ *uncountable noun*
lueur *(feminine)* : **the glow of the fire** la lueur du feu

▨ *verb*
1. rougeoyer : **the fire was glowing** le feu rougeoyait
2. rayonner : **she's glowing with health** elle rayonne de santé.

glue [glu:] *noun & verb*

▨ *noun*
colle *(feminine)* : **a tube of glue** un tube de colle

▨ *verb*
coller : **he glued the two pieces together** il a collé les deux morceaux
➤ **he's glued to the television** il est collé devant la télé.

gnome [nəʊm] *noun*

gnome *(masculine)*
➤ **a garden gnome** un nain de jardin.

go [gəʊ] *verb & noun*

▨ *verb (past tense* went *& past participle* gone*)*
1. aller : **I'm going to Australia** je vais en Australie ; **let's go!** allons-y ! ; **he has gone to the dentist** il est allé chez le dentiste ; **we went for a walk** nous sommes allés nous promener ; **how's it going?** comment ça va ?
2. partir : **the train has gone** le train est parti ; **we're going on vacation** nous partons en vacances ; **ready, steady, go!** à vos marques, prêts, partez !
3. devenir : **he went mad** il est devenu fou

There is often a single verb in French to translate 'go' + adjective:

she went red elle a rougi ; **her hair has gone white** ses cheveux ont blanchi
4. passer : **time goes quickly** le temps passe vite
5. se passer : **the party went well** la fête s'est bien passée
6. marcher : **the car won't go** la voiture ne marche pas
➤ **to be going to do** aller faire : **it's going to rain** il va pleuvoir ; **what are you going to do?** qu'est-ce que tu vas faire ? ; **I'm going to phone my parents** je vais appeler mes parents

go around , **go round** *UK phrasal verb*

to go around the shops faire les magasins ; **to go around the museum** visiter le musée

go away *phrasal verb*

partir : **she's gone away** elle est partie
➤ **go away!** allez-vous-en ! OR va-t'en !

go back *phrasal verb*

retourner : **I went back to the shop** je suis retourné au magasin
➤ **to go back home** rentrer chez soi : **Tim has gone back home** Tim est rentré chez lui
➤ **to go back to sleep** se rendormir
➤ **to go back to work** reprendre le travail

go down *phrasal verb*

1. descendre : **she has gone down to the cellar** elle est descendue à la cave ; **we went down the hill** nous avons descendu la pente
2. baisser : **prices have gone down** les prix ont baissé

go in *phrasal verb*

entrer : **Sam knocked on the door and went in** Sam a frappé à la porte et est entré

go off *phrasal verb*

1. exploser : **the bomb went off** la bombe a explosé
2. sonner : **the alarm clock went off at 6 am** le réveil a sonné à 6 heures
3. partir : **she went off without me** elle est partie sans moi
4. *UK* tourner : **the milk has gone off** le lait a tourné

go on *phrasal verb*

1. continuer : **they went on talking** ils ont continué à parler OR ils ont continué de parler
2. se passer : **what's going on** qu'est-ce qui se passe ?

go out *phrasal verb*

1. sortir : **I'm going out tonight** je sors ce soir ; **he's going out with Tina** il sort avec Tina
2. s'éteindre : **the lights have gone out** les lumières se sont éteintes

go round *UK phrasal verb* ➤ go around

go up *phrasal verb*

1. monter : **he went up to bed** il est monté se coucher ; **they went up the hill** ils ont monté la pente

2. augmenter : **prices have gone up** les prix ont augmenté

go without *phrasal verb*

se passer de : **we'll have to go without bread** nous devrons nous passer de pain

■ *noun UK*

tour *(masculine)* : **it's your go** c'est ton tour OR c'est à toi

➤ **to have a go** essayer : **have another go!** essaie encore une fois !

goal [gəʊl] *noun*

but *(masculine)* : **he scored a goal** il a marqué un but ; **our goal is to succeed** notre but est de réussir.

goalkeeper [ˈgəʊlˌkiːpəʳ] *noun*

gardien *(masculine)* **de but.**

goat [gəʊt] *noun*

chèvre *(feminine)*.

god [gɒd] *noun*

dieu *(masculine)* : **she believes in God** elle croit en Dieu

➤ **my God!** mon Dieu !

goddaughter [ˈgɒdˌdɔːtəʳ] *noun*

filleule *(feminine)*.

goddess [ˈgɒdɪs] *noun*

déesse *(feminine)* : **Aphrodite is the goddess of love** Aphrodite est la déesse de l'amour.

godfather [ˈgɒdˌfɑːðəʳ] *noun*

parrain *(masculine)*.

godmother [ˈgɒdˌmʌðəʳ] *noun*

marraine *(feminine)*.

godson [ˈgɒdsʌn] *noun*

filleul *(masculine)*.

goes [gəʊz] ➤ go.

goggles [ˈgɒglz] *plural noun*

lunettes *(feminine plural)* : **ski goggles** des lunettes de ski.

gold [gəʊld] *uncountable noun*

or *(masculine)* : **it's made of gold** c'est en or ; **a gold ring** une bague en or

➤ **a gold medal** une médaille d'or
➤ **the gold rush** la ruée vers l'or

➤ **to be as good as gold** être sage comme une image.

golden [ˈgəʊldən] *adjective*

doré.

goldfish [ˈgəʊldfɪʃ] *(plural* goldfish*) noun*

poisson *(masculine)* **rouge.**

goldmine [ˈgəʊldmaɪn] *noun*

mine *(feminine)* **d'or.**

golf [gɒlf] *noun*

golf *(masculine)* : **he plays golf** il joue au golf

➤ **a golf ball** une balle de golf
➤ **a golf club** un club de golf
➤ **a golf course** un terrain de golf.

gone [gɒn] *past participle of* go

he has gone to Paris il est allé à Paris.

good [gʊd] *adjective & noun*

■ *adjective*

I. bon *(feminine* bonne*)* : **it's a really good book** c'est un très bon livre ; **did you have a good vacation?** est-ce que tu as passé de bonnes vacances ? ; **that cake looks good** ce gâteau a l'air bon ; **she's good at French** elle est bonne en français ; **exercise is good for you** l'exercice est bon pour la santé

2. sage : **be good!** sois sage !

3. gentil *(feminine* gentille*)* : **it's good of you to help** c'est gentil à vous de m'aider ; **they were very good to me** ils ont été très gentils avec moi

➤ **to have a good time** s'amuser : **did you have a good time?** tu t'es bien amusé ?
➤ **good morning!** bonjour !
➤ **good afternoon!** bonjour !
➤ **good evening!** bonsoir !
➤ **good night!** bonne nuit !

■ *noun*

bien *(masculine)* : **it'll do you good** ça te fera du bien

➤ **it's no good crying** ça ne sert à rien de pleurer
➤ **for good** pour toujours ; **she left for good** elle est partie pour toujours

goods *plural noun*

marchandises *(feminine plural)*.

goodbye [ˌgʊdˈbaɪ] *exclamation*

au revoir !

good-looking [gʊd'lʊkɪŋ] *adjective*

beau *(feminine* **belle**) : he's very good-looking il est très beau.

goose [guːs] *(plural* geese [giːs]) *noun*

oie *(feminine).*

gooseberry [*UK* 'gʊzbərɪ, *US* 'guːsberɪ]

(plural gooseberries) *noun*
groseille *(feminine)* à maquereau.

gorgeous ['gɔːdʒəs] *adjective*

1. magnifique : what a gorgeous hat! quel chapeau magnifique !
2. superbe : she's gorgeous elle est superbe.

gorilla [gə'rɪlə] *noun*

gorille *(masculine).*

gossip ['gɒsɪp] *noun & verb*

◼ *noun*
1. *(uncountable)* bavardages *(masculine plural)* : that's just gossip ce ne sont que des bavardages
2. commère *(feminine)* : she's a real gossip c'est une vraie commère
◼ *verb*
bavarder
➤ to gossip about somebody faire des commérages sur quelqu'un.

got [gɒt] *past tense & past participle of* get

I got a letter from him j'ai reçu une lettre de lui ; she has just got married elle vient de se marier ➤ have.

gotten *US* ['gɒtn] *past participle of* get

he has gotten married il s'est marié.

government ['gʌvnmənt] *noun*

gouvernement *(masculine).*

grab [græb] *(past tense & past participle* grabbed) *verb*

attraper : he grabbed the rope il a attrapé la corde.

graceful ['greɪsfʊl] *adjective*

gracieux *(feminine* **gracieuse**) : the dancer's movements are graceful les mouvements du danseur sont gracieux.

grade [greɪd] *noun*

1. note *(feminine)* : she got a good grade in chemistry elle a eu une bonne note en chimie

2. *US* classe *(feminine)* : what grade are you in? tu es dans quelle classe ?
➤ grade school *US* l'école *(feminine)* primaire.

gradually ['grædʒʊəlɪ] *adverb*

petit à petit : things gradually got better petit à petit, les choses se sont améliorées.

graduate ['grædʒʊət] *noun*

diplômé *(masculine)*, diplômée *(feminine)* : a university graduate un diplômé de l'université
➤ a high-school graduate *US* un bachelier, une bachelière.

graffiti [grə'fiːtɪ] *uncountable noun*

graffiti *(masculine)* [*plural* graffiti] : there's some graffiti on the wall il y a des graffiti sur le mur.

grain [greɪn] *noun*

grain *(masculine)* : a grain of rice un grain de riz ; a grain of sand un grain de sable.

gram [græm] *noun*

gramme *(masculine)* : she bought 500 grams of flour elle a acheté 500 grammes de farine.

grammar ['græmər] *noun*

grammaire *(feminine).*

grammar school ['græmərskuːl] *noun*

1. *UK* établissement *(masculine)* d'enseignement secondaire
2. *US* école *(feminine)* primaire.

gramme *UK* [græm] *noun*

gramme *(masculine)* : she bought 500 grammes of flour elle a acheté 500 grammes de farine.

grand [grænd] *adjective*

imposant : the town hall is a grand building in the centre of town la mairie est un immeuble imposant situé au centre de la ville
➤ the Grand Canyon le Grand Canyon.

grandad ➤ granddad.

grandchild ['græntʃaɪld] *(plural* grandchildren ['græntʃɪldrən]) *noun*

petit-fils *(masculine)*, petite-fille *(feminine)* :

g

Mrs Evans has four grandchildren Mme Evans a quatre petits-enfants.

granddad , grandad ['grændæd] *noun*

informal
papi *(masculine)*, pépé *(masculine)*.

granddaughter ['græn,dɔːtəʳ] *noun*

petite-fille *(feminine)*.

grandfather ['grænd,fɑːðəʳ] *noun*

grand-père *(masculine)*.

grandma ['grænmɑː] *noun informal*

mamie *(feminine)*, mémé *(feminine)*.

grandmother ['græn,mʌðəʳ] *noun*

grand-mère *(feminine)*.

grandpa ['grænpɑː] *noun informal*

papi *(masculine)*, pépé *(masculine)*.

grandparents ['græn,peərənts] *plural noun*

grands-parents *(masculine plural)*.

grandson ['grænsʌn] *noun*

petit-fils *(masculine)*.

granny ['grænɪ] *(plural* grannies ['græniːz]*)*

noun informal
mamie *(feminine)*, mémé *(feminine)*.

grant [*UK* grɑːnt, *US* grænt] *noun*

bourse *(feminine)* : **he gets a student grant** il a une bourse d'études.

grape [greɪp] *noun*

raisin *(masculine)* : **they were eating grapes** ils mangeaient du raisin ; **do you like grapes?** tu aimes le raisin ?
➤ **a bunch of grapes** une grappe de raisin.

grapefruit ['greɪpfruːt] *noun*

pamplemousse *(masculine)*.

graph [*UK* grɑːf, *US* græf] *noun*

graphique *(masculine)* : **he drew a graph** il a fait un graphique.

grasp [*UK* grɑːsp, *US* græsp] *verb*

saisir : **he grasped my hand** il m'a saisi par la main.

grass [*UK* grɑːs, *US* græs] *noun*

herbe *(feminine)* : **they're sitting on the grass** ils sont assis sur l'herbe
➤ **a grass snake** une couleuvre

➤ **to cut the grass** tondre la pelouse.

grasshopper [*UK* 'grɑːs,hɒpəʳ, *US* 'græs-,hɒpəʳ] *noun*
sauterelle *(feminine)*.

grate [greɪt] *verb*

râper : **pasta with grated cheese** des pâtes avec du fromage râpé.

grateful ['greɪtfʊl] *adjective*

reconnaissant : **I'm very grateful to you** je vous suis très reconnaissant.

grave [greɪv] *noun*

tombe *(feminine)* : **there are flowers on the grave** il y a des fleurs sur la tombe

⚠️ Le mot anglais grave est un faux ami, il ne signifie pas "grave".

graveyard ['greɪvjɑːd] *noun*

cimetière *(masculine)*.

gravy ['greɪvɪ] *uncountable noun*

sauce brune à base de jus de rôti.

gray *US adjective* ➤ grey *UK*.

grease [griːs] *noun*

graisse *(feminine)* : **the mechanic's hands are covered in grease** le mécanicien a les mains pleines de graisse.

greasy ['griːsɪ] *adjective*

1. gras *(feminine* grasse*)* : **my hair is greasy** j'ai les cheveux gras
2. graisseux *(feminine* graisseuse*)* : **a greasy rag** un chiffon graisseux.

great [greɪt] *adjective*

1. grand : **it's a great success** c'est un grand succès
2. *informal* génial, formidable : **he's a great guy** c'est un type génial ; **what a great view!** quelle vue formidable !
➤ **I feel great** je me sens en pleine forme
➤ **a great deal** beaucoup : **he has a great deal of money** il a beaucoup d'argent.

Great Britain ['greɪt'brɪtn] *noun*

la Grande-Bretagne

📖 GREAT BRITAIN
La Grande-Bretagne **(Great Britain)** est le terme géographique désignant l'île qui comprend l'Angleterre, le pays de Galles et

l'Écosse. Le Royaume-Uni (**the United Kingdom**), dont le nom complet est the **United Kingdom of Great Britain and Northern Ireland**, désigne quant à lui le pays composé de la Grande-Bretagne et de l'Irlande du Nord. Cependant, dans la langue de tous les jours, on emploie indifféremment ces deux mots pour désigner la même chose.

great-grandfather [greɪt'grænd,fɑːðəʳ]

noun

arrière-grand-père *(masculine)*.

great-grandmother

[greɪt'græn,mʌðəʳ] *noun*

arrière-grand-mère *(feminine)*.

Greece [griːs] *noun*

la Grèce

In French the names of countries are used with the definite article (**le**), except when they follow the preposition **en**:

Greece is a beautiful country la Grèce est un beau pays ; **the Acropolis is in Greece** l'Acropole est en Grèce ; **she's going to Greece** elle va en Grèce.

greedy ['griːdɪ] *adjective*

1. gourmand : **I want some more cake – don't be greedy!** je veux encore du gâteau – ne sois pas si gourmand !
2. avide : **they're greedy for money** ils sont avides d'argent.

Greek [griːk] *adjective & noun*

◻ *adjective*

grec *(feminine* grecque*)* : **I like Greek yoghurt** j'aime le yaourt grec

◻ *noun*

1. grec *(masculine)* : **he speaks Greek** il parle grec
2. Grec *(masculine)*, Grecque *(feminine)* : **the Greeks** les Grecs

Remember not to use a capital letter for the adjective and the language in French. Only use a capital letter for the inhabitants.

green [griːn] *adjective*

vert : **she has green eyes** elle a les yeux verts
➤ **the lights are green** les feux sont au vert
➤ **green beans** haricots *(masculine plural)* verts

➤ **a green salad** une salade verte
➤ **the Green Party** les Verts.

greengrocer *UK* ['griːn,grəusəʳ] *noun*

marchand *(masculine)* de fruits et légumes : **to go to the greengrocer's** aller chez le marchand de fruits et légumes.

greenhouse ['griːnhaus] *noun*

serre *(feminine)*.

greet [griːt] *verb*

1. saluer : **I greeted him with a wave** je l'ai salué d'un geste de la main
2. accueillir : **she's greeting the guests** elle accueille les invités.

greetings card *UK* ['griːtɪŋzkɑːd], **greeting card** *US* ['griːtɪŋkɑːd] *noun*

carte *(feminine)* de vœux.

grew [gruː] *past tense of* grow

her hair grew quickly ses cheveux ont poussé vite ; **he grew up in Brighton** il a grandi à Brighton.

grey *UK*, **gray** *US* [greɪ] *adjective*

gris : **the sky is grey** le ciel est gris ; **she has grey hair** elle a des cheveux gris.

grief [griːf] *uncountable noun*

chagrin *(masculine)*.

grill [grɪl] *noun & verb*

◻ *noun*

gril *(masculine)* : **he cooked the fish under the grill** il a fait cuire le poisson au gril

◻ *verb*

faire griller : **I grilled the chicken** j'ai fait griller le poulet.

grin [grɪn] *noun & verb*

◻ *noun*

grand sourire *(masculine)* : **he had a grin on his face** il avait un grand sourire

◻ *verb*

sourire : **she was grinning at me** elle me souriait.

grind [graɪnd] *(past tense & past participle* ground*) verb*

moudre : **it's for grinding spices** c'est pour moudre des épices.

grip [grɪp] (*past tense & past participle* gripped)
verb
1. **saisir : I gripped his arm** je lui ai saisi le bras
2. **serrer : she was gripping my hand tightly** elle me serrait la main très fort.

groan [grəʊn] *verb & noun*
■ *verb*
gémir : he groaned with pain il a gémi de douleur
■ *noun*
gémissement *(masculine)* **: I could hear groans** j'entendais des gémissements.

grocer ['grəʊsər] *noun*
épicier *(masculine)*, **épicière** *(feminine)* **: I bought some milk at the grocer's** j'ai acheté du lait chez l'épicier.

groceries ['grəʊsəriz] *plural noun*
provisions *(feminine plural)* **: I went out to get the groceries** je suis sorti acheter les provisions.

groom [gru:m] *noun*
marié *(masculine)*
➤ **the bride and groom** les jeunes mariés.

gross [grəʊs] *adjective*
1. **dégoûtant : his behaviour is really gross** son comportement est vraiment dégoûtant
2. **brut : his gross income** ses revenus bruts.

ground [graʊnd] *noun & adjective*
■ *noun*
1. **sol** *(masculine)* **: I dug a hole in the ground** j'ai creusé un trou dans le sol
2. **terrain** *(masculine)* **: a sports ground** un terrain de sport ; **a camping ground** un terrain de camping
➤ **on the ground** par terre : **I was sitting on the ground** j'étais assis par terre
➤ **the gound floor** *UK* le rez-de-chaussée : **they live in the ground floor** ils habitent au rez-de-chaussée
■ *adjective*
moulu : ground coffee café moulu
➤ **ground beef** *US* steak *(masculine)* haché.

group [gru:p] *noun*
groupe *(masculine)* **: a large group of tourists** un grand groupe de touristes.

grow [grəʊ] (*past tense* grew, *past participle* grown) *verb*

1. **pousser : these plants grow quickly** ces plantes poussent vite
2. **grandir : she has really grown** elle a beaucoup grandi
3. **augmenter : the number of net users has grown** le nombre d'internautes a augmenté
4. **cultiver : we grow a lot of vegetables** nous cultivons beaucoup de légumes
5. **se laisser pousser : she's growing her hair** elle se laisse pousser les cheveux
➤ **to grow bigger** grandir
➤ **it's growing colder** il fait plus froid
➤ **to grow old** vieillir : **he's growing old** il vieillit

grow up *phrasal verb*
➤ **grandir : I grew up in Oxford** j'ai grandi à Oxford
➤ **I want to be a pilot when I grow up** je veux être pilote quand je serai grand.

growl [graʊl] *verb*
grogner : the dog growled le chien a grogné.

grown [grəʊn] *past participle of* grow
he's grown quickly il a grandi vite.

grown-up ['grəʊnʌp] *noun*
adulte *(masculine or feminine)* **: you're a grown-up now** tu es adulte maintenant.

growth [grəʊθ] *noun*
croissance *(feminine)* **: economic growth** la croissance économique.

grumble ['grʌmbl] *verb*
rouspéter : she's always grumbling elle est toujours en train de rouspéter.

grumpy ['grʌmpɪ] *adjective*
grognon *(feminine* grognonne*)* **: a grumpy old man** un vieillard grognon.

grunt [grʌnt] *verb*
grogner : the pigs were grunting les cochons grognaient.

guarantee [ˌgærən'ti:] *noun & verb*
■ *noun*
garantie *(feminine)*
■ *verb*
garantir : I can't guarantee I'll come je ne peux pas te garantir que je viendrai ; **my watch is guaranteed** ma montre est sous garantie.

guard [gɑːd] *noun & verb*

- *noun*

  gardien *(masculine)* : **he's a prison guard** il est gardien de prison

➤ **to be on guard** monter la garde

➤ **a guard dog** un chien de garde

- *verb*

  garder : **the soldiers are guarding the building** les soldats gardent le bâtiment.

guava ['gwɑːvə] *noun*

goyave *(feminine)*.

guess [ges] *noun & verb*

- *noun*

  supposition *(feminine)* : **it's just a guess** ce n'est qu'une supposition

➤ **to have a guess** essayer de deviner

- *verb*

1. **deviner** : **I couldn't guess** je n'ai pas pu deviner ; **guess what I did!** devine ce que j'ai fait !

2. **supposer** : **I guess so** je suppose que oui.

guest [gest] *noun*

invité *(masculine)*, **invitée** *(feminine)* : **we have guests** nous avons des invités.

guesthouse ['gesthaʊs, *plural* 'gesthaʊzɪz] *noun*

pension *(feminine)* **de famille**.

guide [gaɪd] *noun & verb*

- *noun*

  guide *(masculine)* : **he's a tour guide** il est guide

➤ **a guide book** un guide

➤ **a guide dog** un chien d'aveugle

➤ **the Guides** *UK* les éclaireuses OR les guides *(feminine plural)*

- *verb*

  guider : **he guided us to the castle** il nous a guidés jusqu'au château.

guilty ['gɪltɪ] *adjective*

coupable : **he's not guilty of the theft** il n'est pas coupable de ce vol ; **I feel guilty** je me sens coupable.

guinea pig ['gɪnɪpɪg] *noun*

cobaye *(masculine)*, **cochon** *(masculine)* **d'Inde**.

guitar [gɪ'tɑːʳ] *noun*

guitare *(feminine)* : **he plays the guitar** il joue de la guitare.

gum [gʌm] *noun*

chewing-gum *(masculine)* : **a stick of gum** un chewing-gum.

gums [gʌmz] *plural noun*

gencives *(feminine plural)*.

gun [gʌn] *noun*

1. **revolver** *(masculine)* : **he has a gun in his hand** il a un revolver à la main

2. **fusil** *(masculine)* : **he bought a gun for hunting** il a acheté un fusil de chasse.

gunfire ['gʌnfaɪəʳ] *uncountable noun*

coups *(masculine plural)* **de feu** : **we could hear gunfire** on entendait des coups de feu.

gutter ['gʌtəʳ] *noun*

caniveau *(masculine)*.

guy [gaɪ] *noun informal*

type *(masculine)* : **he's a nice guy** c'est un type bien.

Guy Fawkes' Night [gaɪ'fɔːksnaɪt] *noun*

fête célébrée le 5 novembre en Grande-Bretagne

> GUY FAWKES' NIGHT
> Le 5 novembre, les Britanniques célèbrent la **Guy Fawkes' Night** ou **Bonfire Night** en souvenir de la Conspiration des poudres de 1605, durant laquelle un groupe de catholiques mené par Guy Fawkes voulait faire sauter le Parlement. Le complot fut déjoué le 4 novembre et les conspirateurs mis à mort. Les gens allument des feux d'artifice ainsi qu'un grand feu de joie sur lequel on brûle l'effigie de Guy Fawkes.

gym [dʒɪm] *noun*

1. **gymnase** *(masculine)* : **I go to the gym on Mondays** je vais au gymnase le lundi

2. **gym** *(feminine)* : **my gym class is at 3** mon cours de gym est à 3 heures

➤ **gym shoes** chaussures *(feminine plural)* de gym.

gypsy ['dʒɪpsɪ] *(plural* gypsies ['dʒɪpsiːz]*)* *noun*

gitan *(masculine)*, **gitane** *(feminine)*.

g

habit ['hæbɪt] *noun*

habitude *(feminine)* **: she has some bad habits** elle a de mauvaises habitudes ; **you'll soon get into the habit** tu prendras vite l'habitude.

hacker ['hækər] *noun*

pirate *(masculine)* **informatique**.

had [hæd] *past tense & past participle of* have

I had a headache j'avais mal à la tête ; **he has had a lot of problems** il a eu beaucoup de problèmes.

hadn't ['hædnt] = had not

he hadn't got a car il n'avait pas de voiture ; **I hadn't finished** je n'avais pas fini.

hail [heɪl] *noun & verb*

☐ *noun*
grêle *(feminine)*
☐ *verb*
grêler : it's hailing il grêle.

hair [heər] *noun*

1. *(uncountable)* **cheveux** *(masculine plural)* **: she has black hair** elle a les cheveux noirs ; **his hair is very long** ses cheveux sont très longs
2. **poil** *(masculine)* **: the dog's hairs are everywhere** il y a des poils du chien partout
3. **cheveu** *(masculine)* **: there's a hair in my soup** il y a un cheveu dans ma soupe
➤ **to do one's hair** se coiffer **: she's doing her hair** elle se coiffe
➤ **a hair clip** une pince à cheveux.

hairbrush ['heəbrʌʃ] *noun*

brosse *(feminine)* **à cheveux**.

haircut ['heəkʌt] *noun*

coupe *(feminine)* **de cheveux**

➤ **to have a haircut** se faire couper les cheveux.

hairdresser ['heəˌdresər] *noun*

coiffeur *(masculine)*, **coiffeuse** *(feminine)* **: to go to the hairdresser's** aller chez le coiffeur.

hairdryer ['heəˌdraɪər] *noun*

sèche-cheveux *(masculine)* [*plural* **sèche-cheveux**].

hairspray ['heəspreɪ] *noun*

laque *(feminine)*.

hairstyle ['heəstaɪl] *noun*

coiffure *(feminine)* **: she has changed her hairstyle** elle a changé de coiffure.

hairy ['heərɪ] *adjective*

poilu : he has hairy arms il a les bras poilus.

half [*UK* hɑːf, *US* hæf] *noun & adverb*

☐ *noun*
1. **moitié** *(feminine)* **: he ate half of the cake** il a mangé la moitié du gâteau
2. *In time expressions*
an hour and a half une heure et demie ; **half an hour** une demi-heure ; **it's half past three** il est trois heures et demie ; **two and a half years** deux ans et demi
3. **mi-temps** *(feminine)* **: the first half of the match** la première mi-temps du match ; **at half time** à la mi-temps
➤ **to cut something in half** couper quelque chose en deux
➤ **half term** *UK vacances scolaires d'une durée d'une semaine intervenant au milieu d'un trimestre*
☐ *adverb*
à moitié : she's half asleep elle est à moitié endormie ; **she's half Spanish** elle est à moitié espagnole.

halfway [*UK* hɑːf'weɪ, *US* hæf'weɪ] *adverb*

1. **à mi-chemin : halfway between Manchester and London** à mi-chemin entre Manchester et Londres
2. **à la moitié : halfway through the film** à la moitié du film.

hall [hɔːl] *noun*

1. **entrée** *(feminine)*, **vestibule** *(masculine)* **: he hung his coat up in the hall** il a accroché son manteau dans l'entrée
2. **salle** *(feminine)* **: there's a large hall where meetings take place** il y a une grande salle où ont lieu les réunions.

Halloween [ˌhæləʊ'iːn] *noun*

Halloween *(feminine)*

> HALLOWEEN
> Autrefois, on pensait que le 31 octo-bre, veille de la Toussaint, les esprits des morts venaient rendre visite aux vivants. Aujourd'hui, aux États-Unis et en Grande-Bretagne, les en-fants se déguisent en fantômes et en sorcières et confectionnent des lampes à partir de citrouilles (**jack-o'-lanterns**). Ils vont ensuite frapper à la porte de leurs voisins en leur disant « **trick or treat** » (« un tour ou un petit cadeau »), les me-naçant ainsi de leur jouer un tour s'ils ne leur donnent pas de l'argent ou des friandises.

hallway ['hɔːlweɪ] *noun*

vestibule *(masculine)*.

halt [hɔːlt] *noun*

➤ **to come to a halt** s'arrêter : **the car came to a halt** la voiture s'est arrêtée.

ham [hæm] *noun*

jambon *(masculine)* : **a ham sandwich** un sandwich au jambon.

hamburger ['hæmbɜːgər] *noun*

hamburger *(masculine)*.

hammer ['hæmər] *noun*

marteau *(masculine)* [*plural* **marteaux**].

hamster ['hæmstər] *noun*

hamster *(masculine)* : **I have a pet hamster** j'ai un hamster à la maison.

hand [hænd] *noun & verb*

◻ *noun*

1. **main** *(feminine)* : **he writes with his left hand** il écrit de la main gauche

2. **aiguille** *(feminine)* : **the hands of a clock** les aiguilles d'une horloge

➤ **to hold hands** se tenir par la main : **they were holding hands** ils se tenaient par la main

➤ **to give somebody a hand** donner un coup de main à quelqu'un

➤ **hand luggage** bagages *(masculine plural)* à main

◻ *verb*

passer : **can you hand me your pen?** tu peux me passer ton stylo ?

hand in *phrasal verb*

rendre : **they handed in their homework** ils ont rendu leurs devoirs

hand out *phrasal verb*

distribuer : **the teacher handed out the papers** le professeur a distribué les copies

hand over *phrasal verb*

remettre : **I handed the money over to her** je lui ai remis l'argent.

handbag ['hændbæg] *noun*

sac *(masculine)* à main.

handcuffs ['hændkʌfs] *plural noun*

menottes *(feminine plural)* : **they put hand-cuffs on the prisoner** ils ont passé les menot-tes au prisonnier.

handkerchief ['hæŋkətʃɪf] *noun*

mouchoir *(masculine)*.

handle ['hændl] *noun & verb*

◻ *noun*

1. **poignée** *(feminine)* : **he turned the door han-dle** il a tourné la poignée de la porte

2. **anse** *(feminine)* : **hold the cup by the handle** tiens la tasse par l'anse

3. **manche** *(masculine)* : **the handle of the broom has come off** le manche du balai s'est détaché

◻ *verb*

1. **traiter, gérer** : **he handled the crisis well** il a bien géré la crise

2. **s'y prendre avec** : **he knows how to handle people** il sait s'y prendre avec les gens.

handlebars ['hændlbɑːz] *plural noun*

guidon *(masculine)*.

handmade [ˌhænd'meɪd] *adjective*

fait à la main.

handrail ['hændreɪl] *noun*

rampe *(feminine)* : **hold on to the handrail** tiens bien la rampe.

handset ['hændset] *noun*

combiné *(masculine)*.

handsome ['hænsəm] *adjective*

beau *(feminine* **belle***)* : **he's very handsome** il est très beau.

h

handy ['hændɪ] *adjective*

1. **pratique** : **it's a handy little tool** c'est un petit outil très pratique
2. **tout près** : **the shops are handy** les magasins sont tout près.

hang [hæŋ] *(past tense & past participle* hung*)* *verb*

1. **accrocher, suspendre** : **he hung the picture on the wall** il a accroché le tableau au mur
2. **être suspendu** : **the picture is hanging on the wall** le tableau est suspendu au mur
3. *(past tense & past participle* hanged*)* **pendre** : **they hanged the murderer** ils ont pendu l'assassin

hang on *phrasal verb informal*

attendre : **can you hang on a minute?** tu peux attendre une minute ?

hang up *phrasal verb*

1. **accrocher, suspendre** : **hang your coat up** accroche ton manteau ; **they hung the decorations up** ils ont suspendu les décorations
2. **raccrocher** : **after the phone call he hung up** après avoir parlé au téléphone, il a raccroché.

hanger ['hæŋəʳ] *noun*

cintre *(masculine)* : **put your jacket on the hanger** mets ta veste sur le cintre.

hang-gliding [hæŋ'glaɪdɪŋ] *noun*

Deltaplane® *(masculine)* : **he goes hang-gliding** il fait du Deltaplane.

happen ['hæpən] *verb*

se passer : **what's happening?** qu'est-ce qui se passe ? ; **what happened?** qu'est-ce qui s'est passé ? ; **it happened last week** ça s'est passé la semaine dernière

> **what happened to him?** qu'est-ce qui lui est arrivé ? ; **guess what happened to me!** devine ce qui m'est arrivé !
> **I happened to meet him yesterday** je l'ai rencontré hier par hasard.

happier ['hæpɪəʳ] *comparative of* happy

she's happier now elle est plus heureuse maintenant.

happiest ['hæpɪəst] *superlative of* happy

I'm the happiest I've ever been je n'ai jamais été aussi heureux.

happiness ['hæpɪnɪs] *uncountable noun*

bonheur *(masculine)*.

happy ['hæpɪ] *adjective*

heureux *(feminine* heureuse*)* : **I'm very happy to see you** je suis très heureux de te voir ; **Karen looks happy** Karen a l'air heureuse

> **happy birthday!** joyeux anniversaire !
> **Happy Christmas!** joyeux Noël !
> **Happy New Year!** bonne année !

harbour *UK,* **harbor** *US* ['hɑːbəʳ] *noun*

port *(masculine)* : **the ships are in the harbour** les bateaux sont au port.

hard [hɑːd] *adjective & adverb*

■ *adjective*

1. **dur** : **the bed is very hard** le lit est très dur ; **she's very hard on him** elle est très dure avec lui
2. **difficile, dur** : **that's a hard question** c'est une question difficile
> **the hard disk** le disque dur

■ *adverb*

dur : **she works hard** elle travaille dur
> **to try hard** faire de son mieux : **I tried very hard to succeed** j'ai fait de mon mieux pour réussir.

hard-boiled [hɑːd'bɔɪld] *adjective*

> **a hard-boiled egg** un œuf dur.

hardly ['hɑːdlɪ] *adverb*

à peine : **I hardly know him** je le connais à peine
> **hardly ever** presque jamais : **he hardly ever phones** il n'appelle presque jamais.

hardware ['hɑːdweəʳ] *uncountable noun*

matériel *(masculine)*.

hare [heəʳ] *noun*

lièvre *(masculine)*.

harm [hɑːm] *noun & verb*

■ *noun*

mal *(masculine)* : **it won't do him any harm** ça ne lui fera pas de mal

■ *verb*

1. **faire du mal à** : **he wouldn't harm a fly** il ne ferait pas de mal à une mouche
2. **nuire à** : **the gases could harm the environment** les gaz pourraient nuire à l'environnement.

harmful ['hɑːmfʊl] *adjective*

nuisible : **the harmful effects of smoking** les effets nuisibles du tabac.

harmless ['hɑːmlɪs] *adjective*

inoffensif (*feminine* inoffensive) : **these animals are harmless** ces animaux sont inoffensifs.

harmonica [hɑːˈmɒnɪkə] *noun*

harmonica (*masculine*) : **he plays the harmonica** il joue de l'harmonica.

harsh [hɑːʃ] *adjective*

sévère, dur : **it's a harsh punishment** c'est une punition sévère.

harvest ['hɑːvɪst] *noun*

moisson (*feminine*), récolte (*feminine*) : **at harvest time** pendant la moisson.

has [həz, hæz] ➤ have

she has three brothers elle a trois frères ; **he has eaten all the cake** il a mangé tout le gâteau.

hasn't ['hæznt] = has not

it hasn't rained all day il n'a pas plu de la journée ; **he hasn't finished** il n'a pas fini.

hat [hæt] *noun*

chapeau (*masculine*) [*plural* chapeaux] : **she's wearing a big hat** elle porte un grand chapeau.

hate [heɪt] *verb*

détester : **I hate liver** je déteste le foie
➤ **to hate doing something** avoir horreur de faire quelque chose : **he hates getting up early** il a horreur de se lever tôt.

hatred ['heɪtrɪd] *noun*

haine (*feminine*).

haunted ['hɔːntɪd] *adjective*

hanté : **this house is haunted** cette maison est hantée.

have [hæv] (*past tense & past participle* had) *verb*

1. avoir : **I have a dog called Sammy** OR **I've got a dog called Sammy** j'ai un chien qui s'appelle Sammy ; **do you have any brothers?** OR **have you got any brothers?** est-ce que tu as des frères ? ; **Ben has flu** *UK* OR **Ben has got flu** *UK* OR

Ben has the flu *US* Ben a la grippe ; **Rosie has blue eyes** OR **Rosie has got blue eyes** Rosie a les yeux bleus ; **they didn't have time** ils n'ont pas eu le temps

⚠ En anglais britannique, on utilise plus souvent **have got** ou **has got** que **have** ou **has** pour montrer la possession au présent.

2. *When 'have' means 'take', 'eat' or 'drink'*

You should use the French verbs **prendre** (to take), **manger** (to eat) or **boire** (to drink):

I'm going to have a shower je vais prendre une douche ; **I'll have a coffee** je vais prendre un café ; **we had sandwiches for lunch** on a mangé des sandwichs à midi ; **Gary had a beer** Gary a bu une bière

When 'have' is used with certain nouns, you can use a single verb in French to translate 'have' + noun:

to have dinner dîner ; **to have a walk** se promener ; **to have a good time** OR **to have a nice time** s'amuser ; **have a nice time** amuse-toi bien !

3. passer : **we had a nice evening** nous avons passé une bonne soirée ; **we had a week in Tenerife** nous avons passé une semaine à Tenerife

4. *In the perfect tenses*

The past tense of most French verbs is formed using the auxiliary verb **avoir** + past participle:

I've finished my homework j'ai fini mes devoirs ; **have you seen my glasses?** as-tu vu mes lunettes ? ; **she had forgotten to phone** elle avait oublié d'appeler

You must use the auxiliary verb **être** + past participle to form the past tense of verbs of movement (**aller, venir, partir, monter**, etc), verbs that show a change of state (**devenir, mourir**, etc), and reflexive verbs (**se coucher, se lever**, etc). The past participle must agree in gender (masculine or feminine) and number (singular or plural) with the subject of the verb:

she has gone to Egypt elle est allée en Égypte ; **they've arrived at last** ils sont enfin arrivés ; **he has become very rich** il est devenu très riche ; **she has gone to bed** elle s'est couchée ; **have you brushed your teeth?** est-ce que tu t'es brossé les dents ?

h

5. *Obligation* **I have to leave** OR **I've got to leave** je dois partir OR il faut que je parte ; **he had to go to the dentist** il a dû aller chez le dentiste

> To say you 'don't have to', use the construction ne pas être obligé de + infinitive:

you don't have to come tu n'es pas obligé de venir

➤ **to have something done** faire faire quelque chose : **I'm going to have the rugs cleaned** je vais faire nettoyer les tapis ; **Ann had her hair cut** Ann s'est fait couper les cheveux

➤ **to have a party** faire une fête : **I'm having a party on Friday** je vais faire une fête vendredi.

haven't ['hævnt] = have not

I haven't finished yet je n'ai pas encore fini ; **they haven't been to England** ils ne sont pas allés en Angleterre.

hawk [hɔ:k] *noun*

faucon *(masculine)*.

hay [heɪ] *uncountable noun*

foin *(masculine)* : **the cows are eating hay** les vaches mangent du foin

➤ **hay fever** rhume *(masculine)* des foins ; **she has hay fever** elle a le rhume des foins.

hazelnut ['heɪzl,nʌt] *noun*

noisette *(feminine)*.

he [hi:] *pronoun*

il : **he's called John** il s'appelle John ; **he came to see me** il est venu me voir

➤ **he's a clever man** c'est un homme intelligent

➤ **there he is!** le voilà !

➤ **he and I** lui et moi : **he and I went for a swim** lui et moi sommes allés nous baigner.

head [hed] *noun & verb*

1. **tête** *(feminine)* : **my head hurts** j'ai mal à la tête

2. **chef** *(masculine)* : **he's the head of state** c'est le chef de l'État

3. *UK* **directeur** *(masculine)*, **directrice** *(feminine)* : **the head of the school** le directeur de l'école

➤ **heads or tails?** pile ou face ?

head for *phrasal verb*

se diriger vers : **they're heading for the exit** ils se dirigent vers la sortie.

headache ['hedeɪk] *noun*

mal *(masculine)* **de tête** [*plural* **maux de tête**] : **she has a headache** elle a mal à la tête.

headlight ['hedlaɪt] *noun*

phare *(masculine)* : **the driver put the headlights on** le conducteur a allumé ses phares.

headline ['hedlaɪn] *noun*

gros titre *(masculine)* : **to read the headlines** lire les gros titres.

headmaster *UK* [,hed'mɑ:stər] *noun*

directeur *(masculine)* : **he's headmaster of the school** c'est le directeur de l'école.

headmistress *UK* [,hed'mɪstrɪs] *noun*

directrice *(feminine)* : **she's headmistress of the school** c'est la directrice de l'école.

headphones ['hedfəʊnz] *plural noun*

casque *(masculine)* : **she put her headphones on to listen to the music** elle a mis son casque pour écouter la musique.

heal [hi:l] *verb*

1. **se cicatriser** : **the wound is healing** la blessure se cicatrise

2. **guérir** : **this will heal your wounds** ceci guérira tes blessures.

health [helθ] *uncountable noun*

santé *(feminine)* : **he's in good health** il est en bonne santé.

healthy ['helθɪ] *adjective*

1. **en bonne santé** : **she's healthy** elle est en bonne santé

2. **sain** : **he leads a healthy life** il mène une vie saine.

heap [hi:p] *noun*

tas *(masculine)* : **his clothes are lying in a heap** ses vêtements sont par terre en tas.

hear [hɪər] (*past tense & past participle* **heard** [hɜ:d]) *verb*

1. **entendre** : **I can't hear** je n'entends rien ; **she heard a noise** elle a entendu un bruit ; **I heard him laughing** je l'ai entendu rire

2. **apprendre** : **have you heard the news?** tu as appris la nouvelle ? ; **I heard he was ill** j'ai appris qu'il était malade

hear from *phrasal verb*

avoir des nouvelles de : **I haven't heard from her for ages** je n'ai pas eu de ses nouvelles depuis très longtemps

hear of *phrasal verb*

entendre parler de : **I've never heard of him** je n'ai jamais entendu parler de lui.

heart [hɑːt] *noun*

cœur *(masculine)* : **my heart missed a beat** mon cœur a bondi
> **by heart** par cœur : **I know the poem by heart** je connais le poème par cœur
a heart attack une crise cardiaque
> **the ace of hearts** l'as de cœur.

heat [hiːt] *noun & verb*

■ *noun*
chaleur *(feminine)* : **I don't like the heat** je n'aime pas la chaleur
■ *verb*
faire chauffer : **heat the water for ten minutes** faites chauffer l'eau pendant dix minutes

heat up *phrasal verb*

1. faire réchauffer : **I heated up the pizza in the oven** j'ai fait réchauffer la pizza au four
2. faire chauffer : **I heated up the milk** j'ai fait chauffer le lait
3. chauffer : **the water is heating up** l'eau chauffe.

heater ['hiːtər] *noun*

radiateur *(masculine)* : **he turned the heater on** il a allumé le radiateur.

heating ['hiːtɪŋ] *noun*

chauffage *(masculine)* : **he put the heating on** il a mis le chauffage.

heaven ['hevn] *noun*

paradis *(masculine)* : **will he go to heaven?** ira-t-il au paradis ?

heavy ['hevɪ] *(comparative* heavier, *superlative* heaviest) *adjective*

1. lourd : **my luggage is very heavy** mes bagages sont très lourds
2. gros *(feminine* grosse) : **a heavy coat** un gros manteau ; **she has a heavy cold** elle a un gros rhume

3. dense : **the traffic is heavy at weekends** la circulation est dense le week-end
4. chargé : **I had a heavy week** j'ai eu une semaine chargée
> **how heavy is it?** combien ça pèse ? : **how heavy is your bag?** combien pèse ton sac ?

he'd [hiːd]

1. = he had : **he'd already finished** il avait déjà fini ; **he'd gone** il était parti
2. = he would : **he'd like to come too** il aimerait venir lui aussi.

hedge [hedʒ] *noun*

haie *(feminine)* : **there's a hedge around the garden** il y a une haie autour du jardin.

hedgehog ['hedʒhɒg] *noun*

hérisson *(masculine)*.

heel [hiːl] *noun*

talon *(masculine)* : **high-heel shoes** des chaussures à talons hauts.

height [haɪt] *noun*

1. hauteur *(feminine)* : **what is the height of the wall?** quelle est la hauteur du mur ?
2. taille *(feminine)* : **she's of average height** elle est de taille moyenne.

heir [eər] *noun*

héritier *(masculine)*, héritière *(feminine)*.

held [held] *past tense & past participle of* hold

he held my hand il me tenait par la main.

helicopter ['helɪkɒptər] *noun*

hélicoptère *(masculine)*.

hell [hel] *noun*

enfer *(masculine)* : **heaven and hell** le paradis et l'enfer.

he'll [hiːl] = he will

he'll be here soon il va bientôt arriver.

hello , **hullo** *UK* [hə'ləʊ] *exclamation*

1. bonjour ! : **hello, how are you?** bonjour, comment vas-tu ?
2. allô ! : **hello, this is Paul speaking** allô, c'est Paul à l'appareil.

helmet ['helmɪt] *noun*

casque *(masculine)* : **the cyclist is wearing a helmet** le cycliste porte un casque.

h

help [help] *noun, exclamation & verb*

■ *noun*
aide *(feminine)* : **do you need any help?** tu as besoin d'aide ? ; **he asked for help** il a demandé de l'aide

■ *exclamation*
au secours ! : **help, I'm drowning!** au secours, je me noie !

■ *verb*
aider : **can I help you?** je peux t'aider ? ; **can you help me with my homework?** tu peux m'aider à faire mes devoirs ? ; **I helped her clean the car** OR **I helped her to clean the car** je l'ai aidée à nettoyer la voiture
➤ **I can't help it** je n'y peux rien
➤ **he couldn't help laughing** il ne pouvait pas s'empêcher de rire
➤ **help yourself!** servez-vous ! ; **I helped myself to cheese** je me suis servi du fromage.

helpful ['helpful] *adjective*
1. **serviable** : **he's always very helpful** il est toujours très serviable
2. **utile** : **your advice was helpful** tes conseils m'ont été utiles.

helping ['helpɪŋ] *noun*
portion *(feminine)* : **a big helping of stew** une grande portion de ragoût
➤ **to have a second helping** en reprendre OR se resservir : **Graham had a second helping** Graham en a repris OR Graham s'est resservi.

helpline UK ['helplaɪn] *noun*
service *(masculine)* **d'assistance téléphonique**.

hen [hen] *noun*
poule *(feminine)* : **he's feeding the hens** il donne à manger aux poules.

her [hɜːʳ] *pronoun & adjective*

■ *pronoun*
1. *Direct object* **la** (**l'** *before a vowel*) : **can you see her?** est-ce que tu la vois ? ; **call her!** appelle-la ! ; **I didn't see her** je ne l'ai pas vue **he had always loved her** il l'avait toujours aimée

> In tenses like the present perfect or the past perfect, the past participle agrees with the direct object pronoun.

2. *Indirect object* **lui** : **I gave her the flowers**

je lui ai donné les fleurs ; **give them to her!** donne-les-lui !
3. *After a preposition* **elle** : **these chocolates are for her** ces chocolats sont pour elle ; **I'm taller than her** je suis plus grande qu'elle

■ *adjective*
son *(feminine* **sa)** [plural **ses**]

> In French the possessive adjective agrees in gender (masculine or feminine) and number (singular or plural) with the noun that follows. Always use son with nouns that begin with a vowel or a silent 'h':

her father is a doctor son père est médecin ; **her car won't start** sa voiture ne veut pas démarrer ; **she lent me her books** elle m'a prêté ses livres ; **her plate is empty** son assiette est vide

> Use the definite article (le, la or les), not the possessive adjective, with parts of the body:

she closed her eyes elle a fermé les yeux ; **Linda's washing her hair** Linda se lave les cheveux.

herb [*UK* hɜːb, *US* ɜːb] *noun*
herbe *(feminine)*.

herd [hɜːd] *noun*
troupeau *(masculine)* [plural **troupeaux**] : **a herd of sheep** un troupeau de moutons.

here [hɪəʳ] *adverb*
ici : **come here!** viens ici !
➤ **here is** OR **here's** voici : **here's Jeremy** voici Jeremy
➤ **here are** voici : **here are your keys** voici vos clés.

hero ['hɪərəʊ] (plural **heroes**) *noun*
héros *(masculine)* : **he's my hero** c'est mon héros.

heroin ['herəʊɪn] *noun*
héroïne *(feminine)* : **heroin is a dangerous drug** l'héroïne est une drogue dangereuse.

heroine ['herəʊɪn] *noun*
héroïne *(feminine)* : **who is the heroine of the book?** qui est l'héroïne du livre ?

herring ['herɪŋ] *noun*
hareng *(masculine)*.

hers [hɜːz] *pronoun*

1. **le sien** *(feminine* **la sienne***)* [*plural* **les siens, les siennes**]

   In French the possessive pronoun agrees in gender (masculine or feminine) and number (singular or plural) with the noun that follows:

   my dress is blue, hers is red ma robe est bleue, la sienne est rouge

2. **à elle** : **that book's not hers** ce livre n'est pas à elle ; **he's a friend of hers** c'est un ami à elle.

herself [hɜːˈself] *pronoun*

1. **se (s'** *before a vowel)* : **she's washing herself** elle se lave ; **she enjoyed herself** elle s'est amusée

2. **elle-même** : **she made it herself** elle l'a fait elle-même

3. **elle** : **she's pleased with herself** elle est contente d'elle

   ➤ **by herself** toute seule : **Amy is all by herself** Amy est toute seule.

he's [hiːz]

1. = he is : **he's a teacher** il est professeur
2. = he has : **he's got a dog** il a un chien.

hesitate [ˈhezɪteɪt] *verb*

hésiter : **I hesitated for a moment** j'ai hésité un instant ; **don't hesitate to call me!** n'hésite pas à m'appeler !

hi [haɪ] *exclamation informal*

salut ! : **hi, how are you?** salut, tu vas bien ?

hiccup [ˈhɪkʌp] *noun*

hoquet *(masculine)* : **I've got hiccups** j'ai le hoquet.

hid [hɪd] *past tense of* hide

she hid behind the door elle s'est cachée derrière la porte.

hidden [ˈhɪdn] *past participle of* hide

I've hidden the box under the bed j'ai caché la boîte sous le lit.

hide [haɪd] *(past tense* hid, *past participle* hidden*) verb*

1. **cacher** : **hide the presents!** cache les cadeaux !

2. **se cacher** : **she's hiding behind the sofa** elle se cache derrière le canapé.

hide-and-seek [haɪdəndsiːk] *noun*

cache-cache *(masculine)* : **they're playing hide-and-seek** ils jouent à cache-cache.

hi-fi [ˈhaɪfaɪ] *noun*

chaîne *(feminine)* **hi-fi.**

high [haɪ] *adjective*

1. **haut** : **how high is the tower?** la tour fait combien de haut ? ; **it's 6 metres high** ça fait 6 mètres de haut

2. **élevé** : **prices are high in London** les prix sont élevés à Londres

3. **aigu** *(feminine* **aiguë***)* : **she has a high voice** elle a une voix aiguë

   ➤ **the high jump** le saut en hauteur

   ➤ **at high speed** à grande vitesse : **the train travels at high speed** le train roule à grande vitesse

   ➤ **the high street** UK la rue principale OR la grand-rue : **there are a lot of shops on the high street** il y a beaucoup de magasins dans la rue principale.

higher [ˈhaɪər] *comparative of* high

1. **plus haut** : **Harry can jump higher than me** Harry saute plus haut que moi

2. **supérieur** : **a higher number** un nombre supérieur.

highlight [ˈhaɪlaɪt] *noun & verb*

◼ *noun*

clou *(masculine)* : **the speech was the highlight of the evening** le discours a été le clou de la soirée

◼ *verb*

1. **surligner** : **I've highlighted the important words in the book** j'ai surligné les mots importants dans le livre

2. **sélectionner** : **double-click on a word to highlight it** double-cliquez sur un mot pour le sélectionner.

highlighter [ˈhaɪlaɪtər], **highlighter pen** [ˈhaɪlaɪtərpen] *noun*

surligneur *(masculine)*.

high school [ˈhaɪskuːl] *noun*

1. *US* **lycée** *(masculine)* : **he's in high school** il est au lycée

2. *UK* **établissement** *(masculine)* **d'enseignement secondaire (collège et lycée)**

   ➤ School.

h

high-tech, hi-tech [haɪ'tek] *adjective*

sophistiqué : it's a high-tech computer c'est un ordinateur sophistiqué

> **a high-tech industry** une industrie de pointe.

highway *US* ['haɪweɪ] *noun*

autoroute *(feminine)*
> **the highway code** le code de la route.

hijack ['haɪdʒæk] *verb*

détourner : a plane has been hijacked un avion vient d'être détourné.

hike [haɪk] *noun*

randonnée *(feminine)* : **to go on a hike** faire une randonnée.

hiking ['haɪkɪŋ] *uncountable noun*

randonnée *(feminine)* : **to go hiking** faire une randonnée OR faire des randonnées.

hilarious [hɪ'leərɪəs] *adjective*

hilarant : the film was hilarious le film était hilarant.

hill [hɪl] *noun*

colline *(feminine)* : **there's a house on the top of the hill** il y a une maison en haut de la colline ; **they walked up the hill** ils ont gravi la colline.

him [hɪm] *pronoun*

1. *Direct object* **le** (**l'** *before a vowel*) : **I can't see him** je ne le vois pas ; **find him!** trouve-le ! ; **I saw him** je l'ai vu
2. *Indirect object and after preposition* **lui : she gave him a kiss** elle lui a donné un baiser ; **tell him to come** dis-lui de venir ; **these CDs are for him** ces CD sont pour lui ; **I'm taller than him** je suis plus grand que lui.

himself [hɪm'self] *pronoun*

1. **se** (**s'** *before a vowel*) : **he's washing himself** il se lave ; **he has cut himself** il s'est coupé
2. **lui-même : he made it himself** il l'a fait lui-même
3. **lui : Jack's very pleased with himself** Jack est très content de lui
> **by himself** tout seul : **he did it by himself** il l'a fait tout seul.

hip [hɪp] *noun*

hanche *(feminine)*.

hippo ['hɪpəʊ], **hippopotamus** [ˌhɪpə'pɒtəməs] *noun*

hippopotame *(masculine)*.

hire ['haɪəʳ] *verb & noun*

■ *verb*
1. *UK* **louer : we hired a car** nous avons loué une voiture
2. **engager : the factory has hired 20 workers** l'usine a engagé 20 ouvriers
■ *noun UK*
> **for hire** à louer : **this car is for hire** cette voiture est à louer.

his [hɪz] *adjective & pronoun*

■ *adjective*
son *(feminine* **sa)** [*plural* **ses**]

In French the possessive adjective agrees in gender (masculine or feminine) and number (singular or plural) with the noun that follows. Always use **son** with singular nouns that begin with a vowel or a silent 'h':

his brother's called Dan son frère s'appelle Dan ; **his car won't start** sa voiture ne veut pas démarrer ; **his parents are away** ses parents sont absents ; **his plate is empty** son assiette est vide

Use the definite article (**le, la** or **les**), not the possessive adjective, with parts of the body:

he raised his hand il a levé la main ; **he's washing his face** il se lave la figure

■ *pronoun*
1. **le sien** *(masculine)*, **la sienne** *(feminine)* [*plural* **les siens, les siennes**]

In French the possessive pronoun agrees in gender (masculine or feminine) and number (singular or plural) with the noun it replaces:

my shirt is green, his is blue ma chemise est verte, la sienne est bleue
2. **à lui : it's his** c'est à lui ; **he's a friend of his** c'est un ami à lui.

hiss [hɪs] *verb*

siffler : the snake hissed le serpent sifflait.

history ['hɪstərɪ] *noun*

histoire *(feminine)* : **they're studying American history** ils étudient l'histoire des États-Unis.

hit [hɪt] *verb & noun*

■ *verb (past tense & past participle* **hit**)
1. **frapper : she hit him** elle l'a frappé
2. **heurter : the car hit a tree** la voiture a heurté un arbre
3. **renverser : she was hit by a car** elle s'est fait renverser par une voiture
4. **cogner : I hit my knee on the table** je me suis cogné le genou contre la table
5. **atteindre : the bullet hit the target** la balle a atteint la cible
■ *noun*
   succès *(masculine)* **: her book was a big hit** son livre a été un grand succès.

hitchhike ['hɪtʃhaɪk] *verb*

   faire de l'auto-stop, faire du stop : she hitchhiked to Paris elle est allée à Paris en auto-stop.

hi-tech *adjective* ➤ high-tech.

hoarse [hɔːs] *adjective*

   enroué : my voice is hoarse je suis enroué OR j'ai la voix enrouée.

hobby ['hɒbɪ] *(plural* hobbies ['hɒbɪz]) *noun*

   hobby *(masculine)*, **passe-temps** *(masculine)* [*plural* **passe-temps**] **: what are your hobbies?** quels sont tes hobbys ?

hockey ['hɒkɪ] *noun*

1. *UK* **hockey** *(masculine)* **sur gazon : they're playing hockey** ils jouent au hockey sur gazon
2. *US* **hockey** *(masculine)* **sur glace : they're playing hockey** ils jouent au hockey sur glace.

Hogmanay ['hɒgməneɪ] *noun*

   la Saint-Sylvestre en Écosse

   ✍ HOGMANAY
   C'est le nom écossais de la fête du Nouvel An. Traditionnellement, à minuit, les Écossais chantent la chanson **Auld Lang Syne** sur l'air de «ce n'est qu'un au revoir» et vont souhaiter la bonne année à leurs amis en leur apportant un petit morceau de charbon pour leur porter chance.

hold [həʊld] *(past tense & past participle* held) *verb*

1. **tenir : I was holding the key in my hand** je tenais la clé dans ma main
2. **contenir : the bottle holds two litres of water** la bouteille contient deux litres d'eau
3. **avoir : we're holding a meeting tomorrow** nous avons une réunion demain
➤ **to hold one's breath** retenir son souffle : **hold your breath** retiens ton souffle
➤ **please hold the line!** ne quittez pas !
➤ **hold it!** attends !
➤ **to get hold of something**
1. **saisir quelque chose : I got hold of her arm** j'ai saisi son bras
2. **trouver quelque chose : I couldn't get hold of his address** je n'ai pas réussi à trouver son adresse

hold on *phrasal verb*

1. **attendre : hold on a minute!** attends une minute !
2. **s'accrocher : hold on tight!** accroche-toi bien ! ; **to hold on to something** s'accrocher à quelque chose

hold out *phrasal verb*

   tendre : he held out his hand il a tendu la main

hold up *phrasal verb*

1. **lever : she held up her hand** elle a levé la main
2. **retarder : we were held up in a traffic jam** on a été retardés par un embouteillage
3. **attaquer : three men held up the bank** trois hommes ont attaqué la banque.

holdup ['həʊldʌp] *noun*

1. **hold-up** *(masculine)*, **braquage** *(masculine)* **: there was a holdup at the bank** il y a eu un hold-up à la banque
2. **retard** *(masculine)* **: what's the holdup?** pourquoi ce retard ?

hole [həʊl] *noun*

   trou *(masculine)* **: to dig a hole** creuser un trou.

holiday ['hɒlɪdeɪ] *noun*

1. *UK* **vacances** *(feminine plural)* **: they're on holiday** ils sont en vacances ; **I'm going on holiday next week** je pars en vacances la semaine prochaine ; **did you have a nice holiday?** est-ce que tu as passé de bonnes vacances ? ; **the school holidays** les vacances scolaires

h

2. jour (masculine) **férié : 26th December is a holiday in the UK** le 26 décembre est un jour férié au Royaume-Uni

 HOLIDAYS
En dehors de Noël, on compte parmi les principales fêtes britanniques, **Boxing Day**, **Guy Fawkes' Night** (appelée aussi **Bonfire Night**) et **Hogmanay** (la Saint-Sylvestre écossaise). En Irlande on célèbre **Saint Patrick's Day**, la fête nationale. Aux États-Unis, les plus grandes fêtes sont the **Fourth of July** (ou **Independence Day**), **Halloween** et **Thanksgiving**.
Vous trouverez plus d'informations en vous reportant à chacun des encadrés consacrés à ces fêtes.

Holland ['hɒlənd] *noun*

la Hollande

In French the names of countries are used with the definite article (**le**, **l'** or **la**), except when they follow the preposition **en**:

Holland is next to Belgium la Hollande est située à côté de la Belgique ; **I'm going to Holland** je vais en Hollande ; **he lives in Holland** il habite en Hollande.

hollow ['hɒləʊ] *adjective*

creux (*feminine* **creuse**) : **the tree trunk is hollow** le tronc d'arbre est creux.

holly ['hɒlɪ] *noun*

houx (*masculine*) : **they bought some holly for Christmas** ils ont acheté du houx pour Noël.

Hollywood ['hɒlɪwʊd] *noun*

Hollywood (*masculine*)

 HOLLYWOOD
Hollywood est un quartier de Los Angeles en Californie où sont produits la plupart des films nord-américains depuis près d'un siècle et où vivent de nombreuses célébrités. Les premières sociétés de production cinématographique se sont installées en 1908 dans cet endroit encore inconnu, dont le climat privilégié permettait de tourner à l'extérieur toute l'année. Les années 1930 et 1940 furent l'âge d'or d'Hollywood. On surnomme la ville **Tinseltown**. Le mot **tinsel**, qui désigne des guirlandes de Noël bon marché et peu solides, symbolise le caractère clinquant et éphémère de l'univers hollywoodien.

holy ['həʊlɪ] *adjective*

saint.

home [həʊm] *noun & adverb*

■ *noun*
maison (*feminine*)
➤ **a home page** une page d'accueil
■ *adverb*
chez soi, à la maison : she took me home elle m'a ramené chez moi
➤ **at home** chez soi OR à la maison : **Tina's not at home** Tina n'est pas chez elle OR Tina n'est pas à la maison
➤ **make yourself at home!** fais comme chez toi !
➤ **to go home** rentrer chez soi : **I want to go home** j'ai envie de rentrer chez moi ; **James got home late** James est rentré tard.

homeless ['həʊmlɪs] *adjective & noun*

to be homeless être sans abri
➤ **the homeless** les sans abri.

homemade [ˌhəʊm'meɪd] *adjective*

fait maison : he likes homemade cakes il aime les gâteaux faits maison.

homesick ['həʊmsɪk] *adjective*

to be homesick avoir le mal du pays.

homework ['həʊmwɜːk] *uncountable noun*

devoirs (*masculine plural*) : **do you have any homework?** est-ce que tu as des devoirs ? ; **my homework is very easy** mes devoirs sont très faciles.

honest ['ɒnɪst] *adjective*

1. **honnête : she's a very honest person** c'est une personne très honnête
2. **franc** (*feminine* **franche**) : **be honest with me** sois franc avec moi.

honesty ['ɒnɪstɪ] *noun*

honnêteté (*feminine*) : **honesty is the best policy** l'honnêteté paie toujours.

honey ['hʌnɪ] *noun*

miel (*masculine*) : **would you like some honey?** tu veux du miel ?

honeymoon ['hʌnɪmuːn] *noun*

lune (*feminine*) **de miel : they spent their honeymoon in India** ils ont passé leur lune de miel en Inde
➤ **to be on honeymoon** être en voyage de noces.

honour *UK*, **honor** *US* ['ɒnər] *noun*
honneur *(masculine)*.

hood [hʊd] *noun*
1. **capuche** *(feminine)* : **put the hood of your coat up** relève la capuche de ton manteau
2. *US* **capot** *(masculine)* : **the hood of the car** le capot de la voiture.

hoof [huːf, hʊf] *(plural* hoofs OR hooves [huːvz]*) noun*
sabot *(masculine)* : **horses and cows have hooves** les chevaux et les vaches ont des sabots.

hook [hʊk] *noun*
1. **crochet** *(masculine)* : **the picture is hanging on a hook** le tableau est suspendu à un crochet
2. **hameçon** *(masculine)* : **he caught the fish on a hook** il a attrapé le poisson avec un hameçon
3. **agrafe** *(feminine)* : **she fastened the hooks on her dress** elle a agrafé sa robe
➤ **the phone is off the hook** le téléphone est décroché.

hooky *US* [hʊkɪ] *noun informal*
➤ **to play hooky** sécher les cours : **she often plays hooky** elle sèche souvent les cours.

hooray ➤ hurray.

hoot *UK* [huːt] *verb*
klaxonner : **the car hooted** la voiture a klaxonné.

hooter *UK* ['huːtər] *noun*
Klaxon® *(masculine)*.

Hoover® *UK* ['huːvər] *noun*
aspirateur *(masculine)*.

hoover *UK* ['huːvər] *verb*
passer l'aspirateur : **he's hoovering the bedroom** il passe l'aspirateur dans la chambre.

hooves [huːvz] *plural of* hoof.

hop [hɒp] *(past tense & past participle* hopped*) verb*
1. **sauter** : **he hopped over the ditch** il a sauté par-dessus le fossé
2. **sauter à cloche-pied** : **he hopped to the door** il a sauté à cloche-pied jusqu'à la porte.

hope [həʊp] *noun & verb*
■ *noun*
espoir *(masculine)* : **the news gave me hope** cette nouvelle m'a donné de l'espoir
■ *verb*
espérer : **I hope she succeeds** j'espère qu'elle va réussir ; **he was hoping for an answer tonight** il espérait une réponse ce soir ; **I hope to see you soon** j'espère vous revoir bientôt
➤ **I hope so** j'espère bien
➤ **I hope not** j'espère bien que non.

hopeful ['həʊpfʊl] *adjective*
1. **plein d'espoir** : **everybody is hopeful** tout le monde est plein d'espoir
2. **encourageant** : **the news is hopeful** la nouvelle est encourageante.

hopefully ['həʊpfəlɪ] *adverb*
avec un peu de chance : **hopefully, it will be hot tomorrow** avec un peu de chance, il fera chaud demain.

hopeless ['həʊplɪs] *adjective*
1. **désespéré** : **the situation is hopeless** la situation est désespérée
2. **nul** *(feminine* **nulle***)* : **he's hopeless in physics** il est nul en physique.

horizon [hə'raɪzn] *noun*
horizon *(masculine)* : **I can see a ship on the horizon** je vois un bateau à l'horizon.

horn [hɔːn] *noun*
1. **corne** *(feminine)* : **bulls have horns** les taureaux ont des cornes
2. **Klaxon**® : **he sounded the horn** il a klaxonné.

horoscope ['hɒrəskəʊp] *noun*
horoscope *(masculine)* : **what's your horoscope for today?** c'est quoi ton horoscope pour aujourd'hui ?

horrible ['hɒrəbl] *adjective*
affreux, épouvantable : **what a horrible place!** quel endroit affreux ! ; **the weather's horrible** il fait un temps épouvantable.

horror ['hɒrər] *noun*
horreur *(feminine)*
➤ **a horror film** un film d'horreur OR un film d'épouvante.

h

horse [hɔːs] noun

cheval (masculine) [plural chevaux] : **can you ride a horse?** sais-tu monter à cheval ?
➤ **horse racing** courses (feminine plural) de chevaux
➤ **horse riding** l'équitation (feminine) : **she goes horse riding** elle fait de l'équitation.

horseshoe ['hɔːsʃuː] noun

fer (masculine) à cheval : **horseshoes bring good luck** les fers à cheval portent bonheur.

hose [həʊz], **hosepipe** ['həʊzpaɪp] noun

tuyau (masculine) [plural tuyaux] : **a garden hose** un tuyau d'arrosage.

hospital ['hɒspɪtl] noun

hôpital (masculine) : **they took him to the hospital** ils l'ont emmené à l'hôpital
➤ **in hospital** UK OR **in the hospital** US à l'hôpital : **she's in hospital** elle est à l'hôpital.

hostage ['hɒstɪdʒ] noun

otage (masculine or feminine) : **she was taken hostage** on l'a prise en otage.

host [həʊst] noun

hôte (masculine)
➤ **a host family** une famille d'accueil.

hostess ['həʊstes] noun

hôtesse (feminine).

hot [hɒt] adjective

1. chaud : **the water's hot** l'eau est chaude ; **I'm hot** j'ai chaud ; **it's hot** il fait chaud
2. épicé : **he likes hot curries** il aime les currys épicés
➤ **a hot dog** un hot dog.

hotel [həʊ'tel] noun

hôtel (masculine) : **I stayed in a hotel** j'ai logé à l'hôtel.

hour ['aʊəʳ] noun

heure (feminine) : **I waited for two hours** j'ai attendu deux heures
➤ **an hour and a half** une heure et demie
➤ **half an hour** une demi-heure
➤ **a quarter of an hour** un quart d'heure.

house [haʊs, plural 'haʊzɪz] noun

maison (feminine) : **he lives in a small house** il habite une petite maison
➤ **at somebody's house** OR **to somebody's house** chez quelqu'un : **you can stay at my house** tu peux rester chez moi ; **I went to her house** je suis allé chez elle
➤ **the House of Commons** la Chambre des communes
➤ **the House of Lords** la Chambre des lords
➤ **the Houses of Parliament** le Parlement britannique
➤ **the House of Representatives** la Chambre des représentants
➤ Senate, Congress, Political Parties

THE HOUSES OF PARLIAMENT
Le Parlement britannique se trouve dans le palais de Westminster, sur les bords de la Tamise à Londres. Le bâtiment a été construit au milieu du XIXᵉ siècle, après qu'un incendie eut détruit l'ancien palais en 1834. Le Parlement se compose de la Chambre des communes, dont les députés (MPs) sont élus et ont le pouvoir de voter les lois, et de la Chambre des lords (composée de nobles, d'hommes d'Église et de personnes récompensées pour leur mérite), qui a le pouvoir de les approuver.

THE HOUSE OF REPRESENTATIVES
La Chambre des représentants constitue, avec le Sénat, l'organe législatif américain : le Congrès. Ses 435 membres sont élus par le peuple tous les deux ans, proportionnellement à la population de chaque État. Ainsi, le Delaware n'a que deux représentants tandis que la Californie en compte 52. Toute nouvelle loi doit être votée par les membres des deux Chambres du Congrès.

houseplant ['haʊsplɑːnt] noun

plante (feminine) d'appartement.

housewife ['haʊswaɪf] (plural housewives ['haʊswaɪvz]) noun

femme (feminine) au foyer : **she's a housewife** elle est femme au foyer.

housework ['haʊswɜːk] uncountable noun

ménage (masculine) : **he hates doing the housework** il déteste faire le ménage.

housing estate UK ['haʊzɪŋɪ'steɪt], **housing project** US ['haʊzɪŋ'prɒdʒekt] noun

cité (feminine) : **they live on a housing estate** ils habitent une cité.

hovercraft [UK 'hɒvəkrɑːft, US 'hɒvəkræft] noun

aéroglisseur *(masculine)*.

how [haʊ] *adverb*

1. **comment : how are you?** comment allez-vous ? ; **how was the exam?** comment s'est passé l'examen ? ; **tell me how you did it** dis-moi comment tu as fait
2. *With 'much' and 'many'* **combien : how much is it?** c'est combien ? ; **how much money do you have?** combien d'argent as-tu ? ; **how many continents are there?** il y a combien de continents ?
3. *In exclamations* **comme : how pretty you look!** comme tu es belle ! ; **how kind!** comme c'est gentil !

➤ **to know how to do something** savoir faire quelque chose : **I don't know how to drive** je ne sais pas conduire ; **do you know how to ski?** tu sais faire du ski ?

➤ **how long will it take?** combien de temps ça va prendre ?

➤ **how long is the rope?** de quelle longueur est la corde ?

➤ **how old are you?** tu as quel âge ?

however [haʊ'evər] *adverb*

cependant : she worked hard, she didn't pass her exams however elle a beaucoup travaillé, cependant, elle n'a pas réussi ses examens.

howl [haʊl] *verb*

hurler : we heard a dog howling on a entendu un chien hurler.

hug [hʌg] *noun & verb*

■ *noun*
to give somebody a hug serrer quelqu'un dans ses bras

■ *verb*
serrer dans ses bras : I hugged him je l'ai serré dans mes bras.

huge [hjuːdʒ] *adjective*

1. **énorme : elephants are huge animals** les éléphants sont des animaux énormes
2. **immense : a huge building** un bâtiment immense.

hullo *UK exclamation* ➤ hello.

hum [hʌm] *verb*

1. **fredonner : he was humming a tune** il fredonnait un air
2. **bourdonner : we could hear the bees humming** on entendait bourdonner les abeilles.

human ['hjuːmən] *adjective*

humain : we're all human nous sommes tous humains

➤ **a human being** un être humain.

humid ['hjuːmɪd] *adjective*

humide : it's very humid il fait un temps très humide.

humour *UK*, **humor** *US* ['hjuːmər] *noun*

humour *(masculine)* **: Suzanne has a good sense of humour** Suzanne a le sens de l'humour.

hump [hʌmp] *noun*

bosse *(feminine)* **: camels have two humps** les chameaux ont deux bosses.

hunchback ['hʌntʃbæk] *noun*

bossu *(masculine)*, **bossue** *(feminine)* **: he's a hunchback** il est bossu.

hundred ['hʌndrəd] *number*

cent : a hundred dollars cent dollars ; **three hundred** trois cents ; **three hundred and one** trois cent un ; **she's a hundred years old** elle a cent ans

➤ **a hundred and one** cent un

➤ **hundreds of people** des centaines de personnes.

hundredth ['hʌndrətθ] *number*

centième.

hung [hʌŋ] *past tense & past participle of* hang

I hung the picture on the wall j'ai accroché le tableau au mur ; **he hasn't hung his coat up** il n'a pas accroché son manteau.

hunger ['hʌŋgər] *noun*

faim *(feminine)*.

hungry ['hʌŋgrɪ] *adjective*

➤ **to be hungry** avoir faim : **I'm hungry** j'ai faim ; **are you hungry?** tu as faim ?

hunt [hʌnt] *verb*

1. **chasser : they hunt foxes** ils chassent le renard
2. **poursuivre, pourchasser : the police are hunting the murderer** la police poursuit le meurtrier

➤ **to hunt for something** chercher quelque chose : **he's hunting for his keys** il cherche ses clés.

h

hunter ['hʌntəʳ] *noun*

chasseur *(masculine)* : **he's a hunter** il est chasseur.

hunting ['hʌntɪŋ] *uncountable noun*

chasse *(feminine)* : **fox hunting** la chasse au renard ; **to go hunting** aller à la chasse.

hurl [hɜːl] *verb*

lancer : **she hurled the ball into the garden** elle a lancé la balle dans le jardin.

hurray, hooray [hʊ'reɪ] *exclamation*

hourra !

hurricane ['hʌrɪkən] *noun*

ouragan *(masculine)*.

hurry ['hʌrɪ] *noun & verb*

■ *noun*
➤ **to be in a hurry** être pressé : **she's always in a hurry** elle est toujours pressée ; **take your time, I'm not in a hurry** prends ton temps, je ne suis pas pressé
➤ **to do something in a hurry** faire quelque chose en vitesse : **she did her homework in a hurry** elle a fait ses devoirs en vitesse
■ *verb (past tense & past participle* hurried*)*
se dépêcher : **she hurried to catch the bus** elle s'est dépêchée pour attraper le bus

hurry up *phrasal verb*

se dépêcher : **hurry up!** dépêche-toi !

hurt [hɜːt] *verb & adjective*

■ *verb (past tense & past participle* hurt*)*
1. faire mal : **ouch, that hurts!** aïe, ça fait mal ! ; **to hurt somebody** faire mal à quelqu'un ; **stop it, you're hurting me** arrête, tu me fais mal
2. blesser : **what he said hurt me** ce qu'il a dit m'a blessé
➤ **to hurt oneself** se faire mal : **have you hurt yourself?** tu t'es fait mal ? ; **I fell and hurt myself** je suis tombé et je me suis fait mal
➤ **my arm hurts** j'ai mal au bras ; **my head hurts** j'ai mal à la tête
■ *adjective*
blessé : **he's badly hurt** il est grièvement blessé ; **she was hurt that you didn't invite her** elle a été blessée parce que tu ne l'as pas invitée.

husband ['hʌzbənd] *noun*

mari *(masculine)* : **her husband is called Dick** son mari s'appelle Dick.

hut [hʌt] *noun*
1. hutte *(feminine)* : **the tribes live in huts** les tribus vivent dans des huttes
2. cabane *(feminine)* : **there's a hut in the garden** il y a une cabane dans le jardin.

hymn [hɪm] *noun*

hymne *(masculine)*.

hyphen ['haɪfn] *noun*

trait *(masculine)* **d'union** : **"e-mail" is written with a hyphen** « e-mail » s'écrit avec un trait d'union.

I [aɪ] *pronoun*

je (j' *before a vowel or a silent 'h'*) : **I'm called Pauline** je m'appelle Pauline ; **I live in Sydney** j'habite Sydney
➤ **here I am!** me voilà !
➤ **she and I** elle et moi : **she and I went dancing** elle et moi sommes allés danser.

ice [aɪs] *noun*
1. glace *(feminine)* : **the children are skating on the ice** les enfants patinent sur la glace
2. verglas *(masculine)* : **there's ice on the road** il y a du verglas sur la route
3. glaçons *(masculine plural)* : **do you want ice in your drink?** tu veux des glaçons dans ton verre ?
➤ **an ice cube** un glaçon
➤ **ice hockey** hockey *(masculine)* sur glace
➤ **an ice lolly** *UK* une glace à l'eau
➤ **an ice rink** une patinoire.

iceberg ['aɪsbɜːg] *noun*

iceberg *(masculine)*.

ice cream [ˌaɪsˈkriːm] *noun*

glace *(feminine)* : **a chocolate ice cream** une glace au chocolat

➤ **an ice-cream van** une camionnette de marchand de glaces

ICE-CREAM VAN
Traditionnellement, en Grande-Bretagne, le vendeur de glaces ambulant se déplace dans sa camionnette et annonce son arrivée par une petite musique très caractéristique.

Iceland [ˈaɪslənd] *noun*

l'Islande *(feminine)*

In French the names of countries are used with the definite article (le, l' or la), except when they follow the preposition en:

they live in Iceland ils vivent en Islande.

ice-skates [ˈaɪsskeɪts] *plural noun*

patins *(masculine plural)* à glace.

ice-skating [aɪsˈskeɪtɪŋ] *noun*

patinage *(masculine)* : **to go ice-skating** faire du patin à glace.

icicle [ˈaɪsɪkl] *noun*

glaçon *(masculine)* : **there are icicles hanging from the trees** il y a des glaçons suspendues aux arbres.

icing [ˈaɪsɪŋ] *noun*

glaçage *(masculine)* : **a cake with pink icing** un gâteau avec un glaçage rose

➤ **icing sugar** *UK* sucre *(masculine)* glace.

icon [ˈaɪkɒn] *noun*

icône *(feminine)* : **click on the icon to open the program** cliquez sur l'icône pour lancer le programme.

icy [ˈaɪsɪ] *adjective*

1. glacial : **an icy wind** un vent glacial
2. verglacé : **be careful, the road is icy** attention, la route est verglacée.

I'd [aɪd]

1. = I had : **I'd forgotten to send her a card** j'avais oublié de lui envoyer une carte
2. = I would : **I'd like a cup of tea** je voudrais une tasse de thé.

ID [aɪˈdiː] *(abbreviation of* identification*) noun*

pièce *(feminine)* **d'identité** : **do you have any ID?** vous avez une pièce d'identité ?

idea [aɪˈdɪə] *noun*

idée *(feminine)* : **that's a good idea** c'est une bonne idée ; **where is he? – I've no idea** où est-il ? – je n'en ai aucune idée.

ideal [aɪˈdɪəl] *adjective*

idéal *(masculine)* [*plural* idéaux] : **it's an ideal place for a party** c'est l'endroit idéal pour une fête.

identical [aɪˈdentɪkl] *adjective*

identique.

identification [aɪˌdentɪfɪˈkeɪʃn] *uncountable noun*

pièce *(feminine)* **d'identité** : **do you have any identification?** vous avez une pièce d'identité ?

identify [aɪˈdentɪfaɪ] *(past tense & past participle* identified*) verb*

identifier : **they've identified the body** ils ont identifié le corps.

identity [aɪˈdentətɪ] *(plural* identities*) noun*

identité *(feminine)*

➤ **an identity card** une carte d'identité.

idiom [ˈɪdɪəm] *noun*

expression *(feminine)* **idiomatique**.

idiot [ˈɪdɪət] *noun*

idiot *(masculine)*, idiote *(feminine)* : **what an idiot!** quel idiot !

if [ɪf] *conjunction*

si : **you can come if you want** tu peux venir, si tu veux ; **if I knew the answer I'd tell you** si je savais la réponse, je te le dirais ; **I don't know if she's coming** je ne sais pas si elle vient

➤ **if not** sinon
➤ **if only** si seulement ; **if only I could go!** si seulement je pouvais y aller !

ignore [ɪgˈnɔːr] *verb*

1. ne pas tenir compte de : **he ignored my advice** il n'a pas tenu compte de mes conseils
2. faire semblant de ne pas voir, ignorer : **I saw her in the street but she ignored me** je l'ai vue dans la rue mais elle a fait semblant de ne pas me voir.

ill [ɪl] *adjective*

malade : he's very ill il est très malade

➤ **to feel ill** ne pas se sentir bien : **Alan feels ill** Alan ne se sent pas bien

➤ **to be taken ill** tomber malade : **he was taken ill** il est tombé malade.

I'll [aɪl] = I will OR I shall

I'll phone you tomorrow je t'appellerai demain.

illegal [ɪ'liːgl] *adjective*

illégal : it's illegal to drive through a red light il est illégal de griller un feu rouge.

illness [ˈɪlnɪs] *noun*

maladie *(feminine)* : **it's a serious illness** c'est une maladie grave.

illustration [ˌɪlə'streɪʃn] *noun*

illustration *(feminine)* : **there are lots of illustrations in the book** il y a beaucoup d'illustrations dans ce livre.

I'm [aɪm] = I am

I'm very tired je suis très fatigué ; **I'm hungry** j'ai faim.

image [ˈɪmɪdʒ] *noun*

image *(feminine)* : **the company has changed its image** la société a changé d'image.

imagination [ɪˌmædʒɪ'neɪʃn] *noun*

imagination *(feminine)*

➤ **it's all in your imagination!** tout ça, c'est dans ta tête !

imagine [ɪ'mædʒɪn] *verb*

imaginer : imagine a princess beside a lake imagine une princesse au bord d'un lac ; **I imagine he's happy** j'imagine qu'il est heureux.

imitation [ˌɪmɪ'teɪʃn] *noun*

imitation *(feminine)*.

immediate [ɪ'miːdjət] *adjective*

immédiat : I need an immediate answer j'ai besoin d'une réponse immédiate.

immediately [ɪ'miːdjətlɪ] *adverb*

tout de suite, immédiatement : I want to leave immediately je veux partir tout de suite OR je veux partir immédiatement.

immigrant [ˈɪmɪgrənt] *noun*

immigré *(masculine)*, **immigrée** *(feminine)*.

impatient [ɪm'peɪʃnt] *adjective*

impatient : he's impatient to leave il est impatient de partir

➤ **to get impatient** s'impatienter : **she's beginning to get impatient** elle commence à s'impatienter.

import [ɪm'pɔːt] *verb*

importer : they import goods from China ils importent des marchandises de Chine.

importance [ɪm'pɔːtns] *noun*

importance *(feminine)* : **it's a matter of great importance** c'est une question d'une grande importance.

important [ɪm'pɔːtnt] *adjective*

important : she's an important woman c'est une femme importante ; **it's not important** ce n'est pas important.

impossible [ɪm'pɒsəbl] *adjective*

impossible : it's impossible to talk to him c'est impossible de lui parler.

impression [ɪm'preʃn] *noun*

impression *(feminine)* : **she made a good impression** elle a fait bonne impression.

improve [ɪm'pruːv] *verb*

1. **améliorer : she wants to improve her Spanish** elle veut améliorer son espagnol
2. **s'améliorer : the weather's improving** le temps s'améliore
3. **aller mieux : the patient is beginning to improve** le malade commence à aller mieux.

improvement [ɪm'pruːvmənt] *noun*

1. **amélioration** *(feminine)* : **this model is an improvement on the previous one** ce modèle représente une amélioration par rapport au précédent
2. **progrès** *(masculine)* : **there's been an improvement in his work** il a fait des progrès dans son travail.

in [ɪn] *preposition & adverb*

▪ *preposition*

1. **dans : there's a desk in my room** il y a un bureau dans ma chambre ; **put this photo in an envelope** mets cette photo dans une enveloppe ; **in the nineties** dans les années quatre-vingt-dix
2. *With place names*

Use en with a feminine country or continent:

Lisa lives in Ireland Lisa vit en Irlande ; **Darwin is in Australia** Darwin est en Australie

Use au or aux with a masculine country and à with a town or city:

Nigel lives in Japan Nigel vit au Japon ; **Arizona is in the United States** l'Arizona se trouve aux États-Unis ; **he lives in Tokyo** il habite à Tokyo

3. à : **in the countryside** à la campagne ; **in the sun** au soleil ; **it's written in pencil** c'est écrit au crayon

4. en : **the film's in French** le film est en français ; **she's dressed in black** elle est habillée en noir ; **they live in town** ils habitent en ville ; **he's in prison** il est en prison

5. *In time expressions* **my birthday's in May** mon anniversaire est en mai ; **he was born in 1932** il est né en 1932 ; **I woke up in the night** je me suis réveillé pendant la nuit ; **the film starts in ten minutes** le film commence dans dix minutes

6. *With morning, afternoon, evening* **I went for a walk in the afternoon** je me suis promené l'après-midi ; **I'll phone you in the morning** je t'appellerai le matin ; **it's three o'clock in the morning** il est trois heures du matin

7. *With superlatives* de : **Everest is the tallest mountain in the world** l'Everest est la plus haute montagne du monde

■ *adverb*

1. là : **is Dan in?** est-ce que Dan est là ?

2. à la maison : **we had a night in** nous sommes restés à la maison

3. *informal* à la mode : **are hats in?** est-ce que les chapeaux sont à la mode ?

➤ **the tide's in** c'est la marée haute.

inch [ɪntʃ] (*plural* inches [ˈɪntʃɪz]) *noun*

= 2,54 cm : **he has grown a few inches this year** il a grandi de quelques centimètres cette année.

include [ɪnˈkluːd] *verb*

comprendre : **service is included** le service est compris.

including [ɪnˈkluːdɪŋ] *preposition*

1. y compris : **everyone's coming, including Thomas** tout le monde vient, y compris Thomas

2. compris : **that's twenty pounds including service** ça fait vingt livres, service compris.

income [ˈɪŋkʌm] *uncountable noun*

revenu *(masculine)*
➤ **income tax** impôt *(masculine)* sur le revenu.

increase *noun & verb*

■ *noun* [ˈɪnkriːs]
augmentation *(feminine)* : **there's been an increase in the price** il y a eu une augmentation du prix

■ *verb* [ɪnˈkriːs]
augmenter : **the number of users is increasing** le nombre d'utilisateurs augmente ; **they've increased the price** ils ont augmenté le prix.

incredible [ɪnˈkredəbl] *adjective*

incroyable : **that story is incredible** cette histoire est incroyable.

indecisive [ˌɪndɪˈsaɪsɪv] *adjective*

indécis : **she's very indecisive** elle est très indécise.

indeed [ɪnˈdiːd] *adverb*

1. vraiment : **I'm very tired indeed** je suis vraiment très fatigué

2. en effet : **indeed there is a problem** en effet, il y a un problème

➤ **thank you very much indeed** merci infiniment.

independence [ˌɪndɪˈpendəns] *noun*

indépendance *(feminine)*
➤ **Independence Day** fête de l'Indépendance américaine, le 4 juillet
➤ National Holidays.

independent [ˌɪndɪˈpendənt] *adjective*

indépendant.

index [ˈɪndeks] *noun*

index *(masculine)* : **look it up in the index** cherche-le dans l'index
➤ **the index finger** l'index *(masculine)*.

India [ˈɪndjə] *noun*

l'Inde *(feminine)*

In French the names of countries are used with the definite article (**le, la** or **l'**), except when they follow the preposition **en**:

India is a beautiful country l'Inde est un beau pays ; **she's going to India** elle va en Inde ; **he lives in India** il habite en Inde.

Indian ['ɪndjən] *adjective & noun*

■ *adjective*
indien *(feminine* **indienne)**

> The French adjective does not start with a capital letter:

I like Indian cooking j'aime la cuisine indienne

■ *noun*
Indien *(masculine)*, **Indienne** *(feminine)*.

indicate ['ɪndɪkeɪt] *verb*

1. **indiquer** : **he indicated the quickest route** il a indiqué l'itinéraire le plus court
2. *UK* **mettre son clignotant** : **you must indicate before you turn** tu dois mettre ton clignotant avant de tourner.

indicator *UK* ['ɪndɪkeɪtər] *noun*
clignotant *(masculine)*.

indigestion [ˌɪndɪ'dʒestʃn] *uncountable noun*
indigestion *(feminine)* : **he has indigestion** il a une indigestion.

individual [ˌɪndɪ'vɪdʒʊəl] *adjective & noun*

■ *adjective*
individuel *(feminine* **individuelle)** : **an individual room** une chambre individuelle

■ *noun*
individu *(masculine)*.

indoor ['ɪndɔːr] *adjective*

1. **d'intérieur** : **indoor plants** des plantes d'intérieur
2. **en salle** : **indoor sports** les sports en salle
➤ **an indoor pool** une piscine couverte.

indoors [ˌɪn'dɔːz] *adverb*
à l'intérieur : **they're indoors** ils sont à l'intérieur
➤ **to go indoors** OR **to come indoors** rentrer : **come indoors, it's raining** rentre, il pleut.

industrial [ɪn'dʌstrɪəl] *adjective*
industriel *(feminine* **industrielle)** : **an industrial zone** une zone industrielle.

industry ['ɪndəstrɪ] *(plural* **industries)** *noun*
industrie *(feminine)* : **he works in the film in-**

dustry il travaille dans l'industrie cinématographique.

infant school *UK* ['ɪnfəntˌskuːl] *noun*
premières années d'école primaire, de 5 à 7 ans.

infection [ɪn'fekʃn] *noun*
infection *(feminine)*
➤ **a throat infection** une angine.

infinitive [ɪn'fɪnɪtɪv] *noun*
infinitif *(feminine)* : **put the verb into the infinitive** mets le verbe à l'infinitif.

infirmary [ɪn'fɜːmərɪ] *(plural* **infirmaries)** *noun*
hôpital *(masculine)*.

inflatable [ɪn'fleɪtəbl] *adjective*
gonflable : **an inflatable toy** un jouet gonflable.

influence ['ɪnflʊəns] *noun & verb*

■ *noun*
influence *(feminine)* : **she has a lot of influence on her brother** elle a beaucoup d'influence sur son frère

■ *verb*
influencer : **don't let him influence you** ne le laisse pas t'influencer.

inform [ɪn'fɔːm] *verb*
informer : **I informed him I was leaving** je l'ai informé de mon départ ; **we were informed that the plane was delayed** on nous a informés que l'avion avait du retard.

informal [ɪn'fɔːml] *adjective*

1. **décontracté** : **an informal atmosphere** une ambiance décontractée
2. **de tous les jours** : **wear informal clothes** mets tes vêtements de tous les jours
3. **familier** *(feminine* **familière)** : **an informal expression** une expression familière.

information [ˌɪnfə'meɪʃn] *uncountable noun*
renseignements *(masculine plural)* : **I'd like some information about train times** je voudrais des renseignements sur les horaires des trains ; **a piece of information** un renseignement
➤ **the information desk** le bureau des renseignements
➤ **the information highway** OR **the information superhighway** l'autoroute de l'information

> **information technology**   l'informatique *(feminine)*.

infrared [ˌɪnfrəˈred] *adjective*

infrarouge : **an infrared beam** un rayon infrarouge.

ingredient [ɪnˈɡriːdjənt] *noun*

ingrédient *(masculine)* : **mix the ingredients together in a bowl** mélangez les ingrédients dans un bol.

inhabitant [ɪnˈhæbɪtənt] *noun*

habitant *(masculine)*, habitante *(feminine)* : **our town has 100,000 inhabitants** notre ville compte 100 000 habitants.

inherit [ɪnˈherɪt] *verb*

hériter de : **he inherited some money from his great-aunt** il a hérité de l'argent de sa grand-tante.

initials [ɪˈnɪʃlz] *plural noun*

initiales *(feminine plural)* : **his initials are GWS** ses initiales sont GWS.

injection [ɪnˈdʒekʃn] *noun*

piqûre *(feminine)*, injection *(feminine)* : **the doctor gave him an injection** le médecin lui a fait une piqûre.

injure [ˈɪndʒəʳ] *verb*

blesser : **he has injured his leg** il s'est blessé à la jambe

 Le verbe anglais to injure est un faux ami, il ne signifie pas "injurier".

injured [ɪnˈdʒəd] *adjective*

blessé : **Herbert is injured** Herbert est blessé

 Injured est un faux ami, il ne signifie pas "injurié".

injury [ˈɪndʒərɪ] *(plural injuries) noun*

blessure *(feminine)* : **he has serious injuries** il a des blessures graves
> **injury time** arrêts *(masculine plural)* de jeu

 Injury est un faux ami, il ne signifie pas "injure".

ink [ɪŋk] *noun*

encre *(feminine)* : **an ink stain** une tache d'encre.

inn [ˈɪn] *noun*

auberge *(feminine)*.

innocent [ˈɪnəsənt] *adjective*

innocent : **he was found innocent** il a été déclaré innocent.

inquire [ɪnˈkwaɪəʳ] *verb*

se renseigner : **to inquire about something** se renseigner sur quelque chose ; **he inquired about the departure times** il s'est renseigné sur les horaires de départ.

inquiry [ɪnˈkwaɪrɪ] *(plural inquiries) noun*

demande *(feminine)* de renseignements : **we've had a lot of inquiries** nous avons eu de nombreuses demandes de renseignements.

insane [ɪnˈseɪn] *adjective*

fou *(feminine folle)* : **he has gone insane** il est devenu fou.

insect [ˈɪnsekt] *noun*

insecte *(masculine)*.

inside [ɪnˈsaɪd] *preposition, adverb, adjective & noun*

▣ *preposition*
à l'intérieur de : **the keys are inside the car** les clés sont à l'intérieur de la voiture ; **don't leave them outside, put them inside the house** ne les laisse pas dehors, mets-les à l'intérieur de la maison

▣ *adverb*
à l'intérieur, dedans : **I've put them inside** je les ai mis à l'intérieur
> **to come inside** OR **to go inside** rentrer : **come inside!** rentre ! ; **let's go inside** rentrons

▣ *adjective*
intérieur : **the inside pages of the book** les pages intérieures du livre

▣ *noun*
intérieur *(masculine)* : **the inside of the box** l'intérieur de la boîte
> **inside out** à l'envers : **your jumper is inside out** ton pull est à l'envers.

insist [ɪnˈsɪst] *verb*

insister : **Ann insisted on coming** Ann a insisté pour venir.

inspect [ɪnˈspekt] *verb*

examiner : **they want to inspect our passports** ils veulent examiner nos passeports.

inspector [ɪnˈspektər] *noun*

inspecteur *(masculine)*, **inspectrice** *(feminine)* : **he's a police inspector** il est inspecteur de police
➤ **a ticket inspector** un contrôleur.

inspire [ɪnˈspaɪər] *verb*

inspirer : **the music inspired me** la musique m'a inspiré.

install, instal *US* [ɪnˈstɔːl] *verb*

installer : **click on the icon to install the program** cliquez sur l'icône pour installer le programme.

instance [ˈɪnstəns] *noun*

➤ **for instance** par exemple.

instant [ˈɪnstənt] *adjective*

immédiat : **the album was an instant success** l'album a eu un succès immédiat
➤ **instant coffee** café *(masculine)* instantané.

instead [ɪnˈsted] *adverb*

plutôt, à la place : **I don't eat meat, I'll have vegetables instead** je ne mange pas de viande, je prendrai plutôt des légumes ; **I don't have any tea, do you want coffee instead?** je n'ai pas de thé, tu veux du café à la place ?
➤ **instead of** au lieu de : **instead of helping us, he got in the way** au lieu de nous aider, il nous a gênés ; **we visited two castles instead of three** nous avons visité deux châteaux au lieu de trois
➤ **instead of somebody** à la place de quelqu'un : **Jenny's going to the meeting instead of me** Jenny va à la réunion à ma place.

instructions [ɪnˈstrʌkʃnz] *plural noun*

1. instructions *(feminine plural)* : **follow my instructions** suivez mes instructions
2. mode *(masculine)* **d'emploi** : **read the instructions before you use the camera** lisez le mode d'emploi avant de vous servir de l'appareil photo.

instructor [ɪnˈstrʌktər] *noun*

moniteur *(masculine)*, **monitrice** *(feminine)* : **he's a driving instructor** il est moniteur d'auto-école.

instrument [ˈɪnstrʊmənt] *noun*

instrument *(masculine)* : **musical instruments** des instruments de musique ; **she plays an instrument** elle joue d'un instrument.

insult *verb & noun*

■ *verb* [ɪnˈsʌlt]
insulter : **he insulted his teacher** il a insulté son professeur
■ *noun* [ˈɪnsʌlt]
insulte *(feminine)* : **the crowd were shouting insults** la foule lançait des insultes.

insurance [ɪnˈʃʊərəns] *noun*

assurance *(feminine)* : **I took out some fire insurance** j'ai pris une assurance contre l'incendie
➤ **an insurance policy** une police d'assurance.

insure [ɪnˈʃʊər] *verb*

assurer : **she insured her car against theft** elle a assuré sa voiture contre le vol.

intelligent [ɪnˈtelɪdʒənt] *adjective*

intelligent : **he's an intelligent boy** c'est un garçon intelligent.

intend [ɪnˈtend] *verb*

avoir l'intention de : **I intend to go to Australia** j'ai l'intention d'aller en Australie
➤ **to be intended for** être destiné à : **that remark was intended for you** cette remarque t'était destinée.

intensive [ɪnˈtensɪv] *adjective*

intensif *(feminine* **intensive)**
➤ **in intensive care** en soins intensifs.

intercom [ˈɪntəkɒm] *noun*

Interphone® *(masculine)* : **she spoke to me on the intercom** elle m'a parlé à l'Interphone.

interest [ˈɪntrəst] *noun & verb*

■ *noun*
intérêt *(masculine)* : **it's in your own interest** c'est dans ton propre intérêt ; **what are your interests?** quels sont tes centres d'intérêt ?
➤ **to take an interest in something** s'intéresser à quelque chose : **she takes an interest in other people** elle s'intéresse aux autres
➤ **to lose interest in something** se désintéresser de quelque chose
■ *verb*
intéresser : **archeology really interests me** l'archéologie m'intéresse beaucoup.

interested ['ɪntrəstɪd] *adjective*

> **to be interested in** s'intéresser à : **Toby is interested in motorbikes** Toby s'intéresse aux motos ; **I'm not interested in that** cela ne m'intéresse pas.

interesting ['ɪntrəstɪŋ] *adjective*

intéressant : **he led an interesting life** il a mené une vie intéressante.

interfere [ˌɪntə'fɪər] *verb*

to interfere in somebody's business se mêler des affaires de quelqu'un
> **don't interfere!** ne t'en mêle pas !
> **he's always interfering** il se mêle toujours de tout.

intermediate [ˌɪntə'miːdjət] *adjective*

moyen *(feminine* **moyenne)** : **he's in the intermediate class** il est dans la classe moyenne.

internal [ɪn't3:nl] *adjective*

interne : **an internal modem** un modem interne.

international [ˌɪntə'næʃənl] *adjective*

international [*plural* **internationaux**] : **she's an international star** c'est une vedette internationale.

Internet, internet ['ɪntənet] *noun*

Internet *(masculine)* : **you'll find the information on the Internet** tu trouveras ces renseignements sur Internet
> **an Internet café** un cybercafé
> **an Internet Service Provider** un fournisseur d'accès.

interpreter [ɪn't3:prɪtər] *noun*

interprète *(masculine or feminine)* : **she's an interpreter** elle est interprète.

interrupt [ˌɪntə'rʌpt] *verb*

interrompre : **she interrupted her teacher** elle a interrompu son professeur.

interruption [ˌɪntə'rʌpʃn] *noun*

interruption *(feminine).*

intersection [ˌɪntə'sekʃn] *noun*

carrefour *(masculine)* : **turn left at the intersection** tourne à gauche au carrefour.

interval ['ɪntəvl] *noun*

1. *UK* **entracte** *(masculine)* : **there's a ten-minute interval after the first half of the**

concert il y a un entracte de dix minutes après la première partie du concert
2. **intervalle** *(masculine)* : **at regular intervals** à intervalles réguliers.

interview ['ɪntəvjuː] *noun & verb*

■ *noun*
1. **entretien** *(masculine)* : **he has a job interview** il passe un entretien professionnel
2. **interview** *(feminine)* : **an interview with Robert De Niro** une interview avec Robert De Niro
■ *verb*
1. **faire passer un entretien à** : **the boss is interviewing the last candidate** le chef fait passer un entretien au dernier candidat
2. **interviewer** : **he interviewed the President** il a interviewé le président.

into ['ɪntʊ] *preposition*
1. **dans** : **he put the book into his bag** il a mis le livre dans son sac
2. **en** : **she translated the letter into Spanish** elle a traduit la lettre en espagnol ; **he cut the cake into three pieces** il a découpé le gâteau en trois parts.

introduce [ˌɪntrə'djuːs] *verb*
1. **présenter** : **she introduced me to her mother** elle m'a présenté à sa mère ; **let me introduce you to Brian** je vous présente Brian
2. **introduire** : **he introduced a new fashion** il a introduit une nouvelle mode.

introduction [ˌɪntrə'dʌkʃn] *noun*

introduction *(feminine)* : **the book has a good introduction** ce livre a une bonne introduction.

invade [ɪn'veɪd] *verb*

envahir : **the town was invaded by tourists** la ville a été envahie par les touristes.

invasion [ɪn'veɪʒn] *noun*

invasion *(feminine)* : **the Roman invasion of Britain** l'invasion de l'Angleterre par les Romains.

invent [ɪn'vent] *verb*

inventer : **who invented the telephone?** qui a inventé le téléphone ?

invention [ɪn'venʃn] *noun*

invention *(feminine).*

inventor [ɪnˈventər] *noun*

inventeur *(masculine)*, inventrice *(feminine)*.

inverted commas *UK* [ɪnˌvɜːtɪdˈkɒməz] *plural noun*

guillemets *(masculine plural)* : **it's in inverted commas** c'est entre guillemets.

investigate [ɪnˈvestɪgeɪt] *verb*

1. enquêter : **the police are investigating** la police enquête OR la police mène l'enquête
2. enquêter sur : **they're investigating the accident** ils enquêtent sur l'accident.

investigation [ɪnˌvestɪˈgeɪʃn] *noun*

enquête *(feminine)* : **a police investigation** une enquête de police.

invisible [ɪnˈvɪzɪbl] *adjective*

invisible.

invitation [ˌɪnvɪˈteɪʃn] *noun*

invitation *(feminine)* : **an invitation to a party** une invitation à une fête ; **a wedding invitation** une invitation à un mariage.

invite [ɪnˈvaɪt] *verb*

inviter : **I invited Tara to my party** j'ai invité Tara à ma fête.

involve [ɪnˈvɒlv] *verb*

1. nécessiter : **it involves a lot of work** cela nécessite beaucoup de travail
2. concerner : **it involves us all** cela nous concerne tous
➤ **to be involved in something**
1. être impliqué dans quelque chose : **he's involved in some nasty business** il est impliqué dans une sale affaire
2. participer à quelque chose : **I'm not involved in the project** je ne participe pas au projet
➤ **she was involved in an accident** elle a eu un accident.

inwards [ˈɪnwədz], **inward** *US* [ˈɪnwəd] *adverb*

vers l'intérieur : **the door opens inwards** la porte s'ouvre vers l'intérieur.

Ireland [ˈaɪələnd] *noun*

l'Irlande *(feminine)*

In French the names of countries are used with the definite article (le, l' or la), except when they follow the preposition en:

Ireland is in Europe l'Irlande fait partie de l'Europe ; **he lives in Ireland** il vit en Irlande ; **I am going to Ireland** je vais en Irlande.

Irish [ˈaɪrɪʃ] *adjective & noun*

■ *adjective*
irlandais : **Sinead is an Irish name** Sinead est un nom irlandais
■ *noun*
irlandais *(masculine)* : **he speaks Irish** il parle irlandais
➤ **the Irish** les Irlandais

Remember not to use a capital letter for the adjective and the language in French. Only use a capital letter for the inhabitants.

iron [ˈaɪən] *noun & verb*

■ *noun*
1. (*uncountable*) fer *(masculine)* : **it's made of iron** c'est en fer ; **an iron bar** une barre de fer
2. fer *(masculine)* à repasser : **the iron is too hot** le fer à repasser est trop chaud
■ *verb*
repasser : **he's ironing his shirt** il repasse sa chemise.

ironing [ˈaɪənɪŋ] *noun*

repassage : **she's doing the ironing** elle fait le repassage
➤ **an ironing board** une planche à repasser OR une table à repasser.

irregular [ɪˈregjʊlər] *adjective*

irrégulier *(feminine* irrégulière*)* : **irregular verbs** les verbes irréguliers.

irritating [ˈɪrɪteɪtɪŋ] *adjective*

agaçant, irritant.

is [ɪz] ➤ be

David is my brother David est mon frère ; **is that your dog?** c'est ton chien ?

island [ˈaɪlənd] *noun*

île *(feminine)*.

Islamic [ɪzˈlæmɪk] *adjective*

islamique.

isle [aɪl] *noun*

île *(feminine)* : **the Isle of Wight** l'île de Wight.

isn't [ˈɪznt] = is not

she **isn't ready** elle n'est pas prête ; **it isn't raining** il ne pleut pas.

issue [ˈɪʃuː] *noun*

1. **numéro** *(masculine)* : **it's the first issue of the magazine** c'est le premier numéro du magazine

2. **question** *(feminine)* : **it's an important issue** c'est une question importante

⚠️ Le mot anglais **issue** est un faux ami, il ne signifie pas "issue".

it [ɪt] *pronoun*

1. *Subject pronoun* **il** *(masculine)*, **elle** *(feminine)*

Use **il** when 'it' stands for a masculine noun and **elle** for a feminine noun:

where's my book? – it's over there où est mon livre ? – il est là-bas ; **do you like my dress? – yes, it's lovely** tu aimes ma robe ? – oui, elle est très jolie

2. *Object pronoun* **le** *(masculine)*, **la** *(feminine)* (**l'** *before a vowel or silent 'h'*)

Use **le** when 'it' stands for a masculine noun and **la** for a feminine noun:

I've got a spare ticket, do you want it? j'ai un billet de trop, tu le veux ? ; **that's my scarf, give it to me!** c'est mon écharpe, donne-la-moi ! ; **I've lost my bag, have you seen it?** j'ai perdu mon sac, tu l'as vu ?

In tenses like the present perfect and the past perfect, the past participle agrees with the direct object pronoun. So if 'it' stands for a feminine noun, you must add an -e to the past participle:

I've got a new car, have you seen it? j'ai une nouvelle voiture, tu l'as vue ?

3. **ce** (**c'** *before a vowel*) : **it's a good film** c'est un bon film ; **it isn't easy!** ce n'est pas facile !

4. **il** : **it's raining** il pleut ; **it's hot today** il fait chaud aujourd'hui ; **what time is it?** quelle heure est-il ? ; **it's ten o'clock** il est dix heures.

IT *(abbreviation of information technology) noun*

informatique *(feminine)* : **she works in IT** elle travaille dans l'informatique.

Italian [ɪˈtæljən] *adjective & noun*

■ *adjective*

italien *(feminine* **italienne***)* : **I like Italian ice cream** j'aime les glaces italiennes

■ *noun*

1. **italien** *(masculine)* : **she speaks Italian** elle parle italien

2. **Italien** *(masculine)*, **Italienne** *(feminine)*

Remember not to use a capital letter for the adjective and the language in French. Only use a capital letter for the inhabitants.

italic [ɪˈtælɪk] *noun*

italique *(masculine)* : **in italics** en italique.

Italy [ˈɪtəlɪ] *noun*

l'Italie *(feminine)*

In French the names of countries are used with the definite article (**le, la** or **l'**), except when they follow the preposition **en**:

Italy is in southern Europe l'Italie est dans le sud de l'Europe ; **he lives in Italy** il habite en Italie ; **we're going to Italy** nous allons en Italie.

itch [ɪtʃ] *verb*

➤ **it itches** ça me démange : **my arm itches** mon bras me démange

➤ **I itch all over** j'ai des démangeaisons partout.

itchy [ˈɪtʃɪ] *adjective*

➤ **I have an itchy nose** j'ai le nez qui me démange

➤ **I'm itchy** j'ai des démangeaisons.

it'd [ˈɪtəd]

1. = it had : **it'd stopped raining** il s'était arrêté de pleuvoir

2. = it would : **it'd be nice if you could come** ce serait sympa si tu pouvais venir.

it'll [ɪtl] = it will

it'll be all right tomorrow ça ira bien demain.

its [ɪts] *adjective*

son *(feminine* **sa***)* [*plural* **ses**]

In French the possessive adjective agrees in gender (masculine or feminine) and number (singular or plural) with the noun that follows:

put the camera back in its case remets l'appareil photo dans son étui ; **the dog gave me its paw** le chien m'a donné sa patte.

it's [ɪts]

1. = it is : **it's my turn to play** c'est à moi de jouer ; **it's raining** il pleut
2. = it has : **it's stopped raining** il s'est arrêté de pleuvoir.

itself [ɪt'self] *pronoun*

1. **se** (s' *before a vowel*) : **the cat is washing itself** le chat se lave ; **the dog has hurt itself** le chien s'est fait mal
2. **lui-même** (*feminine* **elle-même**) : **the town itself is not very big** la ville elle-même n'est pas très grande
➤ **by itself** tout seul : **the door closed by itself** la porte s'est fermée toute seule.

I've [aɪv] = I have

I've decided to leave j'ai décidé de partir ; **I've got two sisters** j'ai deux sœurs.

ivory ['aɪvərɪ] *noun*

ivoire (*masculine*) : **it's made of ivory** c'est en ivoire.

ivy ['aɪvɪ] *noun*

lierre (*masculine*).

jacket ['dʒækɪt] *noun*

veste (*feminine*) : **he's wearing a leather jacket** il porte une veste en cuir
➤ **a jacket potato** une pomme de terre en robe des champs OR une pomme de terre en robe de chambre.

jack-o'-lantern ['dʒækəʊ'læntən] *noun*

1. *lanterne confectionnée à partir d'une citrouille évidée dans laquelle on creuse un visage*
➤ Halloween.

jackpot ['dʒækpɒt] *noun*

gros lot (*masculine*) : **Nasa won the jackpot** Nasa a gagné le gros lot.

jail [dʒeɪl] *noun & verb*

■ *noun*
prison (*feminine*) : **they sent him to jail** ils l'ont mis en prison
■ *verb*
emprisonner : **he was jailed for two years** il a été emprisonné pendant deux ans.

jam [dʒæm] *noun*

1. **confiture** (*feminine*) : **raspberry jam** confiture de framboises
2. **embouteillage** (*masculine*) : **a traffic jam** un embouteillage
➤ **to be in a jam** être dans le pétrin.

Jamaica [dʒə'meɪkə] *noun*

la Jamaïque : **he lives in Jamaica** il habite en Jamaïque

> In French the names of countries are used with the definite article (**le, la,** or **l'**).

Jamaican [dʒə'meɪkn] *adjective & noun*

■ *adjective*
jamaïcain

> The French adjective does not start with a capital letter.

■ *noun*
Jamaïcain (*masculine*), **Jamaïcaine** (*feminine*).

jammed [dʒæmd] *adjective*

bloqué, coincé : **the drawer's jammed** le tiroir est bloqué.

janitor US ['dʒænɪtəʳ] *noun*

concierge (*masculine or feminine*) : **Mr Freeman is a janitor** M. Freeman est concierge.

January ['dʒænjʊərɪ] *noun*

janvier : **in January** en janvier ; **next Janu-**

ary en janvier prochain ; **last January** en janvier dernier

> In French the months of the year do not start with a capital letter.

Japan [dʒə'pæn] *noun*

le Japon

> In French the names of countries are used with the definite article (**le, la** or **l'**). Remember that the French preposition **à** combines with **le** to become **au**:

Japan consists of four islands le Japon est constitué de quatre îles ; **Nigel lives in Japan** Nigel vit au Japon ; **she's going to Japan** elle va au Japon.

Japanese [ˌdʒæpə'niːz] *adjective & noun*

■ *adjective*
japonais : **I like Japanese cooking** j'aime la cuisine japonaise
■ *noun*
japonais *(masculine)* : **they speak Japanese** ils parlent japonais
➤ **the Japanese** les Japonais

> Remember not to use a capital letter for the adjective and the language in French. Only use a capital letter for the inhabitants.

jar [dʒɑːʳ] *noun*

pot *(masculine)* : **a jar of jam** un pot de confiture.

jaw [dʒɔː] *noun*

mâchoire *(feminine)* : **Dan has a square jaw** Dan a une mâchoire carrée.

jazz [dʒæz] *noun*

jazz *(masculine)* : **a jazz band** un orchestre de jazz.

jealous ['dʒeləs] *adjective*

jaloux *(feminine* **jalouse***)*.

jeans [dʒiːnz] *plural noun*

jean *(masculine)* : **a pair of jeans** un jean ; **he's wearing jeans** il porte un jean.

jelly *UK* ['dʒelɪ], **Jell-O**® *US* ['dʒeləʊ] *noun*

gelée *(feminine)* : **the children had jelly for dessert** les enfants ont mangé de la gelée en dessert.

jellyfish ['dʒelɪfɪʃ] *(plural* jellyfish*)* *noun*

méduse *(feminine)*.

jersey ['dʒɜːzɪ] *noun*

pull *(masculine)* : **she's wearing a red jersey** elle porte un pull rouge.

jet [dʒet] *noun*

jet *(masculine)* : **she took a jet to America** elle a pris un jet pour aller en Amérique
➤ **jet lag** *fatigue due au décalage horaire* : **he's suffering from jet lag** il est fatigué à cause du décalage horaire.

Jew [dʒuː] *noun*

Juif *(masculine)*, **Juive** *(feminine)*.

jewel ['dʒuːəl] *noun*

bijou *(masculine)* [*plural* **bijoux**].

jeweller *UK*, **jeweler** *US* ['dʒuːələʳ] *noun*

bijoutier *(masculine)*, **bijoutière** *(feminine)*
➤ **the jeweller's** *UK* OR **the jeweler's** *US* la bijouterie.

jewellery *UK*, **jewelry** *US* ['dʒuːəlrɪ] *noun*

bijoux *(masculine plural)* : **Lady Bagshot has a lot of jewellery** Lady Bagshot a beaucoup de bijoux ; **gold jewellery** des bijoux en or.

Jewish ['dʒuːɪʃ] *adjective*

juif *(feminine* **juive***)*

> The French adjective does not start with a capital letter.

jigsaw ['dʒɪgsɔː], **jigsaw puzzle** ['dʒɪgsɔː'pʌzl] *noun*
puzzle *(masculine)* : **he's doing a jigsaw puzzle** il fait un puzzle.

job [dʒɒb] *noun*

1. **emploi** *(masculine)* : **he has a job in a bookshop** il a un emploi dans une librairie
2. **travail** *(masculine)*, **tâche** *(feminine)* : **you've done a good job** tu as fait du bon travail.

jobless ['dʒɒblɪs] *adjective*

au chômage : **he's jobless** il est au chômage.

jog [dʒɒg] *(past tense & past participle* jogged*)* *verb*

1. **faire du jogging** : **I jog once a week** je fais du jogging une fois par semaine

2. pousser : he jogged my elbow il m'a poussé le coude.

jogging ['dʒɒgɪŋ] *noun*

jogging *(masculine)* **:** I go jogging every day je fais du jogging tous les jours.

join [dʒɔɪn] *verb*

1. **joindre :** you have to join the two ends together il faut joindre les deux bouts
2. **rejoindre :** go ahead and I'll join you later vas-y, je te rejoindrai plus tard
3. **se joindre à :** can I join you? je peux me joindre à vous ?
4. **relier :** join the dots to make a picture relie les points pour faire un dessin
5. **s'inscrire à :** Sally joined the judo club Sally s'est inscrite au club de judo
➤ **to join the army** s'engager dans l'armée
➤ **to join the queue** *UK* faire la queue

join in *phrasal verb*

1. **participer :** Clive wanted to join in Clive voulait participer
2. **participer à :** everyone joined in the conversation tout le monde a participé à la conversation.

joint [dʒɔɪnt] *noun & adjective*

■ *noun*
1. **articulation** *(feminine)* **:** my joints ache in the winter mes articulations me font mal en hiver
2. *UK* **rôti** *(masculine)* **:** we always have a joint for Sunday lunch nous mangeons toujours un rôti le dimanche midi
■ *adjective*
commun, joint : they have a joint account ils ont un compte commun OR ils ont un compte joint.

joke [dʒəʊk] *noun & verb*

■ *noun*
plaisanterie *(feminine)*, **blague** *(feminine)* **:** he told us a joke il nous a raconté une plaisanterie ; they played a joke on Simon ils ont fait une blague à Simon
■ *verb*
plaisanter, blaguer : are you joking? tu plaisantes ?

journalist ['dʒɜːnəlɪst] *noun*

journaliste *(masculine or feminine)* **:** she's a journalist elle est journaliste.

journey ['dʒɜːnɪ] *noun*

1. **voyage** *(masculine)* **:** they went on a long journey ils ont fait un long voyage
2. **trajet** *(masculine)* **:** the journey to school le trajet jusqu'à l'école ; it's an hour's journey on the bus c'est une heure de trajet en bus

> ⚠ **Journey** est un faux ami, il ne signifie pas "journée".

joy [dʒɔɪ] *noun*

joie *(feminine)* **:** the children are jumping for joy les enfants sautent de joie.

joystick ['dʒɔɪstɪk] *noun*

joystick *(masculine)*.

judge [dʒʌdʒ] *noun & verb*

■ *noun*
juge *(masculine)* **:** he's a judge il est juge
■ *verb*
juger : the defendent will be judged tomorrow l'accusé sera jugé demain.

judo ['dʒuːdəʊ] *noun*

judo *(masculine)* **:** he does judo il fait du judo.

jug *UK* [dʒʌg] *noun*

pot *(masculine)* **:** a jug of milk un pot de lait.

juggle ['dʒʌgl] *verb*

jongler : do you know how to juggle? tu sais jongler ?

juice [dʒuːs] *noun*

jus *(masculine)* **:** an orange juice un jus d'orange.

juicy ['dʒuːsɪ] *adjective*

juteux *(feminine* **juteuse)** **:** a juicy orange une orange juteuse.

July [dʒuːˈlaɪ] *noun*

juillet : in July en juillet ; next July en juillet prochain ; last July en juillet dernier

> In French the months of the year do not start with a capital letter.

jumble sale *UK* ['dʒʌmblseɪl] *noun*

vente de charité où sont vendus des articles d'occasion.

jumbo jet ['dʒʌmbəʊdʒet] *noun*

jumbo-jet *(masculine)*, **gros-porteur** *(masculine)* [*plural* **gros-porteurs**].

jump [dʒʌmp] *noun & verb*

■ *noun*

saut *(masculine)* : **the high jump** le saut en hauteur

■ *verb*

1. sauter : **he jumped over the hedge** il a sauté par-dessus la haie ; **she jumped out of the window** elle a sauté par la fenêtre

2. sursauter : **you made me jump** tu m'as fait sursauter.

jumper *UK* ['dʒʌmpəʳ] *noun*

pull *(masculine)* : **he's wearing a blue jumper** il porte un pull bleu.

June [dʒuːn] *noun*

juin : **in June** en juin ; **next June** en juin prochain ; **last June** en juin dernier

> In French the months of the year do not start with a capital letter.

jungle ['dʒʌŋgl] *noun*

jungle *(feminine)* : **these animals live in the jungle** ces animaux vivent dans la jungle.

junior ['dʒuːnjəʳ] *adjective & noun*

■ *adjective*

1. subalterne : **he's a junior employee** c'est un employé subalterne

2. junior : **the junior tennis championship** le championnat de tennis junior

■ *noun*

UK écolier *(masculine)*, écolière *(feminine)* (entre 7 et 11 ans)

➤ **junior school** *UK* école primaire pour les élèves âgés de 7 à 11 ans

➤ **junior high school** *US* dernières années de collège, pour les élèves âgés de 12 à 14 ans.

junk [dʒʌŋk] *uncountable noun*

1. bric-à-brac *(masculine)* : **the house is full of junk** la maison est remplie de bric-à-brac

2. *informal* camelote *(feminine)* : **it's a piece of junk!** c'est de la camelote !

➤ **junk food** nourriture *(feminine)* de mauvaise qualité

➤ **a junk shop** un magasin de brocante.

Jupiter ['dʒuːpɪtəʳ] *noun*

Jupiter *(feminine)* : **Jupiter is the biggest planet in the solar system** Jupiter est la plus grosse planète du système solaire.

jury ['dʒʊərɪ] *(plural* juries*) noun*

jury *(masculine)* : **Mrs Davies is on the jury** Mme Davies fait partie du jury.

just [dʒʌst] *adverb*

1. juste : **it happened just after midnight** ça s'est passé juste après minuit ; **the shop's just after the church** le magasin est juste après l'église ; **we have just enough time** on a juste assez de temps ; **you're just in time!** tu arrives juste à temps ! ; **I'll just have a cup of tea** je prendrai juste une tasse de thé

2. ne ... que : **she's just seven** elle a seulement sept ans OR elle n'a que sept ans ; **just add water** tu n'as qu'à ajouter de l'eau

3. un peu : **I have just over twenty dollars** j'ai un peu plus de vingt dollars

➤ **he just passed his exam** il a réussi son examen de justesse

➤ **to have just done something** venir de faire quelque chose : **he has just left** il vient de partir

➤ **I was just about to leave** j'allais juste partir OR j'étais sur le point de partir

➤ **it's just about ready** c'est presque prêt

➤ **just a minute!** un instant !

justice ['dʒʌstɪs] *noun*

justice *(feminine)*.

kangaroo [ˌkæŋgə'ruː] *noun*

kangourou *(masculine)*.

karate [kə'rɑːtɪ] *noun*

karaté *(masculine)* : **he does karate** il fait du karaté.

kebab [kɪˈbæb] *noun*

brochette *(feminine)* : **lamb kebabs** des brochettes d'agneau
➤ **a doner kebab** un sandwich grec.

keen [kiːn] *adjective*

enthousiaste : **she isn't very keen** elle n'est pas très enthousiaste
➤ **to be keen on something** aimer beaucoup quelque chose : **Alex isn't very keen on rugby** Alex n'aime pas beaucoup le rugby
➤ **to be keen to do something** avoir très envie de faire quelque chose : **I'm keen to see the new film** j'ai très envie de voir le nouveau film.

keep [kiːp] (*past tense & past participle* kept) *verb*

1. **garder** : **keep the change** gardez la monnaie ; **can you keep a secret?** tu sais garder un secret ?
2. **rester** : **we must keep calm** nous devons rester calmes
3. **tenir** : **he kept his promise** il a tenu sa promesse ; **she keeps a diary** elle tient un journal intime
4. **élever** : **they keep chickens** ils élèvent des poules
➤ **to keep doing** OR **to keep on doing**
1. **continuer à faire** : **I kept on working** j'ai continué à travailler
2. **ne pas arrêter de faire** : **she keeps phoning me** elle n'arrête pas de m'appeler
➤ **to keep somebody from doing something** empêcher quelqu'un de faire quelque chose : **nothing will keep me from going** rien ne m'empêchera d'y aller
➤ **to keep somebody waiting** faire attendre quelqu'un : **I'm sorry to keep you waiting** je suis désolé de vous avoir fait attendre
➤ **to keep fit** se maintenir en forme
➤ **to keep quiet** garder le silence : **they kept quiet** ils ont gardé le silence
➤ **keep quiet!** taisez-vous !

keep off *phrasal verb*

'keep off the grass' 'il est interdit de marcher sur la pelouse'

keep out *phrasal verb*

'keep out!' 'défense d'entrer !'

keep up *phrasal verb*

suivre : **don't go so fast, I can't keep up** ne va pas si vite, je n'arrive pas à suivre ; **he**

managed to keep up with the rest of the class il est arrivé à suivre le reste de la classe.

keep-fit *UK* [ˈkiːpfɪt] *noun*

gymnastique *(feminine)* : **she does a lot of keep-fit** elle fait beaucoup de gymnastique ; **keep-fit classes** des cours de gymnastique.

kennel *UK* [ˈkenl] *noun*

niche *(feminine)* : **the dog is in its kennel** le chien est dans sa niche.

kept [kept] *past tense & past participle of* keep

he kept on talking il a continué de parler ; **she has kept my pen** elle a gardé mon stylo.

kerb *UK* [kɜːb] *noun*

bord *(masculine)* **du trottoir.**

ketchup [ˈketʃəp], **catsup** *US* [ˈkætsəp]
uncountable noun
ketchup *(masculine)* : **do you want some ketchup?** tu veux du ketchup ?

kettle [ˈketl] *noun*

bouilloire *(feminine)* : **an electric kettle** une bouilloire électrique
➤ **I'll put the kettle on** je vais mettre l'eau à chauffer.

key [kiː] *noun*

1. **clé** *(feminine)* : **I've lost my keys** j'ai perdu mes clés
2. **touche** *(feminine)* : **the computer keys are dirty** les touches de l'ordinateur sont sales
➤ **a key-ring** un porte-clés.

keyboard [ˈkiːbɔːd] *noun*

clavier *(masculine)* : **we need a new keyboard for the computer** on a besoin d'un nouveau clavier pour l'ordinateur.

keyhole [ˈkiːhəʊl] *noun*

trou *(masculine)* **de serrure** : **she was looking through the keyhole** elle regardait par le trou de la serrure.

keypad [ˈkiːpæd] *noun*

pavé *(masculine)* **numérique.**

khaki [ˈkɑːkɪ] *adjective*

kaki *(invariable)* : **he's wearing khaki shorts** il porte un short kaki.

kick [kɪk] *noun & verb*

■ *noun*
coup *(masculine)* de pied : **he gave me a kick** il m'a donné un coup de pied

■ *verb*
1. donner un coup de pied à : **he kicked me** il m'a donné un coup de pied
2. donner un coup de pied dans : **she kicked the ball** elle a donné un coup de pied dans la balle
3. donner des coups de pied : **stop kicking!** arrête de donner des coups de pied !

kid [kɪd] *noun & verb informal*

■ *noun*
gosse *(masculine or feminine)* : **they have four kids** ils ont quatre gosses ; **he's my kid brother** c'est mon petit frère

■ *verb*
plaisanter : **I'm only kidding!** je plaisante !

kidnap ['kɪdnæp] *(past tense & past participle* kidnapped) *verb*
kidnapper.

kidney ['kɪdnɪ] *noun*
1. rein *(masculine)* : **a kidney disease** une maladie des reins
2. rognon *(masculine)* : **steak and kidney pie** tourte au bœuf et aux rognons
➤ **kidney beans** haricots rouges.

kill [kɪl] *verb*
tuer : **he was killed by a lion** il a été tué par un lion.

kilo ['kiːləʊ] *(abbreviation of* kilogram) *noun*
kilo *(masculine)* : **it costs £2 a kilo** ça coûte 2 livres le kilo.

kilogram , kilogramme *UK* ['kɪləgræm] *noun*
kilogramme *(masculine)*.

kilometre *UK* ['kɪləˌmiːtər], **kilometer** *US* [kɪˈlɒmɪtər] *noun*
kilomètre *(masculine)* : **they're driving at fifty kilometres an hour** ils roulent à cinquante kilomètres à l'heure.

kind [kaɪnd] *adjective & noun*

■ *adjective*
gentil *(feminine* gentille*)* : **she's always kind to me** elle est toujours gentille avec moi

■ *noun*
sorte *(feminine)*, genre *(masculine)* : **it's a kind of bird** c'est une sorte d'oiseau ; **I like all kinds of music** j'aime toutes sortes de musiques ; **I don't like this kind of film** je n'aime pas ce genre de film
➤ **what kind of plant is it?** qu'est-ce que c'est comme plante ?

kindergarten ['kɪndəˌgɑːtn] *noun*
jardin *(masculine)* d'enfants : **she goes to kindergarten** elle va au jardin d'enfants.

kindness ['kaɪndnɪs] *noun*
gentillesse *(feminine)* : **thank you for all your kindness** merci de votre gentillesse.

king [kɪŋ] *noun*
roi *(masculine)* : **King Harold** le roi Harold ; **he lives like a king** il vit comme un roi.

kingdom ['kɪŋdəm] *noun*
1. royaume *(masculine)* : **the United Kingdom** le Royaume-Uni
2. règne : **the animal kingdom** le règne animal.

kiosk ['kiːɒsk] *noun*
kiosque *(masculine)* : **I bought a newspaper from the kiosk** j'ai acheté un journal au kiosque.

kiss [kɪs] *noun & verb*

■ *noun*
baiser *(masculine)* : **she gave her father a kiss** elle a donné un baiser à son père
➤ **love and kisses** grosses bises

■ *verb*
1. embrasser : **she kissed me on the cheek** elle m'a embrassé sur la joue
2. s'embrasser : **they kissed and said goodbye** ils se sont embrassés et se sont dit au revoir.

kit [kɪt] *noun*
1. trousse *(feminine)* : **a first-aid kit** une trousse de secours ; **a tool kit** une trousse à outils
2. *UK* affaires *(feminine plural)* : **I left my football kit in the classroom** j'ai oublié mes affaires de football dans la classe
➤ **a drum kit** *UK* une batterie.

kitchen ['kɪtʃɪn] *noun*
cuisine *(feminine)* : **he's in the kitchen making dinner** il prépare le dîner dans la cuisine.

k

kite [kaɪt] *noun*

cerf-volant *(masculine)* [*plural* **cerfs-volants**] : she's flying a kite elle fait voler un cerf-volant.

kitten ['kɪtn] *noun*

chaton *(masculine)*.

knee [niː] *noun*

genou *(masculine)* [*plural* **genoux**] : she's sitting on his knee elle est assise sur ses genoux ; he was on his knees il était à genoux.

kneel [niːl] (*past tense & past participle* knelt [nelt] OR kneeled [niːld]) *verb*

se mettre à genoux, s'agenouiller : he knelt down il s'est mis à genoux OR il s'est agenouillé ; he was kneeling il était à genoux.

knelt *past tense & past participle of* kneel.

knew [njuː] *past tense of* know

I knew you were right je savais que tu avais raison.

knickers *UK* ['nɪkəz] *plural noun*

culotte *(feminine)* : a pair of green knickers une culotte verte.

knife [naɪf] (*plural* knives [naɪvz]) *noun*

couteau *(masculine)* [*plural* **couteaux**] : a bread knife un couteau à pain.

knight [naɪt] *noun*

1. chevalier *(masculine)* : the Knights of the Round Table les chevaliers de la Table ronde
2. cavalier *(masculine)* : the knight is a piece used in a game of chess le cavalier est une pièce du jeu d'échecs.

knit [nɪt] (*past tense & past participle* knitted) *verb*

tricoter : I knitted a scarf j'ai tricoté une écharpe.

knitting ['nɪtɪŋ] *noun*

tricot *(masculine)* : she does a lot of knitting elle fait beaucoup de tricot
➤ a knitting needle une aiguille à tricoter.

knives *plural of* knife.

knob [nɒb] *noun*

bouton *(masculine)* : a door knob un bouton de porte ; turn the knob to the right tourne le bouton à droite.

knock [nɒk] *noun & verb*

■ *noun*

coup *(masculine)* : give two knocks on the door frappe deux coups à la porte ; I heard a knock at the door j'ai entendu frapper à la porte

■ *verb*

1. frapper : somebody's knocking at the door on frappe à la porte
2. cogner : I knocked my head on the shelf je me suis cogné la tête contre l'étagère
3. enfoncer : he knocked the nail into the wall il a enfoncé le clou dans le mur

knock down *phrasal verb*

renverser : he was knocked down by a car il s'est fait renverser par une voiture

knock out *phrasal verb*

1. assommer : the thief knocked out the guard le voleur a assommé le gardien
2. éliminer : England knocked France out of the tournament l'Angleterre a éliminé la France du tournoi

knock over *phrasal verb*

renverser : I knocked the glass over j'ai renversé le verre.

knot [nɒt] *noun*

nœud *(masculine)* : he tied a knot in the string il a fait un nœud à la ficelle.

know [nəʊ] (*past tense* knew, *past participle* known) *verb*

1. savoir : I know you're right je sais que tu as raison ; he's left – yes, I know il est parti – oui, je sais ; I don't know where he is je ne sais pas où il est ; do you know how to swim? tu sais nager ? ; she doesn't know any English elle ne parle pas un mot d'anglais
2. connaître : do you know Vanessa? tu connais Vanessa ? ; I'm getting to know him je commence à mieux le connaître ; I don't know London very well je ne connais pas très bien Londres

know about *phrasal verb*

1. être au courant de : do you know about the accident? tu es au courant de l'accident ?
2. s'y connaître en : he knows all about computers il s'y connaît en informatique.

know-how ['nəʊhaʊ] *noun*

savoir-faire *(masculine)* : he doesn't have the know-how il n'a pas le savoir-faire.

knowledge ['nɒlɪdʒ] *uncountable noun*

connaissances *(feminine plural)* : **she has a good knowledge of English** elle a de bonnes connaissances en anglais.

known [nəʊn] *past participle of* know

I've known him for years je le connais depuis des années.

lab [læb] *noun informal*

labo *(masculine)* : **a language lab** un laboratoire de langues.

label ['leɪbl] *noun*

étiquette *(feminine)* : **she put a label on her suitcase** elle a mis une étiquette sur sa valise.

labor *US* ['leɪbəʳ] ➤ labour

➤ **Labor Day** la fête du travail
➤ **a labor union** un syndicat

    LABOR DAY
La fête du travail aux États-Unis, **Labor Day**, est célébrée le premier lundi de septembre. C'est un jour férié, qui permet aux Américains de profiter d'un dernier long week-end avant la rentrée scolaire.

laboratory [*UK* lə'bɒrətrɪ, *US* 'læbrə.tɔːrɪ] *(plural* **laboratories***) noun*

laboratoire *(masculine)*.

labour *UK*, **labor** *US* ['leɪbəʳ] *noun*

1. **travail** *(masculine)* : **a labour of love** un travail que l'on fait pour le plaisir
2. **main-d'œuvre** *(feminine)* : **skilled labour** main-d'œuvre qualifiée
➤ **the Labour party** le parti travailliste
   ➤ Political Parties.

lace [leɪs] *noun*

1. **lacet** *(masculine)* : **he tied his laces** il a noué ses lacets
2. **dentelle** *(feminine)* : **a lace tablecloth** une nappe en dentelle.

lack [læk] *noun & verb*

■ *noun*
manque *(masculine)* : **through lack of experience** par manque d'expérience
■ *verb*
manquer de : **she lacks confidence** elle manque d'assurance.

ladder ['lædəʳ] *noun*

échelle *(feminine)* : **she climbed up the ladder** elle est montée sur l'échelle.

lady ['leɪdɪ] *(plural* **ladies***) noun*

dame *(feminine)* : **there's a lady waiting to see you** il y a une dame qui vous attend ; **ladies' clothes** des vêtements pour dames
➤ **Ladies and Gentlemen!** Mesdames, Messieurs !
➤ **the ladies** *UK* OR **the ladies' room** *US* les toilettes pour dames : **where is the ladies?** où sont les toilettes pour dames ?

ladybird *UK* ['leɪdɪbɜːd], **ladybug** *US* ['leɪdɪbʌg] *noun*
coccinelle *(feminine)*.

lager ['lɑːgəʳ] *noun*

bière *(feminine)* **blonde**.

laid [leɪd] *past tense & past participle of* lay

the bird laid an egg l'oiseau a pondu un œuf ; **she hasn't laid the table yet** elle n'a pas encore mis la table.

laid-back ['leɪdbæk] *adjective informal*

relax *(invariable)* : **people are very laid-back in California** les gens sont très relax en Californie.

lain [leɪn] *past participle of* lie

he has lain in bed all day il est resté au lit toute la journée.

lake [leɪk] *noun*

lac *(masculine)* : **Lake Victoria** le lac Victoria.

lamb [læm] *noun*

agneau *(masculine)* [*plural* **agneaux**] : **they had roast lamb for lunch** ils ont mangé de l'agneau rôti à midi.

lame [leɪm] *adjective*

boiteux *(feminine* **boiteuse)* **:** his horse is lame son cheval boite.

lamp [læmp] *noun*

lampe *(feminine)* **:** she put the lamp on elle a allumé la lampe.

lamppost ['læmppəʊst] *noun*

réverbère *(masculine)*.

lampshade ['læmpʃeɪd] *noun*

abat-jour *(masculine)* [*plural* **abat-jour**].

land [lænd] *noun & verb*

▪ *noun*
terre *(feminine)* **:** this land is very fertile cette terre est très fertile ; **they reached land** ils ont touché terre
➤ **a piece of land** un terrain
▪ *verb*
atterrir : the plane lands at 6 o'clock l'avion atterrit à 6 heures.

landing ['lændɪŋ] *noun*

1. **palier** *(masculine)* **:** the bathroom is on the landing la salle de bains est sur le palier
2. **atterrissage** *(masculine)* **:** the pilot made an emergency landing le pilote a fait un atterrissage d'urgence
➤ **a landing card** une carte d'embarquement.

landlady ['lænd,leɪdɪ] *(plural* landladies ['lænd,leɪdɪz]) *noun*
propriétaire *(feminine)*.

landlord ['lændlɔːd] *noun*
propriétaire *(masculine)*.

landscape ['lændskeɪp] *noun*
paysage *(masculine)* **:** the fields and woods of the English landscape les champs et les bois du paysage anglais.

lane [leɪn] *noun*

1. **chemin** *(masculine)* **:** a country lane un chemin de campagne
2. **voie** *(feminine)* **:** this motorway has four lanes cette autoroute a quatre voies.

language ['læŋgwɪdʒ] *noun*

1. **langue** *(feminine)* **:** can you speak a foreign language? tu sais parler une langue étrangère ? ; **he wants to be a language teacher** il veut être professeur de langues

2. **langage** *(masculine)* **:** legal language langage juridique
➤ **a language laboratory** un laboratoire de langues.

lap [læp] *noun*

1. **genoux** *(masculine plural)* **:** the baby is sitting on her lap le bébé est assis sur ses genoux
2. **tour** *(masculine)* **de piste :** the runners did two laps les coureurs ont fait deux tours de piste.

laptop ['læptɒp] *noun*
portable *(masculine)* **:** a laptop computer un ordinateur portable.

large [lɑːdʒ] *adjective*

1. **grand :** London is a very large city Londres est une très grande ville ; **he has a large fortune** il a une grande fortune
2. **gros** *(feminine* **grosse) :** a large book un gros livre ; **they have a large dog** ils ont un gros chien

 Le mot anglais large est un faux ami, il ne signifie pas "large".

lark [lɑːk] *noun*
alouette *(feminine)*.

laser ['leɪzər] *noun*
laser *(masculine)* **:** a laser beam un rayon laser.

last [*UK* lɑːst, *US* læst] *adjective, adverb, noun & verb*

▪ *adjective*
dernier *(feminine* **dernière) :** that's the last time I listen to you! c'est la dernière fois que je t'écoute ! ; **it happened last week** ça s'est passé la semaine dernière ; **Greg arrived last Tuesday** Greg est arrivé mardi dernier
➤ **last name** nom *(masculine)* de famille : what is your last name? quel est votre nom de famille ?
➤ **last night**
1. **hier soir :** I saw him last night je l'ai vu hier soir
2. **la nuit dernière :** I had a bad dream last night j'ai fait un mauvais rêve la nuit dernière
▪ *adverb*
1. **en dernier :** she came last elle est arrivée en dernier OR elle est arrivée la dernière
2. **pour la dernière fois :** I last met her in Paris je l'ai rencontrée pour la dernière fois à Paris

➤ **at last** enfin : **we're home at last** nous sommes enfin à la maison
▪ *noun*
dernier *(masculine)*, **dernière** *(feminine)* : **he's the last in the class** c'est le dernier de la classe ; **they were the last to leave** ils étaient les derniers à partir
➤ **the year before last** il y a deux ans
➤ **the last but one** l'avant-dernier, l'avant-dernière
▪ *verb*
durer : **the film lasted two hours** le film a duré deux heures.

late [leɪt] *adjective & adverb*
1. **en retard** : **I'm sorry I'm late** je suis désolé d'être en retard ; **he arrived late** il est arrivé en retard ; **he was an hour late** il avait une heure de retard OR il était en retard d'une heure ; **the train's late** le train a du retard
2. **tard** : **I went to bed late** je me suis couché tard ; **it's too late** c'est trop tard
➤ **in the late afternoon** en fin d'après-midi : **in late June** fin juin.

lately ['leɪtlɪ] *adverb*
récemment, ces derniers temps : **have you seen him lately?** tu l'as vu ces derniers temps ?

later ['leɪtər] *(comparative of* **late***) adverb*
plus tard : **I'll do it later** je le ferai plus tard ; **I'll see you later!** à plus tard !

latest ['leɪtɪst] *(superlative of* **late***) adjective*
dernier *(feminine* **dernière***)* : **here is the latest news** voici les dernières nouvelles
➤ **at the latest** au plus tard : **it will be ready by tomorrow at the latest** ce sera prêt demain au plus tard.

Latin ['lætɪn] *adjective & noun*
▪ *adjective*
latin
▪ *noun*
latin *(masculine)* : **he's studying Latin** il fait des études de latin
➤ **Latin America** l'Amérique latine : **Peru is in Latin America** le Pérou est en Amérique latine
➤ **Latin American** latino-américain, latino-américaine

> Note that in French the adjective and the language do not start with a capital letter.

laugh [*UK* lɑːf, *US* læf] *noun & verb*
▪ *noun*
rire *(masculine)*
➤ **for a laugh** pour rire OR pour rigoler : **we did it for a laugh** nous l'avons fait pour rigoler
➤ **to have a good laugh** bien rigoler
▪ *verb*
rire : **the audience was laughing** le public riait ; **she burst out laughing** elle a éclaté de rire

laugh at *phrasal verb*
se moquer de : **he was laughing at me** il se moquait de moi.

laughter [*UK* 'lɑːftər, *US* 'læftər] *uncountable noun*
rire *(masculine)*, **rires** *(masculine plural)* : **I can hear laughter** j'entends des rires.

launderette *UK* [lɔːn'dret], **Laundromat®** *US* ['lɔːndrəmæt] *noun*
laverie *(feminine)*.

laundry ['lɔːndrɪ] *uncountable noun*
1. **linge** *(masculine)* : **put the laundry in the basket** mets le linge dans le panier
2. **blanchisserie** *(feminine)* : **there's a laundry next door** il y a une blanchisserie à côté
➤ **to do the laundry** faire la lessive.

lavatory ['lævətrɪ] *(plural* **lavatories***) noun*
toilettes *(feminine plural)* : **where is the lavatory?** où sont les toilettes ?

lavender ['lævəndər] *noun*
lavande *(feminine)*.

law [lɔː] *noun*
1. **loi** *(feminine)* : **we must obey the law** il faut obéir à la loi ; **to break the law** enfreindre la loi
2. **droit** *(masculine)* : **he's studying law** il fait des études de droit
➤ **it's against the law** c'est illégal
➤ **law and order** l'ordre public.

lawn [lɔːn] *noun*
pelouse *(feminine)*, **gazon** *(masculine)* : **she's mowing the lawn** elle tond la pelouse.

lawnmower ['lɔːnˌməʊər] *noun*
tondeuse *(feminine)* **à gazon**.

lawyer ['lɔ:jəʳ] *noun*

avocat *(masculine)*, avocate *(feminine)* :
Cheryl's a lawyer Cheryl est avocate.

lay [leɪ] *verb & verb form*

- *verb (past tense & past participle* laid*)*
poser, mettre : he laid his hand on my
shoulder il a posé sa main sur mon épaule OR
il a mis sa main sur mon épaule
- ➤ to lay the table *UK* mettre la table : can
you lay the table? tu peux mettre la table ?
- ➤ to lay an egg pondre un œuf : the hen laid
an egg la poule a pondu un œuf
- *past tense of* lie
he lay down on the bed il s'est allongé sur le
lit.

layer ['leɪəʳ] *noun*

couche *(feminine)* : there's a thick layer of
snow on the roof il y a une épaisse couche de
neige sur le toit.

lazy ['leɪzɪ] *adjective*

paresseux *(feminine* paresseuse*)* : Arthur's
very lazy Arthur est très paresseux.

lead *verb, noun & adjective*

- *verb* [li:d] *(past tense & past participle* led*)*
1. mener : this path leads to the village ce
chemin mène au village ; France is leading 3
goals to 2 la France mène par 3 buts à 2 ; he
leads a busy life il mène une vie active
2. conduire : she led us into the house elle
nous a conduits dans la maison
- ➤ to lead the way montrer le chemin
- *noun*
1. [li:d] *UK* laisse *(feminine)* : you must keep
your dog on a lead vous devez tenir votre
chien en laisse
2. [li:d] to be in the lead être en tête ; Shadowfax is in the lead Shadowfax est en tête
3. [led] plomb *(masculine)* : the pipes are made
of lead les tuyaux sont en plomb
4. [led] mine *(feminine)* : the lead in a pencil la
mine d'un crayon
- *adjective* [li:d]
he's the lead singer of the Troggs c'est le
chanteur des Troggs.

leader ['li:dəʳ] *noun*

1. chef *(masculine)* : he's the leader of the gang
c'est le chef du gang
2. dirigeant *(masculine)*, dirigeante *(feminine)* :
the leader of the country le dirigeant du pays

3. leader *(masculine)* : the leader of our party le
leader de notre parti.

leaf [li:f] *(plural* leaves [li:vz]*) noun*

feuille *(feminine)* : the trees are losing their
leaves les arbres perdent leurs feuilles.

leaflet ['li:flɪt] *noun*

prospectus *(masculine)*, dépliant *(masculine)*.

league [li:g] *noun*

championnat *(masculine)* : our team is at the
top of the league notre équipe est en tête du
championnat.

leak [li:k] *noun & verb*

- *noun*
fuite *(feminine)* : there has been a gas leak il y
a eu une fuite de gaz
- *verb*
1. fuir : the bucket is leaking le seau fuit
2. prendre l'eau : the boat's leaking le bateau prend l'eau.

lean [li:n] *(past tense & past participle* leaned OR
leant*) verb*
1. appuyer : I leaned the ladder against the
wall j'ai appuyé l'échelle contre le mur ; my
bike is leaning against the wall mon vélo est
appuyé contre le mur
2. s'appuyer : she leaned on the door elle
s'est appuyée contre la porte
3. se pencher : he leaned forward il s'est penché en avant ; don't lean out of the window
ne te penche pas par la fenêtre

lean over *phrasal verb*

se pencher : he leant over to speak to me il
s'est penché vers moi pour me parler.

leant [lent] *past tense & past participle of* lean

he leant on the counter il s'est appuyé au
comptoir.

leap [li:p] *(past tense & past participle* leapt OR
leaped*) verb*
bondir, sauter : the cat leapt on the mouse
le chat a bondi sur la souris ; she leapt out of
bed elle a sauté du lit ; to leap to one's feet
se lever d'un bond.

leapfrog ['li:pfrɒg] *noun*

saute-mouton *(masculine)* : the children are
playing leapfrog les enfants jouent à saute-
mouton.

leapt [lept] *past tense & past participle of* leap

he leapt to his feet il s'est levé d'un bond.

leap year ['liːpjɪərʳ] *noun*

année *(feminine)* **bissextile : there's a leap year every four years** il y a une année bissextile tous les quatre ans.

learn [lɜːn] *(past tense & past participle* learned OR learnt) *verb*

apprendre : we're learning English nous apprenons l'anglais ; **she's learning to swim** OR **she's learning how to swim** elle apprend à nager.

learner ['lɜːnəʳ] *noun*

débutant *(masculine)*, débutante *(feminine)* : **he's a learner** il est débutant.

learnt [lɜːnt] *past tense & past participle of* learn

Phillip learnt Spanish Phillip a appris l'espagnol ; **she has learnt to swim** elle a appris à nager.

least [liːst] *(superlative of* little) *adjective, adverb & pronoun*

■ *adjective*

➤ **the least**

1. **le moins de : he has the least money** c'est lui qui a le moins d'argent
2. **le moindre** *(feminine* **la moindre) : I don't have the least idea** je n'en ai pas la moindre idée

■ *adverb*

➤ **the least**

1. *With verbs* **le moins : I like that one the least** c'est celui-là que j'aime le moins
2. *With adjectives and nouns* **le moins** *(feminine* **la moins)** *[plural* **les moins] : the least expensive restaurant** le restaurant le moins cher ; **the least funny joke** la blague la moins drôle

■ *pronoun*

➤ **the least** le moins : **Sarah ate the least** c'est Sarah qui a mangé le moins

➤ **at least**

1. **au moins : it'll cost at least $100** ça va coûter au moins 100 dollars
2. **du moins : she's never met him, at least that's what she says** elle ne l'a jamais rencontré, du moins c'est ce qu'elle dit

➤ **it's the least I can do** c'est la moindre des choses.

leather ['leðəʳ] *noun*

cuir *(masculine)* : **a leather belt** une ceinture en cuir.

leave [liːv] *verb & noun*

■ *verb (past tense & past participle* left)

1. **partir : I'm leaving tomorrow** je pars demain ; **she has already left** elle est déjà partie
2. **quitter : she left the country this morning** elle a quitté le pays ce matin
3. **laisser : I left the door open** j'ai laissé la porte ouverte ; **leave me alone!** laisse-moi tranquille ! ; **leave the book at home** laisse le livre à la maison
4. **oublier : I've left my umbrella in the café** j'ai oublié mon parapluie au café

leave out *phrasal verb*

oublier : you've left a word out tu as oublié un mot

■ *noun*

1. **congé** *(masculine)* : **the secretary has two days' leave** la secrétaire a deux jours de congé
2. **permission** *(feminine)* : **the soldier is on leave** le soldat est en permission.

leaves *plural of* leaf.

lecture ['lektʃəʳ] *noun*

1. **conférence** *(feminine)* : **he gave a lecture on rock-climbing** il a donné une conférence sur la varappe
2. **cours** *(masculine)* : **he missed his history lecture** il a manqué son cours d'histoire

> ⚠ Le mot anglais **lecture** est un faux ami, il ne signifie pas "lecture".

led [led] *past tense & past participle of* lead

he led me into the garden il m'a conduit dans le jardin ; **she led a happy life** elle a mené une vie heureuse.

leek [liːk] *noun*

poireau *(masculine)* *[plural* poireaux] : **the leek is a national symbol of Wales** le poireau est un emblème national du pays de Galles.

left [left] *adjective, adverb, noun & verb form*

■ *adjective*

gauche : **he took it with his left hand** il l'a pris de la main gauche

■ *adverb*

à gauche : **turn left at the end of the road**
tournez à gauche au bout de la rue

■ *noun*

gauche *(feminine)* : **look to the left** regardez à
gauche ; **you drive on the left in Britain** on
conduit à gauche en Grande-Bretagne

■ *past tense & past participle of* leave

he left at 3 o'clock il est parti à 3 heures ; **she
hasn't left yet** elle n'est pas encore partie

➤ **to be left** rester : **is there any cake left?** est-
ce qu'il reste du gâteau ? ; **do you have any
money left?** il te reste de l'argent ? ; **there's
none left** il n'en reste plus.

left-hand ['lefthænd] *adjective*

de gauche : **the left-hand drawer** le tiroir
de gauche

➤ **on the left-hand side** à gauche.

left-handed [,left'hændɪd] *adjective*

gaucher *(feminine* gauchère*)* : **he's left-
handed** il est gaucher.

left-luggage office *UK* [left'lʌgɪdʒ'ɒfɪs]
noun

consigne *(feminine)* : **leave your luggage in
the left-luggage office** laisse tes bagages à
la consigne.

leftovers ['leftəʊvəʳz] *plural noun*

restes *(masculine plural)* : **I threw away the
leftovers** j'ai jeté les restes.

leg [leg] *noun*

jambe *(feminine)* : **Colin has broken his leg**
Colin s'est cassé la jambe

➤ **to pull somebody's leg**   faire   marcher
quelqu'un : **he's pulling your leg** il te fait
marcher

➤ **a leg of lamb** un gigot d'agneau

➤ **a chicken leg** une cuisse de poulet.

legal ['li:gl] *adjective*

légal [*plural* légaux] : **these activities are
not legal** ces activités ne sont pas légales.

legend ['ledʒənd] *noun*

légende *(feminine)* : **he became a legend** il est
entré dans la légende.

leggings ['legɪŋz] *plural noun*

caleçon *(masculine)* : **she wears leggings to
go jogging** elle porte un caleçon pour faire du
jogging.

leisure [*UK* 'leʒəʳ, *US* 'li:ʒər] *uncountable noun*

loisir *(masculine)*

➤ **a leisure centre** *UK* un centre de loisirs

➤ **leisure time** temps *(masculine)* libre : **what do
you do in your leisure time?** qu'est-ce que tu
fais pendant ton temps libre ?

lemon ['lemən] *noun*

citron *(masculine)* : **a slice of lemon** une rondelle de citron

➤ **lemon juice** jus *(masculine)* de citron.

lemonade [,lemə'neɪd] *noun*

1. *UK* limonade *(feminine)*
2. *US* citronnade *(feminine)*.

lend [lend] (*past tense & past participle* lent) *verb*

prêter

➤ **to lend something to somebody**   prêter
quelque chose à quelqu'un : **can you lend me
your pen?** tu peux me prêter ton stylo ?

length [leŋθ] *noun*

1. longueur *(feminine)* : **what length is it?** ça fait
combien en longueur ? ; **it's five metres in
length** cela fait cinq mètres de long
2. durée *(feminine)* : **the length of a prison sentence** la durée d'une peine de prison.

lens [lenz] (*plural* lenses ['lenzɪz]) *noun*

1. objectif *(masculine)* : **the lens of a camera**
l'objectif d'un appareil photo
2. verre *(masculine)* : **my glasses have thick
lenses** les verres de mes lunettes sont épais
3. verre *(masculine)* de contact, lentille *(feminine)* : **she wears contact lenses** elle porte
des verres de contact.

lent [lent] *past tense & past participle of* lend

he lent me some money il m'a prêté de l'argent ; **I've lent him my book** je lui ai prêté
mon livre.

Lent [lent] *noun*

carême *(masculine)* : **he gave up chocolate for
Lent** il a renoncé au chocolat pendant le carême.

lentil ['lentɪl] *noun*

lentille *(feminine)* : **lentil soup** soupe aux lentilles.

Leo ['li:əʊ] *noun*

Lion *(masculine)* : **I'm a Leo** je suis Lion.

leopard ['lepəd] *noun*

léopard *(masculine)*.

less [les] *(comparative of* little*)* *adjective, adverb &*
pronoun

■ *adjective*
moins de : **I have less money than you** j'ai
moins d'argent que toi

■ *adverb*
moins : **you should eat less** tu devrais manger moins ; **it's less serious than I thought**
c'est moins grave que je ne croyais ; **the more
I see him, the less I like him** plus je le vois,
moins je l'aime

■ *pronoun*
moins : **he'll be here in less than two hours**
il sera là en moins de deux heures ; **he has less
than me** il en a moins que moi ; **they haven't
got much money, but we have even less** ils
n'ont pas beaucoup d'argent, mais nous en
avons encore moins

> When you are referring back to something al-
> ready mentioned, as well as using moins in
> French you have to use the pronoun en. It is
> equivalent to saying 'less of it'.

lesson ['lesn] *noun*

leçon *(feminine)*, cours *(masculine)* : **she's taking English lessons** elle prend des cours d'anglais ; **a driving lesson** une leçon de conduite ; **that'll teach him a lesson!** cela lui servira
de leçon !

let [let] *(past tense & past participle* let*)* *verb*

1. *In suggestions* **let's go!** allons-y ! OR on y
va ! ; **let's go home** rentrons ; **let's go to the
cinema tonight** et si on allait au cinéma ce
soir ?
2. laisser : **to let somebody do something**
laisser quelqu'un faire quelque chose ; **let
me explain** laisse-moi expliquer ; **my parents
won't let me go out** mes parents ne me lais-
seront pas sortir

> **to let go of somebody** OR **something** lâ-
> cher quelqu'un OR quelque chose : **let me go!**
> lâche-moi !

> **to let somebody know something** dire
> quelque chose à quelqu'un : **I'll let you know
> what time I arrive** je te dirai à quelle heure
> j'arrive

> **let us know** tiens-nous au courant

let down *phrasal verb*

laisser tomber : **she let me down at the
last minute** elle m'a laissé tomber à la dernière minute

let in *phrasal verb*

1. faire entrer : **he went to the door and let
them in** il est allé à la porte et les a fait rentrer
2. laisser entrer : **they wouldn't let us in the
club** ils ne nous ont pas laissés entrer dans la
boîte

let off *phrasal verb*

1. ne pas punir : **I'll let you off this time, but
don't do it again** je ne vais pas te punir cette
fois-ci, mais ne recommence pas
2. faire partir, tirer : **they let the fireworks
off** ils ont fait partir les feux d'artifice.

let's [lets] = let us

let's go for a swim allons nager.

letter ['letər] *noun*

lettre *(feminine)* : **I sent him a letter** je lui ai
envoyé une lettre ; **the letters of the alphabet**
les lettres de l'alphabet.

letterbox *UK* ['letəbɒks] *noun*

boîte *(feminine)* aux lettres.

lettuce ['letɪs] *noun*

salade *(feminine)*, laitue *(feminine)* : **she
bought a lettuce** elle a acheté de la salade.

level ['levl] *noun & adjective*

■ *noun*
niveau *(masculine)* [*plural* niveaux] : **they're on
the same level** ils sont au même niveau
■ *adjective*
1. plat : **the ground is level** le terrain est plat
2. à la même hauteur : **the pictures aren't
level** les tableaux ne sont pas à la même hauteur
3. à égalité : **the teams are level after the first
round** les équipes sont à égalité après le premier tour.

lever [*UK* 'liːvər, *US* 'levər] *noun*

levier *(masculine)* : **the gear lever** le levier de
vitesse.

liar ['laɪər] *noun*

menteur *(masculine)*, menteuse *(feminine)* :
he's a liar il est menteur OR c'est un menteur.

liberal ['lɪbərəl] *adjective*

libéral

➤ **the Liberal Democrats** le parti libéral démocrate ➤ Political Parties.

liberty ['lɪbətɪ] *noun*

liberté *(feminine)*.

Libra ['liːbrə] *noun*

Balance *(feminine)* : **she's a Libra** elle est Balance.

librarian [laɪ'breərɪən] *noun*

bibliothécaire *(masculine or feminine)* : **he's a librarian** il est bibliothécaire.

library ['laɪbrərɪ] *(plural* libraries*) noun*

bibliothèque *(feminine)* : **I borrowed a book from the library** j'ai emprunté un livre à la bibliothèque

➤ **a library book** un livre de bibliothèque

 Library est un faux ami, il ne signifie pas "librairie".

licence *UK,* **license** *US* ['laɪsəns] *noun*

permis *(masculine)* : **do you have a driving licence?** tu as ton permis de conduire ?

➤ **a license plate** *US* une plaque d'immatriculation.

lick [lɪk] *verb*

lécher : **the cat's licking its paws** le chat se lèche les pattes.

licorice *US noun* ➤ liquorice *UK.*

lid [lɪd] *noun*

couvercle *(masculine)* : **put the lid back on the saucepan** remets le couvercle sur la casserole.

lie [laɪ] *noun & verb*

◼ *noun*

mensonge *(masculine)* : **it's all lies!** ce ne sont que des mensonges !

➤ **to tell lies** mentir : **he's telling lies** il ment

◼ *verb*

1. *(past tense & past participle* lied, *present participle* lying*)* **mentir** : **you're lying** tu mens ; **she lied to me** elle m'a menti

2. *(past tense* lay, *past participle* lain, *present participle* lying*)* **s'allonger, rester allongé** : **he lay on the grass** il s'est allongé sur l'herbe ; **he**

lay on the beach all day il est resté allongé sur la plage toute la journée

lie down *phrasal verb*

s'allonger, se coucher : **I want to lie down on the bed** je veux m'allonger sur le lit ; **go and lie down** va te coucher

➤ **to be lying down** OR **to be lying** être allongé : **Marcus was lying down** Marcus était allongé ; **she's lying on the sofa** elle est allongée sur le canapé.

life [laɪf] *(plural* lives [laɪvz]*) noun*

vie *(feminine)* : **I've been here all my life** j'ai passé toute ma vie ici ; **you saved my life** tu m'as sauvé la vie ! ; **that's life!** c'est la vie !

➤ **a life belt** une bouée de sauvetage

➤ **a life jacket** *UK* OR **a life preserver** *US* un gilet de sauvetage.

lifeboat ['laɪfbəʊt] *noun*

canot *(masculine)* **de sauvetage.**

lifeguard ['laɪfgɑːd] *noun*

maître *(masculine)* **nageur.**

lift [lɪft] *noun & verb*

◼ *noun UK*

ascenseur *(masculine)* : **I took the lift to the second floor** j'ai pris l'ascenseur pour monter au deuxième étage

➤ **to give somebody a lift** emmener quelqu'un en voiture : **she gave me a lift to school** elle m'a emmenée à l'école en voiture

➤ **can I give you a lift?** je peux te déposer quelque part ?

◼ *verb*

1. **soulever** : **this suitcase is too heavy, I can't lift it** cette valise est trop lourde, je ne peux pas la soulever

2. **lever** : **he lifted his arm** il a levé son bras.

light [laɪt] *adjective, noun & verb*

◼ *adjective*

1. **léger** *(feminine* légère*)* : **it's as light as a feather** c'est léger comme une plume ; **we had a light meal** nous avons pris un repas léger

2. **clair** : **my bedroom is very light** ma chambre est très claire ; **he's wearing a light green shirt** il porte une chemise vert clair

◼ *noun*

1. **lumière** *(feminine)* : **there's not enough light to read by** il n'y a pas assez de lumière pour lire ; **can you switch the light on?** tu peux al-

lumer la lumière ? ; **he switched the light off** il a éteint la lumière

2. **lampe** *(feminine)* : **the light isn't working** la lampe ne marche plus

3. **phare** *(masculine)* : **the driver put his lights on** le conducteur a allumé ses phares

4. **feu** *(masculine)* : **have you got a light?** tu as du feu ? ; **to set light to something** mettre le feu à quelque chose

➤ **traffic lights** feu *(masculine)* : **the lights are red** le feu est au rouge

➤ **a light bulb** une ampoule

■ *verb (past tense & past participle* lit)
allumer : **she lit the candle** elle a allumé la bougie.

lighter ['laɪtəʳ] *noun*

briquet *(masculine)* : **a cigarette lighter** un briquet.

lighthouse ['laɪthaʊs, *plural* 'laɪthaʊzɪz] *noun*

phare *(masculine)* : **there's a lighthouse at the entrance to the harbour** il y a un phare à l'entrée du port.

lightning ['laɪtnɪŋ] *uncountable noun*

éclairs *(masculine plural)* : **there was thunder and lightning** il y avait des coups de tonnerre et des éclairs

➤ **a flash of lightning** un éclair : **I saw a flash of lightning** j'ai vu un éclair

➤ **as quick as lightning** rapide comme l'éclair

➤ **to be struck by lightning** être frappé par la foudre.

like [laɪk] *preposition & verb*

■ *preposition*
comme : **their house is like ours** leur maison est comme la nôtre ; **do it like this** fais-le comme ça

➤ **what's he like?** comment est-il ? : **what's his new girlfriend like?** comment est sa nouvelle copine ?

➤ **what's the weather like?** quel temps fait-il ?

➤ **to look like somebody** ressembler à quelqu'un : **she looks like her sister** elle ressemble à sa sœur

■ *verb*
1. **aimer** : **I like music** j'aime la musique ; **she doesn't like sardines** elle n'aime pas les sardines ; **do you like dancing?** est-ce que tu aimes danser ?

2. **aimer bien** : **she likes him, but she's not in love with him** elle l'aime bien, mais elle n'est pas amoureuse de lui

➤ **if you like** si tu veux

➤ **I would like** OR **I'd like** je voudrais : **I'd like a cup of tea** je voudrais une tasse de thé ; **I'd like to go to Egypt** je voudrais aller en Égypte OR j'aimerais aller en Égypte

➤ **would you like some more cake?** voulez-vous encore un peu de gâteau ? : **would you like to come with us?** est-ce que tu veux venir avec nous ?

likely ['laɪklɪ] *adjective*

probable : **that's not very likely** c'est peu probable

➤ **it's likely to rain** il va probablement pleuvoir.

lilac ['laɪlək] *noun*

lilas *(masculine)*.

lily ['lɪlɪ] (*plural* lilies) *noun*

lis *(masculine)*

➤ **lily of the valley** muguet *(masculine)*.

lime [laɪm] *noun*

citron *(masculine)* **vert** : **lime juice** du jus de citron vert.

limit ['lɪmɪt] *noun & verb*

■ *noun*
limite *(feminine)* : **he knows his limits** il connaît ses limites

■ *verb*
limiter : **we have to try and limit our expenses** il faut essayer de limiter nos dépenses.

limp [lɪmp] *verb & noun*

■ *verb*
boiter : **she's limping** elle boite

■ *noun*
➤ **to have a limp** boiter.

line [laɪn] *noun & verb*

■ *noun*
1. **ligne** *(feminine)* : **draw a straight line** tracez une ligne droite ; **in a straight line** en ligne droite ; **all the lines to London are busy** toutes les lignes pour Londres sont occupées

2. **file** *(feminine)* : **there was a long line of cars** il y avait une longue file de voitures

3. **vers** *(masculine)* : **this poem has ten lines** ce poème comporte dix vers

➤ **to stand in line** *US* faire la queue

➤ **hold the line!** ne quittez pas !

I

to drop somebody a line écrire un mot à quelqu'un : **I dropped her a line** je lui ai écrit un mot

■ verb

1. **border : an avenue lined with trees** une avenue bordée d'arbres

2. **doubler : a coat lined with silk** un manteau doublé de soie

line up *phrasal verb*

faire la queue : **the children are lining up** les enfants font la queue.

linen ['lɪnɪn] *uncountable noun*

1. **lin** *(masculine)* : **linen sheets** des draps en lin

2. **linge** *(masculine)* : **put the dirty linen in the basket** mets le linge sale dans le panier.

link [lɪŋk] *noun & verb*

■ noun

lien *(masculine)* : **there's a link between the two events** il y a un lien entre les deux événements

➤ **a rail link** une liaison ferroviaire

■ verb

1. **relier : the two towns are linked by rail** les deux villes sont reliées par le chemin de fer

2. **lier : the two events are linked** les deux événements sont liés.

lion ['laɪən] *noun*

lion *(masculine)* : **the lion roared** le lion a rugi.

lioness ['laɪənes] *noun*

lionne *(feminine)*.

lip [lɪp] *noun*

lèvre *(feminine)* : **I bit my lip** je me suis mordu la lèvre.

lip-read ['lɪpriːd] *verb*

lire sur les lèvres : **can you lip-read?** tu sais lire sur les lèvres ?

lipstick ['lɪpstɪk] *noun*

rouge *(masculine)* **à lèvres : she's wearing lipstick** elle a du rouge à lèvres.

liquid ['lɪkwɪd] *noun*

liquide *(masculine)*.

liquor *US* ['lɪkər] *noun*

alcool *(masculine)*

➤ **a liquor store** un magasin de vins et spiritueux.

liquorice *UK*, **licorice** *US* ['lɪkərɪs] *noun*

réglisse *(feminine)*.

list [lɪst] *noun & verb*

■ noun

liste *(feminine)* : **her name is on the list** son nom est sur la liste ; **make a list** fais une liste OR dresse une liste

■ verb

faire la liste de : **I've listed the presents to buy** j'ai fait la liste des cadeaux à acheter.

listen ['lɪsn] *verb*

écouter : **listen!** écoute ! ; **listen to me!** écoute-moi ! ; **she's listening to the music** elle écoute la musique.

lit [lɪt] *past tense & past participle of* light

she lit the candle elle a allumé la bougie ; **have you lit the fire?** as-tu allumé le feu ?

liter *US* ➤ litre *UK*.

literature [*UK* 'lɪtrətʃər, *US* 'lɪtərətʃuər] *noun*

littérature *(feminine)*.

litre *UK*, **liter** *US* ['liːtər] *noun*

litre *(masculine)* : **he bought a litre of wine** il a acheté un litre de vin.

litter ['lɪtər] *uncountable noun*

détritus *(masculine plural)*, **ordures** *(feminine plural)*

➤ **a litter bin** *UK* une poubelle.

little ['lɪtl] *adjective & adverb*

■ adjective

1. **petit : a little boy** un petit garçon ; **my little finger** mon petit doigt

2. **peu de : there's very little hope** il y a très peu d'espoir

■ adverb

peu : he eats very little il mange très peu

➤ **a little**

1. **un peu de : I have a little money** j'ai un peu d'argent

2. **un peu : I'm a little hungry** j'ai un peu faim

➤ **a little bit** un petit peu

⚠ Attention à ne pas confondre **little** (peu) et **a little** (un peu).

live *verb & adjective*

■ verb [lɪv]

1. **vivre** : **he lives with his father** il vit avec son père ; **they live together** ils vivent ensemble
2. **habiter** : **Martha lives in Paris** Martha habite Paris OR Martha habite à Paris ; **we live at number 7** nous habitons au numéro 7
- *adjective* [laɪv]
1. **en direct** : **the broadcast is live** l'émission est en direct
2. **vivant** : **experiments on live animals** des expériences sur des animaux vivants.

lively ['laɪvlɪ] *adjective*

1. **plein de vie** : **she's very lively** elle est pleine de vie
2. **animé** : **a lively place** un endroit animé.

liver ['lɪvər] *noun*

foie *(masculine)* : **lamb's liver** du foie d'agneau.

lives *plural of* life.

living ['lɪvɪŋ] *noun*

> **to earn a living** gagner sa vie
> **what do you do for a living?** qu'est-ce que tu fais dans la vie ?

living room ['lɪvɪŋruːm] *noun*

salon *(masculine)*, **salle** *(feminine)* **de séjour**.

lizard ['lɪzəd] *noun*

lézard *(masculine)*.

llama ['lɑːmə] *noun*

lama *(masculine)*.

load [ləʊd] *noun & verb*

- *noun*
  chargement *(masculine)* : **a heavy load** un chargement lourd
> **loads of** *informal* des tas de OR plein de : **there were loads of people at the concert** il y avait des tas de gens au concert ; **he's got loads of money** il a plein d'argent
- *verb*
  charger : **they loaded the luggage into the car** ils ont chargé les valises dans la voiture ; **he loaded the gun** il a chargé le revolver
> **to load a camera** mettre une pellicule dans un appareil photo.

loaf [ləʊf] *(plural* **loaves** [ləʊvz]*) noun*

pain *(masculine)* : **a loaf of bread** un pain.

loan [ləʊn] *noun & verb*

- *noun*
1. **prêt** *(masculine)* : **the bank gave him a loan** la banque lui a accordé un prêt
2. **emprunt** *(masculine)* : **he took out a loan** il a fait un emprunt
- *verb*
  prêter : **he loaned me his camera** il m'a prêté son appareil photo.

loaves *plural of* loaf.

lobby ['lɒbɪ] *(plural* **lobbies***) noun*

hall *(masculine)* : **he's waiting for me in the lobby of the hotel** il m'attend dans le hall de l'hôtel.

lobster ['lɒbstər] *noun*

homard *(masculine)*.

local ['ləʊkl] *adjective*

1. **local** : **a local newspaper** un journal local
2. **du coin, du quartier** : **the local shops** les magasins du quartier ; **the local inhabitants** les gens du coin.

locally ['ləʊkəlɪ] *adverb*

dans le quartier : **she lives locally** elle habite dans le quartier.

location [ləʊ'keɪʃn] *noun*

site *(masculine)*, **endroit** *(masculine)* : **the house is in a beautiful location** la maison est dans un très beau site

⚠ Location est un faux ami, il ne signifie pas "location".

lock [lɒk] *noun & verb*

- *noun*
  serrure *(feminine)* : **she put the key in the lock** elle a mis la clé dans la serrure
- *verb*
  fermer à clé : **she locked the door** elle a fermé la porte à clé

lock in *phrasal verb*

enfermer : **they locked her in her room** ils l'ont enfermée dans sa chambre

lock out *phrasal verb*

enfermer dehors : **I've locked myself out** je me suis enfermé dehors.

locker ['lɒkəʳ] noun

casier (masculine) : **he keeps his books in his locker** il range ses livres dans son casier
➤ **the locker room** le vestiaire.

lodger ['lɒdʒəʳ] noun

locataire (masculine or feminine).

loft [lɒft] noun

grenier (masculine).

log [lɒg] noun & verb

bûche (feminine) : **put a log on the fire** mets une bûche dans le feu
➤ **a log cabin** une cabine en rondins

log in , **log on** phrasal verb

se connecter

log off , **log out** phrasal verb

se déconnecter.

logical ['lɒdʒɪkl] adjective

logique.

lollipop ['lɒlɪpɒp] noun

sucette (feminine).

lolly UK ['lɒlɪ] (plural lollies) noun informal

sucette (feminine)
➤ **an ice lolly** une glace à l'eau.

London ['lʌndən] noun

Londres : **I live in London** j'habite à Londres ; **we're going to London** nous allons à Londres

> LONDON BRIDGE
> Ce pont, qui traverse la Tamise, fut, jusqu'en 1750, le seul pont de Londres. Le London Bridge actuel date seulement de 1973, l'ancien pont ayant été vendu à un homme d'affaires américain et remonté dans l'Arizona.

Londoner ['lʌndənəʳ] noun

Londonien (masculine), Londonienne (feminine).

lonely ['ləʊnlɪ] adjective

1. seul : **she feels lonely** OR **she's lonely** elle se sent seule
2. isolé : **a lonely beach** une plage isolée.

long [lɒŋ] adjective & adverb

■ adjective
long (feminine longue) : **her skirt is too long**

sa jupe est trop longue ; **the fence is ten metres long** la clôture fait dix mètres de long ; **the concert is three hours long** le concert dure trois heures
➤ **a long time** longtemps : **I've been waiting a long time** j'attends depuis longtemps
➤ **it takes a long time** ça prend beaucoup de temps
➤ **it's a long way** c'est loin
➤ **the long jump** le saut en longueur
■ adverb
longtemps : **I didn't wait long** je n'ai pas attendu longtemps
➤ **I won't be long** je n'en ai pas pour longtemps
➤ **how long will it take?** combien de temps cela va-t-il prendre ? : **how long will you be?** tu en as pour combien de temps ?
➤ **how long have you been here?** tu es ici depuis combien de temps ?
➤ **as long as** aussi longtemps que OR tant que : **I'll wait as long as you like** j'attendrai aussi longtemps que tu voudras ; **as long as you are here, you're safe** tant que tu es là, tu ne risques rien
➤ **so long!** au revoir !

loo UK [luː] noun informal

toilettes (feminine plural) : **where's the loo?** où sont les toilettes ?

look [lʊk] noun & verb
■ noun
regard (masculine) : **he gave me a funny look** il m'a lancé un regard bizarre
➤ **to have a look at something** regarder quelque chose : **can I have a look?** je peux regarder ?
■ verb
1. regarder : **don't look!** ne regarde pas !
2. avoir l'air : **you look tired** tu as l'air fatigué ; **she looks cold** elle a l'air d'avoir froid ; **that cake looks good** ce gâteau a l'air bon
➤ **it looks as if it's going to snow** on dirait qu'il va neiger
➤ **to look like somebody** ressembler à quelqu'un : **Frances looks like her mother** Frances ressemble à sa mère

look after phrasal verb

s'occuper de : **he's looking after his little brother** il s'occupe de son petit frère

look around ➤ look round UK

look at *phrasal verb*

regarder : **look at the pictures** regarde les images ; **he looked at her** il l'a regardée

look for *phrasal verb*

chercher : **I'm looking for my keys** je cherche mes clés

look forward to *phrasal verb*

attendre avec impatience : **I'm really looking forward to Christmas** j'attends Noël avec beaucoup d'impatience ; **I look forward to hearing from you** j'espère avoir bientôt de tes nouvelles

look out *phrasal verb*

faire attention : **look out!** attention !

look round *UK*, **look around** *phrasal verb*

1. se retourner : **he looked round when I called him** il s'est retourné quand je l'ai appelé
2. regarder : **I'm just looking round** je regarde seulement
3. visiter : **let's look round the museum** allons visiter le musée

look up *phrasal verb*

1. lever les yeux : **I looked up when he came in** j'ai levé les yeux quand il est entré
2. chercher : **look the word up in a dictionary** cherche ce mot dans un dictionnaire.

loose [luːs] *adjective*

1. desserré : **this screw is loose** la vis est desserrée
2. ample : **loose clothes** des vêtements amples
> **to come loose** se défaire : **the knot has come loose** le nœud s'est défait
> **loose change** de la petite monnaie : **I don't have any loose change** je n'ai pas de petite monnaie.

lord [lɔːd] *noun*

1. seigneur *(masculine)* : **he lives like a lord** il vit comme un seigneur
2. *UK* lord *(masculine)* : **Lord Owen** lord Owen.

lorry *UK* ['lɒrɪ] *(plural* lorries) *noun*

camion *(masculine)*
> **a lorry driver** un camionneur.

lose [luːz] *(past tense & past participle* lost) *verb*

perdre : **I've lost my ticket** j'ai perdu mon billet ; **France lost by three goals to one** la France a perdu par trois buts à un

> **to lose one's way** se perdre : **he lost his way** il s'est perdu.

loser ['luːzər] *noun*

1. perdant *(masculine)*, perdante *(feminine)* : **he's a bad loser** il est mauvais perdant
2. *informal* raté *(masculine)*, ratée *(feminine)* : **he's a real loser** c'est un vrai raté.

loss [lɒs] *noun*

perte *(feminine)*.

lost [lɒst] *adjective & verb form*

■ *adjective*
perdu
> **to get lost** se perdre : **I got lost in the woods** je me suis perdu dans les bois
> **the lost-and-found office** *US* OR **the lost property office** *UK* le bureau des objets trouvés
■ *past tense & past participle of* lose
I lost my key j'ai perdu ma clé.

lot [lɒt] *noun*

> **a lot** beaucoup : **he eats a lot** il mange beaucoup ; **thanks a lot!** merci beaucoup ! ; **he has a lot of friends** il a beaucoup d'amis
> **lots** *informal* beaucoup : **she has lots of money** elle a beaucoup d'argent
> **the lot** tout : **she ate the lot** elle a tout mangé
> **to draw lots** tirer au sort : **they drew lots to see who would go** ils ont tiré au sort pour voir qui irait.

lotion ['ləʊʃn] *noun*

lotion *(feminine)*
> **suntan lotion** crème *(feminine)* solaire.

lottery ['lɒtərɪ] *noun*

loterie *(feminine)* : **she won the lottery** elle a gagné à la loterie.

loud [laʊd] *adjective & adverb*

fort : **the music's too loud** la musique est trop forte ; **can you speak a bit louder?** tu peux parler un peu plus fort ?
> **to read out loud** lire à haute voix
> **out loud** tout haut : **he spoke out loud** il a parlé tout haut.

loudspeaker [ˌlaʊd'spiːkər] *noun*

haut-parleur *(masculine)* [*plural* haut-parleurs].

lounge *UK* [laʊndʒ] *noun*

salon *(masculine)* **: they're watching TV in the lounge** ils regardent la télé dans le salon
> **the departure lounge** la salle d'embarquement.

lousy ['laʊzɪ] *adjective informal*

1. **nul** *(feminine* **nulle)**, **infect : this book's lousy** ce livre est nul ; **the food's lousy** la nourriture est infecte
2. **pourri : the weather's lousy** il fait un temps pourri.

love [lʌv] *noun & verb*

◼ *noun*
amour *(masculine)*
> **a love song** une chanson d'amour
> **to be in love** être amoureux **: he's in love with her** il est amoureux d'elle
> **to fall in love** tomber amoureux **: she fell in love with him** elle est tombée amoureuse de lui
> **give her my love** embrasse-la pour moi
◼ *verb*
1. **aimer : I love you** je t'aime
2. **aimer beaucoup : I'd love to come to your party** j'aimerais beaucoup venir à ta fête
3. **adorer : he loves chocolate** il adore le chocolat ; **I love dancing** j'adore danser.

lovely ['lʌvlɪ] *adjective*

1. **beau** *(feminine* **belle) : that's a lovely dress** c'est une belle robe ; **you look lovely, Claire!** qu'est-ce que tu es belle, Claire !
2. **charmant : he's a lovely man** c'est un homme charmant
3. **délicieux : this tastes lovely** c'est délicieux
> **we had a lovely time** nous nous sommes bien amusés
> **what lovely weather!** qu'est-ce qu'il fait beau !

low [ləʊ] *adjective & adverb*

◼ *adjective*
bas *(feminine* **basse) : the ceiling is very low** le plafond est très bas ; **in a low voice** à voix basse
◼ *adverb*
bas : the plane is flying low l'avion vole bas.

lower ['ləʊəʳ] *adjective, adverb & verb*

◼ *adjective (comparative of* **low)**
inférieur : the lower deck of a ship le pont inférieur d'un navire
◼ *adverb (comparative of* **low)**

plus bas : put the painting a bit lower mets le tableau un peu plus bas
◼ *verb*
baisser : they've lowered the price ils ont baissé le prix.

low-fat ['ləʊfæt] *adjective*

allégé : low-fat yoghurt du yaourt allégé.

luck [lʌk] *uncountable noun*

chance *(feminine)* **: you're in luck** tu as de la chance
> **good luck!** bonne chance !
> **bad luck!** pas de chance !

lucky ['lʌkɪ] *adjective*

> **to be lucky**
1. **avoir de la chance : she's very lucky** elle a beaucoup de chance
2. **porter bonheur : horseshoes are lucky** le fer à cheval porte bonheur
> **a lucky charm** un porte-bonheur.

luggage ['lʌgɪdʒ] *uncountable noun*

bagages *(masculine plural)* **: my luggage is very heavy** mes bagages sont très lourds
> **a luggage rack** un porte-bagages.

lullaby ['lʌləbaɪ] *(plural* **lullabies)** *noun*

berceuse *(feminine)*.

lump [lʌmp] *noun*

1. **morceau** *(masculine)* *[plural* **morceaux] : a lump of sugar** un morceau de sucre
2. **bosse** *(feminine)* **: she has a lump on her forehead** elle a une bosse sur le front.

lunch [lʌntʃ] *noun*

déjeuner *(masculine)* **: what did you have for lunch?** qu'est-ce que tu as mangé au déjeuner ? OR qu'est-ce que tu as mangé à midi ?
> **to have lunch** déjeuner **: we have lunch at one o'clock** nous déjeunons à une heure
> **the lunch hour** la pause de midi.

lunchtime ['lʌntʃtaɪm] *noun*

heure *(feminine)* **du déjeuner : it's nearly lunchtime** c'est bientôt l'heure du déjeuner.

lung [lʌŋ] *noun*

poumon *(masculine)*.

luxury ['lʌkʃərɪ] *noun*

luxe *(masculine)* **: she lives in luxury** elle vit dans le luxe
> **a luxury hotel** un hôtel de luxe.

lying ['laɪɪŋ] ➤ lie.

lyrics ['lɪrɪks] *plural noun*

paroles *(feminine plural)* : **who wrote the lyrics for this song?** qui a écrit les paroles de cette chanson ?

macaroni [ˌmækə'rəʊnɪ] *uncountable noun*

macaronis *(masculine plural)* : **he likes macaroni** il aime les macaronis
➤ **macaroni cheese** gratin *(masculine)* de macaronis.

machine [mə'ʃiːn] *noun*

machine *(feminine)* : **a sewing machine** une machine à coudre
➤ **a machine gun** une mitrailleuse.

mackerel ['mækrəl] *noun*

maquereau *(masculine)*.

mad [mæd] *adjective*

1. fou *(feminine* folle*)* : **he's mad** il est fou ; **you must be going mad** tu deviens fou ; **you're driving me mad!** tu me rends fou !
2. furieux *(feminine* furieuse*)* : **I'm mad at him** je suis furieux contre lui
➤ **to be mad about something** adorer quelque chose ; **he's mad about baseball** il adore le base-ball
➤ **to be mad about somebody** être fou de quelqu'un ; **he's mad about her** il est fou d'elle
➤ **mad-cow disease** maladie *(feminine)* de la vache folle.

madam ['mædəm] *noun*

madame *(feminine)* : **can I help you, madam?** je peux vous aider, madame ?

made [meɪd] *past tense & past participle of* make

I made a mistake j'ai fait une erreur ; **Helen has made a cake** Helen a fait un gâteau.

magazine [ˌmægə'ziːn] *noun*

magazine *(masculine)*, revue *(feminine)* : **a fashion magazine** un magazine de mode.

magic ['mædʒɪk] *noun & adjective*

■ *noun*
magie *(feminine)* : **he appeared as if by magic** il est apparu comme par magie
■ *adjective*
magique : **a magic wand** une baguette magique
➤ **a magic trick** un tour de magie.

magician [mə'dʒɪʃn] *noun*

magicien *(masculine)*, magicienne *(feminine)* : **he's a magician** il est magicien.

magnet ['mægnɪt] *noun*

aimant *(masculine)*.

magnetic [mæg'netɪk] *adjective*

magnétique.

magnificent [mæg'nɪfɪsənt] *adjective*

magnifique.

magnifying glass ['mægnɪfaɪɪŋglɑːs] *noun*

loupe *(feminine)* : **he looked at the spider through a magnifying glass** il examinait l'araignée à la loupe.

magpie ['mægpaɪ] *noun*

pie *(feminine)*.

maid [meɪd] *noun*

domestique *(feminine)*.

maiden name ['meɪdnneɪm] *noun*

nom *(masculine)* de jeune fille.

mail [meɪl] *noun & verb*

■ *noun*
1. courrier *(masculine)* : **has the mail arrived?** est-ce que le courrier est arrivé ? ; **you have mail** vous avez du courrier
2. poste *(feminine)* : **I'll send it by mail** je vais l'envoyer par la poste
■ *verb*
US envoyer : **to mail a letter to somebody** envoyer une lettre à quelqu'un.

mailbox US ['meɪlbɒks] *(plural* mailboxes*)*

noun
boîte *(feminine)* aux lettres : **an electronic mailbox** une boîte aux lettres électronique.

m

mailman *US* ['meɪlmən] (*plural* mailmen ['meɪlmən]) *noun*

facteur *(masculine)* **: the mailman hasn't been by today** le facteur n'est pas passé aujourd'hui.

main [meɪn] *adjective*

principal
- **the main course** le plat principal
- **a main road** une grande route
- **the main street** la rue principale **: the bank's on the main street** la banque se trouve dans la rue principale.

mainly ['meɪnlɪ] *adverb*

principalement.

maize *UK* [meɪz] *uncountable noun*

maïs *(masculine)*.

Majesty ['mædʒəstɪ] (*plural* Majesties) *noun*

majesté *(feminine)* **: Her Majesty the Queen** Sa Majesté la Reine ; **His Majesty the King** Sa Majesté le Roi.

major ['meɪdʒəʳ] *adjective & noun*

■ *adjective*

majeur : it's a major event c'est un événement majeur
- **a major road** une route principale
- **it's of major importance** c'est d'une grande importance

■ *noun*

1. **commandant** *(masculine)* **: Major Johnson** le commandant Johnson
2. *US* **matière** *(feminine)* **principale : I'm a physics major** ma matière principale c'est la physique.

majority [mə'dʒɒrətɪ] (*plural* majorities) *noun*

majorité *(feminine)* **: he won by a big majority** il a gagné avec une forte majorité
- **the majority of people** la majorité des gens OU la plupart des gens.

make [meɪk] *verb & noun*

■ *verb* (*past tense & past participle* **made**)

1. **faire : I made this vase myself** j'ai fait ce vase moi-même ; **don't make any noise** ne fais pas de bruit ; **have you made the bed?** est-ce que tu as fait le lit ? ; **3 and 4 make 7** 3 et 4 font 7 ; **make yourself at home** fais comme chez toi

2. **fabriquer : these cars are made in Italy** ces voitures sont fabriquées en Italie
3. **préparer : to make a meal** préparer un repas
4. **rendre : to make somebody happy** rendre quelqu'un heureux ; **the film made me sad** le film m'a rendu triste
5. **gagner : he makes a lot of money** il gagne beaucoup d'argent
- **to be made of** être en **: is it made of wood?** c'est en bois ? ; **this ring is made of gold** cette bague est en or
- **to make somebody do something**
1. **faire faire quelque chose à quelqu'un : she made me laugh** elle m'a fait rire
2. **obliger quelqu'un à faire quelque chose : he made me open the safe** il m'a obligé à ouvrir le coffre-fort
- **to make do** faire avec ; **we'll have to make do** il faudra faire avec
- **to make do with something** se contenter de quelque chose **: they made do with the leftovers** ils se sont contentés des restes

make out *phrasal verb*

1. **déchiffrer : I can't make out what the inscription says** je n'arrive pas à déchiffrer l'inscription
2. **comprendre : I can't make out what they are saying** je ne comprends pas ce qu'ils disent
3. **prétendre : she's not as rich as she makes out** elle n'est pas aussi riche qu'elle le prétend

make up *phrasal verb*

1. **inventer : he made up an excuse** il a inventé une excuse
2. **se réconcilier : they had an argument, but they've made up now** ils se sont disputés, mais ils se sont réconciliés maintenant
- **to make up one's mind** se décider

make up for *phrasal verb*

1. **compenser : to make up for a loss** compenser une perte
2. **rattraper : we must make up for lost time** il nous faut rattraper le temps perdu

■ *noun*

marque *(feminine)* **: what make of car is that?** cette voiture est de quelle marque ?

make-up ['meɪkʌp] *uncountable noun*

maquillage *(masculine)*
- **a make-up bag** une trousse de maquillage
- **to wear make-up** se maquiller **: Sue**

doesn't wear make-up Sue ne se maquille pas.

male [meɪl] *noun & adjective*

■ *noun*
mâle *(masculine)*
■ *adjective*
1. **mâle** : **a male horse** un cheval mâle
2. **masculin** : **I heard a male voice** j'ai entendu une voix masculine
> **a male nurse** un infirmier
> **a male student** un étudiant.

mall [mɔːl] *noun*

centre *(masculine)* **commercial** : **a shopping mall** un centre commercial.

mammal ['mæml] *noun*

mammifère *(masculine)*.

man [mæn] (*plural* **men** [men]) *noun*

homme *(masculine)* : **he's an old man** c'est un vieil homme ; **a young man** un jeune homme ; **men's clothes** des vêtements *(masculine plural)* d'homme
> **the men's room** *US* les toilettes *(feminine plural)* pour hommes : **where is the men's room?** où sont les toilettes pour hommes ?

manage ['mænɪdʒ] *verb*

1. **se débrouiller, arriver** : **I can manage** je peux me débrouiller ; **can you manage alone?** tu y arrives tout seul ?
2. **diriger, gérer** : **he manages a big company** il dirige une grande entreprise
> **to manage to do something** réussir à faire quelque chose OR arriver à faire quelque chose : **he managed to open the safe** il a réussi à ouvrir le coffre-fort ; **did you manage to carry your suitcase?** tu es arrivé à porter ta valise ?

management ['mænɪdʒmənt] *noun*

1. **gestion** *(feminine)* : **management studies** des études de gestion
2. **direction** *(feminine)* : **the management does not accept responsibility** la direction décline toute responsabilité.

manager ['mænɪdʒəʳ] *noun*

1. **directeur** *(masculine)*, **directrice** *(feminine)* : **the bank manager** le directeur de la banque
2. **gérant** *(masculine)*, **gérante** *(feminine)* : **a shop manager** le gérant d'un magasin
3. **manager** *(masculine)* : **he's the team manager** c'est le manager de l'équipe.

mango ['mæŋgəʊ] *noun*

mangue *(feminine)*.

Manhattan ['mæn‚hætən] *noun*

Manhattan : **Edward lives in Manhattan** Edward habite à Manhattan ; **I'm going to Manhattan** je vais à Manhattan

MANHATTAN
Manhattan, île située entre l'Hudson, l'East River et la rivière de Harlem, constitue le quartier central de la ville de New York. On y trouve **Central Park**, la 5ᵉ Avenue et ses boutiques de luxe, **Broadway** et ses nombreux théâtres, et de célèbres gratte-ciel comme l'**Empire State Building**. Les **Twin Towers** du **World Trade Center** ont été détruites dans l'attentat du 11 septembre 2001.

mankind [mæn'kaɪnd] *noun*

humanité *(feminine)*.

man-made ['mænmeɪd] *adjective*

1. **artificiel** *(feminine* **artificielle)** : **a man-made lake** un lac artificiel
2. **synthétique** : **it's a man-made fabric** c'est un tissu synthétique.

manner ['mænəʳ] *noun*

manière *(feminine)*, **façon** *(feminine)* : **she treated me in a decent manner** elle m'a traité de manière correcte.

manners ['mænəʳz] *plural noun*

manières *(feminine plural)* : **he has very good manners** il a de très bonnes manières.

manor ['mænəʳ] *noun*

manoir *(masculine)* : **they live in a manor house** ils habitent un manoir.

mansion ['mænʃn] *noun*

manoir *(masculine)*.

mantelpiece ['mæntlpiːs] *noun*

cheminée *(feminine)* : **there's a vase on the mantelpiece** il y a un vase sur la cheminée.

manual ['mænjʊəl] *noun*

manuel *(masculine)* : **an instruction manual** un manuel d'utilisation.

m

many ['menɪ] *adjective & pronoun*

■ *adjective*
beaucoup de : **were there many people at the match?** est-ce qu'il y avait beaucoup de gens au match ? ; **she doesn't have many friends** elle n'a pas beaucoup d'amis

■ *pronoun*
beaucoup : **don't eat all the chocolates, there aren't many left** ne mange pas tous les chocolats, il n'en reste pas beaucoup

> When you are referring back to something already mentioned, as well as using **beaucoup** in French you have to use the pronoun **en**. It is like saying 'many of them'.

➤ **how many?**
1. **combien ?** : **how many are there?** il y en a combien ?
2. **combien de ?** : **how many presents did you get?** combien de cadeaux as-tu eu ?
➤ **too many**
1. **trop** : **there's too many** il y en a trop
2. **trop de** : **there are too many people here** il y a trop de monde ici
➤ **as many** autant de : **I don't have as many CDs as my brother** je n'ai pas autant de CD que mon frère
➤ **as many as** autant que : **take as many as you like** prends-en autant que tu veux.

map [mæp] *noun*
1. **carte** *(feminine)* : **a map of Italy** une carte de l'Italie
2. **plan** *(masculine)* : **a map of London** un plan de Londres.

maple ['meɪpl] *noun*
érable *(masculine)* : **the maple leaf is the emblem of Canada** la feuille d'érable est l'emblème du Canada
➤ **maple syrup** sirop *(masculine)* d'érable.

maraca [mə'rækə] *noun*
maraca *(feminine)*.

marathon ['mærəθn] *noun*
marathon *(masculine)* : **Ben's running in the New York marathon** Ben court le marathon de New York.

marble ['mɑːbl] *noun*
1. **marbre** *(masculine)* : **a marble statue** une statue en marbre

2. **bille** *(feminine)* : **they're playing marbles** ils jouent aux billes.

march [mɑːtʃ] *verb*
1. **défiler** : **the protesters marched to the city hall** les manifestants ont défilé jusqu'à la mairie
2. **marcher au pas** : **the soldiers were marching** les soldats marchaient au pas ; **forward march!** en avant, marche !

March [mɑːtʃ] *noun*
mars *(masculine)* : **in March** en mars ; **next March** en mars prochain ; **last March** en mars dernier

> In French the months of the year do not start with a capital letter.

margarine [*UK* ˌmɑːdʒə'riːn, *UK* ˌmɑːgə'riːn, *US* 'mɑːdʒərɪn] *noun*
margarine *(feminine)*.

margin ['mɑːdʒɪn] *noun*
marge *(feminine)* : **he wrote something in the margin** il a écrit quelque chose dans la marge.

mark [mɑːk] *noun & verb*

■ *noun*
1. **tache** *(feminine)* : **there's a mark on your T-shirt** il y a une tache sur ton tee-shirt
2. **marque** *(feminine)* : **there are marks all over his body** il a des marques sur tout le corps
3. *UK* **note** *(feminine)* : **I got a good mark in English** j'ai eu une bonne note en anglais

■ *verb*
1. **marquer** : **X marks the spot** l'endroit est marqué par un X
2. **corriger** : **the teacher has marked our homework** le professeur a corrigé nos devoirs
3. **noter** : **the homework was marked out of twenty** le devoir a été noté sur vingt.

market ['mɑːkɪt] *noun*
marché *(masculine)* : **I'm going to the market** je vais au marché.

marketplace ['mɑːkɪtpleɪs] *noun*
place *(feminine)* **du marché**.

marmalade ['mɑːməleɪd] *noun*
confiture *(feminine)* **d'oranges amères**.

marriage ['mærɪdʒ] *noun*
mariage *(masculine)* : **this is her second marriage** c'est son second mariage.

married ['mærɪd] *adjective*

marié : **are you married?** vous êtes marié ?
➤ **to get married** se marier : **they're getting married** ils vont se marier.

marry ['mærɪ] (*past tense & past participle* married) *verb*

épouser, se marier avec : **will you marry me?** veux-tu m'épouser ? ; **she married Ian Jones** elle s'est mariée avec Ian Jones.

Mars [mɑːz] *noun*

Mars *(feminine)* : **Mars is sometimes called the Red Planet** on surnomme parfois Mars « la planète rouge ».

marvellous *UK*, **marvelous** *US* ['mɑːvələs] *adjective*

merveilleux *(feminine* merveilleuse*)* : **the weather is marvellous** le temps est merveilleux.

marzipan ['mɑːzɪpæn] *noun*

pâte *(feminine)* **d'amandes**.

masculine ['mæskjʊlɪn] *adjective*

masculin.

mashed potatoes [mæʃtpə'teɪtəʊz] *plural noun*

purée *(feminine)* **de pommes de terre**.

mask [*UK* mɑːsk, *US* mæsk] *noun*

masque *(masculine)* : **he's wearing a mask** il porte un masque.

mass [mæs]

◼ *noun*
1. masse *(feminine)* : **a mass of trees** une masse d'arbres
2. messe *(feminine)* : **Catholics go to mass on Sunday** les catholiques vont à la messe le dimanche
◼ *plural noun informal*
➤ **masses of** *UK* des tas de : **Bill has masses of CDs** Bill a des tas de CD.

massage [*UK* 'mæsɑːʒ, *US* mə'sɑːʒ] *noun*

massage *(masculine)* : **can you give me a massage?** tu peux me faire un massage ?

massive ['mæsɪv] *adjective*

énorme : **I saw a massive spider** j'ai vu une araignée énorme.

mast [*UK* mɑːst, *US* mæst] *noun*

mât *(masculine)* : **the boat has three masts** le bateau a trois mâts.

master [*UK* 'mɑːstər, *US* 'mæstər] *noun*

maître *(masculine)* : **the master of the house** le maître de maison.

masterpiece [*UK* 'mɑːstəpiːs, *US* 'mæstərpiːs] *noun*

chef-d'œuvre *(masculine)* [*plural* chefs-d'œuvre].

mat [mæt] *noun*

1. petit tapis *(masculine)* : **an exercise mat** un tapis de gym
2. paillasson *(masculine)* : **wipe your feet on the mat before you come in** essuie tes pieds sur le paillasson avant d'entrer
3. dessous-de-plat *(masculine)* [*plural* dessous-de-plat] : **put the dish on a mat** mets le plat sur un dessous-de-plat
➤ **a place mat** un set de table.

match [mætʃ] *noun & verb*

◼ *noun*
1. match *(masculine)* : **a boxing match** un match de boxe ; **a football match** un match de foot
2. allumette *(feminine)* : **a box of matches** une boîte d'allumettes
◼ *verb*
1. aller avec : **that tie doesn't match your shirt** cette cravate ne va pas avec ta chemise
2. être assortis, aller ensemble : **those socks don't match** ces chaussettes ne sont pas assorties.

matchbox ['mætʃbɒks] (*plural* matchboxes) *noun*

boîte *(feminine)* **d'allumettes**.

matching ['mætʃɪŋ] *adjective*

assorti : **matching dress and shoes** une robe et des chaussures assorties.

mate *UK* [meɪt] *noun informal*

copain *(masculine)*, copine *(feminine)*.

material [mə'tɪərɪəl] *noun*

1. matière *(feminine)* : **raw materials** des matières premières
2. tissu *(masculine)* : **she bought some curtain material** elle a acheté du tissu pour faire des rideaux
3. matériau *(masculine)* [*plural* matériaux] : **building materials** des matériaux de construction.

math *US* ➤ maths *UK*.

mathematics [ˌmæθəˈmætɪks] *uncountable*
noun
mathématiques *(feminine plural)*.

maths *UK* [mæθs], **math** *US* [mæθ] *un-countable* noun *informal*
maths *(feminine plural)* : **I like maths** j'aime les maths ; **maths is fun** les maths, c'est amusant.

matter [ˈmætər] *noun & verb*

◾ *noun*
question *(feminine)* : **it's a matter of time** c'est une question de temps
➤ **as a matter of fact** à vrai dire
➤ **what's the matter?** qu'est-ce qu'il y a ?
➤ **what's the matter with her?** qu'est-ce qu'elle a ?
➤ **there's nothing the matter** tout va bien
◾ *verb*
avoir de l'importance : **it doesn't matter** ça n'a pas d'importance.

mattress [ˈmætrɪs] *noun*
matelas *(masculine)*.

mature [məˈtjʊər] *adjective*
mûr : **he's very mature for his age** il est très mûr pour son âge.

mauve [məʊv] *adjective*
mauve : **Harriet's wearing a mauve dress** Harriet porte une robe mauve.

maximum [ˈmæksɪməm] *adjective & noun*

◾ *adjective*
maximum *(invariable)* : **what's the maximum speed?** quelle est la vitesse maximum ?
◾ *noun*
maximum *(masculine)* : **there'll be a maximum of twenty** il y en aura vingt au maximum.

may [meɪ] *modal verb*
1. *Possibility*

When 'may' is used with another verb to say something is possible, you should use the adverb peut-être in French to translate it:

we may come nous viendrons peut-être ; **it may rain** il va peut-être pleuvoir ; **she may have phoned** elle a peut-être appelé
2. *Asking and giving permission* **pouvoir** :

may I open the window? est-ce que je peux ouvrir la fenêtre ? ; **you may sit down** vous pouvez vous asseoir.

May [meɪ] *noun*
mai *(masculine)* : **in May** en mai ; **next May** en mai prochain ; **last May** en mai dernier
➤ **May Day** le Premier mai

In French the months of the year do not start with a capital letter.

maybe [ˈmeɪbiː] *adverb*
peut-être : **maybe I'll come** je viendrai peut-être ; **maybe you're right** tu as peut-être raison
➤ **maybe not** peut-être pas.

mayonnaise [ˌmeɪəˈneɪz] *noun*
mayonnaise *(feminine)*.

mayor [meər] *noun*
maire *(masculine)* : **he's the mayor of New York** c'est le maire de New York.

maze [meɪz] *noun*
labyrinthe *(masculine)* : **this building is a real maze** cet immeuble est un vrai labyrinthe.

me [miː] *personal pronoun*
1. *Direct and indirect object* **me** (**m'** before a vowel) : **she doesn't know me** elle ne me connaît pas ; **can you hear me?** est-ce que tu m'entends ? ; **he never writes to me** il ne m'écrit jamais

In tenses like the present perfect or the past perfect, the past participle agrees with the direct object pronoun. Add an -e to the past participle if 'me' is feminine:

he saw me il m'a vu OR il m'a vue
2. *In imperatives and after prepositions* **moi** : **give me the book** donne-moi le livre ; **give it to me!** donne-le-moi ! ; **is that for me?** c'est pour moi ? ; **he's smaller than me** il est plus petit que moi.

meal [miːl] *noun*
repas *(masculine)* : **she made a big meal** elle a préparé un grand repas
➤ **enjoy your meal!** bon appétit !

mean [miːn] *adjective & verb*
◾ *adjective*
1. *UK* **avare** : **he's mean, he never buys me**

anything il est avare, il ne m'achète jamais rien

2. **méchant, mesquin : he's always mean to his sister** il est toujours méchant avec sa sœur

■ *verb (past tense & past participle* **meant)**

1. **vouloir dire : what do you mean?** qu'est-ce que tu veux dire ? ; **what does this expression mean?** que veut dire cette expression ? ; **it doesn't mean anything** ça ne veut rien dire

2. **avoir l'intention de : I mean to leave at six o'clock** j'ai l'intention de partir à six heures ; **I didn't mean to hurt you** je ne voulais pas te blesser

➤ **I didn't mean to drop it** je n'ai pas fait exprès de le laisser tomber

➤ **I meant it** j'étais sérieux

➤ **to be meant for** être destiné à : **this present is meant for your sister** ce cadeau est destiné à ta sœur

➤ **to be meant to do** être censé faire : **you were meant to wait for me here** tu étais censé m'attendre ici.

meaning ['miːnɪŋ] *noun*

sens *(masculine)*, **signification** *(feminine)* : **what's the meaning of this word?** quel est le sens de ce mot ?

means [miːnz] *noun*

moyen *(masculine)* : **it's a means to get what he wants** c'est un moyen d'obtenir ce qu'il veut

➤ **by means of** au moyen de : **the thief got in by means of a ladder** le voleur est entré au moyen d'une échelle

➤ **a means of transport** un moyen de transport.

meant [ment] *past tense & past participle of* **mean**

I meant to leave earlier j'avais l'intention de partir plus tôt ; **you were meant to help me** tu étais censé m'aider.

meantime ['miːnˌtaɪm] *noun*

➤ **in the meantime** en attendant.

meanwhile ['miːnˌwaɪl] *adverb*

1. **pendant ce temps : meanwhile, I was out with my friends** pendant ce temps, j'étais sorti avec mes copains

2. **en attendant : meanwhile you can get on with your work** en attendant, tu peux continuer à travailler.

measles ['miːzlz] *noun*

rougeole *(feminine)* : **she has measles** elle a la rougeole.

measure ['meʒəʳ] *verb*

mesurer : she measured the chair with a tape measure elle a mesuré la chaise avec un mètre ; **the room measures 2 metres by 3** la pièce mesure 2 mètres sur 3.

measurement ['meʒəmənt] *noun*

mesure *(feminine)* : **he took my measurements** il a pris mes mesures

➤ **waist measurement** tour *(masculine)* de taille.

meat [miːt] *noun*

viande *(feminine)* : **she doesn't like meat** elle n'aime pas la viande.

mechanic [mɪˈkænɪk] *noun*

mécanicien *(masculine)*, **mécanicienne** *(feminine)* : **he's a mechanic** il est mécanicien.

mechanical [mɪˈkænɪkl] *adjective*

mécanique.

medal ['medl] *noun*

médaille *(feminine)* : **she won a gold medal** elle a gagné une médaille d'or.

media ['miːdjə] *noun*

➤ **the media** les médias : **the event was reported in the media** les médias ont parlé de cet événement

> Le mot **media** peut être suivi d'un verbe au singulier ou au pluriel.

medical ['medɪkl] *adjective & noun*

■ *adjective*
médical : medical treatment traitement médical

➤ **a medical student** un étudiant en médecine, une étudiante en médecine

■ *noun*
visite *(feminine)* **médicale : I had a medical** j'ai passé une visite médicale.

medicine ['medsɪn] *noun*

1. **médecine** *(feminine)* : **Andrew's studying medicine** Andrew fait des études de médecine

m

2. **médicament** *(masculine)* : **I must take my medicine** je dois prendre mes médicaments.

Mediterranean [ˌmedɪtə'reɪnjən] *noun & adjective*

■ *noun*

➤ **the Mediterranean** OR **the Mediterranean sea** la Méditerranée

■ *adjective*

méditerranéen *(feminine* **méditerranéenne)** : **the Mediterranean climate** le climat méditerranéen.

medium ['miːdjəm] *adjective*

moyen *(feminine* **moyenne)** : **he's of medium height** il est de taille moyenne.

medium-sized ['miːdjəmsaɪzd] *adjective*

de taille moyenne : **a medium-sized town** une ville de taille moyenne.

meet [miːt] *(past tense & past participle* met) *verb*

1. **rencontrer** : **I met her at a party** je l'ai rencontrée dans une fête

2. **faire la connaissance de** : **have you met Lisa's brother?** est-ce que tu as fait la connaissance du frère de Lisa ?

3. **se rencontrer** : **we met by chance in the street** nous nous sommes rencontrés par hasard dans la rue

4. **avoir rendez-vous avec** : **I'm meeting Harry tonight** j'ai rendez-vous avec Harry ce soir

5. **se retrouver** : **let's meet in front of the cinema** OR **I'll meet you in front of the cinema** on se retrouve devant le cinéma

6. **chercher** : **I'm going to meet them at the station at 3 o'clock** je vais les chercher à la gare à 3 heures ; **I'll come and meet you** je viendrai te chercher

➤ **pleased to meet you** enchanté de faire votre connaissance.

meeting ['miːtɪŋ] *noun*

1. **réunion** *(feminine)* : **I have a meeting today** j'ai une réunion aujourd'hui

2. **rencontre** *(feminine)* : **this was our first meeting** ça a été notre première rencontre.

megabyte ['megəbaɪt] *noun*

mégaoctet *(masculine)*.

melody ['melədɪ] *(plural* melodies) *noun*

mélodie *(feminine)*.

melon ['melən] *noun*

melon *(masculine)* : **she loves melon** elle adore le melon.

melt [melt] *verb*

fondre : **the butter has melted** le beurre a fondu ; **the ice is melting** la glace est en train de fondre.

member ['membəʳ] *noun*

membre *(masculine)* : **Rita's a member of the chess club** Rita est membre du club d'échecs

➤ **a Member of Congress** US un membre du Congrès

➤ **a Member of Parliament** UK un député
➤ Congress, Houses of Parliament.

memorial [mɪ'mɔːrɪəl] *noun*

monument *(masculine)* : **a war memorial** un monument aux morts.

memorize ['meməraɪz] *verb*

apprendre par cœur, mémoriser : **you must memorize your password** tu dois mémoriser ton mot de passe.

memory ['memərɪ] *(plural* memories) *noun*

1. **mémoire** *(feminine)* : **she has a good memory** elle a une bonne mémoire ; **my new computer has a lot of memory** mon nouvel ordinateur a beaucoup de mémoire

2. **souvenir** *(masculine)* : **I have good memories of that evening** j'ai de bons souvenirs de cette soirée.

men *plural of* man.

mend [mend] *verb*

1. UK **réparer** : **can you mend the radio?** tu peux réparer la radio ?

2. **raccommoder** : **I have some clothes to mend** j'ai des vêtements à raccommoder.

mental ['mentl] *adjective*

mental : **mental arithmetic** le calcul mental.

mention ['menʃn] *verb*

mentionner : **he mentioned your name** il a mentionné votre nom

➤ **thank you! – don't mention it!** merci ! – je vous en prie !

menu ['menjuː] *noun*

menu *(masculine)* : **what's on the menu?** qu'est-ce qu'il y a au menu ? ; **choose Print**

from the File menu sélectionner Imprimer dans le menu Fichier.

meow *US* ➤ miaow *UK*.

Mercury ['mɜːkjʊrɪ] *noun*

Mercure *(feminine)* : **Mercury is the planet that is closest to the sun** Mercure est la planète la plus proche du Soleil.

mercy ['mɜːsɪ] *noun*

pitié *(feminine)* : **he showed no mercy** il n'a eu aucune pitié.

mermaid ['mɜːmeɪd] *noun*

sirène *(feminine)* : **it's a story about a mermaid** c'est l'histoire d'une sirène.

merry ['merɪ] *adjective*

joyeux : **Merry Christmas!** joyeux Noël !

merry-go-round ['merɪɡəʊraʊnd] *noun*

manège *(masculine)* : **to have a go on the merry-go-round** faire un tour de manège.

mess [mes] *uncountable noun & verb*

désordre *(masculine)* : **what a mess!** quel désordre ! ; **my room's in a mess** ma chambre est en désordre ; **the workmen made a mess** les ouvriers ont mis du désordre

mess about *UK*, **mess around** *phrasal verb informal*

1. faire l'imbécile : **stop messing around!** arrête de faire l'imbécile !
2. s'amuser : **the children are messing around in the garden** les enfants s'amusent dans le jardin
3. toucher à : **don't mess around with my guitar** ne touche pas à ma guitare

mess up *phrasal verb informal*

1. mettre en désordre : **he's messed up the kitchen** il a mis la cuisine en désordre
2. gâcher : **that's messed up my plans** ça a gâché mes projets
3. bâcler : **I really messed up my work** j'ai bâclé mon travail.

message ['mesɪdʒ] *noun*

message *(masculine)* : **she sent me a message** elle m'a envoyé un message.

messenger ['mesɪndʒəʳ] *noun*

messager *(masculine)*, **messagère** *(feminine)*.

messy ['mesɪ] *adjective*

1. en désordre : **my room is very messy** ma chambre est tout en désordre
2. désordonné : **you're very messy** tu es très désordonné
3. salissant : **it's a messy job** c'est un travail salissant.

met [met] *past tense & past participle of* meet

I met him in the street je l'ai rencontré dans la rue ; **I haven't met her yet** je n'ai pas encore fait sa connaissance.

metal ['metl] *noun*

métal *(masculine)* : **it's made of metal** c'est en métal.

meter ['miːtəʳ] *noun*

1. compteur *(masculine)* : **a water meter** un compteur d'eau
2. *US* mètre *(masculine)* : **it's two meters long** ça fait deux mètres de long
➤ **a parking meter** un parcmètre.

method ['meθəd] *noun*

méthode *(feminine)* : **we must change our methods** il faut changer nos méthodes.

metre *UK*, **meter** *US* ['miːtəʳ] *noun*

mètre *(masculine)* : **it's four metres long** ça fait quatre mètres de long.

metric ['metrɪk] *adjective*

métrique : **the metric system** le système métrique.

Mexican ['meksɪkn] *adjective & noun*

▢ *adjective*
mexicain

The French adjective does not start with a capital letter:

I like Mexican food j'aime la cuisine mexicaine
▢ *noun*
Mexicain *(masculine)*, **Mexicaine** *(feminine)*.

Mexico ['meksɪkəʊ] *noun*

le Mexique

In French the names of countries are used with the definite article (le, la or l'). Remember that the French preposition à combines with le to become au:

Mexico is in Central America le Mexique est en Amérique centrale ; **I'm going to Mexico**

je vais au Mexique ; **Raoul lives in Mexico** Raoul vit au Mexique

➤ **Mexico City** Mexico : **Mexico City is the capital of Mexico** Mexico est la capitale du Mexique.

miaow *UK* [miːˈaʊ], **meow** *US* [mɪˈaʊ] *verb*

miauler : **the cat's miaowing** le chat miaule.

mice *plural* ➤ mouse.

microchip [ˈmaɪkrəʊtʃɪp] *noun*

puce *(feminine)* : **there's a microchip inside the computer** il y a une puce dans l'ordinateur.

microphone [ˈmaɪkrəfəʊn] *noun*

micro *(masculine)* : **talk into the microphone** parle dans le micro.

microscope [ˈmaɪkrəskəʊp] *noun*

microscope *(masculine)* : **they were looking at something under the microscope** ils examinaient quelque chose au microscope.

microwave [ˈmaɪkrəweɪv], **microwave oven** [ˈmaɪkrəweɪvˈʌvn] *noun*

four *(masculine)* à micro-ondes : **heat it up in the microwave** fais-le chauffer au four à micro-ondes.

midday [mɪdˈdeɪ] *noun*

midi *(masculine)* : **she went out at midday** elle est sortie à midi.

middle [ˈmɪdl] *noun*

milieu *(masculine)* : **it happened in the middle of the night** ça s'est passé au milieu de la nuit ; **the table's in the middle of the room** la table est au milieu de la pièce ; **he sat in the middle chair** il s'est assis sur la chaise du milieu

➤ **the Middle Ages** le Moyen Âge

➤ **the Middle East** le Moyen-Orient : **he's going to the Middle East** il va au Moyen-Orient ; **she lives in the Middle East** elle habite au Moyen-Orient

➤ **middle name** second prénom *(masculine)* : **what is your middle name?** quel est ton second prénom ?

middle-aged [ˈmɪdleɪdʒd] *adjective*

d'une cinquantaine d'années : **she's middle-aged** elle a une cinquantaine d'années.

middle-class [ˈmɪdlklɑːs] *adjective*

bourgeois : **he's very middle-class** il est très bourgeois.

midnight [ˈmɪdnaɪt] *noun*

minuit *(masculine)* : **he came back at midnight** il est rentré à minuit.

might [maɪt] *modal verb*

> When 'might' is used with another verb to say that something is possible, you should use the adverb peut-être in French to translate it:

they might be away ils sont peut-être absents ; **it might snow** il va peut-être neiger ; **she might have got lost** elle s'est peut-être perdue ; **he said he might come** il a dit qu'il allait peut-être venir.

mighty [ˈmaɪtɪ] *adjective*

puissant : **he was a mighty king** c'était un roi puissant.

mike [maɪk] *(abbreviation of* microphone*)* *noun informal*

micro *(masculine)* : **he was talking into the mike** il parlait dans le micro.

mild [maɪld] *adjective*

doux *(feminine* douce*)* : **the climate is very mild** le climat est très doux.

mile [maɪl] *noun*

= 1,6 km : **she was driving at 50 miles an hour** elle roulait à 80 kilomètres à l'heure ; **I walked for miles** j'ai marché pendant des kilomètres OR j'ai fait des kilomètres à pied.

military [ˈmɪlɪtrɪ] *adjective*

militaire : **a military band** une fanfare militaire.

milk [mɪlk] *noun*

lait *(masculine)* : **a glass of milk** un verre de lait ; **would you like milk in your tea?** tu veux du lait dans ton thé ?

➤ **milk chocolate** chocolat *(masculine)* au lait

➤ **a milk shake** un milk-shake.

milkman [ˈmɪlkmən] *(plural* milkmen [ˈmɪlkmən]*)* *noun*

laitier *(masculine)*.

mill [mɪl] *noun*

moulin *(masculine)*.

millennium [mɪ'lenɪəm] (*plural* millennia [mɪ'lenɪə]) noun
millénaire *(masculine)* : **it's the new millennium** c'est le nouveau millénaire.

millimetre *UK*, **millimeter** *US* ['mɪlɪ‚miːtər] noun
millimètre *(masculine)*.

million ['mɪljən] noun
million *(masculine)* : **three millions** trois millions ; **a million dollars** un million de dollars.

millionaire [‚mɪljə'neər] noun
millionnaire *(masculine or feminine)* : **he's a millionaire** il est millionnaire.

mince *UK* [mɪns] noun & verb
■ *noun*
viande *(feminine)* hachée
➤ **mince pie** tartelette garnie d'une pâte de fruits secs
■ *verb*
hacher : **you have to mince the meat** il faut hacher la viande.

mind [maɪnd] noun & verb
■ *noun*
esprit *(masculine)* : **it never crossed my mind** ça ne m'est jamais venu à l'esprit
➤ **to have something on one's mind** être préoccupé : **she has something on her mind** elle est préoccupée
➤ **to make up one's mind** se décider : **have you made up your mind?** tu t'es décidé ?
➤ **to change one's mind** changer d'avis : **she's changed her mind** elle a changé d'avis
■ *verb*
1. faire attention à : **mind the step!** attention à la marche !
2. garder : **could you mind the children this evening?** peux-tu garder les enfants ce soir ?
➤ **I don't mind**
1. ça ne me dérange pas : **I'm sorry about the noise – oh, I don't mind** je suis désolé pour le bruit – oh, ça ne me dérange pas ; **I don't mind waiting** ça ne me dérange pas d'attendre
2. ça m'est égal : **which sandwich do you want? – oh, I don't mind** quel sandwich veux-tu ? – oh, ça m'est égal
➤ **do you mind if I open the window?** est-ce que ça te dérange si j'ouvre la fenêtre ?
➤ **never mind!** ça ne fait rien !

➤ **I wouldn't mind a coffee** je prendrais bien un café
➤ **mind your own business!** occupe-toi de tes affaires !

mine [maɪn] pronoun & noun
■ *possessive pronoun*
1. le mien *(feminine* la mienne*)* [*plural* les miens, les miennes]

> In French the possessive pronoun agrees in gender (masculine or feminine) and number (singular or plural) with the noun it replaces:

his computer's a PC, mine is a Mac son ordinateur c'est un PC, le mien c'est un Mac ; **her dress is blue, mine is red** sa robe est bleue, la mienne est rouge ; **his books are on the table, mine are on the shelf** ses livres sont sur la table, les miens sont sur l'étagère ; **your hands are dirty, mine are clean** tes mains sont sales, les miennes sont propres
2. **is this glass mine?** c'est à moi ce verre ? ; **he's a friend of mine** c'est un ami à moi
■ *noun*
mine *(feminine)* : **a coal mine** une mine de charbon ; **the tank hit a mine** le char a sauté sur une mine.

miner ['maɪnər] noun
mineur *(masculine)* : **he's a miner** il est mineur.

mineral water ['mɪnərəl'wɔːtər] noun
eau *(feminine)* minérale.

miniature [*UK* 'mɪnətʃər, *US* 'mɪnɪətʃuər] *adjective*
miniature : **it's a miniature Eiffel Tower** c'est une tour Eiffel miniature.

minidisc ['mɪnɪdɪsk] noun
MiniDisc® *(masculine)*.

minimum ['mɪnɪməm] noun & adjective
■ *noun*
minimum *(masculine)* : **you have to pay a minimum of $50** il faut payer un minimum de 50 dollars
■ *adjective*
minimum *(invariable)* : **what's the minimum wage?** quel est le salaire minimum ?

miniskirt ['mɪnɪskɜːt] noun
minijupe *(feminine)* : **Clara's wearing a miniskirt** Clara porte une minijupe.

minister ['mɪnɪstə⁣ʳ] *noun*

1. **ministre** *(masculine)* : **the Environment Minister** le ministre de l'Environnement
2. **pasteur** *(masculine)* : **he's a minister in the church** il est pasteur.

ministry ['mɪnɪstrɪ] *noun*

ministère *(masculine)* : **the Ministry of Education** le ministère de l'Éducation.

minivan *US* ['mɪnɪvæn] *noun*

monospace *(masculine)*.

mink [mɪŋk] *(plural* **mink)** *noun*

vison *(masculine)*
➤ **a mink coat** un manteau de vison.

minor ['maɪnə⁣ʳ] *adjective*

mineur : **it's a minor problem** c'est un problème mineur.

minority [maɪ'nɒrətɪ] *(plural* **minorities)** *noun*

minorité *(feminine)* : **we're in a minority** nous sommes en minorité.

mint [mɪnt] *noun*

1. **menthe** *(feminine)* : **he likes mint tea** il aime le thé à la menthe
2. **bonbon** *(masculine)* **à la menthe** : **would you like a mint?** tu veux un bonbon à la menthe ?

minus ['maɪnəs] *preposition*

moins : **20 minus 7 equals 13** 20 moins 7 égale 13 ; **it's minus three degrees** il fait moins trois
➤ **the minus sign** le signe moins.

minute ['mɪnɪt] *noun*

minute *(feminine)* : **he left five minutes ago** il est parti il y a cinq minutes ; **wait a minute!** attends une minute !
➤ **stop this minute!** arrête tout de suite !

mirror ['mɪrə⁣ʳ] *noun*

1. **glace** *(feminine)*, **miroir** *(masculine)* : **he was looking at himself in the mirror** il se regardait dans la glace OR il se regardait dans le miroir
2. **rétroviseur** *(masculine)* : **look in your mirror before you overtake** regarde dans le rétroviseur avant de doubler.

misbehave [ˌmɪsbɪ'heɪv] *verb*

se conduire mal : **they always misbehave in class** ils se conduisent toujours mal en classe.

mischief ['mɪstʃɪf] *uncountable noun*

bêtises *(feminine plural)* : **he's always up to mischief** il fait toujours des bêtises.

miser ['maɪzə⁣ʳ] *noun*

avare *(masculine or feminine)* : **Scrooge is a miser** Scrooge est avare.

miserable ['mɪzrəbl] *adjective*

1. **malheureux** *(feminine* **malheureuse)** : **he looks miserable** il a l'air malheureux
2. **épouvantable** : **the weather's miserable** il fait un temps épouvantable.

misery ['mɪzərɪ] *noun*

1. **malheur** *(masculine)* : **it'll bring nothing but misery** cela ne va apporter que du malheur
2. *UK* **grincheux** *(masculine)*, **grincheuse** *(feminine)* : **he's such a misery!** quel grincheux !

 Misery est un faux ami, il ne signifie pas "misère".

miss [mɪs] *verb*

rater : **I missed the train** j'ai raté le train ; **it's a big house, you can't miss it** c'est une grande maison, tu ne peux pas la rater ; **the film was terrible, you didn't miss anything** le film était nul, tu n'as rien raté
➤ **I miss my family** ma famille me manque : **I miss her** elle me manque ; **I miss you** tu me manques

miss out *UK phrasal verb*

omettre, sauter : **I missed out a word in this sentence** j'ai sauté un mot dans cette phrase.

Miss [mɪs] *noun*

Mademoiselle *(feminine)*, **Mlle** : **can I help you, Miss?** je peux vous aider, mademoiselle ? ; **Miss Janet Pinkerton** Mlle Janet Pinkerton.

missing ['mɪsɪŋ] *adjective*

1. **manquant** : **fill in the missing words** complétez avec les mots manquants
2. **disparu** : **a missing person** une personne disparue
➤ **to be missing**
1. **manquer** : **how many pieces are missing?** il manque combien de pièces ? ; **there's something missing** il manque quelque chose

2. **avoir disparu** : **my watch is missing** ma montre a disparu
➤ **to go missing** disparaître.

mission ['mɪʃn] *noun*

mission *(feminine)* : **our mission is to find him** notre mission est de le trouver.

mist [mɪst] *noun*

brume *(feminine)* : **there's a mist** il y a de la brume.

mistake [mɪ'steɪk] *noun & verb*

◼ *noun*
1. **erreur** *(feminine)* : **it was a big mistake** c'était une grave erreur
2. **faute** *(feminine)* : **a spelling mistake** une faute d'orthographe
➤ **to make a mistake**
1. **se tromper** OR **faire une erreur** : **I'm sorry, I must have made a mistake** je suis désolé, j'ai dû me tromper ; **I made a mistake by telling him** j'ai fait une erreur en le lui disant
2. **faire une faute** : **I made a lot of mistakes in my essay** j'ai fait beaucoup de fautes dans ma rédaction
➤ **by mistake** par erreur : **he took my pen by mistake** il a pris mon stylo par erreur
◼ *verb (past tense* mistook [mɪ'stʊk], *past participle* mistaken [mɪ'steɪkn])*
➤ **to mistake somebody for somebody else** prendre quelqu'un pour quelqu'un d'autre : **I mistook you for your brother** je t'ai pris pour ton frère.

mistaken *past participle of* mistake.

mistletoe ['mɪsltəʊ] *noun*

gui *(masculine)* : **to kiss under the mistletoe** s'embrasser sous le gui.

mistook *past tense of* mistake.

misty ['mɪstɪ] *adjective*

brumeux *(feminine* **brumeuse)** : **it's misty today** le temps est brumeux aujourd'hui.

misunderstand [ˌmɪsʌndə'stænd] *(past tense & past participle* misunderstood [ˌmɪsʌndə'stʊd]) *verb*
mal comprendre : **I misunderstood you** je t'ai mal compris.

misunderstanding [ˌmɪsʌndə'stændɪŋ]

noun

malentendu *(masculine)* : **there's been a misunderstanding** il y a eu un malentendu.

misunderstood *past tense & past participle of* misunderstand.

mix [mɪks] *noun & verb*

◼ *noun*
mélange *(masculine)* : **it's a mix of two cultures** c'est un mélange de deux cultures
➤ **a cake mix** une préparation pour gâteau
◼ *verb*
mélanger : **mix all the ingredients together** mélangez tous les ingrédients

mix up *phrasal verb*

1. **confondre** : **he mixed me up with my brother** il m'a confondu avec mon frère
2. **embrouiller** : **you're mixing me up** tu m'embrouilles ; **I'm getting mixed up** je ne sais plus où j'en suis
3. **mélanger** : **he's mixed up all the photos** il a mélangé toutes les photos.

mixed [mɪkst] *adjective*

1. **assorti** : **a bag of mixed sweets** un sachet de bonbons assortis
2. **mixte** : **it's a mixed school** c'est une école mixte
➤ **a mixed salad** une salade composée.

mixture ['mɪkstʃər] *noun*

mélange *(masculine)* : **it's a mixture of rap and jazz** c'est un mélange de rap et de jazz.

mix-up ['mɪksʌp] *noun*

confusion *(feminine)* : **there's been a mix-up** il y a eu une confusion.

moan [məʊn] *verb*

1. **gémir** : **the patient moaned** le malade a gémi
2. *informal* **râler** : **he's always moaning** il n'arrête pas de râler.

mobile ['məʊbaɪl] *noun & adjective*

portable *(masculine)*
➤ **a mobile phone** un téléphone portable.

mock exam *UK* [mɒkɪg'zæm] *noun*

examen *(masculine)* **blanc**.

model ['mɒdl] *noun*

1. **modèle** *(masculine)* : **it's the latest model** c'est le dernier modèle
2. **maquette** *(feminine)*, **modèle** *(masculine)* **ré-**

duit : **a model plane** une maquette d'avion
OR un modèle réduit d'avion
3. **mannequin** *(masculine)* : **she's a model** elle
est mannequin.

modem ['məʊdem] *noun*

modem *(masculine)*.

modern ['mɒdən] *adjective*

moderne : **the town is very modern** la ville
est très moderne
➤ **modern languages** langues *(feminine plural)*
vivantes.

modest ['mɒdɪst] *adjective*

modeste : **Fred's very modest** Fred est très
modeste.

moldy *US* ➤ **mouldy** *UK*.

mole [məʊl] *noun*

1. **grain** *(masculine)* **de beauté : she has a mole
on her arm** elle a un grain de beauté sur le
bras
2. **taupe** *(feminine)* : **moles live under the
ground** les taupes vivent sous terre.

mom *US* [mɒm] *noun informal*

maman *(feminine)*, **mère** *(feminine)* : **hi, mom!**
bonjour, maman ! ; **his mom's a nurse** sa mère est infirmière.

moment ['məʊmənt] *noun*

moment *(masculine)*, **instant** *(masculine)* : **he's
not here at the moment** il n'est pas là pour le
moment
➤ **wait a moment!** un instant !

mommy *US* ['mɒmɪ] *noun informal*

maman *(feminine)*.

monastery ['mɒnəstrɪ] *(plural* **monasteries)** *noun*

monastère *(masculine)*.

Monday ['mʌndɪ] *noun*

lundi *(masculine)* : **it's Monday today** nous
sommes lundi ; **next Monday** lundi prochain ;
last Monday lundi dernier
➤ **on Monday** lundi : **I'll see you on Monday**
on se voit lundi
➤ **on Mondays** le lundi : **he does judo on
Mondays** il fait du judo le lundi

In French the days of the week do not start with
a capital letter.

money ['mʌnɪ] *uncountable noun*

argent *(masculine)* : **I don't have any money**
je n'ai pas d'argent ; **he makes a lot of money**
il gagne beaucoup d'argent.

mongrel ['mʌngrəl] *noun*

bâtard *(masculine)* : **my dog's a mongrel** mon
chien est un bâtard.

monk [mʌŋk] *noun*

moine *(masculine)* : **he's a monk** il est moine.

monkey ['mʌŋkɪ] *noun*

singe *(masculine)*.

monster ['mɒnstər] *noun*

monstre *(masculine)*.

month [mʌnθ] *noun*

mois *(masculine)* : **this month** ce mois-ci ; **next
month** le mois prochain ; **last month** le mois
dernier ; **we see each other twice a month**
nous nous voyons deux fois par mois.

monument ['mɒnjʊmənt] *noun*

monument *(masculine)* : **it's an ancient
monument** c'est un monument ancien.

moo [muː] *(past tense & past participle* mooed
[muːd]) *verb*
meugler : I can hear the cows mooing j'entends les vaches meugler.

mood [muːd] *noun*

humeur *(feminine)* : **she's in a good mood** elle
est de bonne humeur ; **I'm in a bad mood** je
suis de mauvaise humeur.

moody ['muːdɪ] *adjective*

1. **de mauvaise humeur : you're very moody
today** tu es de très mauvaise humeur aujourd'hui
2. **lunatique : she's a moody person** elle est
lunatique.

moon [muːn] *noun*

lune *(feminine)* : **it's a full moon tonight** c'est
la pleine lune ce soir.

moonlight ['muːnlaɪt] *noun*

clair *(masculine)* **de lune : I went for a walk in
the moonlight** je me suis promené au clair de
lune.

moped ['məʊped] *noun*

Mobylette®*(feminine)* : **she goes to work on a moped** elle va travailler en Mobylette.

moral ['mɒrəl] *adjective & noun*

■ *adjective*
moral : **moral support** un soutien moral
■ *noun*
morale *(feminine)* : **what's the moral of the story?** quelle est la morale de l'histoire ?

morale [mə'rɑːl] *noun*

moral *(masculine)* : **we must try and boost their morale** il faut essayer de leur remonter le moral.

more [mɔːʳ] *adverb, adjective & pronoun*

■ *adverb*
1. plus : **it's more expensive** c'est plus cher ; **she's more intelligent than him** elle est plus intelligente que lui ; **you must come more often** tu dois venir plus souvent ; **Tom reads more than me** Tom lit plus que moi ; **she doesn't live here any more** elle n'habite plus ici
2. davantage, plus : **you must work more** tu dois travailler davantage OR tu dois travailler plus
➤ **once more** encore une fois OR une fois de plus
■ *adjective (comparative of many, much and a lot of)*
1. plus de : **there are more trains in the morning** il y a plus de trains le matin ; **he has more money than me** il a plus d'argent que moi ; **there isn't any more bread** il n'y a plus de pain ; **I need three more tickets** j'ai besoin de trois billets de plus
2. encore de : **would you like some more cake?** voulez-vous encore du gâteau ? ; **three more people arrived** trois autres personnes sont arrivées ; **do you have any more questions?** est-ce que vous avez d'autres questions ?
■ *pronoun (comparative of many, much and a lot)*
1. plus : **it costs more than $100** ça coûte plus de 100 dollars ; **he eats more than I do** il mange plus que moi ; **there aren't any more** il n'y en a plus
2. davantage, plus : **I need more of them** il m'en faut davantage OR il m'en faut plus ; **I like this cake, can I have some more?** j'aime ce gâteau, je peux en prendre encore ?

When you are referring back to something already mentioned, as well as using **plus, davantage** or **encore** in French you have to use the pronoun **en**. It is like saying 'more of them' or 'more of it'.

➤ **more and more**
1. de plus en plus : **she travels more and more** elle voyage de plus en plus
2. de plus en plus de : **I have more and more work** j'ai de plus en plus de travail
➤ **more or less** plus ou moins.

morning ['mɔːnɪŋ] *noun*

1. matin *(masculine)* : **he's not going to school this morning** il ne va pas à l'école ce matin ; **she works in the morning** elle travaille le matin ; **at six o'clock in the morning** à six heures du matin ; **I'll do it in the morning** je le ferai demain matin
2. matinée *(feminine)* : **she stayed in bed all morning** elle est restée au lit toute la matinée
➤ **every morning** tous les matins
➤ **yesterday morning** hier matin
➤ **tomorrow morning** demain matin.

Moscow ['mɒskəʊ] *noun*

Moscou : **he lives in Moscow** il habite à Moscou ; **we're going to Moscow** nous allons à Moscou.

Moslem ➤ Muslim.

mosque [mɒsk] *noun*

mosquée *(feminine)* : **they go to the mosque on Fridays** ils vont à la mosquée le vendredi.

mosquito [mə'skiːtəʊ] *noun*

moustique *(masculine)* : **I'm covered in mosquito bites** je suis couvert de piqûres de moustiques.

most [məʊst] *adverb, adjective & pronoun*

■ *adverb*
the most le plus OR la plus OR les plus ; **the most experienced player in the team** le joueur le plus expérimenté de l'équipe ; **the most beautiful city in the world** la plus belle ville du monde ; **the most expensive tickets** les billets les plus chers
■ *adjective*
1. la plupart de : **most tourists visit the Eiffel Tower** la plupart des touristes visitent la tour Eiffel

2. le plus de : she has most money elle a le plus d'argent ; **who has most sweets?** qui a le plus de bonbons ?

■ *pronoun*

1. la plupart : most of the tourists are American la plupart des touristes sont américains ; **most of them left early** la plupart d'entre eux sont partis tôt

2. le plus : Paul ate the most OR Paul ate most c'est Paul qui a mangé le plus ; **I spent most of the day in bed** j'ai passé la plus grande partie de la journée au lit OR j'ai passé presque toute la journée au lit.

mostly ['məʊstlɪ] *adverb*

surtout : there were lots of customers, mostly young people il y avait beaucoup de clients, surtout des jeunes.

motel [məʊ'tel] *noun*

motel *(masculine)* : we stayed in a motel for the night on a passé la nuit dans un motel.

moth [mɒθ] *noun*

papillon *(masculine)* **de nuit**.

mother ['mʌðər] *noun*

mère *(feminine)*

➤ **Mother's Day** la fête des Mères.

mother-in-law ['mʌðərɪnlɔː] *noun*

belle-mère *(feminine)* [*plural* **belles-mères**].

mother-of-pearl [ˌmʌðərɒv'pɜːl] *noun*

nacre *(feminine)* : a mother-of-pearl necklace un collier en nacre.

motion picture [ˌməʊʃn'pɪktʃər] *noun*

film *(masculine)*.

motivated ['məʊtɪveɪtɪd] *adjective*

motivé : the students are very motivated les étudiants sont très motivés.

motivation [ˌməʊtɪ'veɪʃn] *noun*

motivation *(feminine)*.

motive ['məʊtɪv] *noun*

mobile *(masculine)* : what was the motive for the crime? quel était le mobile du crime ?

motor ['məʊtər] *noun*

moteur *(masculine)* : an electric motor un moteur électrique

➤ **motor racing** course *(feminine)* automobile.

motorbike *UK* ['məʊtəbaɪk] *noun*

moto *(feminine)* : he came on a motorbike il est venu à moto.

motorboat ['məʊtəbəʊt] *noun*

canot *(masculine)* **automobile**.

motorcycle ['məʊtəˌsaɪkl] *noun*

moto *(feminine)* : he's riding a motorcycle il est à moto.

motorcyclist ['məʊtəˌsaɪklɪst] *noun*

motocycliste *(masculine or feminine)*.

motorist *UK* ['məʊtərɪst] *noun*

automobiliste *(masculine or feminine)*.

motorway *UK* ['məʊtəweɪ] *noun*

autoroute *(feminine)*.

motto ['mɒtəʊ] *noun*

devise *(feminine)* : the school motto la devise de l'école.

mouldy *UK*, **moldy** *US* ['məʊldɪ] *adjective*

moisi : the bread is mouldy le pain est moisi

➤ **to go mouldy** moisir : the cake has gone mouldy le gâteau a moisi.

mount [maʊnt] *verb & noun*

■ *verb*

1. monter : Dan mounted his horse Dan a monté son cheval ; **they have mounted a campaign against racism** ils ont monté une campagne contre le racisme

2. augmenter : the cost is mounting le coût augmente

■ *noun*

mont *(masculine)*

➤ **Mount Rushmore** le mont Rushmore

> **MOUNT RUSHMORE**
> Les visages géants de plusieurs présidents des États-Unis (George Washington, Thomas Jefferson, Abraham Lincoln et Theodore Roosevelt) ont été sculptés dans la roche du mont Rushmore, dans l'État du Dakota du Sud, entre 1867 et 1941. Chaque visage mesure 18 mètres de haut.

mountain ['maʊntɪn] *noun*

montagne *(feminine)* : Ben Nevis is the highest mountain in Britain Ben Nevis est la plus haute montagne de Grande-Bretagne

➤ **a mountain bike** un VTT.

mountaineer [ˌmaʊntɪ'nɪər] *noun*

alpiniste *(masculine or feminine)*.

mountaineering [ˌmaʊntɪ'nɪərɪŋ] *uncountable noun*

alpinisme *(masculine)* : **to go mountaineering** faire de l'alpinisme.

mouse [maʊs] *(plural* mice [maɪs]*) noun*

souris *(feminine)*

➤ **he was as quiet as a mouse** il ne faisait pas le moindre bruit

➤ **the mouse button** le bouton de la souris

➤ **a mouse mat** *UK* OR **a mouse pad** *US* un tapis de souris.

mousse [muːs] *noun*

mousse *(feminine)* : **chocolate mousse** mousse au chocolat.

moustache *UK* [mə'stɑːʃ], **mustache** *US* ['mʌstæʃ] *noun*

moustache *(feminine)* : **he has a moustache** il a une moustache.

mouth [maʊθ] *noun*

bouche *(feminine)* : **don't speak with your mouth full!** ne parle pas la bouche pleine ! ; **he didn't open his mouth** il n'a pas ouvert la bouche.

mouth organ ['maʊθ ˌɔːɡən] *noun*

harmonica *(masculine)* : **he plays the mouth organ** il joue de l'harmonica.

move [muːv] *noun & verb*

■ *noun*

1. déménagement *(masculine)* : **the vase broke during the move** le vase s'est cassé pendant le déménagement

➤ **to get a move on** *informal* se dépêcher : **we must get a move on** il faut qu'on se dépêche

2. *In games* tour *(masculine)* : **it's my move** c'est mon tour

■ *verb*

1. bouger : **don't move** ne bouge pas ; **I can't move my arm** je ne peux pas bouger mon bras

2. déplacer : **we must move the furniture to paint the room** il faut déplacer les meubles pour peindre la pièce

3. avancer : **come on, get moving!** allez, avancez ! ; **the mountaineers moved slowly forward** les alpinistes avançaient lentement

4. déménager : **they're moving next week** ils déménagent la semaine prochaine ; **we're**

moving house *UK* nous déménageons ; **we're moving to Brighton** nous allons habiter à Brighton

5. émouvoir : **the film really moved me** le film m'a beaucoup ému ; **she was very moved** elle était très émue

move forward *phrasal verb*

avancer : **the soldiers are moving forward** les soldats avancent

move in *phrasal verb*

emménager : **the new lodger has moved in** le nouveau locataire a emménagé

move off *phrasal verb*

se mettre en route : **the convoy moved off** le convoi s'est mis en route

move out *phrasal verb*

déménager : **he has moved out** il a déménagé

move over *phrasal verb*

se pousser : **move over, I don't have enough room** pousse-toi, je n'ai pas assez de place.

movement ['muːvmənt] *noun*

mouvement *(masculine)* : **she made a sudden movement** elle a fait un mouvement brusque.

movie ['muːvɪ] *noun*

film *(masculine)* : **let's go to a movie** allons voir un film

➤ **the movies** le cinéma : **I went to the movies** je suis allé au cinéma

➤ **a movie camera** une caméra

➤ **a movie theater** *US* un cinéma.

mow [məʊ] *(past tense* mowed [məʊd], *past participle* mowed OR mown [məʊn]*) verb*

tondre : **she's mowing the lawn** elle tond le gazon.

mower ['məʊər] *noun*

tondeuse *(feminine)* à gazon.

mown *past participle of* mow.

MP *UK* [ˌem'piː] *(abbreviation of* Member of Parliament*) noun*

député *(masculine)* : **he's an MP** il est député.

MP3 *UK* [empiː'θriː] *noun*

MP3 *(masculine)* : **to download an MP3** télécharger un MP3.

Mr [ˈmɪstər] *noun*

M., Monsieur *(masculine)* : **Mr Smith has arrived** M. Smith est arrivé.

Mrs [ˈmɪsɪz] *noun*

Mme, Madame *(feminine)* : **Mrs Jones has arrived** Mme Jones est arrivée.

Ms [mɪz] *noun*

Mme, Madame *(feminine)* : **Ms Brown is here to see you** Mme Brown aimerait vous voir.

much [mʌtʃ] *(comparative* more, *superlative* most) *adjective, pronoun & adverb*

■ *adjective*
beaucoup de : **I don't have much time** je n'ai pas beaucoup de temps

■ *pronoun*
beaucoup : **I don't want much** je n'en veux pas beaucoup

> When you are referring back to something already mentioned, as well as using **beaucoup** in French you have to use the pronoun **en**. It is like saying 'much of it'.

■ *adverb*
beaucoup : **she doesn't go out much** elle ne sort pas beaucoup ; **thank you very much** merci beaucoup
> **how much?**
ı. combien ? : **how much does it cost?** combien ça coûte ?
2. combien de ? : **how much money do you have?** combien d'argent as-tu ?
> **too much**
ı. trop : **she talks too much** elle parle trop
2. trop de : **there's too much sugar in my tea** il y a trop de sucre dans mon thé
> **as much** autant : **I don't have as much** je n'en ai pas autant
> **as much as**
ı. autant de : **he doesn't have as much time as I do** il n'a pas autant de temps que moi
2. autant que : **have as much as you like** prends-en autant que tu veux
> **so much**
ı. tellement : **I missed you so much** tu m'as tellement manqué
2. tant de : **he had so much trouble concentrating** il avait tant de mal à se concentrer.

mud [mʌd] *noun*

boue *(feminine)* : **the car's covered in mud** la voiture est couverte de boue.

muddle [ˈmʌdl] *noun & verb*

> **to be in a muddle** être en désordre : **my papers are in a muddle** mes papiers sont en désordre

muddle up *phrasal verb*

ı. mélanger : **you've muddled up my papers** tu as mélangé mes papiers
2. embrouiller : **I'm getting muddled up** je m'embrouille ; **I got the names muddled up** je me suis embrouillé dans les noms.

muddy [ˈmʌdɪ] *adjective*

ı. boueux *(feminine* boueuse*)* : **the ground is very muddy** le terrain est très boueux
2. plein de boue : **my hands are all muddy** mes mains sont pleines de boue.

muesli [ˈmjuːzlɪ] *noun*

muesli *(masculine)*.

mug [mʌg] *noun & verb*

■ *noun*
grande tasse *(feminine)* : **a mug of coffee** une grande tasse de café

■ *verb*
agresser : **she was mugged in the street** elle s'est fait agresser dans la rue.

multimedia [ˌmʌltɪˈmiːdjə] *noun*

multimédia *(masculine)* : **a multimedia computer** un ordinateur multimédia.

multiple-choice test [ˌmʌltɪplˈtʃɔɪstest] *noun*

QCM *(masculine)*.

multiplication [ˌmʌltɪplɪˈkeɪʃn] *noun*

multiplication *(feminine)* : **multiplication sign** signe de multiplication ; **multiplication table** table de multiplication.

multiply [ˈmʌltɪplaɪ] *(past tense & past participle* multiplied) *verb*
multiplier : **what's 3 multiplied by 7?** 3 multiplié par 7 donne quoi ?

mum *UK* [mʌm] *noun informal*

maman *(feminine)*, mère *(feminine)* : **mum, where's my school bag?** maman, où est mon cartable ? ; **his mum's a teacher** sa mère est professeur.

mummy [ˈmʌmɪ] *(plural* mummies) *noun*

1. *UK informal* **maman** *(feminine)* : **good night, mummy** bonne nuit, maman
2. **momie** *(feminine)* : **an Egyptian mummy** une momie égyptienne.

murder ['mɜːdər] *noun & verb*

■ *noun*
meurtre *(masculine)* : **he has been accused of murder** il est accusé de meurtre

■ *verb*
assassiner : **somebody was murdered near the station** quelqu'un a été assassiné près de la gare.

murderer ['mɜːdərər] *noun*

assassin *(masculine)*.

muscle ['mʌsl] *noun*

muscle *(masculine)* : **the stomach muscles** les muscles de l'estomac.

museum [mjuː'ziːəm] *noun*

musée *(masculine)* : **we're going to the museum** nous allons au musée.

mushroom ['mʌʃrʊm] *noun*

champignon *(masculine)*
➤ **mushroom soup** soupe *(feminine)* aux champignons.

music ['mjuːzɪk] *noun*

musique *(feminine)* : **he's listening to music** il écoute de la musique.

musical ['mjuːzɪkl] *noun & adjective*

■ *noun*
comédie *(feminine)* **musicale** : **we're going to see a musical** nous allons voir une comédie musicale

■ *adjective*
➤ **a musical instrument** un instrument de musique : **she plays a musical instrument** elle joue d'un instrument de musique.

musician [mjuː'zɪʃn] *noun*

musicien *(masculine)*, **musicienne** *(feminine)* : **she's a musician** elle est musicienne.

Muslim ['mʊzlɪm], **Moslem** ['mɒzləm]

adjective & noun
■ *adjective*
musulman
■ *noun*
Musulman *(masculine)*, **Musulmane** *(feminine)*

The French adjective does not start with a capital letter.

mussel ['mʌsl] *noun*

moule *(feminine)*.

must [mʌst] *modal verb*

devoir : **I must go** je dois partir OR il faut que je parte ; **you must come and see us** il faut que tu viennes nous voir OR il faut venir nous voir ; **you mustn't tell anyone** tu ne dois le dire à personne ; **you must always read the instructions** il faut toujours lire le mode d'emploi

To make deductions, you use the verb **devoir** in French:

he must be French il doit être français ; **she must have got lost** elle a dû se perdre.

mustache *US* ➤ moustache *UK*.

mustard ['mʌstəd] *noun*

moutarde *(feminine)*.

mustn't ['mʌsnt] = must not

you mustn't go tu ne dois pas y aller.

must've ['mʌstəv] = must have

he must've left already il a déjà dû partir.

mutton ['mʌtn] *noun*

mouton *(masculine)* : **we never eat mutton** nous ne mangeons jamais de mouton.

my [maɪ] *possessive adjective*

mon *(feminine* **ma)** [*plural* **mes**]

In French the possessive adjective agrees in gender (masculine or feminine) and number (singular or plural) with the noun that follows:

my dog is called Cassius mon chien s'appelle Cassius ; **my car won't start** ma voiture ne veut pas démarrer ; **my parents are on holiday** mes parents sont en vacances

Use **mon**, not **ma**, when a feminine noun begins with a vowel or silent 'h':

my plate is empty mon assiette est vide

m

> Use the definite article (**le**, **la**, **l'** or **les**), not the possessive adjective, with parts of the body:

I've broken my leg je me suis cassé la jambe ; **I'm going to wash my hair** je vais me laver les cheveux.

myself [maɪ'self] *pronoun*

1. **me** (**m'** *before a vowel*) : **I'm washing myself** je me lave ; **I'm enjoying myself** je m'amuse
2. **moi-même** : **I asked him myself** je lui ai demandé moi-même
3. **moi** : **I often talk about myself** je parle souvent de moi
> **by myself** tout seul : **I did it by myself** je l'ai fait tout seul.

mysterious [mɪ'stɪərɪəs] *adjective*

mystérieux *(feminine* **mystérieuse)**.

mystery [ˈmɪstərɪ] *(plural* **mysteries)** *noun*

1. **mystère** *(masculine)* : **it's a real mystery** c'est un vrai mystère
2. **roman** *(masculine)* **policier** : **a murder mystery** un roman policier.

myth [mɪθ] *noun*

mythe *(masculine)* : **the Greek myths** les mythes grecs.

mythology [mɪ'θɒlədʒɪ] *noun*

mythologie *(feminine)* : **Greek mythology** la mythologie grecque.

nag [næg] *(past tense & past participle* **nagged)** *verb*

harceler : **stop nagging me** arrête de me harceler.

nail [neɪl] *noun & verb*

■ *noun*

1. **clou** *(masculine)* : **he knocked a nail into the wall** il a planté un clou dans le mur
2. **ongle** *(masculine)* : **he bites his nails** il se ronge les ongles

> **a nail file** une lime à ongles
> **nail polish** OR **nail varnish** vernis *(masculine)* à ongles
■ *verb*

clouer : **she nailed the sign to the door** elle a cloué la pancarte sur la porte.

naked [ˈneɪkɪd] *adjective*

nu : **he was completely naked** il était complètement nu.

name [neɪm] *noun*

nom *(masculine)* : **what's your name?** comment vous appelez-vous ? OR quel est votre nom ? ; **my name is Paul** je m'appelle Paul.

nanny *UK* [ˈnænɪ] *(plural* **nannies)** *noun*

garde *(feminine)* **d'enfants** : **she's a nanny** elle est garde d'enfants.

nap [næp] *noun*

petit somme *(masculine)* : **I had a nap** j'ai fait un petit somme.

napkin [ˈnæpkɪn] *noun*

serviette *(feminine)* : **a paper napkin** une serviette en papier.

nappy *UK* [ˈnæpɪ] *(plural* **nappies)** *noun*

couche *(feminine)* : **he changed the baby's nappy** il a changé la couche du bébé.

narrow [ˈnærəʊ] *adjective*

étroit : **this street is very narrow** cette rue est très étroite.

nasty [*UK* ˈnɑːstɪ, *US* ˈnæstɪ] *adjective*

1. **mauvais** : **this cheese has a nasty taste** ce fromage a mauvais goût
2. **méchant** : **she was nasty to him** elle a été méchante avec lui.

nation [ˈneɪʃn] *noun*

nation *(feminine)*.

national [ˈnæʃənl] *adjective*

national
> **the national anthem** l'hymne *(masculine)* national
> **the National Health Service** *UK* la Sécurité sociale britannique.

nationality [ˌnæʃəˈnælətɪ] *(plural* **nationalities)** *noun*

nationalité *(feminine)* : **what nationality are you?** vous êtes de quelle nationalité ?

native ['neɪtɪv] *adjective*
1. **natal** : **Spain is his native country** l'Espagne est son pays natal
2. **maternel** *(feminine* **maternelle***)* : **English is my native language** ma langue maternelle est l'anglais ; **a native English speaker** une personne de langue maternelle anglaise.

natural ['nætʃrəl] *adjective*
naturel *(feminine* **naturelle***)* : **the natural world** le monde naturel ; **it's quite natural** c'est tout à fait naturel.

naturally ['nætʃrəlɪ] *adverb*
1. **naturellement** : **naturally, I was angry** naturellement, j'étais en colère
2. **de nature** : **she's naturally generous** elle est généreuse de nature.

nature ['neɪtʃər] *noun*
nature *(feminine)* : **I love nature** j'aime la nature ; **he has a very kind nature** il est très gentil de nature
➤ **a nature reserve** une réserve naturelle.

naughty ['nɔːtɪ] *adjective*
vilain, méchant : **he's a naughty boy!** c'est un vilain garçon !

nauseous [*UK* 'nɔːsjəs, *US* 'nɔːʃəs] *adjective*
to feel nauseous avoir la nausée.

navel ['neɪvl] *noun*
nombril *(masculine)*.

navy ['neɪvɪ] *noun & adjective*
◼ *noun*
marine *(feminine)* : **he's in the navy** il est dans la marine
◼ *adjective*
bleu marine *(invariable)* : **she's wearing a navy skirt** elle porte une jupe bleu marine
➤ **navy blue** bleu marine.

near [nɪər] *preposition, adverb & adjective*
◼ *preposition*
près de : **there's a supermarket near the school** il y a un supermarché près de l'école ; **is there a restaurant near here?** y a-t-il un restaurant près d'ici ?
➤ **near to** près de
◼ *adverb*
près : **don't sit so near** ne t'assieds pas si près

◼ *adjective*
proche : **the station is very near** la gare est toute proche ; **where is the nearest hospital?** où est l'hôpital le plus proche ? ; **in the near future** dans un proche avenir.

nearby [nɪə'baɪ] *adjective & adverb*
◼ *adjective*
proche : **there was a fire in a nearby village** il y a eu un incendie dans un village proche
◼ *adverb*
tout près : **there's a school nearby** il y a une école tout près d'ici.

nearly ['nɪəlɪ] *adverb*
presque : **it's nearly 8 o'clock** il est presque 8 heures
➤ **I nearly fell** j'ai failli tomber
➤ **I nearly cried** j'étais sur le point de pleurer.

nearsighted *US* ['nɪərsaɪtɪd] *adjective*
myope : **she's nearsighted** elle est myope.

neat [niːt] *adjective*
1. **bien rangé** : **the house is very neat** la maison est très bien rangée
2. **soigné** : **his work is always neat** son travail est toujours très soigné
3. *US informal* **super** *(invariable)* : **that was a neat movie!** le film était super !

neatly ['niːtlɪ] *adverb*
soigneusement : **she writes very neatly** elle écrit très soigneusement.

necessary [*UK* 'nesəsrɪ, *US* 'nesəserɪ] *adjective*
nécessaire : **is it really necessary?** est-ce vraiment nécessaire ?

neck [nek] *noun*
cou *(masculine)* : **she has a scarf round her neck** elle a une écharpe autour du cou.

necklace ['neklɪs] *noun*
collier *(masculine)* : **she's wearing a gold necklace** elle porte un collier en or.

nectarine ['nektərɪn] *noun*
nectarine *(feminine)*.

need [niːd] *noun & verb*
◼ *noun*
besoin *(masculine)* : **to be in need of something** avoir besoin de quelque chose

> **there's no need** ce n'est pas la peine :
  there's no need to phone ce n'est pas la
  peine d'appeler

■ *verb*

1. *avoir besoin de* : **he needs a new bike** il a
   besoin d'un nouveau vélo ; **I need to get
   some sleep** j'ai besoin de dormir ; **the car
   needs washing** la voiture a besoin d'être la-
   vée

2. *When 'need' means 'have to'* **I need to
   leave right away** je dois partir tout de suite
   OR il faut que je parte tout de suite ; **do we
   need to show our passports?** est-ce que
   nous devons montrer nos passeports OR faut-il
   que nous montrions nos passeports ?

   To translate 'needn't' or 'don't need to', you can
   use the French construction ne pas être obligé de
   faire quelque chose when you want to say that
   somebody is not obliged to do something, or the
   impersonal construction ce n'est pas la peine de
   faire quelque chose to say that it's not worth
   doing something:

   you don't need to wait OR **you needn't wait**
   tu n'es pas obligé d'attendre ; **we needn't
   hurry** ce n'est pas la peine qu'on se dépêche.

needle ['niːdl] *noun*

   aiguille *(feminine)* : **you need a needle and
   thread** il te faut une aiguille et du fil.

needn't ['niːdnt] = need not

   you needn't come tu n'es pas obligé de venir.

negative ['negətɪv] *adjective & noun*

■ *adjective*
   négatif *(feminine* **négative***)* : **we got a negative answer** nous avons eu une réponse négative

■ *noun*
   négatif *(masculine)* : **he made a photo from
   the negative** il a fait une photo à partir du négatif.

negotiation [nɪˌɡəʊʃɪ'eɪʃn] *noun*

   négociation *(feminine)*.

neigh [neɪ] *verb*

   hennir : **the horse neighed** le cheval a henni.

neighbour *UK*, **neighbor** *US* ['neɪbər]
   noun
   voisin *(masculine)*, **voisine** *(feminine)* : **he**

doesn't like his neighbours il n'aime pas ses
voisins.

neighbourhood *UK*, **neighborhood**
US ['neɪbəhʊd] *noun*
   quartier *(masculine)* : **there are a lot of restaurants in the neighbourhood** il y a beaucoup de restaurants dans le quartier.

neither ['naɪðər, 'niːðər] *conjunction, adjective & pronoun*

■ *conjunction*

1. *ni* : **it's neither good nor bad** ce n'est ni bon
   ni mauvais ; **he's neither English nor American** il n'est ni anglais ni américain

2. *non plus* : **he doesn't know and neither
   does she** il ne le sait pas et elle non plus ; **she
   can't swim – neither can I** elle ne sait pas nager – moi non plus

■ *adjective & pronoun*
   aucun des deux, ni l'un ni l'autre : **neither
   book is any good** aucun des deux livres n'est
   bon ; **neither of them came** aucun des deux
   n'est venu OR ni l'un ni l'autre n'est venu ;
   which dress do you want? – neither quelle
   robe veux-tu ? – ni l'une ni l'autre OR quelle robe veux-tu ? – aucune des deux.

neon ['niːɒn] *noun*

   néon *(masculine)*
> **neon lights** néons *(masculine plural)*.

nephew ['nefjuː] *noun*

   neveu *(masculine)* [*plural* **neveux**].

Neptune [*UK* 'neptjuːn, *US* 'neptuːn] *noun*

   Neptune *(feminine)* : **Neptune was discovered in 1846** Neptune a été découverte en
   1846.

nerve [nɜːv] *noun*

1. **nerf** *(masculine)* : **she had an attack of nerves**
   elle a fait une crise de nerfs

2. **courage** *(masculine)* : **he didn't have the
   nerve to tell her the truth** il n'a pas eu le courage de lui dire la vérité

3. *informal* **culot** *(masculine)* : **what a nerve!** quel
   culot !

> **to get on somebody's nerves**   énerver
  quelqu'un : **he gets on my nerves** il m'énerve.

nervous ['nɜːvəs] *adjective*

   nerveux *(feminine* **nerveuse***)* : **a nervous
   breakdown** une dépression nerveuse ; **you're
   making me nervous** tu me rends nerveux

➤ **to be nervous**

1. **avoir le trac** : actors are often nervous be-fore they go on stage les acteurs ont souvent le trac avant de monter sur scène

2. **avoir peur** : **I'm nervous when I go to the dentist** j'ai peur quand je vais chez le den-tiste ; **I'm nervous about speaking in public** j'ai peur de parler en public.

nest [nest] *noun*

nid *(masculine)* : **a bird's nest** un nid d'oiseau.

net [net] *noun*

filet *(masculine)*

➤ **a fishing net** un filet de pêche

➤ **the Net** le Net : **she's surfing the Net** elle surfe sur le Net.

netball *UK* ['netbɔːl] *noun*

net-ball *(masculine)* : **they're playing netball** ils jouent au net-ball.

Netherlands ['neðələndz] *plural noun*

➤ **the Netherlands** les Pays-Bas *(masculine plural)*.

> Remember that the French preposition **à** com-bines with the definite article **les** to become **aux**:

they're going to the Netherlands ils vont aux Pays-Bas ; **he lives in the Netherlands** il vit aux Pays-Bas.

nettle ['netl] *noun*

ortie *(feminine)*.

network ['netwɜːk] *noun*

réseau *(masculine)* [*plural* **réseaux**] : **a com-puter network** un réseau informatique.

never ['nevər] *adverb*

1. **ne ... jamais**

> To translate 'never' in a sentence use **ne** (or **n'** be-fore a vowel) in front of the verb or auxiliary verb, and **jamais** after the verb or the auxiliary verb:

he never drinks il ne boit jamais ; **I've never been to Rome** je ne suis jamais allé à Rome

2. **jamais** : **will you tell me your secret? – never!** tu vas me dire ton secret ? – jamais ! ; **never again** plus jamais

➤ **never mind!** ça ne fait rien !

new [*UK* njuː, *US* nuː] *adjective*

1. **nouveau** *(feminine* **nouvelle***)* : **this is my new address** ceci est ma nouvelle adresse ; **Harriet has a new boyfriend** Harriet a un nouveau co-pain ; **there's a new moon** c'est la nouvelle lune

2. **neuf** *(feminine* **neuve***)* : **I've got a brand new bike** j'ai un vélo tout neuf

➤ **what's new?** quoi de neuf ?

newborn [*UK* 'njuːbɔːn, *US* 'nuːbɔːn] *ad-jective*

nouveau-né : **a newborn baby** un nouveau-né.

newcomer [*UK* 'njuːˌkʌmər, *US* 'nuːˈkʌmər] *noun*

nouveau venu *(masculine)*, **nouvelle venue** *(feminine)*.

news [*UK* njuːz, *US* nuːz] *uncountable noun*

1. **nouvelle** *(feminine)*, **nouvelles** *(feminine plu-ral)* : **a piece of news** une nouvelle ; **I have some good news** j'ai une bonne nouvelle ; **what bad news!** quelle mauvaise nouvelle ! ; **do you have any news from him?** est-ce que tu as de ses nouvelles ?

2. **informations** *(feminine plural)*, **actualités** *(feminine plural)* : **he's listening to the news on the radio** il écoute les informations à la radio ; **I heard it on the news** je l'ai entendu aux in-formations.

newsagent *UK* ['njuːzeɪdʒənt], **news-dealer** *US* ['nuːzdiːlər] *noun*

marchand *(masculine)* **de journaux** : **he's a newsagent** il est marchand de journaux.

newspaper [*UK* 'njuːzˌpeɪpər, *US* 'nuːzˈpeɪpər] *noun*

journal *(masculine)* [*plural* **journaux**] : **Moira's reading the newspaper** Moira lit le journal.

newsstand [*UK* 'njuːzstænd, *US* 'nuːzstænd] *noun*

kiosque *(masculine)* **à journaux**.

New Year [*UK* njuːˈjɪər, *US* nuːˈjɪər] *noun*

the New Year le Nouvel An

➤ **Happy New Year!** bonne année !

➤ **New Year's Day** le jour de l'an

➤ **New Year's Eve** la Saint-Sylvestre

➤ **a New Year's Eve party** un réveillon du jour de l'an.

New Zealand [*UK* njuːˈziːlənd, *US* nuːˈziːlənd] *noun*

la Nouvelle-Zélande

> In French the names of countries are used with the definite article (**le**, **l'** or **la**), except when they follow the preposition **en**:

n

Wellington is the capital of New Zealand Wellington est la capitale de la Nouvelle-Zélande ; **they're going to New Zealand** ils vont en Nouvelle-Zélande ; **David lives in New Zealand** David vit en Nouvelle-Zélande.

New Zealander [*UK* njuːˈziːləndər, *US* nuːˈziːləndər] *noun*
Néo-Zélandais *(masculine)*, **Néo-Zélandaise** *(feminine)*.

next [nekst] *adjective & adverb*

■ *adjective*

1. **prochain : the match is next week** le match aura lieu la semaine prochaine ; **I'll see you next Tuesday** on se voit mardi prochain ; **we're going to Jamaica next year** nous allons en Jamaïque l'année prochaine ; **I'll go with you next time** je viendrai avec toi la prochaine fois
2. **suivant : it's on the next page** c'est à la page suivante ; **next, please!** au suivant !
3. **d'à côté : who's in the next room?** qui est dans la chambre d'à côté ?
> **the next day** le lendemain : **the next day she came to see me** le lendemain elle est venue me voir

■ *adverb*

1. **ensuite : what happened next?** qu'est-ce qui s'est passé ensuite ?
2. **la prochaine fois : when I see him next I'll tell him** la prochaine fois que je le verrai je lui dirai
> **next door** à côté : **they live next door** ils habitent à côté ; **our next-door neighbours** nos voisins d'à côté
> **next to** à côté de : **the bank is next to the bookshop** la banque est à côté de la librairie
> **next to nothing** presque rien.

NHS [ˌeneɪtʃˈes] *(abbreviation of* National Health Service*) noun*
sécurité sociale britannique.

nice [naɪs] *adjective*

1. **gentil** *(feminine* **gentille**)*, **sympathique : Mrs Thompson is very nice** Madame Thompson est très gentille
2. **joli : that's a nice dress** c'est une jolie robe
3. **beau** *(feminine* **belle**) : **it's a nice day** il fait beau aujourd'hui
4. **bon** *(feminine* **bonne**) : **the meal was nice** le repas était bon
> **have a nice time!** amusez-vous bien !

nicely [ˈnaɪslɪ] *adverb*

1. **bien : she was nicely dressed** elle était bien habillée
2. **gentiment : ask nicely!** demande gentiment !

nickel *US* [ˈnɪkl] *noun*
pièce *(feminine)* **de cinq cents.**

nickname [ˈnɪkneɪm] *noun*
surnom *(masculine)* : **do you have a nickname?** tu as un surnom ?

niece [niːs] *noun*
nièce *(feminine)*.

night [naɪt] *noun*

1. **nuit** *(feminine)* : **did you have a good night?** tu as passé une bonne nuit ? ; **he stayed out all night** il n'est pas rentré de la nuit ; **we danced all night** nous avons dansé toute la nuit
2. **soir** *(masculine)* : **it happened last night at 6 o'clock** ça s'est passé hier soir à 6 heures ; **what did you do last night?** qu'est-ce que tu as fait hier soir ?
> **at night** la nuit : **badgers come out at night** les blaireaux sortent la nuit
> **to have an early night** se coucher de bonne heure
> **to have a late night** se coucher tard
> **good night!** bonne nuit !

nightclub [ˈnaɪtklʌb] *noun*
boîte *(feminine)* **de nuit : we're going to a nightclub** nous allons en boîte.

nightie [ˈnaɪtɪ] *noun informal*
chemise *(feminine)* **de nuit : she was in her nightie** elle était en chemise de nuit.

nightingale [ˈnaɪtɪŋgeɪl] *noun*
rossignol *(masculine)*.

nightmare [ˈnaɪtmeər] *noun*
cauchemar *(masculine)* : **I had a nightmare** j'ai fait un cauchemar.

nighttime [ˈnaɪttaɪm] *noun*
nuit *(feminine)* : **it's very noisy at nighttime** il y a beaucoup de bruit la nuit.

nil *UK* [nɪl] *noun*
zéro *(masculine)* : **they won three nil** ils ont gagné trois à zéro.

nine [naɪn] *number*

neuf : **there are nine girls in the group** il y a neuf filles dans le groupe ; **Bill's nine** Bill a neuf ans ; **she went out at nine** elle est sortie à neuf heures.

nineteen [ˌnaɪnˈtiːn] *number*

dix-neuf : **Chantal is nineteen** Chantal a dix-neuf ans.

nineteenth [ˌnaɪnˈtiːnθ] *number*

dix-neuvième : **it's her nineteenth birthday** c'est son dix-neuvième anniversaire
> **it's the nineteenth of May** *UK* OR **it's May nineteenth** *US* nous sommes le dix-neuf mai.

ninety ['naɪntɪ] *number*

quatre-vingt-dix : **she's ninety** elle a quatre-vingt-dix ans
> **ninety-one** quatre-vingt-onze
> **ninety-two** quatre-vingt-douze.

ninth [naɪnθ] *number*

neuvième : **on the ninth floor** au neuvième étage
> **it's the ninth of October** *UK* OR **it's October ninth** *US* nous sommes le neuf octobre.

no [nəʊ] *adverb & adjective*

■ *adverb*
non : **do you like seafood? – no, I don't** est-ce que tu aimes les fruits de mer ? – non ; **no thank you** non merci

■ *adjective*
pas de, aucun : **she has no money** elle n'a pas d'argent ; **there are no buses on Sundays** il n'y a pas de bus le dimanche ; **there's no hope** il n'y a aucun espoir.

nobody ['nəʊbədɪ], **no one** ['nəʊwʌn] *pronoun*

personne : **who did you see? – nobody!** qui as-tu vu ? – personne !

> When there is a verb in the sentence, you must use the negative ne (or n' before a vowel) together with **personne**. The ne comes before the verb or the auxiliary verb:

nobody came personne n'est venu ; **there's nobody in the room** il n'y a personne dans la pièce.

nod [nɒd] (*past tense & past participle* **nodded**) *verb*

faire un signe de tête : **he didn't say hello, but he nodded to me** il ne m'a pas dit bonjour, mais il m'a salué d'un signe de tête ; **I asked him if he was coming and he nodded** je lui ai demandé s'il venait et il a fait signe que oui.

noise [nɔɪz] *uncountable noun*

bruit *(masculine)* : **you're making too much noise** tu fais trop de bruit.

noisy ['nɔɪzɪ] *adjective*

bruyant : **your computer is very noisy** ton ordinateur est très bruyant.

none [nʌn] *pronoun*

1. **aucun** : **how many cards have you got left? – none** il te reste combien de cartes ? – aucune

> In French, when there is a verb in a sentence, you must put the negative ne (or n' before a vowel) between the subject and the verb:

none of the pictures is for sale aucun des tableaux n'est à vendre ; **none of us won** aucun de nous n'a gagné

2. *With uncountable nouns* **have you got any money? – no, none at all** est-ce que tu as de l'argent ? – non, je n'en ai pas du tout ; **there's none left** il n'y en a plus OR il n'en reste plus.

nonsense ['nɒnsəns] *uncountable noun*

bêtises *(feminine plural)* : **you're talking nonsense** tu dis des bêtises
> **nonsense!** n'importe quoi !

nonsmoker [ˌnɒnˈsməʊkəʳ] *noun*

non-fumeur *(masculine)*, **non-fumeuse** *(feminine)*.

nonstop [ˌnɒnˈstɒp] *adjective & adverb*

■ *adjective*
direct : **a nonstop flight** un vol direct
■ *adverb*
sans arrêt : **I'm working nonstop** je travaille sans arrêt.

noodles ['nuːdlz] *plural noun*

nouilles *(feminine plural)* : **egg noodles** nouilles aux œufs.

noon [nuːn] *noun*

midi : **we're meeting at noon** on a rendez-vous à midi.

no one *pronoun* ➤ nobody.

nor ['nɔːʳ] *conjunction*

ni : **neither Fred nor Lucy is coming** ni Fred ni Lucy ne viennent.

normal ['nɔːml] *adjective*

normal : **that's quite normal** c'est tout à fait normal

➤ **at the normal time** à l'heure habituelle.

normally ['nɔːməlɪ] *adverb*

normalement : **normally I get up at 7 o'clock** normalement, je me lève à 7 heures.

Normandy ['nɔːməndɪ] *noun*

la Normandie : **he lives in Normandy** il vit en Normandie.

north [nɔːθ] *noun, adjective & adverb*

■ *noun*

nord *(masculine)* : **Manchester is in the north of England** Manchester est dans le nord de l'Angleterre

■ *adjective*

nord *(invariable)* : **the north coast** la côte nord

■ *adverb*

vers le nord : **we are going north** nous allons vers le nord

➤ **north of** au nord de : **Boston is north of New York** Boston est au nord de New York

➤ **North America** l'Amérique *(feminine)* du Nord : **San Diego is in North America** San Diego est en Amérique du Nord

➤ **the North Pole** le pôle Nord

➤ **the North Sea** la mer du Nord.

northeast [ˌnɔːθ'iːst] *noun*

nord-est *(masculine)* : **Hannah lives in northeast London** Hannah habite au nord-est de Londres.

northern ['nɔːðən] *adjective*

du nord : **Northern Europe** l'Europe *(feminine)* du Nord

➤ **Northern Ireland** l'Irlande *(feminine)* du Nord : **they live in Northern Ireland** ils vivent en Irlande du Nord.

northwest [ˌnɔːθ'west] *noun*

nord-ouest *(masculine)* : **we live in the north-west of the country** nous vivons dans le nord-ouest du pays.

Norwegian [nɔː'wiːdʒən] *adjective & noun*

■ *adjective*

norvégien *(feminine* **norvégienne***)*

■ *noun*

1. norvégien *(masculine)* : **she speaks Norwegian** elle parle norvégien

2. Norvégien *(masculine)*, Norvégienne *(feminine)*

Remember not to use a capital letter for the adjective and the language in French. Only use a capital letter for the inhabitants.

nose [nəʊz] *noun*

nez *(masculine)* : **he's got a big nose** il a un gros nez

➤ **to blow one's nose** se moucher : **blow your nose!** mouche-toi !

nosebleed ['nəʊzbliːd] *noun*

➤ **to have a nosebleed** saigner du nez : **she's got a nosebleed** elle saigne du nez.

nosey ➤ nosy.

nostril ['nɒstrəl] *noun*

narine *(feminine)*.

nosy, nosey ['nəʊzɪ] *adjective*

indiscret *(feminine* **indiscrète***)* : **nosy neighbours** des voisins indiscrets

➤ **don't be so nosy!** occupe-toi de tes affaires !

not [nɒt] *adverb*

1. ne ... pas

To make a negative in French you use ne (or n' before a vowel) in front of the verb or the auxiliary verb, and pas after the verb or the auxiliary verb:

he's not coming il ne vient pas ; **I don't think so** je ne crois pas ; **Hank didn't come** Hank n'est pas venu.

2. pas : **are you coming or not?** tu viens ou pas ? ; **do you go out on Saturday nights? – not always!** tu sors le samedi soir ? – pas toujours !

➤ **I'm afraid not** je crains que non

➤ **I hope not** j'espère que non

➤ **not at all** pas du tout : **do you mind? – not at all!** ça te dérange ? – pas du tout !

➤ **not really** pas vraiment : **do you want to**

come? – not really tu veux venir ? – pas vraiment

> **not yet** pas encore ; **are you ready? – not yet!** tu es prêt ? – pas encore !

note [nəʊt] noun & verb

■ noun

1. note *(feminine)* : **she's taking notes** elle prend des notes
2. mot *(masculine)* : **I sent him a note** je lui ai envoyé un mot
3. *UK* billet *(masculine)* de banque : **she gave me a ten-pound note** elle m'a donné un billet de dix livres

■ verb

noter : **to note something down** noter quelque chose ; **I noted the answers in my exercise book** j'ai noté les réponses dans mon cahier

note down *phrasal verb*

noter : **I'll note it down** je vais le noter.

notebook ['nəʊtbʊk] noun

1. carnet *(masculine)*, calepin *(masculine)*
2. *US* cahier *(masculine)*.

notepad ['nəʊtpæd] noun

bloc-notes *(masculine)*.

nothing ['nʌθɪŋ] pronoun

1. ne ... rien

> To translate 'nothing' in a sentence, use ne (or n' before a vowel) in front of the verb or the auxiliary verb, and rien after the verb:

I've got nothing to do je n'ai rien à faire ; **she has nothing left** elle n'a plus rien

2. rien : **did you see anything? – no, nothing!** tu as vu quelque chose ? – non, rien !
> **nothing at all** rien du tout
> **for nothing** pour rien : **I didn't pay for it, I got it for nothing** je ne l'ai pas payé, je l'ai eu pour rien
> **to have nothing on** être tout nu.

notice ['nəʊtɪs] noun & verb

■ noun

affiche *(feminine)* : **they've put up a notice** ils ont mis une affiche
> **don't take any notice!** ne fais pas attention !
> **he took no notice of her** il n'a pas fait attention à elle

■ verb

remarquer : **I didn't notice you there** je ne t'ai pas remarqué.

noticeboard *UK* ['nəʊtɪsbɔːd] noun

panneau *(masculine)* d'affichage.

nought *UK* [nɔːt] number

zéro *(masculine)* : **nought point five** zéro virgule cinq.

noun [naʊn] noun

nom *(masculine)* : **'dog', 'London', 'happiness' are all nouns** « chien », « Londres », « bonheur » sont tous des noms.

novel ['nɒvl] noun

roman *(masculine)* : **Katie's reading a novel** Katie lit un roman.

novelist ['nɒvəlɪst] noun

romancier *(masculine)*, romancière *(feminine)* : **Agatha Christie is a famous novelist** Agatha Christie est une romancière célèbre.

November [nə'vembər] noun

novembre : **in November** en novembre ; **next November** en novembre prochain ; **last November** en novembre dernier

> In French the months of the year do not start with a capital letter.

now [naʊ] adverb

maintenant : **what shall we do now?** qu'est-ce qu'on fait maintenant ? ; **from now on** à partir de maintenant
> **any time now** d'un moment à l'autre : **I'm expecting her any time now** je l'attends d'un moment à l'autre
> **just now** OR **right now** tout de suite : **I can't do it just now** je ne peux pas le faire tout de suite
> **I saw him just now** je viens de le voir
> **he should be there by now** il devrait déjà être là
> **now and then** OR **now and again** de temps en temps
> **now, let's see** bon, voyons.

nowadays ['naʊədeɪz] adverb

de nos jours, aujourd'hui : **a lot of people work on computers nowadays** beaucoup de gens travaillent sur ordinateur de nos jours.

n

nowhere ['nəʊweər] *adverb*

nulle part : where are you going? – nowhere où vas-tu ? – nulle part

> To translate 'nowhere' in a sentence, you must use the negative ne (or n' before a vowel) in front of the verb:

she goes nowhere without him elle ne va nulle part sans lui

➤ **there's nowhere to sit down** il n'y a pas d'endroit pour s'asseoir

➤ **nowhere near** loin de : **Manchester is nowhere near London** Manchester est loin de Londres.

nuclear [*UK* 'njuːklɪər, *US* 'nuːklɪər] *adjective*

nucléaire : a nuclear bomb une bombe nucléaire ; **nuclear power** l'énergie nucléaire

➤ **a nuclear power station** une centrale nucléaire.

nude [*UK* njuːd, *US* nuːd] *adjective & noun*

■ *adjective*
nu : they were completely nude ils étaient complètement nus

■ *noun*
➤ **in the nude** tout nu : **he was in the nude** il était tout nu.

nudge [nʌdʒ] *verb*

donner un coup de coude à : she nudged me elle m'a donné un coup de coude.

nuisance [*UK* 'njuːsns, *US* 'nuːsns] *noun*

➤ **that's a real nuisance** c'est vraiment embêtant : **it's a nuisance having to go** c'est embêtant de devoir y aller

➤ **he's such a nuisance** il est vraiment casse-pieds.

numb [nʌm] *adjective*

engourdi : my hand has gone numb ma main s'est engourdie.

number ['nʌmbər] *noun*

1. **numéro** *(masculine)* : **what's your telephone number?** quel est ton numéro de téléphone ? ; **we live at number 20** nous habitons au numéro 20 OR nous habitons au 20

2. **nombre** *(masculine)* : **odd numbers and even numbers** les nombres impairs et les nombres pairs ; **a large number of people** un grand nombre de personnes

3. **chiffre** *(masculine)* : **your password should contain letters and numbers** ton mot de passe devrait comprendre des chiffres et des lettres ; **the numbers on the keyboard** les chiffres sur le clavier

➤ **Number Ten** *résidence officielle du Premier Ministre britannique* ➤ Downing Street.

numberplate *UK* ['nʌmbəpleɪt] *noun*

plaque *(feminine)* **d'immatriculation.**

numeral [*UK* 'njuːmərəl, *US* 'nuːmərəl] *noun*

chiffre *(masculine)* : **Roman numerals** chiffres romains.

nun [nʌn] *noun*

religieuse *(feminine)*.

nurse [nɜːs] *noun*

infirmier *(masculine)*, **infirmière** *(feminine)* : **Sue's a nurse** Sue est infirmière

➤ **a male nurse** un infirmier.

nursery ['nɜːsəri] *(plural nurseries) noun*

garderie *(feminine)*, **crèche** *(feminine)*

➤ **a nursery rhyme** une comptine

➤ **a nursery school** une école maternelle : **they go to nursery school** ils vont à l'école maternelle OR ils vont à la maternelle.

nut [nʌt] *noun*

1. « *Nut* » *est un terme général désignant les fruits à coquille tels que les noix, les noisettes, les cacahuètes*

> There is no single word to translate 'nut' into French. You must specify which kind of nut you mean: a peanut une cacahuète, a hazelnut une noisette, a walnut une noix.

2. **écrou** *(masculine)* : **nuts and bolts** des écrous et des boulons.

NYC *abbreviation of* New York City.

nylon ['naɪlɒn] *noun*

Nylon® *(masculine)* : **a nylon shirt** une chemise en Nylon.

oak [əʊk] *noun*

chêne *(masculine)* : **an oak tree** un chêne ; **an oak table** une table en chêne.

oar [ɔːʳ] *noun*

aviron *(masculine)*, **rame** *(feminine)*.

oasis [əʊ'eɪsɪs] *(plural* oases [əʊ'eɪsiːz]*) noun*

oasis *(feminine)* [*plural* **oasis**].

oats [əʊts] *plural noun*

avoine *(feminine)* : **porridge oats** flocons d'avoine.

obedient [ə'biːdɪənt] *adjective*

obéissant : **Fido's a very obedient dog** Fido est un chien très obéissant.

obey [ə'beɪ] *verb*

obéir à : **she has always obeyed her parents** elle a toujours obéi à ses parents ; **you must obey the rules** il faut obéir aux règles.

object ['ɒbdʒɪkt] *noun*

objet *(masculine)* : **what's that strange object?** qu'est-ce que c'est que cet objet bizarre ?

oblong ['ɒblɒŋ] *adjective*

rectangulaire : **an oblong table** une table rectangulaire.

oboe ['əʊbəʊ] *noun*

hautbois *(masculine)* : **she plays the oboe** elle joue du hautbois.

observant [əb'zɜːvənt] *adjective*

observateur *(feminine* **observatrice***)* : **you're very observant** tu es très observateur.

observe [əb'zɜːv] *verb*

observer.

obsessed [əb'sest] *adjective*

obsédé : **she's obsessed with the idea** elle est obsédée par cette idée.

obstacle ['ɒbstəkl] *noun*

obstacle *(masculine)* : **an obstacle race** une course d'obstacles.

obtain [əb'teɪn] *verb*

obtenir : **he obtained permission to leave** il a obtenu la permission de partir.

obvious ['ɒbvɪəs] *adjective*

évident : **it's obvious he's lying** c'est évident qu'il ment.

obviously ['ɒbvɪəslɪ] *adverb*

1. évidemment : **she's obviously right** évidemment, elle a raison
2. manifestement : **he's obviously ill** il est manifestement malade.

occasion [ə'keɪʒn] *noun*

1. occasion *(feminine)* : **on several occasions** à plusieurs occasions OR à plusieurs reprises
2. événement *(masculine)* : **it's an important occasion** c'est un événement important
> **on this ocasion** cette fois-ci : **on this occasion I must say no** cette fois-ci je dois dire non.

occasionally [ə'keɪʒnəlɪ] *adverb*

de temps en temps : **I see him occasionally** je le vois de temps en temps.

occupation [ˌɒkjʊ'peɪʃn] *noun*

travail *(masculine)*, **métier** *(masculine)* : **what is his occupation?** qu'est-ce qu'il fait comme travail ? OR qu'est-ce qu'il fait comme métier ?

occupied ['ɒkjʊpaɪd] *adjective*

occupé : **is this seat occupied?** est-ce que cette place est occupée ?

occur [ə'kɜːʳ] *(past tense & past participle* occurred*) verb*

avoir lieu : **this incident occurred yesterday** l'incident a eu lieu hier
> **to occur to somebody** venir à l'esprit de quelqu'un : **that never occurred to me** cela ne m'était jamais venu à l'esprit.

ocean ['əʊʃn] *noun*

océan *(masculine)* : **the Atlantic Ocean** l'océan Atlantique.

c

o'clock [ə'klɒk] *adverb*

it's three o'clock il est trois heures ; **at two o'clock** à deux heures

⚠️ En anglais, dans la langue courante, on n'utilise que les chiffres 1 à 12 pour indiquer l'heure. Ainsi **2 o'clock** veut aussi bien dire 2 heures de l'après-midi que 2 heures du matin.

October [ɒk'təʊbəʳ] *noun*

octobre *(masculine)* : **in October** en octobre ; **next October** en octobre prochain ; **last October** en octobre dernier

In French the months of the year do not start with a capital letter.

octopus ['ɒktəpəs] *noun*

pieuvre *(feminine)*.

odd [ɒd] *adjective*

1. **bizarre** : **that's very odd** c'est très bizarre
2. **impair** : **five is an odd number** cinq est un nombre impair
3. **dépareillé** : **he's wearing odd socks** ses chaussettes sont dépareillées.

of [əv, ɒv] *preposition*

1. **de** (d' *before a vowel or silent 'h'*)

Remember that **de + le = du** and **de + les = des** :

in the centre of London dans le centre de Londres ; **he ate half of the cake** il a mangé la moitié du gâteau ; **two of the boys are French** deux des garçons sont français ; **there are thousands of people** il y a des milliers de personnes ; **a bit of money** un peu d'argent ; **a kilo of apples** un kilo de pommes ; **a cup of coffee** une tasse de café ; **some of them left early** certains d'entre eux sont partis tôt

When 'of it' or 'of them' are used to refer back to something already mentioned, they are translated by **en** :

have some more cake, there's lots of it prends encore un peu de gâteau, il y en a beaucoup ; **how many cups are there? – there are seven of them** il y a combien de tasses ? – il y en a sept

You do not use **en** when 'of them' refers to people :

there are seven of us nous sommes sept ; **there were lots of them** ils étaient nombreux
2. *Saying what something is made of* **en** : **a ring of gold** une bague en or ; **it's made of silver** c'est en argent
3. *Giving the date*

'Of' is not translated in French when you say which day of the month it is :

the 14ᵗʰ of February le 14 février
4. *US Telling the time* **it's quarter of four** il est quatre heures moins le quart.

off [ɒf, *US* ɔːf] *adverb, preposition & adjective*

▪ *adverb*
I'm off je m'en vais ; **the town is 50 miles off** la ville est à 80 kilomètres ; **he took a week off** il a pris une semaine de congé ; **it's my day off** c'est mon jour de congé ; **he turned the light off** il a éteint la lumière ; **turn the tap off** ferme le robinet ; **there's £10 off** il y a une réduction de 10 livres

▪ *preposition*
he got off the bus il est descendu du bus ; **she took the book off the shelf** elle a pris le livre sur l'étagère ; **the island is just off the coast** l'île est près de la côte ; **he's off work** il ne travaille pas ; **she's off school** *UK* elle est absente de l'école

▪ *adjective*
1. **éteint** : **the lights are off** les lumières sont éteintes ; **is the TV off?** est-ce que la télé est éteinte ?
2. *UK* **tourné** : **the milk's off** le lait a tourné
3. *UK* **avarié** : **this meat is off** cette viande est avariée
4. **annulé** : **the match is off** le match est annulé
5. **absent** : **he's off this week** il est absent cette semaine.

offence *UK*, **offense** *US* [ə'fens] *noun*

délit *(masculine)* : **he committed an offence** il a commis un délit
➤ **to take offence** se vexer.

offend [ə'fend] *verb*

offenser : **I didn't mean to offend you** je ne voulais pas t'offenser.

offense *US* ➤ offence *UK*.

offer [UK ˈɒfəʳ, US ˈɔːfəʳ] *noun & verb*

■ *noun*

offre *(feminine)*, **proposition** *(feminine)* : **this is my last offer** c'est ma dernière offre OR c'est ma dernière proposition

➤ **it's on special offer** c'est en promotion

■ *verb*

1. **proposer** : **she offered to come with me** elle m'a proposé de m'accompagner ; **he has been offered a job** on lui a proposé un poste

2. **offrir** : **I offered her something to drink** je lui ai offert quelque chose à boire ; **he offered the old lady his arm** il a offert son bras à la vieille dame

> ⚠ Le verbe anglais **to offer** est un faux ami. Il ne signifie pas "offrir" au sens de donner un cadeau ou d'inviter.

office [UK ˈɒfɪs, US ˈɔːfɪs] *noun*

bureau *(masculine)* [*plural* **bureaux**] : **Bill works in an office** Bill travaille dans un bureau ; **he's at the office** il est au bureau

➤ **an office block** UK OR **an office building** un immeuble de bureaux.

officer [UK ˈɒfɪsəʳ, US ˈɔːfɪsəʳ] *noun*

officier *(masculine)* : **he's an officer in the army** il est officier dans l'armée

➤ **a police officer** un agent de police.

official [əˈfɪʃl] *adjective*

officiel *(feminine* **officielle)** : **an official announcement** une annonce officielle.

off-licence UK [ɒfˈlaɪsənslaɪəns] *noun*

marchand *(masculine)* **de vins et spiritueux**.

off-line, offline [UK ˌɒfˈlaɪn, US ɔːfˈlaɪn] *adjective*

non connecté : **I'm off-line** je ne suis pas connecté ; **to go off-line** se déconnecter.

offside [UK ˌɒfˈsaɪd, US ɔːfˈsaɪd] *adjective*

hors jeu *(invariable)* : **Giggs was offside** Giggs était hors jeu.

often [UK ˈɒfn, UK ˈɒftn, US ˈɔːfn] *adverb*

souvent : **she often plays tennis** elle joue souvent au tennis

➤ **how often?** tous les combien ? : **how often do you see her?** tu la vois tous les combien ?

oh [əʊ] *exclamation*

oh ! : oh, it's you! oh, c'est toi !

oil [ɔɪl] *noun*

1. **huile** *(feminine)* : **sardines in oil** des sardines à l'huile ; **I've put oil into the engine** j'ai mis de l'huile dans le moteur

2. **pétrole** *(masculine)* : **they've found oil in the area** ils ont trouvé du pétrole dans cette région

➤ **an oil slick** une marée noire

➤ **an oil well** un puits de pétrole.

ointment [ˈɔɪntmənt] *noun*

pommade *(feminine)* : **put this ointment on your skin** passe-toi cette pommade sur la peau.

OK, okay [ˌəʊˈkeɪ] *adjective*

1. **d'accord** : **do you want to come? – OK!** tu veux venir ? – d'accord ! ; **I'll see you tomorrow, OK?** on se voit demain, d'accord ?

2. **bien** *(invariable)* : **how are you? – I'm OK!** comment vas-tu ? – je vais bien ! ; **I like your brother, he's OK** j'aime bien ton frère, il est bien

3. **pas mal** *(invariable)* : **how was the film? – it was OK** comment as-tu trouvé le film ? – c'était pas mal

➤ **are you OK?** ça va ?

➤ **is that OK with you?** ça te va ?

➤ **is it OK if I leave now?** ça va si je pars maintenant ?

old [əʊld] *adjective*

1. **vieux** *(feminine* **vieille)** *(before vowel or silent 'h'* **vieil)** : **it's an old house** c'est une vieille maison ; **he's an old man** c'est un vieil homme OR c'est un vieillard ; **she's an old woman** c'est une vieille femme

2. **ancien** *(feminine* **ancienne)** : **that's my old school** c'est mon ancienne école

➤ **how old are you?** quel âge as-tu ?

➤ **I'm 13 years old** j'ai 13 ans

➤ **old age** la vieillesse

➤ **an old age pensioner** UK un retraité, une retraitée

➤ **old people** les personnes *(feminine plural)* âgées.

older [ˈəʊldəʳ] *(comparative of* **old)** *adjective*

1. **aîné** : **she's my older sister** c'est ma sœur aînée

2. **plus âgé** : **she's older than me** elle est plus âgée que moi ; **he's three years older than me** il a trois ans de plus que moi.

o

oldest [ˈəʊldəst] (*superlative of* **old**) *adjective*

1. aîné : **she's the oldest daughter in the family** c'est la fille aînée de la famille
2. le plus vieux *(feminine* la plus vieille*)* : **it's the oldest church in the town** c'est la plus vieille église de la ville.

old-fashioned [ˌəʊldˈfæʃnd] *adjective*

1. démodé : **that coat is old-fashioned** ce manteau est démodé
2. vieux jeu *(invariable)* : **she's very old-fashioned** elle est très vieux jeu.

olive [ˈɒlɪv] *noun*

olive *(feminine)* : **green olives and black olives** des olives vertes et des olives noires
➤ **olive oil** huile *(feminine)* d'olive
➤ **an olive tree** un olivier.

Olympic [əˈlɪmpɪk] *adjective*

olympique : **an Olympic champion** un champion olympique
➤ **the Olympics** OR **the Olympic Games** les jeux Olympiques.

omelette , **omelet** *US* [ˈɒmlɪt] *noun*

omelette *(feminine)* : **a mushroom omelette** une omelette aux champignons.

on [ɒn] *preposition, adverb & adjective*

■ *preposition*

1. sur : **he's sitting on a chair** il est assis sur une chaise ; **the map's on the table** le plan est sur la table ; **a book on Australia** un livre sur l'Australie ; **the information is on disk** les données sont sur disquette ; **I don't have money on me** je n'ai pas d'argent sur moi
2. à : **we went on foot** nous y sommes allés à pied ; **my house is on the left** ma maison est à gauche ; **there's a picture on the wall** il y a un tableau au mur ; **his coat is hanging on a nail** son manteau est accroché à un clou ; **she has a ring on her finger** elle a une bague au doigt ; **what's on TV?** qu'est-ce qu'il y a à la télé ? ; **she's on the phone** elle est au téléphone
3. *In time expressions*

> With the days of the week and in dates 'on' is not translated in French:

I'm coming on Thursday je viens jeudi ; **he left on May 17th** il est parti le 17 mai ; **I'm having a party on my birthday** je fais une fête le jour de mon anniversaire
4. en : **I've got this album on CD** j'ai cet album

en CD ; **is the film out on video?** est-ce que le film est sorti en vidéo ?

■ *adverb*

put the lid on mets le couvercle ; **I'm going to put a sweater on** je vais mettre un pull ; **she had her glasses on** elle portait ses lunettes ; **he has nothing on** il est tout nu ; **what's on at the Ritz?** qu'est-ce qui passe au Ritz ? ; **put the radio on** allume la radio

■ *adjective*

1. allumé : **the lights are on** les lumières sont allumées
2. en marche : **the washing machine is on** le lave-linge est en marche
3. ouvert : **the tap is on** le robinet est ouvert.

once [wʌns] *adverb*

1. une fois : **once a day** une fois par jour
2. autrefois : **this part of the city was once a village** ce quartier était autrefois un village
➤ **once again** OR **once more** encore une fois
➤ **once and for all** une fois pour toutes : **we'll have to solve this problem once and for all** il faudra résoudre ce problème une fois pour toutes
➤ **once in a while** de temps en temps : **he comes to see me once in a while** il vient me voir de temps en temps
➤ **once upon a time** il était une fois : **once upon a time there was a beautiful princess** il était une fois une belle princesse
➤ **at once**
1. tout de suite : **I must leave at once** je dois partir tout de suite
2. en même temps : **don't all speak at once** ne parlez pas tous en même temps.

one [wʌn] *number & pronoun*

■ *number*

un *(feminine* une*)* : **one day** un jour ; **one, two, three, go!** un, deux, trois, partez ! ; **we have one dog and two cats** nous avons un chien et deux chats ; **there's only one plate** il n'y a qu'une assiette OR il y a seulement une assiette
➤ **one hundred** cent

■ *pronoun*

1. un *(feminine* une*)* : **one of those books is mine** un de ces livres est à moi ; **one of the girls is Mexican** une de ces filles est mexicaine

> When you are referring back to something already mentioned, as well as using un or une in French, you have to use the pronoun en. It is like saying 'one of them':

do you need a stamp? – **no, I've got one** tu as besoin d'un timbre ? – non, j'en ai un ; **I have two caps, you can have one** j'ai deux casquettes, tu peux en prendre une

2. *Referring to a particular person or thing*

> The translation depends on the word that precedes 'one' and will be masculine or feminine depending on the gender of the thing or person you are talking about:

which one? lequel ? OR laquelle ? ; **this one, not that one** celui-ci, pas celui-là OR celle-ci, pas celle-là ; **this bike is better than the old one** ce vélo est mieux que l'ancien OR cette bicyclette est mieux que l'ancienne

3. *Impersonal pronoun* **on** : **one never knows** on ne sait jamais

> **they love one another** ils s'aiment.

oneself [wʌn'self] *pronoun*

1. **se** (**s'** *before a vowel*) : **to wash oneself** se laver ; **to enjoy oneself** s'amuser

2. **soi-même** : **to do something oneself** faire quelque chose soi-même

3. **soi** : **to talk about oneself** parler de soi

> **by oneself** tout seul, toute seule.

one-way [ˌwʌn'weɪ] *adjective*

> **a one-way street** une rue à sens unique

> **a one-way ticket** un aller simple.

onion ['ʌnjən] *noun*

oignon *(masculine)* :

> **onion soup** soupe *(feminine)* à l'oignon.

online, on-line ['ɒnlaɪn] *adjective & adverb*

■ *adjective*
en ligne, connecté : **online help** aide en ligne ; **she's online** elle est connectée

> **to go online** se connecter

■ *adverb*
en ligne : **to shop online** faire des achats en ligne.

only ['əʊnlɪ] *adjective & adverb*

■ *adjective*
seul : **he's the only friend I have** c'est le seul ami que j'aie

> **he's an only child** il est fils unique

> **she's an only child** elle est fille unique

■ *adverb*
1. **ne ... que, seulement**

> In sentences with a verb, the negative **ne** (or **n'** before a vowel) is often used before the verb or auxiliary verb, and **que** after to translate 'only':

she only reads science-fiction elle ne lit que de la science-fiction OR elle lit seulement de la science-fiction ; **there are only three seats left** il ne reste que trois places OR il reste seulement trois places

2. **seulement** : **how much do you have left?** – **only twenty euros** il te reste combien ? – vingt euros seulement ; **he's not only tall but he's good-looking too** non seulement il est grand mais en plus il est beau.

onto, on to ['ɒntuː] *preposition*

sur : **he jumped onto the horse** il a sauté sur le cheval ; **the house looks onto the park** la maison donne sur le parc.

onwards ['ɒnwədz], **onward** *US* ['ɒnwəd] *adverb*

à partir de : **from Monday onwards** à partir de lundi ; **from now onwards** désormais, à partir de maintenant.

open ['əʊpn] *adjective, verb & noun*

■ *adjective*
ouvert : **the door's open** la porte est ouverte

> **wide open** grand ouvert, grande ouverte : **he left the window wide open** il a laissé la fenêtre grande ouverte

■ *verb*
1. **ouvrir** : **I opened the door** j'ai ouvert la porte ; **open the window!** ouvre la fenêtre ! ; **the shops open at 9 o'clock** les magasins ouvrent à 9 heures

2. **s'ouvrir** : **the door opened and I walked in** la porte s'est ouverte et je suis entré

■ *noun*
> **out in the open**
1. **à la belle étoile** : **we slept out in the open** nous avons dormi à la belle étoile

2. **au grand air** : **we could eat out in the open** on pourrait manger au grand air.

opera ['ɒpərə] *noun*

opéra *(masculine)* : **The Magic Flute is an opera by Mozart** La Flûte enchantée est un opéra de Mozart

> **the opera house** l'opéra.

operate ['ɒpəreɪt] *verb*

1. **faire fonctionner** : **he can't operate the**

O

washing machine il ne sait pas faire fonctionner la machine à laver

2. **opérer : to operate on somebody** opérer
quelqu'un.

operation [,ɒpə'reɪʃn] *noun*

opération *(feminine)*
➤ **to have an operation** se faire opérer : **I
had an operation** je me suis fait opérer.

operator ['ɒpəreɪtər] *noun*

opérateur *(masculine)*, opératrice *(feminine)*
➤ **a switchboard operator** un standardiste,
une standardiste
➤ **a tour operator** un tour-opérateur.

opinion [ə'pɪnjən] *noun*

avis *(masculine)*, opinion *(feminine)* : **that's my
opinion** c'est mon avis ; **it's a matter of
opinion** chacun son opinion
➤ **in my opinion** à mon avis
➤ **an opinion poll** un sondage.

opponent [ə'pəʊnənt] *noun*

adversaire *(masculine or feminine)*.

opportunity [*UK* ,ɒpə'tjuːnətɪ, *US* ɒpər-
'tuːnətɪ] (*plural* **opportunities**) *noun*

occasion *(feminine)* : **it will give you the opportunity to travel** cela te donnera l'occasion
de voyager.

opposed [ə'pəʊzd] *adjective*

➤ **to be opposed to something** être contre
quelque chose : **she's opposed to fox hunting** elle est contre la chasse au renard.

opposite ['ɒpəzɪt] *preposition, adjective, adverb & noun*

■ *preposition*
en face de : **the school is opposite the station** l'école est en face de la gare
■ *adjective*
opposé : **he went in the opposite direction**
il est allé dans la direction opposée
➤ **on the opposite side of the room**   de
l'autre côté de la pièce
➤ **the opposite sex** l'autre sexe *(masculine)*
■ *adverb*
en face : **I live opposite** j'habite en face
■ *noun*
contraire *(masculine)* : **the opposite of 'sad' is
'happy'** le contraire de « triste » est « heureux » ; **he always does the opposite to
what he is told** il fait toujours le contraire de
ce qu'on lui dit de faire.

opposition [,ɒpə'zɪʃn] *noun*

opposition *(feminine)*.

optician [ɒp'tɪʃn] *noun*

opticien *(masculine)*, opticienne *(feminine)* :
Mrs Clarke's an optician Mme Clarke est opticienne.

optimistic [,ɒptɪ'mɪstɪk] *adjective*

optimiste : **I'm not very optimistic** je ne
suis pas très optimiste.

option ['ɒpʃn] *noun*

choix *(masculine)* : **I have no option** je n'ai pas
le choix.

optional ['ɒpʃənl] *adjective*

facultatif *(feminine* **facultative***)* : **the German
class is optional** le cours d'allemand est facultatif
➤ **optional extras** accessoires *(masculine plural)*
en option.

or [ɔːr] *conjunction*

1. ou : **do you want tea or coffee?** tu veux du
thé ou du café ? ; **are you coming or not?** tu
viens ou pas ?
2. ni : **I can't come today or tomorrow** je ne
peux venir ni aujourd'hui ni demain ; **he
couldn't eat or sleep** il ne pouvait ni manger
ni dormir
3. sinon : **hurry up or we'll miss the train**
dépêche-toi sinon on va rater le train.

oral ['ɔːrəl] *adjective*

oral [*plural* **oraux**]
➤ **an oral exam** un oral.

orange ['ɒrɪndʒ] *noun & adjective*

■ *noun*
orange *(feminine)* : **an orange juice** un jus
d'orange
➤ **an orange tree** un oranger
■ *adjective*
orange *(invariable)* : **Bob's wearing an orange
shirt** Bob porte une chemise orange.

orchard ['ɔːtʃəd] *noun*

verger *(masculine)* : **an apple orchard** une
pommeraie OR un verger de pommes.

orchestra ['ɔːkɪstrə] *noun*

orchestre *(masculine)* : **she plays in an orchestra** elle joue dans un orchestre.

order [ˈɔːdəʳ] *noun & verb*

■ *noun*

1. **ordre** *(masculine)* : **he gave me an order** il m'a donné un ordre ; **the names are in alphabetical order** les noms sont dans l'ordre alphabétique ; **I hope everything is in order** j'espère que tout est en ordre

2. **commande** *(feminine)* : **the waiter took our order** le serveur a pris notre commande

➤ **out of order** en panne : **the lift is out of order** l'ascenseur est en panne

➤ **in order to** pour : **he came back home in order to see his parents** il est revenu pour voir ses parents

■ *verb*

1. **ordonner à** : **she ordered me to leave** elle m'a ordonné de partir

2. **commander** : **Oliver ordered fish** Oliver a commandé du poisson.

ordinary [*UK* ˈɔːdənrɪ, *US* ˈɔːdənerɪ] *adjective*

1. **ordinaire** : **it was an ordinary day** c'était un jour ordinaire ; **it's out of the ordinary** ça sort de l'ordinaire

2. **comme les autres** : **Austin's just an ordinary guy** Austin est un type comme les autres.

organ [ˈɔːgən] *noun*

orgue *(masculine)* : **he plays the organ** il joue de l'orgue.

organic [ɔːˈgænɪk] *adjective*

biologique, bio *(invariable)* : **organic food** des produits biologiques OR des produits bio.

organization , organisation *UK* [ˌɔːgənaɪˈzeɪʃn] *noun*

organisation *(feminine)* : **the Red Cross is an international organization** la Croix-Rouge est une organisation internationale.

organize , organise *UK* [ˈɔːgənaɪz] *verb*

organiser : **we're going to organize a trip to Canada** on va organiser un voyage au Canada.

original [ɒˈrɪdʒənl] *adjective*

1. **original** [*plural* **originaux**] : **it's an original idea** c'est une idée originale

2. **premier** *(feminine* **première***)* : **who were the original inhabitants of the country?** qui étaient les premiers habitants du pays ?

originally [əˈrɪdʒənəlɪ] *adverb*

à l'origine : **Covent Garden was originally a fruit and vegetable market** Covent Garden était à l'origine un marché aux fruits et légumes.

ornament [ˈɔːnəmənt] *noun*

bibelot *(masculine)* : **there are ornaments on the mantelpiece** il y a des bibelots sur la cheminée.

orphan [ˈɔːfn] *noun*

orphelin *(masculine)*, **orpheline** *(feminine)* : **she's an orphan** elle est orpheline.

orphanage [ˈɔːfənɪdʒ] *noun*

orphelinat *(masculine)*.

ostrich [ˈɒstrɪtʃ] *(plural* **ostriches***) noun*

autruche *(feminine)* : **ostriches can't fly** les autruches ne volent pas.

other [ˈʌðəʳ] *adjective & pronoun*

1. **autre** : **the other shirt is dirty** l'autre chemise est sale ; **I saw Darren the other day** j'ai vu Darren l'autre jour

2. **d'autres** : **they had other problems** ils avaient d'autres problèmes

➤ **the other one** l'autre : **I'll take the other one** je prendrai l'autre

➤ **the others** les autres : **the others are not coming** les autres ne viennent pas.

otherwise [ˈʌðəwaɪz] *conjunction & adverb*

■ *conjunction*

sinon : **go now, otherwise you'll miss your train** pars maintenant, sinon tu vas rater ton train

■ *adverb*

autrement : **we couldn't do otherwise** on ne pouvait pas faire autrement.

ouch [aʊtʃ] *exclamation*

aïe ! : **ouch, that hurts!** aïe, ça fait mal !

ought [ɔːt] *auxiliary verb*

> 'Ought' is translated by the verb **devoir** in the conditional tense:

you ought to go to the dentist tu devrais aller chez le dentiste ; **they ought to be here soon** ils devraient bientôt arriver ; **she ought to have come** elle aurait dû venir.

ounce [aʊns] *noun*

= 28,35 g : **add four ounces of chocolate** ajoutez 100 grammes de chocolat.

our ['aʊəʳ] *adjective*

notre [*plural* **nos**]

> In French the possessive adjective agrees in gender (masculine or feminine) and number (singular or plural) with the noun that follows:

our dog is called Sammy notre chien s'appelle Sammy ; **our cousins live in Canada** nos cousins vivent au Canada

> Use the definite article (**le**, **la** or **les**), not the possessive adjective, with parts of the body:

we brushed our teeth nous nous sommes brossé les dents.

ours ['aʊəz] *possessive pronoun*

1. **le nôtre** *(feminine* **la nôtre)** [*plural* **les nôtres**]

> In French the possessive pronoun agrees in gender (masculine or feminine) and number (singular or plural) with the noun that follows:

their house is big, ours is small leur maison est grande, la nôtre est petite ; **their books are new, ours are old** leurs livres sont neufs, les nôtres sont vieux

2. **à nous : this book isn't ours** ce livre n'est pas à nous ; **he's a friend of ours** c'est un ami à nous.

ourselves [aʊə'selvz] *plural pronoun*

1. **nous : we're enjoying ourselves** nous nous amusons
2. **nous-mêmes : we asked him ourselves** nous le lui avons demandé nous-mêmes.
> **by ourselves** tout seuls, toutes seules.

out [aʊt] *adverb & preposition*

1. **dehors : it's hot out** il fait chaud dehors

> When 'out' means 'outside' or 'out of the house', it is often not translated in French:

they're out in the garden ils sont dans le jardin ; **come out here** viens ici ; **she's out** elle est sortie OR elle n'est pas là ; **I'm going out** je sors ; **he ran out** il est sorti en courant
2. **éteint : the lights are out** les lumières sont éteintes
3. **démodé, plus à la mode : tartan is out this year** le tartan n'est plus à la mode cette année
> **the tide's out** c'est la marée basse

out of *preposition*

1. *With verbs of motion* **he walked out of the room** il est sorti de la pièce ; **she came out of the house** elle est sortie de la maison ; **get out of here!** sors d'ici ! ; **she jumped out of bed** elle a sauté hors du lit
2. **dans : he took a book out of his bag** il a pris un livre dans son sac ; **we drank out of china cups** nous avons bu dans des tasses en porcelaine
3. **par : she did it out of love** elle l'a fait par amour
4. **sur : ten out of twenty** dix sur vingt.

outdoor ['aʊtdɔːʳ] *adjective*

1. **en plein air : an outdoor swimming pool** une piscine en plein air
2. **de plein air : outdoor sports** les sports de plein air.

outdoors [aʊt'dɔːz] *adverb*

dehors : we had lunch outdoors nous avons déjeuné dehors.

outer ['aʊtəʳ] *adjective*

extérieur : the outer wall le mur extérieur
> **outer space** cosmos *(masculine)*.

outfit ['aʊtfɪt] *noun*

tenue *(feminine)* **: that's a nice outfit** c'est une jolie tenue
> **a cowboy outfit** une panoplie de cow-boy.

outing ['aʊtɪŋ] *noun*

sortie *(feminine)* **: we're going on a school outing** nous faisons une sortie scolaire.

outlaw ['aʊtlɔː] *noun*

hors-la-loi *(masculine)* [*plural* **hors-la-loi**] **: Robin Hood was an outlaw** Robin des bois était un hors-la-loi.

outline ['aʊtlaɪn] *noun*

silhouette *(feminine)* **: you can see the outline of the tower** on voit la silhouette de la tour.

out-of-date ['aʊtɒvdeɪt] *adjective*

périmé : your ticket is out-of-date votre billet est périmé.

outrageous [aʊt'reɪdʒəs] *adjective*

1. **scandaleux** *(feminine* **scandaleuse)** **: he said some outrageous things** il a prononcé des paroles scandaleuses

2. extravagant : an outrageous hat un chapeau extravagant
3. exorbitant : outrageous prices des prix exorbitants.

outside ['aʊtsaɪd, ˌaʊt'saɪd] *preposition, adverb, adjective & noun*

■ *preposition*
en dehors de : she lives outside the city elle vit en dehors de la ville ; **it's outside office hours** c'est en dehors des heures de bureau
■ *adverb* [ˌaʊt'saɪd]
dehors : wait for me outside attends-moi dehors
■ *adjective*
extérieur : the outside walls les murs extérieurs
■ *noun*
extérieur *(masculine)* **: the outside of the box is red** l'extérieur de la boîte est rouge.

outskirts ['aʊtskɜːts] *plural noun*
banlieue *(feminine)* **: they live on the outskirts of Edinburgh** ils habitent la banlieue d'Édimbourg.

oval ['əʊvl] *adjective & noun*
■ *adjective*
ovale : an oval window une fenêtre ovale
■ *noun*
ovale *(masculine)*
> **the Oval Office** le bureau du président des États-Unis à la Maison-Blanche.

oven ['ʌvn] *noun*
four *(masculine)* **: put the chicken in the oven** mets le poulet au four.

over ['əʊvəʳ] *preposition, adverb & adjective*
■ *preposition*
1. au-dessus de : there's a light over the table il y a une lampe au-dessus de la table
2. sur : put a cloth over the table mets une nappe sur la table
3. par-dessus : he jumped over the fence il a sauté par-dessus la clôture
4. plus de : she's over forty elle a plus de quarante ans
5. pendant : it happened over the Christmas holidays cela s'est passé pendant les fêtes de Noël
■ *adverb*
1. chez soi : I invited him over je l'ai invité chez moi
2. plus : five dollars or over cinq dollars ou plus

■ *adjective*
terminé : the exams are over les examens sont terminés
> **over here** par ici : **the shop's over here** le magasin est par ici
> **over there** là-bas : **look over there** regarde là-bas
> **over the road** en face : **they live over the road** ils habitent en face
> **all over**
1. partout : there's coffee all over the carpet il y a du café partout sur la moquette
2. fini : it's all over c'est fini.

overalls ['əʊvərɔːlz] *plural noun*
bleu *(masculine)* **de travail : a pair of overalls** un bleu de travail.

overcame *past tense of* overcome.

overcharge [ˌəʊvə'tʃɑːdʒ] *verb*
faire payer trop cher : I've been overcharged on m'a fait payer trop cher.

overcome [ˌəʊvə'kʌm] (*past tense* overcame [ˌəʊvə'keɪm], *past participle* overcome) *verb*
surmonter : she tried to overcome the problem elle a essayé de surmonter le problème.

overlook [ˌəʊvə'lʊk] *verb*
1. donner sur : our room overlooks the sea notre chambre donne sur la mer
2. négliger : she overlooked an important detail elle a négligé un détail important.

overnight [ˌəʊvə'naɪt] *adverb*
1. la nuit : he stayed overnight il est resté la nuit
2. du jour au lendemain : she changed overnight elle a changé du jour au lendemain.

overseas *adjective & adverb*
■ *adjective* ['əʊvəsiːz]
étranger *(feminine* **étrangère)** **: they are overseas students** ce sont des étudiants étrangers
■ *adverb* [ˌəʊvə'siːz]
à l'étranger : she lives overseas elle habite à l'étranger.

oversleep [ˌəʊvə'sliːp] (*past tense & past participle* overslept [ˌəʊvə'slept]) *verb*
ne pas se réveiller à temps : I overslept je ne me suis pas réveillé à temps.

overslept *past tense & past participle of* over-sleep.

overtake *UK* [ˌəʊvə'teɪk] (*past tense* over-took, *past participle* overtaken [ˌəʊvə'teɪkn]) *verb*

doubler : **the cyclist is trying to overtake the bus** le cycliste essaie de doubler le bus.

overtaken *UK past participle of* overtake.

overtime ['əʊvətaɪm] *uncountable noun*

heures *(feminine plural)* supplémentaires : **she's doing overtime** elle fait des heures supplémentaires.

overtook *UK* [ˌəʊvə'tʊk] *past tense of* over-take

he overtook on a bend il a doublé dans un virage.

owe [əʊ] *verb*

devoir : **I owe him fifty euros** je lui dois cinquante euros.

owl [aʊl] *noun*

hibou *(masculine)* [*plural* hiboux]
➤ **a snowy owl** une chouette blanche.

own [əʊn] *adjective & verb*

■ *adjective*
propre : **do you have your own bike?** tu as ton propre vélo ? ; **I saw it with my own eyes** je l'ai vu de mes propres yeux
➤ **a house of my own** une maison à moi
➤ **on one's own** tout seul, toute seule : **I'll do it on my own** je le ferai tout seul
■ *verb*
avoir, posséder : **she owns a car** elle a une voiture

own up *phrasal verb*

avouer : **he owned up to taking the money** il a avoué avoir pris l'argent.

owner ['əʊnər] *noun*

propriétaire *(masculine or feminine)*.

ox [ɒks] (*plural* oxen ['ɒksn]) *noun*

bœuf : **as strong as an ox** fort comme un bœuf.

oxygen ['ɒksɪdʒən] *noun*

oxygène *(masculine)*
➤ **an oxygen mask** un masque à oxygène.

oyster ['ɔɪstər] *noun*

huître *(feminine)*.

oz *abbreviation of* ounce & ounces.

ozone ['əʊzəʊn] *noun*

ozone *(masculine)*
➤ **the ozone layer** la couche d'ozone.

p *UK* [piː] *(abbreviation of* penny & pence)
it costs 20p ça coûte 20 pence.

pace [peɪs] *noun & verb*

■ *noun*
1. allure *(feminine)* : **she's walking at a brisk pace** elle marche à vive allure
2. rythme *(masculine)* : **he couldn't take the pace** il n'arrivait pas à suivre le rythme
■ *verb*
➤ **to pace up and down** faire les cent pas.

Pacific [pə'sɪfɪk] *noun*

the Pacific le Pacifique ; **the Pacific Ocean** l'océan Pacifique.

pacifier *US* ['pæsɪfaɪər] *noun*

tétine *(feminine)* : **the baby dropped his pacifier** le bébé a laissé tomber sa tétine.

pack [pæk] *noun & verb*

■ *noun*
1. paquet *(masculine)* : **a pack of cigarettes** un paquet de cigarettes
2. meute *(feminine)* : **a pack of wolves** une meute de loups
➤ **a pack of cards** un jeu de cartes

■ *verb*
1. **faire ses bagages, faire sa valise : I haven't packed yet** je n'ai pas encore fait mes bagages OR je n'ai pas encore fait ma valise ; **he packed his bags** il a fait ses bagages OR il a fait sa valise
2. **mettre dans sa valise : I forgot to pack my toothbrush** j'ai oublié de mettre ma brosse à dents dans ma valise.

package ['pækɪdʒ] *noun*

paquet *(masculine)* : **the postman has left a package for you** le facteur a laissé un paquet pour toi
➤ **a package holiday** un voyage organisé
➤ **a package deal** un forfait.

packed [pækt] *adjective*

bondé : the train was packed le train était bondé
➤ **a packed lunch** *UK* un panier-repas.

packet ['pækɪt] *noun*

paquet *(masculine)* : **she bought a packet of biscuits** elle a acheté un paquet de biscuits.

paddle ['pædl] *noun & verb*

■ *noun*
1. **pagaie** *(feminine)* : **he dropped his paddle into the water** il a laissé tomber sa pagaie dans l'eau
2. *US* **raquette** *(feminine)* **de ping-pong**
➤ **to go for a paddle** faire trempette
■ *verb*
faire trempette : to paddle in the sea faire trempette dans la mer
➤ **to paddle a canoe** pagayer : **he was paddling the canoe** il pagayait.

paddling pool *UK* ['pædlɪŋpuːl] *noun*

pataugeoire *(feminine)*.

padlock ['pædlɒk] *noun*

cadenas *(masculine)* : **he put a padlock on his bike** il a mis un cadenas sur son vélo.

page [peɪdʒ] *noun*

page *(feminine)* : **turn the page** tournez la page.

paid [peɪd] *adjective & verb form*

■ *adjective*
1. **rémunéré : it's paid work** c'est du travail rémunéré
2. **payé : they don't get paid holidays** ils n'ont

pas de congés payés ; **they are well paid** ils sont bien payés
■ *past tense & past participle of* pay
she paid a lot of money for it elle l'a payé cher.

pain [peɪn] *noun*

douleur *(feminine)* : **a sharp pain** une douleur aiguë
➤ **are you in pain?** tu as mal ?
➤ **I have a pain in my arm** j'ai mal au bras
➤ **she's in a lot of pain** elle a très mal
➤ **he's a real pain** *informal* il est pénible.

painful ['peɪnfʊl] *adjective*

douloureux *(feminine* **douloureuse***)* : **this burn is painful** cette brûlure est douloureuse.

paint [peɪnt] *noun & verb*

■ *noun*
peinture *(feminine)* : **'wet paint'** 'peinture fraîche'
■ *verb*
peindre : he paints landscapes il peint des paysages.

paintbrush ['peɪntbrʌʃ] *noun*

pinceau *(masculine)* [plural **pinceaux**].

painter ['peɪntər] *noun*

peintre *(masculine)* : **Vincent's a painter** Vincent est peintre.

painting ['peɪntɪŋ] *noun*

1. **peinture** *(feminine)* : **she likes painting** elle aime la peinture
2. **tableau** *(masculine)* [plural **tableaux**] : **it's a painting by Monet** c'est un tableau de Monet.

pair [peər] *noun*

paire *(feminine)* : **a pair of shoes** une paire de chaussures
➤ **a pair of trousers** *UK* OR **a pair of pants** *US* un pantalon.

pajamas *US* ➤ pyjamas *UK*.

Pakistan [*UK* ˌpɑːkɪˈstɑːn, *US* ˈpækɪstæn] *noun*
le Pakistan

In French the names of countries are used with the definite article (le, la or l'). Remember that the French preposition à combines with le to become au:

Pakistan is north of India le Pakistan est au nord de l'Inde ; **she's going to Pakistan** elle va au Pakistan ; **he lives in Pakistan** il habite au Pakistan.

Pakistani [UK ˌpɑːkɪˈstɑːnɪ, US pækɪˈstænɪ] *adjective & noun*

■ *adjective*
pakistanais

■ *noun*
Pakistanais *(masculine)*, **Pakistanaise** *(feminine)*

> Remember not to use a capital letter for the adjective in French.

pal [pæl] *noun informal*

copain *(masculine)*, **copine** *(feminine)*.

palace ['pælɪs] *noun*

palais *(masculine)* : **the king lives in a palace** le roi vit dans un palais.

pale [peɪl] *adjective*

pâle : **you're very pale** tu es tout pâle ; **to go pale** pâlir OR devenir pâle ; **pale blue** bleu pâle.

palm [pɑːm] *noun*

1. **paume** *(feminine)* : **she was holding an egg in the palm of her hand** elle tenait un œuf dans la paume de sa main
2. **palmier** *(masculine)* : **a palm tree** un palmier.

pamphlet ['pæmflɪt] *noun*

brochure *(feminine)*.

pan [pæn] *noun*

casserole *(feminine)* : **put the water into the pan** mets l'eau dans la casserole.

pancake ['pænkeɪk] *noun*

crêpe *(feminine)*
➤ **as flat as a pancake** plat comme une galette

> PANCAKE DAY
> **Pancake Day**, appelé aussi **Shrove Tuesday**, est le terme désignant mardi gras. Ce jour-là, la plupart des Britanniques mangent des crêpes (**pancakes**). Selon la tradition, il s'agit du dernier jour avant le début du carême. On organise des courses (**pancake race**) dans lesquelles les participants se poursuivent tout en faisant sauter une crêpe dans une poêle à frire.

panda ['pændə] *noun*

panda *(masculine)*.

pane [peɪn] *noun*

vitre *(feminine)* : **a pane of glass** une vitre.

panic ['pænɪk] *noun & verb*

■ *noun*
panique *(feminine)*
■ *verb (past tense & past participle* panicked)
paniquer : **he panicked** il a paniqué ; **don't panic!** pas de panique !

pant [pænt] *verb*

haleter : **the dog's panting** le chien halète.

panties ['pæntɪz] *plural noun*

culotte *(feminine)*, **slip** *(masculine)* : **a pair of panties** une culotte.

pantomime UK ['pæntəmaɪm] *noun*

spectacle traditionnel de Noël en Grande-Bretagne

> PANTOMIME
> La **pantomime** est un spectacle pour enfants joué au moment des fêtes de Noël. Généralement inspirée d'un conte de fées connu, elle combine comédie bouffonne et chansons. Certains personnages types apparaissent dans toutes les pièces : la **pantomime dame**, la vieille dame comique, rôle toujours tenu par un homme, et le **principal boy**, le héros incarné par une femme. Le public participe au spectacle en chantant, en huant les méchants lorsqu'ils entrent en scène ou en prononçant certaines répliques (**Behind you !**, **Oh yes he is !** ou **Oh no he isn't !**).

pants [pænts] *plural noun*

1. *UK* **slip** *(masculine)* : **a pair of pants** un slip
2. *US* **pantalon** *(masculine)* : **a pair of pants** un pantalon.

pantyhose US ['pæntɪhəʊz] *plural noun*

collant *(masculine)*.

paper ['peɪpər] *noun*

1. **papier** *(masculine)* : **he wrote the number on a piece of paper** il a écrit le numéro sur un bout de papier ; **a paper bag** un sac en papier
2. **journal** *(masculine)* [*plural* **journaux**] : **Dudley's reading the paper** Dudley lit le journal
➤ **an exam paper** une épreuve écrite
➤ **a paper clip** un trombone : **he put the**

pages together with a paper clip il a attaché les feuilles avec un trombone

➤ **the paper shop** UK le marchand de journaux.

paperback ['peɪpəbæk] noun

livre (masculine) de poche : a paperback book un livre de poche.

parachute ['pærəʃuːt] noun

parachute (masculine) : he came down in a parachute il est descendu en parachute.

parade [pə'reɪd] noun

défilé (masculine) : a fashion parade un défilé de mode.

paradise ['pærədaɪs] noun

paradis (masculine) : it's paradise here c'est le paradis ici.

paragraph ['pærəgrɑːf] noun

paragraphe (masculine)
➤ to start a new paragraph aller à la ligne.

parakeet US ['pærəkiːt] noun

perruche (feminine).

parallel ['pærəlel] adjective

parallèle : parallel lines des lignes parallèles.

paralysed UK, **paralyzed** US ['pærəlaɪzd] adjective

paralysé : she's paralysed in both legs elle est paralysée des deux jambes.

parcel UK ['pɑːsl] noun

colis (masculine) : I got a parcel through the post j'ai reçu un colis par la poste.

pardon ['pɑːdn] noun

➤ **pardon?** OR I beg your pardon? pardon ?
➤ I beg your pardon! je vous demande pardon.

parentheses [pə'renθɪsiːz] plural noun

parenthèses (feminine plural) : in parentheses entre parenthèses.

parents ['peərənts] plural noun

parents (masculine plural) : ask your parents demandez à vos parents.

Paris ['pærɪs] noun

Paris : we're going to Paris nous allons à Paris ; Helen lives in Paris Helen habite à Paris.

Parisian [UK pə'rɪzjən, US pə'rɪːʒən] adjective & noun

■ adjective
parisien (feminine parisienne)
■ noun
Parisien (masculine), Parisienne (feminine).

park [pɑːk] noun & verb

■ noun
parc (masculine) : they went for a walk in the park ils sont allés se promener dans le parc
■ verb
1. se garer : where can we park? où est-ce qu'on peut se garer ?
2. garer : I parked the car j'ai garé la voiture.

parking ['pɑːkɪŋ] uncountable noun

stationnement (masculine) : 'no parking' 'stationnement interdit'
➤ a parking lot US un parking : the car's in the parking lot la voiture est au parking
➤ a parking meter un parcmètre
➤ a parking ticket une contravention

⚠ Le mot anglais parking est un faux ami, il ne signifie pas "parc de stationnement".

parliament ['pɑːləmənt] noun

parlement (masculine).

parrot ['pærət] noun

perroquet (masculine).

parsley ['pɑːslɪ] noun

persil (masculine) : parsley is an herb le persil est une herbe.

part [pɑːt] noun & verb

■ noun
1. partie (feminine) : I like parts of the book j'aime certaines parties du livre ; to be part of something faire partie de quelque chose
2. rôle (masculine) : he plays a big part in the play il a un rôle important dans la pièce
3. pièce (feminine) : spare parts for a car des pièces de rechange pour une voiture
4. US raie (feminine) : he has a middle part il a la raie au milieu
➤ to take part in something participer à quelque chose : he took part in the race il a participé à la course
■ verb
se quitter : they parted at the gates ils se sont quittés à la porte
➤ to part one's hair se faire une raie : she

parts her hair in the middle elle se fait une raie au milieu

part with *phrasal verb*

se séparer de : **I had to part with my favourite photo** j'ai dû me séparer de ma photo préférée.

participle ['pɑ:tɪsɪpl] *noun*

participe *(masculine)* : **the past participle** le participe passé.

particular [pə'tɪkjʊlə^r] *adjective*

particulier *(feminine* **particulière)** : **are you looking for something in particular?** est-ce que vous cherchez quelque chose de particulier ?

particularly [pə'tɪkjʊləlɪ] *adverb*

particulièrement : **not particularly** pas particulièrement.

parting *UK* ['pɑ:tɪŋ] *noun*

raie *(feminine)* : **he has a middle parting** il a la raie au milieu.

partner ['pɑ:tnə^r] *noun*

partenaire *(masculine or feminine)*

➤ **a business partner** un associé, une associée.

part-time ['pɑ:ttaɪm] *adjective & adverb*

à temps partiel : **he has a part-time job** il a un travail à temps partiel ; **she works part-time** elle travaille à temps partiel.

party ['pɑ:tɪ] *(plural* **parties)** *noun*

1. fête *(feminine)*, soirée *(feminine)* : **we're having a party** nous allons faire une fête ; **a birthday party** une fête d'anniversaire ; **a Christmas party** une fête de Noël
2. parti *(masculine)* : **the Labour party** le parti travailliste ; **the Democratic party** le parti démocrate
3. groupe *(masculine)* : **a party of tourists** un groupe de touristes.

pass [*UK* pɑ:s, *US* pæs] *noun & verb*

■ *noun*

1. laissez-passer *(masculine)* [*plural* **laissez-passer**] : **you need a pass to get in** il faut un laissez-passer pour entrer
2. carte *(feminine)* d'abonnement : **a bus pass** une carte d'abonnement de bus
3. *In sports* passe *(feminine)* : **he made a pass to Owen** il a fait une passe à Owen

4. col *(masculine)* : **a mountain pass** un col de montagne
➤ **to get a pass** *UK* être reçu : **I got a pass in history** j'ai été reçu en histoire
➤ **a boarding pass** une carte d'embarquement
■ *verb*
1. passer : **can you pass me the salt?** tu peux me passer le sel ? ; **pass me the paper** passe-moi le journal ; **what's the capital of Poland? – pass!** quelle est la capitale de la Pologne ? – je passe ! ; **let me pass!** laissez-moi passer ! ; **they played cards to pass the time** ils ont joué aux cartes pour passer le temps ; **the evening passed quickly** la soirée est passée vite

> When **pass** has a direct object (to pass something), the past tense in French is formed with the verb **avoir** + past participle (I passed the pen to Mark j'ai passé le stylo à Mark). When the verb **passer** has no object and means 'to go past', you use **être** + past participle to form the past tense (the time passed quickly **le temps est passé vite**).

2. passer devant : **I pass the museum on my way to school** je passe devant le musée en allant à l'école
3. doubler, dépasser : **he passed the car in front** il a doublé la voiture qui était devant
4. croiser : **to pass somebody in the street** croiser quelqu'un dans la rue
5. réussir, réussir à : **he passed his exam** il a réussi ses examens OR il a réussi à ses examens ; **to pass one's driving test** avoir son permis de conduire
6. réussir, être reçu : **I got my exam results – did you pass?** j'ai eu le résultat des examens – tu as été reçu ? OR tu as réussi ?

> You must be careful not to translate 'to pass an exam' with the French verb **passer**: passer un examen means to take an exam.

7. voter : **the law was passed** la loi a été votée
➤ **to pass the ball to somebody** faire une passe à quelqu'un : **he passed the ball to Cantona** il a fait une passe à Cantona

pass on *phrasal verb*

transmettre : **can you pass the message on?** tu peux transmettre le message ?

pass out *phrasal verb*

s'évanouir : **she passed out** elle s'est évanouie.

passage ['pæsɪdʒ] *noun*

1. **passage** *(masculine)* : **it's an interesting passage of the book** c'est un passage intéressant du livre
2. **couloir** *(masculine)* : **he was walking along the passage** il longeait le couloir.

passenger ['pæsɪndʒər] *noun*

passager *(masculine)*, **passagère** *(feminine)*.

passerby [UK ˌpɑːsə'baɪ, US ˌpæsər'baɪ] *(plural* passersby [UK ˌpɑːsəz'baɪ, US ˌpæsərz'baɪ]*) noun*

passant *(masculine)*, **passante** *(feminine)*.

passion ['pæʃn] *noun*

passion *(feminine)* : **she has a passion for music** ella a la passion de la musique
> **passion fruit** fruit *(masculine)* de la passion.

passive ['pæsɪv] *adjective & noun*

■ *adjective*
passif *(feminine* **passive)***

■ *noun*
passif *(masculine)* : **in the passive** au passif.

Passover [UK 'pɑːsˌəʊvər, US 'pæsˌəʊvər] *noun*

la **Pâque juive**.

passport [UK 'pɑːspɔːt, US 'pæspɔːt] *noun*

passeport *(masculine)* : **passport control** le contrôle des passeports.

password [UK 'pɑːswɜːd, US 'pæswɜːd] *noun*

mot *(masculine)* **de passe** : **what's the password?** quel est le mot de passe ?

past [UK pɑːst, US pæst] *noun, adjective & preposition*

■ *noun*
passé *(masculine)* : **she often thinks about the past** elle pense souvent au passé
> **in the past** dans le passé OR autrefois : **there are more students now than in the past** il y a plus d'étudiants maintenant qu'autrefois
■ *adjective*
1. **dernier** *(feminine* **dernière)** : **during the past few days** ces derniers jours
2. **passé** : **the past tense** le passé ; **in the past tense** au passé
■ *preposition*
1. **devant** : **we drove past the school** on est passé devant l'école en voiture ; **she walked**

past my desk elle est passée devant mon bureau
2. **après** : **it's just past the church** c'est juste après l'église
> **it's ten past six** il est six heures dix
> **it's half past eight** il est huit heures et demie.

pasta ['pæstə] *uncountable noun*

pâtes *(feminine plural)* : **pasta with tomato sauce** des pâtes à la sauce tomate.

pastime [UK 'pɑːstaɪm, US 'pæstaɪm] *noun*

passe-temps *(masculine)* [*plural* **passe-temps**] : **my favourite pastime is swimming** mon passe-temps favori est la natation.

pastry ['peɪstrɪ] *noun*

1. *(plural* **pastries)** **pâtisserie** *(feminine)* : **would you like a pastry?** vous aimeriez une pâtisserie ?
2. *(uncountable)* **pâte** *(feminine)* : **she's making pastry for an apple pie** elle prépare de la pâte pour une tarte aux pommes.

pat [pæt] *(past tense & past participle* **patted)** *verb*

1. **tapoter** : **I patted the baby on the cheek** j'ai tapoté le bébé sur la joue
2. **caresser** : **can I pat your dog?** je peux caresser ton chien ?

patch [pætʃ] *(plural* **patches** ['pætʃɪz]*) noun*

1. **pièce** *(feminine)* : **jeans with patches on the knees** un jean avec des pièces aux genoux
2. **bandeau** *(masculine)* [*plural* **bandeaux**] : **the pirate's wearing a patch over his eye** le pirate a un bandeau sur l'œil
> **icy patches** plaques *(feminine plural)* de verglas
> **to be going through a bad patch** traverser une mauvaise passe.

path [UK pɑːθ, US pæθ, *plural UK* pɑːðz, *US* pæðz] *noun*

1. **chemin** *(masculine)*, **sentier** *(masculine)* : **this path leads to the river** ce chemin mène à la rivière
2. **allée** *(feminine)* : **she walked up the garden path** elle a remonté l'allée du jardin.

pathetic [pə'θetɪk] *adjective*

lamentable : **a pathetic excuse** une excuse lamentable ; **that's pathetic!** c'est lamentable !

patience ['peɪʃns] *noun*

patience *(feminine)* : **she has a lot of patience** elle a beaucoup de patience.

patient ['peɪʃnt] *adjective & noun*

◼ *adjective*
patient : **Peter's not very patient** Peter n'est pas très patient

◼ *noun*
patient *(masculine)*, **patiente** *(feminine)*, **malade** *(masculine or feminine)*.

patiently ['peɪʃntlɪ] *adverb*

patiemment : **he's waiting patiently** il attend patiemment.

patriotic [*UK* ˌpætrɪ'ɒtɪk, *US* ˌpeɪtrɪ'ɒtɪk] *adjective*
patriote.

patrol [pə'trəʊl] *noun*

patrouille *(feminine)* : **the soldiers are on patrol** les soldats sont en patrouille
➤ **a patrol car** une voiture de police.

pattern ['pætən] *noun*

motif *(masculine)*, **dessin** *(masculine)* : **I like the pattern on your dress** j'aime le motif sur ta robe.

pause [pɔːz] *noun*

pause *(feminine)* : **let's have a five-minute pause** faisons une pause de cinq minutes.

pavement ['peɪvmənt] *noun*

1. *UK* trottoir *(masculine)* : **walk on the pavement** marche sur le trottoir
2. *US* chaussée *(feminine)* : **the car skidded on the icy pavement** la voiture a dérapé sur la chaussée verglacée.

paw [pɔː] *noun*

patte *(feminine)* : **the dog gave his paw** le chien a donné sa patte.

pay [peɪ] *(past tense & past participle* paid*) verb*

payer : **I'll pay the bill** je vais payer l'addition ; **he's paid by the week** il est payé à la semaine
➤ **to pay attention** faire attention : **I wasn't paying attention** je ne faisais pas attention
➤ **to pay somebody a visit** rendre visite à quelqu'un : **he paid me a visit** il m'a rendu visite

pay back | *phrasal verb*

rembourser : **I'll pay you back later** je te rembourserai plus tard

pay for | *phrasal verb*

payer : **I've already paid for the meal** j'ai déjà payé le repas ; **he paid 20 euros for that shirt** il a payé cette chemise 20 euros.

payment ['peɪmənt] *noun*

paiement *(masculine)*.

payphone ['peɪfəʊn] *noun*

téléphone *(masculine)* **public**.

PC [ˌpiː'siː] *(abbreviation of* personal computer*) noun*
PC *(masculine)*.

PE [ˌpiː'iː] *(abbreviation of* physical education*) noun*
EPS *(feminine)* : **we have PE on Fridays** nous avons EPS le vendredi.

pea [piː] *noun*

petit pois *(masculine)* : **I like peas** j'aime les petits pois.

peace [piːs] *uncountable noun*

paix *(feminine)* : **they made peace** ils ont fait la paix
➤ **to leave somebody in peace** laisser quelqu'un tranquille
➤ **I want some peace and quiet** je veux un peu de calme.

peaceful ['piːsfʊl] *adjective*

1. paisible : **it's very peaceful in the country** c'est très paisible à la campagne
2. pacifique : **the demonstration was peaceful** la manifestation était pacifique.

peach [piːtʃ] *(plural* peaches ['piːtʃɪz]*) noun*

pêche *(feminine)* : **James is eating a peach** James mange une pêche.

peacock ['piːkɒk] *noun*

paon *(masculine)* : **as proud as a peacock** fier comme un paon.

peak [piːk] *noun*

sommet *(masculine)*, **cime** *(feminine)* : **he reached the peak of the mountain** il a atteint le sommet de la montagne
➤ **the peak season** la haute saison
➤ **at peak time**
1. *On TV* aux heures de grande écoute

2. **aux heures de pointe : the traffic is bad at peak time** on circule mal aux heures de pointe.

peanut ['piːnʌt] *noun*

cacahuète *(feminine)*
➤ **peanut butter** beurre *(masculine)* de cacahuètes.

pear [peəʳ] *noun*

poire *(feminine)*
➤ **a pear tree** un poirier.

pearl [pɜːl] *noun*

perle *(feminine)* : **a pearl necklace** un collier de perles.

pebble ['pebl] *noun*

caillou *(masculine)* [*plural* **cailloux**]
➤ **a pebble beach** une plage de galets.

peculiar [pɪ'kjuːljəʳ] *adjective*

bizarre : it has a peculiar smell ça a une odeur bizarre.

pedal ['pedl] *noun & verb*

◾ *noun*
pédale *(feminine)* : **put your foot on the pedal** mets le pied sur la pédale
◾ *verb*
pédaler : you have to pedal harder when you go up a hill il faut pédaler plus fort lorsqu'on grimpe une colline.

pedestrian [pɪ'destrɪən] *noun*

piéton *(masculine)*, **piétonne** *(feminine)* : **this road is for pedestrians only** cette rue est réservée aux piétons
➤ **a pedestrian crossing** *UK* un passage pour piétons
➤ **a pedestrian precinct** *UK* OR **a pedestrian zone** *US* une zone piétonne OR une zone piétonnière.

pee [piː] *noun informal*

pipi *(masculine)* : **to have a pee** faire pipi.

peek ➤ peep.

peel [piːl] *noun & verb*

◾ *noun*
1. **peau** *(feminine)* : **take the apple peel off** enlève la peau de ta pomme
2. **écorce** *(feminine)* : **add some orange peel** ajoutez de l'écorce d'orange

◾ *verb*
1. **éplucher : he's peeling the potatoes** il épluche les pommes de terre
2. **peler : my skin is peeling** je pèle

peel off *phrasal verb*

détacher : peel the label off détache l'étiquette.

peep [piːp], **peek** [piːk] *noun & verb*

◾ *noun*
coup *(masculine)* **d'œil : to have a peep** jeter un coup d'œil
◾ *verb*
jeter un coup d'œil
➤ **no peeping!** défense de regarder !

peg [peg] *noun*

1. *UK* **pince** *(feminine)* **à linge : hang up the sheets with these pegs** suspends les draps avec ces pinces à linge
2. **portemanteau** *(masculine)* [*plural* **portemanteaux** *(feminine)*] : **put your coat on the peg** mets ton manteau au portemanteau.

pelican ['pelɪkən] *noun*

pélican *(masculine)*.

pen [pen] *noun*

stylo *(masculine)* : **an ink pen** un stylo à encre
➤ **a pen pal** un correspondant, une correspondante : **my pen pal's called Paul** mon correspondant s'appelle Paul.

penalty ['penltɪ] (*plural* **penalties**) *noun*

1. **peine** *(feminine)* : **the death penalty** la peine de mort
2. *In football* **penalty** *(masculine)*
3. *In rugby* **pénalité** *(feminine)*.

pence *UK* [pens] *plural of* **penny**

a 50-pence piece une pièce de 50 pence.

pencil ['pensl] *noun*

crayon *(masculine)* : **write your name in pencil** écris ton nom au crayon
➤ **a pencil case** une trousse
➤ **a pencil sharpener** un taille-crayon.

pendant ['pendənt] *noun*

pendentif *(masculine)* : **she's wearing a pendant** elle porte un pendentif

 Le mot anglais **pendant** est un faux ami, il ne signifie pas "pendant".

penfriend *UK* ['penfrend] *noun*

correspondant *(masculine)*, **correspondante** *(feminine)* : **my penfriend is called Christine** ma correspondante s'appelle Christine.

penguin ['peŋgwɪn] *noun*

manchot *(masculine)*.

penknife ['pennaɪf] *(plural* penknives ['pennaɪvz]) *noun*

canif *(masculine)*.

penny ['penɪ] *noun*

1. *(plural* pence) penny *(masculine)* : **she dropped a penny on the floor** elle a laissé tomber un penny par terre ; **it costs fifty pence** ça coûte cinquante pence

2. *US (plural* pennies) cent : **can you give me a few pennies?** tu peux me donner quelques cents ?

pension ['penʃn] *noun*

retraite *(feminine)* : **you'll get a pension when you are 60** tu toucheras une retraite quand tu auras 60 ans

⚠️ Le mot anglais **pension** ne signifie pas "pension" au sens de "pensionnat".

pensioner *UK* ['penʃənər] *noun*

retraité *(masculine)*, **retraitée** *(feminine)* : **he's an old-age pensioner** il est retraité.

Pentagon ['pentəgən] *noun*

the Pentagon le Pentagone

 THE PENTAGON
L'édifice du Pentagone, ainsi nommé en raison de sa forme, et qui se trouve près de la ville de Washington, est le siège du ministère américain de la Défense. On parle souvent du **Pentagon** pour parler du pouvoir militaire américain en général. Une partie du Pentagone a été détruite dans l'attentat du 11 septembre 2001.

penthouse ['penthaʊs, *plural* 'penthaʊzɪz] *noun*

appartement de luxe au dernier étage d'un immeuble.

people ['piːpl] *plural noun*

1. **gens** *(masculine plural)* : **they're nice people** ce sont des gens sympas ; **a lot of people think I'm mad** beaucoup de gens pensent que je suis fou ; **there are a lot of people here** il y a beaucoup de monde

2. **personnes** *(feminine plural)* : **there's enough room for ten people** il y a de la place pour dix personnes

➤ **people say that ...** on dit que ... : **people say that he's mean** on dit qu'il est avare

➤ **English people** les Anglais

➤ **French people** les Français

➤ **Irish people** les Irlandais

➤ **a people carrier** un monospace.

pepper ['pepər] *noun*

1. **poivre** *(masculine)* : **salt and pepper** le sel et le poivre

2. **poivron** *(masculine)* : **red, yellow and green peppers** des poivrons rouges, jaunes et verts.

peppermint ['pepəmɪnt] *noun*

bonbon *(masculine)* à la menthe.

per [pɜːr] *preposition*

par : **it's £10 per person** c'est 10 livres par personne

➤ **it costs 2 euros per kilo** ça coûte 2 euros le kilo

➤ **he's paid $15 per hour** il est payé 15 dollars de l'heure.

per cent, percent [pɜːrˈsent] *adverb*

pour cent : **20 percent of the students are absent** 20 pour cent des étudiants sont absents.

perfect ['pɜːfɪkt] *adjective*

parfait : **the weather's perfect** le temps est parfait.

perfectly ['pɜːfɪktlɪ] *adverb*

parfaitement : **I'm perfectly happy** je suis parfaitement heureux.

perform [pəˈfɔːm] *verb*

1. **jouer** : **he's performing in a play** il joue dans une pièce ; **the team performed well** l'équipe a bien joué

2. **exécuter, accomplir** : **a computer can perform several tasks at once** un ordinateur peut exécuter plusieurs tâches à la fois.

performance [pəˈfɔːməns] *noun*

1. **spectacle** *(masculine)* : **the performance lasts two hours** le spectacle dure deux heures

2. **performance** *(feminine)* : **the team's performance was excellent** les performances de l'équipe étaient excellentes

3. **interprétation** (feminine) : **I liked his performance of Romeo** j'ai bien aimé son interprétation de Roméo

⚠️ Le mot anglais **performance** couvre plus de sens que le mot français "performance".

perfume [ˈpɜːfjuːm] noun

parfum (masculine) : **she's wearing perfume** elle a mis du parfum.

perhaps [pəˈhæps] adverb

peut-être : **perhaps you're right** tu as peut-être raison OR peut-être que tu as raison
➤ **perhaps not** peut-être pas.

period [ˈpɪərɪəd] noun

1. **période** (feminine) : **a long period of drought** une longue période de sécheresse
2. **cours** (masculine) : **I have a history period next** j'ai un cours d'histoire maintenant
3. **règles** (feminine plural) : **she has her period** elle a ses règles
4. US **point** (masculine) : **don't forget the period at the end of the sentence** n'oublie pas de mettre le point à la fin de la phrase.

perm [pɜːm] noun

permanente (feminine) : **she's going to have a perm** elle va se faire faire une permanente.

permanent [ˈpɜːmənənt] adjective & noun

▪ adjective
permanent : **a permanent exhibition** une exposition permanente
▪ noun US
permanente (feminine) : **to have a permanent** se faire faire une permanente.

permission [pəˈmɪʃn] noun

permission (feminine) : **she gave me permission to leave** elle m'a donné la permission de partir.

permit noun & verb

▪ noun [ˈpɜːmɪt]
permis (masculine) : **a work permit** un permis de travail
▪ verb [pəˈmɪt] (past tense & past participle permitted)
permettre à : **her parents won't permit her to travel alone** ses parents ne lui permettront pas de voyager seule

➤ **smoking is not permitted** il est interdit de fumer.

person [ˈpɜːsn] (plural people) noun

personne (feminine) : **there's room for one more person** il y a de la place pour une autre personne ; **she came to see me in person** elle est venue me voir en personne ; **it's $20 per person** c'est 20 dollars par personne
➤ **she's a nice person** c'est quelqu'un de sympathique.

personal [ˈpɜːsənl] adjective

personnel (feminine **personnelle**) : **it's a personal letter** c'est une lettre personnelle ; **your personal belongings** tes effets personnels OR tes affaires
➤ **a personal stereo** un baladeur.

personality [ˌpɜːsəˈnælətɪ] (plural personalities) noun

personnalité (feminine) : **he has a strong personality** il a une forte personnalité.

persuade [pəˈsweɪd] verb

persuader : **he persuaded me to go** il m'a persuadé d'y aller ; **I persuaded him not to go out** je l'ai persuadé de ne pas sortir.

pessimistic [ˌpesɪˈmɪstɪk] adjective

pessimiste.

pet [pet] noun

1. **animal** (masculine) **familier** : **have you got any pets?** tu as des animaux familiers ? ; **we have a pet rabbit at home** nous avons un lapin à la maison
2. **chouchou** (masculine), **chouchoute** (feminine) : **he's the teacher's pet** c'est le chouchou du professeur
➤ **a pet shop** une animalerie.

petal [ˈpetl] noun

pétale (masculine) : **the rose is losing its petals** la rose perd ses pétales.

petrol UK [ˈpetrəl] noun

essence (feminine) : **I've run out of petrol** je suis en panne d'essence

⚠️ **Petrol** est un faux ami, il ne signifie pas "pétrole".

pharmacy [ˈfɑːməsɪ] (plural pharmacies) noun

pharmacie *(feminine)* : **I'm going to the pharmacy** je vais à la pharmacie.

pheasant ['feznt] *noun*

faisan *(masculine)*.

philosopher [fɪ'lɒsəfəʳ] *noun*

philosophe *(masculine or feminine)* : **Plato was a Greek philosopher** Platon était un philosophe grec.

philosophy [fɪ'lɒsəfɪ] *noun*

philosophie *(feminine)* : **she's studying philosophy** elle fait des études de philosophie.

phobia ['fəʊbjə] *noun*

phobie *(feminine)* : **she has a phobia about spiders** elle a la phobie des araignées.

phone [fəʊn] *noun & verb*

◼ *noun*

téléphone *(masculine)* : **where's the phone?** où est le téléphone ?

➤ **on the phone** au téléphone : **Fred's on the phone** Fred est au téléphone

➤ **the phone book** l'annuaire *(masculine)* : **look up the number in the phone book** cherche le numéro dans l'annuaire

➤ **a phone booth** OR **a phone box** UK une cabine téléphonique

➤ **a phone call** un coup de fil : **he made a phone call** il a passé un coup de fil

➤ **a phone number** un numéro de téléphone : **what's your phone number?** quel est ton numéro de téléphone ?

◼ *verb*

1. **appeler, téléphoner à** : **I phoned my uncle** j'ai appelé mon oncle OR j'ai téléphoné à mon oncle

2. **appeler, téléphoner** : **your parents phoned** tes parents ont appelé OR tes parents ont téléphoné

phone back *phrasal verb*

rappeler : **I'll phone back tonight** je rappellerai ce soir.

phonecard UK ['fəʊnkɑːd] *noun*

carte *(feminine)* **de téléphone**.

phoney, phony ['fəʊnɪ] *adjective*

faux *(feminine* **fausse)** : **it's a phoney name** c'est un faux nom.

photo ['fəʊtəʊ] *noun*

photo *(feminine)* : **he took a photo** il a pris une photo

➤ **to take a photo of somebody** OR **something** prendre quelqu'un OR quelque chose en photo : **he took a photo of me** il m'a pris en photo.

photocopy ['fəʊtəʊ͵kɒpɪ] *noun & verb*

◼ *noun*

photocopie *(feminine)* : **I'll make a photocopy of the document** je vais faire une photocopie du document

◼ *verb* (*past tense & past participle* photocopied)

photocopier : **I photocopied the letter** j'ai photocopié la lettre.

photograph [UK 'fəʊtəgrɑːf, US 'fəʊtəgræf] *noun*

photographie *(feminine)*, **photo** *(feminine)* : **she was taking photographs** elle prenait des photographies

➤ **to take a photograph of somebody** OR **something** prendre quelqu'un OR quelque chose en photo

⚠ Photograph est un faux ami, il ne signifie pas "photographe".

photographer [fə'tɒgrəfəʳ] *noun*

photographe *(masculine or feminine)* : **she's a photographer** elle est photographe.

photography [fə'tɒgrəfɪ] *noun*

photographie *(feminine)*, **photo** *(feminine)* : **I do a lot of photography** je fais de la photo.

phrase [freɪz] *noun*

expression *(feminine)*

➤ **a phrase book** un guide de conversation.

physical ['fɪzɪkl] *adjective*

physique : **he does a lot of physical exercise** il fait beaucoup d'exercice physique ; **physical education** l'éducation physique.

physician US [fɪ'zɪʃn] *noun*

médecin : **he's a physician** il est médecin.

physics ['fɪzɪks] *uncountable noun*

physique *(feminine)* : **physics is my favourite subject** la physique est ma matière préférée.

pianist ['pɪənɪst] *noun*

pianiste *(masculine or feminine)* : **Mary's a pianist** Mary est pianiste.

piano [pɪ'ænəʊ] *noun*

piano *(masculine)* : **Pete plays the piano** Pete joue du piano.

pick [pɪk] *noun & verb*

■ *noun*

➤ **to take one's pick** faire son choix : **take your pick!** fais ton choix !

➤ **an ice pick** un pic à glace

■ *verb*

1. **choisir** : **pick a card** choisis une carte ; **I picked the green shirt** j'ai choisi la chemise verte

2. **cueillir** : **she's picking flowers** elle cueille des fleurs

➤ **to pick a fight** chercher la bagarre

➤ **to pick one's nose** se décrotter le nez

pick on *phrasal verb*

s'en prendre à, harceler : **they're always picking on him in school** ils s'en prennent tout le temps à lui à l'école

pick up *phrasal verb*

1. **ramasser** : **he bent down and picked up the coin** il s'est penché pour ramasser la pièce

2. **chercher** : **I'll come and pick you up at the station** je viendrai te chercher à la gare

3. **apprendre** : **she has picked up a bit of Italian** elle a appris quelques mots d'italien.

pickle ['pɪkl] *noun*

1. *UK* **pickles** *(masculine plural)*

2. *US* **cornichon** *(masculine)*.

pickpocket ['pɪk‚pɒkɪt] *noun*

pickpocket *(masculine)* : **beware of pickpockets** attention aux pickpockets.

picnic ['pɪknɪk] *noun*

pique-nique *(masculine)* [*plural* **pique-niques**] : **we're going on a picnic** nous allons en pique-nique ; **to have a picnic** faire un pique-nique OR pique-niquer.

picture ['pɪktʃər] *noun*

1. **tableau** *(masculine)* [*plural* **tableaux**] : **there were pictures on the wall** il y avait des tableaux au mur

2. **photo** *(feminine)* : **I took a picture of him** je l'ai pris en photo

3. **dessin** *(masculine)* : **she's drawing a picture** elle fait un dessin ; **she's drawing a picture of a horse** elle dessine un cheval

4. **illustration** *(feminine)* : **are there any pictures in this book?** est-ce qu'il y a des illustrations dans ce livre ?

pie [paɪ] *noun*

1. **tarte** *(feminine)* : **an apple pie** une tarte aux pommes

2. *UK* **tourte** *(feminine)* : **a chicken pie** une tourte au poulet.

piece [piːs] *noun*

1. **morceau** *(masculine)* [*plural* **morceaux**] : **a piece of bread** un morceau de main ; **it's in pieces** c'est en morceaux ; **it fell to pieces** c'est tombé en morceaux

2. **pièce** *(feminine)* : **I've lost a piece of the jigsaw** j'ai perdu une pièce du puzzle

➤ **to take something to pieces** démonter quelque chose

➤ **a piece of furniture** un meuble

➤ **a piece of advice** un conseil

➤ **a piece of information** un renseignement.

pierced [pɪəst] *adjective*

percé : **she has pierced ears** elle a les oreilles percées.

pig [pɪg] *noun*

1. **cochon** *(masculine)* : **they keep pigs on the farm** ils élèvent des cochons à la ferme

2. *informal* **goinfre** *(masculine or feminine)* : **you greedy pig!** quel goinfre !

pigeon ['pɪdʒɪn] *noun*

pigeon *(masculine)*.

piggyback ['pɪgɪbæk] *noun*

➤ **to give somebody a piggyback** porter quelqu'un sur son dos : **he gave me a piggyback** il m'a porté sur son dos.

piggybank ['pɪgɪbæŋk] *noun*

tirelire *(feminine)*.

pigtail ['pɪgteɪl] *noun*

natte *(feminine)* : **she wears pigtails** elle porte des nattes.

pile [paɪl] *noun & verb*

■ *noun*

1. **tas** *(masculine)* : **she left her clothes in a pile on the floor** elle a laissé ses vêtements en tas par terre

2. **pile** *(feminine)* : **there was a pile of books on his desk** il y avait une pile de livres sur son bureau ; **put these coins into piles** mets ces pièces en pile

■ *verb*

1. **empiler** : **he neatly piled his clothes on the bed** il a soigneusement empilé ses vêtements sur le lit

p

2. entasser : **I piled the toys into the box** j'ai entassé les jouets dans la boîte

pile up *phrasal verb*

1. s'entasser, s'empiler : **the dirty plates are piling up in the sink** les assiettes sales s'entassent dans l'évier

2. s'accumuler : **the work is piling up** le travail s'accumule.

pill [pɪl] *noun*

pilule *(feminine)* : **he swallowed the pill** il a avalé la pilule.

pillar ['pɪləʳ] *noun*

pilier *(masculine)* : **marble pillars** des piliers en marbre

➤ **a pillar box** *UK* une boîte aux lettres.

pillow ['pɪləʊ] *noun*

oreiller *(masculine)*.

pillowcase ['pɪləʊkeɪs] *noun*

taie *(feminine)* **d'oreiller**.

pilot ['paɪlət] *noun*

pilote *(masculine)* : **Ted's father is a pilot** le père de Ted est pilote.

pin [pɪn] *noun*

épingle *(feminine)* : **she pricked herself with a pin** elle s'est piquée avec une épingle

➤ **to have pins and needles** avoir des fourmis : **I've got pins and needles** j'ai des fourmis.

PIN [pɪn], **PIN number** [pɪn'nʌmbəʳ] *(abbreviation of* personal identification number*) noun*

code *(masculine)* **confidentiel**.

pinball ['pɪnbɔːl] *noun*

flipper *(masculine)* : **they are playing pinball** ils jouent au flipper

➤ **a pinball machine** un flipper.

pinch [pɪntʃ] *verb*

1. pincer : **she pinched me on the arm** elle m'a pincé le bras

2. *UK informal* piquer : **somebody has pinched my bike** quelqu'un m'a piqué mon vélo.

pine [paɪn] *noun*

pin *(masculine)* : **a pine tree** un pin ; **a pine table** une table en pin.

pineapple ['paɪnæpl] *noun*

ananas *(masculine)* : **pineapple juice** du jus d'ananas.

pink [pɪŋk] *adjective*

rose : **she's wearing a pink skirt** elle porte une jupe rose ; **bright pink** rose vif.

pint [paɪnt] *noun*

1. pinte *(feminine)* : **it costs 50p a pint** ça coûte 50 pence la pinte

2. *UK* bière *(feminine)* : **he went out for a pint** il est allé boire une bière

➤ **a pint of milk** un demi-litre de lait.

pipe [paɪp] *noun*

1. tuyau *(masculine)* [*plural* **tuyaux**] : **the pipes have frozen** les tuyaux ont gelé

2. pipe *(feminine)* : **he smokes a pipe** il fume la pipe.

pirate ['paɪrət] *noun*

pirate *(masculine)* : **he's a pirate** il est pirate.

Pisces ['paɪsiːz] *noun*

Poissons *(masculine plural)* : **he's a Pisces** il est Poissons.

pistol ['pɪstl] *noun*

pistolet *(masculine)*.

pitch *UK* [pɪtʃ] *(plural* pitches*) noun*

terrain *(masculine)* : **a football pitch** un terrain de foot.

pitcher *US* ['pɪtʃəʳ] *noun*

pot *(masculine)* : **a pitcher of milk** un pot de lait.

pity ['pɪtɪ] *noun & verb*

◼ *noun*

1. pitié *(feminine)* : **she took pity on them** elle a eu pitié d'eux

2. dommage *(masculine)* : **what a pity!** quel dommage ! ; **it's a pity you didn't see it** c'est dommage que tu ne l'aies pas vu

◼ *verb*

plaindre : **I pity him** je le plains.

pizza ['piːtsə] *noun*

pizza *(feminine)*

➤ **a pizza parlour** *UK* OR **a pizza parlor** *US* une pizzeria.

place [pleɪs] *noun & verb*

◼ *noun*

1. endroit *(masculine)* : **it's a nice place to live**

c'est un endroit agréable pour vivre ; **I hope this is the right place** j'espère que c'est le bon endroit

2. **lieu** *(masculine)* [*plural* **lieux**] : **place of birth** lieu de naissance ; **put it in a safe place** mets-le dans un lieu sûr

3. **place** *(feminine)* : **can you save me a place?** tu peux me garder une place ? ; **a parking place** une place de parking ; **this book isn't in the right place** ce livre n'est pas à sa place

➤ **my place** chez moi : **come over to my place** viens chez moi ; **let's meet at Justin's place** retrouvons-nous chez Justin

➤ **to change places** changer de place : **can I change places with you?** je peux changer de place avec toi ?

➤ **to take place** avoir lieu : **when did the match take place?** quand le match a-t-il eu lieu ?

➤ **all over the place** partout : **he spilled tea all over the place** il a renversé du thé partout

■ *verb*

placer, mettre : **place your hands on the table** placez vos mains sur la table OR mettez vos mains sur la table.

plain [pleɪn] *adjective & noun*

■ *adjective*

1. **simple** : **he likes plain cooking** il aime la cuisine simple

2. **uni** : **he's wearing a plain tie** il porte une cravate unie ; **a plain blue shirt** une chemise toute bleue

3. **évident** : **it's plain that he's lying** il est évident qu'il ment

4. **nature** *(invariable)* : **a plain yoghurt** un yaourt nature

5. **quelconque** : **she's rather plain** elle est plutôt quelconque

■ *noun*

plaine *(feminine)* : **the Great Plains in the United States** les Grandes Plaines aux États-Unis.

plait [plæt] *noun*

natte *(feminine)* : **Ruby wears plaits** Ruby porte des nattes.

plan [plæn] *noun & verb*

■ *noun*

1. **projet** *(masculine)* : **what are your plans for the future?** quels sont tes projets pour l'avenir ? ; **he has made plans to go to India** il a projeté de partir en Inde

2. **plan** *(masculine)* : **she drew a plan of the house** elle a dessiné le plan de la maison

➤ **everything went according to plan** tout s'est passé comme prévu

■ *verb*

1. **préparer** : **they're planning a surprise** ils préparent une surprise

2. **organiser** : **we must plan the expedition** il faut organiser l'expédition

➤ **to plan to do something** avoir l'intention de faire quelque chose : **I'm planning to go to America** j'ai l'intention d'aller en Amérique.

plane [pleɪn] *noun*

avion *(masculine)* : **I took a plane** j'ai pris l'avion

➤ **by plane** en avion : **we went to Rome by plane** nous sommes allés à Rome en avion.

planet ['plænɪt] *noun*

planète *(feminine)* : **there are nine planets in the solar system** il y a neuf planètes dans le système solaire.

planning ['plænɪŋ] *uncountable noun*

préparation *(feminine)* : **lessons need a lot of planning** les cours exigent beaucoup de préparation

> ⚠ Le mot anglais **planning** est un faux ami, il ne signifie pas "planning".

plant [*UK* plɑːnt, *US* plænt] *noun & verb*

■ *noun*

plante *(feminine)* : **I must water the plants** je dois arroser les plantes

■ *verb*

planter : **we are going to plant an apple tree** nous allons planter un pommier.

plaster [*UK* 'plɑːstər, *US* 'plæstər] *noun*

1. **plâtre** *(masculine)* : **his arm is in plaster** il a le bras dans le plâtre

2. *UK* **pansement** *(masculine)* : **she had a plaster on her finger** elle avait un pansement au doigt.

plastic ['plæstɪk] *noun & adjective*

■ *noun*

plastique *(masculine)* : **it's made out of plastic** c'est en plastique

■ *adjective*

en plastique : **a plastic bag** un sac en plastique.

plate [pleɪt] *noun*

assiette *(feminine)* : **a plate of spaghetti** une assiette de spaghettis.

platform ['plætfɔːm] *noun*

quai *(masculine)* : **the passengers are waiting on platform 9** les passagers attendent sur le quai numéro 9.

play [pleɪ] *noun & verb*

■ *noun*

pièce *(feminine)* : **she's acting in a play** elle joue dans une pièce ; **Macbeth is a play by Shakespeare** Macbeth est une pièce de Shakespeare

➤ **a play on words** un jeu de mots

■ *verb*

1. **jouer : they're playing in the park** ils jouent dans le parc ; **she played an important part** elle a joué un rôle important

2. **jouer à : they're playing tennis** ils jouent au tennis ; **do you want to play chess?** tu veux jouer aux échecs ?

3. **jouer de : can you play the guitar?** tu sais jouer de la guitare ?

4. **jouer contre : we're playing a team from Manchester** nous allons jouer contre une équipe de Manchester

5. **passer, mettre : let's play a CD** passons un CD OR mettons un CD.

player ['pleɪər] *noun*

joueur *(masculine)*, **joueuse** *(feminine)* : **he's a football player** c'est un joueur de tennis

➤ **a piano player** un pianiste, une pianiste : **she's a piano player** elle est pianiste.

playful ['pleɪfʊl] *adjective*

joueur *(feminine* **joueuse)* : **the kitten is very playful** le chaton est très joueur.

playground ['pleɪɡraʊnd] *noun*

1. **cour** *(feminine)* **de récréation : a school playground** une cour de récréation

2. **terrain** *(masculine)* **de jeux : there's a playground in the park** il y a un terrain de jeux dans le parc.

play-off *US* ['pleɪɒf] *noun*

finale *(feminine)* **de championnat.**

pleasant ['pleznt] *adjective*

agréable.

please [pliːz] *adverb & verb*

■ *adverb*

s'il vous plaît

When you are speaking to a close friend, you can also use s'il te plaît:

can you tell me the time, please? vous avez l'heure, s'il vous plaît ? ; **please, tell me!** dis-le-moi, s'il te plaît !

■ *verb*

faire plaisir à : you can't please all the people all the time on ne peut pas faire plaisir à tout le monde

➤ **do as you please!** OR **please yourself!** fais comme tu veux ! OR comme tu veux !

pleased [pliːzd] *adjective*

content : she's not very pleased elle n'est pas très contente ; **I'm pleased with the results** je suis content des résultats

➤ **pleased to meet you!** enchanté !

pleasure ['pleʒər] *noun*

plaisir *(masculine)* : **she does it for pleasure** elle le fait par plaisir

➤ **my pleasure!** je vous en prie ! : **thank you for your help – my pleasure!** merci de votre aide – je vous en prie !

plenty ['plentɪ] *pronoun*

beaucoup : we have plenty of time nous avons beaucoup de temps ; **there's plenty to eat** il y a beaucoup à manger

➤ **that's plenty** c'est bien assez OR c'est largement assez.

plimsoll *UK* ['plɪmsəl] *noun*

tennis *(feminine)* : **you have to wear plimsolls in the gym** il faut mettre des tennis dans le gymnase.

plot [plɒt] *noun & verb*

■ *noun*

1. **complot** *(masculine)* : **the plot to kill the president failed** le complot pour tuer le président a échoué

2. **intrigue** *(feminine)* : **the film has a complicated plot** l'intrigue du film est compliquée

■ *verb*

comploter : they're plotting against the king ils complotent contre le roi.

plough *UK*, **plow** *US* [plaʊ] *noun & verb*

■ *noun*

charrue *(feminine)*

■ *verb*

labourer : the farmer's ploughing the field le fermier laboure le champ.

ploughman's lunch *UK* ['plaumənz-
lʌntʃ] *noun*

assiette de pain, fromage et pickles.

plow *US* ➤ plough *UK*.

plug [plʌg] *noun & verb*

1. **prise** *(feminine)*, **prise** *(feminine)* **de courant :
pull out the plug of the TV** débranche la prise
de la télé
2. **bonde** *(feminine)* : **I pulled the plug out of
the sink** j'ai retiré la bonde de l'évier

plug in *phrasal verb* (*past tense & past participle*
plugged in)
brancher : she plugged the television in
elle a branché la télévision.

plum [plʌm] *noun*

prune *(feminine)* : **plum jam** confiture de prunes
➤ **a plum tree** un prunier.

plumber ['plʌmər] *noun*

plombier *(masculine)* : **he's a plumber** il est
plombier.

plural ['pluərəl] *noun*

pluriel *(masculine)* : **in the plural** au pluriel.

plus [plʌs] *preposition*

plus : 10 plus 5 equals 15 10 plus 5 égale 15
➤ **the plus sign** le signe plus.

Pluto ['pluːtəu] *noun*

Pluton *(feminine)* : **Pluto is the smallest
planet** Pluton est la plus petite des planètes.

p.m. [ˌpiːˈem] *adverb*

de l'après-midi : at 3 p.m. à 3 heures de
l'après-midi OR à 15 heures

In France people often give the time using the
24-hour clock.

poached ['pəutʃɪd] *adjective*

poché : poached eggs des œufs pochés.

pocket ['pɒkɪt] *noun*

poche *(feminine)* : **he put his keys in his
pocket** il a mis ses clés dans sa poche ; **she
had her hands in her pockets** elle avait les
mains dans les poches
➤ **pocket money** argent *(masculine)* de poche.

pocketbook *US* ['pɒkɪtbuk] *noun*

sac *(masculine)* **à main : somebody stole her
pocketbook** quelqu'un lui a pris son sac à
main.

poem ['pəuɪm] *noun*

poème *(masculine)*.

poet ['pəuɪt] *noun*

poète *(masculine)*.

poetry ['pəuɪtrɪ] *noun*

poésie *(feminine)* : **do you like poetry?** est-ce
que tu aimes la poésie ?

point [pɔɪnt] *noun & verb*

■ *noun*

1. **pointe** *(feminine)* : **the point of a knife** la pointe d'un couteau ; **a stick with a sharp point**
un bâton au bout très pointu
2. **endroit** *(masculine)*, **point** *(masculine)* : **the
point where the river divides** l'endroit où la
rivière se sépare en deux ; **a meeting point** un
point de rencontre
3. **moment** *(masculine)* : **at that point, the police arrived** à ce moment-là, la police est arrivée
4. **remarque** *(feminine)* : **to make a point** faire
une remarque
5. **point** *(masculine)* : **he insisted on this point** il
a insisté sur ce point
6. **intérêt** *(masculine)* : **what's the point of the
game?** quel est l'intérêt du jeu ? ; **what's the
point of buying a new car?** quel est l'intérêt
d'acheter une nouvelle voiture ? ; **I don't see
the point of going** je ne vois pas l'intérêt d'y
aller ; **what's the point?** quel intérêt ? OR à
quoi bon ?
7. *In scores* **point** *(masculine)* : **you get two
points for each correct answer** chaque réponse correcte rapporte deux points
8. *In decimals* **virgule** *(feminine)* : **two point
seven** deux virgule sept

Decimals are given with a comma and not with a
point in French: 2.7 is written 2,7.

➤ **point of view** point *(masculine)* de vue :
what's your point of view? quel est ton point
de vue ?
➤ **to get to the point** OR **to come to the
point** aller droit au fait
➤ **the point is that ...** le fait est que ... : **the
point is that he shouldn't have gone** le fait
est qu'il n'aurait pas dû y aller

p

➤ **to miss the point** ne pas comprendre
➤ **that's not the point!** là n'est pas la question ! OR il ne s'agit pas de cela !
➤ **there's no point** ça ne sert à rien : **there's no point in waiting** ça ne sert à rien d'attendre
➤ **to be on the point of doing something** être sur le point de faire quelque chose : **I was on the point of leaving** j'étais sur le point de partir

■ *verb*
1. **montrer du doigt, indiquer du doigt** : **she pointed at the tower** elle a montré la tour du doigt OR elle a indiqué la tour du doigt ; **it's rude to point** c'est impoli de montrer les gens du doigt
2. **indiquer** : **the signpost points south** le poteau indique le sud
3. **braquer** : **he pointed the gun at the guard** il a braqué le revolver sur le gardien

point out *phrasal verb*

1. **montrer** : **he pointed out the opera house to me** il m'a montré l'opéra
2. **faire remarquer** : **he pointed out that no one had paid** il a fait remarquer que personne n'avait payé.

pointed ['pɔɪntɪd] *adjective*

pointu : **he's wearing pointed shoes** il porte des chaussures pointues.

pointless ['pɔɪntlɪs] *adjective*

inutile : **it's pointless trying** il est inutile d'essayer OR ça ne sert à rien d'essayer.

poison ['pɔɪzn] *noun & verb*

■ *noun*
poison *(masculine)* : **arsenic is a poison** l'arsenic est un poison
■ *verb*
empoisonner : **a poisoned arrow** une flèche empoisonnée.

poisonous ['pɔɪznəs] *adjective*

1. **toxique** : **these gases are poisonous** ces gaz sont toxiques
2. **vénéneux** *(feminine* **vénéneuse)** : **these mushrooms are poisonous** ces champignons sont vénéneux
3. **venimeux** *(feminine* **venimeuse)** : **it's a poisonous snake** c'est un serpent venimeux.

poke [pəʊk] *verb*

➤ **to poke somebody** donner un coup à quelqu'un : **she poked me in the ribs** elle m'a donné un coup dans les côtes
➤ **to poke something** donner un coup dans quelque chose : **he poked the leaves with a stick** il a donné un coup de bâton dans les feuilles.

poker ['pəʊkər] *noun*

poker *(masculine)* : **they're playing poker** ils jouent au poker.

polar bear ['pəʊlərbeər] *noun*

ours *(masculine)* **polaire**.

pole [pəʊl] *noun*

poteau *(masculine)* [*plural* **poteaux**] : **he stuck a pole in the ground** il a enfoncé un poteau dans le sol
➤ **a ski pole** un bâton de ski
➤ **the pole vault** le saut à la perche
➤ **the North Pole** le pôle Nord
➤ **the South Pole** le pôle Sud.

police [pə'liːs] *plural noun*

police *(feminine)* : **call the police!** appelez la police ! ; **the police are on their way** la police arrive
➤ **a police car** une voiture de police
➤ **a police officer** un policier, une femme policier
➤ **the police station** le commissariat.

policeman [pə'liːsmən] *(plural* policemen [pə'liːsmən]*)* *noun*

policier *(masculine)*, **agent** *(masculine)* **de police** : **Robert's a policeman** Robert est policier.

policewoman [pə'liːsˌwʊmən] *(plural* policewomen [pə'liːsˌwɪmɪn]*)* *noun*

femme *(feminine)* **policier** : **she's a policewoman** elle est femme policier.

polish ['pɒlɪʃ] *noun & verb*

■ *noun*
cire *(feminine)* : **furniture polish** de la cire pour les meubles
➤ **shoe polish** cirage *(masculine)*
➤ **to give something a polish** cirer quelque chose
■ *verb*
1. **cirer** : **he's polishing his shoes** il cire ses chaussures
2. **faire briller** : **he's polishing the silver** il fait briller l'argenterie.

polite [pə'laɪt] *adjective*

poli : **he's very polite** il est très poli.

political [pə'lɪtɪkl] *adjective*

politique

> POLITICAL PARTIES
> En Grande-Bretagne et aux États-Unis, il y a beaucoup moins de grands partis politiques qu'en France. En Grande-Bretagne, les deux principaux partis sont le **Conservative Party** (parti des conservateurs, dont l'emblème est une torche bleue) et le **Labour Party** (parti travailliste, dont l'emblème est une rose rouge) ; il y a également le **Liberal Democratic Party** (parti libéral, dont l'emblème est un oiseau jaune) ainsi que des partis nationalistes en Écosse, au pays de Galles et en Irlande du Nord.
> Aux États-Unis, les deux grands partis sont le **Democratic Party** (parti démocrate, dont l'emblème est un âne !) et le **Republican Party**, plus conservateur (parti républicain, dont l'emblème est un éléphant !).

politically correct [pə'lɪtɪklɪ kərekt] *adjective*

politiquement correct.

politician [ˌpɒlɪ'tɪʃn] *noun*

homme *(masculine)* politique, femme *(feminine)* politique : **he's a politician** c'est un homme politique.

politics ['pɒlətɪks] *uncountable noun*

politique *(feminine)* : **she's interested in politics** elle s'intéresse à la politique.

poll [pəʊl] *noun*

sondage *(masculine)* : **an opinion poll** un sondage d'opinion.

pollen ['pɒlən] *noun*

pollen *(masculine)* : **the pollen count** le taux de pollen.

pollute [pə'luːt] *verb*

polluer : **this river is polluted** cette rivière est polluée.

pollution [pə'luːʃn] *uncountable noun*

pollution *(feminine)*.

polo neck *UK* ['pəʊləʊnek] *noun*

col *(masculine)* roulé : **a polo-neck sweater** un pull à col roulé.

pomegranate ['pɒmɪˌgrænɪt] *noun*

grenade *(feminine)* : **pomegranates have red flesh** les grenades ont la chair rouge.

pond [pɒnd] *noun*

mare *(feminine)* : **there are a lot of fish in the pond** il y a plein de poissons dans la mare
> **a garden pond** un bassin de jardin.

pony ['pəʊnɪ] *(plural* ponies*) noun*

poney *(masculine)*.

ponytail ['pəʊnɪteɪl] *noun*

queue-de-cheval *(feminine)* : **she put her hair in a ponytail** elle s'est fait une queue-de-cheval.

poodle ['puːdl] *noun*

caniche *(masculine)*.

pool [puːl] *noun*

1. piscine *(feminine)* : **he's swimming in the pool** il nage dans la piscine
2. bassin *(masculine)* : **a rock pool** un bassin dans les rochers
3. billard *(masculine)* américain : **they're playing pool** ils jouent au billard américain
> **the pools** *UK* le loto sportif.

poor [pɔːr] *adjective*

1. pauvre : **they are very poor** ils sont très pauvres ; **the poor boy!** le pauvre garçon !
2. médiocre : **the results are poor** les résultats sont médiocres.

pop [pɒp] *adjective, noun & verb*

■ *adjective*
pop *(invariable)* : **do you like pop music?** tu aimes la musique pop ? ; **a pop concert** un concert pop ; **a pop group** un groupe pop
■ *noun*
1. pop *(feminine)* : **she likes listening to pop** elle aime bien écouter de la pop
2. soda *(masculine)* : **a bottle of pop** une bouteille de soda
3. *US informal* père *(masculine)*, papa *(masculine)* : **her pop's over 100** son père a plus de 100 ans
■ *verb (past tense & past participle* popped*)*
1. faire éclater : **he popped the balloon** il a fait éclater le ballon
2. aller : **she popped over to her uncle's** elle est allée chez son oncle

pop in *phrasal verb*

passer : **I'll pop in and see you** je passerai te voir.

p

popcorn ['pɒpkɔ:n] *uncountable noun*

pop-corn *(masculine)* : **he's eating popcorn** il mange du pop-corn.

pope [pəʊp] *noun*

pape *(masculine)*.

poppy ['pɒpɪ] *(plural* **poppies)** *noun*

coquelicot *(masculine)*.

popular ['pɒpjʊləʳ] *adjective*

populaire : **Janet's very popular** Janet est très populaire.

population [ˌpɒpjʊ'leɪʃn] *noun*

population *(feminine)* : **what is the population of France?** quelle est la population de la France ?

porch [pɔ:tʃ] *noun*

1. *US* véranda *(feminine)* : **let's sit outside on the porch** allons nous asseoir sous la véranda
2. *UK* porche *(masculine)* : **leave your boots in the porch** laisse tes bottes sous le porche.

pork [pɔ:k] *noun*

porc *(masculine)* : **a pork chop** une côtelette de porc.

porridge ['pɒrɪdʒ] *uncountable noun*

porridge *(masculine)* : **he has porridge for breakfast** il mange du porridge au petit déjeuner.

port [pɔ:t] *noun*

1. port *(masculine)* : **Dover is a port** Douvres est un port
2. porto *(masculine)* : **a glass of port** un verre de porto.

portable ['pɔ:təbl] *adjective*

portable : **they have a portable TV** ils ont une télévision portable.

porter ['pɔ:təʳ] *noun*

1. porteur *(masculine)* : **the porter took our luggage** le porteur a pris nos bagages
2. *UK* portier *(masculine)* : **the hotel porter will get you a taxi** le portier de l'hôtel va vous trouver un taxi.

portion ['pɔ:ʃn] *noun*

portion *(feminine)* : **he was eating a big portion of spaghetti** il mangeait une grosse portion de spaghettis.

portrait ['pɔ:treɪt] *noun*

portrait *(masculine)* : **he painted a portrait of his father** il a fait le portrait de son père.

Portugal ['pɔ:tʃʊgl] *noun*

le Portugal

> In French the names of countries are used with the definite article (le, la or l'). Remember that the French preposition à combines with le to become au:

Portugal is a republic le Portugal est une république ; **she's going to Portugal** elle va au Portugal ; **he lives in Portugal** il vit au Portugal.

Portuguese [ˌpɔ:tʃʊ'gi:z] *adjective & noun*

▪ *adjective*

portugais : **I like Portuguese wine** j'aime le vin portugais

▪ *noun*

portugais *(masculine)* : **she speaks Portuguese** elle parle portugais

➤ **the Portuguese** les Portugais

> Remember not to use a capital letter for the adjective and the language in French. Only use a capital letter for the inhabitants.

posh [pɒʃ] *adjective informal*

1. chic *(invariable)* : **it's a posh hotel** c'est un hôtel chic
2. snob *(invariable)* : **she has a posh accent** elle a un accent snob.

position [pə'zɪʃn] *noun*

1. position *(feminine)* : **he changed position** il a changé de position
2. situation *(feminine)* : **I'm in a difficult position** je suis dans une situation difficile
3. poste *(masculine)* : **what position does Beckham play?** à quel poste joue Beckham ?
➤ **to be in position** être en place
➤ **to get into position** se mettre en place OR prendre position.

positive ['pɒzətɪv] *adjective*

1. positif *(feminine* **positive)** : **he has a positive attitude** il a une attitude positive
2. sûr, certain : **I'm positive about it** j'en suis sûr OR j'en suis certain.

possessions [pə'zeʃnz] *plural noun*

affaires *(feminine plural)* : **she took all her possessions with her** elle a pris toutes ses affaires.

possibility [ˌpɒsəˈbɪlətɪ] *(plural possibilities)* *noun*

possibilité *(feminine)* : **that's a possibility** c'est une possibilité.

possible [ˈpɒsəbl] *adjective*

possible : **come and see me as soon as possible** viens me voir dès que possible ; **as quickly as possible** le plus vite possible ; **is it possible to change the tickets?** est-il possible de changer les billets ?

possibly [ˈpɒsəblɪ] *adverb*

1. peut-être : **will you finish today? – possibly** tu vas finir aujourd'hui ? – peut-être
2. vraiment : **I can't possibly accept your money** je ne peux vraiment pas accepter ton argent.

post [pəʊst] *noun & verb*

■ *noun*
1. poteau *(masculine)* [*plural* **poteaux**] : **the net is fixed between two posts** le filet est attaché entre deux poteaux
2. *UK* courrier *(masculine)* : **there's some post for you** il y a du courrier pour toi
3. *UK* poste *(feminine)* : **he sent it by post** il l'a envoyé par la poste
➤ **the post office** la poste OR le bureau de poste : **where is the post office?** où est la poste ? OR où est le bureau de poste ?

■ *verb*
1. *UK* poster, mettre à la poste : **she posted the letter** elle a posté la lettre OR elle a mis la lettre à la poste
2. afficher : **he posted a message on the site** il a affiché un message sur le site.

postbox *UK* [ˈpəʊstbɒks] *(plural postboxes)* *noun*

boîte *(feminine)* **aux lettres**.

postcard [ˈpəʊstkɑːd] *noun*

carte *(feminine)* **postale** : **I got a postcard from my friend** j'ai reçu une carte postale de mon ami.

postcode *UK* [ˈpəʊstkəʊd] *noun*

code *(masculine)* **postal** : **what is your postcode?** quel est votre code postal ?

poster [ˈpəʊstər] *noun*
1. affiche *(feminine)* : **they put up posters advertising the concert** ils ont mis des affiches pour annoncer le concert
2. poster *(masculine)* : **a poster of Mick Jagger** un poster de Mick Jagger.

postman *UK* [ˈpəʊstmən] *(plural postmen* [ˈpəʊstmən]*)* *noun*
facteur *(masculine)* : **has the postman been?** est-ce que le facteur est passé ?

postpone [ˌpəʊstˈpəʊn] *verb*

reporter : **the meeting has been postponed** la réunion a été reportée.

potato [pəˈteɪtəʊ] *(plural potatoes)* *noun*

pomme de terre *(feminine)* : **roast potatoes** des pommes de terre rôties.

pottery [ˈpɒtərɪ] *uncountable noun*

poterie *(feminine)*
➤ **a piece of pottery** une poterie.

poultry [ˈpəʊltrɪ] *uncountable noun*

volaille *(feminine)*.

pound [paʊnd] *noun*
1. *(abbreviation £)* livre *(feminine)* : **a pound coin** une pièce d'une livre
2. *(abbreviation lb)* = 453,6 grammes : **it weighs about two pounds** ça pèse environ un kilo.

pour [pɔːr] *verb*

verser : **she poured the water into the glass** elle a versé l'eau dans le verre ; **he poured her a drink** il lui a versé à boire
➤ **it's pouring** OR **it's pouring with rain** il pleut à verse.

poverty [ˈpɒvətɪ] *noun*
pauvreté *(feminine)*.

powder [ˈpaʊdər] *noun*
poudre *(feminine)*.

power [ˈpaʊər] *noun*
1. pouvoir *(masculine)* : **a new party is in power** un nouveau parti est au pouvoir ; **to take power** prendre le pouvoir

p

2. puissance *(feminine)* **: the military power of a country** la puissance militaire d'un pays ; **the power of the explosion knocked him off his feet** la puissance de l'explosion l'a fait tomber

3. énergie *(feminine)* **: nuclear power** l'énergie nucléaire

4. courant *(masculine)* **: there has been a power cut** il y a eu une coupure de courant

➤ **a power station** OR **a power plant** une centrale électrique.

powerful ['paʊəfʊl] *adjective*

puissant : it's a very powerful computer c'est un ordinateur très puissant.

practical ['præktɪkl] *adjective*

pratique : she's very practical elle est très pratique

➤ **a practical joke** une farce ; **he played a practical joke on his teacher** il a fait une farce à son professeur.

practice ['præktɪs] *noun & verb*

◾ *noun*

1. entraînement *(masculine)* **: she's out of practice** elle manque d'entraînement ; **I've got football practice tonight** j'ai entraînement de foot ce soir

2. exercices *(masculine plural)* **: he's doing his piano practice** il fait ses exercices au piano

➤ **in practice** en pratique

◾ *verb US* ➤ **practise** *UK*.

practise *UK*, **practice** *US* ['præktɪs] *verb*

1. s'entraîner : the team practises every Saturday l'équipe s'entraîne tous les samedis

2. s'exercer : to be a good pianist you must practise every day pour être bon pianiste, il faut s'exercer tous les jours

3. travailler : he practises the guitar twice a week il travaille la guitare deux fois par semaine

4. pratiquer : can I practise my French on you? est-ce que je peux pratiquer mon français avec toi ?

praise [preɪz] *noun & verb*

◾ *uncountable noun*

éloges *(masculine plural)* **: you deserve all this praise** tu mérites tous ces éloges

◾ *verb*

faire l'éloge de : they praised our school ils ont fait l'éloge de notre école.

pram *UK* [præm] *noun*

landau *(masculine)* **: the baby is sleeping in his pram** le bébé dort dans son landau.

prawn [prɔːn] *noun*

crevette *(feminine)* **rose : a prawn cocktail** une salade de crevettes.

pray [preɪ] *verb*

prier : they prayed to God ils ont prié Dieu.

prayer [preəʳ] *noun*

prière *(feminine)* **: she was saying her prayers** elle faisait sa prière.

precaution [prɪ'kɔːʃn] *noun*

précaution *(feminine)* **: we must take precautions** il faut prendre des précautions.

precinct *UK* ['priːsɪŋkt] *noun*

➤ **a pedestrian precinct** une zone piétonne

➤ **a shopping precinct** un centre commercial.

precious ['preʃəs] *adjective*

précieux *(feminine* **précieuse)** **: precious stones** des pierres précieuses

➤ **they're very precious to me** je tiens beaucoup à eux.

precise [prɪ'saɪs] *adjective*

précis : what's the precise time? quelle est l'heure précise ?

precisely [prɪ'saɪslɪ] *adverb*

précisément

➤ **at seven o'clock precisely** à sept heures précises.

predict [prɪ'dɪkt] *verb*

prédire : we can't predict the future on ne peut pas prédire l'avenir.

prefect *UK* ['priːfekt] *noun*

élève de terminale chargé de la surveillance.

prefer [prɪ'fɜːʳ] *verb*

préférer : which one do you prefer? lequel préfères-tu ? ; **she prefers French to Spanish** elle préfère le français à l'espagnol ; **I prefer to leave** je préfère partir.

pregnant ['pregnənt] *adjective*

enceinte : **she's seven months pregnant** elle est enceinte de sept mois.

prehistoric [,pri:hɪ'stɒrɪk] *adjective*

préhistorique : **prehistoric animals** des animaux préhistoriques.

prejudice ['predʒʊdɪs] *noun*

préjugé *(masculine)* : **he has a prejudice against her** il a un préjugé contre elle ; **racial prejudice** des préjugés raciaux.

prejudiced ['predʒʊdɪst] *adjective*

➤ **to be prejudiced** avoir des préjugés.

preparation [,prepə'reɪʃn] *noun*

préparation *(feminine)*
➤ **to make preparations** faire des préparatifs : **they're making preparations for their trip** ils font des préparatifs pour leur voyage.

prepare [prɪ'peəʳ] *verb*

1. préparer : **she's preparing the meal** elle prépare le repas ; **she's preparing for her exam** elle prépare son examen
2. se préparer : **they're preparing to leave** ils se préparent à partir.

prepared [prɪ'peəd] *adjective*

prêt : **are you prepared to do it?** tu es prêt à le faire ? ; **Harry was prepared for anything** Harry était prêt à tout.

preposition [,prepə'zɪʃn] *noun*

préposition *(feminine)*.

preppy, preppie *US* ['prepɪ] *adjective informal*

BCBG *(invariable)* : **preppy clothes** des vêtements BCBG.

prescription [prɪ'skrɪpʃn] *noun*

ordonnance *(feminine)* : **you can only get this medicine on prescription** ce médicament n'est vendu que sur ordonnance.

present *adjective, noun & verb*

■ *adjective* ['preznt]
1. **actual** *(feminine* **actuelle)** : **in the present circumstances** dans les circonstances actuelles
2. présent : **I was present at the meeting** j'étais présent à la réunion
➤ **the present tense** le présent : **put the verb in the present tense** mets le verbe au présent

■ *noun* ['preznt]
1. cadeau *(masculine)* [*plural* cadeaux] : **he gave me a birthday present** il m'a offert un cadeau d'anniversaire
2. présent *(masculine)* : **to live in the present** vivre dans le présent
➤ **at present** actuellement
➤ **for the present** pour le moment
■ *verb* [prɪ'zent]
1. présenter : **who presents the programme?** qui présente l'émission ?
2. remettre : **they presented her with a medal** on lui a remis une médaille.

presenter *UK* [prɪ'zentəʳ] *noun*

présentateur *(masculine)*, présentatrice *(feminine)* : **he's a television presenter** il est présentateur de télévision.

president ['prezɪdənt] *noun*

président *(masculine)*, présidente *(feminine)* : **he's the president of the United States** il est président des États-Unis.

press [pres] *noun & verb*

■ *noun*
presse *(feminine)* : **the national press** la presse nationale
■ *verb*
1. appuyer sur : **you have to press the button** il faut appuyer sur le bouton
2. appuyer : **press harder** appuie plus fort.

press-up *UK* ['presʌp] *noun*

pompe *(feminine)* : **he does ten press-ups every day** il fait dix pompes chaque jour.

pressure ['preʃəʳ] *noun*

pression *(feminine)* : **she's under pressure** elle est sous pression ; **to put pressure on somebody** faire pression sur quelqu'un.

presume [*UK* prɪ'zju:m, *US* prɪ'zu:m] *verb*

supposer : **I presume you're right** je suppose que tu as raison.

pretend [prɪ'tend] *verb*

faire semblant : **I was just pretending** je faisais semblant ; **he pretended to be surprised** il a fait semblant d'être surpris

 Pretend est un faux ami, il ne signifie pas "prétendre".

p

pretty ['prɪtɪ] *adjective & adverb*

◼ *adjective*
joli : what a pretty dress! quelle jolie robe !
◼ *adverb*
plutôt : the book was pretty good le livre était plutôt bien.

prevent [prɪ'vent] *verb*
empêcher
➤ **to prevent somebody from doing something** empêcher quelqu'un de faire quelque chose : **she tried to prevent me from coming in** elle a essayé de m'empêcher d'entrer.

previous ['priːvjəs] *adjective*
précédent : it happened on the previous Tuesday cela s'est passé le mardi précédent.

prey [preɪ] *noun*
proie *(feminine)*
➤ **a bird of prey** un oiseau de proie.

price [praɪs] *noun*
prix *(masculine)* : **what price did you pay?** quel est le prix que tu as payé ?
➤ **the price list** la liste des prix
➤ **a price tag** une étiquette.

prick [prɪk] *verb*
piquer : she pricked her finger elle s'est piqué le doigt.

prickly ['prɪklɪ] *adjective*
épineux *(feminine* **épineuse)* : **this cactus is prickly** ce cactus est épineux.

pride [praɪd] *uncountable noun*
1. **fierté** *(feminine)* : **she looked at her daughter with pride** elle a regardé sa fille avec fierté
2. **amour-propre** *(masculine)* : **it hurt his pride** cela l'a blessé dans son amour-propre
➤ **to take pride in somebody** OR **something** être fier de quelqu'un OR quelque chose : **she takes pride in her daughter** elle est fière de sa fille.

priest [priːst] *noun*
prêtre *(masculine)* : **he's a priest** il est prêtre.

primary ['praɪmərɪ] *adjective*
primaire
➤ **a primary school** une école primaire : **he goes to primary school** il va à l'école primaire.

prime minister [praɪm'mɪnɪstəʳ] *noun*
Premier ministre *(masculine)*.

prince [prɪns] *noun*
prince *(masculine)* : **the Prince of Wales** le prince de Galles ; **Prince Charles** le prince Charles ; **Prince Charming** le prince charmant.

princess [prɪn'ses] *noun*
princesse *(feminine)* : **Princess Anne** la princesse Anne.

principal ['prɪnsəpl] *adjective & noun*
◼ *adjective*
principal : that's the principal reason c'est la raison principale
◼ *noun*
directeur *(masculine)*, **directrice** *(feminine)* : **the teacher sent him to see the principal** le professeur l'a envoyé chez le directeur.

principle ['prɪnsəpl] *noun*
principe *(masculine)* : **in principle** en principe.

print [prɪnt] *noun & verb*
◼ *noun*
1. **caractères** *(masculine plural)* : **it's written in large print** c'est écrit en gros caractères
2. **épreuve** *(feminine)* : **I want to make a print from the negative** je veux tirer une épreuve du négatif
3. **empreinte** *(feminine)* : **the police took his prints** la police a pris ses empreintes
◼ *verb*
1. **imprimer : I printed out the letter** j'ai imprimé la lettre
2. **écrire en caractères d'imprimerie : print your name** écrivez votre nom en caractères d'imprimerie.

printer ['prɪntəʳ] *noun*
imprimante *(feminine)* : **turn the printer on** allumez l'imprimante.

prison ['prɪzn] *noun*
prison *(feminine)* : **they sent him to prison** ils l'ont mis en prison ; **she's in prison** elle est en prison.

prisoner ['prɪznəʳ] *noun*
prisonnier *(masculine)*, **prisonnière** *(feminine)* : **he was taken prisoner** il a été fait prisonnier
➤ **a prisoner of war** un prisonnier de guerre, une prisonnière de guerre.

private ['praɪvɪt] *adjective & noun*

■ *adjective*

1. **privé** : **he doesn't talk about his private life** il ne parle pas de sa vie privée
2. **personnel** *(feminine* **personnelle***)* : **a private letter** une lettre personnelle
3. **particulier** *(feminine* **particulière***)* : **they have private lessons** ils prennent des cours particuliers

➤ **a private detective** un détective privé

➤ **private property** propriété *(feminine)* privée

➤ **a private school** une école privée

■ *noun*

1. **privé** *(masculine)* : **can I talk to you in private?** je peux te parler en privé ?
2. **simple soldat** *(masculine)* : **Private Jones** soldat Jones.

privately ['praɪvɪtlɪ] *adverb*

en privé : **she told me privately** elle me l'a dit en privé.

privilege ['prɪvɪlɪdʒ] *noun*

privilège *(masculine)* : **that's a real privilege** c'est un vrai privilège.

prize [praɪz] *noun*

prix *(masculine)* : **she won first prize** elle a gagné le premier prix.

prizewinner ['praɪzˌwɪnəʳ] *noun*

1. **gagnant** *(masculine)*, **gagnante** *(feminine)* : **a lottery prizewinner** un gagnant au loto
2. **lauréat** *(masculine)*, **lauréate** *(feminine)* : **a Nobel prizewinner** un lauréat du prix Nobel.

probably ['prɒbəblɪ] *adverb*

probablement : **probably not** probablement pas ; **he'll probably come tonight** il viendra probablement ce soir.

problem ['prɒbləm] *noun*

problème *(masculine)* : **what's the problem?** quel est le problème ? ; **to cause problems** poser des problèmes

➤ **no problem!** pas de problème !

process ['prəʊses] *noun & verb*

■ *noun*

processus *(masculine)* : **the peace process** le processus de paix

➤ **to be in the process of doing something** être en train de faire quelque chose : **she's in the process of painting the house** elle est en train de peindre la maison

■ *verb*

traiter : **the computer can process a lot of data** l'ordinateur peut traiter beaucoup de données.

produce [*UK* prə'djuːs, *US* prə'duːs] *verb*

1. **produire** : **these toys are produced in China** ces jouets sont produits en Chine
2. *UK* **mettre en scène** : **he produced a play by Shakespeare** il a mis en scène une pièce de Shakespeare.

producer [*UK* prə'djuːsəʳ, *US* prə'duːsəʳ] *noun*

1. **producteur** *(masculine)*, **productrice** *(feminine)* : **he's a television producer** il est producteur de télévision
2. *UK* **metteur** *(masculine)* **en scène** : **he's a producer of plays** il est metteur en scène.

product ['prɒdʌkt] *noun*

produit *(masculine)* : **this is a new product** ceci est un nouveau produit.

profession [prə'feʃn] *noun*

profession *(feminine)* : **what is your profession?** quelle est votre profession ?

professional [prə'feʃənl] *adjective & noun*

■ *adjective*

professionnel *(feminine* **professionnelle***)* : **he's a professional photographer** c'est un photographe professionnel

■ *noun*

professionnel *(masculine)*, **professionnelle** *(feminine)* : **she's a professional** c'est une professionnelle.

professor [prə'fesəʳ] *noun*

professeur *(masculine)* **d'université** : **he's a professor** il est professeur d'université.

profit ['prɒfɪt] *noun*

bénéfice *(masculine)* : **they made a profit** ils ont fait un bénéfice.

program ['prəʊgræm] *noun & verb*

■ *noun*

1. **programme** *(masculine)* : **a computer program** un programme informatique
2. *US* ➤ **programme** *UK*

■ *verb (past tense & past participle* **programmed***)*
programmer : **do you know how to program a computer?** tu sais programmer un ordinateur ?

programme *UK*, **program** *US* ['prəʊgræm] *noun*

P

1. **émission** *(feminine)* **: a TV programme** une émission de télévision
2. **programme** *(masculine)* **: what's your programme for tonight?** quel est ton programme pour ce soir ?

progress ['prəυgres] *uncountable noun*

progrès *(masculine)* **: you can't stop progress** on ne peut pas arrêter le progrès ; **we're making progress** nous faisons des progrès.

project ['prɒdʒekt] *noun*

1. **projet** *(masculine)* **: there's a project to build a new bridge** il y a un projet de construction d'un nouveau pont
2. **dossier** *(masculine)* **: we're doing a project on rainforests** nous préparons un dossier sur les forêts tropicales
➤ **a housing project** *US* une cité HLM.

promise ['prɒmɪs] *noun & verb*

■ *noun*

promesse *(feminine)* **: Tanya kept her promise** Tanya a tenu sa promesse

■ *verb*

promettre **: he promised me some money** il m'a promis de l'argent ; **I promised to help her** j'ai promis de l'aider.

promote [prə'məυt] *verb*

➤ **to be promoted** être promu ; **I've been promoted** j'ai été promu.

promotion [prə'məυʃn] *noun*

promotion *(feminine)*, **avancement** *(masculine)* **: she got promotion** elle a été promue.

pronoun ['prəυnaυn] *noun*

pronom *(masculine)* **: 'he' is a personal pronoun** « il » est un pronom personnel.

pronunciation [prəˌnʌnsɪ'eɪʃn] *noun*

prononciation *(feminine)* **: her pronunciation is very good** elle a une très bonne prononciation.

proof [pruːf] *uncountable noun*

preuve *(feminine)* **: there's no proof** il n'y a aucune preuve ; **do you have any proof?** avez-vous des preuves ?

proper ['prɒpə'] *adjective*

1. **bon** *(feminine* **bonne)* **: I'll show you the proper way to do it** je te montrerai la bonne façon de le faire ; **the lamp isn't in the proper place** la lampe n'est pas à la bonne place

2. **vrai : that's not a proper meal** ce n'est pas un vrai repas
3. **convenable : this behaviour isn't proper** ce comportement n'est pas convenable

 Proper est un faux ami, il ne signifie pas "propre".

properly ['prɒpəlɪ] *adverb*

1. **comme il faut, correctement : you're not doing it properly** tu ne le fais pas comme il faut
2. **convenablement : eat properly** mange convenablement.

property ['prɒpətɪ] *(plural* **properties)** *noun*

propriété *(feminine)* **: private property** propriété privée
➤ **personal property** biens *(masculine plural)* personnels
➤ **public property** bien *(masculine)* public
➤ **that's my property** ça m'appartient.

proposal [prə'pəυzl] *noun*

proposition *(feminine)* **: she made a proposal** elle a fait une proposition.

propose [prə'pəυz] *verb*

proposer **: he proposed changing the name of the company** il a proposé de changer le nom de la société
➤ **to propose to do something** avoir l'intention de faire quelque chose **: what do you propose to do?** qu'as-tu l'intention de faire ?
➤ **to propose to somebody** demander quelqu'un en mariage.

prospects ['prɒspekts] *plural noun*

perspectives *(feminine plural)* **: the job has good prospects** c'est un travail qui offre des perspectives d'avenir.

protect [prə'tekt] *verb*

protéger **: these glasses protect your eyes from the sun** ces lunettes protègent les yeux du soleil.

protection [prə'tekʃn] *noun*

protection *(feminine)*.

protein ['prəυtiːn] *noun*

protéine *(feminine)* **: meat and fish contain protein** la viande et le poisson contiennent des protéines.

protest *noun & verb*

■ *noun* ['prəʊtest]

protestation *(feminine)* : **she did it as a sign of protest** elle l'a fait en signe de protestation

■ *verb* [prə'test]

protester : **many people are protesting against these measures** beaucoup de gens protestent contre ces mesures.

Protestant ['prɒtɪstənt] *adjective & noun*

protestant.

protester [prə'testər] *noun*

manifestant *(masculine)*, **manifestante** *(feminine)* : **there are a lot of protesters in the street** il y a beaucoup de manifestants dans la rue.

proud [praʊd] *adjective*

fier *(feminine* **fière***)* : **he's proud of his son** il est fier de son fils.

prove [pruːv] (*past participle* proved OR proven ['pruːvn]) *verb*

prouver : **I can't prove he's lying** je ne peux pas prouver qu'il ment.

proverb ['prɒvɜːb] *noun*

proverbe *(masculine)*.

provide [prə'vaɪd] *verb*

fournir

➤ **to provide somebody with something** fournir quelque chose à quelqu'un : **he provided me with an explanation** il m'a fourni une explication.

provided [prə'vaɪdɪd] *conjunction*

à condition que : **she'll do the work provided they pay her** elle fera le travail à condition qu'on la paie.

prune [pruːn] *noun*

pruneau *(masculine)* [*plural* **pruneaux**]

 Le mot anglais **prune** est un faux ami, il ne signifie pas "prune".

pseudonym [*UK* 'sjuːdənɪm, *US* 'suːdənɪm] *noun*

pseudonyme *(masculine)*.

psychiatrist [saɪ'kaɪətrɪst] *noun*

psychiatre *(masculine or feminine)* : **she's a psychiatrist** elle est psychiatre.

psychologist [saɪ'kɒlədʒɪst] *noun*

psychologue *(masculine or feminine)* : **he's a psychologist** il est psychologue.

pub *UK* [pʌb] *noun*

pub *(masculine)* : **they went to the pub for a drink** ils sont allés boire un verre au pub

 PUB
Même les plus petits villages en Grande-Bretagne ont leur pub. Les pubs sont très différents des cafés français. Les horaires d'ouverture sont très stricts : de 11 heures à 23 heures en général. On y boit le plus souvent de la bière et les mineurs n'ont généralement pas le droit d'y entrer. Certains pubs servent également des repas et acceptent les familles.

 Le mot anglais **pub** est un faux ami, il ne signifie pas "pub" au sens de "publicité".

public ['pʌblɪk] *adjective & noun*

■ *adjective*

public *(feminine* **publique***)* : **this is a public place** ceci est un lieu public

➤ **a public holiday** *UK* un jour férié

➤ **public opinion** l'opinion *(feminine)* publique

➤ **a public school**

1. *UK* une école privée

2. *US* une école publique

➤ **public transport** transports *(masculine plural)* en commun

■ *noun*

➤ **the public** le public : **the museum isn't open to the public today** le musée n'est pas ouvert au public aujourd'hui

➤ **in public** en public : **I don't like singing in public** je n'aime pas chanter en public.

publicity [pʌb'lɪsɪtɪ] *uncountable noun*

publicité *(feminine)* : **the film got a lot of publicity** on a fait beaucoup de publicité autour de ce film.

publish ['pʌblɪʃ] *verb*

publier.

pudding ['pʊdɪŋ] *noun*

1. *UK* **dessert** *(masculine)* : **what's for pudding?** qu'est-ce qu'il y a comme dessert ?

2. **pudding** *(masculine)* : **bread-and-butter pudding** pudding au pain

➤ **rice pudding** riz *(masculine)* au lait

➤ **black pudding** *UK* boudin *(masculine)* noir.

p

puddle ['pʌdl] *noun*

flaque *(feminine)* **d'eau : he stepped in a puddle** il a marché dans une flaque d'eau.

puff [pʌf] *verb*

1. **souffler : he was puffing and panting** il soufflait comme un bœuf
2. **tirer sur : he was puffing on a cigarette** il tirait sur une cigarette.

pull [pʊl] *verb*

tirer : he pulled her hair il lui a tiré les cheveux ; **she was pulling on the rope** elle tirait sur la corde ; **pull hard!** tirez fort !

➤ **to pull a muscle** se froisser un muscle

➤ **to pull somebody's leg** faire marcher quelqu'un : **you're pulling my leg!** tu me fais marcher !

pull down *phrasal verb*

1. **démolir : they pulled down the old building** on a démoli le vieil immeuble
2. **baisser : pull the blind down** baisse le store

pull in *phrasal verb*

s'arrêter : the bus pulled in le bus s'est arrêté

pull out *phrasal verb*

1. **arracher : the dentist pulled his tooth out** le dentiste lui a arraché une dent
2. **retirer : he pulled something out of his pocket** il a sorti quelque chose de sa poche

pull through *phrasal verb*

s'en sortir : don't worry, she'll pull through ne t'inquiète pas, elle s'en sortira

pull up *phrasal verb*

1. **remonter : he pulled his socks up** il a remonté ses chaussettes
2. **s'arrêter : a car pulled up in front of the house** une voiture s'est arrêtée devant la maison.

pullover ['pʊl,əʊvər] *noun*

pull *(masculine)* **: put your pullover on** mets ton pull.

pulse [pʌls] *noun*

pouls *(masculine)* **: the doctor took my pulse** le médecin a pris mon pouls.

pump [pʌmp] *noun & verb*

■ *noun*

pompe *(feminine)* **: a bicycle pump** une pompe à vélo ; **a petrol pump** *UK* OR **a gas pump** *US* une pompe à essence

■ *verb*

pomper : he pumped the water out of the pond il a pompé l'eau du bassin

pump up *phrasal verb*

gonfler : he's pumping up the tyres il gonfle les pneus.

pumpkin ['pʌmpkɪn] *noun*

potiron *(masculine)*, **citrouille** *(feminine)* **: a pumpkin pie** une tarte au potiron.

punch [pʌntʃ] *noun & verb*

■ *noun*

1. **coup** *(masculine)* **de poing : he gave me a punch** il m'a donné un coup de poing
2. **punch** *(masculine)* **: a glass of punch** un verre de punch

■ *verb*

1. **donner un coup de poing à : she punched him** elle lui a donné un coup de poing
2. **poinçonner : he punched my ticket** il a poinçonné mon billet.

punctuation [,pʌŋktʃʊ'eɪʃn] *noun*

ponctuation *(feminine)* **: punctuation marks** des signes de ponctuation.

puncture *UK* ['pʌŋktʃər] *noun*

crevaison *(feminine)* **: he repaired the puncture** il a réparé la crevaison

➤ **to have a puncture** crever : **I have a puncture** j'ai crevé.

punish ['pʌnɪʃ] *verb*

punir : they punished him for being late ils l'ont puni pour être arrivé en retard.

punishment ['pʌnɪʃmənt] *noun*

punition *(feminine)* **: he was sent to bed as a punishment** on l'a envoyé se coucher pour le punir.

pupil ['pjuːpl] *noun*

élève *(masculine or feminine)* **: there are 600 pupils in the school** il y a 600 élèves dans l'école.

puppet ['pʌpɪt] *noun*

marionnette *(feminine)* **: a puppet show** un spectacle de marionnettes.

puppy ['pʌpɪ] *(plural* puppies*) noun*

chiot *(masculine)* **: they have a dog and two puppies** ils ont un chien et deux chiots.

purchase [ˈpɜːtʃəs] *verb*

  acheter.

pure [pjʊər] *adjective*

  pur : **it's pure orange juice** c'est du pur jus d'orange ; **it's made of pure silk** c'est en pure soie.

purple [ˈpɜːpl] *adjective*

  violet *(feminine* violette*)* : **Pat's wearing a purple dress** Pat porte une robe violette.

purpose [ˈpɜːpəs] *noun*

  but *(masculine)* : **what's the purpose of your visit?** quel est le but de votre visite ?
  ➤ **on purpose** exprès : **I didn't do it on purpose** je ne l'ai pas fait exprès.

purr [pɜːr] *verb*

  ronronner : **the cat's purring** le chat ronronne.

purse [pɜːs] *noun*

  1. *UK* porte-monnaie *(masculine)* [*plural* portemonnaie] : **she took some money out of her purse** elle a pris de l'argent dans son porte-monnaie
  2. *US* sac *(masculine)* à main : **she took a book out of her purse** elle a sorti un livre de son sac à main.

push [pʊʃ] *verb*

  1. pousser : **we broke down and I had to push the car** on est tombés en panne et j'ai dû pousser la voiture ; **don't push!** ne poussez pas !
  2. appuyer sur : **I pushed the button** j'ai appuyé sur le bouton

push in *phrasal verb*

  resquiller : **there was a long queue so they pushed in** il y avait une longue queue, alors ils ont resquillé.

pushchair *UK* [ˈpʊʃtʃeər] *noun*

  poussette *(feminine)*.

push-up [ˈpʊʃʌp] *noun*

  pompe *(feminine)* : **he does ten push-ups a day** il fait dix pompes par jour.

put [pʊt] (*past tense & past participle* put) *verb*

  1. mettre : **put the plates on the table** mets les assiettes sur la table ; **put it over there** mets-le là-bas ; **he put his arm around her** il a mis son bras autour d'elle ; **that's put him in a bad mood** ça l'a mis de mauvaise humeur

  2. dire : **I don't know how to put it** je ne sais pas comment le dire
  3. investir : **Hamish put a lot of money into the project** Hamish a investi beaucoup d'argent dans le projet
  ➤ **to put a lot of effort into something** faire beaucoup d'efforts pour quelque chose
  ➤ **to put the clocks back** passer à l'heure d'hiver
  ➤ **to put the clocks forward** passer à l'heure d'été

put away *phrasal verb*

  ranger : **she put all her things away** elle a rangé toutes ses affaires

put back *phrasal verb*

  remettre : **put the scissors back when you've finished with them** remets les ciseaux quand tu auras fini avec

put down *phrasal verb*

  poser : **he put the gun down** il a posé son arme
  ➤ **to put the phone down** raccrocher : **he put the phone down on me** il m'a raccroché au nez

put off *phrasal verb*

  1. remettre à plus tard : **the party has been put off** ils ont remis la fête à plus tard
  2. dissuader : **she tried to put him off taking the job** elle a essayé de le dissuader d'accepter le poste
  3. dégoûter : **it put me off mussels for life** ça m'a définitivement dégoûté des moules
  4. *UK* déranger : **stop laughing, you're putting me off** arrête de rire, tu me déranges
  5. éteindre : **she put the TV off** elle a éteint la télé

put on *phrasal verb*

  1. mettre : **she put her hat on** elle a mis son chapeau ; **Sandra put a CD on** Sandra a mis un CD ; **put some sun cream on** mets de la crème solaire
  2. allumer : **put the TV on** allume la télé ; **I'll put the light on** je vais allumer
  3. prendre : **I've put on weight** j'ai pris du poids OR j'ai grossi
  4. monter : **we're putting on a Christmas show** nous montons un spectacle de Noël
  5. *informal* faire marcher : **you're putting me on** tu me fais marcher
  ➤ **to put the brakes on** freiner
  ➤ **he's putting it on** il fait semblant

p

put out *phrasal verb*

1. **éteindre : put the lights out** éteins les lumières
2. **tendre : he put his hand out** il a tendu la main
3. **sortir : I'll put the rubbish out** je vais sortir la poubelle
4. **déranger : I don't want to put you out** je ne veux pas te déranger
> **to be put out** être contrarié : **he was really put out** il était vraiment contrarié

put up *phrasal verb*

1. **ériger : they put up a statue of Joan of Arc** ils ont érigé une statue de Jeanne d'Arc
2. **monter : where shall we put the tent up?** où allons-nous monter la tente ?
3. **mettre : Perry put some posters up on his bedroom wall** Perry a mis des posters au mur de sa chambre
4. *UK* **augmenter : they've put their prices up** ils ont augmenté leurs prix
5. **héberger : can you put me up for the night?** tu peux m'héberger pour la nuit ?
> **to put one's hand up** lever la main : **put your hand up if you know the answer** lève la main si tu connais la réponse

put up with *phrasal verb*

supporter : I won't put up with this kind of behaviour je ne supporterai pas ce genre de comportement.

puzzle ['pʌzl] *noun*

1. **casse-tête** *(masculine)* *[plural* **casse-tête***]* : **a Chinese puzzle** un casse-tête chinois
2. **mystère** *(masculine)* : **that's a real puzzle** c'est un vrai mystère
> **a crossword puzzle** mots *(masculine plural)* croisés : **he's doing a crossword puzzle** il fait des mots croisés
> **a jigsaw puzzle** un puzzle.

puzzled ['pʌzld] *adjective*

perplexe : I'm puzzled je suis perplexe ; **he looks puzzled** il a l'air perplexe.

pyjamas *UK*, **pajamas** *US* [pə'dʒɑːməz]
plural noun
pyjama *(masculine)* : **he was in his pyjamas** il était en pyjama
> **a pair of pyjamas** un pyjama.

pyramid ['pɪrəmɪd] *noun*
pyramide *(feminine)*.

quack [kwæk] *verb*
cancaner : quack, quack! coin-coin !

qualification [ˌkwɒlɪfɪ'keɪʃn] *noun*
diplôme *(masculine)* : **list your academic qualifications** indiquez vos diplômes scolaires et universitaires.

qualified ['kwɒlɪfaɪd] *adjective*
diplômé : he's a qualified teacher c'est un professeur diplômé.

qualify ['kwɒlɪfaɪ] *(past tense & past participle* **qualified***) verb*

1. **obtenir son diplôme : she qualified as a nurse in May** elle a obtenu son diplôme d'infirmière en mai
2. **se qualifier : our team finally qualified** notre équipe s'est enfin qualifiée.

quality ['kwɒlətɪ] *(plural* **qualities***) noun*
qualité *(feminine)* : **it's very good quality** c'est de la très bonne qualité.

quantity ['kwɒntətɪ] *(plural* **quantities***)*
noun
quantité *(feminine)* : **he has a large quantity of books** il a une grande quantité de livres ; **he ate vast quantities of cherries** il a mangé des quantités de cerises.

quarrel ['kwɒrəl]
■ *noun*
dispute *(feminine)* : **they had a quarrel** ils se sont disputés
■ *verb (past tense & past participle* **quarrelled** *UK* OR **quarreled** *US)*
se disputer : we quarrelled all morning nous nous sommes disputés toute la matinée.

quarter ['kwɔːtəʳ] *noun*

1. **quart** *(masculine)* : **he ate three quarters of the cake** il a mangé les trois quarts du gâteau ; **a quarter of an hour** un quart d'heure ; **three quarters of an hour** trois quarts d'heure ; **it's quarter past two** *UK* OR **it's a quarter after two** *US* il est deux heures et quart ; **it's quarter to two** *UK* OR **it's a quarter of two** *US* il est deux heures moins le quart
2. *US* **pièce** *(feminine)* **de 25 cents** : **this candy cost a quarter** ce bonbon a coûté 25 cents.

quarterfinal ['kwɔːtəʳ'faɪnl] *noun*

quart *(masculine)* **de finale**.

quay [kiː] *noun*

quai *(masculine)*.

queasy ['kwiːzɪ] *adjective*

> **to feel queasy** avoir mal au cœur : **she feels a bit queasy** elle a mal au cœur.

queen [kwiːn] *noun*

reine *(feminine)* : **Queen Elizabeth** la reine Élisabeth ; **the Queen of England** la reine d'Angleterre ; **the Queen Mother** la reine mère.

query ['kwɪərɪ] *(plural* queries*) noun*

question *(feminine)* : **do you have any queries?** est-ce que tu as des questions ?

question ['kwestʃn] *noun & verb*

■ *noun*
question *(feminine)* : **I asked the teacher a question** j'ai posé une question au professeur ; **he answered all the questions** il a répondu à toutes les questions

> **that's out of the question** c'est hors de question

> **a question mark** un point d'interrogation
■ *verb*
interroger : **the police want to question him** la police veut l'interroger.

queue *UK* [kjuː] *noun & verb*

■ *noun*
queue *(feminine)* : **there's a long queue** il y a une longue queue
■ *verb*
faire la queue : **we're queuing for tickets** nous faisons la queue pour les billets.

quick [kwɪk] *adjective & adverb*

■ *adjective*
rapide : **you were quick!** tu as été rapide ! ;

he made a quick decision il a pris une décision rapide

> **she's a quick worker** elle travaille vite

> **to make a quick phone call** passer un petit coup de fil

> **be quick!** dépêche-toi !
■ *adverb*
vite : **quick, here he comes!** vite, il arrive !

> **as quick as a flash** avec la rapidité de l'éclair.

quickly ['kwɪklɪ] *adverb*

vite, rapidement : **he's walking quickly** il marche vite OR il marche rapidement.

quiet ['kwaɪət] *adjective*

1. **tranquille** : **a quiet street** une rue tranquille ; **we had a quiet evening** on a passé une soirée tranquille
2. **silencieux** *(feminine* silencieuse*)* : **it's a very quiet engine** c'est un moteur très silencieux
3. **bas** *(feminine* basse*)* : **she spoke in a quiet voice** elle a parlé à voix basse

> **be quiet!** tais-toi !

> **quiet everybody!** silence !

> **you're very quiet** tu ne dis pas grand-chose

> **to keep quiet** ne rien dire : **keep quiet about the party** ne dis rien au sujet de la fête.

quietly ['kwaɪətlɪ] *adverb*

1. **silencieusement** : **Harry left the room quietly** Harry a quitté la pièce silencieusement
2. **doucement** : **he speaks very quietly** il parle très doucement.

quilt [kwɪlt] *noun*

couette *(feminine)*.

quince [kwɪns] *noun*

coing *(masculine)*.

quit [kwɪt] *(past tense & past participle* quit OR quitted*) verb*

1. **quitter** : **she has quit her job** elle a quitté son emploi
2. **démissionner** : **he had a good job but he quit** il avait un bon emploi mais il a démissionné
3. **arrêter de** : **I've quit smoking** j'ai arrêté de fumer.

quite [kwaɪt] *adverb*

1. **assez, plutôt** : **she's quite pretty** elle est assez jolie ; **I'm quite hungry** j'ai plutôt faim
2. **tout à fait** : **you're quite right!** tu as tout à

q

fait raison ! ; **I'm not quite ready** je ne suis pas tout à fait prêt.

quits [kwɪts] *plural noun*

quitte : **we're quits** nous sommes quittes ; **double or quits!** quitte ou double !

quiz [kwɪz] (*plural* quizzes ['kwɪzɪz]) *noun*

1. jeu-concours *(masculine)* : **a TV quiz** un jeu télévisé
2. *US* interrogation *(feminine)* écrite : **the teacher gave us a quiz** le professeur nous a donné une interrogation écrite.

quotation [kwəʊ'teɪʃn] *noun*

citation *(feminine)* : **it's a quotation from Shakespeare** c'est une citation de Shakespeare
➤ **quotation marks** guillemets *(masculine plural)* : **in quotation marks** entre guillemets.

quote [kwəʊt] *noun & verb*

■ *noun*
citation *(feminine)* : **it's a quote from Oscar Wilde** c'est une citation d'Oscar Wilde
➤ **quotes** guillemets *(masculine plural)* : **in quotes** entre guillemets
■ *verb*
citer : **she quoted Homer** elle a cité Homère.

rabbi ['ræbaɪ] *noun*

rabbin *(masculine)* : **he's a rabbi** il est rabbin.

rabbit ['ræbɪt] *noun*

lapin *(masculine)* : **Hannah has a pet rabbit called Dillon** Hannah a un lapin qui s'appelle Dillon
➤ **a rabbit hutch** un clapier.

race [reɪs] *noun & verb*

■ *noun*
1. course *(feminine)* : **she won the race** elle a gagné la course

2. race *(feminine)* : **the human race** la race humaine
➤ **a race car** *US* une voiture de course
➤ **a race driver** *US* un pilote de course
■ *verb*
1. courir : **she raced to the door** elle a couru jusqu'à la porte ; **he raced out** il est sorti en courant
2. faire la course avec : **I'll race you** je fais la course avec toi.

racecourse *UK* ['reɪskɔːs] *noun*

champ *(masculine)* **de courses**.

racehorse ['reɪshɔːs] *noun*

cheval *(masculine)* **de course**.

racetrack ['reɪstræk] *noun*

piste *(feminine)* : **we were watching the cars on the racetrack** nous regardions les voitures sur la piste.

racing car *UK* ['reɪsɪŋkɑːʳ] *noun*

voiture *(feminine)* **de course**.

racing driver *UK* ['reɪsɪŋ'draɪvəʳ] *noun*

pilote *(masculine)* **de course**.

racism ['reɪsɪzm] *noun*

racisme *(masculine)*.

racist ['reɪsɪst] *adjective*

raciste.

rack [ræk] *noun*

porte-bagages *(masculine)* [*plural* porte-bagages].

racket ['rækɪt] *noun*

1. raquette *(feminine)* : **a tennis racket** une raquette de tennis
2. *informal* boucan *(masculine)* : **they're making a racket** ils font du boucan.

racquet ['rækɪt] *noun*

raquette *(feminine)* : **a tennis racquet** une raquette de tennis.

radiator ['reɪdɪeɪtəʳ] *noun*

radiateur *(masculine)* : **put the radiator on** allume le radiateur.

radio ['reɪdɪəʊ] *noun*

radio *(feminine)* : **I heard it on the radio** je l'ai entendu à la radio
➤ **a radio station** une station de radio.

radish ['rædɪʃ] (*plural* radishes) *noun*

radis (*masculine*).

rag [ræg] *noun*

chiffon (*masculine*) : **an oily rag** un chiffon graisseux

rags *plural noun*

guenilles (*feminine plural*) : **he was dressed in rags** il était en guenilles.

rage [reɪdʒ] *noun*

rage (*feminine*)
➤ **to be in a rage** être furieux : **she was in a rage** elle était furieuse
➤ **it's all the rage** ça fait fureur.

raid [reɪd] *noun & verb*

■ *noun*
1. **raid** (*masculine*) : **a bombing raid** un raid aérien
2. **descente** (*feminine*) : **a police raid** une descente de police
3. *UK* **hold-up** (*masculine invariable*) : **a bank raid** un hold-up dans une banque
■ *verb*
1. faire une descente dans : **the police raided their offices** la police a fait une descente dans leurs bureaux
2. faire une razzia sur : **he raided the fridge in the middle of the night** il a fait une razzia dans le frigo en pleine nuit
3. *UK* faire un hold-up dans : **thieves raided the bank** des voleurs ont fait un hold-up dans la banque.

rail [reɪl] *noun*

1. rampe (*feminine*) : **hold on to the rail when you come downstairs** tiens la rampe lorsque tu descends
2. garde-fou (*masculine*) : **the rail on the bridge** le garde-fou du pont
3. rail (*masculine*) : **the train left the rails** le train a quitté les rails
➤ **by rail** en train.

railings ['reɪlɪŋz] *plural noun*

grille (*feminine*) : **the park has railings around it** il y a une grille autour du parc.

railway *UK* ['reɪlweɪ], **railroad** *US* ['reɪlrəʊd] *noun*

chemin (*masculine*) **de fer**
➤ **a railway line** une ligne de chemin de fer
➤ **a railway station** une gare : **could you tell me where the railway station is?** pouvez-vous m'indiquer où se trouve la gare ?
➤ **a railway track** une voie ferrée.

rain [reɪn] *noun & verb*

■ *noun*
pluie (*feminine*) : **don't stand in the rain** ne reste pas sous la pluie
➤ **I'll take a rain check on that** *US* ce n'est que partie remise
■ *verb*
pleuvoir : **it's raining** il pleut ; **it's raining hard** il pleut à verse.

rainbow ['reɪnbəʊ] *noun*

arc-en-ciel (*masculine*) [*plural* arcs-en-ciel] : **how many colours are there in a rainbow?** il y a combien de couleurs dans un arc-en-ciel ?

raincoat ['reɪnkəʊt] *noun*

imperméable (*masculine*) : **he's got a raincoat on** il porte un imperméable.

rainforest ['reɪnfɒrɪst] *noun*

forêt (*feminine*) **tropicale humide** : **the rainforests of Brazil** les forêts tropicales du Brésil.

raise [reɪz] *verb & noun*

■ *verb*
1. lever : **she raised her hand** elle a levé la main ; **they raised the barrier** ils ont levé la barrière
2. augmenter : **they've raised their prices** ils ont augmenté leurs prix
3. améliorer : **we must raise standards** il faut améliorer le niveau
4. élever : **the children were raised in Canada** les enfants ont été élevés au Canada
➤ **to raise one's voice** élever la voix : **she raised her voice to make herself heard** elle a élevé la voix pour se faire entendre
➤ **to raise money** collecter des fonds : **the school is trying to raise money** l'école essaie de collecter des fonds
■ *noun US*
augmentation (*feminine*) : **all the staff got a raise** tous les employés ont eu une augmentation.

r

245

raisin ['reɪzn] *noun*

raisin *(masculine)* **sec : she's eating raisins** elle mange des raisins secs

 Le mot anglais **raisin** est un faux ami, il ne signifie pas "raisin".

rambling ['ræmblɪŋ] *uncountable noun*

randonnée *(feminine)* **: to go rambling** faire de la randonnée.

ran [ræn] *past tense of* run

he ran towards the door il a couru vers la porte.

ranch [*UK* rɑːntʃ, *US* ræntʃ] *(plural* ranches) *noun*

ranch *(masculine)*.

random ['rændəm] *adjective*

➤ **at random** au hasard : **choose a number at random** choisis un numéro au hasard.

rang [ræŋ] *past tense of* ring

your sister rang last night ta sœur a téléphoné hier soir.

range [reɪndʒ] *noun & verb*

■ *noun*

1. **gamme** *(feminine)*, **choix** *(masculine)* **: a car from the top of the range** une voiture dans le haut de gamme ; **there is a wide range of sizes** il y a un grand choix de tailles

2. **éventail** *(masculine)* **: price range** éventail des prix

3. **portée** *(feminine)* **: the target's out of range** la cible est hors de portée

4. *US* **cuisinière** *(feminine)* **: they bought a new range** ils ont acheté une nouvelle cuisinière

➤ **a mountain range** une chaîne de montagnes

■ *verb*

➤ **to range from ... to ...** varier de ... à ... : **prices range from 50 euros to 500 euros** les prix varient de 50 euros à 500 euros.

rank [ræŋk] *noun & verb*

■ *noun*

1. **grade** *(masculine)* **: the rank of colonel is above captain** le grade de colonel est au-dessus de celui de capitaine

2. **rang** *(masculine)* **: the soldiers broke ranks** les soldats ont rompu les rangs

➤ **a taxi rank** *UK* une station de taxis

■ *verb*

classer : he's ranked second in the world il est classé deuxième au niveau mondial.

rap [ræp] *noun*

rap *(masculine)* **: a rap singer** un chanteur de rap, une chanteuse de rap.

rare [reəʳ] *adjective*

1. **rare : this is a rare animal** c'est un animal rare

2. **saignant : I'd like my steak rare** je voudrais mon steak saignant.

rarely ['reəlɪ] *adverb*

rarement : she rarely goes out elle sort rarement.

rash [ræʃ] *noun*

éruption *(feminine)* **: he came out in a rash** il a eu une éruption.

raspberry [*UK* 'rɑːzbərɪ, *US* 'ræzberɪ] *(plural* raspberries) *noun*

framboise *(feminine)* **: a raspberry ice cream** une glace à la framboise ; **a raspberry tart** une tarte aux framboises.

rat [ræt] *noun*

rat *(masculine)* **: a water rat** un rat d'eau.

rate [reɪt] *noun*

1. **taux** *(masculine)* **: the birth rate** le taux de natalité ; **interest rates are low** les taux d'intérêt sont bas

2. **tarif** *(masculine)* **: are there special rates for children?** y a-t-il des tarifs spéciaux pour les enfants ?

rather [*UK* 'rɑːðəʳ, *US* 'ræðəʳ] *adverb*

plutôt : it's rather expensive c'est plutôt cher

➤ **rather than** plutôt que : **it's a comedy rather than a thriller** c'est une comédie plutôt qu'un thriller ; **he did it alone rather than asking for help** il l'a fait tout seul plutôt que de demander de l'aide

➤ **I'd rather leave** je préférerais partir OR j'aimerais mieux partir

➤ **she'd rather not go** elle préférerait ne pas y aller OR elle aimerait mieux ne pas y aller

➤ **would you rather wait?** préférez-vous attendre ?

⚠️ I would rather, she would rather etc se contractent en **I'd rather, she'd rather**, etc. Attention à ne pas confondre avec **I'd better**, la contraction de **I had better** qui signifie "je ferais mieux de".

rattle ['rætl] *noun*

hochet *(masculine)* : **the baby dropped its rattle** le bébé a laissé tomber son hochet.

rattlesnake ['rætlsneɪk] *noun*

serpent *(masculine)* à sonnette : **rattlesnakes are poisonous** les serpents à sonnette sont venimeux.

raw [rɔː] *adjective*

cru : **a raw carrot** une carotte crue

➤ **raw materials** matières *(feminine plural)* premières.

ray [reɪ] *noun*

rayon *(masculine)* : **the sun's rays** les rayons du soleil.

razor ['reɪzər] *noun*

rasoir *(masculine)*

➤ **a razor blade** une lame de rasoir.

Rd *abbreviation of* road.

reach [riːtʃ] *verb & noun*

▪ *verb*

1. arriver à : **we reached Paris before dark** nous sommes arrivés à Paris avant la nuit ; **the snow reached the window** la neige arrivait à la fenêtre

2. atteindre : **I can't reach the book on the top shelf** je n'arrive pas à atteindre le livre sur l'étagère du haut ; **they have reached the summit** ils ont atteint le sommet

3. toucher : **can you reach the ceiling?** tu peux toucher le plafond ?

4. parvenir à : **they've reached a decision** ils sont parvenus à une décision

5. joindre : **you can reach me on this number** tu peux me joindre à ce numéro

▪ *noun*

➤ **within reach** à portée de main : **the telephone is within reach** le téléphone est à portée de main

➤ **within easy reach** à proximité : **the school is within easy reach of my house** l'école est à proximité de ma maison

➤ **out of reach** hors de portée : **the radio is out of reach** la radio est hors de portée

reach out *phrasal verb*

tendre la main : **he reached out and touched her arm** il a tendu la main et lui a touché le bras.

react [rɪ'ækt] *verb*

réagir : **he didn't react** il n'a pas réagi.

reaction [rɪ'ækʃn] *noun*

réaction *(feminine)*.

read [riːd] *(past tense & past participle* read [red]*)* *verb*

lire : **she's reading a comic** elle lit une BD ; **have you read this book?** tu as lu ce livre ?

read out *phrasal verb*

lire à haute voix : **she read a poem out in class** elle a lu un poème à haute voix devant la classe.

reading ['riːdɪŋ] *uncountable noun*

lecture *(feminine)* : **reading is my favourite hobby** la lecture est mon passe-temps préféré.

ready ['redɪ] *adjective*

prêt : **are you ready to go?** tu es prêt à partir ? ; **she's always ready to help** elle est toujours prête à aider

➤ **to get ready** se préparer : **she's getting ready to leave** elle se prépare à partir

➤ **to get something ready** préparer quelque chose : **he's getting lunch ready** il prépare le déjeuner.

real ['rɪəl] *adjective*

1. vrai : **that's not the real reason** ce n'est pas la vraie raison ; **it's made of real leather** c'est en véritable cuir.

2. véritable : **it's real gold** c'est de l'or véritable ; **he's a real crook** c'est un véritable escroc

3. réel : **the real world** le monde réel

➤ **real estate** *US* l'immobilier *(masculine)* : **her father's in real estate** son père travaille dans l'immobilier.

realistic [ˌrɪə'lɪstɪk] *adjective*

réaliste.

reality [rɪ'ælətɪ] *noun*

réalité *(feminine)*.

r

realize , **realise** UK ['rɪəlaɪz] *verb*

se rendre compte de : **he realized his mistake** il s'est rendu compte de son erreur ; **I didn't realize what the time was** je ne me suis pas rendu compte de l'heure.

really ['rɪəlɪ] *adverb*

vraiment : **it's really late** il est vraiment tard ; **are you really going to Australia?** tu pars vraiment en Australie ? ; **not really** pas vraiment

➤ **really?**
1. ah bon ? : **I saw Graham today – oh really?** j'ai vu Graham aujourd'hui – ah bon ?
2. c'est vrai ? : **Ann won the lottery! – really?!** Ann a gagné au loto ! – c'est vrai ? !

rear [rɪər] *adjective & noun*

▢ *adjective*
arrière (*invariable*) : **the rear wheels** les roues arrière

▢ *noun*
arrière (*masculine*) : **I was sitting at the rear of the bus** j'étais assis à l'arrière du bus.

reason ['riːzn] *noun*

raison (*feminine*) : **that's the reason why she left** c'est la raison pour laquelle elle est partie.

reasonable ['riːznəbl] *adjective*
1. raisonnable : **be reasonable!** sois raisonnable !
2. honnête : **the food's reasonable** la cuisine est honnête.

reasonably ['riːznəblɪ] *adverb*

assez : **she's reasonably happy** elle est assez heureuse

➤ **reasonably good** honnête : **the food's reasonably good** la cuisine est honnête.

reassure [ˌriːə'ʃʊər] *verb*

rassurer : **I tried to reassure her** j'ai essayé de la rassurer.

receipt [rɪ'siːt] *noun*

reçu (*masculine*) : **I'd like a receipt, please** je voudrais un reçu, s'il vous plaît.

receive [rɪ'siːv] *verb*

recevoir : **I received a letter this morning** j'ai reçu une lettre ce matin.

receiver [rɪ'siːvər] *noun*

combiné (*masculine*) : **he picked up the re-ceiver and said 'hello!'** il a décroché le combiné et a dit « allô ! ».

recent ['riːsnt] *adjective*

récent : **it's a recent model** c'est un modèle récent.

recently ['riːsntlɪ] *adverb*

récemment : **I met him recently** je l'ai rencontré récemment

➤ **until recently** jusqu'à ces derniers temps : **until recently he lived in London** il a vécu à Londres jusqu'à ces derniers temps.

reception [rɪ'sepʃn] *noun*

réception (*feminine*) : **leave your key at the reception** laisse ta clé à la réception ; **we're going to a reception tonight** nous allons à une réception ce soir

➤ **the reception desk** la réception.

receptionist [rɪ'sepʃənɪst] *noun*

réceptionniste (*masculine or feminine*) : **she's a receptionist** elle est réceptionniste.

recess US ['riːses] *noun*

récréation (*feminine*) : **it's recess time** c'est l'heure de la récré.

recipe ['resɪpɪ] *noun*

recette (*feminine*) : **do you know the recipe for lasagne?** tu connais la recette des lasagnes ?

reckon ['rekn] *verb*
1. estimer : **the age of the earth is reckoned at 4,600 million years** l'âge de la Terre est estimé à 4600 millions d'années
2. penser : **I reckon you're right** je pense que tu as raison ; **what do you reckon?** qu'est-ce que tu en penses ?

recognize , **recognise** UK ['rekəgnaɪz] *verb*

reconnaître : **I didn't recognize you** je ne t'ai pas reconnu.

recommend [ˌrekə'mend] *verb*

recommander : **he recommended this book to me** il m'a recommandé ce livre.

record *noun & verb*

▢ *noun* ['rekɔːd]
1. record (*masculine*) : **she has broken the world record** elle a battu le record du monde
2. disque (*masculine*) : **I like listening to old records** j'aime écouter de vieux disques

➤ **a record player** un tourne-disque
➤ **a criminal record** un casier judiciaire
➤ **to keep a record of something**   noter quelque chose : **keep a record of your expenses** note tous tes frais
■ *verb* [rɪˈkɔːd]
   enregistrer : I've recorded the movie j'ai enregistré le film

records *plural noun*

   archives *(feminine plural)* : **I'll look it up in the records** je vais chercher dans les archives.

recorded delivery *UK* [rɪˈkɔːdɪdɪˈlɪ-vərɪ] *noun*

   to send something by recorded delivery envoyer quelque chose en recommandé.

recorder [rɪˈkɔːdəʳ] *noun*

   flûte *(feminine)* **à bec : he plays the recorder** il joue de la flûte à bec.

recording [rɪˈkɔːdɪŋ] *noun*

   enregistrement *(masculine)* : **this is a bad recording** l'enregistrement est mauvais.

recover [rɪˈkʌvəʳ] *verb*

   se remettre : she's recovering from the flu elle se remet de la grippe.

recovery [rɪˈkʌvərɪ] *noun*

   rétablissement *(masculine)* : **best wishes for a quick recovery!** je fais des vœux pour votre prompt rétablissement !

rectangle [ˈrekˌtæŋgl] *noun*

   rectangle *(masculine)*.

recycle [ˌriːˈsaɪkl] *verb*

   recycler : we recycle bottles and newspapers nous recyclons les bouteilles et les journaux ; **recycled paper** du papier recyclé.

recycling [ˌriːˈsaɪklɪŋ] *uncountable noun*

   recyclage *(masculine)* : **a recycling facility** une installation de recyclage.

red [red] *adjective*

1. **rouge : a red apple** une pomme rouge ; **a bright red hat** un chapeau rouge vif
2. **roux** *(feminine* **rousse)** : **she has red hair** elle a les cheveux roux
➤ **the Red Cross** la Croix-Rouge
➤ **a red light** un feu rouge : **he went through a red light** il a brûlé un feu rouge
➤ **to go red** devenir rouge OR rougir.

redhead [ˈredhed] *noun*

   roux *(masculine)*, **rousse** *(feminine)* : **she's a redhead** elle est rousse.

redo [ˌriːˈduː] *(past tense* **redid**, *past participle* **redone)** *verb*

   refaire : she redid her homework elle a refait son devoir.

reduce [*UK* rɪˈdjuːs, *US* rɪˈduːs] *verb*

   réduire : they've reduced the price on a réduit le prix.

reduction [rɪˈdʌkʃn] *noun*

   réduction *(feminine)* : **he gave me a 10% reduction** il m'a fait une réduction de 10 %.

redundant *UK* [rɪˈdʌndənt] *adjective*

➤ **to be made redundant** être licencié : **all the staff were made redundant** tout le personnel a été licencié.

reef [riːf] *noun*

   récif *(masculine)* : **a coral reef** un récif de corail ; **the Great Barrier Reef** la Grande Barrière.

refer [rɪˈfɜːʳ] *(past tense & past participle* **referred)** *verb*

➤ **to refer to** faire allusion à : **I don't know what you're referring to** je ne sais pas à quoi vous faites allusion.

referee [ˌrefəˈriː] *noun*

   arbitre *(masculine)* : **the referee blew his whistle** l'arbitre a donné un coup de sifflet.

reference [ˈrefrəns] *noun*

1. **allusion** *(feminine)* : **she made a reference to her family** elle a fait une allusion à sa famille
2. **références** *(feminine plural)* : **could you give me a reference for the job?** pouvez-vous me fournir vos références pour le poste ?
➤ **a reference book** un ouvrage de référence
➤ **a reference number**   une   référence : **what's your reference number?** quelle est votre référence ?

reflection [rɪˈflekʃn] *noun*

1. **reflet** *(masculine)* : **I can see my reflection in the mirror** je vois mon reflet dans la glace
2. **réflexion** *(feminine)* : **on reflection I don't think it's a good idea** à la réflexion, je ne crois pas que ce soit une bonne idée.

r

reflex ['riːfleks] *noun*

réflexe *(masculine)* : **he has good reflexes** il a de bons réflexes.

reflexive [rɪ'fleksɪv] *adjective*

réfléchi : **"to wash oneself" is a reflexive verb** « se laver » est un verbe réfléchi.

refreshing [rɪ'freʃɪŋ] *adjective*

rafraîchissant : **a refreshing drink** une boisson rafraîchissante.

refrigerator [rɪ'frɪdʒəreɪtər] *noun*

réfrigérateur *(masculine)* : **put the butter back in the refrigerator** remets le beurre dans le réfrigérateur.

refugee [ˌrefjʊ'dʒiː] *noun*

réfugié *(masculine)*, réfugiée *(feminine)*.

refund *noun & verb*

■ *noun* ['riːfʌnd]
remboursement *(masculine)* : **to get a refund** se faire rembourser
■ *verb* [rɪ'fʌnd]
rembourser : **they refunded me** ils m'ont remboursé.

refuse *verb & noun*

■ *verb* [rɪ'fjuːz]
refuser : **I refuse to do it** je refuse de le faire
■ *noun* ['refjuːs]
ordures *(feminine plural)* : **they collect the refuse every Tuesday** ils ramassent les ordures tous les mardis.

regard [rɪ'gɑːd] *verb*

considérer : **I regard her as my sister** je la considère comme ma sœur ; **he's regarded as the best player in the world** on le considère comme le meilleur joueur du monde.

regards [rɪ'gɑːdz] *plural noun*

amitiés *(feminine plural)* : **give her my regards** faites-lui mes amitiés ; **he sends his regards** il vous envoie ses amitiés.

region ['riːdʒən] *noun*

région : **a mountainous region** une région montagneuse.

register ['redʒɪstər] *noun & verb*

■ *noun*
registre *(masculine)* : **she signed the register** elle a signé le registre
➤ **the school register** le cahier des absences de l'école
➤ **to take the register** faire l'appel : **the teacher took the register** le professeur a fait l'appel
■ *verb*
1. **s'inscrire** : **she wants to register for a Spanish course** elle veut s'inscrire à un cours d'espagnol
2. *UK* faire enregistrer : **we must register our luggage** nous devons faire enregistrer nos bagages.

registered letter [ˌredʒɪstəd'letər] *noun*

lettre *(feminine)* recommandée : **I got a registered letter this morning** j'ai reçu une lettre recommandée ce matin.

registered trademark [ˌredʒɪstəd'treɪd-mɑːk] *noun*

marque *(feminine)* déposée.

registration number *UK* [ˌredʒɪ'streɪʃn'nʌmbər] *noun*

numéro *(masculine)* d'immatriculation : **what is your car's registration number?** quel est le numéro d'immatriculation de votre voiture ?

regret [rɪ'gret] *noun & verb*

■ *noun*
regret *(masculine)* : **do you have any regrets?** as-tu des regrets ?
■ *verb*
regretter : **he regrets having lied** il regrette d'avoir menti ; **you'll regret it!** tu vas le regretter !

regular ['regjʊlər] *adjective*

1. régulier *(feminine* régulière*)* : **at regular intervals** à intervalles réguliers ; **we have regular meetings** nous avons des réunions régulières
2. habituel *(feminine* habituelle*)* : **I'll see you at the regular time** on se voit à l'heure habituelle ; **he's a regular customer** c'est un habitué
3. normal : **a regular portion of fries** une portion de frites normale.

regularly ['regjʊlǝlɪ] *adverb*

régulièrement : **we meet regularly** on se réunit régulièrement.

regulations [ˌregjʊ'leɪʃnz] *plural noun*

règlement *(masculine)* : **it's against the regulations** c'est contraire au règlement.

rehearsal [rɪ'hɜːsl] *noun*

répétition *(feminine)* : **there's a rehearsal for the play tonight** il y a une répétition ce soir.

rehearse [rɪ'hɜːs] *verb*

répéter : **we're rehearsing the play this afternoon** nous répétons la pièce cet après-midi.

reign [reɪn] *noun*

règne *(masculine)* : **it was during the reign of Henry VIII** c'était sous le règne d'Henri VIII.

reindeer ['reɪnˌdɪǝʳ] *(plural* reindeer*) noun*

renne *(masculine)* : **there's a reindeer on the Christmas card** il y a un renne sur la carte de Noël.

reins [reɪnz] *plural noun*

rênes *(feminine plural)* : **she was holding the horse's reins** elle tenait les rênes du cheval.

reject [rɪ'dʒekt] *verb*

1. rejeter : **they rejected my offer** ils ont rejeté mon offre
2. refuser : **her qualifications were good but they rejected her** elle avait de bons diplômes mais on l'a refusée.

related [rɪ'leɪtɪd] *adjective*

1. apparenté : **they're related** ils sont apparentés
2. lié : **the two problems aren't related** les deux problèmes ne sont pas liés.

relation [rɪ'leɪʃn] *noun*

1. parent *(masculine)*, parente *(feminine)* : **he's a distant relation of my mother** c'est un parent éloigné de ma mère ; **Vicky has relations in Miami** Vicky a de la famille à Miami
2. rapport *(masculine)* : **there's no relation between these two ideas** il n'y a aucun rapport entre ces deux idées ; **the two countries have good relations** les deux pays ont de bonnes relations.

relationship [rɪ'leɪʃnʃɪp] *noun*

relations *(feminine plural)* : **they have a good relationship** ils ont de bonnes relations.

relative ['relǝtɪv] *noun*

parent *(masculine)*, parente *(feminine)* : **she's a relative of mine** c'est une parente ; **he has relatives in Dublin** il a de la famille à Dublin.

relax [rɪ'læks] *verb*

se détendre : **you need to relax** tu as besoin de te détendre
➤ **relax, everything will be fine!** ne t'en fais pas, tout ira bien !

relaxation [ˌriːlæk'seɪʃn] *noun*

détente *(feminine)* : **a week of relaxation** une semaine de détente ; **what do you do for relaxation?** qu'est-ce que tu fais pour te détendre ?

relaxed [rɪ'lækst] *adjective*

détendu, décontracté : **he's very relaxed** il est très détendu OR il est très décontracté.

relaxing [rɪ'læksɪŋ] *adjective*

reposant : **it was a relaxing weekend** c'était un week-end reposant.

relay ['riːleɪ], **relay race** ['riːleɪreɪs] *noun*

course *(feminine)* de relais.

release [rɪ'liːs] *noun & verb*

■ *noun*
1. libération *(feminine)* : **the release of the hostages** la libération des otages
2. sortie *(feminine)* : **the film is out on release next week** le film sort la semaine prochaine
➤ **a new release** un nouveau disque : **his new release is called "No Good Blues"** son nouveau disque s'appelle « No Good Blues »
➤ **a press release** un communiqué de presse
■ *verb*
1. libérer : **they released the prisoners** ils ont libéré les prisonniers
2. sortir : **they've just released a new album** ils viennent de sortir un nouvel album.

reliable [rɪ'laɪǝbl] *adjective*

fiable : **he's very reliable** il est très fiable ; **a reliable computer** un ordinateur fiable.

relief [rɪ'liːf] *noun*

soulagement *(masculine)* : **what a relief!** quel soulagement !

 Le mot anglais **relief** est un faux ami, il ne signifie pas "relief".

relieve [rɪ'liːv] *verb*

soulager : **it relieves the pain** cela soulage la douleur.

religion [rɪ'lɪdʒn] *noun*

religion *(feminine)* : **there are many different religions** il y a beaucoup de religions différentes.

religious [rɪ'lɪdʒəs] *adjective*

1. **religieux** *(feminine* **religieuse***)* : **what are your religious beliefs?** quelles sont vos croyances religieuses ?
2. **croyant** : **she's very religious** elle est très croyante.

reluctant [rɪ'lʌktənt] *adjective*

peu enthousiaste : **he's very reluctant** il est très peu enthousiaste

> **to be reluctant to do something** être peu disposé à faire quelque chose.

reluctantly [rɪ'lʌktəntlɪ] *adverb*

à contrecœur : **he turned off the radio reluctantly** il a éteint la radio à contrecœur.

rely [rɪ'laɪ] *(past tense & past participle* **relied***) verb*

> **to rely on** compter sur ; **can I rely on you?** je peux compter sur toi ?

remain [rɪ'meɪn] *verb*

rester : **he remained at home** il est resté à la maison ; **that remains to be seen** cela reste à voir.

remaining [rɪ'meɪnɪŋ] *adjective*

the remaining pupils chose Spanish le reste des élèves a choisi l'espagnol.

remains [rɪ'meɪnz] *plural noun*

1. **restes** *(masculine plural)* : **the remains of the meal** les restes du repas ; **they found human remains** ils ont découvert des restes humains
2. **vestiges** *(masculine plural)* : **the remains of an ancient city** les vestiges d'une ville ancienne.

remark [rɪ'mɑːk] *noun*

remarque *(feminine)* : **I didn't like that remark** je n'ai pas aimé cette remarque.

remarkable [rɪ'mɑːkəbl] *adjective*

remarquable : **she's a remarkable woman** c'est une femme remarquable.

remember [rɪ'membə^r] *verb*

1. **se souvenir de, se rappeler** : **I remember what happened** je me souviens de ce qui s'est passé OR je me rappelle ce qui s'est passé ; **she doesn't remember me** elle ne se souvient pas de moi ; **I remember seeing her yesterday** je me souviens l'avoir vue hier
2. **se souvenir, se rappeler** : **I don't remember** je ne me souviens pas OR je ne me rappelle pas

> **to remember to do something** ne pas oublier de faire quelque chose : **remember to take your umbrella** n'oublie pas de prendre ton parapluie.

remind [rɪ'maɪnd] *verb*

> **to remind somebody of something** rappeler quelque chose à quelqu'un : **you remind me of my brother** tu me rappelles mon frère OR tu me fais penser à mon frère

> **to remind somebody to do something** rappeler à quelqu'un de faire quelque chose : **remind me to phone David** rappelle-moi d'appeler David.

remote [rɪ'məʊt] *adjective*

isolé : **it's a remote town in the north of Scotland** c'est une ville isolée du nord de l'Écosse

> **the remote control** la télécommande.

remove [rɪ'muːv] *verb*

1. **enlever** : **he removed the plates** il a enlevé les assiettes
2. **faire partir** : **it's a product for removing stains** c'est un produit pour faire partir les taches.

renew [*UK* rɪ'njuː, *US* rɪ'nuː] *verb*

renouveler : **I must renew my passport** je dois renouveler mon passeport.

rent [rent] *noun & verb*

■ *noun*

loyer *(masculine)* : **how much is the rent?** le loyer est de combien ?

■ verb
louer : they rented a house for the summer ils ont loué une maison pour l'été ; she rented her house to students elle a loué sa maison à des étudiants

> **'for rent'** 'à louer'.

rental ['rentl] noun & adjective

■ noun
location (feminine) : car rental la location de voitures

■ adjective
de location : a rental car une voiture de location.

repair [rɪ'peəʳ] noun & verb

■ noun
réparation (feminine) : the repairs cost 50 euros les réparations ont coûté 50 euros

■ verb
réparer : he repaired the television il a réparé la télévision ; to get the car repaired faire réparer la voiture.

repeat [rɪ'piːt] verb & noun

■ verb
répéter : don't repeat what I'm telling you ne répète pas ce que je te dis

■ noun
rediffusion (feminine) : this programme is a repeat cette émission est une rediffusion.

replace [rɪ'pleɪs] verb

1. **remplacer** : I replaced the broken window j'ai remplacé la vitre cassée
2. **remettre** : replace the book on the shelf remets le livre sur l'étagère.

reply [rɪ'plaɪ] noun & verb

■ noun
réponse (feminine) : we're waiting for a reply nous attendons une réponse

■ verb (past tense & past participle replied)
répondre : what did you reply? qu'est-ce que tu as répondu ?

report [rɪ'pɔːt] noun & verb

■ noun
1. **rapport** (masculine) : I read the police report j'ai lu le rapport de police
2. **reportage** (masculine) : we read the report in the paper nous avons lu le reportage dans le journal
3. UK **bulletin** (masculine) **scolaire** : he got a good report il a eu un bon bulletin
4. **compte-rendu** (masculine) : we wrote a re-port on the environment nous avons fait un compte-rendu sur l'environnement

> **a report card** US un bulletin scolaire ; she has a good report card elle a un bon bulletin

■ verb
1. **signaler** : we reported the accident to the police nous avons signalé l'accident à la police
2. **annoncer** : the news was reported in the paper la nouvelle a été annoncée dans le journal
3. **se présenter** : report to my office présentez-vous à mon bureau.

reporter [rɪ'pɔːtəʳ] noun
reporter (masculine) : he's a reporter il est reporter.

represent [ˌreprɪ'zent] verb
représenter : the dotted line represents the border le pointillé représente la frontière.

reptile ['reptaɪl] noun
reptile (masculine) : crocodiles are reptiles les crocodiles sont des reptiles.

republic [rɪ'pʌblɪk] noun
république (feminine) : France is a republic la France est une république.

Republican [rɪ'pʌblɪkən] adjective & noun

■ adjective
républicain : the Republican Party le parti républicain

■ noun
républicain (masculine), **républicaine** (feminine).

request [rɪ'kwest] noun & verb

■ noun
demande (feminine) : they made a request ils ont fait une demande

■ verb
demander : I requested him not to smoke je lui ai demandé de ne pas fumer.

require [rɪ'kwaɪəʳ] verb
1. **avoir besoin de** : call me if you require anything appelez-moi si vous avez besoin de quoi que ce soit
2. **nécessiter, requérir** : this work requires a lot of concentration ce travail nécessite beaucoup de concentration.

resat UK [ˌriː'sæt] past tense & past participle of resit
he resat the exam il a repassé l'examen.

r

rescue ['reskju:] *noun & verb*

■ *noun*

secours *(masculine)* **: he came to my rescue** il est venu à mon secours

➤ **a rescue operation** une opération de sauvetage

➤ **the rescue services** les services *(masculine plural)* de secours

➤ **a rescue team** une équipe de secours OR une équipe de sauvetage

■ *verb*

sauver : they rescued her from the fire ils l'ont sauvée de l'incendie.

research [‚rɪ'sɜːtʃ, 'riːsɜːtʃ] *uncountable noun*

recherche *(feminine)* **: he's doing research on genetics** il fait de la recherche en génétique.

researcher [rɪ'sɜːtʃəʳ, 'riːsɜːtʃəʳ] *noun*

chercheur *(masculine)*, **chercheuse** *(feminine)*.

reservation [‚rezə'veɪʃn] *noun*

réservation *(feminine)* **: I've made a reservation for tonight** j'ai fait une réservation pour ce soir.

reserve [rɪ'zɜːv] *noun & verb*

■ *noun*

1. **réserve** *(feminine)* **: keep some water in reserve** garde de l'eau en réserve ; **a nature reserve** une réserve naturelle

2. **remplaçant** *(masculine)*, **remplaçante** *(feminine)* **: he's the reserve for the match** il est remplaçant dans ce match

■ *verb*

réserver : she has reserved two seats on the plane elle a réservé deux places dans l'avion.

residence ['rezɪdəns] *noun*

résidence *(feminine)* **: the president's official residence** la résidence officielle du président

➤ **a residence permit** un permis de séjour.

resident ['rezɪdənt] *noun*

➤ **the residents of the town** les habitants *(masculine plural)* de la ville

➤ **the residents of the street** les riverains *(masculine plural)*

➤ **the hotel residents** les clients *(masculine plural)* de l'hôtel.

resign [rɪ'zaɪn] *verb*

démissionner : he resigned from his job il a démissionné.

resist [rɪ'zɪst] *verb*

résister à : he can't resist chocolate il ne peut pas résister au chocolat ; **I just couldn't resist** je n'ai pas pu résister.

resit *UK* [‚riː'sɪt] *(past tense & past participle* resat) *verb*

repasser : I've got to resit the exam je dois repasser l'examen.

resort [rɪ'zɔːt] *noun*

1. **station** *(feminine)* **: a seaside resort** une station balnéaire ; **a ski resort** une station de sports d'hiver

2. **recours** *(masculine)* **: as a last resort** en dernier recours.

resource [rɪ'sɔːs] *noun*

ressource *(feminine)* **: natural resources** des ressources naturelles.

respect [rɪ'spekt] *noun & verb*

■ *noun*

respect *(masculine)* **: he has no respect for his parents** il n'a aucun respect pour ses parents

■ *verb*

respecter : everybody respects her tout le monde la respecte.

responsibility [rɪˌspɒnsə'bɪlətɪ] *noun*

responsabilité *(feminine)* **: he accepted responsibility for it** il en a accepté la responsabilité.

responsible [rɪ'spɒnsəbl] *adjective*

responsable : she's responsible for the accident elle est responsable de l'accident

➤ **a responsible job** un poste à responsabilités.

rest [rest] *noun & verb*

■ *noun*

repos *(masculine)* **: I need some rest** j'ai besoin de repos ; **she had a rest** elle s'est reposée

➤ **the rest**

1. **le reste : the rest of the book was more interesting** le reste du livre était plus intéressant

2. **les autres : the rest of them have gone home** les autres sont rentrés chez eux

➤ **the rest room** *US* les toilettes *(feminine plural)* **: where is the rest room?** où sont les toilettes ?

■ *verb*

1. **se reposer : I want to rest for a few minutes** je veux me reposer quelques minutes ; **sit down and rest your legs** assieds-toi et repose-toi les jambes

2. appuyer : **she rested her bike against the wall** elle a appuyé son vélo contre le mur
3. être appuyé : **the ladder's resting against the tree** l'échelle est appuyée contre l'arbre.

restaurant ['restərɒnt] *noun*

restaurant *(masculine)* : **we're going to a restaurant tonight** nous allons au restaurant ce soir ; **an Indian restaurant** un restaurant indien.

result [rɪ'zʌlt] *noun*

résultat *(masculine)* : **we're waiting for the exam results** nous attendons les résultats de l'examen.

résumé *US* [*UK* 'rezjuːmeɪ, *US* 'rezuːmeɪ] *noun*

CV *(masculine)*, curriculum vitae *(masculine)*.

retire [rɪ'taɪər] *verb*

prendre sa retraite : **she retired at 60** elle a pris sa retraite à 60 ans.

return [rɪ'tɜːn] *noun & verb*

■ *noun*
1. retour *(masculine)* : **I will phone on my return from Paris** j'appellerai à mon retour de Paris
2. *UK* aller-retour *(masculine)* [*plural* allers-retours] : **I'd like a return to London** je voudrais un aller-retour pour Londres
➤ **a return match** un match retour
➤ **the return journey** le voyage de retour
➤ **a return ticket** *UK* un aller-retour
➤ **in return** en échange : **what do you want in return?** que veux-tu en échange ?
➤ **many happy returns!** bon anniversaire !
■ *verb*
1. revenir : **he returned an hour later** il est revenu une heure plus tard
2. retourner : **she returned to the office** elle est retournée au bureau
3. rendre : **he returned the book I lent him** il m'a rendu le livre que je lui avais prêté
4. rapporter : **I forgot to return the video** j'ai oublié de rapporter la cassette vidéo
5. remettre : **he returned the book to the shelf** il a remis le livre sur l'étagère
➤ **to return home** rentrer : **when did she return home from her trip?** quand est-elle rentrée de voyage ?

reunion [ˌriː'juːnjən] *noun*

réunion *(feminine)* : **a family reunion** une réunion de famille

> Reunion est un faux ami, il ne signifie pas "réunion" au sens de "assemblée professionnelle".

reveal [rɪ'viːl] *verb*

révéler : **she revealed my secret** elle a révélé mon secret.

revenge [rɪ'vendʒ] *noun*

vengeance *(feminine)*
➤ **to take revenge** OR **to get one's revenge** se venger : **I'll get my revenge** je vais me venger : **he took revenge on us** il s'est vengé de nous.

reverse [rɪ'vɜːs] *noun, adjective & verb*

■ *noun*
1. marche *(feminine)* arrière : **you're in reverse** tu es en marche arrière ; **put the car into reverse** passe la marche arrière
2. contraire *(masculine)* : **he did the reverse of what I told him to do** il a fait le contraire de ce que je lui ai dit de faire
■ *adjective*
inverse : **in reverse order** dans l'ordre inverse
➤ **in reverse gear** en marche arrière
■ *verb*
faire marche arrière : **the car reversed** la voiture a fait marche arrière
➤ **to reverse the charges** *UK* appeler en PCV.

review [rɪ'vjuː] *noun*

critique *(feminine)* : **the film got good reviews** le film a eu de bonnes critiques.

revise *UK* [rɪ'vaɪz] *verb*

réviser : **they're revising for their exams** ils révisent pour leurs examens.

revision [rɪ'vɪʒn] *uncountable noun*

révision *(feminine)* : **I must do some revision** je dois faire des révisions.

revolting [rɪ'vəʊltɪŋ] *adjective*

dégoûtant : **the meat was revolting** la viande était dégoûtante.

revolution [ˌrevə'luːʃn] *noun*

révolution *(feminine)* : **the French Revolution** la Révolution française.

r

revolver [rɪ'vɒlvə'] noun

revolver (masculine) : **he took out his revolver** il a sorti son revolver.

reward [rɪ'wɔːd] noun & verb

■ noun
récompense (feminine) : **they're offering a reward** ils offrent une récompense

■ verb
récompenser : **he was rewarded for his efforts** il a été récompensé pour ses efforts.

rewind [ˌriː'waɪnd] (past tense & past participle rewound [ˌriː'waʊnd]) verb
rembobiner : **rewind the tape** rembobine la cassette.

Rhine [raɪn] noun

➤ **the Rhine** le Rhin.

rhinoceros [raɪ'nɒsərəs] noun
rhinocéros (masculine).

rhubarb ['ruːbɑːb] uncountable noun
rhubarbe (feminine) : **a rhubarb tart** une tarte à la rhubarbe.

rhyme [raɪm] noun & verb

■ noun
1. rime (feminine) : **try and find a rhyme for 'please'** essaie de trouver un mot qui rime avec « please »
2. poème (masculine) : **I've made up a little rhyme** j'ai composé un petit poème
■ verb
rimer : **'bad' rhymes with 'mad'** « bad » rime avec « mad ».

rhythm ['rɪðm] noun
rythme (masculine).

rib [rɪb] noun
côte (feminine) : **human beings have twelve pairs of ribs** les êtres humains ont douze paires de côtes.

ribbon ['rɪbən] noun
ruban (masculine) : **she put a ribbon round the parcel** elle a mis un ruban autour du paquet.

rice [raɪs] uncountable noun
riz (masculine) : **brown rice** riz complet ; **boiled rice** riz nature
➤ **rice pudding** riz (masculine) au lait.

rich [rɪtʃ] adjective & noun

■ adjective
riche : **he's very rich** il est très riche
■ noun
➤ **the rich** les riches.

rid [rɪd] (past tense & past participle rid) verb
➤ **to get rid of something** se débarrasser de quelque chose : **he got rid of his old toys** il s'est débarrassé de ses vieux jouets.

ridden ['rɪdn] past participle of ride
have you ever ridden a horse? es-tu déjà monté à cheval ?

riddle ['rɪdl] noun
devinette (feminine) : **he asked me a riddle** il m'a posé une devinette.

ride [raɪd] noun & verb

■ noun
promenade (feminine), tour (masculine) : **he went for a ride on his horse** il est allé faire une promenade à cheval ; **she went for a ride on her bike** elle a fait une promenade à vélo ; **we went for a ride in the car** nous avons fait un tour en voiture
➤ **to give somebody a ride** conduire quelqu'un quelque part : **can you give me a ride to the station?** tu peux me conduire à la gare ?

■ verb (past tense rode, past participle ridden)
1. monter à cheval : **can you ride?** tu sais monter à cheval ?
2. aller : **she rides her bike to school** elle va à l'école à vélo ; **we rode to the top of the mountain** nous sommes allés jusqu'en haut de la montagne
➤ **to ride a bike** faire du vélo : **can you ride a bike?** tu sais faire du vélo ? ; **Katie's riding her bike** Katie fait du vélo.

rider ['raɪdə'] noun
cavalier (masculine), cavalière (feminine) : **he's a good rider** c'est un bon cavalier.

ridiculous [rɪ'dɪkjʊləs] adjective
ridicule : **you look ridiculous in that hat** tu as l'air ridicule avec ce chapeau.

riding ['raɪdɪŋ] uncountable noun
équitation (feminine) : **she goes riding every weekend** elle fait de l'équitation tous les week-ends
➤ **a riding school** une école d'équitation.

rifle ['raɪfl] *noun*

fusil *(masculine)* : **a hunting rifle** un fusil de chasse.

right [raɪt] *adjective, adverb, noun & exclamation*

■ *adjective*

1. **droit** : **give me your right hand** donne-moi ta main droite ; **a right angle** un angle droit

2. **bon** *(feminine* **bonne***)* : **that's the right answer** c'est la bonne réponse ; **is that the right size?** c'est la bonne taille ?

3. **exact, juste** : **do you have the right time?** tu as l'heure exacte ?

4. **bien** : **it's not right to steal** ce n'est pas bien de voler

➤ **to be right** avoir raison : **you're quite right** tu as tout à fait raison ; **she was right to tell the truth** elle a eu raison de dire la vérité

➤ **that's right** c'est ça : **are you going to Turkey? – yes, that's right** tu pars en Turquie ? – oui, c'est ça

■ *adverb*

1. **à droite** : **turn right at the corner of the street** tournez à droite au coin de la rue

2. **correctement** : **she got the question right** elle a répondu correctement à la question

3. **tout** : **go right to the end of the corridor** allez tout au bout du couloir

4. **tout de suite** : **it happened right after Christmas** cela s'est passé juste après Noël

➤ **right now** OR **right away** tout de suite : **leave right now** pars tout de suite

■ *noun*

1. **droite** *(feminine)* : **you drive on the right in France** on conduit à droite en France ; **look to the right** regarde à droite

2. **droit** *(masculine)* : **you have the right to refuse** tu as le droit de refuser ; **human rights** les droits de l'homme

3. **bien** *(masculine)* : **he can't tell right from wrong** il ne sait pas distinguer le bien du mal

➤ **right of way** la priorité : **you have the right of way** tu as la priorité

■ *exclamation*

bon ! : **right, let's stop now!** bon, on va s'arrêter là !

right-hand ['raɪthænd] *adjective*

de droite : **the right-hand drawer** le tiroir de droite

➤ **on the right-hand side** à droite : **it's on the right-hand side** c'est à droite.

right-handed [raɪt'hændɪd] *adjective*

droitier *(feminine* **droitière***)* : **she's right-handed** elle est droitière.

ring [rɪŋ] *noun & verb*

■ *noun*

1. **anneau** *(masculine)* [*plural* **anneaux**] : **she had a ring in her nose** elle avait un anneau dans le nez

2. **bague** *(feminine)* : **she has a diamond ring on her finger** elle a une bague en diamants au doigt ; **an engagement ring** une bague de fiançailles ; **a wedding ring** une alliance

3. **cercle** *(masculine)* : **they stood in a ring** ils ont formé un cercle

4. **ring** *(masculine)* : **the boxers climbed into the ring** les boxeurs sont montés sur le ring

5. **piste** *(feminine)* : **the clowns came into the circus ring** les clowns sont entrés sur la piste du cirque

➤ **to give somebody a ring** appeler quelqu'un : **I'll give you a ring tomorrow** je t'appelle demain

➤ **there was a ring at the door** quelqu'un a sonné à la porte

➤ **a ring binder** un classeur à anneaux

■ *verb* (*past tense* rang, *past participle* rung)

1. *UK* **téléphoner, appeler** : **he forgot to ring** il a oublié de téléphoner

2. *UK* **appeler, téléphoner à** : **I'll ring you tonight** je t'appellerai ce soir

3. **sonner** : **the phone's ringing** le téléphone sonne

➤ **to ring the doorbell** sonner à la porte OR sonner : **somebody rang the doorbell** quelqu'un a sonné

ring back *UK phrasal verb*

rappeler : **I'll ring you back tomorrow** je te rappellerai demain

ring up *UK phrasal verb*

appeler, téléphoner à : **he rang me up last night** il m'a appelé hier soir OR il m'a téléphoné hier soir.

rink [rɪŋk] *noun*

➤ **an ice rink** une patinoire

➤ **a roller-skating rink** une piste pour rollers.

rinse [rɪns] *verb*

rincer : **she's rinsing her hair** elle se rince les cheveux.

r

riot ['raɪət] *noun*

émeute *(feminine)* : **there were riots in the town** il y a eu des émeutes dans la ville.

rip [rɪp] (*past tense & past participle* ripped) *verb*

1. déchirer : **he ripped his shirt** il a déchiré sa chemise
2. se déchirer : **my coat has ripped** mon manteau s'est déchiré
3. arracher : **he ripped the poster off the wall** il a arraché le poster du mur.

ripe [raɪp] *adjective*

mûr : **these bananas are very ripe** ces bananes sont très mûres.

rip-off *noun informal*

arnaque *(feminine)* : **that's a rip-off!** c'est de l'arnaque !

rise [raɪz] *noun & verb*

▪ *noun*

1. hausse *(feminine)*, augmentation *(feminine)* : **temperatures are on the rise** les températures sont en hausse ; **there has been a rise in prices** les prix ont augmenté
2. *UK* augmentation *(feminine)* : **a pay rise** une augmentation de salaire ; **Colin has just had a pay rise** Colin vient d'être augmenté

▪ *verb* (*past tense* rose, *past participle* risen)

1. monter, augmenter : **prices are rising** les prix montent OR les prix augmentent
2. se lever : **the sun rises in the east** le soleil se lève à l'est
3. s'élever : **Everest rises to 8,848 metres** l'Everest s'élève à 8 848 mètres ; **there's smoke rising from the chimney** de la fumée s'élève de la cheminée.

risk [rɪsk] *noun*

risque *(masculine)* : **he doesn't like taking risks** il n'aime pas prendre des risques.

risky ['rɪskɪ] *adjective*

risqué : **it's too risky** c'est trop risqué.

rival ['raɪvl] *noun*

rival *(masculine)*, rivale *(feminine)*.

river ['rɪvəʳ] *noun*

1. rivière *(feminine)* : **they were swimming in the river** ils se baignaient dans la rivière
2. fleuve *(masculine)* : **the Missouri is the longest river in North America** le Missouri est le plus long fleuve d'Amérique du Nord

➤ **the river Thames** la Tamise
➤ **the Mississippi River** le Mississippi

> You should use the French word **fleuve** for major rivers that flow into the sea and **rivière** for smaller rivers.

Riviera [ˌrɪvɪ'eərə] *noun*

➤ **the French Riviera** la Côte d'Azur : **Cannes is on the French Riviera** Cannes est sur la Côte d'Azur
➤ **the Italian Riviera** la Riviera italienne.

road [rəʊd] *noun*

1. route *(feminine)* : **we took the road from London to Bristol** nous avons pris la route de Londres à Bristol
2. rue *(feminine)* : **he lives on the other side of the road** il habite de l'autre côté de la rue
➤ **a road map** une carte routière
➤ **a road sign** un panneau de signalisation
➤ **road works** travaux *(masculine plural)*.

roar [rɔːʳ] *verb*

rugir : **the lion roared** le lion a rugi.

roast [rəʊst] *adjective*

rôti : **a roast chicken** un poulet rôti ; **roast beef** un rôti de bœuf

> ROAST
> Le déjeuner du dimanche en Grande-Bretagne se compose traditionnellement d'un rôti, le **roast beef** (rôti de bœuf) par exemple, accompagné de **Yorkshire pudding** (pâte à frire cuite dans la graisse de ce rôti de bœuf), de pommes de terre rôties, de légumes et de **gravy** (sauce brune à base de jus de rôti).

rob [rɒb] (*past tense & past participle* robbed) *verb*

1. voler : **I've been robbed** on m'a volé
2. dévaliser : **somebody robbed the bank** quelqu'un a dévalisé la banque.

robber ['rɒbəʳ] *noun*

voleur *(masculine)*, voleuse *(feminine)*
➤ **a bank robber** un cambrioleur de banque.

robbery ['rɒbərɪ] (*plural* robberies) *noun*

vol *(masculine)* : **there have been several robberies in the area** il y a eu plusieurs vols dans le quartier

➤ **a bank robbery** un hold-up.

robin ['rɒbɪn] *noun*

rouge-gorge *(masculine)* [*plural* **rouges-gorges**]
➤ **Robin Hood** Robin des bois.

robot ['rəʊbɒt] *noun*

robot *(masculine)*.

rock [rɒk] *noun*

1. **roche** *(feminine)* : **they drilled through the rock** ils ont foré la roche
2. **rocher** *(masculine)* : **there's a pile of rocks at the foot of the cliff** il y a un tas de rochers au pied de la falaise
3. **pierre** *(feminine)* : **he threw a rock at me** il m'a lancé une pierre
4. **rock** *(masculine)* : **Susie loves rock music** Susie adore la musique rock
➤ **rock and roll** rock and roll *(masculine)*
➤ **a rock band** un groupe de rock
➤ **a rock star** une rock star
➤ **rock climbing** varappe *(feminine)* : **to go rock climbing** faire de la varappe.

rocket ['rɒkɪt] *noun*

fusée *(feminine)* : **they sent a rocket into space** ils ont lancé une fusée dans l'espace.

rocking chair ['rɒkɪntʃeəʳ] *noun*

fauteuil *(masculine)* **à bascule** : **grandpa is sitting in his rocking chair** grand-père est assis dans son fauteuil à bascule.

rocking horse ['rɒkɪŋhɔːs] *noun*

cheval *(masculine)* **à bascule**.

rocky ['rɒkɪ] *adjective*

rocailleux *(feminine* **rocailleuse)** : **a rocky path** un chemin rocailleux
➤ **the Rocky Mountains** OR **the Rockies** les montagnes Rocheuses OR les Rocheuses

ROCKY MOUNTAINS
Les montagnes Rocheuses, surnommées les **Rockies**, constituent la chaîne de montagnes la plus grande d'Amérique du Nord. Elles s'étendent sur plus de 4 800 kilomètres depuis le Canada jusqu'à la frontière avec le Mexique, en passant par huit États des États-Unis. Le sommet le plus élevé est le Mont Elbert, dans le Colorado (4 402 mètres).

rod [rɒd] *noun*

➤ **a fishing rod** une canne à pêche.

rode [rəʊd] *past tense of* ride

she rode to school on her bike elle est allée à l'école à vélo.

rodeo ['rəʊdɪəʊ] *noun*

rodéo *(masculine)*

RODEO
Les rodéos sont des spectacles très appréciés, en particulier dans l'ouest des États-Unis. Des cow-boys démontrent leur talent de dresseurs et gagnent des prix en montant des chevaux, des vaches et des taureaux sauvages, et en attrapant des vaches et des taureaux avec un lasso. Le premier rodéo a eu lieu en Arizona en 1888.

role [rəʊl] *noun*

rôle *(masculine)* : **he has an important role** il a un rôle important.

roll [rəʊl] *noun & verb*

■ *noun*
1. **rouleau** *(masculine)* [*plural* **rouleaux**] : **a roll of toilet paper** un rouleau de papier toilette
2. **petit pain** *(masculine)* : **a bread roll** un petit pain
■ *verb*
rouler : **the ball rolled under the chair** la balle a roulé sous la chaise

roll up *phrasal verb*

1. **rouler** : **she rolled up the map** elle a roulé la carte
2. **retrousser** : **Danny rolled up his sleeves** Danny a retroussé ses manches.

roller ['rəʊləʳ] *noun*

1. **rouleau** *(masculine)* [*plural* **rouleaux**] : **a road roller** un rouleau compresseur
2. **bigoudi** *(masculine)* : **her hair is in rollers** elle est en bigoudis

 Le mot anglais **roller** est un faux ami, il ne signifie pas "roller".

Rollerblades® ['rəʊləbleɪdz] *plural noun*

rollers *(masculine plural)* : **a pair of Rollerblades** une paire de rollers.

rollerblading [ˈrəʊləbleɪdɪŋ] *uncountable*
noun
roller *(masculine)* : **to go rollerblading** faire du roller.

roller coaster [ˈrəʊləˈkəʊstəʳ] *noun*
montagnes *(feminine plural)* **russes** : **let's go on the roller coaster** allons faire un tour sur les montagnes russes.

roller skates [ˈrəʊləˈskeɪts] *plural noun*
patins *(masculine plural)* **à roulettes** : **a pair of roller skates** une paire de patins à roulettes.

roller-skating [ˈrəʊləˈskeɪtɪŋ] *uncountable*
noun
patin *(masculine)* **à roulettes** : **to go roller-skating** faire du patin à roulettes.

Roman [ˈrəʊmən] *adjective & noun*
■ *adjective*
romain

> The French adjective does not start with a capital letter:

the Roman empire l'empire romain ; **Roman numerals** les chiffres romains
■ *noun*
Romain *(masculine)*, **Romaine** *(feminine)* : **the Romans came to Britain in 55 BC** les Romains sont arrivés en Grande-Bretagne en 55 av. J.-C.

Roman Catholic [ˈrəʊmənˈkæθlɪk] *adjective & noun*
catholique *(masculine or feminine)* : **he's a Roman Catholic** il est catholique.

romance [rəʊˈmæns] *noun*
1. **amour** *(masculine)* : **a holiday romance** un amour de vacances
2. **côté romantique** *(masculine)* : **the romance of travel** le côté romantique des voyages
3. **roman d'amour** *(masculine)* : **she likes reading romances** elle aime lire des romans d'amour.

romantic [rəʊˈmæntɪk] *adjective*
romantique : **he's very romantic** il est très romantique.

roof [ruːf] *noun*
toit *(masculine)* : **the cat climbed onto the roof** le chat est monté sur le toit

> **a roof rack** *UK* une galerie : **they put the bikes on the roof rack** ils ont mis les vélos sur la galerie.

room [ruːm, rʊm] *noun*
1. **pièce** *(feminine)* : **there are five rooms in our house** il y a cinq pièces dans notre maison
2. **chambre** *(feminine)* : **she went up to her room** elle est montée dans sa chambre
3. **salle** *(feminine)* : **the school has a large room for concerts** l'école a une grande salle pour les concerts
4. **place** *(feminine)* : **can you make some room?** tu peux faire de la place ? ; **the boxes take up a lot of room** les boîtes prennent beaucoup de place.

root [ruːt] *noun*
racine *(feminine)* : **the roots of the tree are very deep** les racines de l'arbre sont très profondes

> **root beer** *US* boisson gazeuse sans alcool aux extraits de plantes.

rope [rəʊp] *noun*
corde *(feminine)* : **I tied it with a rope** je l'ai attaché avec une corde.

rose [rəʊz] *noun & verb form*
■ *noun*
rose *(feminine)* : **he gave her a bunch of red roses** il lui a offert un bouquet de roses rouges ; **the red rose is the emblem of England** la rose rouge est l'emblème de l'Angleterre
■ *past tense of* **rise**
the balloon rose into the air le ballon s'est élevé dans les airs.

rot [rɒt] *(past tense & past participle* **rotted***)* *verb*
pourrir : **this melon will rot if you don't eat it** ce melon va pourrir si tu ne le manges pas.

rotten [ˈrɒtn] *adjective*
1. **pourri** : **rotten bananas** des bananes pourries
2. *informal* **nul** *(feminine* **nulle***)* : **it was a rotten party** la fête était nulle
3. *informal* **mal fichu** : **I feel rotten this morning** je me sens mal fichu ce matin

> **that was a rotten thing to do!** c'est vache d'avoir fait ça !
> **what rotten weather!** quel temps pourri !

rough [rʌf] *adjective*

1. **rugueux** *(feminine **rugueuse**)* : **a rough surface** une surface rugueuse
2. **a rough road** une route cahoteuse
3. **agité** : **the sea is rough** la mer est agitée
4. **brutal** : **he's very rough with his sister** il est très brutal avec sa sœur
5. **dur, rude** : **he has had a rough life** il a eu une vie dure ; **the conditions were rough** les conditions étaient rudes OR les conditions étaient dures
6. **mal fréquenté** : **it's a rough neighbourhood** c'est un quartier mal fréquenté
7. **approximatif** *(feminine **approximative**)* : **this is a rough figure** c'est un chiffre approximatif
➤ **a rough copy** un brouillon.

roughly ['rʌflɪ] *adverb*

1. **à peu près** : **she won roughly 200 euros** elle a gagné à peu près 200 euros
2. **brutalement** : **he treats her roughly** il la traite brutalement.

round [raʊnd] *adjective, preposition, adverb & noun*

■ *adjective*
rond : **a round window** une fenêtre ronde
➤ **a round trip** un aller-retour : **I'd like a round trip between Boston and New York** je voudrais un aller-retour Boston-New York
■ *preposition UK*
autour de : **they're sitting round the table** ils sont assis autour de la table
➤ **it's just round the corner** c'est juste au coin de la rue
➤ **round here** par ici OR dans le coin
■ *adverb UK*
autour : **there are mountains all round** il y a des montagnes tout autour
➤ **round about** vers : **I'll be there round about 8** je serai là vers 8 heures
➤ **to turn round** se retourner
➤ **come round and see us** passez nous voir OR venez nous voir
■ *noun*
1. **série** *(feminine)* : **a round of talks** une série de négociations
2. **manche** : **in the first round of the competition** dans la première manche du concours
3. *In boxing* **round** *(masculine)* : **he was knocked out in the first round** il a été mis K-O au premier round
4. **tournée** : **the postman is doing his round** le facteur fait sa tournée
➤ **a round of ammunition** une cartouche
➤ **to give somebody a round of applause**

applaudir quelqu'un : **he got a round of applause** on l'a applaudi
➤ **a round of drinks** une tournée : **it's my round** c'est ma tournée.

roundabout *UK* ['raʊndəbaʊt] *noun*

1. **rond-point** *(masculine)* [*plural* **ronds-points**] : **to drive round a roundabout** faire le tour d'un rond-point
2. **manège** *(masculine)* : **the children had a go on the roundabout** les enfants ont fait un tour de manège.

rounders *UK* ['raʊndəz] *plural noun*

sport proche du baseball qui se pratique en Grande-Bretagne.

route [ruːt] *noun*

1. **itinéraire** *(masculine)*, **chemin** *(masculine)* : **they're planning the route** ils décident de l'itinéraire ; **the quickest route to Boston** le chemin le plus court pour aller à Boston
2. *US* **autoroute** *(feminine)* : **Route 66** l'autoroute 66.

routine [ruːˈtiːn] *noun*

1. **routine** *(feminine)* : **Thomas hates routine** Thomas déteste la routine
2. **habitudes** *(feminine plural)* : **it's part of my daily routine** ça fait partie de mes habitudes.

row *noun & verb*

■ *noun*
1. [rəʊ] **rangée** *(feminine)* : **a row of houses** une rangée de maisons
2. [rəʊ] **rang** *(masculine)* : **they are sitting in the second row** ils sont assis au deuxième rang
3. [rəʊ] : **in a row** d'affilée ; **he phoned her three times in a row** il lui a téléphoné trois fois d'affilée
4. [raʊ] **dispute** *(feminine)* : **they had a row** ils se sont disputés
5. [raʊ] **vacarme** *(masculine)* : **the class was making a terrible row** les élèves de la classe faisaient un vacarme épouvantable
■ *verb* [rəʊ]
1. **ramer** : **we're rowing against the current** nous ramons à contre-courant ; **they rowed across the river** ils ont traversé le fleuve à la rame
2. **faire de l'aviron** : **he rows every Saturday** il fait de l'aviron tous les samedis.

r

rowboat *US* ['rəubəut] *noun*

canot *(masculine)* **à rames**.

rowdy ['raʊdɪ] *adjective*

chahuteur *(feminine* **chahuteuse)* : **a rowdy class** une classe chahuteuse.

rowing ['rəʊɪŋ] *uncountable noun*

aviron *(masculine)* : **we go rowing once a week** nous faisons de l'aviron une fois par semaine

➤ **a rowing boat** *UK* un canot à rames.

royal ['rɔɪəl] *adjective*

royal *[plural* **royaux)** : **the royal family** la famille royale.

rub [rʌb] *(past tense & past participle* **rubbed)** *verb*

frotter : **don't rub so hard** ne frotte pas si fort ; **he rubbed his eyes** il s'est frotté les yeux

rub out *phrasal verb*

effacer : **she rubbed the word out** elle a effacé le mot.

rubber ['rʌbər] *noun*

1. **caoutchouc** *(masculine)* : **it's made of rubber** c'est en caoutchouc ; **a rubber ball** une balle en caoutchouc
2. *UK* **gomme** *(feminine)* : **can I borrow your rubber?** je peux t'emprunter ta gomme ?
➤ **a rubber band** un élastique.

rubbish *UK* ['rʌbɪʃ] *uncountable noun*

1. **ordures** *(feminine plural)* : **they collect the rubbish on Wednesdays** ils ramassent les ordures le mercredi
2. **camelote** *(feminine)* : **these shops sell a lot of rubbish** ces magasins vendent beaucoup de camelote
3. **bêtises** *(feminine plural)* : **you're talking rubbish!** tu dis des bêtises !
➤ **the film was rubbish** le film était nul
➤ **a rubbish bin** une poubelle
➤ **the rubbish dump** la décharge publique.

ruby ['ru:bɪ] *noun*

rubis *(masculine)* : **a ruby necklace** un collier de rubis ; **a ruby ring** une bague en rubis.

rucksack ['rʌksæk] *noun*

sac *(masculine)* **à dos**.

rude [ru:d] *adjective*

1. **impoli** : **she was rude to her mother** elle était impolie avec sa mère ; **it's rude to talk with your mouth full** c'est impoli de parler la bouche pleine
2. **grossier** *(feminine* **grossière)* : **a rude joke** une blague grossière ; **a rude word** un gros mot.

rug [rʌg] *noun*

tapis *(masculine)* : **there's a rug in front of the fireplace** il y a un tapis devant la cheminée.

rugby ['rʌgbɪ] *noun*

rugby *(masculine)* : **they're playing rugby** ils jouent au rugby.

ruin ['ru:ɪn] *verb & noun*

◼ *verb*

1. **abîmer** : **she ruined her blouse** elle a abîmé son chemisier
2. **gâcher** : **he ruined my party** il a gâché ma fête
3. **ruiner** : **the crash ruined him** le krach l'a ruiné
◼ *noun*

ruine *(feminine)* : **they have found the ruins of an old castle** ils ont découvert les ruines d'un vieux château
➤ **in ruins** en ruine OR en ruines.

rule [ru:l] *noun*

◼ *noun*

règle *(feminine)* : **what are the rules of the game?** quelles sont les règles du jeu ? ; **he broke the rules** il n'a pas respecté les règles
➤ **it's against the rules** c'est contraire au règlement
◼ *verb*

gouverner : **who is going to rule the country?** qui va gouverner le pays ?

rule out *phrasal verb*

exclure : **we can't rule out the possibility** nous ne pouvons pas exclure cette possibilité.

ruler ['ru:lər] *noun*

1. **règle** *(feminine)* : **use a ruler to measure the line** utilise une règle pour mesurer la ligne
2. **chef** *(masculine)* **d'État** : **the ruler of the country** le chef de l'État.

rum [rʌm] *noun*

rhum *(masculine)*.

rumour *UK*, **rumor** *US* ['ruːmər] *noun*

rumeur *(feminine)* : **it's just a rumour** ce n'est qu'une rumeur.

run [rʌn] *noun & verb*

◾ *noun*

1. **course** *(feminine)* **à pied** : **a five-mile run** une course à pied de huit kilomètres
2. **tour** *(masculine)* : **they went for a run in the car** ils ont fait un tour en voiture
3. **série** *(feminine)* : **a run of hits** une série de succès
4. *In cricket and baseball* **point** *(masculine)* : **he scored 4 runs** il a marqué 4 points
5. **piste** *(feminine)* : **a ski run** une piste de ski
▸ **to go for a run** aller courir : **she goes for a run every morning** elle va courir tous les matins
▸ **in the long run** à long terme
◾ *verb (past tense* **ran**, *past participle* **run)**

1. **courir** : **she ran 5 miles** elle a couru 8 kilomètres ; **he runs fast** il court vite ; **he ran in the 100 metres** il a couru le 100 mètres

> When 'run' is followed by a preposition like 'up', 'down' or 'across', it is often translated by another verb in French that shows the direction (**monter** = to go up, **descendre** = to go down or **traverser** = to cross) with **en courant** (= running) added at the end of the sentence:

he ran up the stairs il a monté l'escalier en courant ; **they're running down the hill** ils descendent la colline en courant ; **she ran across the road** elle a traversé la rue en courant
2. **diriger** : **she runs a big company** elle dirige une grande entreprise
3. **organiser** : **they run classes in computing** ils organisent des cours d'informatique
4. **faire couler** : **I'll run the bath** je vais faire couler le bain
5. **couler** : **my nose is running** j'ai le nez qui coule ; **you left the tap running** tu as laissé couler le robinet OR tu as laissé le robinet ouvert
6. **marcher, tourner** : **the bus runs on gas** le bus marche au gaz ; **the engine is running** le moteur tourne
7. **circuler** : **the trains don't run on Sundays** les trains ne circulent pas le dimanche
8. **déteindre** : **my T-shirt has run in the wash** mon tee-shirt a déteint au lavage
9. **filer** : **her tights have run** son collant a filé
10. **passer** : **she ran her hand through her hair** elle a passé la main dans ses cheveux

11. **conduire** : **he offered to run me to the station** il a proposé de me conduire à la gare
12. *US* **être candidat** : **Bush is running for president** Bush est candidat à la présidence

run away *phrasal verb*

s'enfuir : **the thieves ran away** les voleurs se sont enfuis
▸ **to run away from home** faire une fugue

run out *phrasal verb*

s'épuiser : **their supplies ran out** leurs provisions se sont épuisées
▸ **time's running out** il ne reste plus beaucoup de temps
▸ **I've run out of money** je n'ai plus d'argent

run over *phrasal verb*

renverser, écraser : **he was run over by a bus** il s'est fait renverser par un bus OR il s'est fait écraser par un bus ; **to get run over** se faire renverser OR se faire écraser.

rung *UK* [rʌŋ] *past participle of* **ring**

she hasn't rung me yet elle ne m'a pas encore téléphoné.

runner ['rʌnər] *noun*

coureur *(masculine)*, **coureuse** *(feminine)* : **there are ten runners in this race** il y a dix coureurs dans cette course.

runner bean *UK* [ˌrʌnərˈbiːn] *noun*

haricot *(masculine)* **vert**.

runner-up ['rʌnərˈʌp] *noun*

deuxième *(masculine or feminine)* : **she was runner-up in her category** elle a fini deuxième dans sa catégorie.

running ['rʌnɪŋ] *adjective & noun*

◾ *adjective*
de suite : **it happened three weeks running** cela s'est produit trois semaines de suite
◾ *uncountable noun*
course *(feminine)* **à pied** : **he goes running every day** il fait de la course à pied tous les jours.

runny ['rʌnɪ] *adjective*

▸ **to have a runny nose** avoir le nez qui coule : **I've got a runny nose** j'ai le nez qui coule.

runway ['rʌnweɪ] *noun*

piste *(feminine)* : **the plane is on the runway** l'avion est sur la piste.

r

rush [rʌʃ] *noun & verb*

◾ *noun*

hâte *(feminine)* : **to do something in a rush** faire quelque chose à la hâte

➤ **to be in a rush** être pressé : **I'm in a rush!** je suis pressé !

➤ **the rush hour** les heures de pointe

◾ *verb*

1. **se dépêcher** : **you'll have to rush if you want to catch the train** il faut que tu te dépêches si tu veux attraper le train

2. **se précipiter** : **I rushed towards the exit** je me suis précipité vers la sortie

3. **faire à la hâte** : **don't rush your work** ne fais pas ton travail à la hâte

➤ **she was rushed to hospital** elle a été transportée d'urgence à l'hôpital.

Russia [ˈrʌʃə] *noun*

la Russie

> In French the names of countries are used with the definite article (**le, la** or **l'**), except when they follow the preposition **en**:
>
> **the capital of Russia is Moscow** la capitale de la Russie est Moscou ; **they live in Russia** ils vivent en Russie ; **have you ever been to Russia?** tu es déjà allé en Russie ?

Russian [ˈrʌʃn] *adjective & noun*

◾ *adjective*

russe : **the Russian revolution** la révolution russe

◾ *noun*

1. **russe** *(masculine)* : **she speaks Russian** elle parle russe

2. **Russe** *(masculine or feminine)* : **the Russians** les Russes

> Remember not to use a capital letter for the adjective and the language in French. Only use a capital letter for the inhabitants.

rust [rʌst] *noun*

rouille *(feminine)* : **your bike is covered in rust** ton vélo est plein de rouille.

rusty [ˈrʌstɪ] *adjective*

rouillé : **a rusty old nail** un vieux clou rouillé ; **her Italian is rusty** son italien est rouillé.

rye [raɪ] *noun*

seigle *(masculine)* : **rye bread** pain de seigle.

sack [sæk] *noun & verb*

◾ *noun*

sac *(masculine)* : **a sack of potatoes** un sac de pommes de terre

➤ **to get the sack** *UK* être renvoyé

◾ *verb UK*

renvoyer : **he's been sacked** il a été renvoyé.

sad [sæd] *adjective*

triste : **she looks sad** elle a l'air triste.

saddle [ˈsædl] *noun*

selle *(feminine)* : **the cowboy climbed into the saddle** le cow-boy s'est mis en selle.

sadly [ˈsædlɪ] *adverb*

1. **tristement** : **he looked at me sadly** il m'a regardé tristement

2. **malheureusement** : **sadly she died** malheureusement elle est morte.

sadness [ˈsædnɪs] *noun*

tristesse *(feminine)* : **he was full of sadness** il éprouvait une grande tristesse.

safe [seɪf] *adjective & noun*

◾ *adjective*

1. **sans danger** : **it's safe to swim here** on peut se baigner ici sans danger

2. **hors de danger** : **he's safe now** il est hors de danger maintenant

3. **sain et sauf** *(feminine **saine et sauve**)* : **he came home safe** il est rentré sain et sauf

4. **sûr** : **this ladder isn't very safe** cette échelle n'est pas très sûre

5. **prudent** : **he's a safe driver** c'est un conducteur prudent

➤ **to feel safe** se sentir en sécurité

➤ **to be in a safe place** être en lieu sûr : **the jewels are in a safe place** les bijoux sont en lieu sûr

> **it's not safe** c'est dangereux

■ *noun*

coffre-fort *(masculine)* [*plural* **coffres-forts**] : **there's a lot of money in the safe** il y a beaucoup d'argent dans le coffre-fort.

safety ['seɪftɪ] *noun*

sécurité *(feminine)*

> **a safety belt** une ceinture de sécurité
> **a safety pin** une épingle de sûreté.

Sagittarius [ˌsædʒɪ'teərɪəs] *noun*

Sagittaire *(masculine)* : **Terry's a Sagittarius** Terry est Sagittaire.

said [sed] *past tense & past participle of* say

I said you were right j'ai dit que tu avais raison ; **she hasn't said anything** elle n'a rien dit.

sail [seɪl] *noun & verb*

■ *noun*

voile *(feminine)* : **a ship in full sail** un navire toutes voiles dehors

> **to set sail** prendre la mer : **they set sail at dawn** ils ont pris la mer à l'aube

■ *verb*

1. **naviguer** : **the boat is sailing to America** le bateau navigue vers l'Amérique
2. **prendre la mer** : **we sail tomorrow** nous prenons la mer demain.

sailboard *US* ['seɪlbɔːd] *noun*

planche *(feminine)* **à voile** : **you can hire the sailboards on the beach** on peut louer des planches à voile sur la plage.

sailboat *US* [seɪlbəʊt] *noun*

voilier *(masculine)*.

sailing ['seɪlɪŋ] *uncountable noun*

la voile : **he goes sailing at weekends** il fait de la voile le week-end

> **a sailing boat** *UK* un voilier.

sailor ['seɪlər] *noun*

marin *(masculine)* : **he's a sailor** il est marin.

saint [seɪnt] *noun*

saint *(masculine)*, **sainte** *(feminine)* : **Saint Catherine** sainte Catherine

> **Saint Andrew's Day** la Saint-André
> **Saint David's Day** la Saint-David
> **Saint Patrick's Day** la Saint-Patrick

SAINT ANDREW'S DAY & SAINT DAVID'S DAY

Le 1ᵉʳ mars, jour de la Saint-David, le saint patron du pays de Galles, on célèbre la fête nationale galloise. Beaucoup de Gallois portent pour l'occasion une jonquille à leur veste. En Écosse, la fête nationale est célébrée le 30 novembre, jour de la Saint-André, le saint patron écossais.

Le 1ᵉʳ mars et le 30 novembre ne sont cependant pas des jours fériés et ces fêtes ne sont pas de la même ampleur que la Saint-Patrick en Irlande.

SAINT PATRICK'S DAY

Le 17 mars est le jour de la Saint-Patrick, le saint patron de l'Irlande. Les Irlandais et les personnes d'origine irlandaise vivant à l'étranger accrochent un trèfle (l'emblème de l'Irlande) à leur veste ou s'habillent en vert (couleur qui symbolise l'Irlande). De grands défilés sont organisés à Dublin, Boston, Chicago, New York et Sydney.

sake [seɪk] *noun*

> **for somebody's sake** pour quelqu'un : **do it for my sake** fais-le pour moi.

salad ['sæləd] *noun*

salade *(feminine)* : **do you want some salad?** tu veux de la salade ? ; **a chicken salad** une salade au poulet

> **salad cream** *UK* sorte de mayonnaise douce
> **salad dressing** vinaigrette *(feminine)*.

salary ['sælərɪ] (*plural* salaries) *noun*

salaire *(masculine)*.

sale [seɪl] *noun*

soldes *(masculine plural)* : **Bloomingdale's is having a sale** il y a des soldes chez Bloomingdale's

> **in the sales** *UK* OR **on sale** *US* en solde : **I bought this coat in the sales** j'ai acheté ce manteau en solde

> **on sale** *UK* en vente : **it's on sale in all the bookshops** c'est en vente dans toutes les librairies

> **for sale** à vendre : **their house is for sale** leur maison est à vendre.

sales assistant *UK* ['seɪlzə'sɪstənt],

salesclerk *US* ['seɪlzklɜːrk] *noun*

vendeur *(masculine)*, **vendeuse** *(feminine)* : **he's a sales assistant** il est vendeur.

S

salesman ['seɪlzmən] (plural salesmen ['seɪlzmən]) noun
1. **représentant** (masculine) **de commerce :** he's an insurance salesman il est représentant en assurances
2. **vendeur** (masculine) **:** he's a salesman in a department store il est vendeur dans un grand magasin.

salmon ['sæmən] noun
saumon (masculine) **: smoked salmon** saumon fumé.

salon ['sælɒn] noun
salon (masculine) **: a beauty salon** un salon de beauté.

salt [sɔːlt, sɒlt] noun
sel (masculine) **: can you pass me the salt?** tu peux me passer le sel ?

salty ['sɔːltɪ] adjective
salé : it's too salty c'est trop salé.

salute [sə'luːt] verb
saluer : the general saluted le général a salué.

same [seɪm] adjective & pronoun
même : she's wearing the same sweater as I am elle porte le même pull que moi ; **we left at the same time** nous sommes partis en même temps
➤ **the same**
1. **le même** (feminine **la même**) [plural **les mêmes**] **: she has the same one as me** elle a le même que moi
2. **la même chose : I'll have the same as you** je prendrai la même chose que toi
➤ **to look the same** se ressembler : **they all look the same** ils se ressemblent tous
➤ **it's not the same** ce n'est pas pareil
➤ **thanks all the same** merci tout de même.

sand [sænd] uncountable noun
sable (masculine)
➤ **a sand castle** un château de sable : **she's building sand castles** elle fait des châteaux de sable
➤ **a sand dune** une dune.

sandal ['sændl] noun
sandale (feminine) **: she's wearing sandals** elle porte des sandales.

sandwich [UK 'sænwɪdʒ, US 'sænwɪtʃ] (plural sandwiches) noun
sandwich (masculine) **: a cheese sandwich** un sandwich au fromage.

sang [sæŋ] past tense of sing
he sang a song il a chanté une chanson.

sanitary towel UK ['sænɪtrɪ'taʊəl], **sanitary napkin** US ['sænɪtrɪ'næpkɪn] noun
serviette (feminine) **hygiénique**.

sank [sæŋk] past tense of sink
the boat sank le bateau a sombré.

Santa Claus ['sæntə‚klɔːz] noun
le père Noël : do you believe in Santa Claus? tu crois au père Noël ?

sardine [sɑː'diːn] noun
sardine (feminine) **: a tin of sardines** une boîte de sardines.

sat [sæt] past tense & past participle of sit
he sat down il s'est assis.

satchel ['sætʃəl] noun
cartable (masculine).

satellite ['sætəlaɪt] noun
satellite (masculine) **: satellite TV** la télévision par satellite
➤ **a satellite dish** une antenne parabolique.

satisfied ['sætɪsfaɪd] adjective
satisfait : I'm not satisfied with your work je ne suis pas satisfait de ton travail.

Saturday ['sætədɪ] noun
samedi (masculine) **: it's Saturday today** nous sommes samedi ; **next Saturday** samedi prochain ; **last Saturday** samedi dernier
➤ **on Saturday** samedi : **I'll see you on Saturday** on se voit samedi
➤ **on Saturdays** le samedi : **he comes to see me on Saturdays** il vient me voir le samedi

In French the days of the week do not start with a capital letter.

sauce [sɔːs] noun
sauce (feminine) **: tomato sauce** sauce tomate.

saucepan ['sɔːspən] noun
casserole (feminine) **: she's cooking rice in a

saucepan elle fait cuire du riz dans une casse-role.

sauna ['sɔːnə] *noun*

sauna *(masculine)* : **he had a sauna** il est allé au sauna.

sausage ['sɒsɪdʒ] *noun*

saucisse *(feminine)*
➤ **a sausage roll** *UK* un feuilleté à la saucisse.

save [seɪv] *verb*

1. sauver : **she saved my life** elle m'a sauvé la vie

2. mettre de côté : **I've saved a hundred pounds** j'ai mis cent livres de côté

3. économiser : **we must try and save water** il faut économiser l'eau ; **you'll save $2** tu feras une économie de 2 dollars

4. garder : **he saved the cake for later** il a gardé le gâteau pour plus tard

5. sauvegarder : **I've saved my file onto a floppy** j'ai sauvegardé mon fichier sur une disquette
➤ **to save time** gagner du temps : **that will save you a lot of time** cela te fera gagner beaucoup de temps

save up *phrasal verb*

mettre de l'argent de côté : **he's saving up to buy a guitar** il met de l'argent de côté pour s'acheter une guitare.

savings ['seɪvɪŋz] *plural noun*

économies *(feminine plural)* : **she has spent all her savings** elle a dépensé toutes ses économies.

savoury *UK,* **savory** *US* ['seɪvərɪ] *adjective*

salé : **I prefer savoury foods to sweet foods** je préfère le salé au sucré.

saw [sɔː] *noun, verb & verb form*

■ *noun*
scie *(feminine)* : **a power saw** une scie mécanique

■ *verb (past tense* sawed, *past participle* sawn *UK OR* sawed *US)*
scier : **he sawed the plank in half** il a scié la planche en deux

■ *past tense of* see
I saw him yesterday je l'ai vu hier.

sawn *UK* [sɔːn] *past participle of* saw

he's sawn the plank il a scié la planche.

saxophone ['sæksəfəʊn] *noun*

saxophone *(masculine)* : **she plays the saxophone** elle joue du saxophone.

say [seɪ] *(past tense & past participle* said*) verb*

dire : **what did you say?** qu'est-ce que tu as dit ? ; **I said I was tired** j'ai dit que j'étais fatigué
➤ **could you say that again?** pouvez-vous répéter ?

saying ['seɪɪŋ] *noun*

dicton *(masculine)* : **it's a well-known saying** c'est un dicton connu.

scale [skeɪl] *noun*

1. échelle *(feminine)* : **this map has a scale of 1/100** cette carte est à l'échelle 1/100

2. ampleur *(feminine)* : **the scale of the damage** l'ampleur des dégâts

3. gamme *(feminine)* : **she's practising her scales** elle fait ses gammes

scales *plural noun*

balance *(feminine)* : **put your luggage on the scales** mets tes bagages sur la balance
➤ **bathroom scales** pèse-personne *(masculine)*.

scampi ['skæmpɪ] *uncountable noun*

scampi *(masculine plural)* : **scampi and chips** des scampi avec des frites.

scan [skæn] *noun & verb*

■ *noun*
scanner *(masculine)* : **she had a scanner** elle a passé un scanner

■ *verb (past tense & past participle* scanned*)*
scanner : **I scanned the photo** j'ai passé la photo au scanner.

scandal ['skændl] *noun*

scandale *(masculine)* : **it caused a scandal** cela a provoqué un scandale.

scanner ['skænər] *noun*

scanner *(masculine)* : **put the photo in the scanner** mets la photo dans le scanner.

scar [skɑːr] *noun*

cicatrice *(feminine)* : **he has a scar on his arm** il a une cicatrice au bras.

scare [skeər] *noun & verb*

■ *noun*

S

peur *(feminine)* : **you gave me a scare** tu m'as
fait peur
➤ **a bomb scare** une alerte à la bombe
▪ *verb*
faire peur à : she scares me elle me fait peur.

scarecrow ['skeəkrəʊ] *noun*

épouvantail *(masculine)*.

scared ['skeəd] *adjective*

➤ **to be scared** avoir peur : **I was scared of
him** j'avais peur de lui ; **I'm not scared of flying** je n'ai pas peur de prendre l'avion.

scarf [skɑːf] *(plural* scarfs [skɑːfs] OR
scarves [skɑːvz]) *noun*
1. **écharpe** *(feminine)* : **a woolen scarf** une
écharpe en laine
2. **foulard** *(masculine)* : **a silk scarf** un foulard en
soie

> There are two ways of translating 'scarf' into
> French. Use **écharpe** for a long scarf and **foulard**
> for a square scarf.

scarves *plural of* scarf.

scary [skeərɪ] *adjective informal*

➤ **to be scary** faire peur : **it's a scary film**
c'est un film qui fait peur.

scene [siːn] *noun*
1. **scène** *(feminine)* : **act 3, scene 2** acte 3, scène
2 ; **there is a very funny scene in the film** il y
a une scène très amusante dans le film
2. **lieu** *(masculine)* *[plural* lieux] : **the scene of the
crime** le lieu du crime
➤ **on the scene** sur les lieux : **the police were
quickly on the scene** la police est vite arrivée
sur les lieux
➤ **behind the scenes** dans les coulisses.

scenery ['siːnərɪ] *uncountable noun*

paysage *(masculine)* : **I love the scenery in
this part of the country** j'adore le paysage
dans cette région.

schedule [*UK* 'ʃedjuːl, *US* 'skedʒʊl] *noun*

programme *(masculine)* : **I have a busy
schedule** j'ai un programme chargé
➤ **we're on schedule** nous sommes à l'heure
➤ **we're ahead of schedule** nous sommes
en avance
➤ **we're behind schedule** nous sommes en
retard.

scheme [skiːm] *noun*

1. **projet** *(masculine)* : **a scheme for recycling
papers** un projet de recyclage de journaux
2. **combine** *(feminine)* : **it's a scheme to make
money** c'est une combine pour faire de l'argent.

scholarship ['skɒləʃɪp] *noun*

bourse *(feminine)* : **he got a scholarship** il a
obtenu une bourse.

school [skuːl] *noun*

1. **école** *(feminine)* : **all children have to go to
school up to the age of 16** tous les enfants
doivent aller à l'école jusqu'à l'âge de 16 ans
2. *School for children between 11 and 14*
collège *(masculine)*
3. *School for children between 15 and 18*
lycée *(masculine)*
➤ **a school bus** un car de ramassage scolaire
➤ **the school year** l'année scolaire

SCHOOL
En Grande-Bretagne, les enfants vont
d'abord à la **primary school**, de 5 ans à 11 ans, ou
à la **infant school**, de 5 à 7 ans, puis à la **junior
school**, de 7 à 11 ans. Les élèves âgés de 11 à
16 ans (ou de 11 à 18 ans) fréquentent l'école secondaire, la **secondary school**.
Aux États-Unis, les enfants vont d'abord à l'**elementary school** (ou **grade school** ou **grammar
school**) de 6 à 12 ans, puis à la **junior high school**, de
12 à 14 ans, et ensuite à la **high school** à partir de
14 ans. Le C.P. correspond au **year 1** en Grande-
Bretagne et au **1st grade** aux États-Unis. L'équivalent de la terminale est le **year 13** en Grande-
Bretagne et le **12th grade** aux États-Unis.
Dans les deux pays, les écoles privées (**private
schools**) sont assez répandues. Attention, en
Grande-Bretagne, les plus prestigieuses d'entre
elles sont appelées **public schools** ! Les écoles publiques sont appelées **state schools** en Grande-
Bretagne et **public schools** aux États-Unis.

schoolbook ['skuːlbʊk] *noun*

livre *(masculine)* **scolaire** : **don't forget your
schoolbooks** n'oublie pas tes livres de classe.

schoolchildren ['skuːltʃɪldrən] *plural noun*

écoliers *(masculine plural)*.

science ['saɪəns] *noun*

science *(feminine)* : **science and technology**
science et technologie ; **Chris wants to study
science** Chris veut étudier les sciences

> **science fiction** science-fiction *(feminine)* : **it's a science fiction book** c'est un livre de science-fiction.

scientific [ˌsaɪən'tɪfɪk] *adjective*

scientifique : **this method isn't very scientific** cette méthode n'est pas très scientifique.

scientist ['saɪəntɪst] *noun*

scientifique *(masculine or feminine)* : **she's a scientist** c'est une scientifique.

scissors ['sɪzəz] *plural noun*

ciseaux *(masculine plural)* : **have you got any scissors?** est-ce que tu as des ciseaux ?
> **a pair of scissors** une paire de ciseaux.

scone *UK* [skɒn] *noun*

scone *(masculine)* : **scones, jam and cream are a speciality in Devon** les scones avec de la confiture et de la crème sont une des spécialités du Devon.

scoop [skuːp] *noun*

boule *(feminine)* : **three scoops of ice cream** trois boules de glace.

scooter ['skuːtər] *noun*

1. **trottinette** *(feminine)* : **a lot of peole use scooters to get around** beaucoup de gens se déplacent en trottinette
2. **scooter** *(masculine)* : **he prefers a scooter to a motorcycle** il préfère le scooter à la moto.

score [skɔːr] *noun & verb*

■ *noun*
score *(masculine)* : **what's the score?** où en est le score ?

■ *verb*
marquer : **he scored a goal** il a marqué un but ; **they haven't scored yet** ils n'ont pas encore marqué.

Scorpio ['skɔːpɪəʊ] *noun*

Scorpion *(masculine)* : **Patrick's a Scorpio** Patrick est Scorpion.

scorpion ['skɔːpjən] *noun*

scorpion *(masculine)* : **some scorpion bites can be fatal** la piqûre de certains scorpions peut être mortelle.

Scot [skɒt] *noun*

Écossais *(masculine)*, **Écossaise** *(feminine)*.

Scotland ['skɒtlənd] *noun*

l'Écosse *(feminine)*

In French the names of countries are used with the definite article (**le la** or **l'**), except when they follow the preposition **en**:

Scotland is part of the United Kingdom l'Écosse fait partie du Royaume-Uni ; **Loch Ness is in Scotland** le Loch Ness se trouve en Écosse ; **Mary's going to Scotland** Mary va en Écosse.

Scottish ['skɒtɪʃ] *adjective*

écossais

The French adjective does not start with a capital letter:

the Scottish Parliament le parlement écossais.

scout [skaʊt] *noun*

scout *(masculine)* : **he's a scout** il est scout.

scrambled eggs ['skræmbldegz] *plural noun*

œufs *(masculine plural)* **brouillés** : **he has scrambled eggs in the morning** il mange des œufs brouillés le matin.

scrap paper *UK* [skræp'peɪpər], **scratch paper** *US* [skrætʃ'peɪpər] *noun*

papier *(masculine)* **brouillon** .

scratch [skrætʃ] *noun & verb*

■ *noun*
1. **égratignure** *(feminine)* : **my legs are covered with scratches** mes jambes sont couvertes d'égratignures
2. **rayure** *(feminine)* : **there's a scratch on this CD** ce CD est rayé
> **to start from scratch** partir de zéro : **we'll just have to start from scratch** il faut partir de zéro

■ *verb*
1. **gratter** : **can you scratch my back?** est-ce que tu peux me gratter le dos ?
2. **se gratter** : **don't scratch** ne te gratte pas ; **he was scratching his leg** il se grattait la jambe
3. **griffer** : **the cat scratched my hand** le chat m'a griffé la main.

scratch paper *US* > scrap paper.

scream [skriːm] *noun & verb*

■ *noun*

S

cri (*masculine*) : **I could hear screams** j'entendais des cris
- *verb*

  crier : **she screamed when the vampire appeared** elle a crié quand le vampire est apparu.

screen [skri:n] *noun*

écran (*masculine*) : **it's a good film to see on the big screen** c'est un bon film à voir sur le grand écran ; **Pauline corrects her work on screen** Pauline corrige son travail à l'écran.
➤ **a screen saver** un économiseur d'écran.

screw [skru:] *noun & verb*
- *noun*

  vis (*feminine*) : **he went to buy some screws** il est allé acheter des vis
- *verb*

  visser : **you have to screw the mirror to the wall** il faut visser la glace au mur ; **I screwed the top on the bottle** j'ai vissé le bouchon de la bouteille.

screwdriver ['skru:ˌdraɪvəʳ] *noun*

tournevis (*masculine*).

scroll [skrəʊl] *verb*

faire dérouler : **scroll down to the end of the document** fais dérouler le document jusqu'à la fin.

scruffy ['skrʌfɪ] *adjective*

négligé : **he looks scruffy** il a un air négligé.

sculptor ['skʌlptəʳ] *noun*

sculpteur (*masculine*) : **Rodin was a sculptor** Rodin était sculpteur.

sculpture ['skʌlptʃəʳ] *noun*

sculpture (*feminine*) : **an exhibition of modern sculptures** une exposition de sculptures modernes.

sea [si:] *noun*

mer (*feminine*) : **I like swimming in the sea** j'aime bien nager dans la mer
➤ **by the sea** au bord de la mer : **St Ives is by the sea** St Ives est au bord de la mer.

seafood ['si:fu:d] *uncountable noun*

fruits (*masculine plural*) **de mer** : **Frances loves seafood** Frances adore les fruits de mer.

seagull ['si:gʌl] *noun*

mouette (*feminine*) : **seagulls live by the sea or by rivers** les mouettes vivent au bord de la mer ou au bord des fleuves.

seal [si:l] *noun & verb*
- *noun*

  phoque (*masculine*) : **seals are mammals that live in cold waters** les phoques sont des mammifères qui vivent dans les eaux froides
- *verb*

  cacheter : **have you sealed the envelope yet?** as-tu cacheté l'enveloppe ?

search [sɜ:tʃ] *noun & verb*
- *noun*

1. (*plural* searches) fouille (*feminine*) : **the police carried out a search** la police a procédé à une fouille

2. recherches (*feminine plural*) : **there was a search for the missing boy** on a fait des recherches pour retrouver le garçon porté disparu
➤ **a search engine** un moteur de recherche
➤ **a search party** une équipe de secours
- *verb*

1. fouiller : **the police searched the house** la police a fouillé la maison

2. chercher dans : **we searched the whole town** nous avons cherché partout dans la ville ; **I searched my bag** j'ai cherché dans mon sac

search for *phrasal verb*

chercher : **I'm searching for my keys** je cherche mes clés.

seashell ['si:ʃel] *noun*

coquillage (*masculine*) : **she collected a lot of seashells** elle a ramassé beaucoup de coquillages.

seasick ['si:sɪk] *adjective*
➤ **to be seasick** avoir le mal de mer : **she was seasick** elle a eu le mal de mer.

seaside ['si:saɪd] *noun*

le bord de la mer : **we're going to the seaside** nous allons au bord de la mer.

season ['si:zn] *noun*

saison (*feminine*) : **it's the rainy season** c'est la saison des pluies
➤ **a season ticket** une carte d'abonnement : **I'm going to get a season ticket** je vais prendre un abonnement.

seat [si:t] *noun*

1. siège (*masculine*) : **your bag's on the back seat of the car** ton sac est sur le siège arrière de la voiture

2. place *(feminine)* : **is this seat free?** est-ce que cette place est libre ? ; **I've reserved two seats for the play** j'ai réservé deux places pour la pièce

➤ **a seat belt** une ceinture de sécurité : **fasten your seat belts** attachez vos ceintures de sécurité.

seaweed ['siːwiːd] *uncountable noun*

algues *(feminine plural)* : **seaweed grows at the bottom of rivers, lakes and the sea** les algues poussent au fond des fleuves, des lacs et de la mer.

second ['sekənd] *adjective & noun*

■ *adjective*

deuxième : **that's the second time he has rung** c'est la deuxième fois qu'il appelle

➤ **it's the second of June** *UK* OR **it's June second** *US* nous sommes le deux juin

➤ **on the second floor**

1. *UK* au deuxième étage

2. *US* au premier étage

➤ **to come second** arriver deuxième : **he came second in the marathon** il est arrivé deuxième au marathon

■ *noun*

seconde *(feminine)* : **wait a second!** attendez une seconde !

➤ **to have seconds** se resservir : **can I have seconds?** je peux me resservir ?

secondary school [*UK* 'sekəndrɪskuːl, *US* 'sekənderɪskuːl] *noun*

école *(feminine)* secondaire.

second-class [ˌsekənd'klɑːs] *adjective*

de seconde classe : **a second-class ticket** un billet de seconde classe ; **we travelled second-class** nous avons voyagé en seconde classe

➤ **second-class mail** courrier *(masculine)* à tarif réduit.

second-hand [ˌsekənd'hænd] *adjective & adverb*

d'occasion : **it's a second-hand bike** c'est un vélo d'occasion ; **I bought it second-hand** je l'ai acheté d'occasion.

secret ['siːkrɪt] *adjective & noun*

■ *adjective*

secret *(feminine* secrète*)* : **it's a secret meeting place** c'est un lieu de rendez-vous secret

■ *noun*

secret *(masculine)* : **he can't keep a secret** il ne sait pas garder un secret

➤ **we met in secret** nous nous sommes retrouvés en secret.

secretary [*UK* 'sekrətrɪ, *US* 'sekrəterɪ] *(plural* secretaries*)* noun

secrétaire *(masculine or feminine)* : **Penny's a secretary** Penny est secrétaire.

section ['sekʃn] *noun*

1. partie *(feminine)* : **there are three sections to the newspaper** le journal a trois parties

2. rayon *(masculine)* : **where is the food section of the store?** où est le rayon alimentation du magasin ?

security [sɪ'kjʊərətɪ] *noun*

sécurité *(feminine)* : **security at the airport has been tightened** la sécurité à l'aéroport a été renforcée

➤ **a security guard** un garde.

see [siː] *(past tense* saw, *past participle* seen*)* verb

voir : **I saw Jack yesterday** j'ai vu Jack hier ; **have you seen any good films recently?** as-tu vu de bons films récemment ? ; **I can't see** je ne vois rien ; **I'll see what I can do** je vais voir ce que je peux faire

➤ **we'll see** on verra

➤ **see you soon!** à bientôt !

➤ **see you!** salut !

see off *phrasal verb*

dire au revoir à : **he saw me off at the airport** il est venu me dire au revoir à l'aéroport

see to *phrasal verb*

s'occuper de : **I can't close the door – I'll see to it** je n'arrive pas à fermer la porte – je m'en occuperai.

seed [siːd] *noun*

1. graine *(feminine)* : **she planted some sunflower seeds** elle a planté des graines de tournesol

2. tête *(feminine)* de série : **he's number two seed in the tournament** il est tête de série numéro deux au tournoi.

seek [siːk] *(past tense & past participle* sought*)* verb

chercher : **we're seeking a solution** nous cherchons une solution.

seem [siːm] *verb*

1. sembler : **you seem to be having problems**

tu sembles avoir des problèmes ; **there seems
to be a delay** il semble qu'il y ait du retard
2. **avoir l'air : she seems sad** elle a l'air triste ;
they seem bored ils ont l'air de s'ennuyer.

seen [siːn] *past participle of* see

I have never seen an elephant je n'ai jamais
vu d'éléphant.

seesaw ['siːsɔː] *noun*

bascule *(feminine)* : **the children were playing on the seesaw** les enfants jouaient à la
bascule.

Seine [seɪn] *noun*

Seine *(feminine)* : **the Seine flows through the
heart of Paris** la Seine coule au cœur de Paris.

seize [siːz] *verb*

saisir : she seized my arm elle m'a saisi le
bras.

select [sɪ'lekt] *adjective*

**sélectionner : she selected the CD she
wanted** elle a sélectionné le CD qu'elle voulait.

selection [sɪ'lekʃn] *noun*

1. **sélection** *(feminine)* : **you've made a good
selection** tu as fait une bonne sélection
2. **choix** *(masculine)* : **there's a good selection of
food in the market** ils ont un bon choix de
fruits au marché.

self-confident [ˌself'kɒnfɪdənt] *adjective*

sûr de soi : Kim's very self-confident Kim
est très sûre d'elle.

self-conscious [ˌself'kɒnʃəs] *adjective*

**mal à l'aise : I feel very self-conscious in
my red hat** je me sens très mal à l'aise avec
mon chapeau rouge.

self-control [ˌselfkən'trəʊl] *noun*

sang-froid *(masculine invariable)* : **he lost his
self-control** il a perdu son sang-froid.

self-defence *UK*, **self-defense** [ˌself-
dɪ'fens] *noun*

autodéfense *(feminine)* : **a course in self-
defence** un cours d'autodéfense
➤ **in self-defence** en état de légitime défense : **she shot him in self-defence** elle a tiré
sur lui en état de légitime défense.

selfish ['selfɪʃ] *adjective*

égoïste : he's very selfish il est très égoïste.

self-service [ˌself'sɜːvɪs] *noun*

self-service *(masculine)* : **it's a self-service**
c'est un self-service
➤ **a self-service restaurant** un restaurant
self-service
➤ **a self-service shop** un libre-service.

sell [sel] *(past tense & past participle* sold*)* *verb*

1. **vendre : he's trying to sell his computer** il
essaie de vendre son ordinateur ; **I sold him
my bike** je lui ai vendu mon vélo ; **she sold it
for 100 pounds** elle l'a vendu 100 livres
2. **se vendre : his book is selling well** son livre
se vend bien

sell out *phrasal verb*

all the tickets are sold out tous les billets
sont vendus ; **we're sold out of coffee** nous
n'avons plus de café.

Sellotape® *UK* ['seləteɪp] *noun*

Scotch® : **have you got any Sellotape?** est-
ce que tu as du Scotch ?

semester *US* [sɪ'mestə^r] *noun*

semestre *(masculine)* : **the course lasts two
semesters** le cours dure deux semestres.

semicircle ['semɪsɜːkl] *noun*

demi-cercle *(masculine)*.

semicolon [ˌsemɪ'kəʊlən] *noun*

point-virgule *(masculine)* : **a semicolon is
used to separate parts of a long sentence**
on utilise le point-virgule pour séparer les parties d'une longue phrase.

semidetached house *UK* [ˌsemɪ-
dɪ'tætʃthaʊs] *noun*
maison *(feminine)* **jumelée : they live in a
semidetached house** ils habitent dans une
maison jumelée.

semifinal [ˌsemɪ'faɪnl] *noun*

demi-finale *(feminine)* : **Ireland are in the
semifinal** l'Irlande est en demi-finale.

Senate *US* ['senɪt] *noun*

the Senate le Sénat

SENATE
Le Sénat constitue, avec la Chambre
des représentants, l'organe législatif américain :
le Congrès. Les 100 sénateurs (deux par État)
sont élus pour six ans. Toute nouvelle loi doit être
votée par les membres des deux Chambres du

Congrès, mais le Sénat détient davantage de pouvoir en matière de politique étrangère.

senator *US* ['senətər] *noun*

sénateur *(masculine)* : **he's the senator of New York** c'est le sénateur de New York.

send [send] *(past tense & past participle* sent) *verb*

envoyer : **he sent me a letter** il m'a envoyé une lettre

> **send them my love** embrasse-les pour moi
> **to send somebody home** renvoyer quelqu'un chez lui

send back *phrasal verb*

renvoyer : **if you don't want it, you can send it back** si tu ne le veux pas, tu peux le renvoyer

send for *phrasal verb*

appeler, faire venir : **I sent for the doctor** j'ai appelé le médecin OR j'ai fait venir le médecin

send off *phrasal verb*

expulser : **Lomu has been sent off** Lomu a été expulsé.

senior ['si:njər] *adjective & noun*

■ *adjective*

haut placé : **these are senior people in the government** ce sont des gens haut placés dans le gouvernement

> **a senior citizen** une personne âgée
> **senior pupils** *UK élèves des grandes classes*
> **senior year** *US* terminale *(feminine)* : **Raoul's in his senior year** Raoul est en terminale

■ *noun*

> **the seniors**
1. *UK* les élèves des grandes classes
2. *US* les élèves de terminale.

sense [sens] *noun*

1. sens *(masculine)* : **what you say doesn't make sense** ce que tu dis n'a pas de sens ; **the five senses** les cinq sens
2. bon sens : **you have no sense** tu manques de bon sens

> **that makes sense** c'est logique : **he's leaving – that makes sense** il part – c'est logique
> **a sense of humour** le sens de l'humour : **she doesn't have a sense of humour** elle n'a aucun sens de l'humour

> **the sense of smell** l'odorat *(masculine)*
> **the sense of touch** le toucher.

sensible ['sensəbl] *adjective*

raisonnable : **she's very sensible** elle est très raisonnable

⚠ Le mot anglais **sensible** est un faux ami, il ne signifie pas "sensible".

sensitive ['sensɪtɪv] *adjective*

sensible : **he's a sensitive boy** c'est un garçon sensible

> **to be sensitive about something** être susceptible à propos de quelque chose : **she's sensitive about her weight** elle est susceptible à propos de son poids.

sent [sent] *past tense & past participle of* send

I sent my brother a birthday card j'ai envoyé une carte d'anniversaire à mon frère ; **she hasn't sent me the invitation back yet** elle ne m'a pas encore renvoyé l'invitation.

sentence ['sentəns] *noun & verb*

■ *noun*

phrase *(feminine)* : **a sentence should begin with a capital letter and end with a full stop** une phrase doit commencer par une majuscule et finir par un point

■ *verb*

condamner : **he was sentenced to five years in prison** on l'a condamné à cinq ans de prison.

separate *adjective & verb*

■ *adjective* ['seprət]

1. autre : **put it in a separate envelope** mets-le dans une autre enveloppe
2. différent : **these are two separate issues** ce sont deux problèmes différents
3. séparé : **can we have separate receipts?** pouvons-nous avoir des reçus séparés ?
4. à soi : **she has a separate room** elle a sa propre chambre ; **we have our separate rooms** nous avons chacun notre chambre

■ *verb* ['separeɪt]

1. séparer : **they separated the boys from the girls** ils ont séparé les garçons des filles
2. se séparer : **they separated after ten years of marriage** ils se sont séparés après dix ans de mariage.

September [sep'tembər] *noun*

septembre *(masculine)* : **school starts in Sep-**

tember l'école commence en septembre ;
next September en septembre prochain ; **last
September** en septembre dernier

> In French the months of the year do not start with
> a capital letter.

sequel ['si:kwəl] *noun*

suite *(feminine)* : **have you seen the sequel to
the film?** as-tu vu la suite du film ?

sergeant ['sɑːdʒənt] *noun*

1. **sergent** *(masculine)* : **he's a sergeant in the
army** il est sergent dans l'armée de terre
2. **brigadier** *(masculine)* : **he's a police sergeant**
il est brigadier.

serial ['sɪərɪəl] *noun*

feuilleton *(masculine)* : **it's a TV serial** c'est un
feuilleton télévisé.

series ['sɪəriːz] *(plural* series*) noun*

série *(feminine)* : **we've had a series of problems** nous avons eu une série de problèmes
> **The World Series** *US* le championnat de
base-ball.

serious ['sɪərɪəs] *adjective*

1. **sérieux** *(feminine* **sérieuse***)* : **he always looks
serious** il a toujours l'air sérieux
2. **grave** : **she has a serious illness** elle a une
maladie grave.

seriously ['sɪərɪəslɪ] *adverb*

1. **sérieusement** : **seriously, what do you
think?** sérieusement, qu'est-ce que tu en
penses ?
2. **grièvement** : **he was seriously injured** il a
été grièvement blessé.

serve [sɜːv] *verb*

servir : **dinner is served at 7 o'clock** le dîner
est servi à 7 heures ; **it's Williams to serve**
c'est à Williams de servir
> **that serves you right** c'est bien fait pour
toi.

service ['sɜːvɪs] *noun*

1. **service** *(masculine)* : **the service is good in
this restaurant** le service est bien dans ce restaurant ; **service is included** le service est
compris
2. **révision** *(feminine)* : **I'm going to take the car
for a service** je vais emmener la voiture à la
révision
> **a service provider** un fournisseur d'accès

> **a service station** une station-service.

session ['seʃn] *noun*

séance *(feminine)* : **a recording session** une
séance d'enregistrement.

set [set] *noun, adjective & verb*

▪ *noun*
1. **jeu** *(masculine)* [*plural* **jeux**] : **a set of keys** un jeu
de clés ; **a chess set** un jeu d'échecs
2. **collection** *(feminine)* : **a set of encyclopedias**
une collection d'encyclopédies
3. **service** *(masculine)* : **a china dinner set** un
service de table en porcelaine
4. *In tennis* **set** *(masculine)* : **Sampras won the
first set** Sampras a gagné le premier set
> **a television set** un poste de télévision
▪ *adjective*
1. **fixe** : **a set menu** un menu à prix fixe
2. **prêt** : **they were set to leave** ils étaient prêts
à partir
▪ *verb* (*past tense & past participle* **set**)
1. **poser, mettre** : **she set the vase on the
table** elle a posé le vase sur la table ; **he set
his bike against the wall** il a mis son vélo
contre le mur
2. **mettre** : **I'll set the alarm for 6 a.m.** je vais
mettre le réveil à 6 heures ; **set the oven at
150** mets le four à 150
3. **programmer** : **have you set the video?** as-
tu programmé le magnétoscope ?
4. **fixer** : **let's set a time and a place** fixons une
heure et un endroit
5. **établir** : **he set a new world record** il a établi un nouveau record mondial
6. **se coucher** : **the sun's setting** le soleil se
couche
> **to set somebody free** libérer quelqu'un
> **to set something on fire** mettre le feu à
quelque chose
> **to set something going** mettre quelque
chose en marche
> **to set the table** mettre le couvert OR mettre
la table
> **to set a trap** tendre un piège
> **the film's set in Casablanca** le film se dé-
roule à Casablanca

set off *phrasal verb*

1. **partir, se mettre en route** : **they set off at
dawn** ils sont partis à l'aube OR ils se sont mis
en route à l'aube
2. **faire partir** : **they set some fireworks off** ils
ont fait partir des feux d'artifice

3. faire exploser : **they set the bomb off** ils ont fait exploser la bombe

4. déclencher : **the burglar set the alarm off** le cambrioleur a déclenché l'alarme

set out *phrasal verb*

partir, se mettre en route

set up *phrasal verb*

1. créer : **he set up a new business** il a créé une nouvelle entreprise

2. installer : **he set the computer up in his room** il a installé l'ordinateur dans sa chambre

3. monter : **set the tent up in the garden** monte la tente dans le jardin.

set square ['setskweə^r] *noun*

équerre *(feminine)*.

settee [se'ti:] *noun*

canapé *(masculine)* : **he was sitting on the settee** il était assis sur le canapé.

settle ['setl] *verb*

1. régler : **we settled the argument** nous avons réglé la dispute ; **may I settle the bill?** je peux régler l'addition ?

2. s'installer : **they settled in Canada** ils se sont installés au Canada

➤ **that's settled** c'est décidé

settle down *phrasal verb*

1. se calmer : **settle down!** calmez-vous !

2. s'installer : **she settled down in the arm-chair** elle s'est installée dans le fauteuil.

seven ['sevn] *number*

sept : **the seven wonders of the word** les sept merveilles du monde ; **she's seven** elle a sept ans ; **he went out at seven** il est sorti à sept heures.

seventeen [ˌsevn'ti:n] *number*

dix-sept : **there are seventeen girls in the class** il y a dix-sept filles dans la classe ; **she's seventeen** elle a dix-sept ans.

seventeenth [ˌsevn'ti:nθ] *number*

dix-septième : **it's her seventeenth birthday** c'est son dix-septième anniversaire

➤ **it's the seventeenth of May** *UK* or **it's May seventeenth** *US* nous sommes le dix-sept mai.

seventh ['sevnθ] *number*

septième : **on the seventh floor** au septième étage

➤ **it's the seventh of November** *UK* or **it's November seventh** *US* nous sommes le sept novembre.

seventy ['sevntɪ] *number*

soixante-dix : **she's seventy** elle a soixante-dix ans

➤ **seventy-one** soixante-et-onze

➤ **seventy-two** soixante-douze.

several ['sevrəl] *adjective & pronoun*

■ *adjective*

plusieurs : **she called me several times** elle m'a appelé plusieurs fois

■ *pronoun*

plusieurs : **he ate several of them** il en a mangé plusieurs.

sew [səʊ] (*past tense* sewed, *past participle* sewn or sewed) *verb*

coudre : **do you know how to sew?** tu sais coudre ? ; **she sewed the button on** elle a cousu le bouton.

sewing ['səʊŋ] *uncountable noun*

couture *(feminine)*

➤ **a sewing machine** une machine à coudre.

sewn [səʊn] *past participle of* sew

he hasn't sewn the button on il n'a pas cousu le bouton.

sex [seks] *noun*

sexe *(masculine)* : **there were young people of both sexes** il y avait des jeunes gens des deux sexes

➤ **to have sex** avoir des rapports sexuels

➤ **to have sex with somebody** coucher avec quelqu'un.

sexist ['seksɪst] *adjective*

sexiste : **don't be sexist** ne sois pas sexiste.

sexy ['seksɪ] *adjective*

informal sexy *(invariable)* : **she was wearing a sexy dress** elle portait une robe sexy.

shade [ʃeɪd] *noun*

1. ombre *(feminine)* : **I was sitting in the shade** j'étais assis à l'ombre ; **it's 30 degrees in the shade** il fait 30 degrés à l'ombre

2. teinte *(feminine)* : **choose another shade of green** choisis une autre teinte de vert.

shadow ['ʃædəʊ] *noun*

ombre *(feminine)* : **I saw a shadow on the wall** j'ai vu une ombre sur le mur.

S

shake [ʃeɪk] (*past tense* shook, *past participle* shaken) *verb*

1. **secouer : shake the tree to make the apples fall** secouez l'arbre pour faire tomber les pommes

2. **agiter : you have to shake the bottle first** il faut d'abord agiter la bouteille

3. **trembler : my legs are shaking** j'ai les jambes qui tremblent ; **she's shaking with cold** elle tremble de froid

➤ **to shake hands with somebody** serrer la main à quelqu'un : **we shook hands** nous nous sommes serré la main

➤ **to shake one's head** faire non de la tête : **I asked if she was coming and she shook her head** je lui ai demandé si elle venait et elle a fait non de la tête.

shaken [ˈʃeɪkn] *past participle of* shake

I've shaken the rug j'ai secoué le tapis ; **have you shaken the orange juice?** as-tu agité le jus d'orange ?

Shakespeare [ˈʃeɪkspɪəʳ] *noun*

Shakespeare

> SHAKESPEARE
> Le dramaturge et poète William Shakespeare (1564-1616), né à Stratford-upon-Avon, est considéré comme le plus grand écrivain de la langue anglaise. Parmi ses pièces les plus célèbres, on peut citer ses tragédies **Hamlet, Macbeth, Romeo and Juliet** (Roméo et Juliette), ses comédies **A Midsummer Night's Dream** (Le Songe d'une nuit d'été), ou **Much Ado about Nothing** (Beaucoup de bruit pour rien) ou encore ses œuvres historiques **Julius Caesar** (Jules César) et **Richard III**. Shakespeare, à la fois auteur dramatique et comédien, jouait dans ses propres pièces.

shall [ʃəl, ʃæl] *verb*

1. *The future tense* **I shall see him tomorrow** je le verrai demain ; **we shall be late** nous serons en retard

2. *Making suggestions* **shall I open the window?** est-ce que j'ouvre la fenêtre ? OR j'ouvre la fenêtre ? ; **shall we have a game of tennis?** et si on jouait au tennis ? ; **let's go, shall we?** on y va ?

shallow [ˈʃæləʊ] *adjective*

peu profond : the river is shallow here la rivière est peu profonde ici.

shame [ʃeɪm] *noun*

honte *(feminine)* : **he put me to shame** il m'a fait honte

➤ **it's a shame** c'est dommage : **it's a shame that you lost** c'est dommage que tu aies perdu

➤ **what a shame!** quel dommage !

shampoo [ʃæmˈpuː] *noun*

shampooing *(masculine)* : **she bought some shampoo** elle a acheté du shampooing.

shamrock [ˈʃæmrɒk] *noun*

trèfle *(masculine)* : **the shamrock is an emblem of the Republic of Ireland** le trèfle est l'un des emblèmes de la République d'Irlande.

shan't *UK* [ʃɑːnt] = shall not

I shan't be long je n'en ai pas pour longtemps ; **we shan't be able to come** nous ne pourrons pas venir.

shape [ʃeɪp] *noun*

forme *(feminine)* : **a cake in the shape of a heart** un gâteau en forme de cœur

➤ **to be in good shape** être en forme : **he's in good shape** il est en forme.

share [ʃeəʳ] *noun & verb*

■ *noun*
part *(feminine)* : **I didn't get my share** je n'ai pas eu ma part

■ *verb*
partager : I share a room with him je partage une chambre avec lui ; **we shared the cake** nous avons partagé le gâteau.

shares [ʃeəʳz] *plural noun*

actions *(feminine plural)* : **we have shares in the company** nous avons des actions dans la société.

shark [ʃɑːk] *noun*

requin *(masculine)* : **these waters are full of sharks** ces eaux sont pleines de requins ; **not all sharks are dangerous** tous les requins ne sont pas dangereux.

sharp [ʃɑːp] *adjective & adverb*

■ *adjective*

1. **tranchant : a sharp knife** un couteau tranchant

2. **pointu : a sharp needle** une aiguille pointue

3. **brusque : a sharp rise in prices** une brusque hausse des prix

4. **intelligent : he's very sharp** il est très intelligent

■ *adverb*
at eight o'clock sharp à huit heures pile.

shave [ʃeɪv] *noun & verb*

■ *noun*
to have a shave se raser ; **you need a shave** tu as besoin de te raser

■ *verb*
se raser : **he shaves every day** il se rase tous les jours ; **he shaved off his beard** il s'est rasé la barbe.

shaver [ˈʃeɪvər] *noun*
rasoir *(masculine)* : **an electric shaver** un rasoir électrique.

shaving cream [ˈʃeɪvɪŋkriːm] *noun*
crème *(feminine)* à raser.

shaving foam [ˈʃeɪvɪŋfəʊm] *noun*
mousse *(feminine)* à raser.

shawl [ʃɔːl] *noun*
châle *(masculine)* : **she's wearing a shawl** elle porte un châle.

she [ʃiː] *pronoun*
elle : **she's called Eileen** elle s'appelle Eileen ; **she came to see me** elle est venue me voir
➤ **she's a clever woman** c'est une femme intelligente
➤ **there she is!** la voilà !

shed [ʃed] *noun*
remise *(feminine)* : **there's a shed in the garden** il y a une remise dans le jardin.

she'd [ʃɪd, ʃiːd]
1. = **she had** : **she'd forgotten to bring her camera** elle avait oublié d'amener son appareil photo
2. = **she would** : **she'd like to come with us** elle aimerait venir avec nous.

sheep [ʃiːp] *(plural* **sheep***) noun*
mouton *(masculine)* : **there are a lot of sheep in New Zealand** il y a beaucoup de moutons en Nouvelle-Zélande.

sheet [ʃiːt] *noun*
1. drap *(masculine)* : **the sheets are clean** les draps sont propres
2. feuille *(feminine)* : **give me a sheet of paper** passe-moi une feuille de papier.

shelf [ʃelf] *(plural* **shelves** [ʃelvz]*) noun*
1. étagère *(feminine)* : **I put the book on the shelf** j'ai posé le livre sur l'étagère
2. rayon *(masculine)* : **the supermarket shelves are empty** les rayons du supermarché sont vides.

shell [ʃel] *noun*
1. coquillage *(masculine)* : **there are lots of shells on the beach** il y a beaucoup de coquillages sur la plage
2. carapace *(feminine)* : **the turtle has a very big shell** la tortue a une très grande carapace
3. coquille *(feminine)* : **the shell of the egg** la coquille de l'œuf
4. obus *(masculine)* : **the shell exploded in the field** l'obus a explosé dans le champ.

she'll [ʃiːl] = **she will** OR **she shall**
she'll be here soon elle va bientôt arriver.

shelter [ˈʃeltər] *noun & verb*

■ *noun*
abri *(masculine)* : **we were looking for shelter** nous cherchions un abri
➤ **to take shelter** se mettre à l'abri : **he took shelter from the storm** il s'est mis à l'abri de la tempête

■ *verb*
se mettre à l'abri : **where can we shelter from the rain?** où est-ce qu'on peut se mettre à l'abri de la pluie ?

shelves *plural of* **shelf**.

shepherd [ˈʃepəd] *noun*
berger *(masculine)*.

shepherd's pie [ˈʃepədzˈpaɪ] *noun*
hachis *(masculine)* **Parmentier**.

sheriff *US* [ˈʃerif] *noun*
shérif *(masculine)* : **he's the sheriff of Great Rock** c'est le shérif de Great Rock.

she's [ʃiːz]
1. = **she is** : **she's happy to be here** elle est contente d'être ici
2. = **she has** : **she's taken my pen** elle a pris mon stylo.

shield [ʃiːld] *noun*
bouclier *(masculine)* : **the soldiers used shields to protect themselves** les soldats utilisaient des boucliers pour se protéger.

S

shin [ʃɪn] *noun*

tibia *(masculine)* : **I've hurt my shin** je me suis fait mal au tibia.

shine [ʃaɪn] *(past tense & past participle* shone) *verb*

briller : **the sun is shining** le soleil brille

➤ **to shine a torch on something** diriger une lampe sur quelque chose : **she shone the torch on the bush** elle a dirigé la lampe sur le buisson.

shiny ['ʃaɪnɪ] *adjective*

brillant : **a shiny metal object** un objet métallique brillant.

ship [ʃɪp] *noun*

navire *(masculine)* : **the ship sank** le navire a coulé

➤ **we went by ship** nous avons pris le bateau

➤ **a sailing ship** un bateau à voiles.

shipwreck ['ʃɪprek] *noun*

naufrage *(masculine)* : **they died in a shipwreck** ils ont péri dans un naufrage.

shipwrecked ['ʃɪprekt] *adjective*

➤ **to be shipwrecked** faire naufrage : **we were shipwrecked close to the coast of Africa** nous avons fait naufrage près de la côte africaine.

shirt [ʃɜːt] *noun*

chemise *(feminine)* : **he was wearing a shirt and tie** il portait une chemise et une cravate.

shiver ['ʃɪvəʳ] *verb*

1. grelotter : **it's so cold she's shivering** il fait si froid qu'elle grelotte

2. frissonner : **she heard the scream and shivered** elle a frissonné en entendant le cri.

shock [ʃɒk] *noun & verb*

■ *noun*

1. choc *(masculine)* : **I got a shock when I heard the news** j'ai eu un choc quand j'ai appris la nouvelle

2. décharge *(feminine)* : **he got an electric shock** il a reçu une décharge électrique

■ *verb*

1. choquer : **his behaviour shocked me** OR **I was shocked by his behaviour** son comportement m'a choqué

2. bouleverser : **her death shocked us** sa mort nous a bouleversés.

shocking ['ʃɒkɪŋ] *adjective*

choquant : **his attitude is shocking** son attitude est choquante.

shoe [ʃuː] *noun*

chaussure *(feminine)* : **put your shoes on!** mets tes chaussures ! ; **I took my shoes off** j'ai enlevé mes chaussures

➤ **a pair of shoes** une paire de chaussures

➤ **a shoe shop** un magasin de chaussures.

shoelace ['ʃuːleɪs] *noun*

lacet *(masculine)* : **your shoelace is undone** ton lacet est défait.

shone [ʃɒn] *past tense & past participle of* shine

the sun shone all day le soleil a brillé toute la journée.

shook [ʃʊk] *past tense of* shake

she shook the blanket elle a secoué la couverture ; **he shook his head** il a fait non de la tête.

shoot [ʃuːt] *(past tense & past participle* shot) *verb*

1. tirer : **where did you learn to shoot?** où as-tu appris à tirer ?

2. tuer d'un coup de feu : **he was shot and killed in a robbery** il a été tué d'un coup de feu dans un hold-up

3. fusiller : **they shot him at dawn** ils l'ont fusillé à l'aube

4. tourner : **they shot the film in New Zealand** ils ont tourné le film en Nouvelle-Zélande

➤ **she was shot in the arm** elle a reçu une balle dans le bras.

shop [ʃɒp] *noun*

magasin *(masculine)* : **I'm going to the shop to buy some milk** je vais au magasin acheter du lait

➤ **a shop assistant** *UK* un vendeur, une vendeuse : **she's a shop assistant** elle est vendeuse

➤ **a shop window** une vitrine : **she was looking in the shop window** elle regardait dans la vitrine.

shopkeeper *UK* ['ʃɒpˌkiːpəʳ] *noun*

commerçant *(masculine)*, commerçante *(feminine)* : **her father's a shopkeeper** son père est commerçant.

shopping ['ʃɒpɪŋ] *uncountable noun*

courses *(feminine plural)*

➤ **to go shopping** aller faire les courses : **he**

goes shopping every Friday il va faire les courses tous les vendredis

➤ a shopping bag un sac à provisions

➤ a shopping centre *UK* OR a shopping center OR a shopping mall *US* un centre commercial.

shore [ʃɔːʳ] *noun*

rivage *(masculine)* : **we were walking on the shore** on se promenait sur le rivage.

short [ʃɔːt] *adjective*

1. **court** : **Sam has short hair** Sam a les cheveux courts ; **it's a short film** c'est un film court
2. **petit** : **he's very short** il est très petit
➤ **Dan is short for Daniel** Dan est le diminutif de Daniel ; **they call him Bob for short** Bob est son diminutif.

shortcut [ˈʃɔːtkʌt] *noun*

raccourci *(masculine)* : **she took the shortcut** elle a pris le raccourci

➤ **a shortcut key** une touche de raccourci.

shortly [ˈʃɔːtlɪ] *adverb*

bientôt : **I'll see you again shortly** je te reverrai bientôt.

shorts [ʃɔːts] *plural noun*

short *(masculine)* : **he was wearing shorts** il portait un short

➤ **in shorts** en short : **he was in shorts** il était en short.

shortsighted *UK* [ˌʃɔːtˈsaɪtɪd] *adjective*

myope : **he's shortsighted** il est myope.

shot [ʃɒt] *noun & verb form*

▢ *noun*

1. **coup** *(masculine)* **de feu** : **we heard shots** nous avons entendu des coups de feu
2. **photo** *(feminine)* : **this is a nice shot** c'est une bonne photo
➤ **good shot!** bien joué !
▢ *past tense & past participle of* shoot
he shot the bird il a tiré sur l'oiseau ; **he was shot in the leg** il a reçu une balle dans la jambe.

shotgun [ˈʃɒtɡʌn] *noun*

fusil *(masculine)* **de chasse**.

should [ʃʊd] *verb*

'Should' is translated by the verb **devoir** in the conditional tense:

you should go tu devrais y aller ; **should I phone him?** est-ce que je devrais l'appeler ? ; **she should be home soon** elle devrait bientôt être de retour ; **they should have won the match** ils auraient dû gagner le match.

shoulder [ˈʃəʊldəʳ] *noun*

épaule *(feminine)* : **he put his arm around her shoulder** il a mis son bras autour de son épaule

➤ **a shoulder bag** un sac à bandoulière.

shouldn't [ˈʃʊdnt] = should not

I shouldn't be here je ne devrais pas être ici ; **you shouldn't have come** tu n'aurais pas dû venir.

should've [ˈʃʊdəv] = should have

you should've waited tu aurais dû attendre.

shout [ʃaʊt] *noun & verb*

▢ *noun*
cri *(masculine)* : **I heard a shout** j'ai entendu un cri
▢ *verb*
crier : **stop shouting** arrête de crier ; **he was shouting at me** il criait après moi.

show [ʃəʊ] *noun & verb*

▢ *noun*

1. **spectacle** *(masculine)* : **we're going to see a show on Broadway** nous allons voir un spectacle à Broadway
2. **émission** *(feminine)* : **it's a live television show** c'est une émission de télévision en direct
3. **exposition** *(feminine)* : **an art show** une exposition d'art
▢ *verb* (*past tense* showed [ʃəʊd], *past participle* shown [ʃəʊn] OR showed)
1. **montrer** : **I showed them the photos** je leur ai montré les photos ; **he showed me how to do it** il m'a montré comment faire
2. **indiquer** : **can you show me the way?** pouvez-vous m'indiquer le chemin ?
3. **faire preuve de** : **they showed a lot of courage** ils ont fait preuve de beaucoup de courage
4. **passer** : **they are going to show the film tomorrow** ils vont passer le film demain

show off *phrasal verb*

frimer : **he's always showing off** il n'arrête pas de frimer

S

show up phrasal verb

arriver : **she hasn't shown up yet** elle n'est pas encore arrivée.

shower [ˈʃaʊəʳ] noun

1. **douche** (feminine) : **he's in the shower** il est sous la douche

2. **averse** (feminine) : **it's not raining much, it's only a shower** il ne pleut pas beaucoup, ce n'est qu'une averse

➤ **to have a shower** prendre une douche : **I'm going to have a shower** je vais prendre une douche.

shown [ʃəʊn] past participle of show

he has shown me the photos il m'a montré les photos.

show-off [ˈʃəʊɒf] noun

frimeur (masculine), **frimeuse** (feminine) : **he's a show-off** c'est un frimeur.

shrank [ʃræŋk] past tense of shrink

my jeans shrank mon jean a rétréci.

shrimp [ʃrɪmp] noun

crevette (feminine) : **a shrimp cocktail** un cocktail de crevettes.

shrink [ʃrɪŋk] (past tense shrank, past participle shrunk) verb

rétrécir : **this material shrinks** ce tissu rétrécit.

Shrove Tuesday [UK ˌʃrəʊvˈtjuːzdɪ, US ˌʃrəʊvˈtuːzdɪ] noun
Mardi (masculine) **gras**.

shrug [ʃrʌg] (past tense & past participle shrugged) verb

➤ **to shrug one's shoulders** hausser les épaules : **he shrugged his shoulders** il a haussé les épaules.

shrunk [ʃrʌŋk] past participle of shrink

this dress has shrunk cette robe a rétréci.

shuffle [ˈʃʌfl] verb

➤ **to shuffle the cards** battre les cartes.

shut [ʃʌt] adjective & verb

▪ adjective
fermé : **the window is shut** la fenêtre est fermée

▪ verb (past tense & past participle shut)
1. **fermer** : **she shut the door** elle a fermé la porte ; **the bank shuts at four** la banque ferme à quatre heures

2. **se fermer** : **the door shut behind me** la porte s'est fermée derrière moi

shut up phrasal verb

se taire : **will you shut up!** tais-toi !

shutter [ˈʃʌtəʳ] noun

volet (masculine) : **close the shutters** fermez les volets.

shuttle [ˈʃʌtl] adjective

navette (feminine) : **a space shuttle** une navette spatiale.

shy [ʃaɪ] adjective

timide : **he's very shy** il est très timide.

sick [sɪk] adjective

malade : **he's not at school because he's sick** il n'est pas à l'école parce qu'il est malade

➤ **to be sick** UK vomir : **she was sick** elle a vomi

➤ **to feel sick** UK avoir envie de vomir : **do you feel sick?** tu as envie de vomir ?

➤ **to be sick of something** informal en avoir marre de quelque chose : **I'm sick of your lies** j'en ai marre de tes mensonges.

side [saɪd] noun

1. **côté** (masculine) : **the school is on the other side of the road** l'école est de l'autre côté de la rue ; **his dog stood by his side** son chien se tenait à côté de lui

2. **bord** (masculine) : **there's a house by the side of the river** il y a une maison au bord de la rivière

3. **équipe** (feminine) : **our side won the match** notre équipe a gagné le match

➤ **side by side** côte à côte : **they were walking side by side** ils marchaient côte à côte

➤ **to be on somebody's side** être du côté de quelqu'un : **are you on my side?** tu es de mon côté ?

➤ **to take sides** prendre parti.

sideboard [ˈsaɪdbɔːd] noun

buffet (masculine) : **she put the plates in the sideboard** elle a rangé les assiettes dans le buffet.

sideboards UK [ˈsaɪdbɔːdz], **sideburns** [ˈsaɪdbɜːnz] plural noun

pattes (feminine plural) : **he has sideburns** il a des pattes.

sidewalk *US* ['saɪdwɔːk] *noun*

trottoir *(masculine)* : **I was walking on the sidewalk** je marchais sur le trottoir.

sideways ['saɪdweɪz] *adverb*

de côté : **crabs walk sideways** les crabes marchent de côté.

sigh [saɪ] *noun & verb*

▪ *noun*
soupir *(masculine)* : **he gave a sigh of relief** il a poussé un soupir de soulagement
▪ *verb*
soupirer.

sight [saɪt] *noun*

vue *(feminine)* : **I have good sight** j'ai une bonne vue ; **he faints at the sight of blood** il s'évanouit à la vue du sang ; **I've lost sight of her** je l'ai perdue de vue ; **at first sight** à première vue

➤ **out of sight** hors de vue : **I can't see him, he's out of sight** je ne le vois pas, il est hors de vue

➤ **to catch sight of** apercevoir : **I caught sight of the pyramids** j'ai aperçu les pyramides

➤ **I know him by sight** je le connais de vue

➤ **what a funny sight!** quel tableau !

sights [saɪts] *plural noun*

attractions *(feminine plural)* **touristiques** : **we went to see the sights of Sydney** nous sommes allés visiter Sydney.

sightseeing ['saɪtˌsiːɪŋ] *noun*

tourisme *(masculine)* : **let's go sightseeing** allons faire du tourisme.

sign [saɪn] *noun & verb*

▪ *noun*
I. **signe** *(masculine)* : **Harry made a sign to me** Harry m'a fait signe ; **the victory sign** le signe de la victoire
2. **panneau** *(masculine)* [*plural* **panneaux**] : **follow the signs to the station** suivez les panneaux qui indiquent la gare
▪ *verb*
signer : **can you sign here, please?** pouvez-vous signer ici, s'il vous plaît ?

signal ['sɪgnl] *noun*

signal *(masculine)* : **the teacher gave them the signal to start** le professeur leur a donné le signal du départ.

signature ['sɪgnətʃər] *noun*

signature *(feminine)* : **I can't read the signature** je n'arrive pas à lire la signature.

significant [sɪg'nɪfɪkənt] *adjective*

important : **it's a significant discovery** c'est une découverte importante.

signpost ['saɪnpəʊst] *noun*

panneau *(masculine)* **indicateur** [*plural* **panneaux indicateurs**] : **there's a signpost pointing to the village** il y a un panneau qui indique le village.

Sikh [siːk] *adjective & noun*

▪ *adjective*
sikh *(invariable)*

> The French adjective does not start with a capital letter:

the Sikh religion la religion sikh
▪ *noun*
Sikh *(masculine or feminine)* : **Tarseem's a Sikh** Tarseem est Sikh.

silence ['saɪləns] *noun*

silence *(masculine)* : **a sudden noise broke the silence** un bruit soudain a rompu le silence.

silent ['saɪlənt] *adjective*

silencieux *(masculine)*, **silencieuse** *(feminine)* : **they kept silent** ils sont restés silencieux
➤ **a silent film** un film muet.

silicon chip [ˌsɪlɪkən'tʃɪp] *noun*

puce *(feminine)* **électronique** : **silicon chips carry a complicated electronic circuit** les puces électroniques comportent des circuits électroniques compliqués.

silk [sɪlk] *noun*

soie *(feminine)* : **it's made of silk** c'est en soie
➤ **a silk blouse** un chemisier en soie.

silly ['sɪlɪ] *adjective*

bête : **don't be silly!** ne sois pas bête !

silver ['sɪlvər] *adjective*

argent *(masculine)* : **it's made of silver** c'est en argent
➤ **a silver bracelet** un bracelet en argent.

similar ['sɪmɪlər] *adjective*

semblable : **these two bags are similar** ces deux sacs sont semblables
➤ **to be similar to something** ressembler à

S

quelque chose : **her coat's similar to mine**
son manteau ressemble au mien.

simple ['sɪmpl] *adjective*

simple : **it's a simple question** c'est une
question simple.

sin [sɪn] *noun*

péché *(masculine)* : **it's a sin to lie** mentir est
un péché.

since [sɪns] *preposition, conjunction & adverb*

■ *preposition*

depuis : **it's been raining since Sunday** il
pleut depuis dimanche ; **I've lived in France
since 1990** je vis en France depuis 1990 ;
she'd been waiting since 7 p.m. elle attendait depuis 7 heures ; **I haven't seen him
since last year** je ne l'ai pas vu depuis l'année
dernière

> The tenses used in French with **depuis** are not al-
> ways the same as those used with 'since' in Eng-
> lish. In positive sentences the French use the
> present tense where we use the present perfect
> to show that something is still going on, and the
> imperfect where we use the past perfect.

■ *conjunction*

1. **depuis que** : **I've known him since I was 10**
je le connais depuis que j'ai 10 ans
2. **comme, puisque** : **since it's raining, we
might as well stay at home** comme il pleut,
autant rester à la maison OR puisqu'il pleut,
autant rester à la maison
■ *adverb*
depuis : **I haven't seen her since** je ne l'ai
pas vue depuis.

sincere [sɪn'sɪər] *adjective*

sincère.

sincerely [sɪn'sɪəlɪ] *adverb*

> **Yours sincerely** *UK* OR **Sincerely yours**
US veuillez agréer, Madame, Monsieur, mes
salutations distinguées.

sing [sɪŋ] *(past tense* sang, *past participle* sung*)*
verb
chanter : **he sang a song** il a chanté une
chanson ; **she sings well** elle chante bien.

singer ['sɪŋər] *noun*

chanteur *(masculine)*, chanteuse *(feminine)* :
he's a singer il est chanteur.

singing ['sɪŋɪŋ] *uncountable noun*

chant *(masculine)* : **singing lessons** des cours
de chant.

single ['sɪŋgl] *adjective & noun*

■ *adjective*
1. **seul** : **there isn't a single book in their house**
il n'y a pas un seul livre dans leur maison
2. **célibataire** : **she's single** elle est célibataire
■ *noun*
1. **single** *(masculine)* : **their latest single is on
the album** leur dernier single est sur l'album
2. *UK* **aller** *(masculine)* **simple** : **can I have a
single to Birmingham, please?** un aller sim-
ple pour Birmingham, s'il vous plaît
> **a single bed** un lit à une place
> **the single currency** la monnaie unique
> **in single file** en file indienne : **they were
walking in single file** ils étaient en file indienne
> **a single parent** un père célibataire, une
mère célibataire : **she's a single parent** elle
est mère célibataire
> **a single ticket** *UK* un billet simple : **a sin-
gle ticket to Cambridge** un billet simple pour
Cambridge
> **the men's singles** le simple hommes.

singular ['sɪŋgjʊlər] *noun*

singulier *(masculine)* : **put this noun in the
singular** mettez ce nom au singulier.

sink [sɪŋk] *noun & verb*

■ *noun*
1. **évier** *(masculine)* : **the dishes are in the sink** la
vaisselle est dans l'évier
2. **lavabo** *(masculine)* : **she was washing her
hands in the bathroom sink** elle se lavait les
mains dans le lavabo de la salle de bain
■ *verb (past tense* sank, *past participle* sunk*)*
1. **couler** : **the Titanic sank in 1912** le Titanic a
coulé en 1912
2. **s'enfoncer** : **our feet sank into the mud** nos
pieds se sont enfoncés dans la boue.

sip [sɪp] *(past tense & past participle* sipped
[sɪpt]*) verb*
boire à petites gorgées : **he was sipping
his orange juice** il buvait son jus d'orange à
petites gorgées.

sir [sɜːr] *noun*

monsieur *(masculine)* : **excuse me, sir**
excusez-moi, monsieur ; **yes, sir!** oui, monsieur !

➤ **Dear Sir, ...** Monsieur, ...

sister [ˈsɪstəʳ] *noun*

sœur *(feminine)* : **he has two sisters** il a deux sœurs.

sister-in-law [ˈsɪstəʳɪnlɔː] *noun*

belle-sœur *(feminine)* [*plural* belles-sœurs].

sit [sɪt] (*past tense & past participle* sat, *present participle* sitting) *verb*

1. s'asseoir : **come and sit here** viens t'asseoir ici

2. *UK* passer : **he sat the exam last week** il a passé l'examen la semaine dernière

➤ **to be sitting** être assis : **Vicky was sitting on the floor** Vicky était assise par terre

sit down *phrasal verb*

s'asseoir : **sit down!** assieds-toi ! ; **he sat down in the armchair** il s'est assis dans le fauteuil.

site [saɪt] *noun*

1. site *(masculine)* : **have you visited the BBC site?** tu as visité le site de la BBC ? ; **an archaeological site** un site archéologique

2. chantier *(masculine)* : **Bill works on a building site** Bill travaille sur un chantier.

sitting room [ˈsɪtɪŋruːm] *noun*

salon *(masculine)* : **there's a television in the sitting room** il y a une télévision dans le salon.

situation [ˌsɪtjʊˈeɪʃn] *noun*

situation *(feminine)* : **we're in a difficult situation** nous sommes dans une situation difficile.

six [sɪks] *number*

six : **there are six states in Australia** l'Australie a six États ; **he's six** il a six ans ; **we went out at six** nous sommes sortis à six heures.

sixteen [sɪksˈtiːn] *number*

seize : **there are sixteen boys in the class** il y a seize garçons dans la classe ; **he's sixteen** il a seize ans.

sixteenth [sɪksˈtiːnθ] *number*

seizième : **it's his sixteenth birthday** c'est son seizième anniversaire

➤ **it's the sixteenth of June** *UK* OR **it's June sixteenth** *US* nous sommes le seize juin.

sixth [sɪksθ] *number*

sixième : **on the sixth floor** au sixième étage

➤ **it's the sixth of January** *UK* OR **it's January sixth** *US* nous sommes le six janvier

➤ **the sixth form** *UK* la classe de terminale : **she's in the sixth form** elle est en terminale.

sixty [ˈsɪkstɪ] *number*

soixante : **she's sixty** elle a soixante ans

➤ **sixty-one** soixante et un

➤ **sixty-two** soixante-deux.

size [saɪz] *noun*

1. taille *(feminine)* : **the two rooms are the same size** les deux pièces sont de la même taille ; **what size are you?** quelle taille faites-vous ? ; **I'm a size 40** je fais du 40

2. pointure *(feminine)* : **what shoe size do you take?** vous faites quelle pointure ? OR vous chaussez du combien ? ; **I take a size 5 shoe** je chausse du 38.

skate [skeɪt] *noun*

patin *(masculine)* : **I'm getting some new skates** je vais avoir de nouveaux patins.

skateboard [ˈskeɪtbɔːd] *noun*

skateboard *(masculine)*.

skating [ˈskeɪtɪŋ] *noun*

➤ **to go skating** faire du patin à glace : **we go skating on the lake in winter** nous faisons du patin à glace sur le lac en hiver

➤ **a skating rink** une patinoire.

skeleton [ˈskelɪtn] *noun*

squelette *(masculine)* : **there's a skeleton in the cupboard** il y a un squelette dans le placard.

sketch [sketʃ] *noun & verb*

◾ *noun*

croquis *(masculine)* : **I drew a sketch** j'ai fait un croquis

◾ *verb*

faire un croquis de : **he sketched the Eiffel Tower** il a fait un croquis de la tour Eiffel.

sketchpad [ˈsketʃpæd] *noun*

bloc *(masculine)* à croquis.

ski [skiː] *noun & verb*

◾ *noun*

ski *(masculine)* : **he's wearing skis** il porte des skis

➤ **ski boots** chaussures *(feminine plural)* de ski

S

➤ **a ski lift** un remonte-pente : **let's take the ski lift** prenons le remonte-pente
➤ **a ski pole** un bâton de ski
➤ **a ski slope** une piste de ski
■ *verb* (*past tense & past participle* skied, *present participle* skiing)
skier : she's learning how to ski elle apprend à skier.

skid [skɪd] (*past tense & past participle* skidded)
verb
déraper.

skier ['skiːəʳ] *noun*
skieur (*masculine*), **skieuse** (*feminine*) : **she's a good skier** elle est bonne skieuse.

skies *plural of* sky.

skiing ['skiːɪŋ] *uncountable noun*
ski (*masculine*) : **he's having skiing lessons** il prend des leçons de ski
➤ **to go skiing** faire du ski : **they go skiing every week** ils font du ski toutes les semaines.

skilful *UK*, **skillful** *US* ['skɪlfʊl] *adjective*
adroit : he's a skilful player c'est un joueur adroit.

skill [skɪl] *noun*
1. **habileté** (*feminine*) : **a surgeon needs great skill** un chirurgien doit faire preuve d'une grande habileté
2. **compétence** (*feminine*) : **she has many skills** elle a de nombreuses compétences.

skillful *US* ➤ skilful *UK*.

skimmed milk ['skɪmdmɪlk] *noun*
lait (*masculine*) **écrémé : a bottle of skimmed milk, please** une bouteille de lait écrémé, s'il vous plaît.

skin [skɪn] *noun*
peau (*feminine*) : **she has fair skin** elle a la peau claire
➤ **a banana skin** une peau de banane.

skinny ['skɪnɪ] *adjective*
maigre : he's too skinny il est trop maigre.

skin-tight ['skɪntaɪt] *adjective*
moulant : she was wearing skin-tight jeans elle portait un jean moulant.

skip [skɪp] (*past tense & past participle* skipped [skɪpt]) *verb*

1. **sauter : she skipped breakfast** elle a sauté le petit déjeuner
2. **sécher : he skipped his class** il a séché son cours
3. *UK* **sauter à la corde : can you skip?** tu sais sauter à la corde ?

skipping rope *UK* ['skɪpɪŋrəʊp] *noun*
corde (*feminine*) **à sauter.**

skirt [skɜːt] *noun*
jupe (*feminine*) : **Diana's wearing a red skirt** Diana porte une jupe rouge.

skull [skʌl] *noun*
crâne (*masculine*) : **this helmet is to protect your skull** ce casque sert à te protéger le crâne.

sky [skaɪ] (*plural* skies [skaɪz]) *noun*
ciel (*masculine*) : **the sky's blue** le ciel est bleu ; **look in the sky** regarde dans le ciel
➤ **sky blue** bleu ciel : **the walls are sky blue** les murs sont bleu ciel.

skylight ['skaɪlaɪt] *noun*
lucarne (*feminine*).

skyscraper ['skaɪˌskreɪpəʳ] *noun*
gratte-ciel (*masculine*) [*plural* gratte-ciel] : **the skyscrapers of New York** les gratte-ciel de New York.

slam [slæm] (*past tense & past participle* slammed [slæmd]) *verb*
claquer : I slammed the door j'ai claqué la porte ; **the door slammed** la porte a claqué.

slang [slæŋ] *noun*
argot (*masculine*) : **it's a slang word** c'est un mot d'argot.

slap [slæp] *noun & verb*
■ *noun*
gifle (*feminine*) : **he gave me a slap in the face** il m'a donné une gifle
■ *verb* (*past tense & past participle* slapped [slæpt])
gifler : I slapped him in the face je l'ai giflé.

slate [sleɪt] *noun*
ardoise (*feminine*) : **the roof is made of slate** le toit est en ardoise.

slave [sleɪv] *noun*
esclave (*masculine or feminine*) : **there were**

slaves at that time il y avait des esclaves à cette époque-là.

slavery ['sleɪvərɪ] *noun*

esclavage *(masculine)* : **slavery was abolished in 1833 in Britain and in 1865 in the US** l'esclavage fut aboli en 1833 en Grande-Bretagne et en 1865 aux États-Unis.

sledge *UK* [sledʒ], **sled** *US* [sled] *noun*

luge *(feminine)* : **they came down the hill in a sledge** ils ont descendu la colline en luge.

sleep [sliːp] *noun & verb*

▪ *noun*
sommeil *(masculine)* : **I need some sleep** j'ai besoin de sommeil

▪ *verb (past tense & past participle* slept*)*
1. dormir : **she's sleeping** elle dort ; **did you sleep well?** tu as bien dormi ?
2. coucher : **we slept at the Imperial** nous avons couché à l'Imperial

➤ **to go to sleep** s'endormir : **he went to sleep straightaway** il s'est endormi tout de suite

sleep in *phrasal verb*

faire la grasse matinée

sleep over *phrasal verb*

passer la nuit chez quelqu'un : **I slept over at Patty's house** j'ai passé la nuit chez Patty.

sleeping bag ['sliːpɪŋbæg] *noun*

sac *(masculine)* de couchage : **don't forget your sleeping bag** n'oublie pas ton sac de couchage.

sleepy ['sliːpɪ] *adjective*

➤ **to be sleepy** OR **to feel sleepy** avoir sommeil : **I feel sleepy** j'ai sommeil.

sleeve [sliːv] *noun*

manche *(feminine)* : **he rolled up his sleeves** il a retroussé ses manches.

slender ['slendər] *adjective*

mince : **she has slender legs** elle a des jambes minces.

slept [slept] *past tense & past participle of* sleep

he slept until one o'clock il a dormi jusqu'à une heure ; **I haven't slept all night** je n'ai pas dormi de la nuit.

slice [slaɪs] *noun & verb*

▪ *noun*
tranche *(feminine)* : **he cut a slice of bread** il a coupé une tranche de pain

▪ *verb*
couper en tranches : **can you slice the bread?** tu peux couper le pain en tranches ?

slide [slaɪd] *noun & verb*

▪ *noun*
1. toboggan *(masculine)* : **the children are playing on the slide** les enfants jouent sur le toboggan
2. diapositive *(feminine)* : **they showed us their slides** ils nous ont montré leurs diapositives
3. *UK* barrette *(feminine)* : **she's wearing a slide in her hair** elle porte une barrette dans les cheveux

▪ *verb (past tense & past participle* slid [slɪd]*)*
glisser : **he was sliding on the ice** il glissait sur la glace ; **she slid the letter under the door** elle a glissé la lettre sous la porte.

slight [slaɪt] *adjective*

léger *(feminine* légère*)* : **there has been a slight improvement** il y a eu une légère amélioration.

slightly ['slaɪtlɪ] *adverb*

légèrement : **I feel slightly better** je me sens légèrement mieux.

slim [slɪm] *adjective*

mince : **Nicole's very slim** Nicole est très mince.

sling [slɪŋ] *noun*

écharpe *(feminine)* : **his arm is in a sling** il a le bras en écharpe.

slip [slɪp] *noun & verb*

▪ *noun*
erreur *(feminine)* : **I made a slip when I mentioned his name** j'ai fait une erreur quand j'ai dit son nom

➤ **a slip of paper** un bout de papier : **I wrote it on a slip of paper** je l'ai noté sur un bout de papier

▪ *verb (past tense & past participle* slipped [slɪpt]*)*
glisser : **I slipped on the floor** j'ai glissé sur le sol ; **he slipped some money into my pocket** il a glissé de l'argent dans ma poche.

S

slipper [ˈslɪpəʳ] *noun*

pantoufle *(feminine)*, **chausson** *(masculine)* : **he put on his slippers** il a mis ses pantoufles.

slope [sləʊp] *noun*

pente *(feminine)* : **it's a very steep slope** c'est une pente très raide.

slot [slɒt] *noun*

fente *(feminine)* : **put your money in the slot** mets ton argent dans la fente
➤ **a slot machine**
1. *UK* **un distributeur automatique** : **you can buy a sandwich from the slot machine** tu peux acheter un sandwich dans le distributeur automatique
2. **une machine à sous** : **you don't win much money from slot machines** on ne gagne pas beaucoup d'argent dans les machines à sous.

slow [sləʊ] *adjective, adverb & verb*

◼ *adjective*
lent : **this bus is very slow** ce bus est très lent
➤ **my watch is slow** ma montre retarde : **my watch is five minutes slow** ma montre retarde de cinq minutes
➤ **in slow motion** au ralenti
◼ *adverb*
lentement : **we're going slow** nous allons lentement

slow down *phrasal verb*

ralentir : **you're driving too fast, slow down** tu conduis trop vite, ralentis.

slowly [ˈsləʊlɪ] *adverb*

lentement : **I was walking slowly** je marchais lentement.

smack [smæk] *noun & verb*

◼ *noun*
fessée *(feminine)* : **she gave him a smack** elle lui a donné une fessée
◼ *verb*
donner une fessée à : **she smacked him on the bottom** elle lui a donné une fessée
➤ **to smack somebody in the face** donner une gifle à quelqu'un.

small [smɔːl] *adjective*

petit : **they live in a small village** ils habitent un petit village
➤ **small change** petite monnaie *(feminine)* : **do you have any small change?** vous avez de la monnaie ?

smart [smɑːt] *adjective*

1. *UK* **chic** *(invariable)* : **you look smart** tu es chic ; **we went to a smart restaurant** nous sommes allés dans un restaurant chic
2. **intelligent** : **children are smarter than they used to be** les enfants sont plus intelligents qu'avant.

smash [smæʃ] *noun*

1. casser : **he smashed a window** il a cassé une vitre
2. **se casser** : **the glass smashed on the floor** le verre s'est cassé sur le sol.

smell [smel] *noun & verb*

◼ *noun*
odeur *(feminine)* : **I love the smell of cut grass** j'adore l'odeur de l'herbe coupée
➤ **the sense of smell** l'odorat *(masculine)*
◼ *verb (past tense & past participle* **smelt** *OR* **smelled**)
1. sentir : **I can smell gas** ça sent le gaz ; **that cake smells good** ce gâteau sent bon ; **it smells of coffee** ça sent le café
2. **sentir mauvais** : **your socks smell!** tes chaussettes sentent mauvais !

smelly [ˈsmelɪ] *adjective*

qui sent mauvais : **your feet are smelly** tes pieds sentent mauvais.

smelt [smelt] *past tense & past participle of* smell

he smelt the flowers il a senti les fleurs.

smile [smaɪl] *noun & verb*

◼ *noun*
sourire *(masculine)* : **he gave me a big smile** il m'a fait un grand sourire
◼ *verb*
sourire : **she smiled at me** elle m'a souri.

smiley [ˈsmaɪlɪ] *noun*

émoticon *(masculine)*, **smiley** *(masculine)*.

smoke [sməʊk] *noun & verb*

◼ *noun*
fumée *(feminine)* : **the room is full of smoke** la pièce est remplie de fumée
◼ *verb*
fumer : **he was smoking a cigarette** il fumait une cigarette ; **I don't smoke** je ne fume pas.

smoker [ˈsməʊkəʳ] *noun*

fumeur *(masculine)*, **fumeuse** *(feminine)* : **he's a heavy smoker** c'est un gros fumeur.

smoking ['sməʊkɪŋ] *noun*

tabagisme *(masculine)* : **there is no cure for smoking** il n'y a aucun remède contre le tabagisme

➤ **'no smoking'** 'défense de fumer'.

smooth [smuːð] *adjective*

lisse : **he has smooth skin** il a la peau lisse.

SMS [esemes] *(abbreviation of* Short Message Service*) noun*
SMS *(masculine)*.

snack [snæk] *noun*

en-cas *(masculine)* [*plural* **en-cas**]
➤ **to have a snack** manger un morceau
➤ **a snack bar** un snack.

snail [sneɪl] *noun*

escargot *(masculine)* : **at a snail's pace** à une allure d'escargot.

snake [sneɪk] *noun*

serpent *(masculine)* : **snakes are reptiles** les serpents sont des reptiles.

snap [snæp] (*past tense & past participle* snapped [snæpt]) *verb*

1. **casser net** : **the rope snapped** la corde a cassé net
2. **casser** : **I snapped the branch in two** j'ai cassé la branche en deux.

snatch [snætʃ] *verb*

arracher : **he snatched my bag from my hands** il m'a arraché mon sac des mains.

sneakers ['sniːkəz] *plural noun*

tennis *(masculine plural)* : **Ben's wearing sneakers** Ben porte des tennis.

sneeze [sniːz] *noun*

éternuer : **I sneezed** j'ai éternué ; **it made me sneeze** ça m'a fait éternuer.

sniff [snɪf] *verb*

renifler : **I could hear him sniffing** je l'entendais renifler ; **the dog sniffed the bone** le chien reniflait l'os.

snob [snɒb] *noun*

snob *(masculine or feminine)* : **you're a snob** tu es snob.

snobbish ['snɒbɪʃ] *adjective*

snob *(invariable)* : **they're really snobbish** ils sont très snob.

snore [snɔːʳ] *verb*

ronfler : **he snores at night** il ronfle la nuit.

snorkel ['snɔːkl] *noun*

tuba *(masculine)*.

snorkelling *UK*, **snorkeling** *US* ['snɔːklɪŋ] *noun*

➤ **to go snorkelling** faire de la plongée avec un tuba.

snow [snəʊ] *noun & verb*

■ *noun*
neige *(feminine)* : **there's snow on the top of the mountains** il y a de la neige sur le sommet des montagnes

■ *verb*
neiger : **it's snowing** il neige.

snowball ['snəʊbɔːl] *noun*

boule *(feminine)* **de neige** : **they were throwing snowballs at each other** ils se lançaient des boules de neige.

snowboard ['snəʊˌbɔːd] *noun*

planche *(feminine)* **de snowboard**.

snowboarding ['snəʊˌbɔːdɪŋ] *noun*

snowboard *(masculine)* : **to go snowboarding** faire du snowboard.

snowman ['snəʊmæn] (*plural* snowmen ['snəʊmen]) *noun*
bonhomme *(masculine)* **de neige** : **they made a snowman** ils ont fait un bonhomme de neige.

so [səʊ] *adverb & conjunction*

■ *adverb*
1. **si, tellement** : **she's so beautiful!** elle est si belle ! ; **don't be so stupid!** ne pas sois si bête ! ; **the bag is so heavy I can't lift it** le sac est tellement lourd que je n'arrive pas à le soulever OR le sac est si lourd que je n'arrive pas à le soulever
2. **aussi** : **he's American and so is she** il est américain et elle aussi ; **she has a dog and so do I** elle a un chien et moi aussi
3. *With* `think`, `hope`, `say`, `suppose` **I don't think so** je ne pense pas ; **I think so** je pense que oui ; **I hope so** j'espère bien ; **if you say so** si tu le dis ; **I suppose so** je suppose
➤ **so far** jusqu'ici : **so far I haven't made any mistakes** jusqu'ici je n'ai pas fait de fautes
➤ **so many**
1. **tant de** OR **tellement de** : **she has so many**

friends! elle a tant d'amis ! OR elle a tellement d'amis !

2. **autant de** : **I've never seen so many people** je n'ai jamais vu autant de gens

➤ **so much**

1. **tant de** OR **tellement de** : **I have so much work!** j'ai tant de travail ! OR j'ai tellement de travail !

2. **autant de** : **I've never seen so much money** je n'ai jamais vu autant d'argent

3. **tellement** : **I love you so much** je t'aime tellement

➤ **or so** environ OR à peu près : **thirty or so** environ trente OR à peu près trente

■ *conjunction*

donc, alors : **I'll be on vacation, so I won't be able to come** je serai en vacances, donc je ne pourrai pas venir ; **my bike was broken so I repaired it** mon vélo était cassé, alors je l'ai réparé ; **so what's the point then?** alors à quoi bon ? ; **so what?** et alors ?

➤ **so long!** au revoir !

➤ **so that** pour que : **he worked hard so that everything would be ready in time** il a travaillé dur pour que tout soit prêt à temps.

soak ['səʊk] *verb*

tremper : **I got soaked** j'ai été trempé.

soaking ['səʊkɪŋ] *adjective*

trempé : **I'm soaking** OR **I'm soaking wet** je suis trempé.

soap [səʊp] *noun*

savon *(masculine)* : **a bar of soap** une savonnette

➤ **a soap opera** un soap opera.

soccer ['sɒkəʳ] *noun*

football *(masculine)* : **I play soccer every Saturday** je joue au football tous les samedis

➤ **a soccer player** un joueur de football.

social ['səʊʃl] *adjective*

social : **the social sciences** les sciences sociales ; **the social services** les services sociaux

➤ **social security** l'aide *(feminine)* sociale : **he's on social security** il reçoit l'aide sociale.

society [sə'saɪətɪ] *(plural* **societies)** *noun*

1. **société** *(feminine)* : **we live in a multicultural society** nous vivons dans une société multiculturelle

2. **club** *(masculine)* : **Chantal is in the drama society** Chantal est membre du club de théâtre.

sock [sɒk] *noun*

chaussette *(feminine)* : **he's wearing black socks** il porte des chaussettes noires.

soda *US* ['səʊdə] *noun*

soda *(masculine)* : **Cheryl's drinking a soda** Cheryl boit un soda.

soda water ['səʊdə'wɔːtəʳ] *noun*

eau *(feminine)* **de Seltz**.

sofa ['səʊfə] *noun*

canapé *(masculine)* : **he's sitting on the sofa** il est assis sur le canapé.

soft [sɒft] *adjective*

1. **doux** *(feminine* **douce)** : **the baby has soft skin** le bébé a la peau douce

2. **mou** *(feminine* **molle)** : **the butter is soft** le beurre est mou

3. **moelleux** : **a nice soft bed** un lit moelleux

4. **souple** : **a soft leather bag** un sac en cuir souple

➤ **a soft drink** une boisson non alcoolisée.

softly ['sɒftlɪ] *adverb*

doucement : **she was singing softly** elle chantait doucement.

software ['sɒftweəʳ] *uncountable noun*

logiciel *(masculine)* : **the computer comes with a lot of software** l'ordinateur est vendu avec beaucoup de logiciels.

soggy ['sɒgɪ] *adjective*

1. **trempé, détrempé** : **my socks are all soggy** mes chaussettes sont toutes trempées ; **the ground is soggy** le sol est détrempé

2. **pâteux** *(feminine* **pâteuse)** : **these crisps have gone soggy** ces chips sont pâteuses.

soil [sɔɪl] *noun*

terre *(feminine)*, **sol** *(masculine)* : **the soil is red in Australia** la terre est rouge en Australie ; **you should plant it in damp soil** tu devrais le planter dans un sol humide.

solar ['səʊləʳ] *adjective*

solaire : **solar energy** l'énergie solaire.

sold [səʊld] *past tense & past participle of* **sell**

he sold his bike il a vendu son vélo ; **we haven't sold the house yet** nous n'avons pas encore vendu la maison.

soldier ['səʊldʒəʳ] *noun*

soldat *(masculine)* : **he's a soldier** il est soldat.

sole [səʊl] *noun*

semelle *(feminine)* : **there's a hole in the sole of my shoe** il y a un trou dans la semelle de ma chaussure.

solicitor *UK* [sə'lɪsɪtəʳ] *noun*

notaire *(masculine)* : **he's a solicitor** il est notaire.

solid ['sɒlɪd] *adjective*

1. solide : **the bridge is very solid** le pont est très solide
2. massif *(feminine* massive*)* : **he wears a solid gold chain** il porte une chaîne en or massif.

solution [sə'luːʃn] *noun*

solution *(feminine)* : **we're trying to find a solution** nous essayons de trouver une solution.

solve [sɒlv] *verb*

résoudre : **he has solved the problem** il a résolu le problème.

some [sʌm] *adjective, pronoun & adverb*

■ *adjective*

1. du *(feminine* de la*, before a vowel or silent 'h'* de l'*, plural* des*)* : **do you want some tea?** tu veux du thé ? ; **I bought some meat** j'ai acheté de la viande ; **he gave me some money** il m'a donné de l'argent ; **let's go and buy some sweets** allons acheter des bonbons ; **I want to get some new shoes** je veux acheter de nouvelles chaussures
2. certain : **some swans are black** certains cygnes sont noirs ; **some people like his music** certains aiment sa musique OR il y en a qui aiment sa musique
➤ **some day** un de ces jours
■ *pronoun*

1. en : **that cake looks nice, can I have some?** ce gâteau a l'air bon, je peux en prendre ? ; **I've got lots of comics, do you want some?** j'ai beaucoup de BD, tu en veux ?
2. certains : **some are red, some are blue** certains sont rouges, d'autres sont bleus ; **I bought a kilo of oranges, some of them were bad** j'ai acheté un kilo d'oranges, certaines étaient pourries ; **some of them left early** certains d'entre eux sont partis tôt
■ *adverb*

quelque, environ : **there were some 7,000 people at the concert** il y avait quelque 7000 personnes au concert OR il y avait environ 7000 personnes au concert.

somebody ['sʌmbədɪ], **someone** ['sʌmwʌn] *pronoun*

quelqu'un : **somebody came to see you** quelqu'un est passé te voir ; **he's somebody famous** c'est quelqu'un de célèbre ; **somebody else** quelqu'un d'autre.

someday ['sʌmdeɪ] *adverb*

un jour : **someday I'll be rich and famous** un jour, je serai riche et célèbre.

somehow ['sʌmhaʊ] *adverb*

1. d'une manière ou d'une autre : **I'll do it somehow** je le ferai d'une manière ou d'une autre
2. je ne sais pas pourquoi : **somehow, I don't think he'll come back** je ne sais pas pourquoi, mais je crois qu'il ne reviendra pas.

someone *pronoun* ➤ somebody.

someplace *US adverb* ➤ somewhere.

something ['sʌmθɪŋ] *pronoun*

quelque chose : **I have something in my eye** j'ai quelque chose dans l'œil ; **don't just stand there, do something!** ne reste pas là, fais quelque chose ! ; **would you like something to drink?** tu veux quelque chose à boire ? ; **something odd happened** il s'est passé quelque chose de bizarre
➤ **I'll have something else** je vais prendre autre chose
➤ **that was something else!** c'était vraiment quelque chose !
➤ **he's something else!** il est génial !

sometime ['sʌmtaɪm] *adverb*

un de ces jours : **come and see me sometime** viens me voir un de ces jours ; **I'll see you sometime next week** je te reverrai dans le courant de la semaine prochaine.

sometimes ['sʌmtaɪmz] *adverb*

quelquefois, parfois : **she sometimes writes to me** elle m'écrit quelquefois ; **sometimes I make mistakes** parfois, je fais des erreurs.

somewhere ['sʌmweəʳ], **someplace** *US* ['sʌmpleɪs] *adverb*

1. quelque part : **they live somewhere in Scotland** ils vivent quelque part en Écosse
2. un endroit où : **I'm looking for somewhere to live** je cherche un endroit où habiter

S

➤ **somewhere else** ailleurs : **let's go some-where else** allons ailleurs.

son [sʌn] *noun*

fils *(masculine)* : **they have three sons** ils ont trois fils ; **he's my son** c'est mon fils.

song [sɒŋ] *noun*

chanson *(feminine)* : **he was singing a love song** il chantait une chanson d'amour.

son-in-law [ˈsʌnɪnlɔː] *noun*

gendre *(masculine)* : **he's my son-in-law** c'est mon gendre.

soon [suːn] *adverb*

1. **bientôt** : **he'll soon be here** il sera bientôt là ; **I'll see you soon!** à bientôt !
2. **vite** : **write soon!** écris-moi vite !
3. **tôt** : **she came too soon** elle est arrivée trop tôt

➤ **soon after** peu après : **she left soon after** elle est partie peu après

➤ **as soon as** dès que : **I'll tell you as soon as he leaves** je te le dirai dès qu'il partira

➤ **as soon as possible** dès que possible : **leave as soon as possible** pars dès que possible

➤ **I'll be back soon!** je reviens tout de suite !

sooner [ˈsuːnəʳ] *(comparative of* **soon***) adverb*

plus tôt : **you should have come sooner** tu aurais dû venir plus tôt

➤ **sooner or later** tôt ou tard : **sooner or later you'll have to tell me** tôt ou tard, tu devras me le dire.

sorcerer [ˈsɔːsərəʳ] *noun*

sorcier *(masculine)* : **he's a sorcerer** c'est un sorcier.

sore [sɔːʳ] *adjective*

1. **douloureux** *(feminine* **douloureuse***)* : **this burn on my hand is really sore** cette brûlure à la main est vraiment douloureuse
2. *US informal* **fâché** : **he's sore at me** il est fâché contre moi

➤ **to have a sore throat** avoir mal à la gorge ; **she has a sore throat** elle a mal à la gorge.

sorrow [ˈsɒrəʊ] *noun*

peine *(feminine)* : **his death caused me great sorrow** sa mort m'a fait beaucoup de peine.

sorry [ˈsɒrɪ] *adjective*

désolé : **I'm really sorry, I have to go** je suis

vraiment désolé, je dois partir ; **I'm sorry I'm late** je suis désolé d'être en retard

➤ **sorry!** pardon !
➤ **sorry?** pardon ? : **sorry? what did you say?** pardon ? qu'est-ce que tu as dit ?
➤ **you'll be sorry!** tu vas le regretter !
➤ **say sorry to your sister** demande pardon à ta sœur
➤ **he said he was sorry** il a présenté ses excuses
➤ **to feel sorry for somebody** plaindre quelqu'un : **I feel sorry for him** je le plains.

sort [sɔːt] *noun & verb*

◾ *noun*

sorte *(feminine)* : **it's a sort of radio** c'est une sorte de radio ; **there were all sorts of people** il y avait des gens de toutes sortes

➤ **what sort of car is that?** qu'est-ce que c'est comme voiture ?

◾ *verb*

trier : **the computer sorts the words in alphabetical order** l'ordinateur trie les mots par ordre alphabétique

sort out *phrasal verb*

1. *UK* **ranger** : **I'm going to sort out my room** je vais ranger ma chambre
2. **régler** : **he managed to sort the problem out** il a réussi à régler le problème ; **is everything sorted out?** tout est réglé ?
3. *UK* **s'occuper de** : **I'll sort the tickets out** je m'occuperai des billets.

sought [sɔːt] *past tense & past participle of* seek

they sought a solution ils ont cherché une solution.

soul [səʊl] *noun*

âme *(feminine)*.

sound [saʊnd] *noun & verb*

◾ *noun*

1. **son** *(masculine)* : **I recognized the sound of her voice** j'ai reconnu le son de sa voix ; **turn the sound up** monte le son
2. **bruit** *(masculine)* : **I heard a sound** j'ai entendu un bruit ; **try not to make a sound** essaie de ne pas faire de bruit

➤ **sound effects** bruitage *(masculine)*

◾ *verb*

1. **sonner** : **they sounded the alarm** on a sonné l'alarme ; **this wall sounds hollow** ce mur sonne creux
2. **avoir l'air, sembler** : **he sounds happy** il a

l'air heureux ; **it sounds as if they have a problem** ils ont l'air d'avoir un problème

➤ **that sounds like a good idea** ça m'a l'air d'être une bonne idée

➤ **to sound one's horn** klaxonner : **he sounded his horn** il a klaxonné.

soundtrack ['saʊndtræk] *noun*

bande *(feminine)* **originale** : **I bought the soundtrack to the film** j'ai acheté la bande originale du film.

soup [suːp] *noun*

soupe *(feminine)* : **a bowl of onion soup** un bol de soupe à l'oignon.

sour ['saʊəʳ] *adjective*

aigre : **this yoghurt tastes sour** ce yaourt a un goût aigre

➤ **the milk has gone sour** le lait a tourné.

source [sɔːs] *noun*

source *(feminine)* : **the Internet is a good source of information** Internet est une bonne source d'informations.

south [saʊθ] *noun, adjective & adverb*

▢ *noun*
sud *(masculine)* : **Ashford is in the south of England** Ashford est dans le sud de l'Angleterre

▢ *adjective*
sud *(invariable)* : **Bournemouth is on the south coast** Bournemouth est sur la côte sud

▢ *adverb*
vers le sud : **a lot of birds fly south in the winter** beaucoup d'oiseaux partent vers le sud en hiver

➤ **south of** au sud de : **Orléans is south of Paris** Orléans est au sud de Paris.

South Africa [ˌsaʊθ'æfrɪkə] *noun*

l'Afrique *(feminine)* **du Sud**

> In French the names of countries are used with the definite article (le, la or l'), except when they follow the preposition en:

Nelson Mandela became the first black president of South Africa in 1994 Nelson Mandela est devenu le premier président noir de l'Afrique du Sud en 1994 ; **Durban is in South Africa** Durban se trouve en Afrique du Sud ; **they are going to South Africa** ils vont en Afrique du Sud.

South African [ˌsaʊθ'æfrɪkən] *adjective & noun*

▢ *adjective*
sud-africain

> The French adjective does not start with a capital letter:

the South African rugby team is called the Springboks l'équipe sud-africaine de rugby s'appelle les Springboks

▢ *noun*
Sud-Africain *(masculine)*, **Sud-Africaine** *(feminine)*.

South America [ˌsaʊθə'merɪkə] *noun*

l'Amérique *(feminine)* **du Sud**

> In French the names of countries are used with the definite article (le, la or l'), except when they follow the preposition en:

South America is part of the American continent l'Amérique du Sud fait partie du continent américain ; **the Andes are in South America** les Andes se trouvent en Amérique du Sud ; **they are going to South America** ils vont en Amérique du Sud.

South American [ˌsaʊθə'merɪkn] *adjective & noun*

▢ *adjective*
sud-américain

> The French adjective does not start with a capital letter:

I like South American music j'aime la musique sud-américaine

▢ *noun*
Sud-Américain *(masculine)*, **Sud-Américaine** *(feminine)*.

southeast [ˌsaʊθ'iːst] *noun*

sud-est *(masculine)* : **Kent is in the southeast of England** le Kent est dans le sud-est de l'Angleterre.

southwest [ˌsaʊθ'west] *noun*

sud-ouest *(masculine)* : **Cornwall is in the southwest of England** la Cornouailles est dans le sud-ouest de l'Angleterre.

souvenir [ˌsuːvə'nɪəʳ] *noun*

souvenir *(masculine)* : **he bought a lot of souvenirs in Madrid** il a acheté beaucoup de souvenirs à Madrid.

S

soya ['sɔɪə] *noun*

soja *(masculine)* : **soya beans** des graines de soja.

soy sauce [ˌsɔɪ'sɔːs] *noun*

sauce *(feminine)* **soja**.

space [speɪs] *noun*

1. espace *(masculine)* : **who was the first man in space?** qui a été le premier homme dans l'espace ? ; **leave a space for corrections** laissez un espace pour les corrections

2. place *(feminine)* : **there's not enough space for a bed** il n'y a pas assez de place pour un lit ; **the table takes up a lot of space** la table prend beaucoup de place ; **can you make some space for me?** tu peux me faire de la place ?

> **a parking space** une place de parking
> **to stare into space** regarder dans le vide
> **a space shuttle** une navette spatiale.

spaceship ['speɪsʃɪp] *noun*

vaisseau *(masculine)* **spatial** : **they sent a spaceship to Mars** ils ont envoyé un vaisseau spatial sur Mars.

spacesuit ['speɪssuːt] *noun*

combinaison *(feminine)* **spatiale** : **they were wearing spacesuits** ils portaient des combinaisons spatiales.

spade [speɪd] *noun*

1. pelle *(feminine)* : **the children were playing with their buckets and spades on the beach** les enfants jouaient sur la plage avec leurs seaux et leurs pelles

2. pique *(feminine)* : **the queen of spades** la reine de pique.

spaghetti [spə'getɪ] *uncountable noun*

spaghettis *(masculine plural)* : **she loves spaghetti** elle adore les spaghettis.

Spain [speɪn] *noun*

l'Espagne *(feminine)*

In French the names of countries are used with the definite article (le, la or l'), except when they follow the preposition en:

Spain joined the European Union in 1986 l'Espagne est entrée dans l'Union européenne en 1986 ; **Montse lives in Spain** Montse vit en Espagne ; **I'm going to Spain** je vais en Espagne.

Spanish ['spænɪʃ] *adjective & noun*

■ *adjective*

espagnol : **sangria is a Spanish drink** la sangria est une boisson espagnole

■ *noun*

espagnol *(masculine)* : **she speaks Spanish** elle parle espagnol

> **the Spanish** les Espagnols

Remember not to use a capital letter for the adjective and the language in French. Only use a capital letter for the inhabitants.

spanner UK ['spænər] *noun*

clé *(feminine)* : **he used a spanner to tighten the nut** il a utilisé une clé pour serrer l'écrou.

spare [speər] *adjective & verb*

■ *adjective*

1. en trop : **I've got a spare ticket** j'ai un billet en trop

2. libre, disponible : **there's a spare seat at the back** il y a une place de libre à l'arrière

3. de rechange : **bring a spare jumper** apporte un pull de rechange

> **a spare part** une pièce détachée OR une pièce de rechange
> **a spare room** une chambre d'amis : **we have a spare room** nous avons une chambre d'amis
> **spare time** temps *(masculine)* libre : **I don't have any spare time** je n'ai pas de temps libre
> **a spare wheel** une roue de secours

■ *verb*

> **can you spare a few minutes?** vous auriez quelques minutes ?
> **I can't spare the time** je n'ai pas le temps
> **I arrived with a minute to spare** je suis arrivé avec une minute d'avance.

sparkling ['spɑːklɪŋ] *adjective*

pétillant : **a bottle of sparkling water** une bouteille d'eau pétillante

> **sparkling wine** vin *(masculine)* mousseux ; **a glass of sparkling wine** un verre de vin mousseux.

sparrow ['spærəʊ] *noun*

moineau *(masculine)* [*plural* **moineaux**] : **there are a lot of sparrows in cities** il y a beaucoup de moineaux dans les villes.

spat [spæt] *past tense & past participle of* spit

he spat on the floor il a craché par terre.

speak [spiːk] (*past tense* **spoke**, *past participle* **spoken**) *verb*

parler : do you speak English? est-ce que vous parlez anglais ? ; **Sandra speaks French** Sandra parle français ; **speak more slowly** parlez plus lentement ; **I spoke to my parents about the party** j'ai parlé de la fête à mes parents ; **can I speak to Henry, please?** pourrais-je parler à Henry, s'il vous plaît ?

➤ **who's speaking?** qui est à l'appareil ?

➤ **this is Kate speaking** c'est Kate.

speaker ['spiːkə^r] *noun*

enceinte *(feminine)* : **don't put the speakers too close together** ne mets pas les enceintes trop près l'une de l'autre

➤ **he's an English speaker** c'est un anglophone.

special ['speʃl] *adjective*

1. **spécial : you need special shoes to run in** il vous faut des chaussures spéciales pour la course

2. **particulier** *(feminine* **particulière)** : **this is a special case** c'est un cas particulier

3. **cher** *(feminine* **chère)** : **this ring is very special to me** cette bague m'est très chère.

specialist ['speʃəlɪst] *noun*

spécialiste *(masculine or feminine)*.

speciality *UK* [ˌspeʃɪ'ælətɪ] (*plural* **specialities**), **specialty** *US* ['speʃltɪ] (*plural* **specialties**) *noun*

spécialité *(feminine)* : **haggis is a Scottish speciality** le haggis est une spécialité écossaise.

specially ['speʃəlɪ] *adverb*

1. **spécialement : I came specially to see you** je suis venu spécialement pour te voir

2. **particulièrement : it's dangerous, specially at night** c'est dangereux, particulièrement la nuit.

specialty *US noun* ➤ **speciality** *UK*.

species ['spiːʃiːz] (*plural* **species**) *noun*

espèce *(feminine)* : **this species is extinct** cette espèce a disparu.

spectacles *UK* ['spektəklz] *noun*

lunettes *(feminine plural)* : **Harry wears spectacles** Harry porte des lunettes

⚠ Le mot anglais **spectacles** est un faux ami, il ne signifie pas "spectacles".

spectacular [spek'tækjʊlə^r] *adjective*

spectaculaire : the waterfall is a spectacular sight cette chute d'eau est spectaculaire.

spectator [spek'teɪtə^r] *noun*

spectateur *(masculine)*, **spectatrice** *(feminine)*.

sped [sped] *past tense & past participle of* **speed**

they sped along the road ils ont descendu la rue à toute allure.

speech [spiːtʃ] *noun*

discours *(masculine)* : **he gave a speech** il a fait un discours.

speed [spiːd] *noun & verb*

◼ *noun*

vitesse *(feminine)* : **at the speed of light** à la vitesse de la lumière

➤ **at top speed** à toute vitesse ; **they were driving at top speed** ils roulaient à toute vitesse

➤ **the speed limit** la limitation de vitesse ; **the speed limit is 50 miles an hour** la vitesse est limitée à 80 kilomètres à l'heure

◼ *verb* (*past tense & past participle* **sped** OR **speeded**)

1. **rouler trop vite : the driver was speeding** le conducteur roulait trop vite

2. **aller à toute allure : the car sped away** la voiture est partie à toute allure

speed up *phrasal verb*

aller plus vite : can you speed up a bit? tu peux aller un peu plus vite ?

speedboat ['spiːdbəʊt] *noun*

hors-bord *(masculine)* *(plural* **hors-bord)**.

speeding ['spiːdɪŋ] *uncountable noun*

excès *(masculine)* **de vitesse : he was fined for speeding** il a eu une amende pour excès de vitesse.

speedometer [spɪ'dɒmɪtə^r] *noun*

compteur *(masculine)* : **his speedometer is broken** son compteur est cassé.

spell [spel] *noun & verb*

◼ *noun*

➤ **to cast a spell on somebody** OR **to put a spell on somebody** jeter un sort à quelqu'un : **the sorcerer cast a spell on him** le sorcier lui a jeté un sort

S

■ verb (*past tense & past participle* spelled OR spelt UK)

1. **écrire : how do you spell that?** comment ça s'écrit ?
2. **épeler : could you spell your name for me?** vous pouvez épeler votre nom ?

spell-checker ['speltʃekər] *noun*

correcteur *(masculine)* **d'orthographe.**

spelling ['spelɪŋ] *noun*

orthographe *(feminine)* **: a spelling mistake** une faute d'orthographe.

spelt UK [spelt] *past tense & past participle of* spell

I spelt it wrong je l'ai mal écrit.

spend [spend] (*past tense & past participle* spent) *verb*

1. **dépenser : how much did you spend?** tu as dépensé combien ?
2. **passer : I'd like to spend a few days in New York** j'aimerais passer quelques jours à New York.

spent [spent] *past tense & past participle of* spend

I spent a lot of money j'ai dépensé beaucoup d'argent ; **she has spent two days there** elle y a passé deux jours.

spice [spaɪs] *noun*

épice *(feminine)* **: pepper and cinnamon are spices** le poivre et la cannelle sont des épices.

spicy ['spaɪsɪ] *adjective*

épicé **: this curry is very spicy** ce curry est très épicé.

spider ['spaɪdər] *noun*

araignée *(feminine)* **: he's afraid of spiders** il a peur des araignées.

spill [spɪl] (*past tense & past participle* spilled OR spilt UK) *verb*

1. **renverser : I spilled the water** j'ai renversé l'eau
2. **se répandre : the milk spilled on the floor** le lait s'est répandu par terre.

spilt UK [spɪlt] *past tense & past participle of* spill

he spilt the orange juice il a renversé le jus d'orange.

spin [spɪn] (*past tense & past participle* spun) *verb*

1. **tourner : the planet spins on its axis** la planète tourne sur son axe

2. **faire tourner : he spun the wheel** il a fait tourner la roue
➤ **my head is spinning** j'ai la tête qui tourne

spin around , **spin round** UK *phrasal verb*

1. **tourner : the moon spins around the earth** la Lune tourne autour de la Terre
2. **se retourner : she suddenly spun round** elle s'est retournée brusquement.

spinach [UK 'spɪnɪdʒ, US 'spɪnɪtʃ] *uncountable noun*

épinards *(masculine plural)* **: Popeye eats a lot of spinach** Popeye mange beaucoup d'épinards.

spine [spaɪn] *noun*

colonne *(feminine)* **vertébrale : the spine forms the central part of the skeleton** la colonne vertébrale est la partie centrale du squelette.

spiral staircase ['spaɪərəl'steɪkeɪs] *noun*

escalier *(masculine)* **en colimaçon.**

spire ['spaɪər] *noun*

flèche *(feminine)* **: from here you can see the church spire** d'ici, on voit la flèche de l'église.

spit [spɪt] (*past tense & past participle* spat OR spit US) *verb*

cracher **: he spat at me** il m'a craché dessus ; **she spat the mushroom out** elle a craché le champignon.

spite [spaɪt] *noun*

➤ **in spite of** malgré **: in spite of the rain, they went for a long walk** malgré la pluie, ils ont fait une longue promenade.

splash [splæʃ] *noun & verb*

■ *noun*

plouf *(masculine)* **: I heard a loud splash** j'ai entendu un grand plouf

■ *verb*

éclabousser **: you splashed me** tu m'as éclaboussé.

splendid ['splendɪd] *adjective*

splendide **: what splendid weather!** quel temps splendide !

splinter ['splɪntər] *noun*

écharde *(feminine)* **: I've got a splinter in my finger** j'ai une écharde dans le doigt.

split [splɪt] (*past tense & past participle* split) *verb*

1. **fendre : he split some wood for the fire** il a fendu du bois pour faire du feu
2. **se fendre : the frame has split** le cadre s'est fendu
3. **déchirer : I've split my shorts** j'ai déchiré mon short
4. **se déchirer : her dress split open** sa robe s'est déchirée
5. **répartir : let's split the work** on va répartir le travail
6. **diviser : he split the class into two groups** il a divisé la classe en deux groupes

split up *phrasal verb*

se séparer : the band split up last year le groupe s'est séparé l'année dernière.

spoil [spɔɪl] (*past tense & past participle* spoiled OR spoilt) *verb*

1. **gâcher : you spoilt my party** tu as gâché ma fête
2. **abîmer : that ink stain has spoiled my tie** cette tache d'encre a abîmé ma cravate
3. **gâter : they've spoilt their daughter** ils ont gâté leur fille.

spoiled [spɔɪld], **spoilt** [spɔɪlt] *adjective*

gâté : he's a spoiled child c'est un enfant gâté.

spoke [spəʊk] *noun & verb form*

◾ *noun*
rayon *(masculine)* **: the spokes of a wheel** les rayons d'une roue
◾ *past tense of* speak
she spoke to him elle lui a parlé.

spoken ['spəʊkn] *past participle of* speak

I haven't spoken to him je ne lui ai pas parlé.

sponge [spʌndʒ] *noun*

éponge *(feminine)* **: she wiped the table with a sponge** elle a passé un coup d'éponge sur la table
> **a sponge cake** un gâteau de Savoie.

sponsored walk *UK* [ˌspɒnsəd'wɔːk] *noun*

marche en faveur d'une œuvre de charité.

spooky ['spuːkɪ] *adjective informal*

sinistre : a spooky old house une vieille maison sinistre.

spoon [spuːn] *noun*

cuillère *(feminine)* **: a dessert spoon** une cuillère à dessert.

spoonful ['spuːnfʊl] *noun*

cuillerée *(feminine)* **: add a spoonful of lemon juice** ajoutez une cuillerée de jus de citron.

sport [spɔːt] *noun*

sport *(masculine)* **: they play a lot of sport** ils font beaucoup de sport
> **he's a bad sport** il est mauvais joueur
> **a sports car** une voiture de sport
> **a sports ground** un terrain de sport.

sportsman ['spɔːtsmən] (*plural* sportsmen ['spɔːtsmən]) *noun*

sportif *(masculine)* **: he's a sportsman** c'est un sportif.

sportswoman ['spɔːtswʊmən] (*plural* sportswomen ['spɔːtswɪmɪn]) *noun*
sportive *(feminine)* **: she's a sportswoman** c'est une sportive.

sporty ['spɔːtɪ] *adjective*

sportif *(feminine* sportive*)* **: he's not very sporty** il n'est pas très sportif.

spot [spɒt] *noun & verb*

◾ *noun*
1. **tache** *(feminine)* **: a grease spot** une tache de graisse
2. **pois** *(masculine)* **: a shirt with red spots** une chemise à pois rouges
3. *UK* **bouton** *(masculine)* **: he's got a few spots on his face** il a quelques boutons sur le visage
4. **endroit** *(masculine)* **: I know a nice spot where we can eat** je connais un endroit agréable où l'on peut manger
◾ *verb*
apercevoir : I spotted her in the distance je l'ai aperçue au loin.

spotlight ['spɒtlaɪt] *noun*

projecteur *(masculine)*, **spot** *(masculine)* **: he's in the spotlight** il est sous le feu des projecteurs.

sprain [spreɪn] *verb*

> **to sprain one's ankle** se faire une entorse à la cheville : **I've sprained my ankle** je me suis fait une entorse à la cheville.

S

spray [spreɪ] *noun & verb*

■ *noun*
  bombe *(feminine)* : **an insect spray** une bombe insecticide
■ *verb*
1. **vaporiser** : **she sprayed perfume in her hair** elle a vaporisé du parfum dans ses cheveux
2. **pulvériser** : **they're spraying the crops** ils pulvérisent les récoltes
3. **écrire à la bombe** : **somebody has sprayed a poem on the wall** quelqu'un a écrit un poème à la bombe sur le mur.

spread [spred] *(past tense & past participle* spread*) verb*
1. **étaler** : **he spread butter on the bread** il a étalé du beurre sur le pain ; **she spread the blanket on the ground** elle a étalé la couverture par terre
2. **déployer** : **the bird spread its wings** l'oiseau a déployé ses ailes
3. **répandre** : **we must spread the news** il faut répandre la nouvelle
4. **se propager** : **the news spread fast** la nouvelle s'est propagée rapidement ; **the fire is beginning to spread** l'incendie commence à se propager

spread out *phrasal verb*
  se disperser : **the search party spread out** l'équipe de secours s'est dispersée.

spring [sprɪŋ] *noun*
1. **printemps** *(masculine)* : **plants begin to grow again in the spring** les plantes renaissent au printemps
2. **ressort** *(masculine)* : **this bed has a spring mattress** ce lit a un matelas à ressorts
3. **source** *(feminine)* : **the water comes from a mountain spring** l'eau vient d'une source de montagne.

spring onion *UK* [sprɪŋˈʌnjən] *noun*
  ciboule *(feminine)*.

springtime [ˈsprɪŋtaɪm] *uncountable noun*
  printemps *(masculine)* : **the swallows start to come back in springtime** les hirondelles commencent à revenir au printemps.

sprouts [sprauts] *plural noun*
➤ **Brussels sprouts** choux *(masculine plural)* de Bruxelles.

spun [spʌn] *past tense & past participle of* spin
  the top spun very fast la toupie a tourné très vite.

spy [spaɪ] *noun & verb*

■ *noun*
  espion *(masculine)*, **espionne** *(feminine)* : **he's a spy** c'est un espion
➤ **a spy film** un film d'espionnage
■ *verb*
  faire de l'espionnage
➤ **to spy on somebody** espionner quelqu'un.

square [skweəʳ] *adjective & noun*

■ *adjective*
  carré : **the box is square** la boîte est carrée ; **two square metres** *UK* OR **two square meters** *US* deux mètres carrés
■ *noun*
1. **carré** *(masculine)* : **it's a square not a circle** c'est un carré, pas un cercle
2. **place** *(feminine)* : **the hotel is near the market square** l'hôtel est près de la place du marché
➤ **the town square** la grand-place.

squash [skwɒʃ] *noun & verb*

■ *noun*
1. **squash** *(masculine)* : **they're playing squash** ils jouent au squash
2. **courge** *(feminine)* : **he doesn't like eating squash** il n'aime pas les courges
➤ **orange squash** *UK* orangeade *(feminine)*
➤ **lemon squash** *UK* citronnade *(feminine)*
■ *verb*
  écraser : **he squashed my hat** il a écrasé mon chapeau ; **you're squashing me!** tu m'écrases !

squeeze [skwiːz] *verb*
1. **presser** : **she squeezed the sponge** elle a pressé l'éponge ; **a glass of freshly squeezed orange juice** une orange pressée
2. **serrer** : **I squeezed her hand** je lui ai serré la main
3. **réussir à faire entrer** : **I squeezed my things into the suitcase** j'ai réussi à faire entrer mes affaires dans la valise.

squirrel [*UK* ˈskwɪrəl, *US* ˈskwɜːrəl] *noun*
  écureuil *(masculine)*.

St
1. *(abbreviation of* street*)* **13 Barrow St** 13 Barrow St
2. *(abbreviation of* saint*)* **St David** St David.

stab [stæb] *(past tense & past participle* stabbed*)*
  verb

poignarder : **he was stabbed in the street** il a été poignardé dans la rue.

stable ['steɪbl] *noun*

écurie *(feminine)* : **the horses are in the stable** les chevaux sont dans l'écurie.

stack [stæk] *noun*

pile *(feminine)* : **there's a stack of newspapers on the floor** il y a une pile de journaux par terre.

stadium ['steɪdjəm] *(plural* stadiums OR stadia ['steɪdjə]) *noun*

stade *(masculine)* : **the stadium holds 40,000 people** il y a 40 000 places dans le stade.

staff [stɑːf] *noun*

1. personnel *(masculine)* : **the staff of our firm** le personnel de notre entreprise
2. *UK* professeurs *(masculine plural)* : **the staff of our school** les professeurs de notre école.

stage [steɪdʒ] *noun*

1. scène *(feminine)* : **the actors are on the stage** les acteurs sont sur scène
2. étape *(feminine)* : **we are doing this by stages** nous faisons cela par étapes
➤ **at this stage** à ce stade

⚠ Le mot anglais **stage** est un faux ami, il ne signifie pas "stage".

stagger ['stægər] *verb*

tituber : **he was so drunk he was staggering** il avait tellement bu qu'il titubait.

stain [steɪn] *noun & verb*

■ *noun*
tache *(feminine)* : **there's a stain on your jacket** il y a une tache sur ta veste
■ *verb*
tacher : **my jacket is stained** ma veste est tachée.

stair [steər] *noun*

marche *(feminine)* : **he's sitting on the bottom stair** il est assis sur la première marche.

staircase ['steəkeɪs] *noun*

escalier *(masculine)* : **there are two staircases** il y a deux escaliers.

stairs [steəʳz] *plural noun*

escalier *(masculine)* : **she went down the stairs** elle a descendu l'escalier.

stale [steɪl] *adjective*

rassis : **the bread is stale** le pain est rassis.

stammer ['stæmər] *verb*

bégayer : **she stammers** elle bégaie.

stamp [stæmp] *noun & verb*

■ *noun*
1. timbre *(masculine)* : **he stuck on the stamp** il a collé le timbre ; **a stamp album** un album de timbres
2. tampon *(masculine)* : **a rubber stamp** un tampon
■ *verb*
tamponner : **they stamped my passport** ils ont tamponné mon passeport
➤ **to stamp one's foot** taper du pied : **she stamped her foot in rage** en rage, elle tapait du pied.

stand [stænd] *noun & verb*

■ *noun*
1. stand *(masculine)* : **we have a stand at the exhibition** nous avons un stand à l'exposition
2. tribune *(feminine)* : **the stands in a stadium** les tribunes d'un stade
➤ **a newspaper stand** un kiosque à journaux
➤ **a taxi stand** une station de taxis
➤ **an umbrella stand** un porte-parapluies
■ *verb (past tense & past participle* stood)
1. être debout, se tenir debout : **he was standing** il était debout OR il se tenait debout ; **she's standing by the door** elle est debout près de la porte OR elle se tient debout près de la porte
2. se lever : **everyone stood when the judge came in** tout le monde s'est levé quand le juge est entré
3. se trouver : **the house stands in a valley** la maison se trouve dans une vallée
4. supporter : **I can't stand racism** je ne supporte pas le racisme
➤ **stand still!** ne bouge pas ! OR reste tranquille !

stand for *phrasal verb*

1. vouloir dire : **what does FAQ stand for?** que veut dire FAQ ?
2. tolérer : **I won't stand for this behaviour!** je ne tolérerai pas ce genre de comportement ! **stand out** *verb*

ressortir : **the colours stand out against the background** les couleurs ressortent sur le fond

S

➤ **she stands out in a crowd** on la remarque dans la foule

stand up *phrasal verb*

se lever : **stand up!** levez-vous ! ; **she stood up when I came in** elle s'est levée quand je suis entré

stand up for *phrasal verb*

défendre : **he stands up for his little brother** il défend son petit frère.

standard ['stændəd] *noun & adjective*

▪ *noun*
1. **niveau** *(masculine)* : **the standard is very high** le niveau est très élevé
2. **valeur** *(masculine)* : **his parents have strict standards** ses parents ont des valeurs strictes
➤ **the standard of living** le niveau de vie : **they have a high standard of living** ils ont un niveau de vie élevé
➤ **he has high standards** il est très exigeant
▪ *adjective*
1. **ordinaire** : **it's a standard hotel room** c'est une chambre d'hôtel ordinaire
2. **standard** *(invariable)* : **this is the standard size** c'est la taille standard.

stank [stæŋk] *past tense of* stink

the fish stank le poisson puait.

staple ['steɪpl] *noun & verb*

▪ *noun*
agrafe *(feminine)* : **the staple has come out** l'agrafe s'est détachée
▪ *verb*
agrafer : **I stapled the sheets together** j'ai agrafé les feuilles.

stapler ['steɪplə^r] *noun*

agrafeuse *(feminine)* : **have you got a stapler?** est-ce que tu as une agrafeuse ?

star [stɑ:^r] *noun & verb*

▪ *noun*
1. **étoile** *(feminine)* : **there are lots of stars tonight** il y a beaucoup d'étoiles ce soir
2. **vedette** *(feminine)*, **star** *(feminine)* : **he's an international star** c'est une star internationale
➤ **to read one's stars** lire son horoscope : **she reads her stars in the newspaper every day** elle lit son horoscope dans le journal tous les jours

▪ *verb*
1. **avoir pour vedette** : **the film starred Mel Gibson** le film avait pour vedette Mel Gibson
2. **être la vedette** : **Julia Roberts stars in this film** Julia Roberts est la vedette de ce film

stare [steə^r] *verb*

dévisager, regarder fixement : **he stared at me** il m'a regardé fixement ; **it's not nice to stare at people** ça ne se fait pas de dévisager les gens.

stark naked [stɑ:k'neɪkɪd] *adjective*

tout nu : **he was stark naked** il était tout nu.

Stars and Stripes ['stɑ:^rzəndstraɪps] *noun*

the Stars and Stripes la bannière étoilée.

> 📖 **THE STARS AND STRIPES**
> C'est l'un des nombreux noms donnés par les Américains à leur drapeau. Les cinquante étoiles (**stars**) représentent les cinquante États du pays. Les treize rayures (**stripes**) rouges et blanches symbolisent les treize premières colonies qui furent les premiers États des États-Unis. Les Américains sont très fiers de leur drapeau et beaucoup en mettent un à l'entrée de leur maison.

start [stɑ:t] *noun & verb*

▪ *noun*
début *(masculine)* : **it's a start** c'est un début ; **at the start of the film** au début du film
▪ *verb*
1. **commencer** : **the film starts at four o'clock** le film commence à quatre heures
2. **démarrer** : **the car won't start** la voiture ne veut pas démarrer
3. **mettre en marche** : **can you start the washing machine?** tu peux mettre en marche la machine à laver ?
4. **créer** : **he wants to start a business** il veut créer une entreprise
➤ **to start again** recommencer
➤ **to start to do something** OR **to start doing something** commencer à faire quelque chose OR se mettre à faire quelque chose : **he started working** il a commencé à travailler ; **she started crying** OR **she started to cry** elle s'est mise à pleurer

start off, **start out** *phrasal verb*

partir : **we started out at dawn** nous sommes partis à l'aube.

starter *UK* ['stɑːtəʳ] *noun*

hors-d'œuvre *(masculine)* [*plural* hors-d'œuvre] : **do you want a starter?** tu veux un hors-d'œuvre ?

startle ['stɑːtl] *verb*

faire sursauter : **you startled me** tu m'as fait sursauter.

starve [stɑːv] *verb*

mourir de faim : **millions of people are starving all over the world** des millions de gens meurent de faim dans le monde entier
➤ **I'm starving** je meurs de faim.

state [steɪt] *noun*

1. état *(masculine)* : **she's in a state of shock** elle est en état de choc ; **he's not in a fit state to drive** il n'est pas en état de conduire
2. État *(masculine)* : **the head of state** le chef de l'État ; **what are the member states of the European Union?** quels sont les États membres de l'Union européenne ? ; **Alaska is the biggest state in the United States** l'Alaska est le plus vaste État des États-Unis
➤ **the States** les États-Unis : **Vic lives in the States** Vic vit aux États-Unis ; **we're going to the States** nous allons aux États-Unis.

statement ['steɪtmənt] *noun*

déclaration *(feminine)*.

station ['steɪʃn] *noun*

gare *(feminine)* : **I'll meet you at the station** je viendrai te chercher à la gare
➤ **a radio station** une radio : **I often listen to this radio station** j'écoute souvent cette radio
➤ **a bus station** une gare routière
➤ **a railway station** *UK* OR **a train station** *US* une gare
➤ **a tube station** *UK* OR **a subway station** *US* une station de métro
➤ **the police station** le commissariat de police
➤ **a station wagon** un break : **he drives a station wagon** il a un break.

stationery ['steɪʃnərɪ] *uncountable noun*

papier *(masculine)* et enveloppes *(feminine plural)* : **I bought some stationery** j'ai acheté du papier et des enveloppes
➤ **a stationery shop** *UK* OR **a stationery store** *US* une papeterie.

statue ['stætʃuː] *noun*

statue *(feminine)* : **there's a statue of Nelson in Trafalgar Square** il y a une statue de Nelson à Trafalgar Square
➤ **the Statue of Liberty** la statue de la Liberté

> 📖 THE STATUE OF LIBERTY
> La statue de la Liberté est située sur une petite île, **Liberty Island**, à l'entrée du port de New York. Elle représente une femme portant un flambeau qui symbolise la liberté. La France en fit cadeau aux États-Unis en 1884 pour commémorer les révolutions américaine et française. Pour les immigrés qui arrivaient en bateau aux États-Unis, cette statue était le symbole d'une vie nouvelle, du rêve américain.

stay [steɪ] *noun & verb*

■ *noun*

séjour *(masculine)* : **I enjoyed my stay in Montreal** j'ai passé un séjour agréable à Montréal

■ *verb*

1. rester : **stay here!** reste ici ! ; **I'll stay at home** je vais rester à la maison ; **she stayed awake all night** elle est restée éveillée toute la nuit ; **he stayed for a week** il est resté une semaine ; **we stayed in Athens for a few days** nous avons passé quelques jours à Athènes
2. loger : **I stayed with friends** j'étais logé chez des amis ; **I stayed in a hotel** j'étais logé à l'hôtel OR je suis descendu à l'hôtel
➤ **to stay the night** passer la nuit : **do you want to stay the night?** tu veux passer la nuit ici ?

stay away *phrasal verb*

ne pas s'approcher : **stay away from the door** ne t'approche pas de la porte

stay in *phrasal verb*

rester chez soi : **she stayed in yesterday** elle est restée chez elle hier

stay out *phrasal verb*

ne pas rentrer : **he stayed out all night** il n'est pas rentré de la nuit

stay up *phrasal verb*

ne pas se coucher : **she stayed up all night** elle ne s'est pas couchée cette nuit ; **I stayed up late** je me suis couché tard.

steady ['stedɪ] *adjective*

1. régulier *(feminine* régulière*)* : **we're making**

S

steady progress nous faisons des progrès réguliers

2. **stable : the chair isn't very steady** la chaise n'est pas très stable ; **she has a steady job** elle a un emploi stable

3. **ferme : he has steady hands** il a les mains fermes.

steak [steɪk] *noun*

steak *(masculine)* **: I like my steak well done** j'aime le steak bien cuit.

steal [stiːl] *(past tense* stole, *past participle* stolen) *verb*

voler : someone stole my bag on m'a volé mon sac.

steam [stiːm] *noun*

I. **vapeur** *(feminine)* **: a steam engine** une locomotive à vapeur

2. **buée** *(feminine)* **: there's steam on the window** il y a de la buée sur la vitre.

steel [stiːl] *uncountable noun*

acier *(masculine)* **: a steel ladder** une échelle en acier.

steep [stiːp] *adjective*

I. **raide : the stairs are steep** l'escalier est raide

2. **escarpé : it's a steep hill** c'est une colline escarpée.

steering wheel [ˈstɪərɪŋwiːl] *noun*

volant *(masculine)* **: he was at the steering wheel** il était au volant.

step [step] *noun & verb*

◾ *noun*

I. **pas** *(masculine)* **: she took one step backwards** elle a reculé d'un pas

2. **marche** *(feminine)* **: he was sitting on the step** il était assis sur la marche

◾ *verb* (*past tense & past participle* stepped)
marcher : he stepped on an ant il a marché sur une fourmi

step forward *phrasal verb*

avancer : can you step forward a bit? tu peux avancer un peu ?

stepbrother [ˈstepˌbrʌðəʳ] *noun*

demi-frère *(masculine)* **: he's my stepbrother** c'est mon demi-frère.

stepdaughter [ˈstepˌdɔːtəʳ] *noun*

belle-fille *(feminine)* [*plural* **belles-filles**] **: she's my stepdaughter** c'est ma belle-fille.

stepfather [ˈstepˌfɑːðəʳ] *noun*

beau-père *(masculine)* [*plural* **beaux-pères**] **: he's my stepfather** c'est mon beau-père.

stepladder [ˈstepˌlædəʳ] *noun*

escabeau *(masculine)* **: he fell off the stepladder** il est tombé de l'escabeau.

stepmother [ˈstepˌmʌðəʳ] *noun*

belle-mère *(feminine)* [*plural* **belles-mères**] **: she's my stepmother** c'est ma belle-mère.

stepsister [ˈstepˌsɪstəʳ] *noun*

demi-sœur *(feminine)* **: she's my stepsister** c'est ma demi-sœur.

stepson [ˈstepsʌn] *noun*

beau-fils *(masculine)* [*plural* **beaux-fils**] **: he's my stepson** c'est mon beau-fils.

stereo [ˈsterɪəʊ] (*plural* stereos) *noun*

chaîne *(feminine)* **hi-fi : he bought a new stereo system** il s'est acheté une nouvelle chaîne hi-fi

➤ **a personal stereo** un Walkman® OR un baladeur.

stew [*UK* stjuː, *US* stuː] *noun*

ragoût *(masculine)* **: a beef stew** un ragoût de bœuf.

stick [stɪk] *noun & verb*

◾ *noun*

I. **bâton** *(masculine)* **: he hit the tree with a stick** il a frappé l'arbre avec un bâton

2. **canne** *(feminine)* **: she was walking with a stick** elle marchait à l'aide d'une canne

◾ *verb* (*past tense & past participle* stuck)

I. **coller : I stuck the stamps on the envelope** j'ai collé les timbres sur l'enveloppe ; **the label won't stick** l'étiquette ne colle pas

2. **planter : he stuck the penknife into the wood** il a planté son canif dans le bois

3. *informal* **mettre : stick your bag over there** mets ton sac là-bas

stick out *phrasal verb*

dépasser : your shirt is sticking out ta chemise dépasse

➤ **to stick one's tongue out** tirer la langue : **he stuck his tongue out** il a tiré la langue.

sticker ['stɪkəʳ] *noun*

autocollant *(masculine)* : **her case is covered in stickers** sa valise est couverte d'autocollants.

sticky ['stɪkɪ] *adjective*

1. poisseux *(feminine* poisseuse*)* : **my hands are sticky** j'ai les mains poisseuses
2. adhésif *(feminine* adhésive*)* : **a sticky label** une étiquette adhésive.

stiff [stɪf] *adjective*

1. rigide, raide : **stiff cardboard** du carton rigide
2. dur : **it was a stiff exam** l'examen a été dur ; **this drawer is stiff** ce tiroir est dur à ouvrir
> **to be stiff** avoir des courbatures : **I'm stiff all over** j'ai des courbatures partout
> **to have a stiff neck** avoir un torticolis
> **he's bored stiff** *informal* il s'ennuie à mourir
> **she's scared stiff** *informal* elle est morte de peur.

still [stɪl] *adverb & adjective*

■ *adverb*

1. encore : **are you still at this address?** tu es encore à cette adresse ? ; **that's better still** c'est encore mieux
2. quand même : **he's very lazy but she still likes him** il est très paresseux mais elle l'aime bien quand même

■ *adjective*

immobile : **the lizard was very still** le lézard était immobile
> **to keep still** ne pas bouger : **she won't keep still** elle n'arrête pas de bouger
> **sit still!** restez tranquilles !

sting [stɪŋ] *noun & verb*

■ *noun*

piqûre *(feminine)* : **a bee sting** une piqûre d'abeille

■ *verb (past tense & past participle* stung*)*

piquer : **a bee has stung me** je me suis fait piquer par une abeille.

stink [stɪŋk] *(past tense* stank*, past participle* stunk*) verb*

puer : **it stinks in here!** ça pue ici !

stir [stɜːʳ] *(past tense & past participle* stirred*) verb*

remuer : **stir the eggs and sugar together** remuez les œufs avec le sucre.

stitch [stɪtʃ] *noun & verb*

■ *noun*

1. point *(masculine)* : **you can see the stitches on the hem** les points de l'ourlet sont apparents
2. point *(masculine)* de suture : **he had three stitches in his arm** on lui a fait trois points de suture au bras
> **I've got a stitch** j'ai un point de côté

■ *verb*

recoudre : **she stitched the button back on** elle a recousu le bouton.

stock [stɒk] *noun*

1. réserve *(feminine)* : **we have a stock of canned food at home** on a une réserve de conserves à la maison
2. bouillon *(masculine)* : **chicken stock** du bouillon de poulet
> **in stock** en stock
> **we are out of stock** nous sommes en rupture de stock
> **the stock exchange** OR **the stock market** la Bourse.

stocking ['stɒkɪŋ] *noun*

bas *(masculine)* : **she's wearing silk stockings** elle porte des bas en soie.

stole [stəʊl] *past tense of* steal

he stole a lot of money il a volé beaucoup d'argent.

stolen ['stəʊln] *past participle of* steal

my car has been stolen on m'a volé ma voiture.

stomach ['stʌmək] *noun*

estomac *(masculine)* : **you shouldn't work on an empty stomach** tu ne devrais pas travailler l'estomac vide.

stomachache ['stʌməkeɪk] *noun*

to have stomachache *UK* OR **to have a stomachache** *US* avoir mal au ventre ; **I've got stomachache** j'ai mal au ventre.

stone [stəʊn] *noun*

1. pierre *(feminine)* : **she threw a stone at the window** elle a lancé une pierre contre la fenêtre ; **a stone wall** un mur en pierre ; **opals are precious stones** les opales sont des pierres précieuses
2. *UK* noyau *(masculine)* : **cherries have stones** les cerises ont des noyaux
3. *(plural* stone*)UK* = 6,348 kg : **she weighs ten stone** elle pèse environ soixante kilos.

S

stood [stʊd] *past tense & past participle of* stand

she stood up elle s'est levée ; this tree has stood here for hundreds of years cet arbre est là depuis des centaines d'années.

stool [stuːl] *noun*

tabouret *(masculine)* : she's sitting on a stool elle est assise sur un tabouret.

stop [stɒp] *noun & verb*

■ *noun*

arrêt *(masculine)* : where's the next stop? où est le prochain arrêt ? ; a bus stop un arrêt de bus

➤ to come to a stop s'arrêter : the train came to a stop le train s'est arrêté

■ *verb (past tense & past participle* stopped)

1. arrêter : she stopped the car elle a arrêté la voiture ; we'll stop at four o'clock on va arrêter à quatre heures

2. s'arrêter : my watch has stopped ma montre s'est arrêtée ; the bus stopped in front of the school le bus s'est arrêté devant le lycée

➤ to stop doing something arrêter de faire quelque chose : it has stopped raining at last il s'est enfin arrêté de pleuvoir

➤ to stop somebody doing something empêcher quelqu'un de faire quelque chose : I tried to stop him leaving j'ai essayé de l'empêcher de partir.

stopwatch [ˈstɒpwɒtʃ] *noun*

chronomètre *(masculine)* : the referee looked at his stopwatch l'arbitre a regardé son chronomètre.

store [stɔːr] *noun & verb*

■ *noun*

magasin *(masculine)* : he went into the store on the corner il est allé au magasin du coin

a department store un grand magasin

■ *verb*

1. entreposer : we store wine in the cellar nous entreposons du vin dans la cave

2. mémoriser : the latest computers can store even more information les derniers ordinateurs peuvent mémoriser encore plus de données.

storekeeper *US* [ˈstɔːˌkiːpər] *noun*

commerçant *(masculine)*, commerçante *(feminine)* : he's a storekeeper il est commerçant.

storey *UK* (plural storeys), **story** *US* (plural stories) [ˈstɔːrɪ] *noun*

étage *(masculine)* : the building has ten storeys c'est un immeuble de dix étages.

stork [stɔːk] *noun*

cigogne *(feminine)*.

storm [stɔːm] *noun*

orage *(masculine)*, tempête *(feminine)* : there's going to be a storm un orage va éclater OR il va y avoir une tempête.

stormy [ˈstɔːmɪ] *adjective*

orageux *(feminine* orageuse*)* : it's stormy today le temps est orageux aujourd'hui.

story [ˈstɔːrɪ] (plural stories) *noun*

1. histoire *(feminine)* : she told us a story elle nous a raconté une histoire ; a ghost story une histoire de fantômes

2. *US* ➤ storey *UK*

a fairy story un conte de fées.

straight [streɪt] *adjective & adverb*

■ *adjective*

1. droit : draw a straight line tracez une ligne droite ; stand up straight tenez-vous droit

2. raide : he has straight hair il a les cheveux raides

3. franc : he's always very straight with me il est toujours très franc avec moi

■ *adverb*

1. directement : he went straight to the police il est allé directement à la police

2. droit : walk straight ahead marchez droit devant vous

3. tout de suite : it happened straight after that cela s'est passé tout de suite après.

straightaway [ˌstreɪtəˈweɪ] *adverb*

tout de suite : I want to leave straightaway je veux partir tout de suite.

straightforward [ˌstreɪtˈfɔːwəd] *adjective*

simple : it's very straightforward, all you do is press here c'est très simple, tu n'as qu'à appuyer ici.

strain [streɪn] *verb*

➤ to strain a muscle se froisser un muscle : he strained a muscle il s'est froissé un muscle

➤ to strain one's eyes se fatiguer les yeux : don't strain your eyes ne te fatigue pas les yeux.

strange [streɪndʒ] *adjective*

1. étrange, bizarre : it's strange that she's

late c'est étrange qu'elle soit en retard ; **she's a strange woman** c'est une femme bizarre
2. **inconnu** : **there are a lot of strange faces** il y a de nombreux visages inconnus ; **in a strange town** dans une ville inconnue.

stranger ['streɪndʒər] *noun*

inconnu *(masculine)*, **inconnue** *(feminine)* : **he's a complete stranger** c'est un parfait inconnu.

strangle ['stræŋgl] *verb*

étrangler : **the murderer strangled her** l'assassin l'a étranglée.

strap [stræp] *noun*

1. **bretelle** *(feminine)* : **my bra strap is broken** la bretelle de mon soutien-gorge est cassée
2. **courroie** *(feminine)* : **there's a strap around my suitcase** il y a une courroie autour de ma valise
3. **bracelet** *(masculine)* : **I need a new strap for my watch** il me faut un nouveau bracelet pour ma montre.

Stratford-upon-Avon [ˌstrætfərdəpɒn-ˈeɪvn] *noun*

Stratford-upon-Avon

> STRATFORD-UPON-AVON
> C'est dans cette ville du centre de l'Angleterre qu'est né le dramaturge William Shakespeare. Elle est devenue un haut lieu du théâtre et la troupe de la **Royal Shakespeare Company** interprète régulièrement les œuvres de ce grand écrivain.

straw [strɔ:] *noun*

paille *(feminine)* : **there's straw all over the floor** il y a de la paille par terre ; **he was drinking through a straw** il buvait avec une paille.

strawberry ['strɔ:bərɪ] *(plural* strawberries*) noun*

fraise *(feminine)* : **strawberries and cream** des fraises à la crème
> **a strawberry ice cream** une glace à la fraise
> **strawberry jam** confiture *(feminine)* de fraises
> **a strawberry tart** une tarte aux fraises.

stream [stri:m] *noun*

ruisseau *(masculine)* : **we crossed the stream** nous avons traversé le ruisseau.

street [stri:t] *noun*

rue *(feminine)* : **cross the street at the lights** traversez la rue au feu rouge ; **he lives further down the street** il habite plus loin dans la rue
> **a street lamp** OR **a street light** un réverbère.

streetcar *US* ['stri:tkɑ:r] *noun*

tramway *(masculine)* : **there are streetcars in San Francisco** il y a des tramways à San Francisco.

streetwise ['stri:twaɪz] *adjective*

dégourdi : **these kids are very streetwise** ces enfants sont très dégourdis.

strength [streŋθ] *noun*

force *(feminine)* : **I don't have the strength to get up** je n'ai pas la force de me lever.

stress [stres] *noun*

1. **stress** *(masculine)* : **he's under a lot of stress** il est très stressé
2. **accent** *(masculine)* : **the stress is on the first syllable** l'accent est sur la première syllabe.

stressed ['stresd] *adjective*

stressé : **she's stressed** elle est stressée.

stretch [stretʃ] *verb*

1. **s'étirer** : **she woke up and stretched** elle s'est réveillée et s'est étirée
2. **tendre** : **they stretched the net between the two poles** ils ont tendu le filet entre les deux poteaux ; **stretch your arms towards the ceiling** tendez les bras vers le plafond
> **to stretch one's legs** se dégourdir les jambes : **I went outside to stretch my legs** je suis sorti pour me dégourdir les jambes

stretch out *phrasal verb*

1. **tendre** : **she stretched her hand out to take it** elle a tendu la main pour le prendre
2. **allonger** : **he stretched his legs out** il a allongé ses jambes
3. **s'allonger** : **they stretched out on the grass** ils se sont allongés sur l'herbe.

stretcher ['stretʃər] *noun*

brancard *(masculine)* : **they carried her on a stretcher** ils l'ont emmenée sur un brancard.

strict [strɪkt] *adjective*

strict : **his parents are very strict** ses parents sont très stricts.

S

strike [straɪk] *noun & verb*

■ *noun*
grève *(feminine)*
➤ **to be on strike** être en grève
➤ **to go on strike** faire grève
■ *verb (past tense & past participle* struck*)*
1. **frapper : someone struck me** on m'a frappé ; **I was struck by her beauty** j'ai été frappé par sa beauté
2. **sonner : the clock struck six** l'horloge a sonné six heures
3. **heurter : the car struck a tree** la voiture a heurté un arbre
➤ **to strike a match** frotter une allumette : **she struck a match** elle a frotté une allumette.

string [strɪŋ] *noun*
1. **ficelle** *(feminine)* : **I tied the package with string** j'ai attaché le paquet avec de la ficelle
2. **corde** *(feminine)* : **the guitar has a broken string** la guitare a une corde cassée
➤ **a piece of string** un bout de ficelle.

strip [strɪp] *noun & verb*
■ *noun*
bande *(feminine)* : **a strip of paper** une bande de papier
■ *verb (past tense & past participle* stripped, *present participle* stripping*)*
se déshabiller : he stripped and had a shower il s'est déshabillé et il a pris une douche.

stripe [straɪp] *noun*
rayure *(feminine)* : **there are red and green stripes on her dress** il y a des rayures rouges et vertes sur sa robe.

striped [straɪpt] *adjective*
à rayures : Dick's wearing a striped shirt Dick porte une chemise à rayures.

stroke [strəʊk] *noun & verb*
■ *noun*
1. **coup** *(masculine)* : **a stroke of lightning** un coup de foudre
2. **attaque** *(feminine)* : **he had a stroke** il a eu une attaque
➤ **a stroke of luck** un coup de chance
■ *verb*
caresser : she was stroking the cat elle caressait le chat.

stroll [strəʊl] *noun & verb*
■ *noun*
petite promenade *(feminine)* : **we're going for a stroll** on va faire une petite promenade
■ *verb*
se promener : they were strolling through the park ils se promenaient dans le parc.

stroller *US* ['strəʊləʳ] *noun*
poussette *(feminine)* : **she was pushing the baby in the stroller** elle promenait son bébé dans sa poussette.

strong [strɒŋ] *adjective*
1. **fort : Hercules was very strong** Hercule était très fort ; **she likes her coffee strong** elle aime le café fort ; **as strong as an ox** fort comme un bœuf
2. **solide : a strong pair of shoes** des chaussures solides.

struck [strʌk] *past tense & past participle of* strike
the clock struck six l'horloge a sonné six heures ; **I was struck by the size of the building** j'ai été frappé par la taille de l'immeuble.

structure ['strʌktʃəʳ] *noun*
structure *(feminine)*.

struggle ['strʌgl] *noun & verb*
■ *noun*
lutte *(feminine)* : **a struggle to survive** une lutte pour survivre
■ *verb*
1. **se battre : he struggled to survive in the jungle** il s'est battu pour survivre dans la jungle
2. **se débattre : she struggled to get free** elle s'est débattue pour se libérer
3. **avoir du mal : how are you getting on? – we're struggling** comment ça va ? – on a beaucoup de mal ; **he's struggling to finish his homework** il a du mal à finir ses devoirs.

stubborn ['stʌbən] *adjective*
têtu : he's very stubborn il est très têtu ; **as stubborn as a mule** têtu comme une mule.

stuck [stʌk] *adjective & verb form*
■ *adjective*
1. **coincé : the window is stuck** la fenêtre est coincée
2. **bloqué : we're stuck in a snowstorm** nous sommes bloqués dans une tempête de neige
➤ **to get stuck** rester coincé : **my arm got stuck** mon bras est resté coincé

past tense & past participle of stick
she stuck the photo in the album elle a collé la photo dans l'album ; **have you stuck the stamp on?** as-tu collé le timbre ?

stuck-up ['stʌkʌp] *adjective informal*

snob *(invariable)* : **she's really stuck-up** elle est vraiment snob.

student [*UK* 'stjuːdnt, *US* 'stuːdnt] *noun*

étudiant *(masculine)*, **étudiante** *(feminine)* : **he's a student** il est étudiant.

studio [*UK* 'stjuːdɪəʊ, *US* 'stuːdɪəʊ] *(plural* studios) *noun*

1. **studio** *(masculine)* : **a television studio** un studio de télévision
2. **atelier** *(masculine)* : **a painter's studio** un atelier de peintre
➤ **a studio flat** *UK* OR **a studio apartment** *US* un studio.

study ['stʌdɪ] *noun & verb*

noun *(plural* **studies**)
étude *(feminine)* : **he wants to continue his studies** il veut continuer ses études

verb
faire des études de : Flora's studying Spanish Flora fait des études d'espagnol
➤ **to study for an exam** préparer un examen : **I'm studying for my exam** je prépare mon examen.

stuff [stʌf] *noun & verb informal*

noun
1. **truc** *(masculine)*, **trucs** *(masculine plural)* : **what's that stuff you're eating?** c'est quoi, ce truc que tu manges ? ; **what's all this stuff on the table?** c'est quoi, tous ces trucs sur la table ?
2. **affaires** *(feminine plural)* : **don't forget to take your stuff with you** n'oublie pas de prendre tes affaires

verb
fourrer : he stuffed the key into his pocket il a fourré la clé dans sa poche.

stuffy ['stʌfɪ] *adjective*

mal aéré : the room is stuffy cette pièce est mal aérée.

stumble ['stʌmbl] *verb*

trébucher : she stumbled down the stairs elle a trébuché en descendant l'escalier.

stung [stʌŋ] *past tense & past participle of* sting

the nettles stung me je me suis fait piquer par

les orties ; **have you ever been stung by a wasp?** est-ce que tu t'es déjà fait piquer par une guêpe ?

stunk [stʌŋk] *past participle of* stink

it has always stunk here ça a toujours pué ici.

stunned ['stʌnd] *adjective*

abasourdi : he was stunned by the news la nouvelle l'a abasourdi.

stunning ['stʌnɪŋ] *adjective*

1. **stupéfiant : it's stunning news** cette nouvelle est stupéfiante
2. **splendide : the scenery is stunning** le paysage est splendide.

stunt [stʌnt] *noun*

cascade *(feminine)*
➤ **a stunt man** un cascadeur.

stupid [*UK* 'stjuːpɪd, *US* 'stuːpɪd] *adjective*

bête : he's very stupid il est très bête.

stutter ['stʌtər] *verb*

bégayer : she stutters elle bégaie.

style [staɪl] *noun*

1. **style** *(masculine)* : **a new style of sportswear** un nouveau style de vêtements de sport
2. **classe** *(feminine)* : **James Bond has a lot of style** James Bond a beaucoup de classe.

subject ['sʌbdʒekt] *noun*

1. **sujet** *(masculine)* : **what's the subject of the book?** quel est le sujet du livre ?
2. **matière** *(feminine)* : **history is my favourite subject** l'histoire est ma matière préférée.

submarine [ˌsʌbməˈriːn] *noun*

sous-marin *(masculine)*.

subscription [səbˈskrɪpʃn] *noun*

abonnement *(masculine)*
➤ **to take out a subscription to a magazine** s'abonner à un magazine.

substance ['sʌbstəns] *noun*

substance *(feminine)* : **a sticky substance** une substance poisseuse.

substitute [*UK* 'sʌbstɪtjuːt, *US* 'sʌbstɪtuːt] *noun*

remplaçant *(masculine)* : **the teams can have three substitutes** les équipes ont droit à trois remplaçants.

S

subtitle ['sʌb,taɪtl] *noun*

sous-titre *(masculine)* : **I can't read the subtitles** je n'arrive pas à lire les sous-titres.

subtle ['sʌtl] *adjective*

subtil : **there's a subtle difference between the two** il y a une différence subtile entre les deux.

subtract [səb'trækt] *verb*

ôter : **subtract 78 from 100** ôtez 78 de 100.

suburb ['sʌbɜːb] *noun*

banlieue *(feminine)* : **Wanstead is a suburb of London** Wanstead est une banlieue de Londres

➤ **the suburbs** la banlieue : **they live in the suburbs** ils habitent en banlieue.

subway ['sʌbweɪ] *noun*

1. *UK* passage *(masculine)* souterrain : **you have to walk through the subway to cross the road** il faut prendre le passage souterrain pour traverser la route

2. *US* métro *(masculine)* : **it's best to take the subway into Manhattan** il vaut mieux prendre le métro jusqu'à Manhattan.

succeed [sək'siːd] *verb*

réussir : **you have to work hard to succeed** il faut travailler dur pour réussir ; **he succeeded in getting a place at Oxford** il a réussi à être admis à l'université d'Oxford.

success [sək'ses] *noun*

succès *(masculine)* : **it's a great success** c'est un grand succès.

successful [sək'sesfʊl] *adjective*

1. réussi : **it was a successful evening** la soirée était très réussie

2. à succès : **it's a successful book** c'est un livre a succès

➤ **to be successful** réussir : **she's successful in whatever she does** elle réussit tout ce qu'elle entreprend.

successfully [sək'sesfʊlɪ] *adverb*

avec succès : **he finished his studies successfully** il a terminé ses études avec succès.

such [sʌtʃ] *adjective & adverb*

1. tel *(feminine* telle*)* : **it was such a surprise** ça a été une telle surprise ; **such situations are common** de telles situations sont courantes ;

in such cases dans des cas pareils OR dans de tels cas

2. tellement : **it's such a pity** c'est tellement dommage ; **why are you in such a hurry?** pourquoi es-tu tellement pressé ? ; **he has such a lot of books** il a tellement de livres ; **I waited such a long time** j'ai attendu tellement longtemps

3. si : **it's such a beautiful view!** c'est une si belle vue ! ; **he's such a clever man** c'est un homme si intelligent ; **I've never seen such a big dog** je n'ai jamais vu un si grand chien

➤ **there's no such thing** ça n'existe pas

➤ **such as** tel que OR comme : **animals such as lions and tigers** des animaux tels que les lions et les tigres OR des animaux comme les lions et les tigres.

suck [sʌk] *verb*

sucer : **he's sucking his thumb** il suce son pouce.

sudden ['sʌdn] *adjective*

soudain : **there was a sudden shower** il y a eu une averse soudaine

➤ **all of a sudden** tout à coup ; **all of a sudden she got angry** tout à coup, elle s'est mise en colère.

suddenly ['sʌdnlɪ] *adverb*

1. tout à coup : **suddenly he left** tout à coup, il est parti

2. subitement : **she died suddenly** elle est morte subitement.

suede [sweɪd] *uncountable noun*

daim *(masculine)* : **a suede coat** un manteau en daim.

suffer ['sʌfər] *verb*

souffrir : **he's really suffering** il souffre beaucoup

➤ **to be suffering from a cold** avoir un rhume.

sugar ['ʃʊgər] *noun*

sucre *(masculine)* : **how many sugars do you want in your tea?** tu veux combien de sucres dans ton thé ? ; **I don't take sugar** je ne prends pas de sucre.

suggest [*UK* sə'dʒest, *US* sə'gʒest] *verb*

suggérer : **what do you suggest?** qu'est-ce que tu suggères ? ; **I suggest you leave now** je suggère que tu partes maintenant.

suggestion [*UK* sə'dʒestʃn, *US* səg-'dʒestʃn] *noun*

suggestion *(feminine)* : **can I make a suggestion?** est-ce que je peux faire une suggestion ?

suicide ['suɪsaɪd] *noun*

suicide *(masculine)*

➤ **to commit suicide** se suicider : **she committed suicide** elle s'est suicidée.

suit [suːt] *noun & verb*

▣ *noun*

1. **costume** *(masculine)* : **he's wearing a suit** il porte un costume
2. **tailleur** *(masculine)* : **she's wearing a suit** elle porte un tailleur

▣ *verb*

1. **aller à** : **that skirt suits you** cette jupe te va bien
2. **convenir à** : **does Monday suit you?** est-ce que lundi te convient ?
3. **arranger** : **it suits me to leave straightaway** ça m'arrange de partir tout de suite

➤ **suit yourself!** comme vous voulez !

suitable ['suːtəbl] *adjective*

qui convient : **that dress isn't suitable for the occasion** cette robe ne convient pas pour la circonstance.

suitcase ['suːtkeɪs] *noun*

valise *(feminine)* : **I've lost my suitcase** j'ai perdu ma valise ; **I'm going to pack my suitcase** je vais faire ma valise.

suite [swiːt] *noun*

suite *(feminine)* : **they have a suite at the Ritz** ils ont une suite au Ritz.

sulk [sʌlk] *verb*

bouder : **she's sulking** elle boude.

sultana [səl'tɑːnə] *noun*

raisin *(masculine)* **de Smyrne.**

sum [sʌm] *noun & verb*

1. **somme** *(feminine)* : **that's a large sum of money** c'est une grosse somme d'argent
2. **calcul** *(masculine)* : **I can't do the sum** je ne peux pas faire le calcul ; **he's good at sums** il est fort en calcul

sum up *phrasal verb*

résumer : **let's sum up** résumons.

summary ['sʌmərɪ] *(plural* summaries) *noun*

résumé *(masculine)* : **give me a summary of the book** fais-moi un résumé du livre.

summer ['sʌmər] *noun*

été *(masculine)* : **in the summer** en été OR l'été ; **they go to Corsica every summer** ils passent tous leurs étés en Corse

➤ **a summer camp** *US* une colonie de vacances

➤ **summer clothes** vêtements *(masculine plural)* d'été

➤ **the summer holidays** *UK* OR **the summer vacations** *US* les vacances *(feminine plural)* d'été.

summertime ['sʌmətaɪm] *uncountable noun*

été *(masculine)* : **it happened in the summertime** cela s'est passé en été.

summit ['sʌmɪt] *noun*

sommet *(masculine)* : **Edmund Hillary and Tenzing Norgay reached the summit of Everest in 1953** Edmund Hillary et Tenzing Norgay ont atteint le sommet de l'Everest en 1953.

sun [sʌn] *noun*

soleil *(masculine)* : **the sun's shining** le soleil brille

➤ **in the sun** au soleil : **I don't want to go out in the sun** je ne veux pas me mettre au soleil.

sunbathe ['sʌnbeɪð] *verb*

se faire bronzer : **she was sunbathing on the beach** elle se faisait bronzer sur la plage.

sunburn ['sʌnbɜːn] *uncountable noun*

coup *(masculine)* **de soleil** : **I have sunburn on my arms** j'ai des coups de soleil sur les bras.

sunburnt ['sʌnbɜːnt], **sunburned** ['sʌnbɜːnd] *adjective*

➤ **to be sunburnt** OR **sunburned** avoir des coups de soleil : **look how sunburnt he is** regarde les coups de soleil qu'il a pris.

Sunday ['sʌndɪ] *noun*

dimanche *(masculine)* : **it's Sunday today** nous sommes dimanche ; **next Sunday** dimanche prochain ; **last Sunday** dimanche dernier

➤ **on Sunday** dimanche : **I'll see you on Sunday** je te reverrai dimanche

➤ **on Sundays** le dimanche : **he comes to see me on Sundays** il vient me voir le dimanche

S

➤ **to be in one's Sunday best** être endimanché.

sundown US ['sʌndaʊn] *uncountable noun*

coucher *(masculine)* **de soleil : they stopped work at sundown** ils ont arrêté de travailler au coucher du soleil.

sunflower ['sʌn,flaʊəʳ] *noun*

tournesol *(masculine)* : **sunflowers turn to face the sun** les tournesols se tournent vers le soleil.

sung [sʌŋ] *past participle of* sing

he has sung every song he knows il a chanté toutes les chansons qu'il connaissait.

sunglasses ['sʌn,glɑːsɪz] *plural noun*

lunettes *(feminine plural)* **de soleil : she's wearing sunglasses** elle porte des lunettes de soleil.

sunk [sʌŋk] *past participle of* sink

the ship has sunk le navire a coulé.

sunlight ['sʌnlaɪt] *uncountable noun*

lumière *(feminine)* **du soleil : in the sunlight** au soleil.

sunny ['sʌnɪ] *adjective*

ensoleillé : **it was a sunny day** c'était une journée ensoleillée
➤ **it's sunny** il y a du soleil.

sunrise ['sʌnraɪz] *noun*

lever *(masculine)* **du soleil : I woke up before sunrise** je me suis réveillé avant le lever du soleil.

sunset ['sʌnset] *noun*

coucher *(masculine)* **du soleil : I came home after sunset** je suis rentré après le coucher du soleil.

sunshine ['sʌnʃaɪn] *uncountable noun*

soleil *(masculine)* : **there isn't much sunshine today** il n'y a pas beaucoup de soleil aujourd'hui.

suntan ['sʌntæn] *noun*

bronzage *(masculine)* : **she has a nice suntan** elle a un joli bronzage
➤ **suntan lotion** lait *(masculine)* solaire : **put on some more suntan lotion** remets du lait solaire.

super ['suːpəʳ] *adjective informal*

super *(invariable)* : **it's a super film** c'est un film super
➤ **the Super Bowl** US le championnat de football américain

✎   THE SUPER BOWL

Le **Super Bowl** est l'un des événements sportifs les plus importants aux États-Unis. C'est la finale de football américain qui oppose les deux meilleures équipes professionnelles. Elle a lieu chaque année à la fin janvier et des millions d'Américains suivent sa retransmission à la télévision.

---

superhighway US ['suːpə,haɪweɪ] *noun*

autoroute *(feminine)*
➤ **information superhighway** l'autoroute *(feminine)* de l'information.

superior [suːˈpɪərɪəʳ] *adjective*

supérieur : **goods of superior quality** des produits de qualité supérieure.

supermarket ['suːpə,mɑːkɪt] *noun*

supermarché *(masculine)* : **we went to the supermarket** nous sommes allés au supermarché.

supernatural [,suːpəˈnætʃrəl] *adjective*

surnaturel *(feminine* surnaturelle*)* : **she has supernatural powers** elle a des pouvoirs surnaturels.

superstitious [,suːpəˈstɪʃəs] *adjective*

superstitieux *(feminine* superstitieuse*)* : **are you superstitious?** es-tu superstitieux ?

superstore ['suːpəstɔːʳ] *noun*

hypermarché *(masculine)* : **they have opened a superstore** ils ont ouvert un hypermarché.

supper ['sʌpəʳ] *noun*

dîner *(masculine)* : **we had fish for supper** on a mangé du poisson au dîner
➤ **to have supper** dîner.

supply [səˈplaɪ] *noun & verb*

■ *noun (plural* supplies*)*
provision *(feminine)* : **they got in a supply of wood** ils ont fait des provisions de bois ; **the supplies are running out** les provisions commencent à manquer
➤ **supply and demand** l'offre *(feminine)* et la demande

verb (*past tense & past participle* supplied)
fournir : the school supplies pencils l'école fournit des crayons

➤ **to supply someone with something**
fournir quelque chose à quelqu'un : **I supplied him with the details** je lui ai fourni les détails

> ⚠ Le verbe anglais **to supply** est un faux ami. Il ne signifie pas "supplier".

support [sə'pɔːt] *noun & verb*

▪ *noun*
soutien *(masculine)* : **thanks to their support, he was elected mayor** grâce à leur soutien, il a été élu maire

▪ *verb*
1. **soutenir : I will always support you** je te soutiendrai toujours
2. **être un supporter de : she supports Manchester United** c'est une supporter de Manchester United

> ⚠ Le verbe anglais **to support** est un faux ami. Il ne signifie pas "supporter" au sens de "tolérer".

supporter [sə'pɔːtər] *noun*
1. **partisan** *(masculine)*, **partisane** *(feminine)* : **he's a supporter of feminism** c'est un partisan du féminisme
2. **supporter : he's a Leeds supporter** c'est un supporter de Leeds.

suppose [sə'pəʊz] *verb*
1. **supposer : I suppose he'll come tomorrow** je suppose qu'il viendra demain

➤ **suppose you were rich ...** imagine que tu sois riche ...
2. **penser : do you suppose he'll pass his exam?** tu penses qu'il va être reçu à l'examen ?

➤ **I suppose so** je suppose que oui
➤ **to be supposed to do something** être censé faire quelque chose : **we are supposed to wait here** on est censés attendre ici.

sure [ʃʊər] *adjective*
sûr : are you sure she'll come? tu es sûr qu'elle viendra ? ; **I'm sure** je suis sûr ; **I'm not sure** je ne suis pas sûr

➤ **they are sure to be late** ils vont sûrement être en retard
➤ **for sure!** bien sûr !

➤ **to make sure** s'assurer : **make sure you get the right train** assure-toi que tu prends le bon train ; **make sure you don't forget!** surtout n'oublie pas !

surely [ˈʃʊəlɪ] *adverb*
1. **quand même : surely she didn't do that** elle n'a quand même pas fait ça
2. **sûrement : slowly but surely** lentement mais sûrement.

surf [sɜːf] *verb*
surfer : he spends hours surfing the Net il passe des heures à surfer sur le web.

surface [ˈsɜːfɪs] *noun*
surface *(feminine)* : **I can see something on the surface of the water** je vois quelque chose à la surface de l'eau.

surfboard [ˈsɜːfbɔːd] *noun*
planche *(feminine)* **de surf**.

surfing [ˈsɜːfɪŋ] *uncountable noun*
surf *(masculine)* : **to go surfing** faire du surf ; **she goes surfing every weekend** elle fait du surf tous les week-ends.

surgeon [ˈsɜːdʒən] *noun*
chirurgien *(masculine)* : **Tina's father is a surgeon** le père de Tina est chirurgien.

surname [ˈsɜːneɪm] *noun*
nom *(masculine)* **de famille : what's your surname?** quel est votre nom de famille ?

> ⚠ **Surname** est un faux ami, il ne signifie pas "surnom".

surprise [sə'praɪz] *noun & verb*

▪ *noun*
surprise *(feminine)* : **what a surprise!** quelle surprise !
▪ *verb*
surprendre : that surprises me cela me surprend.

surprised [sə'praɪzd] *adjective*
surpris : I'm surprised at his behaviour je suis surpris de son comportement ; **he was surprised to see me** il a été surpris de me voir.

surprising [sə'praɪzɪŋ] *adjective*
surprenant : that's not surprising ce n'est pas surprenant.

surrender [sə'rendər] noun

se rendre : **the soldiers surrendered** les soldats se sont rendus.

surround [sə'raʊnd] verb

1. entourer : **the house is surrounded by a wall** la maison est entourée d'un mur
2. cerner : **the police surrounded the building** la police a cerné l'immeuble.

survey ['sɜːveɪ] noun

sondage (masculine).

survive [sə'vaɪv] verb

survivre : **two people survived** deux personnes ont survécu.

survivor [sə'vaɪvər] noun

survivant (masculine), **survivante** (feminine) : **are there any survivors?** y a-t-il des survivants ?

suspect noun & verb

■ noun ['sʌspekt]
suspect (masculine), **suspecte** (feminine) : **he's a suspect** c'est un suspect
■ verb [sə'spekt]
soupçonner : **they suspect her of stealing the diamond** ils la soupçonnent d'avoir volé le diamant.

suspenders US [sə'spendəz] plural noun

bretelles (feminine plural) : **he wears suspenders to keep his pants up** il met des bretelles pour retenir son pantalon.

suspense [sə'spens] uncountable noun

suspense (masculine) : **the film was full of suspense** il y avait beaucoup de suspense dans ce film.

suspicion [sə'spɪʃn] noun

soupçon : **do you have any suspicions?** tu as des soupçons ?

suspicious [sə'spɪʃəs] adjective

1. méfiant : **he became suspicious** il est devenu méfiant
2. louche : **she looks very suspicious** elle a vraiment l'air louche
➤ **to be suspicious of somebody** se méfier de quelqu'un.

swallow ['swɒləʊ] noun & verb

■ noun
hirondelle (feminine) : **swallows migrate to**

Africa in the winter les hirondelles migrent vers l'Afrique en hiver
■ verb
avaler : **she swallowed the pill** elle a avalé la pilule.

swam [swæm] past tense of swim

I swam across the lake j'ai traversé le lac à la nage.

swamp [swɒmp] noun

marais (masculine) : **there are alligators in this swamp** il y a des alligators dans ce marais.

swan [swɒn] noun

cygne (masculine).

swap, swop US [swɒp] (past tense & past participle swapped OR swopped, present participle swapping OR swopping) verb

échanger : **let's swap jackets** échangeons nos vestes ; **they swapped seats** ils ont échangé leurs places ; **I swapped my bike for a scooter** j'ai échangé mon vélo contre une trottinette.

swear [sweər] (past tense swore, past participle sworn) verb

jurer : **don't swear** ne jure pas ; **I swear I'm telling the truth** je jure que je dis la vérité
➤ **to swear at somebody** injurier quelqu'un.

swearword ['sweəwɜːd] noun

gros mot (masculine), **juron** (masculine) : **don't say that, it's a swearword** ne dis pas ça, c'est un gros mot.

sweat [swet] noun & verb

■ uncountable noun
sueur (feminine) : **I'm covered in sweat** je suis couvert de sueur OR je suis en nage
■ verb
transpirer, suer : **I'm sweating** je transpire.

sweater ['swetər] noun

pull (masculine) : **he's wearing a red sweater** il porte un pull rouge.

sweatshirt ['swetʃɜːt] noun

sweat-shirt (masculine) : **she's wearing a green sweatshirt** elle porte un sweat-shirt vert.

Swedish ['swiːdɪʃ] adjective & noun

■ adjective
suédois : **he bought a Swedish car** il a acheté une voiture suédoise

■ *noun*
suédois *(masculine)* : **he speaks Swedish** il parle suédois
➤ **the Swedish** les Suédois

> Remember not to use a capital letter for the adjective and the language in French. Only use a capital letter for the inhabitants.

sweep [swiːp] *(past tense & past participle* swept*)*
noun
balayer : **he's sweeping the floor** il balaie le sol.

sweet [swiːt] *adjective & noun*

■ *adjective*
1. **sucré** : **the cake is too sweet** le gâteau est trop sucré
2. **gentil** *(feminine* **gentille***)* : **she's very sweet** elle est très gentille
3. **doux** *(feminine* **douce***)* : **a sweet voice** une voix douce
4. **mignon** *(feminine* **mignonne***)* : **what a sweet little baby!** quel mignon petit bébé !
➤ **sweet dreams!** fais de beaux rêves !
➤ **a sweet potato** une patate douce
■ *noun UK*
1. **bonbon** *(masculine)* : **she loves sweets** elle adore les bonbons
2. **dessert** *(masculine)* : **what's for sweet?** qu'est-ce qu'on a comme dessert ?
➤ **a sweet shop** une confiserie.

sweetcorn ['swiːtkɔːn] *uncountable noun*
maïs *(masculine)*.

swell [swel] *(past tense* swelled, *past participle* swollen OR swelled) *verb*
enfler, gonfler : **my lip has started to swell** ma lèvre s'est mise à enfler

swell up *phrasal verb*
enfler, gonfler : **her face has swollen up** son visage a enflé.

swept [swept] *past tense & past participle of* sweep
she swept the floor elle a balayé le sol ; **have you swept under the table?** as-tu balayé sous la table ?

swerve [swɜːv] *verb*
faire une embardée : **she swerved to avoid the child** elle a fait une embardée pour éviter l'enfant.

swim [swɪm] *noun & verb*

■ *noun*
➤ **to go for a swim** OR **to have a swim** aller se baigner
■ *verb (past tense* swam, *past participle* swum*)*
nager : **can you swim?** tu sais nager ?

swimmer ['swɪmər] *noun*
nageur *(masculine)*, **nageuse** *(feminine)* : **he's a good swimmer** c'est un bon nageur.

swimming ['swɪmɪŋ] *uncountable noun*
natation *(feminine)* : **I love swimming** j'adore la natation
➤ **to go swimming**
1. **aller se baigner** : **he goes swimming in the sea every morning** il va se baigner dans la mer tous les matins
2. **aller à la piscine** : **she goes swimming in the pool every morning** elle va à la piscine tous les matins
➤ **a swimming costume** *UK* un maillot de bain : **she's wearing a swimming costume** elle est en maillot de bain
➤ **a swimming pool** une piscine
➤ **swimming trunks** maillot *(masculine)* de bain : **he's wearing swimming trunks** il est en maillot de bain.

swimsuit ['swɪmsuːt] *noun*
maillot *(masculine)* **de bain**.

swing [swɪŋ] *noun & verb*

■ *noun*
balançoire *(feminine)* : **there are swings in the park** il y a des balançoires dans le parc
■ *verb (past tense & past participle* swung*)*
1. **se balancer** : **the monkeys were swinging in the trees** les singes se balançaient dans les arbres
2. **balancer** : **he was swinging his arms** il balançait ses bras.

Swiss [swɪs] *adjective & noun*

■ *adjective*
suisse

> The French adjective does not start with a capital letter:

a Swiss army knife un couteau suisse

S

■ noun
Suisse *(masculine or feminine)* : **the Swiss** les Suisses.

switch [swɪtʃ] *noun & verb*

■ *noun (plural* switches*)*
1. **bouton** *(masculine)* : **turn the switch on the radio** tourne le bouton de la radio
2. **interrupteur** *(masculine)* : **where's the light switch?** où est l'interrupteur ?

■ *verb*
1. **échanger** : **I switched the red one for the blue one** j'ai échangé le rouge contre le bleu
2. **changer de** : **let's switch places** changeons de place

switch off *phrasal verb*
1. **éteindre** : **I switched off the light** j'ai éteint la lumière
2. **arrêter** : **he switched off the engine** il a arrêté le moteur

switch on *phrasal verb*
1. **allumer** : **she switched the light on** elle a allumé la lumière
2. **mettre en marche** : **I switched the engine on** j'ai mis le moteur en marche.

Switzerland ['swɪtsələnd] *noun*

la Suisse

> In French the names of countries are used with the definite article (**le**, **la** or **l'**), except when they follow the preposition **en**:

Switzerland has four official languages la Suisse a quatre langues officielles ; **Lake Geneva is in Switzerland** le lac Léman se trouve en Suisse ; **she's going to Switzerland** elle va en Suisse.

swollen ['swəʊln] *adjective & verb form*

■ *adjective*
enflé : **she has a swollen arm** elle a le bras enflé

■ *past participle of* swell
his leg has swollen sa jambe a enflé.

swop ➤ swap.

sword [sɔːd] *noun*

épée *(feminine)* : **they used to fight with swords** ils combattaient à l'épée.

swore [swɔːʳ] *past tense of* swear

he swore he would help me il a juré qu'il m'aiderait.

sworn [swɔːn] *past participle of* swear

he has sworn he wasn't lying il a juré qu'il ne mentait pas.

swot UK [swɒt] *noun informal*

bûcheur *(masculine)*, **bûcheuse** *(feminine)* : **he's a real swot** c'est un vrai bûcheur.

swum [swʌm] *past participle of* swim

I've swum in the Pacific and in the Atlantic j'ai nagé dans le Pacifique et l'Atlantique.

swung [swʌŋ] *past tense & past participle of* swing
he swung his bag to and fro il balançait son sac.

syllable ['sɪləbl] *noun*

syllabe *(feminine)* : **'happiness' has three syllables** le mot « happiness » a trois syllabes.

syllabus ['sɪləbəs] *(plural* syllabuses*) noun*

programme *(masculine)* : **Spanish isn't on the syllabus any more** l'espagnol ne fait plus partie du programme.

symbol ['sɪmbl] *noun*

symbole *(masculine)* : **the white dove is a symbol of peace** la colombe blanche est un symbole de la paix.

sympathetic [ˌsɪmpə'θetɪk] *adjective*

compatissant : **they were very sympathetic** ils se sont montrés très compatissants

> ⚠ Sympathetic est un faux ami, il ne signifie pas "sympathique".

sympathy ['sɪmpəθɪ] *uncountable noun*

compassion *(feminine)* : **he has no sympathy for them** il n'a aucune compassion pour eux

> ⚠ Sympathy est un faux ami, il ne signifie pas "sympathie".

synagogue ['sɪnəgɒg] *noun*

synagogue *(feminine)*

syrup ['sɪrəp] *uncountable noun*

sirop *(masculine)* : **a cough syrup** un sirop contre la toux ; **maple syrup** sirop d'érable.

system ['sɪstəm] *noun*

système *(masculine)* : **it's a very good system** c'est un très bon système.

table ['teɪbl] *noun*

table *(feminine)* : **the plates are on the table** les assiettes sont sur la table ; **the guests are sitting at the table** les invités sont à table

> **to lay the table** OR **to set the table** mettre le couvert : **shall I set the table?** je mets le couvert ?
> **table tennis** ping-pong *(masculine)* : **they're playing table tennis** ils jouent au ping-pong.

tablecloth ['teɪblklɒθ] *noun*

nappe *(feminine)* : **put a tablecloth on the table** mets une nappe sur la table.

tablespoon ['teɪblspuːn] *noun*

grande cuillère *(feminine)*, **cuillère** *(feminine)* **à soupe**

> **a tablespoon of sugar** une cuillerée à soupe de sucre.

tablet ['tæblɪt] *noun*

comprimé *(masculine)* : **take one tablet every four hours** prenez un comprimé toutes les quatre heures.

tackle ['tækl] *verb*

1. *In football* **tacler**
2. *In rugby and American football* **plaquer**
> **to tackle a problem** s'attaquer à un problème.

tadpole ['tædpəʊl] *noun*

têtard *(masculine)*.

tag [tæg] *noun*

étiquette *(feminine)* : **what's the price on the tag?** quel est le prix indiqué sur l'étiquette ?

tail [teɪl] *noun*

queue *(feminine)* : **the dog's wagging its tail** le chien remue la queue

> **heads or tails?** pile ou face ?

tailor ['teɪlər] *noun*

tailleur *(masculine)* : **he's a tailor** il est tailleur.

take ['teɪk] *(past tense* **took**, *past participle* **taken**) *verb*

1. **prendre** : **let's take the bus** prenons le bus ; **he took my bike** il a pris mon vélo ; **take the book off the shelf** prends le livre sur l'étagère ; **I haven't taken my medicine** je n'ai pas pris mes médicaments ; **I took a lot of photos** j'ai pris beaucoup de photos ; **I'm going to take a shower** je vais prendre une douche
2. **emporter** : **we took a picnic with us** nous avons emporté un pique-nique
3. **amener** : **take the chairs into the garden** amène les chaises dans le jardin
4. **apporter** : **they took her some flowers** ils lui ont apporté des fleurs
5. **emmener** : **he took me to the movies** il m'a emmenée au cinéma ; **to take somebody home** raccompagner quelqu'un OR ramener quelqu'un chez lui ?
6. **passer** : **to take an exam** passer un examen
7. **accepter** : **they don't take credit cards** ils n'acceptent pas les cartes de crédit
8. **faire** : **what size do you take?** quelle taille faites-vous ? ; **what shoe size do you take?** quelle pointure faites-vous ? OR vous chaussez du combien ?
9. **supporter** : **he can't take criticism** il ne supporte pas la critique
10. *When 'take' means 'require'* **it takes patience** il faut de la patience ; **it takes two hours to get there** il faut deux heures pour y aller ; **how long will it take?** il faut combien de temps ? ; **it took us two days to finish** nous avons mis deux jours pour terminer

take after *phrasal verb*

tenir de : **she takes after her grandmother** elle tient de sa grand-mère

take apart *phrasal verb*

démonter : **Jack took the car apart** Jack a démonté la voiture

take away *phrasal verb*

1. **enlever, emporter** : **she took the plates away** elle a enlevé les assiettes ; **a chicken curry to take away** un curry de poulet à emporter
2. **emmener** : **the police took him away** la police l'a emmené

take back *phrasal verb*

rapporter : **I took the jeans back to the shop** j'ai rapporté le jean au magasin

take down *phrasal verb*

1. **démonter : they took the tent down** ils ont démonté la tente
2. **enlever : she took the poster down** elle a enlevé le poster
3. **noter : he took down her name and address** il a noté son nom et son adresse

take off *phrasal verb*

1. **décoller : the plane takes off at 5 a.m.** l'avion décolle à 5 heures
2. **enlever : she took her shoes off** elle a enlevé ses chaussures
➤ **to take one's clothes off** se déshabiller : **he took his clothes off** il s'est déshabillé

take out *phrasal verb*

1. **sortir : he took the gun out of the drawer** il a sorti l'arme du tiroir
2. **retirer : I'm going to take some money out of the bank** je vais retirer de l'argent à la banque
➤ **to take somebody out to dinner** emmener quelqu'un dîner

take up *phrasal verb*

1. **se mettre à : he's taken up golf** il s'est mis au golf
2. **prendre : that box takes up too much room** ce carton prend trop de place.

takeaway *UK* ['teɪkə,weɪ], **takeout** *US* ['teɪkaʊt] *noun*

1. **plat** *(masculine)* **à emporter : let's get a takeaway** allons acheter un plat à emporter
2. **restaurant** *(masculine)* **qui vend des plats à emporter : let's look for a takeaway** cherchons un restaurant qui vend des plats à emporter.

take-off ['teɪkɒf] *noun*

décollage *(masculine)* **: passengers must wear their seatbelts during take-off** les passagers doivent attacher leur ceinture pendant le décollage.

tale [teɪl] *noun*

conte *(masculine)* **: she like fairy tales** elle aime les contes de fées.

talent ['telənt] *noun*

talent *(masculine)* **: Alan has a lot of talent** Alan a beaucoup de talent.

talk [tɔːk] *noun & verb*

■ *noun*

1. **conversation** *(feminine)* **: I had a talk with my dad** j'ai eu une conversation avec mon père
2. **exposé** *(masculine)* **: he gave a talk on the environment** il a fait un exposé sur l'environnement

■ *verb*

parler : my parrot never stops talking mon perroquet n'arrête pas de parler ; **he's talking to his girlfriend** il parle à sa copine ; **we talked about the future** nous avons parlé de l'avenir.

tall [tɔːl] *adjective*

1. **grand : Thomas is very tall** Thomas est très grand
2. **haut : the building is tall** l'immeuble est haut
➤ **how tall are you?** combien mesurez-vous ? : **she's five feet tall** elle mesure 1,50 mètre
➤ **how tall is the Eiffel Tower?** quelle est la hauteur de la tour Eiffel ? : **it's 1052 feet tall** elle fait 321 mètres de haut.

tambourine [tæmbə'riːn] *noun*

tambourin *(masculine)* **: she plays the tambourine** elle joue du tambourin.

tame [teɪm] *adjective*

apprivoisé : Hannah has a tame toad at home Hannah a un crapaud apprivoisé à la maison.

tan [tæn] *noun*

bronzage *(masculine)* **: what a great tan!** quel beau bronzage !
➤ **to have a tan** être bronzé.

tangerine [,tændʒə'riːn] *noun*

mandarine *(feminine)*.

tangle ['tæŋgl] *noun*

➤ **to be in a tangle** être emmêlé : **my hair's in a tangle** mes cheveux sont emmêlés
➤ **to get in a tangle** s'emmêler : **the wires have got in a tangle** les fils se sont emmêlés.

tank [tæŋk] *noun*

1. **réservoir** *(masculine)* : **the fuel tank is empty** le réservoir d'essence est vide
2. **char** *(masculine)* **d'assaut** : **there are a lot of tanks on the border** il y a beaucoup de chars d'assaut à la frontière
➤ **a fish tank** un aquarium.

tanned [tænd] *adjective*

bronzé : **you're very tanned** tu es bien bronzé.

tap [tæp] *noun & verb*

■ *noun*
1. **robinet** *(masculine)* : **turn the tap on** ouvre le robinet ; **turn the tap off** ferme le robinet
2. **petite tape** *(feminine)* : **I felt a tap on my arm** j'ai senti une petite tape sur le bras
■ *verb (past tense & past participle* tapped*)*
taper, tapoter : **someone tapped me on the shoulder** quelqu'un m'a tapé sur l'épaule ; **he was tapping his fingers on the table** il tapotait sur la table.

tape [teɪp] *noun & verb*

■ *noun*
1. **cassette** *(feminine)* **vidéo** : **do you have a blank tape to record this film?** tu as une cassette vierge pour enregistrer ce film ?
2. **cassette** *(feminine)* : **we listened to a Beatles tape** nous avons écouté une cassette des Beatles
3. **bande** *(feminine)* **magnétique** : **you can record sounds and pictures on a tape** on peut enregistrer des sons et des images sur une bande magnétique
4. **ruban** *(masculine)* **adhésif** : **stick this down with tape** colle-le avec du ruban adhésif
➤ **on tape**
1. **sur cassette** : **I've got some good music on tape** j'ai de la bonne musique sur cassette
2. **sur cassette vidéo** : **I've got 'Star Wars' on tape** j'ai enregistré « la Guerre des étoiles » sur cassette vidéo
➤ **a tape recorder** un magnétophone
■ *verb*
enregistrer : **I taped the film** j'ai enregistré le film.

tape measure [teɪp'meʒə'] *noun*

mètre *(masculine)* : **I measured the length with a tape measure** j'ai mesuré la longueur avec un mètre.

target ['tɑːgɪt] *noun*

cible *(feminine)* : **you've hit the target!** tu as atteint la cible !

tart *UK* [tɑːt] *noun*

tarte *(feminine)* : **an apple tart** une tarte aux pommes.

tartan ['tɑːtn] *noun*

tartan *(masculine)* : **Scottish clans each have their own tartan** les clans écossais ont chacun leur propre tartan.

task [*UK* tɑːsk, *US* tæsk] *noun*

travail *(masculine)*, **tâche** *(feminine)* : **it's a difficult task** c'est un travail difficile OR c'est une tâche difficile.

taste [teɪst] *noun & verb*

■ *noun*
goût *(masculine)* : **this fish has a funny taste** ce poisson a un drôle de goût
➤ **have a taste of it!** goûte-moi ça !
➤ **to have good taste** avoir du goût OR avoir bon goût
■ *verb*
1. **goûter** : **taste this delicious soup** goûte cette soupe délicieuse
2. **avoir du goût** : **it tastes delicious** ça a un goût délicieux
➤ **to taste like something** OR **to taste of something** avoir un goût de quelque chose : **it tastes like honey** ça a un goût de miel ; **it tastes of salmon** ça a un goût de saumon.

tasteless ['teɪstlɪs] *adjective*

1. **fade** : **this soup is tasteless** cette soupe est fade
2. **de mauvais goût** : **a tasteless joke** une plaisanterie de mauvais goût.

tasty ['teɪstɪ] *adjective*

délicieux *(feminine* **délicieuse)** : **the meal is very tasty** le repas est délicieux.

tattoo [tə'tuː] *(plural* tattoos*) noun*

tatouage *(masculine)* : **he has a tattoo on his arm** il a un tatouage sur le bras.

taught [tɔːt] *past tense & past participle of* teach

he taught me how to swim il m'a appris à nager ; **you haven't taught her anything** tu ne lui as rien appris.

Taurus [ˈtɔːrəs] noun

Taureau (masculine) : **I'm a Taurus** je suis Taureau.

tax [tæks] noun

1. **impôts** (masculine plural) : **we all have to pay tax** tout le monde doit payer des impôts
2. **taxe** (feminine) : **there's a tax on imports** il y a une taxe sur les importations.

taxi [ˈtæksɪ] noun

taxi (masculine) : **let's take a taxi** prenons un taxi

➤ **a taxi driver** un chauffeur de taxi : **he's a taxi driver** il est chauffeur de taxi

➤ **a taxi rank** UK OR **a taxi stand** US une station de taxis.

tea [tiː] uncountable noun

1. **thé** (masculine) : **I'd like a cup of tea** je voudrais une tasse de thé
2. UK **goûter** (masculine) : **what time is tea?** le goûter est à quelle heure ?

➤ **a tea towel** UK un torchon ; **she was drying the dishes with a tea towel** il essuyait la vaisselle avec un torchon.

teabag [ˈtiːbæg] noun

sachet (masculine) de thé.

teach [tiːtʃ] (past tense & past participle **taught**) verb

1. **apprendre** : **I'm teaching him to ski** je lui apprends à skier ; **my brother is teaching me Spanish** mon frère m'apprend l'espagnol
2. **enseigner** : **she teaches English** elle enseigne l'anglais ; **he teaches in a high school** il enseigne dans un lycée.

teacher [ˈtiːtʃər] noun

1. **professeur** (masculine or feminine) : **he's a teacher in a high school** il est professeur dans un lycée
2. **instituteur** (masculine), **institutrice** (feminine) : **she's a teacher in a primary school** elle est institutrice dans une école primaire.

teacup [ˈtiːkʌp] noun

tasse (feminine) de thé.

team [tiːm] noun

équipe (feminine) : **he's in the football team** il fait partie de l'équipe de football.

teapot [ˈtiːpɒt] noun

théière (feminine).

tear noun & verb

■ noun [tɪər]

1. **larme** (feminine) : **he was in tears** il était en larmes
2. **déchirure** (feminine) : **can you mend this tear?** tu peux réparer cette déchirure ?

■ verb [teər] (past tense & past participle **torn**)

1. **déchirer** : **I tore my skirt** j'ai déchiré ma jupe
2. **se déchirer** : **this cloth tears very easily** ce tissu se déchire très facilement

tear down phrasal verb

démolir : **they're going to tear the old factory down** ils vont démolir la vieille usine

tear out phrasal verb

arracher : **I tore the page out** j'ai arraché la page

tear up phrasal verb

déchirer : **he tore up the letter** il a déchiré la lettre.

tease [tiːz] verb

taquiner : **he's always teasing his little brother** il n'arrête pas de taquiner son petit frère.

teaspoon [ˈtiːspuːn] noun

petite cuillère (feminine), cuillère (feminine) à café : **I need a teaspoon for my coffee** j'ai besoin d'une petite cuillère pour mon café

➤ **add one teaspoon of sugar** ajoutez une cuillerée à café de sucre.

technical [ˈteknɪkl] adjective

technique : **we have some technical problems** nous avons des problèmes techniques.

technique [tekˈniːk] noun

technique (feminine) : **a new technique for making electronic chips** une nouvelle technique de fabrication de puces électroniques.

techno [ˈteknəʊ] noun

techno (feminine) : **Yvonne likes techno** Yvonne aime la techno.

technological [ˌteknəˈlɒdʒɪkl] adjective

technologique : **technological progress** des progrès technologiques.

technology [tekˈnɒlədʒɪ] noun

technologie (feminine) : **it's a new technology** c'est une nouvelle technologie.

teddy bear ['tedɪbeəʳ] *noun*

ours *(masculine)* en peluche : **she loves her teddy bear** elle adore son ours en peluche.

teenage ['tiːneɪdʒ] *adjective*

1. **adolescent** : **he has a teenage son** il a un fils adolescent
2. **pour les jeunes** : **it's a teenage magazine** c'est un magazine pour les jeunes.

teenager ['tiːnˌeɪdʒəʳ] *noun*

adolescent *(masculine)*, adolescente *(feminine)* : **he's a teenager** il est adolescent.

teens [tiːnz] *plural noun*

adolescence *(feminine)*
> **to be in one's teens** être adolescent : **he's in his teens** il est adolescent.

teeth *plural of* tooth.

tel. *(abbreviation of* telephone*)*

tél.

telephone ['telɪfəʊn] *noun*

téléphone *(masculine)* : **the telephone's ringing** le téléphone sonne ; **he answered the telephone** il a répondu au téléphone
> **to be on the telephone** être au téléphone : **she's on the telephone at the moment** elle est au téléphone
> **the telephone book** OR **the telephone directory** l'annuaire *(masculine)*
> **a telephone booth** OR **a telephone box** *UK* une cabine téléphonique : **I'm looking for a telephone box** je cherche une cabine téléphonique
> **a telephone call** un appel téléphonique OR un coup de téléphone : **there's a telephone call for you** on te demande au téléphone
> **a telephone number** un numéro de téléphone : **what's your telephone number?** quel est ton numéro de téléphone ?

telescope ['telɪskəʊp] *noun*

télescope *(masculine)* : **look through the telescope** regarde dans le télescope.

television ['telɪˌvɪʒn] *noun*

télévision *(feminine)* : **I saw it on television** je l'ai vu à la télévision ; **put the television on** mets la télévision
> **a television programme** un programme télé
> **a television set** un poste de télévision OR un téléviseur.

tell [tel] *(past tense & past participle* told*) verb*

dire : **tell me what you did** dis-moi ce que tu as fait ; **I told him I would be late** je lui ai dit que je serais en retard ; **did you tell me the truth?** tu m'as dit la vérité ? ; **can you tell me the time?** tu peux me dire quelle heure il est ?
> **to tell somebody about something** parler à quelqu'un de quelque chose : **I told her about my problems** je lui ai parlé de mes problèmes
> **to tell somebody to do something** dire à quelqu'un de faire quelque chose : **he told me to wait for him here** il m'a dit de l'attendre ici
> **to tell a story** raconter une histoire : **I'm going to tell you a story** je vais vous raconter une histoire
> **to know how to tell the time** savoir lire l'heure : **he can't tell the time** il ne sait pas lire l'heure
> **to tell the difference between** distinguer : **she can't tell the difference between me and my brother** elle n'arrive pas à nous distinguer mon frère et moi

tell off *phrasal verb*

gronder : **my teacher told me off** ma maîtresse m'a grondé.

telly *UK* ['telɪ] *(abbreviation of* television*) noun*

informal télé *(feminine)* : **she's watching telly** elle regarde la télé
> **on telly** à la télé ; **what's on telly?** qu'est-ce qu'il y a à la télé ?

temper ['tempəʳ] *noun*

caractère *(masculine)* : **she has an awful temper** elle a un sale caractère
> **to be in a bad temper** être de mauvaise humeur : **he's in a bad temper** il est de mauvaise humeur
> **to lose one's temper** se mettre en colère : **I lost my temper** je me suis mis en colère.

temperature ['temprətʃəʳ] *noun*

température *(feminine)* : **what is the temperature outside?** quelle température fait-il dehors ? ; **I took her temperature** j'ai pris sa température ; **he has a temperature** il a de la température OR il a de la fièvre.

temple ['templ] *noun*

temple *(masculine)* : **a Greek temple** un temple grec.

t

temporary ['tempərəri] *adjective*

temporaire, provisoire : **she has a temporary job** elle a un travail temporaire.

tempt [tempt] *verb*

tenter : **I'm tempted to say no** je suis tenté de dire non.

tempting ['temptɪŋ] *adjective*

tentant : **it's very tempting** c'est très tentant.

ten [ten] *number*

dix : **the Ten Commandments** les dix commandements ; **she's ten** elle a dix ans ; **he went out at ten** il est sorti à dix heures.

tenant ['tenənt] *noun*

locataire *(masculine or feminine)*.

tend [tend] *verb*

➤ **to tend to do something** avoir tendance à faire quelque chose : **she tends to get up late** elle a tendance à se lever tard.

tender ['tendəʳ] *adjective*

tendre : **the meat is nice and tender** la viande est bien tendre.

tennis ['tenɪs] *noun*

tennis *(masculine)* : **she's playing tennis** elle joue au tennis ; **a game of tennis** une partie de tennis

➤ **a tennis ball** une balle de tennis

➤ **a tennis court** un court de tennis

➤ **a tennis racket** une raquette de tennis

➤ **tennis shoes** tennis *(feminine plural)*

 Le mot anglais **tennis** n'est jamais utilisé au sens de "chaussure de tennis".

tense [tens] *adjective*

tendu : **the atmosphere is tense** l'ambiance est tendue.

tension ['tenʃn] *noun*

tension *(feminine)* : **there's a lot of tension between them** il y a beaucoup de tensions entre eux.

tent [tent] *noun*

tente *(feminine)* : **they put their tent up near the river** ils ont monté leur tente près de la rivière.

tenth [tenθ] *number*

dixième : **on the tenth floor** au dixième étage

➤ **it's the tenth of November** *UK* OR **it's November tenth** *US* nous sommes le dix novembre.

term [tɜːm] *noun*

1. *UK* trimestre *(masculine)* : **there are three terms in the school year** l'année scolaire comprend trois trimestres

2. terme *(masculine)* : **it's a technical term** c'est un terme technique

➤ **to be on good terms with somebody** être en bons termes avec quelqu'un

➤ **to come to terms with something** arriver à accepter quelque chose.

terminal ['tɜːmɪnl] *noun*

aérogare *(feminine)* : **there are three terminals at the airport** il y a trois aérogares à l'aéroport

➤ **the bus terminal** le terminus.

terrace ['terəs] *noun*

terrasse *(feminine)* : **we were sitting on the terrace** nous étions assis sur la terrasse.

terraced house *UK* ['terəshaʊs] *noun*

maison située dans une rangée de maisons attenantes.

terrible ['terəbl] *adjective*

atroce : **the weather is terrible** il fait un temps atroce.

terribly ['terəblɪ] *adverb*

terriblement : **he's terribly disappointed** il est terriblement déçu

➤ **I'm terribly sorry** je suis vraiment désolé.

terrific [tə'rɪfɪk] *adjective informal*

formidable : **it's a terrific book** c'est un livre formidable.

terrified ['terɪfaɪd] *adjective*

terrifié

➤ **to be terrified of** avoir une peur panique de : **she's terrified of the dentist** elle a une peur panique du dentiste.

territory [*UK* 'terətrɪ, *US* 'terɪtɔːrɪ] *(plural territories) noun*

territoire *(masculine)*.

terrorism ['terərɪzm] *noun*

terrorisme *(masculine)*.

terrorist ['terərɪst] *noun*

terroriste *(masculine or feminine)* : **a terrorist attack** un attentat terroriste.

test [test] *noun & verb*

■ *noun*

1. **test** *(masculine)* : **they are doing tests on the new drug** ils effectuent des tests sur la nouvelle drogue

2. **contrôle** *(masculine)*, **interrogation** *(feminine)* : **we had a test this morning** on a eu un contrôle ce matin OR on a eu une interrogation ce matin

3. **analyse** *(feminine)* : **a blood test** une analyse de sang

4. **essai** *(masculine)* : **nuclear tests** des essais nucléaires

➤ **a test tube** une éprouvette

➤ **an eye test** un examen de la vue

➤ **I'm taking my driving test** je passe mon permis de conduire

■ *verb*

1. **essayer** : **I'd like to test the computer before I buy it** je voudrais essayer l'ordinateur avant de l'acheter

2. **interroger** : **the teacher tested us on irregular verbs** le professeur nous a interrogés sur les verbes irréguliers

3. **tester** : **they have to test the new product** ils doivent tester le nouveau produit.

text [tekst] *noun*

texte *(masculine)* : **a text file** un fichier texte.

textbook ['tekstbʊk] *noun*

manuel *(masculine)* : **a biology textbook** un manuel de biologie.

text-message [tekst'mesɪdʒ] *noun*

texto *(masculine)* : **he sent me a text-message** il m'a envoyé un texto.

Thames [temz] *noun*

the Thames OR **the River Thames** la Tamise ; **the Thames flows through London to the North Sea** la Tamise coule à Londres et se jette dans la mer du Nord.

than [ðən, ðæn] *conjunction*

1. **que** : **Tina's taller than Ted** Tina est plus grande que Ted ; **I've got less than you** OR **I've got less than you have** j'en ai moins que toi

2. *With quantities* **de** : **it costs less than $50** ça coûte moins de 50 dollars ; **he stayed more than three months** il est resté plus de trois mois.

thank [θæŋk] *verb*

remercier : **I'd like to thank you for your help** j'aimerais vous remercier de votre aide

➤ **thank you!** merci ! : **thank you very much!** merci beaucoup ! ; **thank you for your help!** merci pour votre aide !

➤ **thank God!** Dieu merci ! !

thanks [θæŋks] *exclamation & noun*

➤ **thanks!** merci ! : **thanks a lot!** merci beaucoup ! ; **thanks for everything!** merci pour tout ! ; **thanks for coming!** merci d'être venu !

➤ **thanks to** grâce à : **I succeeded thanks to you** j'ai réussi grâce à toi.

Thanksgiving *US* ['θæŋks,gɪvɪŋ] *noun*

Thanksgiving

THANKSGIVING
Le quatrième jeudi de novembre, les Américains se retrouvent en famille pour fêter **Thanksgiving**, l'une des plus importantes fêtes aux États-Unis. On y célèbre l'installation des premiers colons britanniques en Amérique, qui en 1621 remercièrent Dieu après leur première récolte de maïs. Le repas traditionnel se compose de dinde rôtie servie avec une sauce aux airelles (**cranberry sauce**) accompagnée de patates douces, puis d'une tarte au potiron (**pumpkin pie**).

that [ðæt] *adjective, pronoun, conjunction & adverb*

■ *adjective* (*plural* **those**)

ce (*before vowel* **cet**, *feminine* **cette**) : **give me that book** donne-moi ce livre ; **that soup is cold** cette soupe est froide ; **I don't like that man** je n'aime pas cet homme

'This' and 'that' are both translated by ce in French, so if you want to insist on 'that one' as opposed to 'this one', you should add -là to the noun:

I prefer that CD je préfère ce CD-là ; **I don't want this dress, I want that one** je ne veux pas cette robe-ci, je veux celle-là

■ *pronoun*

1. **ce** (**c'** *before a vowel*), **cela, ça** : **who's that?** qui est-ce ? ; **is that Janet?** c'est Janet ? ; **what's that?** qu'est-ce que c'est ? ; **that's my brother** c'est mon frère ; **that's not true** ce n'est pas vrai

2. *cela* : **I don't want this, I want that** je ne veux pas ceci, je veux cela

■ *relative pronoun*

1. *Subject of the verb* **qui** : **where's the path that leads to the wood?** où est le chemin qui mène au bois ?

2. *Object of the verb* **que** (**qu'** *before a vowel*) : **show me the CD that you bought** montre-moi le CD que tu as acheté ; **the man that he saw** l'homme qu'il a vu

3. *With a preposition* **lequel**

> Use **lequel** when 'that' refers to a masculine noun, **laquelle** for a feminine noun, **lesquels** for masculine plurals and **lesquelles** for feminine plurals:

the chair that he was sitting on collapsed la chaise sur laquelle il était assis s'est effondrée ; **the boys that he's talking to are his cousins** les garçons avec lesquels il parle sont ses cousins

■ *conjunction*

que (**qu'** *before a vowel*) : **she said that she was coming** elle a dit qu'elle venait

■ *adverb*

si : **it's not that bad** ce n'est pas si mal que ça.

that's [ðæts]

1. = **that is** : **that's John** c'est John ; **that's not my dog** ce n'est pas mon chien

2. = **that has** : **that's got nothing to do with it** ça n'a rien à voir.

the [ðə, ðɪ, ðiː] *definite article*

le *(masculine)*, **la** *(feminine)*, **l'** (*before a vowel or silent 'h'*) [*plural* **les**]

> The definite article must agree in gender (masculine or feminine) and number (singular or plural) with the noun it precedes:

give me the book donne-moi le livre ; **look at the sea** regarde la mer ; **the man left** l'homme est parti ; **where are the children?** où sont les enfants ?

> When you say 'of the' or 'to the' in French, the prepositions **de** and **à** combine with **le** or **les** to make one word : **de + le = du, de + les = des, à + le = au, à + les = aux**:

I can't remember the name of the village je ne me souviens pas du nom du village ; **she gave the ball to the dog** elle a donné la balle au chien.

theatre *UK*, theater *US* ['θɪətər] *noun*

théâtre *(masculine)* : **we're going to the theatre** nous allons au théâtre.

theft [θeft] *noun*

vol *(masculine)* : **they accused him of theft** ils l'ont accusé de vol.

their [ðeər] *possessive adjective*

leur [*plural* **leurs**] : **their house is in the countryside** leur maison est à la campagne ; **their parents are doctors** leurs parents sont médecins

> Use the definite article (**le, la** or **les**), not the possessive adjective, with parts of the body:

they closed their eyes ils ont fermé les yeux ; **they're brushing their teeth** ils se brossent les dents.

theirs [ðeəz] *possessive pronoun*

1. **le leur** *(feminine* **la leur***)* [*plural* **les leurs**]

> In French the possessive pronoun agrees in gender (masculine or feminine) and number (singular or plural) with the noun it replaces:

our dog is big, theirs is small notre chien est grand, le leur est petit ; **your books are here, theirs are on the table** vos livres sont ici, les leurs sont sur la table

2. **à eux** : **those books aren't theirs** ces livres ne sont pas à eux ; **he's a friend of theirs** c'est un ami à eux.

them [ðəm, ðem] *pronoun*

1. *Direct object* **les** : **I can't see them** je ne les vois pas ; **find them!** trouve-les !

> In tenses like the present perfect and the past perfect, the past participle agrees with the direct object pronoun. Add an **-s** if 'them' stands for masculine people or things or a mixture of masculine and feminine. Add **-es** if 'them' stands for feminine people or things:

I saw them je les ai vus OR je les ai vues

2. *Indirect object* **leur** : **she gave them a kiss** elle leur a donné un baiser ; **tell them to come** dis-leur de venir

3. *After a preposition* **eux** *(masculine)*, **elles** *(feminine)* : **I'm going with them** je vais avec eux.

theme [θiːm] *noun*

thème *(masculine)* : **what's the main theme of the festival?** quel est le thème du festival ?
➤ **a theme park** un parc à thème.

themselves [ðem'selvz] *pronoun*

1. se (s'*before a vowel*) : **the boys are washing themselves** les garçons se lavent ; **they're enjoying themselves** ils s'amusent
2. eux-mêmes *(feminine* elles-mêmes*)* : **they made it themselves** ils l'ont fait eux-mêmes
3. eux *(feminine* elles*)* : **they often talk about themselves** ils parlent souvent d'eux
➤ **by themselves** tout seuls *(feminine* toutes seules*)* : **they did it by themselves** ils l'ont fait tout seuls.

then [ðen] *adverb*

1. alors, à cette époque : **we lived in London then** nous habitions alors Londres OR nous habitions Londres à cette époque
2. puis, ensuite : **I had dinner then I went to bed** j'ai dîné, puis je me suis couché OR j'ai dîné, et ensuite je me suis couché
3. alors : **it's too sweet – don't drink it then** c'est trop sucré – alors ne le bois pas.

there [ðeəʳ] *pronoun & adverb*

■ *pronoun*
➤ **there is** OR **there are** il y a : **there's a message for you** il y a un message pour toi ; **there are a lot of people here** il y a beaucoup de gens ici ; **there isn't any bread** il n'y a pas de pain ; **there was a storm** il y a eu un orage
■ *adverb*
1. là : **put it there** mets-le là ; **is Jerry there?** est-ce que Jerry est là ?
2. y : **I'm going there next week** j'y vais la semaine prochaine
➤ **there he is!** le voilà ! : **there they are!** les voilà !

therefore ['ðeəfɔːʳ] *adverb*

donc : **he's only 15 and therefore can't drive** il n'a que 15 ans, donc il ne peut pas conduire.

there's [ðeəz]

1. = there is : **there's a lamp in the corner** il y a une lampe dans le coin
2. = there has : **there's been a lot of rain recently** on a eu beaucoup de pluie ces derniers temps.

thermometer [θə'mɒmɪtəʳ] *noun*

thermomètre *(masculine)* : **the thermometer says 29°** le thermomètre indique 29°.

these [ðiːz] *(plural of* this*)* *adjective & pronoun*

■ *adjective*
ces : **these photos are mine** ces photos sont à moi

> 'These' and 'those' are both translated by ces in French, so if you want to insist on 'these ones' as opposed to 'those', you should add -ci to the noun:

I prefer these flowers je préfère ces fleurs-ci
■ *pronoun*
1. ce (c' *before a vowel*) : **these are my books** ce sont mes livres ; **what are these?** qu'est-ce que c'est ?
2. ceux-ci *(masculine)*, celles-ci *(feminine)* : **which shoes do you want, these or those?** quelles chaussures veux-tu, celles-ci ou celles-là ?

they [ðeɪ] *pronoun*

ils *(masculine)*, elles *(feminine)*

> French nouns are either masculine or feminine. Remember to use ils for masculine subjects and elles for feminine subjects. When 'they' includes male and female, use ils:

they're American ils sont américains OR elles sont américaines ; **where are my glasses? – they're on the table** où sont mes lunettes ? – elles sont sur la table
➤ **here they are!** les voilà !
➤ **they're nice people** ce sont des gens sympas.

they'd [ðeɪd]

1. = they had : **they'd finished their homework** ils avaient fini leurs devoirs
2. = they would : **they'd like to see you** ils aimeraient te voir.

they'll [ðeɪl] = they shall OR they will

they'll be here soon ils seront bientôt là.

they're [ðeəʳ] = they are

they're late ils sont en retard.

they've [ðeɪv] = they have

they've eaten all the cake ils ont mangé tout le gâteau ; **they've left already** ils sont déjà partis.

thick [θɪk] *adjective*

épais *(feminine* épaisse*)* : **it's a thick book** c'est

un livre épais ; **the walls are 15 centimetres thick** les murs ont 15 centimètres d'épaisseur.

thief [θiːf] (*plural* thieves [θiːvz]) *noun*

voleur *(masculine)*, **voleuse** *(feminine)* : **he's a thief** c'est un voleur.

thigh [θaɪ] *noun*

cuisse *(feminine)* : **skaters have muscular thighs** les patineurs ont des cuisses musclées.

thin [θɪn] *adjective*

1. **maigre** : **he's too thin** il est trop maigre
2. **mince** : **she has thin lips** elle a des lèvres minces
3. **fin** : **a thin slice of lemon** une fine tranche de citron.

thing [θɪŋ] *noun*

1. **chose** *(feminine)* : **he has a lot of things to do** il a beaucoup de choses à faire ; **you must take things as they come** il faut prendre les choses comme elles viennent
2. **truc** *(masculine)* : **what's this thing?** c'est quoi, ce truc ?
> **my things** mes affaires : **don't forget your things** n'oublie pas tes affaires
> **I can't see a thing** je n'y vois rien
> **the poor thing!** le pauvre ! OR la pauvre !

think [θɪŋk] (*past tense & past participle* thought) *verb*

1. **penser** : **what do you think?** qu'est-ce que tu en penses ? ; **I think you're mad** je pense que tu es fou
2. **imaginer** : **think how life will be in ten years** imagine comment sera la vie dans dix ans
3. **réfléchir** : **think carefully before you make a decision** réfléchis bien avant de prendre une décision
> **I think so** je pense que oui OR je pense

think about *phrasal verb*

1. **penser à** : **what are you thinking about?** à quoi tu penses ? ; **I'm thinking about the party** je pense à la fête
2. **penser de** : **what did you think about the film?** qu'as-tu pensé du film ?
3. **réfléchir à** : **I'll think about what you said** je réfléchirai à ce que tu m'as dit ; **I'll think about it** j'y réfléchirai

think of *phrasal verb*

penser de : **what do you think of her?** que penses-tu d'elle ?

third [θɜːd] *adjective & noun*

■ *adjective*
troisième : **third time lucky** la troisième fois sera la bonne
■ *noun*
tiers *(masculine)* : **he ate a third of the cake** il a mangé un tiers du gâteau
> **it's the third of November** *UK* OR **it's November third** *US* nous sommes le trois novembre
> **the Third World** le tiers-monde.

thirst [θɜːst] *noun*

soif *(feminine)* : **I'm dying of thirst** je meurs de soif.

thirsty ['θɜːstɪ] *adjective*

> **to be thirsty** avoir soif : **I'm thirsty** j'ai soif.

thirteen [ˌθɜː'tiːn] *number*

treize : **thirteen is my lucky number** le chiffre treize me porte bonheur ; **she's thirteen** elle a treize ans.

thirteenth [ˌθɜː'tiːnθ] *number*

treizième
> **it's the thirteenth of April** *UK* OR **it's April thirteenth** *US* on est le treize avril.

thirtieth ['θɜːtɪəθ] *number*

trentième
> **it's the thirtieth of December** *UK* OR **it's December thirtieth** *US* on est le trente décembre.

thirty ['θɜːtɪ] *number*

trente : **she's thirty** elle a trente ans
> **thirty-one** trente et un
> **thirty-two** trente-deux.

this [ðɪs] (*plural* these) *adjective, pronoun & adverb*

■ *adjective*
ce (*before vowel* **cet**, *feminine* **cette**) : **he left this morning** il est parti ce matin ; **this soup is cold** cette soupe est froide ; **I'll see you this afternoon** on se voit cet après-midi

'This' and 'that' are both translated by ce in French, so if you want to insist on 'this one' as opposed to 'that one', you should add -ci to the noun:

I prefer this CD je préfère ce CD-ci ; **I don't want that dress, I want this one** je ne veux pas cette robe-là, je veux celle-ci
■ *pronoun*
1. **ce** (**c'** *before a vowel*), **ceci** : **this is for you** c'est

pour toi OR ceci est pour toi ; **who's this?** qui est-ce ? ; **what's this?** qu'est-ce que c'est ?

2. **ceci** : **do you really want this?** tu veux vraiment ceci ?

➤ **this is Jackie Brown**

1. *Introducing somebody* je vous présente Jackie Brown

2. *On the phone* Jackie Brown à l'appareil

■ *adverb*

comme ça : **it was this big** c'était grand comme ça.

thistle ['θɪsl] *noun*

chardon *(masculine)* : **the thistle is the emblem of Scotland** le chardon est l'emblème de l'Écosse.

thong [θɒŋ] *noun*

tong *(feminine)* : **he's wearing thongs** il porte des tongs.

thorn [θɔːn] *noun*

épine *(feminine)* : **there are a lot of thorns on this rose bush** ce rosier a beaucoup d'épines.

thorough ['θʌrə] *adjective*

minutieux *(feminine* **minutieuse***)* : **he's thorough in his work** il est minutieux dans son travail.

thoroughly ['θʌrəlɪ] *adverb*

1. **complètement** : **I thoroughly agree** je suis complètement d'accord

2. **à fond** : **he studied this case thoroughly** il a étudié ce dossier à fond.

those [ðəʊz] *(plural of* that*) adjective & pronoun*

■ *adjective*

ces : **those photos are mine** ces photos sont à moi

> 'These' and 'those' are both translated by **ces** in French, so if you want to insist on 'those ones' as opposed to 'these', you should add **-là** to the noun:
>
> **I prefer those flowers** je préfère ces fleurs-là

■ *pronoun*

1. **ce** (**c'** *before a vowel*) : **those are my books** ce sont mes livres ; **what are those?** qu'est-ce que c'est ?

2. **ceux-là** *(masculine)*, **celles-là** *(feminine)* : **I don't want these books, I want those** je ne veux pas ces livres-ci, je veux ceux-là ; **these flowers are nice, but those are nicer** ces fleurs sont jolies, mais celles-là sont plus jolies

3. **ceux** : **those who want to come should put**

their hand up ceux qui veulent venir doivent lever la main.

though [ðəʊ] *conjunction & adverb*

■ *conjunction*

bien que : **though the car's old, it's still in good condition** bien que la voiture soit vieille, elle est encore en bon état

■ *adverb*

pourtant : **we lost! – it was a good game though** on a perdu ! – c'était pourtant un bon match.

thought [θɔːt] *noun & verb form*

■ *noun*

1. **pensée** *(feminine)* : **she was lost in her thoughts** elle était perdue dans ses pensées

2. **idée** *(feminine)* : **he had an interesting thought** il a eu une idée intéressante

■ *past tense & past participle of* think

I thought you were right je pensais que tu avais raison ; **I hadn't thought about it** je n'y avais pas pensé.

thousand ['θaʊznd] *number*

mille : **it costs a thousand euros** cela coûte mille euros

➤ **a thousand and one** mille un

➤ **thousands of** des milliers de : **there were thousands of people** il y avait des milliers de gens.

thread [θred] *noun*

fil *(masculine)* : **a needle and thread** une aiguille et du fil.

threat [θret] *noun*

menace *(feminine)* : **is that a threat?** c'est une menace ?

threaten ['θretn] *verb*

menacer : **she threatened to leave the team** elle a menacé de quitter l'équipe.

three [θriː] *number*

trois : **you get three chances** tu as trois chances ; **she's three** elle a trois ans ; **he went out at three** il est sorti à trois heures.

three-D [ˌθriːˈdiː], **three-dimensional** [ˌθriːdɪˈmenʃənl] *adjective*

à trois dimensions : **a three-dimensional object** un objet à trois dimensions

➤ **a film in three-D** un film en trois dimensions.

t

threw [θru:] *past tense of* throw

he threw the ball to me il m'a lancé la balle.

thrill [θrɪl] *noun & verb*

▪ *noun*
frisson *(masculine)* : **seeing Everest was a real thrill** voir l'Everest m'a donné le frisson
➤ **what a thrill!** quelle émotion !

▪ *verb*
ravir : **I was thrilled to see her again** j'ai été ravi de la revoir.

thriller ['θrɪlər] *noun*

thriller *(masculine)*.

throat [θrəʊt] *noun*

gorge *(feminine)* : **I have a sore throat** j'ai mal à la gorge.

throne [θrəʊn] *noun*

trône *(masculine)* : **Queen Elizabeth came to the throne in 1952** la reine Élisabeth est montée sur le trône en 1952.

through , thru *US* [θru:] *preposition & adverb*

▪ *preposition*
1. à travers : **you can see through the curtains** on voit à travers les rideaux ; **the bullet went through the wall** la balle est passée à travers le mur ; **we went through the park** nous avons traversé le parc
2. par : **the road goes through a tunnel** la route passe par un tunnel ; **she was looking through the window** elle regardait par la fenêtre ; **he came in through the back door** il est entré par la porte de derrière ; **I got the job through a friend** j'ai eu le poste par un ami
3. pendant : **she talked all through the film** elle a parlé pendant tout le film
➤ **to go through a red light** brûler un feu rouge
➤ **Monday through Friday** *US* du lundi au vendredi

▪ *adverb*
à travers : **the arrow went right through** la flèche est passée au travers
➤ **to get through** passer : **you'll have to move, I can't get through** il faut que tu bouges, je ne peux pas passer
➤ **to get through to somebody** joindre quelqu'un or avoir quelqu'un
➤ **I can't get through to him on the phone** je n'arrive pas à le joindre au téléphone or je n'arrive pas à l'avoir au téléphone

➤ **to let somebody through** laisser passer quelqu'un.

throughout [θru:'aʊt] *preposition*

1. pendant : **he slept throughout the meeting** il a dormi pendant toute la réunion
2. partout dans : **throughout the house** partout dans la maison
➤ **throughout France** dans toute la France.

throw [θrəʊ] (*past tense* threw, *past participle* thrown) *verb*

1. lancer : **throw me the ball!** lance-moi le ballon !
2. jeter : **they were throwing stones at the police** ils jetaient des pierres sur la police ; **he threw a book at me** il m'a jeté un livre à la figure
➤ **to throw a party** organiser une fête

throw away *phrasal verb*

jeter : **I threw my ticket away** j'ai jeté mon billet

throw out *phrasal verb*

1. jeter : **I'm going to throw this stale bread out** je vais jeter ce pain rassis
2. mettre à la porte : **they threw him out** ils l'ont mis à la porte

throw up *phrasal verb*

vomir : **he threw up** il a vomi.

thrown [θrəʊn] *past participle of* throw

have you thrown the paper away? est-ce que tu as jeté le journal ?

thru *US* ➤ through.

thumb [θʌm] *noun*

pouce *(masculine)* : **she hurt her thumb** elle s'est fait mal au pouce.

thumbtack *US* ['θʌmtæk] *noun*

punaise *(feminine)* : **put up the poster with thumbtacks** fixe l'affiche au mur avec des punaises.

thump [θʌmp] *verb*

donner un coup de poing à : **he thumped the bad guy** il a donné un coup de poing au méchant.

thunder ['θʌndər] *uncountable noun*

tonnerre *(masculine)* : **I can hear thunder** j'entends le tonnerre ; **there was a clap of thunder** il y a eu un coup de tonnerre.

thunderstorm ['θʌndəstɔːm] *noun*

orage *(masculine)* : **we were caught in a thunderstorm** nous avons été surpris par un orage.

Thursday ['θɜːzdɪ] *noun*

jeudi *(masculine)* : **it's Thursday today** nous sommes jeudi ; **next Thursday** jeudi prochain ; **last Thursday** jeudi dernier
> **on Thursday** jeudi : **I'll see you on Thursday** je te reverrai jeudi
> **on Thursdays** le jeudi : **he comes to see me on Thursdays** il vient me voir le jeudi

In French the days of the week do not start with a capital letter.

tick [tɪk] *noun & verb*

■ *noun UK*
to mark something with a tick cocher quelque chose ; **put a tick in the box** cochez la case
■ *verb*
cocher : **tick here** cochez ici.

ticket ['tɪkɪt] *noun*

billet *(masculine)* : **a plane ticket** un billet d'avion ; **I've got two tickets for the concert** j'ai deux billets pour le concert
> **a parking ticket** un P.-V.
> **a ticket machine** un distributeur de titres de transport
> **the ticket office** le guichet.

tickle ['tɪkl] *verb*

chatouiller : **that tickles!** ça chatouille !

tide [taɪd] *noun*

marée *(feminine)* : **it's high tide** OR **the tide is in** c'est marée haute ; **it's low tide** OR **the tide is out** c'est marée basse.

tidy ['taɪdɪ] *adjective & verb*

■ *adjective*
1. bien rangé, en ordre : **my room is tidy** ma chambre est bien rangée OR ma chambre est en ordre
2. soigné : **her hair is always tidy** ses cheveux sont toujours soignés
3. ordonné : **he's very tidy** il est très ordonné
■ *verb (past tense & past participle* tidied*)*
ranger : **he's tidying his room** il range sa chambre

tidy up *phrasal verb*

ranger : **help me to tidy up** aide-moi à ranger.

tie [taɪ] *noun & verb*

■ *noun*
1. cravate *(feminine)* : **he's wearing a tie** il porte une cravate
2. match *(masculine)* nul : **who won the game? – it was a tie** qui a gagné ? – ils ont fait match nul
■ *verb (present participle* tying*)*
1. attacher : **they tied his hands to the chair** ils lui ont attaché les mains à la chaise ; **tie the rope around the tree** attache la corde autour de l'arbre
2. nouer : **he tied his scarf round his neck** il a noué son écharpe autour de son cou ; **tie your shoe laces** noue tes lacets
> **to tie a knot** faire un nœud : **she tied a knot in her handkerchief** elle a fait un nœud à son mouchoir

tie up *phrasal verb*

1. ficeler : **she tied the package up with ribbon** elle a ficelé le paquet avec du ruban
2. attacher : **they tied up the prisoner** ils ont attaché le prisonnier.

tiger ['taɪgəʳ] *noun*

tigre *(masculine)* : **tigers come from Asia** les tigres viennent d'Asie.

tight [taɪt] *adjective*

1. serré : **this dress is too tight** cette robe est trop serrée ; **the screw is tight** la vis est serrée
2. moulant : **she was wearing tight jeans** elle portait un jean moulant.

tighten ['taɪtn] *verb*

resserrer, serrer : **he tightened the screw** il a resserré la vis.

tightly ['taɪtlɪ] *adverb*

to hold something tightly serrer quelque chose ; **she was holding my hand tightly** elle me serrait la main.

tights [taɪts] *plural noun*

collant *(masculine)* : **she's wearing black tights** elle porte un collant noir.

tile [taɪl] *noun*

1. tuile *(feminine)* : **a tile fell off the roof** une tuile est tombée du toit
2. carreau *(masculine)* [*plural* **carreaux**] : **the floor and the walls in the bathroom are covered in blue tiles** le sol et les murs de la salle de bains sont recouverts de carreaux bleus.

till [tɪl] *noun, preposition & conjunction*

■ *noun*

caisse *(feminine)* : **pay at the till** payez à la caisse

■ *preposition*

1. **jusqu'à** : **we'll play till six** on va jouer jusqu'à six heures

2. **avant** : **she won't come till tomorrow** elle ne viendra pas avant demain

■ *conjunction*

jusqu'à ce que

> The conjunction **jusqu'à ce que** is followed by a verb in the subjunctive:

I'll stay here till he comes je resterai ici jusqu'à ce qu'il vienne

➤ **till now** jusqu'à maintenant.

time [taɪm] *noun*

1. **temps** *(masculine)* : **I don't have time** je n'ai pas le temps ; **take your time** prends ton temps ; **you're just in time for lunch** tu arrives juste à temps pour déjeuner ; **all the time** tout le temps ; **from time to time** de temps en temps ; **most of the time** la plupart du temps

2. **heure** *(feminine)* : **what time is it?** quelle heure est-il ? ; **the train's on time** le train est à l'heure

3. **époque** *(feminine)* : **in Roman times** à l'époque romaine

4. **moment** *(masculine)* : **you've come at the right time** tu es arrivé au bon moment ; **for the time being** pour le moment

5. **fois** *(feminine)* : **how many times have you seen the film?** combien de fois as-tu vu le film ? ; **the first time I saw you** la première fois que je t'ai vu ; **four times a year** quatre fois par an ; **four at a time** quatre à la fois ; **6 times 7 is 42** 6 fois 7 égalent 42

➤ **a long time** longtemps : **we waited for a long time** on a attendu longtemps ; **I've been here for a long time** ça fait longtemps que je suis là

➤ **it's time for bed** c'est l'heure d'aller au lit

➤ **it's time to go** il est temps de partir

➤ **it's about time he left** il est grand temps qu'il parte

➤ **to have a good time** s'amuser : **I had a really good time at the party** je me suis bien amusé à la fête

➤ **in a week's time** dans une semaine.

timetable ['taɪmˌteɪbl] *noun*

1. *UK* **emploi** *(masculine)* **du temps** : **according to my timetable I have geography this afternoon** d'après mon emploi du temps j'ai géo cet après-midi

2. **horaire** *(masculine)* : **check the timetable to see when the next train is** vérifie l'horaire pour voir à quelle heure est le prochain train ; **bus timetable** horaire de bus.

tin [tɪn] *noun*

1. *UK* **boîte** *(feminine)* **de conserve** : **a tin of sardines** une boîte de sardines

2. *(uncountable)* **étain** *(masculine)* : **it's made of tin** c'est en étain

➤ **a tin can** une boîte de conserve

➤ **a tin opener** *UK* un ouvre-boîtes [*plural* ouvre-boîtes].

tinfoil ['tɪnfɔɪl] *uncountable noun*

papier *(masculine)* **aluminium, papier** *(masculine)* **alu** : **the sandwiches are wrapped in tinfoil** les sandwichs sont enveloppés dans du papier alu.

tinsel ['tɪnsl] *uncountable noun*

guirlandes *(feminine plural)* **de Noël** : **the Christmas tree is covered in tinsel** l'arbre de Noël est couvert de guirlandes.

tiny ['taɪnɪ] *adjective*

minuscule.

tip [tɪp] *noun & verb*

■ *noun*

1. **bout** *(masculine)* : **the tips of your fingers** le bout des doigts

2. **pourboire** *(masculine)* : **I gave the waiter a tip** j'ai donné un pourboire au serveur

3. **conseil** *(masculine)* : **safety tips** des conseils de sécurité

4. *UK* **décharge** *(feminine)* : **you must take your rubbish to the tip** tu dois porter les poubelles à la décharge

➤ **it's on the tip of my tongue** je l'ai sur le bout de la langue

■ *verb (past tense & past participle* **tipped***)*

donner un pourboire à : **she tipped the waiter** elle a donné un pourboire au serveur

tip over *phrasal verb*

1. **renverser** : **she tipped the bottle over** elle a renversé la bouteille

2. **se renverser** : **the glass tipped over** le verre s'est renversé.

tiptoe ['tɪptəʊ] *noun*

➤ **on tiptoe** sur la pointe des pieds ; **he was**

walking on tiptoe il marchait sur la pointe des pieds.

tire *US noun* ➤ tyre *UK*.

tired ['taɪəd] *adjective*

fatigué : **he's very tired** il est très fatigué

➤ **to be tired of something** en avoir assez de quelque chose ; **I'm tired of all these arguments** j'en ai assez de toutes ces disputes ; **he's tired of waiting** il en a assez d'attendre.

tiring ['taɪərɪŋ] *adjective*

fatigant : **this work is tiring** ce travail est fatigant.

tissue ['tɪʃuː] *noun*

mouchoir *(masculine)* **en papier : can you give me a tissue?** tu peux me donner un mouchoir en papier ?

title ['taɪtl] *noun*

titre *(masculine)* : **what's the title of the film?** quel est le titre du film ?

to [tə, tʊ, tuː] *preposition*

1. à : **do you want to go to the beach?** tu veux aller à la plage ? ; **let's go to London** allons à Londres ; **I spoke to my teacher** j'ai parlé à mon professeur ; **she wrote to her brother** elle a écrit à son frère ; **from 9 to 5** de 9 heures à 17 heures

> The French preposition à combines with the definite articles le and les to form au and aux:

he's gone to the shop il est allé au magasin ; **give these bones to the dogs** donne ces os aux chiens

2. *With countries and continents*

> You use au with a country that is masculine and aux with a masculine plural. Use en with feminine countries and with continents:

Karen's going to Japan Karen va au Japon ; **Kevin's going to the United States** Kevin va aux États-Unis ; **I'd like to go to Ireland** j'aimerais aller en Irlande ; **they've gone to Australia** ils sont allés en Australie

3. chez

> When you are referring to somebody's office, shop or house use chez:

I'm going to the dentist je vais chez le dentiste ; **he went to John's house** il est allé chez John

4. jusqu'à : **count to 10** comptez jusqu'à 10

5. *Telling the time* moins : **it's quarter to four** il est quatre heures moins le quart ; **it's ten to seven** il est sept heures moins dix

6. *With infinitives*

> When 'to' is used as part of an infinitive after certain verbs (begin to do, try to do, want to do), it is usually translated by à or de depending on the verb used in French:

she began to sing elle a commencé à chanter ; **he tried to help me** il a essayé de m'aider ; **I want to go to bed** je veux aller me coucher

> When 'to' is used after an adjective (easy to do, hard to do), it is usually translated by à and by de when the infinitive has an object:

it's easy to understand c'est facile à comprendre ; **it's hard to believe** c'est difficile à croire ; **it's hard to understand him** il est difficile de le comprendre ; **it's not easy to talk to him** ce n'est pas facile de lui parler

> When 'to' means 'in order to', it is translated by pour:

he worked hard to pass his exam il a travaillé dur pour réussir son examen ; **she's gone to town to buy a coat** elle est allée en ville pour acheter un manteau.

toad [təʊd] *noun*

crapaud *(masculine)* : **toads belong to the same family as frogs** les crapauds font partie de la même famille que les grenouilles.

toadstool ['təʊdstuːl] *noun*

champignon *(masculine)* **vénéneux**.

toast [təʊst] *noun*

pain *(masculine)* **grillé : I have toast for breakfast** je mange du pain grillé au petit déjeuner ; **cheese on toast** du fromage fondu sur du pain grillé

> **a piece of toast** une tartine grillée

> **to drink a toast to somebody** boire à la santé de quelqu'un : **let's drink a toast to Gareth** buvons à la santé de Gareth.

toasted sandwich [ˌtəʊstɪd'sænwɪdʒ] *noun*

sandwich *(masculine)* **grillé**.

toaster ['təʊstər] *noun*

grille-pain *(masculine)* [*plural* **grille-pain**].

tobacco [tə'bækəʊ] *noun*

tabac *(masculine)*.

tobacconist *UK* [tə'bækənɪst] *noun*

bureau *(masculine)* de tabac.

toboggan [tə'bɒgən] *noun*

luge *(feminine)* : **she came down the slope on a toboggan** elle a descendu la piste en luge.

today [tə'deɪ] *adverb*

aujourd'hui : **what did you do today?** qu'est-ce que tu as fait aujourd'hui ? ; **what day is it today?** quel jour sommes-nous aujourd'hui ? ; **today's paper** le journal d'aujourd'hui.

toe [təʊ] *noun*

orteil *(masculine)*, **doigt** *(masculine)* **de pied** : **I banged my toe** je me suis cogné l'orteil.

toffee *UK* ['tɒfɪ] *noun*

caramel *(masculine)* : **she bought some toffees** elle a acheté des caramels.

together [tə'geðər] *adverb*

ensemble : **they arrived together** ils sont arrivés ensemble ; **stick close together** restez ensemble ; **those colours don't go together** ces couleurs ne vont pas ensemble
➤ **together with** avec : **together with the CD, you get a booklet** avec le CD tu as un livret.

toilet ['tɔɪlɪt] *noun*

toilettes *(feminine plural)* : **where are the toilets?** où sont les toilettes ? ; **he went to the toilet** il est allé aux toilettes
➤ **a toilet bag** une trousse de toilette
➤ **toilet paper** papier *(masculine)* hygiénique
➤ **a toilet roll** un rouleau de papier hygiénique.

toiletries ['tɔɪlɪtrɪz] *plural noun*

articles *(masculine plural)* de toilette.

token ['təʊkn] *noun*

➤ **a book token** un chèque-livre
➤ **a gift token** un chèque-cadeau
➤ **a record token** un chèque-disque.

told [təʊld] *past tense & past participle of* **tell**

I told you je te l'ai dit ; **I haven't told anybody** je n'ai rien dit à personne.

toll [təʊl] *noun*

péage *(masculine)* : **you have to pay a toll at the bridge** il y a un péage au pont.

toll-free *US* ['təʊlfriː] *adverb*

➤ **to call toll-free** appeler un numéro vert : **I called toll-free** j'ai appelé le numéro vert.

tomato [*UK* tə'mɑːtəʊ, *US* tə'meɪtəʊ] (*plural* **tomatoes**) *noun*

tomate *(feminine)* : **a tomato salad** une salade de tomates
➤ **tomato sauce** sauce *(feminine)* tomate.

tomb [tuːm] *noun*

tombeau *(masculine)* [*plural* **tombeaux**], **tombe** *(feminine)* : **the pharaohs' tombs** les tombeaux des pharaons.

tomboy ['tɒmbɔɪ] *noun*

garçon *(masculine)* manqué : **Claire's a real tomboy** Claire est un vrai garçon manqué.

tomorrow [tə'mɒrəʊ] *adverb*

demain : **I'll do it tomorrow** je le ferai demain ; **what are you doing tomorrow?** qu'est-ce que tu fais demain ?
➤ **tomorrow morning** demain matin
➤ **tomorrow evening** demain soir
➤ **the day after tomorrow** après-demain : **I'll come over the day after tomorrow** je passerai après-demain.

ton [tʌn] (*plural* **ton** OR **tons**) *noun*

tonne *(feminine)* : **it weighs a ton** ça pèse une tonne
➤ **tons of** *informal* des tas de ; **she has tons of friends** elle a des tas d'amis.

tone [təʊn] *noun*

1. ton *(masculine)* : **don't speak to me in that tone** ne me parle pas sur ce ton
2. sonnerie *(feminine)* : **the ring tones on a mobile phone** les types de sonneries d'un téléphone portable
3. tonalité *(feminine)* : **the phone isn't working, there's no tone** le téléphone ne marche pas, il n'y a pas de tonalité
➤ **speak after the tone** parlez après le signal sonore.

tongue [tʌŋ] *noun*

langue *(feminine)* : she stuck her tongue out at me elle m'a tiré la langue.

tonight [tə'naɪt] *adverb*

1. ce soir : I'm going out tonight je sors ce soir
2. cette nuit : I'll sleep downstairs tonight je vais coucher en bas cette nuit.

tonne [tʌn] *(plural* tonne OR tonnes*) noun*

tonne *(feminine)*.

tonsillitis [ˌtɒnsɪ'laɪtɪs] *noun*

angine *(feminine)* : he has tonsillitis il a une angine.

tonsils ['tɒnslz] *plural noun*

amygdales *(feminine plural)* : he had his tonsils out il s'est fait opérer des amygdales.

too [tuː] *adverb*

1. aussi : are you coming too? tu viens aussi ? ; I'm hungry – me too j'ai faim – moi aussi
2. trop : it's too late il est trop tard
  > too many trop de : there are too many people il y a trop de gens
  > too much

1. trop de : don't drink too much coffee ne bois pas trop de café
2. trop : you talk too much tu parles trop.

took [tʊk] *past tense of* take

I took a shower j'ai pris une douche.

tool [tuːl] *noun*

outil *(masculine)*
  > a tool box une boîte à outils.

tooth [tuːθ] *(plural* teeth [tiːθ]*) noun*

dent *(feminine)* : she's brushing her teeth elle se brosse les dents.

toothache ['tuːθeɪk] *noun*

mal *(masculine)* de dents : he has toothache UK OR he has a toothache US il a mal aux dents.

toothbrush ['tuːθbrʌʃ] *(plural* toothbrushes*) noun*

brosse *(feminine)* à dents.

toothpaste ['tuːθpeɪst] *noun*

dentifrice *(masculine)* : a tube of toothpaste un tube de dentifrice.

top [tɒp] *noun & adjective*

▪ *noun*

1. sommet *(masculine)*, haut *(masculine)* : at the top of the mountain au sommet de la montagne OR en haut de la montagne
2. haut *(masculine)* : at the top of the page en haut de la page ; at the top of the stairs en haut de l'escalier ; she's wearing a pretty top elle porte un joli haut
3. dessus *(masculine)* : she polished the top of the table elle a ciré le dessus de la table
4. bouchon *(masculine)* : a bottle with a screw top une bouteille avec un bouchon à vis
5. couvercle *(masculine)* : put the top back on the jar remets le couvercle sur le pot
6. capuchon *(masculine)* : I've lost my pen top j'ai perdu le capuchon de mon stylo
  > a pyjama top une veste de pyjama
  > on top of
1. sur : he was sitting on top of the table il était assis sur la table
2. en plus de : on top of that, he's stupid en plus de cela, il est bête
  > he's at the top of the class c'est le premier de la classe
  > on top dessus : a cake with a cherry on top un gâteau avec une cerise dessus
▪ *adjective*
1. du haut : the top drawer le tiroir du haut
2. dernier *(feminine* dernière*)* : the top stair la dernière marche
3. grand : he's a top tennis player c'est un grand joueur de tennis
  > the top floor le dernier étage : they live on the top floor ils habitent au dernier étage
  > a top hat un haut-de-forme [*plural* hauts-de-forme]
  > to get top marks avoir d'excellentes notes.

topic ['tɒpɪk] *noun*

sujet *(masculine)* : the main topic of conversation le principal sujet de conversation.

topping ['tɒpɪŋ] *noun*

garniture *(feminine)* : what toppings do you want on your pizza? qu'est-ce que vous voulez comme garniture sur votre pizza ?

top-secret [ˌtɒp'siːkrɪt] *adjective*

top secret *(invariable)* : top-secret information des informations top secret.

torch UK [tɔːtʃ] *(plural* torches*) noun*

lampe *(feminine)* de poche : he shone his torch on me il a braqué sa lampe de poche sur moi.

t

tore [tɔːʳ] *past tense of* **tear**

he tore the paper to bits il a déchiré le papier.

torn [tɔːn] *past participle of* **tear**

my skirt is torn ma jupe est déchirée.

tornado [tɔː'neɪdəʊ] (*plural* tornadoes OR tornados) noun
tornade (*feminine*).

tortoise ['tɔːtəs] noun

tortue (*feminine*) : they have a pet tortoise ils ont une tortue à la maison.

toss [tɒs] verb

lancer : he tossed me the ball il m'a lancé la balle

➤ to toss a coin jouer à pile ou face : let's toss a coin jouons à pile ou face

toss away , **toss out** phrasal verb

jeter : you can toss those old magazines out tu peux jeter ces vieux magazines.

total ['təʊtl] noun & adjective

◼ noun
total (*masculine*) : it costs a total of 200 euros cela fait un total de 200 euros
➤ in total au total
◼ adjective
total : the total price le prix total.

totally ['təʊtəlɪ] adverb

totalement.

touch [tʌtʃ] noun & verb

◼ noun
toucher (*masculine*) : the sense of touch le toucher ; it's soft to the touch c'est doux au toucher
➤ to keep in touch with somebody rester en contact avec quelqu'un
➤ to get in touch with somebody prendre contact avec quelqu'un OR contacter quelqu'un : I got in touch with him j'ai pris contact avec lui OR je l'ai contacté
➤ to lose touch with somebody perdre quelqu'un de vue : I lost touch with them je les ai perdus de vue
◼ verb
1. toucher : I touched his hand je lui ai touché la main
2. toucher à : don't touch that computer ne touche pas à cet ordinateur.

touchdown ['tʌtʃdaʊn] noun

essai (*masculine*) : he scored a touchdown il a marqué un essai.

tough [tʌf] adjective

1. dur : the meat is tough la viande est dure ; it's a tough life la vie est dure
2. solide : he's wearing tough shoes il porte des chaussures solides
3. difficile : it's a tough problem c'est un problème difficile
4. dangereux (*feminine* dangereuse) : this is a tough neighbourhood c'est un quartier dangereux
➤ tough luck! pas de chance !

tour [tʊəʳ] noun

1. voyage (*masculine*) : we went on a tour of Spain nous avons fait un voyage en Espagne
2. visite (*feminine*) : a guided tour une visite guidée ; I went on a tour of the museum j'ai fait la visite du musée
3. tournée (*feminine*) : Britney Spears is on tour Britney Spears est en tournée.

tourism ['tʊərɪzm] noun

tourisme (*masculine*).

tourist ['tʊərɪst] noun

touriste (*masculine or feminine*)
➤ a tourist office OR a tourist information office un office de tourisme.

tournament ['tɔːnəmənt] noun

tournoi (*masculine*) : a chess tournament un tournoi d'échecs.

towards [tə'wɔːdz], **toward** US [tə'wɔːd] preposition

1. vers : he was walking towards me il avançait vers moi
2. avec, envers : she was very kind towards us elle a été très gentille avec nous.

towel ['taʊəl] noun

serviette (*feminine*) : a bath towel une serviette de bain ; a beach towel une serviette de plage.

tower ['taʊəʳ] noun

tour (*feminine*) : the Eiffel Tower was built in 1889 la tour Eiffel fut construite en 1889

> **a tower block** *UK* une tour d'habitation

 TOWER OF LONDON
Ce célèbre monument de Londres est un ancien château fort où ont vécu de nombreux rois et reines d'Angleterre. Il a aussi servi de prison pour ceux qui s'opposaient au roi ou à la reine. Aujourd'hui c'est un musée et on vient surtout y voir les bijoux de la famille royale (**the Crown Jewels**) et les fameux gardes surnommés les **Beefeaters**.

town [taʊn] *noun*

ville *(feminine)* : **he lives in a small town** il habite une petite ville ; **we went into town** nous sommes allées en ville
> **the town centre** *UK* le centre-ville : **we're going to the town centre** nous allons au centre-ville
> **the town hall** la mairie : **the town hall is on the main square** la mairie est sur la grand-place.

toy [tɔɪ] *noun*

jouet *(masculine)*
> **a toy shop** *UK* OR **a toy store** *US* un magasin de jouets.

track [træk] *noun*

1. **sentier** *(masculine)* : **a mountain track** un sentier de montagne
2. **piste** *(feminine)* : **he did three laps around the track** il a fait trois tours de piste
3. **morceau** *(masculine)* [*plural* **morceaux**] : **can I listen to the next track?** je peux écouter le morceau suivant ?
4. **trace** *(feminine)* : **the tyre tracks led to the river** les traces de pneu menaient à la rivière
> **a railway track** *UK* OR **a railroad track** *US* une voie ferrée.

tracksuit ['træksuːt] *noun*

survêtement *(masculine)* : **he's wearing a tracksuit** il porte un survêtement.

tractor ['træktər] *noun*

tracteur *(masculine)*.

trade [treɪd] *noun*

1. **métier** *(masculine)* : **he's a chef by trade** il est chef de son métier
2. **commerce** *(masculine)* : **international trade** le commerce international
> **a trade union** *UK* un syndicat.

trademark ['treɪdmɑːk] *noun*

marque *(feminine)* : **a registered trademark** une marque déposée.

tradition [trə'dɪʃn] *noun*

tradition *(feminine)* : **it's a tradition to kiss under the mistletoe** c'est une tradition de s'embrasser sous le gui.

traditional [trə'dɪʃənl] *adjective*

traditionnel *(feminine* **traditionnelle**) : **a traditional Christmas dinner** un réveillon de Noël traditionnel.

traffic ['træfɪk] *uncountable noun*

circulation *(feminine)* : **there's a lot of traffic** il y a beaucoup de circulation
> **a traffic circle** *US* un rond-point [*plural* **ronds-points**]
> **a traffic jam** un embouteillage : **we got caught in a traffic jam** nous nous sommes retrouvés bloqués dans un embouteillage
> **the traffic lights** les feux OR les feux de signalisation : **stop at the traffic lights** arrêtez-vous aux feux
> **a traffic warden** *UK* un contractuel, une contractuelle.

tragedy ['trædʒədɪ] (*plural* **tragedies**) *noun*

tragédie *(feminine)*.

trail [treɪl] *noun*

piste *(feminine)* : **we are on their trail** nous sommes sur leur piste.

trailer ['treɪlər] *noun*

1. **bande-annonce** *(feminine)* [*plural* **bandes-annonces**] : **I liked the trailer for the film** j'ai bien aimé la bande-annonce du film
2. **remorque** *(feminine)* : **the car was pulling a trailer** la voiture tirait une remorque
3. *US* **caravane** *(feminine)* : **they live in a trailer** ils habitent dans une caravane.

train [treɪn] *noun & verb*

■ *noun*
train *(masculine)* : **I went to Paris by train** je suis allé à Paris en train
■ *verb*
1. **former** : **he is training a new assistant** il est en train de former un nouvel assistant
2. **suivre une formation** : **she's training as a doctor** elle suit une formation de médecin
3. **s'entraîner** : **he's training for the race** il s'entraîne pour la course.

trainer ['treɪnə'] *noun*

entraîneur *(masculine)* : **the Irish team have a new trainer** l'équipe irlandaise a un nouvel entraîneur.

trainers *UK* ['treɪnə'z] *plural noun*

chaussures *(feminine plural)* **de sport, tennis** *(feminine plural)* : **he's wearing trainers** il porte des chaussures de sport OR il porte des tennis.

training ['treɪnɪŋ] *uncountable noun*

1. **formation** *(feminine)* : **he did his training in Spain** il a fait sa formation en Espagne
2. **entraînement** *(masculine)* : **she's out of training** elle manque d'entraînement
> **to be in training** s'entraîner : **he's in training for the tournament** il s'entraîne pour le tournoi.

tram *UK* [træm] *noun*

tramway *(masculine)*, **tram** *(masculine)* : **there are trams in Amsterdam** il y a des tramways à Amsterdam.

tramp [træmp] *noun*

clochard *(masculine)*, **clocharde** *(feminine)*.

trampoline ['træmpəliːn] *noun*

trampoline *(masculine)*.

translate [træns'leɪt] *verb*

traduire : **can you translate this letter into English?** tu peux traduire cette lettre en anglais ?

translation [træns'leɪʃn] *noun*

traduction *(feminine)*.

translator [træns'leɪtə'] *noun*

traducteur *(masculine)*, **traductrice** *(feminine)* : **she's a translator** elle est traductrice.

transparent [træns'pærənt] *adjective*

transparent : **glass is transparent** le verre est transparent.

transport *noun & verb*

■ *noun* ['trænspɔːt]
transport *(masculine)* : **his only means of transport is his bike** son seul moyen de transport, c'est le vélo ; **I always use public transport** j'utilise toujours les transports en commun
■ *verb* [træn'spɔːt]
transporter : **the soldiers were transport-ed by helicopter** les soldats ont été transportés en hélicoptère.

transportation *US* [ˌtrænspɔː'teɪʃn] *noun*

transport *(masculine)* : **we went by public transportation** nous avons pris les transports en commun.

trap [træp] *noun & verb*

■ *noun*
piège *(masculine)* : **it's a trap** c'est un piège
■ *verb (past tense & past participle* **trapped***)*
1. **coincer** : **I'm trapped, I can't get out** je suis coincé, je ne peux pas sortir
2. **prendre au piège** : **the hunters trapped the lion** les chasseurs ont pris le lion au piège.

trash *US* [træʃ] *uncountable noun*

ordures *(feminine plural)* : **there's a pile of trash in the corner** il y a un tas d'ordures dans le coin
> **put it in the trash** mets-le à la poubelle
> **put the trash out** sors la poubelle.

trashcan *US* ['træʃkæn] *noun*

poubelle *(feminine)*.

travel ['trævl] *noun & verb*

■ *uncountable noun*
voyages *(masculine plural)* : **travel broadens the mind** les voyages ouvrent l'esprit
> **a travel agency** une agence de voyages
> **to get travel sick** avoir le mal des transports
■ *verb (past tense & past participle* travelled *UK* OR traveled *US*)
1. **voyager** : **he travels a lot** il voyage beaucoup
2. **faire** : **I've travelled thirty miles** j'ai fait cinquante kilomètres.

traveller *UK*, **traveler** *US* ['trævlə'] *noun*

voyageur *(masculine)*, **voyageuse** *(feminine)*
> **a traveller's cheque** *UK* OR **a traveler's check** *US* un chèque de voyage : **I'd like to change some traveller's cheques** je voudrais changer des chèques de voyage.

tray [treɪ] *noun*

plateau *(masculine)* [*plural* **plateaux**] : **put the plates on a tray** mets les assiettes sur un plateau.

tread [tred] (*past tense* trod, *past participle* trodden) *verb* marcher : **don't tread on the carpet** ne marche pas sur le tapis.

treasure ['treʒəʳ] *uncountable noun*

trésor *(masculine)* : **they found treasure on the shipwreck** ils ont découvert un trésor dans l'épave.

treat [tri:t] *verb & noun*

■ *verb*

traiter : **she treats him well** elle le traite bien

➤ **to treat somebody to something** offrir quelque chose à quelqu'un : **he treated me to an ice cream** il m'a offert une glace

■ *noun*

1. **petit cadeau** *(masculine)* : **I've bought you a treat** je t'ai acheté un petit cadeau

2. **régal** *(masculine)* : **the meal was a real treat** le repas était un vrai régal

3. **plaisir** *(masculine)* : **it was a treat to see you again** c'était un plaisir de te revoir

➤ **it's my treat** c'est moi qui paie.

treatment ['tri:tmənt] *noun*

traitement *(masculine)* : **he's having treatment at the hospital** il suit un traitement à l'hôpital.

treaty ['tri:tɪ] *(plural* treaties*)* *noun*

traité *(masculine)* : **a peace treaty** un traité de paix.

tree [tri:] *noun*

arbre *(masculine)* : **we sat under a tree** nous nous sommes assis sous un arbre

➤ **a family tree** un arbre généalogique

➤ **a tree trunk** un tronc d'arbre.

tremble ['trembl] *verb*

trembler : **I was trembling all over** je tremblais de partout.

trend [trend] *noun*

1. **mode** *(feminine)* : **the latest trends** la dernière mode ; **he has set a new trend** il a lancé une nouvelle mode

2. **tendance** *(feminine)* : **a new trend in music** une nouvelle tendance en musique.

trendy ['trendɪ] *adjective informal*

branché : **we went to a trendy club** nous sommes allés dans une boîte branchée.

trial ['traɪəl] *noun*

procès *(masculine)* : **he pleaded guilty at the trial** il a plaidé coupable au procès

➤ **to go on trial** passer en justice.

triangle ['traɪæŋgl] *noun*

triangle *(masculine)* : **the Bermuda triangle** le triangle des Bermudes.

tribe [traɪb] *noun*

tribu *(feminine)* : **an Amazonian tribe** une tribu amazonienne.

trick [trɪk] *noun & verb*

■ *noun*

1. **tour** *(masculine)* : **he played a trick on his brother** il a joué un tour à son frère ; **a conjuring trick** un tour de passe-passe

2. **truc** *(masculine)* : **there's a trick to opening the door** il y a un truc pour ouvrir la porte

3. **ruse** *(feminine)* : **it was a trick to get him to open the door** c'était une ruse pour lui faire ouvrir la porte

■ *verb*

rouler : **you tricked me** tu m'as roulé.

tried [traɪd] *past tense & past participle of* try

I tried to phone j'ai essayé d'appeler ; **have you ever tried sushi?** est-ce que tu as déjà essayé les sushis ? OR est-ce que tu as déjà goûté les sushis ?

trigger ['trɪgəʳ] *noun*

gâchette *(feminine)* : **she pulled the trigger** elle a appuyé sur la gâchette.

trim [trɪm] *noun & verb*

■ *noun*

coupe *(feminine)* **d'entretien**

■ *verb (past tense & past participle* trimmed*)*

couper : **I need to have my hair trimmed** j'ai besoin de me faire couper un peu les cheveux.

trip [trɪp] *noun & verb*

■ *noun*

1. **voyage** *(masculine)* : **they went on a trip to Italy** ils ont fait un voyage en Italie ; **a school trip** un voyage scolaire

2. **excursion** *(feminine)* : **we're going on a trip to the seaside** nous allons en excursion au bord de la mer

■ *verb (past tense & past participle* tripped*)*

trébucher : **I tripped and fell** j'ai trébuché et je suis tombé.

trod [trɒd] *past tense of* tread

she trod on my foot elle m'a marché sur le pied.

t

trodden ['trɒdn] *past participle of* tread

I've trodden in something horrible j'ai marché dans quelque chose de dégoûtant.

trolley *UK* ['trɒlɪ] (*plural* trolleys) *noun*

chariot (*masculine*) : **a shopping trolley** un chariot OR un Caddie®.

trombone [trɒm'bəʊn] *noun*

trombone (*masculine*) : **he plays the trombone** il joue du trombone

⚠ Le mot anglais **trombone** ne signifie pas "trombone" au sens de "attache pour le papier".

trophy ['trəʊfɪ] (*plural* trophies) *noun*

trophée (*masculine*) : **she won a trophy** elle a gagné un trophée.

tropical ['trɒpɪkl] *adjective*

tropical [*plural* tropicaux] : **a tropical rainforest** une forêt tropicale.

trot [trɒt] (*past tense & past participle* trotted) *verb*

trotter : **the horses were trotting round the field** les chevaux trottaient dans le pré.

trouble ['trʌbl] *noun & verb*

▧ *uncountable noun*

1. ennuis (*masculine plural*) : **he made a lot of trouble for me** il m'a causé beaucoup d'ennuis

2. problème (*masculine*) : **that's the trouble** c'est ça le problème

3. mal (*masculine*), peine (*feminine*) : **she went to a lot of trouble** elle s'est donné beaucoup de peine OR elle s'est donné beaucoup de mal ; **he has gone to a lot of trouble to help me** il s'est donné beaucoup de mal pour m'aider

➤ **to be in trouble** avoir des ennuis : **he's in a lot of trouble** il a beaucoup d'ennuis

➤ **to get into trouble** s'attirer des ennuis : **I don't want to get into trouble** je ne veux pas m'attirer d'ennuis

➤ **to have trouble doing something** avoir du mal à faire quelque chose : **I had trouble writing my essay** j'ai eu du mal à écrire ma rédaction

➤ **what's the trouble?** qu'est-ce qu'il y a ?

▧ *verb*

déranger : **I'm sorry to trouble you** excusez-moi de vous déranger.

trousers *UK* ['traʊzəz] *plural noun*

pantalon (*masculine*) : **Paul's wearing red trousers** Paul porte un pantalon rouge

➤ **a pair of trousers** un pantalon : **a new pair of trousers** un pantalon neuf.

trout [traʊt] *noun*

truite (*feminine*).

truant *UK* ['truːənt] *noun*

➤ **to play truant** sécher les cours ; **he often plays truant** il sèche souvent les cours.

truck [trʌk] *noun*

camion (*masculine*)

➤ **a truck driver** un camionneur OR un routier : **he's a truck driver** il est camionneur OR il est routier.

trucker *US* ['trʌkər] *noun*

camionneur (*masculine*), routier (*masculine*) : **he's a trucker** il est camionneur OR il est routier.

true ['truː] *adjective*

vrai : **it's true** c'est vrai

➤ **to come true** se réaliser : **her dream came true** son rêve s'est réalisé.

trumpet ['trʌmpɪt] *noun*

trompette (*feminine*) : **Louis plays the trumpet** Louis joue de la trompette.

trunk [trʌŋk] *noun*

1. tronc (*masculine*) : **a tree trunk** un tronc d'arbre

2. trompe (*feminine*) : **elephants suck up water with their trunks** les éléphants aspirent l'eau avec leur trompe

3. malle (*feminine*) : **he packed his trunk** il a fait sa malle

4. *US* coffre (*masculine*) : **put your bags into the trunk of the car** mets tes valises dans le coffre de la voiture.

trunks [trʌŋks] *plural noun*

maillot (*masculine*) de bain : **he's wearing swimming trunks** il porte un maillot de bain.

trust [trʌst] *noun & verb*

▧ *uncountable noun*
confiance (*feminine*)

▧ *verb*
faire confiance à quelqu'un : **I trust you** je te fais confiance.

truth [truːθ] *noun*

vérité *(feminine)* : **he's telling the truth** il dit la vérité.

try [traɪ] *noun & verb*

◼ *noun*

essai *(masculine)* : **I'll give it a try** je vais essayer ; **Lomu scored a try** Lomu a marqué un essai

◼ *verb (past tense & past participle* tried)

1. **essayer** : **try this new recipe** essaie cette nouvelle recette ; **I tried to open the door** j'ai essayé d'ouvrir la porte ; **she tried phoning him** elle a essayé de l'appeler

2. **goûter** : **try a bit of this cake** goûte un peu de ce gâteau

➤ **to try one's best** OR **to try one's hardest** faire de son mieux

try on | *phrasal verb*

essayer : **try this hat on** essaie ce chapeau.

T-shirt ['tiːʃɜːt] *noun*

tee-shirt *(masculine)* : **Billy's wearing a T-shirt** Billy porte un tee-shirt.

tube [*UK* tjuːb, *US* tuːb] *noun*

tube *(masculine)* : **a tube of toothpaste** un tube de dentifrice

➤ **the tube** *UK* le métro ; **let's take the tube** prenons le métro.

Tuesday [*UK* 'tjuːzdɪ, *US* 'tuːzdɪ] *noun*

mardi *(masculine)* : **it's Tuesday today** nous sommes mardi ; **next Tuesday** mardi prochain ; **last Tuesday** mardi dernier

➤ **on Tuesday** mardi : **I'll see you on Tuesday** on se voit mardi

➤ **on Tuesdays** le mardi : **he comes to see me on Tuesdays** il vient me voir le mardi

> In French the days of the week do not start with a capital letter.

tulip [*UK* 'tjuːlɪp, *US* 'tuːlɪp] *noun*

tulipe *(feminine)* : **Holland is famous for its tulips** la Hollande est célèbre pour ses tulipes.

tummy ['tʌmɪ] *noun informal*

ventre *(masculine)* : **to have tummy ache** *UK* OR **to have a tummy ache** *US* avoir mal au ventre.

tuna [*UK* 'tjuːnə, *US* 'tuːnə] *(plural* tuna OR tunas) *noun*

thon *(masculine)* : **tuna in oil** du thon à l'huile.

tune [*UK* tjuːn, *US* tuːn] *noun*

air *(masculine)* : **I don't know the words, but I'll sing you the tune** je ne connais pas les paroles, mais je vais te chanter l'air

➤ **out of tune** faux : **he's singing out of tune** il chante faux.

tunnel ['tʌnl] *noun*

tunnel *(masculine)* : **we went through the tunnel** nous avons traversé le tunnel.

Turk [tɜːk] *noun*

Turc *(masculine)*, **Turque** *(feminine)*.

turkey ['tɜːkɪ] *(plural* turkeys) *noun*

dinde *(feminine)* : **people eat turkey on Christmas Day in Britain and at Thanksgiving in the US** les gens mangent de la dinde le jour de Noël en Grande-Bretagne et à Thanksgiving aux États-Unis.

Turkey ['tɜːkɪ] *noun*

la Turquie

> In French the names of countries are used with the definite article (**le, la** or **l'**), except when they follow the preposition **en**:

Turkey lies in two continents la Turquie est à cheval sur deux continents ; **Istanbul is in Turkey** Istanbul se trouve en Turquie ; **I'd like to go to Turkey** j'aimerais aller en Turquie.

Turkish ['tɜːkɪʃ] *adjective & noun*

◼ *adjective*

turc *(feminine* turque) : **a Turkish coffee** un café turc

◼ *noun*

turc *(masculine)* : **he speaks Turkish** il parle turc

➤ **the Turkish** les Turcs

> Remember not to use a capital letter for the adjective and the language in French. Only use a capital letter for the inhabitants.

turn ['tɜːn] *noun & verb*

◼ *noun*

1. **tour** *(masculine)* : **wait your turn** attends ton tour ; **it's my turn** c'est mon tour ; **it's your turn to wash the dishes** c'est à toi de faire la vaisselle OR c'est ton tour de faire la vaisselle

2. **tournant** *(masculine)*, **virage** *(masculine)* : **there's a turn in the road** il y a un tournant OR il y a un virage

t

➤ **to take it in turns to do something** *UK* OR **to take turns at doing something** *US* faire quelque chose à tour de rôle

■ *verb*

1. **tourner** : **turn left at the lights** tournez à gauche aux feux ; **turn the knob to the right** tourne le bouton vers la droite
2. **se retourner** : **he turned and spoke to me** il s'est retourné et m'a parlé
3. **devenir** : **she turned pale** elle est devenue pâle OR elle a pâli ; **the apples turned red** les pommes sont devenues rouges ; **he turned red** il a rougi

turn around , **turn round** *UK phrasal verb*

1. **se retourner** : **he turned around when I came in** il s'est retourné quand je suis entrée
2. **faire demi-tour** : **the car turned around** OR **he turned the car around** il a fait demi-tour
3. **tourner** : **the wheel turned around** la roue a tourné
4. **tourner dans l'autre sens** : **they turned the table around** ils ont tourné la table dans l'autre sens

turn back *phrasal verb*

faire demi-tour : **we walked for an hour and then turned back** nous avons marché pendant une heure et puis nous avons fait demi-tour

turn down *phrasal verb*

rejeter : **they turned my offer down** ils ont rejeté mon offre

turn into *phrasal verb*

1. **changer en, transformer en** : **the witch turned the prince into a frog** la sorcière a changé le prince en grenouille OR la sorcière a transformé le prince en grenouille
2. **se transformer en** : **the caterpillar turned into a butterfly** la chenille s'est transformée en papillon

turn off *phrasal verb*

éteindre : **turn the TV off** éteins la télé

turn on *phrasal verb*

allumer : **turn the radio on** allume la radio ; **he turned the light on** il a allumé la lumière

turn over *phrasal verb*

1. **retourner** : **he turned his cards over** il a retourné ses cartes
2. **se retourner** : **she turned over and went back to sleep** elle s'est retournée et s'est rendormie
3. *UK* **changer de chaîne** : **this film is no good, let's turn over** ce film est nul, changeons de chaîne

turn round *UK phrasal verb* ➤ turn around

turn up *phrasal verb*

1. **mettre plus fort** : **turn the music up** mets la musique plus fort
2. **venir, arriver** : **he didn't turn up** il n'est pas venu ; **don't worry, it'll turn up** ne t'inquiète pas, tu vas le retrouver.

turnip ['tɜːnɪp] *noun*

navet *(masculine)*.

turnpike *US* ['tɜːnpaɪk] *noun*

autoroute *(feminine)* **à péage**.

turquoise ['tɜːkwɔɪz] *adjective*

turquoise.

turtle ['tɜːtl] *(plural* turtle OR turtles) *noun*

1. **tortue** *(feminine)* **marine** : **there's a big turtle on the beach** il y a une grande tortue marine sur la plage
2. *US* **tortue** *(feminine)* : **he keeps a pet turtle** il a une tortue à la maison.

tusk [tʌsk] *noun*

défense *(feminine)* : **elephants have ivory tusks** les éléphants ont des défenses en ivoire.

TV [ˌtiːˈviː] *(abbreviation of* television*) noun*

télé *(feminine)* : **they're watching TV** ils regardent la télé ; **put the TV on** allume la télé ; **what's on TV?** qu'est-ce qu'il y a à la télé ?

twelfth [twelfθ] *numeral*

douzième : **on the twelfth floor** au douzième étage

➤ **it's the twelfth of November** *UK* OR **it's November twelfth** *US* nous sommes le douze novembre.

twelve [twelv] *numeral*

douze : **the twelve apostles** les douze apôtres ; **she's twelve** elle a douze ans ; **I'll meet you at twelve** on se retrouve à midi ; **it's twelve o'clock at night** il est minuit.

twentieth ['twentɪəθ] *number*

vingtième : **in the twentieth century** au vingtième siècle

> **it's the twentieth of May** *UK* OR **it's May twentieth** *US* nous sommes le vingt mai.

twenty ['twentɪ] *number*

vingt : **it's twenty to four** il est quatre heures moins vingt ; **she's twenty** elle a vingt ans
> **twenty-one** vingt et un
> **twenty-first** vingt-et-unième : **the twenty-first century** le vingt-et-unième siècle.

twice [twaɪs] *adverb*

deux fois : **I go swimming twice a week** je vais à la piscine deux fois par semaine ; **she earns twice as much as him** elle gagne deux fois plus que lui.

twig [twɪg] *noun*

brindille *(feminine)*.

twin [twɪn] *noun*

jumeau *(masculine)*, **jumelle** *(feminine)* [*plural* jumeaux] : **they are twins** ils sont jumeaux ; **his twin brother** son frère jumeau ; **she's my twin sister** c'est ma sœur jumelle.

twinned *UK* [twɪnt] *adjective*

jumelé : **our town is twinned with Cannes** notre ville est jumelée avec Cannes.

twist [twɪst] *verb*

1. **tordre** : **he twisted my arm** il m'a tordu le bras
2. **tourner** : **I twisted the knob to the left** j'ai tourné le bouton vers la gauche
3. **enrouler** : **twist the thread round the bobbin** enroule le fil autour la bobine
> **to get twisted** s'entortiller : **the cable has got twisted** le câble s'est entortillé
> **to twist one's ankle** se tordre la cheville : **I twisted my ankle** je me suis tordu la cheville.

two [tuː] *number*

deux : **I cut the paper in two** j'ai coupé le papier en deux ; **she's two** elle a deux ans ; **he left at two** il est parti à deux heures.

type [taɪp] *noun & verb*

■ *noun*
1. **sorte** *(feminine)*, **type** *(masculine)* : **there are different types of houses** il y a plusieurs sortes de maisons OR il y a plusieurs types de maisons
2. **modèle** *(masculine)* : **what type of computer do you have?** quel modèle d'ordinateur as-tu ?
■ *verb*
taper : **he typed the letter** il a tapé la lettre.

typewriter ['taɪpˌraɪtər] *noun*

machine *(feminine)* **à écrire**.

typical ['tɪpɪkl] *adjective*

typique : **can you describe a typical Englishman?** tu peux décrire un Anglais typique ?
> **that's typical of him** c'est bien de lui OR c'est bien son genre.

tyre *UK*, **tire** *US* ['taɪər] *noun*

pneu *(masculine)* : **he pumped up the tyres** il a gonflé les pneus.

UFO *(abbreviation of* unidentified flying object*) noun*
OVNI *(masculine)* : **do you believe in UFOs?** tu crois aux OVNI ?

ugly ['ʌglɪ] *adjective*

laid : **the house is very ugly** la maison est très laide.

UK [ˌjuːˈkeɪ] *(abbreviation of* United Kingdom*) noun*
the UK le Royaume-Uni ; **she lives in the UK** elle habite au Royaume-Uni ; **I'm going to the UK** je vais au Royaume-Uni.

umbrella [ʌmˈbrelə] *noun*

parapluie *(masculine)* : **he put up his umbrella** il a ouvert son parapluie.

umpire ['ʌmpaɪər] *noun*

arbitre *(masculine)*.

UN [juːˈen] *(abbreviation of* United Nations*) noun*
the UN l'ONU.

unable [ʌnˈeɪbl] *adjective*
> **to be unable to do something**
1. **ne pas pouvoir faire quelque chose** : **he was unable to help me** il ne pouvait pas m'aider
2. **ne pas savoir faire quelque chose** : **she's unable to read** elle ne sait pas lire.

u

unbearable [ʌn'beərəbl] *adjective*

insupportable.

unbelievable [ˌʌnbɪ'liːvəbl] *adjective*

incroyable : what happened is unbelievable ce qui est arrivé est incroyable.

uncle ['ʌŋkl] *noun*

oncle *(masculine)* : my uncle lives in Australia mon oncle habite en Australie.

uncomfortable [ˌʌn'kʌmftəbl] *adjective*

inconfortable

➤ to be uncomfortable ne pas être confortable : this chair is really uncomfortable cette chaise n'est pas du tout confortable

➤ to feel uncomfortable se sentir mal à l'aise : I felt very uncomfortable at the party je me sentais très mal à l'aise à la fête.

under ['ʌndər] *preposition & adverb*

▣ *preposition*

1. sous : the dog's under the sofa le chien est sous le canapé

2. moins de : a game for children under five un jeu pour les enfants de moins de cinq ans

➤ it's under there c'est là-dessous

▣ *adverb*

1. en dessous, dessous : he saw the bed and crawled under il a vu le lit et s'est glissé en dessous OR il a vu le lit et s'est glissé dessous

2. au-dessous : children of ten and under des enfants de dix ans et au-dessous

3. moins : under $10 moins de 10 dollars.

underground ['ʌndəgraund] *adjective & noun*

▣ *adjective*

souterrain : an underground passage un passage souterrain

▣ *noun UK*

the underground le métro ; we took the underground nous avons pris le métro.

underline [ˌʌndə'laɪn] *verb*

souligner : he underlined the heading il a souligné le titre.

underneath [ˌʌndə'niːθ] *preposition & adverb*

▣ *preposition*

sous : I looked underneath the chair j'ai regardé sous la chaise

▣ *adverb*

dessous : I bent down and looked underneath je me suis baissé et j'ai regardé dessous.

underpants ['ʌndəpænts] *plural noun*

slip *(masculine)* : a pair of blue underpants un slip bleu.

underpass *US* ['ʌndəpɑːs] *noun*

passage *(masculine)* souterrain.

undershirt *US* ['ʌndəʃɜːt] *noun*

maillot *(masculine)* de corps.

understand [ˌʌndə'stænd] *(past tense & past participle* understood*) verb*

comprendre : do you understand? vous comprenez ? ; I don't understand Spanish je ne comprends pas l'espagnol.

understood [ˌʌndə'stʊd] *past tense & past participle of* understand

I understood everything he said j'ai compris tout ce qu'il a dit ; is that understood? c'est compris ?

underwater [ˌʌndə'wɔːtər] *adjective & adverb*

▣ *adjective*

sous-marin : an underwater camera une caméra sous-marine

▣ *adverb*

sous l'eau : he can swim underwater il sait nager sous l'eau.

underwear ['ʌndəweər] *uncountable noun*

sous-vêtements *(masculine plural)*.

undid [ˌʌn'dɪd] *past tense of* undo

he undid the buttons il a défait les boutons.

undo [ˌʌn'duː] *(past tense* undid*, past participle* undone*) verb*

défaire : I can't undo this knot je n'arrive pas à défaire ce nœud.

undone [ˌʌn'dʌn] *adjective & past participle of* undo

défait

➤ to come undone se défaire : the knot has come undone le nœud s'est défait.

undress [ˌʌn'dres] *verb*

se déshabiller

➤ to get undressed se déshabiller : he got undressed il s'est déshabillé.

unemployed [ˌʌnɪm'plɔɪd] *adjective*

au chômage : they're unemployed ils sont au chômage

➤ the unemployed les chômeurs *(masculine plural)* OR les sans-emploi *(masculine plural)*.

unemployment [ˌʌnɪm'plɔɪmənt] *noun*

chômage *(masculine)*
➤ **unemployment benefit** *UK* OR **unemployment compensation** *US* allocation *(feminine)* de chômage.

unexpected [ˌʌnɪk'spektɪd] *adjective*

inattendu : I got an unexpected telephone call j'ai reçu un coup de téléphone inattendu.

unexpectedly [ˌʌnɪk'spektɪdlɪ] *adverb*

à l'improviste : he came unexpectedly il est venu à l'improviste.

unfair [ˌʌn'feəʳ] *adjective*

injuste.

unfortunately [ʌn'fɔːtʃnətlɪ] *adverb*

malheureusement : unfortunately, there isn't any cake left malheureusement, il ne reste plus de gâteau.

unfriendly [ˌʌn'frendlɪ] *adjective*

pas aimable : he's very unfriendly il n'est pas du tout aimable.

unhappy [ʌn'hæpɪ] *adjective*

malheureux *(feminine* **malheureuse)** **: he looks unhappy** il a l'air malheureux.

unhealthy [ʌn'helθɪ] *adjective*

1. **maladif** *(feminine* **maladive)** **: he looks really unhealthy** il a l'air vraiment maladif.
2. **malsain : it's an unhealthy climate** c'est un climat malsain.

unidentified flying object [ˌʌnaɪ'dentɪfaɪdˌflaɪɪŋ'ɒbdʒɪkt] *noun*

objet *(masculine)* **volant non identifié.**

uniform ['juːnɪfɔːm] *noun*

uniforme *(masculine)* **: he's wearing the school uniform** il porte l'uniforme de l'école.

union ['juːnjən] *noun*

syndicat *(masculine)* **: they belong to a union** ils appartiennent à un syndicat
➤ **the Union Jack** le drapeau britannique

THE UNION JACK
Le drapeau officiel du Royaume-Uni est appelé **the Union Jack** ou **the Union Flag.** Les croix de saint Georges, de saint André et de saint Patrick y représentent respectivement l'Angleterre, l'Écosse et l'Irlande du Nord. Le pays de Galles, bien qu'il fasse partie du Royaume-Uni, a son propre drapeau, représentant un dragon rouge sur fond vert et blanc.

unit ['juːnɪt] *noun*

unité *(feminine)* **: a metre is a unit of measurement** le mètre est une unité de mesure ; **an army unit** une unité de l'armée
➤ **a kitchen unit** un élément de cuisine.

United Kingdom [juːˌnaɪtɪd'kɪŋdəm] *noun*

➤ **the United Kingdom** le Royaume-Uni

Remember that the French preposition à combines with le to become au:

we live in the United Kingdom nous habitons au Royaume-Uni ; **she's going to the United Kingdom** elle va au Royaume-Uni
➤ Great Britain.

United Nations [juːˌnaɪtɪd'neɪʃnz] *plural noun*

➤ **the United Nations** les Nations *(feminine plural)* unies.

United States [juːˌnaɪtɪd'steɪts] *noun*

➤ **the United States** les États-Unis *(masculine plural)*.

Remember that the French preposition à combines with le to become au:

they live in the United States ils habitent aux États-Unis ; **have you ever been to the United States?** tu es déjà allé aux États-Unis ?

universe ['juːnɪvɜːs] *noun*

univers *(masculine)* **: there are different theories on how the universe began** il y a différentes théories sur l'origine de l'univers.

university [ˌjuːnɪ'vɜːsətɪ] *(plural* universities) *noun*

université *(feminine)*, **fac** *(feminine)* **: he goes to university** *UK* OR **he goes to the university** *US* il va à l'université OR il va à la fac ; **my sister's at university** *UK* OR **my sister's at the university** *US* ma sœur est à l'université OR ma sœur est à la fac ; **he's a university student** il est étudiant.

unkind [ʌn'kaɪnd] *adjective*

pas gentil *(feminine* **pas gentille)** **: he's unkind to his sister** il n'est pas gentil avec sa sœur.

unleaded [ˌʌn'ledɪd] *adjective*

sans plomb : **unleaded petrol** *UK* OR **unleaded gas** *US* essence sans plomb.

unless [ən'les] *conjunction*

1. à moins que : **I'll stay here unless he comes** je resterai ici à moins qu'il vienne
2. à moins de : **you won't pass unless you work hard** tu ne réussiras pas à moins de beaucoup travailler.

unlike [ˌʌn'laɪk] *preposition*

contrairement à : **unlike other systems, this one is easy to install** contrairement à d'autres systèmes, celui-ci est facile à installer.

unlikely [ʌn'laɪklɪ] *adjective*

peu probable : **he's unlikely to win** il est peu probable qu'il gagne.

unlock [ˌʌn'lɒk] *verb*

ouvrir : **I can't unlock the door** je n'arrive pas à ouvrir la porte.

unlucky [ʌn'lʌkɪ] *adjective*

> **to be unlucky**
1. ne pas avoir de chance : **he's so unlucky** il n'a vraiment pas de chance
2. porter malheur : **it's unlucky to walk underneath a ladder** ça porte malheur de passer sous une échelle.

unpack [ˌʌn'pæk] *verb*

1. défaire : **we unpacked our suitcases** nous avons défait nos valises
2. déballer : **I unpacked my clothes** j'ai déballé mes vêtements
3. défaire ses bagages : **I'm unpacking** je défais mes bagages.

unpleasant [ʌn'pleznt] *adjective*

désagréable : **he was really unpleasant** il a été vraiment désagréable.

untidy [ʌn'taɪdɪ] *adjective*

1. en désordre : **your room is untidy** ta chambre est en désordre
2. désordonné : **Nick is very untidy** Nick est très désordonné
3. négligé : **he looks untidy** il est négligé.

untie [ˌʌn'taɪ] *(present participle* untying*) verb*

1. défaire : **I untied the knot** j'ai défait le nœud

2. détacher : **they untied the prisoner** ils ont détaché le prisonnier.

until [ən'tɪl] *preposition & conjunction*

▪ *preposition*
1. jusqu'à : **we'll play until six o'clock** on va jouer jusqu'à six heures ; **until now** jusqu'à maintenant
2. avant : **she won't come until tomorrow** elle ne viendra pas avant demain
▪ *conjunction*
1. jusqu'à ce que : **I'll stay here until he comes** je resterai ici jusqu'à ce qu'il vienne
2. avant que : **I won't accept until you've checked everything** je n'accepterai pas avant que tu aies tout vérifié.

unusual [ʌn'juːʒl] *adjective*

1. peu commun, inhabituel : **an unusual colour** une couleur peu commune OR une couleur inhabituelle
2. original : **she wears unusual clothes** elle a des tenues originales

The expression **il est rare que** is followed by a verb in the subjunctive:

> **it's unusual for her to be late** il est rare qu'elle soit en retard.

unwilling [ʌn'wɪlɪŋ] *adjective*

> **to be unwilling to do something** ne pas vouloir faire quelque chose : **she was unwilling to come** elle ne voulait pas venir.

unwrap [ˌʌn'ræp] *(past tense & past participle* unwrapped*) verb*

déballer : **she unwrapped her presents** elle a déballé ses cadeaux.

up [ʌp] *adverb, preposition & adjective*

▪ *adverb*
en haut : **don't look up** ne regarde pas en haut OR ne regarde pas vers le haut ; **up at the top of the house** tout en haut de la maison ; **it's up here** c'est là-haut ; **I'm coming up** je monte ; **to walk up and down** aller et venir OR faire les cent pas
▪ *preposition*
the house is up the hill la maison est en haut de la colline ; **the cat's up the tree** le chat est dans l'arbre ; **he's up the ladder** il est sur l'échelle ; **their house is just up the road** leur maison est un peu plus loin dans la rue

When 'up' is used with a verb of movement in English (to come up or to go up), you often use a verb alone in French to translate it (**monter**):

she went up the stairs elle a monté l'escalier ; **they ran up the road** ils ont remonté la rue en courant

➤ **up to** jusqu'à : **the water came up to my knees** l'eau m'arrivait jusqu'aux genoux ; **up to 30 people** jusqu'à 30 personnes

➤ **it's up to you** c'est à toi de décider

➤ **I don't feel up to going out** je n'ai pas le courage de sortir

➤ **what's he up to?** qu'est-ce qu'il fabrique ?

➤ **he's up to something** il mijote quelque chose

■ *adjective*

I was up at dawn je me suis levé à l'aube ; **is she up?** est-ce qu'elle est levée ? ; **time's up!** c'est l'heure ! ; **what's up?** *informal* qu'est-ce qu'il y a ?

upbringing ['ʌpˌbrɪŋɪŋ] *uncountable noun*

éducation *(feminine)* : **she had a strict upbringing** elle a eu une éducation stricte.

update [ʌp'deɪt] *verb*

mettre à jour : **I updated the file** j'ai mis le fichier à jour.

uphill [ʌp'hɪl] *adverb*

➤ **to go uphill** monter : **the path goes uphill** le sentier monte ; **we ran uphill** nous avons monté la pente en courant.

upon [ə'pɒn] *preposition* ➤ **on.**

upper ['ʌpəʳ] *adjective*

supérieur : **the upper lip** la lèvre supérieure
➤ **the upper classes** l'aristocratie *(feminine)* et la haute bourgeoisie.

upright [ʌp'raɪt] *adjective & adverb*

droit : **stand upright!** tiens-toi droit !

upset [ʌp'set] *adjective & verb*

■ *adjective*

1. **triste** : **she was very upset at the news** elle a été très triste en apprenant la nouvelle

2. **vexé** : **you're not upset, are you?** tu n'es pas vexé ?

➤ **to have an upset stomach** avoir l'estomac dérangé

■ *verb (past tense & past participle* upset)

1. **faire de la peine à** : **it upsets me to think about it** ça me fait de la peine d'y penser

2. **contrarier** : **this decision will upset a lot of people** cette décision va contrarier beaucoup de gens

3. **déranger** : **this has upset my plans** cela a dérangé mes projets

4. **renverser** : **I upset some coffee** j'ai renversé du café.

upside down [ʌpsaɪd'daʊn] *adverb*

à l'envers : **the picture is upside down** le tableau est à l'envers.

upstairs [ʌp'steəz] *adverb & adjective*

■ *adverb*

en haut : **wait for me upstairs** attends-moi en haut

■ *adjective*

d'en haut : **the upstairs rooms** les chambres d'en haut

➤ **to come upstairs** OR **to go upstairs** monter : **can you come upstairs?** tu peux monter ?

up-to-date [ʌptə'deɪt] *adjective*

1. **à jour** : **the data is up-to-date** les données sont à jour

2. **moderne** : **an up-to-date computer** un ordinateur moderne.

upwards ['ʌpwədz], **upward** *US* ['ʌpwəd] *adverb*

vers le haut : **we looked upwards** nous avons regardé vers le haut.

urgent ['ɜːdʒənt] *adjective*

urgent : **I must speak to you, it's urgent** je dois te parler, c'est urgent.

us [ʌs] *pronoun*

nous : **she phones us every week** elle nous appelle chaque semaine ; **is that for us?** c'est pour nous ?

In tenses like the present perfect and the past perfect, the past participle agrees with the direct object pronoun. Add an **-s** if 'us' is masculine or a mixture of masculine and feminine. Add **-es** if 'us' is feminine.

he helped us il nous a aidés OR il nous a aidées.

US [ˌjuː'es] *(abbreviation of* United States) *noun*

➤ **the US** les États-Unis *(masculine plural)* OR les USA *(masculine plural).*

USA [ˌjuːesˈeɪ] *(abbreviation of* United States of America*) noun*

➤ **the USA** les États-Unis *(masculine plural)* OR les USA *(masculine plural)* : **Scott lives in the USA** Scott habite aux États-Unis ; **I'm going to the USA** je vais aux États-Unis.

use *noun & verb*

◼ *noun* [juːs]

1. **utilisation** *(feminine)*, **emploi** *(masculine)* : **there's a ban on the use of certain products** l'utilisation de certains produits est interdite ; **it's ready for use** c'est prêt à l'emploi

2. **usage** *(masculine)* : **for my own use** pour mon usage personnel ; **this machine has many uses** cette machine a de nombreux usages

➤ **to be of use** être utile

➤ **to be in use** être utilisé

➤ **the elevator is out of use** l'ascenseur est hors service

➤ **it's no use** ça ne sert à rien

➤ **what's the use?** à quoi bon ?

◼ *verb* [juːz]

utiliser, se servir de : **I used a new method** j'ai utilisé une nouvelle méthode ; **she uses vinegar to clean the windows** elle se sert de vinaigre pour laver les fenêtres OR elle utilise du vinaigre pour laver les fenêtres ; **he used me** il s'est servi de moi

➤ **can I use your phone?** je peux téléphoner ?

➤ **I used to live in Quebec** j'habitais au Québec avant.

used *adjective*

1. [juːzd] d'occasion : **a used car** une voiture d'occasion

2. [juːst]

➤ **to be used to doing something** avoir l'habitude de faire quelque chose : **I'm used to going to bed late** j'ai l'habitude de me coucher tard ; **I'm used to it** j'ai l'habitude

➤ **to get used to doing something** s'habituer à faire quelque chose : **you'll get used to getting up early** tu t'habitueras à te lever tôt

useful ['juːsfʊl] *adjective*

utile : **take the guidebook, it could be useful** prends le guide, ça pourrait être utile.

useless ['juːslɪs] *adjective*

1. inutile : **a useless piece of information** un renseignement inutile

2. **nul** *(feminine* **nulle***)* : **he's completely useless** il est complètement nul

➤ **it's useless** ça ne sert à rien : **it's useless asking her** ça ne sert à rien de lui demander.

user ['juːzər] *noun*

utilisateur *(masculine)*, utilisatrice *(feminine)*.

user-friendly ['juːzərˈfrendlɪ] *adjective*

convivial : **this system is very user-friendly** ce système est très convivial.

usual ['juːʒəl] *adjective*

habituel *(feminine* **habituelle***)* : **we'll meet at the usual time** on se retrouve à l'heure habituelle

➤ **as usual** comme d'habitude : **she arrived early, as usual** elle est arrivée de bonne heure, comme d'habitude

➤ **later than usual** plus tard que d'habitude.

usually ['juːʒəlɪ] *adverb*

d'habitude : **she usually leaves the house at nine** d'habitude, elle quitte la maison à neuf heures.

utensil [juːˈtensl] *noun*

ustensile *(masculine)* : **kitchen utensils** des ustensiles de cuisine.

vacant ['veɪkənt] *adjective*

libre : **is this seat vacant?** est-ce que cette place est libre ?

vacation *US* [vəˈkeɪʃn] *uncountable noun*

vacances *(feminine plural)* : **they spent their vacation in Greece** ils ont passé leurs vacances en Grèce

➤ **on vacation** en vacances : **she's on vacation** elle est en vacances ; **where are you going on vacation?** où est-ce que tu pars en vacances ?

vacuum ['vækjʊəm] *verb & noun*

- *verb*
  passer l'aspirateur dans : **he's vacuuming the hall** il passe l'aspirateur dans l'entrée
- *noun*
  aspirateur *(masculine)*
  ➤ **a vacuum cleaner** un aspirateur.

vain [veɪn] *adjective*

vaniteux *(feminine* vaniteuse) : **he's very vain** il est très vaniteux
➤ **in vain** en vain : **I tried in vain to help him** j'ai essayé en vain de l'aider.

valentine card ['væləntaɪnkɑːd] *noun*

carte *(feminine)* de la Saint-Valentin.

Valentine's Day ['væləntaɪnzdeɪ] *noun*

la Saint-Valentin.

valid ['vælɪ] *adjective*

valable : **your ticket isn't valid** votre billet n'est pas valable.

valley ['vælɪ] *noun*

vallée *(feminine)* : **the Thames valley** la vallée de la Tamise.

valuable ['væljʊəbl] *adjective*

1. de grande valeur : **a valuable necklace** un collier de grande valeur
2. précieux *(feminine* précieuse) : **your advice has been very valuable** vos conseils ont été très précieux.

valuables ['væljʊəblz] *plural noun*

objets *(masculine plural)* de valeur : **she keeps her valuables in a safe** elle garde ses objets de valeur dans un coffre-fort.

value ['væljuː] *noun*

valeur *(feminine)* : **the value of their house has doubled** la valeur de leur maison a doublé.

van [væn] *noun*

camionnette *(feminine)*.

vanilla [və'nɪlə] *noun*

vanille *(feminine)* : **a vanilla ice cream** une glace à la vanille.

vanish ['vænɪʃ] *verb*

disparaître : **he vanished** il a disparu.

variety [və'raɪətɪ] *(plural* varieties) *noun*

variété *(feminine)* : **there are many different varieties of flowers** il y a beaucoup de variétés différentes de fleurs
➤ **there's a wide variety of dishes on the menu** il y a tout un choix de plats au menu.

various ['veərɪəs] *adjective*

divers : **for various reasons** pour diverses raisons.

varnish ['vɑːnɪʃ] *noun*

vernis *(masculine)* : **nail varnish** du vernis à ongles.

vary ['veərɪ] *(past tense & past participle* varied)
verb

varier : **the weather varies from day to day** le temps varie d'un jour à l'autre.

vase [*UK* vɑːz, *US* veɪz] *noun*

vase *(masculine)* : **I put the flowers in the vase** j'ai mis les fleurs dans le vase.

veal [viːl] *uncountable noun*

veau *(masculine)* : **do you eat veal?** tu manges du veau ?

vegan ['viːgən] *noun*

végétalien *(masculine)*, végétalienne *(feminine)* : **he's a vegan** il est végétalien.

vegetable ['vedʒtəbl] *noun*

légume *(masculine)* : **vegetable soup** soupe *(feminine)* aux légumes.

vegetarian [ˌvedʒɪ'teərɪən] *noun*

végétarien *(masculine)*, végétarienne *(feminine)* : **I'm a vegetarian** je suis végétarien.

vehicle ['viːɪkl] *noun*

véhicule *(masculine)*.

veil [veɪl] *noun*

voile *(masculine)* : **she's wearing a veil** elle porte le voile.

vein [veɪn] *noun*

veine *(feminine)* : **veins carry blood to the heart** les veines amènent le sang jusqu'au cœur.

velvet ['velvɪt] *noun*

velours *(masculine)* : **a velvet skirt** une jupe en velours.

vending machine ['vendɪŋmə'ʃiːn] *noun*

distributeur *(masculine)* **automatique** : **I bought some chocolate from the vending machine** j'ai acheté du chocolat au distributeur automatique.

verb [vɜːb] *noun*

verbe *(masculine)*.

verse [vɜːs] *noun*

1. **strophe** *(feminine)* : **the poem has three verses** le poème a trois strophes
2. **couplet** *(masculine)* : **the song has four verses** la chanson a quatre couplets.

version ['vɜːʃn] *noun*

version *(feminine)* : **there are two versions of the story** il y a deux versions de cette histoire.

versus ['vɜːsəs] *preposition*

contre : **Barcelona versus Liverpool** Barcelone contre Liverpool.

vertical ['vɜːtɪkl] *adjective*

vertical : **a vertical line** une ligne verticale.

very ['verɪ] *adverb*

très : **he's very happy** il est très heureux ; **it's not very good** ce n'est pas très bon
> **very much** beaucoup : **I like him very much** je l'aime beaucoup.

vest [vest] *noun*

1. *UK* **maillot** *(masculine)* **de corps** : **he's wearing a vest under his shirt** il porte un maillot de corps sous sa chemise
2. *US* **gilet** *(masculine)* : **he's wearing a suit and a vest** il porte un costume avec un gilet.

vet [vet], **veterinarian** *US* [ˌvetərɪ-'neərɪən] *noun*

vétérinaire *(masculine or feminine)* : **he's a vet** il est vétérinaire ; **we're taking the dog to the vet** on emmène le chien chez le vétérinaire.

via ['vaɪə] *preposition*

en passant : **you can go to Sydney via Los Angeles** on peut aller à Sydney en passant par Los Angeles.

vicar ['vɪkər] *noun*

pasteur *(masculine)* : **he's a vicar** il est pasteur.

vicious ['vɪʃəs] *adjective*

violent : **a vicious attack** une agression violente

⚠ Vicious est un faux ami, il ne signifie pas "vicieux".

victim ['vɪktɪm] *noun*

victime *(feminine)*.

victory ['vɪktərɪ] *(plural* victories*) noun*

victoire *(feminine)* : **they're sure of victory** ils sont sûrs de remporter la victoire.

video ['vɪdɪəʊ] *noun*

1. **vidéo** *(feminine)* : **they're watching a video** ils regardent une vidéo
2. **cassette** *(feminine)* **vidéo** : **put the video back in the box** remets la cassette dans la boîte
3. **magnétoscope** *(masculine)* : **put the video on** allume le magnétoscope
4. **clip** *(masculine)* : **Madonna's latest video** le dernier clip de Madonna
> **on video** en vidéo : **the film's out on video** le film est sorti en vidéo
> **a video camera** une caméra vidéo
> **a video cassette** une cassette vidéo
> **a video game** un jeu vidéo [*plural* jeux vidéo]
> **a video shop** *UK* OR **a video store** *US* un vidéoclub : **I got a film from the video shop** j'ai pris un film au vidéoclub
> **a video recorder** un magnétoscope.

view [vjuː] *noun*

1. **vue** *(feminine)* : **there's a great view from the top of the Eiffel Tower** il y a une très belle vue du haut de la tour Eiffel
2. **avis** *(masculine)* : **what is your view on the subject?** quel est votre avis sur le sujet ? ; **in my view he's the best singer of all** à mon avis c'est le meilleur chanteur de tous.

viewer ['vjuːər] *noun*

téléspectateur *(masculine)*, **téléspectatrice** *(feminine)* : **the programme attracts millions of viewers** l'émission attire des millions de téléspectateurs.

village ['vɪlɪdʒ] *noun*

village *(masculine)* : **they live in a village** ils habitent un village.

vine [vaɪn] *noun*

vigne *(feminine)* : **grapes grow on vines** le raisin pousse sur la vigne.

vinegar ['vɪnɪgər] *noun*

vinaigre *(masculine)*.

vineyard ['vɪnjəd] *noun*

vignoble *(masculine)* : **there are lots of vineyards in France** il y a beaucoup de vignobles en France.

violence ['vaɪələns] *noun*

violence *(feminine)*.

violent ['vaɪələnt] *adjective*

violent : **he's a violent man** c'est un homme violent.

violin [ˌvaɪə'lɪn] *noun*

violon *(masculine)* : **she plays the violin** elle joue du violon.

violinist [ˌvaɪə'lɪnɪst] *noun*

violoniste *(masculine or feminine)* : **he's a violinist** il est violoniste.

Virgo ['vɜːgəʊ] *noun*

Vierge *(feminine)* : **I'm a Virgo** je suis Vierge.

virus ['vaɪrəs] *(plural* viruses*) noun*

virus *(masculine)* : **he's caught a virus** il a attrapé un virus ; **a computer virus** un virus informatique.

visa ['viːzə] *noun*

visa *(masculine)* : **you need a visa to go to some countries** il faut un visa pour aller dans certains pays.

visit ['vɪzɪt] *noun & verb*

■ *noun*
1. visite *(feminine)* : **I paid a visit to my uncle** j'ai rendu visite à mon oncle
2. séjour *(masculine)* : **they went on a visit to California** ils ont fait un séjour en Californie
■ *verb*
1. rendre visite à : **I visited my uncle** j'ai rendu visite à mon oncle
2. visiter : **we visited the museum** nous avons visité le musée.

visitor ['vɪzɪtər] *noun*

1. invité *(masculine)*, invitée *(feminine)* : **we have visitors tomorrow** nous avons des invités demain

2. visiteur *(masculine)*, visiteuse *(feminine)* : **the park attracts a lot of visitors** le parc attire un grand nombre de visiteurs.

vitamin [*UK* 'vɪtəmɪn, *US* 'vaɪtəmɪn] *noun*

vitamine *(feminine)* : **citrus fruit is full of vitamin C** les agrumes contiennent beaucoup de vitamine C.

vocabulary [və'kæbjʊlərɪ] *(plural* vocabularies*) noun*

vocabulaire *(masculine)*.

voice [vɔɪs] *noun*

voix *(feminine)* : **he has a deep voice** il a une voix grave
> **she has a loud voice** elle parle fort
> **voice mail** messagerie *(feminine)* vocale.

volcano [vɒl'keɪnəʊ] *(plural* volcanoes OR volcanos*) noun*

volcan *(masculine)* : **the volcano erupted** le volcan est entré en éruption.

volleyball ['vɒlɪbɔːl] *noun*

volley-ball *(masculine)* : **they're playing volleyball** ils jouent au volley-ball.

volume ['vɒljuːm] *noun*

volume *(masculine)* : **can you turn the volume up?** tu peux augmenter le volume ?

voluntary ['vɒləntrɪ] *adjective*

1. volontaire : **a voluntary contribution** une contribution volontaire
2. bénévole : **she does voluntary work** elle fait du travail bénévole OR elle fait du bénévolat.

volunteer [ˌvɒlən'tɪər] *noun & verb*

■ *noun*
1. volontaire *(masculine or feminine)* : **these soldiers are volunteers** ces soldats sont des volontaires
2. bénévole *(masculine or feminine)* : **they don't get paid, they're volunteers** on ne les paie pas, ce sont des bénévoles
■ *verb*
to volunteer to do something se porter volontaire pour faire quelque chose ; **he volunteered to help us** il s'est porté volontaire pour nous aider.

vomit ['vɒmɪt] *verb*

vomir : **he vomited** il a vomi.

vote [vəʊt] *noun & verb*

■ *noun*
1. **vote** *(masculine)* **: they organized a vote** ils ont organisé un vote
2. **voix** *(feminine)* **: they won by 20 votes to 4** ils ont gagné par 20 voix contre 4
3. **droit** *(masculine)* **de vote : women got the vote in Britain in 1888** les femmes britanniques ont obtenu le droit de vote en 1888
■ *verb*
voter : he voted for the Green party il a voté pour les Verts.

voucher ['vaʊtʃəʳ] *noun*

bon *(masculine)* **: a voucher for a free drink** un bon pour une boisson gratuite
➤ **a gift voucher** un chèque-cadeau.

vowel ['vaʊəl] *noun*

voyelle *(feminine)* **: there are five vowels in English** il y a cinq voyelles en anglais.

vulture ['vʌltʃəʳ] *noun*

vautour *(masculine)*.

wade *US* [weɪd] *verb*

patauger : they're wading in the stream ils pataugent dans le ruisseau.

wading pool *US* ['weɪdɪŋpuːl] *noun*

pataugeoire *(feminine)*.

waffle ['wɒfl] *noun*

gaufre *(feminine)*.

wag [wæg] *(past tense & past participle* wagged*)* *verb*

remuer : the dog's wagging its tail le chien remue la queue.

wage [weɪdʒ] *noun*

salaire *(masculine)* **: the wages are good** le salaire est bon.

waist [weɪst] *noun*

taille *(feminine)* **: she has a small waist** elle a la taille fine.

waistcoat *UK* ['weɪskəʊt] *noun*

gilet *(masculine)* **: he's wearing a suit and waistcoat** il porte un costume et un gilet.

wait [weɪt] *noun & verb*

■ *noun*
attente *(feminine)* **: it was a long wait** l'attente a été longue
■ *verb*
attendre : we waited a long time nous avons attendu longtemps **; wait a minute!** attends une minute ! **; I waited till he had left** OR **I waited for him to leave** j'ai attendu qu'il soit parti
➤ **I can't wait to see you** j'ai hâte de te revoir
➤ **to keep somebody waiting** faire attendre quelqu'un **: I'm sorry to keep you waiting** je suis désolé de te faire attendre

wait for *phrasal verb*

attendre : wait for me! attends-moi ! **; he's waiting for the bus** il attend le bus.

waiter ['weɪtəʳ] *noun*

serveur *(masculine)* **: he's a waiter** il est serveur.

waiting room ['weɪtɪŋruːm] *noun*

salle *(feminine)* **d'attente**.

waitress ['weɪtrɪs] *noun*

serveuse *(feminine)* **: she's a waitress** elle est serveuse.

wake [weɪk] *(past tense* woke, *past participle* woken*)* *verb*

réveiller : wake me at six réveille-moi à six heures

wake up *phrasal verb*

1. **réveiller : can you wake me up in the morning?** peux-tu me réveiller demain matin ?
2. **se réveiller : I woke up at seven** je me suis réveillé à sept heures.

Wales [weɪlz] *noun*

le pays de Galles

> In French the names of countries are used with the definite article (le, la or l'). Remember that the French preposition à combines with le to become au :

Wales is in the west of Britain le pays de Galles est à l'ouest de la Grande-Bretagne ; **they**

live in Wales ils habitent au pays de Galles ;
he's going to Wales il va au pays de Galles.

walk [wɔːk] *noun & verb*

■ *noun*

promenade *(feminine)* : **let's go for a walk** allons faire une promenade

➤ **it's a long walk** c'est loin à pied

➤ **it's a five-minute walk** c'est à cinq minutes à pied

■ *verb*

1. marcher : **we walked for hours** nous avons marché pendant des heures

2. aller à pied : **I always walk to school** je vais toujours à l'école à pied

3. se promener : **we walked along the beach** nous nous sommes promenés le long de la plage

4. faire à pied : **we've walked three miles** nous avons fait cinq kilomètres à pied

➤ **to walk the dog** promener le chien

walk out | *phrasal verb*

partir : **he just got up and walked out** il s'est levé et il est parti.

walking ['wɔːkɪŋ] *uncountable noun*

marche *(feminine)* à pied : **walking is a good form of exercise** la marche à pied est un bon exercice

➤ **walking shoes** chaussures *(feminine plural)* de marche

➤ **a walking stick** une canne.

Walkman® ['wɔːkmən] *noun*

baladeur *(masculine)*, **Walkman**® *(masculine)* : **he's listening to his Walkman** il écoute son baladeur.

wall [wɔːl] *noun*

mur *(masculine)* : **he jumped over the wall** il a sauté par-dessus le mur.

wallet ['wɒlɪt] *noun*

portefeuille *(masculine)* : **he has a leather wallet** il a un portefeuille en cuir.

wallpaper ['wɔːlˌpeɪpər] *noun*

papier *(masculine)* peint.

Wall Street ['wɔːlstriːt] *noun*

Wall Street *(masculine)* : **Wall Street is the financial district of New York** Wall Street est le quartier financier de New York.

walnut ['wɔːlnʌt] *noun*

noix *(feminine)*.

wand [wɒnd] *noun*

baguette *(feminine)* : **a magic wand** une baguette magique.

wander ['wɒndər] *verb*

flâner : **we wandered around the town** nous avons flâné dans la ville.

want [wɒnt] *verb*

vouloir : **do you want some tea?** tu veux du thé ? ; **I want to go to the cinema** je veux aller au cinéma

➤ **to want somebody to do something** vouloir que quelqu'un fasse quelque chose : **she wants me to stay** elle veut que je reste

The verb that follows **vouloir que** is in the subjunctive.

➤ **the want ads** *US* les petites annonces.

wanted ['wɒntɪd] *adjective*

➤ **he's wanted by the police** il est recherché par la police

➤ **you're wanted in the kitchen** on te demande à la cuisine.

war [wɔːr] *noun*

guerre *(feminine)* : **the Second World War** la Seconde Guerre mondiale ; **the two countries are at war** les deux pays sont en guerre.

wardrobe ['wɔːdrəʊb] *noun*

armoire *(feminine)* : **put your coat in the wardrobe** mets ton manteau dans l'armoire.

warehouse ['weəhaʊs, *plural* 'weəhaʊzɪz]
noun

entrepôt *(masculine)*.

warm [wɔːm] *adjective & verb*

1. chaud : **the water is warm** l'eau est chaude

2. chaleureux *(feminine* chaleureuse*)* : **he got a warm welcome** il a reçu un accueil chaleureux

➤ **I'm warm** j'ai chaud ; **are you warm enough?** tu as assez chaud ?

➤ **it's warm today** il fait chaud aujourd'hui

warm up | *phrasal verb*

1. réchauffer, faire réchauffer : **I'll warm up some apple pie** je vais réchauffer de la tarte aux pommes OR je vais faire réchauffer de la tarte aux pommes

2. se réchauffer : **come and warm up in front of the fire** viens te réchauffer devant le feu

w

3. s'échauffer : the athletes are warming up les athlètes s'échauffent.

warmth [wɔ:mθ] *noun*

chaleur *(feminine)*.

warn [wɔ:n] *verb*

prévenir, avertir : I warned you je t'avais prévenu ; I warned you not to speak to him je t'avais averti qu'il ne fallait pas lui parler.

warning ['wɔ:nɪŋ] *noun*

avertissement *(masculine)* : this is my final warning c'est mon dernier avertissement.

warranty ['wɒrəntɪ] *(plural* warranties*)* *noun*

garantie *(feminine)* : the computer is still under warranty l'ordinateur est encore sous garantie.

wart [wɔ:t] *noun*

verrue *(feminine)* : she has a wart on her neck elle a une verrue au cou.

was [wəz, wɒz] *past tense of* be

he was late yesterday il était en retard hier ; I was waiting for you je t'attendais.

wash [wɒʃ] *noun & verb*

■ *noun*

➤ **to have a wash** *UK* se laver : he had a wash il s'est lavé

■ *verb*

1. laver : he's washing his clothes il lave ses vêtements

2. se laver : I'm washing je me lave ; she washed her hands elle s'est lavé les mains ; he's washing his hair il se lave les cheveux

wash up *phrasal verb*

1. *UK* faire la vaisselle : can you wash up? tu peux faire la vaisselle ?

2. *US* se laver : go and wash up before dinner va te laver avant de manger.

washbasin *UK* ['wɒʃ,beɪsn], **washbowl** *US* ['wɒʃbəʊl] *noun*

lavabo *(masculine)*.

washing ['wɒʃɪŋ] *uncountable noun*

linge *(masculine)* : dirty washing du linge sale
➤ **to do the washing** faire la lessive
➤ **a washing line** *UK* une corde à linge
➤ **a washing machine** une machine à laver
➤ **washing powder** *UK* lessive *(feminine)* ; a packet of washing powder un paquet de lessive.

washing-up *UK* ['wɒʃɪŋʌp] *noun*

vaisselle *(feminine)* : he's doing the washing-up il fait la vaisselle
➤ **washing-up liquid** liquide *(masculine)* vaisselle.

washroom *US* ['wɒʃrʊm] *noun*

toilettes *(feminine plural)* : where is the washroom? où sont les toilettes ?

wasn't [wɒznt] = was not

I wasn't at home last night je n'étais pas chez moi hier soir ; he wasn't paying attention il ne faisait pas attention.

wasp [wɒsp] *noun*

guêpe *(feminine)* : he was stung by a wasp il s'est fait piquer par une guêpe.

waste [weɪst] *noun & verb*

■ *uncountable noun*

1. gaspillage *(masculine)* : what a waste! quel gaspillage !

2. déchets *(masculine plural)* : industrial waste les déchets industriels
➤ **it's a waste of time** c'est une perte de temps

■ *verb*

1. gaspiller : he wastes money il gaspille son argent

2. perdre : he wastes a lot of time il perd beaucoup de temps.

wastebasket *US* ['weɪst,bɑ:skɪt], **wastepaper basket** [,weɪst'peɪpər,bɑ:skɪt] *noun*

corbeille *(feminine)* à papier.

watch [wɒtʃ] *noun & verb*

■ *noun*

montre *(feminine)* : my watch has stopped ma montre s'est arrêtée

■ *verb*

1. regarder : they're watching television ils regardent la télévision

2. surveiller : I'm watching their luggage for them je surveille leurs bagages

watch out *phrasal verb*

faire attention : watch out, there's a car coming! fais attention, il y a une voiture !

water ['wɔːtəʳ] *noun & verb*

■ *noun*

eau *(feminine)* : **can I have a glass of water?** tu peux me donner un verre d'eau ?

■ *verb*

arroser : **remember to water the flowers** n'oublie pas d'arroser les fleurs

> **my eyes are watering** j'ai les yeux qui pleurent

> **my mouth's watering** j'en ai l'eau à la bouche.

waterfall ['wɔːtəfɔːl] *noun*

chute *(feminine)* **d'eau**, cascade *(feminine)*.

watermelon ['wɔːtəˌmelən] *noun*

pastèque *(feminine)*.

waterproof ['wɔːtəpruːf] *adjective*

1. imperméable : **a waterproof jacket** une veste imperméable

2. étanche : **a waterproof watch** une montre étanche.

water-skiing ['wɔːtəʳskiːɪŋ] *uncountable noun*

ski *(masculine)* nautique : **they go water-skiing** ils font du ski nautique.

wave [weɪv] *noun & verb*

■ *noun*

1. vague *(feminine)* : **the waves are big today** il y a de grosses vagues aujourd'hui

2. signe *(masculine)* : **he gave me a wave** il m'a fait un signe de la main

■ *verb*

1. faire un signe de la main : **he waved to me when he saw me** il m'a fait un signe de la main quand il m'a vu

2. agiter : **the children are waving flags** les enfants agitent des drapeaux

> **to wave goodbye** faire au revoir de la main : **I waved goodbye to them** je leur ai fait au revoir de la main

> **to wave a wand** donner un coup de baguette magique.

wax [wæks] *uncountable noun*

cire *(feminine)* : **candles are made of wax** les bougies sont faites de cire.

waxworks ['wækswɔːks] *noun*

musée *(masculine)* de cire.

way [weɪ] *noun*

1. façon *(feminine)*, manière *(feminine)* : **I like the**

way she dresses j'aime bien sa façon de s'habiller ; **in the same way** de la même façon OR de la même manière ; **in a way** d'une certaine manière OR d'une certaine façon

2. chemin : **can you tell me the way to the museum?** vous pouvez m'indiquer le chemin pour aller au musée ? ; **the quickest way to the town** le chemin le plus court pour aller en ville ; **it's on my way** c'est sur mon chemin ; **we stopped on the way** nous nous sommes arrêtés en route

> **he got his own way** il a obtenu ce qu'il voulait

> **the way in** l'entrée *(feminine)*

> **the way out** la sortie

> **to be in the way** gêner : **you're in the way** tu gênes

> **to get out of the way** s'écarter : **get out of the way!** écartez-vous !

> **he's on his way** il arrive

> **it's a long way** c'est loin

> **which way is it?** c'est par où ?

> **this way**

1. par ici : **the hotel's this way** l'hôtel est par ici ; **look this way** regarde par ici

2. comme ça : **you do it this way** tu le fais comme ça

> **that way**

1. par là : **he went that way** il est allé par là

2. comme ça : **don't do it that way** ne fais pas comme ça

> **is this the right way?** est-ce que c'est bien par ici ? OR est-ce que c'est bien la bonne direction ?

> **he went the wrong way** il est parti dans la mauvaise direction

> **you're not doing it the right way** OR **you're doing it the wrong way** ce n'est pas comme ça qu'il faut faire OR tu t'y prends mal

> **the wrong way around** à l'envers : **your hat's the wrong way around** ton chapeau est à l'envers

> **the wrong way up** à l'envers

> **no way!** pas question !

WC [ˌdʌbljuːˈsiː] *noun*

W-C *(masculine plural)* : **where's the W-C?** où sont les WC ?

we [wiː] *pronoun*

nous : **we live in Toronto** nous habitons à Toronto ; **are we late?** nous sommes en retard ?

In informal French the pronoun **on** is often used to translate 'we':

we're going to the cinema nous allons au cinéma OR on va au cinéma.

weak [wiːk] *adjective*

faible : **I feel weak** je me sens faible.

wealthy ['welθɪ] *adjective*

riche

> **the wealthy** les riches *(masculine plural)*.

weapon ['wepən] *noun*

arme *(feminine)* : **she's carrying a weapon** elle porte une arme.

wear [weə^r] *(past tense* wore, *past participle* worn) *verb*

1. **porter** : **Carol's wearing a dress** Carol porte une robe
2. **mettre** : **what are you going to wear?** qu'est-ce que tu vas mettre ?

wear out *phrasal verb*

1. **user** : **I've worn out my shoes** j'ai usé mes chaussures
2. **s'user** : **my shoes wear out quickly** mes chaussures s'usent vite
3. **épuiser** : **that journey has worn me out** ce voyage m'a épuisé.

weather ['weðə^r] *uncountable noun*

temps *(masculine)* : **what's the weather like?** quel temps fait-il ? ; **the weather is awful** il fait un temps affreux ; **the weather is fine** il fait beau

> **the weather forecast** la météo : **what's the weather forecast?** que dit la météo ?

web [web] *noun*

toile *(feminine)* : **a spider's web** une toile d'araignée

> **the Web** le Web OR la Toile : **I found his address on the Web** j'ai trouvé son adresse sur le Web OR j'ai trouvé son adresse sur la Toile
> **a web page** OR **a Web page** une page Web.

website ['websaɪt] *noun*

site *(masculine)* **Web** : **have you visited the Larousse website?** as-tu visité le site Web de Larousse ?

we'd [wiːd]

1. = we had : **we'd already finished** nous avions déjà fini

2. = we would : **we'd like to book a room** nous voudrions réserver une chambre.

wedding ['wedɪŋ] *noun*

mariage *(masculine)*

> **a wedding anniversary** un anniversaire de mariage
> **a wedding cake** une pièce montée
> **a wedding dress** une robe de mariée
> **a wedding ring** une alliance.

Wednesday ['wenzdɪ] *noun*

mercredi *(masculine)* : **it's Wednesday today** nous sommes mercredi ; **next Wednesday** mercredi prochain ; **last Wednesday** mercredi dernier

> **on Wednesday** mercredi : **I'll see you on Wednesday** on se voit mercredi
> **on Wednesdays** le mercredi : **she has a French class on Wednesdays** elle a un cours de français le mercredi

In French the days of the week do not start with a capital letter.

weed [wiːd] *noun*

mauvaise herbe *(feminine)* : **I'm going to dig up the weeds** je vais arracher les mauvaises herbes.

week [wiːk] *noun*

semaine *(feminine)* : **in a week's time** dans une semaine ; **this week** cette semaine ; **next week** la semaine prochaine ; **last week** la semaine dernière

> **a week on Saturday** *UK* OR **a week from Saturday** *US* samedi en huit.

weekend [ˌwiːk'end] *noun*

week-end *(masculine)* : **what are you doing this weekend?** qu'est-ce que tu fais ce weekend ? ; **next weekend** le week-end prochain ; **last week-end** le week-end dernier

> **at the weekend** *UK* OR **on the weekend** *US* le week-end : **I'll see you at the weekend** on se voit ce week-end.

weep [wiːp] *(past tense & past participle* wept) *verb*

pleurer : **she started weeping** elle a commencé à pleurer.

weigh [weɪ] *verb*

peser : **she weighs 40 kilos** elle pèse 40 kilos ; **can you weigh these apples?** vous pouvez peser ces pommes ? ; **I'm going to weigh myself** je vais me peser.

weight [weɪt] *noun*

poids *(masculine)*

> **to put on weight** grossir OR prendre du poids : **I've put on weight** j'ai grossi OR j'ai pris du poids
> **to lose weight** maigrir OR perdre du poids : **she lost weight** elle a maigri OR elle a perdu du poids.

weird [wɪəd] *adjective*

bizarre : **it's a weird film** c'est un film bizarre.

welcome ['welkəm] *noun, verb & adjective*

▪ *noun*
accueil *(masculine)* : **they gave me a warm welcome** ils m'ont fait un accueil chaleureux

▪ *verb*
accueillir : **they welcomed me with open arms** ils m'ont accueilli à bras ouverts

▪ *adjective*
bienvenu : **you're always welcome** vous êtes toujours le bienvenu ici
> **welcome!** bienvenue ! OR soyez le bienvenu ! : **welcome to England!** bienvenue en Angleterre !
> **thank you! — you're welcome!** merci ! – il n'y a pas de quoi ! OR merci ! – de rien !

we'll [wiːl] = **we shall** OR **we will**

we'll come around later on passera plus tard ; **we'll see you later** on se voit plus tard.

well [wel] *adjective, adverb, noun & exclamation*

▪ *adjective*
(comparative **better)** bien : **I'm very well, thank you** je vais très bien, merci ; **all is well** tout va bien

▪ *adverb*
(superlative **best)** bien : **the party went well** la fête s'est bien passée ; **she sings really well** elle chante vraiment bien ; **the work's well done** le travail est bien fait
> **well done!** bravo !
> **as well** aussi : **he came as well** il est venu aussi
> **I might as well go** je ferais aussi bien d'y aller
> **as well as** ainsi que : **they sell records as well as CDs** ils vendent des disques ainsi que des CD

▪ *noun*
puits *(masculine)* : **an oil well** un puits de pétrole

▪ *exclamation*
1. **eh bien ! : oh well, never mind!** eh bien, tant pis ! ; **well, who was it?** eh bien, c'était qui ?
2. **tiens !, ça alors ! : well, well, well!** tiens, tiens ! ; **well, look who it is!** ça alors, regarde qui est là !

well-behaved [welbɪ'heɪvd] *adjective*

sage : **the children were well-behaved** les enfants étaient sages.

wellingtons *UK* ['welɪŋtənz], **welling-ton boots** *UK* [ˌwelɪŋtən'buːts] *plural noun*

bottes *(feminine plural)* en caoutchouc : **they're wearing wellingtons** ils portent des bottes en caoutchouc.

well-known [ˌwel'nəʊn] *adjective*

connu : **it's a well-known restaurant** c'est un restaurant connu.

well-off [wel'ɒf] *adjective*

aisé : **his family is well-off** sa famille est aisée.

Welsh [welʃ] *adjective & noun*

▪ *adjective*
gallois : **a Welsh choir** une chorale galloise
▪ *noun*
gallois *(masculine)* : **he speaks Welsh** il parle gallois
> **the Welsh** les Gallois *(masculine plural)*

> Remember not to use a capital letter for the adjectives and the language in French. Only use a capital letter for the inhabitants.

went [went] *past tense of* **go**

he went to Texas last year il est allé au Texas l'année dernière.

wept [wept] *past tense & past participle of* **weep**

she wept elle a pleuré.

were [wɜːʳ] *past tense of* **be**

were you at the party? tu étais à la fête ? ; **we were late** nous étions en retard ; **they were listening to music** ils écoutaient de la musique.

we're [wɪəʳ] = **we are**

we're late nous sommes en retard ; **we're not coming with you** nous ne venons pas avec vous.

weren't [wɜːnt] = **were not**

we weren't ready nous n'étions pas prêts ; **you weren't listening to me** tu ne m'écoutais pas.

west [west] *noun, adjective & adverb*

■ *noun*
ouest *(masculine)* : **the sun sets in the west** le soleil se couche à l'ouest

■ *adjective*
ouest *(invariable)* : **San Francisco is on the west coast** San Francisco est sur la côte ouest

■ *adverb*
vers l'ouest : **go west** allez vers l'ouest

➤ **west of** à l'ouest de : **Chicago is west of Detroit** Chicago est à l'ouest de Detroit

➤ **the West End** le West End

➤ **the West Indies** les Antilles *(feminine plural)* : **Cuba is in the West Indies** Cuba se trouve aux Antilles

> 📖 THE WEST END
> Le **West End** (la partie ouest du centre de Londres) est un quartier très animé et touristique au cœur de la capitale britannique. On y trouve de nombreux magasins, beaucoup de cinémas, de restaurants et de théâtres où l'on joue des pièces et des comédies musicales. Le **West End** comprend le quartier très vivant de **Soho**, **Oxford Street** et ses grands magasins, **Chinatown** (le quartier chinois), **Leicester Square** et ses cinémas, ainsi que **Picadilly Circus**, célèbre place où se dresse la statue d'Éros.

western ['westən] *adjective & noun*

■ *adjective*
de l'ouest : **Western Europe** l'Europe *(feminine)* de l'Ouest

■ *noun*
western *(masculine)* : **he prefers westerns to thrillers** il préfère les westerns aux thrillers

Westminster ['westmɪnstəʳ] *noun*
Westminster

> 📖 WESTMINSTER
> Westminster est le nom du quartier dans le centre de Londres où se trouvent le Parlement britannique et le Palais de Buckingham. On parle souvent de Westminster pour parler du Parlement lui-même.

> 📖 WESTMINSTER ABBEY
> L'abbaye de Westminster, située au centre de Londres, est l'un des monuments les plus célèbres de Grande-Bretagne. Cette immense église gothique a été construite aux XIIIe et XIVe siècles. C'est là que sont couronnés tous les monarques d'Angleterre depuis Guillaume le

Conquérant. L'église renferme les tombeaux des rois, des reines et des grands hommes britanniques.

wet [wet] *adjective*

1. **mouillé** : **my hair's wet** j'ai les cheveux mouillés

2. **pluvieux** *(feminine* **pluvieuse)** : **the weather is wet** le temps est pluvieux

➤ **to get wet** se mouiller : **I got wet** je me suis mouillé

➤ **to get something wet** mouiller quelque chose : **I've got my shirt wet** j'ai mouillé ma chemise.

we've [wiːv] = we have
we've eaten all the cakes nous avons mangé tous les gâteaux ; **we've arrived in Seattle** nous sommes arrivés à Seattle.

whale [weɪl] *noun*
baleine *(feminine)* : **whales are mammals** les baleines sont des mammifères.

what [wɒt] *adjective, pronoun & exclamation*

■ *adjective*
quel *(feminine* **quelle)** *[plural* **quels, quelles]** : **what colour is it?** c'est de quelle couleur ? ; **what time is it?** quelle heure est-il ? ; **what books do you want?** quels livres veux-tu ? ; **what a pity!** quel dommage ! ; **what lovely flowers!** quelles jolies fleurs !

■ *pronoun*

1. *In questions*

> Use **qu'est-ce qui** (or **qu'est-ce qu'** before an 'i') when 'what' is the subject of the verb that follows and **qu'est-ce que** or **que** (**qu'est-ce qu'** and **qu'** before a vowel) when it is the object:

what's happening? qu'est-ce qui se passe ? OR que se passe-t-il ? ; **what happened?** qu'est-ce qui s'est passé ? OR qu'est-ce qui est arrivé ? ; **what's wrong?** qu'est-ce qu'il y a ? OR qu'y a-t-il ? ; **what's that?** qu'est-ce que c'est ? ; **what are you doing?** qu'est-ce que tu fais ? OR que fais-tu ? ; **what has he done?** qu'est-ce qu'il a fait ? OR qu'a-t-il fait ?

> With prepositions you should use **quoi**:

what are they talking about? de quoi parlent-ils ? ; **what are you thinking about?** à quoi penses-tu ?

2. *In relative clauses*

Use **ce qui** (**ce qu'** before an 'i') when 'what' introduces the subject of the following verb, and **ce que** (or **ce qu'** before a vowel) when it introduces the object:

I saw what happened j'ai vu ce qui s'est passé OR j'ai vu ce qui est arrivé ; **you can't always get what you want** on ne peut pas toujours avoir ce que l'on veut ; **tell me what she said** dis-moi ce qu'elle a dit

➤ **what about going out for a meal?** et si on allait au restaurant ?

➤ **what about me?** et moi alors ?

➤ **what is it about?** il s'agit de quoi ? OR de quoi s'agit-il ?

■ *exclamation*

what! comment ! OR quoi ! ; **what?** quoi ?

whatever [wɒt'evər] *pronoun & adjective*

■ *pronoun*

1. **quoi que : whatever happens, don't tell Joe** quoi qu'il arrive, ne dis rien à Joe

2. **tout ce que : I'll do whatever I can** je ferai tout ce que je peux

■ *adjective*

1. **quel que soit** *(feminine* **quelle que soit)** **: whatever decision you make, I'll support you** quelle que soit la décision que tu prendras, je te soutiendrai

2. **tout le : take whatever books you want** prends tous les livres que tu veux ; **take whatever money you need** tu peux prendre tout l'argent que tu veux.

wheat [wiːt] *noun*

blé *(masculine)* **: wheat fields** des champs de blé.

wheel [wiːl] *noun*

1. **roue** *(feminine)* **: bicycles have two wheels** les vélos ont deux roues

2. **volant** *(masculine)* **: who was behind the wheel?** qui était au volant ?

wheelbarrow ['wiːlˌbærəʊ] *noun*

brouette *(feminine)*.

wheelchair ['wiːlˌtʃeər] *noun*

fauteuil *(masculine)* **roulant.**

when [wen] *adverb & conjunction*

■ *adverb*

quand : when are you going? quand est-ce que tu pars ? OR tu pars quand ? OR quand pars-tu ? ; **tell me when you're coming** dis-moi quand tu viens ; **when does the train ar-**

rive? quand est-ce que le train arrive ? OR à quelle heure est-ce que le train arrive ?

■ *conjunction*

quand : he visited me when I lived in Paris il m'a rendu visite quand j'habitais Paris ; **I'll tell her when she gets here** je lui dirai quand elle arrivera ; **I'll buy you a car when you are 18** je t'achèterai une voiture quand tu auras 18 ans

Note that the verb that follows 'quand' is in the future tense in French.

whenever [wen'evər] *conjunction*

1. **quand : come whenever you like** viens quand tu veux

2. **à chaque fois que : whenever I see them we argue** à chaque fois que je les vois on se dispute.

where [weər] *adverb & conjunction*

■ *adverb*

où : where is the station? où est la gare ? ; **where are you going?** où vas-tu ? OR où est-ce que tu vas ? ; **tell me where you hid it** dis-moi où tu l'as caché

■ *conjunction*

où : this is the village where I grew up c'est le village où j'ai grandi.

wherever [weər'evər] *conjunction*

1. **là où, où : sit wherever you want** assieds-toi là où tu veux OR assieds-toi où tu veux

2. **partout où, où que : he'll follow you wherever you go** il te suivra partout où tu iras OR il te suivra où que tu ailles.

whether ['weðər] *conjunction*

si : I don't know whether she's coming je ne sais pas si elle vient.

which [wɪtʃ] *adjective & pronoun*

■ *adjective*

quel *(feminine* **quelle)** *[plural* **quels, quelles]** **: which bike is yours?** quel vélo est le tien ? ; **which flowers do you like?** quelles fleurs aimes-tu ?

➤ **which one?** lequel ? OR laquelle ? : **there are two bags, which one is yours?** il y a deux sacs, lequel est le tien ?

■ *pronoun*

1. *In questions* **lequel** *(masculine)*, **laquelle** *(feminine)* *[plural* **lesquels, lesquelles]** **: out of the two dresses, which do you prefer?** des deux robes, laquelle préfères-tu ?

2. *In relative clauses*

Use **qui** (or **qu'** before 'i') when 'which' introduces the subject of the following verb, and **que** (or **qu'** before a vowel) when it introduces the object:

houses which are on the beach cost more les maisons qui sont sur la plage coûtent plus cher ; **the book which you lent me was good** le livre que tu m'as prêté était bien

When 'which' is used with a preposition it is translated by **lequel, laquelle, lesquels** or **lesquelles** depending on the gender (masculine or feminine) and the number (singular or plural) of the noun it refers to:

the chair on which he was sitting la chaise sur laquelle il était assis.

while [waɪl] *conjunction & noun*

▪ *conjunction*
1. **pendant que** : **I was reading while you were sleeping** je lisais pendant que tu dormais
2. **alors que** : **he likes to got out while his brother prefers to watch TV** il aime sortir alors que son frère préfère regarder la télé
▪ *noun*
   moment *(masculine)* : **let's stay here for a while** restons ici un moment
▷ **after a while** au bout d'un moment : **after a while he got tired** au bout d'un moment il s'est fatigué.

whip [wɪp] *noun & verb*

▪ *noun*
   fouet *(masculine)*
▪ *verb*
   fouetter : **she whipped her horse** elle a fouetté son cheval.

whipped cream ['wɪptkriːm] *noun*

   crème *(feminine)* **fouettée**.

whiskers ['wɪskəᵣz] *plural noun*

   moustaches *(feminine plural)* : **cats have whiskers** les chats ont des moustaches.

whisper ['wɪspəʳ] *verb*

   chuchoter : **she whispered something to me** elle m'a chuchoté quelque chose.

whistle ['wɪsl] *noun & verb*

▪ *noun*
   sifflet *(masculine)* : **the referee blew his whistle** l'arbitre a donné un coup de sifflet
▪ *verb*
   siffler : **can you whistle?** tu sais siffler ?

white [waɪt] *adjective*

   blanc : **a white shirt** une chemise blanche
▷ **white coffee** *UK* café *(masculine)* au lait
▷ **a white lie** un pieux mensonge
▷ **the White House** la Maison-Blanche.

Whitehall ['waɪthɔːl] *noun*

   rue de Londres, centre administratif du gouvernement britannique.

who [huː] *pronoun*

   qui : **who are you?** qui êtes-vous ? ; **who are you talking about?** de qui parles-tu ? ; **I don't know who she is** je ne sais pas qui c'est ; **she's the woman who lives in that big house** c'est la femme qui habite cette grande maison.

who'd [huːd]

1. = **who had** : **who'd closed the door?** qui avait fermé la porte ?
2. = **who would** : **who'd like to come?** qui voudrait venir ?

whoever [huːˈevəʳ] *pronoun*

1. **qui** : **you can invite whoever you like** tu peux inviter qui tu veux
2. **celui qui** : **whoever wins will get this cup** celui qui gagnera aura cette coupe.

whole [həʊl] *adjective & noun*

▪ *adjective*
   tout, entier *(feminine* **entière***)* : **I spent the whole day reading** j'ai passé toute la journée à lire OR j'ai passé la journée entière à lire ; **she ate the whole cake** elle a mangé tout le gâteau OR elle a mangé le gâteau entier
▪ *noun*
   tout *(masculine)*
▷ **the whole of** tout : **the whole of the summer** tout l'été ; **the whole of London is talking about it** tout Londres en parle
▷ **on the whole** dans l'ensemble.

wholemeal bread *UK* ['həʊlmiːlbred], **wholewheat bread** *US* ['həʊlwiːt- bred] *noun*
   pain *(masculine)* **complet**.

who'll [huːl] = **who will** OR **who shall**
   who'll be there? qui sera là ?

whom [huːm] *pronoun*

1. **qui** : **to whom it may concern** à qui de droit
2. **que** (**qu'** *before a vowel*) : **the man whom she married** l'homme qu'elle a épousé.

who're ['hu:ər] = **who are**

who're you? qui êtes-vous ?

who's [hu:z] *noun*

1. = **who is** : **who's that man?** c'est qui cet homme ?
2. = **who has** : **who's left the door open?** qui a laissé la porte ouverte ?

whose [hu:z] *adjective & pronoun*

1. à qui : **whose car is this?** à qui est cette voiture ? ; **whose is it?** c'est à qui ?
2. dont : **that's the boy whose father is an astronaut** c'est le garçon dont le père est astronaute.

who've [hu:v] = **who have**

the people **who've just left** les gens qui viennent de partir.

why [waɪ] *adverb*

pourquoi : **why did you lie?** pourquoi as-tu menti ? OR pourquoi est-ce que tu as menti ? ; **why don't you come too?** pourquoi est-ce que tu ne viens pas avec nous ? ; **I don't know why he said that** je ne sais pas pourquoi il a dit ça ; **I haven't done my homework – why not?** je n'ai pas fait mes devoirs – pourquoi ? ; **do you want to go out? – OK, why not?** tu veux sortir ? – oui, pourquoi pas ?

wicked ['wɪkɪd] *adjective*

1. méchant : **he's a wicked man** c'est un homme méchant
2. *informal* génial : **it's a wicked song** c'est une chanson géniale.

wide [waɪd] *adjective & adverb*

■ *adjective*

1. large : **a wide road** une rue large ; **how wide is the river?** quelle est la largeur de la rivière ? ; **it's nine metres wide** ça fait neuf mètres de large
2. grand : **a wide choice** un grand choix
■ *adverb*
open wide! ouvrez grand la bouche !
➤ **wide awake** complètement réveillé : **she's wide awake** elle est complètement réveillée
➤ **wide open** grand ouvert : **the window's wide open** la fenêtre est grande ouverte.

widow ['wɪdəʊ] *noun*

veuve *(feminine)* : **she's a widow** elle est veuve.

widower ['wɪdəʊər] *noun*

veuf *(masculine)* : **he's a widower** il est veuf.

width [wɪdθ] *noun*

largeur *(feminine)* : **what's the width of the room?** quelle est la largeur de la pièce ?

wife [waɪf] *(plural* wives [waɪvz]*) noun*

femme *(feminine)* : **she's my wife** c'est ma femme.

wig [wɪg] *noun*

perruque *(feminine)* : **he's wearing a wig** il porte une perruque.

wild [waɪld] *adjective*

1. sauvage : **wild animals** des animaux sauvages
2. fou *(feminine* folle*)* : **that noise is driving me wild** ce bruit me rend fou.

will ['wɪl] *verb & noun*

■ *verb (negative* **won't***)*

1. *The future tense* **I'll help you** je t'aiderai ; **when will you phone?** quand est-ce que tu appelleras ? ; **she'll be cross** elle sera fâchée ; **will we be there on time?** est-ce que nous serons à l'heure ?

> In spoken French you can use the present tense of the verb aller + infinitive to talk about the very near future:

I'll do it now je vais le faire maintenant ; **it will make a change** ça va changer un peu
2. *In invitations and requests* **vouloir** : **will you have some more cake?** voulez-vous encore du gâteau ? ; **will you close the window?** veux-tu fermer la fenêtre ?
➤ **he won't help me** il refuse de m'aider
➤ **the car won't start** la voiture ne veut pas démarrer
➤ **that'll be your father** ça doit être ton père
■ *noun*
1. volonté *(feminine)* : **she has a strong will** elle a beaucoup de volonté
2. testament *(masculine)* : **to make a will** faire son testament
➤ **against one's will** contre son gré.

willing ['wɪlɪŋ] *adjective*

➤ **to be willing to do something** être prêt à faire quelque chose : **I'm willing to help you** je suis prêt à t'aider.

win [wɪn] *(past tense & past participle* won*) noun*

gagner : **I'm going to win** je vais gagner ; **she won the race** elle a gagné à la course.

W

wind *noun & verb*

▨ *noun* [wɪnd]

vent : there's a strong wind il y a beaucoup de vent

➤ **a wind instrument** un instrument à vent

▨ *verb* [waɪnd] (*past tense & past participle* **wound**)

1. **enrouler : wind the rope around the pole** enroule la corde autour du poteau
2. **serpenter : the road winds through the valley** la route serpente à travers la vallée
3. **remonter : I forgot to wind the clock** j'ai oublié de remonter l'horloge

wind up *phrasal verb*

se retrouver : he wound up in jail il s'est retrouvé en prison.

windmill ['wɪndmɪl] *noun*

moulin *(masculine)* **à vent : there's a windmill on the hill** il y a un moulin à vent sur la colline.

window ['wɪndəʊ] *noun*

1. **fenêtre** *(feminine)* **: open the window** ouvre la fenêtre
2. **vitre** *(feminine)* **: he's cleaning the car windows** il lave les vitres de la voiture ; **he broke a window** il a cassé une vitre
3. **vitrine** *(feminine)* **: she's looking in the shop window** elle regarde dans la vitrine.

windscreen *UK* ['wɪndskriːn], **windshield** *US* ['wɪndʃiːld] *noun*

pare-brise *(masculine)* [*plural* **pare-brise**]

➤ **windscreen wipers** *UK* OR **windshield wipers** *US* essuie-glaces *(masculine plural)*.

windsurfing ['wɪndˌsɜːfɪŋ] *noun*

planche *(feminine)* **à voile : he goes windsurfing at weekends** il fait de la planche à voile le week-end.

windy ['wɪndɪ] *adjective*

➤ **it's windy** il y a du vent.

wine [waɪn] *noun*

vin *(masculine)* **: a glass of red wine** un verre de vin rouge.

wineglass ['waɪnglɑːs] *noun*

verre *(masculine)* **à vin.**

wing [wɪŋ] *noun*

aile *(feminine)* **: pelicans have large wings** les pélicans ont de grandes ailes.

wink [wɪŋk] *verb*

faire un clin d'œil : he winked at me il m'a fait un clin d'œil.

winner ['wɪnər] *noun*

gagnant *(masculine)*, **gagnante** *(feminine)*.

winter ['wɪntər] *noun*

hiver *(masculine)* **: it's cold in winter** il fait froid en hiver

➤ **winter sports** sports *(masculine plural)* d'hiver.

wintertime ['wɪntətaɪm] *uncountable noun*

hiver *(masculine)* **: in wintertime** en hiver.

wipe [waɪp] *verb*

essuyer : he's wiping the table il essuie la table ; **wipe your feet!** essuie-toi les pieds !

wipe up *phrasal verb*

essuyer : she wiped up the coffee elle a essuyé le café.

wire ['waɪər] *noun*

1. **fil** *(masculine)* **de fer : a barbed-wire fence** une clôture en fil de fer
2. **fil** *(masculine)* **: somebody cut the telephone wires** quelqu'un a coupé les fils téléphoniques.

wisdom ['wɪzdəm] *noun*

sagesse *(feminine)* **: a wisdom tooth** une dent de sagesse.

wise [waɪz] *adjective*

sage : he's a very wise man c'est un homme très sage

➤ **a wise guy** *informal* un petit malin.

wish [wɪʃ] *noun & verb*

▨ *noun* (*plural* **wishes**)

1. **souhait** *(masculine)*, **désir** *(masculine)* **: his wish came true** son souhait s'est réalisé
2. **vœu** *(masculine)* [*plural* **vœux**] **: she closed her eyes and made a wish** elle a fermé les yeux et a fait un vœu ; **best wishes!** meilleurs vœux !

▨ *verb*

souhaiter : you can stay here if you wish vous pouvez rester si vous le souhaitez ; **he wished me a happy birthday** il m'a souhaité un bon anniversaire

➤ **I wish I had a yacht!** si seulement j'avais un yacht !

➤ **I wish you were here** j'aimerais que tu sois là.

witch [wɪtʃ] (*plural* witches) *noun*

sorcière *(feminine)* : **she's a witch** c'est une sorcière.

with [wɪð] *preposition*

1. avec : **I danced with Mary** j'ai dansé avec Mary ; **Tom came with us** Tom est venu avec nous ; **with pleasure** avec plaisir ; **I cut it with a knife** je l'ai coupé avec un couteau

2. *In descriptions* à [*plural* aux] : **the man with the blue eyes** l'homme aux yeux bleus ; **the girl with the red hat** la fille au chapeau rouge

3. de : **she was trembling with fear** elle tremblait de peur ; **they screamed with laughter** ils hurlaient de rire

4. chez : **I'm staying with my uncle** je loge chez mon oncle.

within [wɪ'ðɪn] *preposition*

1. en moins de : **the doctor came within ten minutes** le médecin est venu en moins de dix minutes

2. à moins de : **we're within thirty miles of Paris** nous sommes à moins de cinquante kilomètres de Paris

3. à l'intérieur de, dans : **the house is situated within a large property** la maison est située dans une grande propriété.

without [wɪð'aʊt] *preposition*

sans : **I won't go without you** je n'irai pas sans toi ; **he left without saying goodbye** il est parti sans dire au revoir

> **to go without something** OR **to do without something** se passer de quelque chose : **we can't go without water** on ne peut pas se passer d'eau.

witness ['wɪtnɪs] (*plural* witnesses) *noun*

témoin *(masculine)*.

witty ['wɪtɪ] *adjective*

spirituel *(feminine* spirituelle*)* : **he's very witty** il est très spirituel.

wives *plural of* wife.

wizard ['wɪzəd] *noun*

sorcier *(masculine)* : **Gandalf is a wizard** Gandalf est un sorcier.

woke [wəʊk] *past tense of* wake

he woke up at seven il s'est réveillé à sept heures.

woken ['wəʊkn] *past participle of* wake

she hasn't woken up yet elle ne s'est pas encore réveillée.

wolf [wʊlf] (*plural* wolves [wʊlvz]) *noun*

loup *(masculine)* : **wolves live in packs** les loups vivent en meute.

woman ['wʊmən] (*plural* women ['wɪmɪn]) *noun*

femme *(feminine)* : **she's a nice young woman** c'est une jeune femme sympa

> **a woman doctor** une femme médecin.

won [wʌn] *past tense & past participle of* win

she won the race elle a gagné la course ; **have you won?** as-tu gagné ?

wonder ['wʌndər] *noun & verb*

■ *noun*

merveille *(feminine)* : **the seven wonders of the world** les sept merveilles du monde

> **no wonder!** ce n'est pas étonnant ! : **no wonder you're tired!** ce n'est pas étonnant que tu sois fatigué !

The expression *ce n'est pas étonnant que* is followed by a verb in the subjunctive.

■ *verb*

se demander : **I wonder what he's doing** je me demande ce qu'il fait ; **I wonder where Tom is** je me demande où est Tom.

wonderful ['wʌndəfʊl] *adjective*

merveilleux *(feminine* merveilleuse*)* : **we had a wonderful holiday** on a passé des vacances merveilleuses ; **it was a wonderful party** c'était une soirée formidable.

won't [wəʊnt] = will not **I won't tell anybody** je ne le dirai à personne ; **they won't come** ils ne viendront pas.

wood [wʊd] *noun*

bois *(masculine)* : **the table is made of wood** la table est en bois ; **there's a wood nearby** il y a un bois près d'ici.

wooden ['wʊdn] *adjective*

en bois : **it's a wooden table** c'est une table en bois.

wool [wʊl] *noun*

laine *(feminine)* : **it's made of wool** c'est en laine.

W

woollen *UK*, **woolen** *US* ['wʊlən] *adjective*

en laine : **a woolen jacket** une veste en laine.

word [wɜːd] *noun*

1. mot *(masculine)* : **she didn't say a word** elle n'a pas dit un mot ; **what does this word mean?** que signifie ce mot ? OR que veut dire ce mot ?
2. parole *(feminine)* : **you gave me your word** tu m'as donné ta parole ; **do you know the words to this song?** tu connais les paroles de cette chanson ?
> **to have a word with somebody** parler à quelqu'un : **I'm going to have a word with your teacher** je vais parler à ton professeur
> **word processing** traitement *(masculine)* de texte.

wore [wɔːʳ] *past tense of* wear

she wore red shoes elle portait des chaussures rouges.

work [wɜːk] *noun & verb*

● *noun*

1. travail *(masculine)* : **I have a lot of work to do** j'ai beaucoup de travail ; **she's not here, she's at work** elle n'est pas là, elle est au travail ; **he's gone to work** il est allé au travail
2. œuvre *(feminine)* : **the complete works of Shakespeare** les œuvres complètes de Shakespeare
> **a work of art** une œuvre d'art
> **to be out of work** être au chômage
■ *verb*

1. travailler : **where do you work?** où est-ce que vous travaillez ? ; **she works very hard** elle travaille très dur
2. marcher : **the TV isn't working** la télé ne marche pas
3. faire marcher : **I can't work this machine** je n'arrive pas à faire marcher cette machine

work out *phrasal verb*

1. trouver : **I've worked out the answer** j'ai trouvé la réponse
2. résoudre : **have you worked out the problem?** as-tu résolu le problème ?
3. calculer : **I'll work out the total** je vais calculer le total
4. comprendre : **I can't work it out** je ne comprends pas
5. se passer : **everything worked out well** tout s'est bien passé

6. faire de l'exercice : **he works out every morning** il fait de l'exercice tous les matins.

worker ['wɜːkəʳ] *noun*

> **an office worker** un employé de bureau, une employée de bureau
> **an factory worker** un ouvrier, une ouvrière.

working-class ['wɜːkɪŋ] *adjective*

ouvrier *(feminine* ouvrière*)* : **it's a working-class neighbourhood** c'est un quartier ouvrier.

workman ['wɜːkmən] *(plural* workmen ['wɜːkmən]*) noun*

ouvrier *(masculine)*.

workshop ['wɜːkʃɒp] *noun*

atelier *(masculine)* : **a drama workshop** un atelier de théâtre.

workstation ['wɜːkˌsteɪʃn] *noun*

poste *(masculine)* de travail.

world [wɜːld] *noun*

monde *(masculine)* : **Russia is the biggest country in the world** la Russie est le plus vaste pays du monde ; **I've travelled all over the world** j'ai voyagé dans le monde entier
> **the world champion** le champion du monde, la championne du monde
> **the World Cup** la Coupe du Monde
> **the First World War** la Première Guerre mondiale
> **the Second World War** la Deuxième Guerre mondiale.

worm [wɜːm] *noun*

ver *(masculine)* : **birds eat worms** les oiseaux mangent des vers.

worn [wɔːn] *adjective & verb form*

■ *adjective*
usé : **the carpet is worn** le tapis est usé
> **worn out**
1. complètement usé : **my shoes are worn out** mes chaussures sont complètement usées
2. épuisé : **I'm worn out** je suis épuisé
■ *past participle of* wear
he has never worn this tie il n'a jamais porté cette cravate.

worried ['wʌrɪd] *adjective*

inquiet *(feminine* inquiète*)* : **you look worried** tu as l'air inquiet

➤ **to be worried about something** OR
somebody s'inquiéter pour quelque chose
OR quelqu'un : **I'm very worried about him** je
m'inquiète beaucoup pour lui
➤ **I'm worried sick** je suis fou d'inquiétude.

worry ['wʌrɪ] *noun & verb*

■ *noun* (*plural* **worries**)
souci (*masculine*) : **he has a lot of worries** il a
beaucoup de soucis
■ *verb*
1. (*past tense & past participle* worried) **s'inquiéter** : **you worry too much** tu t'inquiètes trop ;
he's worrying about the exams il s'inquiète
pour les examens ; **don't worry!** ne t'inquiète
pas ! OR ne t'en fais pas !
2. **inquiéter** : **the situation worries me** la situation m'inquiète.

worse [wɜːs] *adjective & verb*

■ *adjective* (*comparative of* **bad**)
1. **pire** : **it could have been worse** cela aurait
pu être pire ; **it's worse than ever** c'est pire
que jamais
2. **plus mal** : **the patient is worse today** le
malade va plus mal aujourd'hui ; **I feel
worse than before** je me sens plus mal
qu'avant
➤ **to get worse** empirer : **things are getting
worse** les choses empirent
■ *adverb* (*comparative of* **badly**)
plus mal : **he sings worse than I thought** il
chante plus mal que je ne pensais.

worst [wɜːst] *adjective, adverb & noun*

■ *adjective* (*superlative of* **bad**)
1. **plus mauvais** : **it's the worst film I've ever
seen** c'est le plus mauvais film que j'aie jamais
vu
2. **pire** : **it was the worst place to have a picnic** c'était le pire endroit pour un pique-nique ; **the worst thing is the heat** le pire
c'est la chaleur
■ *adverb* (*superlative of* **badly**)
le plus mal : **he plays worst** c'est lui qui joue
le plus mal
■ *noun*
➤ **the worst** le pire (*feminine* **la pire**) [*plural* **les
pires**] : **of all the players I know, you're the
worst** de tous les joueurs que je connais, c'est
toi le pire
➤ **at worst** au pire : **at worst you'll be an hour
late** au pire tu arriveras avec une heure de retard.

worth [wɜːθ] *noun & adjective*

■ *noun*
valeur (*feminine*) : **a jewel of great worth** un
bijou d'une grande valeur
➤ **I have 10 dollars' worth of change** j'ai
pour 10 dollars de monnaie
■ *adjective*
➤ **to be worth doing something** valoir la
peine de faire quelque chose : **it's worth
reading the book** ça vaut la peine de lire le livre ; **it isn't worth waiting** ça ne vaut pas la
peine d'attendre ; **Las Vegas is worth a visit**
Las Vegas vaut la peine d'être visité
➤ **it's worth it** ça vaut la peine.

would ['wʊd] (*negative* **wouldn't**) *verb*

> 'Would' is usually translated by a verb in the conditional tense in French:

if I won the lottery, I would buy a sports car
si je gagnais au loto, j'achèterais une voiture
de sport ; **if I were you, I wouldn't do it** à ta
place, je ne le ferais pas ; **we would have
missed the train if we'd waited** nous aurions
raté le train si nous avions attendu ; **she said
she would come** elle a dit qu'elle viendrait
➤ **would you like another cake?** voulez-vous un autre gâteau ?
➤ **I'd like a cup of tea** je voudrais une tasse
de thé
➤ **we'd really like to see you** nous aimerions vraiment te voir
➤ **the car wouldn't start** la voiture ne voulait pas démarrer.

wouldn't ['wʊdnt] = **would not**

> **I wouldn't do it, even if you paid me** je ne le
ferais pas même si tu me payais ; **the car
wouldn't start** la voiture ne voulait pas démarrer.

would've ['wʊdəv] = **would have**

> **I would've helped you, if you'd asked** je
t'aurais aidé si tu me l'avais demandé.

wound *noun & verb*

■ *noun* [wuːnd]
blessure (*feminine*) : **he has a wound on his
leg** il a une blessure à la jambe
■ *verb* [wuːnd]
blesser : **she was wounded in the arm** elle a
été blessée au bras
■ *past tense & past participle of* **wind** [waʊnd]

W

she wound the thread around her finger elle a enroulé le fil autour de son doigt.

wrap [ræp] (*past tense & past participle* wrapped) *verb*

1. **emballer** : **he's wrapping the presents** il emballe les cadeaux
2. **envelopper** : **she wrapped herself in a blanket** elle s'est enveloppée dans une couverture
3. **enrouler** : **he wrapped his scarf around his neck** il a enroulé son écharpe autour de son cou.

wrapping paper ['ræpɪŋpeɪpəʳ] *uncountable noun*

papier *(masculine)* **cadeau**.

wreck [rek] *noun & verb*

◾ *noun*

épave *(feminine)* : **we found the wreck of a car** nous avons trouvé une épave de voiture

◾ *verb*

1. **détruire** : **the bomb wrecked the village** la bombe a détruit le village
2. **gâcher** : **the weather has wrecked all our plans** le temps a gâché tous nos projets.

wrestler ['resləʳ] *noun*

lutteur *(masculine)*, **lutteuse** *(feminine)* : **he's a wrestler** il est lutteur.

wrestling ['reslɪŋ] *uncountable noun*

lutte *(feminine)* : **a wrestling match** un match de lutte.

wrinkle ['rɪŋkl] *noun*

ride *(feminine)*.

wrinkled ['rɪŋkld] *adjective*

ridé : **her face is wrinkled** son visage est ridé.

wrist [rɪst] *noun*

poignet *(masculine)* : **she broke her wrist** elle s'est cassé le poignet.

write [raɪt] (*past tense* wrote, *past participle* written) *verb*

écrire : **she's writing a letter** elle écrit une lettre ; **write to me!** écris-moi ! ; **they write to each other** ils s'écrivent

write back *phrasal verb*

répondre : **I sent her a letter but she didn't**

write back je lui ai envoyé une lettre mais elle n'a pas répondu

write down *phrasal verb*

noter : **he wrote down everything I said** il a noté tout ce que je lui ai dit.

writer ['raɪtəʳ] *noun*

écrivain *(masculine)* : **I'd like to be a writer** j'aimerais être écrivain.

writing ['raɪtɪŋ] *uncountable noun*

écriture *(feminine)* : **she has nice writing** elle a une belle écriture

➤ **writing paper** papier *(masculine)* à lettres.

written ['rɪtn] *past participle of* write

have you written to Louise? est-ce que tu as écrit à Louise ?

wrong [rɒŋ] *adjective & adverb*

◾ *adjective*

1. **mauvais** : **they went in the wrong direction** ils sont allés dans la mauvaise direction ; **that's the wrong answer** c'est la mauvaise réponse ; **it's the wrong address** ce n'est pas la bonne adresse
2. **faux** *(feminine* **fausse)** : **your calculations are wrong** tes calculs sont faux
➤ **to be wrong** avoir tort : **you're wrong** tu as tort
➤ **you have the wrong number** vous vous trompez de numéro
➤ **what's wrong?** qu'est-ce qui ne va pas ?
➤ **there's something wrong with my bike** mon vélo ne marche pas bien

◾ *adverb*

mal : **she wrote my name wrong** elle a mal écrit mon nom
➤ **to get something wrong** se tromper de quelque chose : **you've got the wrong date** tu t'es trompé de date
➤ **to go wrong**
1. **se tromper** : **I've gone wrong again** je me suis encore trompé
2. **mal tourner** : **my plans have gone wrong** mes projets ont mal tourné
3. **ne plus marcher** : **the radio has gone wrong** la radio ne marche plus.

wrote [rəʊt] *past tense of* write

she wrote a poem elle a écrit un poème.

Xmas *(abbreviation of* Christmas*) noun*

Noël *(masculine)*.

X-ray ['eksreɪ] *noun & verb*

◼ *noun*
radio *(feminine)* : **he needs to have an X-ray** il doit passer une radio

◼ *verb*
faire une radio de : **they X-rayed her leg** ils lui ont fait une radio de la jambe.

xylophone ['zaɪləfəʊn] *noun*

xylophone *(masculine)*.

yacht [jɒt] *noun*

yacht *(masculine)*.

yard [jɑːd] *noun*

1. cour *(feminine)* : **the house has a small yard** la maison a une petite cour
2. *US* jardin *(masculine)* : **the children are playing in the yard** les enfants jouent dans le jardin
3. = 91,44 cm.

yawn [jɔːn] *verb*

bâiller : **he's yawning** il bâille.

year [jɪəʳ] *noun*

1. année *(feminine)* : **we waited a whole year** nous avons attendu toute une année ; **the school year** l'année scolaire
2. an *(masculine)* : **she's 21 years old** elle a 21 ans ; **the New Year** le Nouvel An
➤ **last year** l'an dernier OR l'année dernière
➤ **next year** l'an prochain OR l'année prochaine.

yell [jel] *verb*

hurler : **she was yelling** elle hurlait.

yellow ['jeləʊ] *adjective*

jaune : **she was wearing a yellow dress** elle portait une robe jaune.

yes [jes] *adverb*

1. oui : **are you tired? – yes, I am** tu es fatigué ? – oui ; **would you like some cake? – yes, please** veux-tu du gâteau ? – oui, s'il vous plaît
2. *In reply to a negative question* si : **aren't you hungry? – yes, I am!** tu n'as pas faim ? – si !

yesterday ['jestədɪ] *adverb*

hier : **I saw her yesterday** je l'ai vue hier
➤ **yesterday morning** hier matin
➤ **yesterday evening** hier soir
➤ **the day before yesterday** avant-hier : **he came home the day before yesterday** il est rentré avant-hier.

yet [jet] *adverb*

1. encore : **I haven't seen them yet** je ne les ai pas encore vus
2. déjà : **have they finished yet?** est-ce qu'ils ont déjà fini ?
➤ **not yet** pas encore ; **has she arrived? – no, not yet** est-elle arivée ? – non, pas encore.

yoga ['jəʊgə] *noun*

yoga *(masculine)* : **she practices yoga** elle fait du yoga.

yoghurt, yogurt ['jɒgət] *noun*

yaourt *(masculine)* : **a vanilla yoghurt** un yaourt à la vanille.

yolk [jəʊk] *noun*

jaune *(masculine)* d'œuf : **add the yolk of one egg** ajoutez un jaune d'œuf.

y

you [juː] *pronoun*

1.

> In French there are two ways to translate 'you'. When you are talking to somebody you don't know, you use **vous**. This is known as the polite form. When you are talking to somebody you know well, your friends or your family, you can use the more informal pronoun **tu** (or **te** or **toi**). When you are talking to more than one person, you must use the plural form **vous**.

Subject of a verb **tu, vous** : **what do you do?** qu'est-ce que vous faites dans la vie ? ; **would you like some tea?** voulez-vous du thé ? ; **what are you doing?** qu'est-ce que tu fais ? ; **you're always complaining** tu n'arrêtes pas de te plaindre ; **do you all want to come?** vous voulez tous venir ? ; **you two are late** vous êtes en retard tous les deux

2. *Object of a verb* **te** (**t'** *before a vowel*), **vous** : **do I know you?** je vous connais ? ; **I'll ring you tonight** je t'appellerai ce soir OR je vous appellerai ce soir ; **I gave it to you** je te l'ai donné OR je vous l'ai donné

> In tenses like the present perfect and the past perfect, the past participle agrees with the direct object pronoun. Add an -e if 'you' is feminine, add -s if 'you' is masculine plural or mixed gender, and add -es if it is feminine plural:

hello Jane, I phoned you yesterday salut Jane, je t'ai appelée hier

3. *After a preposition* **toi, vous** : **this is for you** c'est pour toi OR c'est pour vous ; **we're going without you** nous irons sans toi OR nous irons sans vous

4. *Impersonal pronoun* **on** : **you can't always get what you want** on ne peut pas toujours avoir ce qu'on veut ; **exercise is good for you** l'exercice est bon pour la santé.

you'd [juːd]

1. = **you had** : **you'd already finished** tu avais déjà fini

2. = **you would** : **you'd be silly to say no** tu serais bête de refuser.

you'll [juːl] = **you will**

> **you'll be late** tu vas être en retard.

young [jʌŋ] *adjective*

> **jeune** : **he's very young** il est très jeune
>
> ➤ **young people** les jeunes.

younger ['jʌŋgər] (*comparative of* young) *adjective*

> **plus jeune** : **he's younger than me** il est plus jeune que moi ; **my younger brother** mon plus jeune frère.

youngest ['jʌŋgɪst] (*superlative of* young) *adjective*

> **le plus jeune** : **he's the youngest child in the family** c'est le plus jeune enfant de la famille ; **my youngest brother** le plus jeune de mes frères.

your [jɔːr] *adjective*

> **ton** (*feminine* **ta** OR **ton** *before a vowel*) [*plural* **tes**], **votre** [*plural* **vos**]

> The possessive adjective must agree in gender (masculine or feminine) and number (singular or plural) with the noun that follows. Use **ton** (**ta** or **tes**) to translate 'your' when you are talking to somebody you know well and use **votre** (or **vos**) when you are talking to more than one person or to somebody you don't know.

your dog bit me ton chien m'a mordu OR votre chien m'a mordu ; **I like your car** j'aime bien ta voiture OR j'aime bien votre voiture ; **can I listen to your CDs?** je peux écouter tes CD ? OR je peux écouter vos CD ? ; **pass me your plate** passe-moi ton assiette OR passez-moi votre assiette

> Use the definite article (**le**, **la** or **les**), not the possessive adjective, with parts of the body:

close your eyes ferme les yeux OR fermez les yeux ; **have you washed your hands?** est-ce que tu t'es lavé les mains ? OR est-ce que vous vous êtes lavé les mains ?

you're [jɔːr] = **you are**

> **you're going to be late** tu vas être en retard.

yours [jɔːz] *pronoun*

1. **le tien** (*feminine* **la tienne**) [*plural* **les tiens, les tiennes**], **le vôtre** (*feminine* **la vôtre**) [*plural* **les vôtres**]

> The possessive pronoun must agree in gender (masculine or feminine) and number (singular or plural) with the noun it replaces. Use **le tien** (**la tienne, les tiens** or **les tiennes**) to translate 'yours' when you are talking to somebody you know well and use **le vôtre** (**la vôtre** or **les vôtres**) when you are talking to more than one person or to somebody you don't know:

my bike has ten gears, yours has twelve

mon vélo a dix vitesses, le tien en a douze OR mon vélo a dix vitesses, le vôtre en a douze ; **her shoes are red, yours are green** ses chaussures sont rouges, les tiennes sont vertes OR ses chaussures sont rouges, les vôtres sont vertes
2. **à toi**, **à vous** ; **is this yours?** c'est à toi ? OR c'est à vous ?

yourself [jɔːˈself] *pronoun*

1. **te** (**t'** *before a vowel*), **vous** ; **don't cut yourself** ne te coupe pas OR ne vous coupez pas ; **are you enjoying yourself?** est-ce que tu t'amuses ? OR est-ce que vous vous amusez ?
2. **toi-même, vous-même** ; **did you make that yourself?** tu l'as fait toi-même ? OR vous l'avez fait vous-même ?
3. **toi, vous** ; **keep it to yourself** garde ça pour toi OR gardez ça pour vous
➤ **by yourself** tout seul : **were you by yourself?** tu étais tout seul ? OR vous étiez tout seul ?

> Use **te, toi-même** or **toi** to translate 'yourself' when you are talking to somebody you know well and use **vous** or **vous-même** when you are talking to more than one person or to somebody you don't know.

yourselves [jɔːˈselvz] *pronoun*

1. **vous** : **help yourselves!** servez-vous !
2. **vous-mêmes** : **do it yourselves** faites-le vous-mêmes
➤ **by yourselves** tout seuls : **were you by yourselves?** vous étiez tout seuls ?

youth [juːθ] *noun*

1. (*uncountable*) **jeunesse** (*feminine*) : **in his youth** dans sa jeunesse
2. (*plural* **youths**) **jeune** (*masculine or feminine*) : **a gang of youths** une bande de jeunes
➤ **the youth of today** les jeunes d'aujourd'hui
➤ **a youth club** une maison de jeunes
➤ **a youth hostel** une auberge de jeunesse.

you've [juːv] = **you have**

you've forgotten to lay the table tu as oublié de mettre le couvert.

zebra [*UK* ˈzebrə, *US* ˈziːbrə] *noun*

zèbre (*masculine*) : **zebras come from Africa** les zèbres sont originaires d'Afrique
➤ **a zebra crossing** *UK* un passage pour piétons.

zero [ˈzɪərəʊ] *noun*

zéro (*masculine*) : **the temperature is below zero** la température est au-dessous de zéro ; **the Yankees won 16 to zero** les Yankees ont gagné 16 à zéro.

zip *UK* [zɪp], **zipper** *US* [ˈzɪpər] *noun*

fermeture (*feminine*) **Éclair®** : **can you do my zip up?** tu peux remonter ma fermeture ?
➤ **the zip code** *US* le code postal.

zodiac [ˈzəʊdɪæk] *noun*

zodiaque (*masculine*) : **what are the twelve signs of the zodiac?** quels sont les douze signes du zodiaque ?

zone [zəʊn] *noun*

zone (*feminine*).

zoo [zuː] *noun*

zoo (*masculine*) : **we're going to the zoo** nous allons au zoo.

zucchini *US* [zuːˈkiːnɪ] (*plural* zucchini) *noun*

courgette (*masculine*).

Z

Verbes irréguliers anglais

Infinitive	Past Tense	Past Participle
awake	awoke	awoken
be	was, were	been
bear	bore	born *(also borne)*
beat	beat	beaten
become	became	become
begin	began	begun
bend	bent	bent
bet	bet *(also betted)*	bet *(also betted)*
bite	bit	bitten
bleed	bled	bled
blow	blew	blown
break	broke	broken
breed	bred	bred
bring	brought	brought
build	built	built
burn	burnt *(also burned)*	burnt *(also burned)*
burst	burst	burst
buy	bought	bought
can	could	-
catch	caught	caught
choose	chose	chosen
cling	clung	clung
come	came	come
cost	cost	cost
creep	crept	crept
cut	cut	cut
deal	dealt	dealt
dig	dug	dug
do	did	done
draw	drew	drawn
dream	dreamed *(also dreamt)*	dreamed *(also dreamt)*
drink	drank	drunk
drive	drove	driven
eat	ate	eaten
fall	fell	fallen
feed	fed	fed
feel	felt	felt
fight	fought	fought
find	found	found
fling	flung	flung
fly	flew	flown
forbid	forbade	forbidden
forget	forgot	forgotten
freeze	froze	frozen
get	got	got *(US gotten)*
give	gave	given

Verbes irréguliers anglais

Infinitive	Past Tense	Past Participle
go	went	gone
grind	ground	ground
grow	grew	grown
hang	hung *(also hanged)*	hung *(also hanged)*
have	had	had
hear	heard	heard
hide	hid	hidden
hit	hit	hit
hold	held	held
hurt	hurt	hurt
keep	kept	kept
kneel	knelt *(also kneeled)*	knelt *(also kneeled)*
know	knew	known
lay	laid	laid
lead	led	led
lean	leant *(also leaned)*	leant *(also leaned)*
leap	leapt *(also leaped)*	leapt *(also leaped)*
learn	learnt *(also learned)*	learnt *(also learned)*
leave	left	left
lend	lent	lent
let	let	let
lie	lay	lain
light	lit *(also lighted)*	lit *(also lighted)*
lose	lost	lost
make	made	made
may	might	-
mean	meant	meant
meet	met	met
mistake	mistook	mistaken
mow	mowed	mown *(also mowed)*
pay	paid	paid
put	put	put
quit	quit *(also quitted)*	quit *(also quitted)*
read	read	read
rid	rid	rid
ride	rode	ridden
ring	rang	rung
rise	rose	risen
run	ran	run
saw	sawed	sawn
say	said	said
see	saw	seen
seek	sought	sought
sell	sold	sold
send	sent	sent
set	set	set
shake	shook	shaken

Verbes irréguliers anglais

Infinitive	Past Tense	Past Participle
shall	should	-
shine	shone	shone
shoot	shot	shot
show	showed	shown
shrink	shrank	shrunk
shut	shut	shut
sing	sang	sung
sink	sank	sunk
sit	sat	sat
sleep	slept	slept
slide	slid	slid
sling	slung	slung
smell	smelt *(also smelled)*	smelt *(also smelled)*
speak	spoke	spoken
speed	sped *(also speeded)*	sped *(also speeded)*
spell	spelt *(also spelled)*	spelt *(also spelled)*
spend	spent	spent
spill	spilt *(also spilled)*	spilt *(also spilled)*
spin	spun	spun
spit	spat	spat
split	split	split
spoil	spoiled *(also spoilt)*	spoiled *(also spoilt)*
spread	spread	spread
stand	stood	stood
steal	stole	stolen
stick	stuck	stuck
sting	stung	stung
stink	stank	stunk
strike	struck	struck *(also stricken)*
swear	swore	sworn
sweep	swept	swept
swell	swelled	swollen *(also swelled)*
swim	swam	swum
swing	swung	swung
take	took	taken
teach	taught	taught
tear	tore	torn
tell	told	told
think	thought	thought
throw	threw	thrown
wake	woke *(also waked)*	woken *(also waked)*
wear	wore	worn
weep	wept	wept
win	won	won
wind	wound	wound
write	wrote	written

Imprimé en France par Mame Imprimeurs à Tours
n° 06022158 n° projet 11003454 Dépôt légal mars 2006